THE  ENCYCLOPEDIA OF HEAVY ROCK

COLIN LARKIN

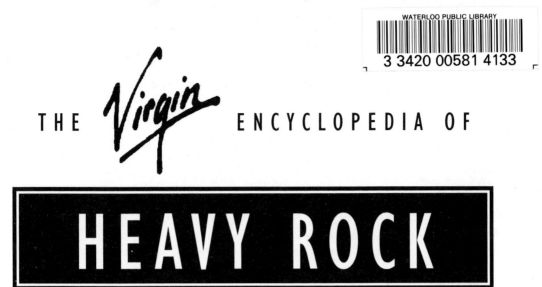

Virgin

IN ASSOCIATION WITH MUZE UK LTD.

Dedicated To Bruce, Baker and Clapton

First published in Great Britain in 1999 by
VIRGIN BOOKS
an imprint of Virgin Publishing Ltd
Thames Wharf Studios, Rainville Road
London W6 9HT

A catalogue record for this book is available from the British Library

ISBN 0 7535 0257 7

Written, edited and produced by
MUZE UK Ltd
to whom all editorial enquiries should be sent
Iron Bridge House, 3 Bridge Approach, Chalk Farm, London NW1 8BD
e-mail: colin@muze.co.uk. http://www.muze.com
Editor In Chief: Colin Larkin
Production Editor: Susan Pipe
Research Assistant: Nic Oliver
Editorial Assistant: Sarah Lavelle
Typographic Design Consultants: Roger Kohn & Acu
Special thanks to Trev Huxley, Tony Laudico, Paul Zullo
and all the Klugettes at Muze Inc.,
and to Rob Shreeve of Virgin Publishing.
Typeset by Midnight Lamp Studios
Printed and bound in Great Britain by Butler & Tanner Ltd, Frome and London

INTRODUCTION

The Virgin Encyclopedia Of Heavy Rock is one in the major series of books taken from the multi-volume *Encyclopedia Of Popular Music*. Other titles already available are:

The Virgin Encyclopedia Of Fifties Music
The Virgin Encyclopedia Of Sixties Music
The Virgin Encyclopedia Of Seventies Music
The Virgin Encyclopedia Of Eighties Music
The Virgin Encyclopedia Of Popular Music (Concise)
The Virgin Encyclopedia Of Indie & New Wave
The Virgin Encyclopedia Of The Blues
The Virgin Encyclopedia Of R&B And Soul
The Virgin Encyclopedia Of Reggae
The Virgin Encyclopedia Of Country Music
The Virgin Encyclopedia Of Dance Music
The Virgin All Time Top 1000 Albums

We decided this time to revert to the older, and now more accepted genre, Heavy Rock, in place of the seemingly outdated Heavy Metal moniker.

Metal fans may throw up their arms in despair, but most magazines catering for this music will now include good old fashioned heavy rock, grunge and alternative rock. Coming up with a suitable title this time, was easy.

I am old enough to remember all the first wave of heavy rock bands. In those days, we thought it was heavy blues; I recall many dozens of gigs at the old Marquee Club in Wardour Street, London. Queuing for hours, always in the rain or freezing cold. Bands like Free, Blodwyn Pig, High Tide, Spooky Tooth, Taste and Ten Years After shook the walls of that grubby establishment. Over in Ameica at that time, Cream and Hendrix were wowing the youth, and credible counterparts like Iron Butterfly, Grand Funk Railroad, Mountain and Steppenwolf were playing a similar hybrid. The key instrument is the solid body electric guitar, and where would our ears be without it. Gibson and Fender sales went through the roof as a new generation discovered something that was beyond rock 'n' roll.

I hope I have done the genre proud. There is a lot of metal, a bit of heavy prog, a lot of hardcore, a bit of punk, a sprinkle of grunge and a lot of that twiddly stuff with amazing guitar solos. The drum solos sadly are still as boring as ever, but the Fender Twin Reverb still sounds like nothing else on earth.

ENTRY STYLE

Albums, EPs (extended play 45s), newspapers, magazines, television programmes, films and stage musicals are referred to in italics. All song titles appear in single quotes. We spell rock 'n' roll like this. There are two main reasons for spelling rock 'n' roll with 'n' as opposed to 'n'. First, historical precedent: when the term was first coined in the 50s, the popular spelling was 'n'. Second, the 'n' is not simply an abbreviation of 'and' (in which case 'n' would apply) but a phonetic representation of n as a sound. The ' ', therefore, serve as inverted commas rather than as apostrophes. The further reading section at the end of each entry has been expanded to give the reader a much wider choice of available books. These are not necessarily recommended titles but we have attempted to leave out any publication that has little or no merit.

We have also started to add videos at the ends of the entries. Again, this is an area that is expanding faster than we can easily cope with, but there are many items in the videography and further items in the filmography, which is another new section we have decided to include. Release dates in keeping with albums attempt to show the release date in the country of origin. We have also tried to include both US and UK titles where applicable.

ALBUM RATING

Due to many requests from our readers we have now decided to rate all albums. All new releases are reviewed either by myself or by our team of contributors. We also take into consideration the review ratings of the leading music journals and critics' opinions.

Our system is slightly different to most 5 Star ratings in that we rate according to the artist in question's work. Therefore, a 4 Star album from Metallica may have the overall edge over a 4 Star album by Savage.

Our ratings are carefully made, and consequently you will find we are very sparing with 5 Star and 1 Star albums.

★★★★★

Outstanding in every way. A classic and therefore strongly recommended. No comprehensive record collection should be without this album.

★★★★

Excellent. A high standard album from this artist and therefore highly recommended.

★★★

Good. By the artist's usual standards and therefore recommended.

★★

Disappointing. Flawed or lacking in some way.

Poor. An album to avoid unless you are a completist.

PLAGIARISM

In maintaining the largest text database of popular music in the world we are naturally protective of its content. We license to approved licensees only. It is both flattering and irritating to see our work reproduced without credit. Time and time again over the past few years I have read an obituary, when suddenly: hang on, I wrote that line. Secondly, it has come to our notice that other companies attempting to produce their own rock or pop encyclopedias use our material as a core. Flattering this might also be, but highly illegal. We have therefore dropped a few more textual 'depth charges' in addition to the original ones. Be warned.

ACKNOWLEDGEMENTS

Our in-house editorial team is lean and efficient. Our EPM Database is now a fully grown child and needs only regular food, attention and love. Thanks to the MUZE UK team and their continuing efficiency. Susan Pipe (her train is always on time), Nic Oliver (his train is always late) and Sarah Lavelle (she used to get the bus), and the screaching solo of Roger Kohn's parrot, Acu. Our outside contributors are further reduced in number, as we now write and amend all our existing text. However, we could not function without the continuing efforts and dedication of Big John Martland and Alex Ogg.

Other past contributors' work may appear in this volume and I acknowledge with thanks once again; Simon Adams, Mike Atherton, Gavin Badderley, Alan Balfour, Michael Barnett, Essi Berilian, Johnny Black, Chris Blackford, Pamela Boniface, Keith Briggs, Michael Ian Burgess, Paul M. Brown, Tony Burke, Alan Clayson, Tom Collier, Paul Cross, Bill Dahl, Norman Darwen, Roy Davenport, Peter Doggett, Kevin Eden, John Eley, Lars Fahlin, Tim Footman, Per Gardin, Ian Garlinge, Mike Gavin, Andy Hamilton, Mark Hodkinson, Mike Hughes, Mark Jones, Simon Jones, Ian Kenyon, Dave Laing, Paul Lewis, Bernd Matheja, Chris May, Dave McAleer, Ian McCann, David McDonald, York Membery, Greg Moffitt, Nick Morgan, Michael Newman, Lyndon Noon, Zbigniew Nowara, James Nye, Ken Orton, Ian Peel, Dave Penny, John Reed, Emma Rees, Lionel Robinson, Johnny Rogan, Alan Rowett,Roy Sheridan, Dave Sissons, Steve Smith, Mitch Solomons, Jon Staines, Mike Stephenson, Sam Sutherland, Jeff Tamarkin, Ray Templeton, Gerard Tierney, Adrian T'Vell, Pete Wadeson, Ben Watson, Pete Watson, Simon Williams and Dave Wilson

Record company press offices are often bombarded with my requests for biogs and review copies. Theirs is a thankless task, but thanks anyway to them all. Thanks for the co-operation of all our colleagues at Virgin Publishing under the guidance of Rob Shreeve, in particular to ultimate rock chick, Roz Scott.

To our publicity aces, the quite heavy Pete Bassett, not to forget his road crew the Bassettes; Milly Willy, Emma Morris and Helen Winchcombe. To Kathy Huxley, who has been known to enjoy a bit of heavy rock in her time. To our owners at Muze Inc., who continue to feed the smooth running of the UK operation and are the business partners I always knew I wanted but never knew where to find. To all colleagues at the office on 304 Hudson Street in New York. In particular to the completely settled Tony Laudico, the casually cool Paul Zullo, Silvia Kessel, Steve 'Figures' Figard, Marc 'Rotosound Strings' Miller, Gary 'the tireless roadie' Geller, Raisa Howe, Chris Bugbee, Jim Allen, David Gil de Rubio (down by the schoolyard), Kim Osorio, Ric Hollander, Stephen Parker, Paul Parreirra, Terry Vinyard, Deborah Freedman, Scott 'nice beard', Lehr, Amanda Denhoff, Thom Pappalardo, Jannett Diaz, Tracey Brandon, Ed 'gentleman' Moore, Marci 'have you got a light' Weisler, Igor Leyzerzon, and Solomon Sabel. And some new Muze chums: The highly helpful Phil Fletcher, Matt 'would you buy a used car from this man' Puccini, Bill 'get your haircut' Schmitt, Mike Doustan, Duncan 'mine's a pint' Ledwith, Gail 'you guys!' Niovitch, Bernadette Eliott, and all the other Klugettes who pass me in the lift and always have a smile..

And to the laid back genius, Trev Huxley. Finally to my musically consistent tin lids, always ready to hear something new as well as my old Iron Butterfly and Spooky Tooth albums.

Colin Larkin, December 1998

A Foot In Coldwater

This prolific rock band produced four albums during their five-year career. Canadian in origin, they comprised Alex Machin (vocals), Paul Naumann (guitar), Bob Horne (keyboards), Hugh Leggat (bass) and Danny Taylor (drums). Concentrating on a traditional approach to songwriting, their work was characterized by Machin's expressive vocals and Naumann's melodic guitar lines. Leggat went on to form the Rolling Stones-influenced Private Eye, and later, a progressive outfit under his own surname.

● ALBUMS: *A Foot In Coldwater* (Love 1972)★★★, *Second Foot In Coldwater* (Love 1973)★★★, *All Around Us* (Elektra 1974)★★★, *Breaking Through* (Anthem 1977)★★★.

A II Z

This band from Manchester, England, made a small but significant contribution to the New Wave Of British Heavy Metal. Formed in 1979, they featured vocalist Dave Owens, guitarist Gary Owens, bassist Cam Campbell and drummer Karl Reti. After signing to Polydor Records and releasing the much-hyped 'No Fun After Midnight', they secured support slots to Girlschool and Black Sabbath. However, after the release of a poorly produced live album, their Iron Maiden and Samson-styled material met with increasing apathy and they disbanded. Gary Owens went on to play with Tytan, after auditioning, unsuccessfully, for Girl. In 1981 the Owens brothers re-formed the band with Tony Backhouse (bass) and ex-Tora Tora drummer Simon Wright (b. 19 June 1963). They released one single, 'I'm The One Who Loves You'. Late in 1982, Simon Wright also joined Tytan, and subsequently replaced Phil Rudd in AC/DC.

● ALBUMS: *The Witch Of Berkeley - Live* (Polydor 1980)★★.

A.C.

Formed in Boston, Massachusetts, USA, in 1988, A.C.'s career has proved as unconventional as the white-knuckle noise they produce. Their first record was a split 7-inch single in 1988, followed by a number of limited pressing singles and EPs (the best of which was the *Morbid Florist* EP), and compilation appearances. There was also a scarcely credible 7-inch with 5,345 'tracks' on it. They quickly earned themselves a reputation for what even veteran thrash metal observers decried as 'merely noise'. Spokesperson Seth admitted in the 90s that they 'broke up because our old guitarist didn't know how to play anything else on guitar'. They soon re-formed, however, with a new, more able guitarist, and a contract with Earache Records for *Everyone Should Be Killed* (only 58 songs, this time), which was described by the band itself as sounding: 'like a vacuum cleaner with us screaming over it'. *Top 40 Hits* was a little more restrained still, though dire production merely exacerbated the inaccessibility. However, cover versions of Elton John's 'I'm Still Standing' and the theme from the US television programme *The A-Team* offered light relief. The best things about the unrelentingly dreary *40 More Reasons To Hate Us* and *I Like It When You Die* were the album titles.

● ALBUMS: *Everyone Should Be Killed* (Earache 1994)★★, *Top 40 Hits* (Earache 1995)★★, *40 More Reasons To Hate Us* (Earache 1996)★★, *I Like It When You Die* (Earache 1997)★★.

Aaron, Lee

Canadian vocalist Lee Aaron (b. Karen Lynn Greening, 21 July 1962, Belleville, Ontario, Canada) first achieved notoriety by naïvely posing nude for a magazine on the advice of an unscrupulous manager, and consequently faced a struggle to prove that she had more to offer than looks alone. *The Lee Aaron Project*, recorded with backing from Triumph's Rik Emmett, Santers, Frank Soda and Moxy, was a positive step, displaying the powerful, husky Aaron voice, although the sometimes clichéd lyrics left a little to be desired. However, domestic interest resulted in a contract with Attic Records, and *Metal Queen* improved on the debut as Aaron worked with guitarists John Albani (ex-Wrabit) and George Bernhardt (ex-Hanover Fist) to produce more suitable material, the former becoming Aaron's long-term songwriting partner. *Call Of The Wild* moved in a more sophisticated direction, although Bob Ezrin's production sounded a little dated, and confident shows both headlining and supporting Bon Jovi helped Aaron to maintain her high European profile. *Lee Aaron* realized her potential at last, with Peter Coleman's sympathetic production and Aaron and Albani's work with songwriters such as Joe Lynn Turner resulting in a classy and accessible album that finally brought some domestic success. *Bodyrock* achieved Canadian double platinum sales as Aaron continued in what was a more comfortable style, and *Some Girls Do* consolidated her Canadian status, although the lack of a worldwide record contract denied her wider fame.

● ALBUMS: *The Lee Aaron Project* (Fantasy 1982)★★, *Metal Queen* (Attic 1984)★★★★, *Call Of The Wild* (Attic 1985)★★★, *Lee Aaron* (Attic 1987)★★★★, *Bodyrock* (Attic 1989)★★★, *Some Girls Do* (Attic 1991)★★★, *Emotional Rain* (Hipchic 1994)★★★.

● COMPILATIONS: *Powerline: The Best Of Lee Aaron* (Attic 1992)★★★.

● VIDEOS: *Danger Zone* (Hendring Music Video 1987), *Metal Queen* (Hendring Music Video 1991).

Aaronsrod

Angelo Jensen formed the heavy metal band Aaronsrod in 1984. Originating in Hawaii, USA, the group comprised Brian Spalding (guitar), Neil Delaforce (vocals, guitar), Edward Dysarz (bass, vocals) and Gerard Gonsalves (drums). Jensen, originally from Italy, was brought up in a vaudeville family. He made his debut at six years old and found performing to be such an exhilarating experience that he was determined to embark on a similar career. *Illusions Kill*, released in 1987, was a solid statement, culling influences from Iron Maiden and Def Leppard to a more American sound, typical of Mötley Crüe. Despite their promise, Aaronsrod remained unsuccessful, their only major break coming as support act to Ratt.

● ALBUMS: *Illusions Kill* (Roadrunner 1987)★★★.

AB/CD

Calling themselves AB/CD, a pun on the Australian group AC/DC, this Swedish rock group was formed by students Braijan (vocals), Bengus (guitar), Nalcolm (guitar), Clim (bass) and Raijmon Left (drums). They assembled in 1986 for a one-off performance at an end-of-term college party. The resemblance to AC/DC went beyond a similarity in name, extending to a propensity for heavy, good-time rock. An astute record producer brought them into the studio to record an album that was released on the Doremi label. Although the set was well received and the group was evidently talented, fears of court action by the Australian group scared off prospective overseas offers. Reluctant to perform under any other name and thus ruin the joke, the group disbanded within a year.

● ALBUMS: *Victim Of Rock* (Doremi 1986)★★★.

Abattoir

Inaugurated during 1983 in Los Angeles, California, USA, this heavy rock group was formed by Mel Sanchez (bass), Mark Caro (guitar) and Juan Garcia (guitar). With the later addition of 'Danger' Wayne (drums) and Rawl Preston (lead vocals), they performed their first concert at the Los Angeles Troubadour. By the time of Abattoir's debut studio recordings, Preston had been replaced by an ex-member of Sceptre, John Cyriis. One of the songs from this session, 'Screams From The Grave', found its way onto the compilation *Metal Massacre IV*. The result was a series of tours supporting top-flight metal acts such as W.A.S.P. and Metallica. However, by this time, the line-up had undergone some changes, with Danny Amaya replacing Wayne on drums, and disenchantment about Abattoir's progression had led to the departure of Cyriis and Garcia, who later re-emerged with their own band, Agent Steel. With the replacement guitarist Danny Olivero and singer Steve Gaines, the group continued with the recording of their debut album, *Vicious Attack*. The group suffered yet more personnel changes when Gaines left to join Bloodlust. In his place, Mike Towers' contributions developed a more subdued sound, which manifested itself on their second album. By 1988, founder-member Mel Sanchez had joined Garcia's new group, Evil Dead, signalling the demise of Abattoir.

● ALBUMS: *Vicious Attack* (Roadrunner 1985)★★, *The Only Safe Place* (Noise 1986)★★★.

Above All

Comprising Tony Maddocks (vocals), Hallam Foster (bass), Ben Doyle (guitar) and Mark Harpley (drums), rock band Above All, from Southend, Essex, England, take their primary influence from the US hardcore scene of the mid-80s and later. In particular, they have adopted that movement's 'straight-edge' creed, which insists on abstinence from drink, drugs and other artificial stimulants. Musically, they betray an obvious musical debt to American bands such as Minor Threat and Sick Of It All, but the energy of their live performances has seen them win many converts among the metal music press. In 1996 they embarked on sessions for their debut album, with former Fudge Tunnel guitarist Alex Newport acting as executive producer. Foster was replaced by Dan Carter in June 1996.

● ALBUMS: *Domain* (Roadrunner 1996)★★★.

Absu

This Texas black-metal act (although they prefer the term 'Mythological Occult Music'), led by the Emperor Proscriptor Magikus (percussion, voices), was formed in 1989 'under the moon and equinox'. The initial line-up recorded the *Temples Of Offal* EP in November 1991, after which Magikus joined Megas, along with Daviel Athron Mysticia from the band. Influenced by progressive rock as well as US and German death metal, they released their debut album in April 1993, its full title reading *Barathrum: Visita Interiora Terrae Rectificando Invenies Occultul Lapidem* (Latin for 'visiting the insides of the earth', or the abyss). Absu is the word for 'abyss' in ancient Sumerian myths, and Magikus's lyrics draw extensively from world mythology. Daviel was subsequently replaced by Shaftiel (voices, guitar), though Magikus (who is also employed as an accountant for a computer firm) remains the central figure.

● ALBUMS: *Barathrum: V.I.T.R.I.O.L.* (Osmose 1993)★★★, *The Sun Of Tiphareth* (Osmose 1995)★★★, *The Third Storm Of Cythraul* (Osmose 1997)★★★.

AC/DC

This theatrical Australian hard rock band was formed in 1973 by Malcolm Young (b. 6 January 1953, Glasgow, Scotland; rhythm guitar) after the demise of his previous outfit, the Velvet Underground (no relation to the US group). Young, whose elder brother George had already achieved stardom in Australia as a member of the Easybeats, also enlisted his younger brother, Angus Young (b. 31 March 1959, Glasgow, Scotland; guitar). Their sister later suggested that Angus wear his school uniform on stage, a gimmick that rapidly became their trademark. The two brothers made their debut appearance in a bar in Sydney on 31 December 1973, along with Dave Evans (vocals), Larry Van Knedt (bass) and Colin Burgess (drums). In 1974, the Young brothers and Evans moved to Melbourne, where Mark Evans (b. 2 March 1956, Melbourne, Australia; bass) and Phil Rudd (b. 19 May 1954, Melbourne, Australia; drums) joined the band. Another immigrant from the UK, Bon Scott (b. Ronald Scott, 9 July 1946, Kirriemuir, Scotland, d. 19 February 1980, London, England; vocals), graduated from being the band's chauffeur to becoming their vocalist when Dave Evans refused to go on stage one night in September 1974. (Evans went on to form Rabbit, releasing two albums for CBS Records in Australia, before joining Hot Cockerel in 1984 and releasing *David Evans And Thunder Down Under* in 1986.) Scott had previously recorded with two Australian outfits, pop group the Valentines (1966-68) and rockers Fraternity (1970-74). Indeed, after he emigrated from Scotland in 1951, he had also spent five consecutive years as drum champion (under-17 section) with the Perth Pipe Band. After such a wholesome start, a prison conviction for assault and battery indicated a more volatile side to his nature, and also resulted in him being refused admission to the army. In 1965 he joined the Spectors, before the aforementioned periods with the Valentines and Fraternity. The AC/DC line-up that welcomed him had already recorded a solitary single, 'Can I Sit Next To You?', but it was his voice that graced their first two albums, *High Voltage* and *TNT*. Both sets were produced by George Young and his writing partner, another former Easybeat, Harry Vanda. Neither set was issued outside Australia, though Atlantic Records in Britain did offer a selection of material from both records under the title *High Voltage* in 1976. These albums established the group as a major draw in their native territory, and brought them to the attention of Atlantic, who promptly relocated the band to London in January 1976. However, bassist Mark Evans was replaced by Cliff Williams (b. 14 December 1949, Romford, Essex, England; ex-Home) in June 1977 after the former tired of touring. He went on to Finch/Contraband, then a variety of bands including Swanee, Heaven, Best and Party Boys. Once AC/DC began to tour outside Australia, the band quickly amassed a cult following, as much for the unashamed gimmickry of its live show as for its furious, frequently risqué brand of hard rock. *Let There Be Rock* broke them as a chart act in the UK, with its contents including the perennial crowd-pleaser, 'Whole Lotta Rosie'. However, it was *Highway To Hell* in 1979 that established them as international stars. This, the band's first album with producer Mutt Lange, also proved to be their last with Bon Scott. On 19 February 1980, after a night of heavy drinking, he was left unconscious in a friend's car, and was later found to be dead, having choked on his own vomit. The coroner recorded a verdict of death by misadventure.

Scott's death threatened the band's future, but his replacement, former Geordie lead singer Brian Johnson (b. 5 October 1947, Newcastle, England), proved more than equal to the task. His first album with the band, *Back In Black*, reached number 1 in the UK and Australia, and spawned the UK number 15 single 'Rock 'n' Roll Ain't Noise Pollution'. That album was certified as having sold 12 million copies in the USA by March 1996. In 1981 *For Those About To Rock (We Salute You)* was released, the band topped the bill at the Donington Festival and also achieved two Top 20 UK singles ('Let's Get It Up' and 'For Those About To Rock (We Salute You)'). After *Flick Of The Switch* in 1983, drummer Phil Rudd left the band to become a helicopter pilot in New Zealand, and was replaced by Simon Wright (b. 19 June 1963; ex-A II Z and Tytan) - who in turn departed to join Dio in 1990. His replacement was Chris Slade (b. 30 October 1946; ex-Manfred Mann's Earth Band; Firm; and Gary Moore). In keeping with their superstar status, AC/DC maintained an increasingly relaxed schedule through the 80s, touring to support each carefully spaced album release. There were further 'casualties', however. When Malcolm Young was unfit to tour in 1988 his cousin, Stevie Young (ex-Starfighters), temporarily deputized. Paul Greg also stepped in for Cliff Williams on the US leg of their 1991 tour. A year earlier, *The Razor's Edge* had been one of the more successful albums of their later career, producing a Top 20 UK hit, 'Thunderstruck'. In 1992 they issued a live album, while the attendant single, 'Highway To Hell', made the UK Top 20. With Brian Johnson long having buried the ghost of Bon Scott, the band showed no signs of varying its winning musical formula. *Ballbreaker* in 1995 marked a powerful return after a lengthy break. The *Bonfire* box set was a fitting memorial to Bon Scott.

● ALBUMS: *High Voltage* Australia only (Albert 1975)★★, *TNT* Australia only (Albert 1975)★★, *High Voltage* (Atlantic 1976)★★, *Dirty Deeds Done Dirt Cheap* (Atlantic 1976)★★★, *Let There Be Rock* (Atlantic 1977)★★★★, *Powerage* (Atlantic 1978)★★★, *If You Want Blood, You've Got It* (Atlantic 1978)★★★, *Highway To Hell* (Atlantic 1979)★★★★, *Back In Black* (Atlantic 1980)★★★★, *For Those About To Rock (We Salute You)* (Atlantic 1981)★★★★, *Flick Of The Switch* (Atlantic 1983)★★, *'74 Jailbreak* mini-album (Atlantic 1984)★★, *Fly On The Wall* (Atlantic 1985)★★, *Who Made Who* (Atco 1986)★★★, *Blow Up Your Video* (Atlantic 1988)★★, *The Razor's Edge* (Atco 1990)★★★, *Live* (Atco 1992)★★, *Ballbreaker* (Atlantic 1995)★★★.

● COMPILATIONS: *Box Set 1* (EMI 1987)★★★, *Box Set 2* (EMI 1987)★★★, *Bonfire* 4-CD box set (EMI 1997)★★★★.

● VIDEOS: *Let There Be Rock* (Warner Home Video 1986), *Fly On The Wall* (Atlantic 1986), *High Voltage* (Virgin Vision 1988), *Who Made Who* (Warner Music Video 1991), *Live* (1992), *No Bull: Live At The Plaza Del Toros* (Warner 1996).

● FURTHER READING: *The AC/DC Story*, Paul Ezra. *AC/DC*, Malcolm Dome. *AC/DC: Hell Ain't No Bad Place To Be*, Richard Bunton. *AC/DC: An Illustrated Collectors Guide Volumes 1 & 2*, Chris Tesch. *AC/DC Illustrated Biography*, Mark Putterford. *Shock To The System*, Mark Putterford. *HM Photo Book*, no author listed. *The World's Most Electrifying Rock 'n' Roll Band*, Malcolm Dome (ed.). *Highway To Hell: The Life And Times Of AC/DC Legend Bon Scott*, Clinton Walker. *AC/DC: The World's Heaviest Rock*, Martin Huxley.

ACCEPT

This German heavy rock quintet originally comprised Udo Dirkschneider on vocals, guitarists Jan Kommet and Wolf Hoffman, drummer Frank Friedrich and bassist Peter Baltes. Formed in 1977, their power metal sound was characterized by Dirkschneider's guttural howl and the speed drumming of Stefan Kaufmann, who replaced Friedrich after the band's debut album. *Breaker* also featured guitarist Jorg Fischer, who left following a support tour to Judas Priest (although he did return briefly in the late 80s). *Restless And Wild*, from 1983, epitomized their blitzing style. This had an undeniable influence on the thrash movement that developed during the late 80s, though *Metal Heart* adopted a more melodic approach. Unhappy with this style, Dirkschneider left and formed his own outfit, Udo. A series of replacement vocalists came and went, including Rob Armitage (ex-Baby Tuckoo), David Reece and Jim Stacey (Stacey stepped in to complete tracks on *Eat The Heat* after Reece and Baltes had a physical confrontation on tour in the USA). Several lacklustre albums were released during these years that received little critical acclaim or commercial reward. Internal problems persisted, with Kaufmann contracting a muscular disease and being replaced by Ken Mary (House Of Lords). However, the band eventually disintegrated in 1989. Reece went on to form Bangalore Choir while old sparring partner Baltes contributed to Dokken. The band reunited in the 90s with a revised line-up including Dirkschneider, Hoffman, Baltes and Kaufmann.

● ALBUMS: *Accept* (Brain 1979)★★★, *I'm A Rebel* (Logo 1980)★★★, *Breaker* (Brain 1981)★★★, *Restless And Wild* (Heavy Metal 1983)★★★, *Balls To The Wall* (Portrait 1984)★★★, *Metal Heart* (Portrait 1985)★★★, *Kaizoku-Ban* (Portrait 1986)★★, *Russian Roulette* (Portrait 1986)★★★, *Eat The Heat* (RCA 1989)★★, *Staying A Life: Live*

In Japan (Epic 1990)★★★, *Objection Overruled* (RCA 1993)★★★, *Death Row* (Pavement 1995)★★★, *Steel Glove* (Castle 1996)★★, *Predator* (Sweat Shop 1997)★★★, *The Final Chapter* (CMC International 1998)★★★
● COMPILATIONS: *Best Of Accept* (Metronome 1983)★★★, *Accept* (Portrait 1986)★★★, *Hungry Years* (Razor 1991)★★★, *The Collection* (Castle 1991)★★★, *Steel Glove: The Collection* (Castle 1995)★★★, *All Areas Worldwide* (GUN 1998)★★.

ACCUSER

Derivative German heavy metal quartet, obviously influenced by Slayer and Metallica. The group was formed in 1986 by vocalist/bassist Eberhard Weyel and drummer Volker Borchert after leaving Breaker. Following a period of unsuccessful formations (including utilizing Thomas Kircher on bass), they finally recruited guitarists Frank Thomas (ex-Expect No Mercy) and Rene Schutz to record *The Conviction*. This was a powerful, if unoriginal, album, working to a set of rules and guidelines that had been drawn up by others. *Experimental Errors*, a mini-album, followed two years later. *Who Dominates Who?* continued the rigidly formularized approach, and their European tour with Mucky Pup the same year met mainly with indifference.
● ALBUMS: *The Conviction* (Atom 1987)★★★, *Experimental Errors* mini-album (Atom 1988)★★, *Who Dominates Who?* (Atom 1989)★★, *Taken By The Throat* (No Bull 1995)★★★.

ACE LANE

This UK heavy metal group was formed in 1982 by ex-Gaskin bassist Stef Prokopczuk and vocalist Mick Clarke. With drummer Roy Whyke and guitarists Gary Sleet and Paul Brook completing the line-up, they released *See You In Heaven* the following year. This featured identikit hard rock songs, distinguished by some blistering guitarwork from Sleet and Brook. Failing to secure significant sales, they were condemned to obscurity, and subsequently split.
● ALBUMS: *See You In Heaven* (Mausoleum 1983)★★.

ACHERON

Based in Florida, USA, Acheron were part of the Satanic black metal movement of the early 90s. The group's leader, guitarist and vocalist Vincent Crowley, founded the anti-Christian youth movement, the Order of the Evil Eye. Musically, the band displayed obvious death-metal roots, with their rapid hammering guitars and guttural vocal style. However, they distinguished themselves from the increasing number of Satanic metal acts appearing during the early 90s by the authenticity of their material. Much of this derives from the involvement of the Reverend Peter Gilmore, a priest in the notorious Church of Satan, who contributed not only advice on the infernal content of the lyrics, but also provided the atmospheric keyboard introductions that link the songs on Acheron's albums. *Hail Victory* constitutes an expanded version of *Satanic Victory*, adding eight songs and nine intros to the original.
● ALBUMS: *Rites Of The Black Mass* (Turbo 1992)★★, *Satanic Victory* (Turbo 1994)★★★, *Hail Victory* (Turbo 1994)★★★, *Lex Talionis* (Turbo 1995)★★★.

ACID

This Belgian heavy metal group was formed in 1980, but their material received little attention abroad. The original line-up consisted of Kate (vocals), Demon (guitar), Dizzy Lizzy (guitar), T-Bone (bass) and Anvill (drums). Their stylistic origins owed much to Previous Page, and their derivative thrash was reminiscent of Motörhead. They released their albums independently, but Kate's leather-clad dominatrix stage persona failed to earn them an appreciative audience outside of Belgium.
● ALBUMS: *Acid* (Giant 1983)★★, *Maniac* (Megaton 1983)★★, *Engine Beast* (Giant 1985)★★, *Don't Lose Your Temper* (SPV 1989)★★.

ACID BATH

This Louisiana-based metal outfit is fronted by Dax Riggs (vocals), whose music reflects the atmosphere of the swamplands. The band's material also exhibits a strong affection for the underworld and, particularly, the art of the serial killer: their debut album, produced by DRI guitarist Spike Cassidy, featured a painting by mass murderer John Wayne Gacy on its cover. Its title was described by Riggs as describing 'the state of mind you get to when you're high - the point where you're capable of just floating away from whatever connects you to the world'.
● ALBUMS: *When The Kite String Pops* (Roadrunner 1995)★★★, *Paegan Terrorism Tactics* (Rotten 1997)★★.

ACID REIGN

This heavy metal band was formed in Harrogate, Yorkshire, England, in 1987, and the original line-up consisted of H (vocals), Kev (guitar), Gaz

Jennings (guitar), Ian Gangwer (bass) and Mark Ramsey Wharton (drums). A demo tape persuaded the Music For Nations subsidiary label, Under One Flag, to sign them. Their debut, 1988's *Moshkinstein*, was a blend of Anthrax-style riffing with the band's own basic metal sound. They became popular on the UK club circuit with their quirky stage antics and down-to-earth attitude. *The Fear*, released in 1989, was thrash metal performed with humour. However, shortly after its release Jennings and Gangwer were replaced by Mac (ex-Holoslade bassist) and Adam Lehan (ex-Lord Crucifer guitarist). They continued to tour extensively, including support slots with Nuclear Assault and Exodus in Europe. They then re-recorded 'Humanoi', a track from the previous album, as well as releasing a cover version of Blondie's hit 'Hanging On The Telephone' (originally recorded by the Nerves). Their second album, *Obnoxious*, was a major musical departure, confirming their songwriting maturity. It was not, however, well received by fans of their previous releases, and, feeling disillusioned following the departure of Lehan and then Kev (the latter to Lawnmower Deth), the band split in October 1991. Under One Flag released a compilation, *The Worst Of Acid Reign*, made up of previously unreleased material, and live and demo tracks. Meanwhile, Lehan and Wharton joined Jennings in Cathedral.

● ALBUMS: *Moshkinstein* mini-album (Under One Flag 1988)★★★, *The Fear* (Under One Flag 1989)★★★★, *Obnoxious* (Music For Nations 1990)★★.

● COMPILATIONS: *The Worst Of Acid Reign* (Under One Flag 1991)★★★.

Acrophet

A thrash metal band from Brookfield, Wisconsin, USA, Acrophet were formed in 1986 by guitarist Dave Pellino. He was joined by Dave Bauman (vocals, bass), Todd Saike (guitar) and Jason Mooney (drums). Although the band were technically competent, originality was not their strong suit. Nevertheless, inspired by Anthrax, Slayer and Megadeth, they managed to release a self-produced demo within a year of formation, and by the autumn of 1988, *Corrupt Minds* was released. This brought them a little attention, and was followed by *Faded Glory* in April 1990. Although this album revealed Acrophet to be a tighter outfit, the same progression was not evident in their songwriting.

● ALBUMS: *Corrupt Minds* (Roadrunner 1988)★★, *Faded Glory* (Roadrunner 1990)★★★.

AD

Kerry Livgren (b. 18 September 1949, Kansas, USA; guitar, vocals) wasted little time after leaving Kansas before embarking on a solo career and putting together AD. Alongside Michael Gleason (vocals, keyboards), Dave Hope (bass) and Dennis Holt (drums), Livgren used the platform to peddle his new-found Christian beliefs (which had been a factor in the dissolution of Kansas). Though his solo releases also continued, Livgren proved more prolific as the leading light behind this group, who recorded in a soft rock/AOR vein. Much of the interest in this output, however, which often ventures into Yes/orchestral rock territory, is from recalcitrant former Kansas fans. That constituency would have been pleased to see the inclusion of 'Portrait' (drawn from *Point Of Know Return*, Kansas's 1977 album) on *Reconstructions*. That album also saw the introduction of vocalist Warren Ham. AD should not be confused with the 90s rap/rock group of similar name.

● ALBUMS: *Time Line* (Columbia 1984)★★, *Art Of State* (Columbia 1985)★★, *Reconstructions* (Sparrow 1987)★★★, *Prime Mover* (Sparrow 1988)★★.

Adam Bomb

This pop-metal outfit was heavily influenced by Bon Jovi and Europe. Their sex-symbol vocalist, Adam Brenner (ex-TKO), persuaded guitarist Jimmy Crespo (ex-Flame; Aerosmith), drummer Sandy Slavin (ex-Riot) and bassist Phil Feit to join forces and record *Fatal Attraction* in 1985. *Pure S.E.X.* emerged in 1990 to indifferent reviews, much of it consisting of leftover material from the first album.

● ALBUMS: *Fatal Attraction* (Geffen 1985)★★★, *Pure S.E.X.* (FM Revolver 1990)★★.

Adams, Bryan

b. Bryan Guy Adams, 5 November 1959, Kingston, Ontario, Canada. Bryan Adams has grown to be the most popular mainstream Canadian rocker of the late 80s and 90s. His solo career commenced in 1978 (having previously worked with Sweeney Todd) when he began writing songs with Jim Vallance, a former member of Prism, who was keen to retire from live work but not from songwriting. Some of these early collaborations were recorded by Loverboy, Bachman Turner Overdrive, Bonnie Tyler and others. In 1979 Adams signed a contract with A&M Records' Rondor Music, assembling a band that included Vallance on drums, plus

Ken Scott (lead guitar) and Dave Taylor (bass). Their debut single, 'Let Me Take You Dancing', was followed by a self-titled album (which featured a cameo from Jeff 'Skunk' Baxter of Steely Dan), although neither charted. He spent 1982 touring with Foreigner (whose Lou Gramm guested on the forthcoming album), the Kinks and Loverboy. The resultant *You Want It, You Got It* scraped into the lower regions of the US charts. A third album, *Cuts Like A Knife*, released in 1983, was Adams' breakthrough, reaching number 8 and going platinum in the USA (although it did not chart in the UK until three years later). It saw Vallance leave, to be replaced by Mickey Curry, though he maintained his songwriting partnership with Adams. The first single from the album, 'Straight From The Heart', also made the US Top 10 with the help of MTV airplay, and two follow-up singles, 'Cuts Like A Knife' and 'This Time', reached the Top 20 and Top 30, respectively. Adams' fourth album, *Reckless*, was issued towards the end of 1984 and topped the *Billboard* album chart. It also gave him his first major UK chart placing, reaching number 7, while the singles 'Run To You' (US number 6/UK number 11) and 'Somebody' (US number 11/UK number 35) further established Adams as a hitmaker. He enjoyed a US number 1 in mid-1985 with 'Heaven', the b-side of which was 'Diana', a tribute to the UK princess, which helped to create the tabloid headline 'Princess Di Flirts With Canadian Rock Star'. Adams was introduced by actor Jack Nicholson at the July 1985 Live Aid concert in Philadelphia, though UK audiences had to cope with transmission problems. He also co-wrote (with Vallance) and helped to perform the Canadian benefit record for Ethiopia, 'Tears Are Not Enough'. The defiant and celebratory 'Summer Of '69' returned him to the Top 10 in the USA and he ended a successful year by duetting with Tina Turner on 'It's Only Love' (though there was one further, bizarre release in December, when he coupled the festive 'Christmas Time' with 'Reggae Christmas'). His fifth album, *Into The Fire*, released in March 1987, became a Top 10 hit in both the USA and UK, boasting songs of a more political bent, informed by Adams' charity work and tours in support of Amnesty International (he is also a staunch vegetarian). It also saw the final effort of the Adams/Vallance songwriting partnership, and the end of a five-album tenure with producer Bob Clearmountain. 'Heat Of The Night' provided Adams with his fifth US Top 10 hit, although subsequent single releases fared less well. Indeed, the late 80s proved a comparatively tranquil time for the artist, as he took stock of his career and waited for a window in producer Mutt Lange's diary. He did, however, contribute to records by Mötley Crüe, Belinda Carlisle, Charlie Sexton and others. In 1988 he guested at the Nelson Mandela birthday party concert at Wembley Stadium in London, and in 1990 appeared with Roger Waters and others at the special Berlin performance of *The Wall*. All this was eclipsed, however, by his contribution to the 1991 Kevin Costner movie, *Robin Hood: Prince Of Thieves*. '(Everything I Do) I Do It For You' was a phenomenal chart success, topping the UK singles listings for an incredible 16 weeks, the longest run since Frankie Laine's 18-week domination with 'I Believe' back in 1953; it also sold three million copies and hit the number 1 position in the USA, becoming the best-selling single of that year. Its follow-up, 'Can't Stop This Thing We Started' (US number 2/UK number 11), and another powerful ballad, 'Thought I'd Died And Gone To Heaven' (US number 13/UK number 8), also charted strongly. The aforementioned singles featured on his hugely successful 1991 album, *Waking Up The Neighbours*, which underwent no less than 18 months in production before topping the UK charts. 'Please Forgive Me' extended Adams's run of UK/US Top 10 successes in late 1993. It was followed by 'All For Love', a collaboration with Sting and Rod Stewart for the 1993 movie *The Three Musketeers*, which became another major hit on both sides of the Atlantic (US number 1, UK number 2). In 1994 he undertook a major tour of South-East Asia (in the process becoming the first Western hard rock artist to visit Vietnam since the end of the war there) and bought a house in London. His latter-day commercial breakthrough may have diminished his stature in the eyes of those fans who once made up the main constituency of his followers, but as a performer and songwriter the greater body of his work remains firmly within the rock tradition. Those who do subscribe to the fact that he is a 'rocker' must have been perplexed by the Spanish tempo and lightweight Lange/Adams/Kamen song, 'Have You Ever Really Loved A Woman' (from the film *Don Juan de Marco*), which topped a number of charts around the world in the summer of 1995. Adams' finances may have been secure but his credibility as a hard-edged rocker was debatable, as the groover from Vancouver was now much smoother. The *18 'Til I Die* album attempted to restore his rocker image with limited success.

● ALBUMS: *Bryan Adams* (A&M 1980)★★★, *You Want It, You Got It* (A&M 1981)★★, *Cuts Like A Knife* (A&M 1983)★★, *Reckless* (A&M

1984)★★★★, *Into The Fire* (A&M 1987)★★★, *Live! Live! Live!* (A&M 1989)★★, *Waking Up The Neighbours* (A&M 1991)★★★, *18 'Til I Die* (A&M 1996)★★, *Unplugged* (A&M 1997)★★, *On A Day Like Today* (A&M 1998).

● COMPILATIONS: *So Far So Good* (A&M 1993)★★★★.

● VIDEOS: *Reckless* (A&M 1984), *So Far So Good And More* (A&M 1994), *MTV Unplugged* (Vision 1998).

● FURTHER READING: *Bryan Adams: The Inside Story*, Hugh Gregory. *The Illustrated Biography*, Sandy Robertson. *Bryan Adams: A Fretted Biography*, Mark Duffett. *Bryan Adams: Everything He Does*, Sorelle Saidman.

ADAMS, S.A.

One of metal's unsung underground warriors, Adams first started fusing punk with hard rock in the Fury, whose career stretched over four years and three line-ups. Previous band members have included Rick Rubin (producer), Mike Nach (Wicked Maraya) and Mike Portnoy (Dream Theater). Recording credits also add Raven, Manowar, Pro-Pain, Type O Negative and Coroner to his list of achievements. Turning solo, Adams took pains to emphasize to the press his determination to enlist musicians interested in carving their own musical niche, rather than reinterpreting prevalent trends. To this effect, he eventually found 'Big Bad Bill' Janusz (bass) and Rocky D (drums, ex-Fury) to back his guitar and potent vocals. However, this line-up only gelled after the release of his debut album, *Exiled On Green Street*, which saw him accompanied solely by a four-track and a DAT machine. The new group toured the east coast of the USA before securing a contract with Rock The Nation Records. In the summer of 1994 they recorded, then re-recorded, the album *Redemption*, and included in the process a mail-order-only CD that featured studio out-takes and live versions.

● ALBUMS: *Exiled On Green Street* (1993)★★★, *Redemption* (RTN 1994)★★★.

ADDICT

London, England rock quartet Addict arrived in 1998 with critical comparisons to Led Zeppelin, Nirvana and Bush ringing in their ears, one magazine citing them as 'one of Britrock's brightest hopes'. Singer Mark Aston conceded to the press that he could 'understand the references . . . and there is a certain substance to our work which is there in the bands we get compared to.' The rest of the band comprises James Denham (bass), Nikolaj Juel (b. Denmark, guitar) and latecomer Luke Bullen (drums). Their debut album for Richard Branson's new V2 label certainly revealed a diversity of sound and approach. Recorded in London with Dave Bianco, previously producer with the Henry Rollins Band and Red Hot Chili Peppers, the album's contents ranged stylistically from the title track's psychedelic nuances to the straightforward rock attack of 'Monsterside' and 'Dust'. The latter effort became the group's first single and took as its subject matter a difficult former relationship, though the woman concerned had the honour of becoming Aston's bride in 1998 as the group set out on a 12-month touring stint.

● ALBUMS: *Stones* (V2 1998)★★★.

ADOLESCENTS

The first line-up of the early 80s hardcore band the Adolescents, from Fullerton, Orange County, California, USA, comprised Frank Agnew (rhythm guitar), Rikk Agnew (lead guitar), Casey Royer (drums, vocals), Tony 'Montana' Brandenburg (vocals) and Steve 'Soto' Rodgers (bass, vocals). Brandenburg formed the band, enlisting the Agnews and Royer, who were all formerly members of Social Distortion. Rikk Agnew had, in addition, formerly played with several Los Angeles bands including the Detours, while Rodgers had been part of Agent Orange. Following a flirtation with Posh Boy Records (the 'Amoeba' single, of which only 15 copies were pressed), the band's debut emerged on Frontier Records in 1981. Immediately afterwards, the band collapsed. Rikk Agnew went on to release a solo album for Frontier the following year, which largely consisted of songs written for the intended second Adolescents album. Afterwards, he played with both Christian Death and TSOL. The Adolescents re-formed for reunion gigs in 1986 and effectively became an active unit once more. *Brats In Battalions*, released on the group's own label, included guitarist Alfie Agnew deputizing for brother Frank on a powerful punk/metal hybrid. The line-up switched for *Balboa Fun*Zone*, but the songwriting of the remaining original members, Agnew and Rodgers, was seen to its best advantage. It was followed by a live album drawn from concerts recorded five years apart. Agnew's second solo effort, credited to Rikk Agnew's Yard Sale, featured his returning two brothers, Alfie and Frank. The Adolescents finally called it a day in 1989, though further reunions are feasible given the band's previous record.

● ALBUMS: *Adolescents* (Frontier 1981)★★★,

Brats In Battalions (SOS 1987)★★★, *Balboa Fun*Zone* (Triple X 1988)★★★★, *Live 1981 and 1986* (Triple X 1989)★★★.
Solo: Rikk Agnew *All By Myself* (Frontier 1982)★★★, as Rikk Agnew's Yard Sale *Emotional Vomit* (Triple X 1990)★★★.

ADRENALIN

This sophisticated AOR outfit, influenced by Styx, Foreigner and Journey, was founded by the Romeo and Pastoria brothers in 1984. The seven-piece band comprised Marc Gilbert (vocals), Flash (guitar), Michael Romeo (guitar), Jimmy Romeo (saxophone), Marc Pastoria (keyboards), Bruce Schafer (bass) and Brian Pastoria (drums). Adrenalin were signed by MCA and released two credible, melodic rock albums. The title track of *Road Of The Gypsy* was also included on the *Iron Eagle* film soundtrack. Success, however, eluded the band and they were dropped by their label in 1987. That year also saw the departure of Gilbert and Flash, with ex-Grand Funk Railroad vocalist and guitarist Mark Farner (b. 29 September 1948, Flint, Michigan, USA) stepping in as replacement. As Grand Funk songs started to appear in their live set, so the band eventually became known as Mark Farner And Adrenalin. Unable to secure a recording contract or attract media attention, Farner left the following year, with Joey Hammody taking over as the new vocalist soon afterwards.

● ALBUMS: *American Heart* (MCA 1985)★★, *Road Of The Gypsy* (MCA 1986)★★★.

ADRENALIN OD

Formed in October 1981 in New Jersey, USA, the hardcore band Adrenalin OD originally comprised Paul Richard (vocals), Jack Steeples (bass), Dave Scott (drums) and Jim Foster (guitar). Following their 1983 debut (the six-track *Let's Barbeque With Adrenalin OD* EP, for their own Buy Our Records label), Foster was replaced by Bruce Wingate on guitar. *The Wacky Hi-Jinks Of Adrenalin OD* delighted in song titles such as 'A.O.D. Vs Godzilla' and 'Middle Aged Whore', and featured rousing three-minute punk pop songs. The logical progression was to tackle 'A.O.D. Vs Son Of Godzilla' on the follow-up, 1986's *Humungousfungusamongus*, and that is exactly what the band did, this time with the aid of hugely improved studio technique. The Ramones' producer Daniel Rey joined the band in time for *Cruisin' With Elvis In Bigfoot's UFO*, which continued the group's preoccupation with monster movies and other offbeat subjects, notably 'Bulemic Food Fight' and 'Something About ... Amy Carter'. By this point the band had slowed down their sound, now relying on a more conventional, yet still energized, rock 'n' roll platform. Produced by Andy Shernoff (Dictators/Wild Kingdom), *Ishtar* did not advance on previous gains, despite the band tackling Queen's 'Sheer Heart Attack' (they had previously covered the same band's 'We Will Rock You' on a 1985 split EP with Bedlam). The band have continued recording into the 90s.

● ALBUMS: *Let's Barbecue With Adrenalin OD* mini-album (Buy Our Records 1983)★★, *The Wacky Hi-Jinks Of Adrenalin OD* (Buy Our Records 1984)★★, *Humungousfungusamongus* (Buy Our Records 1986)★★★, *Cruising With Elvis In Bigfoot's UFO* (Buy Our Records 1988)★★★, *Ishtar* (Restless 1990)★★, *Theme From An I* (Buy Our Records 1992)★★, *Sittin' Pretty* (Grand Theft Auto 1996)★★.

AEROSMITH

One of the USA's most popular hard-rock acts, Aerosmith were formed in 1970 when vocalist Steven Tyler (b. Steven Victor Tallarico, 26 March 1948, New York, USA; vocals) met Joe Perry (b. Anthony Joseph Perry, 10 September 1950, Boston, Massachusetts, USA; guitar) while the latter was working in a Sunapee, New Hampshire ice cream parlour, the Anchorage. Tyler was in the area visiting the family-owned holiday resort, Trow-Rico. Perry, then playing in the Jam Band, invited Tyler (who had previously released one single, 'When I Needed You', with his own band Chain Reaction, and another, 'You Should Have Been Here Yesterday', with William Proud And The Strangeurs) to join him in a Cream-styled rock combo. Together with fellow Jam Band member Tom Hamilton (b. 31 December 1951, Colorado Springs, Colorado, USA; bass) and new recruits Joey Kramer (b. 21 June 1950, New York, USA; drums) and Ray Tabano (guitar), the group's founding line-up was complete. However, Tabano was quickly replaced by the former member of Justin Tyme, Earth Inc., Teapot Dome and Cymbals Of Resistance, Brad Whitford (b. 23 February 1952, Winchester, Massachusetts, USA). After playing their first gig at the Nipmuc Regional High School, the band took the name Aerosmith (rejecting other early monikers including 'Hookers'). Their popularity throughout the Boston area grew rapidly, and a triumphant gig at Max's Kansas City, witnessed by Clive Davis, led to a recording contract with Columbia/CBS Records. In 1973 Aerosmith secured a minor chart placing with their self-titled debut album. Although its attendant single, 'Dream On', initially peaked at number 59, it became a Top 10 hit in April 1976. *Get Your Wings* inaugurated a fruitful working relationship with producer Jack Douglas. Nationwide tours established the quintet as a major attraction, a position consolidated by the highly successful *Toys In The Attic*, which has now sold in excess of six million copies worldwide. A fourth album, *Rocks*, achieved platinum status within months of its release. Aerosmith maintained their pre-eminent position with *Draw The Line* and the powerful *Live! Bootleg*, but despite popular acclaim, they failed to gain the approbation of many critics who dubbed the group 'derivative', particularly of Led Zeppelin. Tyler's physical resemblance to Mick Jagger, and his foil-like relationship with guitarist Perry, also inspired comparisons with the Rolling Stones, with whom they shared several musical reference points. In 1978 the group undertook a US tour of smaller, more intimate venues in an attempt to decelerate their rigorous schedule. They appeared in the ill-fated *Sgt. Pepper's Lonely Hearts Club Band* film (as the Future Villain band), and although their rousing version of 'Come Together' reached the US Top 30, tension between Tyler and Perry proved irreconcilable. The guitarist left the group following the release of the disappointing *Night In The Ruts* and subsequently founded the Joe Perry Project. Jimmy Crespo joined Aerosmith in 1980, but the following year Brad Whitford left to pursue a new career with former Ted Nugent band member, guitarist Derek St. Holmes. Newcomer Rick Dufay debuted on *Rock In A Hard Place*, but this lacklustre set failed to capture the fire of the group's classic recordings. Contact between the group and Perry and Whitford was re-established during a 1984 tour. Antagonisms were set aside, and the following year, the quintet's most enduring line-up was performing together again. The first fruits of a lucrative new contract with Geffen Records, the Ted Templeman-produced *Done With Mirrors* was a tentative first step, after which Tyler and Perry underwent a successful rehabilitation programme to rid themselves of drug and alcohol dependency, synonymous with the group's hedonistic lifestyle. In 1986 they accompanied rappers Run DMC on 'Walk This Way', an Aerosmith song from *Toys In The Attic* and a former US Top 10 entry in its own right. The collaboration was an international hit, rekindling interest in Aerosmith's career, with the following year's 'Dude (Looks Like A Lady)' reaching number 14 in the US charts. Recorded with producer Bruce Fairbairn, *Permanent Vacation* became one of their best-selling albums, and the first to make an impression in the UK, while the highly acclaimed *Pump* and *Get A Grip* (also produced by Fairbairn) emphasized their revitalization. Fêted by a new generation of acts, including Guns N'Roses, the quintet are now seen as elder statesmen, but recent recordings show them leading by example. Those wishing to immerse themselves in this extraordinary band should invest in the impressive 13-CD box set *Box Of Fire*, which comes complete with rare bonus tracks and a free, ready-to-strike match! *Big Ones* was a well-chosen compilation, satisfying long-term fans, but more importantly, it introduced a younger audience to a dinosaur group who still sound fresh and exciting, have refused to compromise and certainly have not 'gone soft'. The band returned to Columbia Records in the mid-90s and spent an age recording *Nine Lives*. In Tyler's words, 'this album has taken me as far as I've ever wanted to go and gotten me back again'. It was worth the wait, bearing all the usual trademarks, and yet sounding strangely fresh. The hit single 'Falling In Love (Is Hard On The Knees)' preceded its release in February 1997. Although Tyler has reached his half-century, he still seems ageless on stage - even Jagger and Bruce Springsteen seem jaded compared to this rock 'n' roll ballet-dancer, apparently still in his prime. In September 1998, the band achieved their first ever US number 1 with the Diane Warren-penned 'I Don't Want To Miss A Thing', taken from the soundtrack of the movie *Armageddon*.

● ALBUMS: *Aerosmith* (Columbia 1973)★★★, *Get Your Wings* (Columbia 1974)★★★, *Toys In The Attic* (Columbia 1975)★★★★, *Rocks* (Columbia 1976)★★★★, *Draw The Line* (Columbia 1977)★★★, *Live! Bootleg* (Columbia 1978)★★★, *Night In The Ruts* (Columbia 1979)★★, *Rock In A Hard Place* (Columbia 1982)★★, *Done With Mirrors* (Geffen 1985)★★★, *Permanent Vacation* (Geffen 1987)★★★, *Pump* (Geffen 1989)★★★★, *Get A Grip* (Geffen 1993)★★★★, *Nine Lives* (Columbia 1997)★★★★, *A Little South Of Sanity* (Columbia 1998)★★★★.

● COMPILATIONS: *Aerosmith's Greatest Hits* (Columbia 1980)★★★★, *Classics Live!* (Columbia 1986)★★, *Classics Live II* (Columbia 1987)★★★, *Gems* (Columbia 1988)★★★, *Anthology* (Raw Power/Castle 1988)★★, *Pandora's Box* box set (Columbia 1991)★★★, *Big Ones* (Geffen 1994)★★★★, *Box Of Fire* 13-CD box set (Columbia 1994)★★★★, *Classics Live Complete* (Columbia 1998)★★★.

● VIDEOS: *Video Scrapbook* (Hendring Music

Video 1988), *Live Texas Jam '78* (CMV Enterprises 1989), *Things That Go Pump In The Night* (Warner Music Video 1990), *The Making Of Pump* (Sony Music Video 1991), *Big Ones You Can Look At* (1994).

● FURTHER READING: *The Fall And Rise Of Aerosmith*, Mark Putterford. *Live!*, Mark Putterford. *Get A Grip*, Aerosmith. *Toys In The Attic: The Rise, Fall And Rise Of Aerosmith*, Martin Huxley. *What It Takes*, Dave Bowler and Brian Dray. *Dream On: Living On The Edge With Steven Tyler*, Cyrinda Foxe-Tyler and Danny Fields. *Walk This Way: The Autobiography Of Aerosmith*, Aerosmith and Stephen Davis.

AFGHAN WHIGS

From Cincinnati, Ohio, and original stalwarts of the Sub Pop Records empire, in the 90s Afghan Whigs were widely classified as favoured proponents of grunge, although there are considerable traditional elements to their music. Their *Uptown Avondale* EP, for example, was a collection of classic soul cover versions, while as early as *Up In It*, they were bastardizing country rock on tracks such as 'Son Of The South'. The band numbers Rick McCollum (b. 14 July 1965, Kentucky, USA; guitar), Steven Earle (b. 28 March 1966, Cincinnati, USA; drums) and John Curley (b. 15 March 1965, Trenton, New Jersey, USA; bass), alongside the distinctive vocals ('I think Camel cigarettes are a big influence on my voice') of frontman Greg Dulli (b. 11 May 1965, Ohio, USA; vocals, guitar). With his origins in Hamilton, a steel-town 30 miles outside Cincinnati, Dulli abandoned his film course in an attempt to pick up acting parts (apparently making it into the last 50 at the auditions for *The Breakfast Club*'s 'weirdo'). He first met bassist Curley in jail, where they were being held overnight for, respectively, urinating in front of a police officer and drug-dealing. When Afghan Whigs provoked the interest of the major labels, Dulli insisted that he produce their records and direct their videos (in fact, before signing, Dulli had handled band management). Elektra Records agreed to his conditions, and to financing a movie project. Their major label debut, *Gentlemen*, concerned familiar Afghan Whigs subjects: alienation and the seedier side of life. One of the songs, 'My Curse', was so personal that Dulli could not sing it himself - instead employing Marcy Mays of Scrawl. Marketing the album also became the subject of a College Music Journal seminar. Earle was subsequently replaced by Paul Buchignani. In 1994 Dulli was part of the supergroup who recorded a soundtrack for *Backbeat*, the Stuart Sutcliffe (Beatles) biopic, singing as John Lennon. Other band members were Mike Mills (R.E.M.), Don Fleming (Gumball), Dave Grohl (Nirvana and Foo Fighters) and Thurston Moore (Sonic Youth). Dulli also covered Barry White's 'Can't Get Enough Of Your Love' for the soundtrack to *Beautiful Girls*. *Black Love* confirmed the soul influence, and featured cover versions of Marvin Gaye's 'Let's Get It On' and the Who's 'Quadrophenia'.

● ALBUMS: *Big Top Halloween* (Ultrasuede 1988)★★★, *Up In It* (Sub Pop 1990)★★★, *Congregation* (Sub Pop 1992)★★★, *Gentlemen* (Sub Pop/Elektra 1994)★★★, *What Jail Is Like* mini-album (Sub Pop/Elektra 1994)★★, *Black Love* (Sub Pop/Elektra 1996)★★★, *1965* (Columbia 1998).

AFTER HOURS

This British heavy rock band, based in Southampton, was formed from the ashes of XS and Love Attack. Comprising John Francis (vocals), Tim Payne (guitar), Rick Young (keyboards), Martin Walls (bass) and Mark Addison (drums), After Hours specialized in melodic pomp/AOR, although tougher edges were also occasionally apparent. *Take Off*, their debut, was an excellent collection of songs in the Foreigner/Whitesnake tradition. Afterwards, the line-up fluctuated to accommodate Andy Nye (keyboards, ex-MSG) and Alan Jackman (drums, ex-Outfield), until further sightings became increasingly rare.

● ALBUMS: *Take Off* (FM Revolver 1988)★★★.

AFTERMATH

This lacklustre heavy metal band originated from Tucson, Arizona, USA, and were formed by vocalist Richard Shayka and guitarist Cliff Finney in 1984. Enlisting the services of John E. January (guitar), Joe Nutt (bass) and Rick Von Glahn (drums), they recorded a self-titled eight-track demo that was rejected by many major labels in the USA. However, newly formed Dutch label Mushroom signed them in 1988. *Don't Cheer Me Up* materialized the same year, a derivative collection of melodic metal, with the occasional anthemic number and power ballad included. This Aftermath was a different band to the Chicago doom metal merchants who had two songs issued on the *Metal Forces* album in the UK.

● ALBUMS: *Don't Cheer Me Up* (Mushroom 1988)★★.

AGENT

This Canadian heavy rock quintet was formed in Vancouver in 1981, by the three-man nucleus of Bob Smart (guitar), Craig Zurba (keyboards) and Andre Kunkel (bass). After a series of short-lived line-ups, they stabilized with the addition of vocalist Rick Livingstone and drummer Dave Allen in 1983. They attracted the interest of Virgin Records after winning a 'Battle Of The Bands' contest, and were approached by ex-Doobie Brothers Jeff 'Skunk' Baxter, who produced their debut album. Influenced by Foreigner, Styx, Kansas and Loverboy, their style was commercial, though unspectacular, melodic rock.

● ALBUMS: *Agent* (Virgin 1986)★★.

AGENT ORANGE

Named after the chemical defoliant so chillingly used by the USA in the Vietnam War, Agent Orange were one of a number of bands formed in the highly active 'So-Cal' hardcore scene of Fullerton, Orange County, Los Angeles. The original line-up comprised Mike Palm (vocals, guitar), Steve 'Soto' Rodgers (bass) and Scott Miller (drums). However, Rodgers left early in their development to form another local punk attraction, the Adolescents. His replacement was James Levesque. The band's first important supporter was KROQ disc jockey Rodney Bingenheimer, who was fundamental to the promotion of many similar outfits. Their debut release, the *Bloodstains* EP, was the only one to feature Rodgers, and its title track was the first song the fledgling group wrote. Afterwards, they signed to prominent local label Posh Boy Records, run by Robbie Fields. The subsequent debut album showed the band rising above the usual three-chord bluster of hardcore with a melodic approach that recalled 60s surf instrumental bands (the Ventures being the most obvious influence). However, the group stormed out of the studio near to the album's completion, complaining about being 'produced' and Fields' behaviour in general, leaving engineer David Hines and Jay Lansford (of Simpletones, Stepmothers and Channel 3 fame) to finish off the recordings. The *Bitchin' Summer EP* was one of the first skate/surf punk crossover items, with three energized surf guitar instrumentals establishing the group's future direction. Various problems delayed the next release until the group signed with Enigma Records for 1984's *When You Least Expect It ... EP*, which saw a conscious and largely unsuccessful attempt to accommodate a more disciplined, polished sound, a mistake compounded by a pointless cover version of Jefferson Airplane's 'Somebody To Love'. However, all the elements came together for *This Is The Voice* - the overdriven guitar mesh now allied to first-rate songwriting and delivery. This time the cover of 'Dangerman' was fine, but subordinate to the Agent Orange originals. Levesque had been replaced by Brent Liles (ex-Social Distortion) a year later, although they have been largely quiet since, save for a 1991 live album and various reissues.

● ALBUMS: *Living In Darkness* (Posh Boy 1981)★★, *This Is The Voice* (Enigma 1986)★★★, *Real Live Sound* (Restless 1991)★★.

AGENT STEEL

This heavy metal unit was formed in Los Angeles, California, USA, and had existed in various guises since the early 80s. The most popular line-up consisted of John Cyriis (vocals, ex-Abattoir), Juan Garcia (guitar, ex-Abattoir), Bernie Versye (guitar), Michael Zaputil (bass) and Chuck Profus (drums). Signing to Combat Records, the band released their debut, *Operation Redeye*, in 1985, but it was the same year's *Skeptics Apocalypse* that was most popular with both music press and public. However, the group experienced difficulty with their record label and internal wrangles owing to Cyriis's reputed eccentricity. With label problems resolved, the band released an EP entitled *Mad Locust Rising*, and quickly followed this with their finest recording, the trash-fixated *Unstoppable Force*. However, they experienced further disruption when Cyriis decided he wanted to relocate the band to Florida. The rest of the group were less than delighted with the provisional change in locale and left (or rather, stayed). Cyriis continued with various musicians in the new location, but was never able to match previous standards. Disillusioned, he dissolved the group in 1988, and, after a brief tenure alongside Profus in Pontius Prophet, has since left the music business. Garcia joined Evil Dead.

● ALBUMS: *Operation Redeye* (Combat 1985)★★, *Skeptics Apocalypse* (Combat 1985)★★★, *Unstoppable Force* (Music For Nations 1987)★★★.

● VIDEOS: *Mad Locust Rising* (Jettisoundz 1989).

AGENTZ

Led by Patrick Dubs (vocals) and Jose Ferro (bass) and completed by John Cappadona (drums), Jason Sabo (guitar) and Tommy Tindall (keyboards), Agentz specialized in a harder-edged AOR sound, reminiscent of Visitor or Saint. Despite the obvious quality of the material on offer, Agentz were sadly restricted by the budget available for the production (performed by Ferro and Dubs), and unlike Saint or Bystander, the lack of gloss generated on a shoestring remains the overriding impression of their album.

● ALBUMS: *Stick To Your Guns* (Dream 1987)★★.

AGNES STRANGE

Agnes Strange, a hard rock/blues group based in Southampton, Hampshire, England, formed in the mid-70s and quickly acquired a recording contract with Birds Nest Records - an affiliate label distributed by Pye Records. Comprising Alan Green (bass), Dave Rodwell (drums) and John Westwood (guitar, vocals), they made their debut in 1975 with *Strange Flavour*, a perfunctory but expertly played collection of original rock songs that failed to bring them to the attention of the mainstream. They broke up shortly thereafter, though members of the band remained active on the Hampshire club scene.

● ALBUMS: *Strange Flavour* (Birds Nest 1975)★★★.

AGNOSTIC FRONT

Originally comprising Roger Miret (vocals), Alex Kinon (guitar), Vinnie Stigma (guitar), Rob Kabula (bass) and Louie Beatto (drums), Agnostic Front were the epitome of New York hardcore bands of the mid-80s. Growing up onstage at CBGB's, like many of that scene's participants, as their career progressed they adopted elements that instead identified them more with the heavy metal scene. Politically not the most circumspect of bands, even by hard rock's standards, their avowed right-wing stance and staunch nationalism served to set them apart from other punk and hardcore bands. Miret spat out the lyrics with quite remarkable ferocity (he apparently spent his spare time breeding pit bull terriers). Following *Cause For Alarm*, Jimmy Merrick replaced Beatto on drums, while guitarist Matt Henderson joined for *One Voice*. This featured lyrics written by Miret during an 18-month prison sentence on drugs charges. Temporary vocalist Alan Peters went on to join Crawlpappy on his release. Although their reputation grew over the years, little changed in Agnostic Front's musical formula, their principal strength always remaining the live arena. They played their last live show together at CBGB's on 20 December 1992. Miret's younger brother, Freddy Cricien, meanwhile, formed Madball with other former members of Agnostic Front.

● ALBUMS: *Victim In Pain* (Rat Cage 1984)★★, *Cause For Alarm* (Combat Core 1986)★★★, *Liberty & Justice For...* (Combat 1987)★★★, *Live At CBGB* (In-Effect/Relativity 1989)★★, *One Voice* (Relativity 1991)★★★, *Last Warning* (Relativity 1993)★★★, *Something's Gotta Give* (Epitaph 1998)★★★.

AIR RAID

This short-lived US quartet specialized in sophisticated and melodic symphonic rock. The band originated in 1980 and featured Arthur Offen (vocals, keyboards), Rick Hinkle (guitar), Tommy Walker (bass) and Rick Brown (drums). Their self-titled debut, released in 1981, was strongly reminiscent of Styx and Journey. Technically, the group were proficient, but they lacked the necessary spark of originality to make any real impact. Failing to attract media attention, they disbanded shortly after the album was released.

● ALBUMS: *Air Raid* (20th Century 1981)★★.

AIREY, DON

Airey is a talented UK keyboard player, who contributed to a wide range of bands and projects during the 70s and 80s. Unable to make a long-term commitment (or, perhaps, to find the right musicians with whom to work), he has made short-lived appearances with Colosseum II, Rainbow, Ozzy Osbourne, Whitesnake, Black Sabbath, MSG, Alaska, Jethro Tull and Gary Moore. In 1986 he decided to concentrate on a solo project. *K2* was an ambitious concept album centred on the mystique of the second highest mountain in the world, and the dangers of climbing it. With the help of Gary Moore, Cozy Powell and Colin Blunstone, the album came to life, but appealed more to new-age music aficionados than to serious rock fans.

● ALBUMS: *K2, Tales Of Triumph And Agony* (MCA 1986)★★.

AIRBORNE

This US AOR band released a single album in 1979 before going their separate ways, although some members found commercial success elsewhere. Consisting of Larry Stewart (vocals, guitar, keyboards), Mike Baird (drums), Beau Hill (vocals, guitar, keyboards), David Zychek (vocals, guitar) and John Pierce (vocals, bass), the album remains one of the better examples of late 70s American AOR. Despite an accent on radio-friendly hooks in the likes of 'No Exception To The Rule' and 'Wastin' My Time', the pristine vocal harmonies that epitomize the genre and a highly polished production from DeVore and Olsen, the album was, perhaps surprisingly, a failure and no second album was forthcoming. Hill joined Shanghai before finding his *métier* as a producer (particularly with Ratt), and Baird went on to become one of AOR's most sought-after session drummers, enjoying stints with Van Stephenson, Giant and Journey.

● ALBUMS: *Airborne* (Columbia 1979)★★★.

AIRRACE

This British heavy rock quintet was formed in 1983 by vocalist Keith Murrell and guitarist Laurie Mansworth. Recruiting Jim Reid (bass), Jason Bonham (b. 1967, England; drums) and Toby Sadler (keyboards), they signed to Atlantic Records the same year. The band's most striking feature was the highly accomplished vocal style of Murrell. His powerful Lou Gramm-like singing led to obvious Foreigner comparisons, but in an approbatory rather than critical sense. Their Beau Hill-produced debut, released in 1984, flopped, but remains a classic of the melodic rock genre. The band split up soon after its release, with Murrell joining Mama's Boys and Bonham (son of Led Zeppelin's John Bonham) forming Virginia Wolf, then Bonham. Mansworth resurrected Airrace in 1986 with a new line-up, but the band quickly vanished again.

● ALBUMS: *Shaft Of Light* (Atlantic 1984)★★★.

ALASKA

This UK heavy rock unit was the phoenix that rose from the ashes of Bernie Marsden's S.O.S. Marsden, also a veteran of Babe Ruth, Wild Turkey and Whitesnake, was joined by Robert Hawthorn (vocals), Brian Badhams (bass, piano), Richard Bailey (keyboards) and John Marter (drums, ex-Mr. Big; Marillion). The band produced symphonic rock with pomp and circumstance, Hawthorn's vocals contrasting subtly with Marsden's blues-influenced style. The band's first big break came in 1984, when they supported Manowar at the Headbanger's Ball in Holland. After two albums, Alaska disintegrated, with Marsden joining the MGM, who split up before releasing any material. Alaska's 'Headlines' was used in a UK television commercial in 1988 for the *Sunday Sport* newspaper and was reissued as a single, but failed to reach the charts.

● ALBUMS: *Heart Of The Storm* (Music For Nations 1984)★★★, *The Pack* (Music For Nations 1985)★★.

● VIDEOS: *Alaska Alive* (Virgin Vision 1990).

ALBINI, STEVE

b. USA. Though he first rose to prominence as a musician, Albini's most high-profile work has come as a producer in the 90s. His first band was the caustic Big Black - powered by Albini's monolithic guitar playing, which took punk rock to its logical conclusion. That band's work is worth assessing in terms of Albini's later production work, in particular the low mixing of the vocals that became a feature of his subsequent output. After Big Black he formed Rapeman - an impressive band whose short career was continually overshadowed by the 'offence' its name caused. In the meantime, Albini was establishing a second career as a producer. Artists including the Pixies, Wedding Present, PJ Harvey and Nirvana all prospered from his employment. Although he often insisted he was merely a 'good engineer', the evidence of records such as *Surfer Rosa* (Pixies), *In Utero* (Nirvana) and *Rid Of Me* (PJ Harvey) argued against such modesty. He also remained one of American underground music's most controversial figures, attacking figures in the mainstream such as Urge Overkill (another of his previous production assignments) and many others for what he considered a lack of integrity. Another tenet of his Big Black days - that of a preference for vinyl over CD, which he once famously christened 'the rich man's eight-track', was maintained. He continued to insist that most of his productions were completed merely to 'pay the rent', and he took particular relish in charging exorbitant fees for artists signed to major record labels, allowing him to work with favoured artists (Scrawl, Jesus Lizard, etc.) for comparatively trivial sums. After the demise of Rapeman he regularly stated to the press how much he missed being part of a band, and it therefore came as little surprise when he formed the typically uncompromising Shellac in 1993.

ALCATRAZZ

This American band were heavy metal exponents in the Deep Purple tradition. Formed by ex-MSG and Rainbow vocalist Graham Bonnet (b. 12 December 1947, Skegness, Lincolnshire, England) in 1983, the initial line-up featured virtuoso guitarist Yngwie Malmsteen (b. 30 June 1963, Sweden), former New England members Jimmy Waldo (keyboards) and Gary Shea (bass), plus former Alice Cooper drummer Jan Uvena. *No Parole From Rock 'n' Roll* was chest-thumping hard rock in the David Coverdale/Ronnie James Dio style, complete with intricately textured and classically influenced guitar breaks. Steve Vai (b. 6 June 1960, Long Island, New York, USA; ex-Frank Zappa) replaced Malmsteen after a disappointing live album to record 1985's *Disturbing The Peace*. This was a disjointed affair comprising a mixture of heavy rock and instrumental showcase numbers. Vai joined David Lee Roth's band in 1986, with ex-Axis guitarist Danny Johnson replacing him. *Dangerous Games* followed but was poorly received, lacking both power and direction. The band broke up in 1987 with Johnson forming Private Life and Bonnet teaming up with guitarist Chris Impelliteri.

● ALBUMS: *No Parole From Rock 'n' Roll* (Rockshire 1983)★★★, *Live Sentence* (Rockshire 1984)★★, *Disturbing The Peace* (Capitol 1985)★★★, *Dangerous Games* (Capitol 1986)★★.

ALEXA

Discovered by Paul Sabu (Only Child; Sabu), this Switzerland-born, USA-based vocalist (b. Alexa Anastasia) combined hard rock overtures with pop hooks. Sabu produced her debut album, which invited comparisons to Lita Ford and Lee Aaron, but was unable to sell in sufficient numbers to attract wider interest.

● ALBUMS: *Alexa* (Savage 1989)★★.

ALIAS (CANADA)

Comprising ex-members of Heart in Roger Fisher (b. 14 February 1950; guitar), Steve Fossen (b. 15 November 1949; bass) and Michael Derosier (b. 24 August 1951, Canada; drums) and a posse of ex-Sherriff men, Freddy Curci (vocals) and Steve De Marchi (keyboards), Alias were a largely unheralded supergroup when their debut was released in 1990. Under the production wing of Rick Neigher (ex-Avalon) and with songs penned mainly by the band, with some input from outside writers such as Jeff Paris and Fee Waybill (ex-Tubes), they made an immediate impact in the US charts, enjoying hit singles with 'Waiting For Love' and 'More Than Words Can Say'. Featuring the distinctive vocal style of Curci, Alias bore similarities to both bands from which membership had been drawn, as well as the most successful AOR bands of the 80s, Journey and Foreigner. Commercial success was not enough, however, to ensure a second album, and in 1994 Curci returned with a solo album, *Dreamer's Road*, on EMI Records, which marked a disappointing move away from his rock roots to a smooth and sophisticated balladic approach.

● ALBUMS: *Alias* (EMI 1990)★★★.

ALIAS (USA)

This hard rock band was formed in Sarasota, Florida, USA, in March 1985, and was originally called Blitz. The band comprised Mark Severns (guitar), Phil Arnt (percussion), Carl Hayden (vocals) and Dirk Van Tilborg (bass, keyboards), who met while playing in local cover bands. Combining diverse influences ranging from Frank Zappa to Weather Report, as well as more traditional metal outfits (Scorpions, Dokken), they recorded their first demo in July 1985. Signing to Grudge Records in February 1987, their debut mini-album was released six months later. Relocating to Los Angeles in 1989 the group backed several major artists, including Ace Frehley, White Lion and Night Ranger. However, it was seven years before the release of a second album in 1994, which attempted to build 'classic metal' songs around clean production and exemplary playing technique. They should not be confused with the Canadian Alias, inaugurated by former members of Sherriff.

● ALBUMS: *Alias* mini-album (Grudge 1987)★★, *Metal To Infinity* (RTN 1990)★★★.

ALICE COOPER

b. Vincent Damon Furnier, 4 February 1948, Detroit, Michigan, USA. Alice Cooper became known as the 'master of shock rock' during the 70s and remained a popular hard-rock artist into the 90s. The Furnier family moved to Phoenix, Arizona, where Vincent began writing songs while in junior high school. Inspired by a dream to become as famous as the Beatles and Rolling Stones, Furnier formed a group in the early 60s called the Earwigs. By 1965 their name had changed to the Spiders and then the Nazz (no relation to Todd Rundgren's band of the same name). Both the Spiders and Nazz played at local dances and recorded singles that were moderately popular regionally. In 1968, the Nazz, which also included Mike Bruce (b. 21 November 1948, California, USA; lead guitar), Dennis Dunaway (b. 15 March 1946, California, USA; bass), Glen Buxton (b. 17 June 1947, Washington, DC, USA, d. 18 October 1997, Iowa, USA; guitar) and Neal Smith (b. 10 January 1946, Washington, USA; drums), changed its name to Alice Cooper, reportedly due to Furnier's belief that he was the reincarnation of a 17th-century witch of that name. The name Alice Cooper was also attached to Furnier, who invented an androgynous, outrageously attired persona to attract attention. The band played deliberately abrasive rock music with the intention of shocking and even alienating those attending its concerts. In 1969 the Alice Cooper band found a kindred spirit in Frank Zappa, who signed them to his new Straight Records label. The group recorded two albums, *Pretties For You* and *Easy Action*, before switching to Straight's parent label, Warner Brothers Records, in 1970. By that time, Cooper had adopted more extreme tactics in his live performances, using a guillotine and electric chair as stage props and a live snake as part of his wardrobe. The finishing touch was the thick, black eye make-up that dripped down his face, affording him his trademark demonic appearance. As the group and its singer built a reputation as a bizarre live act, their records began to sell in greater quantities. In 1971 'Eighteen' was their first single to reach the US charts, at number 21. Cooper's commercial breakthrough came the following year with the rebellious 'School's Out' single and album, both of which made the US Top 10, with the single topping the UK chart. A streak of bestselling albums followed: the number 1 *Billion Dollar Babies*, then *Muscle Of Love*, *Alice Cooper's Greatest Hits* and *Welcome To My Nightmare*, all of which reached the US Top 10. The last was his first true solo album following the dissolution of the band, and Cooper officially adopted the Alice Cooper name as his own.

In contrast to his professional image, the offstage Cooper became a Hollywood celebrity, playing golf and appearing on television talk shows, as well as developing a strong friendship with Groucho Marx, with whom he planned a television series. In tribute to the legendary comedian he purchased one of the 'O's from the famous Hollywood sign and dedicated it to his memory. The late 70s saw him appearing in films such as *Sextette* and *Sgt. Pepper's Lonely Hearts Club Band*. In 1978 Cooper admitted to chronic alcoholism and entered a New York hospital for treatment. *From The Inside*, with songs co-written by Bernie Taupin, reflected on the experience. His band continued touring, and between 1979 and 1982, it featured ex-Iron Butterfly lead guitarist Mike Pinera. Cooper continued recording into the early 80s with diminishing results. In 1986, after a four-year recording absence, he signed to MCA Records, but none of his albums for that label reached the US charts. A 1989 set, *Trash*, his first for Epic Records, returned him to the Top 40 and yielded a Top 10 single, 'Poison', his first in 12 years. *Hey Stoopid* found him accompanied by Joe Satriani, Steve Vai and Slash and Axl Rose from Guns N'Roses, while his 90s tours saw Cooper drawing a new, younger audience who considered him a heavy metal pioneer. This impression was immortalized by Cooper's appearance in the 1992 film *Wayne's World*, wherein the haphazard protagonists kneel before their idol proclaiming that they are 'not worthy'. In recent times, Neal Smith has become a property agent; Bruce is still a songwriter but is bitter about the past - he became an author with the publication of *No More Mr Nice Guy*. Buxton lived in Iowa and was plagued by ill health until his death in 1997, while Dunaway runs a craft shop with his wife in Connecticut.

● ALBUMS: *Pretties For You* (Straight 1969)★★★, *Easy Action* (Straight 1970)★★, *Love It To Death* (Warners 1971)★★★★, *Killer* (Warners 1971)★★★, *School's Out* (Warners 1972)★★★★, *Billion Dollar Babies* (Warners 1973)★★★★, *Muscle Of Love* (Warners 1973)★★, *Welcome To My Nightmare* (Anchor 1975)★★★, *Alice Cooper Goes To Hell* (Warners 1976)★★, *Lace And Whiskey* (Warners 1977)★, *The Alice Cooper Show* (Warners 1977)★★, *From The Inside* (Warners 1978)★, *Flush The Fashion* (Warners 1980)★, *Special Forces* (Warners 1981)★, *Zipper Catches The Skin* (Warners 1982)★, *Dada* (Warners 1983)★, *Live In Toronto* (Breakaway 1984)★, *Constrictor* (MCA 1986)★★, *Raise Your Fist And Yell* (MCA 1987)★★, *Trash* (Epic 1989)★★, *Hey Stoopid* (Epic 1991)★★, *Live At The Whiskey A Go Go* (Edsel 1992)★★, *The Last Temptation* (Epic 1994)★★, *A Fistful Of Alice* (Guardian 1997)★★.

● COMPILATIONS: *School Days* (Warners 1973)★★★, *Alice Cooper's Greatest Hits* (Warners 1974)★★★★, *Freak Out Song* (Castle 1986)★★★, *Beast Of* (Warners 1989)★★★★, *Classicks* (Epic 1995)★★★, *Freedom For Frankenstein: Hits & Pieces 1984-'91* (Raven 1998)★★★.

● VIDEOS: *The Nightmare Returns* (Hendring Music Video 1987), *Welcome To My Nightmare* (Hendring Music Video 1988), *Alice Cooper Trashes The World* (CMV Enterprises 1990), *Box Set* (Hendring Music Video 1990), *Prime Cuts* (Castle Music Pictures 1991).

● FURTHER READING: *Alice Cooper*, Steve Demorest. *Me: Alice: The Autobiography Of Alice Cooper*, Alice Cooper with Steven Gaines. *Rolling Stone Scrapbook: Alice Cooper*, Rolling Stone. *No More Mr Nice Guy: The Inside Story Of The Alice Cooper Group*, Michael Bruce with Michael James.

● FILMS: *Wayne's World* (1992).

Alice In Chains

Formed in 1987 in Seattle, USA, by Layne Staley (b. 22 August 1967, Kirkland, Washington, USA;

vocals) and Jerry Cantrell (b. 18 March 1966, Tacoma, Washington, USA; vocals, guitar) with Mike Starr (bass) and Sean Kinney (b. 27 June 1966, Seattle, Washington, USA; drums), Alice In Chains developed a sound that mixed Black Sabbath-style riffing with Staley and Cantrell's unconventional vocal arrangements and strong songwriting. Cantrell had drifted from his home in Tacoma to Seattle, homing in on a musician's collective entitled the Music Bank. He brought in the rhythm section of Kinney and Starr, before Staley was recruited from a local funk metal act. After dispensing with their early moniker, 'Fuck', the group became Alice In Chains, a name invented by Staley for 'a parody heavy metal band that dressed in drag'. The group won a major recording contract despite some record executives being scared off by Staley's aggressive performance at an early showcase.

Facelift received excellent reviews, but took off slowly, boosted by US touring with Van Halen, the difficult opening slot on the US Clash Of The Titans tour, featuring Slayer, Anthrax and Megadeth, and European dates with Megadeth and the Almighty. 'Man In The Box' became an MTV favourite, and the album went gold in the autumn of 1991, just as Nirvana's success began to make Seattle headline news. The band released the gentler *Sap*, featuring guests from Heart, Soundgarden and Mudhoney, before recording their second full album. *Dirt* was a dark, cathartic work with many personal lyrics, including 'Rooster', which described Cantrell's father's Vietnam War experiences and became a live centrepiece. However, critical attention focused on a sequence of songs referring to Staley's past heroin problems, descending from the initial high of 'Junkhead' ('We are an elite race of our own/The stoners, junkies and freaks'), through depths of addiction, to the realization of the need to break away from dependency in 'Angry Chair' ('Little boy made a mistake/Pink cloud has now turned to gray'). Despite the controversy, *Dirt* was deservedly acclaimed, and was the critics' album of the year in many metal magazines, entering the US charts at number 6. 'Would?' became a hit, boosted by an appearance playing the song in the movie *Singles*, and the band supported Ozzy Osbourne in the USA, with Staley in a wheelchair for the early dates, having broken his foot, before Starr's departure. Ex-Ozzy Osbourne bassist Michael Inez (b. 14 May 1966, San Francisco, California, USA) stepped in, and the band embarked on a sell-out tour of Europe and the USA. The cancellation of European stadium shows supporting Metallica in mid-1993, owing to exhaustion, led to speculation about a setback in Staley's recovery, but Alice In Chains returned in fine style, contributing to the *Last Action Hero* soundtrack and playing superbly on the third Lollapalooza tour. In early 1994 *Jar Of Flies* became the first EP to top the US album charts, entering at number 1. Staley put together a side-project, Mad Season, with Pearl Jam's Mike McCready and Barrett Martin from Screaming Trees, amid rumours that Alice In Chains had split. These rumours were exacerbated by the return of Staley's misfortunes in August 1994 when gigs, including Woodstock II, were cancelled, as a result of further 'health problems'. Amid continuing rumours of drug abuse the band managed a further album in 1995 that boasted some excellent moments. In 1996, the band performed their first concert in over three years, performing for MTV on an *Unplugged* special. Rumours about their future resurfaced when Cantrell released a solo album in April 1998.

● ALBUMS: *Facelift* (Columbia 1990)★★★, *Sap* mini-album (Columbia 1992)★★★, *Dirt* (Columbia 1992)★★★★, *Jar Of Flies* mini-album (Columbia 1993)★★★★, *Alice In Chains* (Columbia 1995)★★★, *MTV Unplugged Live* (Sony 1996)★★★.

Solo: Jerry Cantrell *Boggy Depot* (Columbia 1998)★★.

● VIDEOS: *Live Facelift* (Sony Music Video 1994), *Nona Weisbaum* (Columbia 1995), *The Nona Tapes* (Sony Music Video 1996), *MTV Unplugged* (Sony Music Video 1996).

ALIEN (SWEDEN)

This melodic hard-rock band was formed in Sweden in 1986. Assimilating influences such as Survivor, Styx, Foreigner, Kansas and Journey, they delivered a highly polished, if rather derivative, debut album in 1988. Earlier, they had reached number 1 in Sweden with a cover version of the old Graham Bonnet hit, 'Only One Woman'. Original vocalist Jim Jidhad was replaced by the ex-Madison frontman Peter Sandberg soon after the album was released. The remainder of the band included Tony Borg (guitar), Ken Sandin (bass), Jimmy Wandroph (keyboards) and Toby Tarrach (drums).

● ALBUMS: *Alien* (Virgin 1988)★★★★, *Shiftin' Gear* (Virgin 1990)★★★, *Crash* (Megarock Records 1995)★★.

Alien (USA)

This metal band from New York, USA, consisted of Frank Starr (vocals), Rik Kristi (guitar), Damien 'The Beast' Harlow (bass), Roxann Harlow (drums) and Brian Fair (guitar). They remained together just long enough to release a solitary mini-album, which was overshadowed by the news that Damien Harlow had been charged with murder during an attempted burglary. Kristi later joined ex-Steeler bass player Rik Fox on the west coast.

● ALBUMS: *Cosmic Fantasy* mini-album (Mongol Horde 1983)★★.

Alienoid

One of an increasing number of Asian bands attempting to replicate the sounds of imported American heavy metal, Malaysia's Alienoid are a septet who sing entirely in Cantonese. Influenced in the main by the Beyond and China's Tang Dynasty, the group were first spotted in 1994 at the Canto-Rock Contest. The impression they made there led to a recording contract through Eric Yeoh of PolyGram Records. Together with two other contemporary Malaysian rock bands, Barabastelles and Baby Amps, Alienoid made their debut on the compilation album *Canto-Rock Kaki*, released in 1995. Its success prompted the record label to issue Alienoid's self-titled debut the following year.

● ALBUMS: *Alienoid* (PolyGram 1996)★★★.

Alkatrazz

This group was formed in Maidstone, Kent, England, in 1980 by vocalist Craig Stevens and guitarist Bob Jenner. This heavy metal band should not be confused with the 70s pub rock band Alkatraz (who released one album, *Doing A Moonlight*, in 1976). Recruiting the services of Gary Bevan (bass) and Nicko Parsons (drums), they signed to RCA Records as one of the hopefuls of the New Wave Of British Heavy Metal movement. *Young Blood* featured hard rock reminiscent of UFO. Unable to make a breakthrough, however, they switched to an American-sounding AOR approach with *Radio 5*. This drive for commercial success also failed and RCA dropped them soon after the album was released.

● ALBUMS: *Young Blood* (RCA 1981)★★★, *Radio 5* (RCA 1982)★★.

Alliance

This short-lived, American melodic rock quintet was formed in 1980 by the talented vocalist Mark Bucchare, with guitarist Pat Hand, keyboardist Mark Heckert, bassist Bradley Davidson and drummer David Pridemore completing the line-up. Their music was characterized by note-perfect harmonies, razor-sharp arrangements and understated guitarwork. Their self-titled debut, however, lacked both the image and real direction necessary to elevate them above the numerous other Styx/Kansas/Journey clones around at the time. Disillusioned by the lack of recognition and label support, they disbanded the following year.

● ALBUMS: *Alliance* (Handshake 1982)★★.

Allied Forces

Formed in 1983, Allied Forces were a Dutch hard rock quintet from the province of Brabant, and featured Ronnie Gershwin (vocals), Marc Gershwin (guitar), Harold Cucken (guitar), Steven Highwood (bass) and Pete Van de Sluice (drums). They built up a solid reputation touring the European circuit as support for Anvil and TNT. Following a series of delays, *The Day After* was eventually released in 1987 on the German Flametrader label, produced by ex-Vandenberg bassist Dick Kemper. They acknowledged a variety of influences, including Golden Earring, Scorpions and Europe, but managed to maintain their own originality. Highwood and Cucken quit in 1988, with Ferry Schmuter stepping in to take over on bass.

● ALBUMS: *The Day After* (Flametrader 1987)★★★.

Allies

This US group was formed from the ashes of the religious pomp-rock outfit, the Sweet Comfort Band, in 1983. The members were Bob Carlisle (vocals, guitar), Randy Thomas (guitar, keyboards), Kenny Williams (keyboards, saxophone, vocals), Matthew Chapman (bass) and Jim Erickson (drums); Sam Scott (vocals, keyboards) also appeared on the first album. Their first two albums are fine examples of melodic Christian rock in a Kansas/Stryper vein. 1987's *Shoulder To Shoulder* saw the band diversifying their approach, with blues, funk and soul influences being given more prominence in their compositions. The album was a disappointment, judged by many critics to be overloaded with nondescript power-ballads. *Long Way To Paradise* tried unsuccessfully to recapture the ground lost by this change in style, but was let down by weak material.

● ALBUMS: *Allies* (Light 1984)★★★, *Virtues* (Light 1985)★★★, *Shoulder To Shoulder* (Dayspring 1987)★★, *Long Way To Paradise* (Dayspring 1987)★★

ALLMAN BROTHERS BAND

Formed in Macon, Georgia, USA, in 1969 by guitarist Duane Allman (b. Howard Duane Allman, 20 November 1946, Nashville, Tennessee, USA, d. 29 October 1971, Macon, Georgia, USA), the band included brother Gregg Allman (b. Gregory Lenoir Allman, 8 December 1947, Nashville, Tennessee, USA; keyboards, vocals), Forrest Richard 'Dickie' Betts (b. 12 December 1943, West Palm Beach, Florida, USA; guitar), Raymond Berry Oakley (b. 4 April 1948, Chicago, Illinois, USA, d. 11 November 1972; bass), Butch Trucks (b. Claude Hudson Trucks Jnr., Jacksonville, Florida, USA; drums) and Jai 'Jaimoe' Johanny Johanson (b. John Lee Johnson, 8 July 1944, Ocean Springs, Mississippi, USA; drums). The above line-up was an amalgamation of the members of several southern-based aspirants, of which the Hour Glass was the most prolific. The latter pop/soul ensemble featured Duane and Gregg Allman, and broke up when demo tapes for a projected third album were rejected by their record company. Duane then found employment at the Fame studio where he participated in several sessions prior to instigating this new sextet. The Allman Brothers established themselves as a popular live attraction and their first two albums, *The Allman Brothers Band* and *Idlewild South*, were marked by strong blues-based roots and an exciting rhythmic drive. Nevertheless, it was a sensational two-album set, *Live At The Fillmore East*, that showcased the group's emotional fire. 'Whipping Post', a 22-minute *tour de force*, remains one of rock music's definitive improvisational performances. The set brought the band to the brink of stardom, while Duane's reputation as an outstanding slide guitarist was further enhanced by his contribution to *Layla And Other Assorted Love Songs*, the seminal Derek And The Dominos album. Unfortunately, tragedy struck on 29 October 1971 when this gifted musician was killed in a motorcycle accident. The remaining members completed *Eat A Peach*, which consisted of live and studio material, before embarking on a more mellow direction with *Brothers And Sisters*, a style best exemplified by the album's hit single, 'Ramblin' Man'. A second pianist, Chuck Leavell (b. 1950, Tuscaloosa, Alabama, USA), was added to the line-up, but just as the group recovered its momentum, Berry Oakley was killed in an accident chillingly similar to that of his former colleague on 11 November 1972. Not surprisingly, the Allman Brothers seemed deflated, and subsequent releases failed to match the fire of those first recordings. Their power was further diminished by several offshoot projects. Gregg Allman (who later married Cher twice) and Dickie Betts embarked on solo careers while Leavell, Johanson and new bassist Lamar Williams (b. 1947, Hansboro, Mississippi, USA, d. 25 January 1983, a victim of cancer) formed Sea Level. The Allmans broke up acrimoniously in 1976 following a notorious drugs trial in which Gregg testified against a former road manager. Although the other members vowed never to work with the vocalist again, a reconstituted 1978 line-up included Allman, Betts and Trucks. *Enlightened Rogues* was a commercial success, but subsequent albums fared less well and in 1982 the Allman Brothers Band split for a second time. A new incarnation appeared in 1989 with a line-up of Gregg Allman (vocals, organ), Betts (vocals, lead guitar), Warren Haynes (vocals, slide and lead guitar), Allen Woody (bass), Johnny Neel (keyboards), Trucks (drums) and Mark Quinones (percussion). This much-heralded reunion spawned a credible release: *Seven Turns*. Neel left the band and the remaining sextet made *Shades Of Two Worlds*. Quinones (congas and percussion) joined for *An Evening With The Allman Brothers Band* in 1992. Their 1994 album, *Where It All Begins*, was recorded effectively live in the studio, with production once more by Allman Brothers veteran Tom Dowd. Nevertheless, it is the work displayed on their first five albums that remains among the finest guitar music recorded during the late 60s and early 70s, in particular for the skilful interplay between two gifted, imaginative players.

● ALBUMS: *The Allman Brothers Band* (Capricorn 1969)★★★★, *Idlewild South* (Capricorn 1970)★★★★, *Live At The Fillmore East* (Capricorn 1971)★★★★, *Eat A Peach* (Capricorn 1972)★★★, *Brothers And Sisters* (Capricorn 1973)★★★, *Win, Lose Or Draw* (Capricorn 1975)★★★, *Wipe The Windows, Check The Oil, Dollar Gas* (Capricorn 1976)★, *Enlightened Rogues* (Capricorn 1979)★★★, *Reach For The Sky* (Arista 1980)★★, *Brothers Of The Road* (Arista 1981)★★, *Live At Ludlow Garage 1970* (PolyGram 1990)★★★, *Seven Turns* (Epic 1990)★★★, *Shades Of Two Worlds* (Epic 1991)★★★, *An Evening With The Allman Brothers Band* (Epic 1992)★★★, *The Fillmore Concerts* (Polydor 1993)★★★★, *Where It All Begins* (Epic 1994)★★★, *2nd Set* (Epic 1995)★★, *Twenty* (SPV 1997)★★.

● COMPILATIONS: *The Road Goes On Forever* (Capricorn 1975)★★★, *The Best Of The Allman Brothers Band* (Polydor 1981)★★★, *Dreams* 4-CD box set (Polydor 1989)★★★★, *A Decade Of Hits*

1969-1979 (PolyGram 1991)★★★, *Madness Of The West* (Camden 1998)★★, *Mycology* (Epic 1998)★★.
● VIDEOS: *Brothers Of The Road* (RCA/Columbia 1988), *Live At Great Woods* (1993).
● FURTHER READING: *The Allman Brothers: A Biography In Words And Pictures*, Tom Nolan. *Midnight Riders: The Story Of The Allman Brothers Band*, Scott Freeman.

ALLMAN, DUANE

b. Howard Duane Allman, 20 November 1946, Nashville, Tennessee, USA, d. 29 October 1971, Macon, Georgia, USA. One of rock's most inventive and respected guitarists, Allman initially garnered attention as a member of the Allman Joys. This promising group was succeeded by the Hour Glass who recorded two albums prior to their demise when their record company rejected their final recordings. However, Allman's playing had impressed Rick Hall, owner of the renowned Fame studio, who booked the young musician for a forthcoming session with soul singer Wilson Pickett. The resultant album, *Hey Jude* (1969), was both a commercial and artistic success, and Allman was invited to join the studio's in-house team. The guitarist made several distinctive appearances over the ensuing months. He was featured on releases by Aretha Franklin, King Curtis, Clarence Carter, Otis Rush and Boz Scaggs, but grew frustrated with this limiting role. During one of his periodic visits back home to Florida, he joined a group of local musicians which became the Allman Brothers Band with the addition of his brother Gregg. Despite the deserved success this unit achieved, Duane Allman continued his cameo appearances, the most exceptional of which was his contribution to the Derek And The Dominos classic, *Layla And Other Assorted Love Songs*. Here he displayed a joyous empathy playing slide guitar alongside fellow guitarist Eric Clapton, which resulted in one of rock's truly essential sets. However, despite the offer of a permanent slot, Allman preferred to remain with his own group. In the summer of 1971, the Allman Brothers began work on their fourth album, *Eat A Peach*, but, tired from constant touring, they took a break midway though the sessions. On 29 October, in an effort to avoid a collision with a truck, Allman crashed his motorcycle and died following three hours of intensive surgery. This tragic accident robbed music of one of its exceptional talents, whose all-too-brief legacy reveals an individual of rare skill and humility.
● COMPILATIONS: *Duane & Gregg Allman* recorded 1968 (Bold 1972)★★★, *Duane Allman: An Anthology* (Capricorn 1972)★★★★, *Early Allman* recorded 1966 (Dial 1973)★★★, *Duane Allman: An Anthology, Volume II* (Capricorn 1974)★★★★, *Best Of Duane Allman* (Capricorn 1979)★★★.

ALLMAN, GREGG

b. Gregory Lenoir Allman, 8 December 1947, Nashville, Tennessee, USA. A founder-member of the Allman Brothers Band, Gregg Allman embarked on a solo career in 1973 following a hiatus in the group's progress. *Laid Back*, his debut album, highlighted the singer's measured, bluesy approach and featured a version of 'Midnight Rider', a staple part of the early Allmans repertoire. A double set, *The Gregg Allman Tour*, documented the in-concert work of his band, while *Playin' Up A Storm* consolidated the artist's identity outside the parent group. Relations had been severed in 1976 during a drug trial when, under a promise of immunity, Allman had testified against a former road manager. His highly publicized marriage to Cher resulted in the couple's *Two The Hard Way* album, but the relationship was short-lived. For the next few years Allman struggled against various chemical dependencies, but a reconstituted Allman Brothers temporarily stabilized his personal life. When the group broke up in 1982, the singer established a new Gregg Allman Band but a continuing battle with alcoholism hampered its progress. Allman re-emerged in 1987 with *I'm No Angel*, determined to revive his career. This made the US Top 30 and his own Allman Brothers Band had further success with *Just Before The Bullets Fly* in 1988, prior to the full-scale reunion of the original band. Allman returned to recording in 1997 with the endearing, bluesy *Searching For Simplicity*.
● ALBUMS: *Laid Back* (Capricorn 1973)★★★, *The Gregg Allman Tour* (Capricorn 1974)★★★, *Playin' Up A Storm* (Capricorn 1977)★★★, with Cher as Allman And Woman *Two The Hard Way* (Warners 1977)★, *I'm No Angel* (Epic 1987)★★, *Just Before The Bullets Fly* (Epic 1988)★★, *Searching For Simplicity* (Epic 1997)★★★.
● COMPILATIONS: *Duane & Gregg Allman* recorded 1968 (Bold 1972)★★★, *One More Try: An Anthology* (PolyGram 1997)★★★★.
● VIDEOS: *One Way Out* (Hendring Music Video 1990), *This Country's Rockin'* (1993).

ALMIGHTY

This Scottish hard rock quartet was formed in 1988 by vocalist and guitarist Ricky Warwick (husband of Vanessa, hostess of *Headbanger's Ball* on MTV), guitarist Tantrum, bassist Floyd London and drummer Stumpy Munroe. Along with Little Angels, Quireboys and the Dogs D'Amour, the Almighty spearheaded a revival in British heavy rock during the late 80s, drawing their inspiration from bands such as the Cult, Ramones and Motörhead. Signing to Polydor in 1989, they released *Blood, Fire And Love* to widespread critical acclaim. The title was changed from *Blood, Fire And Roses* to avoid any possible confusion with Guns N'Roses. This was swiftly followed by a perfunctory live mini-album, which included a cover version of Bachman Turner Overdrive's standard, 'You Ain't Seen Nothin' Yet'. *Soul Destruction* reaffirmed the development in the group's songwriting abilities. It spawned the UK Top 20 hit 'Free 'n' Easy', and gained them recognition throughout Europe. However, internal tensions led to the dismissal of Tantrum, with Canadian Peter Friesen, whom the band had met during his time in Alice Cooper's band, filling the gap. The band broke from recording sessions to open the 1992 Donington Monsters Of Rock Festival with a fiery performance, a recording of which was released with initial copies of *Powertrippin'*. Mark Dodson's production gave the band a heavier sound, drawing Metallica and Soundgarden comparisons, yet retaining the Almighty's characteristic aggressive delivery, while a more mature lyrical approach enhanced the band's already strong songwriting platform. Single success with 'Addiction' was followed by heavy touring as the band supported Iron Maiden across Europe, played stadium dates with Metallica, and took on a gruelling club trek to lay the groundwork in the USA. On their return, the Almighty headlined one of the most acclaimed UK tours of 1993 with the Wildhearts and Kerbdog in tow. However, despite a UK Top 5 placing for *Powertrippin'*, the band were faced with demands for new material from Polydor within four months of its release. This led to a parting of the ways, with the Almighty sacking manager Tommy Tee and signing to Chrysalis Records in early 1994. Relocated in London, the debut album for their new label was produced by Chris Sheldon (responsible for Therapy?'s *Troublegum*). *Just Add Life* included two co-writing ventures between Warwick and former members of the Ruts. The band issued an anti-government single in 1996, 'All Sussed Out', which urged fans not to vote Conservative at the next general election. Warwick left in 1996 and the band folded soon afterwards.

● ALBUMS: *Blood, Fire And Love* (Polydor 1989)★★★, *Blood, Fire And Love - Live* (Polydor 1990)★★, *Soul Destruction* (Polydor 1991)★★★, *Powertrippin'* (Polydor 1993)★★★, *Crank* (Chrysalis 1994)★★★, *Just Add Life* (Chrysalis 1996)★★.

● VIDEOS: *Soul Destruction Live* (PolyGram Music Video 1991).

Alpha Centauri

This talented but little-known Canadian heavy rock quintet was formed in 1976 by Kurt Smith (vocals, guitar) and Jesse Redmon (keyboards, vocals). With Garth Hannum (bass, vocals) and Randy Thompson completing the line-up, they specialized in highly dramatic, often grandiose arrangements, awash with keyboards, but punctuated in places by some fierce guitarwork. Their self-titled debut was an undiscovered gem of the pomp-rock genre. Released as a limited edition, it is still much sought after by collectors.

● ALBUMS: *Alpha Centauri* (Salt 1977)★★★.

Altar Of The King

Formed in April 1991 in San Francisco, USA, as Now Hear This, this hard rock group first met at the auditions for lead singer Bogdan Jablonski's previous band, Warsaw, at Jackson St. Studios. This process saw the group evolve to include Bob Coons (guitar; brother of Laaz Rockit's vocalist), Tony Anthony (bass; once auditioned for Metallica) and Steve Quartarola (drums, ex-Black Ice; Vise; Cry Wolf; Lust). Jablonski had been singing in Bay Area bands for over ten years, and had studied under Barbra Streisand's and Frank Sinatra's vocal coach, Judy Davis. He had also sung background vocals for Testament. The group played their first shows soon after this line-up was in place, recording their material at Fantasy Studios in Berkeley in 1993 for release as a demo (which saw the band's original name, *Now Hear This*, revived as its title). This was touted around until the band secured a contract with European label Rock The Nation. In 1994 the tracks were remixed for release at Trax East Studios in New Jersey, while the group supported the likes of Primus, Helix and others on the road.

● ALBUMS: *Altar Of The King* (RTN 1994)★★★.

Amboy Dukes

Originally from Detroit, Michigan, USA, the Amboy Dukes - John Drake (vocals), Ted Nugent (b. 13 December 1949, Detroit, Michigan, USA; lead guitar), Steve Farmer (rhythm guitar), Rick Lorber (keyboards), Bill White (bass) and Dave Palmer (drums) - achieved notoriety for their rendition of 'Journey To The Center Of The Mind', which featured Nugent's snarling guitar and reached the US Top 20. The brashness of their version of Them's 'Baby Please Don't Go' set the tone for the group's subsequent albums on which Farmer's rather pretentious lyrics often undermined the music on offer. The band were highly competent on instrumentals, however, such as the evocative 'Scottish Tea'. Frequent changes in personnel (Drake, Lorber and White were replaced, in turn, by Rusty Day, Andy Solomon and Greg Arama) made little difference to the Amboy Dukes' development, as the group increasingly became an outlet for Nugent's pyrotechnics. He unveiled a new line-up in 1974 with *Call Of The Wild*, the first of two albums recorded for Frank Zappa's DiscReet label. The guitarist then abandoned the band's name altogether and embarked on a solo career.

● ALBUMS: *The Amboy Dukes* (Mainstream 1967)★★★, *Journey To The Center Of Your Mind* (Mainstream 1968)★★★, *Migrations* (Mainstream 1969)★★★, *Marriage On The Rocks* (Polydor 1969)★★, *Survival Of The Fittest/Live* (Polydor 1971)★★, as Ted Nugent And The Amboy Dukes *Call Of The Wild* (DiscReet 1974)★★, as Ted Nugent And The Amboy Dukes *Tooth, Fang And Claw* (DiscReet 1975)★★.

● COMPILATIONS: *The Best Of The Original Amboy Dukes* (Mainstream 1969)★★★.

AMERICADE

This New York hard rock quartet was put together by the De Marigny brothers in 1981. Vocalist P.J. and guitarist Gerard teamed up with ex-Rachel duo Nick Sadano (bass) and Walt Woodward III (drums). Sadano was replaced by Dave Spitz (brother of Dan, the Anthrax guitarist) before any material was recorded. Meanwhile, they gained a reputation for covering Van Halen numbers at high velocity. They split in 1984, but Gerard De Marigny resurrected the name in 1989 with ex-Malice vocalist Mark Weitz, bassist Greg Smith (ex-W.O.W.) and Paul Cammarata on drums.

● ALBUMS: *American Metal* (Adem 1982)★★★.

AMERICAN ANGEL

Comprising Rocco Fury (vocals), Petey D. (guitar), Danny Monchek (guitar), Steve Evetts (bass) and Eric Nilla (drums), US hard rock band American Angel were late 80s underachievers whose melodic rock never attracted an audience. Their self-titled album for Grudge Records was a competent but uninspired set on which Fury's songwriting failed to back up the group's obvious professionalism.

● ALBUMS: *American Angel* (Grudge 1989)★★.

AMERICAN NOISE

An obscure AOR guitar group from the USA, American Noise recorded just one album in 1980. However, that self-titled collection is considered to be something of a minor classic among rock cognoscenti, with the bombastic 'Running Through The Night' earning particular praise. However, shortly afterwards, Craig Balzer (vocals, guitar) and Bruce Balzer (guitar) - the brothers who formed the band - elected to dissolve the group. They and George Stipl (keyboards), Jerry Moran (keyboards), Greg Holt (bass) and Tommy Rich (drums) disappeared from the music scene thereafter.

● ALBUMS: *American Noise* (Planet 1980)★★★.

AMERICAN TEARS

Initially comprising Mark Mangold (vocals, keyboards), Tommy Gunn (drums) and Greg Baze (bass), 70s US rock band American Tears specialized in a rather formless take on the pomp rock of Yes and Journey. The group's debut, *Branded Bad*, and follow-up collection, *Tear Gas*, lacked both the power and musical versatility to give substance to Mangold's ambitious songwriting. Sensing this, *Powerhouse* was recorded with an almost completely different line-up - with Craig Brooks on vocals and guitar, Kirk Powers on bass and Glen Kithcart on drums in addition to Mangold. The results were a vast improvement, and prefaced the singer's later, more convincing work with Touch, who re-recorded two songs from *Powerhouse* for their 1980 debut. Kithcart and Brooks also joined Touch, but when their debut effort was not followed up, Mangold moved on once again to work as a session musician and Michael Bolton collaborator.

● ALBUMS: *Branded Bad* (Columbia 1974)★★, *Tear Gas* (Columbia 1975)★★, *Powerhouse* (Columbia 1976)★★★.

AMORPHIS

Formed in Helsinki, Finland, in 1990, Amorphis was originally conceived by guitarist Esa Holopinen and drummer/synthesizer player Jan Rechberger, who recruited vocalist and guitarist Tomi Koivusaari and bass player Olli-Pekka Laine. On the strength of their demo tape they secured a multi-album recording contract with Relapse Records, famed for their catalogue of American grind bands. In December 1991 the band recorded six tracks for a shared album with labelmates Incantation, but the record was never actually released. Two songs from this session did see the light of day, however, as part of a limited edition 7-inch EP. In May 1992 the quartet travelled to Stockholm, Sweden, to record 11 tracks for their debut album, *The Karelian Isthmus*, with engineer/producer Tomas Skogsberg. A crushing demonstration of state-of-the-art death metal, the dramatic atmosphere of the songs was further enhanced by the addition of keyboard player Kasper Martenson. In the wake of the album's success, Relapse elected to release the abandoned split LP session as part of its Underground series as *Privilege Of Evil*. In September 1993 Amorphis returned to Stockholm to record 10 further tracks for their second full-length album, *Tales From The Thousand Lakes*. As the title suggested, this incorporated elements of 70s progressive rock, with the theme being a historical tribute to Finland and to the national epic, *Kalevala*. In 1995 Rechberger was replaced on drums by Pekka Kasari. The following year's *Elegy* also featured vocalist Pasi Koskinen.

● ALBUMS: *The Karelian Isthmus* (Relapse/Nuclear Blast 1992)★★★, *Privilege Of Evil* mini-album (Relapse 1993)★★, *Tales From The Thousand Lakes* (Relapse/Nuclear Blast 1993)★★★, *Elegy* (Nuclear Blast 1996)★★★, *My Kantele* (Relapse 1997)★★★.

ANATHEMA

Formed in Liverpool, England, in the summer of 1990, doom metal band Anathema owe much to early 70s Black Sabbath, most notably their low, ominous riffs. Combined with this is the influence of 90s death metal, particularly the abrasive guitar and vocals. Perhaps the oddest element of Anathema's sound is their poetic romanticism, most evident in their lyrics and the occasional use of the angelic tones of a female vocalist, Ruth, to complement lead singer Darren White. The results of this odd hybrid are surprisingly effective and Anathema enjoy a strong cult following among doom metal fans. Their four-track demo, *An Illiad Of Woes*, was released in November 1990 under their original title, Pagan Angel. A second demo, *All Faith Is Lost*, recorded at MA Studios, was released in July 1991. In its wake, they cut a limited edition single, 'They Die'/'Crestfallen', for the Swiss label Witchunt. Eventually, the band earned a contract with the musically sympathetic Peaceville Records, initially contributing one track, 'Lovelorn Rhapsody', to the *Volume 4* compilation. The *Crestfallen* EP was sufficiently well received to warrant an album the following year. However, in 1995 White left the band, leaving behind the mini-album *Pentecost III* as his epitaph. Alhough only five tracks long, it has a full 40 minutes duration. Slow, melancholy and heavy, Anathema boast a depth often missing from standard heavy metal. White formed Blood Divine in 1996.

● ALBUMS: *Serenades* (Peaceville 1993)★★★, *Pentecost III* mini-album (Peaceville 1995)★★★, *The Silent Enigma* (Peaceville 1995)★★★, *Eternity* (Peaceville 1996)★★★, *Alternative 4* (Peaceville 1998)★★★★.

ANDERSON, ANGRY

b. Gary Anderson, Australia. As the diminutive, bald-headed frontman of Rose Tattoo, Anderson was the voice for many young, aggressive males from Melbourne's working-class, industrialized western suburbs. The Tatts, as they were affectionately known, and the earlier Buster Brown, were obtrusive rock 'n' roll bands, utilizing Chuck Berry-styled riffs under the abrasive shouting of Anderson. The Buster Brown album was ignored at the time of its release in 1974, as the image of a tough, macho band did not sit well with radio programmers; it is now a much sought-after collector's item. Rose Tattoo, each player having a rose tattooed somewhere on his body, had a similar image. However, because the band's membership was more fluid, its sound changed with the times and it became a more modern-sounding band that had something to say about social justice and the environment. Rose Tattoo featured many highly regarded players from other Sydney heavy rock bands, such as guitarists Tim Gaze, Chris Turner and Peter Wells, and bassists Lobby Loyde and Steve Balbi. While some of the band's work gained airplay, the unit nevertheless gradually disintegrated. *Beats From A Single Drum* (1987), released under the band's name, was effectively Anderson's solo debut. Later, Anderson was successful with his solo single 'Suddenly', a ballad sung at the fictional, soap-opera wedding of teenage heart-throbs Kylie Minogue and Jason Donovan in *Neighbours*. Anderson, who wanted to broaden his audience while still being committed to his ideals, branched out into media and television work. However, his solo album, recorded in the USA with studio musicians, did not have the impact for which he had hoped.

● ALBUMS: *Blood From Stone* (Music For Nations 1991)★★.

ANGEL

Formed in Washington, DC, this band are perhaps more widely recalled for their outrageous image and stage shows than for their musical prowess.

Their self-titled debut, recorded with a line-up of Frank DiMino (vocals), Edwin Lionel 'Punky' Meadows (guitar, ex-BUC), Greg Giuffria (keyboards), Mickey Jones (bass, ex-BUC) and Barry Brandt (drums), was an excellent slab of heavy pomp rock, with lengthy songs swathed in Giuffria's atmospheric keyboards and featuring the long-time stage favourite, 'Tower'. *Helluva Band* continued in a similar vein, although the longest track, 'The Fortune', was exceptional, and thus tended to obscure the rest of the material. The band's famous white satin stage clothing made its debut on the album sleeve. *On Earth As It Is In Heaven* saw a distinct change in musical direction, as the band adopted a pop-rock sound, and introduced a clever logo that read identically when upside down, but poor production let down the album. *White Hot*, with Felix Robinson replacing Jones, was helped by Eddie Leonetti's more sympathetic production, and produced minor US hits in 'I Ain't Gonna Eat Out My Heart Anymore' and 'The Winter Song'. Leonetti subsequently produced *Sinful* and the in-concert set *Live Without A Net*, which had been recorded on the *White Hot* tour and suffered from the lack of material drawn from *Sinful*. Angel's record sales never quite reflected their popularity as a live act, and a legal dispute with PolyGram prompted the band's break-up in 1981. Giuffria had some success with Giuffria and House Of Lords, and Robinson appeared in an early White Lion line-up and played with 707.

● ALBUMS: *Angel* (Casablanca 1975)★★★, *Helluva Band* (Casablanca 1976)★★★, *On Earth As It Is In Heaven* (Casablanca 1977)★★, *White Hot* (Casablanca 1977)★★★, *Sinful* (Casablanca 1979)★★, *Live Without A Net* (Casablanca 1980)★★.

● COMPILATIONS: *Can You Feel It* (PolyGram 1989)★★★, *Anthology* (Casablanca 1992)★★★.

ANGELS

During the late 70s and early 80s, the Angels, formed in 1975, were Australia's most successful rock band, enjoying massive record sales for both singles and albums, and also having the distinction of being the top live act in the country. The group was based around the brothers John (guitar) and Rick Brewster (guitar) with Doc Neeson (vocals), who had played together in jug and rock 'n' roll revival bands such as the Keystone Angels in Adelaide since 1971. The line-up was completed by Chris Bailey (bass) and Graham Bidstrup (drums). The Angels toured incessantly, culminating in an extended tour of the USA where they were known as Angel City. Their no-nonsense, go-getting rock was not particularly innovative, but they worked hard to captivate their audiences at every opportunity, writing lyrics that were concise and anthemic. However, the band made little headway in America and, as with so many others, their audience in Australia tired of them, ignoring subsequent album releases. Personnel changes during the 80s included a new rhythm section comprising Brent Eccles (drums) and Jim Hilbun (bass), and the departure of original member John Brewster, replaced by Bob Spencer (ex-Skyhooks). However, unlike lesser outfits, the Angels continued working and gradually won over a new audience, supporting Guns N'Roses at Los Angeles's Whiskey in 1988, with only Neeson and Rick Brewster remaining from the original line-up. Once again becoming hugely popular in their native country, they achieved an Australian number 1 album for the first time in 1990. *Beyond Salvation* was recorded in Memphis, Tennessee with Led Zeppelin/ZZ Top producer Terry Manning, and featured new bassist James Morley. Spencer and Morley left after *Red Back Fever*, allowing the return of Hilbun and John Brewster. Following a lengthy hiatus the band issued their comeback single, 1996's 'Call That Living', and a new album in 1998.

● ALBUMS: *The Angels* (Albert 1977)★★★, *Face To Face* (Epic 1978)★★★, *No Exit* (Albert 1979)★★★, *Darkroom* (Epic 1980)★★★, *Night Attack* (Epic 1982)★★, *Watch The Red* (Columbia 1983)★★, *Two Minute Warning* (MCA 1984)★★★, *The Howling* (MCA 1986)★★★, *Liveline* (MCA 1988)★★, *Beyond Salvation* (Chrysalis 1990)★★★, *Red Back Fever* (1991)★★★, *Skin And Bone* (1998)★★★.

● COMPILATIONS: *Greatest Hits* (1979)★★★.

ANGELS WITH DIRTY FACES

Taking their name from an old Sham 69 rallying call, Angels With Dirty Faces formed in the northwest of England in early 1991, the line-up consisting of Simon Gibbs (vocals), Jason Woolley (guitar), Jeremy Dykes (bass) and Paul Roscrow (drums). Their debut release was a self-financed mini-album, *A Little Taste*, which was warmly received in the UK. After undertaking many gigs through 1992-93 they signed to RTN subsidiary Blue Flame and released an album the following year.

● ALBUMS: *Sounds Of The World Turning* (Blue Flame 1994)★★★.

ANGELWITCH

One of the first rock groups to be associated with the New Wave Of British Heavy Metal movement that originated in 1979, Angelwitch, a power trio put together by guitar virtuoso Kevin Heybourne, also featured Kevin Riddles (bass) and Dave Dufort (drums; Dufort's sister, Denise, occupied the same position in Girlschool). Their debut album drew heavily on satanic and witchcraft imagery and combined this with doom-laden riffs and vitriolic guitar breaks. Their only chart success was with 'Sweet Danger', which reached number 75 in the UK chart for just one week in June 1980. Soon after the release of *Angelwitch* the band split up, but Heybourne retained the name and enlisted Dave Hogg and Pete Gordelier on drums and bass, respectively, plus vocalist Dave Tattum. After two uninspiring albums they ground to a halt, but Heybourne resurrected the band in 1989 with drummer Spencer Holman and bassist Grant Dennis for a one-off album, recorded live in Los Angeles.

● ALBUMS: *Angelwitch* (Bronze 1980)★★★, *Screaming And Bleeding* (Rock Machine 1985)★★, *Frontal Assault* (Killerwatt 1986)★★, *Screamin' Assault* (Killerwatt 1988)★★, *Live* (Music For Nations 1990)★★.

● COMPILATIONS: *Doctor Phibes* (Raw Power 1986)★★★.

ANNIHILATOR

This heavy metal band is a vehicle for the talents of classically trained Canadian guitarist Jeff Waters (b. Ottawa, Canada). Annihilator set the underground scene alight with a demo entitled 'Phantasmagoria', before relocating to Vancouver and releasing their debut, *Alice In Hell*. This was a *tour de force* of intricate thrash, with all the guitars and bass parts played by Waters, who also produced and wrote the material, with Randy Rampage (vocals, ex-D.O.A.) and Ray Hartmann (drums); the line-up was augmented by Anthony Greenham (guitar) and Wayne Darley (bass) after the recording. The sizzling guitarwork helped the record to become, at the time, the best-selling debut in the history of Roadrunner Records. The band subsequently suffered from an unstable line-up, with Greenham being replaced almost immediately by Dave Scott Davis, while Rampage departed when touring was complete, with ex-Omen frontman Coburn Pharr stepping in. *Never, Neverland* was another excellent effort, displaying rather more lyrical maturity than the debut, and a new version of 'Phantasmagoria'. Band stability remained an issue, and Davis's departure on the eve of a European tour as guests of Judas Priest caused problems due to the sheer complexity of the material, but the group nevertheless managed to produce creditable performances. After a lengthy break, Annihilator returned with new guitarist Neil Goldberg and another vocalist, Aaron Randall. *Set The World On Fire*, though less well received by the metal press than previous offerings, revealed some promising progression beyond thrash boundaries into more melodic spaces, and sold well. The remixed and unreleased tracks compilation *Bag Of Tricks* was the band's last release for Roadrunner. *King Of The Kill* saw Waters take over lead vocals and featured Randy Black on drums, later adding Dave Davis (guitar) and Cam Dixon (bass). *Refresh The Demon* was Waters' weakest album to date, but the follow-up, *Remains*, introduced an interesting new industrial direction to his sound.

● ALBUMS: *Alice In Hell* (Roadrunner 1989)★★★, *Never, Neverland* (Roadrunner 1990)★★★, *Set The World On Fire* (Roadrunner 1993)★★, *King Of The Kill* (Music For Nations 1994)★★★, *Refresh The Demon* (Music For Nations 1996)★★, *In Command (Live 1989-1990)* (Roadrunner 1996)★★★, *Remains* (Music For Nations 1997)★★★.

● COMPILATIONS: *Bag Of Tricks* (Roadrunner 1994)★★★.

ANTHEM

This Japanese group, formed in 1981, specialized in cloning western rock music. After numerous personnel changes, the 1990 line-up comprised Elizo Sakamoto (vocals), Hiroya Fukada (guitar), Nuoto Ski Bata (bass) and Tahamasa Ohuchi (drums), none of whom were original members. Influenced by the style and melodies of UFO, Thin Lizzy, Kiss and, more recently, Megadeth, they produced a series of solid albums. *Bound To Break* was produced by Chris Tsangarides and was a major success in the Far East.

● ALBUMS: *Anthem* mini-album (Medusa 1985)★★★, *Tightrope* (Medusa 1986)★★★, *Bound To Break* (Medusa 1987)★★★, *Gypsy Ways* (Medusa 1988)★★★.

ANTHRAX

This New York-based thrash metal outfit came to prominence in 1982 with a line-up comprising Scott 'Not' Ian (b. Scott Rosenfeld, 31 December 1963; rhythm guitar), Neil Turbin (vocals), Dan Spitz (lead guitar), Dan Lilker (bass; replaced by

Frank Bello in 1983) and Charlie Benante (drums). Managed by Johnny Z, head of the independent Megaforce Records, the quintet released *Fistful Of Metal* in 1984. Despite its tasteless sleeve, the album garnered fair reviews and was a small but steady seller. For a time, Ian, Lilker and Benante were also part of Stormtroopers Of Death (SOD, who were revived briefly in 1991), a hardcore band with a satirical outlook, and Lilker subsequently left Anthrax to pursue a similar direction with Nuclear Assault. Turbin also departed, with his initial replacement, Matt Fallon, being quickly succeeded by Joey Belladonna (b. 30 October 1960, Oswego, New York, USA). This line-up released the *Armed And Dangerous* EP in 1985, and their increasing popularity led to a contract with Island Records. *Spreading The Disease* was deservedly well received, and the band's European profile was raised considerably by their support slot on Metallica's Damage Inc tour. *Among The Living*, co-produced by the band with Eddie Kramer, established Anthrax as a major force in the speed metal scene, producing UK hits in 'I Am The Law' and 'Indians', and their riotously entertaining live shows made them many friends among press and public alike. A humorous rap song, 'I'm The Man', became both a hit and a favourite encore. However, *State Of Euphoria* was a disappointing, patchy affair, with the group suffering an undeserved media backlash over their image. Sterling live work restored their reputation, with Anthrax's commitment to expanding their audiences' musical tastes demonstrated by their choice of UK support acts, Living Colour and Kings X. *Persistence Of Time* showed a return to form, and was a dark and relentless work that produced another hit in the shape of a cover version of Joe Jackson's 'Got The Time'. Classed by the band as an EP, *Attack Of The Killer B's* was essentially a collection of b-sides for the curious fan, but became one of Anthrax's most popular albums, with the hit collaboration with Public Enemy, 'Bring The Noise', leading to the two bands touring together in a co-headlining package. Shortly after the band signed a new contract with Elektra Records, Belladonna was fired, with ex-Armored Saint frontman John Bush stepping in. *Sound Of White Noise* was hailed as the band's finest hour, a post-thrash *tour de force* of power metal with bursts of hardcore speed. Bush's creative input helped Ian and Benante to write some of their best work, while Dave Jerden's production updated and re-energized the Anthrax sound. In 1994 Bush established his own R&B offshoot, Ho Cake, which included former Armored Saint personnel Joey Vera (bass) and Jeff Duncan (guitar), as well as Shawn Duncan (drums), Tony Silbert (keyboards) and Bruce Fernandez (ex-Dread Zeppelin). In 1995 Anthrax began work on *Stomp 442*, an unremittingly brutal collection of hardcore and metal produced by the Butcher Brothers (best known for their work with Urge Overkill). However, Spitz was ejected from the band just prior to recording and his guitar parts were played instead by his former guitar technician, Paul Cook, Pantera's Dimebag Darrell, and the group's drummer, Charlie Benante. In 1998 Ian guested on Tricky's *Angels With Dirty Faces*, shortly before Anthrax broke a three-year silence with *Volume 8 - The Threat Is Real*.

● ALBUMS: *Fistful Of Metal* (Megaforce 1984)★★, *Spreading The Disease* (Island/Megaforce 1986)★★★★, *Among The Living* (Island/Megaforce 1987)★★★, *State Of Euphoria* (Island/Megaforce 1988)★★, *Persistence Of Time* (Island/Megaforce 1990)★★★★, *Attack Of The Killer B's* (Island/Megaforce 1991)★★★, *Sound Of White Noise* (Elektra 1993)★★★★, *Live - The Island Years* (Island 1994)★★★, *Stomp 442* (Elektra 1995)★★, *Volume 8 - The Threat Is Real* (Tommy Boy 1998)★★★.

● COMPILATIONS: *Moshers 1986-1991* (Connoisseur Collection 1998)★★★★.

● VIDEOS: *Oidivnikufesin N.F.V.* (Island Visual Arts 1988), *Persistence Through Time* (Island Visual Arts 1990), *Through Time* (PolyGram Music Video 1991), *N.F.V.* (PolyGram Music Video 1991).

Anti-Nowhere League

Leading lights in the early 80s UK punk scene, along with contemporaries G.B.H. and the Exploited, this quartet from Tunbridge Wells, Kent, England, flaunted their talents in biker leather, chains and hardcore obscenity. Led by Animal (b. Nick Karmer; vocals) and Magoo (guitar), their catalogue of sexual outrage veered from the satirical to the genuinely offensive, with a string of four-letter words, rabid misogyny and the glorification of bestiality. Their most memorable moment was a thrashy rerun of Ralph McTell's 'Streets Of London', which replaced the song's folksy sentiments with the barbed, snarling rhetoric of the gutter. Thousands of copies of the single were seized and destroyed by the police as the b-side, 'So What', was deemed obscene. This action, however, could not prevent the group reaching number 1 in the UK Independent singles charts, a feat accomplished a further three times in 1982 with 'I Hate People', 'Woman' and 'For You'. As their punkish appeal receded, the group abbreviated their name to the League and turned into a punk/metal hybrid in keeping with their biker image. Surprisingly, the results were not as appalling as might have been imagined, with *The Perfect Crime* boasting several fine songs, not least the almost subtle '(I Don't Believe) This Is My England'. The group disbanded in 1988 but there have been several revivals, including the one-off 1989 reunion recorded for release as *Live And Loud*. Anti-Nowhere League bounced back with their 1997 album, *Scum*, which featured such treats as 'Fucked Up And Wasted' and a dubious cover version of Cher's 'Gypsies, Tramps And Thieves'.

● ALBUMS: *We Are ... The League* (WXYZ 1982)★★, *Live In Yugoslavia* (ID 1983)★★, as The League *The Perfect Crime* (GWR 1987)★★★, *Live And Loud* (Link 1990)★★, *Scum* (SPV 1997)★★, *Return To Yugoslavia* (Knock Out 1998)★★.

● COMPILATIONS: *Long Live The League* (Dojo 1986)★★★.

Anvil

Formerly known as Lips, Anvil were a Canadian group from Toronto who made an impression on the speed-metal rock scene during the early 80s. The group comprised frontman Lips (vocals, guitar), who had lent his name to the group's previous incarnation, Dave Allison (guitar), Ian Dickson (bass) and Robb Reiner (drums). The band were technically excellent, playing at breakneck speed and with an intensity that few of their peers could equal. Their first three albums were exemplary, with *Metal On Metal* containing the strongest material. Following a series of legal disputes with their label, as well as internal conflicts concerning musical differences, there was a four-year gap between successive studio albums. *Backwaxed* was a compilation, released against the band's wishes, that featured songs they had recorded but rejected. *Strength Of Steel*, released in 1987, was a satisfactory comeback; however, it was overshadowed by the concurrent work of Slayer, Megadeth and Metallica. This was ironic, given that Anvil were acknowledged as having had a profound influence on these bands during their formative years. 1988's *Pound For Pound* was followed by a compilation of live material, before Allison left the band the following year.

● ALBUMS: *Hard 'n' Heavy* (Attic 1981)★★★, *Metal On Metal* (Attic 1982)★★★, *Forged In Fire* (Attic 1983)★★★, *Strength Of Steel* (Attic 1987)★★★, *Pound For Pound* (Metal Blade 1988)★★★, *Past And Present - Live* (Roadrunner 1989)★★, *Plugged In Permanent* (Massacre 1996)★★★, *Absolutely No Alternative* (Massacre 1998)★★★.

● COMPILATIONS: *Backwaxed* (Attic 1985)★★.

APB

(see Pyle, Artimus, Band)

Apes, Pigs And Spacemen

This mid-90s British heavy metal band took their name from what they considered to be a gap in Charles Darwin's rationale - the theory of evolution not accounting for a 30-million-year gap in fossil records, nor explaining why humans use only 10% of their brain capacity. The answer, for this Surrey, England-based quartet, was that 'An advanced life form came to earth from space and mated with what we consider a lower life-form, an ape. The offspring became what we now call humanity'. The pig element, meanwhile, arrived because 'we're now growing organs in pigs for the purpose of being transplanted into humans. But we eat pigs . . .'. Such elementary logic was reflected in the musical dynamic of the band, fronted by lead singer and thinker Paul Miro, who was backed by friends Sam, Kettle and Bart. Within a year of their formation in 1993 they were putting the finishing touches to a debut EP, *Antiseptic*, produced by Simon Efemey of Wildhearts, Helmet and Pantera fame. The same producer was recalled for their excellent 1995 debut album, produced at Jacobs Studios in Surrey. This highly varied selection included highlights such as 'Open Season' and 'Great Place', establishing the group at the forefront of a revival in UK metal alongside groups such as Reef and Bush.

● ALBUMS: *Transfusion* (Music For Nations 1995)★★★★, *Snapshot* (Music For Nations 1997)★★★.

Apocalypse

Apocalypse were the most important heavy metal outfit to emerge from Switzerland after Celtic Frost. Comprising Carlos R. Sprenger (vocals), Julien Brocher (guitar), Pierre Alain Zurcher (guitar), Jean Claude Schneider (bass) and Andre Domenjoz (drums), their central influence came from speed metal bands such as Slayer. Formed in 1984, a series of short-lived line-ups ensued before stability was achieved and they secured a contract with Under One Flag. Their debut album was mixed by Metallica supremo Flemming Rasmussen and featured high-energy power metal, although the sound was ultimately flawed by insubstantial vocals. They should not be confused with any of the several other pop and rock acts who have used the name Apocalypse.

● ALBUMS: *Apocalypse* (Under One Flag 1988)★★★.

Apocalyptica

A highly unusual development even by the esoteric standards of Finland's popular music industry, Apocalyptica comprise four classically trained cellists from the Sibelius Academy in Helsinki who interpret heavy-metal classics. Their debut album consisted entirely of Metallica songs - and was not, apparently, intended as a joke. Instead, the quartet attempted to recreate the urgency and bombast of such Metallica standards as 'Enter Sandman' and 'Master Of Puppets' by rearranging them for cello. The group, founded by Eicca Toppinen, Max Lilja, Antero Manninen and Paavo Lotjonen, were drawn together because of what Toppinen describes as 'our love of metal. We wanted to see how metal would work classically, and I especially wanted to try Metallica songs, as they've been a favourite of mine for more than 10 years.' The group was founded in 1993, playing a number of acoustic shows before graduating to an amplified show at a Helsinki hard rock club in the early months of 1996. The idea to record their set was the result of an approach by audience member Kari Hunninen, now the group's manager, who took them to his Mercury Records subsidiary label, Zen Garden. After the album's release, Apocalyptica achieved another of their dreams when they became support band to Metallica's two shows in Helsinki in November 1996.

● ALBUMS: *Plays Metallica By Four Cellos* (Zen Garden/Mercury 1996)★★★.

Apocrypha

From Las Vegas, USA, Apocrypha was the brainchild of techno-wizard rock guitarist Tony Fredianelli. The band's music was characterized by his intricate guitarwork, which combined classical and rock styles to startling effect. Formed in 1988, the original line-up featured Fredianelli, Steve Plocica (vocals), Chip Chrovian (guitar), Al Rumley (bass) and Mike Poe (drums). *Forgotten Scroll* and *Eyes Of Time* were excellent speed-metal albums, but were somewhat lacking in variety. Breck Smith and Dave Schiller replaced Rumley and Poe, respectively, before the band recorded *Area 54*. Released in 1990, it revealed an outfit who had matured considerably as songwriters. Seemingly well equipped to compete with artists such as Megadeth and Metallica, the group, nevertheless, ground to a halt soon afterwards.

● ALBUMS: *Forgotten Scroll* (Roadrunner 1988)★★★, *Eyes Of Time* (Roadrunner 1989)★★★, *Area 54* (Roadrunner 1990)★★★.

Appice, Carmine

b. 15 December 1946, Staten Island, New York, USA. This talented and versatile drummer originally played in small bands on the New York bar circuit. He was a member of the Vagrants, whom he left with guitarist Vince Martell (b. 11 November 1945, Bronx, New York, USA) to join the Pigeons with Tim Bogert (b. 27 August 1944, Richfield, New Jersey, USA; bass, vocals) and Mark Stein (b. 11 March 1947, Bayonne, New Jersey, USA; keyboards, vocals). In December 1966 this foursome renamed themselves Vanilla Fudge, a band perhaps best remembered for the ambitious *The Beat Goes On*, one track of which was an attempt to chart the entire history of popular music in just 12 minutes. Vanilla Fudge disbanded in 1970, and Appice and Bogert went on to form Cactus. This was an exciting project that came to an end in 1972 with the formation of the fifth Jeff Beck group, which Appice and Bogert joined. Appice had intended to make this career move earlier, in July 1968, but Beck had been involved in a car crash. In January 1973 the band became the hard rock trio Beck, Bogert And Appice, a combination of extremely able musicians whose personalities nonetheless clashed, leading to the band breaking up early in 1974. Throughout the 70s and early 80s, Appice was a session drummer, playing for notables such as Rod Stewart and Ozzy Osbourne. He demonstrated songwriting ability by co-writing 'Da Ya Think I'm Sexy?' with Stewart in 1978. During the 80s Appice released a disappointing solo album on Stewart's Riva label and re-formed Vanilla Fudge no less than three times. It seemed, however, that the band had had its day, with 1984's *Mystery* failing to chart. He formed King Kobra in 1985, who released three albums before Appice left to join John Syke's Blue Murder project in 1989.

● ALBUMS: *Carmen Appice* (Riva 1982)★★.

April Wine

Formed in 1969 in Montreal, Quebec, this hard rock group became an immediate success, going on to make inroads in the American market after establishing itself as a platinum act in Canada. Through fluctuating line-ups they arrived at steady membership by the late 70s, including original lead singer Myles Goodwyn (b. 23 June 1948, Halifax,

Nova Scotia, Canada), Brian Greenway (b. 1 October 1951; guitar), Gary Moffet (b. 22 June 1949; guitar), Steve Lang (b. 24 March 1949; bass) and Jerry Mercer (b. 27 April 1939; drums). Among their early admirers were former Young Rascals members Dino Danelli and Gene Cornish, who produced early material for the group. The line-up for their first album had featured Goodwyn on guitar and vocals, David Henman on guitar, Jim Clench on bass and Richie Henman on drums. *Electric Jewels* saw the line-up change, with Gary Moffet joining on guitar and Jerry Mercer on drums to replace the Henman brothers. Clench was replaced on *The Whole World's Goin' Crazy* by Steve Lang, with Greenway added as third guitarist in time for *First Glance*. Despite uneven album performances, April Wine placed three Top 40 singles and five albums in the US charts, their greatest commercial successes coming with the gold album *Harder .. Faster* and the platinum *The Nature Of The Beast*. The group broke up in the mid-80s with Goodwyn going on to record a solo album. They reformed at the turn of the new decade, touring and releasing 1993's *Attitude*.

● ALBUMS: *April Wine* (Aquarius 1972)★★, *On Record* (Aquarius 1973)★★, *Electric Jewels* (Aquarius 1974)★★, *Live* (Aquarius 1975)★★, *Stand Back* (Aquarius 1975)★★, *The Whole World's Goin' Crazy* (London 1976)★★★, *Live At The El Mocambo* (London 1977)★★, *First Glance* (Capitol 1978)★★, *Harder ... Faster* (Capitol 1979)★★★, *The Nature Of The Beast* (Capitol 1981)★★★, *Power Play* (Capitol 1982)★★, *Animal Grace* (Capitol 1984)★★, *Walking Through Fire* (Capitol 1985)★★, *Attitude* (Fre 1993)★★★.
Solo: Myles Goodwyn *Myles Goodwyn* (Atlantic 1988)★★.

● COMPILATIONS: *Greatest Hits* (Aquarius 1979)★★★, *Wine Collection* box set (1994)★★★.

● VIDEOS: *Live In London* (PMI 1986).

Arc Angel

Arc Angel was the brainchild of vocalist and drummer Jeff Cannata and lyricist/guitarist Michael Soldan. Enlisting the services of numerous session musicians, notably Jay Johnson (guitar), Jim Gregory (bass), and Jeff Bova (keyboards), their music was characterized by multi-layered guitar-synthesizer arrangements, infused with melody and delivered with precision. From 1988 onwards, Cannata dropped the Arc Angel moniker in favour of releasing material under his own name.

● ALBUMS: *Arc Angel* (Portrait 1983)★★★

Arcade

As the US heavy rock group Ratt began to disintegrate, vocalist Stephen Pearcy was quick to join a new project with old friend Fred Coury (drums, ex-Cinderella). From beginnings as a Pearcy solo project, a band soon evolved under the name Taboo, later changing to Arcade, with the recruitment of bassist Michael Andrews, ex-Sea Hags guitarist Frankie Wilsey (aka Wilsex), and ex-Michael Monroe guitarist Johnny Angel, who was later replaced by Donnie Syracuse. *Arcade* (titled *Calm Before The Storm* in Europe) was a big, brash, hard rock affair, investigating areas where Pearcy felt his old act had failed to go, with the vocalist making a conscious effort to change his vocal style. Both *Arcade* and a lengthy US club tour did well despite difficult times for hard rock in the face of grunge. *A/2* showed a harder approach - experimental moves with alternative flavours added to the heavy arena-metal dominated by Wilsex and Syracuse's guitar onslaught, although Pearcy's vocals reverted to his former style. Pearcy departed to form Vertex in 1996.

● ALBUMS: *Arcade* aka *Calm Before The Storm* (Epic 1993)★★★, *A/2* (Epic 1994)★★.

Archers Of Loaf

Formed in the USA in 1992 when singer Eric Bachmann met guitarist Eric Johnson on a bus in Chapel Hill, North Carolina, the Archers Of Loaf quickly distinguished themselves with a healthy disrespect for pomposity and grandeur in their decidedly low-fi recordings. With the addition of fellow University of Carolina students Mark Price (drums) and Matt Gentling (bass), they recorded a debut single, 'Wrong', that earned them a contract with San Francisco label Alias. The Archers name itself was something of a giveaway, an impression of a band given to self-depreciation confirmed with the arrival of a single entitled 'Toast', which included the line: 'She's an indie rocker, and nothing's gonna stop her'. This was housed on the group's well-received debut album, *Icky Mettle*, a collection of obtuse musical ideas and defiant lyrical cheek. After the release of a five-track EP, *Archers Of Loaf Vs The Greatest Of All Time*, they earned recognition for their fine performance at 1994's Reading Festival and for rejecting the attentions of the big record labels (including Madonna's Maverick), before starting work on a second album. *Vee Vee* continued the thread of their debut with the superior 'Underachievers March And Fight Song' leading from the rear. *The Speed Of*

Cattle was a credible hotch-potch of potato peelings, b-sides and even a BBC *Peel Session* recording.
● ALBUMS: *Icky Mettle* (Alias 1993)★★★, *Vee Vee* (Alias 1995)★★★, *All The Nation's Airports* (Alias/Elektra 1996)★★★.
Solo: Eric Bachman *Barry Black* (Alias 1995)★★.
● COMPILATIONS: *The Speed Of Cattle* (Alias 1996)★★★.

Armored Saint

This Los Angeles heavy metal quintet was formed in 1981. The band originally comprised John Bush (vocals), Dave Prichard (guitar), Phil E. Sandoval (guitar), Joey Vera (bass) and Gonzo (drums). Their incessant gigging around the Los Angeles bar and club circuit led to them contributing a track to the *Metal Massacre II* compilation album. This, in turn, attracted the attention of Chrysalis Records, who signed them in 1984. *March Of The Saint* appeared the same year to widespread apathy. Poor production resulted in the band's dynamic energy being totally dissipated in a muddy wall of noise. They moved away from the one-dimensional thrash approach on their next two albums, with John Bush's powerful vocal style giving them a strong identity. Sandoval left to form Megattack during the recording of the second album. The band continued as a four-piece for some time, before Jeff Duncan (ex-Odin) was drafted in as replacement. With no commercial success after three albums, their contract with Chrysalis ended. The band returned with an excellent live album on Metal Blade Records, followed almost three years later by *Symbol Of Salvation*, their most accomplished work to date. Duncan was superseded by Alan Barlam (ex-Hellion) in 1989, and sadly, Dave Prichard died of leukaemia on 27 February 1990. In 1992 Bush left to replace Joey Belladonna in Anthrax and the rest of the band dispersed (though Vera and Duncan reunited with Bush in his side-project, Ho Cake). Vera also released a solo album for Metal Blade in 1994, which featured a guest appearance from Bush.
● ALBUMS: *March Of The Saint* (Chrysalis 1984)★★, *Delirious Nomad* (Chrysalis 1985)★★★, *Raising Fear* (Chrysalis 1987)★★★, *Saints Will Conquer - Live* (Metal Blade/Enigma 1988)★★★, *Symbol Of Salvation* (Metal Blade/Enigma 1991)★★★.
Solo: Joey Vera *A Thousand Faces* (Metal Blade 1994)★★.
● VIDEOS: *A Trip Thru Red Times* (Video For Nations 1989).

Artch

This Norwegian heavy metal quintet was formed in Sarpsborg, Norway, during 1982, by bassist Bernt A. Jansen and guitarist Cato Olsen. It took a three-year search to find the right musicians to complete the line-up, with drummer Jorn Jamissen, guitarist Geir Nilssen and vocalist Espen Hoss finally meeting the original duo's requirements. Hoss was killed in a motorcycle crash, and a replacement was eventually found in Icelandic-born Eirikur Hauksson. Influenced by Black Sabbath, Candlemass, Celtic Frost and Deep Purple, their debut album assimilated all these elements within a dense, melodic framework. Brutal riffs, anthemic choruses and grandiose arrangements were the order of the day. The album received a favourable response, but the band were reluctant to promote it with a full-scale tour. Little has been heard of them since.
● ALBUMS: *Another Return* (Metal Blade 1988)★★★, *For The Sake Of Mankind* (Metal Blade 1990)★★★.

Artillery

This Danish heavy metal band was formed in 1982 by the guitarist brothers Michael and Morten Stutzer. After several line-ups, vocalist Flemming Rodsdorf, bassist Peter Torsland and drummer Carter Nielsen were recruited. Influenced by Slayer and Anvil, the band specialized in somewhat formulaic thrash-metal, and recorded three workmanlike albums.
● ALBUMS: *Fear Of Tomorrow* (Roadrunner 1985)★★★, *Terror Squad* (Roadrunner 1986)★★, *By Inheritance* (Roadrunner 1990)★★.

ASAP

The acronym stands for Adrian Smith And Project. This heavy metal unit started off as a sideline interest for the Iron Maiden guitarist, under the unlikely moniker The Entire Population Of Hackney, after a jam session at the Marquee Club in 1986. He intended to use it as an outlet for more conventional songs that did not fit into the Maiden concept. Recruiting guitarists Andy Barnett (who had formerly worked alongside Smith in Urchin) and Dave Colwell, bassist Robin Clayton, keyboardist Richard Young and drummer Zak Starkey (son of Ringo Starr), they recorded *Silver And Gold* in 1989. Smith decided to leave Iron Maiden at this point to concentrate fully on his solo career. His output, however, proved uninspiring and *Silver And Gold* sold poorly. Smith was next seen as a guest with Iron Maiden at the Donington Festival in 1992, before forming a new band called the Untouchables. However, they did not record, and he subsequently concentrated on writing new material.

● ALBUMS: *Silver And Gold* (EMI 1989)★★.

Ash

Ash are a highly touted young guitar band from Downpatrick, County Down, Northern Ireland, who first began to make headway into the mainstream in 1994. Playing sprightly, youthful punk-pop, the members' average age was only 17 when they released their debut record. Rick 'Rock' McMurray (b. 11 July 1975, Larne, Co. Antrim, Northern Ireland; drums), Tim Wheeler (b. 4 January 1977, Downpatrick, Co. Down, Northern Ireland; vocals, guitar) and Mark Hamilton (b. 21 March 1977, England; bass) were still studying for their A-levels when that single, 'Jack Named The Planets', was released in a limited edition of 1,000 copies. Both radio and press were immediately wooed by their snappy, commercial sound. Their appeal easily translated to an American alternative climate, where every A&R executive was searching for a new Green Day, and tantalizing offers followed to sign with either Warner/Reprise Records (who eventually attained their signatures) or Interscope Records. The band elected to fly to Los Angeles and let their hosts squabble and indulge them beyond any expectations that a young UK indie band had a right to entertain. In the UK they signed to Infectious Records, though they first had to negotiate a series of prolonged discussions between record label executives, parents and headmasters. Following a seven-song mini-album in late 1994, their topical fourth single, 'Kung Fu', featured a cover picture of Manchester United's Eric Cantona executing his famous 'kung fu' assault on a Crystal Palace fan. It was recorded in Wales with Oasis producer Owen Morris: 'We wanted to write a really crap Ramones song and it was meant to be the b-side but it turned out too good', they surmised. In its wake, 'Girl From Mars' became a major national hit, debuting at number 11 in the UK charts. It was followed by 'Angel Interceptor', a term lifted from the animated children's series *Captain Scarlet*, but which apparently referred to 'missing someone sexually.' Their long-playing debut proper came in 1996 during which they graced the UK Top 10 with the singles 'Goldfinger' and 'Oh Yeah'. Titled *1977*, many considered this to be a dedication to the punk scene that evidently remained their pivotal influence, yet in actuality, it referred to Wheeler and Hamilton's year of birth, the same year that the film *Star Wars* was released and Elvis Presley died. It rose straight to number 1 in the UK charts. By that time, the group had opted for a more elaborate sound, inspired by recent listening to Phil Spector and the Beach Boys. However, other recognizable themes remained, such as science-fiction television, with another tribute to *Star Wars* on 'Darkside Lightside'. They added a new member in August 1997 when guitarist Charlotte Hatherley (b. Charlotte Franklin Hatherley, 20 June 1979) joined from Nightnurse, and returned to the UK Top 10 in October with the title song of the film *A Life Less Ordinary*. Introduced by the frenetic single 'Jesus Says', 1998's *Nu-Clear Sounds* saw the band move towards a harder-edged American alternative sound with considerable maturity.

● ALBUMS: *Trailer* mini-album (Infectious 1994)★★★, *1977* (Infectious 1996)★★★★, *Live At The Wireless* (Death Star 1997)★★★, *Nu-Clear Sounds* (Infectious 1998)★★★★.

● FURTHER READING: *Ash 1977-97*, Charles Porter.

Ashphalt Ballet

This US heavy metal/'biker-rock' outfit were heavily influenced by the Cult, Lynyrd Skynyrd and Aerosmith (their name is derived from a description of a motorcyclist crashing and skidding along the road at high speed). Fronted by gravel-throated vocalist Gary Jefferies, they soon built up a small but loyal following through incessant gigging on the Los Angeles bar and club circuit. Formed in San Diego in 1988, the line-up was completed by Danny Clarke (guitar), Julius J. Ulrich (guitar), Terry Phillips (bass) and Mikki Kiner (drums). Jeffries was ex-Broken Rule, while the other members of the band had worked together as Mistreated. Their debut for Virgin in 1992 epitomized their no-nonsense, raunchy rock 'n' roll style.

● ALBUMS: *Ashphalt Ballet* (Virgin 1992)★★★, *Pigs* (Capitol 1993)★★★.

Asia

A supergroup consisting of well-known musicians from British art-rock bands, Asia formed in early 1981 and included John Wetton (b. 12 July 1949, Willingdon, Derbyshire, England; vocals), keyboardist Geoff Downes, Steve Howe (b. 8 April 1947, London, England; guitar) and Carl Palmer (b. 20 March 1947, Birmingham, West Midlands, England; drums, percussion). At the time, Wetton had recently left the English progressive band UK, Howe and Downes had just abandoned Yes and Palmer had left Emerson, Lake And Palmer. The group's self-titled debut album was released a year later and, although dismissed by critics as unadventurous and overly commercial, it topped the US album charts for nine weeks, becoming one of the year's bestsellers. A single, 'Heat Of The Moment', also reached the US Top 5. Neither fared as well in the group's homeland. A follow-up single, 'Only Time Will Tell', was a moderate US success. The group released its second album, *Alpha*, in 1983 and although it was a Top 10 hit in the USA, as was the single 'Don't Cry', its sales failed to match those of the debut. Wetton then left the group, to be replaced by Greg Lake (b. 10 November 1948, Bournemouth, Dorset, England), another Emerson, Lake And Palmer alumnus. As testament to the residual affection for the band, a live television concert from Japan drew over 20 million US viewers in late 1983. In late 1985 Wetton rejoined the band and a third album, *Astra*, was released. However, its comparatively low chart position precipitated the band's dissolution. By early 1990 Howe had left to join a regenerated Yes, with Pat Thrall, an ex-Pat Travers Band member, moving in to take his place. *Then And Now*, released the same year, was a mixture of six earlier recordings and four new songs. The group then moved from European label Musidisc to a new home on Music For Nations subsidiary Bullet Proof.

● ALBUMS: *Asia* (Geffen 1982)★★★, *Alpha* (Geffen 1983)★★, *Astra* (Geffen 1985)★★, *Then & Now* (Geffen 1990)★★, *Live In Moscow* (Rhino 1992)★★, *Aqua* (Musidisc 1992)★★, *Aria* (Bullet Proof 1994)★★.

● COMPILATIONS: *Anthology* (Reef 1998)★★.

● VIDEOS: *Asia In Asia* (Vestron Music Video 1984), *Asia (Live)* (Virgin Vision 1991).

At The Gates

This heavy thrash quintet from Gothenburg, Sweden, started with a generic approach to their music and eventually became noted for their innate ability to write catchy death-metal tunes. Formed in late 1990, the band comprised Tomas Lindeberg (b. 16 October 1972; vocals), Jonas Bjorler (b. 26 February 1973; bass), Anders Bjorler (b. 26 February 1973; guitar), Adrian Erlandsson (b. 27 October 1970; drums) and Alf Svensson (guitar), who recorded their first release, the *Gardens Of Grief* EP, for the Dolores label. Having thus established their death metal credentials they embarked on a prolonged bout of touring with a variety of other heavyweight acts, such as Massacre and Immolation. After signing to Peaceville Records for their first album, *The Red In The Sky Is Ours*, further touring ensued with My Dying Bride, before they released*With Fear I Kiss The Burning Darkness* in August 1993. Replacing Svensson with Martin Larsson (b. 28 February 1973; guitar), they gradually established a reputation as not only one of the most talented bands on the death metal scene, but also as one of the hardest-working live units. With *Terminal Spirit Disease* the band gained widespread acclaim for their ability to create music of penetrating intensity suffused with melody. Their reputation preceding them, there followed further UK and European touring with My Dying Bride and Anathema, before they finally headlined their own shows. A move to Earache Records resulted in arguably their most complete and accessible album, *Slaughter Of The Soul*. Once again the songs were brutal, raw and boasted a sense of melody lacking among most other bands of the genre. Yet more touring followed, this time in the USA, while the album was nominated in the Best Hard Rock category at the Swedish Grammy Awards, and the video for the lead track, 'Blinded By Fear', became one of the most heavily played clips on MTV's Headbanger's Ball. Unfortunately, their industrious attitude proved to be their undoing, as the extreme touring schedule put the band under huge pressure, resulting in the main songwriting team of the two Bjorler brothers splitting in 1996. The remainder of the band felt that they could not continue and At The Gates splintered into a number of separate fledgling projects. The Bjorler brothers and Erlandsson were reunited in Haunted.

● ALBUMS: *The Red In The Sky Is Ours* (Peaceville 1991)★★★, *With Fear I Kiss The Burning Darkness* (Peaceville 1992)★★★, *Terminal Spirit Disease* (Peaceville 1994)★★★, *Slaughter Of The Soul* (Earache 1995)★★★.

Atheist

Formerly known as Ravage, this US heavy metal band changed its name to Atheist in 1987 when the line-up of Randy Burke (guitar), Roger Patterson (bass), Kelly Shaeffer (vocals, guitar) and Steve Flynn (drums) was established. From amateurish origins, the band developed into a powerful and accomplished 'death-metal' outfit. Playing at breakneck speed, their sound was characterized by Shaeffer's gurgling vocal style. They released a debut album to favourable reviews, and built up a loyal following in their native state of Florida.

● ALBUMS: *Piece Of Time* (Metal Blade

1990)★★★, *Unquestionable Presence* (Metal Blade 1991)★★★, *Elements* (Metal Blade 1993)★★★.

Atilla (Netherlands)

This Dutch power-trio was put together in 1984 by former Wells Fargo members Herbie Vanderloo (vocals, guitar) and Arjen Michaels. With the addition of drummer Ton Holtewes, they recorded a mini-album the following year. Although musically sound, the songs were let down by Vanderloo's amateurish vocal style, which lacked power, range and conviction. Two more thrash-orientated albums followed, with 1989's *Triad* containing their strongest material.

● ALBUMS: *Weapons Of Extermination* mini-album (1985)★★, *Violent Streets* (1988)★★, *Triad* (1989)★★★.

Atilla (USA)

This speed-metal trio from New York, USA, was formed by guitarist John De Leon in 1983. Enlisting the services of vocalist/bassist Vincent Paul and drummer A.T. Soldier, they made their vinyl debut with a track on Mausoleum's sampler album, *Metal Over America*, in 1985. *Rolling Thunder*, produced by Rods drummer Carl Canedy, was released the following year, but made little impact. It featured an uninspired fusion of hard-rock and thrash, including a version of the Alice Cooper classic, 'School's Out'. The band disintegrated shortly after the album's release.

● ALBUMS: *Rolling Thunder* (Mausoleum 1986)★★.

Atlantic

Firmly in the classic AOR tradition, Atlantic musicians Phil Bates (lead vocals, guitar, keyboards), Simon Harrison (guitar, keyboards), Glen Williams (keyboards), Chris Taylor (keyboards), Paul Hoare (bass) and Andy Van Evans (guitar) represent an unfashionably large musical nucleus, complicated by the fact that drummer Andy Duncan does not play live, being replaced on such occasions by Phil Ridden. The group was formed in the summer of 1991 when Harrison was working on a television pilot theme song. He discovered his kindred spirit Bates in his quest for a suitable backing singer. The latter had already performed session tracks for Billy Ocean, Long John Baldry and producer Tony Visconti, while his own bands, Trickster and Quill, had supported ELO and Boston. His many session commissions included an appearance on the *Gladiators* television theme tune. His recent history up to the formation of Atlantic had also seen him singing with ELO Part 2. Together with an assembly line of local musicians, plus producer Colin Thurston (Duran Duran) and session drummer Duncan (Trevor Horn, Simple Minds), the duo concocted a set of AOR rock and power ballads, released by the Music For Nations label. A touring band was assembled, while a single, 'Every Beat Of My Heart', was used to promote the album.

● ALBUMS: *Power* (Music For Nations 1994)★★★.

Atom Seed

This London-based quartet formed in 1989 with a line-up of Paul Cunningham (vocals), Simon James (guitar), Chris Dale (bass - the original bass player, Chris Huxter, departed to form New England) and Amir (drums), and quickly established a reputation as one of Britain's hardest-working and most exciting live bands. Signing to FM Revolver in 1990, Atom Seed released the *I Don't Want To Talk About It* EP, before making their full debut with *Get In Line.* Faith No More and Red Hot Chili Peppers were obvious reference points for *Get In Line*'s remarkably mature material, and the lively delivery retained all the youthful energy of their live shows. With a subsequent major contract with London, the Atom Seed's future seemed bright, despite Amir's departure, with Jerry Hawkins replacing him. However, the band spent considerable time writing and demoing new material for London, who seemed disappointed with the performance of the reissued debut and single 'Rebel', and both their live profile and enthusiasm dwindled as a result. *The Dead Happy* EP was Atom Seed's sole London release before they were dropped, and the disillusioned band broke up. A second album, *Hard Sell Paranoia*, remains unreleased.

● ALBUMS: *Get In Line* (FM Revolver 1990)★★★★.

Atomic Rooster

Formed in 1969 at the height of the UK progressive rock boom, the original Rooster line-up comprised Vincent Crane (b. 21 May 1943, Reading, Berkshire, England, d. 14 February 1989; organ), Nick Graham (bass) and Carl Palmer (b. 20 March 1947, Birmingham, West Midlands, England; drums). Crane and Palmer had just departed from the chart-topping Crazy World Of Arthur Brown and it was assumed that their new group would achieve sustained success. After only one album, however, the unit fragmented, with Graham joining Skin Alley and Palmer founding Emerson, Lake And Palmer. Crane soldiered on with new members John DuCann (guitar, vocals, ex-Andromeda) and

Paul Hammond (drums), featured on the album *Death Walks Behind You*. Their excursions into hard rock produced two riff-laden yet catchy UK hit singles - 'Tomorrow Night' (number 11, Febuary 1971) and 'The Devil's Answer' (number 4, July 1971), as Crane adopted the Ray Manzarek (Doors) style of using keyboards to record bass parts. With assistance from Pete French of Cactus, the trio recorded their third album, *In Hearing Of*, but just when they seemed settled, they split. DuCann and Hammond joined Bullet, then Hardstuff, and French formed Leafhound. The irrepressible Crane refused to concede defeat and recruited new members, guitarist Steve Bolton, bassist Bill Smith and drummer Rick Parnell (son of the orchestra leader, Jack Parnell). The new line-up was completed by the famed singer Chris Farlowe (b. John Henry Deighton, 13 October 1940, Islington, London, England). A dramatic musical shift towards blue-eyed soul won few new fans, however, and Crane finally dissolved the band in 1974. Thereafter, he collaborated with former colleague Arthur Brown, but could not resist reviving the fossilized Rooster in 1979 (the same year he teamed up with Crane once more for the 'Don't Be A Dummy' Lee Cooper jeans advertisement, backed by members of Gillan and Status Quo). After two anti-climactic albums with new drummer Preston Hayman, and then a returning Hammond, Crane finally killed off his creation. The final Atomic Rooster studio album included guest stints from David Gilmour (Pink Floyd), Bernie Torme and John Mazarolli on guitars in place of DuCann. In 1983 Crane accepted an invitation to record and tour with Dexys Midnight Runners and appeared on their acclaimed 1985 album *Don't Stand Me Down*. He had been suffering from depression for some time when he took his own life in 1989.

● ALBUMS: *Atomic Rooster* (B&C 1970)★★, *Death Walks Behind You* (B&C 1970)★★, *In Hearing Of* (Pegasus 1971)★★★, *Made In England* (Dawn 1972)★★, *Nice 'N' Greasy* (Dawn 1973)★, *Atomic Rooster* (EMI 1980)★, *Headline News* (Towerbell 1983)★.

● COMPILATIONS: *Assortment* (B&C 1974)★★, *Home To Roost* (Mooncrest 1977)★★, *The Devil Hits Back* (Demi Monde 1989)★★, *BBC In Concert* (Windsong 1994)★★.

Atomkraft

After a series of false starts and four years of frustration, UK heavy metal band Atomkraft finally secured a recording contract with Neat Records in 1985. They were among the first British thrash-metal bands, and built a solid reputation supporting labelmates Venom. The band comprised Tony Dolan (guitar), Rob Matthews (guitar), D.C. Rage (bass), Ged Wolf (drums), and vocalist Ian Swift (ex-Avenger). By the time *Future Warriors* emerged in 1985, their one-dimensional thrashing sounded rather dated in comparison with the new American outfits that had recently appeared. After a further two average releases, Atomkraft split, with Dolan going on to join the revamped Venom in 1989.

● ALBUMS: *Future Warriors* (Neat 1985)★★★, *Queen Of Death* (Neat 1986)★★, *Conductors Of Noise* (Neat 1987)★★.

Atrophy

This speed metal outfit hailed from Tucson, Arizona, USA. The band was formed in 1987 by vocalist Brian Zimmerman and guitarist Chris Lykins. Recruiting Rick Skowron (guitar), James Gulotta (bass) and Tim Kelly (drums), they recorded a demo album, *Chemical Dependency*, the same year. This attracted the attention of thrash specialists Roadrunner Records, who immediately recognized them as a band with great potential. *Socialized Hate* was an impressive debut, featuring heavy-duty riffing, screaming guitars and thoughtful lyrics. Their second album saw some musical progression, with the material showing a greater awareness of melody and a slightly less extreme approach.

● ALBUMS: *Socialized Hate* (Roadrunner 1988)★★★, *Violent By Nature* (Roadrunner 1990)★★★.

August Redmoon

This Californian heavy rock quartet was formed in 1980 by drummer Dave Young. With the addition of vocalist Michael Henry, Greg Winslow (bass) and Ray Winslow (guitar), they adopted a traditional approach to hard rock. Incorporating influences of Kiss, Van Halen and Aerosmith, plus an added 'speed-metal' element, they recorded *Fools Are Never Alone* in 1982. Following a long line of management and label disputes, the band changed its name to Terracuda in 1984, but split before entering a recording studio. Henry, Young and Gary Winslow went on to form Eden.

● ALBUMS: *Fools Are Never Alone* (1982)★★.

Autograph

Autograph were formed in Los Angeles, California, USA, in 1983 by vocalist Steve Plunkett and bassist Randy Rand. With the addition of Steve Lynch (guitar), Steven Isham (keyboards) and Keni Richards (drums), the band signed to RCA Records the following year. Comprising five exceptionally talented musicians, they delivered a strong combination of sophisticated and melodic AOR that had enormous pop-metal crossover potential. 'Turn Up The Radio', from their debut *Sign In Please*, became a belated US Top 50 hit in 1985, with the album eventually peaking at number 29 in the *Billboard* chart. Two further excellent albums were released, with 1987's *Loud And Clear* representing the pinnacle of the band's creativity. Isham quit in 1988 to start a new project with ex-Dio guitarist Craig Goldie. Autograph continued as a four-piece, but failed to attract media attention or repeat their initial success. They subsequently became disillusioned and disbanded in 1989, having failed to realize their potential. Richards joined Dirty White Boy.

● ALBUMS: *Sign In Please* (RCA 1984)★★★, *That's The Stuff* (RCA 1985)★★★, *Loud And Clear* (RCA 1987)★★★.

Autopsy

Drummer/vocalist Chris Reifert formed this death metal act with guitarist Danny Coralles and Eric Cutler in Florida, USA, after his involvement with Death on *Scream Bloody Gore*. Sadus bassist Steve DiGiorgio guested on *Severed Survival* before Ken Sovari was recruited for a European tour with Bolt Thrower and Pestilence; he was then replaced by Cutler's brother, Steve. The *Retribution For The Dead* EP and *Mental Funeral* saw Autopsy continue in their sludgy death vein with gore-laden lyrics. *Fiend For Blood* again featured DiGiorgio, before Josh Barohn (ex-Suffocation) was recruited as bassist. *Acts Of The Unspeakable* continued the grisly lyrical approach, but encountered problems over gruesome cover artwork, with album covers being destroyed by Australian authorities and similar T-shirts confiscated by German customs. *Shitfun* found the group trawling familiar territory, with song titles such as 'Bowel Ripper', 'Burnt To A Fuck' and 'Excremental Ecstasy'.

● ALBUMS: *Severed Survival* (Peaceville 1989)★★★, *Mental Funeral* (Peaceville 1991)★★, *Fiend For Blood* mini-album (Peaceville 1992)★★, *Acts Of The Unspeakable* (Peaceville 1992)★★, *Shitfun* (Peaceville 1995)★★★.

Avalon

This Dutch heavy metal quintet was formed in 1984 by guitarist Jack Pisters and vocalist Richard Muermans. Recruiting Maarten Huiskamp (keyboards), Erik Fox (bass) and Jacques Kraal (drums), the band specialized in combining the hard-driving rock style of Iron Maiden with very intricate and off-beat guitarwork that at times verged on the *avant garde*. They released an excellent mini-album in 1986 on the independent Dynamo label. This focused attention on the band's imaginative lyrics and futuristic guitar sound. Unfortunately, as soon as the album appeared the band underwent several personnel changes, prompting its eventual demise. This Avalon should not be confused with either the Capitol Records recording artists from the USA, the London recording artists from Canada, or the folk artists, all of whom share the same name.

● ALBUMS: *The Third Move* mini-album (Dynamo 1986)★★★.

Avatar

Formerly known as Metropolis, the heavy metal group Avatar was formed in Florida, USA, in 1978 by the Oliva brothers. Comprising Jon Oliva (vocals, guitar, keyboards), Criss Oliva (guitar), Steve 'Doc' Wacholz (drums) and Keith Collins (bass), they specialized in hard-edged power-metal, with melodic undercurrents. The most distinctive elements of their sound were Jon Oliva's soaring vocals and Chris Oliva's razor-sharp guitar runs. They made their vinyl debut with *City Beneath The Surface*, a three-track EP of brutal and uncompromising metal at its very best. They subsequently changed their name to Savatage and went on to achieve international recognition and success. The EP is now highly valued by collectors of American heavy metal.

Avenger (Germany)

This hi-tech thrash metal quartet originated in Herne, West Germany. Formed in 1984, the band comprised Peter Wagner (vocals, bass), Thomas Gruning (guitar), Jochen Schroeder (guitar) and Jorg Michael (drums). The band's debut album combined a speed-metal style with intricate Rush-like bridges and interludes. The songs were complex and technically proficient but were let down somewhat by the vocals, which lacked both power and range. After the release of the mini-album *Depraved To Black*, they became known as Rage and enjoyed critical acclaim throughout Europe.

● ALBUMS: *Prayer Of Steel* (Wishbone 1985)★★, *Depraved To Black* mini-album (Wishbone 1985)★★★.

AVENGER (UK)

This Newcastle-based, speed-metal outfit was formed by ex-Blitzkrieg duo Brian Ross (vocals) and Mick Moore (bass). With the addition of Gary Young (drums) and Lee Cheetam (guitar), they recorded the single 'Too Wild To Tame', before Ross switched places with Satan's vocalist Ian Swift. *Bloodsports* followed, a prime example of the New Wave Of British Heavy Metal and notable for some inspired guitarwork from Cheetam. A series of guitarists arrived and departed in rapid succession, with American Greg Reiter eventually being recruited on a permanent basis. *Killer Elite* was followed by a disastrous American tour. Returning to England, Swift left to join Atomkraft and the band fell apart.

● ALBUMS: *Blood Sports* (Neat 1984)★★★, *Killer Elite* (Neat 1985)★★.

AVIARY

This short-lived, esoteric UK art-rock band was formed in 1978 by Brad Love (vocals, keyboards) and Toby Bowen (guitar). With the recruitment of Paul Madden (keyboards), Ken Steimonts (bass, vocals) and Richard Bryans (drums), the line-up was complete. Assimilating influences as diverse as Yes, Queen, the Beatles and classical music, they recorded an overblown debut characterized by high-pitched vocals and harmonies. Unable to attract favourable media attention, the band split soon after the album was released. Brad Love went on to record a solo album in 1982.

● ALBUMS: *Aviary* (Epic 1979)★★.

AVIATOR

This New York hard rock quartet was formed in 1984 by guitarist Richie Cerniglia and drummer Michael Ricciardelli (ex-Network and Barnaby Bye). With the addition of vocalist Ernie White and bassist Steve Vitale, they signed to RCA Records in 1986. Influenced by Bon Jovi, Europe and Thin Lizzy, their highly commercial debut album was produced by Neil Kernon. The songs were identikit pop-metal, and the band struggled to establish their own image. The album sold poorly and Aviator were subsequently dropped by RCA. A series of line-up changes ensued, but the band was unable to secure another recording contract. By the 90s the group had split, although former members were involved in an independently packaged CD release of their album that included a number of additional demo tracks.

● ALBUMS: *Aviator* (RCA 1987)★★.

AXE

The rock band Babyface consisted of Edgar Riley (vocals), Bobby Barth (guitar), Mike Turpin (bass) and Bob Miles (drums); in 1979 they recruited Mike Osborne (b. 22 December 1979, d. 21 July 1984) as second guitarist and Teddy Mueller as the replacement for Miles on drums, and changed their name to Axe. Purveying highly sophisticated pomp-rock, they established a loyal following in the USA and released three superbly crafted albums. However, in 1984 vocalist Osborne was killed in a car crash. The band dissolved itself, with Barth joining Blackfoot for a short period in 1985, before re-forming Axe in 1989 with ex-UFO drummer Andy Parker.

● ALBUMS: *Axe* (MCA 1979)★★★, *Living On The Edge* (MCA 1980)★★★, *Offering* (Atco 1981)★★★.

AXE VICTIMS

A German hard rock group of the mid-80s, Axe Victims comprised Tom Bohn (guitar), Frank Fanfare (vocals), Rowland Hag (guitar), Martin Roco (drums) and Holgar George (bass). Recording for Mausoleum Records, they issued two creditable melodic rock albums in 1984 and 1985. *Hypnotised* was the better effort, with tracks such as 'Shoot From The Stars' refining the group's self-evident AC/DC influence. However, it was their final recording, as public and critical apathy combined to ensure their early exit from the music scene.

● ALBUMS: *Another Victim* (Mausoleum 1984)★★, *Hypnotised* (Mausoleum 1985)★★★.

AXEWITCH

This Swedish heavy metal quartet originated in Stockholm in 1981. The initial line-up comprised Anders Wallentoft (vocals), Magnus Jarls (guitar), Mikael Johansson (guitar), Tommy Brage (bass) and Mats Johansson (drums). They started life as a doomy thrash-metal outfit, but, unable to attract press coverage, they decided on a radical change in direction. *Hooked On High Heels* saw the band sporting fashionable clothes, expensive hairstyles and a much more commercial approach similar to Mötley Crüe. However, the record-buying public was not impressed and the album sold poorly. The band split shortly afterwards.

● ALBUMS: *The Lord Of Flies* (Neon 1983)★★, *Visions Of The Past* (Neon 1984)★★, *Hooked On High Heels* (Neon 1985)★★.

Axis

This US power-trio was formed by ex-Derringer duo Danny Johnson (guitar, vocals) and Vinnie Appice (drums). With the addition of bassist Jay Davis, they recorded *It's A Circus World* in 1978. This was a derivative hard-rock album that drew on the early 70s as a source of inspiration. The band disintegrated soon after the album's release, with Appice joining Black Sabbath and later Dio. Johnson replaced Steve Vai in Alcatrazz, then teamed up with Davis again in Private Life. He later formed Danny Johnson And The Bandits.

● ALBUMS: *It's A Circus World* (RCA 1978)★★.

Axxis

This highly competent German hard rock quartet comprised Walter Pietsch (guitar, vocals), Bernhard Weiss (guitar, vocals), Werner Kleinhans (bass) and Richard Michalski (drums, vocals). Their diverse style recalled Boston and Black Sabbath and also Europe and the Scorpions. Axxis released *Kingdom Of The Night* in 1986 to favourable reviews and supported Black Sabbath on their European tour the same year. They were unable to transform this into album sales, however, as the band lacked both consistency and real direction.

● ALBUMS: *Kingdom Of The Night* (Parlophone 1986)★★★.

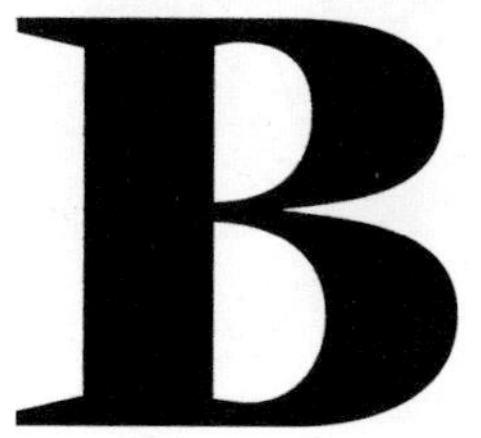

B'zz

Formed from the ashes of heavy metal 'biker-band' Boyzz, this US group featured Michael Tafoya (guitar), David Angel (bass) and Anatole Halinkovich (keyboards). With the recruitment of Tom Holland (vocals) and Steve Riley (drums), they rejected their previous Hells Angels image and concentrated instead on pop-metal. Their debut album, released in 1982, fused elements of Kiss, Cheap Trick and Foreigner, but met with little success. The band disintegrated when Holland left to form a new outfit under his own name. Riley went on to play with W.A.S.P.

● ALBUMS: *Get Up* (Epic 1982)★★.

B.L.O.W.

Something of a mid-90s supergroup, hard rock band b.l.o.w. were formed in 1994 by Dave Gooding (vocals, ex-No Sweat), brothers Bruce (b. 10 May 1968, Berwick-upon-Tweed, Scotland; guitar) and Jimmy Dickinson (keyboards, both ex-Little Angels), Mark Richardson (drums) and final recruit, Nick Boyes (bass). Based in Surrey, England, their first demo exceeded expectations, even given their pedigree, and included a more psychedelic/pop-influenced approach than might have been anticipated. A cover version of Peter Tosh's 'Legalise It' typified their eclectic and much-admired live set throughout 1994. This style was partly a conscious decision on behalf of the former Little Angels members, who wanted a more fluid environment for their songwriting and performances. In the summer of 1995, Richardson departed to join Skunk Anansie, after he was recruited during a drunken exchange at that year's *Kerrang!* awards ceremony.

● ALBUMS: *Man And Goat Alike* mini-album (Cottage Industries 1995)★★★, *Pigs* (Cottage Industries 1996)★★★.

Babe Ruth

Formed in Hatfield, Hertfordshire, England, in 1971, this engaging progressive rock group was originally named Shacklock after founding guitarist Alan Shacklock. Janita 'Jenny' Haan (vocals), Chris Holmes (keyboards and organ), Dave Punshon (piano), Dave Hewitt (bass) and Dick Powell (drums) completed the initial line-up, which took its new name from the legendary American baseball player. *First Base*, which included 'Wells Fargo', a popular stage favourite, enhanced the quintet's growing reputation, much of which rested on Haan's raw delivery. However, despite enjoying commercial success in the USA and Canada, where *Amar Cabalero* achieved a gold disc, the group was plagued by personnel problems. Ed Spevock (drums) and Steve Gurl (piano, ex-Wild Turkey) replaced Powell and Punshon, but the departure of Shacklock following the release of *Babe Ruth* proved pivotal. A second Wild Turkey refugee, Bernie Marsden, was added for *Stealin' Home*, but in 1976 the line-up was again undermined by the loss of Haan and Hewitt. Ellie Hope (vocals) and Ray Knott (bass) joined for *Kid's Stuff*, but the group was now bereft of direction and split. Marsden later surfaced in Paice, Ashton And Lord and Whitesnake while Spevock switched to Pete Brown's Piblokto!

● ALBUMS: *First Base* (Harvest 1972)★★★, *Amar Cabalero* (Harvest 1973)★★★, *Babe Ruth* (Harvest 1975)★★★, *Stealin' Home* (Harvest 1975)★★, *Kid's Stuff* (Capitol 1976)★.

● COMPILATIONS: *Grand Slam: The Best Of Babe Ruth* (EMI 1994)★★★.

BABES IN TOYLAND

This hardcore rock trio spearheaded a new wave of US female bands at the turn of the 90s. Their origins can be traced back to 1987, when Kat Bjelland (b. Katherine Bjelland, 9 December 1963, Woodburn, Oregon, USA; vocals, guitar) moved to Minneapolis. Previously, she had played in a band, Sugar Baby Doll, with Courtney Love (Hole) and Jennifer Finch (L7) in San Francisco. The trio was completed by Michelle Leon (bass) and Lori Barbero (b. 27 November 1960, Minneapolis, Minnesota, USA; drums, vocals). They first came to prominence at the legendary singles club at Sub Pop Records, then made a lasting impression on a European support tour with Sonic Youth. A debut album, produced by Jack Endino, was recorded live with the vocals overdubbed. Soon afterwards, WEA A&R representative Tim Carr saw the band live in Minneapolis and was impressed. After signing to the label, they recorded the 1992 mini-album *To Mother*. Bjelland, meanwhile, was busy defending the band within the media, who were attempting to categorize the group alongside other all-girl bands to create a convenient 'movement': 'Men and women play their instruments to a completely different beat. Women are a lot more rhythmic - naturally - than men. It doesn't even have anything to do with music, it all has to do with timing.' In 1992 Leon left the group and was replaced by Maureen Herman (b. 25 July 1966, Chicago, Illinois, USA). *Fontanelle* received excellent reviews throughout the rock and indie press, and a support tour with Faith No More brought them further plaudits, as they signed with their first manager, Debbie Gordon. However, when the group took a break in 1993, press speculation suggested their imminent demise. Lori Barbero formed her own label, Spanish Fly, home of Milk, while Bjelland worked with her husband Stuart Gray, singer with Australian noise outfit Lubricated Goat, on two projects, Crunt and KatSu. Babes In Toyland reconvened in time for the Lollapalooza tour and in 1995 *Nemesisters* was a powerful return to form, with memorable cover versions of Sister Sledge's 'We Are Family' and Eric Carmen's 'All By Myself' sitting well alongside strong original compositions such as 'Memory' and 'Scherezadian 22'. Herman was replaced by Danna Cochran in late 1996.

● ALBUMS: *Spanking Machine* (Twin Tone 1990)★★, *To Mother* mini-album (Reprise/WEA 1991)★★, *The Peel Sessions* (Strange Fruit 1992)★★★, *Fontanelle* (Reprise/WEA 1992)★★★★, *Painkillers* (Reprise/WEA 1993)★★★, *Nemesisters* (Reprise/WEA 1995)★★★★.

● FURTHER READING: *Babes In Toyland: The Making And Selling Of A Rock And Roll Band*, Neal Karlen.

BABY ANIMALS

This Australian indie-metal quartet was formed in 1990 by vocalist Suzi Demarchi and guitarist Dave Leslie. Recruiting bassist Eddie Parise and drummer Frank Delenza, they released their first album on the Imago label in February 1992. Influenced by Heart, the Pretenders, AC/DC, INXS and Siouxsie And The Banshees, their sound was characterized by Demarchi's provocative growl and Leslie's understated guitarwork. They made a considerable impact in the UK as support band to Bryan Adams on his 1991 tour, but have remained a cult act.

● ALBUMS: *Baby Animals* (Imago 1992)★★★, *Shaved And Dangerous* (Imago 1993)★★★.

BABY CHAOS

This hard rock band, formed in Stewarton, Strathclyde, Scotland, in 1992, were signed by East West Records after appearing on UK television's *The Late Show* in the spring of 1993. Led by the gifted, if erratic, vocalist and guitarist Chris Gordon, the rest of the band originally comprised Bobby Dunn (bass), Davey Greenwood (drums) and Grant McFarlane (guitars). Gordon had studied classical guitar as a child but became frustrated by the lack of opportunities available in Stewarton. The origins of Baby Chaos can be traced to his meeting Dunn, Greenwood and McFarlane at Stewarton Academy. The group spent the next two years driving around Scotland, playing at any venue willing to give them a chance. Then came the fateful appearance on *The Late Show*, at which they were seen by former Happy Mondays manager Nathan McGough, newly installed in an A&R capacity at East West. A series of abrasive rock singles, 'Sperm', 'Buzz', 'Hello Victim' and 'Golden Tooth', followed. A steady rise in profile was achieved with a relentless touring schedule, including nearly 100 gigs with bands such as the Wildhearts (with whom they were frequently compared), Terrorvision and Shed Seven between September 1994 and May 1995. They also toured America with Elastica in support of their *Safe Sex, Designer Drugs & The Death Of Rock 'n' Roll* debut, though, as a result of exhaustion, Greenwood was temporarily replaced by Simon 'Gen' Matthews of Jesus Jones. A second album followed in 1996. *Love Your Self Abuse* shared the debut's affection for rock 'n' roll excess, documenting all manner of seedy pursuits and characters. However, the emotional span of songs such as 'Hello' prevented them from falling into the self-parody that afflicted the end of the Wildhearts' career. Greenwood was forced to leave the band in 1996 on medical advice owing to a heart problem.

● ALBUMS: *Safe Sex, Designer Drugs & The Death Of Rock 'n' Roll* (East West 1994)★★★, *Love Your Self Abuse* (East West 1996)★★★.

BABY TUCKOO

UK heavy metal band Baby Tuckoo were formed in 1983 by ex-Geddes Axe guitarist/keyboard player Andrew Barrott, alongside Rob Armitage (vocals), Neil Saxton (guitar), Paul Smith (bass) and Tony Sugden (drums). They quickly established a following in their home-town of Bradford, and they became part of the second-generation New Wave Of British Heavy Metal movement along with Chrome Molly and Chariot. Signed in 1984 to independent label Ultra Noise, they released an impressive debut album, *First Born*, which embraced British and American influences and drew comparisons with Whitesnake. Nevertheless, they were dropped by their record company soon afterwards. A second album followed in similar musical vein, and they continued to be a popular live attraction. However, the members disbanded Baby Tuckoo in 1986. Rob Armitage joined Accept for a brief spell and Barrott became a member of Chrome Molly.

● ALBUMS: *First Born* (Ultra Noise 1984)★★★, *Force Majeure* (Music For Nations 1985)★★★.

BABYLON AD

Jamey Pacheco (drums), Robert Reid (bass), Ron Freschi (guitar), Danny De La Rosa (guitar) and Derek (vocals) formed this hard rock group in San Francisco, California, USA, in 1987. Originally known as the Persuaders, the group signed a major label contract with Arista Records, on whose advice the band name was changed. Their debut album was a promising collection of cultured, well-produced rock, rendered with melody and purpose. It brought them significant early acclaim in a career that subsequently failed to build on the initial good impressions.

● ALBUMS: *Babylon AD* (Arista 1989)★★★, *Nothing Sacred* (Arista 1992)★★.

BABYS

Considerable attention attended the launch of this much-touted British rock group. John Waite (b. 4 July 1955, Lancaster, Lancashire, England; vocals, bass), Mike Corby (b. 3 July 1955, London, England; guitar, keyboards), Walter 'Wally' Stocker (b. 17 March 1954, London, England; guitar) and former Spontaneous Combustion and Strider member Tony Brock (b. 31 March 1954, Bournemouth, Dorset, England; drums) were promoted as the most promising newcomers of 1976, but while *The Babys* offered a competent blend of pop and rock, similar to that of the Raspberries, it lacked an identifiable sound and image. They were signed to Chrysalis Records on the strength of a video demo directed by Mike Mansfield - a rather unique sales pitch at the time. Obscured by the punk explosion, the quartet looked to the USA for commercial succour over the ensuing years. Jonathan Cain (b. 26 February 1950, Chicago, Illinois, USA) replaced Corby following the release of *Head First*, but although the Babys achieved considerable US success, including two Top 20 singles with 'Isn't It Time' and 'Every Time I Think Of

You', they remained in the shadow of AOR stalwarts Fleetwood Mac, Foreigner and Journey. Ricky Phillips joined as bass player for their final two albums. Waite subsequently embarked on a high-profile solo career, before reuniting with Cain and Phillips in the late 80s 'supergroup' Bad English.

● ALBUMS: *The Babys* (Chrysalis 1976)★★★, *Broken Heart* (Chrysalis 1977)★★★, *Head First* (Chrysalis 1978)★★★, *Union Jacks* (Chrysalis 1980)★★, *On The Edge* (Chrysalis 1980)★★.

● COMPILATIONS: *Anthology* (Chrysalis 1981)★★★, *Unofficial Babys* (NEMS 1982)★★, *The Best Of The Babys* (EMI 1997)★★★.

BACHMAN-TURNER OVERDRIVE

Formed in Vancouver, British Columbia, Canada, in 1972, Bachman-Turner Overdrive was a hard-rock group featuring former Guess Who member Randy Bachman (b. 27 September 1943, Winnipeg, Manitoba, Canada; guitar, lead vocals). Randy Bachman had left the Guess Who in July 1970, recorded a solo album, *Axe*, and, owing to a bout of illness, had to cancel a projected collaboration with former Nice keyboardist Keith Emerson. Bachman subsequently formed Brave Belt with his brother Robbie Bachman, C.F. 'Fred' Turner (b. 16 October 1943, Winnipeg, Manitoba, Canada) and Chad Allan (b. Allan Kobel). Brave Belt recorded two unsuccessful albums for Reprise Records in 1971-72, after which Allan was replaced by another Bachman brother, Tim. In 1972 the new band took its new name, the word 'Overdrive' being borrowed from a trade magazine for truck drivers. They signed to Mercury Records in 1973 and released a self-titled first album which made a minor impact in the USA and at home in Canada. Tim Bachman departed at that point, replaced by Blair Thornton (b. 23 July 1950). After constant touring in the USA, BTO's second album, *Bachman-Turner Overdrive II*, provided their breakthrough, reaching number 4 in the USA and yielding the number 12 hit 'Takin' Care Of Business'. The third album, *Not Fragile*, released in the summer of 1974, topped the US album charts and provided the US number 1/UK number 2 hit single 'You Ain't Seen Nothing Yet', sung with a dramatized stutter by Randy Bachman. *Four Wheel Drive*, the group's 1975 album, was its last Top 10 recording, although the group continued to release singles and albums until the end of the 70s. Randy Bachman departed from the group in 1977 and formed a band called Ironhorse as well as recording solo. He was replaced by Jim Clench, who appeared on the album *Freeways*. The following year the band officially changed its name to BTO but could not revive its earlier fortunes. In 1984, Randy Bachman, Tim Bachman and C.F. Turner regrouped and released a second self-titled album, this time for Compleat Records, that barely scraped the US charts. The group was still touring in the early 90s but had not released any further albums.

● ALBUMS: *Bachman-Turner Overdrive* (Mercury 1973)★★, *Bachman-Turner Overdrive II* (Mercury 1974)★★★, *Not Fragile* (Mercury 1974)★★★★, *Four Wheel Drive* (Mercury 1975)★★★, *Head On* (Mercury 1975)★★, *Freeways* (Mercury 1977)★★, as BTO *Street Action* (Mercury 1978)★, as BTO *Rock N' Roll Nights* (Mercury 1979)★, *Bachman Turner Overdrive* (Compleat 1984)★★, *Live!-Live!-Live!* (Mercury 1986)★★, *King Biscuit Flower Hour* 1974 recording (King Biscuit 1998)★★★.

● COMPILATIONS: *Best Of B.T.O. (So Far)* (Mercury 1976)★★★, *Greatest Hits* (Mercury 1981)★★★, *Greatest Hits Live* (Curb 1990)★★, *The Anthology* (PolyGram 1993)★★★, *The Best Of Bachman-Turner Overdrive Live* (Capitol/Curb 1994)★★, *The Best Of B.T.O. (Remastered Hits)* (Mercury 1998)★★★.

● FURTHER READING: *Bachman Turner Overdrive: Rock Is My Life, This Is My Song: The Authorized Biography*, Martin Melhuish.

BACK STREET CRAWLER

Formed in England during 1975, Back Street Crawler took its name from founder Paul Kossoff's (b. 14 September 1950, Hampstead, London, England, d. 19 March 1976) solo album. The ex-Free guitarist was joined by Terry Wilson-Slessor (vocals), Michael Montgomery (keyboards), Terry Wilson (bass) and Tony Braunagel (drums), but concerts in support of *The Band Played On* were cancelled when the group's leader was hospitalized after a drugs-related seizure. An American tour offered new-found hope, but this optimism was shattered on 19 March 1976 when Kossoff died in his sleep. The band truncated its name to Crawler following the release of *Second Street*. Geoff Whitehorn, formerly of If and Maggie Bell's group, was added on guitar, while John 'Rabbit' Bundrick, another ex-member of Free, replaced Montgomery. Despite minor US chart success, the quintet was unable to escape the legacy of its founder and split following *Snake, Rattle And Roll*.

● ALBUMS: *The Band Plays On* (Atlantic 1975)★★★, *Second Street* (Atlantic 1976)★★★, as Crawler *Crawler* (Epic 1977)★★★, as Crawler *Snake, Rattle And Roll* (Epic 1978)★★

BACKBONE SLIDE

German rock band Backbone Slide are propelled by the powerful vocals of expatriate American Shaun Michaels (b. Atlanta, Georgia, USA), with O.G. (guitars), Kai Portolano (guitars), Achim Gschwend (drums) and Frank Scharfft (bass) completing the line-up. Their fortunes were shaped by former Rolling Stones manager/producer Andrew Loog Oldham, and this fact alone was enough to ensure considerable early press interest. The group's earnest recreation of a rocking Small Faces/Led Zeppelin sound also found favour with the critics, after their recording career was launched with the release of a self-titled debut album in 1995, on European label Mausoleum Records. Produced and engineered by Ed Miller (a veteran of work with the Black Crowes, 38 Special and Georgia Satellites), its potential was increased by the lack of linguistic barriers to international markets through Michaels' trad rock English lyrics.

● ALBUMS: *Backbone Slide* (Mausoleum 1995)★★★.

BAD BOY

The origins of this Milwaukee, USA rock band date back to the mid-70s, when Steve Grimm (guitar, vocals) teamed up with John Marcelli (bass). The first incarnation of Bad Boy had included Lars Hanson (drums) and Joe Luchessie (guitar, keyboards, vocals). The band chemistry was wrong, however, and their debut album was a half-hearted affair. Their second release was a marked improvement, as the band moved in a heavier direction and made greater use of an up-front guitar sound, including Earl Slick (ex-David Bowie). Following a period of inactivity between 1978 and 1982, the band returned with a revamped line-up that saw Xeno (keyboards) and Billy Johnson (drums) alongside Grimm and Marcelli. Unfortunately, they reverted to a melodic pop-rock style. Both albums sold poorly and the band split as a result.

● ALBUMS: *The Band That Made Milwaukee Famous* (United Artists 1977)★★, *Back To Back* (United Artists 1978)★★★, *Private Party* (Indie 1982)★★, *Electric Eyes* (Indie 1984)★★.

BAD BRAINS

This black American hardcore punk and dub reggae outfit originated in 1978, when the band were all playing together in an early fusion outfit. They moved from Washington, DC, to New York where they established a reputation as prime exponents, alongside the Dead Kennedys and Black Flag, of the new 'hardcore' hybrid of punk, based on a barely credible speed of musicianship. The line-up consisted of H.R. (b. Paul Hudson; vocals) and brother Earl Hudson (drums), Dr. Know (guitar) and Darryl Aaron Jenifer (bass). They broke up their sets with dub and reggae outings and attracted a mixed audience, which was certainly one of their objectives: 'We're a gospel group, preaching the word of unity.' It is frustrating that so little studio material remains to document this early period, though the singles 'Pay To Cum' and 'Big Takeover' are regarded as punk classics. More recently, bands such as Living Colour have sung their praises as one of the forerunners of articulate black rock music. They were due to support the Damned in the UK in October 1979, having sold most of their equipment to buy aeroplane tickets. On arrival, however, they were denied work permits. They continued through the 80s, releasing only two full-length albums (*Rock For Light* and *I Against I*), although tension over the band's direction meant that H.R. left to pursue a solo career devoted to reggae music. In May 1988 he was temporarily replaced by ex-Faith No More vocalist Chuck Mosley, while Mackie Jayson (ex-Cro-Mags) took over on drums. The move, which allowed the remaining founding members to gig, was singularly unsuccessful. A major label contract with Epic Records was a commercial disaster, but in 1994 Madonna offered them a place on her Maverick label, with H.R. returning to the fold. *God Of Love*, produced by ex-leader of the Cars, Ric Ocasek, concentrated more on dub and rasta messages than hardcore, but proved again there was still fire in the belly of this group. In 1995 H.R. left the band after assaulting various Bad Brains members before a show on their promotional tour to support *God Of Love*. He was subsequently arrested at the Canadian border and charged with a drugs offence. The band were then dropped by Maverick.

● ALBUMS: *Bad Brains* cassette only (ROIR 1982)★★, *Rock For Light* (PVC 1983)★★★★, *I Against I* (SST 1986)★★★★, *Live* (SST 1988)★★, *Attitude: The ROIR Sessions* (In-Effect 1989)★★★, *Quickness* (Caroline 1989)★★★, *The Youth Are Getting Restless* (Caroline 1990)★★★, *Rise* (Epic 1993)★★★, *God Of Love* (Maverick 1995)★★★, *Black Dots* (Caroline 1996)★★★, *Omega Sessions* 1980 recordings (Victory 1998)★★★.

BAD COMPANY

This solid, highly acclaimed UK heavy rock group formed in 1973, with a line-up comprising Paul Rodgers (b. 17 December 1949, Middlesbrough,

Cleveland, England; vocals), Simon Kirke (b. 28 July 1949, Shrewsbury, Shropshire, England; vocals, drums), Mick Ralphs (b. 31 May 1944, Hereford, Herefordshire, England; vocals, guitar) and Boz Burrell (b. Raymond Burrell, 1946, Lincolnshire, England; bass). With Ralphs (ex-Mott The Hoople) and Rodgers and Kirke (both ex-Free), Bad Company were akin to a blues-based supergroup, with much of their style derived from the traditions established by Free, not least because of Rodgers' distinctive vocals. Their bestselling debut established their sound: strong vocals placed beside tough melody lines and hard riffing. A string of albums through the mid-70s brought them chart success on both sides of the Atlantic, while a series of arduous stadium tours maintained their reputation as an exemplary live act. They achieved singles success with a number of powerful songs (notably, 'Can't Get Enough' and 'Feel Like Makin' Love'), all well produced and faultlessly played, although lyrically they were often pedestrian. A three-year hiatus ended with the release of *Rough Diamonds*, which provided another UK Top 20 album success (US number 26). After nearly a decade of extensive gigging and regular albums, they finally dissolved in 1983. A new version of the group, with former Ted Nugent vocalist Brian Howe replacing Rodgers, was assembled in 1986 for the reunion album *Fame And Fortune*. The band's subsequent releases were mediocre, pale shadows of their first two albums.

The late 80s/early 90s Bad Company model revolved around surviving original members Mick Ralphs and Simon Kirke, and included bassist Rick Wills and rhythm guitarist Dave Colwell. They also enjoyed further US chart success with the singles 'If You Needed Somebody' (number 16, November 1990), 'Walk Through Fire' (number 28, August 1991) and 'How About That' (number 38, September 1992), and the platinum-selling *Here Comes Trouble*. Rodgers' 1993 solo album, *Muddy Waters Blues*, reached the UK Top 50 album charts and included three vintage Bad Company tracks. The group have continued recording into the late 90s with *Company Of Strangers* and *Stories Told And Untold*.

● ALBUMS: *Bad Company* (Island 1974)★★★★, *Straight Shooter* (Island 1975)★★★, *Run With The Pack* (Island 1976)★★, *Burnin' Sky* (Island 1977)★★, *Desolation Angels* (Island 1979)★★★, *Rough Diamonds* (Swan Song 1982)★★, *Fame And Fortune* (Atlantic 1986)★★, *Dangerous Age* (Atlantic 1988)★★, *Holy Water* (Atlantic 1990)★★, *Here Comes Trouble* (Atlantic 1992)★★, *Company Of Strangers* (Atlantic 1995)★★, *Stories Told And Untold* (Atlantic 1996)★★★.

● COMPILATIONS: *10 From 6* (Atlantic 1986)★★★★, *The Best Of Bad Company Live ... What You Hear Is What You Get* (Atco 1993)★★★.

Bad English

Towards the end of the 80s, a new generation of 'supergroups' emerged from the USA, including Mr. Big, Badlands, Damn Yankees, Alias, and, arguably the most successful of them all, Bad English. The group was formed in 1988 by ex-Babys vocalist and successful solo artist John Waite (b. 4 July 1955, Lancaster, Lancashire, England), ex-Santana and Journey guitarist Neal Schon (b. 27 February 1954, San Mateo, California, USA), ex-Babys and Journey keyboard player Jonathan Cain (b. 26 February 1950, Chicago, Illinois, USA), ex-Babys bassist Ricky Phillips, and ex-Wild Dogs drummer Deen Castronovo. Their 1989 self-titled debut album was an instant success in the USA, combining hard-edged, melodic rock with big ballads. It reached the US Top 10, helped on its way by the Dianne Warren-penned 'When I See You Smile', which was a US number 1 hit in 1990 (UK number 61). Success in the UK was not forthcoming and the album barely dented the Top 40, while a similar fate befell the single. The follow-up, *Backlash*, was promoted by the single 'Straight To Your Heart'. Internal disagreements plagued the band, causing them to split soon after its release, with Waite resuming his solo career; Phillips and Castronovo joined the Jimmy Page and David Coverdale project, while Schon and Cain re-formed Journey. Castronovo and Schon also formed Hardline. Despite their short history, Bad English left behind a legacy of high-quality melodic rock that achieved a considerable degree of commercial success.

● ALBUMS: *Bad English* (Epic 1989)★★★, *Backlash* (Epic 1991)★★★.

● VIDEOS: *Bad English* (CMV Enterprises 1990).

Bad News

Originally written by Adrian Edmondson as part of UK television's *The Comic Strip Presents* series in 1982, *Bad News Tour* told the story of an ambitious (but inept) London heavy metal band, on tour and *en route* to Grantham with a television documentary crew. The members were played by Edmondson, as vocalist/guitarist Vim Fuego, Rik Mayall as bassist Colin Grigson, Nigel Planer as dim rhythm guitarist Den Dennis, and Comic Strip co-writer/founder-member Peter Richardson, as drummer Spider Webb. The music and lyrics for the show were put together by Edmondson and composer Simon Brint as a clever parody on the clichés of the UK heavy metal scene. After the success of Rob Reiner's film, *This Is Spinal Tap*, and its subsequent move into legend, Edmondson decided to revive Bad News for another Comic Strip episode, writing a basic storyline that required the band to play a genuine live gig. In 1986, armed with a recording contract with EMI Records, a producer in Queen's Brian May, clever management, and photo sessions by Gerard Mankowitz, they set about recording an album of songs and sketches. The full promotional machinery of interviews, television appearances and a slot at the Donington Festival in August, all used in the film, was set in motion. Four months later, they organized a short tour that included several charity concerts with Iron Maiden. In 1987 *More Bad News* was shown in cinemas as support to another Comic Strip film, *Eat The Rich*, which, incidentally, starred Lemmy from Motörhead. This publicity was boosted by a cover version of Queen's 'Bohemian Rhapsody' on single, and a self-titled debut album. The music was badly received, but in retrospect, revealed itself to be both well constructed and executed. Following the album, they embarked on a two-month tour and released a second single, 'Cashing In On Xmas'. However, by this time the joke had worn too thin for both press and public, and the actors returned to their day jobs. Their name briefly reappeared the following year, when EMI Records released a bootleg album that contained Edmondson-produced out-takes of music and comedy, and a Brian May remix of the 'Christmas' single.

● ALBUMS: *Bad News* (EMI 1987)★★, *Bootleg* (EMI 1988)★★.
● COMPILATIONS: *Collection* (Castle 1994)★★.
● VIDEOS: *Bad News Tour And A Fistful Of Traveller's Cheques* (Virgin Vision 1986), *More Bad News* (Virgin Vision 1987), *Bohemian Rhapsody* (PMI 1987).

BAD RELIGION

This American hardcore band was formed in 1980 in the suburbs of north Los Angeles, California. Their first incarnation comprised Greg Graffin (vocals), Brett Gurewitz (guitar), Jay Lishrout (drums) and Jay Bentley (bass), with the name originating from their mutual distaste for organized religion. Their debut release was the poorly produced EP *Bad Religion*, on Epitaph Records, formed by founder-member Gurewitz. Following several appearances on local compilation albums, Pete Finestone took over as drummer in 1982. The milestone album *How Could Hell Be Any Worse?* was recorded in Hollywood, creating a fair degree of local and national interest. The subsequent *Into The Unknown* proved a minor disaster, disillusioning hardcore fans with the emphasis shifted to slick keyboard textures, though the record itself stands up well. In 1984 there were more changes and Graffin was soon the only surviving member from the previous year, with Greg Hetson and Tim Gallegos taking over guitar and bass, and Pete Finestone returning on drums, while Gurewitz took time out to conquer his drink and drug problems. A comeback EP, *Back To The Known*, revealed a much more purposeful outfit. A long period of inactivity was ended in 1987 when Gurewitz rejoined for a show that Hetson (working with former band Circle Jerks once more) could not attend. New material was written, and *Suffer* was released in 1988 to wide critical acclaim. The band's albums since then have featured intelligent lyrics set against their compelling punk sound. In 1993 the band signed to Atlantic Records, making their major-label debut with the following year's *Stranger Than Fiction*. Despite this, Gurewitz retired in 1994 to spend more time looking after the Epitaph label, which was enjoying success with Offspring and others. The line-up of the band by 1996 was Graffin, Hetson, Brian Baker (guitar), Bentley and Bobby Schayer (drums). *The Gray Race* was an assured release that addressed famine, world disorder and politics without losing grip on the fact that they are out-and-out metal/punks of the finest degree. *Tested* collected powerful live performances from *The Gray Race* tour, but 1998's *No Substance* indicated a group struggling for new ideas.

● ALBUMS: *How Could Hell Be Any Worse?* (Epitaph 1982)★★★★, *Into The Unknown* (Epitaph 1983)★★★, *Suffer* (Epitaph 1988)★★★★, *No Control* (Epitaph 1989)★★★, *Against The Grain* (Epitaph 1990)★★★, *Generator* (Epitaph 1992)★★★, *Recipe For Hate* (Epitaph 1993)★★★, *Stranger Than Fiction* (Atlantic 1994)★★★, *The Gray Race* (Atlantic 1996)★★★★, *Tested* (Epic 1997)★★★, *No Substance* (Atlantic 1998)★★.
● COMPILATIONS: *80-85* (Epitaph 1991)★★★, *All Ages* (Epitaph 1995)★★★.

BAD STEVE

This UK speed metal outfit was founded in 1983 by former Accept members Rubi Rubach (bass), Jan Kommet (guitar) and Frank Friedrich (drums). Recruiting vocalist Phil Magoo (ex-Sin City) and guitarist Akku Becher (ex-Kanaan), they finally secured a contract with Mausoleum Records after being turned down by many major labels in Germany. *Killing The Night* emerged in 1984 and they supported Accept throughout Europe to promote it. The album lacked energy, drive and superior songs, and compared unfavourably to Accept's material, the yardstick by which the band were automatically judged. It failed to sell and the band disintegrated, with Rubach moving on to UDO.

● ALBUMS: *Killing The Night* (Mausoleum 1984)★★.

BADLANDS

This blues-based, UK hard-rock band was formed in 1988 by ex-Black Sabbath and Blue Murder vocalist Ray Gillen (d. 1994) and former Ozzy Osbourne guitarist Jake E. Lee. With the addition of bassist Greg Chaisson and drummer Eric Singer, they signed to Atlantic Records and released a self-titled debut album the following year. Using the early 70s as a source of inspiration, their music invited comparisons with Led Zeppelin, Bad Company, Humble Pie and Free. Singer joined Alice Cooper's band and was replaced by Jeff Martin before the recording of Badlands' second album in 1991. *Voodoo Highway* received widespread critical acclaim, with Gillen's classic soulful vocal style contrasting beautifully with Lee's explosive guitar pyrotechnics. The album oozed class, emotion and energy from every note, and included an inspired cover version of James Taylor's 'Fire And Rain'. Lee went on to form Wicked Alliance.

● ALBUMS: *Badlands* (Atlantic 1989)★★★, *Voodoo Highway* (Atlantic 1991)★★★.

BAKERLOO

Originally the Bakerloo Blues Line, this late 60s power-blues trio from Tamworth, Staffordshire, England, were briefly compared to Cream. Ironically, the band's leader, Dave Clempson (b. 5 September 1949, Tamworth, Staffordshire, England), found himself singing Cream numbers many years later as a member of Jack Bruce's band. The original Bakerloo comprised Clempson (guitar, vocals), Terry Poole (bass) and Keith Baker (drums). Their self-titled album is a collector's item, both as one of the initial Harvest fold-out sleeves and for the music therein. The extended 'Moonshine' gave each member the opportunity to demonstrate his musical dexterity. Clempson was soon tempted away to join Jon Hiseman's Colosseum, and Bakerloo was terminated. Keith Baker re-emerged in one of the early line-ups of Uriah Heep, later teaming up again with Terry Poole in May Blitz.

● ALBUMS: *Bakerloo* (Harvest 1969)★★★.

BALANCE

This US melodic AOR group was formed in 1979 by vocalist Peppy Castro (ex-Wiggy Bits) and session men Doug Katsaros (keyboards) and Bob Kulick (guitarist and older brother of Kiss's Bruce Kulick). Augmented by other hired hands, they debuted in 1981 with a self-titled album that sounded like a three-way amalgam of Toto, Kansas and Journey. As interest grew, the trio enlisted bassist Dennis Feldman and former Brand X drummer Chuck Burgi to stabilize their line-up. *In For The Count*, which followed, assumed a harder direction and incorporated Foreigner influences. Although it attracted an encouraging media response, the album surprisingly failed to take off. Disillusioned, the band went their separate ways in 1982. Bob Kulick subsequently joined Meat Loaf's band prior to forming Skull. In 1987 Kulick, Feldman and Burgi were rumoured to be working together again with former Blue Öyster Cult vocalist Eric Bloom, but no recordings emerged.

● ALBUMS: *Balance* (Portrait 1981)★★, *In For The Count* (Portrait 1982)★★★.

BANDIT

Ostensibly led by guitarist Danny McIntosh, UK hard rock/blues group Bandit formed in the mid-70s. The rest of the line-up included Cliff Williams (b. 14 December 1949, Romford, Essex, England; bass, ex-Home), Jim Diamond (b. 28 September 1951, Glasgow, Scotland; vocals) and Theodore Thunder (drums). However, following the release of their blues-inflected, self-titled debut for Arista Records in 1977, Williams departed for a more lucrative post in AC/DC. Diamond also left, joining PhD. The new line-up featured Tony Lester on bass and Gerry Trew as vocalist, but *Partners In Crime*, for new label Ariola Records, failed to re-establish the group. An unsuccessful attempt to move from their previous roughshod bar-room style to a smooth, American AOR hybrid, it was their final recording.

● ALBUMS: *Bandit* (Arista 1977)★★★, *Partners In Crime* (Ariola 1978)★★.

BANG

While Blue Cheer are widely cited as the group who brought ear-splitting volume to rock music, another early 70s band, known simply and accurately as Bang, were more than capable of blowing a speaker stack or two themselves. Formed by Frank Gilcken (guitar), Frank Ferrara (bass, vocals) and Tony D'Lorio (drums), Bang achieved a mighty din with the release of their self-titled 1972 debut for Capitol Records - especially for a record recorded by a trio. It was somewhat disappointing, therefore, when the group's two subsequent albums retreated from the debut's extremes. Although competent and better produced, neither *Mother/Father* nor *Music* generated the same level of excitement and the group broke up in the mid-70s.

● ALBUMS: *Bang* (Capitol 1972)★★★, *Mother/Father* (Capitol 1973)★★, *Music* (Capitol 1974)★★.

Bang Tango

This Los Angeles, California, USA quintet was assembled in 1987 from the remnants of several local club circuit rock bands. Comprising Joe LeSte (vocals), Mark Knight (guitar), Kyle Stevens (guitar), Kyle Kyle (bass) and Tigg Ketler (drums), they secured a contract with MCA Records. This followed the release of a highly regarded live mini-album that the band partly financed themselves. Initially, they fostered a sleazy, low-life image and incorporated influences such as Aerosmith and the Cult. This manifested itself on *Psycho Cafe*, a refreshingly honest, but slightly offbeat, hard rock album that was characterized by LeSte's laconic vocal style. *Dancin' On Coals*, released in 1991, indicated that the band had matured remarkably in two years. It featured a greater degree of musical sophistication, including soulful and more blues-based material. Apparently poised for international success and recognition, the group left MCA for the Music For Nations independent, revitalizing their career with the self-proclaiming *New Generation*. *Love After Death*, its 1995 follow-up, featured Nicky Hopkins on one of his last session appearances, adding piano to '1000 Goodbyes'.

● ALBUMS: *Live Injection* mini-album (Bang Tango 1987)★★★, *Psycho Cafe* (Mechanic/MCA 1989)★★★, *Dancin' On Coals* (Mechanic/MCA 1991)★★★, *Ain't No Jive ... Live!* (MCA 1992)★★★, *New Generation* (Music For Nations 1994)★★★, *Love After Death* (Music For Nations 1995)★★★.

Bangalore Choir

Heavy metal team Bangalore Choir were named after a torpedo-like explosive device. They were formed in 1991 by former Accept vocalist David Reece, and also feature ex-Razor Maid guitarists Curt Mitchell and John Kirk, plus Ian Mayo (bass) and Jackie Ramos (drums), who were previously with Hurricane Alice. Their collective pedigree had undoubted potential, but *On Target* failed to fulfil it. Reece was a strong frontman, but his phrasing and delivery is closely modelled on David Coverdale and Jon Bon Jovi and the comparison is distracting.

● ALBUMS: *On Target* (Giant 1991)★★.

Banished

This Buffalo, New York, USA-based death metal band rose from the ashes of Baphomet, and released one album in 1991. The name change was prompted by a German group who claimed prior use of the title, and Banished was selected to avert potential legal difficulties. However, their debut material under the new name was not without its problems. Several commentators were struck by the sleeve artwork of their 1993 album, designed by Tim Vigil from Faust Comic Books - unconsciously echoing a sentiment in the spoof 'rockumentary' *This Is Spinal Tap*, their guitarist Tom Frost justified the cover thus: 'It's not like a sexist thing in the sense that it's real. The picture has all women in it, even the demon in the middle is a woman, with a huge strap-on horn...'

● ALBUMS: As Baphomet: *The Dead Shall Inherit* (Deaf 1991)★★. As Banished: *Deliver Me Unto Pain* (Death 1993)★★.

Banshee

Formed in the mid-80s by Tommy Lee Flood (vocals), Terry Dunn (guitar), Bill Westfall (bass) and Ken Burnham (drums), Banshee operated in musical territory somewhere between the New Wave Of British Heavy Metal bands and American power-metal groups - replete with shrieking vocals and unnecessary musical elaboration. Their debut for Roadrunner Records was an uninspired but brash exposition of their craft, and achieved a modicum of praise. It saw them transfer to Atlantic Records subsidiary Titanium, but *Race Against Time* was another disappointing seller and by the turn of the decade, the group members had gone their separate ways.

● ALBUMS: *Cry In The Night* (Roadrunner 1986)★★★, *Race Against Time* (Titanium 1989)★★.

Baron Rojo

This Spanish heavy metal outfit was formed in Madrid in 1980 by the brothers Armando (vocals, guitar) and Carlos (guitar, vocals) de Castro (both ex-Coz). With the addition of former session musicians Jose Luis Campuzano (bass) and Hermes Calabria (drums), they specialized in an early 70s approach, redolent of UFO, Uriah Heep and Black Sabbath. Their appeal was limited in Europe and the USA by the Spanish vocals, but they made some inroads in South America. In an attempt to widen their audience, they recorded an English vocal version of *Volumen Brutal*, but the result was disappointing due to poor phrasing and an awkward lyrical translation (despite the presence of Mel Collins on saxophone and Colin Towns from Gillan on keyboards). They made no attempt to follow fashions and came to be regarded as an anachronistic, but well-respected, curiosity on the international rock scene.

● ALBUMS: *Larga Vida Al Rock And Roll* (Chapa Discos 1981)★★★, *Volumen Brutal* (Chapa Discos 1982)★★★, *Metal Morphosis* (Chapa Discos 1983)★★, *Baron Rojo Vivo* (Chapa Discos 1984)★★, *En Un Lugar De La Marcha* (1985)★★★, *Siempre Estais Alli* (1986)★★★, *Tierra De Nadie* (Zafiro 1987)★★, *No Va Mas!* (Zafiro 1988)★★, *Obstinato* (1989)★★★, *Desafio* (Alex 1993)★★, *Arma Secreta* (Alex 1997)★★, *Concierto Rojo* (Imprint 1998)★★★.

BARREN CROSS

This Christian rock group from California was formed by guitarist Ray Parris and drummer Steve Whitaker in 1981. Enlisting the services of Jim Laverde (bass) and Mike Lee (vocals), they were initially reminiscent of Iron Maiden or Van Halen. *Rock For The King* featured turbo-charged metallic anthems with fluid guitarwork, delivered with steely conviction. Lyrically, the band explored themes such as abortion, drug abuse and terrorism, but explained rather than simply condemned these issues. Later releases saw the band afford greater use of melody, but without compromising their ideals or striving for commercial recognition. *Hotter Than Hell* was a strong live album that fully showcased the band's talents. It provided a much-needed shot in the arm for the credibility of Christian metal, which had suffered adverse press coverage for several years.

● ALBUMS: *Rock For The King* (Starsong 1986)★★★, *Atomic Arena* (Enigma 1987)★★, *State Of Control* (Virgin 1989)★★★, *Hotter Than Hell - Live* (Medusa 1990)★★★.

BARTH, BOBBY

After the disintegration of UK heavy metal band Axe in 1984, lead singer Bobby Barth embarked on a solo career, following a short and fruitless association with Blackfoot. Dispensing with the hard-rock style of his youth, Barth recorded an album of sentimental ballads and middle-of-the-road AOR. The songs featured expansive arrangements that included swathes of keyboards and a brass section. The album made little impact and Barth re-formed Axe in 1989.

● ALBUMS: *Two Hearts-One Beat* (Atco 1986)★★.

BASTARD

This German quartet was formed in Hanover in 1977 by Karl Rothert (bass, vocals) and Keith Kossoff (guitar). With the help of guitarist Uli Meisner and drummer Toto Petticoato, they took the Scorpions, AC/DC and Bad Company as their blueprint for heavy-duty rock 'n' roll. Their first two albums failed to expand on these influences. The live album was an improvement, with the band adding sparkle and character to songs that sounded dull on record.

● ALBUMS: *Back To Nature* (Lava 1978)★★, *Tearing Nights* (Lava 1978)★★, *Live And Alive* (Lava 1980)★★★.

BATHORY

This Swedish satanic-metal project was masterminded by the enigmatic multi-instrumentalist Quothorn. The band originally comprised Quothorn (vocals, guitar), Kothaar (bass) and Vvorthn (drums), but the latter two left after recording just a single track for a heavy metal compilation album. Aided by session musicians, Quothorn decided to continue alone and recorded a series of black metal albums during the latter half of the 80s. He attracted a cult following, many of whom were Satanists, but refrained from taking his music out on the road. *Hammerheart*, released in 1990, was an ambitious concept album based on Viking legend and represented his most (relatively) accessible work to date. Further albums ensued, with 1995's *Octagon* including an unlikely cover version of the Kiss song 'Deuce'.

● ALBUMS: *Bathory* (Under One Flag 1984)★★, *Raise The Dead* (Under One Flag 1984)★★, *The Return* (Under One Flag 1985)★★, *Under The Sign Of The Black Mark* (Under One Flag 1986)★★★, *Blood, Fire, Death* (Under One Flag 1988)★★★, *Hammerheart* (Noise 1990)★★★, *Twilight Of The Gods* (Black Mark 1992)★★★, *Jubileum Volume 1* (Black Mark 1994)★★★, *Jubileum Volume 2* (Black Mark 1994)★★★, *Octagon* (Black Mark 1995)★★★, *Requiem* (Black Mark 1995)★★★, *Blood On Ice* (Black Mark 1996)★★★, *Jubileum Volume 3* (Black Mark 1998)★★★.

Baton Rouge

Originally know as Meridian, Baton Rouge was formed in New Orleans, USA, in 1986 by Kelly Keeling (lead vocals, guitar) and Lance Bulen (lead guitar, vocals), the line-up being completed by Corky McClellan (drums, vocals), Scott Bender (bass, vocals) and David Cremin (keyboards, guitars, vocals). Within a year the band moved away from the covers-orientated Louisiana club circuit to Los Angeles, where two years of songwriting and rehearsal paid off, with a major record contract after only six live shows. *Shake Your Soul*, produced by Jack Ponti, who also wrote with the band, was an album of blues-influenced melodic hard rock, with powerful harmonies, reminiscent of Def Leppard, augmenting Keeling's striking vocals. Extensive US touring, including dates supporting Alannah Myles, coupled with heavy radio airplay for their debut single, 'Walks Like A Woman', allowed the quintet to build up a healthy live following, to the extent that they played a headline show to a crowd of 10,000 in Milwaukee. A slightly heavier approach was adopted for *Lights Out In The Playground*, again produced by (and co-written with) Ponti. This marked the debut of former Keel guitarist Tony Palmucci, who replaced Cremin, but the distinctive Baton Rouge sound remained.

● ALBUMS: *Shake Your Soul* (Atlantic 1990)★★★, *Lights Out In The Playground* (Atlantic 1991)★★★.

Battleaxe

Formed in 1983 in Sunderland, England, Battleaxe made a minor dent on the north-east heavy metal scene after appearing with two tracks on the Guardian compilation album *Roxcalibur*. They quickly followed this exposure with a single, 'Burn This Town'. They maintained a solid line-up with Dave King (vocals), Steve Hardy (guitar), Brian Smith (bass) and Ian McCormack (drums), and eventually signed with Music For Nations, who released both of their albums. With other acts such as Venom and Raven attracting the majority of the attention, Battleaxe split in 1985.

● ALBUMS: *Burn This Town* (Music For Nations 1983)★★★, *Power From The Universe* (Music For Nations 1984)★★.

Battlecry

This Christian rock band was formed in California in 1984 by Dave Chumchal (vocals, guitar, keyboards) and Doug Morris (vocals, guitar). With the recruitment of Robert Kirk Giverink (guitar), Mariko Martinez (keyboards, vocals), Ronald P. Simmons (bass, vocals) and Bret Kik Keys (drums), their sound was heavily laden with keyboards and characterized by high-pitched, note-perfect harmonies. Their sole release was an impressive collection of melodic AOR that paid respect to Yes and Journey's blueprint.

● ALBUMS: *Red, White And Blue* (Greenworld 1986)★★★.

BBM

The potential was greater than the sum of the parts. The power trio of the 90s could have been BBM, had the fiery members of the group stayed together long enough. Gary Moore (b. 4 April 1952, Belfast, Northern Ireland; vocals, guitar), Jack Bruce (b. John Symon Asher, 14 May 1943, Glasgow, Lanarkshire, Scotland; bass, vocals) and Ginger Baker (b. Peter Baker, 19 August 1939, Lewisham, London, England; drums) decided to create a semi-skimmed version of 60s supergroup Cream in the autumn of 1993. Their lone album was highly derivative of some of the songs on Cream's *Disraeli Gears* and *Wheels Of Fire*. 'Waiting In The Wings' owed a debt to the melody and lyrics of 'White Room', even though long-time lyricist Pete Brown was overlooked for this project. 'City Of Gold' was uncannily similar to 'Crossroads' and 'Why Does Love (Have To Go Wrong)?' oozed likeness to 'We're Going Wrong'. Those that had pined for a Cream reunion were somehow placated by this album, and Gary Moore proved quite acceptable with the Gibson Les Paul sound. All three sounded better than ever, and had they been able to continue they could have courted heavy metal and blues in the same way many late 60s bands did. Rumour had it that they had a blistering argument at the end of a media-only performance at London's Marquee Club. No encores were forthcoming at this or any other gig and the band effectively folded, leaving one pretty good album as a legacy.

● ALBUMS: *Around The Next Dream* (Virgin 1994)★★★.

Beau Geste

Beau Geste is the pseudonym of the exceptionally talented Canadian multi-instrumentalist Bryan Hughes. With the aid of session musicians he recorded *Another Night In The City* in 1986. It served as a tribute to Hughes' technical and artistic capabilities, seeing him assume responsibility for writing the material and contributing vocals, bass, keyboards and guitar parts. However, the end result was less than impressive, a melodic AOR album lacking both character and real energy.

● ALBUMS: *Another Night In The City* (1986)★★.

BEAU NASTY

Formed in Los Angeles, California, USA, in the late 80s, Beau Nasty typified the region's fascination with all things bombastic and overwrought. Playing slick, over-produced hard rock, Mark Anthony Fretz (vocals), Brian Young (guitar), George Bernhardt (guitar), Doug Baker (bass) and Mike Terrana (drums) made their debut for WTG Records in 1989 with *Dirty But Well Dressed*. The title was somewhat ironic, given that the songs it contained were all presentation and little substance.

● ALBUMS: *Dirty But Well Dressed* (WTG 1989)★★.

BECK, BOGERT AND APPICE

Plans for guitar virtuoso Jeff Beck (b. 24 June 1944, Wallington, Surrey, England) to form a power trio with the ex-Vanilla Fudge rhythm section were first mooted in 1969. Both the drummer, Carmine Appice (b. 15 December 1946, Staten Island, New York, USA), and bassist Tim Bogert (b. 27 August 1944, Richfield, New Jersey, USA), were dissatisfied with their band at the time. However, these hopes were dashed when Beck was involved in a serious car crash that put him out of action. Meanwhile, Bogert and Appice formed the heavy rock band Cactus, until in 1972, their paths again crossed with Beck and they assembled the heavy rock unit Beck, Bogert And Appice. The self-titled, commercially successful debut was instrumentally superb, but suffered from a lack of songwriting ability and strained vocals. Twenty years later, the album sounds ponderous and is justifiably disowned by the band members.

● ALBUMS: *Beck, Bogert And Appice* (Epic 1973)★★, *Live In Japan* (Epic/Sony 1975)★★.

BECK, JEFF

b. 24 June 1944, Wallington, Surrey, England. As a former choirboy, the young Beck was interested in music from an early age, becoming a competent pianist and guitarist by the age of 11. His first main band was the Tridents, who made a name for themselves locally. After leaving that band, Beck took on the seemingly impossible task of filling the shoes of Eric Clapton, who had recently departed from 60s R&B pioneers the Yardbirds. Clapton had established a fiercely loyal following, but Beck quickly impressed audiences with his amazing guitar pyrotechnics, utilizing feedback and distortion. Beck stayed with the Yardbirds, adding colour and excitement to all their hits, until October 1966. The tension between Beck and joint lead guitarist Jimmy Page was finally resolved during a US tour, when Beck walked out and never returned. His solo career was launched in March 1967 with an unexpected pop single, 'Hi-Ho Silver Lining', wherein his unremarkable voice was heard on a singalong number that was redeemed by his trademark guitar solo. The record was a sizeable hit (UK number 14) and has demonstrated its perennial appeal to party-goers by re-entering the charts on several occasions since. The follow-up, 'Tallyman', was also a minor hit, but Beck's ambitions lay in other directions. From being a singing, guitar-playing pop star, he relaunched a career that led to his becoming one of the world's leading rock guitarists. The Jeff Beck Group, formed in 1968, consisted of Beck, Rod Stewart (vocals), Ron Wood (bass), Nicky Hopkins (piano) and Mickey Waller (drums). This powerhouse group released *Truth*, which became a major success in the USA, resulting in a number of arduous tours. The second album, *Beck-Ola*, enjoyed similar success, although Stewart and Wood had departed for the Faces. Beck also contributed some sparkling guitar and received equal billing with Donovan on the hit single 'Goo Goo Barabajagal (Love Is Hot)', which reached number 12 in the UK charts in July 1969. Beck was hospitalised in August after a car accident, requiring an 18-month period of recuperation. Following his recovery, Beck formed another group with Cozy Powell, Max Middleton and Bob Tench, and recorded two further albums, *Rough And Ready* and *Jeff Beck Group*. Beck was by this time venerated as a serious musician and master of his instrument, figuring highly in various guitarist polls. In 1973 the erratic Beck musical style changed once again, and he formed the trio Beck, Bogert And Appice with the two former members of Vanilla Fudge. Soon afterwards, Beck introduced yet another musical dimension, this time forming an instrumental band. The result was the excellent *Blow By Blow*, considered by many to be his best work. His guitar playing revealed extraordinary technique, combining rock, jazz and blues styles. *Blow By Blow* was a million-seller and its follow-up, *Wired*, enjoyed similar success. Having allied himself with members of the jazz/rock fraternity, Beck teamed up with Jan Hammer for a frantic live album, after which he effectively retired for three years. He returned in 1980 with *There And Back*, and, rejuvenated, found himself riding the album charts once more. During the 80s Beck's appearances were sporadic, although he guested on Tina

Turner's *Private Dancer* and worked with Robert Plant and Jimmy Page on the Honeydrippers' album. The occasional charity function aside, he spent much of his leisure time with automobiles (in one interview, Beck stated that he could just as easily have been a car restorer). In the mid-80s he toured with Rod Stewart and appeared on his hit version of 'People Get Ready', although when Beck's *Flash* arrived in 1985 it proved his least successful album to date. The release of a box set in 1992, chronicling his career, was a fitting tribute to this accomplished guitarist and his numerous guises (the most recent of which had been as guitarist on Spinal Tap's second album). Following an award in 1993 for his theme music (with Jed Stoller) for the Anglia Television production *Frankie's House*, he released *Crazy Legs*, a tribute to the music of Gene Vincent. For this, Beck applied a clean, subdued rock 'n' roll sound, demonstrating once more his absolute mastery of technique. He also made his UK acting debut, playing Brad the serial killer in *The Comic Strip Presents ... Gregory: Diary Of A Nutcase*.

● ALBUMS: *Truth* (EMI 1968)★★★, *Beck-Ola* (EMI 1969)★★, *Rough And Ready* (Epic 1971)★★, *Jeff Beck Group* (Epic 1972)★★, *Blow By Blow* (Epic 1975)★★★★, *Wired* (Epic 1976)★★, with Jan Hammer *Jeff Beck With The Jan Hammer Group Live* (Epic 1977)★, *There And Back* (Epic 1980)★★, *Flash* (Epic 1985)★★, with Terry Bozzio, Tony Hymas *Jeff Beck's Guitar Shop* (Epic 1989)★★, *Crazy Legs* (Epic 1993)★★★.

● COMPILATIONS: *Beckology* CD box set (Epic 1992)★★★★.

BECKER, JASON

This classically trained US guitarist first came to prominence in the late 80s with fellow guitar wizard Marty Friedman in the band Cacophony. Combining blues, rock and classical styles, he built up a reputation for playing at breakneck speed with a melodic intensity and feel that was reminiscent of Alvin Lee. In 1988 he recorded *Perpetual Burn*, a solo instrumental showcase for his remarkable six-string acrobatics. After the recording of Cacophony's second album, Becker accepted David Lee Roth's offer to become permanent replacement for Steve Vai. Becker appeared on Roth's *A Little Ain't Enough* album in 1991, contributing some stunning guitarwork, and silenced the critics' premature suggestions that he would be unable to match his flamboyant predecessor.

● ALBUMS: *Perpetual Burn* (Roadrunner 1988)★★★.

BEDLAM

This UK heavy metal band was formed in 1972 and was originally known as Beast. Bedlam consisted of former Truth singer Frank Aiello (vocals), Dave Ball (b. 30 March 1950; guitar), Dennis Ball (bass) and Cozy Powell (b. Colin Powell, 29 December 1947, England, d. 5 April 1998; drums). Powell and Dave and Dennis Ball were previously members of the Ace Kefford Stand and Big Bertha, but this new act was convened following Powell's tenure with Jeff Beck and Dave Ball's spell in Procol Harum. Despite early optimism, *Bedlam* failed to establish the UK quartet as a commercial proposition and they split in 1974. Powell and Aiello then formed Cozy Powell's Hammer, while their ex-colleagues left music altogether.

● ALBUMS: *Bedlam* (Chrysalis 1973)★★.

BEEFEATER

Formed in Washington, DC, USA, in the mid-80s, this briefly exciting band comprised Tomas Squip Jones (vocals, ex-Red C), Dug E. Bird aka Dug Birdzell (bass, ex-Underground Soldier), Bruce Taylor (drums, ex-Hate From Ignorance; Clear Vision; and Subtle Oppression) and Fred Smith (guitar). Musically, they produced a speedy hybrid of punk and metal blended with jazz and reggae. With all the members coming from different backgrounds, this made for a refreshing change from the traditional hardcore punk sound with which Dischord Records had made their name. Jones, who had drummed in his previous band, was primarily influenced by funk and jazz, Taylor by heavy metal (he had worked with seven or eight such bands previously), Bird by metal and early punk and Smith by jazz, blues and reggae, as well as early DC punk. However, the marriage of influences only survived two albums, although both offered conclusive proof of their talents. Bird and Jones later formed Fidelity Jones.

● ALBUMS: *Plays For Lovers* (Dischord 1985)★★★, *House Burning Down* (Dischord 1987)★★★.

BELFEGORE

One of the lesser-known metal groups to emerge from Germany in the mid-80s, Belfegore recorded a solitary album for a major label, Elektra Records, then disappeared. Comprising Mikel Clauss (vocals), Charly 'T.' Charles (drums) and Raoul Walton (bass), that self-titled collection was a ferocious collage of noise and guitar hooks with eccentric themes and obtuse lyrical statements. Neo-pagan/gothic sentiments abounded, with the group moving liberally from repetitive riffs to more musically sophisticated tracks. *Belfegore* remains one of the classic 'undiscovered' metal records of the period.

● ALBUMS: *Belfegore* (Elektra 1984)★★★.

Benatar, Pat

b. Patricia Andrzejewski, 10 January 1953, Brooklyn, New York, USA. After training as an opera singer, Pat Benatar became a major hitmaker in the early 80s, adept at both mainstream rock and powerful ballads, often focusing on personal relationships and sexual politics. She married Dennis Benatar after graduating from high school and relocated to Virginia. By the 70s she had returned to New York, where she was discovered by Rick Newman in 1979 at the latter's Catch A Rising Star club. With Newman as manager, she signed to Chrysalis Records that year and released her debut album, *In The Heat Of The Night*, produced by Mike Chapman, which became a substantial hit and spawned three US chart singles. Benatar (who retained the name after divorcing) released her second album, *Crimes Of Passion*, in 1980. This collection, which later won a Grammy for Best Female Rock Vocal Performance, rose to number 2 in the US charts, while the hard-rocking 'Hit Me With Your Best Shot' became her first *Billboard* Top 10 single. *Precious Time* was released in 1981 and this time reached number 1 in the USA. Although no Top 10 singles resulted, Benatar won another Grammy for 'Fire And Ice'. In 1982 Benatar married producer Neil Geraldo, who played guitar in her band and wrote most of her material, and released *Get Nervous*, which reached US number 4. The following year, a live album, also featuring two new studio tracks, was released. One of these tracks, 'Love Is A Battlefield', reached number 5 in the USA, the same position attained in 1984 by 'We Belong', from the next album, *Tropico*. The former single eventually became a UK Top 20 hit in 1985, reissued in the wake of the British success of 'We Belong', after initially stalling a year earlier at number 49. Also in 1985, 'Invincible', from the film *Legend Of Billie Jean*, was Benatar's last US Top 10 single of the decade. An album, *Seven The Hard Way*, followed later that year but signalled a decline in Benatar's popularity. Musical inactivity marked the next couple of years as Benatar devoted her attentions to motherhood. A compilation album, *Best Shots*, was released in 1987. Although moderately successful in her homeland, it became a major hit in Europe, putting her into the UK Top 10 album chart for the first time. Since 1988 Benatar has also pursued an acting career. The blues-influenced *True Love* was a commercial and critical disaster, and subsequent albums have seen Benatar struggling to regain lost sales.

● ALBUMS: *In The Heat Of The Night* (Chrysalis 1979)★★★, *Crimes Of Passion* (Chrysalis 1980)★★★, *Precious Time* (Chrysalis 1981)★★, *Get Nervous* (Chrysalis 1982)★★, *Live From Earth* (Chrysalis 1983)★★, *Tropico* (Chrysalis 1984)★★, *Seven The Hard Way* (Chrysalis 1985)★★★, *Wide Awake In Dreamland* (Chrysalis 1988)★★, *True Love* (Chrysalis 1991)★★, *Gravity's Rainbow* (Chrysalis 1993)★★, *Innamorata* (CMC 1997)★★★, *8-15-80* (CMC 1998)★★★.

● COMPILATIONS: *Best Shots* (Chrysalis 1987)★★★, *The Very Best Of Pat Benatar: All Fired Up* (Chrysalis 1994)★★★, *16 Classic Performances* (EMI 1996)★★★.

● VIDEOS: *Hit Videos* (RCA/Columbia 1988), *Best Shots* (Chrysalis Music Video 1988), *Benatar* (RCA/Columbia 1988).

● FURTHER READING: *Benatar*, Doug Magee.

● FILMS: *American Pop* (1981).

Benediction

This death metal band from Birmingham, West Midlands, England, was formed in the late 80s, and featured singer Dave Ingram, with guitarists Darren Brooke and Peter Rew, and bass player Frank Healy. Original vocalist 'Barney' (Mark Greenway) joined Napalm Death, while drummer Ian Treacy quit in late 1993 (for session work, eventually becoming part of Celestial), to be replaced by Paul Brooks, a veteran of several thrash, punk, indie and even reggae bands. Signed to Germany's Nuclear Blast stable, in the 90s European touring with Atheist established the band throughout the continent, with the possible exception of their native country, a fact frequently bemoaned by the group. A half-live affair, *The Grotesque - Ashen Epitaph*, also comprised two new studio tracks, along with material recorded on their well-received European tour. A lifeless fifth album, *The Dreams You Dread*, did little to rectify either the apathy of the record-buying public or the critical perception of the band as underachievers. After a three-year hiatus, *Grind Bastard* went some of the way towards restoring the band's reputation.

● ALBUMS: *Subconscious Terror* (Nuclear Blast 1990)★★★, *Grand Leveller* (Revolver 1991)★★, *Dark Is The Season* (Nuclear Blast 1992)★★, *Transcend The Rubicon* (Nuclear Blast 1993)★★★,

The Grotesque - Ashen Epitaph mini-album (Nuclear Blast 1994)★★, *The Dreams You Dread* (Nuclear Blast 1995)★★, *Grind Bastard* (Nuclear Blast 1998)★★★.

BENGAL TIGERS

This short-lived Australian heavy metal band was formed in Melbourne in 1983 by vocalist Gordon Heald and guitarist Barney Fakhouri. Enlisting Steve Tyler (bass) and Mick Egan (drums, vocals), they released a mini-album on the Mushroom label the following year. Influenced by AC/DC, Iron Maiden and Scorpions, they purveyed clichéd heavy metal that lacked both identity and energy.

● ALBUMS: *Metal Fetish* mini-album (Mushroom 1984)★★.

BETSY

In 1988 Bitch, the Los Angeles-based sado-masochistic band who were obsessed with leather, whips and chains, decided to clean up their act. They changed their name to Betsy and adopted a less extreme angle. The band still comprised Betsy Weiss (vocals), David Carruth (guitar), Ron Cordy (bass) and Robby Settles (drums), but the sexual side of the group's image was played down. Signing to Roadrunner Records, their sole release was not noticeably different from the old Bitch musical style: heavy metal with lacklustre vocals, albeit with less tawdry lyrics. The album sank without trace and they reverted to leather underwear and the Bitch tag within a year.

● ALBUMS: *Betsy* (Roadrunner 1988)★★.

BETTENCOURT, NUNO

b. 20 September 1966, Azores, Portugal. Following the disappointing sales figures for Extreme's *Waiting For The Punchline*, and with the announcement of the departure of lead vocalist Gary Cherone for Van Halen, guitarist Nuno Bettencourt's decision to launch a solo career in 1997 was widely predicted. Staying with Extreme's former label, A&M Records, Bettencourt was keen to take responsibility not only for the music but also the vocals. The result was *Schizophonic*, on which Bettencourt's much-admired guitar pyrotechnics were played down in favour of a darker, more foreboding musical approach. Two of the songs, 'You' and 'Pursuit Of Happiness', were co-written with Cherone, but more representative of the contents was 'Gravity', the first single to be culled from the album.

● ALBUMS: *Schizophonic* (A&M 1997)★★★.

BEYOND

Formed in Derby, England, in 1988, Beyond consisted of John Whitby (vocals), Andy Gatford (guitar), Jim Kersey (bass) and Neil Cooper (drums). Quickly gaining popularity on the live club circuit and obtaining a publishing contract with Island Music, they attracted the attention of EMI Records through some early demos. The band initially signed a year-long development arrangement with the label, during which time they released two singles on the small independent Big Cat Records label - the *Manic Sound Picnic* EP and the single 'No Excuse', both released in 1990. The following year, the band released their first single for the EMI label, 'One Step Too Far'. This was quickly followed by 'Empire' on the relaunched EMI subsidiary Harvest Records. Reminiscent of Jane's Addiction, Voivod and Faith No More, the band's debut album was well received by both the music press and the public. In support of the album they toured the UK and Europe with Living Colour, and an EP, *Raging*, was also added to the band's discography. However, low sales led to the termination of their contract with EMI, although all four members joined forces again in 1995 under the name Gorilla.

● ALBUMS: *Crawl* (Harvest 1991)★★★, *Chasm* (Harvest 1993)★★★.

BIAFRA, JELLO

b. Eric Boucher, 17 June 1958, Denver, Colorado, USA. It took a little time for Biafra to launch his solo career after being emotionally and financially sapped by the demise of his former band, the Dead Kennedys. The drain was primarily due to the torturous legal process after the group were charged with 'distributing harmful matter to minors' over H.R. Giger's painting *Landscape #20* - aka 'Penis Landscape'. When Biafra did resume recording it was initially in the field of spoken word lectures. Both *No More Cocoons* and the ironically titled *High Priest Of Harmful Matter* took this course, the latter explaining in great detail, and no little humour, the forces lined up against him in his trial. Always an articulate songwriter and frontman, Biafra worked well in the environment, with much of the material culled from his live lectures throughout the USA (centred on the theme of artistic censorship by bodies such as the PMRC, who had made Biafra something of a target). Since then Biafra has returned to music, working with a host of artists, generally drawn from the Alternative Tentacles Records roster, a label he set up in the early 80s to house Dead Kennedys product. These have seen Biafra provide the lyrics and distinctive vocals to the musical muscle of NoMeansNo and D.O.A.; the latter teaming fostered the seismic, extended rampage of 'Full Metal Jackoff', one of the artist's finest moments. Biafra also appeared with members of D.O.A. in the *Terminal City Ricochet* film. The recordings conducted with Lard saw him join with Al Jourgensen and Paul Barker of Ministry, with Biafra as acerbic as ever on a cover version of 'They're Coming To Take Me Away' (conducted with the same sort of religious fervour as the Kennedys' versions of 'Rawhide' and 'Viva Las Vegas'). The artist then returned to the spoken word format with *I Blow Minds For A Living*, before another collaboration, this time with renowned anti-redneck country artist Mojo Nixon. In 1994 Biafra was hospitalized with two broken legs after being assaulted at a show by punks who accused him of 'selling out', an action even the PMRC would not have been hysterical enough to pursue.

● ALBUMS: *No More Cocoons* (Alternative Tentacles 1987)★★★, *High Priest Of Harmful Matter - Tales From The Trial* (Alternative Tentacles 1989)★★★, with Lard *The Last Temptation Of Reid* (Alternative Tentacles 1990)★★★, with D.O.A. *Last Scream Of The Missing Neighbors* mini-album (Alternative Tentacles 1990)★★★, with NoMeansNo *The Sky Is Falling And I Want My Mommy* (Alternative Tentacles 1991)★★★, *I Blow Minds For A Living* (Alternative Tentacles 1991)★★★, with Tumor Circus *Tumor Circus* (Alternative Tentacles 1991)★★★, with Mojo Nixon *Prairie Home Invasion* (Alternative Tentacles 1994)★★★, with Lard *Pure Chewing Satisfaction* (Alternative Tentacles 1997)★★★.

Bif Naked

b. 1971, New Delhi, India. Confrontational, tattooed, hard rock singer-songwriter Bif Naked was born to two private-school teachers who quickly gave her up for adoption. She was adopted by two American missionaries, and her childhood was spent in locations including Lexington, Kentucky, USA, and Winnipeg and Manitoba in Canada. Her first group was Jungle Milk, who specialized in rap cover versions of Doris Day songs backed by 10 conga players. She then worked with two of Canada's premier underground bands - Gorilla Gorilla and Chrome Dog. She made her debut with her own band in 1994 with the EP *Fours Songs And A Poem*. It won her instant attention, and heralded a talent that was more fully realized on a full-length album released later that year. With the rest of her band - Randy Black (drums), Rich Priske (bass) and X-Factor (guitar) - the major theme of the lyrics was the politics of sex and love. However, it was her skill in articulating different perspectives on gender issues that really distinguished her - from the male lust expressed in 'Everything' to an account of her own rape ordeal ('Tell On You'). The musical backgrounds ranged from conventional, grinding hard-rock to the seductive hip-hop beats of 'Daddy's Getting Married', a song concerning the remarriage of her father, which became the first single released from the album. She and her band then travelled to the UK for their first British tour, in support of Life Of Agony early in 1996.

● ALBUMS: *Bif Naked* (Plum/A&M 1994)★★★.

Big Black

Initially based in Evanstown, Illinois, USA, Big Black made its recording debut in 1983 with the six-track EP *Lungs*. Fronted by guitarist/vocalist Steve Albini, the group underwent several changes before completing *Bulldozer* the following year. A more settled line-up was formed around Albini, Santiago Durango (guitar) and Dave Riley aka David Lovering (bass) as Big Black began fusing an arresting, distinctive sound, and *Atomizer* (1986) established the trio as one of America's leading independent acts. This powerful, compulsive set included 'Kerosene', a lyrically nihilistic piece equating pyromania with teenage sex as a means of escaping small-town boredom. The combined guitar assault of Albini and Durango was underpinned by Riley's emphatic basswork, which propelled this metallic composition to its violent conclusion. Melvin Belli (guitar) replaced Durango, who left to study law, for *Songs About Fucking*, Big Black's best-known and most popular album. Once again their blend of post-hardcore and post-industrial styles proved exciting, but Albini had now tired of his creation: 'Big Black are dumb, ugly and persistent, just like a wart' - and announced the break-up of the group prior to the record's release. He later became a respected but idiosyncratic producer, working with the Pixies (*Surfer Rosa*), the Breeders (*Pod*) and Tad (*Salt Lick*), before forming a new venture, the controversially named and short-lived Rapeman. When that group shuddered under the weight of criticism at its name (though Albini insisted this was merely a UK phenomenon), he returned to production duties. Undoubtedly the highest profile of these would be PJ Harvey's *Rid Of Me* and Nirvana's *In Utero*. Afterwards Albini returned to a group format with Shellac. Santiago

Durango recorded two EPs as Arsenal.

● ALBUMS: *Atomizer* (Homestead/Blast First 1986)★★★, *Sound Of Impact* live album (Walls Have Ears 1987)★★, *Songs About Fucking* (Touch And Go/Blast First 1987)★★★, *Pigpile* (Blast First 1992)★★★.

● COMPILATIONS: *The Hammer Party* (Homestead/Blast First 1986)★★★, *The Rich Man's Eight-Track Tape* (Homestead/Blast First 1987)★★★.

BIG BROTHER AND THE HOLDING COMPANY

Formed in September 1965, this pivotal San Franciscan rock group evolved out of 'jam' sessions held in the basement of a communal house. The original line-up featured Sam Andrew (b. 18 December 1941, Taft, California, USA; guitar, vocals), Peter Albin (b. 6 June 1944, San Francisco, California, USA; bass, vocals), Dave Eskerson (guitar) and Chuck Jones (drums), but within months the latter pair had been replaced, respectively, by James Gurley (b. *c*.1940, Detroit, Michigan, USA) and Dave Getz (b. 1938, Brooklyn, New York, USA). The restructured quartet initially eschewed formal compositions, preferring a free-form improvisation centred on Gurley's mesmeric finger-picking style, but a degree of discipline gradually evolved. The addition of Texas singer Janis Joplin (b. 19 January 1943, Port Arthur, Texas, USA, d. 4 October 1970, Los Angeles, California, USA) in June 1966 emphasized this new-found direction, and her powerful, blues-soaked delivery provided the perfect foil to the unit's instrumental power. The group rapidly became one of the Bay Area's leading attractions, but they naïvely struck an immoderate recording contract with the Chicago-based Mainstream label. Although marred by poor production, *Big Brother And The Holding Company* nevertheless contains several excellent performances, notably 'Bye Bye Baby' and 'Down On Me'. The quintet rose to national prominence in 1967 following a sensational appearance at the Monterey Pop Festival. Joplin's charismatic performance engendered a prestigious management deal with Albert Grossman, who in turn secured their release from all contractual obligations. Big Brother then switched outlets to Columbia Records, for which they completed *Cheap Thrills* (1968). This exciting album topped the US charts, but despite the inclusion of in-concert favourites 'Piece Of My Heart' and 'Ball And Chain', the recording was fraught with difficulty. Joplin came under increased pressure to opt for a solo career as critics denigrated the musicians' abilities. The group broke up in November 1968 and while Sam Andrew joined the singer in her next venture, Albin and Getz joined Country Joe And The Fish. The following year the latter duo reclaimed the Big Brother name and with the collapse of an interim line-up, re-established the unit with ex-colleagues Andrew and Gurley. Several newcomers, including Nick Gravenites (b. Chicago, Illinois, USA; vocals), Kathi McDonald (vocals), David Schallock (guitar) and Mike Finnegan (piano), augmented the quartet on an informal basis, but despite moments of inspiration, neither *Be A Brother* (1970) nor *How Hard It Is* (1971) recaptured former glories. The group was disbanded in 1972, but reconvened six years later at the one-off Tribal Stomp reunion. In 1987 singer Michelle Bastian joined Getz, Gurley, Andrew and Albin in a fully reconstituted Big Brother line-up, still hoping to assert an independent identity.

● ALBUMS: *Big Brother And The Holding Company* (Mainstream 1967)★★★, *Cheap Thrills* (Columbia 1968)★★★★, *Be A Brother* (Columbia 1970)★★, *How Hard It Is* (Columbia 1971)★, *Cheaper Thrills* recorded 1966 (Made To Last 1984)★★, *Big Brother And The Holding Company Live* recorded 1966 (Rhino 1984)★★, *Live At Winterland '68* (Columbia 1998)★★★.

● COMPILATIONS: *Joseph's Coat* (Edsel 1986)★★.

● VIDEOS: *Comin' Home* (BMG 1992), *Live In Studio: San Francisco '67* (Castle Music Pictures 1992).

● FILMS: *American Pop* (1981).

BIG CHIEF

Founded in Ann Arbor, Michigan, USA, Big Chief's *modus operandi* has been to strip down Motown soul and combine it with MC5 riffs. They consist of Barry Henssler - once memorably described by the UK's *New Musical Express* as providing 'the loudest guitar growl on this planet' - who had previously worked with Detroit hardcore legends the Necros, guitarists Mark Dancey and Phil Dürr (b. Germany), and bass player Matt O'Brien. In September 1994 Big Chief linked up with Detroit singer Thornetta Davis, who had won several blues vocal awards in the 90s. The band had originally recruited her in 1991 to add her voice to two songs on *Face*. She went on to have an even greater impact on several songs that appeared on *Mack Avenue Skullgame*, including the single 'One Born Every Minute', part of a suite of songs originally written for a projected film soundtrack. It led to Big Chief backing Davis on her debut for Sub Pop

Records, *Shout Out*, in 1994, with the title track specially written for her by the band. *Platinum Jive* featured a guest rap from Schoolly D on 'Bona Fide', but again failed to break Big Chief out of the alternative rock ghetto, despite being the first product drawn from a new major label contract with Capitol Records.

● ALBUMS: *Face* (Repulsion 1991)★★★, *Mack Avenue Skullgame* (Sub Pop 1993)★★★, with Thornetta Davis *Shout Out* (Sub Pop 1994)★★★, *Platinum Jive (Greatest Hits 1966-99* (Capitol 1994)★★★.

● COMPILATIONS: *Drive It Off* (Get Hip 1991)★★★.

Big F

This Los Angeles, USA trio comprised Mark Christian (guitar), John Shreve (bass, vocals) and Rob Donin (drums). Their trademark was a 'mind-blowing wall of noise', dominated by crashing drums and screeching feedback, while vocalist Shreve screamed incessantly above the maelstrom. Psychedelia, Jimi Hendrix, the Stooges, the Cult and *avant garde* influences appeared as reference points. Shreve was in fact the alter ego of Berlin's John Crawford. Regardless, the sub-Led Zeppelin riffs and affected stylings of Big F were unlikely to find any success on the scale of 'Take My Breath Away'.

● ALBUMS: *The Big F* (Elektra 1989)★★, *Is* (Chrysalis 1993)★★.

Big House

This Canadian quartet specialized in melodic and hard-edged AOR. They were formed in 1987 by drummer Sjor Throndson and vocalist Jan Ek, who both wanted to prove that Canada had much more to offer than merely Rush and Bryan Adams. Recruiting guitarist K.B. Broc and bassist Jay Scott King, their line-up was finalized in 1989. After incessant gigging in their native Canada, the band were signed by RCA Records. They debuted in 1992 with a self-titled album that incorporated elements of Bon Jovi, Ratt and Aerosmith, and, for a while, looked likely to develop into a major force.

● ALBUMS: *Big House* (Boom Town 1992)★★★.

Billion Dollar Babies

This short-lived group revolved around Mike Bruce (b. 21 November 1948, California, USA; guitar, vocals), Dennis Dunaway (b. 15 March 1946, California, USA; bass) and Neal Smith (b. 10 January 1946, Washington, USA; drums). Founder-members of Alice Cooper, the three were summarily fired in 1974 by lead singer Vincent Furnier, himself known from that time as 'Alice Cooper'. Protracted legal entanglements delayed this riposte, which took its name from one of their former group's bestselling albums. Sessionmen Bob Dolin (keyboards) and Mike Marconi (guitar) completed the line-up, but the resultant album, *Battle Axe*, was a disappointment. Its uncomfortable mix of technology and heavy metal did not prove popular and the quintet was then dissolved. Bruce embarked on a solo career and then teamed up with ex-Angel drummer Barry Brandt to pursue a jazz-orientated path. Dunaway and Smith formed the Flying Tigers while Dolin and Marconi reverted to studio work.

● ALBUMS: *Battle Axe* (Polydor 1977)★★.

Billy Satellite

This Californian heavy metal quartet was formed in 1983 by Monty Byron (guitar, vocals, keyboards) and Danny Chauncey (guitar, keyboards). With bassist Ira Walker and drummer Tom Falletti completing the line-up, they bridged the musical divide between the commercial radio-rock of Boston, and the bluesy southern style of Lynyrd Skynyrd. Signing to EMI Records in 1984, they released only one album before disbanding. Byron and Chauncey went on to join New Frontier and 38 Special, respectively. Eddie Money later covered the band's 'I Wanna Go Back', achieving a major hit in the USA in the process.

● ALBUMS: *Billy Satellite* (Capitol 1984)★★★.

Billy The Kid

This brash pop-metal quartet was formed in Los Angeles, USA, during 1984 by vocalist Stephen Frederick and guitarist Bill L'Kid. With the addition of Jeffrey Velvet (bass) and Randy Delay (ex-Georgia Satellites; drums), they signed a contract with MCA Records the following year. Fusing the energy and flamboyance of Van Halen with the commercial sensibilities of REO Speedwagon, they recorded the impressive *Sworn To Fun* in 1985. Failing to attract media interest, they disbanded soon after the album's release.

● ALBUMS: *Sworn To Fun* (MCA 1985)★★★.

Biohazard

The mean streets of Brooklyn, New York, saw the formation of Biohazard in 1988 by Evan Seinfeld (bass, vocals), Billy Graziedi (guitar, vocals), Bobby Hambel (guitar) and Danny Schuler (drums), and the harsh realities of urban life provide constant lyrical inspiration for this socially and politically aware hardcore band. Modest beginnings supporting the likes of the Cro-Mags and Carnivore at the famous L'Amour club led to an independent debut, *Biohazard*. Constant touring built such a cult following that the band were able to sign to Roadrunner Records for one album, and then secure a major contract with Warner Brothers Records in 1992. *Urban Discipline* was recorded in under two weeks on a tiny budget, but proved to be the band's breakthrough album. Blisteringly heavy, with lyrics to match - 'Black And White And Red All Over' was an anti-racism tirade, intended to dispel a mistakenly applied fascist label stemming from the debut's 'Howard Beach', which concerned a racially motivated Brooklyn murder - the album drew massive praise, as did wild live shows during heavy touring with Kreator in Europe and Sick Of It All in the USA. The band also recorded a well-received track with rappers Onyx for the *Judgement Night* soundtrack. The Warners debut, *State Of The World Address*, was recorded in seven weeks, and demonstrated that major label status did not mean any compromising on Biohazard's part. The album featured a furiously heavy Ed Stasium production and an aggressive performance that attracted a succession of rave reviews. The band embarked on a successful US tour with Pantera and Sepultura as album sales took off. However, a second appearance at the Donington Festival came to a controversially premature end, owing to the stage management's safety worries over Biohazard's penchant for encouraging their audience to join them on stage *en masse*. Further European touring, including several festival dates, was problem-free, with the band reaffirming a deserved reputation for their ferocious live shows, before returning to the USA for dates with House Of Pain and Danzig. Hambel was sacked from the band in November 1995 prior to the recording of *Mata Leáo*. His replacement was Rob Echeverria (b. 15 December 1967, New York, USA; ex-Helmet). *No Holds Barred* was a fierce live album recorded in Europe.

● ALBUMS: *Biohazard* (Maze 1990)★★, *Urban Discipline* (Roadrunner 1992)★★★, *State Of The World Address* (Warners 1994)★★★, *Mata Leáo* (Warners 1996)★★, *No Holds Barred* (Roadrunner 1997)★★★.

Birtha

Birtha were one of the first US all-female bands to attempt to penetrate the exclusively male bastion of heavy rock. Comprising Rosemary Butler (bass, vocals), Sherry Hagler (keyboards), Liver Favela (drums) and Shele Pinizzotto (guitar, vocals), they released two excellent hard-rock albums during the early 70s. They specialized in tight harmonies and performed in a style similar to that of early Uriah Heep, but were, perhaps unjustly, regarded as a novelty at the time. Their tasteless publicity handout during their early 70s UK tour with the Kinks, stating 'Birtha has balls', doubtless did little to alter this image. Along with Fanny, they helped to pave the way for future female rockers such as the Runaways.

● ALBUMS: *Birtha* (Probe 1972)★★★, *Can't Stop The Madness* (Probe 1973)★★.

Bitch (Switzerland)

Bitch were formed in Zurich, Switzerland, in 1979 by the Schmid brothers, Eric (vocals), Jimmy (drums) and Geoffrey (guitar). Adding Marc Portman (guitar) and Roddy Landolt (bass), they combined 70s symphonic rock with a New Wave Of British Heavy Metal approach. Elements of Deep Purple, Krokus, Emerson, Lake And Palmer and Angelwitch were evident in the two albums they released during the early 80s. However, the band's name was always more provocative than their music, and they disappeared from the scene in 1982.

● ALBUMS: *First Bite* (Bellaphon 1980)★★★, *Some Like It Hard* (Bellaphon 1982)★★.

Bitch (USA)

This Los Angeles-based quartet made an impact in 1982 with their debut EP, more as a result of their shock value than because of any originality. Led by female vocalist Betsy Weiss, a former ska singer, they released *Be My Slave*, with David Carruth (guitar), Mark Anthony Wells (bass) and Robby Settles (drums) completing the line-up. With Ron Cordy replacing Wells, it took a further four years before the appropriately titled *The Bitch Is Back* emerged. Regarded with little affection by the mainstream audience, they relaunched themselves as Betsy in 1988, with a cleaner, AOR-like image. This was greeted with indifference and the band became Bitch again within a year, reverting to their original Motörhead/Girlschool metal format.

● ALBUMS: *Damnation Alley* mini-album (Metal Blade 1982)★★, *Be My Slave* (Metal Blade 1983)★★★, *The Bitch Is Back* (Metal Blade 1987)★★.

Bitch Magnet

Formed at Oberlin College, Ohio, in 1986, but based in North Carolina, USA, Bitch Magnet initially specialized in somewhat generic, MC5-

derived garage punk riffs, akin to an agitated Fuzztones, but with less character on display, as evidenced by their debut album, *Star Booty*. More interesting was the follow-up, *Umber*, which offered more distinctive but also more aggressive songwriting. Following this, critics began to make frequent comparisons to Big Black, prompted by the fact that Steve Albini had engineered the group's debut album. *Ben Hur* managed to surpass even its predecessor's squalls of angry noise. The band broke up in 1991 when singer Soo Young left to form Seam. David Grubbs (guitar, ex-Squirrel Bait) returned to his concurrent employment in Bastro.

● ALBUMS: *Star Booty* (Roman Candle/Communion 1988)★★, *Umber* (Communion 1989)★★★, *Ben Hur* (Communion 1990)★★★.

BITCHES SIN

Formed in Cumbria, England, in 1980, during the growth of the New Wave Of British Heavy Metal movement, Bitches Sin comprised Ian Toomey (guitar), Alan Cockburn (vocals), Perry Hodder (bass), Peter Toomey (guitar) and Bill Knowles (drums). Cockburn was later replaced by Frank Quegan, while Mike Frazier took over on bass. Purveying high-energy metallic rock, they combined UFO and Deep Purple influences with modern technology and were occasionally reminiscent of Diamond Head. Their first single, 'Sign Of The Times', achieved success in Holland after it was championed by radio disc jockey Hanneke Kappen. They subsequently contributed a track to a *Heavy Metal Heroes* compilation album, which helped to boost their reputation. A number of personnel changes hindered their progress, however. They released two studio albums, neither of which fulfilled their initial promise, and disbanded before *Invaders* materialized. The Toomey brothers reappeared in 1988 as Flash Point, self-financing the release of a debut album.

● ALBUMS: *Predator* (Heavy Metal 1982)★★★, *Invaders* (King Klassic 1986)★★.

BLACK 'N' BLUE

Formerly known as Boogie Star, Black 'N' Blue were formed in Portland, Oregon, USA, in 1981. After a series of line-up shuffles, the band stabilized with Jaime St. James (vocals), Tommy Thayer (guitar), Jeff Warner (guitar), Patrick Young (bass) and Peter Holmes (drums). Relocating to Los Angeles in 1982, they forged a contract with Geffen Records and delivered their self-titled debut album in 1984. Produced by Dieter Dierks, the album was classic hard rock and sounded surprisingly un-American, shunning the party-metal approach of Ratt and Quiet Riot, and having more in common with the Scorpions and Def Leppard. Failing to attract media attention, the band dropped this approach and attempted to emulate the style of Kiss and Mötley Crüe. With Gene Simmons (Kiss's bassist) producing their third and fourth albums, the accusations of imitation grew even stronger. Failing to find commercial success, the band folded in 1989. Patrick Young went on to Dokken, vocalist James joined Madhouse, Thayer teamed up with Harlow and the remaining pair formed Wet Engine.

● ALBUMS: *Black 'N' Blue* (Geffen 1984)★★★, *Without Love* (Geffen 1985)★★★, *Nasty, Nasty* (Geffen 1986)★★, *In Heat* (Geffen 1988)★★.

BLACK ALICE

Comprising Rob Hartley (vocals), Jamie Page (guitar), Vince Linardi (bass) and Joe Demasi (drums), Australian hard rockers Black Alice specialized in a derivative but highly animated blend of power chords and bellowing vocals from Hartley. Much of the songwriting on the group's sole album was lacking in diversity. Released in Europe before Australia, the group licensed the recording to RCA Records for their domestic market in 1984, but there, too, it failed to sell.

● ALBUMS: *Endangered Species* (Street Tunes 1983)★★★.

BLACK ANGELS

Lacking something in originality (critics noted a particular debt to early Deep Purple), Swiss group the Black Angels went some way towards remedying their shortcomings through sheer energy and self-belief. *Hell Machine*, their 1981 debut for Meteor Records, was the superior of their two efforts, despite some agonizingly clichéd lyrics. Clive Murray (vocals), Harry Stone (keyboards), Andy McKay (guitar), Mark Egg (guitar), Walt Lion (bass) and Brian Irving (drums) attempted to produce a more blended, complex sound for 1984's *Kickdown*, but the resulting tracks lacked the spirit of old. With minimal sales and profound disinterest from European critics, the band had broken up by the following year.

● ALBUMS: *Hell Machine* (Meteor 1981)★★★, *Kickdown* (Gull 1984)★★.

BLACK CROWES

Exposed to a wide variety of music from an early age by their musician father, brothers Chris (b.

Christopher Mark Robinson, 20 December 1966, Atlanta, Georgia, USA; vocals) and Rich Robinson (b. Richard S. Robinson, 24 May 1969, Atlanta, Georgia, USA; guitar) formed the band under the name Mr. Crowe's Garden in 1984. A procession of six bassists and three drummers passed through before the band stabilized with Johnny Colt (b. 1 May 1966, Cherry Point, USA; bass) and Steve Gorman (b. 17 August 1965, Muskegon, Michigan, USA; drums, ex-Mary My Hope). His predecessor, Jeff Sullivan, went on to join Drivin' N' Cryin'. Jeff Cease joined the group as a second guitarist in 1988 from the Nashville band Rumble Circus, to augment and toughen both the songs and the live sound. As the Black Crowes, they were signed to the Def American label by George Drakoulias. Given the heavy nature of other members of the label's roster, such as Slayer and Danzig, the purist rock 'n' roll style of the Crowes was a stark contrast.

Drakoulias produced the debut, *Shake Your Money Maker*, a remarkably mature album from such a young band, blending soul and uncomplicated R&B in a manner reminiscent of vintage Rolling Stones and Humble Pie. Another influence was made obvious by the stirring cover version of Otis Redding's 'Hard to Handle'. The record's highlight was 'She Talks To Angels', an emotive acoustic ballad about the frailties of a drug addict, featuring a superb vocal and highly accomplished lyric from Chris Robinson. The album was released to critical acclaim, and the band went on the road, supporting first Steve Stevens' Atomic Playboys, and then Junkyard in the USA, plus a handful of UK dates as headliners or opening for the Dogs D'Amour. Their live performances drew further Stones comparisons, the band's image being very much rooted in the 70s, and with Chris Robinson's thin frame dominating the stage like a young Mick Jagger. With heavy radio and MTV airplay exposing the Crowes to a wider audience, the first single, 'Jealous Again', reached number 75 in the *Billboard* charts, and the band were invited to fill the prestigious support slot for the final leg of Aerosmith's 'Pump' tour on their return to the USA. Canadian keyboard player Ed Hawrysch, recommended by former Green On Red member Chuck Leavell, who had played on the album, joined the band in early 1991. The band were invited on another high-profile tour as guests of ZZ Top, but their uncompromising attitude led to ZZ Top's management demanding that the Crowes leave the tour following a home-town show in Atlanta, owing to Chris Robinson's persistent, if oblique, criticism of the corporate sponsorship of the tour. Somewhat ironically, the band fired the support act for their subsequent headline shows after discovering that they had made advertisements for a similar major company.

By this stage, the band had achieved a considerable level of chart success, and they joined the European Monsters Of Rock tour, opening at the prestigious Donington Festival in England and culminating in a massive free show in Moscow. Prior to these dates, the band were forced to take a five-week break (their longest in 22 months of touring) when Chris Robinson collapsed, suffering from exhaustion, following an acoustic showcase at Ronnie Scott's club in London. The singer recovered to undertake the tour, plus a UK trek to complete the band's world tour. This ended with further controversy, with Colt and vocalist Robinson becoming embroiled in a fight with a member of the crowd at the Edinburgh Playhouse. Almost immediately after the tour, the band parted company with Jeff Cease, replacing him with former Burning Tree guitarist/vocalist Marc Ford. Rather than rest on their laurels, the band went straight into pre-production for their second album, completing basic tracks in only eight days. Borrowing from the title of an old hymn book, *The Southern Harmony And Musical Companion* was released in the spring of 1992, again to positive reviews. The musical progression of the band, and of the brothers as songwriters, was obvious, with more complex arrangements than the debut, a much greater expanse of sound and the use of female backing singers. New recruit Ford provided superb guitar solos, with one particularly notable lead on 'Sometimes Salvation'. With both the album and opening single 'Remedy' (US number 48, UK number 24) a success, the Black Crowes returned to the road for the High As The Moon tour - a free show in Toronto's G Rose Lord Park drew a 75,000 crowd, with people entering the park at a rate of 1,000 per minute at one point. In 1994 *Amorica* was finally released. A previously completed album (*Tall*) had been scrapped, with only five songs retained, and producer Jack Puig had been brought in to rectify matters. Live shows saw the debut of percussionist Chris Trujillo, and the band achieved another UK success with 'High Head Blues/A Conspiracy' reaching number 25 in Febuary 1995. *Three Snakes And One Charm* was predicted by many to be the band's last album, with numerous personnel changes having interrupted the recording process. Marc Ford left the band in August 1997, and was soon followed by Johnny

Colt; the latter was replaced in early 1998 by Sven Pipien (ex-Mary My Hope).

● ALBUMS: *Shake Your Money Maker* (Def American 1990)★★★, *The Southern Harmony And Musical Companion* (Def American 1992)★★★★, *Amorica* (American 1994)★★★, *Three Snakes And One Charm* (American 1996)★★★.

● COMPILATIONS: *Sho' Nuff* (American 1998)★★★.

● VIDEOS: *Who Killed That Bird On Your Windowsill ... The Movie* (Warner Brothers Video 1993).

● FURTHER READING: *The Black Crowes*, Martin Black.

BLACK FLAG

Formed in 1977 in Los Angeles, California, Black Flag rose to become one of America's leading hardcore groups. The initial line-up - Keith Morris (vocals), Greg Ginn (guitar), Chuck Dukowski (bass) and Brian Migdol (drums) - completed the *Nervous Breakdown* EP in 1978, but the following year Morris left to form the Circle Jerks. Several members joined and left before Henry Rollins (b. 13 February 1961; vocals), Dez Cadenza (guitar) and Robo (drums) joined Ginn and Dukowski for *Damaged*, the group's first full-length album. Originally scheduled for release by MCA Records, the company withdrew support, citing outrageous content, and the set appeared on the quintet's own label, SST Records. This prolific outlet has not only issued every subsequent Black Flag recording, but also has a catalogue that includes Hüsker Dü, Sonic Youth, the Minutemen, the Meat Puppets and Dinosaur Jr. Administered by Ginn and Dukowski, the latter of whom left the group to concentrate his efforts on the label, the company has become one of America's leading, and most influential, independents. Ginn continued to lead Black Flag in tandem with Rollins, and although its rhythm section was subject to change, the music's power remained undiminished. Pivotal albums included *My War* and *In My Head*, while their diversity was showcased on *Family Man*, which contrasted one side of Rollins' spoken word performances with four excellent instrumentals. However, the group split in 1986 following the release of a compulsive live set, *Who's Got The 10 1/2?*, after which Ginn switched his attentions to labelmates Gone. Rollins went on to a successful solo career. The glory days of Black Flag are warmly recalled in one of Rollins' numerous books for his 2.13.61. publishing empire, *Get In The Van*.

● ALBUMS: *Damaged* (SST 1981)★★★★, *My War* (SST 1984)★★★, *Family Man* (SST 1984)★★, *Slip It In* (SST 1984)★★★, *Live '84* (SST 1984)★★, *Loose Nut* (SST 1985)★★, *In My Head* (SST 1985)★★★, *Who's Got The 10 1/2?* (SST 1986)★★★.

● COMPILATIONS: *Everything Went Black* (SST 1982)★★★, *The First Four Years* (SST 1983)★★★★, *Wasted ... Again* (SST 1988)★★★★.

● VIDEOS: *Black Flag Live* (Jettisoundz 1984).

BLACK LACE

In no way connected with the UK cabaret pop group who enjoyed major success with 'Agadoo', this Black Lace were a US heavy metal group of the mid-80s who recorded two albums for Mausoleum Records. Comprising Anthony Fragnito (bass), Carlo Fragnito (guitar), Mary-Ann Scandiffio (vocals) and Steve Werner (drums), the group relied heavily on Scandiffio's vibrato to distinguish them, although the musicianship on both albums was a strong amalgam of hard rock with pop hooks. Sadly, it was not enough to establish them in the mainstream and when *Get It While It's Hot* failed to sell, the group broke up.

● ALBUMS: *Unlaced* (Mausoleum 1984)★★★, *Get It While It's Hot* (Mausoleum 1985)★★★.

BLACK OAK ARKANSAS

A sextet formed in the late 60s, Black Oak Arkansas took its name from the US town and state where singer Jim 'Dandy' Mangrum (b. 30 March 1948) was born. The other members of the group came from nearby towns: Ricky Reynolds (b. 28 October 1948, Manilan, Arkansas, USA; guitar), Stanley Knight (b. 12 February 1949, Little Rock, Arkansas, USA; guitar), Harvey Jett (b. Marion, Arkansas, USA; guitar), Pat Daugherty (b. 11 November 1947, Jonesboro, Arkansas, USA; bass) and drummer Wayne Evans, replaced on the third album by Thomas Aldrich (b. 15 August 1950, Jackson, Mississippi, USA). Before forming the band, the members were part of a gang that shared a house. Initially calling themselves the Knowbody Else, the group recorded an unsuccessful album for Stax Records in 1969. Two years later they changed their name and signed with Atco Records, for whom they recorded a self-titled album that introduced them to the US charts. Touring steadily, this hard rock/southern boogie band built a core following, yet its records never matched its concert appeal. Of the band's 10 US-charting albums between 1971 and 1976, *High On The Hog* proved the most commercially successful, peaking at number 52. It featured the bestselling December

1973 Top 30 single, 'Jim Dandy' (sung by female vocalist Ruby Starr, who reappeared on the *Live! Mutha* album). In 1975, guitarist Jett was replaced by James Henderson (b. 20 May 1954, Jackson, Mississippi, USA), and the following year, after switching to MCA Records, Black Oak Arkansas had one further minor chart single, 'Strong Enough To Be Gentle'. By 1977 only Mangrum remained from the original line-up and although they signed to Capricorn Records, there was no further record success. Mangrum did, however, maintain various touring versions of the group during the 80s, as well as recording a solo album in 1984. The catalogue was reissued in 1995 by Sequel Records.

● ALBUMS: as the Knowbody Else *The Knowbody Else* (Stax 1969)★★, *Black Oak Arkansas* (Atco 1971)★★, *Keep The Faith* (Atco 1972)★★, *If An Angel Came To See You, Would You Make Her Feel At Home?* (Atco 1972)★★, *Raunch 'N' Roll/Live* (Atlantic 1973)★★★, *High On The Hog* (Atco 1973)★★, *Street Party* (Atco 1974)★★, *Ain't Life Grand* (Atco 1975)★★, *X-Rated* (MCA 1975)★, *Live! Mutha* (Atco 1976)★, *Balls Of Fire* (MCA 1976)★, *10 Year Overnight Success* (MCA 1976)★, *Race With The Devil* (Capricorn 1977)★, *I'd Rather Be Sailing* (Capricorn 1978)★, *Black Attack Is Back* (Capricorn 1986)★.
Solo: Jim Dandy *Ready As Hell* (Capricorn 1984)★.

● COMPILATIONS: *The Best Of Black Oak Arkansas* (Atco 1977)★★, *Early Times* (1993)★, *Hot & Nasty: The Best Of* (1993)★★.

Black Rose (UK)

Black Rose were formed in Newcastle, England, in 1983 by vocalist Steve Bardsley and guitarist Chris Watson. With the addition of Mick Thompson (bass) and Malla Smith (drums), they followed a musical direction similar to other north-east bands such as Raven, Venom and Blitzkrieg. After contributing tracks to a number of heavy metal compilation albums, they signed to Bullet Records and released *Boys Will Be Boys* in 1984. Following a Dutch tour to promote the album, Graham Hunter replaced Chris Watson. The band's second album suggested that they had made little musical progress. Pat O'Neill replaced Watson on guitar, but with poorly attended live shows and an ever-diminishing fanbase, the band disintegrated in 1987.

● ALBUMS: *Boys Will Be Boys* (Bullet 1984)★★, *Walk It, How You Talk It* (Neat 1986)★★.

Black Rose (USA)

The US version of Black Rose was formed by singer/actress Cher (b. Cherilyn Sarkarsian La Pier, 20 May 1946, El Centro, California, USA) and guitarist Les Dudek in 1979. Employing the services of Warren Harrison (backing vocals), Ron Ritchotte (guitar), Michael Finnigan (keyboards), Trey Thompson (bass) and Gary Ferguson (drums), they specialized in rock/pop crossover material, with a slight country influence. Their debut (and only) album was highly polished, with slick arrangements and an expensive production. When Cher and Dudek's tempestuous romance ended, Black Rose split. Ritchotte went on to play with Barrage then Steppenwolf.

● ALBUMS: *Black Rose* (Casablanca 1980)★★.

Black Sabbath

Group members Terry 'Geezer' Butler (b. 17 July 1949, Birmingham, England; bass), Tony Iommi (b. Anthony Frank Iommi, 19 February 1948, Birmingham, England; guitar), Bill Ward (b. 5 May 1948, Birmingham, England; drums) and 'Ozzy' Osbourne (b. John Osbourne, 3 December 1948, Aston, Birmingham, England; vocals) were originally known as Earth, changing their name to Black Sabbath in 1969. The band members grew up together in the Midlands, and their name hinted at the heavy, doom-laden and ingenious music they produced. The name had previously been used as a song title by the quartet in their pre-Earth blues band, Polka Tulk, and it was drawn not from a book by the occult writer Denis Wheatley, as is often stated, but from the cult horror film of that title. Nevertheless, many of Sabbath's songs deal with alternative beliefs and practices touched upon in Wheatley's novels. Recording classic albums such as their self-titled debut and *Paranoid* (from which the title track was a surprise UK hit single), the line-up remained unchanged until 1973 when Rick Wakeman (b. 18 May 1949, London, England), keyboard player for Yes, was enlisted to play on *Sabbath Bloody Sabbath*. By 1977 personnel difficulties within the band were beginning to take their toll, and the music was losing some of its earlier orchestral, bombastic sheen, prompting Osbourne to depart for a solo career in January 1979. He was replaced by ex-Savoy Brown member Dave Walker until Ronnie James Dio (b. Ronald Padavona, 10 July 1940, New Hampshire, USA) accepted the job in 1979. Dio had been a central figure in the early 70s band Elf, and spent three years with Ritchie Blackmore's Rainbow. However,

Dio's tenure with the band was short, and he left in 1982 following a disagreement over the mixing of *Live Evil*. The replacement vocalist was Ian Gillan (b. 19 August 1945, Hounslow, Middlesex, England). This Sabbath incarnation was generally regarded as the most disastrous, with *Born Again* failing to capture any of the original vitality of the group. By 1986, Iommi was the only original member of the band, which consisted of Geoff Nichols (b. Birmingham, England; keyboards), who had been the group's keyboard player since 1980 while still a member of Quartz, Glenn Hughes (b. 21 August 1952, Penkridge, Staffordshire, England; vocals), Dave Spitz (b. New York, USA; bass) and Eric Singer (b. Cleveland, Ohio, USA; drums). This was an accomplished line-up, Singer having been a member of the Lita Ford band, and Hughes having worked with Trapeze and Deep Purple. In 1986 the unexpectedly bluesy-sounding *Seventh Star* was released, the lyrics and music for which had been written by Iommi. In the first of a succession of personnel changes, Hughes left the band to be replaced by Ray Gillen (d. 1994), an American singer who failed to make any recordings with them. Tony Martin was the vocalist on 1987's powerful *The Eternal Idol* and 1988's *Headless Cross*, the latter produced by the renowned English drummer Cozy Powell. Martin has intermittently remained with the band since that time and has variously understudied Dio and Osbourne. Dio rejoined in late 1991 to record *Dehumanizer*, but Rob Halford of Judas Priest was forced to stand in for the errant singer the following November at the Pacific Ampithetre in Los Angeles. Dio, having heard of Ozzy Osbourne's plans to reform the original Black Sabbath line-up for a one off performance on his farewell solo tour, refused to take the stage for Black Sabbath's support set. By this time the band was suffering from flagging record sales and declining credibility. Iommi recruited their original bassist, Butler, and attempted to persuade drummer Bill Ward to rejoin. Ward declined, and Cozy Powell was recuperating, having been crushed by his horse, so Vinnie Appice became Sabbath's new drummer. (Bev Bevan of ELO had been part of the band for *Born Again*, and returned at various times - other temporary drummers have included Terry Chimes of the Clash.) Osbourne's attempts to re-form the original group for a 1992 tour faltered when the others demanded equal shares of the spoils. In 1994 a tribute album, *Nativity In Black*, was released, which featured appearances from all four original members in various guises, plus Megadeth, White Zombie, Sepultura, Biohazard, Ugly Kid Joe, Bruce Dickinson, Therapy?, Corrosion Of Conformity and Type O Negative. Spurred by the new interest in the group, the Powell, Iommi and Nichols line-up, with Tony Martin returning as singer and Neil Murray on bass, completed *Forbidden* in 1995. It was recorded in Wales and Los Angeles with Body Count guitarist Ernie-C. producing and Ice-T providing vocals on 'Illusion Of Power'. The line-up in 1996 of this ever-changing unit was Iommi, Martin, Murray and Bobby Rondinelli (drums). Butler formed GZR, but in December 1997 the original line-up of Butler, Iommi, Ward and Osbourne re-formed to play two live shows at the Birmingham NEC. In April, Ward suffered a heart attack, and was replaced by Vinnie Appice.

● ALBUMS: *Black Sabbath* (Vertigo 1970)★★★, *Paranoid* (Vertigo 1970)★★★★, *Master Of Reality* (Vertigo 1971)★★★, *Black Sabbath Vol. 4* (Vertigo 1972)★★★★, *Sabbath Bloody Sabbath* (World Wide Artists 1974)★★★, *Sabotage* (NEMS 1975)★★★, *Technical Ecstasy* (Vertigo 1976)★★★, *Never Say Die!* (Vertigo 1978)★★★, *Heaven And Hell* (Vertigo 1980)★★★★, *Live At Last* (NEMS 1980)★★, *Mob Rules* (Vertigo 1981)★★, *Live Evil* (Vertigo 1982)★★, *Born Again* (Vertigo 1983)★★, *Seventh Star* (Vertigo 1986)★★★, *The Eternal Idol* (Vertigo 1987)★★, *Headless Cross* (IRS 1989)★★, *TYR* (IRS 1990)★★, *Dehumanizer* (IRS 1992)★★, *Cross Purposes* (EMI 1994)★★, *Forbidden* (IRS 1995)★★, *Reunion* (Epic 1998)★★★.

● COMPILATIONS: *We Sold Our Soul For Rock 'n' Roll* (NEMS 1976)★★, *Greatest Hits* (NEMS 1980)★★★, *Collection: Black Sabbath* (Castle 1985)★★★★, *Blackest Sabbath* (Vertigo 1989)★★, *Backtrackin'* (Backtrackin' 1990)★★, *The Ozzy Osbourne Years* 3-CD box set (Essential 1991)★★★★, *Between Heaven And Hell 1970-1983* (Raw Power 1995)★★★, *Sabbath Stones* (IRS 1996)★★, *Under Wheels Of Confusion 1970-1987* 4-CD box set (Essential 1997)★★★★.

● VIDEOS: *Never Say Die* (VCL 1986), *The Black Sabbath Story Volume 1 (1970-1978)* (Castle Music Pictures 1992), *Under Wheels Of Confusion 1970-1987* (Castle Music Pictures 1996).

● FURTHER READING: *Black Sabbath*, Chris Welch.

BLACK SHEEP

This group was formed in New York in 1974 by vocalist Louis Grammatico (b. 2 May 1950, Rochester, New York, USA) and guitarist Donald Mancuso. Recruiting Larry Crozier (keyboards), Bruce Turgon (bass) and Ron Rocco (drums), they signed with Capitol Records the following year. Influenced by Bad Company, Free and Led Zeppelin, they recorded two excellent hard rock albums, characterized by Grammatico's powerful, yet soulful, vocal style. Unable to make an impact, the band split up, with Grammatico changing his name to Lou Gramm and finding considerable success with Foreigner. Turgon, after a spell with Warrior, later helped to co-write Gramm's first solo album.

● ALBUMS: *Black Sheep* (Capitol 1975)★★★, *Encouraging Words* (Capitol 1976)★★★.

BLACK TRAIN JACK

New York hardcore troupe brought up in the CBGB's era, owing obvious stylistic debts to Agnostic Front, Murphy's Law *et al.*, but with more of an ear for melody. The band centres around local legend Ernie Parada, who had previously formed hardcore semi-legends Token Entry, remaining their drummer for several years. Switching to guitar, he was joined in Black Train Jack by former Token Entry roadies Brian (bass) and four-octave, classically trained vocalist Rob. The line-up was completed by Nick (drums), recruited from the group's neighbourhood of Astoria, Queens. They took their name, meanwhile, from a touring incident when all four of them headed off-road in Brian's jeep and ended up in a sewage plant. Henry Rollins' *Hard Volume* was playing from the tape-deck, and as the group emerged, covered from head to foot in sewage, they adapted a line from 'Wreckage' that stated, appropriately: 'You've got a ticket on the black-train, Jack'. Their crunching guitar music was unveiled on a debut album co-produced with manager Anthony Countey, and crossed a street-perspective with the pop sentiments of Bow Wow Wow, or, closer to home, Descendents/All.

● ALBUMS: *No Reward* (Roadrunner 1993)★★★, *You're Not Alone* (Roadrunner 1994)★★★.

BLACK, FRANK

b. Charles Francis Kitteridge III, 1965, Long Beach, California, USA. This US vocalist/guitarist led the Boston-based Pixies under the name Black Francis. When that group underwent an acrimonious split in 1993, Francis embarked on a solo career as Frank Black. His self-titled debut featured assistance from Nick Vincent (drums) and Eric Drew Feldman (guitar, saxophone). The latter, formerly of Captain Beefheart's Magic Band, also produced the set, which featured cameos from fellow Beefheart acolyte Jeff Morris Tepper and ex-Pixies guitarist Joey Santiago. *Frank Black* showed its creator's quirky grasp of pop, from the abrasive 'Los Angeles' to the melodic 'I Hear Ramona Sing'. It also contained a version of Brian Wilson's 'Hang On To Your Ego', which the Beach Boys' leader recast as 'I Know There's An Answer' on *Pet Sounds*. A sprawling double set, *Teenager Of The Year*, ensued, but critical reaction suggested the artist had lost his incisive skills and a year later it was announced he had been dropped by 4AD Records. A new release on Epic Records, preceded by the highly commercial single 'Men In Black' (UK number 37), failed to heighten his reputation and followers continued to revert to praising his work with the Pixies. Backed by the Catholics (Lyle Workman, Dave McCaffrey and Scott Boutier), Black returned to indie cultdom with the rough and ready *Frank Black And The Catholics*.

● ALBUMS: *Frank Black* (4AD 1993)★★★, *Teenager Of The Year* (4AD 1994)★★★★, with Teenage Fanclub *Frank Black & Teenage Fanclub* (Strange Fruit 1995)★★★, *The Cult Of Ray* (Epic 1996)★★★, *Frank Black And The Catholics* (Play It Again Sam 1998)★★★.

BLACKEYED SUSAN

This US hard rock quintet was formed in 1991 by ex-Britny Fox vocalist Dean Davidson. With Erik Levy (bass), Rick Criniti (guitar), Tony Santoro (guitar) and Chris Branco (drums) completing the line-up, the band soon negotiated a contract with Mercury Records. They debuted with *Electric Rattlebone*, a blues-based set of hard rock songs that paid respect to Aerosmith, Humble Pie, Cinderella and the Rolling Stones in more or less equal portions. Although far from original, the material was delivered with conviction. Widely compared to fellow retro-rockers the Black Crowes, they have yet to emulate that level of commercial or artistic achievement.

● ALBUMS: *Electric Rattlebone* (Mercury 1991)★★★.

BLACKFOOT

Southern US rock practitioners Blackfoot initially comprised Rick Medlocke (guitar, vocals), Charlie Hargrett (guitar), Greg Walker (bass) and Jakson Spires (drums, vocals). The quartet shared common origins with Lynyrd Skynyrd (Medlocke co-writing four songs and singing lead on two tracks on the latter's platinum *First And Last*) and in turn offered a similar blues/rock-based sound, centred on their leader's confident playing. Medlocke himself was the grandson of Shorty

Medlocke, a popular Jacksonville, Florida bluegrass musician of the 50s, whose 'Train, Train' was successfully covered by Blackfoot and, in the 90s, Warrant. Rick Medlocke took the name Blackfoot from his own native Indian tradition. Session pianist Jimmy Johnson produced Blackfoot's early work at the revered Muscle Shoals studio, but despite this impressive pedigree, the group was unable to translate an in-concert popularity, especially in the UK, into record sales. *Blackfoot Strikes*, the unit's first release for Atlantic/Atco Records, offered a heavier perspective, while the cream of their early work was captured live on *Highway Song*. After these releases, the group bowed to record company pressure and pursued a more commercial approach that was not always convincing. Ken Hensley (b. 24 August 1945, London, England), formerly of Uriah Heep, joined the line-up for *Siogo* and *Vertical Smiles*, and was eventually replaced by Bobby Barth of Axe, but Blackfoot was disbanded following the latter's release. The name was revived at the end of the decade with a revised line-up, with Medlocke backed by Neal Casal (guitar), Rikki Mayer (bass, ex-Lizzy Borden) and Gunner Ross (drums). However, none of these members remained for Blackfoot's 1994 album with new label Bullet Proof/Music For Nations, with Mark Woerpel (guitar, vocals, ex-Wardrive), Benny Rappa (drums, vocals) and Tim Stunson (bass) stepping in to support the venerable Medlocke. Rappa was replaced by ex-W.A.S.P. drummer Stet Howland for touring.

● ALBUMS: *No Reservations* (Island 1976)★★★, *Flyin' High* (Epic 1977)★★★, *Blackfoot Strikes* (Atco 1978)★★★, *Tomcattin'* (Atco 1980)★★★, *Maurauder* (Atco 1981)★★★, *Highway Song* (Atco 1982)★★★, *Siogo* (Atco 1983)★★★, *Vertical Smiles* (Atco 1984)★★★, *Medicine Man* (Loop 1990)★★, *After The Reign* (Bullet Proof 1994)★★.

● COMPILATIONS: *Rattlesnake Rock 'N' Roll: The Best Of Blackfoot* (Rhino 1995)★★★.

BLACKFOOT SUE

Previously known as Gift and led by twin brothers Tom (bass, keyboards, vocals) and Dave Farmer (drums; both b. 2 March 1952, Birmingham, England), this group was completed by Eddie Galga (b. 4 September 1951, Birmingham, England; lead guitar, keyboards) and Alan Jones (b. 5 January 1950, Birmingham, England; guitar, vocals). The quartet enjoyed a UK Top 5 hit in 1972 with 'Standing In The Road', but although its rhythmic performance appealed successfully to pop and rock audiences, Blackfoot Sue proved unable to maintain such a deft balance. They had a minor hit the same year with 'Sing Don't Speak', but heavier elements displayed on subsequent albums were derided by commentators who viewed the group as a purely 'teeny-bop' attraction. Blackfoot Sue broke up following the release of *Strangers*, which appeared in the middle of the punk boom. Several of the members went on to form the soft-rock group Liner and, in the 80s, Outside Edge.

● ALBUMS: *Nothing To Hide* (Jam 1973)★★, *Gun Running* (Passport 1975)★, *Strangers* (Passport 1977)★.

BLACKMORE, RITCHIE

b. 14 April 1945, Weston-Super-Mare, Avon, England. Guitarist Blackmore spent his early career in Mike Dee And The Jaywalkers before joining Screaming Lord Sutch And His Savages in May 1962. Within months he had switched to the Outlaws, a popular, principally instrumental, group that also served as the studio house band for producer Joe Meek. Blackmore's exciting style was already apparent on the group's releases, notably 'Keep A Knockin''/'Shake With Me', and on sessions for Heinz and Mike Berry. The guitarist briefly joined the former singer's group, the Wild Boys, in 1964, and completed a suitably idiosyncratic solo single, 'Little Brown Jug'/'Getaway', before forging an erratic path as a member of Neil Christian's Crusaders, the Savages (again) and the Roman Empire. When a short-lived act, Mandrake Root, broke up in October 1967, Blackmore opted to live in Hamburg, but the following year was invited back to London to join organist Jon Lord in the embryonic Deep Purple. Although initially envisaged as an 'English Vanilla Fudge', the group quickly became a leading heavy metal act, with Blackmore's powerful, urgent runs an integral part of their attraction. He left the group in 1975, unhappy with their increasingly funk-based sound, and joined forces with the USA-based Elf to form Ritchie Blackmore's Rainbow. This powerful band became a highly popular hard rock attraction, but was blighted by its leader's autocratic demands. Multiple sackings ensued as the guitarist searched for the ideal combination, but such behaviour simply enhanced his temperamental reputation. He was, nevertheless, involved in the Deep Purple reunion, undertaken in 1984, although animosity between the guitarist and vocalist Ian Gillan resulted in the latter's departure. Blackmore finally quit the band in 1994. Blackmore's prowess as a guitar 'hero' is undisputed, while his outstanding technique has influenced everyone from the New Wave Of British Heavy Metal bands to conventional modern rock outfits.

● COMPILATIONS: *Ritchie Blackmore Volume 1: Early Sessions To Rainbow* (1990)★★★, *Ritchie Blackmore Volume 2* (1991)★★, *Session Man* (RPM 1993)★★★, *Take It! - Sessions 63/68* (RPM 1995)★★★.

BLACKOUT

The origins of this Dutch quintet date back to 1983, when Godzilla were assembled from the remnants of the bands Van East and Zenith. Godzilla specialized in mainstream pop-rock material, but switched to 'speed-metal' and changed their name to Blackout in 1984. The band comprised Bas Van Sloten (vocals), Mannes Van Oosten (guitar), Jean Hoffman (guitar), Alfred Dreuge (bass) and Jan Boxem (drums). After securing a contract with Roadrunner Records, they released *Evil Game* the same year. This proved a workmanlike collection of songs, constructed around heavy-duty, quick-fire riffs and dual lead soloing. Failing to make any significant impact, they disappeared from the scene within a year of the album's release.

● ALBUMS: *Evil Game* (Roadrunner 1984)★★.

BLACKTHORNE

This band was assembled by former Balance/Alice Cooper/Meat Loaf guitarist Bob Kulick, with a line-up of former Quiet Riot members Chuck Wright (bass, ex-House Of Lords), Frankie Banali (drums, ex-W.A.S.P.) and Jimmy Waldo (keyboards, ex-Alcatrazz), along with Graham Bonnet (vocals, ex-Rainbow; MSG; Alcatrazz). Such an experienced team inevitably attracted the supergroup tag, but they were keen to play down their collective past to allow the band to be judged on its own merits, and not be viewed as merely a short-term project. The Kulick-produced *Afterlife* saw the band ignore trends and play in a classic hard rock style, with Kulick's powerful guitar lines adding considerable weight to heavy, yet accessible, material that included a reworking of the Rainbow hit, 'All Night Long' (Bonnet felt that the original version was 'not as heavy as it should have been').

● ALBUMS: *Afterlife* (Music For Nations 1993)★★★.

BLACKWYCH

This Irish metal band was put together by the three James brothers in 1985. Comprising vocalist Ciaran, guitarist Declan and bassist Niall, they recruited Bobby Tierney as second guitarist, plus drummer Chris Andralinus to complete their line-up. Influenced by Thin Lizzy, Mama's Boys and the New Wave Of British Heavy Metal, they made their debut on the Irish sampler, *The Green Metal Album*. Under-rehearsed when they entered the studio to record *Out Of Control*, the album proved a rudimentary affair, with flat, tuneless vocals. Reeling from poor reviews, the group split shortly afterwards.

● ALBUMS: *Out Of Control* (Metal Masters 1986)★★.

BLADE RUNNER

Of the few rock bands of any note to emerge from the Humberside region in England (in the two decades that the area was not designated as part of Lincolnshire or Yorkshire), most seemed to draw their principal influence from Status Quo. Blade Runner were no exception, despite the fact that they took their name from a futuristic science fiction film. Comprising Steve Mackay (vocals), Gary Jones (guitar), Mark Wilde (guitar), Mick Cooper (bass) and Gregg Ellis (drums), they made their debut in 1984 with *Hunted* for Ebony Records. It was followed two years later by *Warriors Of Rock*, but with neither record selling substantially, the members of Blade Runner settled back into semi-retirement, with some members remaining active on the local club rock scene.

● ALBUMS: *Hunted* (Ebony 1984)★★, *Warriors Of Rock* (Ebony 1986)★★.

BLESSED DEATH

This American doom/thrash/hardcore outfit was formed in New Jersey in 1984 by vocalist Larry Portelli and guitarist Jeff Anderson. Enlisting the services of Nick Florentino (guitar), Kevin Powelson (bass) and Chris Powleson (drums), they were initially influenced by Black Sabbath, Slayer and Anthrax. *Kill Or Be Killed* highlighted the vocals of Portelli, whose range extended from a low guttural growl to a high-pitched banshee-like screech. Bass-laden riffs, thunderous drums and vitriolic guitar blasts bridged the ground between the doom and thrash metal factions. *Destined For Extinction* incorporated hardcore nuances reminiscent of Bad Brains and Jello Biafra. Produced by Alex Perialas and Raven drummer Rob Hunter, it was heralded as a great achievement, combining excellent sound quality with uncompromising and thought-provoking lyrics. Unfortunately, the positive reviews did not translate into commercial success, and nothing has been heard of the band since.

● ALBUMS: *Kill Or Be Killed* (Megaforce

1986)★★★, *Destined For Extinction* (Roadrunner 1987)★★★.

BLIND DATE

This mysterious US pop-metal quartet first assembled in San Francisco in 1975, with its members employing strange pseudonyms (their original choice of name was Ratz). Featuring Dane Bramage (vocals, bass, keyboards), Brad Billion (guitar, vocals), Arnie Baddie (guitar, vocals) and Pinky Chablis (drums), their music payed homage to Cheap Trick, Kansas and REO Speedwagon. Produced by Jeff Glixman, *Blind Date*, released in 1979, actually comprised songs written four years previously. The instrumental 'Twin Engines' gained a degree of fame after being used as a theme tune to a European radio rock show. The band faded back into obscurity after the album's release, despite signing with the Regency Records label.

● ALBUMS: *Blind Date* (Windsong 1979)★★★.

BLIND FURY

Formerly known as Satan, these UK purveyors of stereotypical black-metal changed their name, personnel and direction in 1984. Based in Newcastle, Blind Fury comprised Lou Taylor (vocals), Steve Ramsey (guitar), Russ Tippins (guitar), Graeme English (bass) and Sean Taylor (drums). Eighteen months of writing and rehearsing led to *Out Of Reach*, a commercial hard rock album that played down their previous associations with witchcraft and the occult. Success proved elusive, however, and they disbanded in 1986. Taylor had periods of activity with Persian Risk and Tour De Force, while the remainder of the band re-formed Satan.

● ALBUMS: *Out Of Reach* (Roadrunner 1985)★★★.

BLIND ILLUSION

This group was formed in Richmond, California, USA, during 1978, by guitarist/vocalist Mike Biederman and bassist Les Claypool. An extensive series of personnel changes ensued over the next 10 years before the band released any product. With the addition of Larry Lalonde (guitar) and Mike Miner (drums), plus the return of Biederman and Claypool from stints with Blue Öyster Cult and Primus, respectively, they finally entered a studio in 1988 to record *The Sane Asylum*. This was a techno-thrash affair, comparable in places to Megadeth and Metallica, but without the bite or ferocity.

● ALBUMS: *The Sane Asylum* (Under One Flag 1988)★★.

BLIND MELON

A US pop-rock band comprising Glen Graham (b. Columbus, Mississippi, USA; drums), Shannon Hoon (b. Lafeyette, Indiana, USA, d. 21 October 1995, New Orleans, Louisiana, USA; vocals), Rogers Stevens (b. West Point, Mississippi, USA; guitar), Christopher Thorn (b. Dover, Pennsylvania; guitar) and Brad Smith (b. West Point, Mississippi, USA; bass), Blind Melon entered the US mainstream in 1993. One of their major claims to fame was introducing the phenomenon of the 'bee girl'. Back in their home base of Columbus, Mississippi, Graham was passing round a snap of his sister, Georgia, appearing in a school play. The band elected to use the shot, which presented young Georgia as an awkward, publicity-shy youngster adorned in a bee-suit, on their debut album. The image would also reappear in the video for their second single, 'No Rain', in June 1992. Directed by Sam Bayer (responsible for Nirvana's 'Smells Like Teen Spirit'), the Bee Girl was portrayed by 10-year-old Heather DeLoach. MTV played the clip relentlessly, helping to boost the fortunes of their album. The young girl became a huge cult icon, beloved of various rock stars including Madonna, while Blind Melon profited greatly from their association with her. Their album had been shipped for several months and was languishing outside the US charts, but it soon re-entered and went on to reach number 3. However, success had not been as instantaneous as many assumed. Smith had long been a dedicated musician, playing drums, baritone saxophone and guitar, the last of which he taught to Stevens. The two had left Columbus in 1989 for Los Angeles, where they met first Hoon, a small-town mischief-maker who had left his sporting ambitions behind when he became involved in the drugs scene, and Thorn, who had formerly played in a local heavy metal band, R.O.T. Together they scoured Hollywood for a drummer and found fellow Mississippi refugee Graham. A demo tape was recorded, and, without their consent, circulated to the major record companies, who began queuing up for their services. This despite the fact that they had an armoury of just five songs. It was Atlantic Records who eventually requested their signatures. They were put to work in a Los Angeles studio, but were distracted by the presence of Hoon's old Indiana friend, Axl Rose, who was recording *Use Your Illusion* with Guns N'Roses. Hoon was invited to add backing vocals, and appeared in the video to 'Don't Cry'. After a support tour to Soundgarden the group relocated to

Durham, North Carolina, to find space and time to finish writing their debut set, before teaming with producer Rick Parashar in Seattle. Afterwards, events overtook them, and by November 1993 *Rolling Stone* magazine was parading them, naked, on their cover. Two years' touring following, including dates at Woodstock II in America and the Glastonbury Festival in England. The pressure to repeat the success of the debut with *Soup* was obvious, but when it finally emerged it was far less accessible than many expected. Recorded in New Orleans during bouts of drug-related non-activity, Hoon confessed in interviews that he could not actually remember making the record. In truth he had passed some of the time between albums in a rehabilitation clinic. The new songs included 'St. Andrew Fall', which concerned suicide, and 'Skinned', about serial killer Ed Gein, who dressed in the skins of his female victims. Some of the effect of this track's lurid subject matter was alleviated by the presence of a kazoo solo. It was generally known that Hoon had unsuccessfully fought heroin addiction for some time, but neither the band nor his family could prise him away for long enough periods for him to complete his rehabilitation programme. He died from a heroin overdose, his body discovered in the band's bus. The final album, *Nico* (named after Hoon's stepdaughter), was released in 1997. It was a sad and patched-together affair that the remaining members felt morally obliged to release.

● ALBUMS: *Blind Melon* (Capitol 1993)★★★★, *Soup* (Capitol 1995)★★, *Nico* (Capitol 1997)★★.

● VIDEOS: *Letters From A Porcupine* (Capitol 1996).

Bliss Band

Taking their moniker from keyboard player/vocalist Paul Bliss's surname, this US hard rock group additionally included Phil Palmer (guitar), Alan Park (keyboards), Andy Brown (bass) and Nigel Elliot (drums). Formed in the mid-70s, they set about perfecting a blend of pomp and AOR, with their leader's operatic vocals and diffident compositions at the forefront of most of their material. They made their debut with *Dinner With Raoul* for Columbia Records in 1978, but much better received was 1979's *Neon Smiles*, which included the group's best song, 'Stagefright'. Nevertheless, poor sales consigned the group to an early grave when Columbia dropped them at the turn of the decade. Paul Bliss subsequently embarked on a low-key solo career.

● ALBUMS: *Dinner With Raoul* (Columbia 1978)★★, *Neon Smiles* (Columbia 1979)★★★.

Blitzkrieg

Not to be confused with the Merseyside punk outfit of the same name and similar period, this UK heavy metal group formed in 1980 around a nucleus of former Satan singer Brian Ross (vocals), with Jim Sirotto (guitar), Mick Moore (bass) and Sean Taylor (drums). However, line-up changes were frequent during their long formative career, which eventually came to fruition in 1985 with the release of *A Time Of Changes* for Neat Records. A confident if uninspiring take on conventional hard rock themes, it was rapidly followed by *Ready For Action* for a new record label, Roadrunner Records. Despite the occasional good review and a strong following in the north of England, the group then surrendered to another round of line-up shuffles and had collapsed completely by the following year. Ross and Moore formed Avenger.

● ALBUMS: *A Time Of Changes* (Neat 1985)★★★, *Ready For Action* (Roadrunner 1985)★★, *Ten* (Neat Metal 1997)★★★, *The Mists Of Avalon* (Neat Metal 1998)★★★.

Blodwyn Pig

During its short life, Blodwyn Pig made a valuable contribution to the British blues boom in the late 60s. The band was formed when Mick Abrahams (b. 7 April 1943, Luton, Bedfordshire, England; guitar) left the fast-rising Jethro Tull in 1969. His energetic and fluid playing blended well with the rest of the band, Jack Lancaster (saxophone), Andy Pyle (bass) and Ron Berg (drums). The fine debut, *Ahead Rings Out*, with its famous pig cover, was a critical success, containing a healthy mixture of various styles of progressive blues. The Tull-influenced 'Ain't Ya Comin Home' and the superb slide guitar of 'Dear Jill' were but two highlights. Lancaster's lengthy 'The Modern Alchemist' showcased his jazz influence and saxophone skills. The band were a prolific live attraction, and Abrahams delighted the crowds with his exceptional showpiece, 'Cats Squirrel', probably the only time that a Cream number had been 'borrowed' and improved upon. Abrahams' solo was superior to Eric Clapton's, although this was a millstone he constantly attempted to shed. The second album showed great moments, notably Abrahams' punchy 'See My Way'. Lancaster's advanced long pieces such as 'San Francisco Sketches' ultimately gave the band a split direction. Abrahams departed and was replaced by Pete Banks (b. 7 July 1947, Barnet, Hertfordshire, England), formerly of Yes, and Larry Wallis. Their direction was now led by

Lancaster and they changed their name to Lancaster's Bomber, and finally, Lancaster, before they crash-landed shortly afterwards. Four years later, Abrahams and Lancaster re-formed Blodwyn Pig, with Pyle and ex-Tull drummer Clive Bunker (b. 12 December 1946, Blackpool, Lancashire, England; drums), but they had hardly started when the signs that their day was long-past became evident. While Lancaster eventually carved out a career as a producer, Abrahams set up his own financial consultancy business. However, Abrahams was not able to forsake the music business for too long and subsequently resurrected the group in the early 90s to play club dates, performing new material, utilizing the services of Dick Heckstall-Smith (b. 26 September 1934, Ludlow, Shropshire, England), plus former Piggies, Clive Bunker and Andy Pyle. In 1993 *Lies* appeared on Abrahams' own label and the informative CD notes contain an invaluable Pete Frame family tree. The line-up of the band in addition to Abrahams comprised: David Lennox, keyboards; Mike Summerland, bass; Jackie Challoner, vocals; and Graham Walker, drums.

● ALBUMS: *Ahead Rings Out* (Chrysalis 1969)★★★★, *Getting To This* (Chrysalis 1970)★★★, *Lies* (A New Day 1993)★★, *All Tore Down* (Indigo 1996)★★, *Live At The Layfayette* (Indigo 1997)★★★.

Blood

Originally named Coming Blood, a moniker so vile even this notoriously unruly collection of characters jettisoned it, UK hardcore punk/heavy metal crossover group the Blood's line-up featured Bill Sykes (vocals), J.J. Manson (guitar), Snake (guitar), Mark Brabbs (drums) and Phil Butcher (keyboards). Combining Motörhead-styled power chords with punk dynamics and irreverence, the group made its debut in March 1983 with 'Meglomania'. A superb, caustic single, played with the velocity of the Damned's 'New Rose', it found supporters in both rock and punk camps. The subsequent album, *False Gestures For A Devious Public*, was just as convincing. Overt humour, as demonstrated on tracks such as 'Gestapo Khazi' and 'Done Some Brain Cells Last Night', did not deflect the band from the potency of their music, but the album's impact was ruined by poor distribution and promotion. Follow-up efforts failed to repair this damage, as the group lost its sense of direction and transmuted into just another heavy metal band.

● ALBUMS: *False Gestures For A Devious Public* (Dorane 1983)★★★, *Se Parare Nex* (Conquest 1985)★★.

● COMPILATIONS: *Full Time Result* (Link 1988)★★★.

Bloodgood

This Christian heavy metal band was formed in Washington, DC, USA, in 1985 by guitarist David Zaffiro and bassist Mike Bloodgood. With Les Carlsen (vocals) and Mark Welling (drums) completing the line-up, they were initially strongly influenced by Iron Maiden and Saxon. However, as time progressed, the band matured and diversified their sound considerably, with their latter albums courting Def Leppard, Whitesnake and Van Halen comparisons. Without doubt, the band were the most credible white metal outfit on the circuit for many years. Kevin Whistler took over on drums from Welling in 1989, and guitarist David Zaffiro recorded a solo album, *The Other Side*, the same year.

● ALBUMS: *Bloodgood* (Frontline 1985)★★★, *Detonation* (Frontline 1987)★★★, *Rock In A Hard Place* (Frontline 1988)★★★, *Out Of Darkness* (Intense 1989)★★★, *Hotter Than Hell* (Roadracer 1990)★★★.

Blue Bludd

Taking as their primary influence US stadium rockers Ratt and UK's Whitesnake, the British Blue Bludd managed to insert a limited amount of their own identity into two albums for Music For Nations Records between 1989 and 1991. Comprising Phil Kane (vocals), Mark Sutcliffe (guitar), Rob Ariss (keyboards), Dave Crawte (bass) and Paul Sutcliffe (drums), the nucleus of the band had previously played together in the group Trespass. *The Big Noise* was an encouraging start, although its slick, heavily stylized sound failed to secure significant sales. That fate also befell *Universal Language* in 1991, though reviews were largely positive.

● ALBUMS: *The Big Noise* (Music For Nations 1989)★★, *Universal Language* (Music For Nations 1991)★★★.

Blue Cheer

San Francisco's Blue Cheer, consisting of Dickie Peterson (b. 1948, Grand Forks, North Dakota, USA; vocals, bass), Leigh Stephens (guitar) and Paul Whaley (drums), harboured dreams of a more conventional direction until seeing Jimi Hendrix perform at the celebrated Monterey Pop Festival. Taking their name from a potent brand of LSD, they made an immediate impact with their uncompromising debut album, *Vincebus Eruptum*, which featured cacophonous interpretations of Eddie Cochran's 'Summertime Blues' (US number 14) and Mose Allison's 'Parchman(t) Farm'. A second set, *Outsideinside*, was completed in the open air when the trio's high volume levels destroyed the studio monitors. Stephens left the group during the sessions for *New! Improved! Blue Cheer*, and his place was taken by former Other Half guitarist Randy Holden; they also added Bruce Stephens (bass), and Holden left during the recording sessions. *Blue Cheer* then unveiled a reconstituted line-up of Peterson, Ralph Burns Kellogg (keyboards), and Norman Mayell (drums, guitar), who replaced Whaley. Stephens was then replaced by former Kak guitarist Gary Yoder, for *The Original Human Being*. It featured the atmospheric, raga-influenced 'Babaji (Twilight Raga)', and is widely acclaimed as the group's most cohesive work. The band was dissolved in 1971 but re-formed in 1979 following an emotional reunion between Peterson and Whaley. This line-up made *The Beast Is Back* in 1985 and added guitarist Tony Rainier. Blue Cheer continued to pursue their original bombastic vision, and *Highlights And Lowlives* coupled the group with Anthrax producer Jack Endino. In the early 90s the band was reappraised, with many of the Seattle grunge rock bands admitting a strong affection for Blue Cheer's groundbreaking work.

● ALBUMS: *Vincebus Eruptum* (Philips 1967)★★★, *Outsideinside* (Philips 1968)★★★, *New! Improved! Blue Cheer* (Philips 1969)★★, *Blue Cheer* (Philips 1969)★★, *The Original Human Being* (Philips 1970)★★★, *Oh! Pleasant Hope* (Philips 1971)★, *The Beast Is Back* (Megaforce 1985)★, *Blitzkrieg Over Nuremberg* (Thunderbolt 1989)★★, *Dining With Sharks* (Nibelung 1991)★★.

● COMPILATIONS: *The Best Of Blue Cheer* (Philips 1982)★★★, *Louder Than God* (Rhino 1986)★★★, *Good Times Are So Hard To Find (The History Of Blue Cheer)* (Mercury 1988)★★★, *Highlights And Lowlives* (Nibelung 1990)★★, *The Beast Is Back: The Megaforce Years* (Megaforce 1996)★★, *Live & Unreleased* (Captain Trip 1996)★★.

Blue Murder

This project was masterminded by ex-Thin Lizzy and Tygers Of Pan Tang guitarist John Sykes, after he left Whitesnake. Enlisting the services of Tony Franklin (ex-Firm) on bass and Cozy Powell on drums (the latter quickly replaced by Carmine Appice), Sykes decided to record as a three-piece outfit. This followed a long and fruitless search for a suitable vocalist to front the band. The material included on their self-titled debut drew heavily on Sykes's Whitesnake legacy, but featured more extended compositions, with sophisticated arrangements and lengthy instrumental breaks. It was criticized upon its release, perhaps prematurely and unfairly, as it did contain a number of competent songs. Franklin quit in 1991 after the recording of tracks for the band's second album.

● ALBUMS: *Blue Murder* (Geffen 1989)★★, *Nothin' But Trouble* (Geffen 1993)★★.

Blue Öyster Cult

The genesis of Blue Öyster Cult lay in the musical ambitions of rock writers Sandy Pearlman and Richard Meltzer. Based in Long Island, New York, the pair put together a group - known variously as the Cows, the Soft White Underbelly and Oaxaca - to perform their original songs. By 1969 the unit, now dubbed the Stalk-Forrest Group, had formed around Eric Bloom (b. 11 December 1944; guitar, vocals), Donald 'Buck Dharma' Roeser (b. 12 November 1947; guitar, vocals), Allen Lanier (b. 25 June 1986; keyboards, guitar), Joe Bouchard (b. 9 November 1948; bass, vocals) and Albert Bouchard (drums). The quintet completed a single, 'What Is Quicksand', before adopting the Blue Öyster Cult appellation. Early releases combined Black Sabbath-styled riffs with obscure lyricism, which engendered an 'intelligent heavy metal' tag. Cryptic titles, including 'A Kiss Before The Redap' and 'OD'd On Life Itself', compounded an image - part biker, part occult - assiduously sculpted by Pearlman, whose clean production technique also removed any emotional inflections. 'Career Of Evil' from *Secret Treaties* - co-written by Patti Smith - showed an increasing grasp of commercial hook-lines, which flourished on the Byrds-sounding international hit, '(Don't Fear) The Reaper'. Smith continued her association with the band on *Agents Of Fortune*, contributing to 'Debbie Denise' and 'The Revenge Of Vera Gemini'. Romantically involved with Allen Lanier, she later added 'Shooting Shark' to the band's repertoire for *The Revolution By Night* and single release. Fantasy writer Michael Moorcock, meanwhile, contributed to *Mirrors* and *Cultosaurus Erectus*. However, the release of the live *Some Enchanted Evening* had already brought the group's most innovative era to an end, despite an unlikely hit single, 'Joan Crawford Has Risen From The Grave', drawn from *Fire Of Unknown Origin*. Sustained by continued in-concert popularity, notably on the *Black And Blue* tour with Black Sabbath, elsewhere predictability had crept into their studio work. Former road crew boss Rick Downey replaced Al Bouchard in 1981, while the following year Roeser completed a solo album as the Cult's own recordings grew less prolific. *Imaginos* in 1988 was the band's reinterpretation of a Bouchard solo album that had never been released. Though of dubious origins, critics welcomed it as the band's best work for several years. Afterwards, Joe Bouchard left the group to form Dead Ringer with Neal Smith (ex-Alice Cooper), Dennis Dunaway, Charlie Huhn and Jay Johnson. In 1992 the group wrote and performed most of the soundtrack to the horror film *Bad Channels*. They reconvened in 1998 for the hard-rocking *Heaven Forbid*, their first studio album in ten years.

● ALBUMS: *Blue Öyster Cult* (Columbia 1971)★★★, *Tyranny And Mutation* (Columbia 1973)★★★, *Secret Treaties* (Columbia 1974)★★, *On Your Feet Or On Your Knees* (Columbia 1975)★★, *Agents Of Fortune* (Columbia 1976)★★★★, *Spectres* (Columbia 1977)★★, *Some Enchanted Evening* (Columbia 1978)★★, *Mirrors* (Columbia 1979)★★, *Cultosaurus Erectus* (Columbia 1980)★★, *Fire Of Unknown Origin* (Columbia 1981)★★, *Extraterrestial Live* (Columbia 1982)★, *The Revolution By Night* (Columbia 1983)★, *Club Ninja* (Columbia 1986)★, *Imaginos* (Columbia 1988)★★★, *Bad Channels* film soundtrack (Moonstone 1992)★★, *Live 1976* (Gopaco 1994)★★★, *Heaven Forbid* (CMC International 1998)★★.

Solo: Donald Roeser *Flat Out* (Portrait 1982)★★.

● COMPILATIONS: *(Don't Fear) The Reaper* (CBS Special Products 1989)★★★, *On Flame With Rock & Roll* (CBS Special Products 1990)★★★, *Career Of Evil: The Metal Years* (Columbia 1990)★★★, *Cult Classic* (Herald 1994)★★★, *Workshop Of The Telescopes* (Columbia/Legacy 1995)★★★★, *Revisited* (Gusto 1996)★★★, *Super Hits* (Columbia/Legacy 1998)★★★.

● VIDEOS: *Live 1976* (Castle Music Pictures 1991).

BLUES TRAVELER

New York, USA blues-rock quartet Blues Traveler are led by singer and harmonica player John Popper (b. 1967, Cleveland, Ohio, USA). Some of the interest in the band in the mid-90s arose from the fact that Popper was a close friend of Eric Schenkman and Chris Barron, putting the pair (who subsequently formed the Spin Doctors) in contact with each other. Like the latter band and another set of friends, Phish, Blues Traveler share an appetite for extended jams, and at their best, the spontaneous musicianship that flows through their live sets can be inspired. Popper first sought to play harmonica after being inspired by the movie *The Blues Brothers*, while at school in Connecticut. He initially intended to become a comedian; his physical appearance has prompted comparisons with actor John Belushi. When Popper moved to Princeton, New Jersey, to attend high school, he met drummer Brendan Hill, the duo calling themselves 'The Blues Band' by 1985. They were eventually joined by the younger, sports-orientated guitarist Chan Kinchla until a knee injury cut short that career. He moved instead to New York, with Hill and Popper. Bass player Bobby Sheehan joined in 1987. Playing low-key gigs at Nightingale's in the East Village, they eventually honed their organic rock into something a little more structured, changing their name to Blues Traveler at the end of the 80s. Recording and selling demo tapes at gigs eventually brought a high-profile visitor to one of their gigs, Bill Graham. Through his influence they found themselves on bills with the Allman Brothers Band and Carlos Santana. Interest from A&M Records followed and the band recorded their debut at the end of 1989, for release early the following year. The band had been befriended at an early stage by Blues Brothers keyboard player Paul Shaffer, who, since his five minutes of celluloid fame, had become bandleader and arranger for the David Letterman television show. Letterman's sponsorship of the band stretched to over a dozen appearances in their first four years of existence, and was paramount in establishing their no-nonsense appeal. The appearances on *Letterman* were part of a huge promotional push that included over 800 gigs in three years. The only setback came in autumn 1992 when Popper was involved in a motorcycle accident which left him with major injuries. *Save His Soul*'s release was consequently delayed, but the incident necessitated a long hiatus from touring, until he took the stage again in April 1993 in a wheelchair.

He continued in this vein for a second H.O.R.D.E. tour (Horizons of Rock Developing Everywhere), an alternative to the Lollapalooza events, with Big Head Todd And The Monsters, among others. A third stint was later undertaken with the Allman Brothers Band, whose Chuck Leavell joined Paul Shaffer in contributing to *Four*. The group then appeared at Woodstock '94, but, true to form, they were unable to stay the whole weekend because of gig commitments elsewhere. They remain a phenomenon in their homeland; *Four* was still in the US charts with 4 million sales two years after its release. *Straight On Till Morning* was eagerly anticipated after the huge success of *Four* and the band managed to get the balance right between rock and blues. The blues harp playing was noticeably spectacular and the longer tracks such as 'Make My Way' and 'Yours' highlighted the band at their best, unlike the throwaway pastiche of 'Felicia' and 'Canadian Rose'.

● ALBUMS: *Blues Traveler* (A&M 1990)★★, *Travelers And Thieves* (A&M 1991)★★★, *On Tour Forever* bonus disc given away free with copies of *Travelers And Thieves* (A&M 1992)★★★, *Save His Soul* (A&M 1993)★★, *Four* (A&M 1994)★★★★, *Live From The Fall* (A&M 1996)★★, *Straight On Till Morning* (A&M 1997)★★★.

Blumfeld

Germany's prime alternative rock band, Hamburg's Blumfeld, comprises Jochen Distelmeyer (vocals, guitar), Eike Bohlken (bass) and Andre Rattay (drums). Their arrival outside of their native market was doubtlessly triggered by the interest shown by Steve Albini and Pavement's Steve Malkmus, the latter inviting them to support on their European tour. Distelmeyer's German lyrics, which predominantly concern politics, culture and society, are densely poetic, and in Germany the group are regarded as intellectuals. The band's raw, pummelling sound is close in construction to American bands such as Sonic Youth and the Pixies, though they also maintain an experimental edge that places them outside of a straightforward alternative rock category.

● ALBUMS: *Blumfeld* (Big Cat 1993)★★★, *L'Etat Et Moi* (Big Cat 1995)★★★.

Bodine

One of the more arresting Dutch traditional metal outfits of the 80s, Bodine released two independent albums in the early 80s before a brief foray with a major label for 1984's *Three Times Running*. Comprising Jay Van Feggelen (vocals), Rheno Xeros (guitar), Armand Hoff (bass) and Gerrad Hatsma (drums), the group's tightly condensed rock sound was ostensibly derivative of groups such as Gillan and Whitesnake, but their better work was imbued with some excellent guitar playing from Xeros, who, as time passed, seemed to be leading the group in a quasi-blues rock direction. Although some fans were concerned about this transition, it proved a shrewd move, judging by the critical reaction afforded their sole major label album for WEA Records in 1984. However, the group were never able to convert press acclaim into sales and by the mid-80s Bodine had collapsed completely.

● ALBUMS: *Bodine* (Rhino 1981)★★★, *Bold As Brass* (Rhino 1982)★★★, *Three Times Running* (WEA 1984)★★★.

Body Count

The Ice-T (b. Tracy Marrow, c.1958, Newark, New Jersey, USA) spin-off metal/hardcore band, who achieved notoriety with the inclusion of the track 'Cop Killer' on their debut Warner Brothers Records album. Other songs included titles such as 'KKK Bitch' and 'Bowels Of The Devil', but it was 'Cop Killer' that effectively ended Ice-T's tenure with his record company, and made him public enemy number one within the American establishment. Body Count made their debut during the inaugural Lollapalooza US festival tour in 1991, preceding the release of the album. The line-up was completed by Ernie-C (guitar), D-Roc (guitar), Mooseman (bass) and Beatmaster V (drums), whom Ice-T knew from Crenshaw High School in South Central Los Angeles. Although occasionally suffering from the misogynistic street language common to much US west coast rap, their material contained forceful anti-drug and anti-racism themes, particularly 'Momma's Gotta Die Tonight', which addressed the issue of institutionalized bigotry being passed down through successive generations. The band continued touring, and were offered the opening slot on the Guns N'Roses/Metallica North American trek, exposing them to a more mainstream audience. In the meantime, the Los Angeles Police Department were taking extreme exception to 'Cop Killer', a song they viewed as dangerous and inflammatory ('I got my twelve gauge sawed off/I got my headlights turned off/I'm 'bout to bust some shots off/I'm 'bout to dust some cops off'). The fury aimed at Ice-T, now officially number 2 in the FBI National Threat list, came thick and fast; Charlton Heston read out the lyrics to 'KKK Bitch' to astonished shareholders at Time Warner's AGM. 'Cop Killer' also appeared in Warners' blockbuster film *Batman Returns*, which consequently faced calls for boycotts. Among the other opponents were Oliver North, President George Bush, and the Texas police force, who called for a nationwide boycott of Time Warner, including their Disneyland complex, thereby threatening to wipe millions off Warners' share value. The pivotal moment came when death threats were received by record company employees, and the U-turn was made; the track was eventually replaced with a spoken word message from former Dead Kennedys frontman and noted anti-censorship lobbyist, Jello Biafra. Undeterred, Ice-T has resolved to continue in authority-tackling mode, and Body Count persist as an ongoing musical concern. Indeed, further albums for new label Virgin offered greater musical depth.

● ALBUMS: *Body Count* (Sire 1992)★★★, *Born Dead* (Virgin 1994)★★★, *Violent Demise: Last Days* (Virgin 1997)★★★.

● FURTHER READING: *The Ice Opinion*, Ice-T and Heidi Seigmund.

Bogert, Tim

b. 27 August 1944, Richfield, New Jersey, USA. Bogert is one of the most distinctive and easily recognized bass players working within the hard rock idiom. He has recorded prolifically as a session player, but he has also enjoyed high-profile group work with artists including Vanilla Fudge, Cactus, Boxer and Pipedream. He embarked on a solo career in 1981 with the release of *Progressions* for Accord Records. This saw him move away from the brutality of his established approach in order to pursue a more complex and thoughtful compositional style. *Master's Brew* featured a guest appearance from Rick Derringer, but proved a less convincing collection of songs than Bogert's debut release. He has subsequently returned to group and session work, though he has also intimated that he may return to his solo projects in the future.

● ALBUMS: *Progressions* (Accord 1981)★★★, *Master's Brew* (Takoma 1983)★★.

Bolin, Tommy

b. 18 April 1951, Sioux City, Iowa, USA, d. 4 December 1976, Miami, Florida, USA. Tommy Bolin was a highly versatile progressive rock guitarist who branched into fusion with considerable success. Bolin became interested in music after seeing Elvis Presley in concert in 1956. He quickly learned to play Presley songs on guitar and won local amateur contests. His first groups, Denny and the Triumphs and American Standard, found little or no success, and Bolin took work backing blues guitarist Lonnie Mack. In 1968 he formed Ethereal Zephyr, later shortened to Zephyr. Signed to Probe Records, their debut release was a US Top 50 album in 1969. Following the failure of their follow-up, Bolin departed and formed the jazz/fusion group Energy with flautist Jeremy Steig, based in Colorado. Bolin also worked on an unreleased Steig album that also featured Jan Hammer and Billy Cobham. The latter then asked Bolin to play guitar on his *Spectrum* album in 1973 (which reputedly inspired Jeff Beck to try his hand at fusion). Having become a 'name' guitarist he was asked to replace Domenic Troiano (who himself had replaced Joe Walsh) in the James Gang. Bolin performed on their 1973 *Bang* album and the following year's *Miami*. After contributing to sessions for jazz drummer Alphonse Mouzon's *Mind Transplant* album, he was hired in 1975 by Deep Purple to replace the departed Ritchie Blackmore. He subsequently wrote and co-wrote many songs for the English hard-rock group's *Come Taste The Band*. During the early stages of that band's dissolution in late 1975 Bolin went solo, recording the critically acclaimed *Teaser* for Nemporer Records and, the following year, *Private Eyes* for Columbia Records. In each case he toured with the Tommy Bolin Band to promote the albums. In December 1976, Bolin was found dead in a Miami hotel room, the victim of a drugs overdose.

● ALBUMS: with Zephyr *Zephyr* (Probe 1969)★★★, *Teaser* (Nemporer 1975)★★★★, *Private Eyes* (Columbia 1976)★★★, *Live At Ebbets Field 1974* (Tommy Bolin Archives 1997)★★★, *Live At Ebbets Field 1976* (Tommy Bolin Archives 1997)★★★, *Live At Northern Lights Recording Studios* (Tommy Bolin Archives 1997)★★.

● COMPILATIONS: *The Ultimate: The Best Of Tommy Bolin* (Geffen 1989)★★★, *From The Archives, Volume 1* (Rhino 1996)★★★, *Bottom Shelf* (Tommy Bolin Archives 1997)★★★, *From The Archives, Volume 2* (Zebra 1998)★★.

Bolt Thrower

Deriving their name from a character in a popular war game story, Bolt Thrower are an extreme 'grindcore' rock band based in Birmingham, England. Comprising Al West (vocals), Gavin Ward (guitar), Barry Thomson (guitar), Jo Bench (bass) and Andy Whale (drums), they released two attention-grabbing demos, 'In Battle There Is No Law' and 'Concessions Of Pain'. They finally managed to gain a recording contract on the strength of their session for BBC disc jockey John Peel, broadcast on Radio 1 in January 1988. The same year, their debut album emerged, featuring an aggressive fusion of hardcore and thrash with indecipherable vocals, this time from replacement vocalist Karl Willets. Titled after their first demo, the contents were housed on the Vinyl Solution label, after which the group moved permanently to Earache Records. *Realm Of Chaos* was the first result of this union, arriving in striking cover art from the

Games Workshop empire that emphasized the band's fondness for both fantasy and militaria. Tours with the musically like-minded Napalm Death, Morbid Angel and Carcass brought these songs of conflict to a progressively wider audience. Their bludgeoning wall of noise was continued on *Warmaster*, by which time the press had developed the tag 'war metal' for Bolt Thrower. More intricate and less obvious was *The IVth Crusade*, with a more melodic style prevalent between aural assaults, and the Games Workshop art dropped in favour of a nineteenth-century painting by Delacroix. The production skills of Colin Richardson also brought new lustre and clarity to the band's sound. However, Bolt Thrower remained unable to change their press stereotyping. Their fourth album for Earache saw Willets and Whale offer their swan-song performances. The remainder of Bolt Thrower elected to continue without them and in late 1994 recruited Martin van Drunen (ex-Asphyx, Pestilence; vocals) and Martin Kearns (drums).

● ALBUMS: *The Peel Sessions EP* (Strange Fruit 1988)★★, *In Battle There Is No Law* (Vinyl Solution 1988)★★★, *Realm Of Chaos* (Earache 1989)★★★, *Warmaster* (Earache 1991)★★, *The IVth Crusade* (Earache 1992)★★★, ... *For Victory* (Earache 1994)★★★.

Bombers

This Australian-based, hard-rock/boogie group was formed in 1989 by ex-Status Quo bassist Alan Lancaster (b. 7 February 1949, Peckham, London, England; bass). Recruiting John Brewster (guitar, harmonica), Steve Crofts (slide guitar), Tyrone Coates (vocals, saxophone) and Peter Heckenberg (drums), they signed to Polydor Records, for whom their *Aim High* arrived in 1990. Musically, the album meandered through territory familiar to fans of Lancaster's former employers, with Coates's pumping saxophone and Crofts' slide guitar adding some individuality to the material. Largely ignored outside of Australia, with the exception of diehard Quo fans, they are nevertheless an accomplished act.

● ALBUMS: *Aim High* (Polydor 1990)★★.

Bon Jovi

This commercial hard rock band was formed in New Jersey, USA, and fronted by Jon Bon Jovi (b. John Francis Bongiovi Jnr., 2 March 1962, Perth Amboy, New Jersey, USA; vocals). His four co-members were Richie Sambora (b. 11 July 1959; guitar, ex-Message), David Bryan (b. David Rashbaum, 7 February 1962, Edison, New Jersey, USA; keyboards), Tico Torres (b. 7 October 1953; drums, ex-Franke And The Knockouts) and Alec John Such (b. 14 November 1956; bass, ex-Message). Bongiovi, of Italian descent, met Rashbaum (ex-Phantom's Opera) at Sayreville High School, where they shared a mutual interest in rock music. They soon joined eight other musicians in the R&B cover band Atlantic City Expressway. When Rashbaum moved to New York to study at the Juilliard School of Music, Bongiovi followed. Charming his way into the Power Station recording studios, which was owned by his cousin Tony, he performed menial tasks for two years before Billy Squier agreed to produce his demo tape. One track, 'Runaway', was played on local radio and appeared on a local artist compilation album (his work would also grace oddities such as the novelty track, 'R2D2 I Wish You A Merry Christmas'). Reunited with Rashbaum, he acquired the services of Sambora, an established session musician, Such (ex-Phantom's Opera) and Torres (ex-Knockouts).

By July 1983, they had a recording contract with PolyGram Records and support slots with Eddie Money and ZZ Top, the latter at Madison Square Garden. Jon Bon Jovi's looks attracted immediate attention for the band, and he turned down the lucrative lead role in the dance film *Footloose* in order to concentrate on his music. Their debut album preceded a headline tour and support slots with the Scorpions, Whitesnake and Kiss. Their second album, *7800 Degrees Fahrenheit*, was greeted with cynicism by the music press, which was already hostile towards the band's manicured image and formularized heavy rock - this mediocre album only fuelled their scorn. The band responded in style: *Slippery When Wet* was the biggest-selling rock album of 1987, although it originally appeared in August 1986. Collaborating with songwriter Desmond Child, three of its tracks - 'Wanted Dead Or Alive', 'You Give Love A Bad Name' and 'Livin' On A Prayer' - were US and European hits. Headlining the Monsters Of Rock shows in Europe, they were joined on stage by Gene Simmons and Paul Stanley (Kiss), Dee Snider (Twisted Sister) and Bruce Dickinson (Iron Maiden) for an encore of 'We're An American Band'. It merely served to emphasize the velocity with which Bon Jovi had reached the top of the rock league. The tour finally finished in Australia after 18 months, while the album sold millions of copies. When *New Jersey* followed, it included 'Living In Sin', a Jon Bon Jovi composition that pointed to his solo future, although the song owed a great debt to his hero Bruce Springsteen. The rest of 1989 was spent on more extensive touring, before the band temporarily retired. As Jon Bon Jovi commented, it was time to 'Ride my bike into the hills, learn how to garden, *anything* except do another Bon Jovi record.' He subsequently concentrated on his solo career, married karate champion Dorothea Hurley and appeared in his first movie, *Young Guns II*, and released a quasi-soundtrack of songs inspired by the film as his debut solo album in 1990. However, the commercial incentive to return to Bon Jovi was inevitably hard to resist. *Keep The Faith*, with a more stripped-down sound, was an impressive album, satisfying critics and anxious fans alike who had patiently waited almost four years for new material. To those who had considered the group a spent commercial force, the success of the slick ballad, 'Always', a chart fixture in 1994, announced no such decline. On the back of its success, Bon Jovi occupied the UK number 1 spot with the compilation set *Crossroad*, amid rumours that bass player Alec John Such was about to be replaced by Huey McDonald. Meanwhile, Bryan released his first solo album, through Phonogram in Japan, and Sambora married Hollywood actress Heather Locklear (ex-*Dynasty*). *These Days* was a typically slick collection of ballads and party rock, and included the hit single 'This Ain't A Love Song'. With their position already secure as one of the world's most popular rock bands, the album lacked ambition, and the band seemed content to provide fans with more of the same old formula.

Their profile had never been greater than in 1995, when, in the annual readers poll of the leading UK metal magazine *Kerrang!*, the band won seven categories, including best band and best album (for *These Days*) and, astonishingly, worst band and worst album (for *These Days*)! *These Days Tour Edition* was a live mini-album released only in Australia. Jon Bon Jovi began to nurture an acting career in the 90s with starring roles in *Moonlight And Valentino* and *The Leading Man*, and enjoyed further solo success with 1997's *Destination Anywhere*.

● ALBUMS: *Bon Jovi* (Mercury 1984)★★, *7800 Degrees Fahrenheit* (Mercury 1985)★★, *Slippery When Wet* (Mercury 1986)★★★★, *New Jersey* (Mercury 1988)★★★, *Keep The Faith* (Mercury 1992)★★★★, *These Days* (Mercury 1995)★★★, *These Days Tour Edition* mini-album (Mercury 1996)★★.

Solo: Jon Bon Jovi *Blaze Of Glory* (PolyGram 1990)★★, *Destination Anywhere* (Mercury 1997)★★★, *The Power Station Years* 1981-83 recordings (Masquerade 1997)★★. David Bryan *On A Full Moon* (Ignition/Mercury 1994)★★. Richie Sambora *Stranger In This Town* (Jambco/Mercury 1991)★★, *Undiscovered Soul* (Mercury 1998)★★★.

● COMPILATIONS: *Crossroad - The Best Of* (Mercury 1994)★★★★.

● VIDEOS: *Breakout* (PolyGram Music Video 1986), *Slippery When Wet* (Channel 5 1988), *New Jersey* (Channel 5 1989), *Dead Or Alive* (PolyGram Music Video 1989), *Access All Areas* (PolyGram Music Video 1990), *Keep The Faith: An Evening With Bon Jovi* (PolyGram Music Video 1993), *Crossroads: The Best Of* (PolyGram Music Video 1994), *Live From London* (PolyGram Music Video 1995).

● FURTHER READING: *Bon Jovi: An Illustrated Biography*, Eddy McSquare. *Faith And Glory*, Malcolm Dome. *Bon Jovi: Runaway*, Dave Bowler and Bryan Dray. *The Illustrated Biography*, Mick Wall. *The Complete Guide To The Music Of Bon Jovi*, Mick Wall and Malcolm Dome. *Bon Jovi*, Neil Jeffries.

BONFIRE

This heavy metal band was formed in Ingolstadt, Germany. They came together in 1985 from the ashes of Cacumen, which had featured Claus Lessmann (vocals) and Hans Ziller (guitar) in their ranks. Other early members of Bonfire included Horst Maier-Thorn (guitar) and a Dominic Huelhorst (drums), who was sacked and replaced temporarily by Ken Mary from House Of Lords. Edgar Patrik (ex-Sinner; Tyran Pace; and Paul Samson) joined in time for their third album, while Thorn was replaced by Angel Schleifer (ex-Pretty Maids; Sinner) in 1988. An early introduction to UK audiences came at 1988's Reading Festival. Afterwards, they completed their third album, *Point Blank*, produced by Michael Wagner, which gave them critical and commercial success in the UK and Europe. Despite this, Ziller departed, leaving the 90s line-up comprising Lessmann, Schleifer, Patrik, Michael Voss (guitar) and Jorg Deisinger (bass). Despite working in a similar vein to the Scorpions, they failed to achieve the same level of crossover appeal. Lessmann split the band in 1993, and teamed up with Ziller once more to form a folk rock group.

● ALBUMS: *Don't Touch That Light* (RCA 1986)★★, *Fireworks* (RCA 1987)★★, *Point Blank* (RCA 1989)★★★, *Knockout* (RCA 1991)★★★.

Bonham

This heavy rock band was founded by Jason Bonham (b. 1967, England), who was given his first drum-kit at the age of four by his father, Led Zeppelin's John Bonham. After playing in local groups, Jason Bonham toured and recorded in 1987 with Jimmy Page and, after his father's death, performed with the surviving members of Led Zeppelin in New York in 1988. After stints with Airrace and Virginia Wolf, he formed his own band with ex-Robert Plant's Honeydrippers guitarist Ian Hatton (b. 1962, Kidderminster, Worcestershire, England), John Smithson (b. 1963, Sussex, England; keyboards, bass) and Daniel MacMaster (b. 1968, Barrie, Ontario, Canada; vocals). The group's first single was 'Wait For You', released in November 1989 and recorded with Alice Cooper's producer Bob Ezrin. The single was augmented by an impressive debut album that took many critics, cynical about the drummer's familial connections, by surprise. A delayed second album was released in 1992, but failed to live up to the promise of the debut.

● ALBUMS: *The Disregard Of Time Keeping* (WTG/Epic 1989)★★★, *Mad Hatter* (WTG 1992)★★.

Bonnet, Graham

b. 12 December 1947, Skegness, Lincolnshire, England. Bonnet first garnered attention in 1968 as one half of the Marbles, who enjoyed a UK Top 5 hit with the emotional 'Only One Woman'. Subsequent singles, both with the group and as a solo act, proved unsuccessful and he later turned to acting, starring in the film *Three For All*. Bonnet resumed recording in 1977 on Ringo Starr's Ring O Records, but although *Graham Bonnet* was not a major seller in Britain, the album achieved gold status in Australia. In 1979 Bonnet replaced Ronnie James Dio in Ritchie Blackmore's Rainbow. With his almost James Dean-like image, the choice of Bonnet as Dio's replacement was the subject of some consternation amongst the group's more traditional heavy metal fans. The singer was featured on *Down To Earth*, one of the group's most popular albums, and also graced the hit singles 'Since You've Been Gone' and 'All Night Long'. However, Rainbow's legendary instability led to Bonnet's departure the following year. He resumed his solo career with *Line Up* in 1981 and earned himself a UK Top 10 single with 'Night Games'. Later, he returned to collectivism by joining MSG for one album, *Assault Attack*, before relocating to the west coast of the USA to become vocalist for Alcatrazz. In 1987 he joined Chris Impelliteri's group, recording the hard rock classic *Stand In Line*. In 1993 he assembled metal 'supergroup' Blackthorne, whose repertoire included an update of 'All Night Long'.

● ALBUMS: *Graham Bonnet* (Ring O 1977)★★★, *Line Up* (Vertigo 1981)★★★.

Bootsauce

This Canadian funk/rap/metal crossover quintet was formed in Montreal in 1989. Comprising Drew Ling (vocals), Pere Fume (guitar), Sonny Greenwich Jr. (guitar), R. Baculis (bass) and Johnny Frappe (replaced Rob Kazenel; drums), the sound they produced was not unlike a three-way hybrid of Earth Wind And Fire, Red Hot Chili Peppers and Weather Report. At times verging on *avant garde* and jazz-rock, they nevertheless possessed an irreverent sense of humour that set them aside from the mainstream. A riotous cover version of Hot Chocolate's 'Every 1's A Winner', together with 'Sex Machine', was released as a single to boost sales of the group's debut album. They moved to Island Records for the lacklustre *Bull*.

● ALBUMS: *The Brown Album* (Next Plateau 1991)★★★, *Bull* (Island 1992)★★.

Boredoms

Based in Yamatsuka, Japan, the Boredoms have borrowed liberally from the US hardcore punk tradition to forge their own climatic rock music. A septet comprising Yoshimi P-We, YY, God Mana, Human Rich Vox Y, Hila Y, Eye Y and No. 1 Y, the group's records combine the musical assault of hardcore with the experimental distorted song structures of the Butthole Surfers. *Onanie Bomb Meets The Sex Pistols*, compiling the first two Japanes releases, featured impenetrable noise and sequences of communal belching. Even more extreme was 1989's *Soul Discharge*, released on Kramer's Shimmy-Disc label, which featured song titles including 'JB Dick + Tin Turner (sic) Pussy Badsmell' and 'Bubblebop Shot'. The music that supported such lyrics offered unremitting musical chaos, akin to Extreme Noise Terror crossed with American no wave and art rock. *Pop Tatari* was once analogized as the 'least commercially viable album released by a major label since *Metal Machine Music*', the Lou Reed album. The group's subsequent records have been comparatively accessible, attracting a cult audience in America and Europe, helped by the group's notorious stage show. Away from the main band Eye performs with his group Hanatarash, and worked with John Zorn on 1996's *Nani Nani*.

● ALBUMS: *Anal By Anal* (Trans 1986)★★, *Osorezan To Stooges Kyo* (Selfish 1988)★★, *Onanie Bomb Meets The Sex Pistols* (Warners 1988)★★, *Soul Discharge* (Shimmy Disc 1989)★★, *Pop Tatari* (Warners/Reprise 1992)★★, *Wow-2* (Avant 1993)★★★, *Super Roots* mini-album (Warners/Reprise 1993)★★, *Chocolate Synthesizer* (Warners/Reprise 1994)★★★, *Super Roots 2* mini-album (Warners 1994)★★, *Super Roots 3* (Warners 1994)★★, *Super Roots 5* (Reprise 1995)★★, *Super Roots 6* (Reprise 1996)★★★.

BORICH, KEVIN

b. New Zealand. Regarded as one of his continent's leading guitarists, Borich came to prominence in Australia with the New Zealand band La De Das in 1976. After a tour of the UK in 1980, several members left, leaving Borich as lead guitarist in a trio that he eventually renamed the Kevin Borich Express. The Express earned a reputation as one of the hardest-working groups in the country, touring and playing incessantly. His style was influenced by Jimi Hendrix and Robin Trower, though his guitarwork often overshadowed his ordinary vocals and songwriting. On album, his talents were not adequately explored, although his guitar-playing on the La De Das' version of 'All Along the Watchtower' was exemplary. An involvement with the hugely popular Party Boys cover band led to the dissolution of his own band in 1983.

● ALBUMS: *Celebration* (Image 1976)★★★, *The Lonely One* (Image 1977)★★★, *Live* (Avenue 1979)★★★, *No Turning Back* (Mercury 1979)★★★, with Renee Geyer *Blues Licence* (1979)★★★, *Angels Hand* (Mercury 1980)★★★, *Kevin Borich Express* (Mercury 1980)★★★, with Dutch Tilders *The Blues Had A Baby And They Called It Rock And Roll* (1981)★★.

● COMPILATIONS: *The Best Of Kevin Borich* (Image 1977)★★★★.

BOSTON

As a result of home-made demos recorded by the enterprising Tom Scholz (b. 10 March 1947, Toledo, Ohio, USA), one of the finest AOR albums of all time was created. The tapes impressed Epic Records and Scholz joined with friends Fran Sheehan (b. 26 March 1949, Boston, Massachusetts, USA; bass), Brad Delp (b. 12 June 1951, Boston, Massachusetts, USA; guitar, vocals), Barry Goudreau (b. 29 November 1951, Boston, Massachusetts, USA; guitar) and Sib Hashian (b. 17 August 1949, Boston, Massachusetts, USA; drums). Adopting the name Boston, their first release was a US Top 3 album that eventually sold 16 million copies in the USA alone, and spent two years in the US charts. The memorable single, 'More Than A Feeling', was an instant classic, containing all the key ingredients of adult-orientated rock: upfront guitar, powerful lead vocal with immaculate harmonies, and heavy bass and drums. Two years later they repeated the formula virtually note for note with *Don't Look Back*, which also topped the US charts. During this time, Scholz, formerly a product designer for the Polaroid Company, invented a mini-amplifier marketed as the Rockman. Goudreau later grew tired of the band's lengthy sabbaticals and released a solo album before quitting to form Orion. Never a prolific band, Boston, in the guise of Scholz and Delp, returned seven years later with *Third Stage*, which spawned two further US hit singles, 'Amanda' (which reached number 1) and 'We're Ready'. Fans wishing to replace worn copies of the previous albums had only to purchase this one, so similar was it to their previous output. It, too, went straight to number 1, giving Boston a record in rock history, by combining the biggest-selling debut album with three number 1 albums and total sales of over 50 million. Scholz then became involved in a long-running court battle against Epic Records over his alleged breach of contract. Scholz won the case, but the ensuing *Walk On*, with Scholz the sole remaining member of the original line-up, was a disappointment.

● ALBUMS: *Boston* (Epic 1976)★★★★, *Don't Look Back* (Epic 1978)★★★, *Third Stage* (MCA 1986)★★★, *Walk On* (MCA 1994)★★.

● COMPILATIONS: *Greatest Hits* (Epic 1997)★★★.

BOULEVARD

This Canadian band was formed in 1984 by ex-session musician Mark Holden (saxophone) and with the addition of David Forbes (vocals), Randy Gould (guitar), Andrew Johns (keyboards), Randy Burgess (bass) and Jerry Adolphe (drums), the line-up was complete. Initially, they pursued a melodic AOR direction, similar to Toto and REO Speedwagon. *Into The Street* marked a move towards a more hard-rock approach, with Bad Company and Bon Jovi influences. They established a solid fanbase in their native Canada, but this success was not translated elsewhere, despite the efforts of Bryan Adams' manager Bruce Allen.

● ALBUMS: *Boulevard* (MCA 1987)★★★, *Into The Street* (MCA 1990)★★★.

BOW WOW
The name translates literally as 'Barking Dog', a fitting title for Japan's finest exponents of melodic heavy metal. Formed in 1976, the band comprised Kyoji Yamamoto (vocals, guitar), Mitsuhiro Saito (vocals, guitar), Kenji Sano (bass) and Toshiri Niimi (drums). Intriguingly, they incorporated classical Japanese musical structures within a framework of westernized hard rock. Influenced by Kiss, Led Zeppelin and Aerosmith, they released a sequence of impressive albums during the late 70s. Characterized by explosive guitarwork and breathtaking arrangements, the only disappointment to western ears was the Japanese vocals, which doubtless restricted their international appeal. On *Asian Volcano*, their eleventh album, released in 1982, the vocals were sung in English for the first time, but the band sounded uncomfortable with the transition. They played the Reading Festival the same year and were afforded an encouraging reception. Two subsequent shows at London's Marquee Club were recorded for the live album *Holy Expedition*, which followed in 1983. At the end of that year the band changed their name to Vow Wow, adding an extra vocalist and keyboard player to pursue a more melodic direction. Lead guitarist Yamamoto has released two solo albums representing an instrumental fusion of classical, rock and jazz styles, *Horizons* and *Electric Cinema* in 1980 and 1982, respectively. Beyond the Far East, success has continued to elude this first-class rock outfit, despite Whitesnake's Neil Murray joining for a short time in 1987.

● ALBUMS: *Bow Wow* (Invitation 1976)★★★, *Signal Fire* (Invitation 1977)★★★, *Charge* (Invitation 1977)★★★, *Super Live* (Invitation 1978)★★★, *Guarantee* (Invitation 1978)★★★, *The Bow Wow* (Invitation 1979)★★★, *Glorious Road* (SMS 1979)★★★, *Telephone* (SMS 1980)★★★, *X Bomber* (SMS 1980)★★★, *Hard Dog* (SMS 1981)★★★, *Asian Volcano* (VAP 1982)★★, *Warning From Stardust* (VAP 1982)★★, *Holy Expedition* (Heavy Metal 1983)★★. As Vow Wow: *Beat Of Metal Motion* (VAP 1984)★★★, *Cyclone* (Eastworld 1985)★★★, *III* (Eastworld 1986)★★★, *Live* (Passport 1987)★★, *V* (Arista 1987)★★★, *VIB* (EMI 1989)★★★, *Helter Skelter* (Arista 1989)★★★.

BOXER
Formed in 1975, Boxer featured two former members of Patto, Michael Patrick McGrath/Mike Patto (b. 22 September 1942, Glasgow, Scotland, d. 4 March 1979; vocals) and Peter 'Ollie' Halsall (b. 14 March 1949, Southport, Merseyside, England, d. 29 May 1992; guitars). The line-up was completed by two experienced musicians, Keith Ellis (bass, ex-Koobas, Juicy Lucy, and Van Der Graaf Generator) and Tony Newman (drums, ex-Sounds Incorporated; Jeff Beck; and May Blitz). *Below The Belt* is better recalled for the controversy surrounding its tasteless 'nude' cover rather than the hard rock unveiled within. The original Boxer broke up when a second album, *Bloodletting*, was withdrawn and not released until 1979. The singer re-established the group in 1977 with Chris Stainton (keyboards, ex-Grease Band), Adrian Fisher (guitar, ex-Sparks), Tim Bogert (b. 27 August 1944, Richfield, New Jersey, USA; bass, ex-Vanilla Fudge) and Eddie Tuduri (drums). Boxer was dissolved following the release of the disappointing *Absolutely*. Mike Patto resumed work with the ad hoc unit Hinkley's Heroes, but died in 1979 following a long battle with throat cancer.

● ALBUMS: *Below The Belt* (Virgin 1975)★★★, *Absolutely* (Epic 1977)★★, *Bloodletting* (Virgin 1979)★★.

BOYZZ
Influenced by Steppenwolf, Black Oak Arkansas and Lynyrd Skynyrd, the US-based Boyzz combined hard-driving rock 'n' roll with southern-style boogie. With a strong biker image, their sole album, *Too Wild To Tame*, featured Dirty Dan Buck (vocals), Anatole Halinkovich (keyboards), Gil Pini (guitar), Mike Tafoya (guitar), David Angel (bass) and Kent Cooper (drums). Unable to translate media interest into record sales, the band disintegrated soon after the album's release. Halinkovich, Tafoya and Angel later went on to form B'zz.

● ALBUMS: *Too Wild To Tame* (Epic 1978)★★★.

BRAD
The involvement of Pearl Jam guitarist Stone Gossard in this project inevitably and unfairly saw Brad tagged as Gossard's solo outing, when in reality, it was a collaboration with two old friends, Pigeonhed/Satchel vocalist and keyboard player Shawn Smith and Satchel drummer Regan Hagar, plus bassist Jeremy Toback. The band was originally called Shame, but Los Angeles musician Brad Wilson held a copyright on the name and was not prepared to give it up - hence, the band cheekily named themselves Brad. They entered the studio with only the album opener, 'Buttercup', written, and wrote, recorded and mixed *Shame* in just 17 days. The result was an enthralling and atmospheric work, blending funk, rock, jazz and soul

with a melancholy lyrical air, and the fact that much of the material stemmed from studio jams gave the album a loose, laid-back feel. Gossard produced a largely understated performance that complemented Smith's piano and organ lines, backed by a solid, economical groove from the rhythm section, while Smith's smoky, soulful vocals added another dimension to the band, and drew comparisons with Prince and Stevie Wonder amid a heap of deserved critical praise. The players reconvened for a less vital second album in 1997, although tracks such as 'Upon My Shoulders' and 'The Day Brings' confirmed Smith's reputation as one of the finest singers of the 90s.

● ALBUMS: *Shame* (Epic 1993)★★★★, *Interiors* (Epic 1997)★★★.

BRATS

This Danish quartet was formed in Copenhagen in 1979 by guitarists Michael Denner and Hank Sherman. Recruiting Yens (bass, vocals) and Monroe (drums), they signed to CBS Records and recorded a debut album the following year. Appropriately titled *1980*, it featured a dozen hard rock tracks, punctuated by some dazzling guitarwork from Denner. The band disintegrated shortly after the album's release, with guitarists Denner and Sherman joining forces with King Diamond (vocals), Timmy Grabber Hansen (bass) and Kim Ruzz to become Mercyful Fate. This corresponded with a change in direction towards satanic heavy metal.

● ALBUMS: *1980* (Columbia 1980)★★.

BREATHLESS

This six-piece melodic AOR band was formed in the US Midwest in 1978. Breathless was assembled by ex-Michael Stanley Band vocalist Jonah Koslen, who, after a successful search, completed the lineup with Alan Greene (guitar), Mark Avsec (keyboards), Bob Benjamin (bass) and drummers Rodney Psycka and Kevin Valentine. They signed to EMI Records in 1979 and released two albums in the space of 18 months. Their lightweight, Kansas meets Toto-style melodic compositions failed to win an appreciative audience. The band split in 1981, with Koslen releasing a solo album, *Aces*, two years later.

● ALBUMS: *Breathless* (EMI 1979)★★, *Nobody Leaves This Song Alive* (EMI 1980)★★.

BRESLAU

This German hard rock quartet was formed in 1981 by vocalist Jutta Weinholt and guitarist Alex Parche. Adding Zweibel Truhol (bass) and Cay Wolf (drums), they recorded their first and only album the following year. Influenced by Iron Maiden, Scorpions and Kiss, *Volksmusik* was notable for Weinholt's powerful and unusual vocal style. The music was derivative, however. Unable to generate any interest, the band disintegrated a few months later. Weinholt reappeared as lead vocalist with Zed Yago.

● ALBUMS: *Volksmusik* (1982)★★.

BRIAR

This pop-rock quartet was formed in Birmingham, England, in 1983 by Kevin Griffiths (vocals, bass) and Daren Underwood (guitar). With Dave Fletcher (guitar) and Dean Cook (drums), they released a self-financed single that was given considerable airplay by BBC Radio 1 disc jockey Peter Powell. A Radio 1 live session was followed by a recording contract with Heavy Metal Records. *Too Young* emerged in 1985, an over-produced affair that was full of lightweight guitar, high-pitched harmonies and anodyne lyrics. The album flopped and the band were forced to return to the club circuit. *Take On The World*, a self-financed cassette, was released in 1986, and eventually resulted in a new contract with CBS Records. Half the album comprised a selection of cover versions, including Richie Valens' 'La Bamba' and Sister Sledge's 'Frankie'.

● ALBUMS: *Too Young* (Heavy Metal 1985)★★, *Take On The World* (Columbia 1986)★★, *Crown Of Thorns* (Columbia 1988)★★.

BRICK LAYER CAKE

US alternative rock band Brick Layer Cake is essentially the vision of one man - Rifle Sport, Breaking Circus and current Shellac drummer Todd Trainer. His activities in this side-band have always been supported by the input of others, however, and he is keen for Brick Layer Cake not to be seen as a tawdry solo project. For 1994's *Tragedy - Tragedy*, the participants included Gerard Boissy (ex-Rifle Sport) and Brian Paulson, a renowned recording engineer who also produced the album. Pitched somewhere between the bleak melancholy of Nick Drake (via Trainer's subdued, detached vocals) and the violent noise convulsions of early Big Black, *Tragedy - Tragedy* proved to be, respectively, as intense and blunt an aural experience as those influences suggested.

● ALBUMS: *Tragedy - Tragedy* (Touch And Go 1994)★★★.

BRICKLIN

This American six-piece rock band was founded by the Bricklin brothers in 1986. Featuring Jake Meyer (vocals, keyboards), Brian Bricklin (guitar, keyboards), Scott Bricklin (vocals, keyboards), Ian Cross (guitar, keyboard, vocals), James Goetz (bass, vocals) and Eddie Bader (drums), the band secured a contract with A&M Records in 1987. Adopting a commercial approach, their music was comparable in style to Toto, Loverboy, It Bites and Kansas. Although technically excellent and superbly produced, their two albums lacked individuality and distinction.

● ALBUMS: *Bricklin* (A&M 1987)★★★, *Bricklin II* (A&M 1989)★★.

BRIGHTON ROCK

This highly popular Canadian band, who followed in the footsteps of Don Dokken and Loverboy, formed in 1984 in Toronto, where they stabilized their line-up with Gredd Fraser (guitar), Gerald McGhee (vocals), Johnny Rogers (keyboards), Stevie Skreeb (bass) and Mark Cavarzan (drums). Recording a self-financed EP to attract attention, they were quickly signed to Warner Brothers Records who reissued the debut. In 1987 they released their first full album, which won critical acclaim - however, it was its successor that put them into the arenas, at least in their native territory. The group eventually disintegrated in 1992 when they failed to convert domestic popularity into worldwide standing.

● ALBUMS: *Young, Wild And Free* (Warners 1987)★★★, *Take A Deep Breath* (Warners 1988)★★★, *Love Machine* (Warners 1991)★★.

BRITNY FOX

This American 'glam-metal' quartet was formed in Philadelphia in 1987 by vocalist 'Dizzy' Dean Davidson (ex-World War III drummer) and former Cinderella guitarist Michael Kelly Smith. With the addition of bassist Billy Childs and ex-Waysted drummer Johnny DiTeodora, they signed to CBS Records and released their debut album the following year. This was a combination of AC/DC, Mötley Crüe and Quiet Riot influences, characterized by Davidson's raucous snarl, and included an inspired cover version of Slade's 'Gudbuy T'Jane', plus nine originals. *Boys In Heat* saw the band mellow a little: the make-up was discarded and replaced with a rough, streetwise rock 'n' roller image. Davidson's vocals were further refined and the material edged, significantly, towards Cinderella's style. Britny Fox toured with Bon Jovi and Alice Cooper, but were unable to convert successful concert performances into album sales. Davidson quit in 1990 and went on to form Blackeyed Susan, with Tommy Paris being drafted in as his replacement almost a year later. *Bite Down Hard* emerged in 1991, with the songs following a much heavier direction. Against expectations, the band looked poised for greater success in the second phase of their career, but it was not to be, and Britny Fox were finally laid to rest in early 1993.

● ALBUMS: *Britny Fox* (Columbia 1988)★★★, *Boys In Heat* (Columbia 1989)★★★, *Bite Down Hard* (East West 1991)★★.

● VIDEOS: *Year Of The Fox* (CMV Enterprises 1989).

BROCAS HELM

Influenced by the New Wave Of British Heavy Metal, Brocas Helm were formed in 1983 and comprised vocalist/guitarist Robbie Wright, bassist Jim Schumacher and drummer Jack Hays. Drawing inspiration from Iron Maiden, Venom and Angelwitch, they specialized in predictable heavy metal adapted from these sources. The emphasis was on up-tempo numbers, which were let down by poor vocals, and they disbanded during 1986.

● ALBUMS: *Into Battle* (First Strike 1984)★★, *Undefeated* (First Strike 1985)★★.

BROKEN BONES

This British hardcore band was formed in Stoke-on-Trent, England, during 1983 by ex-Discharge guitarist Tony 'Bones' Roberts. Recruiting brother Terry on bass, vocalist Nobby and drummer Cliff, they closely followed the metal/punk crossover approach of Bones's former group. With controversial lyrics and a rigidly formularized approach, they have progressed little since their inception. After a period of inactivity, they returned in 1989 with Quiv and D.L. Harris as new faces on lead vocals and bass, respectively. *Losing Control* appeared shortly afterwards, a vitriolic blast of angst-ridden hardcore, but again, little different from previous offerings.

● ALBUMS: *Dem Bones* (Fall Out 1984)★★★, *Live At The 100 Club* (Fall Out 1985)★★★, *Bonecrusher* (Combat Core 1986)★★★, *F.O.A.D.* (Combat Core 1987)★★★, *Losing Control* (Heavy Metal 1989)★★★, *Trader In Death* (Heavy Metal 1990)★★, *Stitched Up* (Music For Nations 1991)★★, *Death Is Imminent* (Cleopatra 1993)★★.

● COMPILATIONS: *Decapitated* (Fall Out

1987)★★★, *Complete Singles* (Cleopatra 1996)★★★.
● VIDEOS: *Live At Leeds* (Jettisoundz 1984).

BROKEN HOPE

Thoroughly brutal musicians based in Illinois, USA, Broken Hope comprises Joe Ptacek (vocals), Jeremy Wagner (guitar), Ed Hughes (bass) and Ryan Stanek (drums). The group was formed in 1989 when Stanek first approached Wagner at a party, with the simple goal of becoming the heaviest of death metal acts on the local scene. Nursing a four-song demo tape, which was traded throughout the fertile underground metal network, the founding members realized an addition to their sound was required and brought in Brian Griffin as second guitarist, who abandoned his budding career as a studio engineer at Wave Digital. It was here that the group entered the studio in the summer of 1990 to record a second demo, which cemented previous impressions and led to several offers from independent labels. They eventually signed with new local label, Grind Core International, for whom they made their long-playing debut in February 1992 with *Swamped In Gore*. However, representatives of the more financially viable Metal Blade Records witnessed the band at the Milwaukee Metalfest VI, and when Broken Hope lost faith in their first home and looked for new offers, Metal Blade stepped in. The resulting *The Bowels Of Repugnance* combined the band's ferocious musicianship with clinical production standards.
● ALBUMS: *Swamped In Gore* (Grind Core International 1992)★★★, *The Bowels Of Repugnance* (Metal Blade 1994)★★★, *Repulsive Conception* (Metal Blade 1995)★★★, *Loathing* (Metal Blade 1997)★★★.

BRONZ

This band were the first to be launched on the US market by the UK-based Bronze Records. The five musicians that co-operated in this marketing ploy were from Bath, England, and were ex-Nightwing vocalist Max Bacon, guitarists Chris Goulstone and Shaun Kirkpatrick, bassist Paul Webb and drummer Carl Matthews. In spite of using four producers and an embarrassingly large budget, their debut album was a ramshackle affair that was inferior to the well-established outfits of the genre. After one album, the band split, with Bacon going on to achieve success with GTR.
● ALBUMS: *Taken By Storm* (Bronze 1984)★★.

BROWN, DANNY JOE, BAND

b. USA. Danny Joe Brown (vocals) elected to pursue a solo career in 1981 after breaking away from Molly Hatchet after their first two albums. Forming his own group, *Danny Joe Brown Band* was recorded with assistance from Bobby Ingram (vocals), Steve Wheeler (guitar), Kenny McVay (guitar), John Galvin (keyboards, vocals), Buzzy Meekins (bass, vocals) and Jimmy Glenn (drums). A mediocre selection of melodic hard rock material, the album failed commercially and the experiment was not repeated, as Brown rejoined Molly Hatchet the following year.
● ALBUMS: *Danny Joe Brown Band* (Epic 1981)★★.

BRUJERIA

In reality, the mysterious Los Angeles-based Brujeria is an extreme death metal side-project for Fear Factory guitarist Dino Cazares and his friends and colleagues. The band name derives from the black magic used by some Mexican drug dealers to inspire fear in religious locals. The publicity surrounding the release of *Matandos Gueros* painted a similar picture, alleging that the band were, in fact, seven psychotic Mexican drug barons, all Satanists, led by vocalist Juan Brujo, and featuring three bassists (Guero Sin Fe, Fantasma, Hongo) for a particularly heavy bottom end. The line-up was completed by Asesino on guitar, Grenudo on drums and the mysterious Jr Hozicon/Director Diabolico. The original album cover featured a photograph of a severed head, allegedly that of another Mexican drug dealer, but it was relegated to the inner sleeve and replaced by a black sleeve that warned of the graphic nature of this and other photographs contained therein. The album itself was a fierce collection of short songs that echoed early Napalm Death and Carcass in style, with lyrics growled exclusively in Spanish. In common with the likes of Stormtroopers Of Death on the New York hardcore scene, the band added a touch of humour and parody to the death/grind network through their deliberately grandiose approach. Meanwhile, suspected contributors such as Cazares, Fear Factory vocalist Burton C. Bell, and Faith No More bassist Bill Gould continued fervently to deny any involvement.
● ALBUMS: *Matandos Gueros* (Roadrunner 1993)★★★, *Raza Odiada* (Roadrunner 1995)★★★.

BRUTAL TRUTH

During a break in activities with Nuclear Assault, bassist Dan Lilker began working with guitarist

Brent McCarty and drummer Scott Lewis to indulge his passion for hardcore. Joined by vocalist Kevin Sharp, the USA-based band created their own brand of high-speed hardcore with industrial and death metal elements. Finding this style more to his liking, Lilker left his old band to concentrate on Brutal Truth (the trio's past work had also included stints with Stormtroopers Of Death, Anthrax, Winter and J.C.T.). Signing with 'grindcore' specialists Earache Records, the band released *Extreme Conditions Demand Extreme Responses*, a collection of exceptionally fast and fierce material with political themes, to a positive reception, and received further good press for their live shows, playing US dates with labelmates Napalm Death, Carcass and Cathedral. A European tour with Fear Factory followed, leaving behind a trail of damaged PA systems, as well as Lewis, who was replaced by Rich Hoak. The group then teamed up with Coventry, England-based techno act Larcency for the 'Perpetual Conversion' single, which also featured a cover version of Black Sabbath's 'Lord Of This World'. The equally venomous *Need To Control* came in an unusual format - a boxed set containing 5-, 6-, 7-, 8- and 9-inch vinyl, with two additional cover versions of Celtic Frost's 'Dethroned Emperor' and Pink Floyd's 'Wish You Were Here'. Lilker also worked part-time in another side-project, Exit-13, as the parent band embarked on a tour of USA, Australia and Japan.

● ALBUMS: *Extreme Conditions Demand Extreme Responses* (Earache 1992)★★★, *Need To Control* (Earache 1994)★★★, *Kill Trend Suicide* mini-album (Relapse 1996)★★★, *Sounds Of The Animal Kingdom* (Relapse 1997)★★★.

BRUTALITY

One of the most popular acts to emerge out of Florida's burgeoning death metal scene, Brutality had actually developed over several years following their formation in 1988. Typically for the genre, they subsisted in the early days through the demo network, although there were also two singles ('Hell On Earth' and 'Sadistic') for the European label Nuclear Blast. These introduced Brutality's trademark sound, aggressive rhythms topped by Scott Reigel's distinctive vocals. The violence of the sound, more fully visited on the debut album *Screams Of Anguish* and the subsequent *When The Sky Turns Black*, was all-encompassing.

● ALBUMS: *Screams Of Anguish* (Nuclear Blast 1993)★★★, *When The Sky Turns Black* (Nuclear Blast 1995)★★★, *In Mourning* (Nuclear Blast 1997)★★★.

BRUZER

Bruzer were a short-lived collaboration between established US musicians playing a mixture of hard rock and techno-pop in the style of Cheap Trick. The line-up comprised Paul Frank (vocals), Jeff Steele (bass), Vinny Appice (drums, ex-Derringer; later Black Sabbath), Mitchell Froom (keyboards, later of Gamma) and Rick Ramirez (guitar, ex-Striker). *Round One*, released in 1982, was well received, but the band splintered before critical interest could be consolidated into commercial success.

● ALBUMS: *Round One* (Handshake 1982)★★★.

BUDGIE

This hard rock group was formed in Cardiff, Wales, by John Burke Shelley (b. 10 April 1947, Cardiff, South Glamorgan, Wales; bass, acoustic guitar, lead vocals) and Ray Phillips (b. 1 March 1949; drums) in 1968. Joined by Tony Bourge (b. 23 November 1948, Cardiff, South Glamorgan, Wales; lead guitar, vocals), the trio established a substantial following on the south Wales college and club circuit and were subsequently signed to MCA Records. Plying their trade in a basic, heavy riffing style, the standard was set with the first single, charmingly entitled 'Crash Course To Brain Surgery'. The vagaries of early 70s British album artwork were typified by the treatment given to Budgie's releases - promotional material depicted ludicrous images of budgerigars variously posed, dressed as a fighter pilot (staring nobly out into the far horizon), a Nazi Gestapo officer, or as a squadron of fighter budgies flying in formation, tearing into combat. Founder-member Phillips quit in 1974 before the recording of their fourth album and was replaced by Pete Boot (b. 30 September 1950, West Bromwich, Staffordshire, England), who in turn departed that year before Steve Williams took over. The exiled drummer formed Ray Phillips' Woman back in Wales, then Tredegar in 1982. With the success of *In For The Kill*, Budgie won over a wider audience, although they remained more popular in mainland Europe during this period. Their sixth album, *If I Was Brittania I'd Waive The Rules*, was their first on A&M Records. *Impeckable* was the last to feature Bourge, who left in 1978, joining Phillips in Tredegar. He was replaced by former George Hatcher Band guitarist John Thomas. The group's popularity grew in the USA, resulting in Budgie touring there for two years, with Rob Kendrick (ex-Trapeze) standing in for Thomas. Returning to Britain, and now signed to RCA Records, Budgie fitted in well with the new heavy rock scene, and despite being without a label for much of the mid-80s, their reputation and influence on a younger generation of musicians brought them consistent work until Shelley dissolved the group in 1988. He subsequently worked with a new trio, Superclarkes. Phillips used the name Six Ton Budgie (inspired by a journalist's comment about the original band) for a new line-up featuring his son, Justin, on guitar, who still play regularly with versions of the former group's standards.

● ALBUMS: *Budgie* (MCA 1971)★★, *Squawk* (MCA 1972)★★, *Never Turn Your Back On A Friend* (MCA 1973)★★, *In For The Kill* (MCA 1974)★★, *Bandolier* (MCA 1975)★★, *If I Was Brittania I'd Waive The Rules* (A&M 1976)★★, *Impeckable* (A&M 1978)★★, *Power Supply* (Active 1980)★★, *Nightflight* (RCA 1981)★★, *Deliver Us From Evil* (RCA 1982)★★.

● COMPILATIONS: *Best Of* (MCA 1976)★★, *An Ecstacy Of Fumbling: The Definitive Anthology* (Repertoire 1996)★★★, *The Best Of* (Half Moon 1997)★★, *Heavier Than Air: Rarest Eggs* (New Millennium 1998)★★★.

BUFFALO

Buffalo emerged in Sydney, Australia, in 1970. Signed by Vertigo Records, the band's albums sold slowly but steadily enough to retain the interest of the label. The group received adverse press owing to the overtly sexist nature of the covers of their first three albums, and also for some of the song lyrics (e.g., 'Skirt Lifter'), which somewhat limited their appeal. Among Australian bands during the 70s, Buffalo were atypical in being as popular in Europe, particularly France, as they were in their homeland. The outfit were musically akin to the likes of Black Sabbath and Deep Purple while retaining their own rock sound, enhanced by Norm Roue's slide guitar playing and the powerful performances of vocalist Dave Tice. Eventually, the dearth of original members led the band to split, after recording five albums. *Dead Forever* achieved gold status three years after release. Bassist Peter Wells played slide guitar in Rose Tattoo with Angry Anderson, while Tice joined original drummer Paul Balbi in the Count Bishops in the UK.

● ALBUMS: *Dead Forever* (Vertigo 1972)★★, *Volcanic Rock* (Vertigo 1973)★★★, *Only Want You For Your Body* (Vertigo 1974)★★, *Mother's Choice* (Vertigo 1976)★★, *Average Rock And Roller* (Vertigo 1977)★★.

● COMPILATIONS: *Best Of* (Vertigo 1980)★★★.

BULLDOZER

This death metal trio was formed in Milan, Italy, during 1984 by classically trained guitarist Andy Panigada and bassist/vocalist A.C. Wild. With the recruitment of drummer Don Andras, they recorded *The Day Of Wrath* in 1985. However, their music was marred by out-of-phase vocals and a muddy production. They built up a small but loyal following, gaining notoriety for their extreme style and bad taste. Two more albums followed in a similar vein, before 1988's *Neurodeli* played down the satanic emphasis of the lyrics. It is unlikely that anything more will be heard from Bulldozer, following Wild's appointment as Metal Master's label representative.

● ALBUMS: *The Day Of Wrath* (Roadrunner 1985)★★, *The Final Separation* (Roadrunner 1986)★★, *IX* (Roadrunner 1987)★★, *Neurodeli* (Roadrunner 1988)★★★.

BULLET

Comprising Klaus Thiel (vocals, guitar), Paul Psilias (guitar), Voker Pechtold (bass) and Mike Lichtenberg (drums), German hard rock band Bullet formed in 1978 and were originally known as Teaser. The group struggled to gain recognition until 1981 when Dieter Dierks of Polydor Records Germany heard one of their demos. The result was *Execution*, the group's 1982 debut album, produced by Dierks. Successfully exported to other European territories, notably the UK, where Bullet secured excellent reviews, it promised a bright future. However, attempts at recording a follow-up over the 1982 Christmas period were fraught with delays and squabbles. Fitty Weinhold replaced Pechtold on bass and by 1983 Psilias had also departed. When *No Mercy* was finally issued in 1984, the group had lost its previous momentum and it was their final release.

● ALBUMS: *Execution* (Polydor 1982)★★★, *No Mercy* (Heavy Metal 1984)★★.

BULLETBOYS

This American hard rock quartet was formed in 1987 by Mike Sweda (guitar, ex-King Kobra) and Marq Torien (vocals, ex-Ratt). They were joined by Lonnie Vincent (bass) and Jimmy D'Anda (drums) and took their musical lead from AC/DC, Van Halen and Montrose. Championed by producer Ted Templeman, they signed to Warner Brothers Records and recorded their debut the following year. Torien's flamboyant persona attracted comparisons with David Lee Roth, while Sweda's guitar effects were based on a style first made famous by Eddie Van Halen. *Freakshow* and *Za-Za* saw the band broaden their musical horizons and incorporate blues and funk influences into the basic hard rock structures. After a brief split, the band reformed in 1997 and began touring and recording again.

● ALBUMS: *Bulletboys* (Warners 1988)★★, *Freakshow* (Warners 1991)★★★, *Za-Za* (Warners 1993)★★★.

BULLSEYE

Although generally marketed as a heavy metal band, US rockers Bullseye imbued their material with pop hooks in a similar manner to both Bon Jovi and Van Halen. Formed in the late 70s by Manna Demagistris (guitar, vocals), Kevin Clougherty (bass, vocals), Thomas Ferrara (guitar), Thomas Graves (keyboards) and Alan Childs (drums), they recorded their sole album in 1979 for Columbia Records. *On Target* was a competently presented, but ultimately unsatisfying, collection of pop rock songs that lacked the musical impact of their evident influences.

● ALBUMS: *On Target* (Columbia 1979)★★.

BULLYRAG

Comprising Robbie Awork (b. *c*.1967; vocals), Stewart Boyle (guitar), Michael Cusick (b *c*.1969; bass), Steve Barney (b. *c*.1970; drums) and Dave Goldring (percussion), Bullyrag formed in Liverpool, Merseyside, England, in January 1995. Their blend of hip-hop and ragga-tinged hard rock found an immediate audience when their first demo was aired on BBC Radio 1, as well as London radio stations GLR and XFM. Within six weeks of formation and after only one live performance (supporting Big Audio Dynamite) Bullyrag were offered a major recording contract, but turned it down in order to give their songwriting time to develop. The offer, with a proposed advance of £250,000, was made by Chris Blackwell of Island Records, who flew the group to Miami with the intention of signing them. They released the *Verdoosh* EP in March 1995, preceding a number of renewed offers from major label A&R executives. They eventually signed with Vertigo Records.

● ALBUMS: *Songs Of Praise* (Vertigo 1998)★★★.

BURNING ROME

Comprising Vicki Thomas (vocals, guitar), Steve Doughterty (guitar), Mickey Shine (bass) and Ron Murray (drums), Burning Rome formed in Los Angeles, California, USA, in the early 80s. The material included on their self-titled debut album for A&M Records in 1982 seemed to signal the group's stylistic confusion - although at times incorporating new wave sentiments, by turns the songs gave way to brash rock guitar. A&M found the group difficult to market and dropped them shortly after the album's release.

● ALBUMS: *Burning Rome* (A&M 1982)★★★.

BURNING TREE

From Los Angeles, USA, this three-piece unit specialized in early 70s blues-based power rock. Marc Ford (guitar, vocals), Mark Dutton (bass, vocals) and Doni Gray (drums) reinvented, rehashed and reinterpreted the riffs, licks and solos first unleashed by artists including Eric Clapton, John Mayall and Jimi Hendrix. Although essentially revivalists who used Cream as a musical template from which to work, Burning Tree celebrated rather than simply duplicated, breathing new life into well-worn arrangements through a combination of sheer conviction and the application of technology. However, it was not enough to bring them the longevity associated with the great blues artists, with Gray joining ex-Quireboys singer Spike in a new project, God's Hotel. Ford went on to join the Black Crowes.

● ALBUMS: *Burning Tree* (Epic 1990)★★★.

BURTNICK, GLEN

After working with Helmet Boy, Jan Hammer and Neal Schon, Burtnick declined the offer to join Bon Jovi in favour of working on a solo career. Securing a contract with A&M Records, he employed session musicians to help to record his debut, *Talking In Code*. A sophisticated and highly polished selection of pop-rock anthems, the album was infused with elements of funk and soul. On *Heroes And Zeroes*, Bruce Hornsby, Anton Fig and Schon made guest appearances, but the songs covered predominantly the same ground as his previous work. In 1990 he joined Styx in place of Tommy Shaw, to record their comeback album, *Edge Of The Century*.

● ALBUMS: *Talking In Code* (A&M 1986)★★★, *Heroes And Zeroes* (A&M 1987)★★.

BURZUM

Founded in 1991 by Norwegian Satanist Count Grishnakh (real name Varg Vikernes), Burzum became one of the leading lights in Scandinavia's black metal revival of the early 90s. Largely a solo project, Grishnakh composes, sings and plays almost all of Burzum's material himself. The project first surfaced under the name of Uruk Hai in

1987. Significantly, the name was drawn from J.R.R. Tolkien's fantasy classic, *The Lord Of The Rings*, in which the Uruk Hai were a particularly brutal tribe of orcs (the subhuman villains of the book). Burzum was the orcish language, while Grishnakh was a treacherous orc who plays a small, but pivotal, role in the proceedings. Count Grishnakh used Tolkien's epic struggle between good and evil as a model for his own brand of Satanism, casting himself among the hordes of darkness. Grishnakh went on to collaborate with Euronymous, godfather of the Scandinavian black metal revival, playing with the latter's band Mayhem, releasing material on his Deathlike Silence label, and playing a leading part in the curious hate cult known as the Black Metal Circle. Meanwhile, Burzum recordings were receiving increasing acclaim on the heavy metal underground, with their tortured mix of overheated guitars, screamed vocals and strange, ambient keyboards. In the spring of 1993, Grishnakh, along with a number of other prominent members of the Black Metal Circle, was arrested for a series of church burnings. Several months later, Grishnakh was arrested for the brutal murder of Euronymous. He was subsequently convicted in 1994, but showed no remorse for his crime, instead relishing the consequent notoriety and publicity. Sentenced to 21 years (the maximum possible under Norwegian law), Grishnakh continues to record increasingly strange and twisted material in jail. Satanism and the works of Tolkien now take a back seat to the right-wing occultism and Viking paganism that are currently his chief obsessions, with many of his lyrics now sung in Old Norse. He managed to record 1997's *Daudi Baldrs* while in prison, using a keyboard and computer.

● ALBUMS: *Burzum* (Deathlike Silence 1992)★★, *Aske* (Deathlike Silence 1993)★★★, *Hvis Lyset Tar Oss* (Misanthropy 1994)★★★, *Det Som Engang Var* (Misanthropy 1994)★★, *Filosofem* (Misanthropy 1996)★★, *Daudi Baldrs* (Misanthropy 1997)★★.

Bush

This contemporary rock band, formed in west London, England, found their initial success in the USA, where college radio was the first to pick up on tracks from their debut album, released on Interscope Records subsidiary Trauma. By the summer of 1995 that record had become a million-seller, while highly promoted UK artists such as Blur and Oasis were still struggling to achieve one tenth of those sales. This was largely attributable to Bush's musical style - generic grunge sitting somewhere between Pearl Jam and Soundgarden. However, Bush had previously spent two years toiling around small London venues, despite being managed by Dave Dorrell, the man behind MARRS' UK number 1, 'Pump Up The Volume'. The songs on *Sixteen Stone* were principally written by vocalist/guitarist Gavin Rossdale (b. 1967, Kilburn, London, England). Rossdale, a former student at Westminster school who had trials for Chelsea Football Club, had previously recorded two singles with his first band Midnight, who also included in their ranks film director David Puttnam's son Sasha. After that group was dropped, he spent six months in California in 1991 - significantly, seeing Nirvana at Los Angeles' Roxy Club during this time. The songs on *Sixteen Stone* dealt with issues as diverse as the bombing of a Covent Garden pub ('Bomb'), death ('Little Things'), religious cults ('Monkey') and sex ('Testosterone'). The rest of the band comprises Dave Parsons (b. 2 July 1962, Uxbridge, London, England; bass, ex-Transvision Vamp), Robin Goodridge (b. 1966, Crawley, Sussex, England; drums, ex-Beautiful People) and Nigel Pulsford (b. 1964, Newport, Gwent, Wales; guitar, ex-King Blank). They made the US connection when disc jockey Gary Crowley passed one of their tapes to Rob Kahane, former manager of George Michael and in the process of setting up his own Trauma Records label. An earlier agreement with the Walt Disney-owned Hollywood Records in 1993 had sundered when Kahane's relations with the label soured. After gaining airplay on Los Angeles' KROQ station in late 1994, particularly for the single 'Everything Zen', interest in the band snowballed. By 1996 this had resulted in three million sales of their debut, at which time they confirmed an intriguing choice of producer for the follow-up set - Steve Albini. Bush are a phenomenon: no UK act with such an indifferent reception in their homeland has experienced such success elsewhere. Their excellent follow-up, *Razorblade Suitcase*, entered the US album chart at number 1 at the end of 1996, and following in the wake was the UK, who finally recognized the band's existence by buying enough copies to put them in the album chart.

● ALBUMS: *Sixteen Stone* (Trauma/Interscope 1995)★★★★, *Razorblade Suitcase* (Trauma 1996)★★★★, *Deconstructed* remixes (Trauma 1997)★★★.

● VIDEOS: *Alleys And Motorways* (Universal/Interscope 1998).

BUSH, STAN

This US singer first came to prominence with the country/rock band Boulder. Bush went solo in 1983, recording a self-titled album that invited comparisons to the sophisticated pop-rock style of Billy Squier and John Parr. He linked up with the band Barrage in 1987 to pursue a more hard rock direction.

● ALBUMS: *Stan Bush* (Columbia 1983)★★★, *Stan Bush & Barrage* (Scotti Bros/Polydor 1987)★★, *Every Beat Of My Heart* (1993)★★.

BUTTHOLE SURFERS

Formerly known as the Ashtray Baby Heads, this maverick quartet from Austin, Texas, USA, made its recording debut in 1983 with a self-titled mini-album (the name Butthole Surfers comes from an early song about beach transvestites). Gibson 'Gibby' Haynes (vocals) Paul Leary Walthall aka Paul Sneef (guitar) and King Coffey (drums) were initially indebted to the punk/hardcore scene, as shown by the startling 'The Shah Sleeps In Lee Harvey's Grave', but other selections were inspired by a variety of sources. Loping melodies, screaming guitar and heavy-metal riffs abound in a catalogue as zany as it is unclassifiable. Lyrically explicit, the group has polarized opinion between those who appreciate their boisterous humour and those deeming them prurient. Having endured a succession of bass players, including Kramer from Shockabilly and Bongwater, the Buttholes secured the permanent services of Jeff Pinker, alias Tooter, alias Pinkus, in 1985. The Surfers' strongest work appears on *Locust Abortion Technician* and *Hairway To Steven*, the former memorably including 'Sweet Loaf', a thinly disguised version of Black Sabbath's 'Sweet Leaf'. On the latter set, tracks are denoted by various simple drawings, including a defecating deer, rather than song titles. In 1991 the release of *Digital Dump*, a house-music project undertaken by Haynes and Pinkus under the Jack Officers epithet, was followed closely by the Buttholes' ninth album, *piouhgd*, which showed that their ability to enrage, bewilder and excite remained as sure as ever. It was marked by a curiously reverential version of Donovan's 'Hurdy Gurdy Man'. In 1991, Pinkus also recorded the frenetic *Cheatos* as Daddy Longhead. This set was closely followed by Paul Leary's excellent solo debut, *The History Of Dogs*, and the band's shock signing to Capitol Records. The delay of *Electriclarryland* was as a result of objections received from the estate of Rodgers And Hammerstein when the band wanted to call the album *Oklahoma!*. It is difficult to be indifferent about this band, it's a simple love or loathe. Tagged as the sickest band in the world, they thrive on their own antics which include simulated sex, urinating and masturbation on stage. This tends to mask their musical ability and commercial potential which *Electriclarryland* clearly demonstrated. Haines also appeared alongside actor Johnny Depp in P, while Coffey recorded 1992's *Pick Up Heaven* as Drain on his own Trance Syndicate label.

● ALBUMS: *Butthole Surfers* (Alternative Tentacles 1983)★★★, *Live PCPPEP* (Alternative Tentacles 1984)★★★, *Psychic ... Powerless ... Another Man's Sac* (Touch And Go 1985)★★★, *Rembrandt Pussyhorse* (Touch And Go 1986)★★★, *Locust Abortion Technician* (Touch And Go 1987)★★★, *Hairway To Steven* (Touch And Go 1988)★★★, *piouhgd* (Rough Trade 1991)★★, *Independent Worm Saloon* (Capitol 1994)★★, *Electriclarryland* (Capitol 1996)★★★★, *After The Astronaut* (Capitol 1998)★★★.

Solo: Paul Leary *The History Of Dogs* (Rough Trade 1991)★★★.

● COMPILATIONS: *Double Live* (Latino Buggerveil 1989)★★★, *The Hole Truth ... And Nothing Butt!* (Trance Syndicate 1995)★★★.

● VIDEOS: *Blind Eye Sees All* (Touch And Go).

BUZZOV.EN

Buzzov.en formed from the ashes of Sewer Puppet in the early 90s. Based in North Carolina and featuring Kirk Fisher (vocals, guitar), Brian Hill (bass) and Ashley Williamson (drums), they played anywhere that would have them, until by 1991 they had raised the money for a studio recording of their first demo tape, *Buttrash*. One of the songs from that demo, 'Wound', was released as a single by a friend setting up his own label. However, the cassette also reached John Yates, founder of San Francisco label Allied Recordings. Yates brought the group into the studio to record the *Wound EP* (although it did not include the song of that name). On the back of this, and with east coast gigs where the music was largely distinguished by its savagery and volume, Buzzov.en embarked on building a cult audience. They completed their debut album in San Francisco with producer Billy Anderson. After experimenting with a second guitarist, the group made Buddy Apostolis a permanent fixture, and embarked on some 200 gigs inside a year. A show at 1993's CMJ Music Convention led to them signing to Roadrunner Records through Monte Conner, and the following year saw them back in the studio with Billy Anderson, recording their second 'studio' album in just nine days (the first had taken only three). Content to play anytime, anywhere, Buzzov.en, with their astonishing GG Allin-inspired stage displays, have yet to capture similar spontaneity and riotousness on record.

● ALBUMS: *To A Frown* (Allied Recordings 1992)★★, *Sore* (Roadrunner 1994)★★★.

● COMPILATIONS: *Music For The Proletariat* (Very Small 1993)★★, *Vinyl Retentive* (Very Small 1993)★★.

BYRON, DAVID

b. David Garrick, 29 January 1947, Epping, Essex, England, d. 28 February 1985. Byron began his musical career as vocalist with the Stalkers, an Essex-based act that, by 1969, had evolved into Uriah Heep. Although subjected to critical denigration, the group became one of the 70s' leading hard rock/heavy metal attractions, thanks in part to the singer's powerful delivery. In 1975, Byron completed a solo album, *Take No Prisoners*, while excessive alcohol consumption put his position within the line-up under increasing pressure. He was fired the following year, but hopes of an artistic rebirth with Rough Diamond proved ill-founded, and this highly touted attraction featuring Dave Clempson broke apart within a year. Bereft of a regular group, he completed *Baby Faced Killer*, but the set appeared during the height of the punk boom, and was not a commercial success. A similar fate befell the ensuing Byron Band, whose ill-focused *On The Rocks* did little to further their leader's progress. They dissolved soon after its release, after which the disconsolate vocalist attempted to sustain his career, with increasingly faltering results. He died in 1985 as a result of a heart attack.

● ALBUMS: *Take No Prisoners* (Bronze 1976)★★, *Baby Faced Killer* (Arista 1978)★, as the Byron Band: *On The Rocks* (Creole 1981)★.

BYSTANDER

This American melodic rock quartet was formed in 1981. Influenced by Loverboy and Kansas, the band comprised Andy Kiely (vocals, bass), Bucky Naughton (guitar, vocals), John E. Allison (guitar, vocals) and Jimmy Callaghan (drums). Allison and Callaghan arrived after the release of their album, replacing Mike Weaver and Stanley Steele. The self-financed *Not So Innocent* was an admirable debut and surpassed the efforts of many of the more well-established acts in the genre.

● ALBUMS: *Not So Innocent* (ABS 1987)★★★.

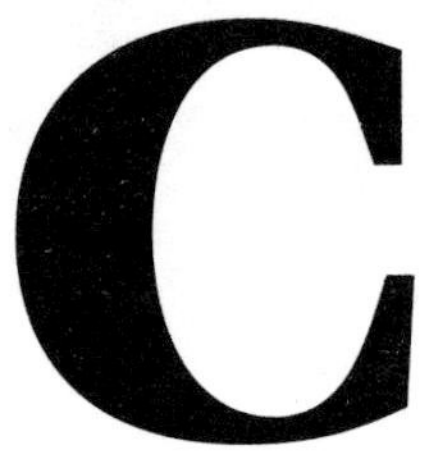

CACOPHONY

This speed metal band was formed in the USA in 1986, and was built around the nucleus of up-and-coming guitar wizards Marty Friedman and Jason Becker. Recruiting drummer Atma Anur and ex-Le Mans vocalist Peter Marrino, they debuted with *Speed Metal Symphony*, a predominantly instrumental album that fused classical, blues and hard rock styles. Friedman and Becker then went on to record individual solo albums in a similar vein, before returning to work with the band. *Go Off!*, released in 1989, saw the arrival of Jimmy O'Shea and Deen Castronovo on bass and drums, respectively. This album reinforced the band's hi-tech instrumental approach, and featured complex passages where the guitars of Friedman and Becker duelled for supremacy. The album was a commercial failure and Cacophony subsequently folded in 1990, with Becker joining Dave Lee Roth and Friedman joining Megadeth.

● ALBUMS: *Speed Metal Symphony* (Shrapnel/Roadrunner 1987)★★★, *Go Off!* (Shrapnel/Roadrunner 1989)★★★.

CADILLAC TRAMPS

From Orange County, California, USA, the Cadillac Tramps did not take too kindly to their press tag of 'bar-drunk brawly blues band', claiming that they offered a much more sophisticated sound - yet that description was close enough to reality to warrant repetition. Comprising Gabby (lead vocals), Brian Coakley (guitar, vocals), Johnny Wickersham (guitar, vocals), Warren Renfrow (bass) and Dieter (drums), they riffed their way to prominence with an acclaimed, sweaty live show that earned a solid reputation for the band on the Southern Californian club circuit. Their admirers include Eddie Vedder of Pearl Jam (who personally filmed one show). Their third album and first for Music For Nations subsidiary Bullet Proof was headed by a title track that concerned Coakley's HIV-positive friend.

● ALBUMS: *It's All Right* (Bullet Proof 1994)★★★.

CALIFORNIA, RANDY

b. Randolph Wolfe, 20 February 1951, Los Angeles, California, USA, d. 2 January 1997. California was best known for his often lustrous rock guitarwork and fine songwriting ability with the west coast band Spirit. He kept the band name alive for nearly 30 years with numerous line-ups. His solo career started in 1972 during one of Spirit's many break-ups, with the perplexing but sometimes brilliant *Captain Kopter And The Fabulous Twirlybirds*. This Jimi Hendrix-inspired outing featured versions of the Beatles' 'Day Tripper' and 'Rain', and Paul Simon's 'Mother And Child Reunion'. The accompanying band featured Ed Cassidy from Spirit and Clit McTorious (alias Noel Redding) playing bass. California went on to make several albums bearing his name, but none appealed to a market outside the loyal cult of kindred spirits. He always needed a band or a 'family' around him, even though he was very direct and opinionated in his work. California, for better or worse, will always be joined at the hip to Spirit, way beyond his tragic death by drowning in 1997, even if most of their time was spent in limbo.

● ALBUMS: *Captain Kopter And The Fabulous Twirlybirds* (Epic 1972)★★★★, *Euro-American* (Beggars Banquet 1982)★★★, *Restless* (Vertigo 1985)★★, *Shattered Dreams* (Line Records 1986)★★.

CANCER

This band emerged from Telford, Shropshire, England, and quickly established themselves as the UK's leading death metal exponents. *To The Gory End* saw the trio of John Walker (vocals, guitar), Ian Buchanan (bass) and Carl Stokes (drums) adopt a traditional death metal sound with suitably gory and offensive imagery, but the addition of American guitarist James Murphy (ex-Death/Obituary) expanded both Cancer's live sound and their approach to songwriting. The Scott Burns-produced *Death Shall Rise* showed considerable progression, but Murphy's continued residence in the USA proved impractical and he departed to form Disincarnate. Barry Savage (b. Barry White) proved to be an able replacement, adding an individual and less Americanized edge to the Cancer sound. The new maturity in evidence on *The Sins Of Mankind* brought not only overdue respect but also a major contract with East West. This made them the first death metal band to sign to a major contract (discounting single territory or distribution contracts afforded Morbid Angel and Carcass). Their first album for East West, *Black Faith*, was the second to be recorded with Simon Efemey. The band split in January 1996.

● ALBUMS: *To The Gory End* (Vinyl Solution 1990)★★★, *Death Shall Rise* (Vinyl Solution 1991)★★, *The Sins Of Mankind* (Vinyl Solution 1993)★★★★, *Black Faith* (East West 1995)★★.

CANDLEBOX

Formed in California, Candlebox consists of Kevin Martin (vocals), Peter Klett (guitar), Bardi Martin (bass) and Scott Mercado (drums), and were widely celebrated as one of the most exciting American rock bands to arrive in the mid-90s. They signed to Madonna's Maverick label and, buoyed by the media interest that accompanies the singer's every move, Candlebox soon found themselves a major success. Both 'Far Behind' and 'You' were hits in the singles chart and in 1995 sales of *Candlebox* reached three million copies in the USA. *Candlebox* was co-produced by Kelly Gray and revealed a band happy to explore territory somewhere between traditional pop-metal and Seattle-styled grunge. This was an assured debut and one that placed the band in the 'anticipated difficult second album' category. *Lucy* was, unfortunately, a major disappointment to fans and critics. Ex-Pearl Jam drummer Dave Krusen replaced Mercado shortly before the recording of a back-to-basics third album, produced by Ron Nevison.

● ALBUMS: *Candlebox* (Maverick/Warners 1994)★★★★, *Lucy* (Maverick 1995)★★, *Happy Pills* (Maverick/Warners 1998)★★★.

CANDLEMASS

This Swedish doom metal quintet formed in 1985, and originally comprised Christian Weberyd (guitar), Klas Bergwall (guitar), Mats Bjorkman (guitar), Leif Edling (bass) and Matz Ekstrom (drums). The band was based around chief songwriter Edling, who had previously played (alongside Weberyd) in Nemesis. Following the release of *Epicus Doomicus Metallicus*, Jan Lindh, Lars Johansson and Messiah Marcolin joined on drums, guitar and vocals respectively. During live performances, Marcolin dressed in a monk's habit, and his deep, bellowing tones added a touch of mystique to the band's style, which combined elements of Black Sabbath, Black Widow and Mercyful Fate. *Nightfall*, their most accomplished work, fused crushing rhythms with delicate, neo-classical interludes to startling effect. *Tales Of Creation* saw the band afforded a larger recording budget with new label Music For Nations. However, their approach had become rather formularized by this stage, and although the album was technically superior to earlier efforts, the songs left a distinct feeling of *déjà vu*. A live album followed in an attempt to recapture lost ground. It soon became apparent that the band were trapped in a creative cul-de-sac, with their initial followers continuing to move on to other things. Marcolin left in 1991, to be replaced by Tomas Vikström (ex-Talk Of The Town). After a further album the band folded, with Edling going on to form Abstrakt Algebra. He reformed Candlemass to record 1998's *Dactylis Glomerata*.

● ALBUMS: *Epicus Doomicus Metallicus* (Black Dragon 1986)★★, *Nightfall* (Metal Blade 1987)★★★★, *Ancient Dreams* (Active 1988)★★★, *Tales Of Creation* (Music For Nations 1989)★★, *Live* (Music For Nations 1990)★★, *Chapter VI* (Music For Nations 1992)★★, *Dactylis Glomerata* (Music For Nations 1998)★★★.

● COMPILATIONS: *As It Is, As It Was* (Music For Nations 1994)★★★.

CANIS MAJOR

Formed in the UK in 1979 but heavily influenced by American pomp rock bands such as Journey and Styx, Canis Major comprised Jacqui Bodimead (vocals), Tony Bodimead (guitar), Mick Groves (guitar), John Pepe (keyboards), Simon Cooper (bass) and Gary Wise (drums). The group released their debut album for JEM Records in 1980. *Butterfly Queen* combined strong songwriting from the Bodimead brother-sister team with fluent musicianship. However, poor promotion and distribution prevented it from making the impact that it deserved. Bodimead subsequently found commercial success as a member of Girlschool.

● ALBUMS: *Butterfly Queen* (JEM 1980)★★★.

CANNATA

Jeff Cannata first came to prominence under the name Arc Angel in 1983. Following five years of producing, arranging and guesting on a variety of projects, he finally took enough time out in 1988 to record *Images Of Forever*. Being responsible for the vocals, guitar, keyboards, bass and drums, the album served as testimony to Cannata's remarkable musical ability. The material invited comparisons with the best works of Boston, Starcastle and Angel, as did a subsequent set released five years later.

● ALBUMS: *Images Of Forever* (Columbia 1988)★★★, *Watching The World* (1993)★★.

CANNIBAL CORPSE

This controversial death metal act was formed in Buffalo, New York, USA, by Chris Barnes (vocals), guitarists Bob Rusay and Jack Owen, Alex Webster (bass) and Paul Mazurkiewicz (drums). The band adopted an almost cartoon-like approach to their material, which stood out even from the extreme grotesqueries of the death scene, and Cannibal Corpse have thrived on the controversy created by offensive song titles such as 'Meat Hook Sodomy', 'Necropedophile' and the infamous 'Entrails Ripped From A Virgin's Cunt'. The band's cover art has not been immune to criticism either, with some retailers refusing to stock both *Butchered At Birth* and *Tomb Of The Mutilated* until the gruesome cover paintings by Vincent Locke (of Dead World Comics) were replaced. Musically, the band have made steady progress from their *Eaten Back To Life* debut, refining a death metal assault to match the song titles, although Rob Barrett (ex-Malevolent Creation) replaced Rusay on *The Bleeding*. The band were also exposed to a major audience with their cameo appearance in the *Ace Ventura: Pet Detective* movie, where they were seen performing 'Hammer Smashed Face'. Barnes was allegedly sacked from the band in 1995, to be replaced on vocals by ex-Monstrosity singer George 'Corpsegrinder' Fisher. The first evidence of his contribution to the band came on 1996's *Vile*, which included familiar lyrical subject matter such as 'Devoured By Vermin' and 'Orgasm Through Torture'.

● ALBUMS: *Eaten Back To Life* (Metal Blade 1990)★★, *Butchered At Birth* (Metal Blade 1991)★★★★, *Tomb Of The Mutilated* (Metal Blade 1992)★★★, *Hammer Smashed Face* mini-album (Metal Blade 1993)★★★★, *The Bleeding* (Metal Blade 1994)★★, *Vile* (Metal Blade 1996)★★★, *Gallery Of Suicide* (Metal Blade 1998)★★★.

CAPTAIN BEYOND

Based in Los Angeles, this Anglo-American 'supergroup' was formed in 1972 around Rod Evans (b. 19 January 1947, Edinburgh, Scotland; vocals, ex-Deep Purple), Bobby Caldwell (drums, ex-Johnny Winter) and two former members of Iron Butterfly, Larry 'Rhino' Rheinhart (b. 7 July 1948, Florida, USA; guitar) and Lee Dorman (b. 19 September 1945, St. Louis, Missouri, USA; bass). Although *Captain Beyond* established the unit's hard-rock style, this initial line-up proved incompatible and Caldwell was replaced by Marty Rodriguez for *Sufficiently Breathless*. The departure of Evans precipitated a lengthy period of inactivity, but in 1976 the remaining trio was joined by Willy Daffern (vocals), Reese Wynans (keyboards, ex-Stevie Ray Vaughan) and Guille Garcia (percussion). This final version broke up following the release of *Dawn Explosion*.

● ALBUMS: *Captain Beyond* (Capricorn 1972)★★, *Sufficiently Breathless* (Capricorn 1973)★★★, *Dawn Explosion* (Capricorn 1977)★★.

CARCASS

This hardcore/death metal group from Liverpool, England, was formed in 1987. The band, all vegetarians, comprised Jeff Walker (vocals, bass, ex-Electro Hippies), Bill Steer (vocals, guitar, ex-Napalm Death) and Ken Owen (drums). The line-up was later enlarged with the addition of a second guitarist, Michael Amott (ex-Carnage). Their approach was characterized by morbid death-grunts over a barrage of chaotic, bass-dominated music. Carcass's lyrical content primarily concerns itself with mutilation, vomiting, putrefaction, intestinal rupturing and steaming entrails - all described in strict medical and anatomical terminology: 'Intenacious, intersecting/Reaving fats from corporal griskin . . . Skeletal groats triturated, desinently exsiccated'. Carcass signed to Columbia Records following *Heartwork*, which dramatically reduced previous 'gore' content, incorporating a more modern image complete with H.R. Giger artwork. They also introduced ex-Devoid guitarist Carlo Regadas (the third such addition since 1990), and toured the UK with Body Count, then the USA with Pitch Shifter. For a band whose appeal initially seemed destined to remain of cult interest, Carcass appeared to be on the threshold of commercial success until Steer departed in late 1995. For a band that were by nature uncompromising and disturbing, but impossible to ignore, Carcass had become too commercial for Steer. His departure signalled the end for the others, Walker and Owen going on to form Black Star.

● ALBUMS: *Reek Of Putrefaction* (Earache 1988)★★★, *Symphonies Of Sickness* (Earache 1989)★★, *Necrotism: Descanting The Insalubrious* (Earache 1991)★★, *Heartwork* (Earache 1993)★★★, *Swansong* (Earrache 1996)★★★.

● COMPILATIONS: *Wake Up And Smell the Carcass* (Earache 1996)★★★.

CARNIVORE

This American heavy metal band was formed by ex-Fallout duo Louie Batteaux (alias Lord Petrus T; drums) and Peter Steele (vocals, bass) in New York in 1983. With the addition of guitarist Keith Alexander, they attracted media interest by basing their image on a *Mad Max*-style post-apocalyptic scenario. Dressed in animal skins, they achieved a degree of notoriety with their racially naïve lyrics. Their songs relied on basic thrash metal with little originality. Marc Piovanetti replaced Alexander on 1987's *Retaliation*, which resulted in a marked improvement in the band's guitar sound. However, this was not sufficient to enable them realistically to compete with first-division acts such as Slayer, Testament or Anthrax. Piovanetti left in 1988, to join Crumbsuckers, while Steele formed Type O Negative.

● ALBUMS: *Carnivore* (Roadrunner 1986)★★, *Retaliation* (Roadrunner 1987)★★★.

CATHEDRAL

This excellent UK doom/grind band was formed by vocalist Lee Dorrian after his departure from Napalm Death, with his bassist friend Mark Griffiths, former Acid Reign guitarists Gaz Jennings and Adam Lehan, and drummer Ben Mockrie. This line-up was in place for the release of a four-track demo, *In Memorium*. Interestingly, this included a cover version of Pentagram's 'All Your Sins' - a band from which Cathedral would later draw members. Dorrian's vocals changed remarkably from his Napalm days to suit a style that drew heavily from early Black Sabbath and late 60s/early 70s underground rock. *Forest Of Equilibrium* was an impressive debut, with ex-Penance/Dream Death drummer Mike Smail standing in for the departed Mockrie. A permanent replacement was then found in Mark Ramsey Wharton (ex-Acid Reign) in time for the *Soul Sacrifice EP*, as Cathedral's live ability was amply demonstrated on the 'Gods Of Grind' UK tour with Carcass, Entombed and Confessor, and dates with Trouble and the Obsessed. A US tour with Brutal Truth, Napalm Death and Carcass followed, and although Griffiths departed, Cathedral signed a US contract with Columbia Records. *The Ethereal Mirror*, produced by Trouble, Danzig and Mick Jagger collaborator Dave Bianco, deservedly received a wealth of critical acclaim, and the band toured the UK with Sleep and Penance in tow before recording the *Statik Majik EP* with Cronos guitarist Mike Hickey guesting on bass. This included the 23-minute epic 'The Voyage Of The Homeless Sapien'. However, Lehan and Wharton left after a US tour with Mercyful Fate, and a new line-up with former Pentagram members Victor Griffin (drums) and Joe Hasselvander (guitar) was assembled for a Black Sabbath support tour. However, personality clashes led to Hasselvander's premature departure. Cathedral re-emerged as a quartet in late 1994 with Dorrian and Jennings joined by Scott Carlson (ex-Repulsion; bass) and Dave Hornyak (drums). *The Carnival Bizarre* was premiered on 8 August 1995 at a location appropriate to its title - the Clink, an ancient dungeon on the banks of the River Thames. It was produced by Kit Woolven (Thin Lizzy/UFO) at Parkgate Studios in Hastings, Sussex, and saw the core duo of Dorrian and Jennings joined by Leo Smee (bass) and Brian Dixon (drums).

● ALBUMS: *Forest Of Equilibrium* (Earache 1991)★★, *The Ethereal Mirror* (Earache 1993)★★★★, *The Carnival Bizarre* (Earache 1995)★★★, *Hopkins (The Witchfinder General)* (Earache 1996)★★★, *Supernatural Birth Machine* (Earache 1996)★★★.

Cats In Boots

This short-lived Japanese-American group was formed when guitarist Takashi 'Jam' Ohashi and bassist Yasuhiro 'Butch' Hatae, of the successful Tokyo-based band Seiki Matsu, recruited vocalist Joel Ellis, a native of Cleveland, Ohio, and drummer Randy Meers, originally from Houston, Texas, from the remains of Los Angeles-based Merry Hoax. The American members relocated to Tokyo to record demos, and these tapes were released as a mini-album that shot to number 1 on the Japanese indie chart. The resultant interest saw the quartet sign to EMI Records. The Mark Opitz-produced *Kicked And Klawed* was a raucous and thoroughly enjoyable debut, with the band's raw, trashy hard rock drawing comparisons with Mötley Crüe, Aerosmith and Vain, and was a huge success in Japan, reaching number 3. However, despite great reviews and considerable MTV airplay, album sales were only moderate elsewhere, and with the almost simultaneous loss of both Ellis and their recording contract, Cats In Boots disintegrated.

● ALBUMS: *Demonstration - East Meets West* mini-album (Bronze 1988)★★, *Kicked And Klawed* (EMI 1989)★★★★.

Celtic Frost

Formed in Switzerland in 1984 from the ashes of the thrash metal-inspired Hellhammer, Celtic Frost's focal point was Thomas Gabriel Warrior (b. Thomas Fischer, guitar, vocals). Together with Martin Eric Ain (bass) and Stephen Priestly (drums), the group's 1984 debut was a thrash metal landmark, with guttural vocals splintering the grim music. Ain was replaced by bassist Dominic Steiner for *To Mega Therion*, while Reed St. Mark was drummer for *Emperor's Return*. Their next album, *Into The Pandemonium*, was Celtic Frost's legacy to the metal world, a major work that has been loosely described as '*avant garde* thrash'. It saw the return of Ain as well as the introduction of second guitarist Ron Marks. *Cold Lake* was much more mainstream and featured the return of Priestly (drums), alongside Curt Victor Bryant (bass) and Oliver Amberg (guitar). Following a glam rock bent, it proved too much of a departure from their natural sound to be a success, and fans deserted them. The band's popularity enjoyed a slight resurgence after the much improved *Vanity/Nemesis*. In the early 90s St. Mark rejoined the band after a spell with Mindfunk, with the promise of new material in the tradition of their early efforts. This never transpired and the band folded, remaining fondly remembered for their pioneering pre-Death Metal influence. A tribute album was issued in 1996. Warrior returned with a new outfit, Appolyon Sun in 1998.

● ALBUMS: *Morbid Tales* (Noise 1984)★★★, *To Mega Therion* (Noise 1985)★★, *Emperor's Return* (Noise 1986)★★★★, *Into The Pandemonium* (Noise 1987)★★★, *Cold Lake* (Noise 1988)★★, *Vanity/Nemesis* (Noise 1990)★★★.

● COMPILATIONS: *The Celtic Frost Story* (EMI 1990)★★★, *Parched With Thirst Am I, And Dying (1984-1992)* (Noise 1992)★★★, various artists tribute album *In Memory Of Celtic* (Dwell 1996)★★★.

● VIDEOS: *Live At Hammersmith Odeon* (Fotodisk Video/Channel 5 1990).

Cement

US band Cement were formed by ex-Faith No More vocalist Chuck Mosley after one too many physical and verbal confrontations with his former employers (apparently, taking to the stage in pyjamas at the Town & Country club on their second UK tour in May 1988 was the last straw). Afterwards, he served time as the replacement for HR in Bad Brains, but this was another ill-starred assignation. He then worked as frontman for Haircuts That Kill before emerging with Cement in 1993. This more permanent outfit was formed in Los Angeles with Sean Maytum (ex-Beer Nuts; guitar), Senon Williams (bass) and Doug Puffy (ex-Pygmy Love Circus; drums). They gigged heavily on the west coast before producing their debut. Critics suggested 'Old Days' from the set may have concerned Faith No More, but this did not detract from a decent hard rock album.

● ALBUMS: *Cement* (Dutch East India 1993)★★★.

CEMETARY

Formed in Sweden in 1989, after two well-received demos (*Incarnation Of Morbidity* and *Articulus Mortis*) Cemetary secured a record contract in 1992. The resultant album, *An Evil Shade Of Grey*, was a competent, but unremarkable, exercise in death metal. *Godless Beauty* saw Cemetary develop beyond the stylistic restraints of the genre, and incorporate new, fresher elements into their sound. Dominant among these were gothic rock influences and sampled dialogue from horror films. The result was a powerful and melodramatic musical exploration of depression and suicide. *Black Vanity* was a continuation of this death metal/gothic rock crossbreed, and featured the line-up of Mathias Lodmalm (vocals, guitar), Anders Iwers (guitar), Thomas Josefesson (bass) and Markus Nordberg (drums).

● ALBUMS: *An Evil Shade Of Grey* (Black Mark 1992)★★, *Godless Beauty* (Black Mark 1993)★★★, *Black Vanity* (Black Mark 1994)★★★, *Sundown* (Black Mark 1996)★★, *Last Confession* (Black Mark 1997)★★★.

CENTAURUS

This US, blues-based rock quartet was formed in Florida, USA, in 1977 by guitar virtuoso Nick Paine. Enlisting the services of Nick Costello (bass), Louis Merlino (vocals) and Joey Belfiore (drums), they took their musical lead primarily from Led Zeppelin and Aerosmith. Paine's guitarwork, certainly, was structured on the style made famous by Jimmy Page. Their sole release was noticeably derivative, but the excellent production and rawness of the band's delivery made it more than worthwhile. They disbanded soon after the album was released, with Costello going on to join Toronto.

● ALBUMS : *Centaurus* (Azra 1978)★★★.

CHAIN REACTION

Not the minor US act from whom Aerosmith drew membership, this Canadian hard rock/techno-pop quartet was formed in 1981 and consisted of Warren Barvour (guitar), Phil Naro (vocals), Ray Lessard (bass) and John Livingston (drums). Influenced by Van Halen, REO Speedwagon and Foreigner, they recorded *X Rated Dream*, a collection of pop-rock anthems that was lifted only by some explosive guitar bursts from Barvour. Naro left to work with Talas in 1983 and the band subsequently disintegrated.

● ALBUMS: *X Rated Dream* (Attic 1982)★★.

CHALLENGER

French hard rock band Challenger formed in 1980 with a line-up comprising Denis Drieu (vocals), Remy Devillard (guitar), Serge Hendrix (guitar; formerly a member of French rock band the Hurricanes), Pierrot Roussel (bass) and Jean-Pierre Pollet (drums). The following year they signed to RCA Records and recorded *First Round*. A formidable record that blended elements of Molly Hatchet and ZZ Top-derived 'southern boogie', it brought them immediate acclaim in mainland European rock circles. However, its failure to attract media attention in either the UK or USA disappointed RCA, who did not renew their contract, and Challenger faded from view.

● ALBUMS: *First Round* (RCA 1981)★★★.

CHAMPION

When David Byron left Rough Diamond in 1977, the remaining band members recruited US vocalist Garry Bell as replacement and changed their name to Champion. With former Humble Pie guitarist Dave Clempson (b. 5 September 1949, Tamworth, Staffordshire, England), ex-Wings drummer Geoff Britton, plus Damon Butcher (keyboards) and Willy Bath (bass) completing the line-up, Champion's music never lived up to the promise suggested by their impressive pedigree. Picked up by Epic Records, they released a self-titled album in 1978 of blues-based rock. Failing to attract media attention, they disbanded shortly after the record was released.

● ALBUMS: *Champion* (Epic 1978)★★.

CHANGE OF SEASONS

This Dutch rock band was founded in 1992, and recorded a demo tape a year later that received the 'demo of the month' award in one of Holland's metal magazines. Other European media were similarly impressed. Signing to Rock The Nation Records shortly thereafter, they re-recorded the songs before travelling to South River, New Jersey, to mix the finished album at Trax East Studios. *Cold Sweat* tapped the alternative sounds of Seattle and the Pearl Jam/Soundgarden axis as its main inspiration, also combining progressive elements drawn from a wider musical vocabulary (press comparisons included Dream Theater).

● ALBUMS: *Cold Sweat* (RTN 1994)★★★.

CHANNEL THREE

This USA-based hardcore band comprised Mike Magrann (vocals, guitar), Kimm Gardner (guitar), Larry Kelly (bass) and Mike Burton (the most permanent of their first four drummers). Residents of the suburban community of Cerritos in south Los Angeles, they originally formed in 1980. Their first release was an EP on Californian label Posh Boy in 1981. One track from this, 'Manzanar', was played heavily by UK disc jockey John Peel, which resulted in Posh Boy's Robbie Fields licensing a three-track EP to No Future Records. This was headed by the title track 'I've Got A Gun'. 'Manzanar' was again present, and concerned Magrann's mother (he is partially of Japanese origin) being sent to a work camp in World War II. In 1982, Jack DeBaun become their new drummer, and *Fear Of Life* was retitled *I've Got A Gun* in the UK with some differences in the track-listing. *After The Lights Go Out* was a superior and more consistent effort, although it failed to recapture the spark of interest that accompanied their first UK single. Ex-Stepmother Jay Lansford strengthened Magrann's songwriting when he joined the band in 1984.

Their 1985 collection for Enigma Records (with Dusty Watson on drums) revealed that the band had comfortably navigated the transition to a more straightforward rock format, without losing that early spark. However, it was to be their last recording. Magrann's summation of their brief existence ran thus: 'Channel 3 was a band formed around friendships, if we weren't playing guitars together we'd probably be bowling or robbing Laundromats together.'

● ALBUMS: *Fear Of Life* (US) *I've Got A Gun* (UK) (Posh Boy/No Future 1982)★★, *After The Lights Go Out* (Posh Boy 1983)★★★, *Last Time I Drank ...* (Enigma 1985)★★★.

CHARIOT

Formed in north London, England, in 1983, Chariot comprised Pete Franklin (vocals, guitar), Scott Biaggi (guitar), John Smith (bass) and Jeff Braithwaite (drums). Recording in a hybrid style that utilized elements of the speed metal sound of bands such as Venom and Slayer, as well as rhythmic touches redolent of the New Wave Of British Heavy Metal groups, they made their debut in 1984 with *The Warrior*. Released on the independent Shades Records label, this project was marred by poor production but otherwise included several promising songs. Gradually extending their appeal beyond the capital, they returned to the studio in 1986 for *Burning Ambitions*. Despite further strong reviews (especially for their live work), it was not enough to help them to cross over into the mainstream and they disbanded shortly afterwards.

● ALBUMS: *The Warrior* (Shades 1984)★★, *Burning Ambitions* (Shades 1986)★★★.

CHARON

Comprising Carsten Sprigode (vocals), Holger Wickens (guitar), Michael Cars (guitar), Eberhard Feldttahn (bass) and Andreas Feldham (drums), German hard rock group Charon formed in Hamburg in 1982. The intuitive guitar interplay between Wickens and Cars dominated their self-titled debut album for Heavy Metal Records, released in 1984. It was followed two years later by the more forceful and better produced *Made In Aluminium* - an obvious attempt to broaden their appeal that failed to produce the desired result. They broke up shortly after its release.

● ALBUMS: *Charon* (Heavy Metal 1984)★★, *Made In Aluminium* (Heavy Metal 1986)★★★.

CHASTAIN, DAVID T.

This highly productive, new-age guitar virtuoso emerged from Cincinnati, USA. As well as releasing solo albums under his own name, he recorded with CJSS and Chastain, to provide outlets for the vast amount of material that he composes. After leaving Spike in 1984 with bassist Mike Skimmerhorn, the duo formed the two semi-permanent outfits CJSS and Chastain, with the latter being a vehicle for the faster, louder and heavier material. With the help of ex-Rude Girl vocalist Leather Leone and drummer Fred Coury, *Mystery Of Illusion* was recorded under the Chastain moniker in 1985. The predominantly up-tempo approach, with raunchy vocals and fluid guitarwork, was well received by the critics, and consequently Chastain became David's major concern. A series of albums followed in quick succession, each one an identikit version of the debut. Eight high-speed rockers and two ballads represented the typical formula. Ken Mary (ex-Alice Cooper) took over the drumstool in 1986 as Chastain's work-rate reached overload. *Instrumental Variations* and *Within The Heat* indicated a move towards a jazz-rock style. *For Those Who Dare* saw Chastain, as a band, back in the studio again, but it rehashed the same formularized approach as before. There is no doubt that David Chastain has sacrificed much of his original credibility in repeatedly releasing average material, though at least his 90s works, *Elegant Seduction*, *Next Planet Please* and the excellent *Acoustic Visions*, have offered some technical respite and variation. *Next Planet Please*, again recorded with regular bass collaborator David Harbour, also saw him utilize a Roland GR-1 guitar synthesizer for the first time. Kate French was the featured vocalist on Chastain's most recent collections, *Sick Society* and *In Dementia*.

● ALBUMS: As David T. Chastain: *The 7th Of Never* (Black Dragon 1987)★★★★, *Instrumental Variations* (Roadrunner 1987)★★★, *Elegant Seduction* (Leviathan 1991)★★★, *Movements Thru Time* (Leviathan 1992)★★★, *Next Planet Please* (Leviathan 1994)★★★, *Acoustic Visions* (Leviathan 1998)★★★. As Chastain: *Mystery Of Illusion* (Shrapnel 1985)★★, *Ruler Of The Wasteland* (Shrapnel 1986)★★, *The Voice Of The Cult* (Roadrunner 1988)★★★, *Within The Heat* (Roadrunner 1989)★★, *For Those Who Dare* (Roadrunner 1990)★★, *Sick Society* (Leviathan 1995)★★★, *In Dementia* (Leviathan 1997)★★★.

Chateaux

A UK hard rock trio of Jrys Mason (vocals, bass), Tim Broughton (guitar) and Chris Dodson (drums), Chateaux recorded three albums for Ebony Records in the mid-80s to critical apathy. There was little wrong with any of them, but the group lacked the songwriting presence to elevate them above the club circuit. *Highly Strung* was their best effort, and featured improved studio technique as well as more polished performances - but Mason's vocals still lacked depth. When he left the band at the end of 1986 Chateaux's career ground to a complete halt.

● ALBUMS: *Chained And Desperate* (Ebony 1983)★★★, *Fire Power* (Ebony 1984)★★, *Highly Strung* (Ebony 1985)★★★.

Cheap 'N' Nasty

This melodic UK rock 'n' roll quartet was formed in 1990 by former Hanoi Rocks guitarist Nasty Suicide (b. Jan Stenfors). Recruiting Alvin Gibbs (bass, ex-UK Subs), Timo Caltio (guitar) and Les Riggs (drums), they signed to China Records the following year. Debuting with *Beautiful Disaster*, the band lacked image and direction, and Suicide seemed uncomfortable in his dual role of guitarist and vocalist. Specializing in mid-paced rockers that relied heavily on vocal harmonies to carry the melody lines, the most distinctive cut was undoubtedly the album's title track. Suicide later returned to a neo-Hanoi Rocks berth in Demolition 23, a new band formed with Sam Yaffa and Michael Monroe.

● ALBUMS: *Beautiful Disaster* (China 1991)★★★.

Cheap Trick

One of rock's most entertaining attractions, Cheap Trick formed in Chicago, Illinois, USA, in 1973. Rick Nielsen (b. 22 December 1946, Rockford, Illinois, USA; guitar, vocals) and Tom Petersson (b. Tom Peterson, 9 May 1950, Rockford, Illinois, USA; bass, vocals) began their careers in various high school bands, before securing a recording contract as members of Fuse. This short-lived outfit folded on completing a debut album, and the duo formed a new group with Thom Mooney and Robert 'Stewkey' Antoni from the recently disbanded Nazz. Mooney was subsequently replaced by drummer Brad Carlson (aka Bun E. Carlos, b. 12 June 1951, Rockford, Illinois, USA), and with the departure of 'Stewkey', the initial Cheap Trick line-up was completed by vocalist Randy 'Xeno' Hogan. He, in turn, was replaced by Robin Zander (b. 23 January 1952, Loves Park, Illinois, USA; guitar, vocals), a former colleague of Carlson's in the short-lived Toons. Relocated to America's Midwest, the quartet embarked on the gruelling bar band circuit before a series of demo tapes secured a recording contract. Although *Cheap Trick* is generally regarded as a disappointment, it introduced the group's inventive flair and striking visual image. The heart-throb good looks of Zander and Petersson clashed with Carlos's seedy garb, while Nielsen's odd-ball costume - baseball cap, bow-tie and monogrammed sweater - compounded this unlikely contrast. Having spent a frenetic period supporting Queen, Journey and Kiss, Cheap Trick completed a second collection within months of their debut. *In Color* offered a smoother sound in which a grasp of melody was allowed to flourish, and established the group's ability to satisfy visceral and cerebral demands. It contained several engaging performances, including 'I Want You To Want Me', 'Hello There' and 'Clock Strikes Ten', each of which became in-concert favourites. *Heaven Tonight* consolidated the group's unique approach, while 'Surrender' offered the consummate Cheap Trick performance, blending the British pop of the Move with the urgent riffing of the best of America's hard rock. *At Budokan* followed a highly successful tour of Japan, and this explosive live set became the quartet's first platinum disc, confirming them as a headline act in their own right. However, *Dream Police* added little to the sound extolled on the previous two studio releases, and, moreover, the title song was originally recorded for the group's debut album. Producer George Martin did little to deflect this sterility on *All Shook Up*, while *Found All The Parts*, a mini-album culled from out-takes, suggested internal problems. A disaffected Petersson left the group in 1982, but although Pete Comita initially took his place, the latter quickly made way for Jon Brant (ex-Ruffians). Neither *One On One*, nor the Todd Rundgren-produced *Next Position Please*, halted Cheap Trick's commercial slide, but *Standing On The Edge* offered hopes of a renaissance. A 1986 recording, 'Mighty Wings', was used on the soundtrack of the successful *Top Gun* movie, while the return of Petersson the same year re-established the group's most successful line-up. *Lap Of Luxury* achieved multi-platinum status when an attendant single, 'The Flame', topped the US chart in 1988, confirming Cheap Trick's dramatic resurrection as a major US act. *Busted* failed to scale similar heights, and their one album for Warner Brothers Records, *Woke Up With A Monster*, was completely overshadowed by the release of a sequel to the *Budokan* album the same year. The band's standing remained high among the new wave of American alternative rockers, however, and they played several dates on the 1996 Lollapalooza tour before signing with the independent label Red Ant. Their second self-titled album followed and marked a return to the thundering power-pop of *In Color* and *Heaven Tonight*. The band's stock is currently high following the release of 1996's 4-CD box set and the complete Budokan concert in 1998.

● ALBUMS: *Cheap Trick* (Epic 1977)★★★, *In Color* (Epic 1977)★★★, *Heaven Tonight* (Epic 1978)★★★★, *At Budokan* (Epic 1979)★★★★, *Dream Police* (Epic 1979)★★★, *Found All The Parts* mini-album (Epic 1980)★★, *All Shook Up* (Epic 1980)★★, *One On One* (Epic 1982)★★, *Next Position Please* (Epic 1983)★★, *Standing On The Edge* (Epic 1985)★★★, *The Doctor* (Epic 1986)★★, *Lap Of Luxury* (Epic 1988)★★★, *Busted* (Epic 1990)★★★, *Woke Up With A Monster* (Warners 1994)★★, *Budokan II* 1978 recording (Epic/Sony 1994)★★, *Cheap Trick* (Red Ant 1997)★★★, *Cheap Trick At Budokan: The Complete Concert* (Columbia/Legacy 1998)★★★★.

● COMPILATIONS: *The Collection* (Castle 1991)★★★★, *Greatest Hits* (Epic 1992)★★★, *Sex, America, Cheap Trick* 4-CD box set (Epic 1996)★★★★.

● VIDEOS: *Every Trick In The Book* (CMV Enterprises 1990).

CHEETAH

Having played in numerous bands since the late 70s, London-born sisters Lyndsay and Chrissie Hammond went to work as music researchers before signing up with the Albert Productions Company in their adopted homeland of Australia. Under the wing of Vanda And Young they began to work on original material with session musicians who had previously backed Maggie Bell in Midnight Flyer. The resulting 1982 album, *Rock N' Roll Women*, was largely ignored for its music content as press attention focused on the fact that they were, indeed, 'Rock N' Roll Women'. Their fate as musicians sealed, not least by their own choice of title, and unable to shake off the public perception of them, the band splintered. Lyndsay later formed Rockhouse but their album remained unreleased.

● ALBUMS: *Rock N' Roll Women* (Epic 1982)★★.

CHILD, DESMOND, AND ROUGE

This commercially minded and chart-orientated US soft rock group was formed in 1975 by keyboardist Desmond Child, backed by an array of musicians. With college friends Maria Vidal, Myriam Naomi Vaille and Diana Grasselli completing the line-up as vocalists, they attracted the interest of Kiss guitarist Paul Stanley. Signing to Capitol Records, their debut album, released in 1979, was a potpourri of styles, including elements of pop, rock, funk, blues and soul. The follow-up, *Runners In The Night*, adopted a more hard rock stance, but also met with indifference. The band became redundant as Child decided to concentrate on writing and production, rather than playing. He has composed for Cher, Michael Bolton, Bon Jovi, Alice Cooper, Kiss and Jimmy Barnes, among others. 'You Give Love A Bad Name' and 'Livin' On A Prayer', co-written with Bon Jovi, and the Kiss million-seller, 'I Was Made For Loving You', have been his greatest successes to date. Child made a return to recording in 1991 for Elektra Records, which, despite the competent performance, again failed to set the charts alight.

● ALBUMS: *Desmond Child And Rouge* (Capitol 1979)★★, *Runners In The Night* (Capitol 1980)★★★. As Desmond Child: *Discipline* (Elektra 1991)★★★.

CHINA

This melodic rock band was formed in Switzerland during 1987 by guitarists Freddy Laurence and Claudio Matteo. Recruiting Math Shiverow (lead vocals), Marc Lynn (bass) and John Dommen (drums), they signed with Phonogram the following year. Influenced by Thin Lizzy, Europe and Scorpions, their self-titled debut appeared in 1988 to a positive media response. It was characterized by Shiverow's high-pitched but note-perfect vocals and the dual guitar attack of Matteo and Laurence. *Sign In The Sky* saw ex-Krokus guitarist Patrick Mason take over on vocals, and Brian Kofmehl replace Lynn on bass. It was a more mature album in several respects, with the songwriting displaying greater depth and a full, crisp production, courtesy of Stephan Galfas. A live mini-album followed, but China failed to receive the recognition that their talents deserved.

● ALBUMS: *China* (Vertigo 1988)★★★, *Sign In The Sky* (Vertigo 1989)★★★★, *Live* mini-album (Vertigo 1990)★★.

China Sky

This group was formed in Florida, USA, in 1987 by ex-Danny Joe Brown and Molly Hatchet guitarist John Ingram. With the addition of vocalist Ron Perry and bassist Richard Smith, they specialized in rough-edged AOR with a southern influence. They recorded a self-titled debut in 1988, which attracted attention due to the fact that 'The Last Romantic Warrior' was reminiscent of Derek And The Dominos' 'Layla'. The band split up soon afterwards.

● ALBUMS: *China Sky* (Parc 1988)★★.

Chinatown

This UK band started life as a glam-rock outfit known as Chinastreet and comprised vocalist Steve Prangell, guitarists Pat Shayler and Danny Gwylym, John Barr (bass) and Steve Hopgood (drums). In 1981 they changed their name to Chinatown and switched to a hard rock style similar to Thin Lizzy and UFO. Their sound was characterized by Prangell's stratospheric vocals and the dual guitar interplay of Shayler and Gwylym. After one album, recorded live, the band split up with only drummer Steve Hopgood resurfacing later. He went on to play with Persian Risk and Paul Di'Anno's Battlezone.

● ALBUMS: *Play It To The Death* (Airship 1981)★★★.

Chocolate Starfish

Led by singer Adam Thompson, Chocolate Starfish are a five-piece hard rock group formed in Melbourne, Australia, in the early 90s. The group has earned an impressive domestic reputation and, increasingly, an international name for their dynamic, theatrical live shows - an obvious critical comparison being Queen. Reportedly having played over 450 times in one 18-month period, the group entered the studio to record their self-titled debut for Virgin Records in 1994. This became a huge success, with the group's boisterous songwriting winning over a huge proportion of the Australian record-buying public and earning platinum status in the process. The follow-up collection was promoted with the release of 'Accidentally Cool'. By entering the ARIA charts at number 4, it ensured *Box* a healthy reception. The album was released in Europe in 1997, at which time the group spent six months based in Paris.

● ALBUMS: *Chocolate Starfish* (Virgin/EMI 1994)★★★, *Box* (Virgin/EMI 1996)★★★.

Chrome Molly

This hard rock/thrash quartet was formed in Leicester, England, during 1984, by vocalist Steve Hawkins and guitarist John Antcliffe. With the addition of Nick Wastell (bass) and Chris Green (drums), they recorded their debut, *You Can't Have It All*, the following year. This was a competent collection of mid-paced rockers. Mark Godfrey replaced Green on drums and Tim Read took over from Antcliffe on lead guitar for the recording of their third album, *Angst*. This collection was afforded a bigger budget, as the band had been picked up by the IRS label. It included an excellent cover version of Squeeze's 'Take Me I'm Yours', but the remainder was much as before. Joined by second guitarist Andrew Barrott (ex-Baby Tuckoo), they secured the support slot on Alice Cooper's 1988 UK tour, including a date at Wembley Arena. Their live reputation was indeed a formidable one, embossed by Hawkins' fetish for placing a cordless microphone down his cycling shorts. However, this did little to stimulate album sales, and Chrome Molly were hastily dropped by their label. Far from disheartened, they began writing new material and eventually secured a contract with Music For Nations. *Slaphead* appeared in 1990, to yet another flat response from the music media, despite an evident increase in quality.

● ALBUMS: *You Can't Have It All* (Powerstation 1985)★★★, *Stick It Out* (Powerstation 1987)★★, *Angst* (I.R.S. 1988)★★★, *Slaphead* (Music For Nations 1990)★★.

Cianide

This death metal band was formed in Chicago, Illinois, USA, by Mike Perun (bass, vocals), Scott Carroll (guitar) and Jeff Kabella (drums). Cianide are a power trio who, like so many others from their genre, made their initial impression with their demo cassette. *Funeral* in 1990 and *Second Life* in 1991 brought their crushing musicianship and steadfast exhortations on the nature of decomposition to the world, until the group went overground in 1992 with *The Dying Truth*. Building on their influences (Hellhammer, Celtic Frost, Venom, Death), *A Descent Into Hell* delivered a further caustic epistle, including a cover version of Canadian death metal crew Slaughter's 'Death Dealer'.

● ALBUMS: *Funeral* (1990)★★★, *Second Life* (1991)★★★, *The Dying Truth* (Century Media 1992)★★★, *A Descent Into Hell* (Bullet Proof 1994)★★★.

CINDERELLA

This Philadelphia-based band was formed in 1983 by guitarist/vocalist Tom Keifer and bassist Eric Brittingham with Michael Kelly Smith (guitar) and Tony Destra (drums), although the latter pair departed in 1985, Smith later forming Britny Fox, and were replaced by Jeff LaBar (ex-White Foxx) and Jody Cortez, respectively. PolyGram Records signed Cinderella on Jon Bon Jovi's recommendation after he witnessed a particularly wild Philadelphia club gig. Fred Coury replaced Cortez after the recording of *Night Songs*, which, while hardly original, ably demonstrated Keifer's songwriting abilities. The band's AC/DC-Aerosmith style proved popular, with raucous live shows helping to make 'Nobody's Fool' a number 13 hit, as the debut album climbed to number 3 in the US charts. *Long Cold Winter* established a more individual sound, as Cinderella adopted a classy blues-rock style that ideally suited Keifer's throaty tones; 'Gypsy Road', 'Don't Know What You Got (Till It's Gone)' (US number 12 in September 1988) and 'Coming Home' continued their ascent. *Heartbreak Station*, featuring R&B elements that gave the album a Rolling Stones feel, was less successful, although 'Shelter Me' provided another Top 40 hit. Coury's departure to Arcade (ex-Shadow King drummer Kevin Valentine briefly replaced him) and throat problems for Keifer necessitated a lengthy break before 1994's *Still Climbing*, a strong comeback that built on the more powerful approach of *Long Cold Winter*, with John Mellencamp drummer Kenny Aaronoff deputizing while Cinderella auditioned new drummers over the Internet. The full-time replacement was Kevin Conway.

● ALBUMS: *Night Songs* (Mercury/PolyGram 1986)★★★, *Long Cold Winter* (Mercury/PolyGram 1988)★★★, *Heartbreak Station* (Mercury/PolyGram 1990)★★★, *Still Climbing* (Mercury/PolyGram 1994)★★.

● COMPILATIONS: *Looking Back* (PolyGram 1997)★★★★, *Bad Attitude 1986-1994* (Connoisseur Collection 1998)★★★★.

● VIDEOS: *Night Songs* (Channel 5 Video 1987).

CINTRON

Taking their moniker from the surname of lead singer and guitarist George Cintron, US hard rock band Cintron additionally comprised Leo Green (bass) and Ray Callahan (drums). The group released its debut EP, *Cintron*, in 1982. It attracted strong reviews for its Black Sabbath-derived power rock and supple rhythmic changes. Despite the good omens, a projected debut album was never released and the group members faded into obscurity, although their EP remains a cult collector's item among hard-rock fans.

CIRCLE JERKS

Formed in Los Angeles, California, USA, in 1980, this powerful hardcore band was founded by vocalist Keith Morris (ex-Black Flag) and guitarist Greg Hetson (ex-Redd Kross, later Bad Religion). Roger (Dowding) Rogerson (bass) and Lucky Lehrer (drums) completed the line-up featured on the quartet's forceful debut album. Their second, *Wild In The Streets*, was initially issued on Police manager Miles Copeland's Step Forward/Faulty label. It featured the services of hardcore's number one drummer, Chuck Biscuits (ex-D.O.A.), but he would leave in 1984 for a career in Danzig. Appearances on several influential 'new music' compilations, including *The Decline Of Western Civilisation* (they also had a starring role in the film of the same name) and *Let Them Eat Jelly Beans* confirmed the Circle Jerks' position at the vanguard of California's virulent hardcore movement. Longstanding members Morris and Hetson remained at the helm of this compulsive group which, by 1985, was fleshed out with the addition of Zander 'Snake' Schloss (bass; later Weirdos and Joe Strummer) and Keith 'Adolph' Clark (drums). *Wönderful*, from the same year, was something of a disappointment, but the Circle Jerks rescued their reputation with the staunch, Dictators-influenced *VI*. After releasing a live anthology the group went their own ways, before unexpectedly returning in the mid-90s to sign with PolyGram Records. The ensuing *Oddities Abnormalities And Curiousities* featured one truly bizarre track, with former teen star

Debbie Gibson providing lead vocals for a thrashy cover version of the Soft Boys' 'I Wanna Destroy You'.

● ALBUMS: *Group Sex* (Frontier 1980)★★★, *Wild In The Streets* (Faulty 1982)★★★, *Golden Shower Of Hits* (LAX 1983)★★, *Wönderful* (Combat Core 1985)★★, *VI* (Relativity 1987)★★★, *Oddities Abnormalities And Curiosities* (Mercury 1995)★★★.

● COMPILATIONS: *Gig* (Relativity 1992)★★★.

Circus Of Power

Emerging from the gutter of New York's late 80s Lower East Side, this heavily tattooed quartet delivered a unique and uncompromising brand of blues-based heavy metal. Alex Mitchell's paint-stripping vocals coupled with Ricky Beck-Mahler's grungy guitar riffs were the band's trademarks, while Gary Sunshine (bass) and Ryan Maher (drums) provided the necessary ammunition in the rhythm section. Distilling influences such as the Dictators, AC/DC, Motörhead and white blues guitarists including Johnny Winter and Rick Derringer, they purveyed solid, raunchy rock 'n' roll, underpinned by a keen sense of melody and dynamics. The lyrical subject matter concerned itself with 'wrong side of the street' narratives, reflecting their origins in the drug-infested Alphabet City community they call home. With three albums for RCA Records behind them and a successful support slot on Black Sabbath's 1990 tour, they remained relatively unknown outside their native New York. RCA consequently dropped the group, which may have been a rash decision, particularly in the light of Columbia Records' decision to step in with a contract.

● ALBUMS: *Circus Of Power* (RCA 1988)★★★, *Still Alive* (RCA 1989)★★, *Vices* (RCA 1990)★★★, *Magic & Madness* (Columbia 1993)★★★.

Cirith Ungol

Taking their name from one of the towers in *Lord Of The Rings*, this gothic heavy metal outfit materialized in 1980. Formed in Ventura, California, USA, the band comprised ex-Titanic duo Jerry Fogle (guitar) and Robert Garven (drums), ex-roadie Tim Baker (vocals) and Greg Lindstrom (bass), the latter eventually replaced by Michael Flint. Characterized by high-pitched vocals and complex, at times cumbersome, arrangements, their style was highly introspective, or less kindly, morbid. Their *Frost And Fire* debut has been referred to by some commentators as 'The Worst Heavy Metal Album Of All Time'. They did progress somewhat, improving song constructions and introducing up-tempo numbers to break the monotony. Nevertheless, success continued to elude them as they struggled to find an audience for their hopelessly outdated brand of fantasy metal.

● ALBUMS: *Frost And Fire* (Liquid Flames 1981)★★, *King Of The Dead* (Roadrunner 1984)★★, *One Foot In Hell* (Roadrunner 1986)★★★, *Paradise Lost* (Restless 1991)★★.

Citizen Kane

Formed in Los Angeles, California, USA, Citizen Kane took their name from the renowned Orson Welles film and comprised John Croswell (vocals), Mark Anderson (guitar), Michael Burton (guitar), Paul Lee (bass) and Chris Olsen (drums). Specializing in competent, mid-paced hard rock, the group made its debut for Rocshire Records in 1982 with the generic *Hot Blooded Rock*. However, when the label folded in 1984 all trace of Citizen Kane disappeared with it.

● ALBUMS: *Hot Blooded Rock* (Rocshire 1982)★★★.

CIV

Formed in New York City in 1995, CIV (pronounced 'sieve' - also the name of the group's singer and leader, Anthony Civocelli) are one of the new generation of hardcore bands from the city. With a line-up completed by Sammy Siegler (drums), Charlie (guitar) and Arthur Smilios (bass), the group took that particular scene by storm with their 1995 debut album, *Set Your Goals*. Their stage performances were also eye-catching, the group favouring sharp suits rather than the army surplus more usually associated with the hardcore fraternity, while the accent on percussion saw them labelled by some as a hardcore version of Adam And The Ants. Each member of the band had previously played with other local bands, most notably Gorilla Biscuits and Youth of Today. CIV were signed by Atlantic Records when A&R executive Mike Gitter saw the group's self-funded 'demo video' for 'Wait One Minute More'. This featured a chat show parody and was regularly aired by MTV. After signing to Atlantic the group consolidated their progress with support dates to L7, Sick Of It All and others. In 1996 the group toured the UK for the first time and released another acclaimed single, 'Choices Made'.

● ALBUMS: *Set Your Goals* (Lava/Atlantic 1995)★★★, *Thirteen Day Getaway* (Atlantic 1998)★★★.

CJSS

This US group was a part-time side project for virtuoso guitarist David T. Chastain. Ably assisted by Mike Skimmerhorn (bass), Les Sharp (drums) and Russell Jenkins (lead vocals), CJSS offered an outlet for Chastain's melodic and more accessible compositions. They recorded two albums during the mid-80s, characterized by impeccable musicianship and inventive guitarwork. In theory, the material still retained enough rough edges to appeal to rock fans but, at the same time, was sophisticated enough to cross over to a mainstream audience. In practice, however, this did not happen and CJSS have been inactive since 1987.

● ALBUMS: *World Gone Mad* (Roadrunner 1986)★★★, *Praise The Loud* (Roadrunner 1986)★★★.

Clarke, 'Fast' Eddie

Highly underrated guitarist Eddie Clarke (b. 5 October 1950, Isleworth, Middlesex, England) will always be remembered for his six years with Motörhead. Clarke had been playing in various bands since 1965 but his big break came in 1973 when he joined Zeus, the group put together by Curtis Knight (the blues/soul man who played with Jimi Hendrix), with whom he remained for 18 months. Following Zeus, he formed Blue Goose along with Nicky Hogarth and Chris Perry. After his departure Blue Goose recorded an album for Anchor Records that included 'Over The Top', a track written by Clarke. His next band, Continuous Performance, formed with Charlie Tumalhi, produced only a handful of demos, a disappointment that led to him quitting music in 1975. It was finally through his friend, drummer Phil Taylor, that he joined Motörhead in 1976. Here he enjoyed worldwide fame as a foil to Lemmy's brutal bass, even taking lead vocal on the blues song 'Step Down' from the *Bomber* album. Clarke played on all of Motörhead's albums between 1977 and 1982. During 1978 (a quiet period for the band) Clarke and Taylor joined vocalist 'Speedy' Keen and Johnny Thunders bassist Billy Wrath in the Muggers, playing a number of gigs under that banner. In 1982 he produced Tank's debut album, *Filth Hounds Of Hades*, guested on Twisted Sister's *Under The Blade* and left Motörhead because of musical differences. He later struck up a partnership with Pete Way (bassist for UFO) and formed Fastway, but Way subsequently accepted an offer to join Ozzy Osbourne, leaving him to form Waysted. Clarke then recruited drummer Jerry Shirley from Humble Pie, vocalist Dave King and bassist Charlie McCracken. This line-up lasted for two years. Further line-ups included ex-Damned/UFO bassist Paul Gray. Eventually, Clarke abandoned the band in favour of solo work and overseeing archive Motörhead releases for Receiver Records.

● ALBUMS: with Phil Taylor *Naughty Old Santa's Xmas Classics* (Receiver 1989)★★★, *It Aint Over Till It's Over* (Chequered Flag 1993)★★★.

Clawfinger

Comprising Jocke Skog (programming), Zak Tell (vocals), Erlend Ottem (guitar) and Bard Torstenson (guitar), Clawfinger formed in 1991 and immediately received international praise for their fluid but powerful alternative rock sound. Their debut single, 1993's 'Nigger', also provoked great controversy. Although the subject matter was profoundly anti-racist, many critics wondered as to the wisdom of its title. The media quickly categorized Clawfinger alongside American groups such as Rage Against The Machine, who similarly combined political activism with a musical scope that ranged from hardcore rap to metal. The group's debut album, *Deaf Dumb Blind*, expanded their repertoire to encompass funk and even jazz flourishes. It was promoted in the USA on tours with Anthrax and Alice In Chains, while Clawfinger remained rooted in their national charts with a joint EP with Swedish rappers Just D. In 1995 the group, now expanded to a six-piece, launched their 'Back To The Basic' European tour, which saw them play in 12 European countries within a few weeks.

● ALBUMS: *Deaf Dumb Blind* (Metal Blade 1993)★★★, *Biggest And The Best* (Coalition 1998)★★★.

Clawhammer

Purveying a music squarely located at the more brutal end of the hardcore punk rock spectrum, Clawhammer were formed in Los Angeles, California, USA, in the mid-80s, taking their name from a Captain Beefheart lyric. Among their earliest releases was a track-by-track cover album cassette of Devo's *Q: Are We Not Men? A: We Are Devo!*. They made their debut in 1989 with the *Poor Robert EP*, followed by a self-titled debut album for Sympathy For The Record Industry a year later. The engaging *Double Pack Whack Attack EP*, meanwhile, included versions of material by Patti Smith, Pere Ubu, Brian Eno and Devo once more. However, it was not until the mid-90s when the band, which features Jon Wahl (vocals, guitar, ex-

Pontiac Brothers), Chris Bagarozzi (guitar), Rob Walther (bass) and Bob Lee (drums), first achieved mainstream prominence. *Pablum*, released on Epitaph Records in 1983, attracted rave reviews, but immediately afterwards they moved away from the label to Interscope Records, though they retained the services of Epitaph head Brett Gurewitz as producer. Their debut for Interscope, *Thank The Holder Uppers*, was another devastating blast of angst-ridden punk blues, with Wahl's unhinged vocals and irresistibly macabre lyrical images holding centrestage.

● ALBUMS: *Get Yer Heh Heh's Out* cassette only (Trigon 1989)★★, *Clawhammer* (Sympathy For The Record Industry 1990)★★★, *Ramwhale* (Sympathy For The Record Industry 1992)★★, *Pablum* (Epitaph 1993)★★★, *Thank The Holder Uppers* (Interscope/Atlantic 1996)★★★.

CLEMPSON, DAVE

b. 5 September 1949, Tamworth, Staffordshire, England. Guitarist Dave 'Clem' Clempson achieved early recognition as a member of Bakerloo, an inventive blues-based trio that completed an excellent album for the Harvest label. In October 1969 he replaced James Litherland in Colosseum with whom he remained for two years. Clempson then joined Humble Pie, whose brand of brash rock contrasted with that of his previous jazz rock employers. *Smokin'* (1972) and *Eat It* (1973) offered his most emphatic work, but by 1975 the quartet was losing its direction. Clempson then formed Strange Brew with bassist Greg Ridely and drummer Cozy Powell, but this short-lived unit dissolved when the latter broke his wrist. Having briefly joined Steve Marriott's All Stars, the guitarist formed Rough Diamond with ex-Uriah Heep singer David Byron. This ill-fated venture collapsed in 1977 with Byron embarking on a solo career. The remaining musicians became known as Champion but Clempson's nomadic path was resumed in 1979 when he departed to join Roger Chapman. During the 80s Clempson played some of his finest work with Jack Bruce and was particularly popular in Germany. In 1994 he was part of *Cities Of The Heart*, the album released to celebrate Bruce's 50th birthday. He is one of the most accomplished rock guitarists to emerge from the late 60s blues boom. His speedy precision playing is faultless, and rarely boring.

CLOVEN HOOF

This UK band, formed in 1979, were strongly influenced by early Kiss records. The personnel took on the pseudonyms of Air, Fire, Earth and Water and dressed in appropriately garish stage costumes. Their actual identities were David Potter (vocals), Steve Rounds (guitar), Les Payne (bass) and Kevin Pountney (drums), and they made their debut with an independently released EP, *The Opening Ritual*. Specializing in kitsch glam-metal, with an underlying satanic element, they recorded an amateurish but charming debut for Neat Records before a live album followed for Moondance Records. Afterwards, the original line-up and band concept disintegrated. The only remaining member, bassist Payne, re-formed the group in 1987 with Russell North (lead vocals), Andy Wood (guitar) and Jon Brown (drums). Rejecting their former image in favour of a hard rock/thrash approach, they signed to FM Revolver Records. *Dominator*, produced by Guy Bidmead (of Motörhead fame) materialized in 1988, but was highly derivative. *A Sultan's Ransom*, which moved further towards a thrash metal style, fared little better and was universally slated by the music press. The band continued, apparently undaunted by such setbacks, until finally sundering in the 90s.

● ALBUMS: *Cloven Hoof* (Neat 1984)★★★, *Live ... Fighting Back* (Moondance 1987)★★, *Dominator* (FM Revolver 1988)★★, *A Sultan's Ransom* (FM Revolver 1989)★★.

CLOVER

Formed in Mill Valley, California, USA, when bassist Johnny Ciambotti joined John McFee (b. 18 November 1953, Santa Cruz, California, USA; guitar, pedal steel guitar, vocals), Alex Call (guitar, vocals) and Mitch Howie (drums) in the Tiny Hearing Aid Company. Having decided on a less cumbersome name, the quartet made its debut as Clover in July 1967 and soon became a popular attraction in the region's thriving dancehalls. *Clover* consolidated their reputation as a feisty bar band, although a primitive production undermined its charm. *Forty-Niner* was a marked improvement, but although its informality was both varied and infectious, the group was unable to break out of its now stifling good-time niche. The band were featured in an early Levis television advertisement singing 'Route 66'. A dispirited Howie left the line-up which was then bolstered by the addition of Huey (Louis) Lewis (b. Hugh Anthony Cregg III, 5 July 1951, New York, USA; vocals, harmonica), Sean Hopper (keyboards, vocals) and Mickey Shine (drums) but fortunes remained unchanged until 1976 when the group came to the UK at the urging of Nick Lowe. Clover quickly became a popular attraction in their adopted homeland, during which time they accompanied Elvis Costello on *My Aim Is True*. However, despite completing two promising albums, Clover were unable to make a significant breakthrough and returned to the USA in 1978 where they folded. McFee subsequently joined the Doobie Brothers while Lewis and Hopper eventually achieved considerable commercial success as Huey Lewis And The News.

● ALBUMS: *Clover* (Fantasy 1970)★★, *Forty-Niner* (Fantasy 1971)★★★, *Unavailable* (Vertigo 1977)★★★, *Love On The Wire* (Vertigo 1977)★★★.

● COMPILATIONS: *Clover Chronicle - The Best Of The Fantasy Years* (DJM 1979)★★★, *The Best Of Clover* (Mercury 1986)★★★.

CLUTCH

This Washington, DC noise-metal quartet was formed in 1991 by childhood friends Neil Fallon (vocals), Tim Sult (guitar), Dan Maines (bass) and Jean-Paul Gaster (drums), and drew from hardcore, metal, punk and industrial traditions for their abrasive, intense sound. The band signed to Earache Records, releasing the *Passive Restraints EP* and establishing their style, and although the EP was not a major commercial success, it brought Clutch to East West Records' attention. *Transnational Speedway League: Anthems, Anecdotes And Undeniable Truths* showed no signs of compromises being made owing to major label status, as Clutch maintained their angry hardcore groove, with a charismatic performance from Fallon. The Clutch live repertoire had grown in stature and confidence since their early European tour with Biohazard, and the band toured with the likes of Fear Factory and Prong. A self-titled 1995 album showed the band to be developing stylistically, and their promising reputation was confirmed when they moved to Columbia Records.

● ALBUMS: *Transnational Speedway League: Anthems, Anecdotes And Undeniable Truths* (East West 1993)★★★, *Clutch* (East West 1995)★★★, *The Elephant Riders* (Columbia 1998)★★★.

COAL CHAMBER

Formed in Los Angeles, California, USA, in 1994, Coal Chamber are led by gruff vocalist Dez Fafara and operate in territory somewhere between the traditional hard riffing of Black Sabbath and the sensationalist techno rock of Marilyn Manson. Fafara met guitarist Miguel 'Meegs' Rascon through a classified ad, and they later added drummer Mike Cox and bassist Rayna Foss, the room-mate of Fafara's future wife. They signed to Roadrunner Records in 1995 after being recommended by Dino Cazares of Fear Factory, and received widespread exposure in the metal press as that label's hottest new property since Machine Head. Their debut attained further strong reviews, despite having been recorded under stressful conditions - on the day recording started, Fafara's wife left him. An already intimidating suite of songs was thus transformed into something of a personal exorcism. Having previously toured with Danzig, they also supported labelmates Machine Head on their 1997 UK tour.

● ALBUMS: *Coal Chamber* (Roadrunner 1997)★★★.

COBRA

This US hard rock quintet was formed in 1982 by guitarist Mandy Meyer and former Target vocalist Jimi Jamison. With the recruitment of Jack Holder (guitar), Tommy Keiser (bass) and Jeff Klaven (drums) they were soon signed by CBS Records. Their music, a fusion of the blues-rock approach of Whitesnake and Bad Company and the heavier, power-metal style of Van Halen and Iron Maiden, was immediately impressive. Legal and contractual problems were instrumental in the band's demise after just one album release. Meyer joined Asia, Jamison teamed up with Survivor and Keiser later appeared in Krokus.

● ALBUMS: *First Strike* (Epic 1983)★★★.

COCKNEY REJECTS

Discovered by Jimmy Pursey of Sham 69, this skinhead group came to the fore in London, England, in 1980 with an irreverent brand of proletarian-focused punk. The group comprised Jefferson Turner (vocals), Vince Riordan (bass, vocals), Micky Geggus (guitar, vocals) and Keith Warrington (drums). Daring and anti-everything, they were virtually a parody of the 'kick over the traces' punk attitude, while also betraying a stubborn parochialism in keeping with their group title. The 'anarchic' contents of their albums were reflected in their garishly tasteless record sleeves. Nevertheless, they had a certain subversive humour, titling their first two albums *Greatest Hits* when the sum of their UK Top 40 achievements rested with 'The Greatest Cockney Ripoff' at number 21 and the West Ham United football anthem, 'I'm Forever Blowing Bubbles', at number 35. On their second album they included the 'Oi! Oi! Oi!' song/chant, thereby giving birth to a musical genre that came to define the brash inarticulacy of skinhead politics. Their gigs during this time also became an interface for working-class culture and the extreme right, and like Sham 69, the Rejects were judged guilty by default. By the time of 1982's *The Wild Ones* the group were veering away from their original punk influences towards heavy metal. Significantly, their new producer was UFO bassist Pete Way. Equally significantly, their career was well on the decline by this point. The group disbanded in 1985 but re-formed to public apathy at the turn of the decade, *Lethal* hardly living up to its title.

● ALBUMS: *Greatest Hits Vol. 1* (Zonophone 1980)★★★, *Greatest Hits Vol. 2* (Zonophone 1980)★★★, *Greatest Hits Vol. 3 (Live And Loud)* (Zonophone 1981)★★, *The Power & The Glory* (Zonophone 1981)★★, *The Wild Ones* (AKA 1982)★★★, *Rock The Wild Side* (Heavy Metal 1984)★★, *Live And Loud!! Bridgehouse Tapes* 1981 recording (Link 1987)★★, *Lethal* (Neat 1990)★★.

● COMPILATIONS: *Unheard Rejects* early unreleased recordings (Wonderful World 1985)★, *We Are The Firm* (Dojo 1986)★★, *The Best Of Cockney Rejects* (Castle 1994)★★★.

Cold Sweat

Following his departure from Keel, US guitarist Marc Ferrari assembled his own band, but not without a series of problems. The initial choice of name, Ferrari, encountered objections from the famous car manufacturers, despite the fact that it was the guitarist's surname, and second choice, Cryin' Shame, clashed with that of a jazz band. Hence, Cold Sweat, from a Thin Lizzy song, was finally adopted. To add to the difficulties, original vocalist Oni Logan was poached by ex-Dokken guitarist George Lynch for his Lynch Mob band. Rory Cathey was recruited to join Ferrari, ex-Waysted guitarist Erik Gamans, bassist Chris McLernon and drummer Anthony White on *Break Out*. While Kevin Beamish's production was a little too clean, the melodic hard-rock material and performances on display were impressive, with some superb guitar interplay between Ferrari and Gamans. Cathey proved his worth as a frontman to complete a talented live act. However, despite some US touring with Dio and their own club dates, the album received little additional promotion, and disappeared. Ferrari later appeared in actress Tia Carrere's backing band in the *Wayne's World* movie.

● ALBUMS: *Break Out* (MCA 1990)★★★.

Come

Formed in 1991, this highly rated quartet centres on musicians already involved in New York's alternative music circuit. Singer/guitarist Thalia Zedek began her recording career with the Dangerous Birds and Uzi, before joining the influential Live Skull. Guitarist Chris Brokaw was formerly drummer in Codeine, while Sean O'Brien (bass) and Arthur Johnson (drums) were both ex-members of the Bar B Q Killers. Come made their debut in August 1991 with 'Car', a slow, menacing performance issued on the Sub Pop Records label. The equally atmospheric 'Fast Piss Blues' succeeded it, backed by a languid version of the Rolling Stones' 'I Got The Blues'. These served as the perfect introduction to *Eleven: Eleven*, rightly lauded as one of 1992's finest releases. The spirit of Patti Smith, Delta blues and the Stooges permeated this startling collection which highlighted Zedek's emotive voice and Brokow's dense guitarwork. A period of seclusion ensued, but Come re-emerged with 1994's powerful second collection, which included further high-calibre recordings in 'Finish Line' and 'Let's Get Lost'. Johnson and O'Brien left the group in 1995, and were replaced by Tara Jane O'Neil (bass) and Kevin Coutlas (drums), both ex-Rodan members. Subsequent albums have failed to scale the heights of their debut, but pay testament to Come's unrelenting musical vision.

● ALBUMS: *Eleven: Eleven* (Matador 1992)★★★★, *Don't Ask, Don't Tell* (Matador 1994)★★★, *Near Life Experience* (Matador 1996)★★★, *Gently Down The Stream* (Matador 1998)★★★.

Company Of Wolves

This US hard rock group, formed in the late 80s, comprised Kyf Brewer (vocals), Steve Conte (guitar), John Conte (bass) and Frankie Larocka (drums; ex-Bryan Adams and John Waite touring bands). Revealing a wide range of influences encompassing Kiss, Aerosmith, Bad Company, Led Zeppelin and David Bowie, these were reprocessed with such frantic energy and attitude that they almost convinced. However, they were dropped by their record company after the release of a solitary album, and subsequently split in 1991.

● ALBUMS: *Company Of Wolves* (Mercury 1990)★★.

Coney Hatch

This Canadian quartet was formed in 1981 by vocalist Carl Dixon and guitarist Steve Shelski. Adapting their name from a north London home for the mentally ill, the line-up was stabilized with the addition of Andy Curran (bass) and Dave Ketchum (drums). They debuted in 1982 with a self-titled album, produced by Max Webster supremo Kim Mitchell. It remains their essential work, featuring a variety of styles from blues-rock to *avant garde* jazz via heavy metal. Dixon's vocals are outstanding, with Shelski's eclectic guitar bursts providing the perfect foil. Barry Connors took over the drumstool after *Outta Hand*, a disappointing and lacklustre follow-up that was not helped by a lifeless production. *Friction* marked a slight return to form, but the band disintegrated before they could capitalize on their success. Occasional reunion gigs still take place in their native territory.

● ALBUMS: *Coney Hatch* (Mercury 1982)★★★, *Outta Hand* (Vertigo 1983)★, *Friction* (Vertigo 1985)★★.

● COMPILATIONS: *Best Of Three* (Anthem 1995)★★★.

● VIDEOS: *Coney Hatch: The Video Single* (PolyGram Music Video 1986).

CONVICT

Canadian hard rockers Convict never escaped the clichés of the genre - leading some to suspect them of being a 'joke' band. However, Terry 'The Can' Browning (vocals, guitar), Kim Kennedy (bass) and Vic Bradley (drums) were perfectly serious in their intent. Their 1985 debut album for Cobra Records, *Go Ahead Make My Day*, balanced conventional hard rock with tedious AOR ballads. Their musical immaturity and lack of songwriting ability led to many stinging reviews in the Canadian press. Unsurprisingly disheartened, Convict folded shortly after its release.

● ALBUMS: *Go Ahead Make My Day* (Cobra 1985)★.

CORONER

Switzerland's premier death metal band Coroner was founded in 1985 by the pseudonymous Ron Royle (vocals), Tommy T. Baron (guitar) and Marquis Marky (drums). They were signed by Noise Records the following year after recording a demo entitled *Death Cult*, which featured guest vocals by Thomas Gabriel Warrior, leader of cult *avant garde* thrash band Celtic Frost. Coroner maintained a close relationship with their countrymen - and now labelmates - over the ensuing years, even roadying for them on Celtic Frost's 1986 US tour. Although Coroner had a less experimental approach to thrash metal than Celtic Frost, a number of intricate and unusual guitar motifs were discernible in their caustic, rapid-fire approach. Of their several albums, *No More Colours* was perhaps the most effective distillation of their anguished, stop-start rhythms and Royle's pained singing. However, Coroner were increasingly sidelined by younger death metal bands after this point. The release of the *Best Of* compilation (featuring remixes, instrumentals and four new tracks) was considered by many to be their swan-song, but they remained active, although lacking the exposure they had once enjoyed.

● ALBUMS: *R.I.P.* (Noise 1987)★★★, *Punishment For Decadence* (Noise 1988)★★, *No More Colour* (Noise 1989)★★★★, *Mental Vortex* (Noise 1991)★★★, *Grin* (Noise 1993)★★.

● COMPILATIONS: *Best Of* (Noise 1995)★★★.

● VIDEOS: *No More Colour Tour '90 (Live In East Berlin)* (Fotodisk Video 1990).

CORROSION OF CONFORMITY

This mid-80s American hardcore crossover band, originally known as No Labels, was formed in Raleigh, North Carolina, USA, in 1982 by Reed Mullin (drums), Woody Weatherman (guitar) and Mike Dean (bass, vocals), and rose to become one of the biggest draws in the American underground with their stunning live shows. *Eye For An Eye*, with vocals supplied by Eric Eyke, separated them from the pack by mixing hardcore speed with Black Sabbath and Deep Purple-influenced power riffing. A more metallic crossover style became evident with *Animosity*, although the group lost neither their aggression nor their hardcore ideals. Following the blistering *Technocracy*, with Simon Bob (ex-Ugly Americans) on vocals, the size of the band's audience expanded with the rise of thrash, but record company problems and the loss of Simon Bob and Dean led to Corrosion Of Conformity's collapse. However, just when it seemed that *Six Songs With Mike Singing* would be their epitaph, Corrosion Of Conformity returned, with Mullin and Weatherman joined by Karl Agell (vocals, ex-School Of Violence), Pepper Keenan (guitar, vocals) and Phil Swisher (bass). Impressive tours with D.R.I. and Danzig helped to gain a new recording contract, and the acclaimed *Blind* saw the band adopt a slower, more melodic, but still fiercely heavy style. It also continued the hardcore lyrical stance of an increasingly politically active band, challenging social, political and ecological issues. Success with 'Vote With A Bullet' and electrifying live shows, including a UK tour supporting Soundgarden, re-established Corrosion Of Conformity as a force, but the departure of Agell and Swisher slowed the momentum once more. *Deliverance*, with Keenan taking lead vocals and Dean back in place, saw the band incorporate ever more diverse influences into their weighty sound, adding southern rock grooves and, perhaps most surprisingly, Thin Lizzy-style guitar harmonies for a varied album that was a considerable departure from their hardcore musical roots. The hardcore image continued to fade as *Wiseblood* demonstrated an excellent grasp of 70s heavy rock.

● ALBUMS: *Eye For An Eye* (No Core 1984)★★★, *Animosity* (Combat 1985)★★★, *Technocracy* mini-album (Combat 1987)★★★, *Six Songs With Mike Singing* mini-album, 1985 recording (Caroline 1988)★★, *Blind* (Combat 1991)★★★, *Deliverance* (Sony 1994)★★★, *Wiseblood* (Sony 1996)★★★.

Coverdale Page

Following Whitesnake's headline appearance at the 1990 Donington Festival, and the comparatively poor sales of *Slip Of The Tongue*, vocalist David Coverdale (b. 22 September 1951, Saltburn-By-The Sea, Cleveland, England) put his band on ice, and had all but retired. Former Led Zeppelin guitarist Jimmy Page (b. James Patrick Page, 9 January 1944, Heston, Middlesex, England) was, however, searching for a singer with whom to work, and Coverdale was suggested by his booking agent during a conversation with Page's manager. The pair met in New York in March 1991, and quickly gelled on personal and professional levels. Their first attempt at writing together produced an album track, 'Absolution Blues', and the duo began writing and recording their debut, enlisting the services of Heart drummer Denny Carmassi and bassists Jorge Casas and Ricky Phillips in the studio. The partnership was viewed rather cynically by sections of the music press as a corporate rock supergroup, and was subject to much speculation on all fronts - 'Legends' was rumoured as a possible band name for some time - before the appearance of the simply titled *Coverdale Page*. The album saw the duo rediscovering their blues-rock roots, and was widely regarded as the finest work produced by either for some time. Majestic ballads such as 'Take Me For A Little While' and the mellow 'Take A Look At Yourself' sat comfortably amid the thunderous hard rock of 'Shake My Tree', 'Waiting On You' and 'Pride And Joy', while the atmospheric delivery of 'Over Now' evoked the epic air of the Zeppelin classic, 'Kashmir'. The album reached the Top 5 on both sides of the Atlantic, and Carmassi's Bonhamesque performance ensured that his services were retained for the live band, along with bassist Guy Pratt and ex-Dave Lee Roth keyboard player Brett Tuggle. However, the band were unable to arrange a financially viable world tour, with promoters sceptical of their drawing power in a poor market for traditional heavy rock, and without that support, album sales dwindled. The group played six shows in Japan in December 1993, successfully mixing Whitesnake and Zeppelin material with Coverdale Page originals, but these performances were the band's swan-song. It seems unlikely that the main protagonists will work together again, especially in view of Page's reunification with Robert Plant.

● ALBUMS: *Coverdale Page* (EMI 1993)★★★.

Coverdale, David

b. 22 September 1951, Saltburn-By-The Sea, Cleveland, England. Coverdale found fame as the venerable singer with UK hard rock stalwarts Deep Purple and Whitesnake. His tenure with Deep Purple lasted from 1973 until March 1976. Moving to Germany, he laid down a vocal track on a multi-artist project organised by Eddie Hardin, released by RCA Records as *Wizard's Convention*. Unable to perform in England for contractual reasons, Coverdale then recorded vocals for both his solo albums in Germany while the backing tracks were laid down in London. The backing musicians who played on these albums were retained for touring purposes, and effectively became the original line-up of Whitesnake. Coverdale remained with Whitesnake thereafter until their dissolution in 1994 when Geffen Records elected not to renew their contract. At that time Coverdale worked with former Led Zeppelin guitarist Jimmy Page on the Coverdale Page project. Inevitably, another Whitesnake re-formation was around the corner. Whitesnake's 1997 comeback album represented a return to Coverdale's R&B heritage. As he told the press on its release, he had tired of the more cartoonish elements of Whitesnake's image: 'I've had enough of the Tarzan impressions. I wanna sing. Less strain on the old Calvins.' Now settled in Lake Tahoe, Nevada, he looks set to remain a fixture in rock's middle-aged hierarchy.

● ALBUMS: *David Coverdale's Whitesnake* (Purple 1977)★★★, *Northwinds* (Purple 1978)★★★.

Cox, Jess

b. England. Well known to followers of UK heavy metal via his involvement with New Wave Of British Heavy Metal group Tygers Of Pan Tang, Cox ended his tenure as that group's singer in 1981. He temporarily joined Lionheart, but that association lasted for only one performance. Afterwards he entered a period of musical non-activity that was eventually broken with the release of his debut solo album, *Third Step*, in 1983. On this collection Cox attempted, largely unsuccessfully, to combine various styles from pop to conventional hard rock, but it was obvious to most critics that he needed fellow musicians to embroider his songwriting.

● ALBUMS: *Third Step* (Neat 1983)★★.

CRAAFT

This German melodic rock quartet was formed in 1984. The line-up consisted of Marcus Schleicher (ex-GMT; guitar), Tommy Keiser (ex-Krokus; bass), Tommy Schneider (drums), Franz Keil (keyboards) and Klaus Luley (vocals; ex-Tokyo), and they provided a breath of fresh air in the mid-80s teutonic rock scene, which was otherwise dominated by identikit speed metal bands. Surprisingly, the band sounded more American than German, combining Night Ranger, Whitesnake and Toto influences to great effect. Luley was a highly talented vocalist, using his considerable range and power to carry the melody lines, while the use of keyboards to fill out the sound is achieved in a subtle and understated fashion. They released two excellent albums, but received little recognition outside Germany.

● ALBUMS: *Craaft* (RCA 1986)★★★, *Second Honeymoon* (RCA 1988)★★.

CRACKJAW

German hard rock band Crackjaw released a single album for local label Steamhammer Records in 1985, but failed to use this as a launch pad to a successful mainstream career. This was disappointing, as the musicianship and songwriting displayed by Stephen Kiergerl (vocals), Holger Eckstein (guitar), Jurgen Schulz (guitar), Gerriot Eisenmenger (bass) and Markus Klinke (drums) on *Night Out* was excellent. Outside of Germany and other central European territories the group's expertly performed melodic hooks never translated into sales and by the following year Crackjaw had folded.

● ALBUMS: *Night Out* (Steamhammer 1985)★★★.

CRADLE OF FILTH

This outlandish band quickly became the most popular UK representatives of the Satanic black metal revival of the early 90s with the release of their formidable 1994 debut, *The Principal Of Evil Made Flesh*. Visually, Cradle Of Filth were evidently influenced by the Scandinavian bands who led the movement, such as Mayhem and Emperor. This influence included adopting the black and white make-up known as 'corpse-paint' and funereal garb, while incorporating displays of fire-breathing and drenching themselves in blood on stage. While the Scandinavian black metal bands have become increasingly interested in the occult, right-wing philosophies of Viking mythology, Cradle Of Filth have a more gothic, quasi-poetic musical outlook. This is evidenced in their darkly poignant lyrics, use of a cello player and the haunting singing of Andrea Mayer (a German Satanist who has since married a member of Emperor). The core of Cradle Of Filth's sound, however, remains a blizzard of apocalyptic guitars and vocals. However, after the successful release of *Supreme Vampiric Evil* the group entered a tumultuous phase, with the loss of group members and several problems with management and their record label. They eventually regrouped in 1996 for the mini-album *Vempire, Or, Dark Phaerytales In Phallustein*, by which time the group incorporated singer Dani Filth as well as Irish keyboard player Damien, guitarist Stuart and guitarist Jared. The new album was released on Cacophonous as a compromise solution to allow them to escape their contract and release a third studio album, *Dusk ... And Her Embrace*, for a new label. Once again it explored at some length their fascination with vampire mythology and Victorian and Medieval romanticism. Ex-Brutality bassist Jeff Acres joined the band in 1995 and guitarist Bryan Hipp departed in early 1996. Cradle Of Filth gained further notoriety (and popularity) by insulting socialite Tara Palmer Tomkinson at the 1998 *Kerrang!* music awards.

● ALBUMS: *The Principle Of Evil Made Flesh* (Cacophonous 1994)★★, *Supreme Vampiric Evil* (Cacophonous 1994)★★★, *Vempire, Or, Dark Phaerytales In Phallustein* mini-album (Cacophonous 1996)★★★, *Dusk ... And Her Embrace* (Music For Nations 1996)★★, *Cruelty And The Beast* (Music For Nations 1998)★★★★.

CRASH 'N' BURN

This Anglo-German hard rock quartet was previously known as Riff. Formed by vocalist William Lennox in 1991, with fellow members Becking (guitar), Thomas (bass) and Brendel (drums), the group was signed by RCA Records, and debuted with *Fever* in 1991. A blues-based heavy rock album, it utilized state-of-the-art recording technology to transpose the group's keen melodies. Replete with promotional single 'Hot Like Fire', it announced a band of considerable flair and energy.

● ALBUMS: *Fever* (RCA 1991)★★★.

CRAWLER

(see Back Street Crawler)

CRAWLEY

Comprising Joel Andersson (vocals), Lawrence West (guitar), Mats Järnil (bass) and Per Johansson (drums), part-American but Swedish-based hard rock unit Crawley formed in 1992. Most of the members had played together since 1986 in sundry under-achieving heavy metal groups. The idea for Crawley was first mooted when Andersson and West began working together in 1987. Subsequently Andersson moved to America (where his family resides) and formed a band named Foreign Legion. He returned to Sweden in 1990, at which time Crawley was officially formed. However, that was not the end of the group's complicated pre-history. Andersson travelled back to the USA to start a car business in Florida while the remaining members concentrated on recording demos. It was not until February 1992 that they were able to tempt their leader back. On the basis of existing demos the group was signed to the Soundfront Record Company almost immediately, and released their debut album, *Addiction*, in the summer of 1992. As well as 10 of their own songs it included a cover version of Jimi Hendrix's 'Freedom'. Prestigious local gigs followed, including an appearance at the 1993 Zeppelin Gala.

● ALBUMS: *Addiction* (Soundfront 1992)★★★.

CREAM

Arguably the most famous trio in rock music, Cream comprised Jack Bruce (b. John Symon Asher, 14 May 1943, Glasgow, Lanarkshire, Scotland; bass, vocals), Eric Clapton (b. Eric Patrick Clapp, 30 March 1945, Ripley, Surrey, England; guitar) and Ginger Baker (b. Peter Baker, 19 August 1939, Lewisham, London, England; drums). In their two and a half years together, Cream made such an impression on fans, critics and musicians as to make them one of the most influential bands since the Beatles. They formed in the height of swinging London during the 60s and were soon thrust into a non-stop turbulent arena, hungry for new and interesting music after the Merseybeat boom had quelled. Cream were promoted in the music press as a pop group, with Clapton from John Mayall's Bluesbreakers, Bruce from Graham Bond and briefly Manfred Mann, and Baker from the Graham Bond Organisation via Alexis Korner's Blues Incorporated. Baker and Bruce had originally played together in the Johnny Burch Octet in 1962. Cream's debut single, 'Wrapping Paper', was a comparatively weird pop song, and made the lower reaches of the charts on the strength of its insistent appeal. This was a paradox to their great strength of jamming and improvisation; each member was already a proven master of their chosen instrument. Their follow-up single, 'I Feel Free', unleashed such energy that it could only be matched by Jimi Hendrix. The debut album *Fresh Cream* confirmed the promise: this band were not what they seemed, another colourful pop group singing songs of tangerine bicycles. With a mixture of blues standards and exciting originals, the album became a record that every credible music fan should own. It reached number 6 in the UK charts. The following year, *Disraeli Gears*, with its distinctive dayglo cover, went even higher, and firmly established Cream in the USA, where they spent most of their touring life. This superb album showed a marked progression from their first, in particular, in the high standard of songwriting from Jack Bruce and his lyricist partner, former beat poet Pete Brown. Landmark songs such as 'Sunshine Of Your Love', 'Strange Brew' and 'SWLABR' (She Was Like A Bearded Rainbow) were performed with precision.

Already rumours of a split prevailed as news filtered back from America of fights and arguments between Baker and Bruce. Meanwhile, their live performances did not reflect the music already released from studio sessions. The long improvisational pieces, based around fairly simple blues structures, were often awesome. Each member had a least one party piece during concerts, Bruce with his frantic harmonica solo on 'Traintime', Baker with his trademark drum solo on 'Toad', and Clapton with his strident vocal and fantastic guitar solo on 'Crossroads'. One disc of the magnificent two-record set, *Wheels Of Fire*, captured Cream live, at their inventive and exploratory best. Just a month after its release, while it sat on top of the US charts, they announced they would disband at the end of the year following two final concerts. The famous Royal Albert Hall farewell concerts were captured on film; the posthumous *Goodbye* reached number 1 in the UK charts and number 2 in the USA, while even some later live scrapings from the bottom of the barrel enjoyed chart success.

The three members came together in 1993 for an emotional one-off performance at the Rock And Roll Hall Of Fame awards in New York, before the CD age finally recognized their contribution in 1997, with the release of an excellent 4-CD box set, *Those Were The Days*. Two CDs from the studio and two from the stage wrap up this brief career, with no stone left unturned. In addition to all of their previously issued material there is the unreleased 'Lawdy Mama', which Bruce claims features the wrongly recorded original bass line of 'Strange Brew'. Another gem is a demo of the Bruce/Brown diamond, 'The Weird Of Hermiston', which later appeared on Bruce's debut solo album, *Songs For A Tailor*. This collection reaffirms their greatness, as three extraordinary musicians fusing their musical personalities together as a unit. Cream came and went almost in the blink of an eye, but left an indelible mark on rock music.

● ALBUMS: *Fresh Cream* (Polydor 1966)★★★★, *Disraeli Gears* (Polydor 1967)★★★★★, *Wheels Of Fire* (Polydor 1968)★★★★, *Goodbye* (Polydor 1969)★★★, *Live Cream* (Polydor 1970)★★★, *Live Cream, Volume 2* (Polydor 1972)★★★.

● COMPILATIONS: *The Best Of Cream* (Polydor 1969)★★★★, *Heavy Cream* (Polydor 1973)★★★, *Strange Brew - The Very Best Of Cream* (Polydor 1986)★★★★, *Those Were The Days* 4-CD box set (Polydor 1997)★★★★★.

● VIDEOS: *Farewell Concert* (Polygram Music Video 1986), *Strange Brew* (Warner Music Video 1992), *Fresh Live Cream* (PolyGram Music Video 1994).

● FURTHER READING: *Cream In Gear (Limited Edition)*, Gered Mankowitz and Robert Whitaker (Photographers). *Strange Brew*, Chris Welch.

CREAMING JESUS

This satirical UK hardcore/metal quintet was formed in 1987 by vocalist Andy and guitarists Richard and Mario. With the addition of drummer Roy and bassist Tally, they signed to the independent Jungle label. Their debut saw chainsaw guitars collide with machine-gun drumming, while the lyrics dealt with contemporary issues such as television evangelists, sexual perverts, childhood anxieties and warmongers. Never big on subtlety, Creaming Jesus have sustained a rudimentary talent over a succession of albums.

● ALBUMS: *Too Fat To Run, Too Stupid To Hide* (Jungle 1990)★★★, *Guilt By Association* (Jungle 1992)★★★, *Chaos For The Converted* (Jungle 1994)★★★, *The End Of An Error* (Jungle 1996)★★★.

CREED

This US blues-based boogie band was formed in 1977 by vocalist Steve Ingle and guitarist Luther Maben. Enlisting the services of Hal Butler (keyboards), James Flynn (bass) and Chip Thomas (drums) they were soon signed by Asylum Records. Their self-titled debut appeared in 1978 and was notable for 'Time And Time Again', an epic southern-style guitar workout, comparable in stature to Lynyrd Skynyrd's 'Freebird'. Unable to attract enough media attention, the band split up shortly after the album's release.

● ALBUMS: *Creed* (Asylum 1978)★★★.

CREEK

Formed in North Carolina, USA, this hard rock band shortened their name from Sugarcreek in 1986 to avoid any association with the country music scene. Comprising Jerry West (guitar, vocals), Rick Lee (keyboards, vocals), Mike Barber (bass), Tim Clark (vocals, percussion) and Lynn Samples (drums), they specialized in highly melodic pomp-rock, making extensive use of four-part vocal harmonies. Influenced by Styx, Kansas and Journey, they have released two exceptional albums on shoestring budgets. In 1987 John Harwell and Robbie Hegler replaced Samples and Barber on drums and bass, respectively.

● ALBUMS: *The Creek* (Music For Nations 1986)★★★★, *Storm The Gate* (Beaver 1989)★★★.

CRIMSON GLORY

Formerly known as Pierced Arrow and Beowolf, this Florida-based heavy metal quintet settled on the name Crimson Glory in 1982. Comprising Midnight (vocals), Jon Drenning (guitar), Ben Jackson (guitar), Jeff Lords (bass) and Dana Burnell (drums), they spent a full three years writing material and developing a sound. They emerged in 1986 with a self-titled debut on Roadrunner Records, which fused the techno-rock of Queensrÿche with the uncompromising power-metal of Iron Maiden. There was also a nod to religious themes, not least in the choice of their name, though the group denied any connection to the 'white metal' movement. The band also sported silver masks to add an element of artistic mystique to their identity. *Transcendence* was an ambitious concept album that explored the themes of destiny, theocracy and philosophy. It received widespread critical acclaim and put the band on the launching pad to international recognition. Internal disputes then led to a line-up reshuffle, with Jackson and Burnell ousted. Ravi Jakhorta was recruited on drums and the band continued as a four-piece. They eventually discarded the masks on *Strange And Beautiful*, their third and most complete work. Here, they incorporated a wider range of influences, added organ and acoustic bridges, and showed an increased awareness of dynamics. Seemingly only a matter of time before the Midnight/Drenning songwriting partnership achieved more significant success, the band's broke up soon after the album's release.

● ALBUMS: *Crimson Glory* (Roadrunner 1986)★★, *Transcendence* (MCA 1988)★★★, *Strange And Beautiful* (Atlantic 1991)★★★★.

Cro-Mags

This US thrash/hardcore band was formed in 1984 by bassist (and sometime singer) Harley Flanagan, a follower of the Hare Krishna doctrine, who nevertheless represented an intimidating, multi-tattooed presence on stage. After a series of false starts, vocalist John 'Bloodclot' Joseph, drummer Mackie Jayson and guitarists Doug Holland (ex-Kraut, who joined in time for *Best Wishes*) and Parris Mitchell Mayhew were recruited to cement the band's line-up. When Joseph left, Flanagan took over vocal duties. They specialized in a fusion of thrash, hardcore and heavy metal, and the influences of Motörhead, the Dead Kennedys and Metallica were apparent on their debut, *The Age Of Quarrel*. They built up a small but loyal cult following, and regularly headlined major hardcore events at New York's CBGB's during the mid-80s. Primarily remarkable for their sheer sonic intensity, the group were at the forefront of a musical genre that became increasingly adopted by the metal fraternity as time wore on. Unlike most, however, Cro-Mags offered lyrical diversity and invention to back up their 'mosh' epics, notably on tracks such as 'The Only One', which delivered a sermon on their leader's religious position. Line-up changes were numerous, the most pertinent of which was Jayson's decision to join Bad Brains. The band broke up while working on *Alpha Omega*, but re-formed with the line-up comprising Flanagan, Holland, Joseph, drummer Dave DiSenzo and guitarist Gabby. Following two more albums (including the completed *Alpha Omega*), the band fell apart again. Following their demise, Joseph formed Both Worlds.

● ALBUMS: *The Age Of Quarrel* (Rock Hotel/Profile 1986)★★★, *Best Wishes* (Profile 1989)★★★, *Alpha Omega* (Century Media 1992)★★★, *Near Death Experience* (Century Media 1993)★★.

Cronos

Named after the group's vocalist and bass player Cronos (b. Conrad Lant, England), this band was formed as a splinter group from English heavy metal band Venom. Cronos and American guitarists Jimmy C. and Mike Hickey were drawn from Venom, with the new group's line-up completed by Chris P. (drums). Relocating to America's east coast in early 1989, the group attempted to build on the formidable reputation afforded Venom in death metal circles. Unfortunately, this new vehicle for Cronos's trademark baleful singing and doom-laden songwriting lacked much of the zest and commitment exhibited in his former group.

● ALBUMS: *Dancin' In The Fire* (Neat 1990)★★, *Venom* (Neat 1995)★★.

Cross

After two solo albums, Roger Taylor (vocals, guitar) sought a new challenge outside the confines of Queen. He formed the Cross in summer 1987 with Clayton Moss (guitar), Spike Edney (keyboards), Peter Noone (bass) and Josh Macrae (drums), concentrating on a low-key pop-rock approach. The group made its debut in September 1987 with 'Cowboys And Indians', a mix of dance and rock music reminiscent of mid-period Queen. *Shove It*, with its title track preceding it as a single, was a nondescript collection of half-hearted rockers that lacked distinction, partly owing to Taylor's limited vocal ability. Ironically, the best track, 'Heaven For Everyone', was delivered by Freddie Mercury, although the single release of the song featured Taylor at the microphone. *Mad, Bad And Dangerous To Know*, a title inspired by the poetry of Byron, was something of a misnomer, though it did feature a more raucous version of the Cross sound than that previously on show. Much of the album had been written by other band members while Taylor was working with Queen, though he did contribute some strong guitarwork and two overtly political songs in 'Old Men (Lay Down)' and 'Final Destination'. Mike Moran assisted on keyboards in place of Edney, unavailable because of touring commitments with Elton John. However, Parlophone Records were losing interest in the group and their third album, *Blue Rock*, was issued only in Germany and Japan. Following the death of Freddie Mercury, extra-curricular work for Taylor included another solo album with further songs of a serious political nature. This activity ruled out any imminent return to the Cross name, and the band played what many considered to be a farewell gig at London's Marquee club in December 1992.

● ALBUMS: *Shove It* (Virgin 1988)★★, *Mad, Bad And Dangerous To Know* (Parlophone 1990)★★, *Blue Rock* (Electrola 1991)★.

CROWBAR

This US quartet emerged in the early 90s as one of the leading lights of the New Orleans extreme metal scene, purveying a sound that blended Black Sabbath/St Vitus-styled heaviness with hardcore aggression. Kirk Windstein (vocals, guitar), Kevin Noonan (guitar), Todd Strange (bass) and Craig Nunenmacher (drums) made their debut with the dark and doom-laden *Obedience Thru Suffering*, after which Noonan was replaced by Matt Thomas, a former bandmate of Pantera frontman Phil Anselmo in Razor White. Anselmo, an old friend who collaborated with Windstein on side-projects such as Down and Both Legs Broken, helped to refine and improve the band's sound with his sympathetic production on *Crowbar*, which included a brutally heavy interpretation of Led Zeppelin's 'No Quarter', adapted stylishly to the Crowbar sound. The band were well received on tour with Paradise Lost in the UK and Pantera in the USA, and released the *Live +1 EP* (which was packaged with *Crowbar* in the UK) before returning to the studio with the stated intention of making *Crowbar* sound 'like Jethro Tull'. In 1995 Jimmy Bowers (ex-Eyehategod) was recruited as the drummer, although *Time Heals Nothing* was recorded by the original line-up. True to form and promise, it provided a thunderous blast of controlled aggression and dark melodicism.

● ALBUMS: *Obedience Thru Suffering* (Grindcore 1992)★★, *Crowbar* (Pavement 1993)★★★, *Time Heals Nothing* (Pavement 1995)★★★, *Broken Glass* (Pavement 1996)★★★, *Odd Fellows Rest* (Mayhem 1998)★★★★.

CROWN OF THORNS

This US heavy metal band (unconnected with the similarly titled IRS Records recording artists) formed in 1991, because 'we just kept bumping into each other on the tour circuit'. Micki Free (guitar, ex-Shalamar) and Jean Beauvoir (b. Chicago, Illinois, USA; vocals, guitar, ex-Plasmatics; Little Steven; Voodoo X and solo) assembled Crown Of Thorns with Michael Page (bass) and Tony Thompson (drums, ex-Power Station). The first song they wrote together, 'Hike It Up', was the stand-out track on their debut mini-album. With production by Kiss's Paul Stanley on five tracks, the collection was not released outside the UK, although the band did tour extensively. Thompson was replaced by Dave 'Hawk' Lopez, and Free (who released a solo album in 1995) by Tommy Lafferty. By 1995 Crown Of Thorns had yet to play their first concert in their native America, but in the UK, after making their debut at London's Marquee in April 1994, they toured almost non-stop and supported Bon Jovi on selected dates. Beauvoir, who turned down work with Prince and Michael Jackson, has also recorded two solo albums and written songs for Kiss and John Waite.

● ALBUMS: *Crown Of Thorns* (1993)★★, *Breakthrough* (Now & Then 1996)★★★, *Mentally Vexed* (Another Planet 1996)★★★.

CRUMBSUCKERS

This New York 'thrashcore' quintet was formed in Long Island in 1983 by vocalist Chris Notaro and guitarist Chuck Lenihan. With the addition of Gary Meskill (bass), Dave Wynn (guitar) and Dan Richardson (drums), they signed to Combat Records and recorded *Life Of Dreams* in 1986. This was an uncompromising blast of hardcore angst with metallic undercurrents, and helped to establish a large cult following for the band. *Beast On My Back* saw Wynn replaced by Ronnie Koebler, as the band moved away from their hardcore roots and entered the thrash metal domain. Marc Piovanetti (ex-Carnivore) and Joe Hegarty replaced Lenihan and Notaro, respectively, in 1989, with the band subsequently changing their name to Heavy Rain. The Crumbsuckers' transition to Metallica and Slayer-like metal was complete. After the band eventually disintegrated, Meskill and Richardson resurfaced in Pro-Pain.

● ALBUMS: *Life Of Dreams* (Combat Core/Rough Justice 1986)★★★, *Beast On My Back* (Combat/Music For Nations 1988)★★★.

CRY OF LOVE

These North Carolina retro-rockers began life in 1989 on the local covers circuit around Raleigh, as a trio of Audley Freed (guitar), Robert Kearns (bass) and Jason Patterson (drums), but did not enjoy any real success until the arrival of vocalist/guitarist Kelly Holland. Cry Of Love (a name taken from a Jimi Hendrix album) quickly signed major recording and management agreements in the wake of his arrival. *Brother* was a classic slice of soulful hard rock, with a sound akin to Free and Bad Company enhanced by atmospheric live takes. Holland produced a performance worthy of Paul Rodgers in his heyday, while the inevitable Hendrix comparisons were heightened by Freed's tasteful lead work. With the success of the Black Crowes reawakening interest in classic rock styles, Cry Of Love's popularity leapt; the superb 'Peace Pipe' reached number 1 on the US

Billboard Album Rock Track chart, while the band produced a series of dazzling live performances on the road with Robert Plant, Lynyrd Skynyrd, Bad Company and ZZ Top. In addition, they continued their own heavy touring schedule, where they freely jammed on extended versions of album material, and preceded their second UK tour with a well-received second stage spot at the 1994 Donington Festival. It therefore came as something of a surprise when Holland departed later that year. He was eventually replaced by Robert Mason, who made his debut on 1997's *Diamonds & Debris*.

● ALBUMS: *Brother* (Columbia 1993)★★★, *Diamonds & Debris* (Sony 1997)★★★.

CRYBABYS

This bluesy rock 'n' roll quartet from the UK was formed in 1991 by former Boys guitarist 'Honest' John Plain. Recruiting Darrell Barth (guitar, vocals), Mark Duncan (bass) and Robbie Rushton (drums), they signed with Receiver Records the same year. Drawing inspiration from Mott The Hoople, Hanoi Rocks and the Georgia Satellites, the Crybabys successfully bridged the gap between punk and rock 'n' roll. Shambolic, chaotic and full of stamina, they debuted with *Where Have All The Good Girls Gone?*. This compared favourably with the best that either the similarly inclined Dogs D'Amour (whom Barth later joined) or Quireboys produced in that period. Barth and Plain later played in Ian Hunter's Dirty Laundry.

● ALBUMS: *Where Have All The Good Girls Gone?* (Receiver 1991)★★★.

CRYPTIC SLAUGHTER

This Californian speed metal quartet was formed in 1985 by vocalist Bill Cook and guitarist Les Evans. Enlisting the services of Rob Nicholson (bass) and Scott Peterson (drums), they specialized in short, abrupt songs that were carried along by warp-speed drumming and relentless riffing. They recorded four albums in total for the Metal Blade and Roadrunner labels between 1986 and 1988, roughly in the mould of all-out thrashers such as D.R.I., Suicidal Tendencies or Gang Green. The band split up in 1990, however, and their passing was scarcely mourned even within that select fraternity.

● ALBUMS: *Convicted* (Metal Blade 1986)★★★, *Money Talks* (Metal Blade 1987)★★, *Stream Of Consciousness* (Roadrunner 1988)★★, *Speak Your Peace* (Metal Blade 1990)★★.

CUBANATE

Confrontational English heavy metal duo, aesthetically likened to the Henry Rollins Band, who managed to attract death threats early in their careers after calling a Belfast audience 'cocksuckers'. The other element of Cubanate's ability to infuriate and upset resides in their musical approach, which utilizes samplers and DAT alongside guitar riffs and hardcore techno percussion (although in their early touring forays with Carcass they were unable to present a further live percussionist and guitarist due to financial restrictions). Marc Heal (vocals/programming) and Phil Barry (guitar), nevertheless, managed to create a not inconsiderable impression on their own, with a musical hybrid similar to, but more extreme than, that engendered by central Europeans Front 242 and KMFDM. This first came to public attention via the striking 'Bodyburn' single on the Berlin based Dynamica label. They offered fuller exposition of this creed on their debut album, recorded in just six days and on a budget of £4,000. Further albums have indicated a greater willingness to experiment with rhythms, without compromising their strikingly intense sound.

● ALBUMS: *Antimatter* (Dynamica 1993)★★★, *Cyberia* (Dynamica 1995)★★★, *Barbarossa* (Dynamica 1996)★★, *Interference* (TVT 1998)★★★.

CULPRIT

This US hard rock quintet, based in Seattle, was formed in 1980 from the ashes of Orpheus and Amethyst. Comprising John DeVol (guitar), Scott Earl (bass), Bud Burrill (drums), Jeff L'Heureux (vocals) and Kjartan Kristoffersen (guitar), they combined the power-metal style of Iron Maiden with the intricate melodic arrangements of Rush. Signing to Mike Varney's Shrapnel label, they debuted with *Guilty As Charged* in 1983. This was favourably received by the music media, and they established a large following throughout Washington state. However, such success was short-lived as the band was beset by drug problems and internal musical disagreements. They finally disintegrated in 1985, and a planned reunion in 1987 failed to reach fruition. Kristoffersen and Earl later joined TKO.

● ALBUMS: *Guilty As Charged* (Shrapnel 1983)★★★.

CULT

Originally known as first Southern Death Cult, then Death Cult, the band was formed by lead singer Ian Astbury (b. 14 May 1962, Heswell, Merseyside, England) in 1981. After a youth spent in Scotland and Canada (where he gained early exposure to the culture of native Indians on the Six Nations Reservation, informing the early stages of the band's career), Astbury moved into a house in Bradford, Yorkshire, and discovered a group rehearsing in the basement. The group's personnel included Haq Quereshi (drums), David 'Buzz' Burrows (guitar) and Barry Jepson (bass). As their vocalist, Astbury oversaw a rapid rise in fortunes, their fifth gig and London debut at the Heaven club attracting a near 2,000-strong audience. Southern Death Cult made their recording debut in December 1982 with the double a-side 'Moya'/'Fatman', and released a self-titled album on Beggars Banquet Records. They supported Bauhaus on tour in early 1983. However, by March the group had folded, Astbury reeling from his perceived image of 'positive punk' spokesman, and the fact that his native Indian concept was being diluted by the group's format. His new band, operating under the truncated name Death Cult, would, he vowed, not become a victim of hype in the same way again (Quereshi, Jepson and Burrows would go on to join Getting The Fear, subsequently becoming Into A Circle before Quereshi re-emerged as the centrepiece of Fun-Da-Mental's 'world dance' ethos under the name Propa-Ghandi). A combination of the single, demo and live tracks was posthumously issued as the sole SDC album. Death Cult comprised the rhythm section of recently deceased gothic band Ritual, namely Ray 'The Reverend' Mondo (drums) and Jamie Stewart (bass), plus guitarist Billy Duffy (b. 12 May 1959, Manchester, England; ex-Ed Banger And The Nosebleeds and Theatre Of Hate). They made their debut in July 1983 with an eponymous four-track 12-inch, at which time Astbury also changed his own name (he had previously been using Ian Lindsay, which, it later transpired, was his mother's maiden name). After an appearance at the Futurama festival Mondo swapped drumming positions with Sex Gang Children's Nigel Preston (d. 7 May 1992), a former colleague of Duffy's in Theatre Of Hate. However, 1984 brought about a second and final name change - with the band feeling that the Death prefix typecast them as a 'gothic' act, they became simply the Cult. They recorded their first album together, *Dreamtime*, for release in September 1984, its sales boosted by a number 1 single in the independent charts with the typically anthemic 'Spiritwalker'.

Another strong effort followed early the next year, 'She Sells Sanctuary', but this was to prove Preston's swan-song. Mark Brzezicki of Big Country helped out on sessions for the forthcoming album until the permanent arrival of Les Warner (b. 13 February 1961), who had previously worked with Johnny Thunders, Julian Lennon and Randy California. The band's major commercial breakthrough came with *Love* in 1985, which comprised fully fledged hard rock song structures and pushed Duffy's guitar lines to the fore. It reached number 4 in the UK, and spawned two UK Top 20 hit singles in the aforementioned 'She Sells Sanctuary' and 'Rain'. *Electric* saw the band's transition to heavy rock completed. There was no disguising the group's source of inspiration, with Led Zeppelin being mentioned in nearly every review. Part-produced by Rick Rubin, *Electric* was a bold and brash statement of intent, if not quite the finished item. It became a success on both sides of the Atlantic, peaking at number 4 and 38 in the UK and US charts, respectively. The gigs to promote it saw the band add bass player Kid 'Haggis' Chaos (b. Mark Manning; ex-Zodiac Mindwarp And The Love Reaction), with Stewart switching to rhythm guitar. Both Haggis and Warner were dispensed with in March 1988, the former joining Four Horsemen. Reduced to a three-piece of Astbury, Stewart and Duffy, the sessions for *Sonic Temple* saw them temporarily recruit the services of drummer Mickey Curry. It was an album that combined the atmospheric passion of *Love* with the unbridled energy of *Electric*, and reached number 3 in the UK and number 10 on the US *Billboard* chart.

A 1989 world tour saw the band augmented by Matt Sorum (b. 19 November 1960, Mission Viejo, California, USA; drums) and Mark Taylor (keyboards; ex-Alarm and Armoury Show). Stewart quit in 1990, while Sorum would go on to a tenure with Guns N'Roses. *Ceremony* was released in 1991, with the help of Charley Drayton (bass) and the returning Mickey Curry. This was a retrogressive collection of songs, that had more in common with *Love* than their previous two albums. Nevertheless, having already established an enormous fanbase, success was virtually guaranteed. *The Pure Cult* compilation duly topped the UK charts in February 1993. *The Cult* saw them reunited with producer Bob Rock, on a set that included the rather clumsy Kurt Cobain tribute 'Sacred Life'. By this time, however, Astbury had departed and later resurfaced with a new band, the Holy Barbarians.

● ALBUMS: as Southern Death Cult *The Southern Death Cult* (Beggars Banquet 1983)★★, *Dreamtime* (Beggars Banquet 1984)★★, *Love* (Beggars Banquet 1985)★★, *Electric* (Beggars Banquet 1987)★★★, *Sonic Temple* (Beggars Banquet 1989)★★★, *Ceremony* (Beggars Banquet 1991)★★, *The Cult* (Beggars Banquet 1994)★★.

● COMPILATIONS: as Southern Death Cult *Complete Recordings* (Situation Two 1991)★★, *Pure Cult* (Beggars Banquet 1993)★★★.

● VIDEOS: *Dreamtime At The Lyceum* (Beggars Banquet 1984), *Electric Love* (Beggars Banquet 1987), *Cult: Video Single* (One Plus One 1987), *Sonic Ceremony* (Beggar's Banquet 1992), *Pure Cult* (1993), *Dreamtime Live At The Lyceum* (Beggars Banquet 1996).

CURRIE, CHERIE

Lead vocalist with the Runaways, Currie (b. 1960, Los Angeles, California, USA) opted for a solo career after the release of *Queens Of Noise* in 1977. Under the wing of Kim Fowley and guitarist Steven T, she recorded *Beauty's Only Skin Deep*, which also featured her sister, Marie, on backing vocals. Released to coincide with the Runaways' *Live In Japan*, it failed to reach the charts and received poor press. Her elusive second album, *Messin' With The Boys*, credited to Cherie And Marie, was a much heavier affair and utilized the talents of session men/Toto members Steve Lukather and Mike Porcaro. The title track was released as a single but ultimately failed to capture the solo success that fellow Runaways Joan Jett and Lita Ford went on to achieve. Currie left the music business in 1980 to become an actress, but after a starring role alongside Jodie Foster and Randy Quaid in the movie *Foxes*, she vanished from the public eye.

● ALBUMS: *Beauty's Only Skin Deep* (Mercury 1978)★★, *Messin' With The Boys* (Capitol 1979)★★★.

● COMPILATIONS: *Young & Wild* (Raven 1998)★★★.

CYCLONE

Formerly known as Centurion, Cyclone were formed in Vilvoorde, Belgium, by vocalist Guido Gevels and guitarist Pascal van Lint in 1981. With the addition of Johnny Kerbush (guitar), Stefan Daamen (bass) and Nicholas Lairin (drums), they initially took their cue from the New Wave Of British Heavy Metal. They later switched to a more thrash-orientated approach, styling themselves on Anthrax. They subsequently negotiated a one-album contract with Roadrunner Records and debuted with *Brutal Destruction* in 1986. The label did not renew the group's contract and Cyclone disbanded the following year.

● ALBUMS: *Brutal Destruction* (Roadrunner 1986)★★.

CYNIC

This death metal act was formed in Florida, USA, in 1987 by guitarist/vocalist Paul Masvidal, guitarist Jason Gobel, bassist Tony Choy, and drummer Sean Reinert, and recorded a number of acclaimed demos where brutal death metal was mixed with highly complex jazz/fusion-style riffs and rhythms. However, until the release of *Focus*, it seemed that the band were destined to be better known for providing session musicians for other bands, as Masvidal and Reinert played on Death's *Human* album and tour, while Choy worked first with Pestilence and then with Atheist, whom he subsequently joined on a permanent basis. *Focus*, with Shawn Malone replacing Choy, was a complex, multi-textured album, displaying some remarkable musicianship without lapsing into self-indulgence, and one reviewer's description of 'King Crimson meets Death' seemed apt. The band were finally able to tour extensively in their own right, although, ironically, a temporary bassist was recruited for some dates due to Malone's music degree study commitments.

● ALBUMS: *Focus* (Roadrunner 1993)★★★.

D'Molls

This Chicago, Illinois-based heavy metal band featured Desi Rexx (vocals, guitar), Billy Dior (drums), S.S. Priest (guitar), Nigel Itson (vocals) and Lizzy Valentine (bass). Their self-titled 1988 debut album caused a stir at the time of its release, with its self-assured Aerosmith-meets-Poison approach. However, the songwriting on the follow-up, *Warped*, was weak and rigidly formularized, lacking the cutting edge of its predecessor. They relocated to Los Angeles, but with poor reviews and sales to match, they disbanded in 1991. Rexx went on to work with former Derringer guitarist Danny Johnson, while Itson joined Millionaire Boys Club.

● ALBUMS: *D'Molls* (Atlantic 1988)★★★, *Warped* (Atlantic 1990)★★, *Beyond D'Valley Of D'Molls!* (Delinquent 1997)★★★.

D.A.D.

Originally known as Disneyland After Dark, D.A.D. came together in Copenhagen, Denmark, in 1985. Comprising Jesper Binzer (vocals, guitar), Jacob A. Binzer (guitar), Stig Pedersen (bass) and Peter L. Jensen (drums), they combined high-energy metallic rock 'n' roll with an irreverent sense of humour, reminiscent of Cheap Trick and ZZ Top at their playful best. After two entertaining and musically competent albums on the independent Mega label, they were signed by Warner Brothers Records in 1989 (reputedly for over $1,000,000) and marketed as their 'next big thing'. Their energetic and eccentric live performances were highly impressive, with scenarios including exploding helmets and instruments, but they failed to generate similar intensity in the studio. Consequently, *No Fuel Left For The Pilgrims* did not live up to the label's advance promotion. *Riskin' It All* emerged in 1991 and proved that the band had not been disillusioned by the press backlash. It was, instead, an excellent hard rock album, sparkling with offbeat energy and their own peculiar, tongue-in-cheek style. *Helpyourselfish* was released in 1995 after 'two and a half years in a rehearsal room', according to Binzen. Song titles such as '(Naked) But Still Stripping' and 'It's When It's Wrong It's Right' continued the band's penchant for more bizarre themes. When Binzon reasoned 'We're toning the circus part down,' he soon put the statement in context: 'But Stig has a new bass like an olive with a toothpick stuck through it. He'll also have a bass stand shaped like a martini glass, and be dressed as a Spanish bullfighter.'

● ALBUMS: *Call Of The Wild* (Mega 1986)★★★, *Disneyland After Dark Draws A Circle* (Mega 1987)★★★, *No Fuel Left For The Pilgrims* (Warners 1989)★★, *Riskin' It All* (Warners 1991)★★★, *Helpyourselfish* (Warners 1995)★★★.

D.C. Star

Formed in Washington, DC, USA, in the early 80s, this hard rock quintet took their prefix from their locale and performed widely in the area long before their songs were released on record. Comprising Henry Farmer (bass), Kenny Talor (vocals), Jeff Avery (keyboards, guitar), Dave Simmons (guitar) and Glenn Jones (drums), their style was one of unreconstructed goodtime rock 'n' roll, considered by the local media to be akin to early Deep Purple. They recorded their debut album, *Rockin' In The Classroom*, for Atlantic Records subsidiary Mirage in 1985, but despite further good reviews this was never followed up.

● ALBUMS: *Rockin' In The Classroom* (Mirage 1985)★★★.

D.R.I.

This thrash metal band was formed in Houston, Texas, USA, in 1982. The band's original line-up consisted of Kurt Brecht (vocals), Spike Cassidy (guitar), Dennis Johnson (bass) and Kurt's brother Eric Brecht (drums). Originally calling themselves Dirty Rotten Imbeciles, they shortened the name to D.R.I. and signed to Roadrunner Records in the UK. In the USA they at first used their own independent label, subsequently signing with Metal Blade/Enigma. Their debut album, *Dirty Rotten LP*, was released in 1984, and preceded the band's relocation to San Francisco. It quickly established D.R.I. at the forefront of their genre, with its vicious mixture of punk, hardcore and thrash metal (Slayer's Dave Lombardo later cited them as a major influence). Before the next album, *Dealing With It!*, founder-member Eric Brecht left the band to be replaced by Felix Griffin, though this was only one of numerous personnel changes during the band's lifetime. D.R.I. continued to bridge punk and metal audiences, even going as far as to call their third album *Crossover*. They eventually moved into a more traditional speed metal style with the release of *4 Of A Kind* in 1988. Perhaps to remind their fans of their 'roots', the band remixed and re-released the *Dirty Rotten LP* in the same year, also including four extra tracks that had originally been released as an EP, *Violent Pacification*, back in 1984. Soon after this, the band encountered problems on a short tour of Mexico when new bass player John Menor was viciously attacked and robbed. However, this did not deter the band from producing their most accomplished album to date, *Thrash Zone*, though it proved to be their swan-song for Metal Blade/Enigma.

● ALBUMS: *Dirty Rotten LP* (Rotten 1984)★★★, *Dealing With It!* (Metal Blade/Enigma 1985)★★★, *Crossover* (Metal Blade/Enigma 1987)★★★, *4 Of A Kind* (Metal Blade/Enigma 1988)★★★, *Thrash Zone* (Metal Blade/Enigma 1989)★★★, *Definition* (Rotten 1992)★★, *Full Speed Ahead* (Rotten 1995)★★★.

● VIDEOS: *Live At The Ritz* (Roadrunner 1989).

DAKOTA

This US melodic rock outfit was formed in Chicago, Illinois, in 1979 by vocalists/guitarists Jerry Hludzik and Billy Kelly. Recruiting Lou Crossa and Jeff Mitchell on keyboards, Bill McMale (bass) and John Robinson (drums), they based their style on the music of Styx, Toto and Kansas. Heavily dominated by keyboards and watertight vocal harmonies, the band released two high-quality studio albums of pomp rock, before disbanding in 1984.

● ALBUMS: *Dakota* (Columbia 1980)★★★, *Runaway* (Columbia 1984)★★★.

DAMIEN THORNE

This American heavy metal quintet was formed in Chicago, Illinois, in 1985 by vocalist Justin Fate and guitarist Ken Starr. The group drew their name from the 'Antichrist' in the book/film *The Omen*. After enlisting the services of Michael Monroe (guitar), Sanders Pate (bass) and Pete Pagonis (drums), they concentrated on a dual guitar approach similar to Judas Priest. They signed to Roadrunner Records and debuted with *Sign Of The Jackal* the following year. Produced by Virgin Steele vocalist David DeFeis, this incorporated Iron Maiden, Def Leppard and Metallica influences, but these were not sufficiently modified or reinterpreted to an extent where they gave the band an identity of their own.

● ALBUMS: *Sign Of The Jackal* (Roadrunner 1986)★★.

DAMN THE MACHINE

Refusing an offer to rejoin Megadeth after playing on the demo sessions for *Rust In Peace*, guitarist Chris Poland subsequently recorded a fine solo effort, *Return To Metalopolis*. Afterwards, he formed Damn The Machine in Los Angeles in 1991 with his drummer brother Mark, bassist Dave Randi, and guitarist/vocalist Dave Clemmons. The band was signed by A&M Records on the strength of a live studio demo. Damn The Machine eschewed Megadeth-style thrash, opting for a progressive blend of traditional power metal and the jazz stylings that Poland had explored in his solo work to produce a complex yet listenable album. However, despite considerable interest and near-universal press support, the band unexpectedly broke up shortly after their debut European dates opening for Dream Theater.

● ALBUMS: *Damn The Machine* (A&M 1993)★★★.

DAMN YANKEES

Formed in 1989, the Damn Yankees were one of several supergroups, including Bad English, to emerge in the USA towards the end of the decade. Ex-Styx guitarist/vocalist Tommy Shaw had already been writing with the larger-than-life guitarist and solo artist Ted Nugent and they were soon joined by Jack Blades on bass and vocals (from the recently demised Night Ranger) and Michael Cartellone, a previously unknown drummer. Warner Brothers beat Geffen Records in the race to sign the band, and their self-titled debut album was released in 1990. The music was hard-edged melodic rock, much heavier than the work of Styx and Night Ranger, with Shaw and Blades handling the bulk of the vocal duties, although Nugent contributed lead vocals to the outrageous 'Piledriver'. The album reached number 13 in the US *Billboard* charts with the help of a Top 5 single - the power ballad 'High Enough', which reached number 3 in September 1990.

Damn Yankees, however, were not simply a record company creation. They could also produce sparkling live performances, gaining a glowing reputation for their shows. These included tantalizing snippets from the respective back catalogues of Styx, Night Ranger and Ted Nugent's solo work. The melodic influence of Shaw and Blades, combined with the melodramatic antics of Nugent, created a highly successful unit in terms of both critical acclaim and commercial success. A second album, *Don't Tread*, climbed to number 22 in

August 1992, but the following year the group called it a day.

● ALBUMS: *Damn Yankees* (Warners 1990)★★★, *Don't Tread* (Warners 1992)★★★.

DANGER DANGER

This melodic and atmospheric US hard rock band were formed in 1988 by former Michael Bolton bassist Bruno Ravel. Enlisting the services of Ted Poley (ex-Prophet vocalist), Kasey Smith (keyboards), Steve West (drums) and Tony Rey (guitar), the band's style lay somewhere between White Lion and Bon Jovi. They were picked up by Imagine Records and debuted with a self-titled album in 1989. Produced by Lance Quinn and Mike Stone, this was an impressive collection of infectious rockers and dynamic power-ballads. Rey left to concentrate on his other project, Saraya, in 1989, and was replaced by Andy Timmons. Signing to Epic Records, they released *Screw It!* in 1992, which built on the solid foundations of their debut, but included a greater element of arrogant street attitude. It signalled considerable crossover potential that, with careful nurturing, might have produced a major songwriting force (despite song titles such as 'Slipped Her The Big One'). However, following touring with Kiss, the band split up, leaving Poley to form his own solo venture, Ted Poley's Bone Machine.

● ALBUMS: *Danger Danger* (Epic 1989)★★, *Screw It!* (Epic 1992)★★★.

DANGEROUS TOYS

This group was formed by ex-Onyx members Scott Dalhover (guitar), Mike Watson (bass) and Mark Geary (drums) in Texas in 1987. With the recruitment of ex-Watchtower vocalist Jason McMaster, the band signed to CBS Records and debuted with a self-titled album in 1989. This revealed strong Guns N'Roses and Aerosmith influences, alongside their previous techno-thrash style. Shortly after the album was released, Danny Aaron was added as second guitarist to add greater flexibility on the road. They achieved minor successes in the US singles market with 'Teas'n, Pleas'n' and 'Scared', the latter a tribute to their idol Alice Cooper. Both reached number 1 on the MTV video chart. Collaborating with Desmond Child, they recorded 'Demon Bell' for inclusion on the soundtrack to the horror movie *Shocker*, following which they supported the Cult and Bonham on a lengthy US west coast tour. *Hellacious Acres* produced further minor successes with 'Gimme No Lip' and 'Line 'Em Up'. Aaron departed in 1992 to be replaced by Paul Lidel (ex-Dirty Looks) in time for the sessions that produced *Pissed*. This album, their first for Music For Nations subsidiary Bullet Proof, was recorded in exactly one month in Los Angeles.

● ALBUMS: *Dangerous Toys* (Columbia 1989)★★★, *Hellacious Acres* (Columbia 1991)★★★, *Pissed* (Bullet Proof 1994)★★★, *The R*tist 4*merly Known As Dangerous Toys* (DMZ 1995)★★.

DANIEL BAND

Canadian heavy metal band formed in 1981 by vocalist/bassist Dan McGabe and guitarist/keyboardist Bill Findlay. The line-up, which remained remarkably stable over the course of the band's career, was completed by Tony Rossi (vocals, guitar) and Matt Delouca (drums). Taking their cue from April Wine, Triumph and Y&T, they specialized in melodic hard rock, with extended guitar and keyboard passages. Unlike many Christian rockers, the religious message was secondary to some excellent music.

● ALBUMS: *On Rock* (Streetlight 1982)★★★, *Straight Ahead* (Refuge 1983)★★★, *Run From The Darkness* (Refuge 1984)★★★, *Rise Up* (Refuge 1986)★★★, *Running Out Of Time* (Refuge 1987)★★★.

DANZIG

US rock band Danzig are largely a vehicle for the lyrical and musical talents of Glenn Danzig (b. 23 June 1959, Lodi, New Jersey, USA). Using musicians from his previous bands, the Misfits and Samhain - guitarist John Christ (b. 19 February 1965, Baltimore, Maryland, USA) and bass player Eerie Von (b. 25 August 1964, Lodi, New Jersey, USA) - plus stylish hardcore veteran Chuck Biscuits on drums (ex-D.O.A.; Black Flag; Circle Jerks), he founded Danzig in 1987 and sold the concept to Rick Rubin's Def American label the following year. The resultant album realized all of the promise shown in Glenn's former projects, producing work with a soulful profundity at which he had previously only hinted. While satanically inclined, Danzig have managed to avoid most of the pitfalls that have plagued other bands who court a devilish image. Younger, more overtly aggressive acts such as Deicide and Slayer presented images dominated by rage and pain, whereas Danzig approached other aspects of the satanic in artfully composed songs, from the seductive to the quietly sinister. However, this subtlety tempered their appeal within the heavy metal fraternity, many of whom demanded a more direct or

traditional approach, and Danzig remained a connoisseur's metal band. Their second release, *Lucifuge*, did little to alter this. None of the elements used were in themselves original - vocals in the style of 50s crooners, rich, black blues guitars, evocative heavy metal riffs - but it was the cunningly seamless way in which they were combined that generated Danzig's dark magic.
A third long-playing release, *How The Gods Kill*, formed a bridge between the high melodrama of heavy metal and the alluring menace of gothic mood. *Black Aria* was a solo project for Glenn Danzig, and was something of a stylistic departure from his previous guitar-based material. It consisted of quasi-classical instrumentals, with one side dedicated to portraying the story of Lucifer's fall from grace. In late 1993 the mainstream rock crowd discovered Danzig through the runaway success of the video for 'Mother' on MTV. 'Mother' was, in fact, a track from their debut, but it took five years for this twisted classic to gain widespread recognition. *Danzig 4* followed and was met with critical accusations that it was a deliberately commercial outing for the band, designed to please their new audience. Indeed, the album contained little of the rousing anthemic rock that had peppered previous albums, but this fourth instalment was still distinctively Danzig (indeed, it echoed Samhain days). Glenn Danzig had long since demonstrated that he could yell up a storm with the Misfits, but this collection proved that he was at his most menacing and creative when he was at his quietest. During touring to support *Danzig 4*, Joey Castillo (b. 30 March 1966, Gardena, California, USA) replaced Biscuits. Danzig, a longstanding comic book fan, founded his own company, Verotix, in 1995, with the intention of publishing adult comics. A new line-up (Danzig, Castillo, vocalist/guitarist Tommy Victor (ex-Prong) and bassist Josh Lazie) recorded *Blackacidevil* in 1996.

● ALBUMS: *Danzig* (Def American/Geffen 1988)★★★, *Danzig II - Lucifuge* (Def American/Geffen 1990)★★★, *How The Gods Kill* (Def American 1992)★★★, *Thrall - Demonsweatlive* (Def American 1993)★★, *Black Aria* (Plan 9 1993)★★, *Danzig 4* (American 1994)★★★, *Blackacidevil* (Hollywood 1996)★★★.

● VIDEOS: *Danzig* (PolyGram Music Video 1992).

DARE

This UK melodic rock quintet was formed in 1987 by ex-Thin Lizzy keyboard player Darren Wharton. The band's name was derived from Wharton's christian name, a suggestion made by Lemmy of Motörhead. Relocating to Manchester after Lizzy's demise, it took Wharton six months to find musicians on his own wavelength. He eventually teamed up with Vinny Burns (guitar), Shelley (bass), James Ross (drums) and Brian Cox (keyboards), taking on vocals and additional keyboards himself. They debuted with *Out Of The Silence* in 1988, a grandiose, keyboard-dominated album, reminiscent of Giuffria, Journey and House Of Lords. The follow-up, *Blood From Stone*, released three years later, adopted an approach rooted in hard rock structures, and featured up-front guitar along with improved vocals from Wharton. Tipped to make a significant impact on the international rock scene, harsh reality intervened as the band became another fixture on 'might have been' lists. Wharton, still playing as Dare, gigs regularly in north Wales and north-west England.

● ALBUMS: *Out Of The Silence* (A&M 1988)★★, *Blood From Stone* (A&M 1991)★★★, *Calm Before The Storm* (MTM 1998)★★★.

DARK ANGEL

Formed in Los Angeles, California, USA, in 1983, Dark Angel specialize in 'ultra-heavy thrash metal'. The original line-up consisted of Don Doty (vocals), Jim Durkin (guitar), Eric Meyer (guitar), Rob Yahn (bass) and Jack Schwarz (drums). Early demos saw the band sign to Axe Killer Records, resulting in the release of *We Have Arrived* in 1984. Unfortunately, this was a clumsy effort that at times made them sound unrehearsed. Soon after its release, Rob Yahn and Jack Schwarz left to be replaced by Mike Gonzalez (bass) and Gene Hoglan (drums), who became the band's chief lyricist. Signing a new contract with Combat Records, they released *Darkness Descends*. This brutally heavy and uncompromising album showed the band to have made the transition into a tight, cohesive unit.
There was a lull in their recording career until they reappeared in 1989 with *Leave Scars*. If anything, this release was even heavier. Featuring new vocalist Ron Rinehart, it also included a cover version of Led Zeppelin's 'Immigrant Song'. The band then embarked on a European tour, recording a live mini-album, *Live Scars*, which was released in 1990 as a stop-gap until the next studio project. The band underwent another line-up shuffle, replacing Jim Durkin with ex-Viking guitarist Brett Eriksen. Together they recorded *Time Does Not Heal*, a turbulent vortex of twisted riffs and savage drums. Definitely not a band for the faint-hearted, Dark

Angel continued to combine unsavoury lyrics with ferocious musicianship, though by that point the impact had waned. Hoglan went on to cause further sonic mayhem in Death.

● ALBUMS: *We Have Arrived* (Axe Killer 1984)★★, *Darkness Descends* (Combat/Under One Flag 1986)★★★, *Leave Scars* (Combat/Under One Flag 1989)★★★, *Live Scars* mini-album (Combat/Under One Flag 1990)★★, *Time Does Not Heal* (Combat/Under One Flag 1991)★★★.

● COMPILATIONS: *Decade Of Chaos* (Combat/Under One Flag 1992)★★★.

DARK HEART

Comprising Alan Clark (guitar), Steve Small (guitar), Colin Bell (bass), Ian Thompson (drums) and Phil Brown (vocals), UK hard rock band Dark Heart formed in 1982. Their first recordings were for the Guardian Records compilation *Pure Overkill*, at which time the group was still known as Tokyo Rose. After changing their name to Dark Heart they signed to Roadrunner Records for 1984's *Shadows Of The Night* - a predictable and unexciting collection, influenced heavily by the New Wave Of British Heavy Metal tradition established by bands such as Samson and Iron Maiden. It failed to sell and when Brown departed, Dark Heart disbanded.

● ALBUMS: *Shadows Of The Night* (Roadrunner 1984)★★.

DARK LORD

This guitar-orientated, hard-rock outfit was formed in Venice, Italy, in 1984 by six-string virtuoso Alex Masi and drummer Sandro Bertoldini. With the addition of vocalist Gable Nalesso and bassist Al Guariento, they released a self-titled mini-album that showcased the talents of Masi, a classically trained guitarist in the style of Yngwie Malmsteen and Steve Vai. *State Of Rock*, another mini-album, followed, and saw the arrival of new bass player Randzo Zulian and vocalist Emanual Jandee. Masi left and relocated to Los Angeles soon after the album's release, joining Sound Barrier, who later became Masi. After two years of inactivity, Jandee and Bertoldni re-formed Dark Lord with Paolo Mufato (guitar) and Alex Favaretto (bass). *It's Nigh' Time* was the result, but it lacked the sophistication and experimentation of Masi's era, and consequently made little impact outside of Italy.

● ALBUMS: *Dark Lord* mini-album (1984)★★★, *State Of Rock* mini-album (1985)★★★, *It's Nigh' Time* (1988)★★.

DARK STAR

Formerly known as Berlin, the band was formed in the Midlands in 1980, during the heyday of the New Wave Of British Heavy Metal. Dark Star comprised Rick Staines (vocals, synthesizer), David Harrison (guitar), Robert Key (guitar), Mark Oseland (bass) and Steve Atkins (drums). They debuted with 'Lady Of Mars', a track on the EMI Records compilation *Metal For Muthas Volume II*. Stylistically, they alternated between pure heavy metal and US pomp-rock and consequently found it difficult to win supporters in either camp. The band ground to a halt shortly after the release of their self-titled debut in 1981. Six years later, Staines, Harrison and Key re-formed the band. With the help of session musicians they recorded *Real To Reel*, but, unable to attract media attention, they disbanded shortly afterwards.

● ALBUMS: *Dark Star* (Avatar 1981)★★, *Real To Reel* (FM Revolver 1987)★★.

DARK WIZARD

Formed in Holland in the early 80s, hard rock band Dark Wizard featured Berto Van Veen (vocals), Marcel de Groot (guitar), Kees Reinders (bass) and Tony White (drums). One of their nation's few contributors to the black metal tradition, Dark Wizard played forceful death metal with oblique, diabolical lyrics. Their first release was the *Devil's Victim* mini-album for Mausoleum Records in 1984. This was followed by their full studio debut, 1985's *Reign Of Evil*. As evidenced by their selection of album titles, the group's lyrical focus remained sharply Satanic. They also hosted a notable live show where costumed skeletons and zombies emerged onstage from coffins - suggesting their dalliance with dark spirits was more entertainment-orientated than many of their peers on the Mausoleum label.

● ALBUMS: *Devil's Victim* mini-album (Mausoleum 1984)★★, *Reign Of Evil* (Mausoleum 1985)★★★.

DARXON

A mainstream hard rock band formed in Germany in the early 80s, Darxon featured Massimo Matteis (vocals), Markus Szart (guitar), Peter Schmidt (bass) and Doinik Hulshorst (drums). Their debut album, *Killed In Action*, drew heavily on the melodic intensity of fellow German bands such as Steeler and Accept (whose guitarist, Jorg Fischer, would produce their third album). *Tokyo* was less derivative, but the band only became a potent force with the advent of 1987's *No Thrills*. By this time, however, Matteis was the only remaining original member and there have been no new releases since.

● ALBUMS: *Killed In Action* (Wishbone 1984)★★, *Tokyo* (Wishbone 1985)★★★, *No Thrills* (Rockport 1987)★★★.

DEAD KENNEDYS

The undoubted kings of US punk, the Dead Kennedys, formed in San Francisco, California, USA, arrived on the 80s music scene with the most vitriolic and ultimately persuasive music ever to marshal the US underground (at least until the arrival of Nirvana). Even today the sight of their name can send the uninitiated into a fit of apoplexy. Originally a quintet with a second guitarist called 6025, the latter left before recordings for the debut album took place, leaving a core group of Jello Biafra (b. Eric Boucher, 17 June 1958, Denver, Colorado, USA; vocals), Klaus Flouride (bass), East Bay Ray Glasser (guitar) and Ted (b. Bruce Slesinger; drums). As soon as they hit a studio the results were extraordinary. Biafra, weaned partially on 70s Brit Punk as well as local San Francisco bands such as Crime and the Nuns, was the consummate frontman, his performances never far away from personal endangerment, including stage-diving and verbally lambasting his audience. He was certainly never destined to be an industry conformist - some of his more celebrated stunts included getting married in a graveyard, running for Mayor of San Francisco (he finished fourth) and allowing the crowd to disrobe him on stage. Lyrically, the Dead Kennedys always went for the jugular but twisted expectations; writing an anti-neutron bomb song called 'Kill The Poor' is a good example of their satire. The band's debut single, 'California Uber Alles', attacked the 'new age' fascism of Californian governor Jerry Brown, a theme developed over a full-blown musical rollercoaster ride. Just as enduring is its follow-up, 'Holiday In Cambodia', which mercilessly parodied college student chic and the indifference to the suffering caused to others by America's foreign policy: 'Playing ethnicky jazz to parade your snazz on your five grand stereo/Bragging that you know how the niggers feel cold and the slum's got so much soul'. 'Too Drunk To Fuck', despite (naturally) a complete absence of airplay, made the UK Top 40 (there were a number of prosecutions linked to those wearing the accompanying T-shirt). Biafra established his own Alternative Tentacles Records after a brief flirtation with Miles Copeland's IRS Records label (Cherry Red Records in the UK), and this has gone on to be a staple of the US alternative record scene, releasing music by both peers and progeny: Hüsker Dü, TSOL, D.O.A., NoMeansNo, Beatnigs and Alice Donut. Slesinger broke away to form the Wolverines at this point, having never been quite in tune with the Kennedys' musical dynamic. His eventual replacement was Darren H. Peligro (ex-Nubs, Speedboys, Hellations, SSI, who had also played guitar with the Jungle Studs and was the drummer for an early incarnation of Red Hot Chili Peppers). If the band's debut album, *Fresh Fruit For Rotting Vegetables*, had followed a broadly traditional musical format, *In God We Trust, Inc.* indulged in full blown thrash. Undoubtedly the long-term inspiration behind literally hundreds of US noise merchants, it certainly took many by surprise with its minimalist adrenaline ('Dog Bite/On My Leg/S'Not Right, S'posed to Beg' practically encompassed the entire lyrics to one song). *Plastic Surgery Disasters* saw the band branch out again. Though it did not share *Fresh Fruit*'s immediacy, there were several stunning songs on offer once more ('Trust Your Mechanic', with Biafra's typically apocalyptic delivery, attacked the values of the service industry, and 'Well Paid Scientist' mocked the career ladder). *Frankenchrist* was more considered, allowing songs such as 'Soup Is Good Food' to bite hard. The cornerstone of the recording was 'Stars And Stripes Of Corruption', which predicted some of Biafra's later solo excursions by relentlessly pursuing a single theme. *Bedtime For Democracy* was the band's final studio recording, and a return to the aggressive speed of the previous mini-album, though without the shock value. Meanwhile, Biafra was on trial for the artwork given away with *Frankenchrist*, a pastiche of American consumerism by H.R. Giger (*Landscape #20* - often referred to as 'Penis Landscape'), which made its point with a depiction of row upon row of male genitalia entering anuses (i.e., everybody fucking everybody else). Long an irritant to the US moral 'guardians', the PMRC now had Biafra in their sights. In truth the band had elected to call it a day anyhow, but there was a long hibernation while Biafra weathered the storm (he was eventually cleared on all counts and the case thrown out of court) before embarking on his next creative phase - an episodic solo career marked by collaborations with D.O.A. and NoMeansNo. Flouride released three albums for Alternative Tentacles, while East Bay Ray formed Scrapyard. The Dead Kennedys' contribution, meanwhile, is best measured not by the number of copy bands who sprung up around the world, but by the enduring quality of their best records and Biafra's admirable and unyielding stance on artistic censorship.

● ALBUMS: *Fresh Fruit For Rotting Vegetables* (IRS/Cherry Red 1980)★★★★, *In God We Trust, Inc.* mini-album (Alternative Tentacles/Faulty Products 1981)★★★, *Plastic Surgery Disasters* (Alternative Tentacles 1982)★★★, *Frankenchrist* (Alternative Tentacles 1985)★★★, *Bedtime For Democracy* (Alternative Tentacles 1986)★★★. Solo: Klaus Flouride *Cha Cha Cha With Mr. Flouride* (Alternative Tentacles 1985)★★, *Because I Say So* (Alternative Tentacles 1988)★★, *The Light Is Flickering* (Alternative Tentacles 1991)★★.

● COMPILATIONS: *Give Me Convenience Or Give Me Death* (Alternative Tentacles 1987)★★★★.

● VIDEOS: *Live In San Francisco* (Hendring Video 1987), *Dead Kennedys Live At DMPO's* (Visionary 1998).

DEAD RINGER

A hard rock group from the USA formed in the late 80s, Dead Ringer featured Charlie Huhn (vocals), Jay Johnson (guitar), Joe Bouchard (b. 9 November 1948; keyboards, ex-Blue Öyster Cult), Dennis Dunaway (bass) and Neal Smith (drums; ex-Alice Cooper). Huhn was formerly vocalist for Victory, but Dead Ringer's sole release, 1989's *Electrocution Of The Heart* debut, suffered from poor production. Songs that were already laboured were further obscured by a thin mix and the result was negligible critical and popular interest - despite a much stronger reputation for their live work.

● ALBUMS: *Electrocution Of The Heart* (Grudge 1989)★★.

DEAF DEALER

This heavy metal band was formed in Jonquiere, Canada, in 1980. The original line-up consisted of Andy La Roche (vocals), Ian Penn (guitar), Marc Hayward (guitar), J.P. Forsyth (bass) and Dan McGregor (drums). Through early demos the band quickly gained popularity on the underground tape-trading scene and also had a track included on the *Metal Massacre IV* compilation album, released on the Metal Blade label in 1983. They then disappeared from the scene until 1985, when they resurfaced as Deaf Dealer with a new vocalist, Michael Flynn. After several false starts on the recording of their debut album, *Keeper Of The Flame* was finally released on Roadrunner Records in 1986. A worthy power metal release, it nevertheless sank without trace amid strong competition from several musically similar outfits. The band tried to persevere, but in the face of such adversity folded in 1987.

● ALBUMS: *Keeper Of The Flame* (Roadrunner 1986)★★★.

DEARLY BEHEADED

This brutal quintet from Stockport, England, formed in early 1993 and comprised Alex Creamer (b. 14 July 1967; vocals), Phil Stevens (b. 30 October 1971; lead guitar), Steve Owens (b. 20 April 1969; rhythm guitar), Tim Preston (b. 8 September 1968; bass) and Bob Ryan (drums). They recorded their first, now-legendary demo, 'We The Unwilling', in Manchester later that year. The band signed initially to East West and recorded their debut EP with producer Simon Efemey. Reluctant to compromise their vision for a record label, they split amicably from East West owing to artistic differences and signed to Music For Nations Records. After two and a half grinding years, their debut EP for the label, *In A Darkened Room*, was eventually released in September 1995. Their ferociously heavy stance soon attracted the attention of metal producer Colin Richardson. An intense period of writing and pre-production followed, with the resulting debut album, *Temptation*, being released in 1996. The classic Black Sabbath influence merged with a tighter Pantera motif to produce an extremely heavy yet melodic album. Subject matter covered the usual metal fare but managed to include a smattering of socially aware lyrics, suggesting that there was more to the music than hollow posturing. Owing to the slightly dated nature of their sound, the album received glowing but not overtly ecstatic reviews from the rock press, although they continued to build their fanbase through regular touring. In early 1997 founding member Phil Stevens had to bow out owing to personal circumstances, leaving the others to work on their follow-up album, *Chamber Of One*.

● ALBUMS: *Temptation* (Music For Nations 1996)★★★, *Chamber Of One* (Music For Nations 1997)★★★.

DEATH

Primarily the brainchild of vocalist/guitarist Chuck Schuldiner, the godfather of the 'death metal' movement, who formed his first embryonic outfit in Florida, USA, in 1983. Through early demos recorded with various local musicians (notably guitarist Rick Rozz and drummer Kam Lee) as Mantas, he secured a recording contract with Combat Records in America, with the provision that the product would also be released in Europe on the Music For Nations subsidiary label Under One Flag. Playing some of the fastest, most aggressive white noise ever recorded, Schuldiner moved the band from Florida to San Francisco, and Death came into existence. The band's history from this point is complicated owing to the sheer number of different musicians who have passed through the Death ranks. For their 1987 debut, *Scream Bloody Gore*, the line-up consisted of Schuldiner (vocals, guitar, bass) and Chris Reifert (drums). The album, as its title implied, was a torrid listening experience, firmly establishing the band as purveyors of musical extremities and the originators of the death metal style, as Schuldiner ground out cinematic riffs to his evocation of night-time terrors. For *Leprosy* the band's line-up expanded to include Schuldiner (vocals, guitar), Rick Rozz (guitar), Terry Butler (bass) and Bill Andrews (drums), with the themes of the debut expanded into less fantastical concerns. By the time of *Spiritual Healing*, Rozz had left the band to be replaced by James Murphy. This third chapter in the group's evolution saw Schuldiner advance a political perspective that blended true crime stories with news reportage, peppered with digs at both the establishment and the evangelist preachers who were beginning to target the group. The band toured Europe as support to Kreator, but on the eve of their departure, frontman Schuldiner left. Against all odds (and common sense), they decided to carry on and undertake this, their most important tour. His replacements for the duration of the exercise were ex-Devastation drummer Louie Carrisalez (handling vocal duties) and ex-Rotting Corpse guitarist Walter Thrashler, both of whom had previously been members of Death's roadcrew. The tour was not a great success, with European fans refusing to accept the group without its figurehead. On their return to America the members soon went their separate ways, with both drummer Bill Andrews and bassist Terry Butler going on to re-form their original band, Massacre. At this point Schuldiner decided to resurrect Death to record what was considered by many to be their best work. Joining him in this new incarnation of the band were Cynic guitarist Paul Masvidal, Sadus bassist Steve DiGiorgio and Cynic drummer Sean Reinert. The album, entitled *Human*, was released in 1991 and unveiled material of a much more varied composition than had previously been the case - even going as far as to include a melodic instrumental track, entitled 'Cosmic Sea'. After its release Schuldiner pledged to assemble a full-time unit from the musicians who had played on the album, with the intention of a European tour in 1992. However, by the following year Gene Hoglan (drums, ex-Dark Angel) and Skott Karino (guitar) had been recruited. For the sessions that produced *Individual Thought Patterns*, however, the supporting cast was Andy Larocque (guitar, ex-King Diamond) plus DiGiorgio (bass) and Hoglan (drums). The album's better moments included two cuts that attacked the music industry ('Overactive Imagination', 'Trapped In A Corner'), and it was produced by Scott Burns.

● ALBUMS: *Scream Bloody Gore* (Combat/Under One Flag 1987)★★★★, *Leprosy* (Combat/Under One Flag 1988)★★★, *Spiritual Healing* (Combat/Under One Flag 1990)★★★, *Human* (Roadrunner 1991)★★★, *Individual Thought Patterns* (Roadrunner 1993)★★, *Symbolic* (Roadrunner 1995)★★★.

● COMPILATIONS: *Fate: The Best Of Death* (Under One Flag 1992)★★★.

DEATH ANGEL

This group was formed in San Francisco, California, USA, the home of the Bay Area 'thrash' phenomenon, in 1982. The band consisted of five cousins, namely Mark Osegueda (vocals), Rob Cavestany (guitar), Gus Pepa (guitar), Dennis Pepa (bass) and Andy Galeon (drums). Their debut, *The Ultra-Violence*, was a brutal blend of high-speed thrash riffs and thunderous drums. The band quickly followed it with *Frolic Through The Park* in 1988, which showed that the band had progressed both musically and lyrically, although many preferred the outright carnage of their opening salvo. Death Angel experienced internal problems but managed to pull through, signing to Geffen Records after touring with Motörhead, and releasing the highly acclaimed *Act III* in 1990. However, while touring to promote the latter album their bus crashed in the early hours of the morning in the middle of the desert between Phoenix and Las Vegas. Drummer and youngest member Andy Galeon was critically hurt, and took more than a year to recover. Unfortunately, their problems escalated with the departure of vocalist Mark Osegueda, who was not prepared to remain inactive during Galeon's recuperation. The other members, with their recovered cousin and drummer, became the Organization.

● ALBUMS: *The Ultra-Violence* (Enigma 1987)★★★, *Frolic Through The Park* (Enigma 1988)★★★, *Fall From Grace: Live* (Enigma 1990)★★★, *Act III* (Geffen 1990)★★★★.

DEATH MASK

Formed in New York, America, in 1985, this heavy metal band consisted of Steven Michaels (vocals), Benny Ransom (guitar), Chris Eichhorn (bass) and Lee Nelson (drums). All had been members of various New York street gangs, and they channelled their aggression into the music. They attracted the attention of Jon-Mikl Thor, the muscle-bound vocalist of the band Thor, who produced their debut album. The band signed to the Killerwatt Records label and released their debut, *Split The Atom*, in 1986. Production duties were handled by Thor and guitarist Steve Price. Unfortunately, the music on offer did not reflect the band's tough street image, being a mixture of mediocre thrash metal and hard rock. Although Thor included one of the album tracks, entitled 'I'm Dangerous', on the soundtrack to his film *Zombie Nightmare*, the band failed to make any impact and soon sank without trace.

● ALBUMS: *Split The Atom* (Killerwatt 1986)★★.

DEDRINGER

Originally titled Deadringer, they formed in late 1977 in Leeds, England, as a competent but average rock group comprising John Hoyle (vocals), Neil Hudson (guitar), Al Scott (rhythm guitar), Lee Flaxington (bass) and Kenny Jones (drums). They built up a small but loyal following throughout 1978 and came to the attention of Virgin Records through their A&R man, who decided to manage them when Virgin failed to sign them. In 1980 they signed to pop/new romantic label DinDisc who issued a handful of singles and an album, before touring in support of Triumph and Gillan. In 1981, following the release of their best single, 'Maxine', they decided to split. A year later, Scott re-formed the group with Neil Garfitt (vocals) and Chris Graham (bass). Armed with a new recording contract with Neat Records, they adopted a more aggressive style typical of bands such as Fist and Tygers Of Pan Tang, but after a second uninspired long-playing collection they fell apart.

● ALBUMS: *Direct Line* (DinDisc 1980)★★★, *Second Arising* (Neat 1983)★★.

DEEP PURPLE

Deep Purple evolved in 1968 following sessions to form a group around former Searchers drummer Chris Curtis (b. Christopher Crummey, 26 August 1941, Oldham, Lancashire, England). Jon Lord (b. 9 June 1941, Leicester, Leicestershire, England; keyboards) and Nick Simper (b. 14 April 1945, Southall, Middlesex, England; bass), veterans, respectively, of the Artwoods and Johnny Kidd And The Pirates, joined guitarist Ritchie Blackmore (b. 14 April 1945, Weston-Super-Mare, Avon, England) in rehearsals for this new act, initially dubbed Roundabout. Curtis dropped out within days, and when Dave Curtis (bass) and Bobby Woodman (drums) also proved incompatible, two members of Maze, Rod Evans (b. 19 January 1947, Edinburgh, Scotland; vocals) and Ian Paice (b. 29 June 1948, Nottingham, Nottinghamshire, England; drums), replaced them. Having adopted the Deep Purple name following a brief Scandinavian tour, the quintet began recording their debut album, which they patterned on US group Vanilla Fudge. *Shades Of Deep Purple* included dramatic rearrangements of well-known songs, including 'Hey Joe' and 'Hush', the latter becoming a Top 5 US hit when issued as a single. Lengthy tours ensued as the group, all but ignored at home, steadfastly courted the burgeoning American concert circuit. *The Book Of Taliesyn* and *Deep Purple* also featured several excellent reworkings, notably 'Kentucky Woman' (Neil Diamond) and 'River Deep Mountain High' (Ike And Tina Turner), but the unit also drew acclaim for its original material and the dramatic interplay between Lord and Blackmore. In July 1969 both Evans and Simper were axed from the line-up, which was then buoyed by the arrival of Ian Gillan (b. 19 August 1945, Hounslow, Middlesex, England; vocals) and Roger Glover (b. 30 November 1945, Brecon, Wales; bass) from the pop group Episode Six. Acknowledged by aficionados as the 'classic' Deep Purple line-up, the reshaped quintet made its album debut on the grandiose *Concerto For Group And Orchestra*, scored by Lord and recorded with the London Philharmonic Orchestra. Its orthodox successor, *Deep Purple In Rock*, established the group as a leading heavy metal attraction and introduced such enduring favourites as 'Speed King' and 'Child In Time'. Gillan's powerful intonation brought a third dimension to their sound and this new-found popularity in the UK was enhanced when an attendant single, 'Black Night', reached number 2. 'Strange Kind Of Woman' followed it into the Top 10, while *Fireball* and *Machine Head* topped the album chart. The latter included the riff-laden 'Smoke On The Water', now lauded as a seminal example of the hard rock oeuvre and a Top 5 hit in America. The album was also the first release on the group's own Purple label. Although the platinum-selling *Made In Japan* captured their live prowess, relations within the band grew increasingly strained, and *Who Do We Think We Are!* marked the end of this highly successful line-up. The departures of Gillan and Glover robbed Deep Purple of an expressive frontman and imaginative arranger, although David Coverdale (b. 22 September 1951, Saltburn-By-The Sea, Cleveland, England; vocals) and Glenn Hughes (b. 21 August 1952, Cannock, Staffordshire, England; bass, ex-Trapeze) brought a new impetus to the act. *Burn* and *Stormbringer* both reached the Top 10, but Blackmore grew increasingly dissatisfied with the group's direction and in May 1975 left to form Rainbow. US guitarist Tommy Bolin (b. 18 April 1951, Sioux City, Iowa, USA, d. 4 December 1976, Miami, Florida, USA), formerly of the James Gang, joined Deep Purple for *Come Taste The Band*, but his jazz/soul style was incompatible with the group's heavy metal sound, and a now-tiring act folded in 1976 following a farewell UK tour. Coverdale then formed Whitesnake, Paice and Lord joined Tony Ashton in Paice, Ashton And Lord, while Bolin died of a heroin overdose within months of Purple's demise. Judicious archive and 'best of' releases kept the group in the public eye, as did the high profile enjoyed by its several ex-members. Pressure for a reunion bore fruit in 1984 when Gillan, Lord, Blackmore, Glover and Paice completed *Perfect Strangers*. A second set, *The House Of Blue Light*, ensued, but recurring animosity between Gillan and Blackmore resulted in the singer's departure following the in-concert *Nobody's Perfect*. Former Rainbow vocalist Joe Lynn Turner was brought into the line-up for 1990's *Slaves And Masters* as Purple steadfastly maintained their revitalized career. Gillan rejoined in 1993 only to quit, yet again, shortly afterwards, while his old sparring partner, Blackmore, also bailed out the following year, to be replaced briefly by Joe Satriani. The line-up that recorded the credible *Purpendicular* in 1996 consisted of Steve Morse on guitar, with Lord, Gillan, Glover and Paice.

● ALBUMS: *Shades Of Deep Purple* (Parlophone 1968)★★, *The Book Of Taliesyn* (Harvest 1969)★★★, *Deep Purple* (Harvest 1969)★★★, *Concerto For Group And Orchestra* (Harvest 1970)★★, *Deep Purple In Rock* (Harvest 1970)★★★★, *Fireball* (Harvest 1971)★★★★, *Machine Head* (Purple 1972)★★★★, *Made In Japan* (Purple 1973)★★★, *Who Do We Think We Are!* (Purple 1973)★★★, *Burn* (Purple 1974)★★★, *Stormbringer* (Purple 1974)★★★, *Come Taste The Band* (Purple 1975)★★★, *Deep Purple Live* (UK) *Made In Europe* (US) (Purple/Warners 1976)★★★, *Deep Purple: Live In London* recorded 1974 (Harvest 1982)★★, *Perfect Strangers* (Polydor 1984)★★★, *The House Of Blue Light* (Polydor 1987)★★★, *Nobody's Perfect* (Polydor 1988)★★, *Slaves And Masters* (RCA 1990)★★, *Knebworth '85* (Connoisseur 1991)★★, *The Battle Rages On* (RCA 1993)★★★, *The Final Battle* (RCA 1994)★★★, *Come Hell Or High Water* (RCA 1994)★★, *On The Wings Of A Russian Foxbat: Live In California 1976* (Connoisseur 1995)★★, *Live At The California Jam* (Mausoleum 1996)★★, *Deep Purple In Concert On The King Biscuit Flower Hour* (King Biscuit 1996)★★★, *Purpendicular* (RCA 1996)★★★, *Mark III, The Final Concerts* (Connoisseur 1996)★★, *Live At The Olmpia '96* (Thames 1997)★★★, *Abandon* (EMI 1998)★★.

● COMPILATIONS: *Purple Passages* (Warners 1972)★★, *24 Carat Purple* (Purple 1975)★★★★, *Last Concert In Japan* (EMI 1977)★★★, *Powerhouse* (Purple 1977)★★★, *When We Rock, We Rock And When We Roll, We Roll* (Warners 1978)★★★★, *Singles: As & Bs* (Harvest 1978)★★★, *The Mark II Purple Singles* (Purple 1979)★★★, *Deepest Purple: The Very Best Of Deep Purple* (Warners 1980)★★★, *The Anthology* (Harvest 1985)★★★★, *Scandinavian Nights* (Connoisseur 1988)★★, *Anthology 2* (EMI 1991)★★, *Knocking At Your Back Door* (Mercury 1992)★★★, *The Best Of Deep Purple In The 80s* (Mercury 1994)★★★, *The Collection* (EMI Gold 1997)★★★★, *Purplexed* (Camden 1998)★★, *30 - The Very Best Of* (EMI 1998)★★★.

● VIDEOS: *California Jam* (BBC Video 1984), *Video Singles* (Channel 5 Video 1987), *Bad Attitude* (PolyGram Music Video 1988), *Concert For Group And Orchestra* (BBC Video 1988), *Deep Purple* (Virgin Vision 1988), *Doing Their Thing* (Castle Music Pictures 1990), *Scandinavian Nights* (Connoisseur Collection 1990).

● FURTHER READING: *Deep Purple: The Illustrated Biography*, Chris Charlesworth.

DEEP SWITCH

Formed in Norwich, England, in late 1985, Deep Switch - Jinx (vocals), Gander (bass), Reverend Nice (guitars) and Simon DeMontford (drums) - played few gigs and received almost no press. It was thanks to the underground fanzine *The Organ* that the band achieved cult status with a blistering review of their only self-financed album. Musically they blended elements of Alice Cooper and Wrathchild (UK) with a sense of humour that stretched the boundaries of taste. One track, 'Pigfeeder', had a clever political theme based on

George Orwell's book, *Animal Farm*. By the time word of the band filtered out of the underground to the likes of heavy metal magazine *Kerrang!* and DJ Tommy Vance at Radio 1 (who played 'Pigfeeder' once), they had split up, with DeMontford joining the Bombshells.

● ALBUMS: *Nine Inches Of God* (Switch 1986)★★★.

DEF LEPPARD

This supremely popular hard rock band was formed in 1977 in Sheffield by Pete Willis (b. 16 February 1960, Sheffield, England; guitar), Rick Savage (b. 2 December 1960, Sheffield, England; bass) and Tony Kenning (drums), as Atomic Mass. They assumed their current name when Joe Elliott (b. 1 August 1959, Sheffield, England; vocals) joined the band. The quartet initially hired a tiny room in a spoon factory, which served as a rehearsal area, for £5 per week. Early in 1978, Willis met another young guitarist, Steve Clark (b. 23 April 1960, Sheffield, England, d. 8 January 1991, London, England), and invited him to join. Clark agreed only on condition that they would play some 'proper' shows, and in July that year Def Leppard debuted at Westfield School before an audience of 150 children. After several gigs, the band voted to dismiss their drummer, replacing him with Frank Noon, who was working with another Sheffield group, the Next Band. In 1979 they recorded a debut EP for Bludgeon Riffola Records, which included 'Ride Into The Sun', 'Getcha Rocks Off' and 'The Overture'. Shortly after its release, Noon returned to the Next Band, and Rick Allen (b. 1 November 1963, Sheffield, England) became Def Leppard's permanent drummer. Later that year, the band supported Sammy Hagar and AC/DC on short UK tours. This generated considerable interest and they were then offered a contract by Vertigo Records. Their Tom Allom-produced debut, *On Through The Night*, was issued in 1980, climbing to number 15 in the UK album charts. The band subsequently staged their first headlining tour of Britain and also visited America for the first time - a move that prompted fans to accuse them of 'selling out', making their displeasure known by throwing cans at the band during their appearance at the Reading Festival that summer. The following year's *High 'N' Dry* was recorded with producer Robert 'Mutt' Lange, and reached number 26 in the UK and number 38 in the USA. *Pyromania* in 1983 saw the first change in the band's line-up since 1979. After missing many pre-production meetings and arriving drunk for a recording session, Pete Willis was sacked and replaced by ex-Girl guitarist Phil Collen (b. 8 December 1957, Hackney, London, England). The album was Def Leppard's most successful to date, climbing to number 2 in the US album charts, but they were unable to build on that momentum. On New Year's Eve 1984, tragedy struck when drummer Rick Allen was involved in a car crash in which he lost his left arm. The band maintained faith in their percussionist, and did not resume work until Allen had perfected a specially designed kit that made it possible for him to play most of the drums with his feet. His recovery severely delayed the recording of *Hysteria*, which was finally released in 1987 and eventually sold a staggering 15 million copies worldwide. It topped both the British and American charts, and produced two Top 5 US singles, 'Armageddon It' and the anthemic 'Pour Some Sugar On Me', and the October 1988 number 1 'Love Bites'. To promote the album, the band embarked on a 14-month world tour, which ended at the Memorial Arena, Seattle, in October 1988. This was destined to be Steve Clark's last show with the band. As they began work on their belated follow-up to *Hysteria*, Clark was found dead in his London flat after consuming a lethal mixture of drugs and alcohol. The rest of the band subsequently revealed that they had spent years trying to divert Clark from his self-abusive lifestyle. Faced once again by tragedy, Def Leppard soldiered manfully through the recording sessions for their fifth album, *Adrenalize*, which was released in March 1992 and immediately scaled the charts, topping the UK and US lists on release (unlike *Hysteria*, which had taken 49 weeks to reach the top in America). Greeted with the usual mixture of critical disdain and public delight (the group's fans had chosen the title), Def Leppard celebrated by performing at the Freddie Mercury tribute concert at Wembley Stadium. This event also introduced replacement guitarist Vivian Campbell (b. 25 August 1962, Belfast, Northern Ireland; ex-Dio; Trinity; Whitesnake; and Shadow King), who had made his debut at a low-key Dublin gig. In 1995 Rick Allen faced the possibility of two years in jail after he was arrested for assaulting his wife in America. In the meantime, a greatest hits package and a new studio collection, *Slang*, were released. In 1996 Joe Elliott appeared in the soccer movie *When Saturday Comes*.

● ALBUMS: *On Through The Night* (Mercury 1980)★★★, *High 'N' Dry* (Mercury 1981)★★★, *Pyromania* (Mercury 1983)★★★★, *Hysteria* (Mercury 1987)★★★★, *Adrenalize* (Mercury

1992)★★★, *Slang* (Mercury 1996)★★★.
● COMPILATIONS: *Retro Active* (Mercury 1993)★★★, *Vault: Def Leppard Greatest Hits 1980-1995* (Mercury 1995)★★★★.
● VIDEOS: *Love Bites* (PolyGram Music Video 1988), *Historia* (PolyGram Music Video 1988), *Rocket* (PolyGram Music Video 1989), *Rock Of Ages* (PolyGram Music Video 1989), *In The Round - In Your Face* (PolyGram Music Video 1989), *Animal* (PolyGram Music Video 1989), *Visualise* (PolyGram Music Video 1993), *Unlock The Rock: Video Archive 1993-1995* (PolyGram Music Video 1995).
● FURTHER READING: *Def Leppard: Animal Instinct*, David Fricke. *Def Leppard*, Jason Rich. *Biographize: The Def Leppard Story*, Dave Dickson.

DEFIANCE

Formed in San Francisco, California, USA, in the late 80s, heavy metal group Defiance comprised Ken Elkington (vocals), Doug Harrington (guitar), Jim Adams (guitar), Mike Kaufmann (bass) and Matt Van der Ende (drums). Influenced by what was known colloquially as the 'Bay Area thrash scene', Defiance began their career playing club dates along the Californian coast. They were signed to Roadrunner Records in 1989, at which time they recorded their debut album, *Product Of Society*. With the exception of the group's dynamic rhythm section, the results were mediocre. The following year's *Void Terra Firma* failed to address the group's songwriting problems, though Steve Esquivel was recruited as the group's new vocalist.
● ALBUMS: *Product Of Society* (Roadrunner 1989)★★, *Void Terra Firma* (Roadrunner 1990)★★, *Beyond Recognition* (Roadrunner 1992)★★.

DEFTONES

An intense, thoroughly contemporary hard rock group, the Deftones comprise Chino Moreno (vocals), Chi Cheng (bass), Stephen Carpenter (guitar) and Abe Cunningham (drums). The group is based in Sacramento, California, USA, where they enjoyed the early sponsorship of local favourites Korn. With that band they also shared a fan community drawn from skateboarders. The members of the group actually met while skateboarding, and their first rehearsals together took place in 1989, where they jammed on rough versions of Danzig's 'Twist Of Cain'. With the line-up complete, they began playing low-key sets, gradually building support within their neighbourhood. The group eventually signed with Madonna's label, Maverick Records, and made their debut in 1995 with *Adrenaline*. The group then toured with Kiss and Ozzy Osbourne, as sales of their debut increased to more than half a million. By now widely championed in both the US and UK metal press, the group began work on their second album, *Around The Fur*, which proved to be an equally solid collection highlighted by the radio favourite 'My Own Summer (Shove It)'.
● ALBUMS: *Adrenaline* (Maverick 1995)★★★, *Around The Fur* (Maverick/Warners 1997)★★★.

DEICIDE

This controversial Satanic metal outfit was formed in 1987 in Florida, USA, as Amon, with the line-up of Glen Benton (bass, vocals), guitarists Eric and Brian Hoffman, and Steve Asheim (drums). The band became notorious owing to their conflict both with the Christian establishment in America, and with animal rights groups, because of Benton's outrageous statements concerning the mutilation of small animals. Repeated bomb threats from the Animal Militia during European tours culminated in an explosion at a Stockholm venue in 1992 during support band Gorefest's set. The fact that the outspoken Benton branded his own forehead with an inverted cross, created an air of evil charisma that *Deicide*'s workmanlike death metal struggled to match. Nevertheless, the publicity helped to establish them as a major death metal act. *Legion* saw considerable progression, with a more focused approach channelling Deicide's aggression into better musicianship and songs. The band subsequently released two raw Amon demos, 'Feasting The Beast' and 'Sacrificial', as *Amon: Feasting The Beast*. *Once Upon The Cross* provided the best evidence to date of the musical talent that lurked somewhere beneath Benton's ludicrous self-aggrandisement. Scott Burns' production added clarity to a once murky sound, propelled by the superbly efficient twin guitars of the Hoffman brothers. Deicide's ability to win converts from the mainstream must still be limited by songs such as 'When Satan Rules His World' and 'Kill The Christian'. In 1997, Benton retracted his claim that he would commit suicide upon reaching the age of 33, saying: 'The whole thing's ridiculous'.
● ALBUMS: *Deicide* (Roadrunner 1990)★★, *Legion* (Roadrunner 1992)★★★, as Amon *Amon: Feasting The Beast* (Roadrunner 1993)★★, *Once Upon The Cross* (Roadrunner 1995)★★★, *Serpents Of The Light* (Roadrunner 1997)★★★.

Demolition 23

New York-based rock band whose rise to prominence was initially sponsored by three of the group members' former occupation - as part of legendary sleaze rockers Hanoi Rocks. That band sundered with the death of drummer Razzle in 1984, since which time Michael Monroe, Nasty Suicide and Sam Yaffa had involved themselves in a variety of solo and group projects. However, none of these proved satisfactory, and in the summer of 1993 Demolition 23 was born. Guitarist Jay Henning joined them for a 10-week residency at the downtown Manhattan club, the Grand. An unusal tenure for a new band, their popularity was confirmed by a set that mixed Hanoi Rocks standards with US punk rock anthems drawn from the Dead Boys, New York Dolls, Heartbreakers, MC5 and the Stooges. Guest performers included Joey Ramone (Ramones), Ian Hunter, Kory Clarke (Warrior Soul) and Sebastian Bach (Skid Row). With the band now established as Monroe (vocals, harmonica), Suicide (guitar), Yaffa (bass) and Jimmy Clark (drums), they recorded their debut album in five days at the Power Station in New York. An important collaborator was Steven Van Zandt, who produced and also co-wrote much of the material. Released in Japan in June 1994, where the Hanoi legacy still burns strong, it was eventually welcomed as a return to form when released in mainland Europe and the USA.

● ALBUMS: *Demolition 23* (Music For Nations 1994)★★★.

Demon

This Midlands, UK-based quintet was formed in the early 80s by vocalist Dave Hill and guitarist Mal Spooner (b. 1945, d. 1985) in the halcyon days of the New Wave Of British Heavy Metal movement. Backed by Les Hunt (guitar), Chris Ellis (bass) and John Wright (drums), after two albums they had outgrown the formularized approach of this genre and diversified into more melodic and mature rock music, fired with passion and a keen sense of dynamics. *The Plague* was designed as a musical equivalent to George Orwell's novel *1984*, a powerful statement of intent on both a musical and lyrical level. *British Standard Approved* and *Heart Of Our Time* followed, consolidating the band's position as the UK's leading exponents of underground melodic rock. Following the death of Mal Spooner in 1985, keyboardist Steve Watts teamed up with Dave Hill as the band's new writing force. Subsequently augmented by Scot Crawford on drums and guitarists Steven Brookes and John Waterhouse, the group went on to release a string of highly polished, atmospheric studio albums and a double live set recorded in Germany. Still struggling to achieve widespread recognition and exposure well into their second decade, it is Demon's commitment to maintaining standards as much as their longevity that distinguishes them.

● ALBUMS: *Night Of The Demon* (Carerre 1981)★★, *The Unexpected Guest* (Carerre 1982)★★, *The Plague* (Carerre 1983)★★★, *British Standard Approved* (Clay 1985)★★★, *Heart Of Our Time* (Clay 1985)★★★, *Breakout* (Clay 1987)★★★, *Taking The World By Storm* (Clay 1989)★★★, *One Helluva Night - Live* (Sonic 1990)★★, *Hold On To The Dream* (Sonic 1991)★★★, *Blow-Out* (Sonic 1992)★★★.

● COMPILATIONS: *Anthology* (Clay 1991)★★★.

Derringer, Rick

b. Richard Zehringer, 5 August 1947, Fort Recovery, Ohio, USA. Originally a member of the chart-topping McCoys ('Hang On Sloopy'), Derringer went on to produce two of their later albums, paving the way for his new career. Along with his brother Randy, Rick formed the nucleus of Johnny Winter's backing group. After producing four of Winter's albums, he joined the Edgar Winter Group and produced their bestselling 1972 album, *They Only Come Out At Night*. Meanwhile, Derringer recorded his first solo album, the heavy metal-tinged *All American Boy*. Vinny Appice (later of Black Sabbath) joined in 1976. Appice, plus band colleagues Danny Johnson (guitar) and Kenny Aaronson (bass), eventually departed to form Axis after the release of *Derringer Live* in 1977. After several albums under the group name Derringer, Rick reverted to solo billing and appeared as guest guitarist on albums by Steely Dan (he was the subject of 'Rikki Don't Lose That Number'), Bette Midler, Todd Rundgren, Donald Fagen, Kiss, Cyndi Lauper, Meat Loaf, Barbra Streisand and 'Weird Al' Yankovic. Afterwards, he turned his attention to production and soundtrack work. However, in the 90s he returned to solo recording, having turned down several previous attempts to lure him: 'They all saw me as some kind of screaming, sweating rock 'n' roller, but I've grown out of that now'. It was Mike Varney at Shrapnel Records who finally won the day, teaming him with bassist and co-producer Kevin Russell for *Back To The Blues* and *Electra Blues*.

● ALBUMS: *All American Boy* (Blue Sky 1973)★★★, *Spring Fever* (Blue Sky 1975)★★,

Derringer (Blue Sky 1976)★★, *Sweet Evil* (Blue Sky 1977)★★, *Derringer Live* (Blue Sky 1977)★★★, *If You Weren't So Romantic, I'd Shoot You* (Columbia 1978)★★, *Guitars And Women* (Columbia 1979)★★, *Face To Face* (Columbia 1980)★★, *Good Dirty Fun* (Passport 1983)★★, *Back To The Blues* (Shrapnel 1993)★★★, *Electra Blues* (Shrapnel 1994)★★★, *Tend The Fire* (Code Blue 1996)★★★, *Blues Deluxe* (Blues Bureau 1998)★★★, *King Biscuit Flower Hour* 1983 recording (King Biscuit 1998)★★★.

● COMPILATIONS: *Rock & Roll Hoochie Coo: The Best Of Rick Derringer* (Sony 1996)★★★★.

Des Barres, Michael

Des Barres was formerly lead vocalist with 70s glam-rockers Silverhead. Before going solo, he was also a short-lived member of Detective and Chequered Past, and made a guest appearance on Gene Simmons' solo album in 1978. Five years on from his debut effort, he replaced Robert Palmer as the vocalist in Power Station in 1985. Both of his solo albums, meanwhile, have been erratic, featuring an *ad hoc* collection of styles and ideas that, while rock-based, are not easily pigeonholed into any particular genre.

● ALBUMS: *I'm Only Human* (Dreamland 1980)★★, *Somebody Up There Likes Me* (Gold Mountain/MCA 1986)★★.

Desire

Comprising Fred Daniel (vocals), Burk Price (guitar), David Svach (bass) and Larry Sexton (drums), Desire was a largely unsuccessful US hard rock group of the early 80s. Price's work on the group's debut album, 1983's *Cry At The Sky*, created some ripples of encouragement in the press, but the group's sound was too limited and formulaic to cultivate a larger audience. After only a handful of cursory promotional gigs the group folded.

● ALBUMS: *Cry At The Sky* (Rock Power 1983)★★.

Destiny

This Swedish melodic rock quintet was formed in 1980 by bassist Stefan Bjornshog. Following multiple short-lived line-up changes, the band finally stabilized in 1984 with Bjornshog plus Magnus Osterman (guitar), John Proden (guitar), Peter Lundgren (drums) and Hakan Ring (vocals). They debuted the following year with *Beyond All Sense*, which comprised an uninspiring collection of identikit Eurorock numbers. Attracting little media interest, Osterman, Proden and Ring quit the band and were replaced by Jorgen Pettersson, Floyd Konstantin (ex-King Diamond) and Zenny Hanson, respectively. This line-up recorded *Atomic Winter*, which was more aggressive and leaned towards the thrash genre. Nevertheless, it fared little better than its predecessor. Konstantin and Pettersson left shortly after the album was recorded, and the band reverted to a four-piece with the addition of Gunnar Kindberg. *Destiny*, released in 1990, was their finest work to date, but the band remain virtually unknown outside their native Sweden.

● ALBUMS: *Beyond All Sense* (1985)★★, *Atomic Winter* (1988)★★★, *Destiny* (1990)★★★, *Nothing Left To Fear* (Music For Nations 1991)★★★.

Destruction

Along with Kreator, this speed metal band was at the forefront of the 80s German thrash scene, although Destruction never quite achieved the former's level of success. Schmier (bass, vocals), Mike (guitar) and Tommy (drums) made a rather raw debut with *Sentence Of Death*, but quickly refined their sound into potent, powerful thrash for the excellent *Infernal Overkill*. Second guitarist Harry joined following the recording of the equally ferocious *Eternal Devastation* to bolster the live sound, although Tommy also departed to be replaced by Olly, and the pair made their debut on the *Mad Butcher EP*. *Release From Agony* saw the band make full use of the extra dimension the second guitar added, although their increasing musical dexterity and more intricate song structures did nothing to temper Destruction's aggression and heaviness, and the band began to extend themselves abroad, playing with Motörhead across Europe and on a few dates of Slayer's US tour. *Live Without Sense* was an adequate display of the band's onstage power, but Destruction's fortunes took a downturn after they supported Celtic Frost on their Cold Lake UK tour. Internal dissent led to Schmier's departure, with the rest of the band electing to pursue a more melodic direction. *Cracked Brain* was recorded with new bassist Chris and stand-in vocalist Andre, but was disappointing. Further credibility was lost with a pointless cover version of the Knack's 'My Sharona', and Destruction soon folded.

● ALBUMS: *Sentence Of Death* mini-album (SPV 1985)★★, *Infernal Overkill* (SPV 1987)★★★, *Eternal Devastation* (SPV 1986)★★★, *Release From Agony* (SPV 1987)★★★, *Live Without Sense* (Noise 1989)★★, *Cracked Brain* (Noise 1990)★★★.

● COMPILATIONS: *The Best Of Destruction* (SPV 1992)★★★.

DETECTIVE

Powerful Anglo-American Led Zeppelin-inspired supergroup fronted by actor and ex-Silverhead vocalist Michael Des Barres and ex-Yes keyboard player Tony Kaye (b. 11 January 1946, Leicester, England). With the addition of Michael Monarch on guitar, Bobby Picket on bass and the powerful drummer Jon Hyde, they soon began to make waves in the clubs of Los Angeles. When Jimmy Page saw them, he signed them to his Swan Song label and immediately put them into the studio. Hyde's drumming proved so John Bonham-like that Page himself undertook most of the production work (under the pseudonym Jimmy Robinson) to do justice to the band's sound. Detective soon built up a reputation among their professional peers but fame eluded them. A second album lacked the direction and production of the first and did little to elevate them into the first division. It did, however, lead them into a starring role for an episode of the American situation comedy series, *WKRP In Cincinnatti*. Des Barres split the band soon afterwards and made a guest appearance on Gene Simmons' solo album before launching his own band in 1980. Monarch joined Meat Loaf's backing band and Kaye later returned to Yes, while Hyde abandoned the music business.

● ALBUMS: *Detective* (Swan Song 1977)★★★, *It Takes One To Know One* (Swan Song 1978)★★, *Live* (Swan Song 1978)★★.

DETENTE

This heavy metal band with a punk attitude was formed in Los Angeles in 1984, by vocalist Dawn Crosby (d. December 1996) and drummer Dennis Butler. Recruiting guitarists Caleb Quinn and Ross Robinson, along with bassist Steve Hochheiser, through small-ad columns, the line-up was complete. They signed to Roadrunner Records and debuted in 1986 with *Recognize No Authority*. Produced by Dana Strum it was characterized by Crosby's vitriolic vocal tirade and the heavy riffing of Quinn and Robinson. The album was not a commercial success and Hochheiser and Robinson left to form Catalepsy. Detente continued with Greg Cekalovich (guitar) and George Robb (bass) and, later, ex-Abattoir guitarist Mike Carlino. By this point, they had changed their name to Fear Of God. The band lost their contract with Roadrunner in 1988 and remained inactive. Crosby died in 1996 after battling with drug and alcohol abuse.

● ALBUMS: *Recognize No Authority* (Roadrunner 1986)★★★.

DI'ANNO'S, PAUL, BATTLEZONE

When Paul Di'Anno (b. 17 May 1959, Chingford, London, England) was unceremoniously asked to leave Iron Maiden, he set about forming his own band. After playing in the American-influenced Lonewolf and Dianno, he put together the first incarnation of the band known as Paul Di'Anno's Battlezone in London, England, in 1985. Joining Di'Anno in this venture were ex-Deep Machine and Tokyo Blade guitarist John Wiggins, John Hurley (guitar), Pete West (bass) and Bob Falck (drums). The band signed to the Raw Power label and released their debut album, *Fighting Back*, in 1986. It marked a welcome return to the style of music for which Di'Anno earned his reputation - hard and fast power metal in the classic British tradition. Tours took the band throughout Europe (where they appeared at the Dynamo Open Air Festival) and America, at the end of which Falck left the band to join Overkill. Around the same time, Hurley also departed. Their replacements were drummer Steve Hopgood and guitarist Graham Bath, both ex-Persian Risk. A label switch preceded the group's second album, and *Children Of Madness* was released by Powerstation in 1987. Slightly Americanized, and harking back to Di'Anno's Lonewolf days, the material was not as strong as the band's previous release. Battlezone soon fell apart, leaving their leader alone to regroup. The band's last line-up comprised Di'Anno (vocals), Graham Bath (guitar), Randy Scott (guitar), Mel Gibbons (bass) and Wayne Hewitt (drums). They gigged but never managed to secure a recording contract and subsequently folded. Di'Anno later appeared as guest vocalist with the re-formed Praying Mantis on a Japanese tour, before putting together Killers with former members of Passion, Jagged Edge and Tank.

● ALBUMS: *Fighting Back* (Raw Power 1986)★★★, *Children Of Madness* (Powerstation 1987)★★.

DIAMOND HEAD

Formed in Stourbridge, England, in 1979, the original line-up of Diamond Head comprised Sean Harris (vocals), Brian Tatler (guitar), Colin Kimberley (bass) and Duncan Scott (drums). The band were one of the pioneers of the New Wave Of British Heavy Metal and their debut single, 'Sweet And Innocent', showcased the band's blues influences and Harris's impressive vocal talents. After gigging extensively, the band recorded a session for the Friday night rock show on BBC Radio 1. 'Play It Loud' and 'Shoot Out The Lights' were both released in 1981 to minor critical acclaim. The press even went as far as to hail the band as the new Led Zeppelin. With interest growing, they decided to self-finance their debut, which they sold through the pages of *Sounds* magazine under the title *Lightning To The Nation*. This was quickly snapped up by the German-based Woolfe Records in the same year, and released on import. The album was full of hard rock, soaring vocals and tasteful guitarwork, and attracted the attention of several major record companies. As a stop-gap, the band released a 12-inch EP, *Diamond Lights*, again on DHM Records, in 1981, before signing to MCA Records. Their first release for the label was an EP, *Four Cuts*, which was quickly followed by their most popular album to date, *Borrowed Time*. Again, the material was Led Zeppelin-style hard rock, and the band also included a couple of re-recorded tracks that had originally appeared on their first album. During sessions for the follow-up, *Canterbury*, both Kimberley and Scott left the band. They were quickly replaced by ex-Streetfighter bassist Merv Goldsworthy (later a member of FM) and drummer Robbie France. The album represented a brave change of direction, still melodic but much more inventive and unconventional. Unfortunately, this change in style was not well received and despite a very successful appearance at the Donington Festival, it flopped, and the group split in 1985. Tatler then remixed their debut album, dropped two of the original tracks and added four previously released single tracks. The result was released under the new title of *Behold The Beginning* in 1986. Tatler went on to form Radio Moscow while Sean Harris teamed up with guitarist Robin George in the ill-fated Notorious album project. Even though Diamond Head were no longer in existence, they retained a healthy press profile owing to the acclaim accorded them by Metallica drummer Lars Ulrich, who made no secret of the fact that the band were one of his main influences and inspired him to begin his musical career. Metallica subsequently recorded a cover version of Diamond Head's old stage favourite, 'Am I Evil'. Early in 1991 Harris and Tatler re-formed Diamond Head with newcomers Eddie Nooham (bass) and Karl Wilcox (drums). The band undertook a short, low-key UK club tour using the name Dead Reckoning, and declared officially that they had re-formed. The first release from this new incarnation was a limited edition 12-inch single, 'Wild On The Streets'. Housed on the newly relaunched Bronze label in 1991 it showed the band had returned in fine form and rediscovered their previous spirit. By the time they had pieced together a new collection (after shelving a projected mini-album the previous year), many of the rock world's biggest names were only too pleased to help out (including Tony Iommi of Black Sabbath, Dave Mustaine of Megadeth, and still-fervent supporter Lars Ulrich). The band finally broke up after the tour to support the release of their final album in 1993.

● ALBUMS: *Lightning To The Nation* (Woolfe 1981)★★★, *Borrowed Time* (MCA 1982)★★★, *Canterbury* (MCA 1983)★★, *Behold The Beginning* (Heavy Metal 1986)★★, *Am I Evil* (FM Revolver 1987)★★★, *Death & Progress* (Bronze 1993)★★★.

● VIDEOS: *Diamond Head* (1981).

DIANNO

This British band was formed in 1982 by ex-Iron Maiden vocalist Paul Di'Anno (17 May 1959, Chingford, London, England; vocals), John Wiggins (guitar), Peter J. Ward (guitar, vocals), Mark Venables (keyboards, vocals), Kevin Browne (bass, vocals) and Mark Stuart (drums). Originally known as Lonewolf, they spent their first year touring Europe playing American-style melodic AOR rock. In 1983 John Wiggins was replaced on guitar by Lee Slater and Lonewolf signed to FM Revolver. Soon after the contract was in place, Lonewolf were forced to change their name following complaints from a group of the same title. On their debut album *Dianno*, they came across as an English band trying to sound American, although their version of Cliff Richard's 'Heart User' was a surprise inclusion. The album did not sell well and at the end of the year Dianno fell apart, with Paul Di'Anno going on to form Paul Di'Anno's Battlezone, then Killers.

● ALBUMS: *Dianno* (FM Revolver 1984)★★.

DICKINSON, BRUCE

b. Paul Bruce Dickinson, 7 August 1958, Worksop, Nottinghamshire, England. Dickinson left the heavy metal group Samson to join pioneering contemporaries Iron Maiden, replacing Paul Di'Anno in 1981. By the following year Dickinson had fully established himself within the line-up through his performances on the road and on 1982's UK number 1 album, *The Number Of The Beast*. Iron Maiden went on to become one of the most popular heavy metal groups in the world, with spectacular live shows and a run of hit singles and albums. At the start of the 90s, Dickinson began to branch out from the group. His aspirations to become a novelist were realized in his comic-novel, *The Adventures Of Lord Iffy Boatrace*, a sub-standard attempt in the style of Tom Sharpe. However, legions of Iron Maiden fans propelled the book into the bestseller lists. In the same year, Dickinson's solo album, *Tattooed Millionaire*, reached number 14 in the UK album charts, while the title track climbed to number 18 in April 1980. A version of Mott The Hoople's 'All The Young Dudes' also reached the UK Top 30. As well as being an accomplished light aeroplane pilot, Dickinson is a keen fencer, at one time having been ranked seventh in the men's foils for Great Britain, serving to reaffirm his reputation as metal's renaissance man. He finally left Iron Maiden in 1993, a year after releasing a second book, *The Missionary Position*. A second solo album for EMI Records followed a year later, sandwiched between his broadcasting duties as a presenter for BBC Radio 1. In 1996 he enlisted the legendary grunge and ex-Nirvana producer Jack Endino for *Bruce Dickinson's Skunkworks*. His touring band during 1996 comprised Alex Dickson (guitar), Alessandro Elena (drums) and Chris Dale (bass). *The Chemical Wedding* was released on Dickinson's own Air Raid label.

● ALBUMS: *Tattooed Millionaire* (EMI 1990)★★★, *Balls To Picasso* (EMI 1994)★★★★, *Alive In Studio A* (EMI 1995)★★, *Bruce Dickinson's Skunkworks* (Raw Power 1996)★★★, *Accident Of Birth* (Raw Power 1997)★★★, *The Chemical Wedding* (Air Raid 1998)★★.

● FURTHER READING: *The Adventures Of Lord Iffy Boatrace*, Bruce Dickinson. *The Missionary Position*, Bruce Dickinson.

DICTATORS

Formed in 1974 in New York City, the Dictators predated by two years the punk rock of bands such as the Ramones and Sex Pistols, yet they exhibited many of that genre's hallmarks from their inception. Purveying loud, three-chord rock without long solos, and drawing their lyrical inspiration and visual images from such disparate facets of popular culture as fast food, professional wrestling, cult movies and late-night television, the Dictators established a devoted fanbase in their home-town and selected hip pockets in the USA and Europe. However, they were unable to succeed commercially and are rarely acknowledged for their pioneering efforts in helping to establish the new rock 'n' roll of the 70s and 80s. The group originally consisted of guitarists Scott 'Top Ten' Kempner and Ross 'The Boss' Funicello, bassist Andy Shernoff and drummer Stu Boy King. Vocalist 'Handsome Dick Manitoba' (b. Richard Blum) guested on the group's debut album and subsequently joined. *The Dictators Go Girl Crazy!* featured original songs by Shernoff with titles such as 'Teengenerate', '(I Live For) Cars And Girls' and a cover version of Sonny And Cher's 'I Got You Babe'. It was released on Epic Records, who dropped the group when the album failed to attract interest. King left after the release of the album and was replaced by Richie Teeter, and bassist Mark 'The Animal' Mendoza also joined at that time, allowing Shernoff to switch to keyboards. The Dictators signed to Asylum/Elektra Records in late 1976 and released *Manifest Destiny*, their only album to chart. Before they recorded their third and final album, *Bloodbrothers*, in 1978, Mendoza left to join heavy metal outfit Twisted Sister. When the third album failed, they were dropped by Elektra and disbanded. The Dictators have reunited several times for single concert dates, one of which was recorded and released as a cassette-only album in 1981, *Fuck 'Em If They Can't Take A Joke*. During the 80s Kempner went on to form the Del Lords, another straight-ahead rock group popular in New York. Manitoba and Shernoff formed the quasi-metal band Manitoba's Wild Kingdom. Ross Funicello joined the short-lived Shakin' Street, before forming Manowar. The Dictators reunited once more in December 1993 to play at the 20th anniversary celebrations for CBGB's.

● ALBUMS: *The Dictators Go Girl Crazy!* (Epic 1975)★★★, *Manifest Destiny* (Asylum 1977)★★★, *Bloodbrothers* (Asylum 1978)★★★, *Fuck 'Em If They Can't Take A Joke* cassette only (ROIR 1981)★★★.

DIE CHEERLEADER

A British four-piece consisting of Rita Blazyca (guitar), Sam Ireland (vocals), Debbie Quargnolo (bass) and lone male member Andy Semple (drums), Die Cheerleader play chunky, punk-edged, hard rock, featuring feisty, semi-surreal songs about relationships and life's many downturns. In the process they have managed to straddle both the heavy metal and indie genres, attracting the attention of journalists from both camps and securing a publishing contract with poet and punk legend Henry Rollins. Tours with well-regarded punk and rock acts Terrorvision, Bad Religion and Iggy Pop helped to establish their reputation as a hard-working, talented live act. *Filth By Association* collected their well-received first three EPs (*D.C.E.P.*, *Saturation* and *69 Hayloft Action*) in updated form, along with two new tracks to complete the package. Rollins later sought to launch them in the USA by arranging a contract with London Records, who released the US-only *Son Of Filth*, an album split between old material remixed by Rollins and new songs produced in London with Steve Mack (ex-That Petrol Emotion).

● ALBUMS: *Filth By Association* (Abstract 1993)★★★, *Son Of Filth* US only (Human Pitbull/London 1995)★★★.

DIE KREUZEN

This punk/thrash band was formed in Milwaukee, Wisconsin, USA, in 1981, their name deriving from the German for 'the crosses'. The band, featuring Dan Kubinski (vocals), Brian Egeness (guitar), Keith Brammer (bass) and Eric Tunison (drums), started life with a highly regarded album of embryonic thrash (incorporating all six tunes from their 1982 debut EP *Cows And Beer*). Since that debut their material has revealed a much stronger inclination towards traditional rock structures, although they were widely congratulated for bringing intelligence and lyrical diversity to the heavy metal sphere. *Century Days*, for example, includes both piano and horns on several tracks, while maintaining an allegiance to the band's traditionally hard sound. Brammer left to join Wreck in 1989. Signed to Chicago independent Touch And Go Records, their 1991 album was produced by Butch Vig (Garbage; Killdozer; Tad; Nirvana).

● ALBUMS: *Die Kreuzen* (Touch & Go 1984)★★★, *October File* (Touch & Go 1986)★★★, *Century Days* (Touch & Go 1988)★★★, *Gone Away* mini-album (Touch & Go 1989)★★★, *Cement* (Touch & Go 1991)★★★.

DIE KRUPPS

German group Die Krupps have been a pioneering force in experimental music ever since they were formed in 1981 by Jurgen Engler (vocals, keyboards, guitars and group spokesman, ex-famed German punk band Male) and Ralf Dorper (ex-Propaganda). Together with Front 242, they formulated the Body Music subgenre of Euro rock, a sound lush in electronics but harsh in execution. Several albums of synthesized material emerged, venerated by a loyal fanbase. However, Engler spent the mid-80s, which were largely quiet for the band, absorbing the new sounds pioneered by Metallica, pushing back the frontiers of metal. When Die Krupps eventually returned in 1992 they added layers of metal guitar. The most famous of two excellent sets in that year was a tribute album to the band who had revolutionized Engler's thinking: 'Metallica were coming to Germany for some dates and I wanted to present something to them because I really admired what they did. So we put together this tape, and that's all it was intended for, but our label heard of it and wanted to put it out . . .' On *The Final Option* Lee Altus (guitar, ex-Heathen) and Darren Minter (drums) were brought in, and Die Krupps adhered to their bleak lyrical themes, notably on 'Crossfire', a reaction to the Yugoslavian conflict. A remix album, with contributions from Gunshot, Jim Martin (ex-Faith No More), Andrew Eldritch (Sisters Of Mercy) and Julian Beeston (Nitzer Ebb, who in 1989 had remodelled the group's classic 'Wahre Arbeit, Wahrer Lohn'), was also unveiled. On *III: Odyssey Of The Mind* the band moved to a new record company and embraced still further the metallic guitar sound, which now subsumed their distinctive hard dance electronics. It was produced by Tony Platt (a veteran of work with Motörhead and the Cult). Engler said of it: 'The guitars are definitely louder on this one. We still get put into different sections in record stores all over the world. In Germany we're in the independent section. In France the techno, and in England in the metal. It's all right, but it's all wrong too. We should be in every section!'

● ALBUMS: *Stahlwerksinfonie* (Zick Zack 1981)★★, *Volle Kraft Voraus* (Warners 1982)★★, *Entering The Arena* (Statik 1984)★★, *Metalle Maschinen Musik 91-81 Past Forward* (Rough Trade 1991)★★★, *One* (Rough Trade 1992)★★★, *Metal For The Masses Part II - A Tribute To Metallica* (Rough Trade 1992)★★★, *The Final Option* (Rough Trade 1993)★★★, *The Final Mixes* (Rough Trade 1994)★★★, *III: Odyssey Of The Mind* (Music For Nations 1995)★★★, *Paradise Now* (Music For Nations 1997)★★★.

● COMPILATIONS: *Die Krupps Box* 3-CD box set (Rough Trade 1993)★★★.

DIE MONSTER DIE

Formed in Athens, Georgia, USA, the original impetus for Die Monster Die (self-described as 'the highest and lowest intellect combined into one mass') came from guitarist/bassist Evan Player's love of the Dead Kennedys' *Fresh Fruit For Rotting Vegetables*. However, the first incarnation of Die Monster Die dispersed in the late 80s, with Player departing for a new life in New York. Drummer and New Orleans native Kenny Sanders also settled in the city around this time, following his calling to 'become a rock star'. The two met through industrial metal outfit Stalwart - when they both left the latter group in 1991, Die Monster Die was reborn. Sanders invited Alice Cohen, from Philadelphia, to sing with the group, having formerly appeared in Shag Motor Pony and the Vels. Cohen also shared bass duties with Player. With Shawn Tracy on second guitar, the group released its first single, 'Planet'/'Backwater Trailer Park Blues'. A series of chaotic live performances ensued, highlighted by garish costumes and outlandish stage behaviour.

DINOSAUR JR

This uncompromising alternative rock band from the university town of Amherst, Massachusetts, USA, was originally called simply Dinosaur. Their musical onslaught eventually dragged them, alongside the Pixies, into the rock mainstream of the late 80s. Both J. Mascis (b. 10 December 1965, Amherst, Massachusetts, USA; vocals, guitar) and Lou Barlow (bass) were formerly in the hardcore band Deep Wound, along with a singer called Charlie. The latter recruited his best friend Murph (b. Patrick Murphy; ex-All White Jury) from Connecticut, and was rewarded by the first line-up of Dinosaur ejecting him and thus becoming a trio. Mascis had by this time switched from drums to guitar to accommodate the new arrival. Mascis, apparently a huge fan of Sham 69 and the UK Oi! movement, had actually known Murphy at high school but they had never been friends. He formed Deep Wound as a response to seeing 999 play live when he was 14 years old. During Dinosaur Jr's career internal rifts never seemed far from the surface, while their leader's monosyllabic press interviews and general disinterest in rock 'n' roll machinations gave the impression of 'genius anchored by lethargy'. SST Records saw them establish their name as a credible underground rock act - *You're Living All Over Me* featured backing vocals from Sonic Youth's Lee Ranaldo. However, their debut album for Homestead had brought them to the attention of ageing hippie group Dinosaur, who insisted the band change their name. Mascis elected to add the suffix Junior. Real recognition came with the release of the huge underground anthem 'Freak Scene', which more than one journalist called the perfect pop single. Its sound was constructed on swathes of guitar and Mascis's laconic vocals, which were reminiscent of Neil Young. However, the parent album (*Bug*) and tour saw Barlow depart (to Sebadoh) and Donna became a temporary replacement. This line-up recorded a version of the Cure's 'Just Like Heaven', which so impressed Robert Smith that it led to joint touring engagements. Soon afterwards they signed to Warner Brothers Records subsidiary Blanco y Negro, remixing their Sub Pop Records track 'The Wagon' as their debut major label release. Subsequent members included Don Fleming (Gumball, etc.), Jay Spiegel and Van Conner (Screaming Trees), while Mascis himself flirted with other bands such as Gobblehoof, Velvet Monkeys and satanic metal band Upside Down Cross, principally as a drummer. By the advent of *Green Mind*, Dinosaur Jr had effectively become the J. Mascis show, with him playing almost all the instruments. Although critically acclaimed, *Where You Been* did not manage to build on the commercial inroads originally made by *Green Mind*. *Without A Sound* included several strong compositions such as 'Feel The Pain' and 'On The Brink', with the bass now played by Mike Johnson (b. 27 August 1965, Grant's Pass, Oregon, USA). Mascis also produced other artists including the Breeders, and wrote the soundtrack for and appeared in Allison Anders' film *Gas Food Lodging*. A new album, *Hand It Over*, was released in March 1997, and proved to be a full-bodied Dinosaur Jr recording that sounded like Mascis was once more committed to his music. While the lyrics were often muddied, Mascis's melodic grunge was very much intact. However, Mascis formally announced the end of Dinosaur Jr in December 1997.

● ALBUMS: as Dinosaur *Dinosaur* (Homestead 1985)★★★, as Dinosaur Jr *You're Living All Over Me* (SST 1987)★★★, *Bug* (SST 1988)★★★★, *Green Mind* (Blanco y Negro/Sire 1991)★★★, *Whatever's Cool With Me* mini-album (Blanco y Negro/Sire 1993)★★, *Where You Been* (Blanco y Negro 1993)★★★★, *Without A Sound* (Blanco y Negro 1994)★★★, *Hand It Over* (Blanco y Negro 1997)★★★.

Solo: J Mascis *Martin + Me* (Baked Goods/Reprise 1996)★★★.

DIO, RONNIE JAMES

b. Ronald Padavona, 10 July 1940, New Hampshire, USA. Dio was raised in New York, USA, and served his musical apprenticeship in the late 50s with school-based bands such as the Vegas Kings, Ronnie And The Rumblers and Ronnie And the Redcaps (one single, 'Lover'/'Conquest', in 1958). From 1961-67 he led Ronnie Dio And the Prophets, not solely as a vocalist, but also playing the piano, bass guitar, and even trumpet. A multi-talented musician, he also acted as a record producer. During that time, the Prophets released at least seven singles, including a gimmick version of

'Love Potion No. 9' that featured the same song on both sides, plus an album. In 1967, with his cousin, David Feinstein, he formed the Electric Elves, who, in 1970, changed their name to Elf. The same year, the entire band was involved in a car crash, in which guitarist Nick Pantas died. Dio took over lead vocals in Elf and played the bass. Elf were discovered by Roger Glover and Ian Paice of Deep Purple in 1972, and the group went on to support Deep Purple on two American tours as well as signing to their Purple label in the UK. In 1975 Glover gave Dio the opportunity to appear on his *The Butterfly Ball*, and the widespread recognition that ensued helped to persuade Ritchie Blackmore, who had already recorded one track, 'Black Sheep Of The Family', with Elf, and recently left Deep Purple himself, to link up with Dio. The remnants of Elf, with the exception of the ousted Steve Edwards, became Rainbow. This saw Dio develop from the honky-tonk influence of his former band to the harder rock of Blackmore and Rainbow. Dio's penchant for writing about supernatural events, thoughts and fantasies also began to emerge at this stage, combining with the succession of often excellent musicians in Rainbow (the former members of Elf had been rapidly discarded) to produce four albums of high quality and enduring appeal. In 1978 Dio left Rainbow, taking his gift for singing and songwriting to Black Sabbath, where he built on the previously phenomenal, but now waning, success of the band, doing much to rejuvenate the flagging supergroup. *Heaven And Hell* arrived alongside the New Wave Of British Heavy Metal, outclassing most of its rivals with its tight, solid, bass-dominated sound and science fiction-themed lyrics. After an acrimonious disagreement over the mixing of *Live Evil*, Dio left in November 1982 to form his own band, Dio, which comprised Vinnie Appice (drums), Jimmy Bain, former bassist with Rainbow and Wild Horses, Vivian Campbell (b. 25 August 1962, Belfast, Northern Ireland; guitar) and Claude Schnell (keyboards). Together, they recorded four albums, with Dio taking on all the lyrics and songwriting himself, allowing his creative muse a completely free rein. While the subject matter remained other worlds, times and beings, the style ranged from anthemic to epic. A lack of direction led to stagnation, and by 1987, when Craig Goldie replaced Campbell, the band was failing. In 1991 Dio renewed his acquaintance with Black Sabbath, joining them for a UK tour and recording *Dehumanizer* with them the following year. However, November saw Judas Priest's Rob Halford stand in for Dio when he refused to appear with the band in California after hearing of Ozzy Osbourne's intention to re-form the original Sabbath line-up as part of his solo farewell tour. Dio, whom some commentators had described as 'the Cliff Richard of heavy metal', simply returned to the studio with yet another incarnation of his eponymous band, releasing further albums and touring extensively into the late 90s.

● ALBUMS: as Ronnie Dio And The Prophets *Dio At Dominos* (Lawn 1963)★★. As Dio: *Holy Diver* (Vertigo 1983)★★★★, *The Last In Line* (Vertigo 1984)★★★, *Sacred Heart* (Vertigo 1985)★★★, *Intermission* (Vertigo 1986)★★★, *Dream Evil* (Vertigo 1987)★★★, *Hey Angel* (Vertigo 1990)★★★, *Lock Up The Wolves* (Vertigo 1990)★★★, *Strange Highways* (Reprise 1994)★★, *Angry Machines* (Mayhem 1996)★★, *Dio's Inferno - Live In Line* (SPV 1998)★★★.

● COMPILATIONS: *Diamonds: The Best Of Dio* (Vertigo 1992)★★★, *Anthology* (Connoisseur Collection 1997)★★★.

● VIDEOS: *Live In Concert* (Channel 5 1986), *Special From The Spectrum* (PolyGram Music Video 1986).

DIRTY LOOKS

Founded in the early 80s by Dutch-born Hendrik Ostergaard, Dirty Looks released three albums on three different independent labels before achieving a major contract with Atlantic Records in 1987. Ostergaard handled both vocals and guitar, ably supported by Paul Lidel (guitar), Jack Pyers (bass) and Gene Barnett (drums). Their major label debut, *Cool From The Wire*, showed the band to be purveyors of straight-ahead, no-nonsense power metal very much in the AC/DC mould. Both the crushing style of guitar riffing and the vocal delivery of Ostergaard made comparisons with the Australian supremos inevitable. However, such was the energy and commitment the band brought to recording and live performances that their indebtness quickly became forgivable. The follow-up, *Turn Of The Screw*, was not as successful, despite critical acclaim. *Bootlegs* saw the band presenting the same style of relentless power boogie, albeit with a return to a smaller label.

● ALBUMS: *Dirty Looks* (Axe Killer 1985)★★, *I Want More* (Storm 1986)★★★, *In Your Face* (Mirroe 1987)★★★, *Cool From The Wire* (Atlantic 1987)★★★, *Turn Of The Screw* (Atlantic 1988)★★, *Bootlegs* (Shrapnel 1991)★★★, *One Bad Leg* (Rockworld/Music For Nations 1995)★★★.

DIRTY TRICKS

This blues-based UK heavy rock outfit was formed in 1974 by vocalist Kenny Stewart and guitarist John Fraser Binnie. With bassist Terry Horbury and drummer John Lee completing the line-up, they drew inspiration from Bad Company, the Faces, Black Sabbath and Deep Purple. However, they never graduated from support status, as their attempt to bridge the divide between hard rock and heavy metal was handicapped by weak material. They released three albums on Polydor Records during the mid-70s that failed to reflect the energy they generated in a live setting. In 1976 Andy Beirne took over the drumstool, but the band was soon overwhelmed by the growing punk movement. Beirne later joined Grand Prix, Terry Horbury teamed up with speed metal outfit Vardis and guitarist John Fraser Binnie was recruited by Rogue Male in 1984.

● ALBUMS: *Dirty Tricks* (Polydor 1975)★★★, *Night Man* (Polydor 1976)★★, *Hit And Run* (Polydor 1977)★★.

DIRTY WHITE BOY

This 'supergroup' was put together by Earl Slick (ex-guitarist with David Bowie, John Waite and John Lennon bands) and David Glen Eisley, former vocalist of Giuffria. Adding ex-Autograph drummer Keni Richards and bassist F. Kirk Alley to the line-up, their style and approach was the antithesis of what one might expect from their collective pedigrees. Throwing caution to the wind, they went for a no-holds-barred, down-and-dirty rock 'n' roll attack with their debut album. Produced by Beau Hill (of Ratt), *Bad Reputation* found these seasoned musicians rediscovering their roots and enjoying themselves in the process. 'Let's Spend Momma's Money', released as a single, also attracted approving glances.

● ALBUMS: *Bad Reputation* (PolyGram 1990)★★★.

DISCHARGE

Many fans would argue that UK band Discharge were the most influential punk band after the Sex Pistols. Certainly, their caustic wall of sound (a million miles away from anything Phil Spector could ever have envisaged when he invented the term) has inspired both punk and metal bands throughout the UK and USA. Discharge were formed in 1978 in Birmingham, England. Like many of the early 80s punk bands, Discharge's line-up was fluid and consisted of people who refused to offer anything other than nicknames to the press - but the nucleus of the band has always been demonic singer Cal (b. Kevin Morris) and long-serving bass player Rainy. Other early members of the band included Bones (guitar) and Rainy's brother Tezz (drums), who was subsequently replaced by Bambi and then Gary. Their debut EP, released in 1980 as the first record on Stoke-On-Trent label Clay Records, preceded their participation on the renowned Apocalypse Now tour, on which they joined such punk luminaries as the Exploited, Chron Gen and Anti-Pasti. In common with each of these bands, Cal's lyrics decried the horrors of war, but they eschewed the melodies pursued, to varying degrees, by the others. They were also closest of these bands to Crass's ideals about cheaply priced records, vegetarianism, and suspicion of the press. Gary Bushell (later a newspaper critic for *The Sun*), whose *Sounds* music paper was alone in documenting the emerging scene, railed at their methodology: 'Umpteen versions of the same pneumatic drill solo . . . awful . . . no tunes, no talent, no fun . . . dull, boring and monotonous . . . the musical equivalent of glue-sniffing.' However, others did not agree, and the band soon built up a considerable following through EPs such as *Realities Of War*, *Why?* and *Fight Back*. Over a full album Discharge could be a uniquely intimidating experience, and their impact dwindled as the 80s progressed. However, the impact of their sonic assaults can still be heard in a thousand or more bands, including practically everything on Earache Records through to mainstream metal bands Guns N'Roses and Metallica.

● ALBUMS: *Hear Nothing, See Nothing, Say Nothing* (Clay 1982)★★★, *Never Again* (Clay 1984)★★★, *Brave New World* (Clay 1986)★★★, *The Nightmare Continues* (Clay 1988)★★★, *Live At City Garden* (Clay 1990)★★, *Shootin' Up The World* (Clay 1994)★★★.

● COMPILATIONS: *Discharge 1980-1986* (Clay 1987)★★★, *Why* (Receiver 1998)★★★.

DISMEMBER

Swedish band Dismember are a product of the increasingly active Scandinavian death metal scene. Like most of their peers, Dismember are rather short on subtlety and originality, but in terms of musical vitriol and intensity, they are a force with which to be reckoned. They have also developed a talent for attracting controversy and outrage, a valuable asset in the shock-hungry death metal genre. Most notably, upon the release of *Like*

An Ever Flowing Stream, several hundred copies were seized at UK customs, as the track 'Skin Her Alive' was deemed obscene. The song dealt with a murder that had taken place in the flat beneath that of vocalist Matti Karki, and the lyrics attempted to explore the thoughts of the killer. Despite widespread mainstream consensus that death metal did not deserve freedom of speech, the album was acquitted of obscenity in court. Dismember continued to flout good taste, dressing their drummer, Fred Estby, as Jesus Christ in a demonic parody of the crucifixion on video shoots and album artwork. *Indecent And Obscene* refers to the attempted prosecution of their debut and comes complete with a track designed to provoke similar outrage, entitled 'Eviscerated (Bitch)'. The group's third album employed a more considered production from Thomas Skogsberg at Sunlight Studios in Sweden, but their lyrical concerns survived intact.

● ALBUMS: *Like An Ever Flowing Stream* (Nuclear Blast 1991)★★, *Indecent And Obscene* (Nuclear Blast 1993)★★, *Massive Killing Capacity* (Nuclear Blast 1995)★★★, *Death Metal* (Nuclear Blast 1997)★★★.

Diving For Pearls

This cult AOR quintet was formed in New York in 1988, when ex-Urgent guitarist Yul Vazquez joined Danny Malone (vocals), Jack Moran (keyboards), David Weeks (bass) and ex-Jean Beauvoir drummer Peter Clemente, taking their unusual name from an Elvis Costello lyric ('Shipbuilding'). The band signed within nine months to Epic Records on a development contract, and were subsequently able to record their full debut. *Diving For Pearls*, produced by David Prater, was received with a wave of acclaim in AOR circles, prompting comparisons to a diverse array of acts for their classy blend of keyboard-flavoured, commercial hard rock, also featuring superb vocals and melancholy lyrics from Malone. However, given minimal promotion, the album simply failed to sell, and Diving For Pearls broke up when they lost their contract. Malone later reappeared in Band Of Angels.

● ALBUMS: *Diving For Pearls* (Epic 1989)★★★.

Dizzy Miss Lizzy

Danish hard rock band Dizzy Miss Lizzy made a huge domestic impact with the release of their self-titled debut album in 1994. Sales of 180,000 units (equivalent to triple platinum status in Denmark) made it the biggest-selling debut of all time in that country. It later won two Danish Grammy awards. The group were also hugely successful in Japan, touring there in 1995 and recording a live album in Osaka, the modestly titled *One Guitar, One Bass And One Drummer - That's Really All It Takes*, for release in that territory. Guitarist/vocalist Tim Christensen took the group back to the studio in November 1996 - this time Abbey Road, London, with producer Nick Foss. On this occasion there were more rough edges left in the final mix, though the album again took the Danish charts by storm, while reaching a mainstream European audience outside of Scandinavia for the first time.

● ALBUMS: *Dizzy Miss Lizzy* (EMI-Medley 1994)★★★, *One Guitar, One Bass And One Drummer - That's Really All It Takes* (EMI Japan 1995)★★★, *Rotator* (EMI-Medley 1996)★★★.

DNA

This US band was a short-lived collaboration between guitarist Rick Derringer (b. Richard Zehringer, 5 August 1947, Fort Recovery, Ohio, USA) and drummer Carmine Appice (b. 15 December 1946, Staten Island, New York, USA). With the assistance of Duane Hitchings (keyboards) and Jimmy Johnson (bass), they released *Party Tested* in 1983. This featured a wide range of styles that included jazz, rock, funk, blues and pop. The playing was beyond criticism, but the songs were devoid of soul, and the album as a whole lacked unity and cohesion. Failing to win support in the media, DNA disintegrated when Carmine Appice accepted an offer to join Ozzy Osbourne's band. He subsequently formed King Kobra.

● ALBUMS: *Party Tested* (Polydor 1983)★★.

DOA

This explosive band was based in Vancouver, Canada, and formed in 1978, before emerging as their country's most popular and influential hardcore act. The line-up featured Joey 'Shithead' Keithley (lead vocals, guitar), Randy Rampage (bass, vocals), Chuck Biscuits (drums) and Brad Kent (guitar, ex-Avengers). Early releases included the *Disco Sucks EP* on their own Sudden Death Records, an incredibly rare artefact. Dave Gregg was added as second guitarist in 1980 to expand the band's sound (Kent was only a temporary member). In the early 80s they toured incessantly, and not only defined their own sound but much of the subsequent 'hardcore' genre. The *Positively DOA EP* and *Hardcore 81* proved hugely important to the development of North American punk. The latter album even gave the movement an identity, not only in name, but as a political agenda. The band's most successful line-up collapsed in 1982. Biscuits left to join the Circle Jerks (and subsequently Black Flag and Danzig), while Randy Rampage went on to a solo career; Greg 'Dimwit' James (drums, ex-Subhumans; Pointed Sticks; actually Chuck Biscuits' elder brother) and Brian 'Wimpy Boy' Goble (bass, vocals, ex-Subhumans) then joined. DOA's product in this incarnation was almost as invigorating. However, the third album realized fully the potential of its two predecessors: *Let's Wreck The Party* was a definitive, hard-rocking, intelligent punk record. After its release, James departed and was replaced on drums by Jon Card (ex-Personality Crisis and SNFU). Chris Prohourn aka 'Humper The Dumper' (guitar, vocals, ex-Red Tide) also joined when Dave Gregg started his own band, Groovaholics. Keithley formed Joey Keithley's Instinct when DOA briefly disbanded, but re-formed the group in 1990 with Goble and new drummer Ken Jensen (d. January 1995). Keithley also appeared as a biker cop alongside old friend Jello Biafra in the film *Terminal City Ricochet*. DOA would subsequently record a ferocious mini-album in tandem with the former Dead Kennedys vocalist. Asked in 1994 if he saw himself as a punk Tom Jones (DOA having covered one of the Welshman's songs), Keithley offered this career summation: 'Well, DOA can't keep going on forever, though some people say it already has, but I gotta think of my career later on in life, y'know, down in Vegas and Reno.' Morbidly compelling, *The Black Spot* commemorated Jensen, who died in a house fire in January 1995, and several other former members and friends of the group who had recently died.

● ALBUMS: *Something Better Change* (Friend's 1980)★★★, *Hardcore '81* (Friend's 1981)★★★, *Let's Wreck The Party* (Alternative Tentacles 1985)★★★★, *True (North) Strong And Free* (Rock Hotel/Profile 1987)★★★, *Murder* (Restless 1990)★★, with Jello Biafra *Last Scream Of The Missing Neighbors* mini-album (Alternative Tentacles 1990)★★★, *Talk Minus Action Equals Zero* (Roadrunner 1990)★★★, *13 Flavours Of Doom* (Alternative Tentacles 1992)★★, *Loggerheads* (Alternative Tentacles 1993)★★★, *The Black Spot* (Essential Noise/Virgin 1995)★★★.

● COMPILATIONS: *Bloodied But Unbowed* (CD Presents 1984)★★★★, *The Dawning Of A New Error* (Alternative Tentacles 1991)★★★.

● VIDEOS: *Assassination Club* (JettiSoundz 1984).

Doc Holliday

Not to be confused with Frank Carillo's band from the early 70s (although both groups were American and played Southern boogie/rock), this version of Doc Holliday formed in 1980 with Bruce Brookshire (guitar, vocals), Rick Skelton (guitar), Eddie Stone (keyboards) and Robert Liggio (drums), and followed the 'heavier' style of Blackfoot, mixed with more obvious influences such as the Outlaws and the Allman Brothers Band. Having released two excellent albums without gaining mass acceptance, they made what fans saw as a mistake in changing musical tack, with an album in 1983 more suited to the listening tastes of Journey or Styx fans. When this, too, failed, they broke up. In 1986 they returned with a harder edge and finally gained overdue attention with *Danger Zone*. *Song For The Outlaw Live* also earned strong reviews, although afterwards they fell silent.

● ALBUMS: *Doc Holliday* (A&M 1981)★★, *Doc Holliday Rides Again* (A&M 1982)★★★, *Hell Bent And Whisky Bound* (A&M 1982)★★★, *Modern Medicine* (A&M 1983)★★, *Danger Zone* (Metal Masters 1986)★★★, *Song For The Outlaw Live* (Loop 1989)★★★.

Doctor Butcher

Doctor Butcher were formed in Florida, USA, in 1992, when Jon Oliva (vocals, ex-Savatage) and guitarist Chris Caffery, who had previously worked together on Savatage's *Gutter Ballet*, began writing and recording together. Joined by John Osborn (drums) and Brian Gregory (bass), the quartet set about rehearsing songs that, unsurprisingly, attracted the attention of Savatage's many fans. However, work was put in abeyance in late 1993 when Jon's brother, Savatage guitar player Criss Oliva, was killed. Jon elected to rejoin his former band to complete their *Handful Of Rain* album in tribute to his brother. He had returned to Doctor Butcher by the summer, however, and set about working on the group's self-titled debut. Bracing classic rock against more contemporary developments (especially evident in its guitar platform), the album was completed at Morrisound Studios in Tampa, Florida. Track titles such as 'The Altar' and 'Season Of The Witch' revealed that Oliva's lyrical focus had shifted little since his Savatage heyday.

● ALBUMS: *Doctor Butcher* (Gun 1995)★★★.

Dog Eat Dog

Formed in New York, USA, Dog Eat Dog are a 90s metal crossover group comprising John Connor (vocals), Dan Nastasi (guitar, vocals), Sean Kilkenny (guitar), David Neabore (bass) and David Maltby (drums). Their earliest releases, the 1993 EP *Warrant*, and 1994 album *All Boro Kings*, were stylistically diverse, combining hip-hop, hardcore and dancehall reggae as well as more traditional rock riffing. The album featured contributions from Darryl Jenifer of Bad Brains, with production by Jason Corsaro (Soundgarden, Danzig, Madonna, etc.). Accused in some quarters of jumping onto Rage Against The Machine's rock/rap bandwagon, the group nevertheless provided an intoxicating blend of forceful music. 'No Fronts' was a caustic reply to their detractors in the press: 'No front, no tricks, no soap-box politics, no guns, just blunts, we kick this just for fun.' Comparisons to Cypress Hill were prompted by the introduction of the Solid Ground hip-hop crew and a brass section. Playing live with both hip-hop (Goats, Onyx) and metal/alternative acts (Biohazard, Bad Brains) further extended their audience. This eclecticism was confirmed by the 1995 release of a remix EP, *No Fronts - The Remixes*, with mixes from Jam Master Jay (Run DMC), the Beatnuts and Phil Greene. Nastasi left the band in 1995 and subsequently formed Number 9 with ex-Hades guitarist Dan Lorenzo, before forming the eponymous Nastasi.

● ALBUMS: *All Boro Kings* (Roadrunner 1994)★★★, *Play Games* (Roadrunner 1996)★★★.

DOGS D'AMOUR

This rock outfit was originally formed in Birmingham, England, during 1983, with a line-up comprising Tyla (guitar), Ned Christie (vocals), Nick Halls (guitar), Carl (bass) and Bam Bam (drums). After making their London debut in April 1983 and recording a track for the Flicknife compilation *Trash On Delivery*, they underwent a rapid series of personnel changes. Halls, Bam Bam and Christie departed, prompting Tyla to assume lead vocal responsibilities. He and Carl recruited replacements Dave Kusworth (guitar) and Paul Hornby (drums). They relocated to Finland, where their hard rock style won them an underground following. After returning to the UK in 1985, further changes in the line-up were underway, with Bam Bam replacing Hornby, while Kusworth departed in favour of the elegantly named Jo-Dog. Later that year, the procession of changes continued with the departure of Carl in favour of Doll By Doll bassist Mark Duncan, and then Mark Drax who lasted until 1987 when Steve James arrived. The group finally broke through with the minor hit 'How Come It Never Rains', and the mini-album *A Graveyard Of Empty Bottles*. The follow-up, 'Satellite Kid', also reached the UK Top 30 in August 1989, as did their album, *Errol Flynn*. The latter met with some resistance in the USA where it was forcibly retitled *The King Of The Thieves*. Having at last stabilized their line-up, Dogs D'Amour failed to establish themselves in the top league of hard rock acts, but continued to tour extensively. During a lull in the early 90s James formed the Last Bandits, while Bam Bam joined the Wildhearts. The group re-formed in 1993 with Darrell Barth (ex-Crybabys) replacing Jo-Dog. However, by 1994 the group had ground to a halt, with Tyla embarking on a solo career with the self-financed *Nocturnal Nomad* in 1998, while Steve James and Bam Bam formed Mary Jane.

● ALBUMS: *The State We're In* (Kumibeat 1984)★★, *The (Un)Authorised Bootleg* (China 1988)★★, *In The Dynamite Jet Saloon* (China 1988)★★★, *A Graveyard Of Empty Bottles* mini-album (China 1989)★★★, *Errol Flynn* (UK) *The King Of The Thieves* (US) (China 1989)★★★, *Straight* (China 1990)★★★, ... *More Uncharted Heights Of Disgrace* (China 1993)★★.

● COMPILATIONS: *Dog's Hits And The Bootleg Album* (China 1991)★★★, *Skeletons - The Best Of The Dogs D'Amour* (Nectar 1997)★★★.

DOKKEN

This Los Angeles, USA band was put together by vocalist Don Dokken. His first break came when producer Dieter Dierks recruited him to supply (eventually unused) back-up vocals on the Scorpions' *Blackout* in 1982. Dierks then allowed Dokken the remaining studio time to produce demos. These rough recordings impressed Carrere Records enough to secure him a contract, and he enlisted the services of guitarist George Lynch, drummer Mick Brown and bassist Juan Croucier (who later left to form Ratt and was replaced by Jeff Pilson) to form the band Dokken. Essentially Dokken's music is an intimate fusion of hard rock, melody and atmospherics. Elektra Records recognized these qualities and signed them in 1982. They remixed and re-released their Carrere debut, *Breaking The Chains*, which made the lower end of the US *Billboard* album charts. Thereafter, Elektra allowed the band a substantial recording budget, with producers Michael Wagener, Geoff Workman, Tom Werman and Roy Thomas Baker being used at different times. The band recorded three excellent studio albums for Elektra (*Back For The Attack* reaching US number 13 in December 1987) before internal disputes between Lynch and Don Dokken led the band to split in 1988. A farewell live album, *Beast From The East*, followed, and provided a fitting epitaph. Lynch went on to form Lynch Mob, while Don Dokken negotiated a solo contract with Geffen Records and released *Up From The Ashes* in 1990. In 1994 Dokken resurrected the band and a live album, *One Live Night*, and a studio album, *Dokken*, followed. This time the group dabbled in harmonic pop as well as hard rock, all of which was accompanied by fairly sombre lyrics. It had started out as a solo set before Mick Brown and Jeff Pilson were enrolled as co-writers. Having been begged by Dokken fans over the preceding years for some form of reunion, they eventually elected to make it permanent. Guitarist George Lynch finally settled his differences with Don Dokken and rejoined in May 1994.

● ALBUMS: *Breaking The Chains* (Carrere 1982)★★★, *Tooth And Nail* (Elektra 1984)★★★, *Under Lock And Key* (Elektra 1985)★★★, *Back For The Attack* (Elektra 1987)★★★, *Beast From The East* (Elektra 1988)★★★, *Back In The Streets* (Repertoire 1989)★★, *One Live Night* (1995)★★, *Dokken* (Geffen 1995)★★, *Shadowlife* (CMC 1997)★★★.

Solo: Don Dokken *Up From The Ashes* (Geffen 1990)★★.

DOLLFACE

This UK hard rock band, formed in autumn 1992, comprises Adrian Portas (b. Sheffield, Yorkshire, England; vocals, guitar), John Alexander (b. Surrey, England; bass), Rob Todd (b. Wales; guitar) and Dave Mage (b. Buckinghamshire, England; drums). Signing to Kill City Records in 1993, they made their debut with the *Methedrine EP*, followed by another four-track collection, *Rock Stars*. This, with endearing songs such as 'Dead Boyfriend' and the ironic title track, brought them to the attention of a media who admired their straightforward approach to dynamic rock. The personal confessions and character studies continued on their debut album, the critically lauded *Giant*. It saw Portas deified, a little prematurely, as 'the last great story-teller in rock 'n' roll'. Support slots with Slash's Snakepit on their UK tour broadened their fanbase further, while Alexander's attempts to charm Polish barmaids on their European tour saw him become a minor celebrity of the gossip columns. However, their impetus stalled in 1995 when Kill City Records collapsed.

They continued to play well-received shows on the London club circuit while searching for a new recording contract. Mage was replaced in July 1996 by ex-Blue Aeroplanes drummer Graham Russell.

● ALBUMS: *Giant* (Kill City Records 1995)★★★★.

DOMAIN

This hard rock band was formed in Germany in 1986 by Bernie Kolbe (vocals, bass) and British expatriate Cliff Jackson (guitar; formerly the leader of UK progressive rock group Epitaph). Originally named Kingdom, the group added guitarist Alex Ritt, keyboard player Voker Sassenberg and drummer Thorstein Preker before releasing their self-titled 1988 debut for Teldec Records. The name-change occured shortly afterwards, owing to confusion with the similarly named US hard rock group Kingdom Come. Their debut album was subsequently repackaged and credited to Domain, with its title extended to *Our Kingdom*. The following year's *Before The Storm* was produced by Albert Bockholt (previously a collaborator with Magnum and Treat) and saw the group continue on its path of experimental but somewhat mannered psychedelic hard rock.

● ALBUMS: *Our Kingdom* (Teldec 1988)★★★, *Before The Storm* (Teldec 1989)★★.

DOMINIQUE, LISA

Dominique is a former beautician and is the sister of guitarist Marino. She started her career in the UK singing in Marino's band, but came to prominence through the pages of *Kerrang!* magazine, appearing regularly as a pin-up. With interest already generated, she decided on a career in the music business and was signed by FM Revolver/Heavy Metal Records. With the help of Marino (guitar), Pete Jupp (drums) and other session musicians, she debuted with *Rock 'N' Roll Lady* in 1989. The album was universally slated by the music media, and Dominique was subsequently dropped. Undaunted by this setback, she signed to Castle Communications and delivered *Lisa Dominique* in 1991. Again, this was not well received in the heavy metal fraternity, or anywhere else for that matter.

● ALBUMS: with Marino *Wanna Keep You Satisfied* (LRM 1985)★★, *Rock 'N' Roll Lady* (FM Revolver 1989)★, *Lisa Dominique* (Essential/Castle 1991)★★.

DON PATROL

Comprising Dille Diedricsson (vocals), Peter Nordholm (guitar), Imre Daun (drums) and Henrik Thomson (keyboards), Don Patrol formed in Sweden in 1990. The base component of their sound was immediately obvious - drawing heavily on the blues their composite hard rock style drew comparisons with artists such as Free, Bad Company and Grand Funk Railroad. In the studio the group have consistently eschewed studio polish in favour of spontaneous, uninhibited performances. The best example of this was their 1990 self-titled debut, which received widespread recognition and airplay. A more complex record, 1992's *A Wire, A Deal And The Devil* was less immediate and ultimately less compelling.

● ALBUMS: *Don Patrol* (Record Station 1990)★★★, *A Wire, A Deal And The Devil* (Record Station 1992)★★.

Done Lying Down

Led by Jeremy Parker (b. Boston, Massachusetts, USA; vocals, guitar), Done Lying Down also consists of English musicians Ali Mac (bass), Glen Young (guitar) and James Sherry (drums). The EP *Heart Of Dirt*, released in 1993, was produced by Membranes/Sensurround leader and journalist John Robb. The three tracks were headed by 'Dissent', a forceful song with a stop-start construction reminiscent of Nirvana (a comparison that stayed with the band throughout their early career). It was awarded Single Of The Week in the *New Musical Express*. In 1994 they released three EPs (*Family Values*, *Negative One Friends* and *Just A Misdemeanour*) that brought some indie chart success, BBC radio sessions with the disc jockey John Peel and video appearances on the UK television show *The Chart Show*. They also toured with Girls Against Boys, Compulsion, Ned's Atomic Dustbin and many others. Their debut album, *John Austin Rutledge*, was named after a friend of Parker's who co-wrote some of the songs: 'All he wanted was a credit, but we decided to name it after him and put his photo on the cover!'. In 1995 the band went to America for their first live shows there, before signing a new contract with Immaterial Records and recording their fifth EP, *Chronic Offender*. Their second album was issued in 1996.

● ALBUMS: *John Austin Rutledge* (Black And White Indians/Abstract 1994)★★★, *Kontrapunkt* (Abstract 1996)★★★.

Donington Festival

Held annually during August at the Castle Donington racetrack in north Leicestershire, England, the Donington Festival has come to represent the highlight of the UK heavy metal calendar. First staged in 1980, Donington was conceived as an alternative to the Reading Festival when the latter moved away from its hard-rock roots to encompass new wave and indie acts. Donington's one-day event, billed 'Monsters Of Rock', generally features at least six top-flight rock bands, with the opening slot reserved for 'talented newcomers'. This has resulted in commercially successful acts such as Mötley Crüe (1984), Cinderella (1987), Thunder (1990) and the Black Crowes (1991) all using the spot as a platform to launch their international careers. Among the headliners, AC/DC have returned three times (1982, 1984, 1991), and Iron Maiden (1988, 1992) and Whitesnake (1983, 1990) twice. Although the festival has encountered fewer public disorder problems than most, in 1988 two attendees were killed during Guns N'Roses' performance when a video screen and supporting scaffolding collapsed at the side of the stage. Two years previously, heavy metal satirists Bad News were 'bottled off' as their caricatures of the heavy metal lifestyle wore thin. In 1992 BBC Radio 1 presented its first live broadcast of the festival in its entirety - with the provision of a 15-second delay before 9pm so engineers could delete any expletives. Though that year's audience fell 10,000 below the 72,500 maximum capacity imposed by safety regulators, Donington continues to be the one annual festival for heavy metal and hard rock fans that remains uncontaminated by the presence of other forms of music.

Doro

b. Dorothee Pesch, 3 June 1964, Dusseldorf, Germany. Pesch, the leading light and vocalist of the German heavy metal band Warlock, dissolved the band after the release of 1987's *Triumph And Agony*. Retaining only bassist Tommy Henriksen, she embarked on a solo career under the name of Doro. To complete the new line-up she recruited guitarist John Devin and drummer Bobby Rondinelli (ex-Rainbow). With Joey Balin as writing partner, *Force Majeure* offered a departure from her previous heavy style, moving towards a more mainstream AOR approach in a bid for commercial success. It featured an embarrassing cover version of Procol Harum's 'A Whiter Shade Of Pale' as the opening track, and fared poorly. Jettisoning the entire band in favour of hired hands, she recorded *Doro* with Gene Simmons (of Kiss) as producer. Musically, this was even further away from her roots, an attempt to achieve chart success that verged on desperation. *Rare Diamonds* was a compilation of older material, giving Doro time for a rethink about her next career move. When she did re-emerge in 1993 with *Angels Never Die*, interest was minimal. *Machine II Machine* featured the producer and songwriter Jack Ponti and it managed to avoid the overt commercial overtones of its forerunners. However, tracks such as 'Tie Me Up' still offered little evidence of songwriting maturity.

● ALBUMS: as Doro And Warlock *Force Majeure* (Vertigo 1989)★★, *Doro* (Vertigo 1990)★★, *Angels Never Die* (Vertigo 1993)★★, *Machine II Machine* (Mercury 1995)★★.

● COMPILATIONS: *Rare Diamonds* (Vertigo 1991)★★.

DOUCETTE

Named after the group's leader Jerry Doucette (vocals, guitar), Canadian hard rock band Doucette comprised Mark Olson (keyboards), Donnie Cummings (bass) and Dure Maxwell (drums). Doucette's skill as Canada's pre-eminent slide guitarist distinguished his group's three albums. The first of these, *Mama Let Him Play*, appeared for Mushroom Records in 1977 and featured eloquent original compositions alongside fluid musicianship. It was followed two years later by *Douce Is Loose*. However, following the release of *Comin' Up Roses* in 1981 the group ceased to be active, although their leader continued to work as a session musician and performed at Canadian clubs throughout the 80s.

● ALBUMS: *Mama Let Him Play* (Mushroom 1977)★★★, *Douce Is Loose* (Mushroom 1979)★★★, *Comin' Up Roses* (Rio 1981)★★.

DOWN

A US heavy metal 'supergroup', Down were formed in the early 90s by Phil Anselmo (vocals; Pantera), Pepper Keenan (guitar; Corrosion Of Conformity), Kirk Windstein (guitar; Crowbar), Todd Strange (bass; Crowbar) and Jimmy Bowers (drums; Crowbar). By the time they released their self-produced debut in 1995, the group had been playing together for four years. Two demos recorded during this time were regularly traded on the underground networks. Forgoing the predicted thrash metal and hardcore influences, *Nola* ventured instead for a 70s rock 'n' roll sound on songs such as 'Lifer' and 'Stone The Crow'. The band returned to the studio for a eagerly awaited follow-up in 1998.

● ALBUMS: *Nola* (Elektra 1995)★★★.

DOWN BY LAW

This Los Angeles, California, USA hardcore rock band were formed in the early 90s by veteran singer Dave Smalley, formerly of DYS, Dag Nasty and All. His compatriots, who by the mid-90s included Tampa Bay, Florida native Sam Williams (guitar, ex-Balance; Slap Of Reality), Angry John (bass, ex-Clay Idols; Leonards) and Danny Westman (drums, ex-Florecene; Spindle), all boasted a similar level of achievement and experience. The group's self-titled debut album from 1991 illustrated their style and outlook - uncompromising rock 'n' roll delivered with pace and a high degree of musical dexterity. It saw them signed to the influential Epitaph Records label where they have remained since. Though subsequent albums have revealed steadily more complex arrangements, Down By Law's work remains thoroughly consistent with the hardcore style. *All Scratched Up!* was introduced by the typically urgent 'Independence Day', the band demonstrating its commitment to vinyl purchasers by providing them with a full side of bonus tracks unavailable on the CD. However, the simplistic nature of too many of the songs argues against the possibility of Down By Law repeating the international success of labelmates such as Rancid or Offspring.

● ALBUMS: *Down By Law* (Epitaph 1991)★★★, *Blue* (Epitaph 1992)★★★, *Punkrockacademyflightsong* (Epitaph 1994)★★★, *All Scratched Up!* (Epitaph 1996)★★★, *Last Of The Sharpshooters* (Epitaph 1997)★★★.

DOWN RIVER NATION

Down River Nation, who comprise Shaun Atkins (vocals), Gizz Butt (guitar), Shop (bass) and Pinch (drums), were formed in Peterborough, Cambridgeshire, England, in 1994. Although they were welcomed in the pages of heavy metal magazines, there was more than a hint of third-generation UK punk rock in their fiery songwriting. This was perhaps unsurprising, as two band members had formerly been in English Dogs, who specialized in a similar brand of molten thrash. However, Down River Nation added a surly brand of funk and dance rhythms, clearly influenced by Urban Dance Squad. Atkins' vocals were also compared to those of Layne Staley of Alice In Chains. The group made their debut in 1995 with a seven-track demo, *Subworld Disciples*, before setting out on tour with Blaggers ITA.

DOWNSET

These fierce and confrontational metal-rappers (usually titled downset.), from the San Fernando Valley/Sylmar area of Los Angeles, originally formed under the name Social Justice in 1986. Immersed in the 90s US independent underground scene, Rey Anthony Oropeza (b. 2 June 1970; 'Messenger'), James Morris (b. 11 April 1974; bass) and Chris Lee (b. 27 January 1975; drums) were the founding members, later joined by guitarists Rogelio 'Roy' Lozano and Brian 'Ares' Schwager (b. 12 December 1973) as they slowly evolved into downset. Typically, the band began by recording and releasing a series of singles and cassettes on a variety of labels, with 'Angel'/'Ritual' (Theologian Records) and 'Our Suffocation' (Abstract Records) being among the best known. Having established a formidable fanbase, the band inevitably attracted major label interest. By early 1993 the band had to compromise their hardcore ethics in order to reach a wider audience; adopting their current name, they opted for Mercury Records. In autumn 1993 they entered Silver Cloud Studios with their friend, mentor and confidant Roy Z as their producer, with the intention of recording an EP. The resultant tracks were so intensely powerful and emotionally charged that they decided to record a full album. The self-titled result was one of the most brutally heavy and intelligent albums to emerge from the Los Angeles underground, with socially aware lyrics rapped in raging hip-hop style; their formative years in LA's violent and poverty-stricken neighbourhoods finally found full release. So impressive was their debut that they were invited to take part on a European tour with Biohazard and Dog Eat Dog, covering 42 shows in 15 countries. Unfortunately, the gruelling schedule proved too much; Lozano eventually left and the band recorded the 1996 follow-up *do we speak a dead language?* as a four-piece. Once again, the music was as uncompromising as the hip-hop, hardcore and graffiti art scenes that inspired it, mirroring their personal growth and cultivated from personal experience.

● ALBUMS: *downset.* (Mercury 1994)★★★★, *do we speak a dead language?* (Mercury 1996)★★★.

DR. MASTERMIND

Formed in the USA during 1986, Dr. Mastermind were part of a new wave of guitar-orientated rock bands. Comprising Kurt James (ex-Steeler and Driver guitarist), Deen Castronovo (drums) and the enigmatic Dr. Mastermind (widely believed to be Matt McCourt; ex-Wild Dogs) on bass and vocals, they were a power trio in every sense of the word. Frenetically paced songs, which never quite degenerated into tuneless thrash, were punctuated by high-octane and complex guitar breaks. After the release of their debut album, Castronovo joined Cacophony, and James left for Turbin. Rick Hosert and Pete Lachman were drafted in as replacements on drums and guitar, respectively, but this new line-up failed to find success.

● ALBUMS: *Dr. Mastermind* (Roadrunner 1986)★★★.

DRAIN

Hard rock band Drain were formed by Maria Sjoholm (vocals), Flavia Canel (guitar), Anna Kjelberg (bass) and Martina Axen (drums) in Stockholm, Sweden, in 1994. They rose to prominence in the UK with a support slot to Fear Factory, whose grim lyrical subject matter and grating, hard-edged music was clearly an influence. Though *Kerrang!* magazine did them few favours by calling them 'the female Alice In Chains', they nevertheless made a strong impression with the release of their first internationally distributed single, 'I Don't Mind'. This was followed by a full album produced by Adam Kvlman. *Horror Wrestling* again drew positive press for its compelling song structures and, in particular, Maria Sjoholm's by turns melodramatic and gentle vocal delivery.

● ALBUMS: *Horror Wrestling* (MVG/EastWest 1996)★★★.

DREAD ZEPPELIN

Novelty hard rock combo featuring an overweight Elvis Presley lookalike from California who led his band through a succession of Led Zeppelin cover versions played in reggae and calypso style. The band's line-up was as bizarre as its theme, and featured the aforementioned TortElvis (b. Greg Tortell; vocals), Jah Paul Jo (b. Carl Haasis; guitar), Fresh Cheese (b. Joe Ramsey; drums), Put-Mon (b. Paul Masselli; bass), Ed Zeppelin (b. Gary Putman; bongos) and Carl Jah (b. Bruce Fernandez; guitar). Formed in January 1989, they supposedly met when TortElvis rammed his milkfloat into the back of the band's car. They predictably attracted media curiosity and enjoyed a minor hit single with 'Your Time Is Gonna Come' from their first album, and then with 'Stairway To Heaven' from the second. Robert Plant was reportedly highly amused at their appearance, though not so the Graceland estate of Elvis Presley. TortElvis left the band in 1992. Fernandez went on to join Anthrax singer John Bush's side project, Ho Cake, while the rest of the band went 'straight'.

● ALBUMS: *Un-Led-Ed* (I.R.S. 1990)★★★, *5,000,000* (I.R.S. 1991)★★.

DREAM THEATER

Dream Theater arrived on the US techno-rock scene in 1988. Initially comprising Berklee College Of Music students John Petrucci (guitar), John Myung (bass) and Mike Portnoy (drums), they subsequently enlisted old schoolfriend Kevin Moore (keyboards) and began to record demos. Along with a contract with MCA Records, they also secured the services of vocalist Charlie Dominici, adopting their new name in favour of original choice Majesty. Their debut album showcased strong material, incorporating elements of Rush, Queensrÿche, and Yngwie Malmsteen, in addition to the English progressive tradition embodied by King Crimson and Genesis. Dynamic, multifaceted hard rock songs, characterized by countless slick time changes and impeccable musicianship, were the band's trademark. The album received a favourable response from the music media, but unfortunately was ignored by the record-buying public. Dismayed at the poor album sales, MCA terminated their contract and Dominici quit shortly afterwards. It took the group a year to extricate themselves from the contract, and a rigorous auditioning process began to find a new singer. The winning candidate was Canadian James LaBrie, formerly of Winter Rose, and also Carl Dixon's replacement in Coney Hatch. After their earlier label and personnel tribulations, their 90s albums saw them regain their initial momentum, with both mainstream and metal critics acknowledging their fluency in meshing a variety of styles around a hard rock core. The band also supported Elton John on his European tour.

● ALBUMS: *When Dream And Day Unite* (MCA 1989)★★, *Images And Words* (Atco 1993)★★★, *Awake* (East West 1994)★★★, *A Change Of Seasons* (East West 1995)★★★, *Falling Into Infinity* (Elektra/Asylum 1997)★★★.

● VIDEOS: *Images And Words* (1994).

DRIVE

This California, USA heavy metal group formed in the mid-80s with a line-up of David Taylor (vocals), Rich Chavez (guitar), Mercy Valdez (guitar), Michael Anthony (bass) and Valentine San Miguel (drums). Critics detected nothing startlingly original about the group's 1988 debut album, *Characters In Time*, which contained songs derived from the Slayer and Anthrax speed-metal tradition. It proved to be their sole release.

● ALBUMS: *Characters In Time* (Rampage 1988)★★★.

DRIVE, SHE SAID

The band was formed in 1986 by the former American Tears, Touch, and Michael Bolton keyboard player Mark Mangold, and previously unknown vocalist/guitarist Al Fritsch. Mangold was also a successful songwriter, co-writing Cher's hit, 'I've Found Someone', along with Bolton. After signing to CBS Records in 1988 their self-titled debut album was released a year later in the USA and featured guest appearances by artists such as multi-instrumentalist Aldo Nova and Bob Kulick of Balance and Meat Loaf fame. The collection of light-edged melodic rock songs, which included a reworking of the Touch classic 'Don't You Know What Love Is', was aimed directly at the American market, but failed to make any significant impact. It sold well on import in the UK, however, prompting the independent Music For Nations label to sign the band for the European market (Mangold reportedly being unhappy at CBS's marketing attempts). The album was subsequently released in the UK in 1990 and was quickly followed by a club tour. *Drivin' Wheel*, a slightly harder-edged album, was released in 1991, preceded by the single 'Think About Love', both of which failed to achieve any significant success. Undeterred by the lack of chart success, they toured the UK with FM in 1992 before embarking on sessions for a third album.

● ALBUMS: *Drive, She Said* (Columbia 1989)★★★, *Drivin' Wheel* (Music For Nations 1991)★★★.

DRIVER

A trio of Peter Glinderman (vocals, guitar), Dennis Coats (bass) and Stephen Roxford (drums), Driver formed in Canada in the mid-70s. Signed to A&M Records, they recorded their debut album, *No Accidents*, in 1977. Featuring well-executed, three-minute rock songs largely composed by Glinderman, with the resourceful deployment of pop hooks, it was a critical success within Canada and also provoked good reviews in the USA. Despite this sales were poor and the group's contract was not renewed.

● ALBUMS: *No Accidents* (A&M 1977)★★★.

DRIVIN' N' CRYIN'

Guitarist/vocalist Kevn Kinney, having relocated to Atlanta, Georgia, USA, after splitting from his old punk band the Prosecutors, met bassist Tim Nielsen in a local club, and the two formed Driving' N' Cryin'. *Scarred But Smarter* was recorded in a week and a half with a real garage rock trio sound, and the band recruited drummer Jeff Sullivan from Mr Crowe's Garden, who later became the Black Crowes, and began to broaden their musical style, incorporating country and R&B influences, while expanding their audience with gruelling club touring. *Whisper Tames The Lion*, by way of contrast to the debut, was rather overproduced, but *Mystery Road*, with a second guitarist in ex-R.E.M. roadie Buren Fowler, was more representative of the band's true sound. However, Driving' N' Cryin' had become musically somewhat schizophrenic at this stage, mixing heavy rockers with country songs, although the latter made little impression within insular US C&W radio circles. *Fly Me Courageous* thus saw a conscious effort to focus on the rock direction of their live shows, and while it met with a mixed reception from reviewers, respectable US sales finally established the band as a force. *Smoke* refined the harder approach with a tough sound and Ramones-like simplicity. Kinney reserved the more acoustic-based material for his solo albums, while Nielsen (Kathleen Turner Overdrive and Toenut) and Sullivan (Kathleen Turner Overdrive) indulged their artistic whims in side projects. Fowler left after *Smoke*, and the band relocated to a new label for 1995's typically eclectic *Wrapped In Sky*.

● ALBUMS: *Scarred But Smarter* (Island 1986)★★★, *Whisper Tames The Lion* (Island 1988)★★★, *Mystery Road* (Island 1989)★★★, *Fly Me Courageous* (Island 1990)★★★★, *Smoke* (Island 1993)★★★, *Wrapped In Sky* (DGC 1995)★★★★.
Solo: Kevin Kinney *MacDougal Blues* (Island 1990)★★★, *Down Out Law* (Mammoth 1994)★★★.

DUARTE, CHRIS, GROUP

Formed in Austin, Texas, USA, the Chris Duarte Group are John Jordan (bass), Brannen Temple (drums) and band leader Chris Duarte (b. 16 February 1963, San Antonio, Texas, USA; guitar, vocals). The release of *Texas Sugar Strat Magik* brought immediate acclaim for the band's gritty, intense southern blues sound, with Duarte singled out for his technique. Indeed, in the 1995 *Guitar World* magazine Readers' Poll, he was voted fourth best blues guitarist behind the much more established and esteemed company of Eric Clapton, Buddy Guy and B.B. King. The group's debut was additionally voted fourth best blues album. Duarte has described the band's sound as 'blues based, but it has that loud aggressive edge that punk had. I liked Dead Kennedys, Sex Pistols, Dead Boys, anything that was hard.' The decision to employ producer Dennis Herring, the former Los Angeles session guitarist previously noted for his work with Camper Van Beethoven and Throwing Muses, was also interesting. Afterwards the album was promoted on US touring dates with Buddy Guy. *Tailspin Headwhack* built on the debut with a stronger blues edge.

● ALBUMS: *Texas Sugar Strat Magik* (Silvertone 1994)★★★, *Tailspin Headwhack* (Silvertone 1997)★★★★.

DUB WAR

A collision of ragga and punk, shot through with steely metallic guitar, Dub War emerged in 1994 as a high-octane, highly political extension of hard rock's new-found ability to merge innovative styles with the old. Formed in Newport, Wales, in 1993, the four-piece comprises Jeff Rose (guitar), Richie Glover (bass), Martin Ford (drums) and Benji (vocals), all of whom come from diverse musical backgrounds. Glover had played in several minor punk bands, while Benji's apprenticeship came in reggae dancehalls, and he had previously worked with Mad Professor. The group made its debut at the end of 1993 with a self-titled 12-inch EP that managed simultaneously to appear in three different *New Musical Express* charts - the 'Vibes', 'Turn Ons' and 'Hardcore' listings. Following a debut mini-album in 1994, they switched to Earache Records for the *Mental EP*, joining Pop Will Eat Itself and Manic Street Preachers on touring engagements. *Mental* featured remixes from Senser, Brand New Heavies and Jamiroquai, and was followed by a further EP, *Gorrit*. Their first full album came in February 1995 with *Pain*, by which time the band had established a strong live following to augment their press profile. *Wrong Side Of Beautiful* was their finest album to date; it was re-released in a new limited edition version the following year, together with a six-track CD of remixes, *Right Side Of Beautiful*.

● ALBUMS: *Dub Warning* mini-album (Words Of Warning 1994)★★★, *Pain* (Earache 1995)★★★, *Words Of Dubwarning* (Words Of Warning 1996)★★★, *Wrong Side Of Beautiful* (Earache 1996)★★★★.

DUKE JUPITER

Formed in Rochester, New York, USA, in the late 70s, hard rock band Duke Jupiter experienced two distinct phases in their career. The first was as a generic AOR group who recorded two unexceptional albums for Mercury Records in 1979 and 1981. In 1982 the original line-up of Marshall

James Styler (vocals, keyboards), Greg Walker (vocals, guitar), George Barajas (bass) and David Corcoran (drums) moved to Coast To Coast Records and revised their style to a much more strident, Aerosmith-derived hard rock sound. The songwriting had also improved, and each of the group's annual studio albums, from *Duke Jupiter 1* onwards, combined accessibility with supple musical power in an attractive manner. The most successful was *White Knuckle Ride*, which reached number 122 in the US *Billboard* charts in June 1984.

● ALBUMS: *Taste The Night* (Mercury 1979)★★, *Band In Blue* (Mercury 1981)★★, *Duke Jupiter 1* (Coast To Coast 1982)★★★, *You Make It Easy* (Coast To Coast 1983)★★★, *White Knuckle Ride* (Morocco 1984)★★★, *The Line Of Your Fire* (Morocco 1985)★★★.

Dumpy's Rusty Nuts

Dumpy (b. Graham Dunnell, July 1949, London, England) had been playing with various bands since the mid-60s. His first big break came in 1977 with new wave outfit the Rivvets. Four years later he returned to his love of blues and formed Dumpy's Rusty Nuts. Taking on guitar and vocals, he was joined by Malcolm McKenzie (bass) and Chris Hussey (drums). Together they recorded the 'Biker Anthem' and 'Just For Kicks', before encountering trouble with BBC Radio 1 who objected to the band's name - for a while 'nuts' became 'bolts'. Dumpy, a natural entertainer, followed the rock traditions started by Jackie Lynton and interspersed the music with jokes, which helped to gain them a cult following in the pubs and clubs. Prior to a major tour with the Blues Band, McKenzie left to join Nuthin' Fancy and was replaced by Jeff Brown. Over the next few years, the band's records sold badly, a situation exacerbated by ever-fluctuating line-ups, with transient personnel including Mark Brabbs (drums, ex-Tank), Alan Fish and Mick Kirton (bass and drums, both ex-Groundhogs), Alan Davey and Danny Thompson (bass and drums, on loan from Hawkwind) and guitarist Mick Grafton from Cloven Hoof. It was Dumpy's connections with Hawkwind that kept him in the public eye, with 1987's *Get Out On The Road* becoming his most successful release, largely owing to guest appearances by Davey, Thompson and Dave Brock from Hawkwind. The band had one last attempt at the big time in October 1990 when they entered the studio to record a cover version of the Jo Jo Gunne classic, 'Run Run Run', with Kim Wilde producer Steve Glenn. The single was to be released to coincide with a major support slot on the Status Quo tour. However, all did not go according to plan - the single only appeared as a promo copy and, under orders, they had to omit much of the humour from their live set. This undermined their unique performing style and rendered them just another blues rock band. Since that time, there have been no new records and they have returned to the pub and club circuit. McKenzie later went on to manage Thunder while Alan Fish formed Egypt.

● ALBUMS: *Somewhere In England* (Landslide 1984)★★★, *Hot Lover* (Gas 1985)★★, *Get Out On The Road* (Metal Masters 1987)★★★, *Firkin Well Live* (Razor 1988)★★.

● VIDEOS: *Live At The Marquee 1986* (1988), *The Vintage Video* (1990), *Live At The Hippodrome 1989* (1990).

Dust

A hard rock band formed in the USA in the early 70s, Dust comprised Richie Wise (vocals, guitar), Kenny Aaronson (bass) and Marc Bell (drums). They launched their career in 1971 with *Dust*, a seamless exposition of standard hard rock traditions (the debt to Led Zeppelin and Jimi Hendrix was clearly audible) with the occasional unusual arrangement. For 1972's *Hard Attack* the group extended the more experimental aspects of their sound, incorporating strings on several songs. However, it was not enough to push the group into the mainstream, and they collapsed shortly after its release. Aaronson subsequently joined Derringer and played with several other rock bands, while Bell worked with the Ramones.

● ALBUMS: *Dust* (Kama Sutra 1971)★★★, *Hard Attack* (Kama Sutra 1972)★★★.

DVC

Formed in the USA in 1980, DVC comprised Bob Forest (guitar, vocals), John Bartle (guitar, vocals), Max Padilla (bass) and John Bollin (drums). Their energetic brand of hard rock encompassed excellent dual guitar interplay and harmonies from Forest and Bartle, but more attention focused on the fact that John Bollin was the brother of the late Tommy Bolin. The group's 1981 self-titled debut for Alfa Records thus attracted substantial press coverage (not least due to the presence of a cover version of Bolin's 'Teaser'), but once the novelty had worn off rock journalists looked elsewhere. In retrospect, this was a minor travesty considering the strength of the group's own compositions.

● ALBUMS: *DVC* (Alfa 1981)★★★.

EARFORCE

A German heavy metal band featuring Mandy Van Baaren (vocals), Burkhard Lipps (vocals), Paco Saval (keyboards, vocals), Tato Gomez (guitar) and Willi Ketzer (drums), Earforce formed in the early 80s. Their debut album, 1982's *Hot Line*, featured an eclectic mix of styles, from Fleetwood Mac-styled folk/blues rock to more assertive hard rock. Many critics suggested that the songs lost something in translation (they relied almost exclusively on English language lyrics), but otherwise the album was a fairly impressive achievement. Despite this, there was never a follow-up, as the band members dispersed to other projects.

● ALBUMS: *Hot Line* (Xenophone 1982)★★★.

EARTHSHAKER

This Japanese heavy metal band was modelled on the styles of Y&T, Deep Purple and Van Halen. Formed by guitarist Shinichiro Ishihara in 1981, even its name was taken from Y&T's third album. After a series of false starts, the band was completed with the addition of Masafumi Nishida (vocals), Takayuki Kai (bass) and Yoshihiro Kudo (drums). Relocating to San Francisco in 1983, they utilized the talents of ex-Gamma keyboardist Mitchell Froom on the following year's *Fugitive* opus. As a consequence the band's sound became less aggressive, which only served to highlight their obvious limitations. They continued to release albums as a four-piece, but made little impact outside their native Japan.

● ALBUMS: *Earthshaker* (Music For Nations 1983)★★, *Fugitive* (Music For Nations 1984)★★★, *Midnight Flight* (Music For Nations 1984)★★★, *Live* (Nexus 1985)★★, *Over The Run* (Eastworld 1986)★★★, *Treachery* (Eastworld 1989)★★★, *Live Best* (Eastworld 1990)★★.

EASY ACTION

Swedish hard rock act Easy Action formed in the early 80s and comprised Zinny Zan (vocals), Chris Lynn (guitar), Kee Marcello (guitar), Alex Tyrome (bass) and Freddy Van Gerber (drums). They made their major label recording debut in 1984 with a powerful self-titled collection that predominantly looked to US radio rock for its inspiration. However, they were dropped by Sire Records because of disappointing sales, and they moved to the independent KGR Records three years later for *That Makes One*. This saw them adopt more contemporary elements such as the 'sleaze rock' of Hanoi Rocks, but overall, the record failed to gel as effectively as their debut. When Marcello left the band to join platinum-sellers Europe, Easy Action foundered.

● ALBUMS: *Easy Action* (Sire 1984)★★★★, *That Makes One* (KGR 1987)★★★.

EF BAND

Comprising John Rich (vocals), Par Ericson (bass, vocals, flute), Benet Fischer (guitar) and Dag Eliason (drums), Swedish hard rockers the Ef Band formed in 1978, originally as a trio. By 1980 they had added Rich to become a quartet. They made their debut one year later with *Last Laughs On You* for Mercury Records. With the New Wave Of British Heavy Metal movement gaining pace in the UK, the Ef Band found ready support for their similar back-to-basics hard rock assault, which also flirted with progressive rock elements. They were included on EMI Records' *Metal For Muthas Volume 1* compilation - one of the agenda-setting releases of the early 80s, and they also supported Rainbow on their Scandinavian tour. However, subsequent releases failed to build on this momentum. Eliason was replaced by Dave Dufort on drums (brother of Denise Dufort of Girlschool) and Rich was replaced by former Nevada Foxx singer Roger Marsden in 1984. The following year's *One Night Stand*, their first release for Mausoleum Records, sounded both dated and tired, and the Ef Band broke up soon after its release.

● ALBUMS: *Last Laughs On You* (Mercury 1981)★★★, *Deep Cut* (Ewita 1983)★★★, *One Night Stand* (Mausoleum 1985)★★.

EINSTEIN

Einstein, a German hard rock band formed in the late 70s, comprised Richard Shoenherz (vocals, keyboards), Christian Kolonovits (vocals, keyboards) and Harmut Pfanmuller (drums). Their music was pitched somewhere between the progressive rock of Emerson, Lake And Palmer and the pomp AOR of Kansas or Journey, but on the evidence of their sole album, *Principles*, released on a major label in 1979, they were less intuitive songwriters and performers than any of those acts. Greeted with disdain bordering on antipathy by reviewers, the group continued for only a few months after its release.

● ALBUMS: *Principles* (WEA 1979)★★.

ELECTRIC ANGELS

Comprising Jonathan Daniel (bass), John Schubert (drums), Ryan Roxie (guitar) and former Candy singer Shane (vocals), US rock band the Electric Angels formed at the end of the 80s. Their blend of guttural, sleazy rock (Hanoi Rocks were an obvious reference point) was premiered on their self-titled Atlantic Records debut in 1990. The producer was Tony Visconti, but even he failed to generate anything of substance from a suite of very average songs.

● ALBUMS: *Electric Angels* (Atlantic 1990)★★.

ELECTRIC BOYS

This Swedish funk-metal band was formed by vocalist/guitarist Conny Bloom (b. Blomquist) and bassist Andy Christell in 1988. As a duo, the pair recorded 'All Lips 'N' Hips', and finding themselves with a domestic hit, completed the band by recruiting guitarist Franco Santunione and drummer Niclas Sigevall. The self-produced *Funk-O-Metal Carpet Ride* was a strong debut, with memorable songs delivered in a heavy punk style with a distinct psychedelic edge. The band replaced five songs on the original version of the debut with new, Bob Rock-produced efforts, and the revised *Funk-O-Metal Carpet Ride* made a considerable impact, emerging as the rock world was opening its collective mind to the likes of Living Colour and Dan Reed Network. The band's colourful image and live shows enhanced their growing reputation. However, the funk-metal bubble had burst by the time that the more heavily psychedelic *Groovus Maximus* appeared, and despite the potential of the Beatles-influenced 'Mary In The Mystery World' (the album was actually recorded at Abbey Road), the Electric Boys struggled, and after a US tour with Mr. Big, Santunione and Sigevall departed. Martin Thomander (guitar) and Thomas Broman (drums, ex-Great King Rat) replaced them on *Freewheelin'*, which abandoned funk in favour of a more 70s-inspired Aerosmith/Led Zeppelin groove, but this impressive comeback could not restore the band's waning fortunes, and they broke up shortly after its release.

● ALBUMS: *Funk-O-Metal Carpet Ride* (Mercury 1989)★★★, *Groovus Maximus* (Mercury 1992)★★, *Freewheelin'* (Music For Nations 1994)★★★.

ELECTRIC HELLFIRE CLUB

The band's name was derived from the English eighteenth-century group of Satanic society swingers known as the Hellfire Club; the band was formed in an attempt to emulate the club's devilish hedonism in a musical (thus 'Electric') form. At the core of the group is the vocalist, synthesizer programmer and Satanist Thomas Thorn. Thorn had previously been in the seminal industrial dance act the Thrill Kill Kult under the name Buck Ryder. In 1991 he had become alienated by their increasingly commercial direction and contemptuous attitude towards darker topics. He left and formed the Electric Hellfire Club with a diverse group of musicians, including the Reverend Doctor Luv (keyboards), Ronny Valeo (guitars) and Janna Flail (drums), who was later replaced on percussion by Richard Frost. All of them brought different influences into the band's sound, from heavy metal and ethnic music, to punk and techno. Thorn's own fascination with 60s psychedelia adds to this cocktail to create a style that is distinctive and colourful. Frivolous and sinister in equal parts, the Electric Hellfire Club are far removed from the clichéd stamping grounds of Satanic rock.

● ALBUMS: *Burn, Baby, Burn!* (Cleopatra 1994)★★★, *Calling Mr. Luv* (Cleopatra 1996)★★★.

ELECTRIC LOVE HOGS

This Los Angeles quintet originated when vocalist John Feldmann and guitarist Donny Campion linked with drummer Bobby Fernandez in a San Diego covers band. The addition of second guitarist Dae Kushner and funk-orientated bassist Kelly LeMieux, who was recruited following a wrong-number phone call, saw the band move towards original material, incorporating LeMieux's slap bass into a trad/speed metal framework for an energetic hybrid style. The band adopted the Electric Love Hogs name as a reaction against the crop of Los Angeles glam bands on the late 80s club scene who they felt were taking the music business too seriously. London Records signed the band without asking them to change their name, and *Electric Love Hogs* was a bright debut, offering a strong, punchy sound courtesy of Mark Dodson (although more interest centred on two tracks produced by Mötley Crüe's Tommy Lee). Nevertheless, the album did not have the individuality to distinguish the band from the funk-metal pack. The band's live work remained impressive as they toured the USA with L.A. Guns and the UK with Ugly Kid Joe before returning to the studio.

● ALBUMS: *Electric Love Hogs* (London 1992)★★★.

ELECTRIC SUN

This German group was formed by Uli Jon Roth (guitar, vocals) after he left the Scorpions in 1978. At first he was assisted by Ule Ritgens on bass and Clive Edwards on drums. The group was quickly signed by the Brain label and released *Earthquake* in 1979. It was a highly spiritual record, with guitarwork that aspired to imitate Jimi Hendrix and the west coast acid rock movement. This fusion of jazz and rock music, however, was let down by Roth's vocals. On *Firewind*, released in 1981, Clive Edwards was replaced by Sidhatta Gautama. The music was improved and featured pieces influenced by the oriental tradition, even though the vocals remained the same. Roth's solo album, *Beyond The Astral Skies*, took four years to complete, but when it was finally released, it revealed a great leap forward. In addition to the jazz rock pieces, there were also neo-classical movements that allowed Roth free reign to indulge his religious beliefs and demonstrate his musical ability and technique. The biggest improvement was in the vocals, with Roth still singing lead but having the support of seven other vocalists.

● ALBUMS: *Earthquake* (Brain 1979)★★, *Firewind* (Brain 1981)★★★.

Solo: Uli Jon Roth *Beyond The Astral Skies* (EMI 1985)★★★.

ELECTRO HIPPIES

This eccentric 'grindcore' outfit formed in Liverpool, England, in 1988. Specializing in low-technology studio techniques, they went on to issue a sequence of albums for Peaceville, and, later, Necrosis. In each case, a distorted, bass-laden barrage was overridden by stomach-churning vocals that consciously lacked both finesse and cohesion. The group's initial line-up included Simon (drums), Dom (bass, vocals) and Andy (guitar, vocals). Chaotic and extreme, Electro Hippies used their platform to chastise the whole recording industry. Their mantle was upheld in the first case by Radio 1 disc jockey John Peel, for whom the group recorded a July 1987 session consisting of nine tracks. Titles such as 'Starve The City (To Feed The Poor)' and 'Mega-Armageddon Death Part 3' summed up both their appeal and limitations.

● ALBUMS: *Peel Sessions* (Strange Fruit 1987)★★★, *The Only Good Punk Is A Dead One* (Peaceville 1988)★★, *Electro Hippies Live* (Peaceville 1989)★★, *Play Loud Or Die* (Necrosis 1989)★★.

● COMPILATIONS: *The Peaceville Recordings* (Peaceville 1989)★★.

ELEND

Led by singer and composer Alexandre Iskandar Hasnaoui, French/Australian group Elend specialize in the performance of baroque orchestral pieces in praise of Lucifer. Though their ambitions may be grand in design, Elend have nevertheless made two fine recordings that are far more musically literate than many of the dark metal bands attempting to incorporate classical elements into their work. The first, *Lecons De Ténébres*, was rooted in traditional black metal sentiments, but for *Les Ténébres Du Dehors* the arrangements were more orchestral in tone and scope. The blend of Hasnaoui's piercing screams with the operatic sopranos of Eve Gabrielle Siskind and Nathalie Barbary certainly produced a disconcerting musical effect in this, the group's second instalment in their attempt to recreate the three masses of the Catholic Officium Tenebarum. The packaging was also distinctive, featuring engravings by Gustave Doré taken from *Paradise Lost*. The complexity of Elend's ideas and music is particularly unusual given that the group are based partially in Australia (where musician Renaud is based) and that their songs are systematically built as the result of overseas tape correspondence. Despite this, the classical training of each member involved in Elend shines through, as does their academic knowledge of the Baroque, Classical and Romantic periods.

● ALBUMS: *Lecons De Ténébres* (Holy 1994)★★★, *Les Ténébres Du Dehors* (Holy 1996)★★★.

ELF

This US heavy rock unit was formed in 1967 by vocalist Ronnie James Dio (b. Ronald Padavona, 10 July 1940, New Hampshire, USA) with cousin Dave Feinstein on guitar, plus Gary Driscoll (drums), Doug Thaler (keyboards) and Nick Pantas (guitar). They worked under the name Electric Elves until 1970 when the entire band was involved in a car crash, in which guitarist Nick Pantas died and Thaler was hospitalized. Mickey Lee Soule (keyboards, guitar) was added to a reshuffled line-up, seen by Roger Glover and Ian Paice of Deep Purple in 1972. A production and recording contract was arranged, with Elf supporting Deep Purple on two American tours. However, the group's bar-room blues and boogie was always more effective live than in the studio (witness the posthumous live album for MGM Records). In 1973 Elf recruited bassist Craig Gruber, allowing Dio to concentrate on vocals. Their guitarist, Feinstein, gave up touring and was replaced first by Doug Thaler, previously keyboard player for the Elves, and then Steve Edwards. From 1974 Mark Nauseef (later Ian Gillan and Thin Lizzy) played percussion for the band. In 1975 Glover offered Dio the opportunity to appear on his project *The Butterfly Ball*, and this gave Dio the widespread recognition he desired. Ritchie Blackmore stepped in to co-opt Elf into his Rainbow project, though after five months only Dio remained as former Elf musicians Gruber, Lee Soule and Driscoll were summarily discarded.

● ALBUMS: *Elf* (Epic 1972)★★★, *LA59* (Purple 1974)★★, *Trying To Burn The Sun* (MGM 1975)★★, *Live* (MGM 1976)★★★.

ELIXIR

This UK heavy metal quintet was formed in the mid-80s and featured Paul Taylor (vocals), Kevin Dobbs (bass), Phil Denton (b. *c.*1962, Luton, Bedfordshire, England; guitar), Norman Gordon (guitar) and Nigel Dobbs (drums). Their debut album, released in 1988, was preceded by a session for the Radio 1 *Friday Rock* show. A second album saw them joined by ex-Iron Maiden drummer Clive Burr (b. 8 March 1957), plus Mark White on bass, replacing the Dobbs brothers. Their stylistic origins date back to the New Wave Of British Heavy Metal, utilizing twin lead guitars to alternate between circular power-riffs and intricate solos. Early Iron Maiden and Def Leppard were strong influences, with their lyrical content split between mythology/epic struggles ('Son Of Odin', etc.) and the equally clichéd themes of sex, violence and drugs. After the band's dissolution Denton returned to playing the clubs with covers band Rough Diamond (not the 70s supergroup).

● ALBUMS: *Elixir* (Goasco 1988)★★★, *Lethal Potion* (Sonic 1990)★★★.

ELOY

This German progressive-space rock band is essentially a vehicle for the creative talents of lead vocalist, guitarist and songwriter Frank Bornemann, with a somewhat unstable backing line-up. The band released their debut, *Inside*, in 1973, and achieved enormous success in Germany with a succession of albums in the vein of Pink Floyd and Yes but with a heavier, guitar-based approach. These usually featured instrumentally complex epics based on Bornemann's science fiction-flavoured concepts, but despite a domestic major label contract, and a consistent English language approach, their early material was not released outside their homeland. Bornemann, at this stage joined by Hannes Filberth (keyboards), Hannes Arkona (keyboards, guitar), Klaus-Peter Matziol (bass) and Fritz Randow (drums), was by now updating the Eloy sound, culminating in the excellent *Metromania*, where modern keyboard textures added colour to more compact, less indulgent songs, but this line-up crumbled as the rhythm section departed. Bornemann was subsequently less prolific as his duties as owner and manager of Hanover's Horus Sound Studios took up more of his time, but Eloy made a comeback with *Destination* and then *The Tide Returns Forever*, with Michael Gerlach's keyboards helping Bornemann to produce an altogether more technical sound along the lines of latter-day Rush while retaining all of Eloy's individual character.

● ALBUMS: *Inside* (Electrola 1973)★★★★, *Floating* (Electrola 1974)★★★, *Power And The Passion* (Electrola 1975)★★★★, *Dawn* (Electrola 1976)★★★, *Oceans* (Electrola 1977)★★★, *Silent Cries, Mighty Echoes* (Electrola 1978)★★★, *Live* (Electrola 1978)★★, *Colours* (Electrola 1983)★★★, *Metromania* (Electrola 1984)★★★★, *Ra* (Electrola 1989)★★, *Destination* (SPV 1993)★★★, *The Tide Returns Forever* (SPV 1995)★★★.

EMERGENCY

German hard rock group Emergency originally comprised Englishman Pete Lovell on vocals plus Frans Limonard (guitar), Jos Anthonissen (bass), Hedwig Spijkers (drums) and Coen Van Hoof (keyboards). Both Anthonissen and Limonard had previously been part of Rancid (not the 90s Californian punk band) while Lovell was a former contributor to Picture. Achieving some momentum in mainland Europe with their expansive stage shows, the group signed to Ariola Records in 1989. Their debut, *Martial Law*, was a competent collection that failed adequately to translate their live popularity into the studio. After its release, Spijkers was replaced by former Highway Chile drummer Ernst Van Ee.

● ALBUMS: *Martial Law* (Ariola 1989)★★.

EMPEROR

Members of the bizarre Norwegian Satanic club known as the Black Metal Circle, led by Euronymous of Mayhem, Emperor form part of the black metal revival of the 90s. Musically, they whip up a cacophonous storm of blistering guitars and bellowed vocals, with aggressive, devilish themes and a few strange, quasi-classical flourishes. In 1993 they released a split CD with Scandinavian pagan heavy metal band Enslaved. In the same year the Black Metal Circle were linked with a series of church burnings in Norway and Samoth, Emperor's sinisterly flamboyant frontman, was arrested in connection with the crimes. He was later released; however, in addition to the arson, Emperor drummer Faust was convicted of the 1992 murder of a homosexual. Despite this, and the murder of fellow black metal Satanist Euronymous, Emperor continue to fly the Scandinavian black metal banner.

● ALBUMS: *Emperor* (Candlelight 1993)★★★, *In the Nightside Eclipse* (Candlelight 1994)★★★, *Anthems To The Welkin At Dusk* (Candlelight 1997)★★★.

ENTOMBED

This Swedish death metal band was formed in Stockholm in 1987 as Nihilist, releasing four acclaimed demos: *Drowned*, *Premature Autopsy*, *But Life Goes On* and *Only Shreds Remain*. After dissolving Nihilist, the band reunited a few days later as Entombed, with a line-up of Lars Goren-Petrov (vocals), Ulf Cederlund (guitar), Alex Hellid (guitar), Lars Rosenburg (bass) and Nicke Andersson (drums). *Left Hand Path* adequately demonstrated the band's potential with an atmospheric and individual sound and live shows were equally impressive. Petrov departed shortly after the debut, but Orvar Safstrom only lasted for one single ('Crawl') before ex-Carnage bassist Johnny Dordevic took over on the well-reviewed *Clandestine*. After an extensive US tour with Morbid Angel, he too was ousted in favour of the returning Petrov for the Gods Of Grind UK jaunt with Carcass, Cathedral and Confessor. The mini-album *Hollowman* was swiftly followed by the hugely impressive *Wolverine Blues* as Entombed continued to ignore death metal convention, establishing themselves as one of the genre's leading acts, and creating more accessible material by incorporating into the fierce death metal framework traditional rock song structures and a rhythmic groove. Entombed's popularity continued to increase as they toured Europe on a frighteningly intense bill with labelmates Napalm Death, while an EP, *Out Of Hand*, saw high-class cover versions of material by Kiss ('God Of Thunder') and Repulsion ('Blackbreath').

● ALBUMS: *Left Hand Path* (Earache 1990)★★★, *Clandestine* (Earache 1991)★★★, *Hollowman* mini-album (Earache 1993)★★, *Wolverine Blues* (Earache 1993)★★★★, *To Ride, Shoot Straight And Speak The Truth* (Music For Nations 1997)★★★, *Entombed* (Earache 1997)★★★.

ENUFF Z'NUFF

This 90s Chicago, USA pop-metal crossover quartet comprised Donnie Vie (vocals), Derek Frigo (guitar, ex-Le Mans), Chip Z'Nuff (bass) and Vikki Foxx (drums). Influences such as Cheap Trick and the Beatles were apparent through the band's extensive use of three-part harmonies, which carried the melody line in many of the songs. On a visual level, they initially appeared as multi-coloured fashion casualties from the early 70s, sporting an ambitious and often dazzling array of sunglasses, waistcoats, boots and accessories (regalia notably paraded on MTV via the video to their minor hit, 'New Thing'). This image was played down following the release of *Strength*, an impressive and mature musical offering that combined infectious hooks, abrasive guitarwork and a sparkling production to dramatic effect. Following Atco's internal problems with Atlantic, the trio moved to Arista Records, though their third album saw them lose Foxx to the Vince Neil Band. The replacement was Ricky Parent (ex-War And Peace). *Tweaked* was criticized for being too derivative.

● ALBUMS: *Enuff Z'Nuff* (Atco 1989)★★★, *Strength* (Atco 1991)★★★, *Animals With Human Intelligence* (Arista 1993)★★, *Tweaked* (Music For Nations 1995)★★, *Seven* (Music For Nations 1997)★★★.

ENVY

Comprising Rhonni Stile (vocals), Gina Stile (guitar), Bill Spencer (bass) and Danny Kapps (drums), hard rock band Envy were formed on the east coast of America in the mid-80s. The group's highly accessible style, with distinctive female harmonies, drew early comparisons to Heart. The carefully constructed songwriting on *Ain't It A Sin* perfectly complemented the sisters' lovelorn lyrics with fluid arrangements and excellent production. However, despite Atlantic Records' self-evident investment in and early enthusiasm for the group, Envy broke up shortly after the album's release.

● ALBUMS: *Ain't It A Sin* (Atlantic 1987)★★★.

EPITAPH

US band Epitaph's career comprises two distinct phases, linked together by founder-member and guitarist/vocalist Cliff Jackson. The first two albums had little to do with their later hard-rock style and featured a jazz-tinged AOR flavour. The band disintegrated in 1975, but Jackson resurrected Epitaph in 1979 with Heinz Glass (guitar), Harvey Janssen (bass), Michael Karch (keyboards) and Fritz Randow (drums). *Return From Reality* adopted an aggressive approach, characterized by the heavy-duty guitarwork of Glass. Karch was fired after the album was released, and *See You In Alaska*, which followed, was surprisingly lightweight compared to its predecessor. *Live* redressed the balance and saw the band in good shape once more. However, internal disputes resulted in the departure of Glass, Randow and Janssen soon after the album's release. Klaus Walz, Norbert Lehmann and Bernie Kolbe were drafted in as replacements on guitar, drums and vocals, respectively, to record *Danger Man* in 1982. Unable to generate renewed interest, the band folded in 1983. Kolbe and Jackson went on to Kingdom (later renamed Domain), while Randow joined Victory.

● ALBUMS: *Outside The Law* (Billingsgate 1974)★★★, *Stop, Look And Listen* (Polydor 1975)★★, *Return From Reality* (Brain 1979)★★★, *See You In Alaska* (Brain 1980)★★, *Live* (Metronome 1981)★★★, *Danger Man* (Metronome 1982)★★★.

Epitaph Records

One of the longest-standing and most successful homes to the USA's constantly evolving alternative rock movement, Epitaph Records was originally started as an in-house label for Los Angeles, California group Bad Religion. In common with that group, Epitaph took several years to rise to the prominence it currently enjoys. Guitarist Brett Gurewitz (b. *c.*1962, USA) formed Epitaph in the early 80s as an outlet for Bad Religion releases. Having recently recovered from crack cocaine addiction, the label at its inception was a long way from the 'greatest rock 'n' roll record company in the world' that Gurewitz envisaged for its future in the mid-90s. By 1993 the label was home to Rancid, No FX, Pennywise and Offspring in addition to Bad Religion, Gurevitz having recently left the band to concentrate on the label, but had sold only 1.5 million records in seven years. That situation changed dramatically with the Offspring's breakthrough early in 1994. Their song 'Come Out And Play (Keep 'Em Separated)' became a major hit on MTV and propelled the accompanying album, *Smash*, to sales of over eight million. Gurewitz was even lionized with an article in *Newsweek* magazine under the headline 'Punk Is His Business'. From a team of six people working in a garage, Epitaph suddenly became a major concern, relocating to new offices in the plush Los Angeles neighbourhood of Silverlake. However, although the success allowed Epitaph to expand its roster, two of its most successful groups, Bad Religion and the Offspring, have jumped ship to a major record label, the latter publicly stating that Gurewitz's 'independent' attitude was just a smokescreen for his corporate interests. Despite this, Rancid followed up the Offspring's success with two further million-selling albums to keep Epitaph a highly profitable concern throughout 1995 and 1996. Whether or not the label will ever achieve the level of success that Gurewitz clearly intends for it is less clear-cut, particularly as his 1996 divorce required him to secure further finance for the label.

Eric Steel Band

A hard-working hard rock band from Chicago, Illinois, USA, the Eric Steel Band comprised Bruce Hansfield (vocals, guitar), Dave Anderson (guitar), Mike Hobson (bass) and Brad Wickham (drums). After coming to prominence on the local Illinois club scene they signed to Megaforce Records in 1984 for the release of *Eric Steel*. Though there was little distinguished about the songwriting on view, the group's natural energy ensured it was greeted as an above-average release. Four years passed before a follow-up collection, *Infectious*, was released by Passport Records. In the interim, the group had lost some of its impetus but, on the evidence of their new songs, none of their vivacity.

● ALBUMS: *Eric Steel* (Megaforce 1984)★★★, *Infectious* (Passport 1988)★★★.

Ethel The Frog

Featuring P. Sheppard (vocals), Tognola (guitar), Hopkinson (bass) and Paul Conyers (drums), Ethel The Frog, taking their name from a *Monty Python* sketch, first came to the public's attention via a track on EMI Records influential *Metal For Muthas Vol. I* compilation in 1980. This album was intended to introduce unsigned British heavy metal bands and is notable for boasting two early Iron Maiden tracks. The concept was very much to advance the New Wave Of British Heavy Metal of which Ethel The Frog was a part. However, their track, 'Fight Back', was disappointingly basic heavy metal. Soon afterwards, they recorded and released their own debut, *Ethel The Frog*, which failed to capture the public's interest and met with critical disdain. Disillusioned, they split in 1980, with Conyers and Tognola moving on to Salem.

● ALBUMS: *Ethel The Frog* (EMI 1980)★★.

EUROPE

A Swedish heavy rock band, Europe achieved international success in the late 80s. In 1982, Joey Tempest (b. 19 August 1963, Stockholm, Sweden; vocals), John Norum (guitar) and John Leven (bass) founded Force in the Stockholm suburb of Upplands-Vasby. After winning a national talent contest, the group recorded two Rush-influenced albums for the Swedish market before signing to Epic Records in 1986. By this time, Norum had left and the renamed Europe included guitarist Kee Marcello (ex-Easy Action), Michael Michaeli (keyboards) and Ian Haughland (drums). The first Epic album was produced by Kevin Elson and included three 1987 hits 'The Final Countdown' (UK number 1/ US number 8), 'Rock The Night' (UK number 12/US number 30), and 'Carrie' (UK number 22/US number 3). *The Final Countdown* went on to triple platinum status, but also set the group a standard they subsequently failed to maintain. However, Europe's continued success in Japan and the USA was assisted by the group's lengthy world tours. Later hits included 'Superstitious' (UK number 34/US number 31, August 1988) from the Ron Nevison-produced second album. *Prisoners In Paradise*, with Beau Hill as producer, sold poorly, despite containing the UK number 28 hit single 'I'll Cry For You'. Joey Tempest signed a solo contract with PolyGram Records in 1994 and released his debut, *A Place To Call Home*, in 1995.

● ALBUMS: *Europe* (Hot 1983)★★, *Wings Of Tomorrow* (Hot 1984)★★★, *The Final Countdown* (Epic 1986)★★★, *Out Of This World* (Epic 1988)★★, *Prisoners In Paradise* (Epic 1991)★★★.
● COMPILATIONS: *Europe 1982 - 1992* (Epic 1993)★★★.

EVERCLEAR

Comprising Art Alexakis (b. 12 April 1962, Los Angeles, California, USA; vocals, guitar), Craig Montoya (b. 14 September 1970; bass, vocals) and Greg Eklund (b. 18 April 1970), who replaced original drummer Scott Cuthbert in 1994. Everclear were formed in Portland, Oregon, in 1991. Alexakis had previously worked as a roadie for a succession of north-west punk bands. Indulging himself in copious quantities of drugs, he only decided to start his own group when a cocaine overdose temporarily stopped his heart. Early comparisons to Nirvana (exacerbated by the singer's blonde hair) went into overdrive when Kurt Cobain publicly stated his approval. They made their debut in 1994 with *World Of Noise*, which included the intriguing 'Sparkle' ('Fire pulls the spirit from the corporate whore/I'm embarrassed by the plaid you wear/If I were you I'd hide behind that stupid bleached blond hair'). Critics were left unsure as to whom the reference concerned, Alexakis or Cobain. It was followed by a mini-album, *White Trash Hell*, again on Fire Records, before a major recording contract with Capitol Records. They were signed by Gary Gersh, who had previously taken both Nirvana and Sonic Youth to Geffen Records. In 1995 they released their first album for the new label, the critically lauded and commercially successful *Sparkle And Fade*. They looked set to repeat this success two years later with the release of the infectious *So Much For The Afterglow*.

● ALBUMS: *World Of Noise* (Fire 1994)★★★, *White Trash Hell* mini-album (Fire 1995)★★★, *Sparkle And Fade* (Capitol 1995)★★★★, *So Much For The Afterglow* (Capitol 1997)★★★.

EVERY MOTHER'S NIGHTMARE

This US 'sleaze-rock' heavy metal band, originating (surprisingly) from the home of country music, Nashville, was formed in 1989 by vocalist Rick Ruhl and guitarist Steve Malone. With the addition of bassist Mark McMurty and drummer Jim Phipps, they signed a contract with Arista Records in 1990. Their self-titled debut, released the same year, combined Kiss, Aerosmith, Tesla and Bon Jovi influences to powerful effect. Their dynamism and musical palate gave the songs a cutting edge that elevated the resultant collection above mere plagiarism.

● ALBUMS: *Every Mother's Nightmare* (Arista 1990)★★★.

EVIL DEAD

After his split with the eccentric Agent Steel in 1988, guitarist Juan Garcia (also ex-Abattoir) went on to form Evil Dead featuring a line-up of Albert Gonzalez (guitar), Phil Fiores (vocals), and Rob Ailinz (drums, ex-Necrophilia). A strong and professional thrash metal act, Evil Dead nevertheless lacked identity or the kind of individuality Agent Steel frontman John Cyriis was able to give his volatile five-piece. In the increasingly crowded thrash and death metal genres, Garcia's act struggled to hold the attention of the young, and somewhat fickle, extreme metal audiences.

● ALBUMS: *Rise Above* (Steamhammer 1988)★★★, *Annihilation Of Civilisation* (Steamhammer 1990)★★.

EVIL SUPERSTARS

Belgium's Evil Superstars, who comprise Mauro Pawlowski (vocals, guitar), Dave Schroyen (drums), Marc Requile (keyboards), Bert Vandebroek (bass) and Tim Vanhamel (guitar), became one of a number of mainland European groups alongside Whale, Bettie Serveert and the Cardigans to procure UK and US audiences in the mid-90s. They recorded their debut EP, *Hairfacts*, in 1995, before touring with Placebo and achieving notoriety for their 'Satan Is In My Ass' single. Encompassing several traditions of music such as jazz, reggae and hard rock, the impression of eclecticism was confirmed by the 1996 release of *Love Is Okay*, which shaped these diverse influences into pop songs of genuine merit and accessibility. *Boogie-Children-R-Us* repeated the formula to lesser effect.

● ALBUMS: *Love Is Okay* (Paradox 1996)★★★, *Boogie-Children-R-Us* (Paradox 1998)★★.

EX

Unconventional Dutch conglomerate formed in 1977 when punk first hit Holland and a variety of like minds came together as a politically active musical and social unit. The Ex were formed from the ashes of two small local bands, and their varied membership has included G.W. Sok (vocals), Terrie Hessels (guitar), Sabien Witteman (drums), Katrin Bornfeld (drums), Jos Kley (vocals), Han Buhrs (vocals), Yoke Laarman (bass), Luc Klaassen (bass), Wineke T. Hart (violin), Kees vanden Haak (saxophone), John van der Weert (vocals, guitar), Nicolette (guitar), Dolf Planteydt (guitar) and Tom Greene (guitar). They were strongly linked to a variety of left-field concerns in general and the Amsterdam squatting movement in particular (they also released a joint live album of a benefit tour for striking British miners). Although the sound started life as strictly agit-prop punk, they later incorporated elements such as Eastern folk music, funk and various other styles. *Scrabbling At The Lock* and *And The Weathermen Shrug Their Shoulders*, for instance, were collaborations with experimental violin player Tom Cora, and they have also recorded with Iraqi Kurdish group Awara. Guests on other works have included Thurston Moore and Lee Ranaldo (Sonic Youth), Jon Langford (Mekons), and the Dog Faced Hermans (whose guitar player, Andy, joined Ex in 1990). Their attitude to the place of rebel music in the scheme of things can best be summised by a statement on the rear of 1985's *Pokkeherrie*: 'Where have all the musicians gone? The ones who made sound disturb, who pulled down the stage, who forged music into a weapon. Where have all the musicians gone? They perform in supermarkets and have their instruments tuned. "Our ears are deaf and our strings are wrapped up in silk. We hurt nobody."' A lowlands equivalent to Fugazi then, but with arguably more stylistic variation. In 1998 they signed to Touch & Go Records in the USA, and began recording with Steve Albini.

● ALBUMS: *Disturbing Domestic Peace* (Verrecords 1980)★★★, *History Is What's Happening* (More DPM 1982)★★★, *Dignity Of Labour* (VGZ 1983)★★★, *Tumult* (FAI 1983)★★★, *Blueprints For A Blackout* (Pig Brother Productions 1983)★★★, *Pokkeherrie* (Pockabilly 1985)★★★, *Too Many Cowboys* (Mordam 1987)★★★, *Live In Wroclaw* cassette only (Red 1987)★★★, *Aural Guerilla* (Ex 1988)★★★, *Joggers And Smoggers* (Ex 1989)★★★, *Dead Fish* mini-album (Ex 1990)★★★, with Dog Faced Hermans *Treat* cassette only (Demon Rage 1990)★★, with Tom Cora *Scrabbling At The Lock* (Ex 1991)★★★★, with Cora *And The Weathermen Shrug Their Shoulders* (Fist Puppet 1993)★★★★, *Mudbird Shivers* (Ex/RecRec 1995)★★★, with various artists *Instant* (Ex 1995)★★★.

● COMPILATIONS: with various artists *Oorwormer* (1982)★★★, *Hands Up! You're Free* (Ex 1988)★★★.

● VIDEOS: *The Ex & Guests - Live At The Bimhuis* (1992), *Terrie, Andy & Friends - Sounds Of Bells* (1995).

EXCALIBUR

This group was formed in Yorkshire, England, in 1981 by Paul McBride (vocals), Paul Solynskyj (b. 27 October 1966, England; guitar), Martin Hawthorn (bass), and Mick Dobson (drums). The band was formed while they were still schoolboys and they would reportedly fall asleep in class after a heavy night's gigging. On finishing school, Excalibur continued to tour heavily, while the members also attempted to hold down day jobs. Conquest Records signed the band in 1985 after an employee heard Excalibur by chance one night. *The Bitter End* mini-album was released in 1985, containing slightly predictable but melodic heavy metal. In 1986 Excalibur expanded to a five-piece with the addition of Steve Blades (b. 20 May 1968, Scotland; guitar, keyboards). This was followed by a session for BBC Radio 1's *Friday Rock Show*, which was broadcast in July 1986 and again in September. The four tracks that the band recorded were later released by Clay Records as the *Hot For Love EP* in

1988. That year saw Excalibur appear on a BBC television programme, *On A Personal Note*, where they performed 'Hot For Love' and 'Running Scared' alongside slots from Def Leppard and Little Angels. Before the year's end, Dobson was replaced by Dave Sykes on drums, while the group supported Uriah Heep for most of their UK tour. In 1989 the band signed to Active Records and immediately began recording a debut album. The first taster was a track entitled 'Carole Ann', an acoustic number that drew comparisons to Bon Jovi. After *One Strange Night* was released to critical acclaim, Excalibur embarked on their first full headlining tour of the UK in February 1990. They supported Saxon on UK and European dates, though there were further personnel changes to endure. Livermore had replaced Martin Hawthorn in 1989, and he now left to make way for Dean Wilson (b. 5 March 1966, England). In 1991 Excalibur were in the studio recording their follow-up album, when Paul McBride announced that he was leaving the band, placing their career on hold.

● ALBUMS: *The Bitter End* mini-album (Conquest 1985)★★★, *One Strange Night* (Active 1990)★★★★.

Exciter (Canada)

Formed in Ottawa, Canada, in 1979 as a three-piece outfit, the band's original line-up consisted of Dan Beehler (drums, vocals), John Ricci (guitar) and Allan Johnson (bass), their name deriving from an old Judas Priest track. An impressive demo attracted the attention of Shrapnel Records, who, as well as featuring the band on an early *U.S. Metal* compilation, also released the demo as an album entitled *Heavy Metal Maniac* in 1983. This was belligerent, Motörhead-influenced power metal and quickly gained the band a strong following in Europe. They then changed labels and released *Violence & Force* for Roadrunner Records in 1984. Produced by ex-Rods drummer Carl Canedy, it was a much more stylish release, benefiting from better production and higher-quality material. By the next release, the band had changed European labels once again. Their third album, *Long Live The Loud*, appeared on the Music For Nations label in 1985. Recorded and produced in London with producer Guy Bidmead, this album did not seem as immediate as previous releases and saw them lose some of their early raw power. However, this did not deter the band from undertaking an extensive European tour in support of the release. Afterwards, Ricci left to be replaced by Brian McPhee, a friend of the band, who added a new dimension to their fourth album, *Unveiling The Wicked*. Unfortunately, even McPhee's excellent guitarwork could not alleviate the sense of weariness in the music, and after a short tour of Brazil the band decided to add a vocalist/frontman to give them a stronger identity. This resulted in the recruitment of Rob Malnati. Once again they changed labels, signing to the small Canadian independent Maze Records. Their last album, *Exciter*, failed to sell and shortly after its release the band sank into obscurity, playing on the local club scene.

● ALBUMS: *Heavy Metal Maniac* (Shrapnel 1983)★★★, *Violence & Force* (Roadrunner 1984)★★★, *Long Live The Loud* (Music For Nations 1985)★★★, *Unveiling The Wicked* (Music For Nations 1986)★★, *Exciter* (Maze/Music For Nations 1988)★★, *Better Live Than Dead* (1993)★★.

Exciter (Netherlands)

Often confused with the Canadian Exciter - a band who made their breakthrough at approximately the same time and worked in the same genre - the Dutch group Exciter comprised Gert Admiral (bass), Marc Karsten (guitar), Marcel Admiral (guitar) and Walter Admiral (drums). The Admiral brothers had played music together since childhood and formed the group in the early 80s. They immediately secured a major label contract with WEA Records who released their self-titled debut album in 1983. A solid but unexciting collection of stylized Euro-metal with moderate collaborative songwriting, it was their sole release. Disappointing sales resulted in WEA dropping the group from their roster by the following year.

● ALBUMS: *Exciter* (WEA 1983)★★.

Exit-13

This environmentally themed 'grind rock' group from Pennsylvania, USA, are a side-project for Brutal Truth bass player Dan Lilker. Joined by Relapse Records co-owner Bill Yurkiewicz (vocals, samples), guitarist Steve O'Donnell and former Brutal Truth drummer Scott Lewis, the band's debut fused traditional doom metal with blues and jazz. An unlikely combination, it saw the record described in one quarter as mixing 'Stevie Ray Vaughan and early Napalm Death'. Yurkiewicz's lyrics continued to explore desperate themes on *Ethos Musick* - the opening track, subtly titled 'Societally Provoked Genocidal Contemplation', opened with the line 'This whole world is fucking sick', before concluding its first verse with

'Insanity frees my mind to wonder, I gleefully ponder humanity's murder'. Elsewhere the group ruminated further on the human race's capacity for self-degradation and cruelty, and the lasting effect of industrial activities on the planet. It certainly provided an intriguing contrast to hear 60s-style idealism braced against some of the 90s' most fearsome noise. A follow-up set continued in 'hemp-fuelled hedonist' vein, though just as interesting was a further side-project, this time featuring Yurkiewicz, O'Donnell, Lilker, Rich Hoak (drums) and Bliss Blood (Pain Teens). The project, titled *Smoking Songs*, saw the ensemble recreate jazz and blues standards of the 30s and 40s.

● ALBUMS: *Ethos Musick* (Relapse/Nuclear Blast 1994)★★★, *Didactic Grind* (Relapse/Nuclear Blast 1995)★★.

EXODUS

Formed in San Francisco, USA, in 1982, Exodus were one of the earliest thrash metal bands. Their first line-up included Metallica guitarist Kirk Hammett, though he did not record with the band. Their first album was a landmark in the thrash arena, with a highly aggressive musical and lyrical approach, dealing with all manner of extremes and brutalities. It was recorded by the line-up of Paul Baloff (vocals), Gary Holt (guitar), Rick Hunolt (guitar), Rob McKillop (bass) and Tom Hunting (drums). Vocalist Steve Sousa replaced Baloff (who formed Piranha) for *Pleasures Of The Flesh*, which was marginally more mellow, but still a daunting proposition. Even after the departure of Hunting, who was replaced by John Tempesta (b. 1964, New York, USA), Exodus continued to record worthy material, but lacked the commercial success of contemporaries such as Metallica and Anthrax. They refused to compromise or waver from their straightforward thrash style, and managed to maintain a level of popularity sufficient to gain a major label record contract. However, their own exodus was confirmed in 1992 after *Force Of Habit* saw them banging their heads against brick walls. The band briefly reunited in 1997 for a live album.

● ALBUMS: *Bonded By Blood* (Music For Nations 1985)★★★, *Pleasures Of The Flesh* (Music For Nations 1987)★★★, *Fabulous Disaster* (Music For Nations 1989)★★, *Impact Is Imminent* (Capitol 1990)★★★, *Good Friendly Violent Fun* (Roadrunner 1991)★★★, *Force Of Habit* (Roadrunner 1992)★★★, *Another Lesson In Violence* (Century Media 1997)★★★.

● COMPILATIONS: *The Best Of Exodus - Lessons In Violence* (Music For Nations 1992)★★★.

EXPLORER

New Jersey, USA band Explorer, formed by Lennie Rizzo (vocals), Kevin Kennedy (guitar), Eddie Lavolpe (guitar), Johnny G. (bass) and Mike Moyer (drums), are symptomatic of the creative nadir experienced by heavy metal by the late 80s. The material on their two albums distilled elements from major sellers such as Iron Maiden, particularly that group's reliance on high-pitched vocals and virtuoso guitar, without ever stamping an original identity on any of their songs. As a result, Explorer's *Symphonies Of Steel* and *Beg, Borrowed And Steal* (a dangerous title given a series of reviews that chastised them for being too derivative) were quickly consigned to the bargain bins by record retailers.

● ALBUMS: *Symphonies Of Steel* (HHH 1984)★★, *Beg, Borrowed And Steal* (Black Dragon 1987)★★.

EXPORT

This UK rock band was formed in 1980 by former Hardstuff vocalist Harry Shaw and guitarist Steve Morris. Enlisting the services of bassist Chris Alderman and drummer Lou Rosenthal, they specialized in Americanized AOR. Their material was characterized by note-perfect harmonies, sterling guitarwork and infectious hooklines similar to Kansas, Starz and REO Speedwagon. After a well-received self-titled debut in 1981, they were picked up by Epic Records, who recognized their enormous potential. Two albums were delivered, with Lance Quinn at the production helm for 1986's *Living In Fear Of A Private Eye*. Surprisingly, the band failed to take off in the USA and Epic dropped them owing to poor sales figures. Steve Morris produced Torino's debut album in 1987, while Export continued to search for a (not forthcoming) new contract.

● ALBUMS: *Export* (His Masters Vice 1980)★★, *Contraband* (Epic 1984)★★, *Living In Fear Of A Private Eye* (Epic 1986)★★.

EXTREME

This Boston quartet comprised Gary Cherone (b. 26 July 1961, Malden, Massachusetts, USA; vocals), Nuno Bettencourt (b. 20 September 1966, Azores, Portugal; guitar), Pat Badger (b. 22 July 1967, Boston, Massachusetts, USA; bass) and Paul Geary (b. 24 July 1961, Medford, Massachusetts, USA; drums). The origins of the band can be traced to local act the Dream, whose sole six-track EP in 1983 featured Cherone and Geary. As Extreme, the original line-up found themselves on television in

1985 via a video clip for 'Mutha (Don't Wanna Go To School Today)', as part of an MTV competition, but it was the arrival of Bettencourt in 1986 and Badger the following year that boosted their career. A recording contract with A&M Records was quickly secured and the band made their vinyl debut with 'Play With Me' for the soundtrack to *Bill And Ted's Excellent Adventure*. The inevitable self-titled debut album followed. Encompassing elements of pop, metal, funk and blues, their song-writing powers were still in their infancy at this stage and although competent, the album met with widespread critical indifference. *Pornograffitti* was a stunning second release, being an ambitious concept affair, subtitled 'A Funked Up Fairy Tale'. 'Get The Funk Out' reached number 19 in the UK charts in June 1991, but the band had already broken through in America in March when the simple acoustic ballad 'More Than Words' topped the charts. The song climbed to UK number 2 in July the same year. 'Hole Hearted' was their only other US success, reaching number 4 later that year, although they would continue to achieve Top 20 singles in the UK until 1995. The band's music was now characterized by Bettencourt's innovative guitarwork, intelligent lyrics and a diverse style that transcended a variety of musical genres. Their appearance at the Freddie Mercury memorial concert in May 1992, which interrupted sessions for *III Sides To Every Story*, gave them considerable exposure beyond the heavy metal fraternity. Prior to the band's appearance at the Donington Festival in the summer of 1994, Mike Mangini (ex-Annihilator) replaced Paul Geary on drums. After the disappointing critical and commercial reaction to 1995's *Waiting For The Punchline*, Bettencourt announced plans to release a solo album through Colorblind, the label he runs through A&M. The band formally broke up in October 1996, with Cherone moving on to become lead singer with Van Halen.

● ALBUMS: *Extreme* (A&M 1989)★★★, *Pornograffitti* (A&M 1990)★★★★, *III Sides To Every Story* (A&M 1992)★★★, *Waiting For The Punchline* (A&M 1995)★★.

● COMPILATIONS: *The Best Of Extreme* (A&M 1998)★★★.

EXTREME NOISE TERROR

A band whose name truly encapsulates their sound, Extreme Noise Terror formed in January 1985 and were signed by Manic Ears Records after their first ever gig. Their debut release was a split album with Chaos U.K., and although there were musical similarities, ENT, along with Napalm Death, were already in the process of twisting traditional punk influences into altogether different shapes. Along with the latter, they became the subject of disc jockey John Peel's interest in 1987, recording a session (one of three) that would eventually see release on Strange Fruit Records. Afterwards, drummer Mick Harris, who had left Napalm Death to replace the group's original drummer, in turn departed, joining Scorn. His replacement was Stick (Tony Dickens), who joined existing members Dean Jones (vocals), Phil Vane (vocals) and Pete Hurley (guitar). Mark Bailey had by now replaced Mark Gardiner, who himself had replaced Jerry Clay, on bass. Touring in Japan preceded the release of *Phonophobia*, while continued Peel sessions brought the group to the attention of the KLF's Bill Drummond. He asked them to record a version of the KLF's '3 A.M. Eternal', with the intention of the band appearing on *Top Of The Pops* live at Christmas to perform the tune (BBC Television, however, decided this was not in the best interests of their audience). Eventually released as a limited edition single, the two bands' paths crossed again in 1992 when the KLF were invited to perform live at the 1992 BRIT Awards. This crazed event, which included the firing of blanks into the audience, has already passed into music industry legend. Back on their own, 1993 saw Extreme Noise Terror touring widely, and the group signed to Earache Records the following year. By this time, the line-up had expanded to include Lee Barrett (bass; also Disgust) replacing Bailey, Ali Firouzbakht (lead guitar), and Pig Killer on drums. Together they released *Retro-bution*, ostensibly a compilation, but nevertheless featuring the new line-up on re-recorded versions of familiar material.

● ALBUMS: split with Chaos UK *Radioactive* (Manic Ears 1985)★★, *A Holocaust In Your Head* (Hurt 1987)★★, *The Peel Sessions* (Strange Fruit 1990)★★★, *Phonophobia* (Vinyl Japan 1992)★★, *Retro-bution* (Earache 1995)★★★, *Damage 381* (Earache 1997)★★.

● VIDEOS: *From One Extreme To The Other* (Jettisoundz 1989).

EYEHATEGOD

Based in New Orleans, Louisiana, USA, Eyehategod, who are led by vocalist Michael Williams (ex-Crawlspace), produce a sound that is a marriage of their two greatest influences, Black Flag and Black Sabbath. The most distinctive element of their sound is Williams' deliberately monotonous vocals, which act as a supplementary instrument rather than a singing voice in the conventional sense. The group initially perceived their job to be one of annoying people, but over three full studio albums they have refined their technique into a convincing and unremittingly intense soundtrack. The group are also well known for their outside activities. Williams is a former writer for US rock magazine *Metal Maniac*, while Brian Patton has concurrently worked with Soylent Green over several years. Joey works with Japanese music and regularly releases underground cassettes of his work. Jimmy Bowers is a member of Down and Crowbar. Mark Schultz is a member of Both Legs Broken with Joe Fazzio of Stressball. After a three-year gap, when many presumed the group had sundered, Eyehategod returned with their third and best album, 1996's *Dopesick*. This was produced, without charge, by Billy Anderson (Neurosis, Sleep) and continued to mine the group's favourite subjects - alienation, pain and depression, informed by the rough neighbourhoods of New Orleans in which the band members grew up.

● ALBUMS: *In The Name Of Suffering* (1992)★★, *Take As Needed For Pain* (1993)★★★, *Dopesick* (1996)★★★★.

Ezo

This Japanese band relocated to Los Angeles, California, immediately after their formation in 1985, in a move deemed necessary in order to achieve wider international exposure. Featuring Masaki (vocals), Shoyo (guitar), Taro (bass) and Hiro (drums), they were retro-rock specialists, drawing heavily on the legacy of Led Zeppelin, UFO and Kiss for their inspiration. Signing to Geffen Records and linking with Kiss bassist Gene Simmons as producer seemed a promising start. However, *Ezo* was unimpressive. The follow-up, *Fire, Fire*, dropped many of the blatant reference points of its predecessor, but ultimately lacked direction, with the band struggling to find its own identity.

● ALBUMS: *Ezo* (Geffen 1987)★★★, *Fire, Fire* (Geffen 1989)★★.

Faith No More

Formed in San Francisco in 1980, Faith No More, titled after a greyhound on which the members had placed a bet, were among the first outfits to experiment with the fusion of funk, thrash and hardcore styles that effectively became a new musical subgenre. The band initially comprised Jim Martin (b. 21 July 1961, Oakland, California, USA; guitar, ex-Vicious Hatred), Roddy Böttum (b. 1 July 1963, Los Angeles, California, USA; keyboards), Bill Gould (b. 24 April 1963, Los Angeles, California, USA; bass), Mike Bordin (b. 27 November 1962, San Francisco, California, USA; drums) and Chuck Mosley (vocals). Böttum had attended the same school as Gould, while Bordin was recruited from his course in tribal rhythm at Berkeley University. Gould had met Mosley on the Los Angeles club circuit in 1980, while Martin had been recommended by Metallica's Cliff Burton. This line-up recorded a low-budget, self-titled debut on the independent Mordam label, followed by the groundbreaking *Introduce Yourself* on Slash, a subsidiary of Warner Brothers Records. It encompassed a variety of styles but exuded a rare warmth and energy, mainly through Mosley's melodramatic vocals, and was well received by the critics (not least for the signature tune 'We Care A Lot'). However, internal disputes led to the firing of Moseley on the eve of widespread press coverage and favourable live reviews, although it had been reported that the band underwent a period when every single member walked out at some point. Mosley went on to gig temporarily with Bad Brains, before putting together his own band, Cement. Against the odds, his replacement, Mike Patton (b. 27 January 1968, Eureka, California, USA), was even more flamboyant and actually more accomplished as a singer (it was also rumoured that Courtney Love of Hole auditioned/rehearsed with the group). *The Real Thing*, the album that followed Patton's recruitment, was a runaway success, with the single 'Epic' reaching number 9 on the *Billboard* chart in June 1990, and denting the UK Top 40. Their style was now both offbeat and unpredictable, yet retained enough melody to remain a commercial proposition. Despite the universal adulation, however, it transpired that offstage, there was still a great deal of acrimony between the band members. *Live At The Brixton Academy* was released as a stop-gap affair, while the band toured for nearly three years on the back of the worldwide success of their most recent studio album. After Patton temporarily defected back to his original, pre-Faith No More outfit, Mr Bungle, the group finally returned with *Angel Dust*. A tougher, less accessible record, in keeping with the group's origins (despite a cover version of the Commodores' 'I'm Easy', which reached UK number 3 in January 1993), it made the US Top 10 and UK number 2 as their commercial ascent continued. However, in 1994, following a good deal of press speculation, the ever-volatile line-up of Faith No More switched again as Jim Martin was ousted in favour of Trey Spruance, who had formerly worked in Mr Bungle. Martin went on to form The Behemoth. Böttum formed Imperial Teen as a side project in 1996. *Album Of The Year* received a mixed reaction, including one or two scathing reviews. The same year they collaborated with Sparks on a bizarre reworking of the latter's 'This Town Ain't Big Enough For The Both Of Us'. In April 1998 they announced that they were disbanding.

● ALBUMS: *Faith No More* (Mordam 1984)★★, *Introduce Yourself* (Slash 1987)★★★★, *The Real Thing* (Slash/Reprise 1989)★★★★, *Live At The Brixton Academy* (Slash/London 1991)★★★, *Angel Dust* (Slash/Reprise 1992)★★, *King For A Day ... Fool For A Lifetime* (Slash/Reprise 1995)★★★, *Album Of The Year* (Slash/Reprise 1997)★★.

● VIDEOS: *Live At Brixton* (London 1990).

● FURTHER READING: *Faith No More: The Real Story*, Steffan Chirazi.

FAITHFUL BREATH

This progressive heavy metal band from Germany has a long and chequered history, dating back to 1974. The initial nucleus of the band comprised Heinz Mikus (guitar, vocals), Horst Stabenow (bass) and Uwe Otto (drums). Influenced by King Crimson and Deep Purple, their debut album was *Fading Beauty* in 1974. This featured intricate arrangements and keyboards, but lacked both melody and memorable hooks. After a lengthy gap and the abandonment of the keyboards, the band concentrated on guitar-orientated hard rock. Three competent albums followed, but each suffered from inexperienced self-production. Successful appearances at two Dutch rock festivals in 1983 attracted the attention of Mausoleum Records. Jurgen Dusterloh took over the drumstool and Andy Bibi Honig was added as a second guitarist for the recording of *Gold 'N' Glory*. Produced by Michael Wagener, it remains the band's finest recorded work. Further line-up changes ensued as the band moved towards the thrash end of the hard rock spectrum. In 1987, they changed their name to Risk, with only Mikus surviving from the original line-up.

● ALBUMS: *Fading Beauty* (Sky 1974)★★, *Back On My Hill* (Sky 1980)★★★, *Rock Lions* (Sky 1981)★★, *Hard Breath* (Sky 1983)★★★, *Gold 'N' Glory* (Mausoleum 1984)★★★★, *SKOL* (Ambush 1985)★★★, *Live* (Noise 1986)★★.

FALSE PROPHETS

'Our aim is to disarm the mechanics of oppression through persistent "making and doing" of words and music in an invocation of the ancient magic which empowers humankind through the massing of voices in sacred speech/song.' With this impressive philosophy in mind, the False Prophets, comprising Stephan Ielpi (vocals), Debra De Salvo (guitar, vocals), Steven Taylor (guitar, vocals), Nick Marden (bass, vocals) and Billy Atwell III (drums, vocals) - burst into life in the early 80s as part of the famed US hardcore scene that also spawned Black Flag and Hüsker Dü. Their hypothesis was intelligence, intellect and knowledge as opposed to the horror-show shock tactics used by many US punk acts. This approach led to a contract with Jello Biafra's Alternative Tentacles Records in 1986, from which sprang *False Prophets* and *Implosion*. These albums showed a willingness to experiment and break away from pure punk thrash-outs. *Invisible People*, on Konkurrel, saw them start the new decade in style, with an innovative fusion of hardcore punk, Latin rhythms, hard rock and polemic sculpted into a uniquely compelling record. They continued their quest for equality and freedom through the 80s with this theory as their cornerstone: 'All music, particularly rock, is ecstatic activity, and ecstasy itself is revolutionary.'

● ALBUMS: *False Prophets* (Alternative Tentacles 1986)★★★, *Implosion* (Alternative Tentacles 1987)★★★, *Invisible People* (Konkurrel 1990)★★★.

FAMILY

Highly respected and nostalgically revered, Family were one of Britain's leading progressive rock bands of the late 60s and early 70s. They were led by the wiry yet vocally demonic Roger Chapman

(b. 8 April 1942, Leicester, England), a man whose stage presence could both transfix and terrify his audience, who would duck from the countless supply of tambourines he destroyed and hurled into the crowd. Chapman was ably supported by Ric Grech (b. 1 November 1945, Bordeaux, France, d. 16 March 1990; violin, bass), Charlie Whitney (b. 24 June 1944, Leicester, England; guitar), Rob Townsend (b. 7 July 1947, Leicester, England; drums) and Jim King (b. Kettering, Northamptonshire, England; flute, saxophone). The band was formed in 1962 and known variously as the Farinas and the Roaring Sixties, finally coming together as Family in 1966 with the arrival of Chapman and Townsend. Their first album, released in 1968, was given extensive exposure on John Peel's influential BBC radio programme, resulting in this Dave Mason-produced collection becoming a major cult record. Chapman's remarkable strangulated vibrato caused heads to turn. Following the release of their most successful album, *Family Entertainment*, they experienced an ever-changing personnel of high pedigree musicians when Ric Grech departed to join Blind Faith in 1969, being replaced by John Weider, who in turn was supplanted by John Wetton (b. 12 July 1949, Willingdon, Derbyshire, England) in 1971, then Jim Cregan in 1972. Poli Palmer (b. John Palmer, 25 May 1943) superseded Jim King in 1969 who was ultimately replaced by Tony Ashton (b. 1 March 1946, Blackburn, Lancashire, England) in 1972.

Throughout this turmoil they maintained a high standard of recorded work and had UK singles success with 'No Mules Fool' (number 29, November 1969), 'Strange Band' (number 11, August 1970), 'In My Own Time' (number 4, July 1971) and the infectious 'Burlesque' (number 13, September 1972). Family disintegrated after their disappointing swan-song, *It's Only A Movie*, with Chapman and Whitney departing to form Streetwalkers. While their stage performances were erratic and unpredictable, the sight of Roger Chapman performing their anthem, 'The Weaver's Answer', on a good night was unforgettable.

● ALBUMS: *Music In A Doll's House* (Reprise 1968)★★★★, *Family Entertainment* (Reprise 1969)★★★★, *A Song For Me* (Reprise 1970)★★★, *Anyway* (Reprise 1970)★★★, *Fearless* (Reprise 1971)★★★★, *Bandstand* (Reprise 1972)★★★★, *It's Only A Movie* (Reprise 1973)★★, *Peel Sessions* mini-album (Strange Fruit 1988)★★, *In Concert* (Windsong 1991)★★★★.

● COMPILATIONS: *Old Songs New Songs* (Reprise 1971)★★★★, *Best Of Family* (Reprise 1974)★★★, *Singles A's and B's* (See For Miles 1991)★★★★.

Fandango (UK)

Comprising Jim Proops (vocals), Pete Parks (vocals, guitar), Nick Simper (b. 14 April 1945, Southall, Middlesex, England; bass) and Ron Penney (drums), much of the initial coverage surrounding UK heavy metal act Fandango concerned their employment of former Deep Purple and Warhorse bass player Nick Simper. Otherwise there was little of note about the group's two albums for Gull Records in 1979 and 1980. Both offered competent but uninspired blues rock, despite Parks' best efforts to lead from the front with some fluent guitarwork. The group were also hampered by the ascendancy of an American band named Fandango - who held the international rights to the name. With the writing clearly on the wall, the group broke up shortly after the release of *Future Times*.

● ALBUMS: *Slipstreaming* (Gull 1979)★★, *Future Times* (Gull 1980)★★.

Fandango (USA)

American melodic hard rock outfit formed in 1976 by vocalist Joe Lynn Turner and guitarist Rick Blakemore. Enlisting the services of Larry Dawson (keyboards), Bob Danyls (bass) and Abe Speller (drums), they signed to RCA Records the following year. They produced four albums in four years, with each successive release featuring more accomplished and memorable compositions. Influenced by Kiss, Journey and Styx, their style was rigidly formularized and geared to US FM radio playlists. The band disintegrated in 1981, with Turner going on to work with Rainbow, Yngwie Malmsteen's Rising Force and Deep Purple, as well as pursuing a solo career. Blakemore was killed in a car crash in the early 80s.

● ALBUMS: *Fandango* (RCA 1977)★★, *One Night Stand* (RCA 1978)★★★, *Last Kiss* (RCA 1979)★★★, *Cadillac* (RCA 1980)★★★★.

Fanny

Warner Brothers Records claimed in 1970 that their recent signing Fanny were the 'first all-female rock group'. They sustained a career for four years on that basis, throwing off all rivals to the throne, including Birtha, whose tasteless publicity handout stated 'Birtha has balls'. Formerly Wild Honey, the name Fanny was suggested by George Harrison to their producer Richard Perry. It was only later in their career that the group realized how risqué their name was internationally. Comprising Jean

Millington (b. 1950, Manila, California, USA; bass, vocals), June Millington (b. 1949, Manila, California, USA; guitar, vocals), Alice DeBuhr (b. 1950, Mason City, Iowa, USA; drums) and Nickey Barclay (b. 1951, Washington, DC, USA; keyboards), their blend of driving hard rock and rock 'n' roll was exciting, although they were always a second division act. They were more popular in the UK where they toured regularly, recording albums at Apple and Olympic studios. June Millington and DeBuhr were replaced in 1974 by Patti Quatro (sister of Suzi Quatro) from the Pleasure Seekers, and Brie Brandt-Howard. None of their albums charted in the UK and their sales in the USA were minimal. Their second album, *Charity Ball* was their best work, giving them a US Top 40 hit with the title song. Todd Rundgren was brought in to produce *Mother's Pride*, but ironically it was as the band were fragmenting in 1975 that they scored their biggest hit 'Butter Boy' (US number 29). June and Jean Millington reunited to form Millington, who released their only album in 1978.

● ALBUMS: *Fanny* (Reprise 1970)★★★, *Charity Ball* (Reprise 1971)★★★, *Fanny Hill* (Reprise 1972)★★★, *Mother's Pride* (Reprise 1973)★★, *Rock 'N' Roll Survivors* (Casablanca 1974)★★.
Solo: Nickey Barclay *Diamond In A Junkyard* (Ariola 1976)★★.

FARGO

This German heavy metal/hard rock band was formed by bass player Peter Khorn in Hanover in 1973. The group earned its initial reputation by supporting bands such as AC/DC and April Wine on their German tours of the late 70s. By 1976 Khron had established a more solid line-up, with the inclusion of Peter Ladwig (guitar, vocals), Mathias Jabs (guitar) and Franky Tolle (drums). Prior to the release of their debut album, however, Jabs accepted an invitation to join the Scorpions and was replaced by Hanno Grossman in 1978. The group's long-forestalled debut, *Wishing Well*, augured well for their future in its effective distillation of melodic rock laced with pop hooks. During touring to promote it, Tolle became exhausted and was replaced on drums by Rudi Kaeding. The group toured throughout Europe in support of *Front Page Lover* in 1981, but inter-band tensions remained. Tolle returned for 1982's *F*, while Tommy Neewton replaced Grossman. The uncertainty of that recording suggested the band's demise was imminent, and rumours proved well founded when no further follow-ups were issued.

● ALBUMS: *Wishing Well* (Harvest 1979)★★★, *No Limit* (Harvest 1980)★★, *Front Page Lover* (Harvest 1981)★★★, *F* (Harvest 1982)★★.

FAST FORWARD

This one-off side project from former UK Stories vocalist Ian Lloyd came to fruition in 1984. With the help of producer Bruce Fairbairn (of Loverboy and Bon Jovi fame) and a series of highly regarded session musicians, the end result was *Living In Fiction*, a highly polished melodic rock album, featuring razor-sharp harmonies, swathes of keyboards and an infectious pop sensibility. Guest appearances included Mick Jones and Lou Gramm from Foreigner and Beau Hill (Ratt producer) on keyboards. Songwriting contributions from Bryan Adams and Jim Vallance added further interest to the project, yet, surprisingly, it was a commercial flop. As a result, plans to record a second album were abandoned.

● ALBUMS: *Living In Fiction* (Island 1984)★★★★.

FASTER PUSSYCAT

The mid-80s Los Angeles glam/sleaze scene that produced Guns N'Roses also saw the formation of Faster Pussycat in 1986, around vocalist Taime Downe and guitarist Mick Cripps - although Cripps later departed for L.A. Guns along with original bassist Kelly Nickels. Downe, formerly co-owner of LA club The Cathouse, recruited guitarists Brent Muscat and Greg Steele, bassist Eric Stacy and drummer Mark Michals, and, with their name deriving from Russ Meyer's film *Faster, Pussycat! Kill! Kill!*, the band signed to Elektra Records in December 1986. *Faster Pussycat* was recorded on a low budget with Poison producer Ric Browde, and was an infectious collection of Aerosmith/Rolling Stones-influenced numbers, with the band's sense of humour shining through in 'Bathroom Wall', 'Don't Change That Song' and 'Babylon'. A UK tour with Guns N'Roses and US dates with Alice Cooper, David Lee Roth and Motörhead helped to build respectable album sales, and the band had matured considerably by the time they recorded *Wake Me When It's Over* with John Jansen. This buried the glam image under a heavier sound and greater lyrical depth, with 'Pulling Weeds' addressing the abortion issue, while the emotive 'House Of Pain' examined the trauma of divorce through a child's eyes. The humour still permeated through, however, on 'Slip Of The Tongue' and 'Where There's A Whip There's A Way'. Michals left in disgrace, jailed on drugs charges, on the eve of a European tour with the Almighty and Dangerous Toys, and Frankie Banali filled in before Brett Bradshaw assumed the drumstool for further US touring with Kiss and Mötley Crüe. *Whipped* showed further progression and a different approach, but emerged into a much-changed musical climate. Despite the quality of the album, Faster Pussycat fell victim to a combination of the recession and the success of the Seattle bands - ironically, Downe was a Seattle native - with Elektra dropping them while they toured America with Kiss. The band split shortly thereafter. Taime Downe was later seen working with Pigface.

● ALBUMS: *Faster Pussycat* (Elektra 1987)★★★, *Wake Me When It's Over* (Elektra 1989)★★★, *Whipped* (Elektra 1991)★★★.

FASTWAY

After quitting Motörhead in May 1982, guitarist 'Fast' Eddie Clarke (b. 5 October 1950, Isleworth, Middlesex, England) went into partnership with bassist Pete Way from UFO, drummer Jerry Shirley from Humble Pie and previously unknown vocalist Dave King. Way left soon afterwards to form Waysted and was replaced by Charlie McCracken. Within a year they had formulated a style far removed from Motörhead and soon drew comparisons to Deep Purple and Led Zeppelin, yet they won few fans despite a strong debut album and a minor hit single with 'Easy Living'. Finding a degree of fame in America boosted their confidence and they recorded a second album with producer Eddie Kramer. Again, this was a good collection, but it remained largely ignored in Europe and unfortunately suffered a similar fate in America, prompting Shirley and McCracken to quit. After a new line-up and a third album, minor success came with the soundtrack to the rock/horror film *Trick Or Treat*, which kept them in the American charts for 11 months. However, they failed to capitalize on this opportunity. Clarke returned to the UK in 1988 and rebuilt the band with Paul Gray (bass, ex-Eddie And The Hot Rods; Damned; UFO), Steve Clarke (drums) and former Joan Jett lyricist Lea Hart on vocals and guitar. *On Target* failed to capture public interest and Clarke and Hart formed a new line-up with American bassist K.B. Bren and a drummer known as 'Riff Raff'. With the addition of members of Girlschool, this line-up recorded *Bad Bad Girls*, which was their last album. Once more the legacy of Motörhead overshadowed Clarke's involvement in Fastway - the failure of the press to view the band as a separate entity was always the rock on which Fastway ran aground, and finally floundered. Clarke subsequently launched a solo career under his own name.

● ALBUMS: *Fastway* (Columbia 1983)★★★, *All Fired Up* (Columbia 1984)★★★, *Waiting For The Roar* (Columbia 1986)★★★, *Trick Or Treat* film soundtrack (Columbia 1986)★★★★, *On Target* (GWR 1988)★★, *Bad Bad Girls* (Legacy 1990)★★.

FATE

Comprising Jeff Limbo (vocals), Hank Shermann (guitar), Pete Steiner (bass) and Bob Lance (drums), Danish hard rock band Fate formed from the remains of Mercyful Fate in the mid-80s. Immediately, the group, ostensibly led by Shermann, moved away from Mercyful Fate's more mythology-based material to a melodic, contemporary metal sound redolent of groups such as Survivor. Despite a major label recording contract with EMI Records, their self-titled debut failed to impress critics. *A Matter Of Attitude*, released in 1987, signalled a refinement of their previous sound, with more upbeat lyrics and melodies akin to Bon Jovi or Van Halen. *Crusin' For A Brusin'* was a more disciplined conventional hard rock effort but again failed to achieve significant export sales outside of Scandinavia.

● ALBUMS: *Fate* (EMI 1986)★★★, *A Matter Of Attitude* (EMI 1987)★★★, *Crusin' For A Brusin'* (EMI 1989)★★★.

FATES WARNING

Formed in Cincinnati, Ohio, USA, in 1982, initially as Misfit, the original line-up of Fates Warning consisted of John Arch (vocals), Jim Matheos (guitar), Victor Arduini (guitar), Joe DiBiase (bass) and Steve Zimmerman (drums). After a couple of early demos the band were invited to contribute a track to the *Metal Massacre V* compilation, released on Metal Blade Records in 1984. The label immediately signed the band to a long-term recording agreement and released the debut album, entitled *Night On Brocken*, in the same year. The album was very reminiscent of early Iron Maiden, both in the compositions and Arch's vocal style. Shortly after its release guitarist Victor Arduini left the band to be replaced by Frank Aresti. The next two albums, *The Spectre Within* and *Awaken The Guardian*, released in 1985 and 1986, respectively, showed the band's music to be more progressive and complex than first impressions had suggested. However, vocalist John Arch was unhappy with the musical direction that Fates Warning had begun to pursue and left, but was soon replaced by Ray Alder, whose voice was better suited to the material. This was most noticeable on *No Exit*. Released in 1988, it was widely recognized as the band's finest work to date, partially thanks to producer Max Norman, who strove for a clean, Queensrÿche-like sound. Soon after its release, Zimmerman left the band to be replaced by Mark Zonder. *Perfect Symmetry* was released in 1989 after the band had completed a couple of rather uneasy European tours. The result was an album that in some places sounded orchestral in its arrangements, and featured Dream Theater keyboard player Kevin Moore as a guest musician. With the next album, *Parallels*, released in 1991, the band returned to their earlier techno-pomp metal influences. It was well received by the press, who were beginning to acknowledge a band who had a lot to offer and deserved more recognition than had previously been awarded them.

● ALBUMS: *Night On Brocken* (Metal Blade 1984)★★★, *The Spectre Within* (Metal Blade 1985)★★, *Awaken The Guardian* (Metal Blade 1986)★★★, *No Exit* (Metal Blade 1988)★★★★, *Perfect Symmetry* (Metal Blade 1989)★★, *Parallels* (Metal Blade 1991)★★★, *A Pleasant Shade Of Grey* (Massacre 1997)★★★.

FEAR FACTORY

This Los Angeles-based band are one of the few truly innovative acts in death metal, mixing industrial-style electronic rhythms and samples with grinding guitars and harsh vocals to create their own brutal soundscape. Formed in late 1991 with the line-up of Burton C. Bell (vocals), Dino Cazares (guitar, who has an additional side project, Brujeria), Andrew Shives (bass) and Raymond Herrera (drums), the band rapidly made an impact with two tracks on the *LA Death Metal* compilation, produced by Faith No More bassist Bill Gould, and subsequently signed to Roadrunner Records. The Colin Richardson-produced *Soul Of A New Machine* established Fear Factory as a genuine death metal force, with a good collection of songs delivered with originality and ferocity. Meanwhile, the band set about developing their live show on their debut tour with Brutal Truth in Europe, followed by US dates with Sick Of It All and Biohazard. *Fear Is The Mind Killer*, a mini-album of remixes by Canadian industrialists Front Line Assembly, demonstrated further dimensions and possibilities available to the Factory sound by adding an industrial dance edge, bringing the band further acclaim. *Demanufacture* was produced by Colin Richardson, but the band were unhappy with the final mix and invited Rhys Fulbert (Front Line Assembly) and Greg Reely (Front Line Assembly, Skinny Puppy) to remix it to reflect the futuristic atmosphere they desired. The bonus tracks on one of the CD formats included a cover version of Agnostic Front's 'Your Mistake', with Madball's Freddy Cricien guesting on vocals. Press response ranked it alongside Therapy?'s *Infernal Love* and White Zombie's *Astro Creep 2000* as one of the definitive noise albums of 1995. In the meantime, singer Bell found work as the vocalist on Black Sabbath bass player Geezer Butler's GZR project. Following a remix album in 1997, the band returned with the brutal metal noisefest *Obsolete*.

● ALBUMS: *Soul Of A New Machine* (Roadrunner 1992)★★★, *Fear Is The Mind Killer* mini-album (Roadrunner 1993)★★★, *Demanufacture* (Roadrunner 1995)★★★★, *Remanufacture (Cloning Technology)* (Roadrunner 1997)★★★, *Obsolete* (Roadrunner 1998)★★★★.

FEEDER

Highly fêted UK alternative rock band Feeder were formed in 1995 by sound engineer Grant Nicholas (guitar, vocals) and John Lee (drums), who had previously played together in Reel and Rain Dancer. They were joined by Japanese bass player Taka Hirose, and began playing under the name of Real. After signing to the Echo label later the same year, the trio changed their name to Feeder and played their first gig in Yeovil, Somerset on 25 May. The band released their debut *Two Colours EP* in November 1995, and built up a substantial live reputation as a support act for Terrorvision and Reef. An acclaimed six-track mini-album, *Swim*, followed in June 1996, but their early singles 'Stereo World' (October 1996), 'Tangerine' (February 1997), 'Cement' (April 1997; UK number 49) and 'Crash' (August 1997; UK number 41) made little progress in the charts. A new song, the dramatically charged 'High', gained heavy airplay on mainstream radio, and entered the UK charts at number 24 in October 1997, with the band finally looking like achieving the success their highly melodic guitar rock deserved. 'High' was included on a reformatted version of their debut long-player *Polythene*, originally released in May 1997. An excellent collection of post-grunge alternative rock, the album saw the band receiving further high praise from the music press.

● ALBUMS: *Swim* mini-album (Echo 1996)★★★, *Polythene* (Echo 1997)★★★★.

FEMME FATALE

This American quintet formed in Alberquerque, New Mexico, in 1987. However, it was not long before they relocated to the bright lights of Los

Angeles in the quest for wider exposure and A&R attention from record companies. Fronted by Lorraine Lewis, they were quickly snapped up by MCA Records, who assigned Jim Faraci (of L.A. Guns fame) as producer. Musically, they strived to corner the same market as Bon Jovi, relying on a pop-metal/hard rock crossover approach. In interviews Lewis repeatedly stated her objective was to be the biggest 'pin up girl' in rock. The band, completed by Mazzi Rawd (guitar), Bill D'Angelo (guitar), Rick Rael (bass) and Bobby Murray (drums), recorded a self-titled debut album that played heavily on their vocalist's sexuality. This approach often overshadowed Lewis's genuine ability, and although it was received favourably by the critics, it was quickly consigned to the bargain bins, while the band disappeared without trace. Lewis went on to work with Roxy Petrucci (ex-Vixen) and Gina Stile (ex-Poison Dollys) in a new all-female outfit.

● ALBUMS: *Femme Fatale* (MCA 1988)★★★.

FIELDS OF THE NEPHILIM

This UK rock group was formed in Stevenage, Hertfordshire, in 1983. The line-up comprised Carl McCoy (vocals), Tony Pettitt (bass), Peter Yates (guitar) and the Wright brothers, Nod (b. Alexander; drums) and Paul (guitar). Their image, that of neo-western desperados, was borrowed from films such as *Once Upon A Time In America* and *The Long Ryders*. They also had a bizarre habit of smothering their predominantly black clothes in flour and/or talcum powder for some of the most hysterically inept videos ever recorded. Their version of goth-rock, tempered with transatlantic overtones, found favour with those already immersed in the sounds of the Sisters Of Mercy and the Mission. Signed to the Situation Two label, Fields Of The Nephilim had two major UK independent hit singles with 'Preacher Man' and 'Blue Water', while their first album, *Dawnrazor*, made a modest showing on the UK album chart. The second set, *The Nephilim*, reached number 14, announcing the group's arrival as one of the principal rock acts of the day. Their devoted following also ensured a showing on the national singles chart, giving them minor hits with 'Moonchild' (also an independent chart number 1), 'Psychonaut' and 'Summerland (Dreamed)'. In October 1991 McCoy left the group, taking the 'Fields Of The Nephilim' name with him. The remaining members vowed to carry on. With the recruitment of a new vocalist, Alan Delaney, they began gigging under the name Rubicon in the summer of 1992, leaving McCoy to unveil his version of the Nephilim (renamed Nefilim). Nod Wright departed to form Swallowed Soul.

● ALBUMS: *Dawnrazor* (Situation 2 1987)★★, *The Nephilim* (Situation 2 1988)★★★, *Elizium* (Beggars Banquet 1990)★★, *Earth Inferno* (Beggars Banquet 1991)★★, *BBC Radio 1 In Concert* (Windsong 1992)★★, *Revelations* (Beggars Banquet 1993)★★.

● VIDEOS: *Forever Remain* (Situation 2 1988), *Morphic Fields* (Situation 2 1989), *Earth Inferno* (Beggars Banquet 1991), *Visionary Heads* (Beggars Banquet 1992), *Revelations* (Beggars Banquet 1993).

FIFTH ANGEL

Formed in Seattle, Washington, USA, in 1985, Fifth Angel comprised Ted Pilot (vocals), Kendall Bechtel (guitar), Ed Archer (guitar), John Macko (bass) and Ken Mary (drums). On the back of promising club dates they came to the attention of Mike Varney, who signed them to his Shrapnel label. A self-titled debut album backed up with touring commitments won them many fans and brought them to the attention of Epic Records, who had the album remixed and reissued in 1988. *Time Will Tell* sold well but the band were unable to live up to expectations and they broke up later that year, with only drummer Mary going on to a degree of success with the Alice Cooper Band and House Of Lords.

● ALBUMS: *Fifth Angel* (Shrapnel 1986)★★★, *Fifth Angel* remix of debut (Epic 1988)★★★, *Time Will Tell* (Epic 1989)★★★.

FIGHT

Inspired by the aggressive new metal sounds of the likes of Pantera, Skid Row and Metallica, the Judas Priest vocalist Rob Halford (b. 25 August 1951, Walsall, England) formed Fight as a solo project to explore material that he felt was inappropriate for Priest, but it eventually led to a bitter and acrimonious split from his old band as they celebrated 20 years together. Taking Priest drummer Scott Travis with him, Halford recruited guitarists Russ Parish (ex-War And Peace) and Brian Tilse and bassist Jay Jay (both ex-Cyanide) for *War Of Words*. While Pantera comparisons were obvious, Fight proved themselves not to be the clone band some had feared, with the intense material given an individual character by Halford's distinctive vocal delivery, and the band delivered with powerful live shows. However, the demanding tour schedule proved too much for Parish, who was replaced by Robbie Lockner for the Anthrax US tour, and then permanently by Mark Chaussee, as Fight performed with Metallica across the USA. The band then released the *Mutations* mini-album, a collection of live tracks and cover versions, including 'Freewheel Burnings', before setting to work on their second album, *A Small Deadly Space*, whose lyrics ranged across subjects such as AIDS, the Holocaust, child abuse and domestic violence.

● ALBUMS: *War Of Words* (Epic 1993)★★★, *Mutations* mini-album (Epic 1994)★★★, *A Small Deadly Space* (Epic 1995)★★★.

FILTER

Brian Liesegang (programming, guitar, keyboards, drums) and Richard Patrick (vocals, guitar, bass, programming, drums, ex-Nine Inch Nails) first hatched the idea of working together during a cross-country trek when they visited the Grand Canyon. Patrick had already been experimenting on an eight-track console in his parents' basement in Cleveland, Ohio, USA. Liesegang, meanwhile, had just finished a degree in philosophy and turned his hand to music himself, experimenting in his own small electronic studio, which was adjacent to that owned by Robert A. Moog (originator of the Moog synthesizer). Occupying his time by investigating the world of computers and their applications to music, he found what he describes as a 'perfect musical match' in Patrick. Both were interested in producing hard electronic music. The line-up of the band was completed for touring purposes by Geno Lenardo (guitar), Matt Walker (drums) and Frank Cavannagh (bass). *Short Bus* was co-produced by Ben Gross (Jane's Addiction, Red Hot Chili Peppers), while the single 'Hey Man Nice Shot' became a staple of college radio. Walker left the band to join the Smashing Pumpkins in August 1996. Liesegang also abandoned the band in September 1997 to pursue a solo career.

● ALBUMS: *Short Bus* (Reprise/Warners 1995)★★★.

FINCH

Comprising Owen Orford (vocals), Bob Spencer (guitar), Tony Strain (bass) and Peter McFarlane (drums), Finch formed in Australia in 1973 and devoted themselves to a conventional but well-observed style of feisty hard rock. Orford had previously been a member of Stillwater, while other members of Finch also included Mark Evans (bass, ex-AC/DC), Chris Jones (guitar), Graham Kennedy (guitar) and Sam Mallet (guitar). They made their debut in 1975 with the single 'And She Sings' for Picture Records, which was followed a year later with a studio collection for Eagle Records which pleased Australian rock critics. However, the group broke up when McFarlane and Orford joined Mark Evans in Contraband. Spencer moved on to Silverhooks.

● ALBUMS: *Thunderbird aka Finch* (Eagle 1976)★★★.

FIONA

b. Fiona Flanagan, New Jersey, USA. Fiona had always harboured ambitions to be a star since her teenage years singing in clubs with various rock bands in New York. Eventually she took the first steps towards achieving that dream by signing a contract with Atlantic Records in 1985, who put her in the studio with guitarist Bobby Messano (ex-Starz), along with session men Donnie Kisselbach (bass), Joey Franco (ex-Good Rats and Twisted Sister; drums) and Benjy King (keyboards). After a false start with production problems, former Good Rats vocalist Peppi Marchello took over. The resulting self-titled album received good press and predictable comparisons to Heart and Pat Benatar ensued. The second album displayed a more mature sound thanks to producer Beau Hill (her boyfriend at the time) and guest appearances from Nile Rodgers, and Kip Winger and Reb Beach from the Alice Cooper band (at the time forming their own unit, Winger). The album featured a poignant cover version of 'Thunder And Lightning' by German singer Chi Coltrane, which, if released as a single, might have provided a much needed hit. She did, however, come to the attention of producer Richard Marquand who cast her in his 1987 movie *Hearts Of Fire*, in which she sang alongside Bob Dylan and actor Rupert Everett. Her last album for Atlantic was greeted with a measure of indifference and her career has remained on hold ever since, despite winning a new contract from Geffen Records.

● ALBUMS: *Fiona* (Atlantic 1985)★★, *Beyond The Page* (Atlantic 1986)★★.

● FILMS: *Hearts Of Fire* (1987).

FIRE MERCHANTS

This hi-tech power trio of well-seasoned session musicians was founded by ex-Andy Summers bassist Doug Lunn. Enlisting John Goodsall (ex-Brand X and Peter Gabriel) on guitar and keyboards, the line-up was eventually completed following a long search for the right drummer. Ex-Frank Zappa and Genesis drummer Chester Thompson was enlisted, allowing the band to stabilize in October 1987. Released two years later, their self-titled debut album was an all-instrumental affair, offering an eclectic fusion of jazz, rock and blues.

● ALBUMS: *Fire Merchants* (Roadrunner 1989)★★★.

FIREHOSE

This propulsive US hardcore trio (usually titled fIREHOSE) was formed by two ex-members of the Minutemen, Mike Watt (vocals, bass) and George Hurley (drums), following the death of the latter group's founding guitarist, David Boon, in 1985. Ed Crawford, aka eD fROMOHIO, completed the new venture's line-up, which made its debut in 1987 with the impressive *Ragin', Full-On*. Although undeniably powerful, the material Firehose offered was less explicit than that of its predecessor, and showed a greater emphasis on melody rather than bluster. Successive releases, *If'n* and *fROMOHIO*, revealed a group that, although bedevilled by inconsistency, was nonetheless capable of inventive, exciting music. At their best these songs merged knowing sarcasm (see 'For The Singer Of REM') with an unreconstructed approach to music making (as on drum solo 'Let The Drummer Have Some'). In 1989, Watt and Hurley also collaborated with Elliott Sharp on the avant-garde *Bootstrappers* project. The group's variety argued against commercial fortune, but the band were still picked up by a major, Columbia Records, in 1991, who released the slightly more disciplined *Flyin' The Flannel* that year. Following the disappointing critical and commercial response to *Mr Machinery Operator*, the group decided to call it a day in 1995.

● ALBUMS: *Ragin', Full-On* (SST 1987)★★★, *If'n* (SST 1988)★★, *fROMOHIO* (SST 1989)★★★, *Flyin' The Flannel* (Columbia 1991)★★★, *Live Totem Pole* mini-album (Columbia 1992)★★, *Mr Machinery Operator* (Columbia 1993)★★.

As Bootstrappers *Bootstrappers* (New Alliance 1989)★★.

FIRESIDE

Fireside were formed in 1992 by Frans Johansson (bass), Per Nordmark (drums), Krisofer Astrom (vocals, guitar) and Pelle Gunnerfeldt (guitar). Based in Lulea, in the far north of Sweden above the Polar Circle, each member of the group had formerly played in sundry local punk and alternative outfits. Their first EPs were released through the small independent label A West Side Fabrication, before they signed to Stockholm-based label Startrec in the spring of 1995. An international recording contract was then secured with American Recordings when Swedish native and American Recordings A&R executive Johan Kugelberg returned home on a holiday trip. With a sound regularly compared to the more muscular end of the alternative rock spectrum (Henry Rollins, Fugazi), the group made its breakthrough with their 1996 Pelle Gunnerfeldt-produced, *Do Not Tailgate*. This won them several Swedish Album Of The Year awards in magazines such as *Aftonbladet*, *Slitz* and *Expressen*. They also won a 1996 Swedish Grammy for Best Hard Rock Band, announcing the start of what many observers have agreed may be a very promising career.

● ALBUMS: *Do Not Tailgate* (Startrec/American 1996)★★★★.

FIRM

It seemed to be a marriage made in heaven when ex-Led Zeppelin guitarist Jimmy Page (b. James Patrick Page, 9 January 1944, Heston, Middlesex, England) and former Free and Bad Company vocalist Paul Rodgers (b. 17 December 1949, Middlesbrough, Cleveland, England) began working together as the Firm in 1984. Enlisting drummer Chris Slade (b. 30 October 1946; ex-Uriah Heep, Manfred Mann) and virtual unknown Tony Franklin on bass (an acquaintance of Page's from work with Roy Harper), the partnership never quite gelled in a manner that matched either protagonist's earlier achievements. However, the band was not without musical merit, with Slade's precise backbeat providing a solid base for Page and the stylish Franklin. On *The Firm*, Rodgers was in fine voice on varied material, from the lengthy and Zeppelinesque 'Midnight Moonlight' to the more commercial strains of 'Radioactive', which was a minor hit, plus a cover version of 'You've Lost That Loving Feeling'. Live dates proved successful, with Page producing his customary show-stopping solo spot, replete with laser effects, although neither Page nor Rodgers were willing to reprise their previous work. *Mean Business* continued in the warm, understated and bluesy style of the debut, but failed to raise the band to new heights, and the Firm split after the subsequent world tour. Page and Rodgers returned to their respective solo careers, while Slade joined AC/DC and Franklin teamed up with John Sykes in Blue Murder.

● ALBUMS: *The Firm* (Atlantic 1985)★★★, *Mean Business* (Atlantic 1986)★★★.

FISH

b. Derek William Dick, 25 April 1958, Dalkeith, Edinburgh, Scotland. Fish acquired his nickname from a landlord who objected to the lengthy periods he spent in the bath. He sang for Nottingham band the Stone Dome before auditioning for progressive rockers Marillion by writing lyrics for their instrumental, 'The Web'. The group established a strong following through constant touring, before releasing their debut single 'Market Square Heroes'. Fish's bombastic vocals, markedly similar to Peter Gabriel, strengthened critics' arguments that Marillion were mere Genesis copyists. Despite this, Marillion went from strength to strength, with Fish structuring a series of elaborately linked concept albums that were still capable of yielding UK hit singles including 'Garden Party' and the melodic ballad 'Kayleigh', which reached number 2 in May 1985. His lyrics were strongly influenced in style and content by the work of Peter Hammill, former leader of progressive 70s group Van Der Graaf Generator, a debt he acknowledged by inviting Hammill to be special guest on Marillion's 1983 tour of Britain. After the success of 1987's *Clutching At Straws*, he began to disagree with the rest of the band about their musical direction and left in 1988 to embark on a solo career; he was replaced by Steve Hogarth. Fish's debut solo album utilized stylistically diverse elements such as folk tunes and brass arrangements, as shown on the UK number 25 single 'Big Wedge', but he also retained a mixture of hard rockers and ballads. In 1989 he worked with Peter Hammill on his opera, *The Fall Of The House Of Usher*, but their voices clashed and Fish was replaced on the project by Andy Bell. A more successful collaboration was the single 'Shortcut To Somewhere', recorded with Genesis keyboard player Tony Banks in 1986. His 1993 release was a desultory album of cover versions, including the Kinks' 'Apeman' and the Moody Blues' 'Question'. Far more satisfying was his 1995 duet with Sam Brown on 'Just Good Friends', and his 1997 album *Sunsets On Empire* put him back in favour.

● ALBUMS: *Vigil In A Wilderness Of Mirrors* (EMI 1990)★★, *Internal Exile* (Polydor 1991)★★, *Songs From The Mirror* (Polydor 1993)★, *Sushi* (Dick Bros 1994)★★★, *Acoustic Session* (Dick Bros 1994)★★★, *Suits* (Dick Bros 1994)★★, *Sunsets On Empire* (Dick Bros 1997)★★★★, *Fortunes Of War* (Dick Bros 1998)★★★.

● COMPILATIONS: *Yin* (Dick Bros 1995)★★★, *Yan* (Dick Bros 1995)★★★.

FISHBONE

This funk metal hybrid from Los Angeles, USA, has now been active for over a decade. Five of the seven band members met through the Los Angeles School Bussing Program, a scheme that encouraged black and white children to visit each other's schools. Although their recorded output is sparse given their longevity, their hard political edge and high-octane rhythmic onslaught is every bit as deserving of mass attention as the Red Hot Chili Peppers or Living Colour. Their line-up boasts Chris 'Maverick Meat' Dowd (b. Christopher Gordon Dowd, 20 September 1965, Las Vegas, Nevada, USA; trombone, keyboards), 'Dirty' Walter Kibby (b. Walter Adam Kibby II, 13 November 1964, Columbus, Ohio, USA; trumpet, horn, vocals), 'Big' John Bigham (b. 3 March 1969, Lidsville, USA), Kendall Jones (b. Kendall Rey Jones, USA; guitar), Philip 'Fish' Fisher (b. 16 July 1967, El Camino, Los Angeles, California, USA; drums - has guested for Little Richard, Bob Dylan and others), John Fisher (b. John Norwood Fisher, 9 December 1965, El Camino, Los Angeles, California, USA; bass) and Angelo Moore (b. Angelo Christopher Moore, 5 November 1965, USA; lead vocals). Norwood was stabbed on stage early in their career when Fishbone played alongside hardcore bands such as the Dead Kennedys (the influence of Bad Brains is obvious in their output). After a debut mini-album, the production expertise of David Kahne saw them touch on a more conventional metal direction, before exposing their true talents for the first time on *Truth And Soul*. This was helped in no small part by the airplay success of a cover version of Curtis Mayfield's 'Freddie's Dead'. Subsequent recordings saw Fishbone branching out and working with rap artists such as the Jungle Brothers, although *The Reality Of My Own Surroundings* had more in common with the hard-spined funk of Sly Stone. 'Fight The Youth' and 'Sunless Saturday' demonstrated a serious angle with socio-political, anti-racist and anti-drug lyrics, in contrast to their lighter side on the humorous 'Naz-Tee May'en'. Fishbone's live shows continued to sell out without a hit to be seen. However, just as transatlantic commercial success beckoned with the *Give A Monkey* ... set, bizarre press stories began to circulate concerning the activities of Jones, who, at the instigation of his father, had left the flock to join a religious cult. The group, whom he had renounced, were accused of attempted kidnap in their attempts to retrieve him. Appearing on 1993's Lollapalooza tour failed to restore the group's diminishing reputation, as did a lacklustre new album in 1996.

● ALBUMS: *Fishbone* mini-album (Columbia

1985)★★, *In Your Face* (Columbia 1986)★★, *Truth And Soul* (Columbia 1988)★★★★, *The Reality Of My Surroundings* (Columbia 1991)★★★, *Give A Monkey A Brain And He'll Swear He's The Centre Of The Universe* (Columbia 1993)★★★, *Chim Chim's Badass Revenge* (Rowdy 1996)★★★.
● COMPILATIONS: *Singles* (Sony Japan 1993)★★★, *Fishbone 101 - Nuttasaurusmeg Fossil Fuelin' The Fonkay* (Columbia/Legacy 1996)★★★.

FIST (CANADA)

This Canadian heavy rock quartet was formed in 1978 by vocalist/guitarist Ron Chenier. After several false starts and numerous line-up changes, the band stabilized with Chenier, plus Laurie Curry (keyboards), Bob Moffat (bass) and Bob Patterson (drums). Influenced by Triumph, Rush and Led Zeppelin, they released five albums of generally average hard rock between 1979 and 1985, with *In The Red* from 1983 being undoubtedly the strongest. This featured the highly talented Dave McDonald on lead vocals instead of Chenier, who lacked both range and power. In order to prevent confusion with the British band Fist, their albums were released under the name Myofist in Europe.
● ALBUMS: *Round One* (TCD 1979)★★★, *Hot Spikes* (A&M 1980)★★★, *Thunder In Rock* (A&M 1982)★★, *In The Red* (A&M 1983)★★★★, *Danger Zone* (A&M 1985)★★★.

FIST (UK)

Formed as Axe in Newcastle-upon-Tyne, England, in 1978, changing their name at the beginning of the following year, the band's original line-up consisted of Keith Satchfield (vocals, guitar), Dave Irwin (guitar), John Wylie (bass) and Harry Hill (drums). They released a couple of mediocre singles via Neat Records in 1979. However, recognizing potential, MCA Records signed the band and released their debut album, *Turn The Hell On*, in 1980. This was a lacklustre affair of standard hard rock and was largely overlooked by both press and public. Fist were subsequently dropped by MCA, and Satchfield left in 1981. Determined to persevere, the band recruited Glenn Coates (vocals) and John Roach (guitar), then re-signed to Neat Records and released their second album, *Back With A Vengeance*, in 1982. Even though this was an improvement on their previous release, it still failed to attract any real interest, and Fist's end was in sight.
● ALBUMS: *Turn The Hell On* (MCA 1980)★★, *Back With A Vengeance* (Neat 1982)★★★.

5X

Japanese hard rock band founded in 1981 by ex-Midnight Cruiser guitarist George Azuma and former Oz vocalist Carmen Maki. With Kinta Moriyama (bass) and Jun Harada (drums) completing the line-up, they adopted a style that incorporated elements of Motörhead, Van Halen and AC/DC, also veering towards thrash metal at times. By their third album, which saw them adopt a slightly altered name that gave their singer more prominent billing, they had moved into mainstream rock territory, and it appeared that vocalist Carmen Maki was striving to become the Japanese equivalent of Heart's Ann Wilson.
● ALBUMS: *Human Targets* (EMI 1982)★★★★, *Live X* (EMI 1982)★★, *Carmen Maki's 5X* (Eastworld 1983)★★★.

FLIPPER

San Francisco hardcore band Flipper formed in 1979 with original members Will Shatter (d. 1987; bass, vocals), Steve DePace (drums), both former members of Negative Trend, Bruce Lose (bass, vocals) and Ted Falconi (guitar), also of Negative Trend, on drums. Following the single 'Love Canal'/'Ha Ha', on Subterranean Records, the group released its debut and best-known album, *Generic*, in 1982. Sporting topical lyrics and both hardcore punk and noise dirges, the collection was instantly recognized as a classic of west coast punk. However, these were no stereotypical three-chord thrashes, the band experimenting instead with the wildly overblown 'Sex Bomb Baby' and the super-minimalist 'Life'. Other albums followed on Subterranean in 1984 and 1986 but failed to match their debut's impact, and the following year Shatter died of an accidental heroin overdose. The three surviving members of Flipper reunited in 1990, resulting in the eventual release of *American Grafishy*. This was the first official release on the new label founded by Henry Rollins and Rick Rubin. Flipper are now cited as being highly influential in the development of Nirvana's sound.
● ALBUMS: *Generic* (Subterranean 1982)★★★★, *Blow 'n Chunks* (ROIR 1984)★★, *Gone Fishin'* (Subterranean 1984)★★★, *American Grafishy* (Def American 1992)★★★, *Live At CBGB's* 1983 recording (Overground 1997)★★★.
● COMPILATIONS: *Public Flipper Limited Live 1980-1985* (Subterranean 1986)★★★, *Sex Bomb Baby!* (Subterranean 1988)★★★★.

FLOCK

Although they were formed in 1966 (Chicago, Illinois, USA) it was not until 1969 that Flock burst upon a most receptive market. CBS Records had successfully taken the lion's share of the progressive boom and for a short time Flock became one of their leading products. The original band comprised Jerry Goodman (violin), Fred Glickstein (guitar, vocals), Tom Webb and Rick Canoff (saxophones), Ron Karpman (drums), Jerry Smith (bass) and Frank Posa (trumpet). Their blend of jazz and rock improvisations soon exhausted audiences as the solos became longer and longer. Jerry Goodman was the outstanding musician, stunning fans with his furious and brilliant electric violin playing. Their version of the Kinks' 'Tired Of Waiting For You' was memorable if only for the fact that they managed to turn a three-minute pop song into a magnum opus lasting, on occasions, over 10 minutes. Goodman left in 1971 to team up with John McLaughlin in the Mahavishnu Orchestra.

● ALBUMS: *The Flock* (Columbia 1969)★★★, *Dinosaur Swamps* (Columbia 1970)★, *Inside Out* (Mercury 1975)★.

● COMPILATIONS: *Flock Rock: The Best Of The Flock* (Columbia 1993)★★★.

FLOODGATE

Formed in New Orleans, USA, in 1994, hard rock band Floodgate quickly earned comparisons to the previous year's 'big thing', Machine Head. Certainly there were similarities in the two groups' sound, Floodgate opting for a no-frills, driving musical approach, without sacrificing melody for bombast. The group comprises Kyle Thomas (vocals, guitar), Steven Fisher (guitar), Kevin Thomas (bass) and Neil Montgomery (drums). The two Thomas brothers had already won notoriety in their former groups (Kyle Thomas having penned Exhorder's 'Slaughter In The Vatican'). Indeed, much of Floodgate's material is written in a profane vein, stated by Kyle Thomas to be a reaction against the suffocating, abusive Roman Catholic school he attended. His other former bands include Armageddon and Raid, while his brother was a member of Acid Bath and Moon Crickets. Kevin also joined Kyle in Exhorder shortly before their early 90s demise. The lyrics on Floodgate's 1996 debut, *Penalty*, were apparently written from Kyle Thomas's memories of his nightmares. Certainly 'Black With Sin' and 'Running With Sodden Legs' spoke volumes about their author's ability to evoke dark, intoxicating imagery without falling into the sort of melodrama or cliché that is common to so many of their peers.

● ALBUMS: *Penalty* (Roadrunner 1996)★★★.

FLOTSAM AND JETSAM

This 'thrash metal' band was formed in Phoenix, Arizona, USA, in 1984 by drummer David Kelly Smith and bassist Jason Newsted (b. 4 March 1963). Adding vocalist Eric A.K. and guitarists Mike Gilbert and Ed Carlson, they debuted with tracks on the *Speed Metal Hell II* and *Metal Massacre IV* compilations. This led to a contract with Roadrunner Records and the release of *Doomsday For The Deceiver* in 1986. Hard, fast and punchy riffs were the band's trademarks, but their progress was hampered by the departure of Newsted to Metallica, shortly after the album's release. Eventually, Troy Gregory was recruited as a permanent replacement and *No Place For Disgrace* emerged in 1988. This sadly revealed that the band had progressed little in two years, and the new material lacked imagination. In an attempt to break into the singles market, they recorded a cover version of Elton John's 'Saturday Night's Alright For Fighting', which failed commercially. Dropped by Roadrunner, they were eventually signed by MCA Records in 1990 and released *When The Storm Comes Down*. Produced by Alex Periallis (of Testament and Anthrax fame), it was aggressive and power-paced, but suffered from an overall monotony of pace and tone.

● ALBUMS: *Doomsday For The Deceiver* (Roadrunner 1986)★★★, *No Place For Disgrace* (Roadrunner 1988)★★, *When The Storm Comes Down* (MCA 1990)★★, *Cuatro* (MCA 1993)★★, *High* (Metal Blade 1997)★★★.

FLYING SQUAD

Formed in Scotland in the mid-70s, Flying Squad were a proficient if unspectacular hard rock group in the gritty, unpretentious vein of Tank or Fastway. Comprising Ian Muir (vocals), Monty McMonagle (guitar), Alex Calder (guitar), George Crossan (bass) and Jim Kelly (drums), they recorded a self-titled debut album in 1978 which was produced by Francis Rossi of Status Quo. Played with agility and imbued with considerable melodic presence, it augured well for the group with Muir's stylish vocals attracting particular praise. However, it was never followed up, and Muir eventually defected to form Waysted (under the pseudonym 'Fin').

● ALBUMS: *Flying Squad* (Columbia 1978)★★★.

FM

FM Radio was pioneered in San Francisco by DJ Tom Donahue at stations KMPX and, later, KSAN. It represented a conscious attempt to reject a Top 40-based playlist in favour of album-orientated acts. By the early 70s, this formula had become common and indeed, many such concerns offered as restrictive an output as their AM counterparts. Released in 1978, *FM* tells the fictional tale of a Los Angeles station, staffed by mavericks, who attempt to remain on air by hijacking a Linda Ronstadt concert, scheduled for their main rival. The film completely fails to question why the founding ethos of FM radio had been subverted, preferring the tiresome 'good versus bad' scenario that has plagued rock films from their inception. Jimmy Buffett, REO Speedwagon and Tom Petty And The Heartbreakers join Ronstadt in contributing musical interludes, while the soundtrack also features material by Steely Dan (who provided the title song), Fleetwood Mac, Boz Scaggs, Joe Walsh, Steve Miller, the Eagles, Foreigner and Foghat. Despite its plot, *FM* enshrines the complacency of AOR music and provides a good explanation for the rise of punk.

FOETUS

You've Got Foetus On Your Breath, Scraping Foetus Off The Wheel, Foetus Interruptus, Foetus Uber Alles, Foetus Inc - all these titles are actually the pseudonym of one person: Australian emigré Jim Thirlwell, alias Jim Foetus and Clint Ruin. After founding his own record company, Self Immolation, in 1980, he set about 'recording works of aggression, insight and inspiration'. Backed with evocatively descriptive musical slogans such as 'positive negativism' and 'bleed now pay later', Foetus released a series of albums, several of which appeared through Stevo's Some Bizzare Records. With stark one-word titles such as *Deaf*, *Ache*, *Hole* and *Nail*, Thirlwell presented a harrowing aural netherworld of death, lust, disease and spiritual decay. In November 1983, Foetus undertook a rare tour, performing with Marc Almond, Nick Cave and Lydia Lunch in the short-lived Immaculate Consumptive. Apart from these soul mates, Foetus has also played live with the Swans' Roli Mossiman as Wiseblood (who released *Dirtdish* in 1986), Lydia Lunch in Stinkfist, and appeared on albums by several artists including The The, Einsturzende Neubauten, Nurse With Wound and Anne Hogan. Thirwell also records instrumental work as Steroid Maximus, releasing *Quilombo* (1991) and *Gonwanaland* (1992) on the Big Cat label. In 1995 Thirlwell announced plans to release his first studio album in seven years. The result was *Gash*, an album that led to a reappraisal of his work as one of the key figures in the development of the 'Industrial' music movement.

● ALBUMS: as You've Got Foetus On Your Breath *Deaf* (Self Immolation 1981)★★★, as You've Got Foetus On Your Breath *Ache* (Self Immolation 1982)★★★, as Scraping Foetus Off The Wheel *Hole* (Self Immolation 1984)★★★, as Scraping Foetus Off The Wheel *Nail* (Self Immolation/Some Bizzare 1985)★★★, as Foetus Interruptus *Thaw* (Self Immolation/Some Bizzare 1988)★★★, as Foetus Corruptus *Rife* (No Label 1989)★★★, as Foetus In Excelsis Corruptus Deluxe *Male* recorded 1990 (Big Cat 1993)★★★, *Gash* (Columbia 1995)★★★, *Boil* (Columbia 1996)★★★.

● COMPILATIONS: as Foetus Inc *Sink* (Self Immolation/Wax Trax! 1989)★★★.

● VIDEOS: *!Male!* (Visionary 1994).

FOGHAT

Although British in origin, Foghat relocated to the USA, where this boogie-blues band built a large following during the 70s. The band originally consisted of 'Lonesome' Dave Peverett (b. 1950, London, England; guitar/vocals), Tony Stevens (b. 12 September 1949, London, England; bass), Roger Earl (b. 1949; drums) and guitarist Rod Price. Peverett, Stevens and Earl had been members of Savoy Brown, the British blues band. They left and immediately settled in the USA with the new unit, where Foghat signed with Bearsville Records, owned by entrepreneurial manager Albert Grossman. Their self-titled debut album reached the US charts, as did the single, a cover of Willie Dixon's blues standard 'I Just Want To Make Love To You'. (A live version sof that song also charted, in 1977.) The group held on to its formula for another dozen albums, each on Bearsville and each a chart item in the USA. Of those, the 1977 live album was the most popular, reaching number 11 on the *Billboard* chart. The band underwent several personnel changes, primarily bassists, with Price being replaced by Erik Cartwright in 1981. In the mid-90s the band were still active, regularly gigging in the USA.

● ALBUMS: *Foghat* i (Bearsville 1972)★★, *Foghat* ii (Bearsville 1973)★★, *Energized* (Bearsville 1974)★★★, *Rock And Roll Outlaws* (Bearsville 1974)★★★, *Fool For The City* (Bearsville 1975)★★, *Night Shift* (Bearsville 1976)★★★, *Foghat Live*

(Bearsville 1977)★★★, *Stone Blue* (Bearsville 1978)★★★, *Boogie Motel* (Bearsville 1979)★★★, *Tight Shoes* (Bearsville 1980)★, *Girls To Chat And Boys To Bounce* (Bearsville 1981)★, *In The Mood For Something Rude* (Bearsville 1982)★, *Zig-Zag Walk* (Bearsville 1983)★, *Return Of The Boogie Man* (Modern 1994)★.
● COMPILATIONS: *The Best Of Foghat* (Rhino 1988)★★★, *The Best Of Foghat, Volume 2* (Rhino 1992)★★★.

FOO FIGHTERS

The Foo Fighters were formed at the end of 1994 by former Scream and Nirvana drummer Dave Grohl (b. 14 January 1969, Warren, Ohio, USA), now switched to guitar and vocals. There was some conjecture that the Nirvana bass player Krist Novoselic would join him in this venture, but Grohl eventually recruited Pat Smear (guitar, ex-Germs and a 'fourth' member of Nirvana during their later career), Nate Mendel (b. 2 December 1968, Seattle, Washington, USA; bass) and William Goldsmith (b. 4 July 1972, Seattle, Washington, USA; drums). The latter pair had previously played with Seattle group Sunny Day Real Estate. Their debut single, 'This Is A Call', was released on Roswell/Capitol Records in June 1995. The Foo Fighters' arrival initiated intense A&R activity, but Grohl opted for Capitol through the auspices of Gary Gersh, who had been Nirvana's A&R representative at Geffen Records. With media expectations weighing heavily on the project, analysis of the group's debut album focused on tracks such as 'I'll Stick Around', which some alleged was an attack on Cobain's widow, Courtney Love. Both the song's title and its lyrical refrain ('I don't owe you anything') seemed to pursue some form of personal exorcism, but it was hard to argue against the sheer impact of Grohl's new canon of songs. Detractors pointed at the similarity to Nirvana in the stop-start construction of several tracks, and Grohl's inability on occasion to match Cobain's evocation of mood. However, the simplicity of execution added greatly to the immediacy of the project. Grohl's original demos had simply been remixed rather than glossed over by a new production, and the result was, on the whole, enthralling. Goldsmith left the group during the recording of their second album and was replaced by Taylor Hawkins from Alanis Morissette's touring band. Although the critics were waiting to pounce on *The Colour And The Shape* it was another hard and tough album of blistering, paced songs, which were lightened by the group's great grasp of melody - songs such as 'Monkey Wrench' and 'My Poor Brain' burst into life in the middle eight. Smear also left the group, and was later replaced by Franz Stahl (ex-Scream). In 1998, Grohl recorded the soundtrack to Paul Schrader's *Touch*.
● ALBUMS: *Foo Fighters* (Roswell/Capitol 1995)★★★★, *The Colour And The Shape* (Roswell/Capitol 1997)★★★★.

FOR LOVE NOT LISA

This guitar-based alternative rock band was formed in Oklahoma, USA in 1990 by guitarist Miles, vocalist/guitarist Mike Lewis, bassist Doug Carrion and drummer Aaron Preston. They relocated to Los Angeles in mid-1991, although they soon moved away from the culture shock of the Hollywood scene, and signed a major recording contract while steering well clear of the notorious pay-to-play clubs. *Merge* was an effective debut, mixing punk and rock influences into a varied style with good songwriting. The band backed up the record with live shows, during which they revealed an experimental side, including Lewis's unusual penchant for ad-libbing most of his lyrics. However, the question on many critics' lips was whether For Love Not Lisa could rise above the glut of major label, grunge-flavoured bands signed in Nirvana and Pearl Jam's wake.
● ALBUMS: *Merge* (East West 1993)★★★.

FORBIDDEN

Originally travelling under the moniker Forbidden Evil, this band was formed in San Francisco, California, in 1985. Its original line-up consisted of Russ Anderson (vocals), Glen Alvelais (guitar), Craig Locicero (guitar), Matt Camacho (bass) and Paul Bostaph (drums). They quickly gained a strong following playing numerous support slots with more established Bay Area bands such as Testament and Exodus. Through their early demos the band signed to Combat Records (product was released in Europe on the Music For Nations subsidiary label, Under One Flag). Their name was truncated to Forbidden while the full title was saved for their debut long-player, *Forbidden Evil*. This arrived in 1988 to critical acclaim within the Bay Area thrash community and some of the mainstream metal magazines. They toured Europe in support of the release during 1989, appearing at the Dynamo Open Air Festival in Holland. This was recorded and the subsequent live album, *Raw Evil At The Dynamo*, was released the same year. During preparation for their next studio album, Glen Alvelais left the band, but was replaced by ex-Militia guitarist Tim Calvert in time for the recordings. *Twisted Into Form*, released in 1990, was again received well by the media, with its blend of hard-hitting thrash metal, cleverly structured songs and excellent guitar interplay. The band's long-term impact was then dealt a blow by a split between Megaforce and Atlantic Records, which left them without an outlet for much of the early 90s (they later signed to German label Gun). On *Distortion* drummer Steve Jacobs joined Camacho, Locicero, Calvert and Anderson on a set that included a cover version of King Crimson's '21st Century Schizoid Man', as well as powerful new originals.

● ALBUMS: *Forbidden Evil* (Metal Blade 1988)★★★, *Raw Evil At The Dynamo* mini-album (Metal Blade 1989)★★★, *Twisted Into Form* (Metal Blade 1990)★★★, *Distortion* (Gun 1994)★★★, *Green* (Gun 1997)★★★.

● COMPILATIONS: *Point Of No Return: The Best Of Forbidden* (Metal Blade 1993)★★★★.

FORD, LITA

b. 23 September 1959, London, England. Ford was one of the original members of the Kim Fowley-conceived Runaways, first joining the band at age 15. In 1980 a disagreement within the ranks over musical direction led to the Runaways' break-up, leaving Ford to explore a solo career on the US glam metal circuit (initially subsidized by her day job as a beautician). Her debut album was recorded for Mercury Records with the assistance of Neil Merryweather on bass, though it was Ford's guitar playing that took centrestage. *Dancin' On The Edge* made a minor impact on the US album charts, reaching number 66, although it was a less slick collection. Almost four years later in 1988 came *Lita*. Housed on RCA Records (a third album for MCA, *The Bride Wore Black*, had been abandoned), it reached the Top 30 and spawned the US number 12 hit, 'Kiss Me Deadly' (April 1988), plus a Top 10 hit with a duet with Ozzy Osbourne, 'Close My Eyes Forever' (March 1989). She later married W.A.S.P. guitarist Chris Holmes, although the marriage did not last. *Stiletto* continued to display Ford's commitment to the formula rock format prevalent in the USA, but she left RCA following disappointing sales for 1991's *Dangerous Curves*.

● ALBUMS: *Out For Blood* (Mercury 1983)★★★, *Dancin' On The Edge* (Mercury 1984)★★, *Lita* (RCA 1988)★★★, *Stiletto* (RCA 1990)★★★, *Dangerous Curves* (RCA 1991)★★, *Black* (ZYX 1995)★★.

● COMPILATIONS: *Best Of* (BMG 1992)★★★.

● VIDEOS: *Lita Live* (BMG Video 1988), *A Midnight Snack* (BMG Video 1990).

FOREIGNER

The band derived its name from the fact that the original members were drawn from both sides of the Atlantic, and this mixture of influences is much in evidence in their music. Mick Jones (b. 27 December 1944, London, England; guitar, vocals) formed the band in 1976, having spent time in Nero And The Gladiators (two minor hits, 'Entry Of The Gladiators' and 'In The Hall Of The Mountain King', in 1961). The rest of the 60s were taken up working as a songwriter and musical director for French singer Johnny Halliday, alongside ex-Gladiator Tommy Brown, with whom Jones also recorded several singles and EPs. During the early 70s he worked with ex-Spooky Tooth keyboardist Gary Wright in Wonderwheel, which led to Jones playing on three albums with the reformed Spooky Tooth. Jones then worked with Leslie West and Ian Lloyd before taking a job as an A&R man, although he never actually signed anyone. Prepared to make one final attempt on the music scene, Jones auditioned musicians, eventually forging a line-up that consisted of Ian McDonald (b. 25 June 1946, London, England; guitar, keyboards, horns, vocals), formerly of King Crimson, Lou Gramm (b. Lou Grammatico, 2 May 1950, Rochester, New York, USA; vocals), who had played with Black Sheep in the early 70s, Dennis Elliott (b. 18 August 1950, London, England; drums), Al Greenwood (b. New York, USA; keyboards) and Edward Gagliardi (b. 13 February 1952, New York, USA; bass). In 1977 the band released *Foreigner*, and in a poll conducted by *Rolling Stone* magazine, emerged as top new artists. The album was an immediate success in America, climbing to number 4 in the *Billboard* chart. Jones and Gramm wrote most of the band's material, including classic tracks such as 'Feels Like The First Time' (US number 4, March 1977) and 'Cold As Ice' (US number 6, July 1977). Despite playing at the Reading Rock Festival in England twice in the 70s, Foreigner had more consistent success in the USA, where 'Hot Blooded' (number 3, July 1978) and 'Double Vision' (number 2, September 1978) were both million sellers. In 1979 Rick Wills (b. England; bass) replaced Gagliardi, having served a musical apprenticeship with King Crimson and Peter Frampton; Gagliardi reportedly 'fell on the floor and passed out' on being told the news. *Head Games*, meanwhile, proved most notable for its 'exploitative' sleeve design, which contrasted with the subtle brand of rock it contained. In 1980 McDonald and Greenwood departed to form Spys, leading to the guest appearances of Thomas Dolby and Junior Walker on the following year's US chart-topping *4*, produced by Mutt Lange. The album also broke the group in the UK, reaching number 5 in July of that year. 'Waiting For A Girl Like You' was the hit single lifted from the album, spending ten weeks at number 2 in the US charts, and providing the group with their first UK Top 10 single. Although it was representative of the band's highly musical approach, taking the form of a wistful yet melodious ballad, it pigeonholed the group as purveyors of the epic AOR song. This reputation was only endorsed in December 1984 by the release of 'I Want To Know What Love Is', which proved to be Foreigner's greatest commercial success. It topped the charts on both sides of the Atlantic and featured the New Jersey Mass Choir backing Gramm's plaintive vocal. *Agent Provocateur*, meanwhile, topped the UK album charts and reached number 4 in America. In the mid-80s the members of Foreigner were engaged in solo projects, and the success of Gramm's *Ready Or Not* in 1987 led to widespread speculation that Foreigner were about to disband. This was not the case, as *Inside Information* proved, though in other respects it was a poor record and a portent of things to come, despite containing the US Top 10 hit singles 'Say You Will' and 'I Don't Want To Live Without You'. In 1989 Gramm enjoyed success with another solo project, *Long Hard Look*, before officially leaving the band in May 1990 to form Shadow King. Jones refused to face the inevitable, and, amid much press sniping, recruited Johnny Edwards (ex-King Kobra) to provide vocals for *Unusual Heat*. In 1992 both Jones and Gramm grasped the nettle and reunited, launching a re-formed Foreigner, though both Wills and Elliott were deemed surplus to requirements. The 1994 model boasted a line-up of Bruce Turgon (bass; a former colleague of Gramm in Black Sheep and Shadow King), Jeff Jacobs (keyboards, ex-Billy Joel circa *Storm Front*) and Mark Schulman (drums), in addition to Jones and Gramm. The band were back on the road during the early part of 1995 to promote *Mr Moonlight*. The album was only a moderate success, even though it was a typical Foreigner record. At their well attended gigs, however, it was still 'Cold As Ice', 'Urgent' and 'I Want To Know What Love Is' that received the biggest cheers. Whether or not their legacy grows further, Foreigner will continue to epitomize better than anybody the classic sound of 'adult orientated rock'.

● ALBUMS: *Foreigner* (Atlantic 1977)★★★, *Double Vision* (Atlantic 1978)★★★, *Head Games* (Atlantic 1979)★★★, *4* (Atlantic 1981)★★★★, *Agent Provocateur* (Atlantic 1985)★★★, *Inside Information* (Atlantic 1987)★★★, *Unusual Heat* (Atlantic 1991)★★★, *Mr Moonlight* (BMG 1994)★★★.
Solo: Mick Jones *Mick Jones* (Atlantic 1989)★★.
● COMPILATIONS: *Records* (Atlantic 1982)★★★★, *The Very Best Of Foreigner* (Atlantic 1992)★★★★, *The Very Best ... And Beyond* (Atlantic 1992)★★★★, *Classic Hits Live* (Atlantic 1993)★★★.
● FILMS: *Footloose* (1984).

44 Magnum

Japanese heavy metal outfit formed in 1977 by vocalist Tatsuya Umehara and guitarist Satoshi Hirorse. With the addition of Hironori Yoshikawa on bass and Satoshi Miyawaki on drums, they persevered for many years in the shadow of higher-profile Japanese bands such as Loudness, Earthshaker and Bow Wow. They eventually secured a record contract in 1982 and debuted with *Danger* the following year. Although the musicianship was competent, their ideas and style were too obviously influenced by British and American acts such as Van Halen, Deep Purple and Led Zeppelin.

● ALBUMS: *Danger* (Moon 1983)★★★, *Street Rock 'n' Roller* (Roadrunner 1984)★★★.

44xes

This techno rock/industrial band was formed in Bremen, Germany, in 1993, originally as Crashcat. By the beginning of 1995 Heiko Grien (vocals), Markus Gronostay (guitar), Raphael Kraft (guitar) and Dietmar Popke (drums) had changed their name to 44xes - pronounced 'forty-four excess'. Their first concert together came at an Amsterdam festival, performing in front of a mixed audience of punks, industrial and metal fans. After the release of their debut mini-album in 1995, boasting a punishing sound reminiscent of a more restrained Nine Inch Nails, they embarked on touring dates with Shihad.

● ALBUMS: *Banish Silence* mini-album (When! Recordings 1995)★★★.

Four Horsemen

This UK heavy metal/rock 'n' roll outfit was formed in 1991 by former Cult bassist Haggis, who in a previous life had been Kid Chaos of Zodiac Mindwarp And The Love Reaction, although his parents have always known him as Mark Manning. Recruiting Frank C. Starr (vocals), Ken 'Dimwit' Montgomery (drums), Dave Lizmi (guitar) and Ben

Pape (bass), they negotiated a contract with Rick Rubin's Def American label (with whom the band's leader had worked during his stint with the Cult). With Haggis on rhythm guitar, their music drew heavily from AC/DC, the Black Crowes and the Georgia Satellites, though most critics seemed unable to see past their Cult affiliations Their debut album, *Nobody Said It Was Easy*, was a powerful collection of heavy-duty rockers based on loud riffs and infectious chorus lines. Like Haggis's former employers, they exaggerated every cliché in the book, yet this approach did not groan under the same weight of lofty ideals and was consequently much more fun. Manning was last sighted in 1994 promoting his book of illustrations, *A Bible Of Dreams*, in conjunction with Bill Drummond of the KLF.

● ALBUMS: *Nobody Said It Was Easy* (Def American 1991)★★★.

FRAMPTON, PETER

b. 22 April 1950, Beckenham, Kent, England. The former 'Face of 1968', with his pin-up good looks as part of the 60s pop group the Herd, Frampton grew his hair longer and joined Humble Pie. His solo career debuted with *Wind Of Change* in 1971, although he immediately set about forming another band, Frampton's Camel, to carry out US concert dates. This formidable unit consisted of Mike Kellie (b. 24 March 1947, Birmingham, England; drums), Rick Wills (bass) and Mickey Gallagher (keyboards), all seasoned players from Spooky Tooth, Cochise and Bell And Arc, respectively. *Frampton* in 1975 was a great success in the USA, while in the UK he was commercially ignored. The following year a double set recorded at Winterland in San Francisco, *Frampton Comes Alive*, scaled the US chart and stayed on top for a total of 10 weeks, in four visits during a record-breaking two-year stay. It also reached number 6 in the UK album chart. The record became the biggest-selling live album in history and to date has sold over 12 million copies. Quite why the record was so successful has perplexed many rock critics. Like Jeff Beck, Frampton perfected the voice tube effect and used this gimmick on 'Show Me The Way', a US number 6 hit in February 1976 (this single was also Frampton's only UK Top 10 entry). The follow-up, *I'm In You*, sold in vast quantities, although compared to the former it was a flop, selling a modest 'several million'. The title-track climbed to number 2 in the US singles chart in May 1977. Again Frampton found little critical acclaim, but his records were selling in vast quantities. He continued to reach younger audiences with aplomb. In 1978 he suffered a near fatal car crash, although his fans were able to see him in the previously filmed *Sgt Pepper's Lonely Hearts Club Band*. Frampton played Billy Shears alongside the Bee Gees in the Robert Stigwood extravaganza that was a commercial and critical disaster. When he returned in 1979 with *Where I Should Be*, his star was dwindling. The album garnered favourable reviews, but it was his last successful record. Even the short-haired image for *Breaking All The Rules* failed, with only America, his loyal base, nudging it into the Top 50. Following *The Art Of Control* Frampton 'disappeared' until 1986, when he was signed to Virgin Records and released the synthesizer-laced *Premonition*. He returned to session work thereafter. Later on in the decade Frampton was found playing guitar with his former school-friend David Bowie on his 1987 release *Never Let Me Down*. In 1991 he was allegedly making plans to re-form Humble Pie with Steve Marriott, but a week after their meeting in New York, Marriott was tragically burnt to death in his home. He diverted his interest to the other great success of his career in 1995 by releasing *Frampton Comes Alive II*.

● ALBUMS: *Wind Of Change* (A&M 1972)★★★, *Frampton's Camel* (A&M 1973)★★★, *Somethin's Happening* (A&M 1974)★★, *Frampton* (A&M 1975)★★, *Frampton Comes Alive!* (A&M 1976)★★★★, *I'm In You* (A&M 1977)★★, *Where I Should Be* (A&M 1979)★★, *Breaking All The Rules* (A&M 1981)★★, *The Art Of Control* (A&M 1982)★★, *Premonition* (Virgin 1986)★, *When All The Pieces Fit* (Atlantic 1989)★★, *Show Me The Way* (1993)★★, *Peter Frampton* (Relativity 1994)★★★, *Frampton Comes Alive II* (El Dorado/IRS 1995)★★.

● COMPILATIONS: *Classics, Voluume 12* (A&M 1989)★★★, *Shine On: A Collection* (A&M 1992)★★★, *Greatest Hits* (A&M 1996)★★★★.

● FURTHER READING: *Frampton!: An Unauthorized Biography*, Susan Katz. *Peter Frampton*, Marsha Daly. *Peter Frampton: A Photo Biography*, Irene Adler.

FREAK OF NATURE

Following the break-up of White Lion, frontman Mike Tramp assembled Freak Of Nature with guitarist Kenny Korade, former White Lion bassist Jerry Best, drummer Johnny Haro and ex-VVSI/House Of Lords guitarist Dennis Chick, a replacement for original member Oliver Steffenson. Away from record company pressures, the band developed a strong collection of melodic rock songs with a distinctly harder edge than White Lion, with Tramp concentrating on introspective, personal lyrics, again in contrast to the simpler themes of his previous group. '92' dealt with a traumatic year in Tramp's personal and professional life, while 'Rescue Me' tackled the difficult subject of his brother's addiction problems. While acquiring recording contracts for Europe and Japan, Freak Of Nature had trouble finding a contract for the USA owing to their unwillingness to compromise. However, they were prepared to be patient and to let their music and growing live reputation break the band. A lengthy touring schedule, taking in the USA, Japan and Europe, from May 1993 made the band many friends, and served to reinforce the idea of Freak Of Nature as a band rather than a Tramp solo project. Late 1994 saw the introduction of new guitarist Marcus Mand in place of Kenny Korade.

● ALBUMS: *Freak Of Nature* (Music For Nations 1993)★★★, *Gathering Of Freaks* (Music For Nations 1994)★★.

FREE

Formed in the midst of 1968's British blues boom, Free originally comprised Paul Rodgers (b. 17 December 1949, Middlesbrough, Cleveland, England; vocals), Paul Kossoff (b. 14 September 1950, Hampstead, London, England, d. 19 March 1976; guitar), Andy Fraser (b. 7 August 1952, London, England; bass) and Simon Kirke (b. 28 July 1949, Shrewsbury, Shropshire, England; drums). Despite their comparative youth, the individual musicians were seasoned performers, particularly Fraser, a former member of John Mayall's Bluesbreakers. Free received early encouragement from Alexis Korner, but having completed an excellent, earthy debut album, *Tons Of Sobs*, the group began honing a more individual style with their second set. The injection of powerful original songs, including 'I'll Be Creeping', showed a maturing talent, while Rodgers' expressive voice and Kossoff's stinging guitar enhanced a growing reputation. The quartet's stylish blues rock reached its commercial peak on *Fire And Water*. This confident collection featured moving ballads - 'Heavy Load', 'Oh I Wept' - and compulsive, uptempo material, the standard-bearer of which was 'All Right Now'. An edited version of this soulful composition reached number 2 in the UK and number 4 in the USA in 1970, since which time the song has become one of pop's most enduring performances, making periodic reappearances in the singles chart. A fourth set, *Highway*, revealed a more mellow perspective, highlighted by an increased use of piano at the expense of Kossoff's guitar. This was the result, in part, of friction within the group, a situation exacerbated when the attendant single, 'The Stealer', failed to emulate its predecessor's success. Free broke up in May 1971, paradoxically in the wake of another hit single, 'My Brother Jake' (UK number 4), but regrouped in January the following year when spin-off projects faltered, although Kossoff and Kirke's amalgamation (Kossoff, Kirke, Tetsu And Rabbit) proved fruitful. A sixth album, *Free At Last*, offered some of the unit's erstwhile fire and included another UK Top 20 entry, 'Little Bit Of Love'. However, Kossoff's increasing ill health and Fraser's departure for the Sharks undermined any new-found confidence. A hastily convened line-up consisting of Rodgers, Kirke, John 'Rabbit' Bundrick (keyboards) and Tetsu Yamauchi (b. 1946, Fukuoka, Japan; bass) undertook a Japanese tour, but although the guitarist rejoined the quartet for several British dates, his contribution to Free's final album, *Heartbreaker*, was muted. Kossoff embarked on a solo career in October 1972, with Wendel Richardson from Osibisa replaced him on a temporary basis. Despite a final Top 10 single, 'Wishing Well', in January 1973 Free had ceased to function by July of that year. Rodgers and Kirke subsequently formed Bad Company.

● ALBUMS: *Tons Of Sobs* (Island 1968)★★★, *Free* (Island 1969)★★★, *Fire And Water* (Island 1970)★★★★, *Highway* (Island 1970)★★★, *Free Live* (Island 1971)★★, *Free At Last* (Island 1972)★★, *Heartbreaker* (Island 1973)★★.

● COMPILATIONS: *The Free Story* (Island 1974)★★★★, *Completely Free* (Island 1982)★★★, *All Right Now* (Island 1991)★★★, *Molton Gold: The Anthology* (Island 1993)★★★★, *Walk In My Shadow - An Introduction* (Island 1998)★★★★.

● VIDEOS: *Free* (Island Visual Arts 1989).

FREHLEY'S COMET

Following drug and alcohol-related problems, US guitarist Ace Frehley (b. Paul Frehley, 22 April 1951, Bronx, New York, USA) left Kiss in December 1982. After a four-year period of rehabilitation, he began writing and playing again, signing to the Megaforce label in 1987. Recruiting Tod Howarth (ex-707; vocals, guitar), John Regan (bass) and Anton Fig (drums), Frehley's Comet was born. With an emphasis on Americanized hard rock, with a commercial edge, their self-titled debut was given a favourable reception from critics and Kiss fans alike. In time, Tod Howarth's creative input began to change the band's sound, pushing them in a more lightweight AOR direction. This was illustrated on *Second Sighting*. Frehley, concerned that this new direction might alienate his loyal fanbase, relieved Tod Howarth of vocal duties on *Trouble Walkin'* (issued as an Ace Frehley solo album), drafting in guitarist Richie Scarlet as replacement. This album was a backward step musically in an attempt to appeal to the same market as Kiss, even employing that band's drummer, Peter Criss, as guest vocalist and covering Paul Stanley's (Kiss guitarist) 'Hide Your Heart'. The rest of the band became frustrated by Frehley's controlling interest and left halfway through the tour to support the album.

● ALBUMS: *Frehley's Comet* (Megaforce 1987)★★★, *Live + 1* (Megaforce 1988)★★, *Second Sighting* (Megaforce 1988)★★★, *Trouble Walkin'* (Megaforce 1989)★★.

● VIDEOS: *Live 4* (Hendring Video 1990).

FREHLEY, ACE

b. Paul Frehley, 22 April 1951, Bronx, New York, USA. Ace Frehley rose to fame as the lead guitarist for premier US hard rock band Kiss during its prime years. Often nicknamed 'Space Ace' by fans, Frehley released his debut solo album in 1978, with albums by the other three members of Kiss also recorded simultaneously. The album, which found the guitarist attempting more diverse musical styles than he was allowed to follow within the context of Kiss, reached the Top 30 and spawned a number 13 single, the Russ Ballard-penned 'New York Groove'. Frehley left Kiss in December 1982 following a near-fatal car accident, and attempted to free himself of a drug habit over the next four years. He formed his own band, Frehley's Comet, in 1987, with whom he recorded three studio albums. He rejoined Kiss on their successful reunion tour in 1996.

● ALBUMS: *Ace Frehley* (Casablanca 1978)★★★.

● COMPILATIONS: *12 Picks* (SPV/Steamhammer 1997)★★★, *Loaded Decks* (SPV 1998)★★★.

FRIEDMAN, MARTY

This technically brilliant USA-born guitarist has a long and impressive pedigree. Stints with Vixen, Hawaii and Cacophony helped to formulate and define his characteristic quick-fire style, before he embarked on a solo career. *Dragon's Kiss* was an impressive instrumental debut, combining heavy-duty riffs and intricate solos with Far Eastern influences and undertones. Friedman later went on to produce speed-metallers Apocrypha, before commencing work on a second solo project. This was put on hold after he accepted an invitation to join Megadeth in February 1990, though it did finally emerge three years later. By *Introduction*, the guitarist had moved on to a spacious, new-age technique, on a set more expansive in tone that anything he had previously recorded in the rock field.

● ALBUMS: *Dragon's Kiss* (Roadrunner 1988)★★★, *Scenes* (Roadrunner 1993)★★, *Introduction* (Roadrunner 1994)★★, *The Obsessions* (Metal Blade 1996)★★★.

FRONT (1)

Comprising Keith Angelino (vocals, guitar), Steven Mark (keyboards), Sean Healy (bass) and Chris Cavill (drums), US hard rock band the Front formed in the early 80s. Their sound combined youthful angst with often irreverent lyrics. However, their self-titled debut album failed to provide evidence of the sort of musical sophistication which could mark them apart from other Cheap Trick imitators such as New England. With independent distribution it failed to make a dent in the mainstream marketplace and the group sundered before a follow-up collection could be considered.

● ALBUMS: *The Front* (Arockolypse 1982)★★.

FRONT (2)

A second US hard rock group to emerge in the 80s under the name the Front, this incarnation comprised Michael Anthony Franano (vocals), Mike Greene (guitar), Bobby Franano (keyboards), Randy Jordan (bass) and Shane (drums). Unlike their namesakes, they specialised in material heavily influenced by the Doors - Michael Anthony Franano's vocals earning him a reputation as a Jim Morrison sound-alike, while his brother's dense keyboard patterns recalled Ray Manzarek's contribution to the same band. Despite a major label recording contract with Columbia Records, they proved unable to break into the mainstream.

● ALBUMS: *The Front* (Columbia 1989)★★★.

FRONT 242

A duo of Patrick Codenys (b. 16 November 1958, Brussels, Belgium; composition, computers, synthesizers, guitars, vocals) and Daniel Bressanutti (b. 27 August 1954, Brussels, Belgium; programming, samples), Front 242 have earned their long-standing reputation within the industrial/*avant garde* community via a largely compelling series of experimental exercises in sound. Originally, Front 242 comprised Codenys alone, for the 1982 single 'Principles', then became a trio with Jean-Luc De

Meyer and Bressanutti. These early releases were more in tune with the elementary synth-pop of artists such as Depeche Mode, and it was not until after the release of *Geography* that they appeared live. A fourth member, Geoff Bellingham, was added for this purpose, although he was later replaced by ex-roadie and concurrent Revolting Cocks member Richard 23. Through the 80s Front 242's became a more distinctive unit, however, with politically motivated samples filtering through the repetition. On the back of an awesome reputation for live events and visuals, they were launched out of cult status by the success of *Official Version*. This introduced the intemperate, militaristic rhythms that became a signature, as well as a diversity enshrined by nods to disco and pop in other tracks. It was not until the advent of *Tyranny For You* that the ingredients were significantly rearranged once more, this time to instil a darker overtone to proceedings (the album emerged at the same time as the Gulf War and proclamations of a New World Order). Influenced by the German anti-rock movement (Can, Neu, Faust), cinema and architecture, the duo (following De Meyer's departure in the 90s) continue to run the Art & Strategy design company and record label.

● ALBUMS: *Geography* (RRE 1982)★★, *No Comment* mini-album (Wax Trax! 1985)★★★, *Official Version* (Wax Trax! 1987)★★★★, *Front By Front* (Wax Trax! 1988)★★★, *Tyranny (for You)* (RRE/Epic 1991)★★★, *Live Target* (Guzzi 1993)★★★, *06:21:03:11 Up Evil* (RRE/Epic 1993)★★★, *05:22:09:12 Off* (RRE/Epic 1993)★★★, *Mut@ge Mix@ge* (RPE 1995)★★★.

● COMPILATIONS: *Backcatalogue* (Wax Trax! 1987)★★★, *Geography 1981-1983* (RRECD 1992)★★★, *No Comment 1984-1985* (RRECD 1992)★★★, *Back Catalogue 1981-1985* (RRECD 1992)★★★, *Official Version 1986-1987* (RRECD 1992)★★★, *Front By Front 1988-1989* (RRECD 1992)★★★.

FU MANCHU

Formed in Orange County, California, USA, Fu Manchu comprised Scott Hill (vocals, guitar), Ruben Romano (drums), Brad Davis (bass) and Eddie Glass (lead guitar). Their debut EP was released in 1990, establishing their headily psychedelic, groove-orientated approach. While many compared them to Kyuss, Fu Manchu preferred to make cryptic references to pharmaceuticals and produce cover images that tied them to older generations of rock bands. *In Search Of ...* , for example, featured a woman in flares preparing to start an illegal drag race, while the album's title derived from a lacklustre science-fiction programme of the 70s. Suitably, Hill has never spent much time perfecting his lyrics, instead using his voice as a fifth instrument to complement the group's dense, rhythmic passages. Glass and Romano both left the band in 1996, replaced by ex-Kyuss Brant Bjork and Bob Balch, respectively.

● ALBUMS: *No One Rides For Free* (Mammoth 1994)★★★, *Daredevil* (Mammoth 1995)★★, *In Search Of ...* (Mammoth 1996)★★, *The Action Is Go* (Mammoth 1998)★★.

FUDGE TUNNEL

UK noise operatives Fudge Tunnel were formed in 1989 by 18-year-old vocalist, guitarist and songwriter Alex Newport when he moved to Nottingham. He quickly sought out sympathizers in the shape of Dave Ryley (bass) and Adrian Parkin (drums). Their first ever release, 1990's *Sex Mammoth EP*, was immediately chosen as Single Of The Week in the *New Musical Express*. Six months later came *The Sweet Sound Of Excess EP*, then touring commitments with Silverfish and Godflesh. In 1991 they gained a permanent home at Earache Records, which culminated in the release of their debut album, which arrived with the self-explanatory title of *Hate Songs In E Minor*. This immensely caustic epistle was released in May 1991 after initial copies, controversially featuring a drawing of a decapitation taken from the John Minnery book *How To Kill*, were confiscated by Nottingham vice police. The acclaim eventually accrued in metal and indie magazines by the Colin Richardson-produced disc was huge, however, with barely a word of dissent and plenty more that earmarked Fudge Tunnel as the ultimate in brutal music. A commercially successful EP, *Teeth* (UK indie chart number 4 - a major landmark for such extreme music), preceded the release of a second album, *Creep Diets*. Despite continued progress, the band were unhappily bracketed with the emerging Seattle 'grunge' sound (which they actually predated) and some of the momentum waned. As well as time spent touring, in 1993 Newport worked with Max Cavalera (Sepultura) on the Nailbomb project. Fudge Tunnel then reconvened at Sawmill Studios in Cornwall for their third album. *The Complicated Futility Of Ignorance* saw the grunge comparisons finally dropped as the group processed a further increase in their already massively violent sound.

● ALBUMS: *Hate Songs In E Minor* (Earache 1991)★★★, *Fudge Cake* comprises *Sex Mammoth*

and *The Sweet Sound Of Excess* EPs (Pigboy/Vinyl Solution 1992)★★, *Creep Diets* (Earache 1993)★★★, *The Complicated Futility Of Ignorance* (Earache 1994)★★★.
● COMPILATIONS: *In A Word* 1990-93 recordings (Earache 1995)★★★.

FUGAZI

The thinking person's modern hardcore band, and vocalist/guitarist Ian MacKaye's most permanent institution since his Minor Threat days. More so than Henry Rollins and, arguably, Jello Biafra, Fugazi have continued and expanded on the arguments of their antecedents. Door prices are kept down, mainstream press interviews are shunned, and they maintain a commitment to all-age shows that shames many bands. They have also been among the first to object publicly to the ridiculous macho ritual of slam-dancing: 'We're about challenging crowds, confronting ourselves and them with new ideas and if I was a teenager now, I would not be doing a dance that's been going on for ten years'. It is a shame that Fugazi's press seems to focus unerringly on MacKaye's Minor Threat connections, as the contribution from his co-lyricist Guy Picciotto (vocals, guitar; ex-Rites Of Spring) deserves to be ranked above that of supporting cast. His more abstract, less direct communiqués blend well with his partner's realism. The other members of the band are Brendan Canty (drums) and Joe Lally (bass), and together they have forged one of the most consistent and challenging discographies within the US underground. Although they have concentrated primarily on touring rather than studio efforts, each of their albums has gone on to sell more than 100,000 copies, produced entirely independently within their own Dischord Records framework. In a rare mainstream music press interview in 1995, MacKaye continued to decry those who would use the guise of punk rock to record for major corporations, commenting on the success of Green Day and Offspring by stating: 'They'll be forgotten, 'cos they're the fucking Ugly Kid Joe's of the 90s'. *Red Medicine* proved just as abrasive and disciplined an exercise as usual.
● ALBUMS: *Fugazi EP* (Dischord 1988)★★★, *Margin Walker EP* (Dischord 1989)★★★, *Repeater* (Dischord 1990)★★★★, *Steady Diet Of Nothing* (Dischord 1991)★★★, *In On The Killtaker* (Dischord 1993)★★★, *Red Medicine* (Dischord 1995)★★★, *End Hits* (Dischord 1998)★★★.
● COMPILATIONS: *13 Songs* first two EPs (Dischord 1988)★★★.

G-FORCE

G-Force was the brainchild of ex-Skid Row, Colosseum II, and Thin Lizzy guitarist Gary Moore (b. 4 April 1952, Belfast, Northern Ireland). After leaving Lizzy shortly after playing on the band's *Black Rose* in 1979, Moore headed for Los Angeles with the intention of forming a new group there. He teamed up with some reputable local musicians and, not wishing at that time to be known as the Gary Moore Band, they chose to travel under the moniker of G-Force. Joining Moore in this project were Tony Newton (vocals), Willie Dee (ex-Pipedream; bass) and Mark Nauseef (drums). The band played some low-key gigs in and around the Los Angeles area and signed to Jet Records, for whom they released their debut album in 1980. A slice of melodic hard rock with definite commercial prospects, it nevertheless flopped. The band folded soon after its release, with Moore resuming his solo career.
● ALBUMS: *G-Force* (Jet 1980)★★★.

G.B.H.

Formerly known as Charged G.B.H. (truncating the name by the release of 1986's *Oh No It's G.B.H. Again! EP*), the band formed just as the initial impetus of the punk movement was petering out in 1980, counting the Exploited and Discharge among their peers. Comprising Cal (b. Colin Abrahall; vocals), Jock Blyth (guitar), Ross (bass) and Wilf (drums), they adopted a violent and aggressive image (G.B.H., of course, standing for 'grievous bodily harm'), sporting multicoloured mohican haircuts and *de rigeur* studded and chained leathers. Musically, they combined influences such as the Ramones and Venom into a hardcore metallic barrage of testosterone-led frustration. With 'smash-the-system' sloganeering in place of lyrics, they were an uncompromising and extreme musical outfit during the early 80s, and exerted some influence on the thrash and hardcore movements that followed. While musically they could be exciting, any enjoyment was downgraded by the poverty of intellect behind the lyrics (notable examples being the anti-feminist tract

'Womb With A View', from *City Baby's Revenge*, or 'Limpwristed', from *Midnight Madness And Beyond*). Furthermore, their success was always limited by an inability to progress musically. Kai replaced Wilf on drums in 1989, as the band veered away from regimented hardcore towards speed metal. This trend continued with the arrival of new bassist Anthony Morgan. Even the mohicans had disappeared on their tour to promote *From Here To Reality*, which the *NME* kindly reviewed as having 'no redeeming features whatsoever'.

● ALBUMS: *Leather, Bristles, Studs And Acne* mini-album (Clay 1981)★★, *City Baby Attacked By Rats* (Clay 1982)★★★, *Live At City Garden* (Clay 1982)★★, *City Baby's Revenge* (Clay 1983)★★★, *Midnight Madness And Beyond* (Rough Justice 1986)★★★, *No Need To Panic!* (Rough Justice 1987)★★, *A Fridge Too Far* (Rough Justice 1989)★★, *From Here To Reality* (Music For Nations 1990)★★, *Church Of The Truly Warped* (Rough Justice 1993)★★, *Punk Junkies* (We Bite 1996)★★.

● COMPILATIONS: *Leather, Bristles, No Survivors And Sick Boys* (Clay 1982)★★★, *The Clay Years 81 - 84* (Clay 1986)★★★, *Diplomatic Immunity* (Clay 1990)★★.

● VIDEOS: *Live At The Ace Brixton* (Jettisoundz 1983), *A Video Too Far* (Video For Nations 1989), *Kawasaki Live* (Visionary 1993).

G.G.F.H.

G.G.F.H. (an acronym for Global Genocide Forget Heaven) consists of two Californians, Brian J. Walls and Ghost. Highly media-literate and pessimistic, G.G.F.H.'s music paints a picture of pain, ignorance and perversity with a palette of harsh electronic music, robotic vocals and sampled dialogue. Their main obsession, however, is the way in which a paranoid establishment creates sensationalist panics to feed to the TV-addicted populace. *Eclipse*, their first full album, concentrated on the media panic around Satanism, with audio samples from talk shows and cheap films as its backdrop. The second album, *Disease*, dropped the Satanic theme in favour of the more generic territory of serial murder, sexual violence and urban alienation. The grinding hum of *Eclipse* was replaced by a lighter, more electronic, though no less disturbing, tone for *Disease*. The grim *Halloween EP*, released in a limited edition in 1991, was re-released in an extended form as their third full album, consisting of demo material recorded between 1986 and 1989.

● ALBUMS: *Eclipse* (Dreamtime 1991)★★, *Disease* (Dreamtime 1993)★★★, *Halloween* (Dreamtime 1994)★★.

GALACTIC COWBOYS

This US metallic art-rock quartet was formed in 1990 by vocalist Ben Huggins and guitarist Dane Sonnier. With the addition of bassist Monty Colvin and drummer Alan Doss, they specialized in complex and densely melodic song structures that typically exceeded the six-minute mark. Combining elements of Kings X, Metallica and Neil Young with state-of-the-art technology, they produced one of 1991's most impressive debut albums. Defying simple categorization, they surprised the listener with what initially seemed the *ad hoc* juxtaposition of incompatible styles. Somehow, the strange fusion worked, manic thrashing giving way to harmonica solos, which in turn were followed by four-part vocal harmonies. The Galactic Cowboys' flair for innovation was further confirmed by 1993's *Space In Your Face*, a second chapter in what promises to be an intriguing career. Following their departure from MCA, they signed to the specialist label Metal Blade and produced a highly commercial album, *Machine Fish*. Sonnier was replaced by Wally Farkas.

● ALBUMS: *Galactic Cowboys* (MCA 1991)★★★★, *Space In Your Face* (MCA 1993)★★★, *Machine Fish* (Metal Blade 1996)★★★, *The Horse That Bud Bought* (Metal Blade 1997)★★★.

GALLAGHER, RORY

b. 2 March 1949, Ballyshannon, Co. Donegal, Eire, d. 15 June 1995. Having served his musical apprenticeship in the Fontana and Impact Showbands, Gallagher put together the original Taste in 1965. This exciting blues-based rock trio rose from regional obscurity to the verge of international fame, but broke up acrimoniously five years later. Gallagher was by then a guitar hero and embarked on a solo voyage supported by Gerry McAvoy (bass) and Wilgar Campbell (drums). He introduced an unpretentious approach, which marked a career that deftly retained all the purpose of the blues without erring on the side of excessive reverence. Gallagher's early influences were Lonnie Donegan, Woody Guthrie, Chuck Berry and Muddy Waters and he strayed very little from those paths. The artist's refreshing blues guitar work, which featured his confident bottleneck playing, was always of interest and by 1972 Gallagher was a major live attraction. Campbell was replaced by Rod De'ath following the release of *Live In Europe*, while Lou Martin was added on keyboards. This line-up remained constant for the next six years and was responsible for Gallagher's major commercial triumphs, *Blueprint* and *Irish Tour '74*. De'ath and Martin left the group in 1978. Former Sensational Alex Harvey Band drummer Ted McKenna joined the ever-present McAvoy but was in turn replaced by Brendan O'Neill. Former Nine Below Zero member and blues harmonica virtuoso Mark Feltham became a full-time 'guest', as Gallagher quietly continued with his career. Shunning the glitzy aspect of the music business, he toured America over 30 times in addition to touring the globe twice. His record sales reached several millions and he retained a fiercely loyal following. He had several opportunities to record with his heroes, such as Donegan, Waters, Jerry Lee Lewis and Albert King, and his love for his homeland resulted in contributions to the work of the Fureys, Davy Spillane and Joe O'Donnell. Gallagher retained his perennial love for the blues, his original Stratocaster guitar (now badly battered) and the respect of many for his uncompromising approach. He died following complications after a liver transplant in 1995.

● ALBUMS: *Rory Gallagher* (Polydor 1971)★★★, *Deuce* (Polydor 1971)★★★, *Live! In Europe* (Polydor 1972)★★★, *Blueprint* (Polydor 1973)★★★★, *Tattoo* (Polydor 1973)★★★★, *Irish Tour '74* (Polydor 1974), *Saint ... And Sinner* (Polydor 1975)★★★, *Against The Grain* (Chrysalis 1975)★★★, *Calling-Card* (Chrysalis 1976)★★★, *Photo Finish* (Chrysalis 1978)★★★, *Top Priority* (Chrysalis 1979)★★★, *Stage Struck* (Chrysalis 1980)★★★, *Jinx* (Chrysalis 1982)★★★, *Defender* (Demon 1987)★★, *Fresh Evidence* (Castle 1990)★★.

● COMPILATIONS: *In The Beginning* (Emerald 1974)★★★, *The Story So Far* (Polydor 1976)★★★, *The Best Years* (1976)★★★, *Best Of Rory Gallagher And Taste* (Razor 1988)★★★★, *Edged In Blue* (Demon 1992)★★★, *Rory Gallagher Boxed* 4-CD box set (1992)★★★.

● VIDEOS: *Live In Cork* (Castle Hendring Video 1989).

GAMMA

After the failure of his solo album, Colorado-born guitarist Ronnie Montrose reunited with former Montrose members Jim Alcivar (keyboards) and Alan Fitzgerald (bass) and, with the addition of Davey Patison on vocals and Skip Gallette on drums, formed Gamma in 1979. Following the release of a debut album, the line-up changed, with another ex-Montrose member, Denny Carmassi, taking over drumming duties, and newcomer Glen Letsch on bass. This new line-up recorded *Gamma 2* - a much stronger album that spawned a hit single in 'Voyager' and a successful tour of America and Europe. Alcivar left soon afterwards to be replaced by Mitchell Froom (ex-Bruzer). Despite being a fine synthesizer player in his own right, his input led to keyboard saturation on the third album, relegating Montrose's perennially excellent guitar-playing to secondary status. Gamma then toured with Foreigner in 1983 but failed to record again as Montrose attempted to re-form the band of his name with original vocalist Sammy Hagar. Davey Pattison later surfaced with Robin Trower, and Montrose, never fulfilling his wish, returned to a solo career.

● ALBUMS: *Gamma* (Elektra 1979)★★, *Gamma 2* (Elektra 1980)★★★★, *Gamma 3* (Elektra 1982)★★★.

GAMMA RAY

After leaving Helloween in 1989, the band he founded, guitarist Kai Hansen teamed up with ex-Tyran Pace vocalist Ralf Scheepers. The intention was to record an album of existing material that had been deemed unsuitable for Hansen's previous band. Joining them for this proposed project were Uwe Wessel (bass), Mathias Burchardt (drums) and a host of guest musicians. Signing to Noise Records they entered the Horus Sound Studios in Germany with producer Tommy Newton. The resulting recordings were released under the Gamma Ray moniker as *Heading For Tomorrow* in 1990. The album was an excellent blend of powerful melodic heavy metal, with song structures reminiscent of Queen. Having proved a favourite with press and public alike, Hanson began to realize the group's potential and decided to form a working unit out of the musicians who had played on the project to tour in support of the album. The fully assembled Gamma Ray consisted of Ralf Scheepers (vocals), Hansen (guitar, vocals), Dirk Schlacter (guiter), Wessel (bass) and Uli Kusch (drums). They toured extensively throughout Europe and Japan where they gained a substantial following, and, as a stop-gap between albums, released an EP of new material, *Heaven Can Wait*. Come the next album, *Sigh No More*, the band were in fine form; extensive touring had disciplined them into a tight, cohesive unit. Though heavier than its predecessor the album boasted high-quality heavy metal with melody and power, serving as a more than worthy encore to their impressive debut. *Land Of The Free*, however, revealed little in the way of progression, relying heavily on Hansen's virtuoso guitar to provide texture for the lacklustre songwriting.

● ALBUMS: *Heading For Tomorrow* (Noise 1990)★★★, *Sigh No More* (Noise 1991)★★★, *Land Of The Free* (Noise 1995)★★.

Ganafoul

Prior to the breakthrough of Trust and Telephone, rated among the best hard rock bands working in France were Ganafoul. Comprising Jack Bon (vocals, guitar), Jean Yves Astier (bass, vocals) and Yves Rotacher (drums), their music relied on the type of 12-bar blues boogie patented by Status Quo. However, their execution of similar material was altogether tougher, drawing equally on the nascent punk tradition for their rhythmic attack. After their 1977 debut, a cheaply produced and packaged but still incendiary collection entitled *Side 3*, Rotacher was replaced on drums by Bernard Antoine, who provided more percussive versatility. Subsequent albums for Crypto Records continued to follow the group's *oeuvre* of stylistically delimited but brutally played hard rock, which found a ready audience on France's late 70s club circuit.

● ALBUMS: *Side 3* (Crypto 1977)★★★, *Full Speed Ahead* (Crypto 1978)★★★★, *Live* (Crypto 1979)★★, *Saturday Night* (Crypto 1980)★★★, *T'as Failli Crever* (Crypto 1981)★★★.

Gang Green

This quartet from Boston, Massachusetts, USA, specializing in a fusion of hardcore and thrash, was put together by guitarist/vocalist Chris Doherty. Although originally formed in 1982, it was the 1985 incarnation that secured a contract with Taang! Records (Doherty had spent some of the intervening period with Jerry's Kids). After numerous line-up changes, a degree of stability was achieved for *You Got It*, with Doherty, plus Brian Bertzger (drums), Fritz Erickson (guitar; replacing Chuck Stilphen), and Joe Gittleman (bass), the latter eventually replaced by ex-DRI member Josh Papp. Extolling the virtues of alcohol and skateboarding, and ridiculing the PMRC at every opportunity, their music was fast, aggressive and occasionally abusive. One career highlight was the mini-album *I81B4U*, where the group's irreverent sense of fun put 'two fingers up' at Van Halen's *OU812*. They also released one record as a skateboard-shaped picture disc. Unable to progress on the songwriting front, their sound, nevertheless, grew louder and more impressive as time wore on, particularly on *Older, Budweiser*, which took their obsession with the eponymous beer to excessive lengths. *Can't Live Without It* was a very loud live album.

● ALBUMS: *Another Wasted Night* (Taang! 1986)★★★, *You Got It* (Roadracer 1987)★★★, *I81B4U* mini-album (Roadracer 1988)★★★, *Older, Budweiser* (Emergo 1989), *Can't Live Without It* (Emergo 1990)★★, *King Of Bands* (Roadrunner 1991)★★★.

Gaskin

UK N.W.O.B.H.M. group Gaskin were led by namesake Paul Gaskin (vocals, guitar, keyboards) with Stef Prokopczuk (bass) and Dave Norman (drums). Formed in Scunthorpe, south Humberside, England, they secured a strong following in the north-east and Midlands club circuit, areas eternally receptive to unpretentious hard rock. Paul Gaskin's singing earned the group comparisons to Rush, though in truth his songwriting was closer in conception to N.W.O.B.H.M. peers such as Tygers Of Pan Tang or Def Leppard. The group recorded two disciplined, well-executed albums for Rondolet Records in the early 80s before disbanding. With Rondolet primarily a punk label, Gaskin felt out of place and with no new offers forthcoming, they had broken up permanently by 1984. Prokopczuk formed the short-lived Ace Lane.

● ALBUMS: *End Of The World* (Rondolet 1981)★★★, *No Way Out* (Rondolet 1982)★★★.

Gaye Bykers On Acid

This UK rock group employed an image that combined traditional biker attire with elements of psychedelia and hippie camp. They were led by the colourful figure of Mary Millington, aka Mary Mary (b. Ian Garfield Hoxley; vocals), alongside Kevin Hyde (drums), Robber (b. Ian Michael Reynolds; bass) and Tony (b. Richard Anthony Horsfall; guitar). They were later complemented by disc jockey William Samuel Ronald Monroe ('Rocket Ronnie'). Mary Mary, who had once come second in Leicester's Alternative Miss Universe competition, was often to be seen in platform shoes and dresses, which fuelled the critics' confusion with regard to the band's name and gender orientation. Their debut album, *Drill Your Own Hole*, required purchasers to do just that, as the record was initially issued without a hole in its centre. After leaving Virgin Records they set up their own label, Naked Brain, quite conceivably because nobody else would have them. Subsequent to the band's demise, which may or may not prove permanent, Hyde instigated a new band, GROWTH, with Jeff (ex-Janitors). Tony teamed up with Brad Bradbury in Camp Collision, while Mary Mary joined ex-members of Killing Joke, Ministry and Public Image Limited in the multi-member outfit Pigface.

The 90s brought a more permanent home for his talents in the shape of Hyperhead, a band he formed with Karl Leiker (ex-Luxuria; Bugblot).

● ALBUMS: *Drill Your Own Hole* (Virgin 1987)★★★, *Stewed To The Gills* (Virgin 1989)★★★, *GrooveDiveSoapDish* (Bleed 1989)★★★, *Cancer Planet Mission* (Naked Brain 1990)★★, as PFX *Pernicious Nonsense* (Naked Brain 1991)★★, *From The Tomb Of The Near Legendary* (1993)★★.

● VIDEOS: *Drill Your Own Hole* (Virgin Vision 1987).

GEDDES AXE

Far from having anything to do with a tribute to Rush's bass player, UK rock band Martin Wilson and Andrew Barrot took their name from a school book titled *Geddex Axe 1921-1922*. Coming together in 1980 with Andy Millard (vocals), Dave Clayton (drums) and Mick Peace (bass), the band decided to follow in the footsteps of fellow Sheffield citizens Def Leppard and record a self-financed EP. Entitled *Return Of The Gods*, it failed to generate the public interest that Def Leppard had aroused. After one further single, 'Sharpen Your Wits', the band underwent a major personnel change, with Barrot joining Baby Tuckoo (and later Chrome Molly), Millard and Clayton quitting, and being replaced with Nick Brown, Tony Rose and John Burke, respectively. A revamped live set included the progressive 'Valley Of The Kings' (sadly unrecorded) and cover versions of Kiss songs. The Bullet label picked up the band and released an improved 12-inch single, 'Escape From New York', but it failed to gain any ground for them and by 1983 they had again broken up.

GENITORTURERS

During the early 90s, sexual fetish trappings - such as rubber and leather garb and increasingly extravagant body piercings - became fashionable. It was no surprise, therefore, that a band surfaced who used elaborate sado-masochistic imagery as the basis for their act. The band in question was the Genitorturers, a Florida, USA death metal band who were discovered by IRS Records when they were looking for acts for a film featuring rock bands with spectacular stage shows. The film project was abandoned, but the Genitorturers secured a contract and recorded their sadist debut, *120 Days Of Genitorture*. The founder, vocalist and core of the band, Gen, is a statuesque dominatrix who is not only a professional body piercer but also works as an organ reclamation technician in a local hospital. She is a persuasive spokesperson for the new piercing ethos, which sees sado-masochism as not only a sexual, but a spiritual and tribal practice. This translates into an unforgettable stage show, featuring everything from whips and chains, to live nipple and genital piercing. Inevitably, the Genitorturers' striking visual aspects rather eclipse their music, which is a somewhat pedestrian blend of power metal and hardcore punk, combined with a few modern touches such as sampled dialogue. Gen's vocals are gruff and assertive, and the whole package is reminiscent of the Plasmatics, the punk posse of another blonde rock sex queen, Wendy O. Williams.

● ALBUMS: *120 Days Of Genitorture* (Under One Flag 1993)★★★, *Sin City* (SPV 1998)★★.

GEORDIE

From the north-east of England, Brian Johnson (b. 5 October 1947, Newcastle, England; vocals), Victor Malcolm (guitar), Tom Hill (bass) and Brian Gibson (drums) started life as a poor man's Slade. Their unconsciously professional style was based on the pop end of the hard rock spectrum, with a stage act that included an audience participation opus, the dialectal 'Geordie's Lost His Liggy', which involved Johnson hoisting Malcolm onto his shoulders. After one single for Regal Zonophone, 'Don't Do That', scraped the hit parade, they were signed by EMI Records, whose faith was justified when 'All Because Of You', from 1973's *Hope You Like It*, reached the UK Top 20. Two lesser entries - 'Can You Do It' and 'Electric Lady' - followed, and the group's albums sold steadily. Geordie's power as a concert attraction outlasted this chart run, and when the going became difficult in the watershed year of 1976-77, the quartet signed off with *Save The World* - a consolidation rather than development of their derivative music. They were remembered not for their hits, but as the *alma mater* of Johnson who, after a lean period in which he was heard in a vacuum cleaner commercial, replaced the late Bon Scott in AC/DC.

● ALBUMS: *Hope You Like It* (EMI 1973)★★★, *Masters Of Rock* (EMI 1974)★★, *Don't Be Fooled By The Name* (EMI 1974)★★, *Save The World* (EMI 1976)★★.

● COMPILATIONS: *Featuring Brian Johnson* (Red Bus 1981)★★.

GEORGE, ROBIN

The style of UK-born guitarist/producer Robin George, despite his geographical origins, is pure US AOR. George began his career with his band Life, who released one single, 'Too Late'. The line-up also included Dave Holland (later of Judas Priest) and Mark Stanway (later of Magnum). He then played guitar in the Byron Band, fronted by one-time Uriah Heep vocalist David Byron. His fine guitarwork can be heard to good effect on their debut album, *On The Rocks* (Creole Records), in 1981, though after a year with them he left to pursue a solo career. He first signed to Arista Records in 1983, cementing the relationship with the release of a single, 'Go Down Fighting', the melodic guitarwork of which quickly brought attention and a reputation as the UK's answer to Billy Squier. Despite this, Arista dropped him and he went on to work in a production capacity with Heavy Metal Records, helping various acts including Wrathchild (UK). In 1984 Bronze Records signed him, and the release of 'Heartline' preceded his first full album, *Dangerous Music* - both releases were noted for their pristine production and the basswork of Pino Pallidino (Paul Young Band). Despite the good auspices, 'Heartline' remained his only real success and was reissued in 1985, again selling well. He remained in production until 1990 when he formed a partnership with ex-Diamond Head vocalist Sean Harris in Notorious. This was an ill-fated project that advanced neither career, and they soon parted. George has since returned to the mixing desk.

● ALBUMS: *Dangerous Music* (Bronze 1984)★★★. With Notorious: *Notorious* (Bronze 1990)★★★.

● VIDEOS: *Dangerous Music* (1985).

Germs

Los Angeles, California, USA punk band the Germs were formed in April 1977. The original members were Darby Crash (b. Paul Beahm; vocals), Pat Smear (guitar), Lorna Doom (bass) and Belinda Carlisle (drums), later of the Go-Gos. She soon left and was replaced by a succession of percussionists, including future X drummer D.J. Bonebrake and Don Bolles of 45 Grave. The group's first single, 'Forming', was issued on What? Records in 1977 and is considered by some to be the first example of the post-punk 'hardcore' genre, later popularized by bands such as Black Flag and the Dead Kennedys. Their next single was issued on Slash Records, which in 1979 released the group's only album, *GI*. The group disbanded in early 1980 but re-formed later that year. A week after their first reunion concert, however, singer Crash died of a heroin overdose. Smear later worked with Nirvana and the Foo Fighters. The catalyst to a thousand US punk bands, though few modelled themselves on Crash's legendary self-destructive nature, the Germs were fated only ever to offer a musical flashpoint rather than a career blueprint. A tribute album was issued in 1996 featuring White Zombie, Courtney Love, the Melvins, Mudhoney and others.

● ALBUMS: *GI* (Slash 1979)★★★, *Germicide - Live At The Whisky* 1977 recording (ROIR 1982)★★, *Rock N' Rule* 1979 recording (XES 1986)★★.

● COMPILATIONS: *What We Do Is Secret* (Slash 1981)★★, *Let The Circle Be Unbroken* (Gasatanka 1985)★★, *Lion's Share* (Ghost O' Darb 1985)★★, *MIA* (Slash 1994)★★.

Giant

Originating from Nashville, USA, Giant developed in the mid-80s when seasoned session guitarist Dann Huff met with keyboard player Alan Pasqua on various projects, notably Whitesnake's *1987* album. However, it was not until 1988 that Giant evolved into a fully fledged unit, with Huff's younger brother, David, joining as drummer and Mike Brignardello on bass (the Huff brothers had formerly been in partnership as part of Christian rockers White Heart). By this time, Dann Huff had taken on lead vocal duties after an unsuccessful search for a suitable singer. Candidates for the job had included the highly successful songwriter and backing vocalist, Tom Kelly. Giant signed to A&M Records in 1988 and released their debut album, *Last Of The Runaways*, in the USA in 1989, a potent brew of hard rock, strong on melody and presentation. It included the Top 10 hit single, 'I'll See You In My Dreams'. The success of the album and single in the USA and impressive sales on import in the UK prompted A&M to give *Last Of The Runaways* a European release in 1990, to a moderate degree of success. This was followed by a series of highly acclaimed club dates around the UK. In 1991, Huff, Pasque and Brignardello played together on Amy Grant's *Heart In Motion*, and prepared material for a new album. However, *Time To Burn* did not feature Pasqua, and though it was again critically lauded, soon after its release Epic, to whom Giant had transferred, dropped the band.

● ALBUMS: *Last Of The Runaways* (A&M 1989)★★★★, *Time To Burn* (Epic 1992)★★★.

Gilgames J

Comprising Frank Van Stijn (vocals), Henry Van Santen (guitar), Gerry Den Hartog (guitar), Jan Vos (bass) and Hans Laponder (drums), Dutch heavy metal band Gilgames J made their debut in 1982 with a track on the compilation album *Metal Clogs*. Two years later they followed it with their debut album for the same label, *Take One*. Self-evidently influenced by other mainland European bands such as the Scorpions and Gamma, their forceful but uninspiring melodic hard rock failed to build an audience beyond the Netherlands, and there was no follow-up.

● ALBUMS: *Take One* (Rave On 1984)★★.

GILLAN, IAN

b. 19 August 1945, Hounslow, Middlesex, England. Heavily influenced by Elvis Presley, vocalist Gillan formed his first band at the age of 16. In 1962 he was invited to join local semi-professional R&B band the Javelins, who eventually disbanded in March 1964. Gillan next formed the Hickies, but abandoned the project to join established soul band Wainwright's Gentlemen. He quickly became unhappy with this group and readily accepted an invitation to join the fully professional outfit Episode Six, in May 1965. A succession of tours and singles failed to produce any domestic chart placings, however, and by early 1969 the band was beginning to disintegrate. In August of the same year, Gillan and Roger Glover were recruited to join Deep Purple, forming the legendary 'Mk II' line-up with Ritchie Blackmore, Jon Lord and Ian Paice. Deep Purple gradually established themselves as a major rock band, helped by their dynamic live show and an aggressive sound, characterized by a mix of long instrumentals and Gillan's powerful vocals. The latter part of 1972 saw Deep Purple, acknowledged as the biggest-selling rock band in the world, enter the *Guinness Book Of Records* as the loudest pop group of their day. Their status was consolidated with the release of the live album *Made In Japan*. In August 1972 Gillan decided to leave the band, but was persuaded to remain with them until June 1973. By the time of his last show with Deep Purple on 28 June, he had already purchased the De Lane Lea studio in London, and it was on this venture that he concentrated after leaving the band, forming Kingsway Studios.

He recorded a solo album in 1974 for the Purple label, to whom he was still signed, but it was rejected as being too radical a musical departure, and has never been released. After a brief attempt to launch Ian Gillan's Shand Grenade, which included Glover, in late 1975, it was the Ian Gillan Band that began recording *Child In Time* in the first days of 1976. The line-up was Gillan, Ray Fenwick (guitar), Mike Moran (keyboards), Mark Nauseef (drums; ex-Elf) and John Gustafson (bass). This first album was much lighter in tone than Deep Purple, but included some excellent songs. The next two albums, now with Colin Towns on keyboards, demonstrated a notable jazz-rock influence, particularly on *Clear Air Turbulence*, which was also distinguished by its striking Chris Foss-designed cover. None of these albums was particularly successful commercially, and after a disappointing tour in spring 1978, Gillan disbanded the group.

Within just a few months of dissolving the Ian Gillan Band, he was back in the studio with a new outfit, inspired by a Towns song, 'Fighting Man'. New members Leon Genocky (drums), Steve Byrd (guitar) and John McCoy (bass) joined Ian Gillan and Towns to record *Gillan* in summer 1978. The lack of a record contract meant that this excellent album was never released in the UK, although several of the tracks did appear on the next album, *Mr. Universe*, recorded early in 1979 with Pete Barnacle on drums. The title track was based on a song of the same name that Ian Gillan had recorded with Episode Six. The album as a whole marked the return of the imposing frontman to solid rock music. In so doing, this collection was instrumental in developing the New Wave Of British Heavy Metal, a label even more applicable to Gillan's subsequent album, *Glory Road*. Now with Bernie Torme on guitar and former Episode Six drummer Mick Underwood, Gillan produced one of his finest albums, the first copies of which contained a second, free album, *For Gillan Fans Only*. After the slightly disappointing *Future Shock*, Torme left to be replaced by guitarist Janick Gers of White Spirit, who featured on *Double Trouble*, a double album comprising one studio and one live album, recorded mainly at the 1981 Reading Rock Festival, at which the band appeared for the third consecutive year, a testimony to their popularity. Summer 1982 saw the release of *Magic*, another album of quality, although sadly also the group's last. After many years of speculation and rumour, a Deep Purple re-formation seemed imminent and Gillan wound up his band amid a certain amount of acrimony and uncertainty, early in 1983. Finding that he had ended Gillan somewhat prematurely, he joined Black Sabbath, a move he claims was motivated by financial necessity. Artistically, the time he spent with this band is deplored by both Gillan and Sabbath fans. After one album and a tour with Sabbath, the much discussed Deep Purple reunion took off and Gillan had his opportunity to escape. After 11 years apart, and all with successful, if turbulent careers during that time, the essential question remained as to whether the various band members would be able to co-operate. A successful tour and a sell-out British concert at the 1985 Knebworth Festival seemed to suggest the reunion had worked, but by the time of the next album, *House Of The Blue Light*, it was clear that the latent tensions within the band were beginning to reappear. Between Deep Purple tours, and adding to the speculation about a break-up, Gillan and Glover recorded an album together; a curious but thoroughly enjoyable collection of material, it seemed to fulfil a need in both musicians to escape from the confines of the parent band. The 1988/9 Deep Purple tour revealed the true extent of the rift between the members, and Gillan's departure was formally announced in May 1989. The collaboration had been effectively finished since January, when he was informed that he need not attend rehearsals for the next album. Gillan's response was to perform a short tour as his alter ego, Garth Rockett, in spring 1989, before recording vocals for the Rock Aid Armenia version of 'Smoke On The Water', in July.

By the end of 1989 Gillan had assembled a band to record a solo album, which he financed himself to escape record company pressures, and recorded under his own name to avoid the politics of group decisions. The line-up featured Steve Morris (guitar), from the Garth Rockett tour, Chris Glen (bass) and Ted McKenna (drums), both formerly of the Michael Schenker Group, Tommy Eyre (keyboards), Mick O'Donoghue (ex-Grand Prix; rhythm guitar) and Dave Lloyd (ex-Nutz, Rage and 2am; backing vocals, percussion). The album, *Naked Thunder*, released in July 1990, was labelled middle-of-the-road by some critics, while Gillan himself described it as 'hard rock with a funky blues feel.' After touring in support of it, Gillan returned to the studio to prepare a second solo album. Now formulating a highly productive partnership with Steve Morris, he recruited Brett Bloomfield (bass) and Leonard Haze (ex-Y&T; drums) and produced an excellent album as a four-piece rock band, blending straightforward music with Gillan's often bizarre sense of humour and offbeat lyrics. *Toolbox* was released in October 1991 to critical acclaim. Gillan rejoined Deep Purple in 1992, undertaking new recording sessions with the band and touring, before yet again quitting. However, the career decision taken in 1994 was indeed a strange one, seeing him reunited with his very first band, the Javelins, for a moribund collection of 60s cover versions. His third solo album, *Dreamcatcher*, was a poor attempt at a more acoustic style. However, Gillan's durability alone makes him a central player in the British rock tradition, despite occasional lapses.

● ALBUMS: as Ian Gillan Band *Child In Time* (Oyster 1976)★★★, *Clear Air Turbulence* (Island 1977)★★, *Scarabus* (Scarabus 1977)★★, *I.G.B. Live At The Budokan* (Island 1978)★★, *Live At The Rainbow* recorded 1977 (Angel Air 1998)★★. As Gillan *Gillan* (Eastworld 1978)★★, *Mr. Universe* (Acrobat 1979)★★, *Glory Road* (Virgin 1980)★★★★, *Future Shock* (Virgin 1981)★★★, *Double Trouble* (Virgin 1982)★★★, *Magic* (Virgin 1982)★★★, *Live At The Budokan* (Virgin 1983)★★, *What I Did On My Vacation* (Virgin 1986)★★, *Live At Reading 1980* (Raw Fruit 1990)★★, *Dead Of Night: The BBC Tapes Volume 1 1979* (RPM 1998)★★, *Unchain Your Brain: The BBC Tapes Volume 2 1980* (RPM 1998)★★. As Garth Rockett *Story Of* (Rock Hard 1990)★★★. With the Javelins *Raving ... With The Javelins* (RPM 1994)★★. As Ian Gillan *Naked Thunder* (East West 1990)★★★, *Toolbox* (East West 1991)★★★, *Dreamcatcher* (Carambi 1997)★★.

● COMPILATIONS: With Episode Six *Put Yourself In My Place* (PRT 1987)★★. With Gillan/Glover *Accidentally On Purpose* (Virgin 1988)★★, *Trouble: The Best Of* (Virgin 1991)★★★, *The Japanese Album* (East West 1993)★★★.

● VIDEOS: *Gillan Live At The Rainbow 1978* (Spectrum 1988), *Ian Gillan Band* (Spectrum 1990), *Ian Gillan Live* (Castle 1992). As Garth Rockett And The Moonshiners *Live* (Fotodisk 1990).

● FURTHER READING: *Child In Time: The Life Story Of The Singer From Deep Purple*, Ian Gillan with David Cohen.

GIRL

A band very much ahead of their time, Girl's lipstick and glam image, portrayed on the cover of their debut, *Sheer Greed*, was quite a shock to the traditional UK heavy metal community during the rise of the New Wave Of British Heavy Metal, despite the existence of more outrageous glam bands in the preceding decade. Recorded with a line-up of Philip Lewis (vocals), Phil Collen (b. 8 December 1957, Hackney, London, England; guitar), brothers Gerry (guitar) and Simon Laffy (bass), and Dave Gaynor (drums), *Sheer Greed* was an impressive slice of sleazy hard rock, but was overshadowed by the band's image and by publicity surrounding Lewis's relationship with actress Britt Ekland. Although the band were a capable live act, and were given great exposure by support slots on major UK tours with the Pat Travers Band and UFO (twice), they failed to capture the public's imagination. *Wasted Youth*, with Pete Barnacle taking over on drums, paled beside the debut, and the band, dispirited, dissolved as Collen was invited to join Def Leppard. A third, currently unreleased album, exists on tape. Lewis later became frontman for L.A. Guns, with whom he re-recorded 'Hollywood Tease', the opening track on *Sheer Greed*, and the success of this band, along with the likes of Poison and Guns N'Roses, suggests that Girl may have met a better fate had they appeared only a few years later.

● ALBUMS: *Sheer Greed* (Jet 1980)★★★, *Wasted Youth* (Jet 1982)★★.

GIRLS AGAINST BOYS

Evocative US alternative rock band Girls Against Boys formed originally in Washington, DC, in 1990, but soon relocated to New York. A quartet of Scott McCloud (vocals, guitar), Alexis Fleisig (drums), Eli Janney (bass, keyboards) and Johnny Temple (bass), had all formerly been part of Dischord Records recording artists Soulside (Janney was that group's sound engineer). Having recorded two albums together, they broke up at the end of the 80s before Janney and McCloud elected to continue working together. This collaboration soon evolved to encompass their former Soulside bandmates in time for their debut *Nineties Vs. Eighties* EP. A debut album, also for Adult Swim Records, followed, before the group moved to Chicago independent Touch And Go Records. Following the release of 'Bulletproof Cupid', they recorded *Venus Luxure No. 1 Baby* for the label in 1993. By now the group's sound had been clearly established, with McCloud's insular, melancholy lyrics driven by the group's distinctive double-bass sound. 1994's *Cruise Yourself* was another acclaimed release, with songs such as '(I) Don't Get A Place' earning particular praise. Again, the group's sound remained somehow foreboding, but McCloud's narratives were maturing rapidly and by this time the band had become popular fixtures on the US alternative rock scene (despite several snipes from puritanical hardcore fans who had formerly supported the band in their original incarnation as Soulside). *House Of GVSB* refined previous musical currents and was just as disquieting an aural experience, with outstanding songs such as 'Vera Cruz' and 'Click Click' twisting sexual themes into startling new shapes. McCloud, ironically, was widely cited as the US underground's latest pin-up - despite the barbed nature of most of his lyrics. The band made their major label debut with 1998's disappointingly pedestrian *Freak*on*ica*.

● ALBUMS: *Nineties Vs. Eighties* mini-album (Adult Swim 1990)★★★, *Tropic Of Scorpio* (Adult Swim 1992)★★★, *Venus Luxure No. 1 Baby* (Touch And Go 1993)★★★★, *Cruise Yourself* (Touch And Go 1994)★★★, *House Of GVSB* (Touch And Go 1996)★★★, *Freak*on*ica* (Geffen 1998)★★.

GIRLSCHOOL

The all-female heavy metal band had its origins in Painted Lady, founded by teenagers Enid Williams (bass, vocals) and Kim McAuliffe (b. 13 April 1959; guitar, vocals). The remaining members of Painted Lady went on to form Tour De Force. After Kelly Johnson (guitar, vocals) and Denise Dufort (drums) had joined in 1978 the name became Girlschool and the independently produced single, 'Take It All Away', for City Records, led to a tour with Motörhead. As a direct result of Lemmy's sponsorship of the band they signed to the Bronze label in 1980, for whom Vic Maile produced the first two albums. There was a minor hit with a revival of Adrian Gurvitz's 'Race With The Devil', a 1968 success for Gun, before the group combined with Motörhead to reach the UK Top 10 as Headgirl with an EP entitled *St Valentine's Day Massacre*. The lead track was a frenetic version of Johnny Kidd's 'Please Don't Touch'. Girlschool had smaller hits later in 1981 with 'Hit And Run' and 'C'mon Let's Go', but soon afterwards a bored Williams was replaced by former Killjoys bass player Gill Weston (introduced to the band by Lemmy). Williams went on to form melodic rockers Framed, record two singles with Sham 69's Dave Parsons, and work on sessions with disco producer Biddu, before joining Moho Pack. Later she also sang, variously, country and opera (appearing in Fay Weldon's *The Small Green Space* and her own opera, *The Waterfall*) and taught performance and vocal skills. Girlschool, meanwhile, persevered, with Slade's Noddy Holder and Jim Lea producing the glam-influenced *Play Dirty*, which found the group opting for a more mainstream rock sound. In 1984 Johnson left the band for an unsuccessful solo career (later abandoning music and taking up sign language to work with the deaf) and Girlschool added guitarist Chris Bonacci and lead singer Jacqui Bodimead from Canis Major. The group also switched visual style towards a more glam rock look as they recorded 'I'm The Leader Of The Gang' with Gary Glitter in 1986. After the departure of Weston in 1987, ex-Rock Goddess bass player Tracey Lamb was enlisted, while McAuliffe left to work with punk singer Beki Bondage and present the cable show *Raw Power*. She also wrote an unpublished script for a rock show with Philthy Taylor of Motörhead, and later formed Strange Girls with Toyah, Dufort and Williams. Girlschool persevered, but split following a Russian tour supporting Black Sabbath. In the 90s McAuliffe re-formed the group with the addition of ex-Flatmates bass player Jackie Carrera.

● ALBUMS: *Demolition* (Bronze 1980)★★, *Hit 'N' Run* (Bronze 1981)★★★, *Screaming Blue Murder* (Bronze 1982)★★★, *Play Dirty* (Bronze 1983)★★★, *Running Wild* (Mercury 1985)★★, *Nightmare At Maple Cross* (GWR 1986)★★, *Take A Bite* (GWR 1988)★★, *Live* (Communiqué 1995)★★, *Race With The Devil (Live)* (Receiver 1998)★★, *Live On The King Biscuit Flower Hour* recorded 1984 (Strange Fruit 1998)★★.

● COMPILATIONS: *Race With The Devil* (Raw Power 1986)★★★, *Cheers You Lot* (Razor 1989)★★, *Collection* (Castle 1991)★★★, *From The Vaults* (Sequel 1994)★★.

● VIDEOS: *Play Dirty Live* (1984), *Bronze Rocks* (1985).

Giuffria

This US band was formed in 1981 by Greg Giuffria (keyboards) when his previous band, Angel, split up. His first step was to secure a good rhythm section consisting of Chuck Wright (bass) and Alan Krigger (drums), and David Glen Eisley (vocals). Rough Cutt guitarist Craig Goldy joined after his former group disintegrated. In 1984 Giuffria's self-titled debut album, released on MCA, demonstrated a melodic rock band that sounded symphonic in places and could have been mistaken for Angel on some tracks. Greg Giuffria referred to their music as 'cinema rock'. After the promotional tour for the album, Goldy left to join Driver and, subsequently, Ronnie James Dio, while Wright returned to session work. They were replaced by Lanny Cordola (guitar) and David Sikes (bass). As a result of these personnel changes, the follow-up album, *Silk And Steel*, was not released until August 1986. This was very much a continuation of their first album - it did not sell in anything like sufficient quantities and in 1987 MCA dropped the group. Giuffria, Cordola, Wright, Ken Mary (drums) and David Glen Eisley attempted to start again. They gained some support from Gene Simmons of Kiss, who had just set up his own record label. However, Simmons insisted that the name be changed to House Of Lords, and that James Christian should replace Eisley on vocals.

● ALBUMS: *Giuffria* (MCA 1984)★★, *Silk And Steel* (MCA 1986)★★.

Glitterbox

Comprising vocalist Jonny Green, guitarist/vocalist Michael Heseltine and drummer Mark Servas, the three members of Glitterbox originally met while attending college lectures in Norwich, Norfolk. In the early 90s they moved to London and shared a flat. With the addition of bass player Tony Holland, they played their first gig together in early 1994. At this stage operating under the name She, they began touring as a fully functioning unit a year later. Demos were produced and, the band claimed, interested parties from American record companies flew over on Concorde to try to sign the band. They elected to join Atlantic Records subsidiary Radar before starting on sessions for their debut album. However, it was then the group encountered the first of a series of problems. A female R&B band signed to Death Row Records, also entitled She, threatened to sue them if they did not change their name. The quartet thus became Glitterbox 'because glitter rhymes with shitter'. Green was then struck down by a serious throat virus. *Tired & Tangled* eventually emerged in 1998, two years after it was originally recorded. The acknowledged influences at work here included Flaming Lips and Afghan Whigs, two groups with a similar 'off-kilter' attitude to hard rock music.

● ALBUMS: *Tied & Tangled* (Radar/Atlantic 1998)★★★.

Glory Bell's Band

From Sweden, Glory Bell's Band was led by Glory North (vocals), a consummate live performer of considerable local reputation. Together with Miguel Santana (guitar), Franco Santuione (guitar), Marks Anderson (guitar, keyboards), Bob Anderson (bass) and Peter Udd (drums), the band made its debut in 1982 with *Dressed In Black*. A solid collection of hard-rock songs distinguished by the presence of three fluent guitarists, early reviews compared the group to Judas Priest. Three years later a follow-up collection was released, but *Century Rendezvous* failed to break the group outside of Scandinavia. No further recordings have been issued.

● ALBUMS: *Dressed In Black* (SOS 1982)★★★, *Century Rendezvous* (SOS 1985)★★.

GLOVER, ROGER

b. 30 November 1945, Brecon, Wales. Bassist Glover's professional musical career began when his group, the Madisons, amalgamated with fellow aspirants the Lightnings to form Episode Six. This popular act released nine singles between 1966 and 1969, but eclectic interests - including harmony pop, MOR and progressive rock-styled instrumentals - engendered a commercial impasse. Frustrated, both Glover and vocalist Ian Gillan then accepted an offer to join Deep Purple, where they enjoyed considerable international acclaim. However, clashes with guitarist Ritchie Blackmore led to Glover's sacking in 1973, although he remained nominal head of A&R at Purple Records, the group's custom-created label. Glover later embarked on a successful career in production with Nazareth, Status Quo, Judas Priest and Rory Gallagher. In 1974 Glover was commissioned to write the music to *The Butterfly Ball*, which in turn inspired a book, illustrated by Alan Aldridge, and film. The album featured the services of David Coverdale, Glenn Hughes and Ronnie James Dio. He recorded a solo album, *Elements*, which again boasted the assistance of vocalist Dio, but Glover surprised several commentators in 1979 by rejoining Blackmore in Rainbow. Any lingering animosity was further undermined in 1984 when both musicians were active in a rekindled Deep Purple which, although unable to recreate the halcyon days of the early 70s, proved to be a much in-demand live attraction.

● ALBUMS: *The Butterfly Ball* (Purple 1975)★★★, *Elements* (Polydor 1978)★★, *Mask* (Polydor 1984)★★, with Ian Gillan *Accidentally On Purpose* (Virgin 1988)★★★.

GODDO

Hard rock band Goddo were formed in Canada in the late 70s after bass player and vocalist Greg Godovitz had left his previous employers, the briefly successful pop band Fludd. Together with Gino Scarpelli (guitar) and Doug Inglis (drums), Goddo allowed him to indulge his twin passions - one for dynamic, gritty rock music and the other for articulate but esoteric lyrics. The group's irreverent sense of humour was celebrated in their album titles as well as lyrics, and each of their three albums for Polydor Records in the late 70s impressed with their musical adventurousness. By the 80s the group had switched to Attic Records, but neither *Pretty Bad Boys* nor the live set, *Live, Best Seat In The House*, managed to secure mainstream success. This was a great pity, as Godovitz remains one of Canada's unsung talents, a genuine maverick in the contemporary recording industry.

● ALBUMS: *Goddo* (Polydor 1977)★★★, *Who Cares* (Polydor 1978)★★★, *An Act Of Goddo* (Polydor 1979)★★, *Pretty Bad Boys* (Attic 1981)★★, *Live, Best Seat In The House* (Attic 1981)★★.

GODFLESH

The Godflesh partnership was inaugurated by Justin Broadrick (guitar, vocals) and G. Christian Green (bass) in 1988, when the former left the venerated (by UK radio presenter John Peel, at least) hardcore industrial trio, Head Of David. Green had formerly served time in industrialists Fall Of Because, and Godflesh were completed by the addition of a drum machine. A self-titled EP was released on the Swordfish label before moving to the more permanent home of Earache Records. By the advent of their debut album, the group had expanded temporarily to include guitarist Paul Neville (also ex-Fall Of Because). With strong critical reaction, they toured with Loop and as part of the Earache Grindcrusher USA package, alongside Napalm Death. Broadrick had actually appeared with the latter as guitarist on side one of the legendary *Scum* album. In 1991 there were three limited edition 12-inches (including one for the Sub Pop empire), which were eventually collected together as the *Slavestate* mini-album. With Neville opting to concentrate on his own project, Cabel Regime, Robert Hampson of Loop stepped in for additional guitar duties on the group's excellently reviewed *Pure*. He would choose to stay at home, however, as the duo embarked on a promotional European tour. In 1993 Broadrick branched out by providing guitar tracks for labelmates Scorn (on their *Vae Solis* debut), and he also produced a 'biomechanical' remix of Pantera's 'Walk'. This 'biomechanical' method is described by Green as involving: 'stripping them (the tracks) down and reconstructing them from scratch with different drum patterns, different vocal lines etc.' Meanwhile, Godflesh's first own-name project in nearly two years, the *Merciless* EP, resurrected an eight-year-old Fall Of Because song. A major new work, *Selfless*, was a stunningly direct and brutal album from a band whose quality threshold has hardly wavered since their inception. *Songs Of Love And Hate* was challenging and provocative and arguably their finest work to date. Drummer Mantia left to join Primus in August 1996.

● ALBUMS: *Streetcleaner* (Earache 1989)★★★,

Slavestate mini-album (Earache 1990)★★★, *Pure* (Earache 1992)★★★, *Selfless* (Earache 1994)★★★, *Songs Of Love And Hate* (Earache 1996)★★★, *Love And Hate In Dub* remix album (Earache 1997).

GODZ

Originating from Cleveland, Ohio, USA, the Godz were a heavy metal band with a strong 'biker' image. Formed in 1977, they featured vocalist/bassist Eric Moore, guitarist Mark Chatfield, drummer Glen Cataline and guitarist/keyboard player Bob Hill. Their first album, produced by Grand Funk's Don Brewer, was an intensely powerful barrage with raw, gutsy vocals filtered through its core, which remains something of a metal minor-classic. *Nothing Is Sacred* was self-produced and featured Cataline on vocals, the most obvious contributory factor to the disappointment it brought on almost every level. The band split soon after the album's release. In 1985 Moore and Chatfield resurrected the name and a new partnership was forged with former Outlaws guitarist Freddy Salem and drummer Kevin Valentine. *I'll Get You Rockin'* materialized, but met with a lacklustre reception. In 1987 most of the album was remixed and re-recorded, with three new tracks added and re-released as *Mongolians*. However hard they have tried, the Godz have never recaptured the energy and excitement generated by their debut.

● ALBUMS: *The Godz* (Millenium 1978)★★★★, *Nothing Is Sacred* (Millenium 1979)★★, *I'll Get You Rockin'* (Heavy Metal 1985)★★, *Mongolians* (Grudge 1987)★★.

GOEDERT, RON

b. USA. Before embarking on a solo career Goedert had previously led White Witch. His new group, which featured Jerry Runyman on guitar, Riff West on bass and Jack West on drums, in addition to his own singing and keyboard playing, continued his fixation with 60s west coast counter-culture. The cover of *Breaking All The Rules* depicted Goedert in huge flared trousers, matching the esotericism of the lyrical contents. Similar to Hawkwind in its employment of far-flung themes, it failed to cultivate a similar niche audience.

● ALBUMS: *Breaking All The Rules* (Polydor 1980)★★.

GOGMAGOG

This group was formed in 1985 in London, England, by Jonathan King, who wanted to create some sort of heavy-metal theatre. At first he attracted the interest of Cozy Powell and John Entwistle, but they elected to concentrate on other projects. The line-up was eventually finalized as Paul Dianno (ex-Iron Maiden; vocals), Clive Burr (ex-Iron Maiden; drums), Pete Willis (ex-Def Leppard; guitar), Janick Gers (ex-White Spirit; guitar) and Neil Murray (ex-Whitesnake; bass), a line-up that saw Gogmagog christened a New Wave Of British Heavy Metal 'supergroup'. To test critical reaction, King put Gogmagog into a studio to record three songs that he had written with Russ Ballard. With these tracks in hand, King visited various major record companies to see if there was any support, and all showed a genuine interest in the project. The only stumbling block was King's insistence on a substantial advance, which saw him universally rejected. The project subsequently disintegrated, and the members of Gogmagog went their separate ways. After the group's demise, a three-track single appeared on Music For Nations subsidiary Food For Thought, entitled 'I Will Be There'. The group's music was in contradiction to the heavy metal tag it was given, being closer to pop, with only a slight nod towards the musicians' rock roots.

GOLDEN EARRING

Formed in the Hague, Netherlands, in 1961 by George Kooymans (b. 11 March 1948, the Hague, Netherlands; guitar, vocals) and Rinus Gerritsen (b. 9 August 1946, the Hague, Netherlands; bass, vocals) along with Hans Van Herwerden (guitar) and Fred Van Der Hilst (drums). The group, initially known as the Golden Earrings, subsequently underwent several changes before they secured a Dutch Top 10 hit with their debut release, 'Please Go' (1965). By this point Kooymans and Gerritsen had been joined by Frans Krassenburg (vocals), Peter De Ronde (guitar) and Jaap Eggermont (drums) and the revitalized line-up became one of the most popular 'nederbeat' attractions. Barry Hay (b. 16 August 1948, Fyzabad, India; lead vocals, flute, saxophone, guitar) replaced Krassenburg in 1966, while De Ronde also left the group as they embraced a more radical direction. The group's first Dutch number 1 hit, 'Dong-Dong-Di-Ki-Di-Gi-Dong', came in 1968 and saw them branching out from their homeland to other European countries as well as a successful tour of the USA. Eggermont left the group to become a producer and was eventually supplanted by Cesar Zuiderwijk (b. 18 July 1948, the Hague, Netherlands) in 1969 as Golden Earring began courting an international audience with their compulsive *Eight Miles High*, which featured an extended version of the famous Byrds song.

After years of experimenting with various music styles, they settled for a straight, hard rock sound and in 1972 Golden Earring were invited to support the Who on a European tour. They were subsequently signed to Track Records and the following year had a Dutch number 1/UK Top 10 hit with 'Radar Love' which subsequently found its way into the US Top 20 in 1974. Despite this, they were curiously unable to secure overseas success, which was not helped by a consistently unstable line-up. Robert Jan Stips augmented the quartet between 1974 and 1976 and on his departure Eelco Gelling joined as supplementary guitarist. By the end of the decade, however, the group had reverted to its basic line-up of Kooymans, Gerritsen, Hay and Zuiderwijk, who continued to forge an imaginative brand of rock and their reputation as a top European live act was reinforced by *Second Live*. With the release of *Cut* in 1982, Golden Earring earned themselves a US Top 10 hit with 'Twilight Zone'. This was followed by a triumphant tour of the USA and Canada, where further chart success was secured with 'Lady Smiles'. With various members able to indulge themselves in solo projects, Golden Earring have deservedly earned themselves respect throughout Europe and America as the Netherlands' longest surviving and successful rock group.

● ALBUMS: *Just Ear-rings* (Polydor 1965)★★★, *Winter Harvest* (Polydor 1966)★★★, *Miracle Mirror* (Polydor 1968)★★★, *On The Double* (Polydor 1969)★★★, *Reflections* (Polydor 1969)★★★, *Highlights From On The Double* (Polydor 1969)★★★, *Eight Miles High* (Polydor 1969)★★★, *Golden Earring (Wall Of Dolls)* (Polydor 1970)★★★, *Golden Earring* Box 5-LP box set (Polydor 1970)★★★★, *Seven Tears* (Polydor 1971)★★★, *Pophistory Vol 16* (Polydor 1971)★★★, *Together* (Polydor 1972)★★★, *Moontan* (Polydor 1973)★★★, *Switch* (Polydor 1975)★★★, *To The Hilt* (Polydor 1975)★★★, *Rock Of The Century* (Polydor 1976)★★★, *Contraband* (Polydor 1976)★★★, *Mad Love* (1977)★★★, *Live* (Polydor 1977)★★★, *Grab It For A Second* (Polydor 1978)★★★, *No Promises ... No Debts* (Polydor 1979)★★★, *Prisoner Of The Night* (Polydor 1980)★★★, *Second Live* (Polydor 1981)★★★, *Cut* (Mercury 1982)★★★, *Live Tracks* (Polydor 1983)★★★, *N.E.W.S. (North East West South)* (21 Records 1984)★★★, *Live And Pictured* (Polydor 1984)★★★, *Something Heavy Going Down - Live From The Twilight Zone* (21 Records 1984)★★★, *The Hole* (21 Records 1986)★★★, *Keeper Of The Flame* (Jaws 1989)★★★, *Bloody Buccaneers* (Columbia 1991)★★★, *The Naked Truth* (Columbia 1992)★★★, *Face It* (Columbia 1994).

Solo: George Kooymans *Jojo* (Polydor 1971)★★, *Solo* (Ring 1987)★★. Barry Hay *Only Parrots, Frogs And Angels* (Polydor 1972)★★★, *Victory Of Bad Taste* (Ring 1987)★★. Rinus Gerritsen and Michel Van Dijk *De G.V.D. Band* (Atlantic 1978)★★, *Labyrinth* (1985)★★.

● COMPILATIONS: *Hits Van De Golden Earrings* (Polydor 1967)★★★, *Greatest Hits* (Polydor 1968)★★★★, *Best Of Golden Earring* (1970)★★★, *Greatest Hits Volume 2* (Polydor 1970)★★★, *Superstarshine Vol. 1* (Polydor 1972)★★★, *Hearring Earring* (1973)★★★, *The Best Of Golden Earring* (Polydor 1974)★★★, *The Best Ten Years: Twenty Hits* (Arcade 1975)★★★, *Fabulous Golden Earring* (Polydor 1976)★★★, *The Golden Earring Story* (1978)★★★, *Greatest Hits Volume 3* (Polydor 1981)★★★, *Just Golden Earrings* (Polydor 1990)★★★, *The Complete Singles Collection 1 1965-1974* (Arcade 1992)★★★★, *The Complete Singles Collection 1975-1991* (Arcade 1992)★★★★.

GOLDFINGER

Goldfinger sprang from a new wave of punk bands formed in California, USA, in the wake of Green Day and the Offspring's international breakthrough. Based in Los Angeles, Goldfinger blend elements of ska and punk (*à la* Rancid and Reel Big Fish) with emocore (as pioneered by Guy Piccoloto's pre-Fugazi group, Rites Of Spring). The group comprises guitarist Charlie Paulson, vocalist/guitarist John Feldmann and rhythm team Darrin Pfeiffer and Simon Williams. In keeping with the traditions of the west coast punk scene (as opposed to its east coast and British counterparts), the group were wary of any 'radical punk' tag: 'Punk was about being different, about being against the establishment. We're on the Warped Tour. We're on MTV. How fucking against the establishment can we possibly be?'. It took Goldfinger some time to break through, however. Rick Rubin of American Records was among many who turned down their demo tape, stating that they were too close in sound to Green Day. Eventually, they signed with Mojo Records. Instead of political subjects, Feldmann's lyrics focus on the time-honoured frustrations of boy-girl relationships - he pointed out that: 'I write what I know. Relationships affect me like the IRA probably affects Bono.' He also confessed that one particular girl provided the inspiration for much of

Goldfinger's debut album; 'Only A Day' was about 'Wishing I could be with her', 'Here In Your Bedroom' about spending time with her, and 'Fuck You And Your Cat' concerned her decision to dump him.

● ALBUMS: *Goldfinger* (Mojo 1997)★★★.

Goo Goo Dolls

This US rock trio, formed in Buffalo, New York, in 1986, consists of bass player and vocalist Robby Takac, guitarist and vocalist Johnny Rzeznik and drummer George Tutuska. The group's first two albums were compared to Cheap Trick and the Replacements. They started doing unlikely cover versions on *Jed*, when the professional crooner Lance Diamond sang guest vocals on a version of Creedence Clearwater Revival's 'Down On The Corner'. He also sang on a version of Prince's 'I Could Never Take The Place Of Your Man' on *Hold Me Up*. Both albums featured unpretentious pop punk songwriting, and the band was now being celebrated by a growing number of fans in the media. Their commercial breakthrough came with 1995's hit single 'Name' and *A Boy Named Goo*, which was produced by Pere Ubu, Hüsker Dü and Sugar accomplice Lou Giordano. Their career showed signs of stalling in 1997 following litigation with their record company Warner Brothers Records and the departure of Tutuska, although 'Iris', taken from the soundtrack of *City Of Angels*, was an endearing radio hit.

● ALBUMS: *Goo Goo Dolls* (Mercenary/Celluloid 1987)★★, *Jed* (Death/Enigma 1989)★★, *Hold Me Up* (Metal Blade/Warners 1990)★★★, *Superstar Car Wash* (Metal Blade/Warners 1993)★★★, *A Boy Named Goo* (Metal Blade/Warners 1995)★★★★, *Dizzy Up The Girl* (Warners 1998)★★★.

Good Rats

This US group was formed while the members were at college in 1964 by Peppi and Mickey Marchello, both from Long Island, New York, USA. Their debut was a mixture of rock 'n' roll and progressive rock. A succession of poor-selling albums coupled with regular changes of record labels hampered their commercial prospects. They broke up for three years during 1969-72. By the time of their fourth and best album - *From Rats To Riches* - (which was later issued on Radar in the UK), the line-up was the gruff-voiced Peppi, Mickey (guitar), John 'the Cat' Gatto (guitar), Lenny Kotke (bass) and Joe Franco (drums). This album was recorded on Long Island in late 1977 with Flo And Eddie (Mark Volman and Howard Kaylan) producing. Although their place in the market was never clear they were essentially a good old-fashioned, basic US rock 'n' roll band.

● ALBUMS: *The Good Rats* (Kapp 1968)★★★, *Tasty* (Rat City 1974)★★, *Rat City In Blue* (Rat City 1976)★★, *From Rats To Riches* (Passport/Radar 1978)★★★, *Rats The Way You Like It - Live* (Passport 1978)★★, *Birth Comes To Us All* (Passport 1978)★★, *Live At Last* (Rat City 1980)★★, *Great American Music* (Great American/Passport 1981)★★.

● COMPILATIONS: *Tasty Seconds* (Uncle Rat Music 1997)★★★.

Goodwin, Myles

When Canadian hard rockers April Wine disintegrated in 1985, lead vocalist Goodwin embarked on a solo career. He immediately divorced himself from the style to which he was accustomed. Forsaking his blues-rock roots, he concentrated on MOR pop/rock with understated guitar and lightweight harmonies. Utilizing the services of session musicians, he recorded a self-titled debut on the Atlantic label in 1988. This failed to win a new audience, and at the same time alienated his former fanbase. The album sank without trace and little has been heard of him since.

● ALBUMS: *Myles Goodwin* (Atlantic 1988)★★.

Gordi

The pre-eminent hard rock group of Yugoslavia in the early 80s, Gordi comprised Zlatko Manojlovic (guitar, vocals), Slobodan Surdlan (bass, vocals) and Gedomir Petrovic (drums). Heavily influenced by British rock music, the sound they offered on their 1981 debut album, *Pakleni Trio*, was close in conception to that of Black Sabbath or Motörhead - albeit without the originality of songwriting. A follow-up collection released the following year, *Kraljica Smrti*, was just as brutal, and managed to secure a cult audience outside of central Europe. Sadly, the group found it difficult to gain work permits to tour outside of the Balkans, and this hampered their original impetus.

● ALBUMS: *Pakleni Trio* (LSY 1981)★★, *Kraljica Smrti* (Jugoton 1982)★★.

Gorefest

Formed in 1989, Dutch band Gorefest have managed to carve a niche for themselves in an increasingly overcrowded death metal genre, making their debut on the underground demo scene with two tapes, *Tangled In Gore* and *Horrors In A Retarded*

Mind. After *Mindloss*, they secured a contract with Nuclear Blast Records and released *False*. Gorefest's material is morbidly metaphysical, and at their best they manage to combine melodic and inventive riffs with an abrasive edge. A popular live band, they released a recording of their performance at 1993's Dynamo Open Air Festival as *The Eindhoven Insanity*, which some argue was the first ever live death metal album. *Erase* represented their most confident outing to date, and featured the line up of Jan-Chris De Koeijer (vocals, bass guitar), Frank Harthoorn (rhythm guitar), Boudewijn Bonebakker (lead, rhythm guitars) and Ed Warby (drums).

● ALBUMS: *Mindloss* (F2000 1991)★★, *False* (Nuclear Blast/Relapse 1992)★★★, *The Eindhoven Insanity* (Nuclear Blast/Relapse 1993)★★, *Erase* (Nuclear Blast/Relapse 1994)★★★★, *Soul Survivor* (Nucear Blast 1996)★★, *Chapter 13* (SPV 1997)★★★.

GORILLA

Formed in Derby, Derbyshire, England, in the mid-90s, experimental hard rock band Gorilla was formed when the Beyond's two albums failed to achieve either strong critical support or healthy sales. John Whitby (vocals), Andy Gatford (guitar), Jim Kersey (bass) and Neil Cooper (drums) added violinist Andy Lingard to complete the new line-up, making their debut in May 1995 with a four-track EP, *Extended Play*, on Embryo Records. A raw self-production, it saw the group receive excellent reviews, although it also marked the departure of Kersey, who had tired of living on the breadline in a fringe rock band.

GORKY PARK

Comprising Nikolai Naskov (vocals), Alex Belov (guitar), Jan Janewkow (guitar), Alexander Minkov (bass) and Sascha Lvov (drums), Russian hard rock band Gorky Park formed in the late 80s. They rose to international prominence at the 1989 Moscow Music And Peace Festival, where they shared a stage with Mötley Crüe, Bon Jovi and Ozzy Osbourne. Those artists were sufficiently impressed by Gorky Park's powerful stage show to spread news of them to the west, eventually resulting in a US release for their self-titled 1989 album. However, once the novelty of a Russian hard rock band had worn off, Gorky Park faced critical and commercial resistance to their unspectacular hard rock presentation.

● ALBUMS: *Gorky Park* (PolyGram 1989)★★.

GOUDREAU, BARRY

b. 29 November 1951, Boston, Massachusetts, USA. The original guitarist with Boston, Goudreau launched his solo career in 1980 following the release of that group's *Don't Look Back*. Much of the impetus behind his self-titled debut collection, which also included contributions from Boston colleagues Brad Delp and Sib Hashian, arose from Goudreau's frustration with Scholz's laborious studio methodology. *Barry Goudreau* reached number 88 in the *Billboard* album charts, an admirable feat for a debut album but a poor performance given the fact that both Boston's previous releases had topped the US charts. After its release he chose not to return to Boston but launched Orion The Hunter instead. They achieved a little success with their self-titled debut album in 1984, but thereafter Goudreau became embroiled in legal proceedings with his former Boston colleague Scholz. In 1991 he regrouped with Delp and Tim Archibald, Brian Mayes and Dave Stefanelli as R.T.Z. (Return To Zero).

● ALBUMS: *Barry Goudreau* (Portrait 1980)★★★.

GRAMM, LOU

Vocalist Lou Gramm (b. Lou Grammatico, 2 May 1950, Rochester, New York, USA) possesses one of the great hard-rock voices, and rose from small beginnings with late 60s group Poor Heart and Black Sheep to fame and fortune with Foreigner. After the enormous success of *Agent Provocateur*, however, Gramm's desire for more upbeat, guitar-based songs led him to write solo material with bassist friend Bruce Turgon. *Ready Or Not* was a satisfying solo debut, proving that Gramm could produce classy AOR material without Foreigner cohort Mick Jones, and produced a surprise hit in 'Midnight Blue'. Gramm returned to the Foreigner fold for *Inside Information*, but solo success had only increased the tension between Jones and the vocalist, and a split was inevitable. Gramm and Turgon worked together again on *Long Hard Look*, producing another US hit in 'Just Between You And Me', and Gramm's departure from Foreigner was confirmed as he embarked on a solo US tour, with Jones drafting in former Wild Horses (USA) vocalist Johnny Edwards for *Unusual Heat*, which ironically returned to the harder style that Gramm had been missing. Gramm subsequently put together the ill-fated Shadow King with Turgon, drummer Kevin Valentine and ex-Dio/Whitesnake guitarist Vivian Campbell. The band barely lasted beyond their first album and live show before

Campbell left to replace the late Steve Clark in Def Leppard and Valentine joined Cinderella. However, Gramm and Jones eventually put their differences behind them, and the vocalist rejoined Foreigner in 1992, taking Turgon along with him.

● ALBUMS: *Ready Or Not* (Atlantic 1987)★★★, *Long Hard Look* (Atlantic 1989)★★.

GRAND FUNK RAILROAD

Formed in 1968, Grand Funk Railroad was the first American heavy rock 'power trio' to achieve massive fame, while alienating another large segment of the rock audience and critics at the same time. The group consisted of guitarist Mark Farner (b. 29 September 1948, Flint, Michigan, USA), bassist Mel Schacher (b. 3 April 1951, Owosso, Michigan, USA) and drummer Don Brewer (b. 3 September 1948, Flint, Michigan, USA). The group was a spin-off of Terry Knight And The Pack, a popular soul-rock group in the Michigan area in the mid-60s. Farner and Brewer had both been members of that band (Brewer had also belonged to the Jazz Masters prior to the Pack). Following a single release on the small Lucky Eleven label, 'I (Who Have Nothin)', which reached number 46 in the US chart, the Pack were joined by Schacher, formerly of ? And The Mysterians. At this point Knight stopped performing to become the band's manager, renaming it Grand Funk Railroad (the name was taken from the Michigan landmark the Grand Trunk Railroad). The new trio signed with Capitol Records in 1969 and immediately began making its name by performing at several large pop festivals. Their first singles reached the charts but Grand Funk soon proved its real strength in the album market. *On Time* reached number 27 in 1969, followed by the number 11 *Grand Funk* in 1970. By the summer of that year they had become a major concert attraction, and their albums routinely reached the Top 10 for the next four years. Of those, 1973's *We're An American Band* was the biggest seller, reaching number 2. The group's huge success is often attributed to the public relations expertise of manager Knight. In 1970, for example, Knight reportedly paid $100,000 for a huge billboard in New York City's Times Square to promote the group's *Closer To Home*, which subsequently became their first Top 10 album, reaching number 6 and spawning the FM radio-staple title track. That promotional campaign backfired with the press, however, which dismissed the band's efforts despite spiralling success with the public. In June 1971, for example, Grand Funk became only the second group (after the Beatles) to sell out New York's Shea Stadium. Their recordings sold in greater quantity even though many radio stations ignored their releases. 1970's *Live Album* reached number 5 and included another concert and radio favourite in Farner's 'Mean Mistreater'. The next year saw the release of *Survival* and *E Pluribus Funk*, the latter most notable for its round album cover. In 1972 the group fired Knight, resulting in a series of lawsuits involving millions of dollars (they hired John Eastman, father of Linda McCartney, as their new manager). In 1973 the group shortened its name officially to Grand Funk, and added a fourth member, keyboardist Craig Frost (b. 20 April 1948, Flint, Michigan, USA). Now produced by Todd Rundgren, they finally cracked the singles market, reaching number 1 with the album title track 'We're An American Band', a celebration of the group's times on the road. In 1974 a major revision of Little Eva's 'Loco-motion' also reached the top (the first time in US chart history that a cover version of a song that had previously reached number 1 also attained that position). In 1975, with their popularity considerably diminished, the group reverted to its original name of Grand Funk Railroad. The following year they signed with MCA Records and recorded *Good Singin', Good Playin'*, produced by Frank Zappa. When it failed to reach the Top 50, Farner left for a solo career. The others stayed together, adding guitarist Billy Elworthy and changing their name to Flint, a group who failed to find commercial success with their solitary album. Grand Funk, this time consisting of Farner, Brewer and bassist Dennis Bellinger, re-formed for two years in 1981-83 and recorded *Grand Funk Lives* and *What's Funk?* for the Full Moon label. Failing to recapture former glories, they split again. Farner returned to his solo career, before joining Adrenalin. Brewer and Frost joined Bob Seger's Silver Bullet Band. The band reunited for a benefit for Bosnian orphans in 1997.

● ALBUMS: *On Time* (Capitol 1969)★★★, *Grand Funk* (Capitol 1970)★★★, *Closer To Home* (Capitol 1970)★★★, *Live* (Capitol 1970)★★, *Survival* (Capitol 1971)★★, *E Pluribus Funk* (Capitol 1971)★★★, *Phoenix* (Capitol 1972)★★★, *We're An American Band* (Capitol 1973)★★★, *Shinin' On* (Capitol 1974)★★, *All The Girls In The World Beware!!!* (Capitol 1974)★★, *Caught In The Act* (MCA 1975)★★, *Good Singin', Good Playin'* (MCA 1976)★★★, *Grand Funk Lives* (Full Moon 1981)★★, *What's Funk?* (Full Moon 1983)★★.

● COMPILATIONS: *Mark, Don & Mel 1969-71* (Capitol 1972)★★, *Grand Funk Hits* (Capitol 1976)★★★, *The Best Of Grand Funk Railroad*

(Capitol 1990)★★★, *More Of The Best Of Grand Funk Railroad* (Capitol 1991)★★, *The Collection* (Castle 1992)★★★.

GRAND PRIX

Ranked alongside Magnum as the UK's most accomplished pomp rock/AOR group, Grand Prix originally comprised Bernie Shaw (vocals), Phil Lanzon (keyboards), Michael O'Donoghue (guitar), Ralph Hood (bass) and Andy Beirne (drums, ex-Dirty Tricks). After an excellent self-titled debut collection for RCA Records in 1980, which highlighted the group's melodic strengths and structured songwriting, Shaw left to join Praying Mantis (and later Stratus). He was replaced by Robin McAuley, who settled into the role for two further albums. *There For No One To See* was an excellent platform for his abilities, but proved to be Grand Prix's final album for RCA. 1983's *Samurai*, was released on Chrysalis Records, but by the early months of 1984 the group had broken up permanently. McAuley subsequently joined the McAuley Shenker Group, while his former band's three records became highly esteemed collector's items among fans of British AOR.

● ALBUMS: *Grand Prix* (RCA 1980)★★★★, *There For No One To See* (RCA 1982)★★★★, *Samurai* (Chrysalis 1983)★★.

GRAVE DIGGER

Originally comprising Chris Boltendahl (vocals), Peter Masson (guitar), C.F. Brank (bass) and Albert Eckardt (drums), German hard rock group Grave Digger suffered from numerous personnel shifts during their career. Formed in 1980, they released their debut six-track demo shortly thereafter, but then broke up before any official releases could be planned. However, offered a contract in 1983 by Noise Records, Boltendahl and Masson re-formed the group with Willi Lackmann on bass and Philipp Seibel on drums. Two of the group's fiery rock tracks were recorded for inclusion on the German *Rock From Hell* sampler compilation, and led to sessions for a debut album. By the time they entered the studio in February 1984, Eckhardt had returned from the original line-up to replace Siebel, and Brank to replace Lackmann. Several European tours were arranged, and by the mid-80s the group had established a strong live reputation in mainland Europe. Rene T. Bone replaced Brank in September 1984, after which time the group's line-up remained relatively stable. However, neither *Witch Hunter* nor *War Games* managed to secure a mainstream audience, and as Noise Records concentrated on developing new acts, Grave Digger faded from prominence.

● ALBUMS: *Heavy Metal Breakdown* (Noise 1984)★★★★, *Witch Hunter* (Noise 1985)★★★, *War Games* (Noise 1986)★★, *Tunes Of War* (Gun 1996)★★★, *Knights Of The Cross* (Gun 1998)★.

GRAVITY KILLS

Modern-day St. Louis, USA, the cradle of the blues, seems an unlikely place to start a band firmly in the Nine Inch Nails style of industrial metal; yet the band's genesis was as unusual as the unlikely setting from which they emerged. The roots of the band can be traced back to late 1995 when the unit of Matt Dudenhoeffer (guitar), Doug Firley (keyboards), Kurt Kerns (bass, drums) and Kern's cousin Jeff Scheel (vocals) decided they wanted one of their tracks to be included on the local radio station compilation album. They produced 'Guilty' in six frantic hours and beat the radio station deadline by half an hour. The single showed an incredible degree of songwriting awareness and boasted a danceable, hypnotic rhythm. Suddenly Gravity Kills were an ongoing concern. On the back of this success, the band supported the Sex Pistols in the USA while material was finished for their first self-titled album. Their frenetic and compelling live performances were soon experienced in Europe as they began a bout of touring. One of their main assets was the presence of a keyboard player not permanently rooted behind banks of hi-tech equipment. Firley's simple stage set-up consisted of industrial-strength tripods built to take his weight, allowing him to become a breathtaking gymnastic blur without missing a beat. To match the bleakness of their first single, the album boasted tracks of tense and dramatic electro-metal which lent itself easily to cinematic interpretation. 'Guilty' was featured in the thriller *Seven*, while the qualities of the other tracks attracted directors as diverse as Rocky Morton (creator of Max Headroom) and Peter Christopherson (Rage Against The Machine video director), to provide visual accompaniment to the brooding tales.

● ALBUMS: *Gravity Kills* (TVT 1996)★★★, *Perversion* (TVT 1998)★★.

GREAT WHITE

This Los Angeles-based heavy metal band was formed in 1981 and comprised Jack Russell (vocals), Mark Kendall (guitar), Lorne Black (bass) and Gary Holland (drums). They adopted a no-frills approach from the start, relying on the music - earthy, honest blues-rock delivered with stunning precision - rather than gimmicks. The band attracted the attention of EMI Records with their self-financed mini-album, *Out Of The Night*, produced by their friend Don Dokken. Unfortunately, the momentum was not maintained and *Stick It*, their EMI debut, was erratic and sold poorly, and the band was subsequently dropped. Far from disillusioned, they funded the recording of *Shot In The Dark* out of their own pockets, which eventually opened the door to a new contract with Capitol Records. Lorne Black and Gary Holland broke ranks at this stage and were replaced by Tony Montana and Audie Desbrow, respectively. Michael Lardie was also added on keyboards to expand the group to a five-piece and add an extra dimension to their sound. Enjoying the benefits of a larger budget, *Once Bitten* received considerable critical acclaim with its more melodic, accessible sound. Sales of the album went on to pass the million mark. *Recovery...Live* payed homage to their roots, being an inspired selection of blues-styled cover versions from the Who, Led Zeppelin, Humble Pie and Jimi Hendrix. *Twice Shy* and *Hooked* have consolidated their success with further platinum awards. *Sail Away* saw the introduction of new bass player Teddy Cook, on an album influenced by Julian Barnes' novel *The History Of The World In Ten And A Half Chapters*.

● ALBUMS: *Out Of The Night* mini-album (Aegan 1982)★★★, *Stick It* (EMI 1984)★★, *Shot In The Dark* (Telegraph 1986)★★★, *Once Bitten* (Capitol 1987)★★★★, *Recovery...Live* (Enigma 1988)★★, *Twice Shy* (Capitol 1989)★★★, *Live In London* (Capitol 1990)★★, *Hooked* (Capitol 1991)★★★★, *Psycho City* (Capitol 1992)★★★, *Sail Away* (RCA 1994)★★★.

GREEN DAY

With alternative rock music going overground in the early 90s, few acts were better positioned to exploit the commercial possibilities than Green Day - Billie Joe Armstrong (b. 17 February 1972, California, USA; vocals, guitar), Mike Dirnt (b. 4 May 1972, California, USA; bass, vocals) and Tre Cool (b. Frank Edwin Wright III, 9 December 1972, Germany; drums, vocals). Armstrong and Dirnt had been playing together since the age of 11 in the refinery town of Rodeo, California, performing in various garage bands. Tre Cool had been in a band called The Lookouts who broke up in 1990, but their final EP, *IV*, featured Billie Joe Armstrong playing guitar and singing backing vocals on three tracks. Armstrong and Dirnt had already formed Sweet Children with ex-Isocracy drummer John Kiffmeyer. Their debut release came on Livermore's Lookout Records in 1989, the *1000 Hours* EP. However, two weeks before release the band informed Livermore that they had changed their name to Green Day, inspired by their fondness for marijuana and by the fact that another local band, Sweet Baby Jesus, had just changed their name to Sweet Baby and signed with Slash/Warner Brothers Records. Their debut album, *39/Smooth*, recorded in a single day, comprised 10 pop punk tracks. Two limited edition EPs followed, one for Lookout, the second for Chicago label Skene Records. Kiffmeyer booked their first national tour, but afterwards left the band to concentrate on college (his only subsequent musical activity came in the Ne'er Do Wells). Cool was asked to fill in, and immediately wrote the comedic 'Dominated Love Song' for *Kerplunk!*, where the 60s pop quotient was reduced in favour of a synthesis of 70s British punk bands the Jam and Stiff Little Fingers. It sold over 50,000 records through word of mouth and underground media support. Afterwards they decided to take the plunge and move to a major label, signing to Warner Brothers subsidiary Reprise Records, despite bigger offers from elsewhere. A&R man Rob Cavallo was also recruited as producer for their third album. *Dookie* gradually stalked the charts, going on to sell over nine million copies in the USA. Their arduous touring schedule was the chief reason for their rise, and was topped off by appearances on the 1994 Lollapalooza package and the revived Woodstock event. The other main factor was the estimable quality of their songwriting. With *Dookie* being so successful, it came as no surprise when the band were nominated in no less than four Grammy categories. In 1995 it was confirmed that they had sold over 10 million albums worldwide, a stunning achievement for a band who have remained faithful to a basic punk pop framework. *Insomniac* had a hard act to follow and was a disappointing collection.

● ALBUMS: *39/Smooth* (Lookout 1990)★★★, *Kerplunk!* (Lookout 1992)★★★, *Dookie* (Reprise 1994)★★★★, *Insomniac* (Reprise 1995)★★, *Nimrod* (WEA 1997)★★.

● COMPILATIONS: *1,039/Smoothed Out Slappy Hours* (Lookout 1991)★★.

GREEN JELLY

Described as 'this year's musical lowpoint' by *Rolling Stone* magazine in 1993, Green Jello ended that same year being forced to change their name to Green Jelly, in order to avoid a lawsuit from

General Foods. Initially conceived as a 'video' band, they rose to fame largely through this medium. Their breakthrough hit certainly boasted excellent animation, but little musical substance, allied as it was to a psychedelic heavy metal version of the popular nursery rhyme, 'Three Little Pigs'. Like their follow-up, a cover version of the Sex Pistols' 'Anarchy In The UK', it was an exercise of limited merit.

● ALBUMS: *Cereal Killer* (Zoo/BMG 1993)★★★, *333* (Zoo/BMG 1994)★.

GREEN RIVER

Seattle band Green River may go down in history as the first 'grunge' band, and were certainly the first to release a record on the Sub Pop label. The band was formed in 1984 with Jeff Ament (ex-Deranged Diction) on bass, drummer Alex Shumway, guitarist and vocalist Mark Arm and former Mr Epp guitarist Steve Turner. The line-up was expanded with the addition of ex-Ducky Boys/March Of Crimes guitarist Stone Gossard, and they began to air their wares on the local north-west scene. By 1985 they had appeared alongside the Melvins on the *Deep Six* compilation album on the C/Z label, released a six-song EP, *Come On Down*, for Homestead, and were playing the same clubs as another local band, Soundgarden. Both bands came to the attention of Sub Pop owner Bruce Pavitt, who decided to expand his cassette-based fanzine into a full record label and worked with them in producing the 12-inch EP *Dry As A Bone*, which was released in June 1987. Turner left soon afterwards and was replaced by another Deranged Diction member, Bruce Fairweather. In May 1988 they released the mini-album *Rehab Doll* (cassette and CD versions added *Dry As A Bone*), but the band was already falling apart due to musical differences between Arm and Ament, which led to them splitting in June. Arm joined Turner with ex-Melvins bassist Matt Lukin and drummer Dan Peters to form Mudhoney. Ament, Gossard and Fairweather regrouped with ex-Malfunkshun vocalist Andrew Wood and drummer Regan Hagar and formed Lords Of The Wasteland, who quickly evolved into Mother Love Bone. After the death of Wood in March 1990, that band fractured, with Gossard and Ament forming the hugely successful Pearl Jam. Green River thus became an important footnote in the development of the 90s' strongest rock movement, although their light was reignited temporarily on 30 November 1993 at the Aladdin Hotel in Las Vegas, when Pearl Jam ended their live set early to make way for a one-off re-formation of Green River, with Gossard, Arm, Turner and Ament joined by Chuck Treece (bassist from Urge Overkill) playing drums.

● ALBUMS: *Rehab Doll* mini-album (Sub Pop 1988)★★★.

GREEN, JACK

b. England. Known to UK rock and pop fans through his involvement with the Pretty Things, Green relocated to Canada to build his solo career. Though now regularly consigned to the 'where are they now?' columns in the UK, a sequence of albums for RCA Records in Canada have produced a cult following in that territory. *Humanesque*, which featured Ritchie Blackmore of Rainbow on one track, and *Essential Logic* are two collections that married melodious pop hooks with Green's own rock guitar licks. *Latest Game* saw him move to FM/Revolver, but distribution of the record in the UK failed to excite much critical interest despite Green's reputation and stature in Canada.

● ALBUMS: *Humanesque* (RCA Canada 1980)★★★, *Essential Logic* (RCA Canada 1981)★★★, *Latest Game* (FM/Revolver 1987)★★.

GREENWAY, BRIAN

b. 1 October 1951, Canada. When Canadian heavy metal band April Wine broke up in 1988 following singer Myles Goodwin's decision to embark on a solo project, his move predicted the future course of former colleague Brian Greenway's career. In reality, Greenway simply did not have the song-writing skills to make it on his own - the vocals on *Serious Business*, his debut album for Atlantic Records in 1988, were laboured and unconvincing, despite the obvious skill of his guitar playing. It proved to be a one-off experiment before Greenway and Goodwin reunited in a re-formed April Wine at the turn of the 90s.

● ALBUMS: *Serious Business* (Atlantic 1988)★★.

GRIFFIN

US rock band Griffin was originally formed in 1981 around a trio of William Rodrick McCay (vocals), Rick Cooper (guitar) and Rick Wagner (drums). However, it was only with the expanded line-up of Yaz (guitar) and Thomas Sprayberry (bass) that the group began to make progress. Signed to Shrapnel/SPV Records in 1985, they made their debut with *Flight Of The Griffin*, a solid hard rock collection with the material consistently accentuating McCay's vocal delivery. Yaz and Sprayberry then left the group, leaving Cooper to double up on bass for Griffin's second album, 1987's *Protectors Of*

The Lair. Once again this failed to expand their audience and the original trio parted soon after its release.

● ALBUMS: *Flight Of The Griffin* (Shrapnel/SPV 1985)★★★, *Protectors Of The Lair* (SPV 1987)★★★.

GRIM REAPER

Formed in 1979, and featuring Steve Grimmett (vocals), Nick Bowcott (guitars), Dave Wanklin (bass) and Lee Hams (drums), Grim Reaper are a typical example of the bands that formed the UK heavy metal revival of the early 80s known as the New Wave Of British Heavy Metal. They epitomized most of the movement's strengths (a fresh, down-to-earth approach, enthusiasm, and powerful but melodic guitar riffs), but also the weaknesses that plagued it (bargain-basement production values and daftly melodramatic lyrics delivered in an inappropriate falsetto). In 1994 one of their videos was dragged out of the crates in the MTV cartoon *Beavis And Butthead*, and was introduced with an incredulous 'Is this Spinal Tap?'. While they flirted with infernal imagery, Grim Reaper were never a Satanic band, as was claimed by some critics (including fundamentalist Christian preachers), and actually suffered from being a little bland. Their debut, *See You In Hell*, was probably Grim Reaper's finest moment, particularly the catchily anthemic title track, and the band enjoyed some success on both sides of the Atlantic during the mid-80s. Ultimately, they could neither repeat nor build on this success, and in 1988 they broke up. Grimmett joined Onslaught, then Lionsheart.

● ALBUMS: *See You In Hell* (Ebony 1983)★★★★, *Fear No Evil* (Ebony 1985)★★, *Rock You In Hell* (MCA 1987)★★.

GRINGOS LOCOS

A Finnish quintet of Richard Johnson (vocals), Ben Granfelt (guitar), Muddy (guitar), Pete Asiala (bass) and Miri Miettinen (drums), Gringos Locos formed in the mid-80s and took their chief inspiration from the southern boogie of Lynyrd Skynyrd and the Georgia Satellites. When their debut album emerged for Phonogram Records in 1987, many were surprised by the authenticity of the sound, given the group's geographical origins. The resultant record also caused a stir in the USA, and Lynyrd Skynyrd producer Tom Dowd was impressed enough to offer to produce the follow-up collection. *Punch Drunk* was released via a new contract with Atlantic Records, and provided further evidence of a group capable of offering accessible, energized interpretations of a foreign sound.

● ALBUMS: *Gringos Locos* (Phonogram 1987)★★★, *Punch Drunk* (Atlantic 1989)★★★.

GROOP DOGDRILL

Founded in Doncaster, Yorkshire, England, Groop Dogdrill comprise drummer Hug, singer/guitarist Pete Spiby and bassist Damo Fowkes. In addition there is a fourth member, roadie Boz, who also writes the group's lyrics. That line-up gives some indication of the lack of convention inherent in the group, made explicit on their ferocious debut album, 1998's *Half Nelson*. Not averse to advising music journalists to 'pull some fanny', Groop Dogdrill quickly gained a reputation as natural successors to the Wildhearts as rock's resident hard-boiled nutcases (at one London support gig to Reef, Fowkes responded to a thrown bottle from the audience by pulling out a flick-knife) - but then, as Fowkes himself pointed out: 'I think we'd be a lot more violent if we didn't do what we do. If I wasn't doing this, I'd be out killing someone. Or hunting small animals.'

● ALBUMS: *Half Nelson* (Beggars Banquet 1998)★★★.

GROPE

Led by guitarist/singer Tue Madsen, Danish extreme metal band Grope chose their name from a friend's suggestion of a moniker with deliberately 'cheap' connotations. Although primarily rooted in the death rock tradition, the group's eclecticism was immediately apparent - a quality that was at least partially engendered by Madsen's 10 years working in a record store. As well as recording a cover version of Björk's 'Army Of Me' in 1995, they also appeared on tribute albums to both Metallica and Slayer. With influences ranging from the hardcore punk scene to traditional metal bands such as Led Zeppelin and Black Sabbath, the group made a bright impression with the release of *Primates* in 1995. Popular throughout mainland European circles despite a lack of promotional leverage, it was quickly followed by *The Fury*. This record's high intensity levels and volume provoked immediate comparisons with Machine Head, which Grope took as a compliment.

● ALBUMS: *Primates* (1995)★★★, *The Fury* (1996)★★★, *Desert Storm* (Diehard 1997)★★.

GROSVENOR, LUTHER

b. 23 December 1949, Evesham, Worcestershire, England. Grosvenor's flowing and biting lead guitar lines were widely heard when he was a member of heavy progressive rockers Spooky Tooth in the late 60s. Tracks such as 'Better By You, Better Than Me' benefited greatly from his memorable riffs. When Spooky Tooth disintegrated, Grosvenor released the obligatory solo album. He became much in demand as a session player and briefly joined Stealers Wheel; consequently, his credible debut *Under Open Skies*, was overlooked. In mid-1973 he joined Mott the Hoople, by which time he had acquired the bizarre moniker 'Ariel Bender'. After less than two years with Mott he left to form the heavier-sounding Widowmaker with Steve Ellis (ex-Love Affair). He drifted out of the music business during the early 90s, but following a session on the Peter Green tribute album *Rattlesnake Guitar* in 1996, Grosvenor evidently became enthused about playing again and recorded a new album in 1996.

● ALBUMS: *Under Open Skies* (Island 1971)★★★, *Floodgates* (Brilliant Recording Co 1996)★★.

GROUNDHOGS

The original Groundhogs emerged in 1963 when struggling UK beat group the Dollarbills opted for a more stylish name; Tony 'T.S.' McPhee (b. 22 March 1944, Humberstone, Lincolnshire, England; guitar), John Cruickshank (vocals, harp), Bob Hall (piano), Pete Cruickshank (b. 2 July 1945, Calcutta, India; bass) and Dave Boorman (drums) also adopted a 'John Lee' prefix in honour of mentor John Lee Hooker, whom the quintet subsequently backed in concert and on record. John Lee's Groundhogs recorded two singles before breaking up in 1966. McPhee completed several solo tracks with producer Mike Vernon before rejoining Pete Cruickshank in Herbal Mixture, a short-lived pseudo-psychedelic group. In 1968 the two musicians formed the core of a re-formed Groundhogs alongside Steve Rye (vocals, harmonica) and Ken Pustelnik (drums). The new unit made its debut with the rudimentary *Scratching The Surface*, but were then reduced to a trio by Rye's departure. A second set, *Blues Obituary*, contained two tracks, 'Mistreated' and 'Express Man', which became in-concert favourites as the group embarked on a more progressive direction. This was confirmed with *Thank Christ For The Bomb*, the Groundhogs' powerful 1970 release, which cemented a growing popularity. McPhee composed the entire set and his enthusiasm for concept albums was maintained with its successor, *Split*, which examined schizophrenia. Arguably the group's definitive work, this uncompromising selection included the stage classic, 'Cherry Red'. Pustelnik left the group following the release of *Who Will Save The World?* in 1972. Former Egg drummer Clive Brooks (b. 28 December 1949, London, England) was an able replacement, but although the Groundhogs continued to enjoy fervent popularity, their subsequent recordings lacked the fire of those early releases. The trio was also beset by managerial problems and broke up in 1975, although McPhee maintained the name for two disappointing releases, *Crosscut Saw* and *Black Diamond*. The guitarist resurrected the Groundhogs sobriquet in 1984 in the wake of interest in an archive release, *Hoggin' The Stage*. Although Pustelnik was one of several musicians McPhee used for touring purposes, the most effective line-up was completed by Dave Anderson on bass, formerly of Hawkwind, and drummer Mike Jones. McPhee has in recent years appeared as a solo performer as part of a 70s nostalgia tour, together with various incarnations of his respected band. The Groundhogs' name endures mainly through a live reputation second to none.

● ALBUMS: *Scratching The Surface* (Liberty 1968)★★, *Blues Obituary* (Liberty 1969)★★★, *Thank Christ For The Bomb* (Liberty 1970)★★★, *Split* (Liberty 1971)★★★★, *Who Will Save The World?* (United Artists 1972)★★★, *Hogwash* (United Artists 1972)★★★, *Solid* (WWA 1974)★★, *Crosscut Saw* (United Artists 1976)★★, *Black Diamond* (United Artists 1976)★★, *Razor's Edge* (Conquest 1985)★★, *Back Against The Wall* (Demi-Monde 1987)★★, *Hogs On The Road* (Demi-Monde 1988)★★, as Tony McPhee's Groundhogs *Who Said Cherry Red?* (Indigo 1996)★★, *Hogs In Wolf's Clothing* (HTD 1998)★★.

● COMPILATIONS: *Groundhogs Best 1969-1972* (United Artists 1974)★★★, *Hoggin' The Stage* (Psycho 1984)★★★, *Moving Fast, Standing Still*, comprises McPhee solo album *2 Sides Of* plus *Razor's Edge* (Raw Power 1986)★★, *No Surrender* (Total 1990)★★, *Classic Album Cuts 1968 - 1976* (1992)★★★, *The Best Of ...* (EMI Gold 1997)★★★, *On Air 1970 - 1972* (Strange Fruit 1998)★★★.

GUN

Gun emerged in the summer of 1989 with a debut album, *Taking On The World*, which saw them acclaimed as one of Scotland's most invigorating modern rock bands. The group comprised Mark Rankin (vocals), Scott Shields (drums) 'Baby' Stafford (guitar) and the Gizzi brothers, Giuliano 'Joolz' (guitar) and Dante (bass). Backed up by a spectacular live show, singles such as 'Better Days', 'Money (Everybody Loves Her)' and 'Inside Out' all reached the UK charts at a time when the *zeitgeist* was geared more to dance music than unrepentant rockers. Following their support to Simple Minds at Wembley Stadium, the group were also the personal choice of Mick Jagger and Keith Richards to support the Rolling Stones on their 1990 *Urban Jungle* UK tour. However, the sight of the Stones' intimidating audience saw Stafford depart to go solo, believing he could never surpass his heroes. Gun recruited Alex Dixon (ex-Midnight Blue) in his stead and pressed on with a second album, *Gallus*, which arrived in 1992 (its title was a Glaswegian term that loosely translates as 'dead cool'). Proffering three further hits in 'Steal Your Fire', 'Higher Ground' and 'Welcome To The Real World', it also boasted a tougher, more muscular songwriting approach. However, when *Swagger* was unveiled in 1994 the group had slimmed down to a four-piece, replacing Shields with Mark Kerr. Recorded in the more rural setting of Wales over a two-week period, it continued its predecessor's back-to-basics approach, with its rock foundation infused with the vigour and excitement of punk. Arguably the worst item, a rock version of Cameo's funk classic 'Word Up', was the first single to be lifted from *Swagger*. It rewarded the group with its biggest single success (Top 10), and opened up the group's more wholesome material for discovery by a new legion of fans. The best tracks on the album included 'Don't Say It's Over', co-written with Jim Vallance, and a rap track, 'Something Worthwhile'. Kerr departed in July 1996.

● ALBUMS: *Taking On The World* (A&M 1989)★★★, *Gallus* (A&M 1992)★★★, *Swagger* (A&M 1994)★★★★, *0141 632 6326* (A&M 1997)★★.

GUNS N'ROSES

The founder-members of the most controversial heavy rock band of the late 80s included Axl Rose (an anagram of Oral Sex) (b. William Bailey, 6 February 1962, Lafayette, Indiana, USA) and Izzy Stradlin (b. Jeffrey Isbell, 8 April 1962, Lafayette, Indiana, USA). Vocalist Rose, who had first sung at the age of five in a church choir, met guitarist Stradlin in Los Angeles in 1984. He changed his name to Rose at the age of 17 when he discovered who his real father was, the Axl prefix coming from a band with whom he had rehearsed in Indiana. With Tracii Guns (guitar) and Rob Gardner (drums), they formed a rock band called, in turn, Rose, Hollywood Rose and L.A. Guns. Soon afterwards, Guns and Gardner left, to be replaced by two members of local band Road Crew, drummer Steven Adler (b. 22 January 1965, Cleveland, Ohio, USA) and guitarist Slash (b. Saul Hudson, 23 July 1965, Stoke-on-Trent, Staffordshire, England), the son of a clothes designer and an album cover artist. With bass player Duff McKagan (b. Michael McKagan, 5 February 1964, Seattle, Washington, USA; ex-Fartz; Fastbacks; Ten Minute Warning; and approximately 30 other north-west bands), the band was renamed Guns N'Roses. Following the disastrous US Hell Tour '85, Guns N'Roses released an EP, *Live?!*@ Like A Suicide*, on the independent Uzi/Suicide label. This brought intense interest from critics and record companies and in 1986 the group signed to Geffen Records, who reissued the EP the following year.

During 1987 they toured extensively, though the group's appetite for self-destruction became readily apparent when Fred Coury of Cinderella was recruited to replace Adler temporarily, after the latter had broken his hand in a brawl. February 1988 also saw the first internal rift when Rose was kicked out, then reinstated, within three days. Their debut, *Appetite For Destruction*, produced by Mike Clink, went on to sell 20 million copies worldwide and reached number 1 in the USA a year after its release date. 'Welcome To The Jungle' was used on the soundtrack of the Clint Eastwood film *Dead Pool*, and reached the Top 30 in the UK. The group's regular live shows in the USA and Europe brought frequent controversy, notably when two fans died during crowd disturbances at the Monsters Of Rock show at Donington, England, in 1988. In 1989 the eight-track album *G N' R Lies* was issued, becoming a big hit on both sides of the Atlantic, as were the singles 'Sweet Child O' Mine' (written about Rose's girlfriend and later wife Erin Everly, daughter of Don Everly), 'Paradise City' and 'Patience'. However, Rose's lyrics for 'One In A Million' were widely criticized for their homophobic sentiments. Although Guns N'Roses appeared at the Farm Aid IV charity concert, their career was littered with incidents involving drugs, drunkenness and public disturbance offences in 1989/90. At times their excesses made the band seem like a caricature of a 60s supergroup, with headlines screaming of Stradlin urinating in public on an aeroplane, Slash and McKagan swearing live on television while collecting trophies at the American Music Awards, and Rose's on-off relationship with Everly. In September 1990 Adler was replaced by Matt Sorum (b. 19 November 1960, Mission Viejo, California, USA) from the Cult. Apparently more restrained in their private life, Guns N'Roses added Dizzy Reed (b. Darren Reed;

keyboards) for a 1991 world tour, where their exciting and unpredictable performances brought favourable comparisons with the heyday of the Rolling Stones. In September the group released the highly publicized pair of albums, *Use Your Illusion I* and *II*, preceded by a version of Bob Dylan's 'Knockin' On Heaven's Door' from the soundtrack of *Days Of Thunder*. Further hit singles, 'You Could Be Mine' (featured in the film *Terminator II*) and 'Don't Cry', followed. The *Illusion* brace immediately sat astride the top two album positions in the *Billboard* chart, the first occasion on which they had been thus dominated since Jim Croce in 1974. Izzy Stradlin found the pressure too much and left late in 1991, going on to form the Ju Ju Hounds. He was replaced by Gilby Clarke (ex-Kill For Thrills). Meanwhile, Slash's growing reputation brought guest appearances on recordings by Dylan and Michael Jackson. He also contributed to tribute albums to Muddy Waters and Les Paul, and subsequently established his own spin-off band, Slash's Snakepit. Guns N'Roses' appearance at the 1992 Freddie Mercury AIDS Benefit concert prompted the reissue of 'Knockin' On Heaven's Door', and while Dylan fans groaned with disbelief, the band's vast following was happy to see its heroes scale the charts shortly after the single's release. While both of their previous albums remained on the US chart, having sold more than four million copies each, it was not until the end of 1993 that any new material emerged. When it arrived, it came in the form of *The Spaghetti Incident*, a much vaunted collection of cover versions with a punk foundation. A perfunctory affair, it was mainly notable for lining the pockets of several long-forgotten musicians (UK Subs, Nazareth, Misfits, Fear, etc.), and for including a song written by mass murderer Charles Manson. The main inspiration behind the project, Duff McKagan, had his debut solo album released at the same time. However, reports of an unhappy camp continued to filter through in 1994, leading to the dismissal of Gilby Clarke towards the end of the year, following his own, highly public, outbursts about Rose. His replacement was Paul Huge, a former flatmate of Rose from his Indiana days. Huge's first recording with the band was a cover version of the Rolling Stones' 'Sympathy For The Devil' for the soundtrack to *Interview With The Vampire*. However, Huge stayed only briefly with the band, as did his replacement, Zakk Wylde (ex-Ozzy Osbourne), who failed to record a single note with the band before falling out irreconcilably with Rose. In May 1995 Izzy Stradlin was reinstated as second guitarist, but by the end of the year Rose and Slash were again at loggerheads and no new album was imminent. Sorum and McKagen, meanwhile, teamed up with guitarist Steve Jones for the spin-off band the Neurotic Outsiders. Slash confirmed Rose's departure in November 1996, although this situation was reversed in February 1997 when Rose allegedly purchased the rights to the Guns N'Roses name. Later in the year, this was seemingly confirmed by the recruitment of Robin Finck, formerly of Nine Inch Nails, to replace Slash.

● ALBUMS: *Appetite For Destruction* (Geffen 1987)★★★★, *G N' R Lies* (Geffen 1989)★★★, *Use Your Illusion I* (Geffen 1991)★★★, *Use Your Illusion II* (Geffen 1991)★★★, *The Spaghetti Incident* (Geffen 1993)★★.

● VIDEOS: *Use Your Illusion I* (1992), *Making Fuckin' Videos Vol 1* (1993), *Making Fuckin' Videos Vol 2* (1993), *The Making Of Estranged - Part IV Of The Trilogy* (1994).

● FURTHER READING: *In Their Own Words*, Mark Putterford. *Appetite For Destruction: The Days Of Guns N'Roses*, Danny Sugerman. *Guns N'Roses: The World's Most Outrageous Hard Rock Band*, Paul Elliot. *The Most Dangerous Band In The World*, Mick Wall. *The Pictures*, George Chin. *Over The Top: The True Story Of ...* , Mark Putterford. *Lowlife In The Fast Lane*, Eddy McSquare. *Live!*, Mick St. Michael.

GWAR

This theatrical shock-rock heavy metal quintet emerged from Richmond, Virginia, USA. Assuming bizarre pseudonyms, they comprised Oderus Urungus (vocals), Balsac, The Jaws Of Death (guitar), Flattus Maximus (guitar), Beefcake The Mighty (bass) and Nippleus Erectus (drums). They are primarily renowned for an outrageous live show that involves the band adorning themselves in hideous *papier mâché* masks and wielding blood-splattered torture implements, with set-pieces including the feigned buggery of a priest with a crucifix. Consequently, their UK tour ground to a halt after just three dates owing to the resulting moral panic. Taken to court in the USA over allegedly displaying a penis as a stage prop (the band suggested, bizarrely, that it was some form of fish), it came as little surprise to learn that the origins of GWAR (apparently, 'God What A Racket') lie in an art school collective. The music, which is rudimentary thrash complete with unintelligable vocals, takes second place to the visuals.

● ALBUMS: *Hell-O* (Shimmy Disc 1988)★★★★,

Scumdogs Of The Universe (Master 1990)★★, *America Must Be Destroyed* (Zorro 1992)★★★, *This Toilet Earth* (Metal Blade 1994)★★, *Ragnarök* (Metal Blade 1995)★★, *Carnival Of Chaos* (Metal Blade 1997)★★★.
● VIDEOS: *The Movie* (1990), *Live From Antartica* (1990), *Phallus In Wonderland* (1992), *Tour De Scum* (1994), *Skulhedface (Metal Blade)* (Metal Blade 1994).

Gypsy Queen

This US heavy metal group from Florida, USA, was fronted by twin sisters Pam and Paula Mattiola (formerly topless stars of *Playboy* magazine). Their debut album featured guitarists Pedro Riera and Bryan Le Mar, bassist Mars Cowling (ex-Pat Travers) and drummer Keith Daniel Cronin, and was produced by Aerosmith supremo Jack Douglas. Mid-paced pop-metal anthems and the occasional power ballad were the order of the day, penned within a very limited musical framework. The album sold poorly and the Mattiola twins fired the entire band, recruiting Scott Migone (guitar), Joey O'Jeda (bass, keyboards) and Kenny Wendland (drums) in their place. A second album recorded in 1989 remains unreleased, delayed by legal complications that eventually saw the twins move to new home Scotti Bros (as Cell Mates).
● ALBUMS: *Gypsy Queen* (Loop 1987)★★.

GZR

Ostensibly a solo vehicle for Geezer Butler (b. Terry Butler, 17 July 1949, Birmingham, England), formerly with Black Sabbath, this 1995 project allowed the bass player to 'blow off some steam' at events taking place in the Black Sabbath camp. The resulting album, *Plastic Planet*, including the scathing 'Giving Up The Ghost'. Lines such as 'You bastardised my intellect/Castrated our conviction' left critics in no doubt as to what Butler thought of Tony Iommi's handling of Black Sabbath affairs. The rest of the album made much less of an impact, with Butler's attempted accommodation of new metal styles frequently falling flat. He had first conceived the idea of a solo album in 1985 but 'couldn't find a singer'. It took him a full decade to realize his ambition with the addition of Burton C. Bell of Fear Factory. The same band invited GZR to support them on their UK dates in 1995.
● ALBUMS: *Plastic Planet* (1995)★★.

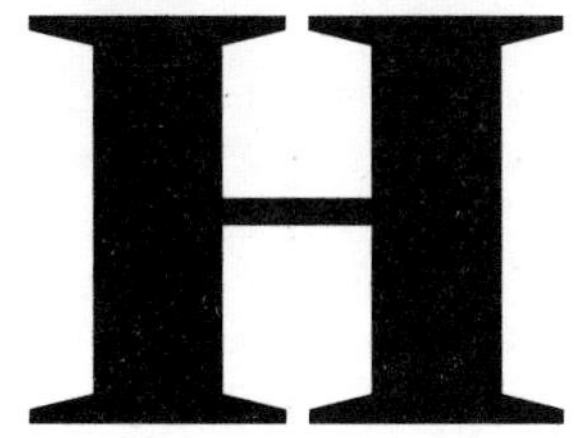

Hagar, Sammy

b. 13 October 1947, Monterey, California, USA. Hagar is a singer, guitarist and songwriter whose father was a professional boxer. Legend has it that Elvis Presley persuaded him not to follow in his father's footsteps, and instead he started out in 60s San Bernardino bands the Fabulous Castillas, Skinny, Justice Brothers and rock band Dust Cloud. He joined Montrose in 1973 (formed by ex-Edgar Winter guitarist Ronnie Montrose) and became a minor rock hero in the Bay Area of San Francisco, in particular acquiring a reputation as a potent live performer. After two albums with Montrose he left to go solo, achieving a string of semi-successful albums and singles. He took with him Bill Church (bass) and added Alan Fitzgerald (keyboards), and later Denny Carmassi (drums, also ex-Montrose). The band attracted good press on support tours with Kiss, Boston and Kansas, but by 1979 Hagar had fashioned a radically altered line-up, with Gary Pihl (guitar), Chuck Ruff (drums) and Geoff Workman (keyboards) joining Hagar and Church. 1983's *Three Lock Box* became their first Top 20 entry, and included 'Your Love Is Driving Me Crazy', which reached number 13 in the singles chart. Hagar then took time out to tour with Journey guitarist Neal Schon, Kenny Aaronson (bass) and Michael Shrieve (drums, ex-Santana), recording a live album under the band's initials HSAS. Under this title they also cut a studio version of Procol Harum's 'Whiter Shade Of Pale'. Returning to solo work, Hagar enjoyed his biggest hit to date with the *Voice Of America* out-take, 'I Can't Drive 55'. In 1985 he surprised many by joining Van Halen, from whom Dave Lee Roth had recently departed. However, he continued to pursue a parallel, if intermittent, solo career which continues to be characterized by a refreshing lack of bombast in a genre not noted for its subtlety. Hagar left Van Halen in 1996.
● ALBUMS: *Nine On A Ten Scale* (Capitol 1976)★★, *Red* (Capitol 1977)★★★, *Musical Chairs* (Capitol 1978)★★★, *All Night Long - Live* (Capitol 1978)★★, *Street Machine* (Capitol 1979)★★★,

Danger Zone (Capitol 1979)★★★, *Live, Loud And Clear* (Capitol 1980)★★, *Standing Hampton* (Geffen 1982)★★★, *Three Lock Box* (Geffen 1983)★★, *Live From London To Long Beach* (Capitol 1983)★★, *VOA* (Geffen 1983)★★★, as Hagar, Schon, Aaronson And Shrieve *Through The Fire* (Geffen 1984)★★, *Sammy Hagar* (Geffen 1987)★★, *Red* (Geffen 1993)★★, *Unboxed* (Geffen 1994)★★, *Marching To Mars* (MCA 1997)★★★.
● COMPILATIONS: *Rematch* (Capitol 1983)★★★, *The Best Of* (Geffen 1993)★★★.
● FILMS: *Footloose* (1984).

HALL, JAMES

b. *c.*1967, USA. Heavy-rock singer-songwriter Hall first cut his teeth on the Nashville country circuit, before moving to Atlanta at the age of 18, where he formed Mary My Hope, known during his activities therein as 'Lynchpin'. He made his first recordings with that band at Curtis Mayfield's studio in 1990, during sessions that produced their debut album, *Museum*. When Mary My Hope hit a 'creative stalemate', Hall formed a new band under his own name with Lynn, a friend from Atlanta, before finding Grant and then Sterling to finalize the line-up in 1993. The group's debut album saw their singer reacquaint himself with his late 70s/early 80s influences, while critics name-checked David Bowie and the Psychedelic Furs as reference points. Recent work aligns him more closely with Black Crowes and Rage Against The Machine.
● ALBUMS: *Love, Sex And Spirit* (Endangered 1995)★★★, *Pleasure Club* (Geffen 1996)★★.

HALLOWS EVE

The first incarnation of the US heavy metal band Hallows Eve dates back to 1984, when the nucleus of Stacy Anderson (vocals), Tommy Stewart (bass) and David Stuart (guitar), plus second guitarist Skellator and drummer Tym Helton, recorded a demo that was included on the *Metal Massacre IV* compilation. Their music from the outset has been extreme, representing one of the far outposts of the rock spectrum via a turbulent, high-speed wall-of-noise. Lyrics dealt with death, reincarnation, torture and mutilation, but the sentiments were usually indecipherable through frantic background thrashing. *Tales Of Terror* was recorded on a low budget but nevertheless featured the band's strongest material. *Death And Insanity* and *Monument*, although aesthetically more satisfying, were more formularized. Stacy Anderson quit in 1988, and the band have been inactive since.
● ALBUMS: *Tales Of Terror* (Roadrunner 1985)★★, *Death And Insanity* (Roadrunner 1986)★★★, *Monument* (Roadrunner 1988)★★★.

HAMM, STUART

This enormously talented bassist from the USA is probably better known as a member of Joe Satriani's touring band, but has also released a series of fine solo recordings. *Radio Free Albemuth* displayed Hamm's virtuoso abilities as he tackled Beethoven's 'Moonlight Sonata' and a Debussy composition, but also aired some fine jazz-rock-flavoured material, showing admirable restraint in only adopting the lead role periodically, and concentrating on superb rhythm playing and song integrity as guests Satriani and Allan Holdsworth added colour. Hamm adopted a funkier element in his playing on *Kings Of Sleep*, with the stunning 'Black Ice' demonstrating a remarkable ability to both drive and enhance a song through his dextrous rhythm-playing. Shotgun Messiah's Harry K Cody added some excellent lead guitar, and worked with Hamm again, along with Eric Johnson, on *The Urge*. Curiously, Hamm's career paralleled that of Satriani in his addition of lead vocals to some tracks on his third album, just as Satriani had done on *Flying In A Blue Dream*, but the album's outstanding piece was a live solo spot, 'Quahogs, Anyone?'. In addition to his own albums and tours, he is a respected session musician, having worked with the likes of Steve Vai. He continues to work periodically with Satriani.
● ALBUMS: *Radio Free Albemuth* (Relativity 1988)★★★★, *Kings Of Sleep* (Relativity 1989)★★★, *The Urge* (Relativity 1991)★★★.

HAMMERHEAD

In league with groups such as Helmet and Unsane, Hammerhead have helped to blur the boundaries between US heavy metal/hard rock and punk/hardcore music. Comprising Paul Erickson (bass), Jeff Mooridian Jnr. (drums) and Paul Sanders (vocals, guitar), the group's corrosive sound properties are best sampled on their 1996 album, *Duh, The Big City*. The latest in a series of singles and albums for the acclaimed independent label Amphetamine Reptile, it was the last release to feature departing frontman Sanders. However, it successfully distilled all of the band's most distinctive qualities - resonant feedback and sonic disharmony playing as large a part as ever in the group's musical equation.
● ALBUMS: *Duh, The Big City* (Amphetamine Reptile 1996)★★★.

Hammersmith

Comprising Doran Beattie (vocals), Dan Lowe (guitar), Jeff Boyne (guitar), Royden Morice (bass) and James Llewellyn (drums), Canadian hard rock group Hammersmith formed following the dissolution of Painter. They recorded a self-titled debut album for Mercury Records in 1975, but soon after its release Boyne was replaced by Craig Blair (guitar) and Llewellyn by Dale Buchner (drums). Their second release, *It's For You*, moved away from the conventional rock patterns of their debut with more esoteric, humorous lyrics and some musical themes borrowed from the progressive rock era. It failed to boost their fortunes, however, and soon after its release the group broke up. Lowe subsequently joined 451°.

● ALBUMS: *Hammersmith* (Mercury 1975)★★★, *It's For You* (Mercury 1976)★★★.

Hand Of Glory

US hard rock band Hand Of Glory are dark Texan romantics with a strong dash of southern gothic. Although they share some musical similarities with the Cult and the Doors, Hand Of Glory have a unique sound. *Far From Kith and Kin*, featured some strong moments, most notably the ironic revolutionary anthem 'Ball And Chain', but lacked identity. With *Here Be Serpents* they blended the magical, the maudlin and the macabre with vitality and wit.

● ALBUMS: *Far From Kith And Kin* (Skyclad 1989)★★, *Here Be Serpents* (Skyclad 1990)★★★.

Handsome Beasts

Hailing from Wolverhampton, England, the Handsome Beasts are the band responsible for launching the Heavy Metal Records label/company after their manager, Paul Birch, was unable to secure them a contract. A thoroughly melodramatic band, perhaps typical of the New Wave Of British Heavy Metal, they were still able to grab the attention of the press thanks to their humungous lead vocalist, Gary Dalloway. He appeared totally naked in a pig sty (complete with pig) for their first album cover. The rest of the band, Paul Robins (guitar), Steve Hough (bass) and Pete Malbassa (drums), were always overshadowed by Dalloway's image, yet they managed to produce some fine recordings that passed totally unmentioned. The only exception was the single 'Sweeties', but again it was because of its cover that publicity was gained. Not surprisingly, the band disintegrated. In 1990 Dalloway (now slimmer) revamped the band, utilizing the 'bad taste' sleeve angle for one last time (a woman and a dog). This tawdry sensationalism was quite rightly given little press coverage and the band finally faded away.

● ALBUMS: *Beastiality* (Heavy Metal 1981)★★, *The Beast Within* (FM Revolver 1990)★★★.

Hannover Fist

Their name a pun on the expression 'hand over fist', this hard rock group was formed in the mid-80s and brought together several veterans of the Canadian metal scene, namely Frank Zrione (vocals), George Bernhardt (guitars), Chris Brockway (guitars), David Applin (bass) and Kim Hunt (drums). Bernhardt was the best-known of the members, having formerly achieved considerable success working with Lee Aaron. Signed to MCA Records in 1985, the group's self-titled debut was heavily promoted by the label, who undoubtedly regretted their investment in the group when they broke up before a supporting tour could be finalized. *Hannover Fist* was thus deleted within weeks of its release, despite strong reviews for its intricate, April Wine-derived style.

● ALBUMS: *Hannover Fist* (MCA 1985)★★★.

Hanoi Rocks

This Finnish heavy rock band was distinguished by their leanings towards 70s glam rock, which they carried off with more style and conviction than any of their peers. Initially the brainchild of Andy McCoy (b. Antti Hulkko) and Michael Monroe (b. Matti Fagerholm) in 1976, the group was not formed until 1980 when singer Monroe enlisted Nasty Suicide (b. Jan Stenfors; guitar), Stefan Piesmack (guitar), Pasi Sti (bass) and Peki Senola (drums). By September, when they recorded their debut album, *Bangkok Shocks, Saigon Shakes, Hanoi Rocks* (initially only released in Scandinavia), the line-up was Monroe, Suicide, McCoy (guitar), Sam Yaffa (b. Sami Takamaki; bass) and Gyp Casino (b. Jesper Sporre; drums). McCoy had previously played with two Finnish punk bands, Briard and Pelle Miljoona Oy. In addition, Suicide had played in Briard, while Yaffa had also been a member of Pelle Miljoona Oy at various times. Hanoi Rocks' debut single - 'I Want You', was released on the Finnish Johanna label in 1980 and preceded the album. The band then travelled to London where they began recording *Oriental Beat*. Soon after it was finished, Casino was sacked (and joined the Road Rats) and replaced by Razzle (b. Nicholas Dingley, 2 December 1963, Isle Of Wight, England), who had previously played with Demon

Preacher and the Dark. In 1983 they were signed to CBS Records and started to attract attention in the British music press. They hit the UK charts for the first and only time in 1984 with a cover version of Creedence Clearwater Revival's 'Up Around The Bend', but the year ended in tragedy. The band were in the USA when Razzle was killed in a car crash on 7 December. The car driver - Vince Neil of Mötley Crüe - was later found guilty of Vehicular Manslaughter. Former Clash drummer Terry Chimes was brought in as a replacement and when Yaffa left (to form Chain Gang, and then join Jetboy), Rene Berg (ex-Idle Flowers) also joined the group. However, Monroe never accepted the loss of Razzle and in early 1985 he informed the band that he intended to quit. Hanoi Rocks played their final gig in May 1985 and Monroe has since embarked on a solo career. Piesmack joined Pelle Miljoona Oy, then abandoned music, and Sti and Senola also left the music scene. McCoy, who had already formed a side-project in 1983 - the Urban Dogs - with Charlie Harper, Alvin Gibbs (UK Subs) and Knox (Vibrators), went on to form the Cherry Bombz with Suicide, Chimes and ex-Toto Coelo vocalist Anita Chellemah. The Cherry Bombz barely lasted a year and the members went on to play in various short-lived outfits, most notably Suicide (with Gibbs once more) in Cheap 'N' Nasty. A near-reunion of Hanoi Rocks, featuring Monroe with Suicide and Sam Yaffa, emerged as Demolition 23 in 1994.

● ALBUMS: *Bangkok Shocks, Saigon Shakes, Hanoi Rocks* (Johanna 1981)★★★, *Oriental Beat* (Johanna 1982)★★★, *Self Destruction Blues* (Johanna 1982)★★★, *Back To Mystery City* (Lick 1983)★★★, *Two Steps From The Move* (Columbia 1984)★★★.

● COMPILATIONS: *All Those Wasted Years* (Johanna 1985)★★, *Rock 'N' Roll Divorce* (Lick 1985)★★, *Best Of Hanoi Rocks* (Lick 1985)★★★, *Dead By Christmas* (Raw Power 1986)★★, *Tracks From A Broken Dream* (Lick 1990)★★★.

● VIDEOS: *All Those Wasted Years* (1988), *The Nottingham Tapes* (1988).

Hansen, Randy

Raised in Seattle, Washington, USA, guitarist Hansen first attracted attention as a member of nightclub act Kid Chrysler And The Cruisers. The group's tongue-in-cheek repertoire encompassed several styles of popular music, but was marked by the musician's imperturbable pastiche of Jimi Hendrix. Having formed a trio, Machine Gun, in 1977, Hansen took his tribute on tour, but achieved a greater notoriety when he contributed Hendrix-influenced effects to the film soundtrack of *Apocalypse Now*. This in turn engendered a management agreement with San Francisco-based entrepreneur David Rubinson, who began promoting his client as an artist in his own right. *Randy Hansen* comprised original material that sadly paled in comparison with that of his mentor. Hendrix's songs still provided the focal point of the guitarist's live act, and in 1984 he reverted completely to the role of imitator by joining drummer Buddy Miles in a revamped version of Band Of Gypsies. The 90s saw Hansen working as part of a tribute revue with original Hendrix bass player Noel Redding.

● ALBUMS: *Randy Hansen* (EMI 1981)★★, *Astral Projection Live* (Shrapnel 1983)★★.

Hard Response

Comprising Tony Triano (vocals), Chris Caputo (guitar), Mark Terranova (bass) and Don DeKay (drums), this group is a powerful representative of the US derivation of hardcore known colloquially as 'emo-core'. With its accent on highly personal, intense songwriting in place of posture and machismo, the description accurately fitted Hard Response. The group formed in 1991, at which time their first demo tape began to circulate and gained them their first shows with Sick Of It All. These appearances gave way to a clutch of support slots with Madball, Dog Eat Dog and the Cro-Mags, and their debut EP, *Mindrape*. Two appearances on east coast compilations enhanced their reputation, before the release of *Single Bullet Theory*, which impressively attached melody and texture to the familiar hardcore assault, with particularly strong vocals from Triano.

● ALBUMS: *Single Bullet Theory* (Gain Ground 1995)★★★.

Hard-Ons

Belligerent punk rock band the Hard-Ons were formed in Sydney, Australia, in 1982, from the ashes of the Plebs and Dead Rats (neither of whom recorded). They were immediately celebrated for their live performances, channelled through Ray Ahn (bass), Peter Black (guitar) and Keish De Silva (drums, vocals). Despite the band members originating in Korea, Yugoslavia and Sri Lanka, early press coverage suggested they might have fascist sympathies. Though there was no foundation for such accusations, their graphic record sleeves and lyrics certainly suggested a nonconformist view of sexual politics. Their recording career began with the limited edition (1,000 copies) *Surfin' On My Face* EP for Vi-Nil Records in 1985. A series of further singles ('Suck'n'Swallow', 'Girl In A Sweater'), fanzine freebies and compilation discs duly appeared. Their debut album, *Smell My Finger*, delighted in the vulgarity suggested by its title, and was issued in America as *The Hard-Ons*, with its crude sleeve drawing amended. *Hot For Your Love, Baby* was repackaged by Vinyl Solution Records in 1988 for European audiences as *The Worst Of The Hard-Ons* (with the addition of their 1987 single, 'All Set To Go'). *Dickcheese* followed, by which time the group's tasteless, primal rock 'n' roll style had been firmly established. After their 1989 studio album, the Hard-Ons also recorded a split 10-inch, eight-song EP with England's Stupids. *Yummy* proved the group's strongest collection of songs thus far, despite a monstrously irreverent cover version of Led Zeppelin's 'Stairway To Heaven'. In 1990 they appeared on the Kiss tribute album *Hard To Believe*. *Dull*'s sleeve parodied Deep Purple's famous *In Rock* artwork, while the accompanying 12-inch single, 'Let There Be Rock', was an entertaining cover version of the AC/DC standard with Henry Rollins guesting on vocals. The title of the group's 1993 album, *Too Far Gone*, proved prophetic, however. Despite vocal contributions from Poison Idea's Jerry A. ('The Blade'), and a tour of the UK in November, it was their final recording.

● ALBUMS: *Smell My Finger* aka *Hard-Ons* (Waterfront 1986)★★, *Hot For Your Love, Baby* aka *The Worst Of The Hard-Ons* (Waterfront 1987)★★, *Dickcheese* (Vinyl Solution 1988)★★, *No Cheese* split mini-album with the Stupids (Vinyl Solution 1988)★★, *Love Is A Battlefield Of Wounded Hearts* (Waterfront 1989)★★★, *Yummy* (Waterfront 1990)★★★, *Dull* (Vinyl Solution 1991)★★★, *Too Far Gone* (Survival 1993)★★.

HARDLINE

This US hard rock act evolved from a songwriting partnership between brothers Johnny and Joey Gioeli (vocals and guitar, respectively, both ex-Brunette) and ex-Santana, Journey and Bad English guitarist Neal Schon. Bad English drummer Deen Castronovo joined, and completed the rhythm section by drafting in childhood friend Todd Jensen (ex-David Lee Roth; bass). *Double Eclipse* was classy American radio rock, with Schon unleashing some of the guitar firepower that had been restricted by Bad English's lighter AOR style, and the band spent some time touring, including US dates supporting Van Halen, before the debut was actually released. However, when Schon, Jensen and Castronovo took considerable time off to act as a backing band on Paul Rodgers' solo tour, the resulting friction split Hardline.

● ALBUMS: *Double Eclipse* (MCA 1992)★★★.

HARDSTUFF

As their name implied, Hardstuff were a UK trio of no-nonsense hard rockers from the early 70s. Comprising John DuCann (vocals/guitar; ex-Atomic Rooster), John Gustafson (vocals/bass) and Paul Hammond (drums), they released two gritty albums for Purple Records (Deep Purple's record label) in 1972 and 1973 before disbanding. Both *Bullet Proof* and *Bolex Dementia* were excellent collections which entertained few commercial considerations in favour of a direct, minimalist rock sound which predicted the later rise of Motörhead.

● ALBUMS: *Bullet Proof* (Purple 1972)★★★★, *Bolex Dementia* (Purple 1973)★★★★.

HARLEQUIN

An underachieving melodic rock act formed in the USA in the late 70s, Harlequin attracted a modicum of interest over a four-album-long career without ever threatening to break into the mainstream. Comprising George Belanger (vocals), Glen Willows (guitar), Gary Golden (keyboards), Ralph James (bass) and David Budzak (drums), they made their debut for Epic Records in 1978 with *Victim Of A Song*. The follow-up, 1980's *Love Crimes*, is widely considered to be their strongest set, with Willows' guitar and Golden's keyboards having moulded a distinctive AOR sound. Subsequent albums failed to produce any showing in the US charts, however, and the group had disbanded by the mid-80s.

● ALBUMS: *Victim Of A Song* (Epic 1978)★★, *Love Crimes* (Epic 1980)★★★, *One False Move* (Epic 1982)★★, *Harlequin* (Epic 1984)★★.

HARRY CREWS

Named after the cult US novelist, Harry Crews was a short-lived project featuring Lydia Lunch (vocals), Kim Gordon (bass, vocals), concurrently of Sonic Youth, and Sadie Mae (drums). In 1988 the group undertook a tour of the UK and Europe, parts of which were preserved on *Naked In Garden Hills*, initially released on Lunch's own Widowspeak label. The album owes much to Lunch's confrontational style, although the tempo is markedly more upbeat than most of her work. Its content is largely inspired by Crews' writings, notably 'Knockout Artist', the title of one of his novels. However, the album does include a virulent version of Sonic Youth's '(She's In A) Bad Mood'. Harry Crews split up in 1988 when the tour was complete.

● ALBUMS: *Naked In Garden Hills* (Widowspeak 1989)★★★.

HATCHER, GEORGE, BAND

b. Florida, USA. Though born in Florida, hard rock vocalist and songwriter George Hatcher was forced to relocate to England to form a permanent backing band. Accompanied by 'Big' John Thomas (guitar), Phil Swan (guitar), Steve Wren (keyboards), Harris Joannou (bass) and Chris Slade (drums), Hatcher enjoyed a glimpse of mainstream success in 1976 by acquiring support slots to Status Quo. The group made its debut for United Artists Records with the release of *Dry Run* later that year. Located in mid-tempo hard rock territory, with Lynyrd Skynyrd an obvious influence, it was well received by UK critics. However, when *Talking Turkey* failed to consolidate the band's commercial position, the group folded. Hatcher was prevented from using the band name by record company litigation, though a further album, *Rich Girl*, did emerge for Shark Records after Hatcher relocated to Germany at the end of the 70s. Thomas subsequently joined Budgie while Slade worked with Uriah Heep, then the Firm and AC/DC.

● ALBUMS: *Dry Run* (United Artists 1976)★★★, *Talking Turkey* (United Artists 1977)★★, *Rich Girl* (Shark 1978)★★.

HAUNTED

Led by intimidating, shaven-headed singer Peter Dolving, hard rock band the Haunted were formed in Stockholm, Sweden, in July 1997. Brothers Anders (rhythm guitar) and Jonas Bjorler (bass) and Adrian Erlandsson (drums) had all previously recorded with At The Gates. Surnameless lead guitarist Jensen formerly played with Séance. Dolving, who spent much of his early life in Seattle, had previously sung on Mary Beats Jane's two well-received albums. The Haunted's debut album was notable for its ostensibly downbeat tone, notably album opener 'Hate Song' and the bleak 'Forensick' – an anti-rape tract. *Kerrang!* acclaimed the record as 'the best (album) to fit the thrash metal tag in aeons.'

● ALBUMS: *The Haunted* (Earache 1998)★★★★.

HAVANA BLACK

A pseudonymous quartet of Guts (vocals), Crazy (guitar), Risto (bass) and J.T. (bass), Finnish heavy metal/blues rock group Havana Black released their domestic debut album in 1988. This was quickly followed by an international release for Capitol Records. The sound on *Indian Warrior* was cited by critics as a direct descendent of the mid-70s work of Bad Company and Humble Pie, though their stage presentation had more in common with the street imagery of fellow countrymen Hanoi Rocks. The majority of the songs were the same as those included on their domestic debut, although some of the lyrics had been sanitized for the American market. It was heavily promoted but fared poorly in a market saturated with fellow 70s revivalist bands such as the Black Crowes and the Quireboys.

● ALBUMS: *Indian Warrior* (Capitol 1989)★★★.

HAVOHEJ

This profane black metal outfit was formed in June 1993, and was led by self-confessed New York Satanist, drum-teacher and graphic artist, Paul Ledney: 'In the days when Venom first appeared there was something very personal about what was going on. You could relate to the music. Now there are just too many trendies jumping on a bandwagon and imitating what they perceive as being the atmosphere of the genre. They all put on make-up and sing about Satan. They believe that alone makes them evil'. Equally influenced by the early punk bands, Ledney put together Havohej as a studio project following the dissolution of his earlier band, Profanatica, when tapes of their first full album together were mysteriously destroyed in the studio (arguably a good thing, given its working title - *The Raping Of The Virgin Mary*). They had previously recorded a split album with Columbian band Massacre for the Osmose label, and a three-track single, 'Unholy Darkness And Impurity'. Like Profanatica, Havohej benefited from the underground tape scene, particularly as many of the songs on the band's debut album were reconstructions of material from Ledney's former outfit. However, by the middle of 1994 Havohej, too, were no more.

● ALBUMS: *Dethrone The God* (Candlelight 1993)★★.

HAWAII

Comprising Eddie Day (vocals), Marty Friedman (guitar), Tom Azcredo (guitar), Joe Galisha (bass) and Jeff Graves (drums), Hawaii were one in a sequence of bands to highlight the virtuoso guitar capabilities of Friedman. After the collapse of Deuce, Vixen (not the all-female quartet) and

Aloha, Friedman formed Hawaii in the early 80s. Three albums emerged for a succession of labels, none quite capturing his true abilities. *The Natives Are Restless* was probably the best example of an uneven discography, but soon after its release Friedman was on the move again. After two albums with Cacophony he moved on to a solo career before joining Megadeth.

● ALBUMS: *One Nation Underground* (Shrapnel 1983)★★, *Loud Wild And Heavy* (Indie 1985)★★, *The Natives Are Restless* (Steamhammer 1985)★★.

HAWKWIND

Befitting a group associated with community and benefit concerts, Hawkwind was founded in the hippie enclave centred on London's Ladbroke Grove during the late 60s. Dave Brock (b. Isleworth, Middlesex, England; guitar, vocals), Nik Turner (b. Oxford, Oxfordshire, England; saxophone, vocals), Mick Slattery (guitar), Dik Mik (b. Richmond, Surrey; electronics), John Harrison (bass) and Terry Ollis (drums) were originally known as Group X, then Hawkwind Zoo, prior to securing a recording contract. Their debut, *Hawkwind*, was produced by Dick Taylor, former guitarist with the Pretty Things, who briefly augmented his new protégés on Slattery's departure. Indeed, Hawkwind underwent many personnel changes, but by 1972 had achieved a core consisting of Brock, Turner, Del Dettmar (b. Thornton Heath, Surrey, England; synthesizer), Lemmy (b. Ian Kilmister, 24 December 1945, Stoke-on-Trent, Staffordshire, England; bass), Simon King (b. Oxford, Oxfordshire, England; drums), Stacia (b. Exeter, Devon, England; dancer) and poet/writer Robert Calvert (b. *c.*1945, Pretoria, South Africa, d. 14 August 1988; vocals). One part-time member was science-fiction writer Michael Moorcock who helped to organize some of Hawkwind's concert appearances and often deputized for Calvert when the latter was indisposed. This role was extended to recording credits on several albums. The group's chemically blurred science-fiction image was emphasized in such titles as *In Search Of Space* and *Space Ritual*. They enjoyed a freak UK pop hit when the compulsive 'Silver Machine' soared to number 3 in July 1972, but this flirtation with a wider audience ended prematurely when a follow-up single, 'Urban Guerilla', was hastily withdrawn in the wake of a terrorist bombing campaign in London. Hawkwind continued to discard personalities; Calvert left and then rejoined, Dettmar was replaced by Simon House (ex-High Tide), but the group lost much of its impetus in 1975 when Lemmy was fired on his arrest on drugs charges during a North American tour. The bassist subsequently formed Motörhead. Although the group enjoyed a period of relative stability following the release of *Astounding Sounds, Amazing Music*, it ended in 1977 with the firing of founder-member Turner and two latter additions, Paul Rudolph (ex-Deviants and Pink Fairies) and Alan Powell. The following year, Simon House left to join David Bowie's band before Brock, Calvert and King assumed a new name, the Hawklords, to avoid legal and contractual complications. The group reverted to its former appellation in 1979, by which time Calvert had resumed his solo career. An undaunted Hawkwind pursued an eccentric path throughout the 80s. Dave Brock remained at the helm of a flurry of associates, including Huw Lloyd Langton, who played guitar on the group's debut album, Tim Blake (synthesizer), Alan Davey (bass) and drummer Ginger Baker. Nik Turner also reappeared in the ranks of a group that has continued to enjoy a committed following, despite the bewildering array of archive releases obscuring the group's contemporary standing. In 1990 they underwent a resurgence in popularity thanks primarily to the growth of the rave culture and their album, *Space Bandits*, reflected this new, young interest. It also saw the return of Simon House and the inclusion for the first time of a female vocalist, Bridgett Wishart (ex-Hippy Slags). However, when their next album started to copy rave ideas, it became obvious that they were running out of inspiration, with *Palace Springs* containing no less than five new versions of early tracks. In 1992 they completed a successful American tour, but on their return fell apart. Eventually reduced to a three-piece (Brock, Davey and drummer Richard Chadwick), they became totally dance/rave-orientated and subsequent releases had little in common with the classic days gone by.

● ALBUMS: *Hawkwind* (Liberty 1970)★★★★, *In Search Of Space* (United Artists 1971)★★★★, *Doremi Fasol Latido* (United Artists 1972)★★, *Space Ritual* (United Artists 1973)★★★★, *Hall Of The Mountain Grill* (United Artists 1974)★★★, *Warrior On The Edge Of Time* (United Artists 1975)★★★, *Astounding Sounds, Amazing Music* (Charisma 1976)★★★, *Quark, Strangeness And Charm* (Charisma 1977)★★, as Hawklords *25 Years On* (Charisma 1978)★★, *PXR5* (Charisma 1979)★★★, *Live 79* (Bronze 1980)★★, *Levitation* (Bronze 1980)★★★, *Sonic Attack* (RCA 1981)★★★, *Church Of Hawkwind* (RCA 1982)★★, *Choose Your Masques* (RCA 1982)★★★, *Zones* (Flicknife

1983)★★★, *Stonehenge: This Is Hawkwind Do Not Panic* (Flicknife 1984)★★, *Bring Me The Head Of Yuri Gagarin* 1973 recording (Demi-Monde 1985)★, *Space Ritual Volume 2* (American Phonograph 1985)★★★, *Chronicle Of The Black Sword* (Flicknife 1985)★★★, *Ridicule* (Obsession 1985)★★★, *Live Chronicles* (GWR 1986)★★★, *Out & Intake* (Flicknife 1987)★★, *The Xenon Codex* (GWR 1988)★★★, *Space Bandits* (GWR 1990)★★★, *Palace Springs* (GWR 1991)★★, *BBC Radio 1 Live In Concert* (Windsong 1991)★★★, *The Friday Rock Show Sessions: Live At Reading '86* (Raw Fruit 1992)★★, *Electric Tepee* (Castle 1992)★★★, *It Is The Business Of The Future To Be Dangerous* (Castle 1993)★★★, *The Business Trip: Live* (Emergency Broadcast Systems 1994)★★, *California Brainstorm* (Iloki/Cyclops 1995)★★★, *Future Reconstructions: Ritual Of The Solstice* (Emergency Broadcast Systems 1996)★★★, *1999 Party - Live At The Chicago Auditorium March 21 1974* (EMI 1997)★★★.

● COMPILATIONS: *Road Hawks* (United Artists 1976)★★★, *Masters Of The Universe* (United Artists 1977)★★★, *Repeat Performance* (Charisma 1980)★★★, *Hawkwind, Friends And Relations* (Flicknife 1982)★, *Twice Upon A Time: Hawkwind, Friends And Relations Volume 2* (Flicknife 1983)★★, *The Text Of Festival (Hawkwind Live 1970-72)* (Illuminated 1983)★★, *Independent Days* mini-album (Flicknife 1984)★★, *Hawkwind, Friends And Relations Volume 3* (Flicknife 1985)★★, *Live 70/73* (Castle/Dojo 1985)★★, *In The Beginning* (Demi-Monde 1985)★★, *Utopia 84* (Mausoleum 1985)★★, *Anthology Volume 1* (Samurai 1985)★★★, *Welcome To The Future* (Mausoleum 1985)★★, *Anthology Volume 2* (Samurai 1986)★★★, *Anthology Volume 3* (Samurai 1986)★★, *Hawkfan 12* (Hawkfan 1986)★★★, *The Hawkwind Collection* (Castle 1986)★★★★, *Angels Of Death* (RCA 1986)★★★, *Independent Days Volume 2* (Flicknife 1986)★★, *Approved History Of Hawkwind* 3-LP set (Samurai 1986)★★★, *British Tribal Music* (Start 1987)★★, *Early Daze (Best Of Hawkwind)* (Thunderbolt 1987)★★, *Spirit Of The Age* (Virgin 1988)★★★, *Best Of Hawkwind, Friends And Relations* (Flicknife 1988)★★★, *Ironstrike* (Avanti 1989)★★, *Night Of The Hawk* (Powerhouse 1989)★★★, *The Best Of And The Rest Of Hawkwind Live* (Action Replay 1990)★★, *Night Riding* (Knight 1990)★★, *Stasis: The UA Years 1971-1975* (EMI 1990)★★★, *Masters Of The Universe* not 1977 UA release (Marble Arch 1991)★★, *Spirit Of The Age* not 1988 Virgin release (Elite 1991)★★, *Anthology* 3-CD set (Castle 1991)★★★, *Mighty Hawkwind Classics 1980-1985* (Anagram 1992)★★★, *The Pychedelic Warlords* (Cleopatra 1992)★★★, *Lord Of Light* (Cleopatra 1993)★★★, *Hawkwind, Friends And Relations, The Rarities* (Anagram 1995)★★★.

● VIDEOS: *Night Of The Hawks* (Jettisoundz 1984), with Roy Harper, Enid *Stonehenge 84* (Jettisoundz 1984), *Chronicle Of The Black Sword* (Jettisoundz 1986), *Live Legends* (Castle 1990), *Promo Collection* (Castle 1992), *Hawkwind: The Solstice At Stonehenge 1984* (1993), *Love In Space 1995* (Visionary 1996).

● FURTHER READING: *This Is Hawkwind, Do Not Panic*, Kris Tait.

HAYWIRE

Canadian hard rock band Haywire comprises Paul MacAuland (vocals), Martin Birt (guitar), David Rashed (keyboards), Ronnie Switzer (bass) and Sean Killbridge (drums). The highlight of their live performances and three studio albums was undoubtedly MacAuland's effervescent vocals, which accompanied studied musical patterns placed firmly within the US AOR radio tradition. Despite achieving platinum saless for *Bad Boys* and *Don't Just Stand There* in Canada, neither record was released in the USA or Europe. 1990's *Nut House* was produced by Stagedolls and TNT collaborator Bjorn Nessjoe and saw them move to a more rough-hewn, basic rock sound akin to early Aerosmith. Once again, it was not released outside Canada and Haywire remain an entirely domestic success story.

● ALBUMS: *Bad Boys* (Attic 1986)★★★★, *Don't Just Stand There* (Attic 1987)★★★★, *Nut House* (Attic 1990)★★.

HAZE

This UK hard rock trio, comprising Paul McMahon (vocals, guitars), Chris McMahon (bass) and Paul Chisnell (drums), specialized in grandiose thematic musical designs that were conversely accompanied by unflattering, low-key production on their 1984 debut. Their studio technique progressed as the band matured, however, and by *Stoat & Bottle*, their intricate musical skills had been matched to a better grasp of songwriting dynamics. Despite this, the album sold no better than its forerunners and Haze disappeared shortly after its release.

● ALBUMS: *C'est La Vie* (Gabadon 1984)★★, *Warts 'n' All* (Pinnacle 1986)★★★, *Stoat & Bottle* (Gabadon 1987)★★★.

HEAD EAST

An example of stubborn belligerence ensuring longevity despite limited musical identity, Head East persevered on the Midwest, USA circuit for several years, releasing a sequence of competent hard rock albums without ever making the transition to international fame that peers such as REO Speedwagon enjoyed. Comprising John Schlitt (vocals), Mike Sommerville (guitar), Roger Boyd (keyboards), Dan Birney (bass) and Steve Huston (drums), after forming in St. Louis, Missouri, they cultivated a highly commercial hard rock sound that made them perfect for AOR radio. Critics were less appreciative of their earnest, hard driving sound (reflected in lyrics which dwelled on domestic and romantic themes), but their live following by the end of the 70s was considerable. Accordingly, their best album of this period was the 1979 *Head East Live!* set, attaining the group's highest chart placing at US number 65. In the early 80s the group attempted to restrain their sound and convert their local popularity into national chart placings, but despite cover versions of material by Russ Ballard, they never made the transition. For *U.S. 1* Schlitt, Sommerville and Birney all left, with their replacements being Dan Odum (vocals), Tony Gross (guitar) and Mark Boatman (bass). Eventually A&M Records, their home since 1975, became frustrated by their lack of national success and dropped the group. One further album emerged for an independent in 1982, but the group broke up following its release. A late 80s reunion saw the release of *Choice Of Weapons*, but this lacked the original spirit of the band and fared poorly.

● ALBUMS: *Flat As A Pancake* (A&M 1975)★★★★, *Get Yourself Up* (A&M 1976)★★★, *Gettin' Lucky* (A&M 1977)★★, *Head East* (A&M 1978)★★★, *Head East Live!* (A&M 1979)★★★, *A Different Kind Of Crazy* (A&M 1979)★★, *U.S. 1* (A&M 1980)★★, *Onwards And Upwards* (Allegiance 1982)★★, *Choice Of Weapons* (Dark Heart 1989)★★.

HEADGIRL

A project conceived by British rock bands Motörhead and Girlschool, both of whom shared the same manager and record company, Bronze. The collaboration arose when Motörhead had to cancel a tour after their drummer, Taylor, broke his neck. They were at a Girlschool recording session when producer Vic Maile suggested that they work together. The result was an EP, *St. Valentine's Day Massacre*, spearheaded by 'Please Don't Touch', a cover version of a Johnny Kidd And The Pirates song from 1960. This was recorded in December 1980 at the Jackson studio, Rickmansworth, Hertfordshire, and its success led to Headgirl (an amalgamation of the names of the two bands) appearing no less than three times on the UK television music programme *Top Of The Pops*.

HEADSWIM

Headswim, who specialize in a virulent brand of funk metal, were formed in Essex, England, in 1992. They consist of ex-Blinder frontman Dan Glendining (b. 11 October 1971, Essex, England; vocals, guitar), Nick Watts (b. 1970; keyboards), Tom Glendining (b. 1970; drums) and Clovis (b. Clovis Dilwood Taylor, 1971; bass). The group's second EP, *Moment Of Union*, drew comparisons with Pearl Jam, Soundgarden and others, and preceded a mini-album, *Tense Moments*. This was the first instalment in a long-term development contract the group had secured with Epic Records/Sony Records. It was followed by *Flood* in October 1994, a much darker, more sombre affair than many had predicted. Their February 1995 single, 'Crawl', reached the Top 60 in the UK, furthering a reputation built on solid touring. The death of the Glendinings' younger brother delayed the follow-up, but the strikingly inventive *Despite Yourself* proved to be worth the wait. The hard-rocking 'Torniquet' was a hit in both America and England.

● ALBUMS: *Tense Moments* mini-album (Epic 1994)★★★, *Flood* (Epic 1994)★★★, *Despite Yourself* (Epic 1998)★★★★.

HEAR 'N' AID

The Hear 'N' Aid project came about after Jimmy Bain and Vivian Campbell of Dio had taken part in a 'Radiothon' held over a weekend by KLOS of Los Angeles for the famine in Africa. Realizing that very few rock stars were involved, they initially contacted Ronnie James Dio to tell him of the project. While Dio attempted to gather more support, Bain and Campbell wrote the score, and Dio produced the lyrics. 'Stars' was recorded over a four-month period in 1986. In addition to the single release, a video was planned and all the sessions were filmed. They ambitiously planned to release an album on which each act would write a track, but this never occurred. Instead, bands donated tracks, most of which were live recordings. Another idea was for a session to be held in London, so that European rock stars could be included, but this, too, was aborted due to lack of participants. Those that did take part included the following: Queensrÿche, Rough Cutt, Iron Maiden, Ted Nugent, Y&T, Spinal Tap, Night Ranger, Twisted Sister, Mötley Crüe, Vanilla Fudge, Dio, Blue Öyster Cult, Don Dokken, Yngwie Malmsteen, Quiet Riot, Judas Priest, King Kobra, W.A.S.P. and Journey.

● ALBUMS: *Hear 'N' Aid* (Vertigo 1986)★★★.

HEART

This durable US rock band features the talents of sisters Ann (b. 19 June 1951, San Diego, California, USA) and Nancy Wilson (b. 16 March 1954, San Francisco, California, USA). The elder sister had released two singles as Ann Wilson And The Daybreaks on a local label in 1967. After a series of unreleased demos she took her sister to Vancouver, Canada, in search of a backing band. There they found bassist Steve Fossen (b. 15 November 1949) and guitarist Roger Fisher (b. 14 February 1950), and Heart was born (two initial monikers, the Army and White Heart, were rejected). After *Dreamboat Annie* emerged on Mushroom Records in 1976, their second single, 'Crazy On You', brought them to public attention. Michael Derosier (b. 24 August 1951, Canada) had previously become the band's first permanent drummer. They maintained their high profile when *Little Queen* and the single, 'Barracuda', became mainstays in the US charts. By the time *Dog And Butterfly* arrived in 1978, the professional relationships within the band had escalated to ones of a more personal nature, with Nancy Wilson dating guitarist Fisher, while sister Ann was involved with his brother, Mike. Mike Fisher, who had once been part of the group's embryonic line-up, had become their unofficial manager. However, before sessions for *Bebe Le Strange* on Epic were complete, the relationships had soured and Roger Fisher left the band, leaving the group bereft of the lead guitar that had previously been so prominent in the group's formula. The guitar parts were covered on tour by Nancy and multi-instrumentalist Howard Leese (b. 13 June 1953, Canada), who became a permanent member. By the time they resurfaced with *Private Audition* in 1983, Fossen and Derosier were also on the verge of departure. Their replacements were Mark Andes (b. 19 February 1948, Philadelphia, USA; ex-Spirit) and Denny Carmassi (ex-Montrose and Sammy Hagar), though their efforts on *Passionworks* were not enough to inspire any kind of revival in Heart's fortunes. Their confidence was bolstered, however, when Ann's duet with Mike Dean (Loverboy) produced 'Almost Paradise...Love Theme From Footloose', which rose to number 7 in the US charts. When Epic allowed their contract to lapse, Heart joined Capitol Records in 1985, seemingly with their career in its death throes. The new label brought about a transformation in the band's image, projecting them as a more rock-orientated concern, but could hardly have expected the turnaround in Heart's fortunes that resulted. *Heart* gave them a number 1 in the USA, and the highly lucrative singles 'What About Love' and 'Never', before 'These Dreams' finally achieved the equivalent number 1 slot in the singles chart. The follow-up, *Bad Animals*, was almost as successful, stalling at number 2. While both Wilson sisters continued to work on soundtrack cuts, the most profitable of which was Ann's duet with Robin Zander (Cheap Trick), 'Surrender To Me', Nancy married *Rolling Stone* writer Cameron Crowe. Heart's success continued with the long-projected *Brigade* in 1990, from which 'All I Wanna Do Is Make Love To You' (written by Robert John 'Mutt' Lange) became a Top 10 hit in the UK and a number 1 in the USA. Both Wilson sisters then became involved in solo projects, while former companions Fossen, Roger Fisher and Derosier embarked on a new dual career with Alias, who had two big US singles hits in 1990. The sisters returned as Heart in 1993, backed by Schuyler Deale (bass), John Purdell (keyboards), Denny Carmassi (drums) and Lease (guitar) and found themselves with another hit on their hands in 'Will You Be There (In The Morning)', which preceded *Desire Walks On*. *The Road Home* was an acoustic live album with production by John Paul Jones, released to mark the band's 20th anniversary.

● ALBUMS: *Dreamboat Annie* (Mushroom 1976)★★★★, *Little Queen* (Portrait 1977)★★★, *Dog And Butterfly* (Portrait 1978)★★★★, *Magazine* (Mushroom 1978)★★, *Bebe Le Strange* (Portrait 1980)★★★, *Greatest Hits/Live* (Portrait 1981)★★★, *Private Audition* (Epic 1982)★★, *Passionworks* (Epic 1983)★★, *Heart* (Capitol 1985)★★, *Bad Animals* (Capitol 1987)★★, *Brigade* (Capitol 1990)★★, *Rock The House Live!* (Capitol 1991)★★, *Desire Walks On* (Capitol 1993)★★, *The Road Home* (Capitol 1995)★★★.

● COMPILATIONS: *Heart Box Set* (Capitol 1990)★★, *Greatest Hits* (Capitol 1997)★★★.

● VIDEOS: *If Looks Could Kill* (PMI/EMI 1988), *The Road Home* (Capitol 1995).

HEARTBREAKERS

The Heartbreakers were formed in New York in 1975 when Richard Hell (b. Richard Myers, 2 October 1949, Lexington, Kentucky, USA), former bassist with Television, joined forces with Johnny Thunders (b. John Anthony Genzale Jnr., 15 July 1952, New York City, New York, USA, d. 23 April 1991, New Orleans, Louisiana, USA; guitar, vocals) and Jerry Nolan (d. 14 January 1992; drums), disaffected members of the New York Dolls. The new act made one live appearance as a trio before adding Walter Lure (guitar, vocals) to the line-up. The original Heartbreakers enjoyed cult popularity, but by the following year the mercurial Hell left to found the Voidoids. Drafting in Billy Rath as his replacement, the quartet later moved to London, eager to embrace its nascent punk movement. They supported the Sex Pistols on the aborted Anarchy tour (December 1976) and were then signed to the ailing Track Records. 'Chinese Rocks', a paean to heroin co-written by Dee Dee Ramone of the Ramones, and the subsequent *L.A.M.F.*, gave an indication of the group's 'wrong side of the tracks' rock 'n' roll strengths, but was marred by Speedy Keen's unfocused production. Nolan left the band in disgust, but returned to fulfil outstanding commitments. The Heartbreakers then severed connections with Track, but having broken up in November 1977, re-formed the following year with new drummer Ty Styx. The name was subsequently dropped and resurrected on several occasions, notably in 1984, but such interludes vied with Thunders' other, equally temporary, outlets, until he was found dead in mysterious circumstances in April 1991.

● ALBUMS: *L.A.M.F.* (Track 1977)★★★★, *Live At Max's Kansas City* (Max's Kansas City 1979)★★, *D.T.K. Live At The Speakeasy* (Jungle 1982)★★, *Live At The Lyceum Ballroom 1984* (ABC 1984)★★, *L.A.M.F. Revisited* remixed version of their debut (Jungle 1984)★★★.

● COMPILATIONS: *D.T.K. - L.A.M.F.* (Jungle 1984)★★★.

HEAVEN

Australian hard rock group Heaven formed in Adelaide in 1979. Relocating to Sydney, the group went through a number of personnel changes before establishing their line-up as Allen Fryer (vocals), Mick Cocks (guitar; ex-Rose Tattoo), Kelly Haese (guitar), Laurie Marlow (bass) and Joe Turter (drums). They made their debut for the local Deluxe Records label in 1982 with *Twilight Of Mischief*, before a US recording contract with RCA Records allowed them to distribute their records internationally. A series of critical comparisons with Cocks' former group Rose Tattoo greeted all three of their releases, though Fryer's vocals did lend the band a distinctive edge. Further line-up shuffles followed the release of *Where Angels Fear To Tread*, with Tommy Dimitroff joining on drums and Mark Cummingham on guitar. *Knockin' On Heaven's Door*, promoted by a single version of the Bob Dylan song, failed to satisfy the critics. The group continued for several more years without attaining any substantial degree of success.

● ALBUMS: *Twilight Of Mischief* (Deluxe 1982/RCA 1983)★★★, *Where Angels Fear To Tread* (Brighton/Columbia 1983)★★★, *Knockin' On Heaven's Door* (Columbia 1985)★★.

HEAVEN'S EDGE

Formed in Philadelphia, USA, contemporary hard rock group Heaven's Edge comprises Mark Evans (vocals), Reggie Wu (guitar), Steven Perry (guitar), G.G. Guidotti (bass) and David Rath (drums). With glam-rock stylings borrowed from America's west coast, early critical comparisons with Winger and Warrant ensued, though the group's self-titled debut album, released for Columbia Records in 1990, failed to elevate them to that level of commercial achievement.

● ALBUMS: *Heaven's Edge* (Columbia 1990)★★.

HEAVY LOAD

Formed in Sweden in the mid-70s, long-running hard rock band Heavy Load originally comprised Stybjoin Wahlquist (vocals), brother Ragne Wahlquist (vocals, guitar), Torbjorn Ragnes Jo (bass) and Eddy Malm (bass). They made their name on the Stockholm club circuit by dint of an elaborate stage show where visual presentation and humour was at least as important as the group's belligerent musical dirges. Stybjoin Wahlquist, in particular, was given to acts of wanton exhibitionism, which earned him a personal following on the domestic rock scene. On record, Heavy Load proved less endearing, with their primal basic metal style rapidly becoming formulaic over the course of four studio albums. Their unintentionally amusing pidgin English lyrics, in particular, weakened the overall effect.

● ALBUMS: *Full Speed At High Level* (HS 1977)★★★, *Metal Conquest* (Thunderload 1981)★★, *Death Or Glory* (Thunderload 1982)★★, *Stronger Than Evil* (Thunderload 1984)★★.

HEAVY METAL

Heavy metal is one of the most consistently popular of musical genres, with individual bands counting their followings in millions. The term's origins lie in Steppenwolf's late 60s single 'Born To Be Wild', and the lyric 'heavy metal thunder', with its imagery of outlaws, hard drinking and macho bikers. This is doubtless the source both of the genre's central appeal and critical derision of the music. The term heavy metal is largely interchangeable with 'hard rock', both describing a music dominated by a traditional guitar, bass and drums line-up with an accent on technique. It is usually accompanied by stylized singing of generally simplistic lyrics. Heavy metal arguably began with Cream, Jimi Hendrix, Black Oak Arkansas, Grand Funk Railroad and Led Zeppelin in the late 60s, continuing through the self-parodying Judas Priest and Manowar, and flourishing with the artistic resurrection brought about by the advent of grunge in the 90s. In between, there have been moments of genuine innovation and excitement, but these have been all but obscured by a clutch of bands whose longevity is synonymous with a style of music unwilling or unable to reinvent itself. After the demise of Led Zeppelin, Black Sabbath remained the genre's most notable champions, although their ability to write songs as singularly stunning as 'Paranoid' is long gone. Other behemoths such as AC/DC, Kiss and the more pop-orientated Status Quo have all suffered a similar fate. It is symptomatic of metal's slow evolution that its first real stylistic departure took a decade to ferment. The development of the New Wave Of British Heavy Metal in 1979 came in partial response to the new authenticity in music propelled by punk. Iron Maiden, Def Leppard and Saxon became metal's new vanguard, but quickly fell victim to the same mistakes made by their forerunners (an inability to write anything other than formulaic material). The N.W.O.B.H.M. acts, rather than redefining metal, seemed content to fulfil its mythology. Thus, Iron Maiden's artwork, with its horror-film imagery and pseudo-mystical lyrics, became the new blueprint for a thousand lesser bands. Saxon's 'Denim And Leather' even eulogized a dress code. Throughout the 80s, heavy metal remained content to celebrate its own orthodoxy. Bands such as Motörhead, whose 'Ace of Spades' is arguably the definitive hard rock single, offered an honourable exception. In the late 80s Bon Jovi succeeded in taking commercial heavy metal to the top of the US charts, but Guns N'Roses, despite a varied output, were a more interesting development. Their confrontational approach and childish tantrums accompanied music that once again sounded vibrant and energized. However, it was the innovative Metallica who ushered metal into the new decade. James Hetfield satisfied the genre's demand for musical virtuosity but brought a wholly new approach to songwriting. Traditional metal groups were gradually outpaced, first by thrash rock, then other variants such as death metal. The resultant furore over 'Satanic' lyrics finally returned metal musicians to their former status as antisocial role models. In the early 90s Nirvana and Seattle grunge were adopted as an extension of the heavy metal community's sphere of influence, even though the groups concerned were not always happy with the comparison. Pearl Jam and Soundgarden, encouraged by heavy exposure on MTV, discovered huge popularity in this manner. However, with groups as diverse as Danzig, Extreme Noise Terror, Death and Nine Inch Nails all attracting large followings, heavy metal has essentially become a repository for various strands of extreme music - a position to which it had aspired, but not occupied, since the early 70s.

● FURTHER READING: *Encyclopedia Metallica: The Bible Of Heavy Metal*, Brian Harrigan and Michael Dome. *The HM A-Z*, Brian Harrigan. *The Power Age*, Ross Halfin. *The International Encyclopedia Of Hard Rock & Heavy Metal*, Tony Jasper. *Masters Of Metal*, Lee Martyn. *Heavy Metal Thunder*, Philip Bashe. *Thrash Metal*, Malcolm Dome. *Stairway To Hell: The 500 Best Heavy Metal Albums In The Universe*, Chuck Eddy. *Guinness Who's Who Of Heavy Metal*, Colin Larkin (ed.). *Headbangers: Worldwide Mega-book Of Heavy Metal Bands*, Mark Hale. *Giants Of Heavy Metal: Authentic Guitar - Tab Edition*, editor not listed. *Running With The Devil: Power, Gender And Madness In Heavy Metal...*, Robert Walser. *Kerrang! Directory Of Heavy Metal: The Indispensable Guide To...*, Neil Jeffries (ed.). *Secrets To Writing Killer Metal Songs*, Troy Stetina and Shauna Joyce. *Metalheads: Heavy Metal Music And Adolescent Alienation*, Jeffrey Jensen Arnett.

HEAVY METAL ARMY

One of the lesser lights of the Japanese hard rock revolution of the early 80s, Heavy Metal Army comprised John Patterson (vocals), Yuki Nakajima (keyboards), Shinki Sugama (guitar), Masahiko Takeuchi (bass) and Eiichi Miyanaga (drums). Featuring several established names in Japanese rock, Heavy Metal Army were initially regarded as a 'supergroup'. Patterson formerly sang with Mariner, while Sugama played guitar with Condition Green. Nakajima was ex-Carmen Maki, Takeuchi ex-Creation and Miyanaga ex-Murasaki. Their 1981 debut album for Nexus Records certainly emphasized their status as rock journeymen, the seasoned performers indulging their individual contributions to the deficit of collaborative songwriting. The group splintered shortly after the record's release, with each member continuing to work with other bands on the Japanese scene.

● ALBUMS: *Heavy Metal Army* (Nexus 1981)★★★.

HEAVY METAL KIDS

Formed in London, England, in 1973, Heavy Metal Kids consisted of Gary Holton (vocals), Mickey Waller (guitar), Ron Thomas (bass) and Keith Boyce (drums). Signing to Atlantic Records, the band released their self-titled debut album in 1974. Quickly gaining popularity on the live club circuit in and around the London area, playing brash street metal, the band followed up with *Anvil Chorus* in 1975. This featured keyboard player Danny Peyronel and the semi-legendary 'Cosmo' on guitar joining the quartet. The album also contained the utterly outrageous 'Call The Cops'. However, Holton's volatile nature caused trouble at various gigs, with him eventually breaking his leg on an ill-fated American tour. Subsequently dropped by Atlantic Records, the band nevertheless released a third and final album. *Kitsch* appeared on RAK Records in 1977, and was again dominated by tough, street metal tunes. It still did not provide the band with the break it needed and they folded shortly after its release. Holton went on to a short-lived solo career that saw him (very) briefly join the Damned, release a solo album in Europe and have a minor hit single with 'Catch A Falling Star' in 1984, before setting out to pursue an acting career. He will be best remembered for his role as Wayne in the television series *Auf Wiedersehen Pet*. He died of a drugs overdose during the filming of the series.

● ALBUMS: *Heavy Metal Kids* (Atlantic 1974)★★, *Anvil Chorus* (Atlantic 1975)★★, *Kitsch* (RAK 1977)★★.

HEAVY PETTIN

This Scottish hard rock quintet was formed in July 1981 when vocalist Steve 'Hamie' Hayman and guitarist Punky Mendoza joined with guitarist Gordon Bonnar, bassist Brian Waugh and drummer Gary Moat, who had been playing together as Weeper. Taking their name from a UFO album, the young band toured the UK heavily, and their impressive three-track demo led to a single, 'Roll The Dice', through Neat Records. This, coupled with a BBC Radio 1 *Friday Rock Show* session, led to a major contract with Polydor. *Lettin' Loose*, produced by Brian May and Queen producer Mack, was a confident display of the band's talents, with their catchy melodic hard rock being favourably compared to Def Leppard, and Heavy Pettin made a big impression on UK tours with Kiss and Ozzy Osbourne. The domestic music press lauded a band who seemed set to follow in Leppard's footsteps, and *Rock Ain't Dead*'s mature songwriting sought to justify that opinion, as the band toured the USA with Kiss, Ozzy, Mötley Crüe and AC/DC. However, it all went wrong for Heavy Pettin during the recording of *The Big Bang*. 'Romeo' was put forward as a candidate for the UK's Eurovision Song Contest entry by Polydor, albeit unsuccessfully, seriously damaging the band's credibility, which they salvaged to some extent on Magnum's UK tour. Polydor shelved the album as 'Romeo' failed to set the charts alight, and a dispirited Heavy Pettin, unhappy with their new pop direction, led by Bonnar's keyboards, split in early 1988. *The Big Bang* was released posthumously the following year.

● ALBUMS: *Lettin' Loose* (Polydor 1983)★★★, *Rock Ain't Dead* (Polydor 1985)★★★, *The Big Bang* (FM Revolver 1989)★★★.

HEIR APPARENT

Formed in Seattle, Washington, USA, in 1984, the band's original line-up consisted of Paul Davidson (vocals), Terry Gorle (guitar), Michael Jackson (keyboards), Derek Peace (bass) and Ray Black (drums). Via early demos they attracted the attention of the French-based Black Dragon Records. This resulted in the band's debut, *Graceful Inheritance*, a worthy slice of Americanized melodic rock, released in 1986. After an uneventful European tour, vocalist Paul Davidson left the band to be replaced by Steve Benito. They also briefly lost bassist Derek Peace to touring partners Savage Grace before he realized his mistake and rejoined. However, all this instability took its toll and the band were dropped by their record company. After several new demos they attracted the attention of Metal Blade Records, which resulted in *One Small Voice* being released in 1989. Shortly afterwards, both Black and Gorle left to be replaced by Gary McCormick and Klaus Derendorf, respectively. However, little was subsequently heard from the band as they disappeared back into the Seattle club scene from which they came.

● ALBUMS: *Graceful Inheritance* (Black Dragon 1986)★★★, *One Small Voice* (Metal Blade 1989)★★.

HELIX

Formed in Ontario, Canada, in 1978, the band's original line-up consisted of Brian Vollmer (vocals), Brent Doerner (guitar), Paul Hackman (guitar), Keith Zurbrigg (bass) and Brian Doerner (drums). Together they released *Breaking Loose* before swapping Brent Doerner and Zurbrigg for Leo Niebudek (guitar) and Mike Vzelac (bass). The resultant *White Lace & Black Leather* was an improvement on their basic hard rock approach, but again met with a less than enthusiastic reception. However, these releases did serve to attract the attention of Capitol Records, who signed the band and released their third album, *No Rest For The Wicked*, in 1983. This featured a line-up bolstered by new drummer Greg Hinz (ex-Starchild), while Niebudek had departed to leave Hackman in sole charge of guitars. Widely judged to be their best album, this was a solid collection of rock songs that sold well. *Walkin' The Razors Edge*, released in 1984, introduced new bassist Daryl Gray. This, their most permanent line-up, went on to record two more albums for Capitol, *Long Way To Heaven* and *Wild In The Streets*, which demonstrated a much more commercial songwriting approach. However, they were dropped when neither managed to produce a breakthrough, though sadder still was Hackman's death in a tour-bus accident during 1992.

● ALBUMS: *Breaking Loose* (H&S 1979)★★, *White Lace & Black Leather* (H&S 1981)★★★, *No Rest For The Wicked* (Capitol 1983)★★, *Walkin' The Razors Edge* (Capitol 1984)★★★, *Long Way To Heaven* (Capitol 1985)★★★, *Wild In The Streets* (Capitol 1987)★★★, *Back For Another Taste* (GWR 1990)★★, *It's Business Doing Pleasure* (1993)★★★.

HELLANBACH

Formed in Newcastle-upon-Tyne, England, in 1980, Hellanbach were one of the many groups to emerge from the New Wave Of British Heavy Metal. The band consisted of Jimmy Brash (vocals), Dave Patton (guitar), Kev Charlton (bass) and Steve Walker (drums). Instead of taking the usual route of making demos to secure a recording contract, the band went straight ahead with recording and releasing a four-track EP at their own expense - like many other N.W.O.B.H.M. groups, adopting the 'do it yourself' punk creed. *Out To Get You* was a heavy yet melodic debut. Hellanbach then kept a low profile until re-emerging on the Neat Records label and releasing their debut album, *Now Hear This*, in 1983. It was afforded a mixed reaction by the press, however, and the comparisons to Van Halen dogged them for the rest of their career. By the time *The Big H* was released in 1984, the band had clearly taken note of the criticisms levelled against them. Again, this was a worthy release from a dedicated band, deftly executed and full of melodic choruses. Owing to a continued lack of media interest, the band quickly folded.

● ALBUMS: *Now Hear This* (Neat 1983)★★★, *The Big H* (Neat 1984)★★★.

HELLCATS

The formation of US rock band the Hellcats came as a direct result of the dissolution of their better-remembered forebears, Starz. Both Michael Lee Smith (vocals) and Richie Ranno (guitar) had been integral members of that group, and formed Hellcats in the early 80s with the assistance of Peter Scance (bass) and Doug Madick (drums), recruited from Prism. Like Starz before them, the group elected to concentrate on a classical American rock style, replete with powerful hooks and adept musicianship. All these qualities were evident on their self-titled 1982 debut, though the release of a follow-up album took several years to negotiate. A bonus track on the less impressive *Hellcats Kids* was a live version of 'Tear It Down', a staple of the Starz live set, which indicated that the five-year break between albums might not have incubated a sufficient number of fresh musical ideas

● ALBUMS: *Hellcats* (Radio 1982)★★★, *Hellcats Kids* (Classic 1987)★★.

HELLHAMMER

Formed in 1982, seminal Swiss extreme heavy metal band Hellhammer toyed with Satanic imagery, but were chiefly concerned with generating morbid intensity. Generally considered to be formless noise at the time, Hellhammer attracted a cult following nonetheless. They appealed to the youthful grass-roots of the heavy metal scene, who coveted the most bombastically abrasive sounds that could be committed to vinyl. Extreme metal cognoscenti often cite Hellhammer as the first true death metal band and their early demos are still regarded as underground classics by some. Nevertheless, they undeniably lacked maturity and

subtlety - as evidenced by the band members' stage names: Satanic Slaughter (b. Thomas Fischer, vocals), Savage Damage (bass) and Bloodhunter (b. Bruce Day; drums). Satanic Slaughter and Savage Damage, under the names Thomas Gabriel Warrior and Martin Eric Ain, respectively, went on to form the better-realized thrash band Celtic Frost in 1984, having recorded only one mini-LP as Hellhammer.
● ALBUMS: *Apocalyptic Raids* (Noise 1984)★★★.

HELLION

From Los Angeles, California, Hellion came together in 1982 and quickly gained support from local radio stations and metal magazines worldwide. The band was the brainchild of vocalist Ann Boleyn, who put together a series of formations before settling on a line-up of Alan Barlam (guitar), Sean Kelly (drums), Ray Schenck (guitar) and Bill Sweet (bass). After releasing their first album on Music For Nations, their heavy approach based on Judas Priest and the Scorpions brought them to the attention of Ronnie James Dio, who used them as a support act and also produced their demos. His wife, Wendy, helped them to secure a full-time management agreement, but the business side took its toll and the band split. Boleyn then convinced them to re-form, which they did, with the exception of Sweet, who was replaced by Dave Dutton. A second mini-album, *Postcards From The Asylum*, featured a cover version of the Judas Priest standard, 'Exciter'. This revitalized the band and they took up a residency at the Troubadour Club in Los Angeles and toured in Europe. In 1987 Boleyn assembled a new line-up with Alex Campbell (bass), Chet Thompson (guitar, sitar) and Greg Pecka (drums). Together they recorded *Screams In The Night*, but once more collapsed following the release. Boleyn subsequently adopted a different career trajectory and began to work on a novel, *Black Dragon*, backed up by a mooted concept album. The book failed to secure her a literary career, although one final album, *The Black Book*, did surface to minimal residual interest.
● ALBUMS: *Hellion* mini-album (Music For Nations 1983)★★★, *Postcards From The Asylum* mini-album (Music For Nations 1988)★★★★, *Screams In The Night* (Music For Nations 1988)★★★, *The Black Book* (Music For Nations 1990)★★.

HELLOISE

A Dutch hard rock group featuring Stan Verbraak (vocals), Ben Blaauw (guitar), Arjan Boogerds (guitar), Marchell Remeeus (bass) and Ernst Van Ee (drums), Helloise recorded two moderate studio collections for major label WEA Records in the mid-80s. Both Blaauw and Van Ee had formerly played with Highway Chile, but Helloise was an altogether more polished, musically complex project. *Cosmogony*, the group's debut, released in 1985, secured strong praise for its musical dynamism and free-flowing rhythms, but sales lagged behind the critical response. That fate also befell *Polarity*, released in 1987, after which WEA lost patience and Van Ee left the group. The group attempted to soldier on, but by the early 90s had become frustrated with a lack of record-company reaction to an allegedly superior set of demo tapes.
● ALBUMS: *Cosmogony* (WEA 1985)★★★★, *Polarity* (WEA 1987)★★.

HELLOWEEN

Formed in 1984 in Hamburg, Germany, from the ashes of local bands Second Hell and Iron Fist, the band's original line-up comprised Kai Hansen (guitar, vocals), Michael Weikath (guitar), Markus Grosskopf (bass) and Ingo Schwichenburg (drums). After having two tracks included on the *Death Metal* compilation album released by Noise Records in 1984, the label issued their self-titled debut mini-album in 1985. This was soon followed by *Walls Of Jericho* and an EP, *Judas*. The band gained a strong following with their unique brand of high-speed power metal. Soon after its release, Helloween decided to add a vocalist/frontman, namely Michael Kiske, a charismatic 18-year-old. *Keeper Of The Seven Keys Part I*, released in 1987, showed the band to be pursuing a much more melodic approach and Kiske proved himself a worthy addition. Helloween then toured Europe relentlessly, building a sizeable following in the process. *Keeper Of The Seven Keys Part II* was released in 1988, together with a successful appearance at the Donington Monsters Of Rock Festival that year. After this came an EP, *Dr. Stein*, but behind the scenes, all was not well. The band had become increasingly unhappy with their record company and started to negotiate with several major labels who had previously shown an interest. As a stop-gap the band released *Live In The UK*, recorded at the Hammersmith Odeon in 1989. Kai Hansen then left to form his own outfit, Gamma Ray. His replacement was Roland Grapow. A protracted legal battle with their record company ensured that it was not until 1990 that the band was back in action. They finally signed to EMI Records and gained major management in the form of the Smallwood/Taylor organization. The band's debut for their new label, *Pink Bubbles Go Ape*, released in 1990, depicted Helloween as a shadow of their former selves, sadly missing Kai Hansen and his songwriting skills. Shortly after the dismissal of Kiske, Ingo Schwichenberg was also given his marching orders due to personal health problems and a clash with Weikath, who was now the main force behind the band. Their replacements were Andi Deris (vocals, ex-Pink Cream 69) and Ulli Kusch (drums), who were in place in time for their Castle/Raw Power debut, *Master Of The Rings*. This became Helloween's most successful album for several years, topping the Japanese charts. 1996's *The Time Of The Oath* featured writing contributions from Weikath, Deris and Kusch, while the group composition 'Mission Motherland' saw the band tackle one of the social problems affecting Germany since the fall of the Berlin wall - refugees. Kiske went solo and released an album, *Instant Charity*, in 1996.

● ALBUMS: *Helloween* mini-album (Noise 1985)★★, *Walls Of Jericho* (Noise 1986)★★, *Keeper Of The Seven Keys Part I* (Noise 1987)★★★, *Keeper Of The Seven Keys Part II* (Noise 1988)★★★, *Live In The UK* (Noise 1989)★★, *Pink Bubbles Go Ape* (EMI 1990)★★, *Chameleon* (EMI 1993)★★, *Master Of The Rings* (Raw Power 1994)★★★, *The Time Of The Oath* (Raw Power 1996)★★★, *Tore Down House* (Mesa 1996)★★, *Better Than Raw* (Raw Power 1998)★★★.

HELMET

Moving to New York City, New York, USA, to pursue a degree in jazz guitar, Page Hamilton (b. 18 May 1960, Portland, Oregon, USA) 'discovered distortion' and new influences such as Big Black, Killing Joke and Sonic Youth during his time with Band Of Susans. The experience led him to form Helmet with fellow Oregon native Henry Bogdan (b. 4 February 1961, Riverside, California, USA; bass), Australian guitarist Peter Mengede and classically schooled drummer John Stanier (b. 2 August 1968, Baltimore, Maryland, USA), a veteran of the Florida hardcore scene. The band's close-cropped, clean-cut anti-image is in deliberate contrast to their brutally heavy music. Hamilton's lyrics draw from his life in New York and roots in Oregon, and are delivered with an angry roar in economical song structures, overlaid with an intense barrage of staccato riffing. The band play with rigid discipline, avoiding the high-speed delivery of many thrash and hardcore bands and generating enormous power as a result. While selling modestly, *Strap It On* created considerable interest in Helmet, and the major label debut, *Meantime*, showed much progression as the band established smoother rhythmic flows without compromising their sound. They toured widely, with Faith No More in the USA and Ministry in Europe, before undertaking headline dates of their own. Helmet subsequently parted company with Mengede, replacing him in mid-1993 with ex-postal worker Rob Echeverria (b. 15 December 1967, New York, USA). Before the release of a third album for new label Atlantic Records/East West, the group recorded 'Just Another Victim' with House Of Pain for the *Judgement Night* soundtrack. *Betty* featured co-production from Todd Ray, plus one track concocted with Butch Vig, 'Milquetoast', which also featured on a soundtrack, this time *The Crow*. The following year, their former label, Amphetamine Reptile, took the opportunity to repackage their back-catalogue, while the band began work on sessions for their fourth studio album. Mengede subsequently formed Handsome. *Aftertaste* was their finest release to date, highly commercial, confident and full of hair-raising chord progressions.

● ALBUMS: *Strap It On* (Amphetamine Reptile 1991)★★★, *Meantime* (Interscope 1992)★★★, *Betty* (East West 1994)★★, *Aftertaste* (Interscope 1997)★★★★.

● COMPILATIONS: *Born Annoying* (Amphetamine Reptile 1995)★★.

HELSTAR

Formed in 1982 in Houston, Texas, USA, the band's original line-up consisted of James Rivera (vocals), Larry Barragan (guitar), Robert Trevin (guitar), Jerry Abarca (bass) and Rene Lima (drums). Owing to an excellent four-track demo recorded in 1983, the band quickly became a favourite on the underground tape-trading scene. Attracting the attention of Combat Records, they released their debut album, *Burning Star*, in 1984. Produced by ex-Rods drummer Carl Canedy, it did not possess the spark of the early demo but was still a worthy slice of power metal. Internal wrangles led to both guitarist Robert Trevin and drummer Rene Lima leaving the band to be replaced by André Corbin and Frank Ferreeira, respectively. A second album, *Remnants Of War*, was released in 1986 and followed closely in the footsteps of its predecessor. The band had been dissatisfied with their record label for some time and both parties separated amicably. Helstar then relocated to Los Angeles where they signed a new recording contract with Metal Blade, the first product of which was *A Distant Thunder* in 1988. The band had by this time developed their own distinctive sound and were attracting many new fans. They toured across America and Europe and on their return to America moved back to Houston. The next album, entitled *Nosferatu*, was a concept affair with vampires as its theme. However, this new approach towards their songwriting did not suit the now distinctive Helstar style and reactions were discouraging. *Multiples Of Black* was produced by Megadeth bass player Dave Ellefson in 1995, after he met the band while they were touring together in 1986. It included an ill-advised cover version of Judas Priest's 'Beyond The Realms Of Death'.

● ALBUMS: *Burning Star* (Music For Nations 1984)★★★, *Remnants Of War* (Noise/Combat 1986)★★★, *A Distant Thunder* (Restless/Metal Blade 1988)★★★, *Nosferatu* (Roadrunner 1989)★★.

HENDRIX, JIMI

b. Johnny Allen Hendrix, 27 November 1942, Seattle, Washington, USA, d. 18 September 1970, London, England. (His father subsequently changed his son's name to James Marshall Hendrix.) More superlatives have been bestowed upon Hendrix than any other rock guitarist. Unquestionably one of music's most influential figures, he brought an unparalleled vision to the art of playing electric guitar. Self-taught (and with the burden of being left-handed with a right-handed guitar), he spent hours absorbing the recorded legacy of southern-blues practitioners, from Robert Johnson to B.B. King. The aspiring musician joined several local R&B bands while still at school, before enlisting as a paratrooper in the 101st Airborne Division. It was during this period that Hendrix met Billy Cox, a bass player with whom he collaborated at several stages during his career. Together they formed the King Kasuals, an in-service attraction later resurrected when both men returned to civilian life. Hendrix was discharged in July 1962 after breaking his right ankle. He began working with various touring revues, backing, among others, the Impressions, Sam Cooke and the Valentinos. He enjoyed lengthier spells with the Isley Brothers, Little Richard and King Curtis, recording with each of these acts, but was unable to adapt to the discipline their performances required. The experience and stagecraft gained during this formative period proved essential to the artist's subsequent development. By 1965 Hendrix was living in New York. In October he joined struggling soul singer Curtis Knight, signing a punitive contract with the latter's manager, Ed Chalpin. This ill-advised decision returned to haunt the guitarist. In June the following year, Hendrix, now calling himself Jimmy James, formed a group initially dubbed the Rainflowers, then Jimmy James And The Blue Flames. The quartet, which also featured future Spirit member Randy California, was appearing at the Cafe Wha? in Greenwich Village when Chas Chandler was advised to see them. The Animals' bassist immediately recognized the guitarist's extraordinary talent and persuaded him to go to London in search of a more receptive audience. Hendrix arrived in England in September 1966. Chandler became his co-manager in partnership with Mike Jeffries (aka Jeffreys), and immediately began auditions for a suitable backing group. Noel Redding (b. 25 December 1945, Folkestone, Kent, England) was selected on bass, having recently failed to join the New Animals, while John 'Mitch' Mitchell (b. 9 July 1947, Ealing, Middlesex, England), a veteran of the Riot Squad and Georgie Fame's Blue Flames, became the trio's drummer. The new group, dubbed the Jimi Hendrix Experience, made its debut the following month at Evereux in France. On returning to England they began a string of club engagements that attracted pop's aristocracy, including Pete Townshend and Eric Clapton. In December the trio released their first single, the understated, resonant 'Hey Joe'. Its UK Top 10 placing encouraged a truly dynamic follow-up in 'Purple Haze'. The latter was memorable for Hendrix's guitar pyrotechnics and a lyric that incorporated the artist's classic line: ''Scuse me while I kiss the sky'. On tour, his trademark Fender Stratocaster and Marshall Amplifier were punished night after night, as the group enhanced its reputation with exceptional live appearances. Here Hendrix drew on black culture and his own heritage to produce a startling visual and aural bombardment. Framed by a halo of long, wiry hair, his slight figure was clad in a bright, rainbow-mocking costume. Although never a demonstrative vocalist, his delivery was curiously effective. Hendrix's playing technique, meanwhile, although still drawing its roots from the blues, encompassed an emotional range far greater than any contemporary guitarist. Rapier-like runs vied with measured solos, matching energy with ingenuity, while a wealth of technical possibilities - distortion, feedback and sheer volume - brought texture to his overall approach. This assault was enhanced by a flamboyant stage persona in which Hendrix used the guitar as a physical appendage. He played his instrument behind his back, between his legs or, in simulated sexual ecstasy, on the floor. Such practices brought criticism from radical quarters, who claimed the artist had become an 'Uncle Tom', employing tricks to ingratiate himself with the white audience - accusations that neglected similar showmanship from generations of black performers, from Charley Patton to 'T-Bone' Walker. Redding's clean, uncluttered basslines provided the backbone to Hendrix's improvisations, while Mitchell's drumming, as instinctive as his leader's guitarwork, was a perfect foil. Their concessions to the pop world now receding, the Experience completed an astonishing debut album that ranged from the apocalyptic vision of 'I Don't Live Today', to the blues of 'Red House' and the funk of 'Fire' and 'Foxy Lady'. Hendrix returned to America in June 1967 to appear, sensationally, at the Monterey Pop Festival. His performance was a musical and visual feast, culminating in a sequence that saw him playing the guitar with his teeth, and then burning the instrument with lighter fuel. He was now fêted in his homeland, and following an ill-advised tour supporting the Monkees, the Experience enjoyed reverential audiences on the country's nascent concert circuit. *Axis: Bold As Love* revealed a new lyrical capability, notably in the title track and the jazz-influenced 'Up From The Skies'. 'Little Wing', a delicate love song bathed in unhurried guitar splashes, offered a gentle perspective, closer to that of the artist's shy, offstage demeanour. Released in December 1967, the collection completed a triumphant year, artistically and commercially, but within months the fragile peace began to collapse. In January 1968 the Experience embarked on a gruelling American tour encompassing 54 concerts in 47 days. Hendrix was by this time tiring of the wild-man image that had brought him initial attention, but he was perceived as diffident by spectators anticipating gimmickry. An impulsive artist, he was unable to disguise below-par performances, while his relationship with Redding grew increasingly fraught as the bassist rebelled against the set patterns he was expected to play. *Electric Ladyland*, the last official Experience album, was released in October. This extravagant double set was initially deemed 'self-indulgent', but is now recognized as a major work. It revealed the guitarist's desire to expand the increasingly limiting trio format, and contributions from members of Traffic (Chris Wood and Steve Winwood) and Jefferson Airplane (Jack Casady) embellished several selections. The collection featured a succession of virtuoso performances - 'Gypsy Eyes', 'Crosstown Traffic' - while the astonishing 'Voodoo Chile (Slight Return)', a posthumous number 1 single, showed how Hendrix had brought rhythm, purpose and mastery to the recently invented wah-wah pedal. *Electric Ladyland* included two UK hits, 'The Burning Of The Midnight Lamp' and 'All Along The Watchtower'. The latter, an urgent restatement of the Bob Dylan song, was particularly impressive, and received the ultimate accolade when the composer adopted Hendrix's interpretation when performing it live on his 1974 tour. Despite such creativity, the guitarist's private and professional life was becoming problematic. He was arrested in Toronto for possessing heroin, but although the charges were later dismissed, the proceedings clouded much of 1969. Chas Chandler had, meanwhile, withdrawn from the managerial partnership and although Redding sought solace with a concurrent group, Fat Mattress, his differences with Hendrix were now irreconcilable. The Experience played its final concert on 29 June 1969; Hendrix subsequently formed Gypsies Sons And Rainbows with Mitchell, Billy Cox (bass), Larry Lee (rhythm guitar), Juma Sultan and Jerry Velez (both percussion). This short-lived unit closed the Woodstock Festival, during which Hendrix performed his famed rendition of the 'Star Spangled Banner'. Perceived by some critics as a political statement, it came as the guitarist was increasingly being subjected to pressures from different causes. In October he formed an all-black group, Band Of Gypsies, with Cox and drummer Buddy Miles, intending to accentuate the African-American dimension in his music. The trio made its debut on 31 December 1969, but its potential was marred by Miles's comparatively flat, pedestrian drumming and unimaginative compositions. Part of the set was issued as *Band Of Gypsies*, but despite the inclusion of the exceptional 'Machine Gun', this inconsistent album was only released to appease former manager Chaplin, who acquired the rights in part-settlement of a miserly early contract. The Band Of Gypsies broke up after a mere three concerts and initially Hendrix confined his efforts to completing the building of his Electric Ladyland recording studio. He then started work on another double set, *First Rays Of The New Rising Sun* (finally released in 1997), and later resumed performing with Cox and Mitchell. His final concerts were largely frustrating, as the aims of the artist and the expectations of his audience grew increasingly separate. His final UK appearance, at the Isle Of Wight festival, encapsulated this dilemma, yet still drew an enthralling performance. The guitarist returned to London following a short European tour. On 18 September 1970, his girlfriend, Monika Danneman, became alarmed when she was unable to rouse him from sleep. An ambulance was called, but Hendrix was pronounced dead on arrival at a nearby hospital. The inquest recorded an open verdict, with death caused by suffocation due to inhalation of vomit. Eric Burdon claimed at the time to possess a suicide note, but this has never been confirmed. Two posthumous releases, *Cry Of Love* and *Rainbow Bridge*, mixed portions of the artist's final recordings with masters from earlier sources. These were fitting tributes, but many others were tawdry cash-ins, recorded in dubious circumstances, mispackaged and mistitled. This imbalance has been redressed of late with the release of archive recordings, but the Hendrix legacy also rests in his prevailing influence on fellow musicians. Many guitarists have imitated his technique; few have mastered it, while none at all have matched him as an inspirational player. In November 1993 a tribute album, *Stone Free*, was released, containing a formidable list of performers including the Pretenders, Eric Clapton, Cure, Jeff Beck, Pat Metheny and Nigel Kennedy, a small testament to the huge influence Hendrix has wielded and will continue to wield as the most inventive rock guitarist of all time. The litigation regarding ownership of his recordings that had been running for many years was resolved in January 1997, when the Hendrix family finally won back the rights from Alan Douglas. This was made possible by the financial weight of Microsoft co-founder Paul Allen, who, in addition to helping with legal expenses, has financed the Jimi Hendrix Museum, which will be located in Seattle. A major reissuing programme took place in 1997, including out-takes from the recording of *Electric Ladyland*. The reissued catalogue on Experience/MCA records is now the definitive and final word.

● ALBUMS: *Are You Experienced?* (Track 1967)★★★★★, *Axis: Bold As Love* (Track 1967)★★★★★, *Electric Ladyland* (Track 1968)★★★★, *Band Of Gypsies* (Track 1970)★★★, shared with Otis Redding *Monterey International Pop Festival* (Reprise 1970)★★★★, *Cry Of Love* (Polydor 1971)★★★, *Experience* (Ember 1971)★, *Isle Of Wight* (Polydor 1971)★★, *Rainbow Bridge* (Reprise 1971)★★, *Hendrix In The West* (Polydor 1971)★★★, *More Experience* (Ember 1972)★, *War Heroes* (Polydor 1972)★★, *Loose Ends* (Polydor 1974)★★, *Crash Landing* (Polydor 1975)★★, *Midnight Lightnin'* (Polydor 1975)★★, *Nine To The Universe* (Polydor 1980)★★, *The Jimi Hendrix Concerts* (Columbia 1982)★★★, *Jimi Plays Monterey* (Polydor 1986)★★★, *Live At Winterland* (Polydor 1987)★★★, *Radio One* (Castle 1988)★★★★, *Live And Unreleased* (Castle 1989)★★★, *First Rays Of The New Rising Sun* (Experience/MCA 1997)★★★, *South Saturn Delta* (Experience 1997)★★★, *Original Soundtrack To The Motion Picture 'Experience'* (Charly 1998)★★.

● COMPILATIONS: *Smash Hits* (Track 1968)★★★★, *The Essential Jimi Hendrix* (Polydor 1978)★★★★, *The Essential Jimi Hendrix Volume Two* (Polydor 1979)★★★, *The Singles Album* (Polydor 1983)★★★★, *Kiss The Sky* (Polydor 1984)★★★, *Cornerstones* (Polydor 1990)★★★, *Blues* (Polydor 1994)★★★, *Exp Over Sweden* (Univibes 1993)★★, *Jimi In Denmark* (Univibes 1995)★★, *BBC Sessions* (Experience/MCA 1998)★★★★.

● VIDEOS: *Jimi Hendrix Plays Berkeley* (Palace Video 1986), *Jimi Plays Monterey* (Virgin Vision 1986), *Jimi Hendrix* (Warner Home Video 1986), *Experience* (Palace Video 1987), *Rainbow Bridge* (Hendring Video 1988), *Live At The Isle Of Wight 1970* (Rhino Home Video 1990), *Jimi Hendrix Live At Monterey* (1994), *Jimi At Woodstock* (BMG 1995), *Jimi At The Atlanta Pop Festival* (BMG 1995), *Jimi Hendrix Experience* (BMG 1995), *Jimi Hendrix Plays The Great Pop Festivals* (BMG 1995).

● FURTHER READING: *Jimi: An Intimate Biography Of Jimi Hendrix*, Curtis Knight. *Jimi Hendrix*, Alain Dister. *Jimi Hendrix: Voodoo Child Of The Aquarian Age*, David Henderson. *Scuze Me While I Kiss The Sky: The Life Of Jimi Hendrix*, David Henderson. *Hendrix: A Biography*, Chris Welch. *Hendrix: An Illustrated Biography*, Victor Sampson. *The Jimi Hendrix Story*, Jerry Hopkins. *Crosstown Traffic: Jimi Hendrix And Post-War Pop*, Charles Shaar Murray. *Jimi Hendrix: Electric Gypsy*, Harry Shapiro and Caesar Glebbeek. *Are You Experienced?*, Noel Redding and Carole Appleby. *The Hendrix Experience*, Mitch Mitchell and John Platt. *And The Man With The Guitar*, Jon Price and Gary Geldeart. *The Jimi Hendrix Experience In 1967 (Limited Edition)*, Gerard Mankowitz and Robert Whitaker (photographers). *Jimi Hendrix: A Visual Documentary, His Life, Loves And Music*, Tony Brown. *Jimi Hendrix: Starchild*, Curtis Knight. *Hendrix: Setting The Record Straight*, John McDermott with Eddie Kramer. *The Illustrated Jimi Hendrix*, Geoffrey Guiliano. *Cherokee Mist - The Lost Writings Of Jimi Hendrix*, Bill Nitopi (compiler). *Voodoo Child: The Illustrated Legend Of Jimi Hendrix*, Martin L. Green and Bill Sienkiewicz. *The Ultimate Experience*, Adrian Boot and Chris Salewicz. *The Lost Writings Of Jimi Hendrix*, Jimi Hendrix. *The Complete Studio Recording Sessions 1963-1970*, John McDermott. *Complete Guide To The Music Of*, John Robertson. *The Inner World Of Jimi Hendrix*, Monika Dannemann. *Jimi Hendrix Experience*, Jerry Hopkins. *Jimi Hendrix: Voices From Home*, Mary Willix. *The Man, The Music, The Memorabilia*, Caesar Glebbeek and Douglas Noble. *Eye Witness: The Illustrated Jimi Hendrix Concerts*, Ben Valkhoff. *Hendrix: The Final Days*, Tony Brown. *The Jimi Hendrix Companion*, Chris Potash (ed.). *Through Gypsy Eyes: My Life, The Sixties And Jimi Hendrix*, Kathy Etchingham.

HENSLEY, KEN

b. 24 August 1945, London, England. A founder-member of the Gods, organist Hensley led this tempestuous Hertfordshire group throughout its four-year history. Mick Taylor and Greg Lake were also members at different times, although both had departed before the release of the unit's two albums *Genesis* (1968) and *To Samuel A Son* (1970). The Gods evolved into Toe Fat with the addition of singer Cliff Bennett, before Hensley left in November 1969 to join Uriah Heep. This much maligned act survived critical denigration to become such a popular attraction that the organist was afforded the luxury of a concurrent solo career. Although *Proud Words On A Dusty Shelf* featured fellow Heep members Gary Thain and Lee Kerslake, it was noticeably mellow in tone which, in part, may account for its commercial failure. *Eager To Please*, a collaboration with Colosseum bassist Mark Clarke, proved even less successful and Hensley temporarily ceased outside activities. He remained with Uriah Heep until 1980 when he was summarily fired. Having completed the disappointing *Free Spirit*, Hensley formed the short-lived Shotgun, before joining US group Blackfoot. He appeared on two releases, *Siogo* (1983) and *Vertical Smiles* (1984), but subsequently switched to session work with W.A.S.P. and Ozzy Osbourne.

● ALBUMS: *Proud Words On A Dusty Shelf* (Bronze 1973)★★★, *Eager To Please* (Bronze 1975)★★, *Free Spirit* (Bronze 1980)★★.

● COMPILATIONS: *From Time To Time* (Viceroy 1994)★★.

HERETIC

Formed in 1984 in Los Angeles, California, USA, the band's original line-up consisted of Julian Mendez (vocals), Brian Korban (guitar), Bobby Marquez (guitar), Dennis O'Hara (bass) and Rick Merrick (drums). Quickly gaining popularity on the club circuit in and around the Los Angeles area, the band attracted the attention of Metal Blade Records. Heretic's debut release for the label was a mini-album, *Torture Knows No Boundaries*, in 1987. This was a worthwhile serving of fast power metal, slightly marred because Julian Mendez's vocals were not ideally suited to the band's hard-hitting approach. To his credit, the singer realized this and left the band, to be replaced by Mike Howe later the same year. On their second outing, the full-length *Breaking Point*, they sounded much more confident. However, when Howe left the band later that year to join Metal Church, a series of vocal replacements could not prevent Heretic folding in 1989.

● ALBUMS: *Torture Knows No Boundaries* mini-album (Metal Blade 1987)★★★, *Breaking Point* (Metal Blade 1988)★★★.

HERITAGE

One of the lesser lights of the N.W.O.B.H.M. explosion, this band from Yorkshire, England, featured Steve Johnson (vocals, guitar), Steve Barratt (vocals, guitar), Fasker Johnson (vocals, bass) and Pete Halliday (drums). Like fellow north England group Gaskin, Heritage signed to the predominantly punk-orientated Rondolet Records, releasing their debut album, *Remorse Code*, in 1982. With literally hundreds of bands attempting to break into the mainstream rock music scene at the same time, most of them located much closer to its epicentre in London, Heritage had neither the songs nor the vision to attach themselves to the bandwagon.

● ALBUMS: *Remorse Code* (Rondolet 1982)★★.

HIGH TIDE

Heavy/psychedelic progressive British band formed in 1969 by Tony Hill (ex-Misunderstood; guitar, vocals, keyboards), Simon House (violin, piano), Roger Hadden (drums, organ) and Peter Pavli (ex-White Rabbit; bass). Signed to the Clearwater production agency, they obtained a recording contract with Liberty Records who were eager to join the progressive rock bandwagon that had been milked dry by other record companies. High Tide was a more than credible debut, complete with Mervyn Peake-styled sleeve illustrations. 'Walking Down Their Outlook' features Hill's Jim Morrison-like vocals although longer tracks such as 'Pushed But Not Forgotten' allowed House and Hill to stretch out and improvise - always a feature of their live performances - with lead guitar and violin competing with each other. They played their first live concert with fellow Clearwater band, Hawkwind. After two albums with Liberty they were dropped, and a poor second album sold badly. After numerous tours they became involved with Arthur Brown, Magic Muscle, and the post-Arthur Brown band, Rustic Hinge. By 1972 Hadden was suffering from mental problems and was placed in hospital where he remains to this day. Hill then went on to work with Drachen Theaker while Pavli and House joined the Third Ear Band. Pavli soon involved himself in a number of musical projects with Robert Calvert and Michael Moorcock; House, meanwhile, joined Hawkwind and later David Bowie's band. In 1987 House and Pavli re-formed High Tide and have overseen various other related projects and releases. Hill released a solo album, *Playing For Time*, in 1991, while House again joined up with Hawkwind and Magic Muscle.

● ALBUMS: *Sea Shanties* (Liberty 1969)★★★★, *High Tide* (Liberty 1970)★★★, *Ancient Gates* (80s)★★, *Interesting Times* (High Tide 1987)★★, *Precious Cargo* (Cobra 1989)★★, *The Flood* (High Tide 1990)★★, *A Fierce Native* (High Tide 1990)★★.
Solo: Tony Hill *Playing For Time* (1991)★★★.

HIGHWAY ROBBERY

A US rock group comprising Don Fracisco (vocals, drums), Michael Stevens (guitar) and John Livingston Tunison (bass), Highway Robbery proved themselves adept musicians and songwriters with the arrival of their 1972 RCA Records debut, *For Love Or Money*. With the lyrics containing multitudinous references to the 60s, Highway Robbery balanced their hippie idealism with thunderous arrangements redolent of early Black Sabbath. The combination was a winning one, but it served to confuse record purchasers and also their record company, who dropped them shortly after the album's release.

● ALBUMS: *For Love Or Money* (RCA 1972)★★.

HIRAX

Hirax first formed in Los Angeles, California, USA, in 1984 - the band's original line-up consisting of Katon W. De Pena (vocals), Scott Owen (guitar), Gary Monardo (bass) and John Tabares (drums). Their promising demos attracted the attention of Metal Blade who included one of the band's tracks on the *Metal Massacre VI* compilation album, released in 1985. A debut album, *Raging Violence*, was released for the same label in 1985. Full of short and ultra-fast thrash metal, it offered nothing very innovative. Shortly after its release, Tabares left the band to be replaced by ex-DRI percussionist Eric Brecht. Their next release was a mini-album, *Hate, Fear And Power*, released in 1986. The material on offer was in the same vein as before, but the production this time around had improved greatly. However, owing to internal band wrangles vocalist Katon W. De Pena left to be replaced by ex-Exodus vocalist Paul Baloff. He, in turn, did not stay long before being replaced himself by Billy Wedgeworth. Unable to maintain a stable line-up, the band folded after recording several more demos in 1988.

● ALBUMS: *Raging Violence* (Metal Blade 1985)★★, *Hate, Fear And Power* (Metal Blade 1986)★★★.

HISSANOL

Hissanol is the solo project inaugurated by former NoMeansNo singer/guitarist Andy Kerr (b. Canada). His debut album was recorded in tandem with old friend Scott Henderson through the postal exchange of tapes between two continents. Sadly, the disjointed nature of the experiment shone through on *4th And Black*. Songs such as 'Angra' and 'Exterminal' lacked none of the imagination shown on previous NoMeansNo records, but much of their considerable musical artistry was missing.

● ALBUMS: *4th And Black* (Alternative Tentacles 1995)★★★, *The Making Of Him* (Alternative Tentacles 1998)★★.

HITTMAN

Comprising Dirk Kennedy (vocals), John Kristen (guitar), Jim Bachie (guitar), Mike Buccell (bass) and Chuck Kory (drums), Hittman formed in New York City, New York, USA, in the mid-80s. Though there was nothing wholly innovative about their debut album for SPV Records, critics throughout the USA and Europe acclaimed it as an exceptional collection of songs in the power metal mould of Savatage or Accept. However, thereafter a series of inter-group squabbles overtook the band, fatally delaying the release of a follow-up collection.

● ALBUMS: *Hittman* (SPV 1988)★★★.

HOLLAND

Despite the name, Holland was a UK heavy metal act from the early 80s who rode briefly on the crest of the N.W.O.B.H.M. Comprising Bob Henman (guitar), Graeme Hutchinson (bass), Kenny Nicholson (guitar) and Marty Day (drums), their name was initially made on the burgeoning demo tape scene, a reputation that eventually led to a recording contract with Ebony Records. However, poor production on *Early Warning* dissipated the critical buzz surrounding the band and they never recovered their footing. The same line-up changed the band's name to Hammer, recording the more impressive *Contract With Hell* two years later.

● ALBUMS: *Early Warning* (Ebony 1984)★★.

HOLOCAUST

Holocaust were formed in Edinburgh, Scotland, in 1978. The original line-up consisted of Gary Lettice (vocals), John Mortimer (guitar), Edward Dudley (guitar), Robin Begg (bass) and Paul Collins (drums). They were signed by Phoenix Records, who released the band's debut, 'Heavy Metal Mania', in 1980. The band's long-playing debut, *The Nightcomers*, arrived a year later. The material on offer was basic hard rock, fuelled by the enthusiasm that the New Wave Of British Heavy Metal had fired. It was to prove a very influential release, Metallica later covering one of the tracks on their *Garage Days Revisited* EP. By 1982 and the release of Holocaust's second single, 'Coming Through', the band was disintegrating. A posthumous live album appeared in 1983, again on Phoenix Records, entitled *Live, Hot Curry & Wine*. Guitarist Edward Dudley left to form Hologram (who recorded one album, also for Phoenix, entitled *Steal The Stars*, in 1982). Hologram, however, proved short-lived as Holocaust re-formed to release a third album, *No Mans Land*, in 1984. Soon after its release the band folded again. With the resurgence of interest in the N.W.O.B.H.M. bands (primarily owing to Metallica cover versions), the band started working together again in 1989.

● ALBUMS: *The Nightcomers* (Phoenix 1981)★★★★, *Live, Hot Curry & Wine* (Phoenix 1983)★★★, *No Mans Land* (Phoenix 1984)★★★, *The Land Of Souls* (Chrome 1990)★★, *Hypnosis Of Birds* (1993)★★, *Covenant* (Neat 1997)★★★.

HOLY MOSES

This thrash metal group from Germany, formed in the mid-80s, comprised Andy Classen (guitar), Sabina Classen (vocals), Reiner Laws (guitar), Thomas Becker (bass) and Ulli Kusch (drums). Their early efforts for the independent domestic label Aaarrg Records saw the group hone its sound into one of the more powerful examples of the speed-metal genre, drawing obvious influence from Slayer and Anthrax. A series of excellent reviews and a growing live reputation led to a contract with WEA Records. Unfortunately, *The New Machine Of Lichenstein*, produced by Anthrax and Testament producer Alex Parialis, showcased a group confused as to whether to pursue the style with which they had earned their reputation, or to produce something more accessible to the mainstream. With the group unable to resolve their direction, it received mixed reviews and their association with WEA was discontinued. They persevered with a further album for an independent label, 1990's *World Chaos*, but by this time they had lost much of their initial momentum.

● ALBUMS: *Queen Of Siam* (Aaarrg 1986)★★★, *Finished With The Dogs* (Aaarrg 1987)★★, *The New Machine Of Lichenstein* (WEA 1989)★★★, *World Chaos* (Virginia 1990)★★★.

HONEYCRACK

Comprising Pete Clarke (bass), Hugo Degenhardt (drums), Mark McCrae (guitar, ex-Rub Ultra), Willie Dowling (keyboards, ex-Grip; Wildhearts) and CJ (b. Chris Jagdhar; vocals, guitar, ex-Tattooed Love Boys; Wildhearts), UK heavy rock band Honeycrack were formed with an agenda that stated 'we have no messages to convey, but we do want to change the world'. The group was conceived in August 1994 after both CJ and Dowling had been ejected from the Wildhearts. Honeycrack's debut single, 'King Of Misery', was released to accompany their first tour of 1995, and was followed by October's 'Sitting At Home'. 'Go Away' followed in February 1996 and became their most successful single to date, entering the UK Top 40 and coinciding with a headlining tour and a four-week residency at London's Splash Cub. The debut album was an exciting and assured set and contained a glut of strong songs in addition to the previous singles. The biggest problem the band experienced was not writing songs or recording them but in choosing a name: 'We busked around for weeks on end, we should be marrying up the notion of something sweet and something dreadfully hard' - hence their sweet harmonies with bone-crunching guitar. The band appeared to have broken up by spring 1997.

● ALBUMS: *Prozaic* (Epic 1996)★★★.

HONEYMOON SUITE

A Canadian hard rock quintet of Johnny Dee (guitar, vocals), Derry Grehan (lead guitar), Dave Betts (drums), Gary Lalonde (bass) and Ray Coburn (keyboards), Honeymoon Suite formed in 1982 and set about establishing the strong club following that accompanied them throughout their career. Their debut release was a self-financed single, 'New Girl Now', which sold in sufficient quantities locally to attract the interest of Warner Brothers Records. Their self-titled debut album for the major was a dextrous, committed example of contemporary Canadian rock music, though some critics considered the lyrics to be banal even by AOR standards. It was followed by two further collections, *The Big Prize* and *Racing After Midnight*, which sold well in Canada without giving the group the impetus to break through across the southern border.

● ALBUMS: *Honeymoon Suite* (Warners 1984)★★, *The Big Prize* (WEA 1986)★★, *Racing After Midnight* (WEA 1988)★★.

HORSE

Based in London, England, Horse combined heavy metal musicianship with some of the lyrical concerns of the punk movement. Comprising Gary Gene (vocals), Marc Perez (guitar), Damon Williams (bass) and Dave Hoyland (drums), after forming in 1988 they embarked on a gruelling circuit of support and club dates to establish their reputation. Their onstage behaviour won them immediate notoriety in London fanzines such as *House Of Dolls*, and by the turn of the 90s some critics were hailing them as the natural successors to the musical and visual excesses of early Motörhead. In truth, their sound owed more to the mysticism of the Cult and the unreconstructed attitude of Guns N'Roses. An American recording contract followed in 1990 with the MCA Records subsidiary Mechanic, Atlantic Records having turned them down for being 'too erratic'. However, the group's debut, *Diesel Power*, was strangely lacking in the feisty qualities that had made the group such an intimidating live spectacle.

● ALBUMS: *Diesel Power* (Mechanic 1990)★★.

HOT TUNA

This US group represented the combination of two members of the Jefferson Airplane, Jack Casady (b. 13 April 1944, Washington, DC, USA; bass) and Jorma Kaukonen (b. 23 December 1940, Washington, DC, USA; guitar, vocals). The group evolved as a part-time extension of the Airplane with Kaukonen and Casady utilizing the services of colleagues Paul Kantner (guitar) and Spencer Dryden (drums) and other guests, displaying their talents as blues musicians. Stage appearances were initially integrated within the Airplane's performances on the same bill. During one of the Airplane's rest periods, the duo began to appear in their own right, often as a rock trio with the then Airplane drummer, Joey Covington. Having had the name Hot Shit rejected (Kaukonen has since refuted this, stating that 'age-old rumors that we planned to call it Hot Shit are completely unfounded'), they settled on Hot Tuna and released a self-titled debut as a duo, with a guest appearance from harmonica player Will Scarlet. The set was drawn largely from traditional blues/ragtime material by Jelly Roll Morton and the Rev. Gary Davis, with Casady's booming and meandering bass lines interplaying superbly with Kaukonen's fluid acoustic guitar. By the time of their second album, another live set, they were a full-blown rock quartet with the addition of violinist 'Papa' John Creach and Sammy Piazza on drums. This line-up displayed the perfect combination of electric and acoustic rock/blues for which Casady and Kaukonen had been looking. Creach had departed by the time *The Phosphorescent Rat* was recorded, and Piazza, who had left to join Stoneground was replaced by Bob Steeler in 1974. The music became progressively louder, so that by the time of their sixth album they sounded like a rumbling heavy rock traditional ragtime blues band. Kaukonen's limited vocal range added to this odd concoction, but throughout all this time the group maintained a hardcore following. In the late 70s the duo split, resulting in Casady embarking on an ill-advised excursion into what was perceived as 'punk' with SVT. Kaukonen continued with a solo career combining both electric and acoustic performances. At best Hot Tuna were excitingly different, at worst they were ponderous and loud. Selected stand-out tracks from their erratic repertoire were 'Mann's Fate' from *Hot Tuna*, 'Keep On Truckin'' and 'Sea Child' from *Burgers*, 'Song From The Stainless Cymbal' from *Hoppkorv*, and 'Hit Single #1' from *America's Choice*. Casady and Kaukonen reunited in the mid-80s, and returned to recording in 1991 with a workmanlike album that found little favour with the record-buying public. Since 1984, Relix Records have released several archival and contemporary live albums.

● ALBUMS: *Hot Tuna* (RCA 1970)★★★, *First Pull Up Then Pull Down* (RCA 1971)★★★, *Burgers* (Grunt 1972)★★★★, *The Phosphorescent Rat* (Grunt 1973)★★, *America's Choice* (Grunt 1975)★★★, *Yellow Fever* (Grunt 1975)★★, *Hoppkorv* (Grunt 1976)★★★, *Double Dose* (Grunt 1978)★★★, *Final Vinyl* (Grunt 1979)★★★, *Splashdown* recorded 1975 (Relix 1985)★★, *Historic Hot Tuna* recorded 1971 (Relix 1985)★★★, *Pair A Dice Found* (Epic 1991)★★, *Live At Sweetwater* (Relix 1992)★★, *Live At Sweetwater*

Two (Relix 1993)★★, *Historic* (Relix 1993)★★, *Classic Electric* recorded 1971 (Relix 1996)★★★, *Classic Acoustic* recorded 1971 (Relix 1996)★★★, *Splashdown Two* (Relix 1997)★★, *Live In Japan: At Stove's Yokohoma City 02/20/97* (Relix 1998)★★.
● COMPILATIONS: *Trimmed And Burning* (Edsel 1994)★★★★, *Hot Tuna In A Can* 5-CD tin (Rhino 1996)★★★★.

HOTEL

This US rock band, formed in the late 70s, was frequently accused of 'taking a hammer to crack a nutshell', to quote one analogy. The assembled ranks of Hotel, who specialized in grandiloquent, multi-layered AOR, included Tommy Caton (guitar, vocals), Marc Phillips (keyboards, vocals), Michael Reid (guitar, vocals), George Creasman (bass, vocals), Lee Bargeon (keyboards, vocals) and Michael Cadenhead (drums, percussion). Their 1979 debut album, released on MCA Records, was a disappointing collection of songs where the focus on unnecessary musical embellishment detracted from the group's songwriting. *Half Moon Silver*, which followed a year later, was an improvement, but it, too, failed to elevate them into the AOR mainstream.
● ALBUMS: *Hotel* (MCA 1979)★★, *Half Moon Silver* (MCA 1980)★★★.

HOUNDS

As predictable as the music of US heavy metal band the Hounds was, its lack of intelligence paled into insignificance compared to their record sleeves. On *Unleashed*, their 1978 debut for Columbia Records, John Hunter (vocals, keyboards), Jim Orkis (guitar), Glen Rupp (guitar), Joe Cuttone (bass) and John Horvath (drums) struck unpleasant macho poses behind salivating, chained dogs. The music contained within struck out aggressively, but with little substance, while the lyrics caused at least one bout of hilarity among the critics subjected to it. *Puttin' On The Dog* continued in the same vein, but by now, Columbia's initial confidence in the group had all but collapsed. Though Spinal Tap have acknowledged that their heavy metal satire was based on the real-life exploits of Uriah Heep, they could just as easily have been inspired by either of the Hounds' record sleeves.
● ALBUMS: *Unleashed* (Columbia 1978)★★, *Puttin' On The Dog* (Columbia 1979★★★.

HOUSE OF LORDS

This five-piece US heavy rock supergroup was put together by ex-Angel keyboardist Gregg Giuffria. Augmented by bassist Chuck Wright (ex-Quiet Riot), drummer Ken Mary (ex-Alice Cooper), vocalist James Christian (ex-Canata) and guitarist Lanny Cordola (ex-Giuffria), the line-up was impressive and promised much. With Giuffria in control, the band pursued an overstated melodic approach with swathes of keyboards, multi-phased harmonies and atmospheric arrangements redolent of mid-70s arena rock. Signing to RCA Records, their debut was recorded with the help of Andy Johns and long-time friend Gene Simmons (Kiss bassist) at the production desk. The result was well received, a state-of-the-art pomp-rock album with a powerful and sparkling sound. Apart from a few support slots on the Scorpions' European tour, the band did not commit themselves to touring in a way that was necessary to stimulate album sales. Lanny Cordola quit as a result, and was replaced by Michael Guy (ex-Fire) before the band entered the studio once more. *Sahara* continued in the same musical vein, but the interest it generated (the album went platinum) was once again allowed to ebb away as the band was still reluctant to tour. Guests included David Glen Eisley, the original Giuffria vocalist, whom Simmons had advised they replace prior to them becoming House Of Lords. They split shortly thereafter, though they did reform to record a new album for the Japanese market. After the band's dissolution, Christian eventually regrouped with both Cordola and Wright to pursue a solo career, releasing his debut album, *Rude Awakening*, on Now & Then Records in 1995. However, it lacked much of the sparkle that had once made the House Of Lords so vital.
● ALBUMS: *House Of Lords* (RCA 1988)★★★, *Sahara* (RCA 1990)★★★.
Solo: James Christian *Rude Awakening* (Now & Then 1995)★★.

HOWE II

After recording a solo instrumental album in 1988, guitarist Greg Howe decided to expand his musical horizons and incorporate his talents within a band framework. Brother Al stepped in as vocalist, with Vern Parsons and Joe Nevolo taking on bass and drum duties, respectively. Released in 1989, their debut album was a highly accomplished work that combined elements of Van Halen and Rising Force; Al Howe's vocals were reminiscent of vintage Dave Lee Roth, while Greg's guitar style was not far removed from that of the Swedish guitarist Yngwie Malmsteen. Their second album built on these solid foundations, but featured more melodic compositions.

● ALBUMS: *High Gear* (Roadrunner 1989)★★★, *Now Hear This* (Roadrunner 1991)★★★★.

HSAS

This US group was formed in the early part of 1984 by Sammy Hagar (vocals) and Neil Schon (guitar). Both were from the San Francisco area and had planned a collaboration for some time. When Hagar had finished promoting his latest solo record and Schon had completed touring with Journey, HSAS was formed. They brought in Peter Schrieve (drums) and Kenny Aaronson (bass), primarily because they shared the same management. They wrote approximately 15 songs during one month and then decided to tour with the set. It was while they were on the road that they recorded two dates in their home-town of San Francisco for their debut album, rather than in the studio. A deal was struck with Sammy Hagar's label, Geffen, and *Through The Fire* was prepared for release. However, American radio was resistant to live records, so most of the crowd noise was removed from the final mix, with the exception of two tracks where the audience actively participated in the songs. Never a permanent band, after the album's release, Hagar returned to his solo career and Schon went back to Journey.

● ALBUMS: *Through The Fire* (Geffen 1984)★★★.

HUGHES, GLENN

b. 21 August 1952, Cannock, Staffordshire, England. Hughes left school at the age of 15 to follow his dream of becoming a musician. He began playing lead guitar with the News in 1967, where he also sang, emulating his heroes Otis Redding and Wilson Pickett. Later he switched to bass guitar, inspired by James Jamerson from the Tamla/Motown Records 'house band'. These influences, married to a love of rock 'n' roll, led him to form Trapeze with Dave Holland (drums) and Mel Galley (guitar). Trapeze signed to the Moody Blues' record label, Threshold Records, and released four albums up to 1973, when Hughes was offered a job with a new Birmingham band, Electric Light Orchestra. However, he declined and in June joined Deep Purple instead. It was with Purple that Hughes made his mark in the UK with his superb singing on *Burn*, where he joined with, and some believe outclassed, their new vocalist David Coverdale. Hughes' influence over the band became a major factor in Ritchie Blackmore's decision to quit, and his association with the band continued until 1976 when he re-formed Trapeze with the original line-up, although this venture failed to tour or record. When they finally began a US tour, Hughes walked out halfway through. The band continued without him while their leader disappeared from public view. Two years later he resurfaced with a solo album before again dropping out of sight. In 1982 he joined with Pat Thrall (guitar, ex-Pat Travers Band) and Quiet Riot drummer Frankie Banali to form Hughes/Thrall, who released one album to a poor reception (although this set went on to achieve 'legendary' status and became one of the most sought-after rock albums of the 80s). After the project fell apart, Hughes worked for a time with Gary Moore, but little came of the collaboration. In 1985 he reunited with Mel Galley and a host of stars to record as the supergroup Phenomena. Although the ensuing concept album was considered obsolete by rock critics, it did serve to put Hughes back on the map, and Tony Iommi, looking for a replacement for Ian Gillan in Black Sabbath, contacted him. Hughes spent less than a year with the band but recorded some fine vocals for *Seventh Star*. He then returned to obscurity and suffered personal problems, but help from an unusual quarter was at hand. Bill Drummond of the KLF was keen to experiment with blending rock and dance music (he had already gained infamy in such matters with Extreme Noise Terror), and in 1991 he coaxed Hughes back into the limelight for the hit single 'America - What Time Is Love?'. This success reanimated the vocalist's efforts and he set about forming a new band that has since enjoyed a small degree of concert success. He has also renewed his partnership with Pat Thrall for a projected second album. A new band, World, was assembled in 1993, although his solo career continues. On *Feel*, he edged closer to AOR balladry.

● ALBUMS: *Play Me Out* (Safari 1978)★★★, *From Now On* (Roadrunner 1994)★★★, *Feel* (SPV 1995)★★, *Addiction* (Steamhammer 1996)★★★.

HUGHES/THRALL

This was a short-lived collaboration between former Deep Purple and Trapeze bassist/vocalist Glenn Hughes and guitarist Pat Thrall, who had previously played with Automatic Man and Pat Travers. With the help of various session drummers, including Frankie Banali (later of Quiet Riot), they recorded an album that fused rock and funk through the use of synthesized guitar effects.

Shortly after the album was released, Thrall went back to session work, while Hughes had stints with Gary Moore, Black Sabbath and Phenomena. In 1987 they worked together again, on the soundtrack of the film *Dragnet*.

● ALBUMS: *Hughes/Thrall* (Epic 1982)★★★.

HUM

Hum were formed in 1989 in Champaign, Illinois, USA, and consist of Jeff Dimpsey (b. 23 May 1967, Illinois, USA; bass), Tim Lash (b. 16 June 1974, Champaign, Illinois, USA; guitar), Bryan St. Pere (b. 2 April 1966, Evergreen Park, Illinois, USA; drums) and Matt Talbott (b. 27 June 1967, Geneseo, Illinois, USA; vocals, guitar). Adhering rigidly to the principles of self-booked touring dates and own-label releases, they have steadily built an international following for their intelligent but caustic musicality and Talbott's engaging, oblique lyrics. After a series of releases on their own 12-Inch Records label, the group signed to UK label Dedicated Records in 1996 in time for the release of their third album, *You'd Prefer An Astronaut*. Produced by Keith Cleversley (Flaming Lips, Spiritualized), it prompted a series of excellent reviews and confirmed Hum's rise as one of the more interesting and entertaining of the mid-90s alternative rock crop.

● ALBUMS: *You'd Prefer An Astronaut* (Dedicated 1996)★★★.

HUMBLE PIE

An early example of the 'supergroup', Humble Pie was formed in April 1969 by Peter Frampton (b. 22 April 1950, Beckenham, Kent, England; guitar, vocals, ex-Herd), Steve Marriott (guitar, vocals, ex-Small Faces) and Greg Ridley (b. 23 October 1947, Cumberland, England; bass, ex-Spooky Tooth). Drummer Jerry Shirley (b. 4 February 1952) completed the original line-up which had a UK Top 5 hit with its debut release, 'Natural Born Bugie'. The quartet's first two albums blended the single's hard-rock style with several acoustic tracks. Having failed to consolidate their early success, Humble Pie abandoned the latter, pastoral direction, precipitating Frampton's departure. He embarked on a prosperous solo career in October 1971, while his former colleagues, now bolstered by former Colosseum guitarist Dave Clempson (b. 5 September 1949, Tamworth, Staffordshire, England), concentrated on wooing US audiences. This period was best captured on *Smokin'*, the group's highest-ranking UK chart album. Humble Pie latterly ran out of inspiration and, unable to escape a musical rut, broke up in March 1975. Marriott then formed Steve Marriott's All Stars, which latterly included both Clempson and Ridley, while Shirley joined a new venture, Natural Gas. Tragically, Marriott died on 20 April 1991, following a fire at his Essex home.

● ALBUMS: *As Safe As Yesterday Is* (Immediate 1969)★★★, *Town And Country* (Immediate 1969)★★★, *Humble Pie* (A&M 1970)★★★, *Rock On* (A&M 1971)★★★, *Performance - Rockin' The Fillmore* (A&M 1972)★★, *Smokin'* (A&M 1972)★★, *Eat It* (A&M 1973)★★, *Thunderbox* (A&M 1974)★, *Street Rats* (A&M 1975)★, *On To Victory* (Jet 1980)★, *Go For The Throat* (Jet 1981)★.

● COMPILATIONS: *Crust Of Humble Pie* (EMI 1975)★★, *The Humble Pie Collection* (Castle 1994)★★★, *Natural Born Boogie* (BBC 1998)★★★.

HURRICANE

Formed in Los Angeles, California, USA, in 1983, this heavy metal band's original line-up consisted of Kelly Hanson (vocals), Robert Sarzo (guitar), Tony Cavazo (bass) and Jay Schellen (drums). Robert Sarzo is the brother of Whitesnake bassist Rudy Sarzo and Tony Cavazo is the brother of Quiet Riot guitarist Carlos Cavazo. Hurricane arrived via a mini-album released in 1986, entitled *Take What You Want*, on Roadrunner Records. It was a fine debut, featuring hard-edged melodic rockers. The band then switched labels, signing to Enigma Records and releasing *Over The Edge*. It failed to sell and during 1989 Robert Sarzo left the band to be replaced by ex-Lion guitarist Doug Aldrich. This line-up went on to record the much improved *Slave To The Thrill*, released in 1990 to critical acclaim.

● ALBUMS: *Take What You Want* mini-album (Roadrunner 1986)★★★, *Over The Edge* (Enigma 1988)★★, *Slave To The Thrill* (Enigma 1990)★★★★.

HUNTER, IAN

b. 3 June 1946, Shrewsbury, Shropshire, England. Having served a musical apprenticeship in several contrasting groups, Hunter was employed as a contract songwriter when approached to audition for a new act recently signed by Island Records. Initially known as Silence, the band took the name Mott The Hoople on his installation and Hunter's gravelly vocals and image-conscious looks - omnipresent dark glasses framed by long Dylanesque curly hair - established the vocalist/pianist as the group's focal point. He remained their driving force until 1974 when, having collapsed from physical exhaustion, he left the now-fractious line-up to begin a career as a solo artist. Late-period Mott guitarist Mick Ronson quit at the same time and the pair agreed to pool resources for particular projects. Ronson produced and played on *Ian Hunter*, which contained the singer's sole UK hit, 'Once Bitten Twice Shy' (number 14, May 1975). Having toured together as Hunter/Ronson with Peter Arnesen (keyboards), Jeff Appleby (bass) and Dennis Elliott (drums), the colleagues embarked on separate paths. *All American Alien Boy* contained contributions from Aynsley Dunbar, David Sanborn and several members of Queen, but despite several promising tracks, the set lacked the artist's erstwhile passion. *Overnight Angels* continued this trend towards musical conservatism, although following a period of seclusion, Hunter aligned himself with the punk movement by producing *The Valley Of The Dolls* for Generation X. *You're Never Alone With A Schizophrenic* marked his reunion with Ronson and subsequent live dates were commemorated on *Ian Hunter Live/Welcome To The Club*, which drew material from their respective careers. Hunter's output during the 80s was minimal, occasionally recording songs for film soundtracks, and in 1990 he resumed his partnership with Ronson on *YUI Orta*. He made an appearance at the 1992 Freddie Mercury AIDS benefit and in 1995 was once again tempted out of retirement to front the all-star band, Ian Hunter's Dirty Laundry, which featured ex-Crybabys Darrell Barth and Honest John Plain, plus Vom (ex-Doctor And The Medics), Casino Steel (ex-Hollywood Brats) and Glen Matlock (ex-Sex Pistols). He released a worthy new studio album, *The Artful Dodger*, in 1997.

● ALBUMS: *Ian Hunter* (Columbia 1975)★★★, *All American Alien Boy* (Columbia 1976)★★, *Overnight Angels* (Columbia 1977)★★, *You're Never Alone With A Schizophrenic* (Chrysalis 1979)★★★, *Ian Hunter Live/Welcome To The Club* (Chrysalis 1980)★★★, *Short Back And Sides* (Chrysalis 1981)★★★, *All Of The Good Ones Are Taken* (Columbia 1983)★★★, with Mick Ronson *YUI Orta* (Mercury 1990)★★★, as Ian Hunter's Dirty Laundry *Ian Hunter's Dirty Laundry* (Norsk 1995)★★★,, as the Hunter Ronson Band *BBC Live In Concert* (Strange Fruit 1995)★★★, *The Artful Dodger* (Citadel 1997)★★★.

● COMPILATIONS: *Shades Of Ian Hunter* (Columbia 1980)★★★★,, *The Very Best Of Ian Hunter* (Columbia 1990)★★★, *The Collection* (Castle 1991)★★★.

● FURTHER READING: *Diary Of A Rock 'N' Roll Star*, Ian Hunter.

Hüsker Dü

Formed in Minneapolis, Minnesota, USA, in 1979, Hüsker Dü were a punk trio consisting of guitarist/vocalist Bob Mould (b. 16 October 1960, Malone, New York, USA), bassist Greg Norton and drummer Grant Hart, whose melding of pop and punk influences inspired thousands of UK, US and European bands. Indeed, it is hard to think of a single other band who have had such a profound impact on modern alternative music as this trio. Taking their name, which means 'Do you remember?', from a Norwegian board game, they started out as an aggressive hardcore thrash band before challenging that genre's restrictions and expanding to other musical formats. Their primary strength, like so many other truly great groups, was in having two songwriting partners (Mould and Hart) who for the entirety of their career fully complemented each other. Their first single, 'Statues', was released on the small Reflex label in 1981. The same year, a debut album, *Land Speed Record,* arrived on New Alliance Records, followed by an EP, *In A Free Land*. *Everything Falls Apart* in 1982 saw them back on Reflex. By the advent of their second EP, *Metal Circus* (now on SST Records), Hüsker Dü had become a critics' favourite in the USA - a rapport that was soon to be exported to their UK brethren. *Zen Arcade* in 1984 brought about a stylistic turning point - a two-record set, it followed a single storyline about a young boy leaving home and finding life even more difficult on his own. A 14-minute closing song, 'Reoccurring Dreams', in which it was revealed that the boy's entire ordeal had been a dream, broke all the rules of punk. A non-album cover version of the Byrds' 'Eight Miles High' followed, and a 1985 album, *New Day Rising*, maintained the trio's reputation as a favourite of critics and college radio stations, with its irresistible quicksilver pop songs. After *Flip Your Wig* the band signed with Warner Brothers Records (there were several other interested parties), with whom they issued *Candy Apple Grey* in 1986 and *Warehouse: Songs And Stories*, another double set, the following year. In December 1987 Hart was dismissed from the group (though there are many conflicting versions of events leading up to this juncture), which summarily disbanded. Mould and Hart continued as solo artists, before Mould formed the equally rumbustious Sugar in 1991.

● ALBUMS: *Land Speed Record* (New Alliance 1981)★★, *Everything Falls Apart* (Reflex 1982)★★, *Metal Circus* mini-album (Reflex/SST 1983)★★★,

Zen Arcade (SST 1984)★★★★, *New Day Rising* (SST 1985)★★★, *Flip Your Wig* (SST 1985)★★★★, *Candy Apple Grey* (Warners 1986)★★★★, *Warehouse: Songs And Stories* (Warners 1987)★★★★, *The Living End* 1987 recording (Warners 1994)★★★.
● COMPILATIONS: *Everything Falls Apart And More* (Warners 1993)★★★★.

HUSTLER

Among the early pioneers of UK hard rock, Hustler comprised Steve Haynes (vocals), Micky Llewellyn (guitar, vocals), Tigger Lyons (bass, vocals), Kenny Daughters (keyboards) and Tony Beard (drums, percussion). At a time when the UK music scene still related anything from the rock field with complex, multi-layered progressive recordings, Hustler seemed somewhat of place with their straightforward rock hooks and 'good-time boogie' style. Nevertheless, both *High Street* and *Play Loud* remain excellent examples of the back-to-basics British rock movement that eventually exploded into the N.W.O.B.H.M. After the group's collapse, Llewellyn joined Mr. Big.
● ALBUMS: *High Street* (Firefly/A&M 1974)★★★, *Play Loud* (Firefly/A&M 1975)★★★.

HYDRA

Based in the southern states of America, hard rock band Hydra formed in the early 70s around a line-up of Wayne Bruce (vocals, guitar), Spencer Kirkpatrick (guitar), Orville Davis (bass) and Steve Pace (drums). Signed to the Allman Brothers and Marshall Tucker Band's record label, Capricorn Records, they made their debut in 1974 with a self-titled collection that drew heavily on Lynyrd Skynyrd's southern boogie tradition, but also added elaborate pop hooks and disciplined rhythmic codas. Songs such as 'Glitter Queen' won them a fervent fanbase, though the subsequent *Land Of Money*, a more abrasive collection, was less successful. By the advent of *Rock The World* Davis had departed to join Rex and the resultant instability stalled the group's progress.
● ALBUMS: *Hydra* (Capricorn 1974)★★★, *Land Of Money* (Capricorn 1975)★★★, *Rock The World* (Polydor 1977)★★.

HYPERHEAD

When the UK band Gaye Bykers On Acid folded, frontman Mary Mary (previously known as Mary Byker, though his real name is Ian Garfield Hoxley) began following a different musical path, working with the experimental industrial collective Pigface, before forming Hyperhead with a long-time friend, American bassist Karl Leiker. Pigface colleagues Martin Atkins (drums, ex-PiL; Killing Joke) and guitarist William Tucker (My Life With The Thrill Kill Kult; Revolting Cocks), along with guitarist Paul Dalloway, contributed to *Metaphasia*, showcasing an unpredictable hybrid style that drew from hard rock, soul, funk, indie pop and industrial for a diverse and interesting album. Mary, Leiker and Dalloway assembled a touring band with guitarist Oscar, drummer Chin and percussionist Keith, and this line-up recorded the *Terminal Fear* EP, which actually preceded *Metaphasia*'s release. Hyperhead established an excellent live reputation, boosted by Keith's sometimes crazed behaviour on stage, adding to the band's unpredictable air.
● ALBUMS: *Metaphasia* (Devotion 1993)★★★.

HYPOCRISY

One of Sweden's more extreme metal concerns, combining a musical intensity that borders on spite and unremittingly dark and violent lyrics. Comprising Peter Tägtgren (vocals, guitar, keyboards), Michael Hedlund (drums) and Lars Szöke (drums), Hypocrisy's reputation was established with *Osculum Obscenum* and European tours with labelmates Brutality. Forthright exponents of black metal, the group's exposition of the mystical and diabolical was conveyed in tracks such as 'Orgy In Blood' and 'The Arrival Of The Demons' on their 1994 opus, *Fourth Dimension*. This saw the trio concentrate on generating the maximum possible power from their riffs, sacrificing some velocity in the process. However, generally superior songwriting (particularly the title track and 'Apocalypse') ensured that they lost nothing in impact. *The Final Chapter*, their ninth release, was dominated by more of the same forceful riffing.
● ALBUMS: *Osculum Obscenum* (Nuclear Blast 1993)★★★, *Fourth Dimension* (Nuclear Blast 1994)★★★★ *The Final Chapter* (Nuclear Blast 1997)★★★.

ICON

Icon were formed in Phoenix, Arizona, USA, in 1981, by schoolfriends Dan Wexler (guitar), Tracy Wallach (bass, backing vocals) and Stephen Clifford (lead vocals). Drummer Pat Dixon and John Aquilino (guitar) joined a couple of months later. Icon spent their first three years playing local bars and recording demo tapes, originally under the name of the Schoolboys. Mike Varney heard the band and subsequently signed them to his Shrapnel label, after which Icon recorded their first album with Varney and Dan Wexler producing. After the sessions were completed, Varney realized that he had a commercial record on his hands, and sold Icon's contract to Capitol Records. In late 1984 *Icon* was released, a dynamic record in the Dokken tradition of melodic heavy metal. Brushing aside poor sales, they returned to the studio in 1985 with producer Eddie Kramer to record the follow-up, *Night Of The Crime*. Capitol dropped them from their roster following further disappointing sales, and Icon returned to Phoenix. At this point, Clifford, who had become a born-again Christian, was replaced by Jerry Harrison. In 1987 Icon released a cassette album, *A More Perfect Union*, which was sold locally and was reissued in 1995 as *An Even More Perfect Union*, also featuring four unissued tracks from the same sessions. Two years later Johnny Zazula heard the tape and signed them to his Megaforce label, which had just negotiated a worldwide distribution agreement with Atlantic Records. In the middle of 1989 Icon were about to start recording when Aquilino left the band. His replacement was Drew Bollmann, a Phoenix native. With Dan Wexler again producing, *Right Between The Eyes* saw Icon deliver their best record to date - again in their familiar AOR/melodic heavy rock vein - it also featured Alice Cooper guesting on two tracks. However, this did not signal Icon's triumphant return. After a short UK tour, Wexler announced their break-up.

● ALBUMS: *Icon* (Capitol 1984)★★★, *Night Of The Crime* (Capitol 1985)★★★, *A More Perfect Union* cassette only (Icon 1987)★★★, *Right Between The Eyes* (Megaforce 1989)★★★, *An Even More Perfect Union* CD reissue of *A More Perfect Union* (Epilogue 1995)★★★.

IGGY POP

b. James Jewel Osterburg, 21 April 1947, Ypsilanti, Michigan, USA. The sinewy 'Godfather Of Punk', Iggy Pop was born just west of Detroit to an English father and raised in nearby Ann Arbor. He first joined bands while at high school, initially as a drummer, most notably with the Iguanas in 1964 where he picked up the nickname Iggy. The following year he joined the Denver blues-styled Prime Movers, but a year later he dropped out of the University of Michigan to travel to Chicago and learn about the blues from former Howlin' Wolf and Paul Butterfield Blues Band drummer Sam Lay. On returning to Detroit as Iggy Stooge, and further inspired after seeing the Doors, he formed the Psychedelic Stooges with Ron Asheton of the Chosen Few. Iggy was vocalist and guitarist, Asheton initially played bass, and they later added Asheton's brother Scott on drums. Before the Chosen Few, Ron Asheton had also been in the Prime Movers with Iggy. The Psychedelic Stooges made their debut on Halloween night 1967, in Ann Arbor. The same year Iggy also made his acting debut in a long-forgotten Françoise De Monierre film that also featured Nico. Meanwhile, Dave Alexander joined on bass and the word 'Psychedelic' was dropped from their name. Ron switched to guitar, leaving Iggy free to concentrate on singing and showmanship. The Stooges were signed to Elektra Records in 1968 by A&R man Danny Fields (later manager of the Ramones). They recorded two albums (the first produced by John Cale) for the label which sold moderately at the time but later became regarded as classics, featuring such quintessential Iggy numbers as 'No Fun' and 'I Wanna Be Your Dog'. Steven MacKay joined on saxophone in 1970 in-between the first and second albums, as did Bill Cheatham on second guitar. Cheatham and Alexander left in August 1970, with Zeke Zettner replacing Alexander and James Williamson replacing Cheatham - but the Stooges broke up not long afterwards as a result of Iggy's heroin problem. Stooge fan David Bowie tried to resurrect Iggy's career and helped him to record *Raw Power* in London in the summer of 1972 (as Iggy and the Stooges, with Williamson on guitar, Scott Thurston on bass, and the Ashetons, who were flown in when no suitable British musicians could be found). The resultant album included the nihilistic anthem 'Search And Destroy'. Bowie's involvement continued (although his management company Mainman withdrew support because of constant drug allegations) as Iggy sailed through stormy seas (including self-admission to a mental hospital). The popular, but poor quality, live *Metallic KO* was released only in France at the time. Iggy Pop live events had long been a legend in the music industry, and it is doubtful whether any other artist has sustained such a high level of abject self-destruction on stage. It was his performance on the British television slot *So It Goes*, for example, that ensured the programme would never air again. After *Raw Power* there were sessions for *Kill City*, although it was not released until 1978, credited then to Iggy Pop and James Williamson. It also featured Thurston, Hunt and Tony Sales, Brian Glascock (ex-Toe Fat and later in the Motels), and others. The Stooges had folded again in 1974 with Ron Asheton forming New Order (not the same as the UK band) and then Destroy All Monsters. Steve MacKay later died from a drugs overdose and Dave Alexander from alcohol abuse. Thurston also joined the Motels. Interest was stirred in Iggy with the arrival of punk, on which his influence was evident (Television recorded the tribute 'Little Johnny Jewel'). In 1977 Bowie produced two studio albums - *The Idiot* and *Lust For Life* - using Hunt and Tony Sales, with Bowie himself, unheralded, playing keyboards. Key tracks from these two seminal albums include 'Night Clubbin'', 'The Passenger' and 'China Girl' (co-written with and later recorded by Bowie). Iggy also returned one of the several favours he owed Bowie by guesting on backing vocals for *Low*. In the late 70s Iggy signed to Arista Records and released some rather average albums with occasional assistance from Glen Matlock (ex-Sex Pistols) and Ivan Kral. He went into (vinyl) exile after 1982's autobiography and the Chris Stein-produced *Zombie Birdhouse*. During his time out of the studio he cleaned up his drug problems and married. He started recording again in 1985, with Steve Jones (ex-Sex Pistols) featuring on the next series of albums. He also developed his acting career (even taking lessons), appearing in *Sid And Nancy*, *The Color Of Money*, *Hardware*, and on television in *Miami Vice*. His big return came in 1986 with the Bowie-produced *Blah Blah Blah* and his first ever UK hit single, 'Real Wild Child', a cover version of Australian Johnny O'Keefe's 50s rocker. His rejuvenated *Brick By Brick* album featured Guns N'Roses guitarist Slash, who co-wrote four of the tracks, while his contribution to the *Red Hot And Blue* AIDS benefit was an endearing duet with Debborah Harry on 'Well Did You Evah?'. This was followed in 1991 by a duet with the B-52's' Kate Pierson, who had also featured on *Brick By Brick*. *American Caesar*, from its jokily self-aggrandizing title onwards, revealed continued creative growth, with longer spaces between albums now producing more worthwhile end results than was the case with his 80s career. Throughout he has remained the consummate live performer, setting a benchmark for at least one generation of rock musicians.

● ALBUMS: *The Idiot* (RCA 1977)★★★★, *Lust For Life* (RCA 1977)★★★★, *TV Eye Live* (RCA 1978)★★, *New Values* (Arista 1979)★★, *Soldier* (Arista 1980)★★, *Party* (Arista 1981)★★, *Zombie Birdhouse* (Animal 1982)★★, *Blah Blah Blah* (A&M 1986)★★★, *Instinct* (A&M 1988)★★, *Brick By Brick* (Virgin 1990)★★★, *American Caesar* (Virgin 1993)★★★, *Naughty Little Doggie* (Virgin 1996)★★★, *Heroin Hates You* recorded 1979 (Other People's Music 1997)★★★, *Live On The King Biscuit Flower Hour* recorded 1988 (King Biscuit 1998)★★★.

● COMPILATIONS: *Choice Cuts* (RCA 1984)★★★, *Compact Hits* (A&M 1988)★★★, *Suck On This!* (Revenge 1993)★★, *Live NYC Ritz '86* (Revenge 1993)★★, *Best Of ... Live* (MCA 1996)★★, *Nude & Rude: The Best Of ...* (Virgin 1996)★★★★, *Pop Music* (BMG/Camden 1996)★★★.

● FURTHER READING: *The Lives And Crimes Of Iggy Pop*, Mike West. *I Need More: The Stooges And Other Stories*, Iggy Pop with Anne Wehrer. *Iggy Pop: The Wild One*, Per Nilsen and Dorothy Sherman. *Neighbourhood Threat: On Tour With Iggy Pop*, Alvin Gibbs.

IMPELLITERI, CHRIS

Impelliteri is a new-age guitarist influenced by a combination of rock and classical music styles. Utilizing a high-speed fretboard technique, he is distinguished by his ability to fit as many notes as possible into the shortest time-span. Moving to Los Angeles in 1986, he first recorded a self-financed mini-album of up-tempo instrumentals. The following year, he formed Impelliteri, which also featured vocalist Graham Bonnet (b. 12 December 1947, Skegness, Lincolnshire, England; ex-MSG and Rainbow), drummer Pat Torpey (ex-Ted Nugent), bassist Chuck Wright (ex-Quiet Riot) and keyboardist Phil Wolfe. Together they recorded the stunning hard rock album, *Stand In Line*. Although it provoked unjustified accusations of plagiarism from Rainbow devotees, the music was powerful, exciting and melodic. However, the band disintegrated shortly after the album's release; Chuck Wright joined House Of Lords and Pat Torpey teamed up with Mr. Big. Impelliteri himself joined forces with ex-Dio keyboard player Claude Schnell and vocalist Mark Weisz in 1990.

● ALBUMS: *Impelliteri* (Polytour 1986)★★★. As Impelliteri: *Stand In Line* (Music For Nations 1988)★★★★.

Imperial Teen

Much of the attention initially surrounding San Francisco, California, USA rock band Imperial Teen focused on the fact that one of its members was concurrent Faith No More keyboard player Roddy Böttum. He put together the band in 1994 as a reaction to the death of two of his friends, his father's terminal cancer and his own heroin addiction. He took over guitar and vocal duties, while he enlisted friends Lynn Perko (drums, ex-Wrecks; Sister Double Happiness), Jone Stebbins (bass, also ex-Wrecks) and Will Schwarz (guitar, vocals). The group's debut album, *Seasick*, was produced by Steve McDonald of Red Kross and featured songs addressing the death of his friend Kurt Cobain ('Butch'), his father ('Luxury') and Courtney Love ('Copafeelia'). However, the emotional scar tissue was hidden deep within an upbeat blend of pop and rock riffs, many of the songs being characterized by the female backing vocals.

● ALBUMS: *Seasick* (Slash/London 1996)★★★.

Incubus Succubus

Incubus Succubus, from Cheltenham, Gloucestershire, England, are a rock band with strong English folk and gothic punk influences. Most of their lyrics revolve around either of two themes - vampirism and the pagan faith of Wicca. The vampiric strand accounts for much of their gothic feel. It is Wicca, however, that dominates their material, with its continuation of the Medieval witchcraft tradition of pre-Christian hunting gods and moon goddesses. Their Wiccan beliefs have attracted a strong following in the UK's pagan subculture, though this has yet to translate into mainstream success. The band (originally known as Children Of The Moon) has had a fluctuating line-up, but the core remains Tony McCormick (ex-Screaming Dead; guitars) and Candia (vocals).

● ALBUMS: *Beltaine* (Nightbreed 1992)★★★, *Belladonna And Aconite* (Nightbreed 1992)★★, *Wytches* (Pagan Media 1994)★★★.

Infectious Grooves

This heavy Los Angeles, USA funk-rock band was founded by the Suicidal Tendencies duo of vocalist Mike Muir and hugely talented bassist Robert Trujillo, with guitarists Adam Siegel (from Excel) and Dean Pleasants and ex-Jane's Addiction drummer Stephen Perkins. The band was deemed more than a side project for Muir and Trujillo, given equal status with Suicidal Tendencies, and the two bands often toured together, necessitating two exhausting sets per night for the pair. The debut established an entirely different sound from the parent band, with a heavy, Red Hot Chili Peppers-style funk attack, with Muir, for once, producing lighter lyrical fare. Stand-out track 'Therapy' featured guest backing vocals from Ozzy Osbourne, who punctuated Muir's vocals with gleeful, manic roars of the title over furious riffing and a potent Trujillo-Perkins rhythm. Perkins left for Porno For Pyros the following year, and Josh Freese stepped in on *Sarsippius' Ark*, an odd collection of previously unreleased songs, live takes, cover versions and new numbers, with spoken interjections from a 'Sarsippius' character. *Groove Family Cyco* was a more conventional set of new material in the same hard funk vein, with Muir taking a satirical lyrical swipe at Rage Against The Machine on 'Do What I Tell Ya!', while adopting his more customary serious lyrical slant. With the break-up of Suicidal in early 1995, it seemed likely that more time would be devoted to Infectious Grooves, although the industrious Muir also formed a punk band, My Head, with Siegel.

● ALBUMS: *The Plague That Makes Your Booty Move ... It's The Infectious Grooves* (Epic 1991)★★★, *Sarsippius' Ark* (Epic 1993)★★, *Groove Family Cyco* (550 Music/Epic 1994)★★★.

Inner City Unit

The weird and wonderful Inner City Unit were formed by ex-Hawkwind member and Oxford-born English eccentric Nik Turner (saxophone, vocals) in 1979, along with Trev Thoms (guitar), Dead Fred Reeves (keyboards), Baz Magneto (bass) and Mick Stupp (drums). Turner's first non-Hawkwind album was with Steve Hillage in 1977, entitled *Sphynx (Xitintoday)* - a set far removed from the punk sound then prevalent, which became a major influence on Inner City Unit. A debut album, *Pass Out*, and two singles, 'Solitary Ashtray' and 'Paradise Beach', appeared on his own Riddle label. In 1981 he moved the band to Avatar for *The Maximum Effect*, which also featured Captain Sensible and comedian Max Wall. Magneto reverted to his real name of Barry Downes to join Weapon and was replaced by Reeves, who doubled up on bass and keyboards. The next album,

Punkadelic, featured reworkings of earlier tracks, but soon afterwards, Turner rejoined Hawkwind. In 1984 Turner re-formed Inner City Unit, with Steve Pond replacing Stupp. Their first album together, *New Anatomy*, produced two firsts: it was the first album on ex-Hawkwind bassist Dave Anderson's new record label, Demi-Monde, and it was also the first album to feature a computer programme on vinyl for the Spectrum system. Inner City Unit then recorded the *Blood And Bone* 12-inch EP and backed it with a video that included the surreal 'Little Black Egg' and a guest appearance from Robert Calvert. A final album, *The President's Tapes*, was received with mass indifference and the band folded. Thoms then formed the Atom Gods and Turner the Fantastic All Stars, before journeying to the USA in 1993 and recording with Pressurehead. He has since worked on new projects with members of Psychic TV.

● ALBUMS: *Pass Out (The 360 Psycho Deleria Sound)* (Riddle 1980)★★★, *The Maximum Effect* (Avatar 1981)★★★, *Punkadelic* (Flicknife 1982)★★, with Robert Calvert *Ersatz* (Pompadour 1982)★★, *New Anatomy* (Demi-Monde 1984)★★★, *The President's Tapes* (Flicknife 1985)★★.

● VIDEOS: *Blood And Bone* (Jettisoundz 1985).

INNER SANCTUM

Formed in late 1979, Inner Sanctum surfaced at the time of the New Wave Of British Heavy Metal but also predated the rise of Metallica, Anthrax and thrash metal by combining traditional hard rock postures with the dark imagery of Black Sabbath. The group's early material, such as 'Streets And Alleys' and 'The Butcher', provided a discernible influence on prototype thrash metal bands Hellhammer, Testament and Coroner. Over the years the core membership of Inner Sanctum has remained two sets of brothers: Mick Pendergast (vocals), Rick Pendergast (guitar), Eric Barbasso (bass) and Adam Barbasso (guitar). The position of drummer has never been quite as secure, however. On the debut, Mike Portnoy, now of Dream Theater, was the drummer. Two further drummers have also recorded with the band, including Jed Hawkins, who together with fellow Inner Sanctum part-timer Dave Ray joined Skyclad in the mid-90s. *12 a.m.* comprised a selection of the 28 tracks the band had been perfecting since their formation, and was re-released as an 'undiscovered classic' by Rock The Nation Records in 1994.

● ALBUMS: *Revenge* (1986)★★★, *R.I.P. - Live* (1988)★★, *12 a.m.* (Rock The Nation 1994)★★★.

INSANE CLOWN POSSE

Formed in Detroit, Michigan, USA. Insane Clown Posse's highly shocking rap/metal fusion and spectacular live performances had, by the time they were signed to a major label in 1997, earnt them both public notoriety and commercial success. Violent J. (b. Joseph Bruce) and Shaggy 2 Dope (b. Joey Ulster) originally performed as the Inner City Posse in the late 80s, releasing the hardcore gangsta rap *Dog Beats* in 1991. Following the underground success of this album, Bruce and Ulster changed their name to Insane Clown Posse and underwent a startling change of image, adopting Kiss-style clown make-up and rapping about the apocalypse. The duo released several albums on their own Psychopathic Records imprint (each claiming to contain a further revelation from the final judgement), and gained a sizeable underground following in the Midwest without the backing of any radio play. They also roused the public ire of several local politicians and moral and religious campaigners, who reacted with shock to the foul-mouthed lyrics, open fires, chainsaws and barely contained violence of the duo's live shows. Jive Records signed the duo and released *The Riddle Box* in 1995, but the album failed to sell. Disney's Hollywood Records signed the band a year later and poured nearly a million dollars into *The Great Milenko*, Insane Clown Posse's 1997 major label debut recorded with guest artists including Slash and Alice Cooper. The label recalled the album only six hours after it was released, however, with the duo's obscene lyrics placing Disney under further pressure from powerful Christian groups. Island Records bought out the Hollywood contract, and re-released the album later in the year with Insane Clown Posse still a permanent fixture in the media pages.

● ALBUMS: *Carnival Of Carnage* (Psychopathic 1992)★★★, *The Ringmaster* (Psychopathic 1994)★★, *The Riddle Box* (Battery 1995)★★, *The Great Milenko* (Hollywood 1997)★★★.

● COMPILATIONS: *Forgotten Freshness* (PSY 1995)★★.

INTO ANOTHER

Proffering a melodic brand of intelligent east coast hard rock, Into Another were formed in New York, USA, in 1990, by Richie Birkenhead, formerly a member of hardcore legends Youth Of Today. Additionally comprising Peter Moses (guitar), Tony Bono (bass, ex-Whiplash) and Drew Thomas (drums), the group made its debut with a self-titled collection in 1991. This, and subsequent EPs such as *Creepy Eepy* and *Herbivore*, established a musical agenda that drew from the psychedelic metal crossover style of Redd Kross and Urge Overkill. By 1996 and the *Seamless* album, the group had been made a priority by their record company and enlisted the services of Pearl Jam/Soundgarden producer Rick Parashar in an attempt to develop a fuller, more polished rock sound. Certainly some of the tracks, such as opener 'Mutate Me', recalled the sound of grunge, but elsewhere Into Another adopted a more cerebral approach, with Birkenhead's lyrics in particular winning critical praise.

● ALBUMS: *Into Another* (Revelation 1991)★★, *Ignaurus* (Revelation 1994)★★★, *Seamless* (Hollywood 1996)★★★.

INTRINSIC

This power-metal quintet from California, USA, was formed in 1983 with guitarists Mike Mellinger and Ron Crawford settling on the rhythm section of Joel Stern (bass) and Chris Binns (drums) in late 1984, with vocalist Garrett Graupner joining the following year. The band refined their fast, Iron Maiden-influenced style on the club scene, playing support slots to the likes of Megadeth and Armored Saint in San Francisco while conversely opening for glam bands in Los Angeles, before releasing *Intrinsic* to enormous critical acclaim. However, the band were held back while they searched for a new vocalist, with Graupner having departed by mutual consent, as both parties felt that his bluesy tones were unsuited to Intrinsic's more aggressive material. David Wayne (ex-Metal Church) stepped in as the band signed a contract with Important Records, who re-released the debut, but was ousted after only five live shows, and the band's continuing search for a vocalist prevented them capitalizing on their good press. A self-financed EP followed, demonstrating again the band's sophisticated guitarwork, but failing to reach the heights of the debut; no new contract ensued, and Intrinsic continued to haul their power demos around record labels.

● ALBUMS: *Intrinsic* (No Wimp 1987)★★★, *Distortion Of Perspective* mini-album (Cheese Flag 1991)★★★.

IOMMI, TONY

b. Anthony Frank Iommi, 19 February 1948, Birmingham, England. A blues/jazz-influenced guitarist, Iommi was eager to escape the mundanity of industrial Birmingham and his job repairing typewriters. A number of small-time bands, including Polka Tulk and Earth, gradually led to the formation of Black Sabbath in 1969, with Iommi on guitar, Ozzy Osbourne (vocals), Terence 'Geezer' Butler (bass) and Bill Ward (drums). It was with Black Sabbath that Iommi established his international reputation as a guitarist of skill and invention. The Black Sabbath sound was built on his devastating riffing, delivered with a fuzzy, distorted guitar tone that became his trademark. He was, and still is, the godfather of the heavy metal riff. Iommi has a unique soloing and rhythm style, and sports an unusual set of plastic finger extensions on his right hand as a result of an accident (he is left-handed). A tall, dark, moustachioed man, he is also famed for his lack of movement on stage. Personal differences between Iommi and Osbourne contributed to the latter's departure from Black Sabbath in 1978, to be replaced by American Ronnie James Dio. After Dio's own departure in 1982, Black Sabbath entered a highly unstable phase, and it was Iommi who held the band together and kept the Black Sabbath name alive. The album *Seventh Star* was released under the heading 'Black Sabbath Featuring Tony Iommi', according to record company wishes. Iommi, however, had intended it to be a solo effort, giving the songs a different emphasis to those from a pure Black Sabbath album.

● ALBUMS: See Black Sabbath.

IRON BUTTERFLY

During the progressive music revolution in the late 60s, one of the most surprising successes was that of Iron Butterfly. The band was formed by Doug Ingle (b. 9 September 1946, Omaha, Nebraska, USA; organ, vocals), who added Ron Bushy (b. 23 September 1941, Washington, DC, USA; drums), Eric Brann (b. 10 August 1950, Boston, Massachusetts, USA; guitar), Lee Dorman (b. 19 September 1945, St. Louis, Missouri, USA; bass, vocals) and, briefly, Danny Weiss. Together, they were arguably the first to amalgamate the terms 'heavy' and 'rock', following the release of their debut in 1968. Their second effort, *In-A-Gadda-Da-Vida* ('In The Garden Of Eden'), became a multi-million-seller and was for a number of years the biggest-selling item in Atlantic Records' catalogue. The album also became the record industry's first platinum disc. The 17-minute title track contained everything a progressive rock fan could want - neo-classical organ with Far East undertones, a solid beat, screeching guitar parts, barbed-wire feedback and an overlong drum solo. Magnificently overwrought at the time, the intervening years have been less kind to its standing. The follow-up, *Ball*, was less of a success, despite being a better collection of songs, notably the invigorating 'It Must Be Love' and the more subtle 'Soul Experience'. Brann departed after a poor live album and was replaced by two guitarists: Larry 'Rhino' Rheinhart (b. 7 July 1948, Florida, USA) and Mike Pinera (b. 29 September 1948, Florida, USA; ex-Cactus; Alice Cooper). However, no further success ensued. *Metamorphosis* was a confused collection, recorded when the band was disintegrating. They re-formed in the mid-70s, delivering two disappointing albums. Another re-formation, this time in 1992, was masterminded by Mike Pinera. A new version of 'In-A-Gadda-Da-Vida' was recorded and Pinera recruited Dorman and Bushy for extensive touring in the USA. By 1993, their legendary second album had sold an astonishing 25 million copies and in 1995 the band re-formed once more for an anniversary tour.

● ALBUMS: *Heavy* (Atco 1968)★★★, *In-A-Gadda-Da-Vida* (Atco 1968)★★★★, *Ball* (Atco 1969)★★★, *Iron Butterfly Live* (Atco 1970)★, *Metamorphosis* (Atco 1970)★★, *Scorching Beauty* (MCA 1975)★★, *Sun And Steel* (MCA 1976)★★★.

● COMPILATIONS: *The Best Of Iron Butterfly: Evolution* (Atco 1971)★★★, *Star Collection* (Atlantic 1973)★★★, *Light And Heavy: The Best Of Iron Butterfly* (Rhino 1993)★★★.

IRON MAIDEN

Formed in London, England, in 1976, Iron Maiden was from the start the brainchild of Steve Harris (b. 12 March 1957, Leytonstone, London, England; bass), formerly a member of pub rockers Smiler. Named after a medieval torture device, the music was suitably heavy and hard on the senses. The heavy metal scene of the late 70s was widely regarded as stagnant, with only a handful of bands proving their ability to survive and produce music of quality. It was at this time that a new breed of young British bands began to emerge. This movement, which began to break cover in 1979 and 1980, was known as the New Wave Of British Heavy Metal, or N.W.O.B.H.M. Iron Maiden were one of the foremost bands in the genre, and many would say its definitive example. Younger and meaner, the N.W.O.B.H.M. bands dealt in faster, more energetic heavy metal than any of their forefathers (punk being an obvious influence). There were several line-up changes in the Iron Maiden ranks in the very early days, and come the release of their debut EP, the group featured Harris, Dave Murray (b. 23 December 1958, London, England; guitar), Paul Di'Anno (b. 17 May 1959, Chingford, London, England; vocals) and Doug Sampson (drums). The group made its live debut at the Cart & Horses Pub in Stratford, east London, in 1977, before honing its sound on the local pub circuit over the ensuing two years. Unable to solicit a response from record companies, the group sent a three-track tape, featuring 'Iron Maiden', 'Prowler' and 'Strange World', to Neal Kay, DJ at north London's hard rock disco, the Kingsbury Bandwagon Soundhouse. Kay's patronage of Iron Maiden won them an instant welcome, which prompted the release of *The Soundhouse Tapes* on the band's own label. In November 1979 the group added second guitarist Tony Parsons to the line-up for two tracks on the *Metal For Muthas* compilation, but by the time the group embarked on sessions for their debut album, he had been replaced by Dennis Stratton (b. 9 November 1954, London, England), and Sampson by Clive Burr (b. 8 March 1957; drums, ex-Samson). A promotional single, 'Running Free', reached number 34 on the UK charts and brought an appearance on BBC Television's *Top Of The Pops*. Refusing to mime, they became the first band since the Who in 1973 to play live on the show. *Iron Maiden* was a roughly produced album, but reached number 4 in the UK album listings on the back of touring stints with Judas Priest and enduringly popular material such as 'Phantom Of The Opera'. *Killers* boasted production superior to that of the first album, and saw Dennis Stratton replaced by guitarist Adrian Smith (b. 27 February 1957). In its wake, Iron Maiden became immensely popular among heavy metal fans, inspiring fanatical devotion, aided by blustering manager Rod Smallwood and apocalyptic mascot Eddie (the latter had been depicted on the cover of 'Sanctuary' standing over Prime Minister Margaret Thatcher's decapitated body).

The release of *Number Of The Beast* was crucial to the development of the band. Without it, Iron Maiden might never have gone on to be such a force in the heavy metal arena. The album was a spectacular success, the sound of a band on the crest of a wave. It was also the debut of former infantryman and new vocalist Bruce Dickinson (b. Paul Bruce Dickinson, 7 August 1958, Worksop, Nottinghamshire, England), replacing Paul Di'Anno (who went on to front Dianno, Paul Di'Anno's Battlezone and Killers). Formerly of Samson, history graduate Dickinson made his live debut with Maiden on 15 November 1981. Singles such as 'Run To The Hills' and 'The Number Of

The Beast' were big UK chart hits, Iron Maiden leaving behind their N.W.O.B.H.M. counterparts in terms of success, just as the movement itself was beginning to peter out. *Piece Of Mind* continued their success and was a major hit in the UK (number 3) and USA (number 14). Clive Burr was replaced by Nicko McBrain on the sessions, formerly drummer with French metal band Trust, who had supported Maiden on their 1981 UK tour (he had also played in Streetwalkers). *Piece Of Mind* was not dissimilar to the previous album, showcasing the strong twin-guitar bite of Murray and Smith, coupled with memorable vocal lines and a sound that perfectly suited their air-punching dynamic. Single offerings, 'Flight of Icarus' and 'The Trooper', were instant hits, as the group undertook two massive tours, the four-month *World Piece* jaunt in 1983, and a *World Slavery* retinue, which included four sell-out dates at London's Hammersmith Odeon a year later. With the arrival of *Powerslave* in November, some critics accused Iron Maiden of conforming to a self-imposed writing formula, and playing safe with tried and tested ideas. Certainly, there was no significant departure from the two previous albums, but it was nonetheless happily consumed by the band's core supporters, who also purchased in sufficient quantities to ensure UK chart hits for 'Aces High' and 'Two Minutes To Midnight'. *Live After Death* was a double-album package of all their best-loved material, recorded live on their gargantuan 11-month world tour. By this time, Iron Maiden had secured themselves an unassailable position within the metal hierachy, their vast popularity spanning all continents. *Somewhere In Time* was a slight departure: it featured more melody than previously, and heralded the use of guitar synthesizers. Their songwriting still shone through and the now obligatory hit singles were easily attained in the shape of 'Wasted Years' and 'Stranger In A Strange Land'. Reaching number 11 in the USA, this was another million-plus seller. Since the mid-80s Maiden had been staging increasingly spectacular live shows, with elaborate lighting effects and stage sets. The *Somewhere In Time* tour (seven months) was no exception, ensuring their continued fame as a live band, which had been the basis for much of their success. A period of comparative inactivity preceded the release of *Seventh Son Of A Seventh Son*, which was very much in the same vein as its predecessor. A concept album, it retained its commercial edge (giving the band their second UK number 1 album) and yielded hit singles in 'Can I Play With Madness', the surprisingly sensitive 'Evil That Men Do' and 'The Clairvoyant'.

After another exhausting mammoth world trek, the band announced their intention to take a well-earned break of at least a year. Speculation abounded that this signalled the dissolution of the band, exacerbated by Dickinson's solo project, *Tattooed Millionaire*, his book, *The Adventures Of Lord Iffy Boatrace*, and EMI Records' policy of re-releasing Maiden's single catalogue in its entirety (on 12-inch). After a considerable hiatus, news of the band surfaced again. Steve Harris felt that the direction pursued on the last two albums had been taken as far as possible, and a return to the style of old was planned. Unhappy with this game plan, Adrian Smith left to be replaced by Janick Gers (b. Hartlepool, Lancashire, England), previously guitarist with White Spirit and Gillan (he had also contributed to Dickinson's solo release). The live show was also scaled down in a return to much smaller venues. *No Prayer For The Dying* was indeed much more like mid-period Iron Maiden, and was predictably well received, bringing enormous UK hit singles with 'Holy Smoke' and 'Bring Your Daughter To The Slaughter'. The latter, previously released in 1989 on the soundtrack to *A Nightmare On Elm Street 5*, had already been awarded the Golden Raspberry Award for Worst Song that year. Nevertheless, it gave Iron Maiden their first ever UK number 1. The obligatory world tour followed. Despite being denounced as 'Satanists' in Chile, 1992 also saw the band debut at number 1 in the UK charts with *Fear Of The Dark*, which housed another major single success in 'Be Quick Or Be Dead' (number 2). However, it was Dickinson's swan-song with the band, who invited demo tapes from new vocalists following the lead singer's announcement that he would depart following current touring engagements. His eventual replacement was Blaze Bayley (b. 1963, Birmingham, West Midlands, England) from Wolfsbane. His debut album was *X-Factor*, and on this and at live gigs (which they only resumed in November 1995), he easily proved his worth. This was a daunting task, having had to learn Maiden's whole catalogue and win over patriotic Dickinson followers. Adrian Smith resurfaced in a new band, Psycho Motel, in 1996.

● ALBUMS: *Iron Maiden* (EMI 1980)★★★, *Killers* (EMI 1981)★★, *Number Of The Beast* (EMI 1982)★★★★, *Piece Of Mind* (EMI 1983)★★★, *Powerslave* (EMI 1984)★★, *Live After Death* (EMI 1985)★★★, *Somewhere In Time* (EMI 1986)★★★, *Seventh Son Of A Seventh Son* (EMI 1988)★★★★, *No Prayer For The Dying* (EMI 1990)★★★, *Fear Of*

The Dark (EMI 1992)★★★, *A Real Live One (Volume One)* (EMI 1993)★★★, *A Real Dead One* (EMI 1993)★★, *Live At Donington '92* (EMI 1993)★★, *The X Factor* (EMI 1995)★★★, *Virtual XI* (EMI 1998)★★★.

● COMPILATIONS: *The Best Of The Beast* (EMI 1996)★★★.

● VIDEOS: *Live At The Rainbow* (PMI/EMI 1984), *Behind The Iron Curtain Video EP* (PMI/EMI 1986), *Live After Death* (PMI/EMI 1986), *Run To The Hills* (Video Collection 1987), *Twelve Wasted Years* (PMI/EMI 1987), *Maiden England* (PMI/EMI 1989), *The First Ten Years (The Videos)* (PMI/EMI 1990), *Raising Hell* (1993), *Donington Live 1992* (1994).

● FURTHER READING: *Running Free: The Official Story Of Iron Maiden*, Garry Bushell and Ross Halfin. *A Photographic History*, Ross Halfin. *What Are We Doing This For?*, Ross Halfin. *Run To The Hills, Iron Maiden: The Official Biography*, Mick Wall.

IRONHORSE

This US group was founded by Randy Bachman, formerly the leader of the Canadian rock group Bachman-Turner Overdrive. The initial line-up comprised Bachman (b. 27 September 1943, Winnipeg, Manitoba, Canada; guitar, vocals), John Pierce (bass), Tom Sparks (guitar, vocals) and Mike Baird (drums). They enjoyed a US Top 40 hit in 1979 with 'Sweet Lui-Louise' and by the time the second album was recorded, the line-up had undergone several alterations, with Ron Foos and Chris Leighton replacing Pierce and Baird, respectively. This largely undistinguished outfit recorded one further album, the title of which neatly summarized the attitude of their critics.

● ALBUMS: *Ironhorse* (Scotti Bros 1979)★★, *Everything Is Grey* (Scotti Bros 1980)★.

IT'S ALIVE

Formed in Stockholm, Sweden, in 1987, It's Alive are a hard rock sextet comprising Martin White (vocals), Per Aldeheim (guitar), Kim Björkegren (guitar), Peter Kahn (bass), John Rosth (keyboards) and Richard Eversand (drums). Describing their sound as 'rock with funk influences', the group grew up listening to dramatic bands such as Kiss and the Sweet. That influence was much in evidence on their breakthrough 1993 single, 'Sing This Blues', which, like other releases, arrived in packaging shot by internationally acclaimed photographer Lennart Nilsson. The concurrent debut album, *Earthquake Visions*, on Cheiron Records (later through Music For Nations in the UK), saw them garner further critical support, including nominations for a Swedish Grammy plus Album Of The Year and Best Breakthrough Act in the country's Zeppelin awards. In its wake, they commenced touring engagements with Kingdom Come. They remain one of the most genuinely innovative groups working on the Scandinavian hard rock circuit.

● ALBUMS: *Earthquake Visions* (Cheiron/Music For Nations 1993)★★★.

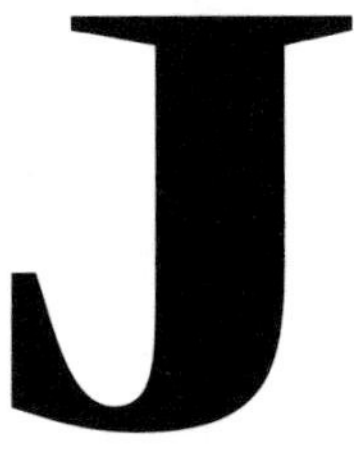

JACKYL

This Atlanta, Georgia-based band was formed in 1990 by the larger-than-life frontman Jesse James Dupree, guitarists Jeff Worley and Jimmy Stiff, bassist Tom Bettini and drummer Chris Worley. The band created an enormous buzz, with a basic AC/DC style that transferred well to the live setting on a heavy touring schedule, and they were quickly signed by John Kalodner to Geffen Records. *Jackyl* courted controversy from the start, enraging feminists with the ludicrously titled 'She Loves My Cock', while Dupree's onstage antics kept the music press busy. During 'The Lumberjack', Dupree soloed on a chainsaw - his father had been so impressed by a club performance with a hired chainsaw that he bought his son a new one - and also regularly indulged his penchant for performing the latter part of the set naked, which resulted in an early departure from a Lynyrd Skynyrd support slot. However, tours with Damn Yankees and, in particular, Aerosmith proved more successful, and *Jackyl* achieved platinum status against the grunge-loaded odds. *Push Comes To Shove* continued in the vein of the debut, and added to the controversy when an advertising hoarding in Nashville was censored (Dupree was displaying his bare buttocks in the band photograph).

● ALBUMS: *Jackyl* (Geffen 1992)★★★, *Push Comes To Shove* (Geffen 1994)★★★, *Night Of The Living Dead* (Music For Nations 1996)★★, *Cut The Crap* (Epic 1997)★★★.

JADE

The first working unit of Jade was formed in Winnipeg, Canada, in 1982. The original line-up consisted of Roxy Lyons (vocals), Pat Belrose (guitar), Terry Rudd (bass) and Dave Samson (drums). The band initially played on the local club circuit in the absence of a genuine rock scene. They decided to relocate to Ottawa where they quickly struck a one-off album contract with the small independent label Zaphia Records. Their debut, *Teasing Eyes*, released in 1984, was a mediocre collection of tired pop rock. Realizing their mistake in choice of locale, they relocated once again, this time to Toronto, where the rock community was much more active. Following disagreements on personal and professional matters, Lyons left the band to be replaced by ex-Aggressor vocalist Sweet Marie Black. The band worked hard on their songwriting, taking a more rock-based approach, and subsequent demos led to them being signed by the Roadrunner label, who released *If You're Man Enough* in 1985. With more rock and less pop, the album nevertheless failed to attract any interest and the band sank back into obscurity in 1986.

● ALBUMS: *Teasing Eyes* (Zaphia 1984)★★★, *If You're Man Enough* (Roadrunner 1985)★★.

JADE WARRIOR

Formed in 1970, USA rock band Jade Warrior centred on the multi-instrumental talents of Tony Duhig (d. November 1990; electric and acoustic guitar, bass, keyboards) and John Field (percussion, flute, guitar, keyboards), previously members of psychedelic-pop group July. Glyn Havard (bass, guitar, vocals) completed the pair's new venture, which, although inspired by oriental motifs, betrayed a greater debt to British progressive rock. Jade Warrior completed three albums for the renowned Vertigo label, the last of which, *Last Autumn's Dream*, introduced Duhig's brother David (guitar) into the line-up. Havard left the group when a fourth set, *Eclipse*, failed to secure a release, while the founding duo began a parallel career as session musicians. Jade Warrior's later releases, issued by Island Records, showed an even greater propensity for experimentation, but failed to elevate the band above cult status. Following six years of inactivity, the group was reassembled for *Horizons*, but the reunion proved short-lived. Tony Duhig succumbed to a fatal heart attack in November 1990.

● ALBUMS: *Jade Warrior* (Vertigo 1971)★★★, *Released* (Vertigo 1971)★★★, *Last Autumn's Dream* (Vertigo 1972)★★, *Floating World* (Island 1974)★★★, *Waves* (Island 1975)★★★, *Kites* (Island 1976)★★★, *The Way Of The Sun* (Island 1978)★★, *Horizons* (1984)★★★.

● COMPILATIONS: *Reflections* (1980)★★★, *Breathing The Storm* (1993)★★★.

JAG PANZER

Formed in Colorado, USA, in 1981, the band's original line-up consisted of the curiously named The Tyrant (vocals), Mark Briody (guitar), John Tetley (bass) and Butch Carlson (drums). Quickly signing to the small independent Azra Records, their debut mini-album, *Jag Panzer*, was released in 1983. Basically a collection of demo tracks, it was a rough and ready affair of straight-ahead power metal-inspired rock. The band decided to add another guitarist to give them an extra dimension, and with this in mind, they relocated to Los Angeles to seek young hopefuls. There they auditioned countless guitarists until Joey Tafolla was finally recruited. With Tafolla in place, they promptly headed back to Colorado to record their first full-length album, *Ample Destruction*, released in 1984 (it was later re-released in 1990 on the Metalcore label). Unfortunately, the album only served to establish the band as a strong underground act with minimal cult status. Dissatisfied with this lack of success, Tafolla left the outfit for a solo career and later went on to play in Alice Cooper's touring band. Shortly after his departure, both The Tyrant and Carlson also left the band. The Tyrant joined Riot, albeit briefly, before forming his own band, Titan Force. This left Briody and Tetley to pick up the pieces and re-form the band. Joining them in this new incarnation of Jag Panzer were Bob Parduba (vocals), Christian Lasage (guitar) and Rikard Stjernqvist (drums). This line-up went on to record an impressive demo that secured them a new recording contract with Auburn Records in 1987, resulting in *Chain Of Command* being released the same year.

● ALBUMS: *Jag Panzer* mini-album (Iron Works 1983)★★, *Ample Destruction* (Iron Works 1984)★★, *Chain Of Command* (Auburn 1987)★★★, *The Fourth Judgement* (Century Media 1997)★★.

Jag Wire

Formed in Los Angeles, California, USA, Jag Wire's origins lay in a band named Sin, a popular attraction on the local rock club scene. Comprising Art Deresh (vocals), Howard Drossin (guitar), Vince Gilbert (keyboards), Joey Cristofanilli (bass) and Carl Elizondo (drums), their initial appearances brought comparisons with groups such as Mötley Crüe and Legs Diamond, leading to a recording contract with local independent Target Records. Their long-playing debut, *Made In Heaven*, followed in 1985. This featured songs rooted in the west-coast glam rock tradition, though the tidy harmonies and anthemic choruses were more forthright than many of their peers. However, it failed to bring the group to the attention of a major label and Jag Wire broke up within a year of its release.

● ALBUMS: *Made In Heaven* (Target 1985)★★★.

Jagged Edge

This UK-based quartet was formed in 1987 by guitarist Myke Gray. A series of personnel changes followed before Andy Robbins (bass), Fabio Del Rio (b. Italy; drums) and Matti Alfonzetti (b. Sweden; vocals, ex-Bam Bam Boys) became the full-time members. Having been picked up by Polydor Records before a singer was even recruited, their debut five-track mini-album was rushed out in 1990. Although it featured some fine guitarwork, complemented by Gray and Alfonzetti's vocals, the songs were weak. *Fuel For Your Soul*, released later the same year, was much better. Intricate solos, power-ballads and hard-driving rock 'n' roll were enhanced by Jeff Glixman's production. However, Jagged Edge split a year later. Gray and Del Rio joined Bruce Dickinson (Jagged Edge had previously been signed to Iron Maiden's management company, Sanctuary). Alfonzetti later led his own band, Skintrade, based in Sweden.

● ALBUMS: *Trouble* mini-album (Polydor 1990)★★, *Fuel For Your Soul* (Polydor 1990)★★★★.

Jaguar

This band was formed in Bristol, England, in 1979, with an original line-up comprising Rob Reiss (vocals), Garry Pepperd (guitar), Jeff Cox (bass) and Chris Lovell (drums). Early demos led to the band having a track included on the *Heavy Metal Heroes* compilation album. The unit subsequently attracted the attention of Neat Records, who released two Jaguar singles, 'Back Street Woman' and 'Axe Crazy', in 1981 and 1982, respectively. The band quickly gained popularity with their New Wave Of British Heavy Metal-rooted speed metal. 'Axe Crazy' was the first single release to feature new vocalist Paul Merrell, who replaced Reiss. Merrell's powerful melodic voice was in fine form for the band's debut album, *Powergames*, again released on Neat in 1983. This was well received, with excellent vocal and guitar work complementing the high-speed power-metal rhythms. The band quickly gained a strong following in Europe, especially in the Netherlands, where they toured extensively. However, this all changed with a drastic shift in musical style on their next album. After switching labels to Roadrunner Records, *This Time* was released in 1984. This saw the band slow down considerably, proffering instead melodic rock, accompanied by the guest keyboards of Larry Dawson. It was an ill-conceived gambit that lost the band many fans. Shortly after its release, drummer Lovell was replaced by Gary Davies. Owing to the adverse press reaction the album received, the band folded in 1985.

● ALBUMS: *Powergames* (Neat 1983)★★★★, *This Time* (Roadrunner 1984)★★.

James Gang

Formed in 1967 in Cleveland, Ohio, USA, the embryonic James Gang was comprised of Glenn Schwartz (guitar, vocals), Tom Kriss (bass, vocals) and Jim Fox (drums, vocals). Schwartz left in April 1969 to join Pacific Gas And Electric, but Joe Walsh proved a more than competent replacement. *Yer Album* blended group originals with excellent interpretations of material drawn from Buffalo Springfield ('Bluebird') and the Yardbirds ('Lost Women'). The group enjoyed the approbation of Pete Townshend, who admired their mature cross-section of British and 'west coast' rock. Kriss was replaced by Dale Peters for *The James Gang Rides Again*, an excellent, imaginative amalgamation of rock, melody and instrumental dexterity. Here Walsh emerged as the group's director, particularly on the second side which also marked his maturation as a songwriter. Keyboards were added to create a dense, yet more fluid sound as the group embraced themes drawn from country and classical music. *Thirds* was another highlight, including the excellent 'Walk Away', but when a retreat to hard rock proved unconvincing, Walsh quit to pursue solo ambitions. He later found fame as a member of the Eagles. Two Canadians - Roy Kenner (vocals) and Dom Troiano (guitar) - joined Fox and Peters for *Straight Shooter* and *Passin' Thru*, but both sets were viewed as disappointing.

Troiano was then replaced by Tommy Bolin (b. 18 April 1951, Sioux City, Iowa, USA, d. 4 December 1976, Miami, Florida, USA), formerly of Zephyr, whose exemplary technique provided new bite and purpose. *Bang*, which featured eight of the newcomer's songs, was a marked improvement, but still lacked the verve and conviction of the Walsh era. *Miami*, released in July 1974, was the final album before Bolin's departure to Deep Purple, following which the James Gang was dissolved. Fox and Peters resurrected the name the following year, adding Bubba Keith (vocals) and Richard Shack (guitar), but finally dropped the name following the undistinguished *Jesse Come Home*.

● ALBUMS: *Yer Album* (BluesWay 1969)★★★, *The James Gang Rides Again* (ABC 1970)★★★★, *Thirds* (ABC 1971)★★★, *James Gang Live In Concert* (ABC 1971)★★★, *Straight Shooter* (ABC 1972)★★, *Passin' Thru'* (ABC 1972)★★, *Bang* (Atco 1974)★★, *Miami* (Atco 1974)★★, *Newborn* (Atco 1975)★★, *Jesse Come Home* (Atco 1976)★★.

● COMPILATIONS: *The Best Of The James Gang Featuring Joe Walsh* (ABC 1973)★★★, *16 Greatest Hits* (ABC 1973)★★★, *The True Story Of The James Gang* (See For Miles 1987)★★★.

JANE'S ADDICTION

This innovative, art-rock quartet was formed in Los Angeles, USA, in 1986, by vocalist Perry Farrell (b. 29 March 1959, Queens, New York, USA). He had formerly starred in the Cure-influenced Psi Com, from whose ranks would also emerge Dino Paredes, while it is rumoured that two other former members joined the Hare Krishna sect. With the addition of guitarist Dave Navarro, bassist Eric A. and drummer Stephen Perkins, Jane's Addiction incorporated elements of punk, rock, folk and funk into a unique and unpredictable soundscape. They debuted with a live album on the independent Triple X label, recorded at Hollywood's Roxy venue, which received widespread critical acclaim, despite a throwaway cover version of Lou Reed's 'Rock 'n Roll' and Farrell's limited stage banter, largely consisting of profanities. Drawing inspiration from the Doors, PiL, Velvet Underground and Faith No More, they set about delivering a hypnotic and thought-provoking blend of intoxicating rhythms, jagged and off-beat guitar lines and high-pitched vocals of mesmeric intensity. *Ritual De Lo Habitual* was a work of depth and complexity that required repeated listening to reveal its hidden melodies, subtle nuances and enigmatic qualities. It included the video-friendly shoplifting narrative, 'Been Caught Stealing'. In the USA, because of censorship of the album's provocative front cover (as with earlier work, featuring a Farrell sculpture), it was released in a plain envelope with the text of the First Amendment written on it. Farrell, meanwhile, helmed the Lollapalooza concert series. Despite widespread media coverage, Jane's Addiction never achieved the commercial breakthrough that their talents deserved, and Farrell dissolved the band in 1992. On his decision to defect to Porno For Pyros, taking drummer Perkins and bass player Martyn Le Noble with him, Farrell concluded: 'What it really boiled down to was, I wasn't getting along with them. I'm not saying whose fault it was. Even though I *know* whose fault it was'. The subject of these slurs, Navarro, went on to join the Red Hot Chili Peppers in 1994. In the summer of 1997 the original band reunited to record together. Two new tracks appeared on a compilation of live material, demos and out-takes.

● ALBUMS: *Jane's Addiction* (Triple X 1987)★★★, *Nothing's Shocking* (Warners 1988)★★★★, *Ritual De Lo Habitual* (Warners 1991)★★★.

● COMPILATIONS: *Kettle Whistle* (Warners 1997)★★★.

JANUS STARK

This late 90s hard rock group are an amalgamation of veterans from the early 80s punk scene. Bass player Shop, drummer Pinch and singer/guitarist Gizz Butt were previously united in one of the many line-ups of the English Dogs. After learning to play guitar at the age of 11, Butt had secured a place in the line-up of Peterborough's Destructors. After his spell with the English Dogs (notably on the album *All The World's A Rage*) he became the Prodigy's live guitarist. At this stage Butt and his two colleagues decided to jump ship from the English Dogs. In order to escape preconceptions, the trio decided to choose a less obvious moniker. 'Janus Stark is the name of a 70s comic character', noted Butt. 'He was quite mystical, with a bit of *James Bond* thrown in.' As well as the change in name, the new group allowed Butt to explore new musical possibilities, leaving behind the English Dogs' more ponderous hardcore racket for a poppier, if still highly energized style.

● ALBUMS: *Great Adventure Cigar* (Earache 1998)★★★.

JEFFERSON AIRPLANE

Along with the Grateful Dead, Jefferson Airplane are regarded as the most successful San Francisco band of the late 60s. The group were formed in

August 1965 by Marty Balin (b. Martyn Jerel Buchwald, 30 January 1942, Cincinnati, Ohio, USA; vocals, guitar). The other members in the original line-up were Paul Kantner (b. 17 March 1941, San Francisco, California, USA; guitar, vocals) and Jorma Kaukonen (b. 23 December 1940, Washington, DC, USA; guitar, vocals). Bob Harvey and Jerry Peloquin gave way to Alexander Skip Spence (b. 18 April 1946, Windsor, Ontario, Canada) and Signe Anderson (b. Signe Toly Anderson, 15 September 1941, Seattle, Washington, USA). Their replacements, Spencer Dryden (b. 7 April 1938, New York, USA; drums) and Jack Casady (b. 13 April 1944, Washington, DC, USA), made up a seminal band that blended folk and rock into what became known as west coast rock. Kantner, already a familiar face on the local folk circuit and Balin, formerly of the Town Criers and co-owner of the Matrix club; soon became highly popular locally, playing gigs and benefits organized by promoter Bill Graham. Eventually they became regulars at the Fillmore Auditorium and the Carousel Ballroom, both a short distance from their communal home in the Haight Ashbury district. Anderson departed shortly after the release of their moderately successful debut *Jefferson Airplane Takes Off* and was replaced in October 1966 by Grace Slick (b. Grace Barnett Wing, 30 October 1939, Evanston, Illinois, USA; vocals). Slick was already well known with her former band, the Great Society, and donated two of their songs, 'White Rabbit' and 'Somebody To Love', to the Airplane. Both titles were on their second influential collection, *Surrealistic Pillow*, and both became US Top 10 hits. They have now achieved classic status as definitive songs from that era. The lyrics of 'White Rabbit' combined the harmless tale of *Alice In Wonderland* with an LSD trip. Their reputation was enhanced by a strong performance at the legendary Monterey Pop Festival in 1967. This national success continued with the erratic *After Bathing At Baxters* and the brilliant *Crown Of Creation*. The latter showed the various writers in the band maturing and developing their own styles. Balin's 'If You Feel', Kaukonen's 'Ice Cream Phoenix' and Slick's tragi-comic 'Lather' gave the record great variety. This album also contained 'Triad', a song their friend David Crosby had been unable to include on a Byrds album. They maintained a busy schedule and released a well-recorded live album, *Bless Its Pointed Little Head*, in 1969. The same year, they appeared at another milestone in musical history: the Woodstock Festival. Later that year they were present at the infamous Altamont Festival, where a group of Hells Angels killed a young spectator and attacked Balin. Slick and Kantner had now become lovers and their hippie ideals and political views were a major influence on *Volunteers*. While it was an excellent album, it marked the decline of Balin's role in the band. Additionally, Dryden departed and the offshoot Hot Tuna began to take up more of Casady and Kaukonen's time. Wizened fiddler Papa John Creach (b. 28 May 1917, Beaver Falls, Pennsylvania, USA, d. 22 February 1994; violin) joined the band full-time in 1970, although he still continued to play with Hot Tuna. Kantner released a concept album, *Blows Against The Empire*, bearing the name Paul Kantner And The Jefferson Starship. The 'Starship' consisted of various Airplane members, plus Jerry Garcia, David Crosby, Graham Nash, *et al*. This majestic album was nominated for the science fiction Hugo Award. Slick, meanwhile, gave birth to a daughter, China, who later in the year graced the cover of Slick And Kantner's *Sunfighter*. Following a greatest hits selection, *Worst Of*, and the departure of Balin, the band released the cleverly packaged *Bark*. Complete with brown paper bag, the album offered some odd moments, notably Slick's 'Never Argue With A German', sung in spoof German, and new drummer Joey Covington's 50s-sounding *a cappella* 'Thunk'. It also marked the first release on their own Grunt label. The disappointing *Long John Silver* was followed by a gutsy live outing, *30 Seconds Over Winterland*. This was the last album to bear their name, although an interesting compilation consisting of single releases and studio out-takes later appeared as *Early Flight*. Hot Tuna became Casady and Kaukonen's main interest and Slick and Kantner released further 'solo' albums. The name change evolved without any fuss, and one of the most inventive bands in history prepared for a relaunch as the Jefferson Starship. Kantner, Balin and Casady regrouped briefly as the KBC Band in 1986. The Airplane title was resurrected in 1989 when Slick, Kaukonen, Casady, Balin and Kantner re-formed and released *Jefferson Airplane* to an indifferent audience. By the early 90s Hot Tuna had re-formed, Kantner was rebuilding his Jefferson Starship and Slick had apparently retired from the music business.

● ALBUMS: *Jefferson Airplane Takes Off* (RCA 1966)★★, *Surrealistic Pillow* (RCA 1967)★★★★, *After Bathing At Baxter's* (RCA 1967)★★★, *Crown Of Creation* (RCA 1968)★★★★, *Bless Its Pointed Little Head* (RCA 1969)★★★, *Volunteers* (RCA 1969)★★★★, *Bark* (Grunt 1971)★★★, *Long John*

Silver (Grunt 1972)★★★, *30 Seconds Over Winterland* (Grunt 1973)★★★, *Jefferson Airplane* (Epic 1989)★, *Live At The Fillmore East* recorded 1968 (RCA 1998)★★★.
● COMPILATIONS: *Worst Of Jefferson Airplane* (RCA 1970)★★★, *Early Flight* (Grunt 1974)★★★, featuring Jefferson Airplane and Jefferson Starship *Flight Log (1966-1976)* (Grunt 1977)★★★★, *The Best Of Jefferson Airplane* (RCA 1980)★★★, *2400 Fulton Street: An Anthology* (RCA 1987)★★★★, *Collection* (Castle 1988)★★★, *White Rabbit & Other Hits* (RCA 1990)★★, *Jefferson Airplane Loves You* 3-CD box set (RCA 1992)★★★, *Journey: The Best Of Jefferson Airplane* (Camden 1996)★★★.
● FURTHER READING: *The Jefferson Airplane And The San Francisco Sound*, Ralph J. Gleason. *Grace Slick - The Biography*, Barbara Rowe.

JEFFERSON STARSHIP

Formerly the Jefferson Airplane, the band evolved into the Jefferson Starship after Paul Kantner (b. 17 March 1941, San Francisco, California, USA; guitar, vocals) had previously released *Blows Against The Empire* in 1970, billed as Paul Kantner And The Jefferson Starship. His fascination with science fiction no doubt led the Airplane to metamorphose into a Starship. The official debut was *Dragonfly* in 1974, which became an immediate success. The band played with a freshness and urgency that had been missing on recent Airplane releases. Joining Kantner on this album were Grace Slick (b. Grace Barnett Wing, 30 October 1939, Chicago, Illinois, USA; vocals), Papa John Creach (b. 28 May 1917, Beaver Falls, Pennsylvania, USA; violin), former Quicksilver Messenger Service bassist David Freiberg (b. 24 August 1938, Boston, Massachusetts, USA; vocals, keyboards), Craig Chaquico (b. 26 September 1954; lead guitar), ex-Turtles member John Barbata (drums) and Pete Sears (bass, keyboards). Among the tracks were 'Ride The Tiger', which was accompanied by an imaginatively graphic, early video and 'Hyperdrive', a Slick magnum opus featuring Chaquico's frantic screaming guitar. Old Airplane fans were delighted to hear Marty Balin guesting on one track with his own composition 'Caroline', and further cheered when he joined the band at the beginning of 1975. *Red Octopus* later that year became their most successful album and ended up selling several million copies and spending a month at the top of the US charts. The flagship track was Balin's beautiful and seemingly innocent 'Miracles', including its oblique reference to cunnilingus with Balin singing 'I had a taste of the real world, when I went down on you' and Slick innocently responding in the background with 'Mmm, don't waste a drop of it, don't ever stop it'. Soon afterwards, Kantner and Slick separated; she moved in with Skip Johnson, the band's lighting engineer, and eventually married him. Later that year Slick was regularly in the news when her drinking problems got out of control. *Spitfire* and *Earth* continued their success, although the band had now become a hard rock outfit. Balin's lighter 'Count On Me' was a US Top 10 hit in 1978. That year, Slick was asked to leave the band, to be allowed to return when she dried out. She was eventually dismissed in 1978, closely followed by Balin, who left towards the end of a turbulent year. He was replaced by Mickey Thomas and further changes were afoot when stalwart drummer Aynsley Dunbar (b. 1946, Liverpool, England) joined in place of Barbata. *Freedom From Point Zero* and the US Top 20 hit 'Jane', at the end of 1979, bore no resemblance to the musical style towards which remaining original member Kantner had attempted to steer them. He suffered a stroke during 1980, but returned the following spring together with a sober Grace Slick. Both *Modern Times* (1981) and *Winds Of Change* (1982), continued the success, although by now the formula was wearing thin. Kantner found his role had diminished and released a solo album later that year. He continued with them throughout the following year, although he was openly very unsettled. Towards the end of 1984 Kantner performed a nostalgic set of old Airplane songs with Balin's band, amid rumours of a Jefferson Airplane reunion. The tension broke in 1985 when, following much acrimony over ownership of the band's name, Kantner was paid off and took with him half of the group's moniker. Kantner claimed the rights to the name, although he no longer wanted to use the title, as his reunion with Balin and Casady in the KBC Band demonstrated. In defiance his former band performed as Starship Jefferson, but shortly afterwards became Starship. Both Thomas and Freiberg left during these antagonistic times, leaving Slick the remaining original member after the incredible changes of the previous few years. The new line-up added Denny Baldwin on drums and recorded *Knee Deep In The Hoopla* in 1985, which became their most successful album since *Red Octopus*. Two singles from the album, 'We Built This City' (written by Bernie Taupin) and 'Sara', both reached number 1 in the USA. The following year they reached the top spot on both sides of the Atlantic with the theme from the film *Mannequin*, 'Nothing's Gonna Stop Us Now'. Their image was now of slick perpetrators of AOR, performing immaculate music for the MTV generation (on which China Kantner was a presenter). Now, having gone full circle, Grace Slick departed in 1989 to join Kaukonen, Casady, Balin and Kantner in . . . the Jefferson Airplane. After Starship broke up in the early 90s, Kantner revived the Jefferson Starship name and by the mid-90s had Balin and Casady in tow. A new live album was issued in 1995, featuring a guest appearance from Slick. *Windows Of Heaven* featured new vocalist Diana Mangano.

● ALBUMS: *Dragonfly* (Grunt 1974)★★★, *Red Octopus* (Grunt 1975)★★★★, *Spitfire* (Grunt 1976)★★★, *Earth* (Grunt 1978)★★, *Freedom At Point Zero* (Grunt 1979)★★, *Modern Times* (RCA 1981)★★, *Winds Of Change* (Grunt 1982)★★, *Nuclear Furniture* (Grunt 1984)★★, as Starship *Knee Deep In The Hoopla* (RCA 1985)★★, as Starship *No Protection* (RCA 1987)★★, as Starship *Love Among The Cannibals* (RCA 1989)★, *Deep Space/Virgin Sky* (Intersound 1995)★, *Live: Miracles* (EMI 1997)★, *Windows Of Heaven* (SPV 1998)★.

● COMPILATIONS: featuring Jefferson Airplane and Jefferson Starship *Flight Log (1966-1976)* (Grunt 1977)★★★★, *Gold* (Grunt 1979)★★★★, *Jefferson Starship: At Their Best* (RCA 1993)★★★, *Collection* (Griffin 1995)★★.

Jepson, Tony, And The Whole Truth

While his former colleagues in Little Angels made quick headway in 1994 as b.l.o.w., UK vocalist Jepson was more stealthily piecing together the rudiments for his own solo career. At the outset he said: 'I do not want to be a pop star again.' Signing to Cottage Industry Records, Jepson recruited former Elvis Costello drummer Pete Thomas, bass player Roger Davis and guitarist Russ Goodwin. The line-up embarked on touring in October 1995 under the name Tony Jepson And The Whole Truth, following the August release of *Ignorance Is Bliss*. Jepson commented: 'I looked long and hard to find the right sort of musicians to work with. The last thing I wanted to do was work with famous people.' The 10-song collection was co-written with guitarist Goodwin, with Jepson taking charge of production in his own barn studio, constructed opposite his home.

● ALBUMS: *Ignorance Is Bliss* (Cottage Industry 1995)★★★.

Jerusalem Slim

When Michael Monroe began working on the follow-up to his *Not Fakin' It* solo album, song-writing work with ex-Billy Idol guitarist Steve Stevens metamorphosed into a full band with the recruitment of drummer Greg Ellis and Monroe's former Hanoi Rocks colleague, bassist Sam Yaffa. However, the guitarist's bombastic style never really gelled with Monroe's more straightforward rock 'n' roll approach, and the band dissolved when Stevens joined ex-Mötley Crüe vocalist Vince Neil's band; this did little to promote an amicable split, as Neil had been driving in the accident in which Monroe and Yaffa's late bandmate Razzle had died. Monroe and Yaffa formed the more satisfying Demolition 23, and publicly disowned the posthumous release of *Jerusalem Slim*, which received universally poor reviews.

● ALBUMS: *Jerusalem Slim* (Mercury 1993)★★★.

Jetboy

This UK glam/sleaze rock quintet featured ex-Hanoi Rocks bassist Sam Yaffa, with Mickey Finn (vocals), Fernie Rod (guitar), Billy Rowe (guitar) and Ron Tostenson (drums) completing the line-up. Applying cosmetic surgery to the riffs of AC/DC, Poison and Aerosmith, they leaned towards the bluesier end of this genre. However, Jetboy failed to add the necessary sparkle to make their material either memorable or commercially accessible. Yaffa quit in 1990 to join forces with former Hanoi Rocks vocalist Michael Monroe, and Jetboy have been inactive since.

● ALBUMS: *Feel The Shake* (MCA 1988)★★, *Damned Nation* (MCA 1990)★★.

Jesus Lizard

Formed in 1989, the Jesus Lizard originally comprised David Yow (vocals), David Sims (bass) - both formerly of the Austin, Texas act Scratch Acid - and Duane Denison (guitar), with the help of a drum machine. *Pure*, their abbreviated debut, maintained the uncompromising style of their former incarnation with its ponderous bass lines, growled vocals and crashing guitar. The set was produced by Steve Albini (ex-Big Black), with whom Sims had worked in the controversially named Rapeman. Albini engineered and co-produced *Head*, on which the Jesus Lizard were joined by drummer Mac McNeilly. The group's sound remained as powerful and compulsive as ever, although some critics detected an artistic impasse. Jesus Lizard would join Nirvana on a joint single that broke the UK charts, but *Down* saw the band maintain a ferocity that deemed them very much a secular concern. They planned to expand their fanbase by signing to Capitol Records in 1995, but *Shot* showed little sign of compromise. The band's strength is as an exciting live act, with frontman Yow as a formidable singer and showman.

● ALBUMS: *Pure* mini-album (Touch & Go 1989)★★★, *Head* (Touch & Go 1990)★★★, *Goat* (Touch & Go 1991)★★★, *Liar* (Touch & Go 1992)★★★, *Show* (Collision Arts/Giant 1994)★★★, *Down* (Touch & Go 1994)★★★, *Shot* (Capitol 1996)★★★, *Blue* (Capitol 1998)★★★.

JETHRO TULL

Jethro Tull was formed in Luton, England, in 1967 when Ian Anderson (b. 10 August 1947, Edinburgh, Scotland; vocals, flute) and Glenn Cornick (b. 24 April 1947, Barrow-in-Furness, Cumbria, England; bass), members of a visiting Blackpool blues group, John Evan's Smash, became acquainted with Mick Abrahams (b. 7 April 1943, Luton, Bedfordshire, England; guitar, vocals) and Clive Bunker (b. 12 December 1946, Blackpool, Lancashire, England; drums), Abrahams' colleague in local attraction McGregor's Engine, completed the original line-up which made its debut in March the following year with 'Sunshine Day'. This commercially minded single, erroneously credited to Jethro Toe, merely hinted at developments about to unfold. A residency at London's famed Marquee club and a sensational appearance at that summer's Sunbury Blues Festival confirmed a growing reputation, while 'Song For Jeffrey', the quartet's first release for the Island label, introduced a more representative sound. Abrahams' rolling blues licks and Anderson's distinctive, stylized voice combined expertly on *This Was* - for many Tull's finest collection. Although the material itself was derivative, the group's approach was highly exciting, with Anderson's propulsive flute playing, modelled on jazzman Raahsan Roland Kirk, particularly effective. The album reached the UK Top 10, largely on the strength of Tull's live reputation in which the singer played an ever-increasing role. His exaggerated gestures, long, wiry hair, ragged coat and distinctive, one-legged stance cultivated a compulsive stage personality to the extent that, for many spectators, Jethro Tull was the name of this extrovert frontman and the other musicians merely his underlings.

This impression gained credence through the group's internal ructions. Mick Abrahams left in November 1968 and formed Blodwyn Pig. When future Black Sabbath guitarist Tony Iommi proved incompatible, Martin Barre (b. 17 November 1946) joined Tull for *Stand Up*, their excellent chart-topping second album. The group was then augmented by John Evan (b. 28 March 1948; keyboards), the first of Anderson's Blackpool associates to be invited into the line-up. *Benefit*, the last outwardly blues-based album, duly followed and this period was also marked by the group's three UK Top 10 singles, 'Living In The Past', 'Sweet Dream' (both 1969) and 'The Witch's Promise' (1970). Cornick then quit to form Wild Turkey and Jeffrey Hammond-Hammond (b. 30 July 1946), already a legend in Tull's lexicon through their debut single, 'Jeffrey Goes To Leicester Square' and 'For Michael Collins, Jeffrey And Me', was brought in for *Aqualung*. Possibly the group's best-known work, this ambitious concept album featured Anderson's musings on organized religion and contained several tracks that remained long-standing favourites, including 'My God' and 'Locomotive Breath'.

Clive Bunker, the last original member, bar Anderson, left in May 1971. A further John Evan-era acolyte, Barriemore Barlow (b. 10 September 1949), replaced him as Jethro Tull entered its most controversial period. Although *Thick As A Brick* topped the US chart and reached number 5 in the UK, critics began questioning Anderson's reliance on obtuse concepts. However, if muted for this release, the press reviled *A Passion Play*, damning it as pretentious, impenetrable and the product of an egotist and his neophytes. Such rancour obviously hurt. Anderson retorted by announcing an indefinite retirement, but continued success in America, where the album became Tull's second chart-topper, doubtless appeased his anger. *War Child*, a US number 2, failed to chart in the UK, although *Minstrel In The Gallery* proved more popular. *Too Old To Rock 'N' Roll, Too Young To Die* marked the departure of Hammond-Hammond in favour of John Glascock (b. 1953, London, England, d. 17 November 1979), formerly of the Gods, Toe Fat and Chicken Shack. Subsequent releases, *Songs From The Wood* and *Heavy Horses*, reflected a more pastoral sound as Anderson abandoned the gauche approach marking many of their predecessors. David Palmer, who orchestrated each Tull album, bar their debut, was added as a second keyboards player as the group embarked on another highly successful phase, culminating in November 1978 when a concert at New York's Madison Square Garden was simultaneously broadcast around the world by satellite. However,

Glascock's premature death in 1979 during heart surgery ushered in a period of uncertainty, culminating in an internal realignment. In 1980 Anderson began a projected solo album, retaining Barre and new bassist Dave Pegg (ex-Fairport Convention), but adding Eddie Jobson (ex-Curved Air and Roxy Music; keyboards) and Marc Craney (drums). Long-time cohorts Barlow, Evan and Palmer were left to pursue their individual paths. The finished product, *A*, was ultimately issued under the Jethro Tull banner and introduced a productive period that saw two more group selections, plus Anderson's solo effort, *Walk Into Light*, issued within a two-year period. Since then Jethro Tull have continued to record and perform live, albeit on a lesser scale, using a nucleus of Anderson, Barre and Pegg. *Catfish Rising* in 1991, although a disappointing album, was a return to their blues roots. *Roots To Branches* was a return to the standard Tull progressive rock album, full of complicated time changes, and fiddly new age and Arabian intros and codas. Squire Anderson has also become a renowned entrepreneur, owning tracts of land on the west coast of Scotland and the highly successful Strathaird Salmon processing plant.

● ALBUMS: *This Was* (Chrysalis 1968)★★★★, *Stand Up* (Chrysalis 1969)★★★★, *Benefit* (Chrysalis 1970)★★★, *Aqualung* (Chrysalis 1971)★★★★, *Thick As A Brick* (Chrysalis 1972)★★★, *A Passion Play* (Chrysalis 1973)★★, *War Child* (Chrysalis 1974)★★, *Minstrel In The Gallery* (Chrysalis 1975)★★★, *Too Old To Rock 'N' Roll Too Young To Die* (Chrysalis 1976)★★★, *Songs From The Wood* (Chrysalis 1977)★★★★, *Heavy Horses* (Chrysalis 1978)★★★, *Live - Bursting Out* (Chrysalis 1978)★★, *Storm Watch* (Chrysalis 1979)★★, *A* (Chrysalis 1980)★★, *The Broadsword And The Beast* (Chrysalis 1982)★★, *Under Wraps* (Chrysalis 1984)★★, *Crest Of A Knave* (Chrysalis 1987)★★★, *Rock Island* (Chrysalis 1989)★★, as the John Evan Band *Live '66* (A New Day 1990)★★, *Live At Hammersmith* (Raw Fruit 1990)★★, *Catfish Rising* (Chrysalis 1991)★★, *A Little Light Music* (Chrysalis 1992)★★, *Nightcap* (Chrysalis 1993)★★, *In Concert* (Windsong 1995)★★★, *Roots To Branches* (Chrysalis 1995)★★. Solo: Ian Anderson *Walk Into Light* (Chrysalis 1983)★★, *Divinities: Twelve Dances With God* (EMI 1995)★★.

● COMPILATIONS: *Living In The Past* (Chrysalis 1972)★★★★, *M.U.: Best Of Jethro Tull* (Chrysalis 1976)★★★, *Repeat, The Best Of Jethro Tull - Volume II* (Chrysalis 1977)★★★, *Original Masters* (Chrysalis 1985)★★★, *20 Years Of Jethro Tull* 3-CD box set (Chrysalis 1988)★★★★, *25th Anniversary Box Set* 4-CD box set (Chrysalis 1992)★★★★, *The Anniversary Collection* (Chrysalis 1993)★★★.

● VIDEOS: *Slipstream* (Chrysalis 1981), *20 Years Of Jethro Tull* (Virgin Video 1988), *25th Anniversary Video* (PMI 1993).

JETT, JOAN, AND THE BLACKHEARTS

b. Joan Larkin, 22 September 1960, Philadelphia, Pennsylvania, USA. Jett was one of the most successful US female singers to emerge from the rock scene of the 70s. She spent most of her childhood in the Baltimore, Maryland area, where she learned guitar as a child, playing along to favourite rock 'n' roll records. In 1972 her family relocated to Los Angeles, where she became enamoured with artists including David Bowie, Suzi Quatro, T. Rex and Gary Glitter. At the age of 15 she began infiltrating the Los Angeles rock scene and formed her first band. Producer Kim Fowley took the group under his wing and named it the Runaways, procuring a record contract with Mercury Records. The group recorded three punk-tinged hard rock albums that were unsuccessful in the USA but hits in Japan, where they recorded a live album. Also successful in England, they recorded their swansong, *And Now ... The Runaways*, in that country in 1979. After the dissolution of the group, Jett moved to New York and teamed up with producer Kenny Laguna, who became her manager. Laguna had previously been involved with a number of 60s bubblegum hits. Laguna produced Jett's first solo album, which was released on the European Ariola label. When no US label picked it up, they issued it themselves and the album sold well, becoming one of the best-selling US independent records of that time. This led to a contract with Neil Bogart's Boardwalk Records, who reissued it as *Bad Reputation*, and saw it reach number 51 in the US charts. With her group the Blackhearts (guitarist Ricky Byrd, bassist Gary Ryan and drummer Lee Crystal), Jett recorded *I Love Rock 'N' Roll* in late 1981, produced by Laguna and Ritchie Cordell. The title track, originally an obscure b-side for UK group the Arrows, became a major hit, largely owing to a big push from MTV, and spent seven weeks at number 1 in the USA in early 1982. The follow-up single, a cover version of Tommy James And The Shondells' 'Crimson And Clover', was itself a Top 10 hit, reaching number 7 in 1982. Also on the album was an update of a Jett song from the Runaways era, 'You're Too Possessive'. With Bogart's death, the group signed to MCA, which then distributed Blackheart Records. However, subsequent outings on that label were not nearly as successful as the Boardwalk releases. *Glorious Results Of A Misspent Youth* again retreated to Jett's past with the Runaways, this time on a revision of 'Cherry Bomb'. *Good Music* saw some intriguing collaborations, with members of the Beach Boys and Darlene Love guesting, and an unlikely rap duet with Scorpio of Grandmaster Flash And The Furious Five. The album also saw the departure of Lee Crystal and Gary Ryan, the former permanently replaced by Thommy Price. Jett, meanwhile, found time to make a second film appearance (following *We're All Crazy Now!*), playing Michael J. Fox's sister in *Light Of Day*; she also sang the Bruce Springsteen-penned theme. *Up Your Alley* brought another hit with 'I Hate Myself For Loving You', before 1990's *The Hit List*, an album of cover versions, which included a duet with Ray Davies on 'Celluloid Heroes'. *Notorious* saw her collaborate with Paul Westerberg of the Replacements on the co-written 'Backlash', but by the advent of *Pure And Simple*, Byrd was no longer a permanent member of the band. This set saw a guest appearance from L7 on a track entitled 'Activity Grrrl', emphasizing Jett's influence on a new generation of female rockers (by this time, Jett had also produced Bikini Kill, in addition to late 70s LA punk band the Germs).

● ALBUMS: *Joan Jett* (Blackheart 1980)★★★, *Bad Reputation* reissue of debut (Boardwalk 1981)★★★, *I Love Rock 'n' Roll* (Boardwalk 1981)★★★★, *Album* (MCA/Blackheart 1983)★★★, *Glorious Results Of A Misspent Youth* (MCA/Blackheart 1984)★★★, *Good Music* (Columbia/Blackheart 1986)★★★, *Up Your Alley* (Columbia/Blackheart 1988)★★★, *The Hit List* (Columbia/Blackheart 1990)★★★, *Notorious* (Epic/Blackheart 1991)★★★, *Pure And Simple* (Blackheart/Warners 1994)★★★.

● COMPILATIONS: *Flashback* (Blackheart 1993)★★★★, *Fit To Be Tied* (Mercury 1997)★★★.

JO JO GUNNE

Formed by Jay Ferguson (b. John Ferguson, 10 May 1947, Burbank, California, USA; vocals, piano) and Mark Andes (b. 19 February 1948, Philadelphia, Pennsylvania, USA; bass, vocals), following their departure from Spirit in 1971. This hard rock quartet was completed by Matthew Andes (guitar, vocals) and Curly Smith (drums). Their contagious debut single 'Run Run Run' was an instant success, reaching number 6 in the UK. Shortly afterwards, Andes was replaced by Jimmy Randall. Unfortunately, they were unable to progress musically, and their four albums all follow a very similar pattern of average hard rock. *Bite Down Hard* is the most powerful album, particularly in 'Rock Around the Symbol' and 'Ready Freddy'. *Jumpin' The Gunne* featured a tacky album cover - with a photo montage depicting the band in bed together watching obese naked females flying through their window. The band broke up in 1974.

● ALBUMS: *Jo Jo Gunne* (Asylum 1972)★★★, *Bite Down Hard* (Asylum 1973)★★★★, *Jumpin' The Gunne* (Asylum 1973)★★, *So ... Where's The Show?* (Asylum 1974)★★.

JOHANSEN, DAVID

b. 9 January 1950, Staten Island, New York, USA. Johansen gained recognition in the early 70s as lead singer of the New York Dolls. A R&B/rock group taking inspiration from the likes of the Rolling Stones, the Dolls' street attitude and outrageous sense of dress thrust them into the glitter/glam scene, although their music had little in common with others of that nature. Prior to joining the Dolls, Johansen joined his first band, the Vagabond Missionaries, in high school. At the age of 17 he moved to Manhattan, New York, and briefly worked with a band called Fast Eddie And The Electric Japs. The Dolls came together in late 1971 and quickly built a devoted audience at New York clubs such as the Mercer Arts Center and Max's Kansas City. They recorded two albums for Mercury Records and held on until late 1976. After their demise they became an inspiration to numerous artists, from the newly forming punk bands such as the Sex Pistols, to Kiss, to the Smiths. Johansen launched a solo career in 1978, recording for Blue Sky Records. Less flamboyant than the Dolls' records, this was a solid rock effort that stressed Johansen's lyrical acumen. He released three other rock/R&B-orientated solo albums for Blue Sky and one for Passport Records before shifting career directions once again. In 1983 Johansen began booking small cabaret concert dates under the name Buster Poindexter, performing a slick, tightly arranged set of vintage R&B numbers, show tunes, and jump blues. Dressing in a formal tuxedo and playing the lounge lizard, Poindexter built a following of his own; he completely gave up his rock act to pursue the new image full-time. He recorded albums as Buster Poindexter, including *Buster Poindexter* (1987) and *Buster Goes Berserk* (1989), the first yielding a chart and club hit in a cover version of Arrow's 1984 soca dance tune, 'Hot, Hot, Hot'. He was still popular as Poindexter in the early 90s, touring with a 10-piece band and packing clubs. He also launched an acting career in the late 80s, appearing in films including *Scrooged* and *Married To The Mob*.

● ALBUMS: *David Johansen* (Blue Sky 1978)★★★, *In Style* (Blue Sky 1979)★★★, *Here Comes The Night* (Blue Sky 1981)★★, *Live It Up* (Blue Sky 1982)★★★, *Sweet Revenge* (Passport 1984)★★★.

● COMPILATIONS: *Crucial Music: The David Johansen Collection* (Columbia/Relativity 1990)★★★.

JOHNNY CRASH

Following the break-up of Tokyo Blade, vocalist Vicki James Wright became disillusioned with the British rock scene and moved to Los Angeles in search of compatible musicians. After a series of false starts, he finally stabilized a line-up of August Worchell and Christopher Stewart (guitars), Andy Rogers (bass) and Stephen Adamo (drums), under the name Johnny Crash. Blatantly parading traditional metal influences such as Mötley Crüe, AC/DC and Kiss, they delivered a high-energy blast of streetwise, blues-based rock 'n' roll on their Tony Platt-produced debut.

● ALBUMS: *Neighbourhood Threat* (WTG 1990)★★.

JONES, STEVE

b. 3 September 1955, London, England. Formerly the guitarist in the Sex Pistols, Jones's basic but powerful style was then employed as part of the underachieving Professionals (with ex-Sex Pistol member Paul Cook). Prior to that he had worked with the Avengers in the USA. He later played a substantial role in the creation of two records: Iggy Pop's *Blah Blah Blah* (1986) and ex-Duran Duran member Andy Taylor's *Thunder* (1987). His first solo venture, however, was a lacklustre affair, with Jones's rough Cockney voice spread thinly over a set that mingled rock numbers with, to the horror of old punks, ballads. The worst offender in this category was the comical version of 'Love Letters'. A capable, fluent man with a rhythm guitar, given a microphone Jones came across as forced and inarticulate, a situation not helped by the clumsy moralism of tracks such as 'Drugs Suck'. Undeterred, Jones proceeded to make the same mistakes a second time with *Fire And Gasoline*. Co-produced and co-written with Ian Astbury of the Cult, and with a vocal contribution from Guns N'Roses' Axl Rose on the Pistols revival track 'Did You No Wrong', it offered further evidence of Jones's decline. Billy Duffy of the Cult even managed to outgun the old stager with his solo on 'Get Ready'. Collectively, the albums offer a sad footnote to the career of one of rock and pop's most influential guitarists. Jones has since worked as part of The Neurotic Outsiders, alongside John Taylor (ex-Duran Duran) and Duff McLagan and Matt Sorum of Guns N'Roses, with the group releasing a self-titled album for Madonna's Maverick label in 1996. The collaboration led to Jones replacing the departed Slash as Guns N'Roses guitarist.

● ALBUMS: *Mercy* (Gold Mountain/MCA 1987)★★, *Fire And Gasoline* (Gold Mountain/MCA 1989)★★.

JOSHUA

This American band was formed by Joshua Pehahia (guitar, vocals) in 1981 after he had left Blind Alley. In the early days the line-up fluctuated wildly, with the exception of singer Stephen Fontaine, who possessed a vocal range of four octaves. Perahia and Fontaine, with two acquaintances, recorded the mini-album*The Hand Is Quicker Than The Eye*, in 1982. The title was suggested by one of the studio engineers, who noticed Perahia's dexterity on the fretboard. After the album's release, Joshua attempted to tour, but frequent personnel changes made this impracticable, and no more than four dates were completed with the same line-up. In 1984 Joshua were signed to Polydor in America with Perahia (guitar, vocals), Ken Tamplin (guitar, vocals), Patrick Bradley (keyboards, vocals), Loren Robinson (bass, vocals), Jo Galletta (drums) and Jeff Fenholt (lead vocals). Perahia produced the album and wrote all the song arrangements. *Surrender* was released in 1985 and offered classy American hard rock, but the European arm of Polydor was not interested, and its European release was handled by FM Revolver. Fenholt was left after the album's completion, while Gregory Valesco joined them as vocalist for touring. Tamplin went on to form his own unit, Shout. Joshua then signed to RCA with completely different personnel: Perahia (guitar, vocals), Bob Rock (lead vocals), Greg Schultz (keyboards, vocals), Emil Lech (bass) and Tim Gehrt (drums). This membership recorded *Intense Defence*, which was slightly more restrained. Bob Rock's input helped to raise the standard of the songwriting and their future looked bright. However, Rock, Schultz and Lech left the band after the recording was finished, and formed their own outfit, Driver.

● ALBUMS: *The Hand Is Quicker Than The Eye* (Olympic 1982)★★★, *Surrender* (Polydor 1985)★★★★, *Intense Defense* (RCA 1988)★★★.

JOURNEY

This US rock group was formed in 1973 by ex-Santana members Neal Schon (b. 27 February 1954, San Mateo, California, USA; guitar) and Gregg Rolie (b. 1948; keyboards), with the assistance of Ross Valory (b. 2 February 1949, San Francisco, USA; bass, ex-Steve Miller band) and Prairie Prince (b. 7 May 1950, Charlotte, North Carolina, USA; drums, ex-Tubes). George Tickner was later added as rhythm guitarist and lead vocalist. On New Year's Eve the same year, they made their live debut in front of 10,000 people at San Fransisco's Winterland. The following day they played to 100,000 at an open-air festival in Hawaii. In February 1974 Prince returned to the Tubes and was replaced by Aynsley Dunbar (b. 10 January 1946, Liverpool, Lancashire, England; ex-Jeff Beck; John Mayall; Frank Zappa, etc.). They initially specialized in jazz-rock, complete with extended and improvised solo spots, a style much in evidence on their first three albums. In 1975 Tickner left (for medical school) and was eventually replaced by ex-Alien Project vocalist Steve Perry (b. 22 January 1953, Hanford, California, USA), following a brief tenure by Robert Fleischmann. The switch to highly sophisticated pomp rock occurred with the recording of *Infinity*, when Roy Thomas Baker was brought in as producer to give the band's sound a punchy and dynamic edge. The album was a huge success, reaching number 21 on the *Billboard* charts and gaining a platinum award. Dunbar was unhappy with this new style and left for Jefferson Starship, to be replaced by Steve Smith (b. 21 August 1954, Los Angeles, California, USA). *Evolution* followed and brought the band their first Top 20 hit, 'Lovin', Touchin', Squeezin''. *Captured* was a live double album that surprised many critics, being far removed from their technically excellent and clinically produced studio releases; instead, it featured cranked-up guitars and raucous hard rock, eventually peaking at number 9 in the US album chart. Founder-member Rolie departed after its release, to be replaced by Jonathan Cain (b. 26 February 1950, Chicago, Illinois, USA), who had previously played with the Babys. Cain's arrival was an important landmark in Journey's career, as his songwriting input added a new dimension to the band's sound. *Escape* represented the pinnacle of the band's success, reaching number 1 and staying in the chart for over a year. It also spawned three US Top 10 hit singles in the form of 'Who's Crying Now', 'Don't Stop Believin'' and 'Open Arms'. The follow-up, *Frontiers*, was also successful, staying at number 2 on the *Billboard* album chart for nine weeks; 'Separate Ways', culled as a single from it, climbed to number 8 in the singles chart. After a series of internal disputes, the band was reduced to a three-man nucleus of Schon, Cain and Perry to record *Raised On Radio* (though they were joined on live dates by Randy Jackson and Mike Baird on drums and bass). This was Journey's last album before Schon and Cain joined forces with John Waite's Bad English in 1988. Smith fronted a fusion band, Vital Information, before teaming up with ex-Journey members Rolie and Valory to form Storm in 1991. Perry concentrated on his long-awaited second solo album. A *Greatest Hits* compilation was posthumously released to mark the band's passing, since which time only a November 1991 reunion to commemorate the death of promoter Bill Graham has seen the core members regroup. This continued with new albums in 1996 and 1997 that saw the band religiously refusing to adapt or change from a style of music that now sounds dated.

● ALBUMS: *Journey* (Columbia 1975)★★★, *Look Into The Future* (Columbia 1976)★★★, *Next* (Columbia 1977)★★★, *Infinity* (Columbia 1978)★★★★, *Evolution* (Columbia 1979)★★★, *Departure* (Columbia 1980)★★★, *Dream After Dream* (Columbia 1980)★★, *Captured* (Columbia 1981)★★★, *Escape* (Columbia 1981)★★★★, *Frontiers* (Columbia 1983)★★★, *Raised On Radio* (Columbia 1986)★★★, *Trial By Fire* (Columbia 1996)★★, *Into The Fire* (Columbia 1997)★★, *Greatest Hits Live* (Columbia 1998)★★.

● COMPILATIONS: *In The Beginning* (Columbia 1979)★★, *Greatest Hits/Best Of Journey* (Columbia 1988)★★★★, *Time* 3-CD box set (Columbia 1992)★★★★.

JUDAS PRIEST

This group was formed in Birmingham, England, in 1969, by guitarist K.K. Downing (b. Kenneth Downing) and close friend, bassist Ian Hill. As another hopeful, struggling young rock band, they played their first gig in Essington in 1971 with a line-up completed by Alan Atkins (vocals) and John Ellis (drums). The name Judas Priest came from Atkins' previous band (who took it from a Bob Dylan song, 'The Ballad Of Frankie Lee And Judas Priest') before he joined up with Hill and Downing. Constant gigging continued, with Alan Moore taking over on drums, only to be replaced at the end of 1971 by Chris Campbell. Most of 1972 was spent on the road in the UK, and in 1973 both Atkins and Campbell departed, leaving the nucleus of Hill and Downing (in 1991 Atkins released a debut solo album that included 'Victim Of Changes', a song he co-wrote in Judas Priest's infancy). At this point, their fortunes took a turn for the better. Vocalist and ex-theatrical lighting engineer Rob Halford (b. 25 August 1951, Walsall, England) and drummer John Hinch, both from the band Hiroshima, joined the unit. More UK shows ensued as their following grew steadily, culminating in the addition of second guitarist Glenn Tipton (b. 25 October 1948; ex-Flying Hat Band). In 1974 they toured abroad for the first time in Germany and the Netherlands, and returned home to a record contract with the small UK label Gull. The band made their vinyl debut with *Rocka Rolla* in September 1974. Disappointed with the recording, the band failed to make any impact, and Hinch left to be replaced by the returning Alan Moore.

In 1975 the band's appearance at the Reading Festival brought them to the attention of a much wider audience. *Sad Wings Of Destiny* was an improvement on the debut, with production assistance from Jeffrey Calvert and Max West. However, despite good reviews, their financial situation remained desperate, and Alan Moore left for the second and final time. A worldwide contract with CBS Records saved the day, and *Sin After Sin* was a strong collection, with Simon Philips sitting in for Moore. The band then visited America for the first time with drummer Les Binks, who appeared on *Stained Class*, an album that showed Priest at a high watermark in their powers. *Killing Machine* yielded the first UK hit single, 'Take On The World', and featured shorter, punchier, but still familiar, rock songs. *Unleashed In The East* was recorded on the 1979 Japanese tour, and in that year, Binks was replaced on drums by Dave Holland of Trapeze. After major tours with both Kiss and AC/DC, Priest's popularity began to gather momentum. *British Steel* smashed into the UK album charts at number 3, and included the hit singles 'Breaking The Law' and 'Living After Midnight'. After appearing at the 1980 Donington Monsters Of Rock festival, they began recording *Point Of Entry*. It provided the hit single 'Hot Rockin', and was followed by sell-out UK and US tours. The period surrounding *Screaming For Vengeance* was phenomenally successful for the band. The hit single, 'You've Got Another Thing Comin'', was followed by a lucrative six-month US tour, with the album achieving platinum status in the USA. *Defenders Of The Faith* offered a similar potent brand of headstrong metal to *Screaming For Vengeance*. *Turbo*, however, proved slightly more commercial and was poorly received, Judas Priest's traditional metal fans reacting with indifference to innovations that included the use of synthesized guitars. *Ram It Down* saw a return to pure heavy metal by comparison, but by this time their popularity had begun to wane. Dave Holland was replaced by Scott Travis (b. Norfolk, Virginia, USA; ex-Racer X) for the return to form that was *Painkiller*. Although no longer universally popular, Priest were still a major live attraction and remained the epitome of heavy metal, with screaming guitars matched by screaming vocalist, and the protagonists clad in studs and black leather. The band were taken to court in 1990 following the suicide attempts of two fans (one successful) in 1985. Both CBS Records and Judas Priest were accused of inciting suicide through the 'backwards messages' in their recording of the Spooky Tooth classic, 'Better By You, Better Than Me'. They were found not guilty in June 1993 after a long court battle, Downing admitting: 'It will be another ten years before I can even spell subliminal'. Soon afterwards, Halford became disheartened with the band and decided to quit. He had temporarily fronted an Ozzy-less Black Sabbath and recorded 'Light Comes Out Of The Black' with Pantera for the *Buffy The Vampire Slayer* soundtrack, as well as working on his Fight project. He debuted with his new band, Halford, in 1996. With new vocalist Ripper Owens, Judas Priest returned to recording with 1997's *Jugulator*.

● ALBUMS: *Rocka Rolla* (Gull 1974)★★, *Sad Wings Of Destiny* (Gull 1976)★★, *Sin After Sin* (Columbia 1977)★★★, *Stained Class* (Columbia 1978)★★★, *Killing Machine* (Columbia 1978)★★, *Live - Unleashed In The East* (Columbia 1979)★★★★, *British Steel* (Columbia 1980)★★★★, *Point Of Entry* (Columbia 1981)★★★, *Screaming For Vengeance* (Columbia 1982)★★★, *Defenders Of The Faith* (Columbia 1984)★★★, *Turbo* (Columbia 1986)★★, *Priest Live* (Columbia 1987)★★, *Ram It Down* (Columbia 1988)★★★, *Painkiller* (Columbia 1990)★★★, *Jugulator* (SPV 1997)★★★, *Concert Classics* (Ranch Life 1998)★★.

● COMPILATIONS: *Best Of* (Gull 1978)★★, *Hero Hero* (Telaeg 1987)★★, *Collection* (Castle 1989)★★★, *Metal Works '73 - '93* (Columbia 1993)★★★★, *Living After Midnight* (Columbia 1997)★★★.

● VIDEOS: *Fuel Of Life* (Columbia 1986), *Judas Priest Live* (Virgin Vision 1987), *Painkiller* (Sony Music Video 1990), *Metal Works 73-93* (1993).

● FURTHER READING: *Heavy Duty*, Steve Gett.

JUICY LUCY

Juicy Lucy was formed in 1969 when three ex-members of the Misunderstood - Ray Owen (vocals), Glen 'Ross' Campbell (steel guitar) and Chris Mercer (tenor saxophone) - were augmented by Neil Hubbard (guitar), Keith Ellis (bass, ex-Van Der Graaf Generator) and Pete Dobson (bass). The sextet enjoyed a surprise hit single with their fiery reading of Bo Diddley's 'Who Do You Love', a track featured on the group's first, and best-known, album. The cover became a sexist classmate of Jimi Hendrix's *Electric Ladyland*, and featured a naked busty woman languishing on a banquet table, amid a glut of various sliced and squashed fruits. Owen was later replaced by former Zoot Money singer Paul Williams, one of several changes afflicting the group. Their brand of blues-rock became more predictable as one by one the original cast dropped out. A fourth album, *Pieces*, was completed by a reshaped unit of Williams, Mick Moody (guitar), Jean Roussal (keyboards) and ex-Blodwyn Pig members Andy Pyle (bass) and Ron Berg (drums), but this was the final line-up of Juicy Lucy, which broke up soon afterwards. A new version of the band appeared in the 90s with Andy Doughty (bass), Mike Jarvis (guitar) and Spencer Blackledge (drums) together with the ever present Owen.

● ALBUMS: *Juicy Lucy* (Vertigo 1969)★★★★, *Lie Back And Enjoy It* (Vertigo 1970)★★, *Get A Whiff A This* (Bronze 1971)★★, *Pieces* (Polydor 1972)★★, *Here She Comes Again* (HTD 1996)★★★.

● COMPILATIONS: *Who Do You Love: The Best Of* (Sequel 1990)★★.

JUGGERNAUT

Formed in Texas, California, USA, in 1985, the band's original line-up consisted of Harlan Glenn (vocals), Eddie Katilius (guitar), Scott Womack (bass) and Bobby Jarzombek (drums). They signed to the Metal Blade Records label and had an early demo track included on the *Metal Massacre VII* compilation album. Their debut long-player, *Baptism Under Fire*, was released in 1986. Their music was as the band's name suggested, traditional heavy metal, with the emphasis on 'heavy'. The outfit received little attention from the media and Glenn left the band to be replaced by Steve Cooper in time for *Trouble Within*. Released in 1987, this similarly made little impact. With any degree of sustained success seemingly beyond them, the band folded in early 1988.

● ALBUMS: *Baptism Under Fire* (Metal Blade 1986)★★★, *Trouble Within* (Metal Blade 1987)★★.

JUNKIE XL

One of the pre-eminent remixers in the field of industrial rock, Tom Holkenborg's tastes were originally informed by his exposure to Vera - his local, world-renowned music venue in Groningen, Holland. Afterwards Holkenborg joined a series of bands, including Nerve (who recorded *Cancer Of Choice* for Play It Again Sam Records). However, he was attracted to the possibilities of dance music and remixing in 1989, while attending the Dutch Lowlands Festival. There he saw metal fans being converted by cutting edge dance music at the dance tent, and he started working on a wholly different batch of raw dance/rock material. Impressed by what they heard of these demo sessions, Roadrunner Records asked him to do a remix for Dog Eat Dog. Fear Factory then invited him to remix tracks for their *Remanufacture* album (he has also worked with Ohio punk band New Bomb Turks). Fear Factory's Dino Cazares offered to play on Junkie XL's debut album to return the compliment, providing all the guitar work. This led Holkenborg to reassess the project, deciding to make Junkie XL a full-time working band. Long-standing friends Rene (drums) and Bas (drums) completed the line-up. Ex-Urban Dance Squad singer Rude Boy (b. Patrick Remington) was brought in to provide raps on two of the tracks on the subsequent debut album, *Saturday Teenage Kick*, and elected to become a full-time member. However, 8,000 copies of the album had to be withdrawn when Bob Mould (Hüsker Dü/Sugar) objected to the uncleared use of a sample of his music.

● ALBUMS: *Saturday Teenage Kick* (Roadrunner 1998)★★★.

JUNKYARD

This five-piece US group was comprised of seasoned Los Angeles club circuit musicians. Formed in 1988, the line-up was David Roach (vocals), Chris Gates and Brian Baker (guitars), Clay Anthony (bass) and Patrick Muzingo (drums). Signing to Geffen Records, their debut offered 'trashy metallic boogie'. Two years later, *Sixes Sevens And Nines* emerged and the songwriting partnership of Roach and Gates had matured considerably, with the emphasis on the music rather than image. Musically, Junkyard sit somewhere between Great White, Dokken and ZZ Top, dealing in abrasive raunch 'n' roll. On their second album, producer Ed Stasium achieved a harder and bluesier sound (somewhat akin to Lynyrd Skynyrd), without pushing the band in a blatantly commercial direction. The group were nevertheless dropped by Geffen in 1992, though they elected to persevere.

● ALBUMS: *Junkyard* (Geffen 1989)★★, *Sixes, Sevens And Nines* (Geffen 1991)★★★.

KANSAS

This US group was formed in 1972 after David Hope (b. *c*.1951, Kansas, USA; bass) and Phil Ehart (b. 1951, Kansas, USA; drums, percussion) changed the name of their band, White Clover, to Kansas, recruiting Kerry Livgren (b. 18 September 1949, Kansas, USA; guitar, vocals), Robert Steinhardt (b. *c*.1951, Michigan, USA; violin, strings, vocals), Steve Walsh (b. *c*.1951, St. Joseph, Missouri, USA; keyboards, vocals) and Richard Williams (b. *c*.1951, Kansas, USA; guitars). Although an American band, Kansas were heavily influenced from the outset by British rock of that era, such as Yes and Genesis, and this was evident in the lyrics of their primary songwriter, Walsh. Kansas released their debut in 1974, and the following two albums attained gold status, guaranteeing the band a high profile in the USA (although no Kansas albums reached the charts in the UK). By 1977 the band had tired of the progressive rock pigeonhole into which the music press was forcing them, and decided to try a more commercial approach. Their popularity was confirmed on 27 June 1978 when they attended a ceremony at Madison Square Gardens in New York, at which the organization UNICEF named the band Deputy Ambassadors of Goodwill. In the early 80s Walsh decided to leave the band after he became unhappy with their increasingly commercial sound. He released the solo set, *Schemer Dreamer*, which featured other members of Kansas. He was replaced by John Elefante (b. *c*.1958, Levittown, New York, USA; keyboards, vocals), who wrote four of the songs on *Vinyl Confessions*. The band split in 1983 following two unsuccessful albums. Livgren and Hope had become born-again Christians, the former releasing *Seeds Of Change*, a commercially disastrous solo effort based on his religious experiences, and then recorded prolifically with AD. In October 1986 Walsh, Ehart and Williams re-formed Kansas with Steve Morse, lately of Dixie Dregs (guitar), and Billy Greer (bass). This reunion was celebrated with the release of *Power*, an album that rejected the jazz-rock feel of earlier releases in favour of a heavier sound. Their first studio album in seven years was released in May 1995.

● ALBUMS: *Kansas* (Kirshner 1974)★★★, *Song For America* (Kirshner 1975)★★★, *Masque* (Kirshner 1976)★★★, *Leftoverture* (Kirshner 1977)★★★, *Point Of Know Return* (Kirshner 1977)★★★★, *Two For The Show* (Kirshner 1978)★★★, *Monolith* (Kirshner 1979)★★★, *Audio-Visions* (Kirshner 1980)★★★, *Vinyl Confessions* (Kirshner 1982)★★, *Drastic Measures* (Columbia 1983)★★, *Power* (MCA 1986)★★, *In The Spirit Of Things* (MCA 1988)★★, *Live At The Whisky* (1993)★, *Freaks Of Nature* (Intersound 1995)★★.

● COMPILATIONS: *The Best Of Kansas* (Columbia 1984)★★★.

KAT

The self-proclaimed 'Great Kat' began her musical career as a classically trained violinist, graduating from the Juilliard School of Music in New York. After six years of solid performance on the instrument, she switched to the guitar and began experimenting with a fusion of classical and rock music. Adopting a high-speed technique, she concentrated on short instrumentals. *Worship Me Or Die* was poorly received, despite Kat's proclamations that it represented 'the first real revolutionary music since Beethoven'. Undaunted, she released *Beethoven On Speed*, which marked a considerable improvement in both musical and production terms. Promoting herself as a grotesque parody of a 'wild woman of rock', this contrivance fell flat with European audiences and, despite her potential to produce an innovative metal/classical crossover album, little has been heard from the artist since.

● ALBUMS: *Worship Me Or Die* (Roadrunner 1987)★★, *Beethoven On Speed* (Roadrunner 1990)★★★★.

KATON, MICHAEL

This acclaimed blues rock guitarist/vocalist grew up in Ipsilanti, Michigan, USA, and his musical family background soon inspired him to take up the guitar. Katon began playing with local bands in clubs and roadhouse bars around Detroit from the age of 15, and spent 20 years paying his dues in classic blues fashion, working with a succession of blues and jazz bands. Subsequently based in Hell, Michigan, he released his solo debut, *Boogie All Over Your Head*, on his own Wild Ass label, with Swedish label Garageland picking up the record in Europe. The straightforward R&B boogie style, gravelly vocals and stylish blues guitar of *Proud To Be Loud* endeared Katon to both the blues and heavy metal crowds, and live shows with Ed Phelps (guitar, harmonica), Johnny Arizona (bass) and Gary Rasmussen (drums) proved to be wild affairs, particularly owing to the guitarist's penchant for four- and five-hour sets. Blues label Provogue were suitably impressed, offering Katon a European contract. Katon gave up drinking to concentrate on his guitar playing, resulting in the harder, more focused *Get On The Boogie Train*, and while his lyrics retained their customary humour, he also produced a fine slice of urban blues in 'Cadillac Assembly Line', a lament for Detroit's declining motor industry. *Rip It Hard* continued in the traditional blues-boogie vein, and while, like many bluesmen, major commercial success evades Katon, he remains a respected guitarist in the field.

● ALBUMS: *Boogie All Over Your Head* (Wild Ass 1985)★★★, *Proud To Be Loud* (Wild Ass 1988)★★★, *Get On The Boogie Train* (Wild Ass 1992)★★★★, *Rip It Hard* (Wild Ass 1994)★★★, *Rub* (Provogue 1996)★★★.

KEEL

US-born vocalist Ron Keel started his career in 1983 with Steeler, who also temporarily featured future guitar hero Yngwie Malmsteen. After one self-titled album on Shrapnel Records, he dissolved the band to go solo. Forming a typical Kiss/Aerosmith-styled band with musicians Brian Jay (guitar), Marc Ferrari (guitar), Kenny Chaisson (bass) and Dwain Miller (drums), Keel obtained the production services of Gene Simmons (Kiss) for a second album that won them many fans. The follow-up, 1986's *The Final Frontier*, featured an all-star line-up including Joan Jett, Michael Des Barres (Silverhead/Detective) and Simmons. The album also spawned a hit single with a cover version of Patti Smith's 'Because The Night'. Moving to MCA in 1987 proved less fruitful and after one album, they switched to an indie label and sundered shortly afterwards. Ferrari sped off and formed Cold Sweat in 1990. In 1991 Keel talked in depth about forming a new act with an all-female band. This has, so far, proved wishful thinking.

● ALBUMS: *Lay Down The Law* (Shrapnel 1984)★★, *The Right To Rock* (Vertigo 1985)★★★, *The Final Frontier* (Vertigo 1986)★★★, *Keel* (MCA 1987)★★, *Larger Than Live* (Mountain Castle 1989)★★★.

KEPONE

Alternative US rock/punk band Kepone are Michael Bishop (bass, vocals), Tim Harris (guitar, vocals) and former Honor Role drummer Seth Harris (later replaced by Ed Trask). Formed in the early 90s, they took their name from the pesticide that was manufactured by the Allied Signal Corporation of Hopewell, Virginia, in the 70s, and caused the company's employees severe neurological damage (this incident was also the subject of a Dead Kennedys song, 'Kepone Factory'). The group's deliberate, anthemic rock style was unveiled with the 1994 release of *Ugly Dance* for Quarterstick Records. A potent collision of punk-pop with the distinctive employment of dual lead vocals, it followed on from the group's excellent 1993 singles, 'Henry' and '295'. The latter single was released on Jello Biafra's (ex-Dead Kennedys) Alternative Tentacles Records - supplying ample evidence of Kepone's original inspiration. *Skin* and *Kepone* were further slices of the band's endearingly offbeat alternative rock.

● ALBUMS: *Ugly Dance* (Quarterstick 1994)★★★, *Skin* (Quarterstick 1995)★★★, *Kepone* (Quarterstick 1997)★★★.

KERBDOG

Irish alternative rock band Kerbdog enjoyed their biggest success to date in 1994 when 'Dummy Crusher' took them into the UK Top 40. Heavily influenced by the more abrasive US bands (Smashing Pumpkins, Helmet, Hüsker Dü, etc.), they received excellent press within the UK hard rock press for their efforts. However, shortly after this initial success they lost original guitarist Billy Dalton, slimming down to a trio led by bassist Colin Fenelley, vocalist/guitarist Cormac Battle and drummer Butler. They re-emerged two years later with an intensive work schedule aimed at recapturing their previous high profile within the hard rock media. New material was initially unveiled on the four-track 1996 EP *JJ's Song*, recorded at the same sessions that produced their follow-up album, *On The Turn*. Garth Richardson, best known for his work with Rage Against The Machine, and partner Joe Barresi, who assisted Richardson on his production work with Jesus Lizard, oversaw production.

● ALBUMS: *Totally Switched* (Vertigo 1994)★★★, *On The Turn* (Fontana 1996)★★.

KIK TRACEE

This US hard rock quintet was formed in 1990 by Stephen Shareux (vocals) and Michael Marquis (guitar). The line-up was completed by the addition of Rob Grad (bass), Gregory Hex (rhythm guitar) and Johnny Douglas (drums). Signed by RCA Records, they debuted in 1991 with *No Rules*, a varied and uncompromising collection of mature rock numbers that included, in an unusual choice of cover material, a version of Simon And Garfunkel's 'Mrs. Robinson'.

● ALBUMS: *No Rules* (RCA 1991)★★★.

KILL FOR THRILLS

Formed in Los Angeles, California, USA, this group delivered a trademark sound best described as 'sleaze rock'. Featuring the talents of Gilby Clarke (vocals, guitar), Jason Nesmith (guitar), Todd Muscat (bass) and David Scott (drums), their 1990 debut, *Dynamite From Nightmare Land*, was a prime example of no-nonsense standard-chord hard rock. The album was produced by Vic Maile and Ric Browde who are renowned, respectively, for their work with Motörhead and Poison.

● ALBUMS: *Dynamite From Nightmare Land* (MCA 1990)★★★.

KILLDOZER

Killdozer were formed in Madison, Wisconsin, USA, and the music of the area was regularly celebrated in their primal country blues. The original line-up featured Michael Gerald (bass, vocals), plus the brothers Dan (guitar) and Bill Hobson (drums). From their formation the trio released a steady stream of albums that often highlighted their distaste at what they saw as the social and political malaise of their native country. They were just as likely to turn the spotlight on small-town weirdness, however, or their singer's rampant confusion about the state of the world. In a respite from this angst, *For Ladies Only* was a project dedicated to cover versions of classic songs of the 70s, including 'One Tin Soldier' and 'Good Lovin' Gone Bad'. Guitarist Paul Zagoras was recruited during the 90s in place of Dan Hobson, during which time Killdozer's formidable output was restrained somewhat due to Gerald sitting accountancy exams (he is a former mathematics teacher). However, the band bounced straight back to form with albums in 1994 and 1995, both featuring further bizarre anecdotes. The band broke up at the end of 1996 with the aptly named 'fuck you we quit tour'.

● ALBUMS: *Intellectuals Are The Shoeshine Boys Of The Ruling Elite* (Bone Air 1984)★★★, *Snakeboy* (Touch & Go 1985)★★★, *Burl* mini-album (Touch & Go 1986)★★★, *Little Baby Buntin'* (Touch & Go 1987)★★★, *Twelve Point Buck* (Touch & Go 1988)★★★, *For Ladies Only* (Touch & Go 1989)★★★, *Uncompromising War On Art Under The Dictatorship Of The Proletariat* (Touch & Go 1994)★★★, *God Hears Pleas Of The Innocent* (Touch & Go 1995)★★★, *The Last Waltz* 1996 recording (Man's Ruin 1997).

● VIDEOS: *Little Baby Buntin' Live* (Jettisoundz 1990).

KILLERS

This UK quintet was founded in 1991 by former Iron Maiden vocalist Paul Di'Anno. Comprising Steve Hopgood (drums), Cliff Evans (guitar, ex-Tank), Gavin Cooper (bass) and Nick Burr (guitar), their approach was firmly rooted in the New Wave Of British Heavy Metal movement of the early 80s. *Murder One*, released in early 1992, was rather anachronistic, sounding virtually identical to early Iron Maiden, though the calibre of the protagonists guaranteed press and public interest.

● ALBUMS: *Murder One* (RCA 1992)★★, *South American Assault: Live* (Magnetic Air 1994)★★.

KILLING JOKE

This immensely powerful post-punk UK band combined a furious rhythm section with near-psychotic performances from Jaz Coleman (b. Jeremy Coleman, Cheltenham, England; vocals, keyboards). The band came about when Coleman, of Egyptian descent, was introduced to Paul Ferguson, then drumming for the Matt Stagger Band. Coleman joined as a keyboard player, before they both left to form their own group. This first incarnation added 'Geordie' (b. K. Walker, Newcastle, England; guitar) and Youth (b. Martin Glover Youth, 27 December 1960, Africa; bass), who had made his first public appearance at the Vortex in 1977 with forgotten punk band the Rage. After relocating to Notting Hill Gate they paid for a rehearsal studio and borrowed money from Coleman's girlfriend to release the *Almost Red EP*. Picked up by UK disc jockey John Peel, the band provided a session that would become the most frequently requested of the thousands he has commissioned. Via Island Records the band were able to set up their own Malicious Damage label, on which they released 'Wardance' in February 1980, notable for its remarkably savage b-side, 'Psyche'. A succession of fine, aggressive singles followed, alongside live appearances with Joy Division. They were in a strong enough position to negotiate a three-album contract with EG, which allowed them to keep the name Malicious Damage for their records. After the release of a typically harsh debut album, the band were banned from a Glasgow gig when council officials took exception to posters depicting Pope Pius giving his blessing to two columns of Hitler's Brown Shirts (a genuine photograph). It was typical of the black humour that pervaded the band, especially on their record sleeves and graphics. After the recording of the third album was completed the band disintegrated when Coleman's fascination with the occult led him to the conclusion that the apocalypse was imminent, and he fled to Iceland. He was followed later by Youth. When Youth returned it was to begin work with Ferguson on a new project, Brilliant. However, having second thoughts, Ferguson became the third Joker to flee to Iceland, taking bass player Paul Raven (ex-Neon Hearts) with him. Brilliant continued with Youth as the only original member. The Killing Joke output from then on lacks something of the menace that had made them so vital. However, *Night Time* combined commercial elements better than most, proffering the UK number 16 hit single 'Love Like Blood' (February 1985). While *Outside The Gate* was basically a Coleman solo album wrongly credited to the band, they returned with their best album for years with 1990's *Extremities, Dirt & Various Repressed Emotions*, which saw the drumming debut of Martin Atkins (b. 3 August 1959, Coventry, England; ex-Public Image Limited). Regardless, the band broke up once more with bitter acrimony flying across the pages of the press the same year. While his former co-conspirators pronounced Killing Joke dead, Coleman pledged to continue under the name. He did just that after a brief sojourn into classical/ethnic music via a collaborative project with Anne Dudley which resulted in *Songs From The Victorious City* released on China Records in 1990. *Pandemonium* saw Youth return to join Geordie and Coleman, with the addition of new drummer Geoff Dugmore. This saw a revitalized Killing Joke, notably on 'Exorcism', recorded in the King's Chamber of the Great Pyramid in Cairo. They were welcomed back by a wide cross-section of critics (or at least, those whom Coleman had not physically assaulted at some point) and friends. Indeed, bands claiming Killing Joke as a direct influence ranged from the Cult, Ministry and Skinny Puppy to Metallica and Soundgarden, while many noticed an uncanny similarity between the band's 'Eighties' and Nirvana's 'Come As You Are'. *Pandemonium* yielded two UK Top 40 singles, 'Millennium' and the title track, and sold in excess of 100,000 copies in the USA where they signed to Zoo Records. Meanwhile, Coleman's secondary career had evolved. In addition to scoring a second symphony alongside Youth and arranging classical interpretations of the music of Pink Floyd, Led Zeppelin and the Who, he became composer in residence for the New Zealand Symphony Orchestra (the country where he spends most of his time). It led to him being hailed by conductor Klaus Tennstedt as 'the new Mahler'. For his part Youth had become one of the UK's top dance remixers, also recording with acts as diverse as Bananarama and Crowded House. He returned to Killing Joke in 1996 for *Democracy* - a cynical snipe at the build-up to election year in the UK.

● ALBUMS: *Killing Joke* (Malicious Damage/EG 1980)★★★★, *what's THIS for ... !* (Malicious Damage/EG 1981)★★★, *Revelations* (Malicious Damage/EG 1982)★★★, *Ha! EP10* (Malicious Damage/EG 1982)★★★, *Fire Dances* (EG 1983)★★★★, *Night Time* (EG/Polydor 1985)★★★, *Brighter Than A Thousand Suns* (EG/Virgin 1986)★★★, *Outside The Gate* (EG/Virgin 1988)★★★, *Extremities, Dirt & Various Repressed Emotions* (Noise International/RCA 1990)★★★★, *Pandemonium* (Big Life/Zoo 1994)★★★, *BBC In Concert* (Strange Fruit/Windsong 1995)★★★, *Democracy* (Zoo 1996)★★★.

● COMPILATIONS: *An Incomplete Collection* (EG 1990)★★★, *Laugh? I Nearly Bought One!* (EG/Caroline 1992)★★★, *Wilful Days* (Blue Plate 1995)★★★.

KING DIAMOND

When popular metal act Mercyful Fate split into two separate factions in March 1985, vocalist King Diamond (b. Kim Bendix Petersen, 14 June 1956, Copenhagen, Denmark), Michael Denner (guitar) and Timi Hansen (bass) decided to pursue their obsession with Satanic heavy metal and the occult, while the others sought a more mainstream direction. King Diamond's music was characterized by supernatural storylines, high-pitched, banshee-like vocals and meandering guitarwork. On live performances, their leader specialized in amateurish theatrical stunts to bring the songs to life. This included face make-up not dissimilar to that worn by Alice Cooper. Since 1985 there have been numerous line-up changes, but the most enduring personnel have included Andy Larocque (guitar, who joined Death, replaced by ex-Madison guitarist Mikael Myllynen, aka Mikael Moon), Pete Blakk (guitar), Hal Patino (bass) and Snowy Shaw (drums). Each successive album has offered ever more complex themes and subplots, resulting in the musical equivalent of a sinister version of Dungeons and Dragons. After the failure of *The Eye*, Diamond resurrected Mercyful Fate in 1993, but returned to his solo career two years later to record *Spider's Lullaby*. His current intention seems to be to keep both careers separate but ongoing.

● ALBUMS: *Fatal Portrait* (Roadrunner 1986)★★★, *Abigail* (Roadrunner 1987)★★★, *Them* (Roadrunner 1988)★★★, *The Dark Sides* (Roadrunner 1988)★★, *Conspiracy* (Roadrunner 1989)★★★, *The Eye* (Roadrunner 1990)★★★, *Spider's Lullaby* (Massacre 1995)★★★, *The Graveyard* (Massacre 1996)★★, *Voodoo* (Massacre 1998)★★★.

KING KOBRA

After departing as the drummer of Ozzy Osbourne's band in 1984, Carmen Appice (b. 15 December 1946, Staten Island, New York, USA) decided to form his own group under the King Kobra moniker. Enlisting the services of four relative unknowns, Mark Free (vocals), David Michael-Phillips (guitar), Mike Sweda (guitar) and Johnny Rod (bass), he negotiated a contract with EMI Records, which eventually resulted in *Ready To Strike* in 1985, a hard rock album full of infectious hooks and pyrotechnic guitar breaks. On the strength of this release they were offered the chance to write the theme music for the film *Iron Eagle*. They changed styles at this juncture, switching to a more sophisticated and lightweight AOR approach. As a result, album sales dried up and they were dropped by their label. Johnny Rod left to join W.A.S.P. and the band disintegrated. A few months later, the nucleus of Appice and Michael-Phillips rebuilt the band with ex-Montrose vocalist Johnny Edwards, Jeff Northrup (guitar) and Larry Hart (bass). They returned to their hard rock origins and released *King Kobra III* on Music For Nations, but it was again poorly received. The band finally became obsolete when Appice joined John Sykes' Blue Murder project in 1989. Edwards later joined Foreigner for their *Unusual Heat* album.

● ALBUMS: *Ready To Strike* (Capitol 1985)★★★★, *Thrill Of A Lifetime* (EMI 1987)★★★, *King Kobra III* (Music For Nations 1988)★★★.

KING OF THE HILL

This St. Louis, Missouri-based four-piece heavy metal outfit began life on the local club circuit as a covers band, with the line-up settling when bassist George Potsos joined Frankie Muriel (vocals), Vito Bono (drums) and Jimmy Griffin (guitar). Initially known as Broken Toyz, the band gradually introduced original material into their set, until the demand for their own songs allowed them to drop the cover versions entirely. They signed a recording contract in 1990, and, having adopted the name King Of The Hill, recorded their self-titled debut with Bang Tango producer Howard Benson. The album mixed party metal in the grand Van Halen style with funk influences, while also touching on AOR, with vocal harmonies that echoed Bon Jovi. The opening single, 'I Do U', did well on MTV, and with major backing from their record label the band spent much of 1991 on the road, touring with White Lion, Trixter, Lynch Mob and Steelheart in the USA, and received a rapturous reception as Extreme's guests on their autumn UK tour. This, the band's first live work outside their own country, served to sharpen their performing abilities, with the charismatic Muriel becoming the visual focus of the band, drawing comparisons to both David Lee Roth and Prince, not least for his multiple costume changes throughout each show. However, despite the fact that King Of The Hill were due to record a second album in early 1992, they seemed to disappear almost overnight.

● ALBUMS: *King Of The Hill* (SBK 1991)★★★.

KINGDOM COME

In 1984 German vocalist Lenny Wolf fronted the Led Zeppelin-inspired Stone Fury, who released *Burns Like A Star*. After they disbanded he returned to Germany and had a rethink. He moved back to America in 1987 with a new plan and found like-minded musicians Danny Stag (guitar), Rick Steier (guitar), Johnny Frank (bass) and James Kottak (drums). He then took his idea to ex-Gentle Giant vocalist Derek Shulman, now working in A&R, who ensured that the new group signed to Polydor Records. Their 1988 album revealed Wolf's great plan: the band had not so much been influenced by, but had totally reproduced Led Zeppelin, from the drum sound of John Bonham to the vocals of Robert Plant. It was a complete facsimile, yet such was the interest in America that the album went gold on advance orders alone. The rock world soon fell into two factions - those who hated it and those who did not. Of their detractors, Robert Plant and John Paul Jones made less than flattering remarks and guitarist Gary Moore was prompted to write the song 'Led Clones' on his *After The War* album later that same year. Wolf lacked the ability to argue his case convincingly and even those who chose to support them began to change sides. Realizing that all was not well, they attempted to be a little more original for the second album, *In Your Face*. This produced a classic rock track in 'Do You Like It', a highly charged song that managed to avoid previous comparisons. However, the title of their final single, 'Overrated', summarized the whole project, and theysummarily disbanded. Lenny Wolf later returned as a solo artist and produced a fine single, 'Shouldn't I', but the ghost of *Kingdom Come* haunted his every move.

● ALBUMS: *Kingdom Come* (Polydor 1988)★★★, *In Your Face* (Polydor 1989)★★.

KINGFISH

Formed in 1974 in San Francisco, California, USA, Kingfish were one of the city's most popular live attractions during the late 70s. Founder-members Matt Kelly (guitar, vocals) and Chris Herold (drums) first worked together in the 60s in the New Delhi River Band. In 1968 they formed Horses who recorded an album for White Whale Records. This group's lead guitarist Bobby Hoddinot joined Kelly and Herold in 1973 in Lonesome Janet, along with Nick Ward (keyboards). When Dave Torbert (bass, ex-New Riders Of The Purple Sage and New Delhi Blues Band) was added to the line-up in 1974, Lonesome Janet became known as Kingfish. Ward died in 1974, after which Grateful Dead guitarist/vocalist Bob Weir joined the remaining musicians, boosting their popularity overnight. *Kingfish* captures their relaxed, bar band style, but it disguised internal disharmony. Weir left soon after its completion and *Live'N'Kicking* featured a four-piece group. Dave Perber replaced Herold for *Trident*, which also introduced newcomers Mike O'Neil (guitar) and Barry Flast (keyboards). Perber then left, and Mark Neilson became the group's third drummer for *Two For The Sun*. Kingfish disbanded officially in 1979, although Kelly and Flast subsequently revived the name during the 80s. *Kingfish* (1985) featured assistance from John Lee Hooker and Mike Bloomfield, as well as Bob Weir, who resumed his association with the group, albeit on a part-time basis. *Live From The Sweetwater* proved their in-concert sparkle had not disappeared.

● ALBUMS: *Kingfish* (Round 1976)★★★, *Live'N'Kicking* (Jet 1977)★★★, *Trident* (Jet 1978)★★, *Two For The Sun* (Krishner 1979)★★, *Kingfish* (Relix 1985)★★, *Live From The Sweetwater* (Relix 1986)★★★.

KINGHORSE

Based in Louisville, Kentucky, USA, Kinghorse are a rock band featuring Sean Garrison (vocals), Kevin Brownstein (drums), Mark Abromavage (guitar) and Mike Bucayu (bass). They attracted a good deal of critical interest after their debut release, not least because they had secured cover artwork from legendary heavy metal artist Pushead (singer for Septic Death, but best known for his work with Metallica), and had Glenn Danzig (of Misfits and Danzig fame) producing. The resultant album was an exercise in heated nihilism and aggressive angst. Potent, painfully gritty and, at times, oddly poignant, Kinghorse were perhaps too unremittingly bleak for most tastes.

● ALBUMS: *Kinghorse* (Caroline 1990)★★★.

KINGS X

Initially known as the Edge and specializing in Top 40 cover versions, Doug Pinnick (bass, vocals), Ty Tabor (guitar) and Jerry Gaskell (drums) relocated to Houston, Texas, USA, in 1985, and were taken under the wing of ZZ Top video producer, Sam Taylor. Under Taylor's guidance, they concentrated on their own material and changed their name to Kings X. After recording demos and being turned down by several major record companies in the USA, they finally secured a contract with the independent Megaforce label. *Out Of The Silent Planet*, with its unique sound and offbeat approach, emerged in 1988 to widespread critical acclaim. Fusing Beatles-style harmonies with hard rock and blues riffs, they encompassed a variety of genres that defied simple pigeonholing. *Gretchen Goes To Nebraska* was an even greater triumph, building on previous strengths, but adding depth in both a technical and lyrical sense. Preferring the 'positive' tag to that of Christian rockers, *Faith, Hope, Love*, released in 1990, scaled even greater heights with its state-of-the-art production and inspired compositions. After a long gap from recording, *Ear Candy* was a pleasant surprise, both in quality and in the fact that their fans had not deserted them.

● ALBUMS: *Out Of The Silent Planet* (Megaforce

1987)★★★, *Gretchen Goes To Nebraska* (Megaforce 1989)★★★★, *Faith, Hope, Love* (Megaforce 1990)★★★★, *King's X* (Atlantic 1992)★★★★, *Dogman* (Atlantic 1994)★★★, *Ear Candy* (Atlantic 1996)★★★.

● COMPILATIONS: *Best Of Kings X* (Atlantic 1998)★★★★.

Kiss

Following the demise of Wicked Lester, Kiss were formed in 1972 by Paul Stanley (b. Paul Eisen, 20 January 1950, Queens, New York, USA; rhythm guitar, vocals) and Gene Simmons (b. Chaim Witz, 25 August 1949, Haifa, Israel; bass, vocals), who went on to recruit Peter Criss (b. Peter Crisscoula, 27 December 1947, Brooklyn, New York, USA; drums, vocals) and Ace Frehley (b. Paul Frehley, 22 April 1951, Bronx, New York, USA; lead guitar, vocals). At their second show at the Hotel Diplomat, Manhattan, in 1973, Flipside producer Bill Aucoin offered the band a management contract, and within two weeks they were signed to Neil Bogart's recently established Casablanca Records. In just over a year, Kiss had released their first three albums with a modicum of success. In the summer of 1975 their fortunes changed with the release of *Alive!*, which spawned their first US hit single, with the reissued live version of 'Rock And Roll All Nite' climbing to number 12 in November. The appeal of Kiss has always been based on their live shows: the garish greasepaint make-up, outrageous costumes and pyrotechnic stage effects, along with their hard-rocking anthems, combined to create what was billed as 'The Greatest Rock 'n' Roll Show On Earth'. Their live reputation engendered a dramatic upsurge in record sales, and *Alive* became their first certified platinum album in the USA. *Destroyer* proved just as successful, and also gave them their first US Top 10 single, earning Peter Criss a major songwriting award for the uncharacteristic ballad, 'Beth'. Subsequent releases, *Rock And Roll Over*, *Love Gun* and *Alive II*, each certified platinum, confirmed the arrival of Kiss as major recording artists. By 1977 Kiss had topped the prestigious Gallup poll as the most popular act in the USA. They had become a marketing dream: Kiss merchandise included make-up kits, masks, board games, and pinball machines. *Marvel Comics* produced two super-hero cartoon books, and a full-length science-fiction film, *Kiss Meet The Phantom Of The Park*, was even produced. The ranks of their fan club, the Kiss Army, had swollen to a six-figure number. In September 1978 all four group members released solo albums on the same day, a feat never before envisaged, let alone matched. At the time, this represented the biggest shipment of albums from one 'unit' to record stores in the history of recorded music. The albums enjoyed varying degrees of success; Ace Frehley's record came out on top and included the US Top 20 hit single, 'New York Groove'. Gene Simmons, whose album featured an impressive line-up of guests including Cher, Donna Summer, Bob Seger and Janis Ian, had a hit single in the UK with 'Radioactive', which reached number 41 in 1978. After the release of *Dynasty* in 1979, which featured the worldwide hit single, 'I Was Made For Lovin' You', cracks appeared in the ranks. Peter Criss left to be replaced by session player Anton Fig, who had previously appeared on Frehley's solo album. Fig played drums on the 1980 release *Unmasked* until a permanent replacement was found in the form of New Yorker Eric Carr (b. 12 July 1950, d. 24 November 1991), who made his first appearance during the world tour of 1980. A fuller introduction came on *Music From The Elder*, an album that represented a radical departure from traditional Kiss music and included several ballads, an orchestra and a choir. It was a brave attempt to break new ground but failed to capture the imagination of the record-buying public. Frehley, increasingly disenchanted with the musical direction of the band, finally left in December 1982. The two albums prior to his departure had featured outside musicians. Bruce Kulick, who had contributed to the studio side of *Alive II* and played on Stanley's solo album, supplied the lead work to the four previously unreleased tracks on the *Killers* compilation of 1982, and Vincent Cusano (later to become Vinnie Vincent) was responsible for lead guitar on the 1982 release, *Creatures Of The Night*. By 1983 the popularity of the band was waning and drastic measures were called for. The legendary make-up that had concealed their true identities for almost 10 years was removed on MTV in the USA. Vinnie Vincent made his first official appearance on *Lick It Up*, an album that provided Kiss with their first Top 10 hit in the UK. The resurgence of the band continued with *Animalize*. Vincent had been replaced by Mark St. John (b. Mark Norton), a seasoned session player and guitar tutor. His association with the band was short-lived, however, as he was struck down by Reiters Syndrome. Bruce Kulick was enlisted as a temporary replacement on the 1984 European Tour, and subsequently became a permanent member when it became apparent that St. John would not be able to continue as a band member.

Further commercial success was achieved with *Asylum* and *Crazy Nights*, the latter featuring their biggest UK hit single, 'Crazy Crazy Nights', which peaked at number 4 in October 1987 and was soon followed by another Top 40 hit single, 'Reason To Live'. *Hot In The Shade* succeeded their third compilation album, *Smashes, Thrashes And Hits*, and included another US hit single, 'Forever', which reached number 8 in February 1990. Work on a new Kiss album with producer Bob Ezrin was delayed following Eric Carr's illness due to complications from cancer. He died on 24 November 1991, in New York, at the age of 41. Despite this setback, Kiss contributed a hit cover version of Argent's classic 'God Gave Rock 'N' Roll To You II' (UK number 4, January 1992) to the soundtrack of the film *Bill And Ted's Bogus Journey*, and brought in replacement drummer Eric Singer (ex-Black Sabbath; Badlands). The album *Revenge* also provided them with their highest charting US album (number 4), and their first Top 10 release since *Dynasty* reached number 9 in 1979. The *Kiss My Ass* tribute album was released in 1994, with contributions from Lenny Kravitz, Stevie Wonder, Garth Brooks, Lemonheads, Faith No More, Dinosaur Jr, Rage Against The Machine and others. The interest in *Kiss My Ass* led to a historic reunion for *MTV Unplugged*. A stable unit with Bruce Kulick (guitar) and Eric Singer (drums), together with Simmons and Stanley, appeared to be on the cards, but Frehley and Criss returned for a reunion tour. So successful was the tour that Kulick and Singer were naturally somewhat annoyed and both quit. Their irritation was further exacerbated by the fact that a new studio album, *Carnival Of Souls*, featured both of them. In 1997 Vincent sued the band, alleging that they owed him royalties. A year later, *Psycho Circus* marked the return of the original line-up to the studio. With a history spanning three decades, Kiss's impact on the consciousness of a generation of music fans, particularly in the USA, remains enormous.

● ALBUMS: *Kiss* (Casablanca 1974)★★★, *Hotter Than Hell* (Casablanca 1974)★★, *Dressed To Kill* (Casablanca 1975)★★★, *Alive!* (Casablanca 1975)★★★, *Destroyer* (Casablanca 1976)★★★★, *Rock And Roll Over* (Casablanca 1976)★★, *Love Gun* (Casablanca 1977)★★★, *Alive II* (Casablanca 1977)★★★, *Dynasty* (Casablanca 1979)★★, *Unmasked* (Casablanca 1980)★★, *Music From The Elder* (Casablanca 1981)★★, *Creatures Of The Night* (Casablanca 1982)★★, *Lick It Up* (Vertigo 1983)★★, *Animalize* (Vertigo 1984)★★, *Asylum* (Vertigo 1985)★★, *Crazy Nights* (Vertigo 1987)★★★, *Hot In The Shade* (Vertigo 1989)★★, *Revenge* (Mercury 1992)★★★, *Alive III* (Mercury 1993)★★, *MTV Unplugged* (Mercury 1996)★★★, *Carnival Of Souls The Final Sessions* (Mercury 1997)★★, *Psycho Circus* (Mercury 1998)★★.

● COMPILATIONS: *The Originals* 3-LP set (Casablanca 1976)★★★, *Originals II* 3-LP set (Casablanca 1978)★★★, *Double Platinum* (Casablanca 1978)★★★, *Killers* (Casablanca 1982)★★★, *Smashes, Thrashes And Hits* (Vertigo 1988)★★★, *Revenge* (Mercury 1992)★★, *You Wanted The Best, You Got The Best* (Mercury 1996)★★★★, *Greatest Kiss* (Mercury 1996)★★★.

● VIDEOS: *Kiss Animalize Live - Uncensored* (Embassy Home Video 1984), *The Phantom Of The Park* (IVS 1987), *Kiss Exposed* (PolyGram Music Video 1987), *Crazy, Crazy Nights* (Channel 5 1988), *Age Of Chance* (Virgin Vision 1988), *X-Treme Close Up* (1992), *Konfidential* (1993), *Kiss My A*** (PolyGram Music Video 1994), *Unplugged* (PolyGram Music Video 1996).

● FURTHER READING: *Kiss*, Robert Duncan. *Still On Fire*, Dave Thomas. *Kiss: The Greatest Rock Show On Earth*, John Swenson. *Kiss: The Real Story Authorized*, Peggy Tomarkin. *Kiss Live*, Mick St. Michael. *Black Diamond: The Unauthorised Biography Of Kiss*, Dale Sherman. *Kiss And Sell: The Making Of A Supergroup*, CK Lendt.

Kiss Of The Gypsy

This melodic hard-rock quintet (formerly known as Fantasia) was formed in Blackpool, Lancashire, England, in 1990, by Tony Mitchell (vocals, guitar) and Martin Talbot (bass). With the addition of Darren Rice (guitar), George Williams (keyboards) and Scott Elliot (drums), they signed to Atlantic the following year. The band's music is blues-rock-based, with a sense of energetic songwriting not dissimilar to that of Bad Company or Whitesnake. Following successful support slots to Winger, Magnum and Great White, the band released their self-titled debut album on the WEA/East West label in 1992, which saw them widely hailed as one of the most promising commercial British groups to emerge since Def Leppard.

● ALBUMS: *Kiss Of The Gypsy* (East West 1992)★★★.

Kix

This US group was formed by Donnie Purnell (bass) and Ronnie Younkins (guitar) in 1980. After experimenting with a number of line-ups, Steve Whiteman (vocals), Brian Forsythe (guitar) and Jimmy Chalfant (drums) were drafted in on a permanent basis. Their style was typical of America's east coast, a brash amalgam of influences that included Mötley Crüe, AC/DC and Kiss, while their live reputation within their native West Virginia was second to none. Securing a contract with Atlantic Records in 1981, their first two albums were rather derivative and poorly promoted. *Midnight Dynamite*, however, produced by Beau Hill (who had previously worked with Ratt), attracted some attention, and the band were given the support slot on Aerosmith's 1985 USA tour. *Blow My Fuse* and *Hot Wire* received a good reception on both sides of the Atlantic, with the band maturing as songwriters and starting to develop an identity of their own.

● ALBUMS: *Atomic Bomb* (Atlantic 1981)★★, *Cool Kids* (Atlantic 1983)★★, *Midnight Dynamite* (Atlantic 1985)★★★, *Blow My Fuse* (Atlantic 1988)★★★★, *Hot Wire* (Atlantic 1991)★★★.

KORN

Hardcore rock band Korn formed in the early 90s in Bakersfield, California, USA, and toured widely, playing over 200 shows before releasing their self-titled debut album for EastWest Records in 1994. Subsequently based in Huntington Beach in California, the quintet, whose members are Jonathan Davis (vocals), Reggie Fieldy Arvizu (bass), James Munky Shaffer (guitar), Brian Welch (guitar, vocals) and David Silveria (drums), released their first single, 'Blind', which was widely shown on late-night MTV shows. The album gave them their commercial breakthrough and saw them cited in *Billboard* magazine as 'the first debut hardcore rock act to top the Heatseekers chart and one of the first to crack the upper half of the *Billboard* 200 in the last two years.' Much of this success arose from the reputation garnered by their live work, which was bolstered by tours alongside House Of Pain, Biohazard, 311, Sick Of It All, Danzig, Marilyn Manson and Megadeth. A second single, 'Shoots And Ladders', featured Davis playing the bagpipes. The Ross Robinson-produced *Life Is Peachy* continued the anger, although further breakthrough success was limited by the explicit lyrics liberally laced throughout. In late 1997 Korn established their own label, Elementree. They also made the news by serving a cease-and-desist order to the assistant principal of a Michigan high school, who had suspended a student for wearing a T-shirt featuring the band's name. The eagerly anticipated *Follow The Leader* was recorded with help from Guns N'Roses collaborator, Steve Thompson. The album was a commercial and critical success, with highlights including 'It's On' and first single 'Got The Life'.

● ALBUMS: *Korn* (Immortal 1995)★★★★, *Life Is Peachy* (Epic 1996)★★★, *Follow The Leader* (Epic 1998)★★★★.

● VIDEOS: *Who Then Now?* (SMV 1997).

KOSSOFF, PAUL

b. 14 September 1950, Hampstead, London, England, d. 19 March 1976. The son of English actor David Kossoff, Paul was an inventive, impassioned guitar player who was initially a member of Black Cat Bones, a late 60s blues band that included drummer Simon Kirke. In 1968, both musicians became founder-members of Free and later worked together in Kossoff, Kirke, Tetsu And Rabbit, a spin-off project that completed a lone album in 1971 during a hiatus in the parent group's career. Free was reactivated in 1972, but Kossoff's tenure during this second phase was blighted by recurring drug and health problems. Absent on portions of several tours, Kossoff finally left the group to pursue a solo career. *Back Street Crawler* contained several excellent performances, notably 'Molten Gold', but it was two years before the guitarist was well enough to resume live work. He accompanied John Martyn on a 1975 tour before assembling a new group, also entitled Back Street Crawler. The quintet completed one album but projected concerts were cancelled when Kossoff suffered a near-fatal heart attack. Specialists forbade an immediate return, but plans were hatched for a series of concerts the following year. However, in March 1976, Paul Kossoff died in his sleep during a flight from Los Angeles to New York. On Jim Capaldi's 1975 solo album, *Short Cut Draw Blood*, two songs were reputedly written in tribute to Kossoff: 'Seagull' and 'Boy With A Problem'; Kossoff had played lead guitar on the latter.

● ALBUMS: *Back Street Crawler* (Island 1973)★★★, *Live In Croydon, June 15th 1975* (Repertoire 1995)★★.

● COMPILATIONS: *Koss* (DJM 1977)★★★, *The Hunter* (Street Tunes 1983)★★, *Leaves In The Wind* (Street Tunes 1983)★★, *Blue Soul* (Island 1986)★★★, *The Collection* (Hit Label 1995)★★★, *Stone Free* (Carlton Sounds 1997)★★★.

KOTZEN, RICHIE

This highly gifted, US-born new-age rock guitar god is very much in the Joe Satriani mould. By the time Kotzen had reached his seventh birthday, he had moved from piano to guitar lessons, and was playing live with his own band, Arthur's Museum, when he entered his teens. Taken under the wing of Mike Varney, he was introduced to bassist Stuart Hamm and ex-Journey drummer Steve Smith, with whom he recorded a solo instrumental album. This showcased Kotzen's inherent ability and feel for the electric guitar, but also highlighted the limitations of rock music without vocals. Realizing this, he formed Fever Dream, a power trio comprising Danny Thompson (bass), Atma Anur (drums) and himself on guitar and vocals. Although the guitar breaks were excellent, there was a paucity of hooks and a scarcity of real tunes. Kotzen went on to replace C.C. Deville in Poison's ranks in 1991.

● ALBUMS: *Richie Kotzen* (Roadruner 1989)★★★, *Fever Dream* (Roadrunner 1990)★★★, *Electric Joy* (Roadrunner 1993)★★.

KRAMER, WAYNE

b. *c.*1949, USA. The rise of Epitaph Records in the 90s was built largely on the success of bands such as the Offspring and Rancid, yet the label also signed a solo artist whose early involvement in Detroit's MC5 had laid the foundations for the whole punk movement. The MC5 played their final gig on 31 December 1972, Kramer subsequently forming Gang War. In the late 80s he began work on an off-Broadway musical, *The Last Words Of Dutch Schultz*, before performing with former members of MC5 in 1992 at a tribute to their recently departed vocalist, Rob Tyner. At the same he recorded his first solo album, *Wayne Kramer's Deathtongue*. However, it was only when he signed with Epitaph that his career once again hit an upswing. Brett Gurevitz, head of Epitaph, told *Music Week* how he managed to recruit Kramer. 'One day the phone rang and a voice said, "This is Wayne Kramer from the MC5, I've got a new record, will you put it out?"' The album concerned, *The Hard Stuff*, became a major critical hit both in Europe and the USA. A follow-up collection, *Dangerous Madness*, saw Kramer indulging further in the loose, raucous guitar technique copied by so many. However, it also included a series of reflective, considered lyrics, especially the sanguine 'God's Worst Nightmare'. *Citizen Wayne* featured more involvement from producer Don Was, but was still an effective and powerful hard rock record.

● ALBUMS: *Wayne Kramer's Deathtongue* (1992)★★, *The Hard Stuff* (Epitaph 1995)★★★, *Dangerous Madness* (Epitaph 1996)★★★, *Citizen Wayne* (Epitaph 1997)★★★.

KRAVITZ, LENNY

b. 26 May 1964, New York, USA. Kravitz's family ties - his Jewish father was a top television producer; his Bahamian mother an actress - suggested a future in showbusiness. As a teenager he attended the Beverly Hills High School where his contemporaries included Slash, later of Guns N' Roses, and Maria McKee of Lone Justice. Kravitz's interest in music flourished in 1987 with the completion of the first of several demos which concluded with an early version of *Let Love Rule*. These recordings engendered a contract with Virgin America, but the company was initially wary of Kravitz's insistence that the finished product should only feature 'real' instruments - guitar, bass, keyboards and drums - rather than digital and computerized passages. Although denigrated in some quarters as merely retrogressive, notably in its indebtedness to Jimi Hendrix, *Let Love Rule* proved highly popular. Kravitz then gained greater success when Madonna recorded 'Justify My Love', a new, rap-influenced composition quite unlike his previous work. In 1991, the artist continued his unconventional path by writing a new arrangement to John Lennon's 'Give Peace A Chance' as a comment on the impending Gulf War. The resultant recording, credited to the Peace Choir, featured several contemporaries, including Yoko Ono and Sean Lennon. The latter also appeared on *Mama Said*, wherein Kravitz's flirtation with 60s and early 70s rock was even more apparent. The set spawned the hit 'It Ain't Over 'Til It's Over'. *Circus* was a stripped-down version of his overall sound and one that displayed his talent as a writer of more contemporary songs, rather than the 60s hybrid flavour of his past work. The belated follow-up, *5*, saw Kravitz embracing digital recording and attempting a more relaxed fusion of soul and hip-hop styles.

● ALBUMS: *Let Love Rule* (Virgin 1989)★★★, *Mama Said* (Virgin 1991)★★★, *Are You Gonna Go My Way?* (Virgin 1993)★★★, *Circus* (Virgin 1995)★★, *5* (Virgin 1998)★★★.

● VIDEOS: *Alive From Planet Earth* (1994)★★★.

KREATOR

Formed in Essen, Germany, in 1984, originally under the name Tormentor, this heavy metal band originally comprised Mille Petroza (guitar, vocals), Rob (bass) and Ventor (drums). Their vicious thrash style was inspired by the filth and industrial pollution problem that Essen, on the River Ruhr, was experiencing. After changing their name to

Kreator, they signed with the German-based Noise Records label, and their debut album, *Endless Pain*, appeared in 1985. Despite roughshod production, it was eagerly purchased by fans of the then fast-growing thrash metal scene. After *Pleasure To Kill*, Kreator grew to become one of the most popular bands of the genre, especially in Europe. Lyrically, they have always dealt with the dark side of life, a theme encapsulated in their slogan, 'Flag Of Hate'. Only in the 90s did they even slightly waver from their established musical path, endearing them to fans who have helped to maintain their place in the crowded and highly competitive field of thrash and death metal. After employing a number of second guitarists, they eventually settled on Frank 'Blackfire' Gosdzik, once with fellow German thrash metallers Sodom. Together with Petrozza, Andreas Herz (bass) and Jürgen 'Jüille' Reil (drums), they toured South America supported by Sick Of It All in 1994. However, by the following year when they signed a new contract with Gun Records, Herz had been replaced by Christian Giesler and Reil by Joe Canglosi (ex-Whiplash). A new album, *Cause For Conflict*, was released in 1995.

● ALBUMS: *Endless Pain* (Noise 1985)★★, *Pleasure To Kill* (Noise 1986)★★★★, *Terrible Certainty* (Noise 1988)★★★, *Out Of The Dark Into The Light* (Noise 1989)★★★, *Extreme Aggression* (Noise 1989)★★★, *Coma Of Souls* (Noise 1990)★★★, *Renewal* (Noise 1992)★★★, *Cause For Conflict* (Gun 1995)★★, *Outcast* (Gun 1997)★★★.

KROKUS

Formed in Soluthurn, Switzerland, Krokus appeared in 1974 playing symphonic rock similar to Yes, Genesis and Emerson, Lake And Palmer. After four years and two rather lacklustre albums, they switched to a hard rock style and dropped the frills in favour of a back-to-basics approach in the mode of AC/DC. The group originally comprised Chris Von Rohr (vocals), Fernando Von Arb (guitar), Jurg Naegeli (bass), Tommy Keiser (guitar) and Freddy Steady (drums). The songs were formulaic numbers based on simple riffs and predictable choruses that were chanted repeatedly. With Von Rohr's voice lacking the necessary vocal range, he stepped down to became the bass player in favour of new arrival 'Maltezer' Marc (b. Marc Storace, Malta; ex-Tea). Naegeli occasionally played keyboards and subsequently took over the technical side of the band. *Metal Rendez-vous* was the turning point in the band's career; released in 1980, it was heavier than anything they had done before and coincided with the resurgence of heavy metal in Britain. They played the Reading Festival in 1980 and were well received, and their next two albums continued with an aggressive approach, though they streamlined their sound to make it more radio-friendly. *Hardware* and *One Vice At A Time* both reached the UK album charts, at numbers 44 and 28, respectively. Before *Headhunter* materialized, a series of personnel changes took place. The most important of these was the replacement of Keiser with ex-roadie Mark Kohler (guitar), while Steve Pace stepped in on drums. Keiser subsequently returned to replace Rohr. Produced by Tom Allom, *Headhunter*'s high-speed, heavy-duty approach propelled it to number 25 in the *Billboard* album charts. Further line-up changes (the temporary addition of ex-Crown guitarist Patrick Mason and the exit, then return of Pace) delayed the release of *The Blitz*, an erratic album that reached number 31 on the US chart mainly on the strength of its predecessor. Since 1985 there has been a continuing downward trend in the band's fortunes, with their personnel in a constant state of flux (Keiser committed suicide in 1986 and guitarist Mandy Meyer joined). Their music has progressed little during the last decade and still relies heavily on the legacy of AC/DC and the Scorpions. In 1995 the band were touring with a line-up of Storace (vocals), Fernando Von Arb (bass), Maurer (guitar), Kohler (guitar) and Steady (drums), and recording sessions followed.

● ALBUMS: *Krokus* (Schmontz 1975)★★, *To You All* (Schmontz 1977)★★, *Painkiller* (Mercury 1978)★★, *Pay It In Metal* (Mercury 1979)★★, *Metal Rendez-vous* (Ariola 1980)★★★, *Hardware* (Ariola 1981)★★★, *One Vice At A Time* (Ariola 1982)★★★, *Headhunter* (Arista 1983)★★★, *The Blitz* (Arista 1984)★★, *Change Of Address* (Arista 1985)★★, *Alive And Screamin'* (Arista 1986)★★, *Heart Attack* (MCA 1987)★★, *Stampede* (Ariola 1990)★★.

KYUSS

Formed in Palm Springs, California, USA, this quartet of schoolfriends mixed their differing tastes to provide a blues-based retro rock sound of stunning heaviness charged with a spiritual air. Vocalist John Garcia's mainstream tastes and bassist Nick Oliveri's metal background blended with guitarist Josh Homme and drummer Brant Bjork's penchant for Black Flag, the Misfits and the Ramones, to produce music with the groove of classic Black Sabbath but with a modern intensity and their own definite identity. Although their early efforts were unpopular in the hardcore-orientated late 80s, the band stuck doggedly with their music and were accepted as tastes broadened in the post-grunge 90s. *Wretch* was a decent debut, but the band found a kindred spirit in Master Of Reality leader Chris Goss, who produced *Blues For The Red Sun*. On the latter, the looser atmosphere and mature material were given extra ambience as Goss captured the band's live power in the studio. Kyuss were suddenly hot property, touring the USA with Danzig and Faith No More, and in Australia with Metallica, although Oliveri departed to be replaced by Scott Reeder from old touring partners the Obsessed. When their label collapsed, distributors Elektra offered Kyuss a contract, and the band collaborated with Goss again on the pounding sludge-rock of *Sky Valley*, with new drummer Alfredo Hernandez replacing the tour-weary Bjork. Goss was again producer for the group's fourth album, which further enhanced their reputation, although the band decided to call it a day later that year. Garcia formed Slo-Burn and Homme formed Gamma Ray. Bjork later joined Fu Manchu in 1996. Homme released a solo album at the end of 1997, *Instrumental Driving Music For Felons*, amid rumours of a Kyuss reunion. *Queens Of The Stone Age* was a collection of their last studio recordings.

● ALBUMS: *Wretch* (Dali-Chameleon 1991)★★★, *Blues For The Red Sun* (Dali-Chameleon 1992)★★★★, *Sky Valley* (Elektra 1994)★★★, *...And The Circus Leaves Town* (Elektra 1995)★★★, *Queens Of The Stone Age* (Man's Ruin 1998)★★.

L.A. Guns

This US group was formed by ex-Guns N'Roses guitarist Tracii Guns and Paul Black in Los Angeles in 1987, though the latter was soon replaced by ex-Girl/Bernie Torme vocalist Phil Lewis. Working on material that was a hybrid of metal, glam and blues-based rock 'n' roll, they signed with PolyGram Records in the USA the following year. With the addition of Mick Cripps (guitar, ex-Faster Pussycat), Kelly Nickels (bass, ex-Faster Pussycat) and Steve Riley (drums, ex-W.A.S.P.) the line-up was complete. However, with Riley arriving too late to appear on their self-titled debut, the group used the services of Nickey Alexander (formerly 'Nicky Beat' of punk legends the Weirdos). *Cocked And Loaded* was a marked improvement on its predecessor; the band had matured as songwriters and Lewis's vocals were stronger and more convincing. *Hollywood Vampires* saw them diversifying musically, but retaining the essential energy and rough edges for which they had become renowned. Touring as support to Skid Row in Europe, it at last looked as though Guns would no longer have to look longingly at the phenomenal success his former band had achieved in his absence. However, it was not to be. As the group disintegrated, Guns went on to form a new outfit, Killing Machine, while Lewis formed Filthy Lucre. However, L.A. Guns were soon re-formed when both these bands failed. *Vicious Circle* continued the vampiric metaphors of the group's previous album with the track 'Crystal Eyes', a song also included on *Hollywood Vampires*. Greeted as a strong return from a group still held in high regard, it was arguably the best recorded work to date by either Guns or Lewis.

● ALBUMS: *L.A. Guns* (PolyGram 1988)★★, *Cocked And Loaded* (PolyGram 1989)★★★, *Hollywood Vampires* (PolyGram 1991)★★★, *Vicious Circle* (PolyGram 1994)★★★.

● VIDEOS: *One More Reason* (1989), *Love, Peace & Geese* (1990).

L7

Guitarist/vocalists Donita Sparks (b. 8 April 1963, Chicago, Illinois, USA) and Suzi Gardner (b. 1 August 1960, Sacramento, California, USA) formed L7 in the mid-80s, linking with Jennifer Finch (b. 5 August 1966, Los Angeles, California, USA; bass, vocals) and trying several drummers, finally finding Dee Plakas (b. 9 November 1960, Chicago, Illinois, USA) after domestic touring to promote *L7*, supporting Bad Religion (drummer on their debut album was Roy Kolltsky). The band's raw punk-metal caught the interest of Sup Pop Records, who released *Smell The Magic*, a raucous, grunge-flavoured blast that further enhanced the band's growing underground reputation. *Bricks Are Heavy* brought major success, with the surprisingly poppy 'Pretend We're Dead' becoming a major hit on both sides of the Atlantic. Subsequently, the band became darlings of the music press with their multicoloured hair and shock-tactic humour - at 1992's Reading Festival, Sparks retaliated against missile throwers by removing her tampon on stage and throwing it into the crowd, and later dropped her shorts during a live television performance on *The Word* - but the band's serious side led them to form Rock For Choice, a pro-abortion women's rights organization that has gathered supporters from Pearl Jam to Corrosion Of Conformity for fund-raising concerts. L7 went on to appear as a band named Camel Lips in a John Waters film, *Serial Mom*, before *Hungry For Stink* picked up where *Bricks Are Heavy* left off, blending serious and humorous lyrics against a still-thunderous musical backdrop. Jennifer Finch departed in the summer of 1996 and formed Lyme. Her replacement was Gail Greenwood from Belly, who provided greater musical diversity on 1997's *The Beauty Process: Triple Platinum*.

● ALBUMS: *L7* (Epitaph 1988)★★★, *Smell The Magic* mini-album (Sup Pop 1990)★★★, *Bricks Are Heavy* (Slash/London 1992)★★★★, *Hungry For Stink* (Slash/London 1994)★★★, *The Beauty Process: Triple Platinum* (Slash/Reprise 1997)★★★.

Laibach

With origins in Trbovlje, Slovenia, Northern Yugoslavia, Laibach's powerful imagery has long been confused with the fascist icons they have tried to deconstruct. They were formed in 1980 by members of the Yugoslavian army, including Tomaz Hostnik (b. 1961, d. 1982; vocals) and Miran Mohar. They acted as the musical arm of the political art movement NSK (Neue Slowenische Kunst - New Slovian Art), conceived in 1980 and formulated in 1984. Laibach form one of three sections of the movement, the others being Irwin (painters) and Scipion Nasice (theatre). Laibach themselves have a constantly fluctuating line-up. However, the nucleus can be identified as Milan Frez, Dejan Knez, Ervin Markosek and Ivan Novak, the latter acting as spokesman after Hostnik had committed suicide. In 1982 they toured outside of their native country for the first time, releasing their first UK single, 'Boji', in 1984. In the mid-80s they recorded Teutonic reworkings of rock classics such as 'Sympathy For The Devil', and appeared on *The South Bank Show*. The 1987 release 'Life Is Life', later covered by Opus, had the unfortunate effect of becoming an anthem for neo-Nazis. Other notable pursuits included the commissioning of a soundtrack to *Macbeth* performed by the German theatre company Deutsches Schauspielhaus. It was played live during performances. In 1988 the band also covered the Beatles' *Let It Be*, bar the title track, in its entirety, in Wagnerian military style. They also released the German-only single '3 Oktober', to celebrate reunification in 1990. Although they have achieved some degree of prominence, any realistic study of Laibach should focus on them as merely one component in a larger and more important artistic movement.

● ALBUMS: *Through Occupied Europe Tour* (Staal 1984)★★, *Laibach* (Skuc 1985)★★★, *Nova Arkopola* (Cherry Red 1985)★★★, *Krst Pod Triglavom-Baptism* (Walter Ulbricht 1986)★★★, *Opus Dei* (Mute 1987)★★★, *Let It Be* (Mute 1988)★★★, *Sympathy For The Devil* mini-album (Mute 1990)★★★, *Macbeth* (Mute 1990)★★★, *Kapital* (Mute 1992)★★★, *Ljubjana Zagreb Beograd* (1993)★★★, *Trans-Slovenia Express* (1994)★★★, *Sarajevo - Occupied Europe NATO Tour 1994-1995* (Mute 1996)★★★, *Jesus Christ Superstars* (Mute 1996)★★★, *MB December 21, 1984* (Mute 1997)★★★.

● COMPILATIONS: *Rekapitulacija 1980 - 1984* (Walter Ulbricht 1985)★★★.

● VIDEOS: *Nato* (Mute 1996).

Last Crack

Last Crack, from Wisconsin, USA, specialized in schizophrenic 'acid-metal', a truly unique aural experience that revelled in the desecration of musical boundaries from thrash to blues, then back through funk, psychedelia and rock 'n' roll. Lead vocalist Buddo Buddo conveyed a mixture of gut-wrenching passion, flamboyance and deranged eccentricity in his caterwauling (his other claim to fame being his penchant for posing naked at photo sessions). The backbeat was equally unpredictable, with guitarists Pablo Schuter and Don Bakken switching and blending styles with consummate ease. Phil Buerstate (drums) and Todd Winger (bass) provided the necessary power in the rhythm section. The latter was replaced by Dave Truehardt in 1990.

● ALBUMS: *Sinister Funkhouse #17* (Roadracer 1989)★★★, *Burning Time* (Roadrunner 1991)★★★.

LAWNMOWER DETH

Lawnmower Deth were a thrash metal parody band from the north of England. Founded in 1987, the combined forces of Qualcast Mutilator (vocals), Mr Flymo (drums), Concorde Faceripper (guitars), Mightymo Destructimo (bass) and Scitzophrenic Sprintmaster (guitar) proved a timely antidote to the more ridiculous excesses of banal bloodlust and po-faced pretension in the thrash and death metal genres. With songs including 'Satan's Trampoline' and 'Can I Cultivate Your Groinal Garden', Lawnmower Deth were characterized by their schoolboy sense of humour. This same infantile sense of fun, stretched to their live shows, with 'gimmicks' such as throwing around buckets of baked beans or dressing in third-rate Robin Hood costumes (a direct satire of the pagan Medieval thrash band Skyclad). Eventually, the joke began to lose its edge, and Lawnmower Deth expanded musically by including snatches of ska and funk in their repertoire, but wound up the band over Christmas 1994.

● ALBUMS: *Quack Em All* (Earache 1988)★★★, *Ooh Crikey Its...* (Earache 1990)★★★, *Return of The Fabulous Metal Bozo Clowns* (Earache 1992)★★, *Billy* (Earache 1994)★★★.

LE GRIFFE

Despite using the French moniker Le Griffe (meaning 'The Claw'), this band was formed in Stoke-on-Trent, Staffordshire, England, in 1980. Le Griffe's original line-up consisted of Chris Hatton (vocals, guitar), Paul Wood (guitar), Tim Blackwood (guitar), Kevin Collier (bass) and Martin Allen (drums). Quickly becoming popular on their local live circuit, the band signed to the (now defunct) Bullet Records label, who released a three-track EP entitled *Fast Bikes* in 1981. The EP was a worthy debut, featuring melodic rockers reminiscent of early Def Leppard coupled with 12-bar Status Quo-style boogie. The band gigged extensively throughout the UK and released a mini-album, *Breaking Strain,* again on the Bullet Records label, in 1984. At the time of its release guitarist Tim Blackwood left the band to be replaced by Amos Sanfillipo, but the band dissolved early in 1985. Collier went on to join Rogue Male.

● ALBUMS: *Breaking Strain* mini-album (Bullet 1984)★★.

LEATHERWOLF

The origins of this Californian quintet date back to 1983 when Michael Olivieri (vocals, guitar), Geoff Gayer (guitar), Carey Howe (guitar), Matt Hurich (bass) and Dean Roberts (drums) were at high school together. Influenced by a range of styles, from hard rock to jazz, they recorded a self-titled, five-track mini-album that attracted the attention of Island Records. Matt Hurich was replaced by Paul Carman before they left to record their second album in the Bahamas, under the guidance of REO Speedwagon producer Kevin Beamish. *Street Ready* avoided the pitfalls of their previous release, and saw the band developing their own identity, as they gingerly ventured into the pop-metal crossover market. Beamish achieved a harder and more powerful sound this time, but with an added dimension of accessibility and the potential for commercial success. Ultimately, however, this remained unrealized, with Leatherwolf disintegrating before the start of the new decade.

● ALBUMS: *Leatherwolf I* (Tropical 1986)★★, *Leatherwolf II* (Island 1987)★★, *Street Ready* (Island 1989)★★★.

LED ZEPPELIN

This pivotal quartet was formed in October 1968 by British guitarist Jimmy Page (b. James Patrick Page, 9 January 1944, Heston, Middlesex, England) following the demise of his former band, the Yardbirds. John Paul Jones (b. John Baldwin, 3 June 1946, Sidcup, Kent, England; bass, keyboards), a respected arranger and session musician, replaced original member Chris Dreja, but hopes to incorporate vocalist Terry Reid floundered on a contractual impasse. The singer unselfishly recommended Robert Plant (b. 20 August 1948, West Bromwich, West Midlands, England), then frontman of struggling Midlands act Hobbstweedle, who in turn introduced drummer John Bonham (b. 31 May 1948, Birmingham, England, d. 25 September 1980), when first choice B.J. Wilson opted to remain with Procol Harum. The quartet gelled immediately and having completed outstanding commitments under the name 'New Yardbirds', became Led Zeppelin following a quip by the Who's Keith Moon, who, when assessing their prospects, remarked that they would probably 'go down like a lead Zeppelin'. Armed with a prestigious contract with Atlantic Records, the group toured the USA supporting Vanilla Fudge prior to the release of their explosive debut, *Led Zeppelin*, which included several exceptional original songs, including 'Good Times, Bad Times', 'Communication Breakdown', 'Dazed And Confused' - a hangover from the Yardbirds' era - and skilled interpretations of R&B standards 'How Many More Times?' and 'You Shook Me'. The set vied with Jeff Beck's *Truth* as the definitive statement of English heavy blues/rock, but Page's meticulous production showed a greater grasp of basic pop dynamics, resulting in a clarity redolent of 50s rock 'n' roll. His staggering dexterity was matched by Plant's expressive, beseeching voice, a combination that flourished on *Led Zeppelin II*. The group was already a headline act, drawing sell-out crowds across the USA, when this propulsive collection confirmed an almost peerless position. The introductory track, 'Whole Lotta Love', a thinly veiled rewrite of Willie Dixon's 'You Need Love', has since become a classic, while 'Livin' Lovin' Maid' and 'Moby Dick', Bonham's exhibition piece, were a staple part of the quartet's early repertoire. Elsewhere, 'Thank You' and 'What Is And What Should Never Be' revealed a greater subtlety, a factor emphasized more fully on *Led Zeppelin III*. Preparation for this set had been undertaken at Bron-Y-Aur cottage in Snowdonia (immortalized in 'Bron-Y-Aur Stomp'), and a resultant pastoral atmosphere permeated the acoustic-based selections 'That's The Way' and 'Tangerine'. 'The Immigrant Song' and 'Gallow's Pole' reasserted the group's traditional fire and the album's release confirmed Led Zeppelin's position as one of the world's leading attractions. In concert, Plant's sexuality and Adonis-like persona provided the perfect foil to Page's more mercurial character, yet both individuals took full command of the stage, the guitarist's versatility matched by his singer's unfettered roar.

Confirmation of the group's ever-burgeoning strengths appeared on *Led Zeppelin IV*, also known as 'Four Symbols', the 'Runes Album' or 'Zoso', in deference to the fact that the set bore no official title. It included the anthemic 'Stairway To Heaven', a group *tour de force*. Arguably the definitive heavy-rock song, it continues to win polls, and the memorable introduction remains every guitar novice's first hurdle. The approbation granted this ambitious piece initially obscured other tracks, but the energetic 'When The Levee Breaks' is now also lauded as a masterpiece, particularly for Bonham's drumming. 'Black Dog' and 'Rock 'N' Roll' saw Zeppelin at their immediate best, while 'The Battle Of Evermore' was marked by a vocal contribution from Sandy Denny. *IV* was certified as having sold 16 million copies in the USA by March 1996. However, the effusive praise this album generated was notably more muted for *Houses Of The Holy*. Critics queried its musically diverse selection - the set embraced folk ballads, reggae and soul - yet when the accustomed power was unleashed, notably on 'No Quarter', the effect was inspiring. A concurrent US tour broke all previous attendance records, the proceeds from which helped to finance an in-concert film, issued in 1976 as *The Song Remains The Same*, and the formation of the group's own record label, Swan Song. Bad Company, the Pretty Things and Maggie Bell were also signed to the company, which served to provide Led Zeppelin with total creative freedom. *Physical Graffiti*, a double set, gave full rein to the quartet's diverse interests, with material ranging from compulsive hard rock ('Custard Pie' and 'Sick Again') to pseudo-mystical experimentation ('Kashmir'). The irrepressible 'Trampled Underfoot' joined an ever-growing lexicon of peerless performances, while 'In My Time Of Dying' showed an undiminished grasp of progressive blues. Sell-out appearances in the UK followed the release, but rehearsals for a projected world tour were abandoned in August 1975 when Plant sustained multiple injuries in a car crash. A new album was prepared during his period of convalescence, although problems over artwork delayed its release. Advance orders alone assured *Presence* platinum status, yet the set was regarded as a disappointment and UK sales were noticeably weaker. The 10-minute maelstrom 'Achilles Last Stand' was indeed a remarkable performance, but the remaining tracks were competent rather than fiery and lacked the accustomed sense of grandeur. In 1977 Led Zeppelin began its rescheduled US tour, but on 26 July news reached Robert Plant that his six-year-old son, Karac, had died of a viral infection. The remaining dates were cancelled amid speculation that the group would break up.

They remained largely inactive for over a year, but late in 1978 they flew to Abba's Polar recording complex in Stockholm. Although lacking the definition of earlier work, *In Through The Out Door* was a strong collection on which John Paul Jones emerged as the unifying factor. Two concerts at Britain's Knebworth Festival were the prelude to a short European tour on which the group unveiled a stripped-down act, inspired, in part, by the punk explosion. Rehearsals were then undertaken for another US tour, but in September 1980, Bonham was found dead following a lengthy drinking bout. On 4 December, Swansong announced that the group had officially retired, although a collection of archive material, *Coda*, was subsequently issued. Jones later became a successful producer, notably with the Mission, while Plant embarked on a highly successful solo career, launched with *Pictures At Eleven*. Page scored the film *Death Wish 2* and, after a brief reunion with Plant and the Honeydrippers project in 1984, he inaugurated the short-lived Firm with Paul Rogers. He then formed the Jimmy Page Band with John Bonham's son, Jason, who in turn drummed with Led Zeppelin on their appearance at Atlantic's 25th Anniversary Concert in 1988. Despite renewed interest in the group's career, particularly in the wake of the retrospective *Remasters*, entreaties to make this a permanent reunion were resisted. However, in 1994 Page and Plant went two-thirds of the way to a reformation with their ironically titled *Unledded* project, though John Paul Jones was conspicuous by his absence (for want of an invitation). The duo cemented the relationship with an album of new Page And Plant material in 1998. Although their commercial success is unquestionable, Led Zeppelin are now rightly recognized as one of the most influential bands of the rock era and their catalogue continues to provide inspiration to successive generations of musicians.

● ALBUMS: *Led Zeppelin* (Atlantic 1969)★★★★, *Led Zeppelin II* (Atlantic 1969)★★★★, *Led Zeppelin III* (Atlantic 1970)★★★★, *Led Zeppelin IV* (Atlantic 1971)★★★★★, *Houses Of The Holy* (Atlantic 1973)★★★★, *Physical Graffiti* (Swan Song 1975)★★★★, *Presence* (Swan Song 1976)★★★, *The Song Remains The Same* film soundtrack (Swan Song 1976)★★, *In Through The Out Door* (Swan Song 1979)★★★, *Coda* (Swan Song 1982)★★, *BBC Sessions* (Atlantic 1997)★★★★.

● COMPILATIONS: *Led Zeppelin* 4-CD box set (Swan Song 1991)★★★★, *Remasters* (Swan Song 1991)★★★★, *Remasters II* (Swan Song 1993)★★★.

● VIDEOS: *The Song Remains The Same* (Warner Home Video 1986).

● FURTHER READING: *Led Zeppelin*, Michael Gross and Robert Plant. *The Led Zeppelin Biography*, Ritchie Yorke. *Led Zeppelin*, Howard Mylett. *Led Zeppelin: In The Light 1968-1980*, Howard Mylett and Richard Bunton. *Led Zeppelin: A Celebration*, Dave Lewis. *Led Zeppelin In Their Own Words*, Paul Kendall. *Led Zeppelin: A Visual Documentary*, Paul Kendall. *Led Zeppelin: The Book*, Jeremy Burston. *Jimmy Page: Tangents Within A Framework*, Howard Mylett. *Led Zeppelin: The Final Acclaim*, Dave Lewis. *Hammer Of The Gods: The Led Zeppelin Saga*, Stephen Davis. *Illustrated Collector's Guide To Led Zeppelin*, Robert Godwin. *Led Zeppelin: Heaven & Hell*, Charles Cross and Erik Flannigan. *Stairway To Heaven*, Richard Cole with Richard Trubo. *Led Zeppelin: Breaking And Making Records*, Ross Clarke. *Led Zeppelin: The Definitive Biography*, Ritchie Yorke. *On Tour With Led Zeppelin*, Howard Mylett (ed.). *Led Zeppelin*, Chris Welch. *The Complete Guide To The Music Of . . .*, Dave Lewis. *Led Zeppelin Live: An Illustrated Exploration Of Underground Tapes*, Luis Rey. *The Making Of: Led Zeppelin IV*, Robert Godwin. *The Photographer's Led Zeppelin*, Ross Halfin (ed.). *The Led Zeppelin Concert File*, Dave Lewis and Simon Pallett. *Led Zeppelin - Dazed And Confused*, Chris Welch.

LEE, ALVIN

b. 19 December 1944, Nottingham, England. Guitarist Lee began his professional career in the Jaybirds, a beat trio popular both locally and in Hamburg, Germany. In 1966, an expanded line-up took a new name, Ten Years After, and in turn became one of Britain's leading blues/rock attractions with Lee's virtuoso solos its main attraction. His outside aspirations surfaced in 1973 with *On The Road To Freedom*, a collaboration with American Mylon LeFevre, which included support from George Harrison, Steve Winwood and Mick Fleetwood. When Ten Years After disbanded the following year, the guitarist formed Alvin Lee & Co. with Neil Hubbard (guitar), Tim Hinkley (keyboards), Mel Collins (saxophone), Alan Spenner (bass) and Ian Wallace (drums). Having recorded the live *In Flight*, Lee made the first of several changes in personnel, but although he and Hinkley were joined by Andy Pyle (bass, ex-Blodwyn Pig) and Bryson Graham (drums) for *Pump Iron!*, the group struggled to find its niche with the advent of punk. Lee toured Europe fronting Ten Years Later (1978-80) and the Alvin Lee Band (1980-81), before founding a new quartet, known simply as Alvin Lee, with Mick Taylor (guitar, ex-John Mayall; Rolling Stones), Fuzzy Samuels (bass, ex-Crosby, Stills, Nash And Young) and Tom Compton (drums). This promising combination promoted *RX-5*, but later disbanded. In 1989, Lee reconvened the original line-up of Ten Years After to record *About Time*. Lee released *Zoom* in 1992 with Sequel

Records, after finding the major companies were not interested. Although offering nothing new, it was a fresh and well-produced record, and featured George Harrison on backing vocals.

● ALBUMS: with Mylon LeFevre *On The Road To Freedom* (Columbia 1973)★★★, *In Flight* (Columbia 1975)★★★, *Pump Iron!* (Columbia 1975)★★, *Rocket Fuel* (Polydor 1978)★★, *Ride On* (Polydor 1979)★★★, *Free Fall* (Avatar 1980)★★, *RX-5* (Avatar 1981)★★★, *Detroit Diesel* (21 Records 1986)★★★, *Zoom* (Sequel 1992)★★, *Nineteen Ninety Four* (Magnum Music 1994)★★, *I Hear You Rockin'* (Viceroy 1994)★★★, *Going Back Home* (Blind Pig 1994)★★★, *Pure Blues* (Chrysalis 1995)★★★, *Sweetheart Of The Blues* (Delmark 1995)★★★, *Braille Blues Daddy* (Justin Time 1995)★★★.

Legs Diamond

Deriving their name from an infamous 20s gangster, Legs Diamond were formed by Michael Diamond (bass) and Jeff Poole (drums) in San Francisco, California, during 1977. Moving to Los Angeles, they recruited Rick Sanford (vocals), Michael Prince (guitar, keyboards) and Roger Romeo (guitar) to consolidate the line-up. Signed by Mercury Records, their debut release was a classy hard rock album influenced by the traditions of Led Zeppelin and Deep Purple. The songs were well constructed, but the album was let down by a weak production. The follow-up was every bit as strong, with the band alternating between brooding and intense power ballads and unabashed rockers. They toured as support to Ted Nugent, Kiss and Styx, but, to their surprise, were dropped by their label shortly afterwards. They subsequently negotiated a contract with the independent Cream label, releasing *Fire Power* in 1978. This marked a change in style to a more AOR-orientated approach, but it was poorly received. The band members, disillusioned, decided to go their separate ways. Six years later, Rick Sanford resurrected Legs Diamond, and after several personnel changes stabilized the line-up with Romeo and Prince joined by new members Dusty Watson (drums) and Mike Christie (bass). Signing to the independent metal specialists Music For Nations, they have delivered several albums of sophisticated hard rock and captured much of the excitement and promise that was not fulfilled the first time around.

● ALBUMS: *Legs Diamond* (Mercury 1977)★★★★, *A Diamond Is A Hard Rock* (Mercury 1977)★★★★, *Fire Power* (Cream 1978)★★★, *Out On Bail* (Music For Nations 1984)★★★, *Land Of The Gun* (Music For Nations 1986)★★★, *Town Bad Girl* (Music For Nations 1990)★★★, *Captured Live* (Music For Nations 1992)★★, *The Wish* (Music For Nations 1994)★★★.

Leviathan

US hard rock quintet Leviathan comprises Jack Aragon (vocals), Ron Skeen (guitar), John Lutzow (guitar), James Escobedo (bass) and Ty Tameus (drums). Formed in Colorado in 1992, they rose to public prominence in the same year with the release of a self-titled, self-financed five-song debut CD. Afterwards, the group accepted a contract with European label Rock The Nation and recorded its first full-length album, *Deepest Secrets Beneath*. Aided by producer Jim Morris (Savatage, Crimson Glory), the group offered a technically precise demonstration of their songwriting skills and power riffs, with an emphasis on textual, neo-progressive structures.

● ALBUMS: *Deepest Secrets Beneath* (RTN 1994)★★★.

Life Of Agony

Formed in Brooklyn, New York, USA, this quartet was formed in 1989 by Alan Robert Goldstein (b. *c.*1972; bass, vocals) and cousins Keith Caputo (b. *c.*1974; vocals, keyboards) and Joseph Zampella (b. *c.*1972; guitar, vocals), otherwise known as Joey Z. They initially recruited Sal Abruscato on drums, but he was later replaced by Daniel Joseph Richardson (b. *c.*1969). Together, they began Life Of Agony as a simple hardcore act, propelled by flaring nostrils and flying sweat, until diminutive lead singer Caputo had singing lessons from vocal coach Don Lawrence (who had previously worked with Mick Jagger, Sebastian Bach from Skid Row and Jon Bon Jovi). The result was a much greater level of dexterity employed in both songwriting and execution by the band, with Goldstein operating as chief lyricist behind Caputo's powerful delivery. Playing on the road in support of Agnostic Front, Biohazard, Fear Factory, Motörhead, Corrosion Of Conformity and Obituary, their debut set for Roadrunner Records represented a conscious attempt to appeal to fans of more melodic metal (comparisons with Stone Temple Pilots were a feature of the critical response). Their second album was released in October 1995, an 11-track selection produced by Steve Thompson. Following the release of their third album, Life Of Agony abandoned plans for a tour of the UK and Europe in autumn 1997, as vocalist Caputo was 'suffering from mental exhaustion and fatigue'. Caputo later announced that he was leaving the band permanently; he was replaced by former Ugly Kid Joe vocalist Whitfield Crane.

● ALBUMS: *River Runs Red* (Roadrunner 1994)★★★, *Ugly* (Roadrunner 1995)★★★, *Soul Searching Sun* (Roadrunner 1997)★★★.

LIFE, SEX AND DEATH

This trio was formed in Los Angeles, USA, during 1991 by demented vocalist and ex-Chicago street hobo Stanley. LSD, as they are often known, are completed by drummer Brian Michael Horak and ex-Enuff Z'Nuff guitarist Alex Kane. Signing to Warner Brothers, they debuted in July 1992 with *The Silent Majority*, which met with a mixed reception. Influences as diverse as Cheap Trick, Sex Pistols, Beatles and Guns N'Roses manifested themselves clearly, but Stanley's rasping yet inherently melodic vocal style gave the band some identity. LSD were certain to earn a degree of notoriety with their provocative album cover and Stanley's outrageous claim to not having washed for over a year, but their critical reception was hardly gleaming either.

● ALBUMS: *The Silent Majority* (Warners 1992)★★.

LILLIAN AXE

This melodic rock quintet, originally from Michigan, USA, comprised Ron Taylor (vocals), Steve Blaze (guitar), Jon Ster (guitar, keyboards), Rob Stratton (bass) and Danny King (drums). Initially known as Stiff, the band were taken under the wing of Ratt guitarist Robbin Crosby before changing their name to Lillian Axe. Produced by Crosby, their debut was a fine amalgam of infectious rockers and hard-edged pop tunes. *Love And War* was even more impressive, featuring extended atmospheric compositions that were both anthemic and memorable. However, the record sold poorly and MCA Records dropped the band from their roster. In 1990 Danny King and Rob Stratton were replaced by Gene Barnett and Darren DeLatta, respectively, after which the Music For Nations independent became their home during the early 90s.

● ALBUMS: *Lillian Axe* (MCA 1988)★★★, *Love And War* (MCA 1989)★★★★, *Poetic Justice* (Music For Nations 1992)★★★, *Psychoschizophrenia* (Music For Nations 1994)★★★.

LIMELIGHT

This UK heavy metal trio, based in Mansfield, Nottinghamshire, was formed by the Scrimshaw brothers - Glen (guitar, keyboards) and Mike (bass, vocals) - with Pat Coleman occupying the drumstool. Limelight specialized in extended melodic compositions of a progressive nature, featuring complex time changes and individual virtuoso sections (similar to Yes, yet also incorporating the contemporary style of the New Wave Of British Heavy Metal). Their one and only album contained strong material, but was let down by low-budget production and weak vocals. The Scrimshaw brothers returned to the pub rock scene, playing mainly pop-rock cover versions.

● ALBUMS: *Limelight* (Future Earth 1980)★★★, *Limited Limelight* remix/reissue of debut (Avatar 1981)★★★.

LIMP BIZKIT

Led by self-confessed 'freak' Fred Durst (b. North Carolina, USA), the son of a policeman, hard rock/hard electro/hip-hop group Limp Bizkit were formed in the mid-90s in Jacksonville, Florida. Completed by guitarist Wes Boorland, bassist Sam Rivers and drummer John Otto, the band were further augmented in 1996 by the services of DJ Lethal (b. Latvia, and the man who wrote the enduring 'Jump Around' rap anthem) when his former employers House Of Pain ran aground. The connection was made originally when Limp Bizkit supported House Of Pain on their final tour. On his move from hip-hop to an (admittedly eclectic) rock sound, he commented: '80% of the drums in rap come from old rock records. People who talk shit about me being white and doing hip-hop better check who the fuck they're sampling!' The group made its debut with *Three Dollar Bill, Y'all$* in 1997, a record that quickly notched up sales in excess of 250,000 as it was adopted by a new generation of MTV rock fans. Durst continued to court celebrity and self-publicity, making guest appearances on albums by Cold, Korn and Soulfly during this period. He also became an A&R executive for his record label, Flip, fellow Jacksonville band Cold being his first signing.

● ALBUMS: *Three Dollar Bill, Y'all$* (Flip 1997)★★★.

LINDENBERG, UDO

b. 17 May 1946, Gronau, Germany. From the 70's *Lindenberg* to the aiming of his output more directly at the English-speaking market in the late

80s, Lindenberg had sales of over 15 million albums in Germany alone. His early career included a spell as drummer in a local jazz group playing mainstream standards such as 'The Shadow Of Your Smile' that later found a place in his vocal repertoire. 'Lover Man (Where Can You Be)' would be performed with no lyrical alterations to reflect what he called his 'flexible' sexuality. Further aspects of David Bowie's artistic presentation were noted in Lindenberg's multi-media concerts which featured wrestlers, trampolinists and similar non-musical support acts. Another influence was a less famous friend, Jean-Jacques Kravetz, whom Udo assisted willingly on three 70s albums. His interest in national left-wing politics manifested itself in active membership of the Green party and its peace movement - with compositions like 'Father You Should Have Killed Hitler' and 'They Don't Need Another Fuehrer' expressing concern over the renaissance of Nazism. This was balanced with the pride apparent in 1984's 'Germans' which lauded Goethe, Kafka, Mozart, Schumann and other cultural icons. Though this single - buttressed by a promotional visit - made ripples in Britain, a duet with Leata Galloway ('Gesang'), 'Berlin', the lighter 'Special Train To Pankow' (portraying a prominent East German leader 'as a closet rock 'n' roller') and other worthy singles together made less worldwide impact than his characteristically controversial appearance, backed by the Panik Orchestra, as his country's representative on Live Aid. Nevertheless, though not neglecting a still huge home following, releases such as 1987's *All Clear!* (which embraced a revival of Steppenwolf's 'Born To Be Wild') demonstrated a continued attempt to woo a wider audience.

● ALBUMS: *Lindenberg* (1971)★★★★, *Daumen Im Wind* (1972)★★★, *Alles Klar Auf Der Andrea Doria* (1973)★★★, *Ball Pompos* (1974)★★★, *Votan Wahnwitz* (1975)★★★, *Das Sind Die Herrn Vom Andern Stern* (1976)★★★, *Galaxo Gang* (1976)★★★, *Sister King Kong* (1977)★★★, *No Panic* (Decca 1977)★★★, *Lindenbergs Rock Revue* (1978)★★, *Droehnland Symponie* (1978)★★★, *Odyssee* (1979)★★★, *Livehaftig* (1979)★★★, *Der Detektiv* (1979)★★★, *Panische Zeiten* (1980)★★★, *Udopia* (1981)★★★, *Intensivstationen* (1982)★★★, *Keule* (1982)★★★, *Lindstarke 10* (1983)★★★, *Gottewrhammerung* (1984)★★★, *Udo Lindenberg Und Das Panik Orchestra* (Teldec 1985)★★, *Feuerlamnd* (1987)★★★, *All Clear!* aka *Alles Klar!* (Teldec 1987)★★★, *Lieder Statt Briefe* (1988)★★★, *CasaNova* (1988)★★★, *Hermine* (1988)★★★, *Bunte Republik Deutschland* (1989)★★★, *Niemandsland* (1990)★★★, *Ich Will Dich Haben* (1991)★★★, *Gustav* (1991)★★★, *Panik-Panther* (1992)★★.

LION

After the demise of the largely overlooked UK hard rock band Tytan, vocalist Kal Swan left England for Los Angeles to assemble his own band. Formed in 1983, Lion consisted of Swan (vocals), Doug Aldrich (guitar), Jerry Best (bass) and ex-Steeler drummer Mark Edwards. The band quickly produced a self-financed EP, *Powerlove* (only available as a Japanese release), which gained them a strong following in the Far East. Owing to the interest being shown in them, primarily through their contributions to the soundtracks of two films, *The Wraith* and *Transformers*, they attracted the attention of the Scotti Brothers label. This resulted in the band's debut, *Dangerous Attraction*, released in 1987. This proved to be a strong, melodic hard rock effort, on which Swan's soaring vocals came to the fore. However, Scotti Brothers failed adequately to promote the record and album sales suffered. The band signed a new recording agreement with Grand Slam Records after disentangling themselves from their former employers, resulting in *Trouble At Angel City* being released in 1989. Unfortunately, soon after the record's release, the band folded owing to drummer Mark Edwards experiencing a debilitating accident and guitarist Doug Aldrich leaving to join Hurricane.

● ALBUMS: *Power Love* Japan only (Lion 1985)★★★★, *Dangerous Attraction* (Scotti Bros 1987)★★★, *Trouble At Angel City* (Grand Slam 1989)★★.

LIONHEART

Formed in 1980 by Dennis Stratton (guitar) on his exit from Iron Maiden, he was joined in this crusade by vocalist Jess Cox (Tygers Of Pan Tang), Frank Noon (Next Band/Def Leppard) on drums, Steve Mann (Liar) on guitar and Rocky Newton (Wildfire) on bass. They made their highly impressive debut one Saturday night at the Marquee, London, but suffered from bad press thanks to criticism of Cox. This led to the cancellation of the next two appearances and saw Cox replaced by Reuben Archer (Lautrec). Noon quit in 1981 to join Paul Di'Anno's band before setting off for Waysted. The nucleus of Stratton, Mann and Newton continued with various line-ups that included drummers Les Binks (Judas Priest) and Clive Edwards (Grand Prix). In 1982 they signed to Heavy Metal

Records but only managed to release one track, on the *Heavy Metal Heroes Vol 2* compilation. That track, 'Lionheart', remains the only representative recording of their early sound, as they later changed their style significantly. With the addition of Chad Brown on vocals and session drummer Robert Jenkins, they went on to record an album with producer Kevin Beamish (REO Speedwagon). This was a slick, Americanized effort that failed to capture the old fans' interest or that of their target audience in the USA. In 1985 they continued with drummer Andy Bierne and Phil Lanzon (keyboards), who had been playing with re-formed glam rockers Sweet. After a while, Lanzon also left and was replaced by Steve Mann from Stratus and new vocalist Keith Murrell. They eventually split up in 1986, with Bierne going into management, Murrell to Mama's Boys and Newton and Mann joining MSG. Stratton later found fame in Japan as part of the British All Stars/Praying Mantis line-up, which featured a number of ex-New Wave Of British Heavy Metal musicians.

● ALBUMS: *Die For Love* (Epic 1984)★★★.

LIONSHEART

Following his departure from UK heavy metal thrashers Onslaught, ex-Grim Reaper vocalist Steve Grimmett set about forming a more melodic band to suit his vocal abilities and musical inclinations, enlisting twin brothers Mark (guitar) and Steve Owers (bass), Graham Collet (keyboards) and Anthony Christmas (drums). Lionsheart signed to Music For Nations, but the Owers brothers departed before the release of their self-titled debut, with illness leaving Mark Owers unable to tour, and they were replaced by Nick Burr (guitar, ex-Killers; Idol Rich) and Zak Bajjon (bass). Lionsheart ignored grunge trends in favour of guitar-driven melodic hard rock with high-quality songwriting, and despite minimal reaction at home and in the USA, the band achieved deserved success in Europe and major status in Japan. *Pride In Tact* saw Lionsheart extending their approach from near-AOR balladry to harder blues-rock, with Burr proving equal to the task of following Mark Owers' performance on the debut.

● ALBUMS: *Lionsheart* (Music For Nation 1993)★★★, *Pride In Tact* (Music For Nations 1994)★★★.

LIQUID JESUS

This experimental Los Angeles-based quintet was formed in 1990 by bassist Johnny Lonely and guitarist Scott Tracey. Adding Todd Rigione (guitar), Buck Murphy (vocals) and John Molo (drums), they gigged incessantly on the LA bar and club circuit. Fusing psychedelic, blues, jazz and metal influences to bizarre extremes, they debuted with an independently released live album. Tipped by some as the next Jane's Addiction, they were signed by Geffen Records in 1991 and delivered *Pour In The Sky*. This pooled their influences of Jimi Hendrix, Led Zeppelin, the Red Hot Chili Peppers and Queen, but accusations of plagiarism were sidestepped by virtue of their totally deranged and unpredictable delivery.

● ALBUMS: *Liquid Jesus Live* (Liquid Jesus 1990)★★★, *Pour In The Sky* (Geffen 1991)★★★.

LITTLE ANGELS

This UK heavy rock quintet was formed in Scarborough, Yorkshire, during 1985, originally under the title Mr Thrud. Comprising Tony Jepson (vocals), Bruce John Dickinson (b. 10 May 1968, Berwick-upon-Tweed, Scotland; guitar), Mark Plunkett (bass), Jimmy Dickinson (keyboards) and Dave Hopper (drums), they were a youthful outfit, whose energy and enthusiasm in the live setting won them a loyal fanbase in their native north-east. Following a series of independent releases, notably the seven-track *Too Posh To Mosh*, they attracted the attention of Polydor Records. *Don't Prey For Me*, which featured new drummer Michael Lee, included a dozen gems of melodic, but roughshod, rock 'n' roll, characterized by Jepson's raucous and charismatic vocals. The big-budget follow-up, mixed by the Steve Thompson/Michael Barbiero partnership, was a disappointment. Abandoning their roots, this set saw them make a concerted attempt to break into the American FM radio market. Internal disputes began to manifest themselves in 1991. Drummer Michael Lee secretly auditioned for the Cult, and was ejected from the band as a result. His replacement was Mark Richardson. *Jam* regained lost ground in 1993, entering the UK charts at number 1 and winning them the support slot on Van Halen's European tour. However, having found their niche, they nevertheless elected to go their separate ways in 1994. The Dickinsons moved on to b.l.o.w.

● ALBUMS: *Too Posh To Mosh* (Powerstation 1987)★★★★, *Don't Prey For Me* (Polydor 1989)★★★★, *Young Gods* (Polydor 1991)★, *Jam* (Polydor 1993)★★★, *Little Of The Past* (Polydor 1994)★★★.

● COMPILATIONS: *Too Posh To Nosh* (Castle 1994)★★★.

● VIDEOS: *Big Bad Video* (1991).

LITTLE CAESAR

A highly underrated R&B-influenced rock band from Los Angeles, Little Caesar made their recorded debut with one track, 'Down To The Wire', on *Street Survivors*, a compilation showcasing the best unsigned local bands. With a line-up of Ron Young (vocals), Apache (guitar, steel guitar), Louren Molinaire (guitar), Fidel Paniagua (bass) and Tom Morris (drums), an EP, *Name Your Poison*, was recorded, helping the band to secure a major contract with Geffen. The self-titled debut, produced by Bob Rock, deservedly received excellent reviews. Packed with good material, from the basic rock 'n' roll of 'Down-N-Dirty' to the more soulful R&B of 'In Your Arms', plus two Motown cover versions in 'Chain Of Fools' and 'I Wish It Would Rain', the album displayed the band's strong songwriting talents and sense of melody, coupled with an emotive performance from the smoky-voiced Young. Despite praise in the press, the album failed to take off. As it was released, Guns N'Roses were gaining enormous mass popularity, and the band's tattooed biker image, unpremeditated though it may have been, allowed many to dismiss them as yet another Guns N'Roses clone band without hearing the evidence. Little was heard from the group for some time, although Young made a cameo appearance in *Terminator 2: Judgement Day*, and 'Down To The Wire' featured on the *Point Break* soundtrack, until they reappeared with ex-David Bowie/Dirty White Boy guitarist Earl Slick replacing the departed Apache for some live shows prior to recording *Influence*. Boasting a harder sound than the debut, the album was another high-quality outing, but despite further good press, sales were again disappointing. When Geffen failed to take up a third-album option, the band split up, with Young going on to front the similarly ill-fated Manic Eden.

● ALBUMS: *Little Caesar* (Geffen 1990)★★★, *Influence* (Geffen 1992)★★★.

LITTLE EGYPT

Claiming their initial notoriety from the fact that lead guitarist and vocalist Nick Rossi is the son of Francis Rossi of Status Quo, Little Egypt formed in the early 90s as a similarly inclined metal/boogie affair. The nepotism extended further: the group supported Quo on their 1993 tour, while Francis, who wrote several of their early songs, also co-produced their debut album. Bob Young, famed for his harmonica contributions to the denim warriors, is their manager. The other members of Little Egypt include Duncan Turmain (guitar, vocals), Dan Eames (drums) and 'Flying' Dave Conti (bass).

● ALBUMS: *Little Egypt* (1994)★★.

LIVE

A US alternative rock band from York, Pennsylvania, Live comprise Ed Kowalczyk (vocals), with Patrick Dahlheimer, Chad Taylor and Chad Gracey. The group was formed from blue-collar friends attending high school because 'we share the same ignorance'. The group's dynamic is one of fraught pop that occasionally expands into full-blown rock mode - with lyrics striking an idealistic tone. This was particularly true of the group's 1991 debut, the largely ignored *Mental Jewelery*, where spiritual overtones were also present. No less intense was the subsequent *Throwing Copper*; however, by this point Kowalczyk's lyrics had developed in a less literal direction: 'I'm more into letting my subconscious write, I want to let go completely, without becoming addicted to anything - which is a danger'. Another danger was a track such as 'Shit Towne', which addressed the populace of home-town York, and did little to ingratiate the band to their old community. The band's unexpected success continued into 1996 when *Throwing Copper* was certified as selling six million copies in the USA alone. *Secret Samadhi* looked set to be equally successful, even though it was an altogether bleaker-sounding record.

● ALBUMS: *Mental Jewelry* (Radioactive 1991)★★, *Throwing Copper* (Radioactive 1994)★★★★, *Secret Samadhi* (Radioactive 1997)★★★.

LIVGREN, KERRY

The former Kansas guitarist (b. 18 September 1949, Kansas, USA) departed the fold in the early 80s to put on record his new-found religious beliefs as a born-again Christian. His debut solo effort saw him keeping a nucleus of Kansas personnel in support, adding the vocals of Ronnie James Dio on a competent set. Afterwards, Livgren indulged in some tepid AOR albums, often allied to grandiose orchestral concepts, both solo and with his spin-off project, AD.

● ALBUMS: *Seeds Of Change* (Kirshner 1980)★★.

LIVING COLOUR

This US rock band was originally formed by Vernon Reid (b. 22 August 1958, London, England; guitar), Muzz Skillings (bass) and William Calhoun (b. 22 July 1964, Brooklyn, New York, USA; drums). Reid had studied performing arts at Manhattan Community College, having moved to New York at the age of two. His first forays were in experimental electric jazz with Defunk, before he formed Living Colour as a trio in 1984. Both Skillings and Calhoun were experienced academic musicians, having studied and received acclaim at City College and Berklee College Of Music, respectively. The line-up was completed by the induction of vocalist Corey Glover (b. 6 November 1964, Brooklyn, New York, USA), who had just finished a role in Oliver Stone's film *Platoon*, and whom Reid had originally encountered at a friend's birthday party. Their first major engagement came when Mick Jagger saw them performing at CBGB's and invited them to the studio for his forthcoming solo album. Jagger's patronage continued as he produced two demos for the band, which secured them a contract with Epic Records. Their debut, *Vivid*, earned them early critical acclaim and rose to number 6 in the US charts. Fusing disparate black musical formats such as jazz, blues and soul, alongside commercial hard rock, its diversity was reflected in the support slots the band acquired to promote it, Cheap Trick, Robert Palmer and Billy Bragg among them. Musically, the band is most closely aligned to the first of that trio, although their political edge mirrors the concerns of Bragg. In 1985 Reid formed the *Black Rock Coalition* pressure movement alongside journalist Greg Tate, and Living Colour grew to be perceived as their nation's most articulate black rock band. Two subsequent singles, 'Cult Of Personality' (which included samples of John F. Kennedy's speeches and won a Grammy award) and 'Open Letter (To A Landlord)', were both provocative but intelligent expressions of urban concerns. The ties with the Rolling Stones remained strong, with Reid collaborating on Keith Richards' solo album. They also joined the Stones on their *Steel Wheels* tour. After sweeping the boards in several Best New Band awards in such magazines as *Rolling Stone*, *Time's Up* was released in 1990, and afforded another Grammy Award. Notable contributions, apart from the omnipresent Jagger, included Little Richard on the controversial 'Elvis Is Dead'. In 1991 worldwide touring established them as a highly potent force in mainstream rock. Following Skillings' departure, bassist Doug Wimbush (b. 22 September 1956, Hartford, Connecticut, USA) from Tackhead joined them for *Stain* which added a sprinkling of studio gimmickry on a number of tracks. The band announced its dissolution early in 1995; Vernon Reid stated: '. . . Living Colour's sense of unity and purpose was growing weaker and fuzzier, I was finding more and more creative satisfaction in my solo projects. Finally it became obvious that I had to give up the band and move on'. An excellent retrospective, *Pride*, was released following their demise. Reid released an impressive solo debut album in 1996.

● ALBUMS: *Vivid* (Epic 1988)★★★★, *Time's Up* (Epic 1990)★★★★, *Stain* (Epic 1993)★★★, *Dread* Japanese live release (Epic 1993)★★★.

● COMPILATIONS: *Pride* (Epic 1995)★★★★.

LIZZY BORDEN

This theatrical heavy rock band formed in Los Angeles in 1983, and took their name from the infamous axe murderess. Utilizing strong sexual and horror imagery, their visual style owed much to Alice Cooper. The group featured Lizzy Borden (vocals), his brother Joey Scott Harges (drums), Mike Kenny (bass) and Tony Matuzak (guitar). Their contribution to the *Metal Massacre IV* compilation impressed Metal Blade boss Brian Slagel enough to offer them a contract. The mini-album *Give 'Em The Axe* emerged in the summer of 1984, followed a year later by *Love You To Pieces*, their official full-length debut. Both were highly derivative of Rainbow/Iron Maiden, with Lizzy's vocals sounding similar to Geoff Tate's of Queensrÿche. Alex Nelson replaced Matuzak on guitar before the recording of *The Murderess Metal Roadshow*. This was a double live collection whose low-tech origins did little to flatter the band. Two more studio albums followed, including the abbreviated *Terror Rising*, which saw Betsy from Bitch duetting on a cover version of the Tubes' kitsch classic, 'Don't Touch Me There'. Gene Allen was added as a second guitarist and Jesse Holmes and Mychal Davis replaced Nelson and Kenny, respectively, before the recording of what is arguably the band's most enduring set, *Visual Lies*. Loosely based around a central theme of illusions, the album was varied and hard-hitting, characterized by infectious hooks, anthemic choruses and smouldering guitar breaks. They played the Reading Festival in 1987 to an indifferent reaction and Lizzy disbanded the group shortly afterwards (Holmes and Allen having already departed, with guitarist Ron Cerito replacing Mike Davis). Concentrating on a solo career, he released the ambitious concept album, *Master Of Disguise*.

● ALBUMS: *Give 'Em The Axe* mini-album (Metal Blade 1984)★★★, *Love You To Pieces* (Metal Blade 1985)★★★, *The Murderess Metal Roadshow* (Roadrunner 1986)★★, *Menace To Society* (Roadrunner 1986)★★★, *Terror Rising* mini-album (Metal Blade 1987)★★★, *Visual Lies* (Roadrunner 1987)★★★★.

Solo: Lizzy Borden *Master Of Disguise* (Roadrunner 1989)★★★.
● COMPILATIONS: *Best Of* (Metal Blade 1994)★★★.
● VIDEOS: *Murdress Metal Roadshow* (1986).

LODESTAR

A group forged after disagreements in the Senser camp over musical direction, Lodestar feature three former members of that 'crustoid, pan-cultural fusioneering' group - Heitham Al-Sayed (vocals), Haggis (bass) and John Morgan (drums). Their line-up completed with the addition of Jules Hodgson (guitar), Lodestar were unequivocally a hard rock band. As Al-Sayed told the press, '. . . a lot of it's a lot less accessible than the Senser stuff. I started to hear music for the melody much more. Our sound is influenced by a lot of old British rock bands and really old American blues stuff.' Their debut album was released by Ultimate Records at the end of 1996 and certainly came as a surprise to old Senser fans, though reviews, particularly in the metal press, were generally good. The one obvious continuity from the past was Al-Sayed's distinctive vocals - whether rapping or singing, his approach remained one of absolute personal conviction.
● ALBUMS: *Lodestar* (Ultimate 1996)★★★.

LONE STAR

This traditional UK hard rock quintet was formed in 1975 by Kenny Driscoll (lead vocals), Tony Smith (guitar), Paul 'Tonka' Chapman (guitar), Pete Hurley (bass) and Dixie Lee (drums). Specializing in dynamic heavy rock, they attracted considerable attention with their Roy Thomas Baker-produced debut, offering an approach and sound not dissimilar to early Queen's pomp/hard rock formula. Driscoll was replaced by John Sloman in 1977 before the release of *Firing On All Six*. This album pushed the dual guitars of Chapman and Smith to the forefront and concentrated on heavier material. Shortly after its release the band disintegrated, with Sloman joining Uriah Heep, Chapman replacing Michael Schenker in UFO and Dixie Lee teaming up with Wild Horses.
● ALBUMS: *Lone Star* (Columbia 1976)★★★, *Firing On All Six* (Columbia 1977)★★★★, *BBC Radio 1 Live* (Windsong 1994)★★★.

LOVE CANAL

Based in Fort Lauderdale, Florida, USA, Love Canal comprise Chad Phoebus (vocals), Stephen Carroll (guitar), George Fotiadis (bass) and Jody Martin (drums). Melding elements of 80s hard rock with its more alternative 90s variants, the group made its debut with two self-released EPs and several appearances on local Florida various artists compilations. One of these, a *Rock The Vote* compilation on Phisst Records that included their single 'Wormhold', led to Love Canal being signed permanently to that label. Their self-produced debut album, *Embers*, followed in the summer of 1995.
● ALBUMS: *Embers* (Phisst 1995)★★★.

LOVE/HATE

This Los Angeles, California-based quartet, formerly known as Data Clan, originally comprised Jizzy Pearl (lead vocals), Jon E. Love (guitar), Skid Rose (bass) and Joey Gold (drums). Proudly dubbing themselves the 'stoopidest band in the world', the new name was first invoked in 1986. With a streetwise attitude and a highly talented frontman, their debut album, produced by Tom Werman, was released to widespread critical acclaim. A hybrid of Guns N'Roses and Mötley Crüe, their songs dealt with the well-worn themes of sex, drugs, drink and rock 'n' roll. It was in a live setting that the band truly excelled, however, playing with genuine commitment and generating real intensity with their brand of funk-infused, jitterbug rock. The visual spectacle of a cross constructed from empty Budwiser cans also appealed. *Wasted In America* confirmed their fans' faith in them and recruited many new converts, but nevertheless saw them dropped by Columbia. They regrouped for *Let's Rumble*, with Love replaced by Darren Housholder, but by this point some of the earlier momentum, if not their native talent, had dispersed. *I'm Not Happy* was a prophetic title, with the band bereft of any new chords.
● ALBUMS: *Blackout In The Red Room* (Columbia 1990)★★★, *Wasted In America* (Columbia 1992)★★★★, *Let's Rumble* (1993)★★, *I'm Not Happy* (SPV 1995★★.

LOVERBOY

Loverboy were formed in Toronto, Canada, in 1980, by Mike Reno (vocals), Paul Dean (guitar), Doug Johnston (keyboards), Scott Smith (bass) and Matthew Frenette (drums). Reno was formerly with Moxy, and Dean and Frenette had been members of Sweetheart, a melodic AOR/heavy rock band. With this pedigree, Loverboy were signed by CBS Records as soon as they were formed. Producer Bruce Fairbairn helped them to record a self-titled album that was to set Loverboy's standard for years to come. It was an American-styled melodic hard rock collection that also dipped into reggae and jazz moods. With the hit singles 'Turn Me Loose' and 'The Kid Is Hot Tonite', *Loverboy* went platinum. After touring, the group re-entered the studio in 1981, with Fairbairn again producing, to record the follow-up, *Get Lucky*. The album lived up to its name by selling over two million copies, helped by the singles chart progress of 'Working For The Weekend'. The only territory where the band had failed to take off was Europe. After further touring Fairbairn produced the multi-platinum *Keep It Up* in 1983, from which 'Hot Girls In Love' charted. Loverboy's inviting blend of melodic AOR had been honed to a fine art, the album's success keeping the band on the road for nearly two years. On *Lovin' Every Minute Of It* they were joined by Tom Allom, best known for his work with Judas Priest. The result was a musically tougher album that proved to be the band's least successful, though it still sold well over a million copies. The title track, released as a single, was written by Def Leppard producer Robert John 'Mutt' Lange. Fairbairn had by now made his name as the producer of Bon Jovi, but returned to the helm for Loverboy's *Wildside*, released in 1987, and their most complete album to date. Bryan Adams, Richie Sambora and Jon Bon Jovi all co-wrote various tracks. 'Notorious' also proved the band's most successful single, achieving platinum status three times over. This was followed by a marathon two-year tour, their longest yet. They did, however, take a break for two months to record tracks with producer Bob Rock before supporting Def Leppard on their European tour in the spring of 1988. Afterwards, Loverboy returned home to Canada and an uncertain future. Dean and Reno announced plans to record solo and this left the rest of the band in limbo. In 1989 a compilation album was released by Columbia, *Big Ones*, which also contained three new tracks that had been recorded with Bob Rock. Later that year, Dean released a solo effort assisted by Loverboy drummer Frenette and Jon Bon Jovi on harmonica. The parent band, meanwhile, have remained inactive.

● ALBUMS: *Loverboy* (Columbia 1980)★★★, *Get Lucky* (Columbia 1981)★★★, *Keep It Up* (Columbia 1983)★★★, *Lovin' Every Minute Of It* (Columbia 1985)★★★, *Wildside* (Columbia 1987)★★★.
Solo: Paul Dean *Hard Core* (Columbia 1989)★★.
● COMPILATIONS: *Big Ones* (Columbia 1989)★★★.

LUNACHICKS

Legend has it that New York's Lunachicks were rescued from a life of street gangs, drinking, idolatry and terrorism against humanity by being discovered by Sonic Youth, who recommended the all-female band to Blast First Records so vociferously that the Lunachicks' debut, *Babysitters On Acid*, was barely recorded before it was let loose upon an unsuspecting public. The 'not-at-all-nice-girls' turned their rebellious behaviour into a stage act. Becky (drums), Squid Sid (bass), Gina (lead guitar) and Sindi (guitar) were the musicians with a taste for excessive volume; Theo was the singer with a predilection for blood-splattered wedding gowns. The Lunachicks can only be described as 'different'. *Binge And Purge* was a marked (and listenable) improvement over their debut. With new drummer Chip on board the band took a backward step with *Jerk Of All Trades*, which lacked the inventiveness of the previous album.

● ALBUMS: *Babysitters On Acid* (Blast First 1990)★★, *Binge Purge* (Blast First 1993)★★★, *Jerk Of All Trades* (Go Kart 1995)★★★, *Pretty Ugly* (Go Kart 1997)★★★.

LUNCH, LYDIA

b. Lydia Koch, 1959, Rochester, New York, USA. The provocative Lydia Lunch was a pivotal figure in New York's 'no wave' scene of the late 70s and has worked with an array of talent since then. After spells with Teenage Jesus And The Jerks and Beirut Slump (the latter were restricted to one US single, 'Try Me'), Lunch opted for the freedom of solo work with 1980's acclaimed *Queen Of Siam* on the Ze label. Her next project, Eight-Eyed Spy, toyed with funk and R&B while retaining her uncompromising vocal style and violent, experimental musical approach. Then came *13:13* on the Ruby label, which benefited from a harder production and more co-ordinated sound. In 1982 she shared a 12-inch EP with the Birthday Party on 4AD Records, *The Agony Is The Ecstasy*, revealing her increasing fascination with the baser instincts of human nature. Members of the Birthday Party also backed her on 'Some Velvet Morning', while Einsturzende Neubauten joined her for 'Thirsty'. This marriage of the New York and Berlin undergrounds was further developed on 'Der Karibische Western', on Zensor with Die Haut. Lunch continued her collaborative ventures in 1983, working with Danish band Sort Sol. *In Limbo*, a 1984 mini-album for Cabaret Voltaire's Doublevision label, reintroduced her to solo work, and she soon founded Widowspeak Productions in 1985 as an outlet to document her work, starting, appropriately, with *The Uncensored Lydia Lunch* cassette. This included 'Daddy Dearest' - a document of the abuse she suffered at the hands of her father. After a project with Michael Gira (Swans), entitled *Hard Rock* (a cassette on Ecstatic Peace), Lunch teamed up with New York art rock pranksters Sonic Youth for 'Death Valley '69', a menacing record concerning the Manson killings, which launched Blast First Records in the UK. An equally sinister solo offering, *The Drowning Of Lady Hamilton*, was followed by a 10-inch EP recorded with No Trend, *Heart Of Darkness*. The next release for Widowspeak was a limited edition box set, *The Intimate Diaries Of The Sexually Insane*, containing a cassette of chronic case histories, a magazine and a book, *Adulterers Anonymous*, co-written by Lunch. The remixed and remastered double album retrospective, *Hysterie*, summarized her work from 1976-86, before she paired with the man behind Foetus and Clint Ruin, Jim Thirlwell, for the awesome Stinkfist project in 1989. The previous year she had formed Harry Crews, an all-female, wall-of-guitar-sound group in which Lunch was joined by Sonic Youth bassist Kim Gordon.

She spent 1993 working on a film script, *Psychomenstruum*. Lunch, in conjunction with her soul mate Thirlwell, has also become known as an avid opponent of censorship. Her own work is uncompromisingly confrontational and lurid, including videos featuring highly explicit sexual activity. The politics of outrage remain her gospel. *Rude Hieroglyphics* was a provocative collaboration with X singer Cervenka.

● ALBUMS: *Queen Of Siam* (Ze 1980)★★★, with 8 Eyed Spy *Live* cassette only (ROIR 1981)★★★, with 8 Eyed Spy *8 Eyed Spy* (Fetish 1981)★★★, *13:13* (Ruby 1982)★★★, with Michael Gira *Hard Rock* cassette only (Ecstatic Peace 1984)★★★, *In Limbo* mini-album (Doublevision 1984)★★★, *The Uncensored Lydia Lunch* cassette only (Widowspeak 1985)★★★, with Lucy Hamilton *The Drowning Of Lucy Hamilton* mini-album (Widowspeak 1985)★★★, *Honeymoon In Red* (Widowspeak 1987)★★★, *Oral Fixation* (Widowspeak 1989)★★★, with Harry Crews *Naked In Garden Hills* (Widowspeak 1989)★★★, *Conspiracy Of Women* (Widowspeak 1991)★★★, with Rowland S. Howard *Shotgun Wedding* (UFO 1991)★★★, with Exene Cervenka *Rude Hieroglyphics* (Rykodisk 1995)★★★, *The Uncensored ... Oral Fixation* (Atavistic 1996)★★★.

● COMPILATIONS: *Hysterie (1976-1986)* (Widowspeak 1986)★★★, *Crimes Against Nature* 3-CD set (Triple X)★★★.

● VIDEOS: *Lydia Lunch: The Gun Is Loaded* (1993).

● FURTHER READING: *Incriminating Evidence*, Lydia Lunch.

LYNCH MOB

Following Dokken's acrimonious split in 1988, guitarist George Lynch and drummer Mick Brown recruited bassist Anthony Esposito and tempted vocalist Oni Logan away from the embryonic Cold Sweat to complete Lynch Mob. *Wicked Sensation* was a decent hard rock debut, carried by Lynch's considerable ability, but youthful vocalist Logan's inexperience began to show through on the road. The band felt particularly uncomfortable when comparing Logan with Geoff Tate during a European tour with Queensrÿche, where the highlight of the set tended to be a rendition of 'Mr Scary', Lynch's Dokken-era instrumental guitar workout. Logan was replaced by another relative unknown, Robert Mason, when touring was complete. *Lynch Mob* incorporated more R&B influences, moving further from the Dokken sound, and this suited Mason's bluesy tones, while the band paid tribute to their influences with a cover version of Queen's 'Tie Your Mother Down'. However, neither album really took off, and Lynch split the band, opting to go solo while Brown rejoined Don Dokken in 1994.

● ALBUMS: *Wicked Sensation* (Elektra 1990)★★★, *Lynch Mob* (Elektra 1992)★★★★.

LYNOTT, PHIL

b. 20 August 1951, Dublin, Eire, d. 4 January 1986. Having enjoyed considerable success in Thin Lizzy, Lynott first recorded solo in 1980, the same year that he married Caroline Crowther, daughter of UK television celebrity Leslie Crowther. Lynott's first single, 'Dear Miss Lonely Hearts', reached number 32 in the UK charts and was followed by an album, *Solo In Soho*. A tribute to Elvis Presley, 'King's Call' also reached number 35. Lynott had to wait until 1982 for his next hit, 'Yellow Pearl', which reached the UK Top 20 after being used as the theme tune to television show *Top Of The Pops*. In the summer of 1983 Thin Lizzy broke up and it was widely anticipated that Lynott would go on to solo fame. A new group, Grand Slam, failed to develop and Lynott's subsequent solo single, 'Nineteen', did not sell.

The last notable instalment in his career came in May 1985 when he partnered Gary Moore on the number 5 hit, 'Out In The Fields'. He played his last gig with Grand Slam at the Marquee in London on 3 December 1985. At the turn of the following year he suffered a drug overdose and, following a week in a coma, died of heart failure, exacerbated by pneumonia.

● ALBUMS: *Solo In Soho* (Vertigo 1981)★★★, *The Phillip Lynott Solo Album* (Vertigo 1992)★★.

● FURTHER READING: *Phillip Lynott: The Rocker*, Mark Putterford. *Songs For While I'm Away*, Phillip Lynott, *My Boy: The Phillip Lynott Story*, Philomena Lynott.

LYNYRD SKYNYRD

Formed in Jacksonville, Florida, in 1964, this US boogie/hard rock band took their (slightly corrupted) name from their Physical Education teacher, Leonard Skinner. The group initially comprised Ronnie Van Zant (b. 15 January 1948, Jacksonville, Florida, USA, d. 20 October 1977; vocals), Gary Rossington (b. 4 December 1951, Jacksonville, Florida, USA; guitar), Allen Collins (b. 19 July 1952, Jacksonville, Florida, USA, d. 23 January 1990; guitar, ex-Mods), Larry Jungstrom (bass) and Bob Burns (drums, ex-Me, You & Him), the quintet meeting through minor league baseball connections. They played together under various names, including Noble Five, Wildcats, Sons Of Satan and My Backyard, releasing one single, 'Need All My Friends', in 1968, before changing their name to Lynyrd Skynyrd.

After playing the southern states during the late 60s they released a second single, 'I've Been Your Fool', in 1971, after recording demos in Sheffield, Alabama. The group were discovered in Atlanta by Al Kooper in 1972 while he was scouting for new talent for his Sounds Of The South label. Signed for $9000, the group's ranks were swollen by the addition of Leon Wilkeson (b. 2 April 1952; bass), who replaced Jungstrom (who went on to work with Van Zant's brother, Donnie, in .38 Special). Kooper produced the group's debut album, *Pronounced Leh-Nerd Skin-Nerd*, which also featured former Strawberry Alarm Clock guitarist Ed King (originally standing in on bass for Wilkeson, who dropped out of the band for six months) and Billy Powell (b. 3 June 1952; keyboards). Their three-guitar line-up attracted a great deal of attention, much of it generated through support slots with the Who, and the combination of blues, honky tonk and boogie proved invigorating. Their momentous anthem, 'Free Bird' (a tribute to Duane Allman), included a superb guitar finale, while its gravity and durability were indicated by frequent reappearances in the charts years later. In 1974 the group enjoyed their biggest US hit with 'Sweet Home Alabama', an amusing and heartfelt response to Neil Young who had criticized the south in his compositions 'Southern Man' and 'Alabama'. After the release of parent album *Second Helping*, drummer Bob Burns was replaced by Artimus Pyle (b. 15 July 1948, Spartanburg, South Carolina, USA). The group were by now renowned as much for their hard living as their music, and Ed King became the first victim of excess when retiring from the band in May 1975 (Van Zant's name was also regularly to be found in the newspapers, through reports of bar brawls and confrontations with the law). *Gimme Back My Bullets* arrived in March of the following year, with production expertise from Tom Dowd.

In September 1976 Rossington was injured in a car crash, while Steve Gaines (b. 14 September 1949, Seneca, Missouri, d. 20 October 1977; guitar) became King's replacement. With their tally of gold discs increasing each year and a series of sell-out tours, the band suffered an irrevocable setback in late 1977. On 20 October, Van Zant, Gaines, his sister Cassie (one of three backing singers) and personal manager Dean Kilpatrick were killed in a plane crash *en route* from Greenville, South Carolina, to Baton Rouge, Louisiana. Rossington, Collins, Powell and Wilkeson were seriously injured, but all recovered. That same month the group's new album, *Street Survivors*, was withdrawn as the sleeve featured an unintentionally macabre design of the band surrounded by flames. With their line-up devastated, the group dispersed and the remaining members went on to join the Rossington-Collins Band (with the exception of Pyle).

In 1987 the name Lynyrd Skynyrd was revived for a 'reunion' tour featuring Rossington, Powell, Pyle, Wilkeson and King, with Ronnie's brother Johnny Van Zant (vocals) and Randell Hall (guitar). One of their performances was later issued as the live double set, *For The Glory Of The South*. Collins had earlier been paralyzed and his girlfriend killed during an automobile accident in 1986. When he died in 1990 from pneumonia, this only helped to confirm Lynyrd Skynyrd's status as a 'tragic' band. However, members were still performing and recording in the early 90s, after disentangling themselves from legal complications over the use of the name caused by objections from Van Zant's widow. The most spectacular aspect of this was a 20th anniversary performance live on cable television in February 1993, with Rossington, Powell,

Wilkeson, King and Johnny Van Zant joined by guests including Peter Frampton, Brett Michaels (Poison), Charlie Daniels and Tom Kiefer (Cinderella), the latter having also written new songs with Rossington. Pyle was conspicuous by his absence, having been charged with the sexual assault of a four-year-old girl the previous year.

● ALBUMS: *Pronounced Leh-Nerd Skin-Nerd* (Sounds Of The South/MCA 1973)★★★★, *Second Helping* (Sounds Of The South/MCA 1974)★★★★, *Nuthin' Fancy* (MCA 1975)★★★, *Gimme Back My Bullets* (MCA 1976)★★, *One More From The Road* (MCA 1976)★★★★, *Street Survivors* (MCA 1977)★★★★, *First And Last* 1970-72 recordings (MCA 1978)★★★, *For The Glory Of The South* (MCA 1987)★★★, *Lynyrd Skynyrd 1991* (MCA 1991)★★★, *The Last Rebel* (MCA 1993)★★★, *Endangered Species* (Capricorn 1995)★★★, *Southern Knights* (CBH 1996)★★★, *Twenty* (SPV 1997)★★, *Live From Steel Town* (SPV 1998)★★★.

● COMPILATIONS: *Gold And Platinum* (MCA 1980)★★★★, *Best Of The Rest* (MCA 1982)★★★, *Legend* (MCA 1987)★★★, *Anthology* (Raw Power 1987)★★★, *Skynyrd's Innyrds* (MCA 1989)★★, *Definitive* 3-CD box set (MCA 1991)★★★★.

● VIDEOS: *Freebird: The Movie* (Cabin Fever 1997), *Lynyrd Skynrd Live: The Concert Video* (CMC Video 1998).

M.A.R.S.

This short-lived UK heavy rock supergroup project was assembled in 1987. Featuring Tony Macalpine (guitar), Tommy Aldridge (drums), Robert Rock (vocals) and Rudi Sarzo (bass), their collective pedigrees promised more than they delivered. Produced by Mike Varney, their sole album would have been indistinguishable from Vinnie Moore's, Tony Macalpine's, Marty Friedman's, Jason Becker's or Greg Howe's instrumental sets, were it not for the additional vocals of Rock. *Project Driver* clearly lacked identity, with the all-too transparent influences of Yngwie Malmsteen and Rainbow unbalancing the collection. The band dissolved soon after the release, with Sarzo and Aldridge joining Whitesnake, Rock taking over vocals in Joshua and Macalpine resuming his solo career.

● ALBUMS: *Project Driver* (Roadrunner 1987)★★.

Macabre

Chicago-based specialists in the field of sick rock, Macabre's chief obsession is with serial killers. The positive response on the fanzine network to their mass murderer-fixated demos demonstrated the degree to which Macabre had tapped into a fascination of the heavy metal underground. During the late 80s, serial killers were becoming the ultimate villains - icons of antisociality - and serial killer T-shirts, magazines and books were doing a brisk trade on the darker fringes of youth culture. In 1987 Macabre released their official debut, the self-financed EP *Grim Reality*, which featured ditties about such deviants as German cannibal Fritz Haarmann and Harvey Glatman, 'the Want Ad killer'. Macabre's material often sounds like punk nursery rhymes: serial killer tributes that drip with black humour and kitsch crudity, delivered with frantic speed, minimal polish and a total disregard for any standards of good taste.

As their career has progressed, their style has veered away from their more punkish roots to include a few death metal flourishes, but is still decidedly rough. With the stable line-up of Dennis the Menace (drums), Corporate Death (vocals, lead guitar) and Nefarious (bass guitar), Macabre

remain a morbid gag of extravagant proportions.
● ALBUMS: *Gloom* (Vinyl Solution 1989)★★★, *Sinister Slaughter* (Nuclear Blast 1992)★★★.

MACALPINE, TONY

Initially trained as a pianist, Tony Macalpine graduated to the electric guitar with an ambition to fuse rock and classical influences into a musical form that would have widespread appeal. Teaming up with ex-Journey drummer Steve Smith and ex-David Lee Roth bassist Billy Sheehan, he recorded *Edge Of Insanity*, which featured a set of classical-jazz-rock fusion instrumental numbers. The album was characterized by Macalpine's ability to improvise and imbue feeling and emotion into songs, even at breakneck speed. He experimented with the idea of forming a straightforward rock band as a consequence, and signed up Tommy Aldridge (drums), Rudi Sarzo (bass) and Robert Rock (vocals) to record *Project Driver* under the M.A.R.S. alias, but the result was a disappointing Rainbow-style collection of hard rock numbers. The band split soon after the release and Macalpine returned to solo status, forming his own Squawk label. He released another all-instrumental album but it was readily apparent, not least to the artist, that he had taken this particular format as far as it could go. On 1990's *Eyes Of The World*, released on Vertigo Records, he added Alan Schorn on lead vocals, Mark Robertson (keyboards), Billy Carmassi (drums) and Mike Jacques (drums) to form Macalpine, the band, specializing in highly polished melodic rock, punctuated by fluid but economical guitar breaks.
● ALBUMS: *Edge Of Insanity* (Roadrunner 1986)★★★★, *Maximum Security* (Vertigo 1987)★★★, *Evolution* (Roadrunner 1995)★★★.

MACC LADS

This trio from Macclesfield, Cheshire, England, comprised pseudonymous chancers The Beater (guitar, vocals), Muttley McLad (bass, vocals) and Chorley The Hord (drums). With a musical brief that incorporated elements of three-chord boogie, metallic riffs and punk, they insulted and entertained their audiences with a barrage of foul-mouthed one-liners and rock 'n' roll rugby songs. Lyrically, they extolled and exaggerated the virtues of the northern, macho, male-dominated pub scene: drinking real ale, 'pulling' women, Chinese takeaways and homophobia. Sample song titles include 'Now He's A Poof', 'Eh Up Let's Sup', 'Dan's Big Log' and 'No Sheep 'Til Buxton'. Releasing a series of albums full of schoolboy humour, they inevitably ran out of ideas. Shunned by nearly every record company and live venue in the land, the Macc Lads' grim philosophy, if such a polysyllabic word is appropriate, endures.
● ALBUMS: *Beer & Sex & Chips 'N' Gravy* (FM Revolver 1985)★★, *Bitter, Fit, Crack* (FM Revolver 1987)★★, *Live At Leeds - The Who?* (FM Revolver 1988)★★, *From Beer To Eternity* (Hectic House 1989)★★, *The Beer Necessities* (Hectic House 1990)★★, *Turtle's Heads* (Hectic House 1991)★★, *Alehouse Rock* (Up Not Down 1994)★★.
● COMPILATIONS: *20 Golden Crates* (1991)★★★.
● VIDEOS: *Come To Brum* (Jettisoundz 1989), *Quality Of Mersey* (ReVision 1990), *Three Bears* (Jettisoundz 1990), *Sex, Pies And Videotape* (Polygram Music Video 1992).

MACHINE HEAD

Formed in Oakland, California, USA, in June 1992, Machine Head comprise Robb Flynn (b. 19 July 1968, Oakland, California, USA; vocals, guitar, ex-Violence), Logan Mader (guitar), Adam Duce (bass) and Chris Kontos (ex-Verbal Abuse; drums). Specializing in angry, violent scenarios, their debut relied heavily on Flynn's 'reflections about the self and some of my personal experiences'. These were accompanied by overdriven guitars in the tradition of a fresh-faced Anthrax, with a level of guile that few had anticipated. European touring with Slayer brought the band rave reviews the following year, before Roadrunner released 'Old', backed by cover versions of hardcore material by Poison Idea and the Cro-Mags. Meanwhile, *Burn My Eyes* picked up third place in *Kerrang!* Magazine's critics' lists for 1994, describing the band as 'the HM discovery of the year'. Kontos left the band in 1995 to work with Testament; his replacement was ex-Sacred Reich Dave McClain. Logan Mader unexpectedly left the band in spring 1998 and was replaced by Ahrue Luster.
● ALBUMS: *Burn My Eyes* (Roadrunner 1994)★★★★, *The More Things Change...* (Roadrunner 1997)★★★.

MAD RIVER

Laurence Hammond (vocals, harmonica), David Robinson (lead guitar), Greg Druian (rhythm guitar), Tom Manning (bass) and Greg Dewey (drums) formed the Mad River Blues Band in 1965. Initially based in Yellow Springs, Ohio, USA, the group subsequently moved to California, by which time Druian had been replaced by Rick Bockner. The quintet, now dubbed simply Mad River, initially struggled to assert themselves, but a privately pressed EP helped to secure a series of gigs at prestigious San Franciscan venues. Mad River's debut album was released in 1968. Although mastered too fast owing to a technical error, it remains an enthralling slice of vintage acid rock, where traces of Country Joe And The Fish and Quicksilver Messenger Service blend with Hammond's reedy, quivering voice. A second album, *Paradise Bar And Grill*, was an altogether different affair. A handful of the tracks echoed the style of that first selection, while others were indebted to C&W, a genre towards which the singer was increasingly drawn. Two haunting acoustic instrumentals and a cameo appearance by the late writer Richard Brautigan completed one of the late 60s' most engaging collections. Mad River broke up soon after its release. Dewey later joined Country Joe And The Fish, and has subsequently played with numerous Bay Area groups. Hammond pursued his love of country music with his Whiplash Band and recorded an engaging album, *Coyote's Dream*, in 1976. The remainder of the group retired from active performance.

● ALBUMS: *Mad River* (Capitol 1968)★★★, *Paradise Bar And Grill* (Capitol 1969)★★★.

Mad Season

Mad Season were formed as a brief offshoot of Pearl Jam when their lead guitarist, Mike McCready, was on holiday in Minneapolis. There he met John Baker Saunder, the bass player with Lamont Cranston. The rest of Mad Season consist of Seattle luminaries Barrett Martin (drums; also Screaming Trees) and Layne Staley (b. 1967, vocals; Alice In Chains). They played their first gig with just three days notice as the Gacy Bunch (a halfway-house name between television serial *The Brady Bunch* and serial killer John Wayne Gacy) at Seattle's Crocodile Cafe. There had still been no proper rehearsals when they played their second gig two weeks later. By the recording of the album they were called Mad Season, which McCready first heard in Surrey when Pearl Jam were mixing their first album. 'It's the time when the psychedelic mushrooms grow. And it's a Hunter S. Thompson thing, and it certainly describes my years of alcohol, so it had stuck in my mind for a long time.' The group's 1995 debut album, *Above*, featured Screaming Trees vocalist Mark Lanegan duetting with Staley. The understated performances from the star personnel helped to create an impressive and relaxed album. Layne Staley's continuing problems led to Mark Lanegan taking over vocal duties on the band's second album.

● ALBUMS: *Above* (Columbia 1995)★★★.
● VIDEOS: *Live At The Moore* (Columbia 1995).

Madam X

One of Madam X's more distinctive songs, 'Come One, Come All', contained the line 'We're bad, we're good, that's all we ever wanted'. Unfortunately for them, most people thought they belonged chiefly in the former category. The group were formed in New York in 1983 by sisters Maxine and Roxy Petrucci on guitar and drums, respectively, along with vocalist Bret Kaiser and bassist Christopher 'Godzilla' Doliber. They subsequently moved to Los Angeles where their brand of glam metal was more readily accepted. In February 1985 they released an anthemic single, 'High In High School', backed with a suitably grandiose video. The single was produced by Rick Derringer who also performed the same task on the album. Both, however, were very average affairs and live shows fell short of the expected excitement. In 1986 Roxy departed to form Vixen and Kaiser quit the scene with ego suitably deflated. Mark McConnell took over the drums while vocal duties were handled by Sebastian Bach. Within the year the band disintegrated, with Doliber forming a wild and heavy band called Godzilla (which failed). Maxine remained in the shadow of her sister, but Bach found stardom with Skid Row.

● ALBUMS: *We Reserve The Right* (Jet 1984)★★★.

Madball

Singer Freddy Cricien (b. Florida, USA), brother of Agnostic Front's Roger Miret, was inevitably influenced by his imposing sibling, and his own band, Madball, operated in a similar, all-out hardcore vein. Cricien had made his debut at an Agnostic Front show at the age of seven, when visiting his New York-based brother, climbing on stage to offer a rendition of the Animals' It's My Life'. Eventually, he moved to the US capital, spending much time at the city's home for hardcore, CBGB's. It was Vinnie Stigma of Agnostic Front who gave him his nickname, 'Madball', after provoking the young Cricien to the point where his face resembled such an object. When Madball was formed, it included Stigma on guitar, with brother Roger on bass and Will Shepler on drums. Their first release, 'Ball Of Destruction', was unveiled in 1989 on In-Effect Records, and is now a genuine rarity. However, there was a three-year gap before a second 7-inch, 'Droppin' Many Suckers', this time released with Wreck-age Records. It prefaced a switch to Roadrunner Records and a long-playing set that, predictably, accented machismo and power over subtlety, but was nevertheless an energizing collection. It saw the debut of the band's current line-up: Cricien (vocals), Shepler (drums), Stigma (guitar), Matt Henderson (guitar) and Hoya (bass).

● ALBUMS: *Set It Off* (Roadrunner 1993)★★★, *Demonstrating My Style* (Roadrunner 1996)★★★, *Look My Way* (Roadrunner 1998)★★.
● COMPILATIONS: *Ball Of Destruction* (Century Media 1996)★★★.

MADDER ROSE

Spuriously lauded on their arrival in 1993 as the 'new Velvet Underground', Manhattan-based New Yorkers Madder Rose comprised Billy Coté (b. New Jersey, USA; guitar), Mary Lorson (vocals), Matt Verta-Ray (bass) and Johnny Kick (b. Chicago; drums, ex-Speedball). The initial ripples were caused by singles such as 'Swim', a yearning, slow-burning torch song reminiscent of Lou Reed's craft. However, they could hardly be described as anyone's 'new young thing', with all of the members aged over 30 at this early stage in their career. Each boasted an interesting, mainly non-musical background. Lorson was an ex-busker and film student, while both Verta-Ray and Kick worked at the Andy Warhol silk-screen factory and met the great man several times (a fact that helped to encourage the Velvet Underground comparisons). Coté had additionally spent much of the 80s working in No/New Wave bands Hammerdoll and Coté Coté, while struggling to overcome his heroin addiction. Cover versions of PiL's 'Rise' and the Cars' 'My Best Friend's Girl' on stage further revealed Madder Rose's diversity, while their debut album was trumpeted by *Melody Maker* magazine as '*the* debut album of 1993'. Released on Atlantic Records' independently distributed subsidiary Seed, production was overseen by Kevin Salem of Dumptruck. Matt Verta-Ray left in February 1994 to concentrate on his own project, Speedball Baby, the departure agreed before the band recorded their second album. He was replaced for *Panic On* by Chris Giammalvo (ex-Eve's Plum), on a set co-produced with Clash/Breeders/Th' Faith Healers veteran, Mark Freegard. This saw Lorson emerge as a songwriting force to rival Coté on some of the album's best numbers, including the appealing 'Foolish Ways'.

● ALBUMS: *Bring It Down* (Seed 1993)★★★★, *Panic On* (Atlantic 1994)★★★.

MAGELLAN

Formed in Vacaville, California, USA, in the mid-80s, Magellan was originally a project put together by brothers Wayne (electric and acoustic guitar) and Trent (lead vocals, keyboards) Gardner. Together with Hal Stringfellow Imbrie (bass, vocals), they set out to reinstate the progressive rock tradition of the 70s, which married riffs to jazz and classical flourishes. This combination was finely executed on their 1991 debut, *Hour Of Restoration*, which added modern, computer-generated possibilities to the equation. August 1993 saw the release of its follow-up, *Impending Ascension*, which earned comparisons to Dream Theater's crafted electro-rock. Opponents of grandiose musical statements were rewarded with much at which to scoff, including quotes drawn from Shakespeare, Poe and Magellan, the explorer from whom the group drew their name. The subject matter was far from trite mysticism, including topics such as virtual reality and social alienation.

● ALBUMS: *Hour Of Restoration* (Magna Carta/Roadrunner 1991)★★★, *Impending Ascension* (Magna Carta/Roadrunner 1993)★★★★, *Test Of Wills* (Roadrunner 1997)★★.

MAGNUM

This Birmingham, England-based pomp rock group was formed in 1972 by Tony Clarkin (guitar), Bob Catley (vocals), Kex Gorin (drums) and Dave Morgan (bass). They remained unsigned, undertaking various engagements, including acting as Del Shannon's backing band, until 1978, when they were signed by Jet Records. By this time Morgan had departed, to be replaced by Colin 'Wally' Lowe, and Richard Baily had joined as keyboard player. Between 1978 and 1980, Magnum released three albums to a moderate degree of success, and toured relentlessly with Judas Priest, Blue Öyster Cult, and Def Leppard. *Chase The Dragon* was released in 1982, with new keyboard player Mark Stanway, and gave them their first Top 20 album; it featured the grandiose pomp of 'Sacred Hour' and 'The Spirit', both of which still feature in their current live set. Following the release of *Eleventh Hour*, problems beset the band: Clarkin became ill, and a dispute with Jet Records ensued. The band fragmented as a result, but the troubles were soon resolved, and a number of low-key club dates persuaded them to continue. FM Revolver Records signed the band in 1985 for *On A StoryTeller's Night*. Its Top 40 success, along with a highly successful tour of the UK, prompted Polydor Records to offer a long-term contract. *Vigilante*, which featured new drummer Mickey Barker, was the first release under the new contract, and was produced by Queen's Roger Taylor. The backing of a major label paid immediate dividends with a Top 30 album and a sell-out UK tour. This success was taken one step further with *Wings Of Heaven* (1988), their first gold album and UK Top 10 hit. Top 40 single success came with 'Days Of No Trust', 'Start Talkin' Love' and 'It Must Have Been Love'. Numerous compilation albums, including *Mirador* and *Anthology*, were released, along with reissues of their now extensive back-catalogue from Jet Records. A two-year gap between official releases resulted in the Keith Olsen-produced *Goodnight L.A.*, and again Top 40 success was achieved with a single, 'Rocking Chair', the album also enjoying Top 10 status. Extensive touring promoted *Goodnight L.A.* and several shows were recorded for a double live set, *The Spirit*. A new contract with EMI Records began with *Rock Art*. After years of struggle and setbacks, Magnum's popularity has been achieved the hard way, by dint of constant touring and a series of high-quality albums. Clarkin was working on a new project with Catley in 1996 following their departure from the group.

● ALBUMS: *Kingdom Of Madness* (Jet 1978)★★★, *Magnum II* (Jet 1979)★★★, *Marauder* (Jet 1980)★★★, *Chase The Dragon* (Jet 1982)★★★, *The Eleventh Hour* (Jet 1983)★★★, *On A StoryTeller's Night* (Polydor 1985)★★★, *Vigilante* (Polydor 1986)★★★, *Wings Of Heaven* (Polydor 1988)★★★★, *Goodnight L.A.* (Polydor 1990), *Invasion - Magnum Live* (Receiver 1990)★★★, *The Spirit* (Polydor 1991)★★★, *Sleepwalking* (Polydor 1992)★★★, *Rock Art* (EMI 1994)★★★, *Firebird* (Spectrum/Polygram 1995)★★★.

● COMPILATIONS: *Anthology* (Raw Power 1986)★★★★, *Collection* (Castle 1990)★★★★, *Box Set* (Castle 1992)★★★, *Chapter And Verse - Best Of* (Polydor 1993)★★★, *Uncorked* (Jet 1994)★★★.

● VIDEOS: *The Sacred Hour Live* (1986), *On The Wings Of Heaven* (1988), *From Midnight To LA* (1990).

Mahogany Rush

Recovering in hospital from a bad drugs experience, Frank Marino (b. 22 August 1954, Canada) claimed he was visited by an apparition of Jimi Hendrix. After leaving hospital he picked up a guitar for the first time and was able to play Hendrix riffs, or so the legend runs. The group was formed in Montreal during 1970 when Marino recruited bassist Paul Harwood and drummer Jim Ayoub to fulfil his wish to work in a power trio format. Their first three albums were derivative in the extreme; every component of Hendrix's unique style had been dismantled, adapted, then rebuilt under new song titles. Nevertheless, they were not dismissed as copyists, but instead revered for paying tribute in such an honest and sincere fashion. By 1976 Marino had started to develop his own style, based on an extension of the Hendrix tricks he had already mastered. This is clearly evident on *Mahogany Rush IV* and *World Anthem*, released in 1976 and 1977, respectively. Eventually he outgrew the comparisons as his own style began to dominate the band's material. The name was amended to Frank Marino and Mahogany Rush, then to Frank Marino, following the release of *What's Next* and the departure of Ayoub.

● ALBUMS: *Maxoom* (Kotai 1971)★★, *Child Of The Novelty* (20th Century 1974)★★, *Strange Universe* (20th Century 1975)★★, *Mahogany Rush IV* (Columbia 1976)★★★, *World Anthem* (Columbia 1977)★★★, *Live* (Columbia 1978)★★★, *Tales Of The Unexpected* (Columbia 1979)★★★, *What's Next* (Columbia 1980)★★★.

Malevolent Creation

Formed in Buffalo, New York, USA, in 1987, it took Malevolent Creation four years to secure a contract and release their official debut for Roadrunner Records. This gore-fixated recording, *The Ten Commandments*, was mixed at Morrisound Studios in Florida by noted extreme metal producer Scott Burns, whose distinctive work had previously more or less defined the death metal sound. Malevolent Creation were initially considered an above average example of an often formulaic genre, and attracted a degree of critical acclaim. They arrived on the death metal scene too late, however, to establish themselves among the front-runners and as its popularity waned, the band found themselves without a contract in 1994. They eventually returned with a new album in 1996, but both *Eternal* and the subsequent *In Cold Blood* proved to be as lacklustre and dated as previous efforts.

● ALBUMS: *The Ten Commandments* (Roadrunner 1991)★★★, *Retribution* (Roadrunner 1992)★★★, *Stillborn* (Roadrunner 1993)★★★, *Eternal* (Bulletproof 1996)★★, *In Cold Blood* (Pavement 1997)★★.

Malice

This Los Angeles band emerged from the local club scene of the early 80s with a sound influenced by

European metal, particularly Judas Priest. Indeed, Malice were widely described as Priest clones, not only for their twin guitar-based sound and James Neal's vocal similarities to Rob Halford, but also for their leather-clad image and guitarist Jay Reynolds' distinct resemblance to KK Downing. Malice, completed by Mick Zane (guitar), Mark Behn (bass) and Peter Laufman (drums), recorded a stunning five-track demo, with producer Michael Wagener, that had independent labels clamouring to release it in its own right, but the band instead signed to Atlantic Records. The demo formed half of *In The Beginning*, with the remaining five tracks produced by Ashley Howe. It was an excellent debut, built on a solid base of power metal guitars, although the Priest comparisons remained obvious. However, cracks were beginning to show by *License To Kill*, as internal conflicts began to divide the band, and the split came in late 1987, as Malice divided into two warring camps. Reynolds later joined Megadeth for a brief period.

● ALBUMS: *In The Beginning* (Atlantic 1985)★★★★, *License To Kill* (Atlantic 1987)★★.

MALMSTEEN, YNGWIE

b. 30 June 1963. This Swedish-born guitar virtuoso was the originator of the high-speed, technically precise, neo-classical style that developed during the 80s. Influenced by Jimi Hendrix, Ritchie Blackmore and Eddie Van Halen, Malmsteen first picked up a guitar at the age of five and had formed his first band, Powerhouse, by the time he entered his teens. At age 14 he formed Rising, named after Rainbow's second album, and recorded a series of demo tapes. One of these was picked up by producer and guitar specialist Mike Varney. Malmsteen was persuaded by Varney to relocate to Los Angeles and join Ron Keel's Steeler as lead guitarist, and went straight into the studio to record the band's debut album. Following this he was approached by Kiss, UFO and Ozzy Osbourne, but declined their offers in favour of teaming up with Graham Bonnet in a new group called Alcatrazz. This association lasted for one studio album and a live set, recorded in Japan. After the dissolution of that band, Malmsteen was immediately offered a solo contract by Polydor Records, just as his reputation and stature were beginning to escalate. He released the self-produced *Rising Force*, utilizing ex-Jethro Tull drummer Barriemore Barlow, vocalist Jeff Scott Soto and keyboardist Jens Johansson. This comprised a mixture of new songs and reworked demo material that had been available for several years. Deciding to work within a band framework once more, but this time exercising tight control, Malmsteen formed Rising Force with Soto and Johansson, plus bassist Marcel Jacob and drummer Anders Johansson. This basic formation recorded two albums, the second of which, *Trilogy*, saw Soto replaced by ex-Ted Nugent vocalist Mark Boals, which showcased Malmsteen's amazing virtuosity and ability to combine speed with melody. Following an 18-month break after a serious road accident involving Malmsteen, Rising Force was resurrected with ex-Rainbow vocalist Joe Lynn Turner. Produced by Jeff Glixman and mixed by the Thompson/Barbiero team, *Odyssey* was released in 1988 to widespread acclaim. At last Malmsteen's guitar pyrotechnics were anchored within commercial hard rock structures. The guitar solos, for once, were economical, and did not detract from the songs. The album reached number 40 on the US *Billboard* album chart and brought many new fans to the guitarist. Eager to capitalize on this success, Malmsteen then issued a disappointing and self-indulgent live album recorded in Leningrad. The momentum was lost and Joe Lynn Turner was dismissed, to be replaced with a Swedish vocalist, Goran Edman. *Eclipse* emerged in 1990 with weak vocals and an unusually restrained Malmsteen on guitar, and it appeared that he was suppressing his real desires and talents in the search for commercial success. *Fire And Ice* debuted at number 1 in the Japanese charts, and introduced new vocalist Mike Vescera. Malmsteen switched back to his old flamboyant style on *No Mercy*, however, which featured classical material and a string orchestra. In 1996 he joined with Jeff Scott Soto as Human Clay to issue their self-titled debut.

● ALBUMS: *Yngwie Malmsteen's Rising Force* (Polydor 1984)★★★, *Marching Out* (Polydor 1985)★★★, *Trilogy* (Polydor 1986)★★★, *Odyssey* (Polydor 1988)★★★, *Live In Leningrad* (Polydor 1989)★★, *Eclipse* (Polydor 1990)★★, *Fire & Ice* (Elektra 1992)★★, *Seventh Sign* (Elektra 1994)★★★, *No Mercy* (CMC International 1994)★★★, *Facing The Animal* (Ranch Life 1998)★★.

● VIDEOS: *Rising Force Live 85* (1989), *Trial By Fire* (1989), *Collection* (1992).

MAMA'S BOYS

The three McManus brothers began their musical careers as folk musicians, playing the local dancehall and club circuit in their native Northern Ireland. After seeing the Irish electric folk-rock outfit Horslips in concert in 1978, they decided to abandon their acoustic guitars and tambourines and become a hard rock power trio with John on vocals and bass, Pat on lead guitar and Tommy on drums. Merging traditional Irish influences with blues and heavy rock, they quickly developed a unique style that echoed Thin Lizzy. Their first two albums contained high-energy boogie and driving blues, but from *Turn It Up* onwards, they began to show a greater awareness of melody and veered towards AOR. Realizing the limitations of John as a vocalist, they expanded to a quartet in 1987, adding ex-Airrace singer Keith Murrell. *Growing Up The Hard Way* followed and was undoubtedly the band's most accomplished album to date, with a sophisticated approach reminiscent of Foreigner. After four years of recording inactivity, *Live Tonite* emerged. Recorded on their 1990 European tour, it featured latest vocalist Mike Wilson, plus four brand new songs. On 16 November 1994 Tommy McManus died of a lung infection following a bone marrow transplant, having for several years been ill with leukaemia.

● ALBUMS: *Official Bootleg* (Pussy 1980)★★★, *Plug It In* (Albion 1982)★★★, *Turn It Up* (Spartan 1983)★★★, *Mama's Boys* (Jive 1984)★★★, *Power And The Passion* (Jive 1985)★★, *Growing Up The Hard Way* (Jive 1987)★★★★, *Live Tonite* (Music For Nations 1991)★★, *Relativity* (CTM 1992)★★★.

MAMMOTH

The prerequisite for joining this appropriately titled UK band was, as legend has it, to weigh in excess of 20 stone. Consequently, potential members were few and far between, but made up in girth what they lacked in number. Vocalist Nicky Moore (ex-Samson) and bassist John McCoy (ex-Gillan) eventually found guitarist Big Mac Baker and drummer 'Tubby' Vinnie Reid large enough for their requirements. The idea behind Mammoth was to present an alternative to 'pouting' rock bands such as Poison and Bon Jovi, with the music, rather than the image, topping the agenda. Unfortunately, due to contractual problems with their record company Jive, their debut album was delayed for 10 months and the interest they generated had evaporated by the time it was released. It comprised a poorly produced but workmanlike selection of hard rock and R&B numbers, with guitarists Bernie Tormé and Kenny Cox guesting on a couple of tracks. The single, 'Can't Take The Hurt Anymore', was included on the soundtrack to *Nightmare On Elm Street 5, The Dream Child*. The band collapsed shortly after the album's release.

● ALBUMS: *Mammoth* (Jive 1988)★★★.

MANHOLE

A contemporary hard rock group from Los Angeles, California, USA, Manhole are led by the distinctive, brazen vocals and confrontational stage persona of singer Tairrie B. Previously a white protégé of rap producer/svengali Eazy-E, her solo debut stalled in 1990 and she elected to concentrate instead on music with a similar thematic ethos but a more aggressive bent. With Scott Ueda (guitar), Rico Villasenor (bass) and Marcelo Palomino (drums), Manhole work in territory widely analogized as 'post-hardcore metal'. Tairrie B continues to rap as well as sing over the backdrop, which also contains trace elements of hip-hop rhythms, but it is doubtful whether those unacquainted with the singer's past would confuse Manhole with anything other than a ferocious hard rock group. They made their debut with the *Victim* EP, a taster for their 1996 debut album, which contained an impassioned condemnation of rape and sexual oppression. *All Is Not Well* followed for Noise International Records in April 1996, with production from Ross Robinson (Korn, Sepultura). It was promoted with support slots on Fear Factory's UK tour. Owing to the prior existence of another group called Manhole, in 1997 the group was forced to change its name to Tura Satana, the name of the leading actress in Russ Meyer's cult film *Faster, Pussycat! Kill! Kill!*.

● ALBUMS: *All Is Not Well* (Noise International 1996)★★.

MANOWAR

This traditionalist heavy metal quartet from the USA (whose motto is 'Death To False Metal') was formed in 1981 by bassist Joey Demaio (a former Black Sabbath roadie) and ex-Shakin' Street and Dictators guitarist Ross 'The Boss' Funicello. Recruiting vocalist Eric Adams and drummer Donnie Hamzik, they decided on an approach that was to be the total antithesis of melodic AOR. Dressed in animal skins, they delivered a brutal series of riffs that were characterized by Adams' barbaric vocals and the dense basswork of Demaio. They debuted in 1982 with *Battle Hymns*, a milestone in the metal genre. With subject material firmly centred on fighting, bloodshed, death and carnage, they came across as a turbo-charged hybrid of Ted Nugent and Black Sabbath. The album was notable for an amazing version of the 'William Tell Overture', played as an electric bass solo, while the voice of actor Orson Welles appeared on 'Dark Avenger'. *Battle Hymns* failed to sell, however, and with the press treating the band as an absurd joke, they were dropped by Liberty Records in 1982. They subsequently signed to Megaforce (Music For Nations in the UK), using their own blood on the contract, their veins opened via a ceremonial dagger. Scott Columbus took over the drum-stool on *Into Glory Ride*, another intensely heavy, chest-beating collection of metal epics. They built up a small yet loyal cult following, but were generally panned by the rock mainstream. Their UK tours in 1983 and 1984 attracted poor audiences, but they had more success in Europe. *Sign Of The Hammer*, released in 1985, featured some excellent guitarwork from Ross The Boss and contained the band's most accessible compositions to date, including the archetypal metal boast, 'All Men Play On 10'. Once again it flopped, and after a rethink they returned two years later with *Fighting The World* (in the meantime, they had entered the *Guinness Book Of Records* for playing live at 160 decibels). On this album they incorporated elements borrowed from Kiss and Judas Priest into their songwriting, but although it was aimed at the rock mainstream, it failed to win many new fans. *Kings Of Metal* was released the following year and met with a similar fate. Disillusioned, Ross The Boss quit in 1988, with Scott Columbus following suit two years later (Ross was replaced by Death Dealer, aka Dave Shankel, Columbus by Rhino). The future of the group is still uncertain. Manowar are colourful, flamboyant and rather kitsch, but, nevertheless, an essential component in the music industry - the perfect antidote to the sometimes conservative rock fraternity.

● ALBUMS: *Battle Hymns* (Liberty 1982)★★★, *Into Glory Ride* (Megaforce 1983)★★★, *Hail To England* (Megaforce 1984)★★★, *Sign Of The Hammer* (Virgin 1985)★★★, *Fighting The World* (Atco 1987)★★, *Kings Of Metal* (Atlantic 1988)★★, *Triumph Of Steel* (Atlantic 1992)★★, *Louder Than Hell* (Geffen 1996)★★.

MANTAS

This short-lived hard rock quartet from the north of England was formed by Mantas after quitting the demonic thrash metallers Venom. Enlisting the help of vocalist Pete Harrison, second guitarist Al Barnes and Keith Nichol on keyboards, their debut and only release comprised nine new originals penned by Mantas. Moving away from the one-dimensional approach of Venom, they straddled the ground between AOR and the more commercial slant of Rainbow, Saxon and Dio. *Winds Of Change* featured computerized drums and extensive use of keyboards, but Harrison's vocals lacked distinction and the material was ultimately dull. The album was ignored by mainstream record purchasers aside from diehard Venom fans. Following a careful rethink, Mantas disbanded the group and rejoined Venom in 1989.

● ALBUMS: *Winds Of Change* (Neat 1988)★★.

MARILLION

Front-runners of the short-lived UK progressive rock revival of the early 80s, Marillion survived unfavourable comparisons with Genesis to become a popular melodic rock group, notching up several successful singles plucked from their grandiose concept albums. The group formed in Aylesbury, Buckinghamshire, originally as Silmarillion, a name taken from the novel by J.R.R. Tolkien. The group featured Doug Irvine (bass), Mick Pointer (b. 22 July 1956; drums), Steve Rothery (b. 25 November 1959, Brampton, South Yorkshire, England; guitar) and Brian Jelliman (keyboards). After recording the instrumental demo, 'The Web', the band recruited Fish (b. Derek William Dick, 25 April 1958, Dalkeith, Edinburgh, Scotland; vocals) and Diz Minnett (bass), and began building a strong following through almost continuous gigging. Before recording their debut, 'Market Square Heroes', Jelliman and Minnitt were replaced by Mark Kelly (b. 9 April 1961; keyboards) and Pete Trewavas (b. 15 January 1959, Middlesbrough, Cleveland, England; bass). Fish wrote all the lyrics for *Script For A Jester's Tear* and became the focal point of the group, often appearing on stage in garish make-up, echoing the style, both visually and vocally, of Genesis's singer Peter Gabriel. In 1983 Pointer was sacked and replaced for brief stints by Andy Ward of Camel, then John Marter and Jonathan Mover, before the arrival of Ian Mosley (b. 16 June 1953, London, England), a veteran of many progressive rock bands, including Curved Air and the Gordon Giltrap band. Marillion's second album embraced a more straightforward hard rock sound and yielded two hits, 'Assassin' and 'Punch And Judy'. 1985's *Misplaced Childhood* was Marillion's biggest-selling album - surprisingly so, as it featured an elaborate concept, being virtually one continuous piece of music based largely on Fish's childhood experiences. 'Kayleigh', a romantic ballad extracted from this mammoth work, reached number 2 in the UK charts. By 1988 Fish was becoming increasingly dissatisfied with the group's musical development and left to pursue a solo career. The live double album *Thieving Magpie* was his last recorded contribution, and provided a fitting overview of the group's past successes. Marillion acquired Steve Hogarth (b. Doncaster, Yorkshire, England), formerly of the Europeans, who made his debut on *Seasons End*, proving himself equal to the daunting task of fronting a well-established band. In the 90s Marillion were as popular as ever, with the ghost of Fish receding into the background. With Hogarth fronting the band, consistent success has continued, including chart status for 'Sympathy', 'The Hollow Man' and 'Alone Again In The Lap Of Luxury'. *Afraid Of Sunlight* tackled the subject of fame, with references to Kurt Cobain, John Lennon and O.J. Simpson, the former American footballer who at the time was on trial for murder. Unusually, for a band rooted in the progressive rock subculture, a genre dominated by the album, Marillion continue to be distinguished as much for their singles as their album releases.

● ALBUMS: *Script For A Jester's Tear* (EMI 1983)★★★, *Fugazi* (EMI 1984)★★, *Real To Reel* (EMI 1984)★, *Misplaced Childhood* (EMI 1985)★★★, *Brief Encounter* (EMI 1986)★★, *Clutching At Straws* (EMI 1987)★★★, *B Sides Themselves* (EMI 1988)★★, *The Thieving Magpie* (EMI 1988)★★, *Seasons End* (EMI 1989)★★★, *Holidays In Eden* (EMI 1991)★★★, *Brave* (EMI 1994)★★★, *Afraid Of Sunlight* (EMI 1995)★★★, *Made Again* (EMI 1996)★★, *This Strange Engine* (Intact/Raw Power 1997)★★★, *Radiation* (Intact 1998)★★.

● COMPILATIONS: *A Singles Collection* (EMI 1992)★★★, *The Best Of Both Worlds* (EMI 1997)★★★.

● VIDEOS: *1982-1986 The Videos* (1986), *Live From Lorely* (1987), *From Stoke Row To Ipanema* (1990), *Brave* (1995).

● FURTHER READING: *Market Square Heroes*, Mick Wall. *Marillion*, Carol Clerk. *The Authorized Story Of Marillion*, Mick Wall. *Marillion: The Script*, Clive Gifford.

MARILYN MANSON

Controversial by design rather than accident, Florida group Marilyn Manson were formed in 1989 with the express intention of 'exploring the limits of censorship'. The original line-up consisted of Manson (b. Brian Warner, 5 January 1969, Canton, Florida, USA; vocals, tape loops), Daisy Berkowitz (guitar), Olivia Newton-Bundy (bass) and Zsa Zsa Speck (keyboards), later joined by Sara Lee Lucas (drums) - all the band members assuming forenames of female icons and surnames of famous murderers. Bundy and Speck were replaced at the end of 1989 by Gidget Gein and Madonna Wayne Gacy (b. Steve Bier), respectively. In keeping with their controversial image, they were the first band to be signed to Trent Reznor (Nine Inch Nails) and John A. Malm Jr's Nothing label. Support slots with the likes of Suicidal Tendencies, Meat Beat Manifesto, Murphy's Law and the Genitorturers brought them considerable local recognition, in the form of the 1993 'Slammy' awards (taking the song of the year nomination for 'Dope Hat') and sundry other baubles (not least, short-heading Gloria Estefan for the Best Local Musician category in *South Florida* Magazine). In December 1993 bassist Gein was replaced by Twiggy Ramirez (b. Jeordie Francis White, 20 June 1971, Florida, USA). Reznor acted as guest musician and executive producer on the group's 1994 debut album, with half of the tracks mixed at the house of the infamous Tate murders by the Manson family (where Nine Inch Nails also recorded). In March 1995 Lucas was replaced on drums by Ginger Fish (b. Kenny Wilson). Berkowitz also departed in June 1996 (he later sued the band for unpaid royalties and breach of contract) and was replaced by Zim Zum (b. Mike Nastasi). *Antichrist Superstar* included the American hit single 'The Beautiful People', and reached number 3 on the *Billboard* album charts. By 1998 they had become one of the biggest bands in the USA,a position aided as much by their notoriety and propensity for upsetting US right-wing and Christian groups as by their music.

● ALBUMS: *Portrait Of An American Family* (Nothing/East West 1994)★★, *Smells Like Children* (MCA 1996)★★, *Antichrist Superstar* (Nothing/Interscope 1996)★★★★, *Remix And Repent* (Nothing/Interscope 1998)★★★, *Mechanical Animals* (Nothing/Interscope 1998)★★★.

● VIDEOS: *Dead To The World* (Nothing/Interscope 1998).

● FURTHER READING: *The Long Hard Road Out Of Hell*, Marilyn Manson with Neil Strauss. *Marilyn Manson - A Biography*, Kurt B. Reighley.

MARINO, FRANK

b. 22 August 1954, Canada. This formidable guitarist obsessively based his style on Jimi Hendrix. Forming Mahogany Rush in 1970 (later known as Frank Marino And Mahogany Rush), he decided to work solely under his own name from 1980 onwards. Playing the Heavy Metal Holocaust Festival in Port Vale during 1981, he was the surprise success of the day, upstaging headliners

Triumph with a truly dazzling display of guitar pyrotechnics and showmanship. *The Power Of Rock 'N' Roll* was the first release under Marino's own name and featured a more aggressive style, coupled with lyrical references to sensitive social and political issues of the time. *Juggernaut* built on this success, but increased the tempo and introduced a greater degree of melody to the material. A four-year break from recording ensued, owing to business and management setbacks, before *Full Circle* appeared in 1986. A stunning double live album was issued two years later, but nothing further appeared until a single-track contribution to the *Guitar Speak Vol.2* album was released in 1990.

● ALBUMS: *The Power Of Rock 'N' Roll* (Columbia 1981)★★★, *Juggernaut* (Columbia 1982)★★★★, *Full Circle* (Maze 1986)★★★★, *Double Live* (Maze 1988)★★★.

MARIONETTE

Formed in the early 80s in Islington, London, Marionette were a four-piece group in the tradition of the New York Dolls and Faces. The main strength of the band, fronted by vocalist Ray Zell, along with Dave Veal on guitar, KK (b. Kevin Matthew) on bass and Pig (b. Adam Honey) on drums, was in their live performances, which at times recalled the punk gigs of the mid- to late 70s. Their first release was *Provocatively Trashy*, a live cassette, after which they ventured into the recording studio for 'My Baby Sucks', which was a proposed single at the time, but did not materialize. By 1985 Zell was making a name for himself as a journalist in the music press, eventually working for *Kerrang!* magazine where he created the long-running cartoon character, Pandora Peroxide. Heavy Metal Records did release one album by them, but UK glam had long since given way to American imports. Zell revived the band at the request of the Quireboys' Spike, who invited Marionette to open for them at the London Dominion in 1988. Zell now seems content to concentrate on writing. Pig married and moved abroad, and Veal works as a school caretaker. KK worked at Wessex Studios as assistant to Bill Price, and later became a freelance engineer and producer, working with EMF, Catherine Wheel, Nymphs and the Wildhearts.

● ALBUMS: *Blonde Secrets And Dark Bombshells* (Heavy Metal 1985)★★★

MARSDEN, BERNIE

This masterly UK guitarist rose to prominence during his stints with Babe Ruth, UFO and Whitesnake. At the turn of the 70s Marsden took time out between Whitesnake projects to record solo material. He was assisted by several noteworthy musicians who included Ian Paice, Cozy Powell, Simon Phillips, Don Airey, Neil Murray and Jack Bruce. The albums featured melodic hard rock, with Marsden successfully handling the vocals as well as some extended guitar workouts. He subsequently formed Bernie Marsden's S.O.S., which later became known as Alaska. Marsden remains an accomplished musician, able to offer enormous variety and depth to heavy rock, although the solo trail was never his most rewarding enterprise.

● ALBUMS: *And About Time Too* (Sunburst 1979)★★★, *Look At Me Now* (Sunburst 1981)★★.

MARSEILLE

This band was formed in London, England, in 1976, ostensibly to record the soundtrack to the Jane Birkin film *The French Way*. The original line-up consisted of Paul Dale (vocals), Neil Buchanan (guitar), Andy Charters (guitar), Steve Dinwoodie (bass) and Keith Knowles (drums). Signing to the now-defunct Mountain Records label, the band released their debut album in 1978. *Red, White And Slightly Blue* was a subtle blend of melodic rock and pop. A couple of tours followed, supporting UFO among others, on whom the band later modelled themselves. This was most noticeable on *Marseille*, where a more traditional hard rock sound was embraced. The group then encountered difficulties when Mountain Records went bankrupt. This left Marseille in limbo, but they resurfaced in 1983 with new personnel and a record contract. The new line-up consisted of ex-Savage Lucy vocalist Sav Pearse, Mark Hays (guitar), Neil Buchanan (guitar), Steve Dinwoodie (bass) and Keith Knowles (drums). They went on to record the band's third and final album, *Touch The Night*, which appeared on the Ultra Noise Records label in 1984. Still failing to make any real impact with either press or public, the band folded soon afterwards.

● ALBUMS: *Red, White And Slightly Blue* (Mountain 1978)★★★, *Marseille* (Mountain 1979)★★★, *Touch The Night* (Ultra Noise 1984)★★.

MARSHALL LAW

This Birmingham, England-based heavy metal quintet comprised Andy Pike (vocals), Dave Martin (guitar), Andy Southwell (guitar), Rog Davis (bass) and Mick Donovan (drums). Following in the tradition of UK rockers such as Judas Priest, Saxon and Iron Maiden, they transposed melody onto infectious, circular power-riffs, cleverly avoiding any monotony by the injection of twin lead guitar solos between rousing choruses. Signing to the Heavy Metal Records label, they released their self-titled debut in 1989 to considerable critical acclaim. Touted as the spearhead of a new revival in traditional UK heavy rock, there was nevertheless a lengthy eight-year gap before the release of *Metal Detector*.

● ALBUMS: *Marshall Law* (Heavy Metal 1989)★★★, *Metal Detector* (Neat Metal 1997)★★★.

MARTIN, ERIC

b. USA. The members of San Francisco, California, USA rock group the Eric Martin Band were drawn from an earlier collective who recorded an independently released album for the local Californian rock underground. With their new billing, giving greater prominence to singer/guitarist and songwriter Eric Martin, they secured a recording contract with CBS Records, which resulted in the release of *Sucker For A Pretty Face* in 1983 - a consummate example of melodic west coast metal. Afterwards, however, Martin took sole billing and dismissed his former colleagues to pursue a solo career with Capitol Records. After a disappointing self-titled solo album in 1985 he returned to form with the release of *I'm Only Fooling Myself* in 1986, though some considered the title to be an accurate reflection of his long-term prospects within the music industry.

● ALBUMS: with the Eric Martin Band *Sucker For A Pretty Face* (CBS 1983)★★★, *Eric Martin* (Capitol 1985)★★★, *I'm Only Fooling Myself* (Capitol 1986)★★.

MASSACRE

Formed in the USA in the mid-80s, Massacre were one of the earliest extreme thrash metal bands, acting as pioneers of a style that was a popular underground phenomenon long before gaining public attention and widespread success. Founder-members Kam Lee (vocals) and Rick Rozz (guitar) had been two-thirds of the first Death line-up with Chuck Schuldiner. When Schuldiner relocated to California, the duo put together Massacre with Terry Butler (bass) and Bill Andrews (drums). Like other early thrash/death metal bands from Florida, they spread their name by recording demo tapes that were sent around the world and traded with various contacts. In the late 80s death metal and extreme thrash were becoming increasingly popular, and bands were much more widespread than when Massacre was formed. After a period of non-activity (with Rozz, Butler and Andrews again joining *Leprosy*-era Death), this new attention provided an opportunity for Massacre to resume work, and they succeeded in gaining a record contract with UK label Earache, whose specialism in extreme music was well established. Their debut album saw Lee and Rozz reunited with Butler and Andrews to record *From Beyond*, a set primarily based on original demo material that had never been given official release. Successful touring in the USA preceded the April 1992 launch of a 12-inch, 'Inhuman Condition', which included a cover version of the Venom standard, 'Warhead', with guest vocals from that band's Cronos. The recording of a second album introduced a new rhythm section in Pete Sison (bass) and Syrus Peters (drums).

● ALBUMS: *From Beyond* (Earache 1991)★★★, *Promise* (Earache 1995)★★★.

MASTERS OF REALITY

This New York, USA-based quartet originally featured Chris Goss (vocals, guitar), Tim Harrington (guitar), Googe (bass) and Vinnie Indrizzo (drums). Deriving their name from the title of Black Sabbath's third album, they fused a diverse array of rock styles into a form that clearly invoked names such as the Doors, Vanilla Fudge, Love and Deep Purple. The group formed as early as 1980, after which they embarked on a long-haul club touring policy that eventually brought them serious attention. With the aid of producer Rick Rubin, who signed them originally to his Def Jam enterprise before it became Def American, they distilled their influences into a potent and powerful sound that had its roots in the 70s but was delivered with the technology of the present. Their self-titled debut was released to widespread critical acclaim in 1989, but fans had to wait another four years for *Sunrise On The Sufferbus*, which featured Ginger Baker alongside the only remaining members, Goss and Googe; the first line-up had imploded following disastrous touring engagements in support of their debut. A live album was released in 1997 that also featured Stone Temple Pilots vocalist Scott Weiland.

● ALBUMS: *Masters Of Reality* (Def American 1989)★★★, *Sunrise On The Sufferbus* (Def American 1993)★★★, *How High The Moon - Live At The Viper Room* (Malicious Vinyl 1997)★★.

MAX AND THE BROADWAY METAL CHOIR

'The Devil gave us Death Metal and God gave us Max': this was the publicity that introduced Maximilan Gelt - a Jewish delicatessen owner from Miami, Florida, in his late 40s. Max was asked by a friend to visit London to see a band, the Broadway Metal Choir, featuring Jan Cyrka (guitar), Kevin Riddles (bass, ex-Angelwitch; Tytan), Kevin Fitzpatrick (keyboards) and Andy Beirne (drums). As they lacked a vocalist, Max offered his services, but after six weeks of touring he broke his leg and returned to Miami. He later returned to London armed with new songs, and together with FM and guitarist Steve Boltz, and backing singers Suzie O'List and Gillian O'Donovan, he recorded 10 tracks of what can only be described as Led Zeppelin fronted by Mel Brooks. The press loved the story but not the finished product and, dejected, Max returned home to face a different type of music. His wife, Shirly, had launched divorce proceedings, claiming his recent obsession with heavy metal music had driven him 'insane'. The rest of the band split, returning to session work, or, in Cyrka's case, to minor guitar 'hero' status.

● ALBUMS: *And God Gave Us Max* (Powerstation 1986)★★.

MAX WEBSTER

This Toronto, Canada-based group was formed by guitarist Kim Mitchell, who had worked with various bands over the years, including MC5 and Alice Cooper. Mitchell was very much the central figure owing to his onstage showmanship and guitar ability. He was backed by Dave Myles on bass, Terry Watkinson on keyboards and Gerry McCracken on drums. The UK proved a hard nut to crack, but they tried hard in 1979 with two albums and a single, 'Paradise Skies', which featured guest appearances from fellow Canadians Rush. For some reason, British audiences turned their back on the band and most of the tour was cancelled. 1980's *Universal Juveniles* brought back some dignity but their career and songwriting was on the wane, and by 1982 they had split up. Mitchell continued as a solo artist.

● ALBUMS: *Hangover* (Mercury 1976)★★★, *High Class In Borrowed Shoes* (Mercury 1977)★★★, *Mutiny Up My Sleeve* (Capitol 1978)★★★, *A Million Vacations* (Capitol 1979)★★★, *Live Magnetic Air* (Capitol 1979)★★, *Universal Juveniles* (Mercury 1980)★★★.

MAY BLITZ

Formed in 1969, May Blitz comprised guitarist James Black and drummer Tony Newman, both veterans of Sounds Incorporated and the Jeff Beck Group. They were subsequently joined by Reid Hudson (bass). *May Blitz* showcased the trio's forceful sound and, in particular, Black's aggressive style, but it failed to emulate the success of stablemates Uriah Heep and Black Sabbath. *The Second Of May* was less satisfying and the group split up soon after its release. Newman subsequently joined Three Man Army and Boxer.

● ALBUMS: *May Blitz* (Vertigo 1970)★★★, *The Second Of May* (Vertigo 1971)★★.

MAY, BRIAN

b. 19 July 1947, Twickenham, Middlesex, England. Best known as the flamboyant and highly original guitarist in Queen, May has also recorded in his own right. In the summer of 1983 he teamed up with Eddie Van Halen (guitar), REO Speedwagon's Alan Gratzer (drums), Fred Mandel (keybords) and Phil Chen (bass) for a supergroup session, which was released under the title *Star Fleet Project*. He subsequently produced the spoof heavy metal group Bad News, as well as the recording of 'Anyone Can Fall In Love' by his actress partner Anita Dobson. He also worked with Steve Hackett, completed a solo album and, in 1991, wrote and recorded the score for a production of Shakespeare's *Macbeth*. Following a commission for an advertisement by the Ford Motor Company in 1991, May released a further single, 'Driven By You', which became a sizeable hit at the end of 1991. He was also one of the prime movers behind the Freddie Mercury AIDS Benefit in 1992, and he has sustained himself admirably as a solo artist in the wake of the latter's death. *Another World* featured the late Cozy Powell on drums but, like its predecessor, was an anonymous MOR collection.

● ALBUMS: *Star Fleet Project* (EMI 1983)★★, *Back To The Light* (EMI 1992)★★, *Live At Brixton* (EMI 1994)★★, *Another World* (Parlophone 1998)★★.

● VIDEOS: *Star Licks* (Star Licks Master Series 1986), *Live At The Brixton Academy* (1994).

● FURTHER READING *Queen & I: The Brian May Story*, Laura Jackson.

MAYHEM

Formed in Norway by Euronymous (real name Oystien Aarseth), who was a young fan of the Satanic black metal played by bands such as Bathory and Venom, Mayhem made their first impact with the 1984 demo *Pure Fucking Armageddon*, which is regarded in underground circles as a classic of extreme metal. The black metal genre was losing popularity, however, along with the leather-and-chains imagery and Satanic lyrics that were its trademark. Rather than follow heavy metal fashion and adopt the hardcore punk or death metal genres that were becoming popular, Euronymous opted to preserve purist black metal. In order to do so, he opened a record shop in Oslo named Helvete (Norwegian for 'Hell') and founded the Deathlike Silence label, both dedicated solely to black metal. In 1987 he released *Deathcrush*, Mayhem's official debut, which featured six songs in 17 and a half minutes of frenzied angst. Then, in 1991, the band's vocalist shot himself (by way of black irony, he went under the stagename 'Dead'). Rather than halting Euronymous's black metal crusade, the tragedy appeared to have redoubled his faith. Mayhem inspired a number of Scandinavian bands to readopt the musical style and imagery of black metal during the early 90s, while Euronymous became an increasingly melodramatic and popular spokesman on the extreme metal underground, with his philosophies of cold hate and spite. A series of Norwegian church burnings in early 1993 were linked to the Black Metal Circle, a cult-like group centred around Euronymous's black metal crusade and dominated by members of bands such as Emperor, Dark Throne and Burzum, all signed to Deathlike Silence. Euronymous revelled in the international publicity. However, on 10 August 1993, he was found, stabbed 25 times, outside his Oslo apartment. Two weeks later, Varg Vikernes (better known by his stage-name of Count Grishnakh) of the band Burzum was arrested for the murder, and convicted the following year. Vikernes had been Euronymous's right-hand man, and it is not apparent whether the murder was committed because of a financial dispute over record royalties, over a woman, or because of darker doctrinal differences between the two. What does seem clear is that Euronymous was consumed by the vivid world of pain and hate he had himself created, while the black metal revival he inspired continues unabated. In 1994 *De Mysteriis Dom Sathanas*, Mayhem's last recording, was released posthumously. Sinisterly, it featured Grishnakh on bass guitar.

● ALBUMS: *Deathcrush* (Deathlike Silence 1987)★★★, *De Mysteriis Dom Sathanas* (Deathlike Silence 1994)★★★.

MC5

Formed in 1964 in Detroit, Michigan, USA, and originally known as the Motor City Five, the group was sundered the following year when its rhythm section left in protest over a new song, 'Back To Comm'. Michael Davis (bass) and Dennis Thompson (drums) joined founder-members Rob Tyner (b. Robert Derminer, 12 December 1944, Detroit, Michigan, USA, d. 18 September 1991; vocals), Wayne Kramer (guitar) and Fred 'Sonic' Smith (b. 1949, d. 4 November 1994; guitar) to pursue the radical direction this experimental composition offered. By 1967 their repertoire included material drawn from R&B, soul and *avant garde* jazz, as well as a series of powerful original songs. Two singles, 'One Of The Guys'/'I Can Only Give You Everything' (1967) and 'Borderline'/'Looking At You' (1968), captured their nascent, high-energy sound as the group embraced the 'street' politics proselytized by mentor/manager John Sinclair. Now linked to this former DJ's Trans Love Commune and White Panther party, the MC5 became Detroit's leading underground act, and a recording contract with the Elektra label resulted in the seminal *Kick Out The Jams*. Recorded live at the city's Grande Ballroom, this turbulent set captured the quintet's extraordinary sound, which, although loud, was never reckless. However, MC5 were dropped from their label's roster following several disagreements, but later emerged anew on Atlantic Records. Rock journalist Jon Landau, later manager of Bruce Springsteen, was invited to produce *Back In The USA*, which, if lacking the dissolute thrill of its predecessor, showed a group able to adapt to studio discipline. 'Tonight', 'Shakin' Street' and a remade 'Lookin' At You' are among the highlights of this excellent set. A third collection, *High Time*, reasserted a desire to experiment, and several local jazz musicians added punch to what nonetheless remains a curiously ill-focused album on which each member, bar Davis, contributed material. A move to Europe, where the group performed and recorded under the aegis of Rohan O'Rahilly, failed to halt dwindling commercial prospects, while the departure of Davis, then Tyner, in 1972, brought the MC5 to an end. Their reputation flourished during the punk phenomenon, during which time each former member enjoyed brief notoriety. Davis later surfaced in Destroy All Monsters, and Sonic Smith married Patti Smith (and was heavily featured on the singer/poet's 'comeback' album, *Dream Of Life*, in 1988). Both Kramer and Tyner attempted to use the

MC5 name for several unrelated projects. They wisely abandoned such practices, leaving intact the legend of one of rock's most uncompromising and exciting acts. In September 1991 Tyner died of a heart attack in the seat of his parked car in his home-town of Ferndale, Michigan. Smith also passed away three years later. Kramer, however, relaunched a solo career in the same year, enlisting several prominent members of the US underground/alternative scene as his new cohorts.

● ALBUMS: *Kick Out The Jams* (Elektra 1969)★★★★, *Back In The USA* (Elektra 1970)★★★, *High Time* (Elektra 1971)★★, *Do It* (Revenge 1987)★★, *Live Detroit 68/69* (Revenge 1988)★.

● COMPILATIONS: *Babes In Arms* cassette only (ROIR 1983)★★★, *Looking At You* (Receiver 1994)★★★, *Power Trip* (Alive 1994)★★★.

McDonald, Brian, Group

This melodic US pop-rock outfit was put together in 1987 by keyboard wizard Brian McDonald. Enlisting the services of Will Hodges (guitar), Andrew G. Wilkes (bass), and D.W. Adams (drums), the group signed to Capitol Records and released *Desperate Business* the same year. Influenced by Nightranger, Bryan Adams and Jeff Paris, the album was a solid musical statement, marred only by McDonald's vocals, which lacked both power and range. However, the set did feature singer/actress Fiona on backing vocals, which helped the cause.

● ALBUMS: *Desperate Business* (Capitol 1987)★★★.

McKagan, Duff

b. Michael McKagan, 5 February 1964, Seattle, Washington, USA. Guns N'Roses' bass player, McKagan has served time in more *ad hoc* bands than anybody can care to remember. It was once said of McKagan that there were few punk/hard rock outfits in Seattle with whom he had not played at some point, with bands including the Fartz, Ten Minute Warning, Thankless Dogs, Silly Killers and Wandering Bandeleros. However, in 1993 McKagan decided to take the big step towards a solo career. Writing and playing most of the instruments, his debut included guest appearances by a fine array of rock's glitterati, Jeff Beck, Lenny Kravitz, Sebastian Bach (Skid Row) among them. There were also appearances from his Guns N'Roses workmates Matt Sorum, Gilby Clarke and Slash, just to prove there were no bad feelings about his foray. Despite the strength of the largely power-pop musical backing, McKagan's lyrics revealed only faint flashes of insight, notably on 'Man In The Meadow', dedicated to his former best friend, Todd Crew, who died of an overdose in 1987. It also disappointed those expecting him to return to his punk roots (he sang half of the tracks on Guns N'Roses punk tribute album, *The Spaghetti Incident*).

● ALBUMS: *Believe In Me* (Geffen 1993)★★★.

Meanstreak

Originating from New York, USA, Meanstreak were formed in 1985 by guitarists Marlene Apuzzo and Rena Sands. Recruiting vocalist Bettina France, bassist Martens Pace and drummer Diane Keyser, they were the first all-female thrash metal band to record an album. Signing to the independent Music For Nations label, they released *Roadkill*, produced by Alex Perialas and ex-Raven drummer Rob Hunter. Recorded within a week, the pressure resulted in a set that betrayed its origins by being both shambolic and ill-focused. The songs, meanwhile, were rigidly formularized and were further scuppered by weak vocals. The album remains of interest to thrash aficionados, but even then, only on a historical rather than musical level.

● ALBUMS: *Roadkill* (Music For Nations 1988)★★.

Meat Loaf

b. Marvin Lee Aday, 27 September 1951, Dallas, Texas, USA. Meat Loaf strongly claims this date of birth, but it has also been suggested as 1947. The name Meat Loaf originated at school, when, aged 13, he was christened 'Meat Loaf' by his football coach, owing to his enormous size and ungainly manner. Two years later his mother died of cancer, and fights with his alcoholic father grew worse. He moved to Los Angeles in 1967 and formed Popcorn Blizzard, a psychedelic rock group that toured the club circuit, opening for acts including the Who, Ted Nugent and the Stooges. In 1969 Meat Loaf successfully auditioned for a role in *Hair*, where he met soul vocalist Stoney. Stoney and Meat Loaf recorded a self-titled album in 1971, which spawned the minor *Billboard* chart hit, 'What You See Is What You Get'. *Hair* closed in New York in 1974, and Meat Loaf found new work in *More Than You Deserve*, a musical written by Jim Steinman, then took the part of Eddie in the film version of *The Rocky Horror Picture Show*. In 1976, he was recruited by Ted Nugent to sing lead vocals on his *Free For All*, after which he joined up with Steinman once more in the famous US satirical comedy outfit, the National Lampoon Roadshow.

Meat Loaf and Steinman struck up a working musical relationship and started composing a grandiose rock opera. After a long search, they found Epic Records and producer Todd Rundgren sympathetic to their ideas and demo tapes. Enlisting the services of Bruce Springsteen's E Street Band, they recorded *Bat Out Of Hell* in 1978. This was pieced together around the high camp of the title track, an operatic horror melodrama that saw Meat Loaf raging against nature, and 'Paradise By The Dashboard Lights', with Ellen Foley providing female accompaniment. The album was ignored for the first six months after release, although Meat Loaf toured extensively, supporting Cheap Trick, among others. Eventually the breakthrough came, and *Bat Out Of Hell* rocketed towards the top of the charts in country after country. It stayed in the UK and US album charts for 395 and 88 weeks, respectively, and sold in excess of 30 million copies worldwide, the third biggest-selling album release of all time. However, with success came misfortune. Meat Loaf split with his manager, David Sonenberg, causing all manner of litigation. He was also drinking heavily, unable to cope with his new-found but barely anticipated stardom, and lost his voice. He lost his songwriter too, as Steinman left for the solo release of what had been mooted as a thematic follow-up to *Bat Out Of Hell - Bad For Good*: 'I spent seven months trying to make a follow-up with him, and it was an infernal nightmare. He had lost his voice, he had lost his house, and he was pretty much losing his mind'. After a three-year gap, during which Meat Loaf voluntarily declared himself bankrupt, the eagerly anticipated follow-up, *Dead Ringer*, was released. Again, it used Steinman's compositions, this time in his absence, and continued where *Bat Out Of Hell* left off, comprising grandiose arrangements, anthemic choruses and spirited rock 'n' roll. The title song made the Top 5 in the UK and the album hit number 1, but it only dented the lower end of the Top 50 *Billboard* album chart. This was, seemingly, the last time Meat Loaf would be able to use Steinman's sympathetic songwriting skills, and the consequent decline in standards undoubtedly handicapped the second phase of his career. Concentrating on Europe, relentless touring helped both *Midnight At The Lost And Found* and *Bad Attitude* to creep into the UK Top 10 album chart. Nevertheless, this represented a significant decline in popularity compared with his Steinman-penned albums. *Blind Before I Stop* saw Meat Loaf teaming up with John Parr for the single 'Rock'n'Roll Mercenaries', which, surprisingly, was not a hit. The album was, however, his strongest post-Steinman release and featured a fine selection of accessible, blues-based hard-rock numbers. In live performances, things had never been better; Meat Loaf's band included Bob Kulick (brother of Kiss guitarist Bruce Kulick, and now of Skull), and ex-Rainbow drummer Chuck Burgi. They delivered an electrifying show that ran for nearly three hours. Recorded at London's Wembley Stadium, *Meat Loaf Live* emerged in 1987, and featured raw and exciting versions of his finest songs. By this time, Meat Loaf was also a veteran of several films, including *Roadie*, *Americathon* and, in the 90s, *Wayne's World* and *Leap Of Faith*. Apart from re-releases and compilations, he maintained a recording silence well into the 90s. However, he signed a new contract with Virgin Records in 1990, and as rumours grew that he was once again working with Steinman, the media bandwagon began to roll. *Bat Out Of Hell II: Back Into Hell*, from its title onwards displayed a calculated, stylistic cloning of its precursor. The public greeted the familiarity with open arms, propelling the first single, 'I'd Do Anything For Love (But I Won't Do That)', to number 1 in both the USA and UK, its parent album performing the same feat. Though critics could point at the formulaic nature of their approach, Meat Loaf had no doubts that by working with Steinman again, he had recaptured the magic. Steinman was noticeably absent from *Welcome To The Neighbourhood*, apart from two old compositions. Instead, the excellent pulp magazine-style package contained songs that sound exactly like Steinman's work, particularly 'I'd Lie For You' and 'If This Is The Last Kiss', both written by Diane Warren.

● ALBUMS: *Bat Out Of Hell* (Epic 1978)★★★★, *Dead Ringer* (Epic 1981)★★★, *Midnight At The Lost And Found* (Epic 1983)★★★, *Bad Attitude* (Arista 1985)★★★, *Blind Before I Stop* (Arista 1986)★★★, *Meat Loaf Live* (Arista 1987)★★★, *Bat Out Of Hell II: Back Into Hell* (Virgin 1993)★★★, *Alive In Hell* (Pure Music 1994)★★★, *Welcome To The Neighbourhood* (Virgin 1995)★★★.

● COMPILATIONS: *Hits Out Of Hell* (Epic 1984)★★★, with Bonnie Tyler *Heaven & Hell* (1993)★★, *Rock'n'Roll Hero* (Pickwick 1994)★★.

● VIDEOS: *Live At Wembley* (Videoform 1984), *Bad Attitude Live* (Virgin Vision 1986), *Hits Out Of Hell* (Epic 1985), *Meat Loaf Live* (MIA 1991), *Bat Out Of Hell II - Picture Show* (1994).

● FURTHER READING: *Meatloaf: Jim Steinman And The Phenomenology Of Excess*, Sandy Robertson.

MEGADETH

This thrash metal quartet was founded in San Francisco, California, USA, by guitarist Dave Mustaine after leaving Metallica in 1983 (he co-wrote four songs on the latter's debut album, though he did not actually appear on it). Recruiting bassist Dave Ellefson, guitarist Chris Poland and drummer Gars Samuelson, Mustaine negotiated a contract with the independent Combat label. Working on a tight budget, Megadeth produced *Killing Is My Business...And Business Is Good* in 1985. This was a ferocious blast of high-energy thrash metal, weakened by a thin production. Nevertheless, Capitol Records, realizing the band's potential, immediately signed them, even though Mustaine was beginning to acquire a reputation for his outspoken and provocative manner. *Peace Sells...But Who's Buying?* was a marked improvement over their debut, both technically and musically. It was characterized by incessant, heavy-duty riffing, bursts of screaming guitar and lyrics that reflected Mustaine's outspoken perception of contemporary social and political issues. In 1988 Mustaine fired Poland and Samuelson (who then formed Fatal Opera), bringing in Jeff Young and Chuck Behler as replacements before the recording of *So Far, So Good...So What!* This built on their aggressive and vitriolic style, and included a cover version of 'Anarchy In The UK', with the Sex Pistols' guitarist Steve Jones making a guest appearance. Following two years of heroin-related problems, and the enforced departure of Poland and Behler, Mustaine reappeared in 1990 with guitar virtuoso Marty Friedman and drummer Nick Menza. *Rust In Peace* was released to widespread critical acclaim, combining an anti-nuclear message with the explosive guitar pyrotechnics of Friedman. *Countdown To Extinction*, meanwhile, was a bruising encounter that entertained more melody in the execution of its theme - that of impending ecological disaster. Reports of Mustaine's drug problems again overshadowed sessions for their sixth album, *Youthanasia*, recorded in Phoenix, Arizona, where three-quarters of the band now live. It was produced by Max Norman (who co-produced *Countdown To Extinction* and mixed *Rust In Peace*). Along with Slayer, Metallica and Anthrax, Megadeth remain at the forefront of the thrash metal genre, despite the vulnerability of their central creative force. In 1998 drummer Nick Menza left the band due to 'health problems'; he was replaced by Jimmy Degrasso.

● ALBUMS: *Killing Is My Business...And Business Is Good* (Megaforce 1985)★★, *Peace Sells ... But Who's Buying?* (Capitol 1986)★★★, *So Far, So Good ... So What!* (Capitol 1988)★★★, *Rust In Peace* (Capitol 1990)★★★★, *Countdown To Extinction* (Capitol 1992)★★★, *Youthanasia* (Capitol 1994)★★★, *Hidden Treasures* (Capitol 1995)★★★, *Cryptic Writings* (Capitol 1997)★★★.

● VIDEOS: *Exposure Of A Dream* (PMI 1993), *Evolver: The Making Of Youthanasia* (Capitol 1995).

MELVINS

The late Kurt Cobain of Nirvana described the US rock band the Melvins as his favourite group. Unsurprising, perhaps, as they are the only other band of note to originate from his home-town of Aberdeen in the USA (though they have since relocated to San Francisco), and he did once roadie for them. Drummer Dale Crover also played with Nirvana for a spell, while Cobain guested on and co-produced *Houdini* for the band. The other members of the Melvins, formed in 1984, were Buzz Osbourne (vocals, guitar) and Lori Beck (bass). Matt Lukin (Mudhoney) was also a floating member. Reputed to be more influenced by the heavy rock angle than many who have fallen under the generic title 'grunge', the Melvins are big fans of Black Sabbath and even released three solo albums in a tribute to the Kiss strategy of similar pretensions. A cover version of Flipper's 'Way Of The World' and 'Sacrifice' sat alongside Alice Cooper's 'Ballad Of Dwight Fry' on the cover album *Lysol*. *Stoner Witch*, their second album for Atlantic Records/East West, saw Crover and Osbourne joined by bass player Mark Deutrom, who had previously produced the band's first two albums. This time, they were working with Garth Richardson of Red Hot Chili Peppers and L7 fame. Two albums with Atlantic failed to break the band into the mainstream and they moved to a subsidiary for *Stag*. It was felt that a smaller label would be more supportive to the band, rather than being lost in the wave of releases from a large label.

● ALBUMS: *Gluey Porch Treatments* (Alchemy 1987)★★★, *Ozma* (Boner 1989)★★, *Bullhead* (Boner 1991)★★, *Lysol* (Boner/Tupelo 1992)★★★, *Houdini* (Atlantic 1993)★★★, *Prick* (Amphetamine Reptile 1994)★★★, *Stoner Witch* (Atlantic 1994)★★★, *Stag* (Mammoth 1996)★★★, *Honky* (Amphetamine Reptile 1997)★★, *Live At The F**ker Club* (Amphetamine 1998)★★.

● COMPILATIONS: *Singles 1-12* (Amphetamine Reptile 1997)★★★.

Mental Hippie Blood

Comprising Michael Oran (vocals), Mikael Jansson (guitar), Jonas Pettersson (guitar), Lake Skoglund (bass) and Anders Odenstrand (drums), Swedish heavy metal band Mental Hippie Blood formed in 1992. Their name gave some clue as to the nature of their music - a brutal collision of 60s psychedelia and acid rock (notably the work of Jimi Hendrix) with contemporary hard rock (especially groups such as Anthrax). The group evolved after Oran returned from a period in the USA and replaced the original singer in a long-running band known as the Glorious Bankrobbers - the original nucleus for the members of Mental Hippie Blood. Their debut album and attendant single, 'Don't Talk', saw the press locate them at the forefront of a new wave of Swedish heavy metal. In particular, their lyrics were celebrated for the complete absence of 'Norse Gods or magic swords'.

● ALBUMS: *Mental Hippie Blood* (MNW 1993)★★★.

Mercyful Fate

This seminal black metal act was formed in Copenhagen, Denmark, in 1980 by vocalist King Diamond (b. Kim Bendix Petersen, 14 June 1956, Copenhagen, Denmark) and guitarist Hank Shermann with Michael Denner (guitar), Timi Grabber Hansen (bass) and Kim Ruzz (drums). The band's first vinyl appearance was with 'Black Funeral' on the *Metallic Storm* compilation, before *A Corpse Without Soul* (aka *Nuns Have No Fun*) saw the full debut of their heavy yet intricate guitar-based approach, and of King Diamond's unique vocal style, which ranged from deep bass growls to falsetto shrieks. *Melissa*, with a name taken from the human skull owned by Diamond and used as a stage prop, fulfilled Mercyful Fate's promise, and the band became one of the mainstays of the black metal underground with their occult lyricism and theatrical approach (though Diamond's facial make-up later prompted legal action from Kiss's Gene Simmons over alleged similarities to his 'God Of Thunder' persona). *Don't Break The Oath* was a more mature work, as the band reaped the benefits of extensive touring with a tighter sound. However, when they regrouped after further successful live work to record a third album, Shermann's determination to pursue a surprising AOR direction saw the band split, with Diamond going on to a solo career with Hansen and Denner in tow, while Shermann formed Fate. The posthumous release of *In The Beginning*, containing the debut mini-album plus BBC session tracks, seemed to be an epitaph for Mercyful Fate. However, the heavier approach of Shermann and Denner's Zoser Mez led to the reformation of the old band, with Ruzz replaced by Morten Nielsen on *In The Shadows*, and by Snowy Shaw on tour (the latter taking up the position permanently).

The record recalled *Don't Break The Oath*'s style, and also featured a guest appearance by Metallica's Lars Ulrich on 'Return Of The Vampire', a song resurrected from the band's second demo in 1982. Before 1994's *Time*, Hansen was replaced on bass by Sharlee D'Angelo, as the group toured the USA with Flotsam & Jetsam and Cathedral (live recordings from which were released as *The Bell Witch* EP). When *Time* did emerge, it provided unexpected diversions, with the Middle-Eastern flavour of 'The Mad Arab' and the serenity of 'Witch's Dance' rubbing shoulders with more traditional Mercyful Fate concerns ('Nightmare Be Thy Name', etc.).

● ALBUMS: *A Corpse Without Soul* mini-album (Rave-On 1982)★★, *Melissa* (Roadrunner 1983)★★★, *Don't Break The Oath* (Roadrunner 1984)★★★, *In The Shadows* (Metal Blade 1993)★★★, *Time* (Metal Blade 1994)★★★.

● COMPILATIONS: *In The Beginning* (Roadrunner 1988)★★, *Return Of The Vampire* (Roadrunner 1992)★★★.

Messiah Force

Formed in Jonquire, Canada, in 1984, the band consisted of Lynn Renaud (vocals), Bastien Deschênes (guitar), Jean Tremblay (guitar), Eric Parisé (bass) and Jean-Francois Boucher (drums). The band was essentially formed from the ashes of two local power metal bands, Exode and Frozen. Utilizing a sound that was reminiscent of early Warlock, the band released their debut, *The Last Day*, on the small independent Haissem Records label in 1987. Though a strong power metal release, the album went largely unnoticed, resulting in the band's demise soon after its release.

● ALBUMS: *The Last Day* (Haissem 1987)★★★.

Metal Church

Formed in Seattle, USA, in 1982, Metal Church initially comprised David Wayne (vocals), Kurt Vanderhoof (guitar), Craig Wells (guitar), Duke Erickson (bass) and Kirk Arrington (drums). Their first album was a phenomenal debut, brimming with energy and promise. The style was the then-evolving thrash metal sound, and Metal Church executed their own brand with precision. *The Dark* was a strong follow-up, but failed to surpass the debut, and Wayne left at this point to be replaced by Mike Howe for the recording of *Blessing In Disguise*, another commendable effort. Vanderhoof then retired from the band's ranks owing to his dislike of touring, and was replaced by John Marshall, previously guitar technician for Metallica. Metal Church have proved to be a consistently excellent band, but have failed to rise to the level of success suggested by their first album. Personnel changes and short tenures with their record companies have undoubtedly contributed to their underachievement.

● ALBUMS: *Metal Church* (Ground Zero 1985)★★★★, *The Dark* (Elektra 1987)★★★, *Blessing In Disguise* (Elektra 1989)★★★, *The Human Factor* (Epic 1991)★★, *Hanging In The Balance* (Blackheart 1994)★★.

METALLICA

The most consistently innovative metal band of the late 80s and early 90s was formed in 1981 in California, USA, by Lars Ulrich (b. 26 December 1963, Copenhagen, Denmark; drums) and James Alan Hetfield (b. 3 August 1963, USA; guitar, vocals) after each separately advertised for fellow musicians in the classified section of American publication *The Recycler*. They recorded their first demo, *No Life Til' Leather*, with Lloyd Grand (guitar), who was replaced in January 1982 by David Mustaine, whose relationship with Ulrich and Hetfield proved unsatisfactory. Jef Warner (guitar) and Ron McGovney (bass) each had a brief tenure with the group, and at the end of 1982 Clifford Lee Burton (b. 10 February 1962, USA, d. 27 September 1986; bass), formerly of Trauma, joined the band, playing his first live performance on 5 March 1983. Mustaine departed to form Megadeth and was replaced by Kirk Hammett (b. 18 November 1962, San Francisco, California, USA; guitar). Hammett, who came to the attention of Ulrich and Hetfield while playing with rock band Exodus, played his first concert with Metallica on 16 April 1983. The Ulrich, Hetfield, Burton and Hammett combination endured until disaster struck the band in the small hours of 27 September 1986, when Metallica's tour bus overturned in Sweden, killing Cliff Burton. During those four years, the group put thrash metal on the map with the aggression and exuberance of their debut, *Kill 'Em All*, the album sleeve of which bore the legend 'Bang that head that doesn't bang'. This served as a template for a whole new breed of metal, though the originators themselves were quick to dispense with their own rulebook. Touring with New Wave Of British Heavy Metal bands Raven and Venom followed, while Music For Nations signed them for European distribution. Although *Ride The Lightning* was not without distinction, notably on 'For Whom The Bell Tolls', it was *Master Of Puppets* that offered further evidence of Metallica's appetite for the epic. Their first album for Elektra in the USA (who had also re-released its predecessor), this was a taut, multi-faceted collection that both raged and lamented with equal conviction. After the death of Burton, the band elected to continue, the remaining three members recruiting Jason Newsted (b. 4 March 1963; bass) of Flotsam And Jetsam. Newsted played his first concert with the band on 8 November 1986. The original partnership of Ulrich and Hetfield, however, remained responsible for Metallica's lyrics and musical direction. The new line-up's first recording together was *The $5.98 EP - Garage Days Revisited* - a collection of cover versions including material from Budgie, Diamond Head, Killing Joke and the Misfits, which also served as a neat summation of the group's influences to date. Sessions for *...And Justice For All* initially began with Guns N'Roses producer Mike Clink at the helm, before the group opted to return to Johnny Zazula, a realtionship they had begun with *Ride The Lightning*. A long and densely constructed effort, this 1988 opus included an appropriately singular spectacular moment in 'One', also released as a single, while elsewhere the barrage of riffs somewhat obscured the usual Metallica artistry. Songs continued to deal with large themes - justice and retribution, insanity, war, religion and relationships, on 1991's *Metallica*. Compared to *Kill 'Em All* nearly a decade previously, however, the group had grown from iconoclastic chaos to thoughtful harmony, hallmarked by sudden and unexpected changes of mood and tempo. The MTV-friendly 'Enter Sandman' broke the band on a stadium level. Constant touring in the wake of the album ensued, along with a regular itinerary of awards ceremonies. There could surely be no more deserving recipients, Metallica having dragged mainstream metal, not so much kicking and screaming as whining and complaining, into a bright new dawn when artistic redundancy seemed inevitable. *Metallica* was certified as having sold nine million copies in the USA by June 1996, and one month later *Load* entered the US charts at number 1. The following year's *Re-Load* collected together more tracks recorded at the *Load* sessions, and featured 60s icon Marianne Faithfull on the first single to be released from the album, 'The Memory Remains'.

● ALBUMS: *Kill 'Em All* (Megaforce 1983)★★★, *Ride The Lightning* (Megaforce 1984)★★, *Master Of Puppets* (Elektra 1986)★★★★, *... And Justice For All* (Elektra 1988)★★★, *Metallica* (Elektra 1991)★★★★, *Live Shit: Binge & Purge* 3-CD set (Elektra 1993)★★★★, *Load* (Mercury 1996)★★★★, *Re-Load* (Vertigo 1997)★★★.

● VIDEOS: *Lick 'Em Up* (PolyGram Music Video 1988), *Home Vid Cliff 'Em All* (Channel 5 1988), *2 Of One* (Channel 5 1989), *A Year And A Half In The Life Of Metallica* (1992), *Live Shit: Binge And Purge* (Elektra Entertainment 1993), *A Year And A Half: Volume 1* (1993), *A Year And A Half: Volume 2* (1993).

● FURTHER READING: *A Visual Documentary*, Mark Putterford. *In Their Own Words*, Mark Putterford. *Metallica Unbound*, K.J. Doughton. *Metallica's Lars Ulrich: An Up-Close Look At The Playing Style Of ...*, Dino Fauci. *Metallica Live!*, Mark Putterford. *Metallica: The Frayed Ends Of Metal*, Chris Crocker. *The Making Of: Metallica's Metallica*, Mick Wall and Malcom Dome. *From Silver To Black*, Ross Halfin.

METHOD OF DESTRUCTION

Following his work in legendary New York hardcore act Stormtroopers Of Death, vocalist Billy Milano formed M.O.D. (as they are commonly known) with Tim McMurtrie (guitar), Ken Ballone (bass) and Keith Davis (drums). The quality of the groove-based hardcore on *USA For MOD* was overshadowed by controversy over apparently racist and near-fascist lyrics, although Milano later explained in an open letter to the press that his aim was to illustrate prejudice by writing from the bigot's perspective in the first person, thus stirring up truly negative reactions to these attitudes in the process. Milano subsequently noted that many of the most contentious lyrics were written by Anthrax's Scott Ian for the SOD. The subsequent tour, while successful, proved unhealthy for MOD, with McMurtrie breaking his leg and continuing in a wheelchair, while Ballone broke his arm, and the line-up split after the tour. Milano was then joined by guitarist Louie Svitek, bassist John Monte (who had toured in place of the injured Ballone) and drummer Tim Mallare for the lyrically lighter *Surfin' MOD*, where Milano's sense of humour shone through, and the new band moved towards a metal/hardcore crossover style. *Gross Misconduct* maintained the quality, although Milano peppered the lyric sheet with explanations as he once more tackled serious subject matter. However, personal problems enforced Milano's departure from the music scene, with Svitek and Monte going on to form Mindfunk. MOD were revived as a trio in 1992 after the SOD reunion, with Milano (adopting the bassist role as he had in his days with the Psychos), drummer Dave Chavarri and the returning McMurtrie on guitar for *Rhythm Of Fear*, sounding like the band had never been away. Despite a rather fluid line-up thereafter, *Devolution* showed that Milano - now rhythm guitarist, with Rob Moscheti on bass - was still producing strong and relevant hardcore to match the likes of Biohazard and Sick Of It All.

● ALBUMS: *USA For MOD* (Megaforce 1987)★★★★, *Surfin' MOD* mini-album (Megaforce 1988)★★★, *Gross Misconduct* (Megaforce 1989)★★★, *Rhythm Of Fear* (Megaforce 1992)★★★★, *Devolution* (Music For Nations 1994)★★★.

MILLER, DONNIE

This American guitarist and singer-songwriter was most widely renowned for his leather-clad biker image. Influenced by Steve Earle, Bruce Springsteen and the old blues masters, he specialized in a laid-back, understated approach, with fluid but economical lead guitar breaks. Signed to Epic Records, he released *One Of The Boys*, ably assisted by Vince Kirk (second guitar), Norman Dahlor (bass), Kurt Carow (keyboards) and Tim 'Kix' Kelly (drums). The album also featured guest appearances from Cyndi Lauper and Tommy Shaw (of Damn Yankees). 'The Devil Wears Lingerie' attracted some attention as a single, with its provocative and sordid promotional video, but it effectively marked the last sighting of the artist.

● ALBUMS: *One Of The Boys* (Epic 1989).

MILLER, STEVE

b. 5 October 1943, Milwaukee, Wisconsin, USA. The young Miller was set on his musical path by having Les Paul as a family friend, and a father who openly encouraged music in the home. His first band, the Marksmen, was with schoolfriend Boz Scaggs; also with Scaggs, he formed the college band the Ardells, and at university they became the Fabulous Night Trains. He moved to Chicago in 1964, and became involved in the local blues scene with Barry Goldberg, resulting in the Goldberg Miller Blues Band. Miller eventually moved to San Francisco in 1966, after hearing about the growing hippie music scene, and formed the Miller Blues Band. Within a year he had built a considerable reputation and as the Steve Miller Band, he signed with Capitol Records for a then unprecedented $50,000, following his appearance at the 1967 Monterey Pop Festival. The band at that time included Boz Scaggs, Lonnie Turner, Jim Peterman and Tim Davis, and it was this line-up that was flown to London to record the Glyn Johns-produced *Children Of The Future*. The album was a critical success although sales were moderate, but it was *Sailor* later that same year that became his *pièce de résistance*. The clear production and memorable songs have lasted well and it remains a critics' favourite. Miller's silky-smooth voice and masterful guitar gave the album a touch of class that many of the other San Francisco rock albums lacked. The atmospheric instrumental 'Song For Our Ancestors' and well-crafted love songs such as 'Dear Mary' and 'Quicksilver Girl' were just three of the many outstanding tracks. Scaggs and Peterman departed after this album, and Miller added the talented Nicky Hopkins on keyboards for *Brave New World*, which completed a trio of albums recorded in London with Johns. The blistering 'My Dark Hour' featured Paul McCartney (as Paul Ramon) on bass, while the epic 'Cow Cow' showed off Hopkins' sensitive piano.

The excellent *Your Saving Grace* maintained the quality of previous albums and repeated the success. Lonnie Turner and Hopkins left at the end of 1969, and Miller replaced Turner with Bobby Winkleman from local band Frumious Bandersnatch. *Number 5* completed a cycle of excellent albums that hovered around similar chart positions, indicating that while Miller was highly popular, he was not expanding his audience. He decided to change the format for *Rock Love*, by having half of the album live. Unfortunately, he chose to record a live set with arguably his weakest band; both Ros Valory and Jack King left within a year and the album sold poorly. Following a European tour, and in an attempt to reverse the trend of the preceding album, he released *Recall The Beginning ... A Journey From Eden*, a perplexing album that showed Miller in a melancholic and lethargic mood; once again, Miller's fortunes declined further with poor sales. After a gap of 18 months, Miller returned with the US chart-topping single 'The Joker', an easily contrived song over a simple riff in which Miller mentioned all references to his various self-titled aliases used in songs over the past years: 'Some people call me the Space Cowboy (*Brave New World*), some call me the Gangster Of Love (*Sailor*), some call me Maurice (*Recall The Beginning*) . . .' The accompanying album was a similar success, stalling at number 2. His future had never looked brighter, but Miller chose to buy a farm and build a recording studio and he effectively vanished. When he reappeared on record three years later, only his loyal fans rated his commercial chances; however, *Fly Like An Eagle* became his best-selling album of all time and provided a major breakthrough in the UK. This record, with its then state-of-the-art recording, won him many new fans, and finally put him in the major league as one of America's biggest acts. Almost as successful was the sister album *Book Of Dreams* (1977); they both gave him a number of major singles including the simplistic 'Rock 'N' Me' and the uplifting 'Jet Airliner'. Miller had now mastered and targeted his audience, with exactly the kind of songs he knew they wanted. Once again, he disappeared from the scene and a new album was not released for almost four years. The return this time was less spectacular. Although *Circle Of Love* contained one side of typical Miller - short, sharp, punchy melodic rock songs - side two was an over-long and self-indulgent epic, 'Macho City'. He once again corrected the fault by responding only six months later, with another US number 1, the catchy 'Abracadabra'. This gave him his second major hit in the UK, almost reaching the coveted top spot in 1982. In the USA, the album climbed near to the top and Miller was left with another million-plus sale. The momentum was lost over the following years, as a live album and *Italian X-Rays* were comparative failures. *Living In The 20th Century* contained a segment consisting of a tribute to Jimmy Reed, with whom Steve had played as a teenager. He opted out of the commercial market with the excellent *Born 2B Blue* in 1989. Together with his old colleague Ben Sidran, Miller paid homage to jazz and blues standards with some exquisite arrangements from Sidran. Songs including Billie Holiday's 'God Bless The Child' and 'Zip-A-Dee-Doo-Dah' were given lazy treatments with Miller's effortless voice, but the record was only a moderate success. In the autumn of 1990, while Miller bided his time with the luxury of deciding what to do next, in the UK Levi's jeans had used 'The Joker' for one of their television advertisements. Capitol quickly released it, and astonishingly, Maurice, the space cowboy, the gangster of love, found himself with his first UK number 1. *Wide River* in 1993 was a return to his basic rock formula but it was not one of his better efforts. In 1996 Seal had a major US hit with a version of 'Fly Like An Eagle' and k.d. lang recorded 'The Joker' in 1997. Miller's collaboration with Paul

McCartney on *Flaming Pie* (1997) was highly publicized. He co-wrote 'Used To Be Bad' and played guitar on what many regard as McCartney's finest post-Beatles work.

● ALBUMS: *Children Of the Future* (Capitol 1968)★★★★, *Sailor* (Capitol 1968)★★★★★, *Brave New World* (Capitol 1969)★★★★, *Your Saving Grace* (Capitol 1969)★★★, *Revolution* film soundtrack 3 tracks only (United Artists 1969)★★, *Number 5* (Capitol 1970)★★★★, *Rock Love* (Capitol 1971)★★, *Recall The Beginning ... A Journey From Eden* (Capitol 1972)★★★, *The Joker* (Capitol 1973)★★★, *Fly Like An Eagle* (Capitol 1976)★★★★, *Book Of Dreams* (Capitol 1977)★★★★, *Circle Of Love* (Capitol 1981)★★★, *Abracadabra* (Capitol 1982)★★★, *Steve Miller Band - Live!* (Capitol 1983)★★, *Italian X Rays* (Capitol 1984)★★, *Living In The 20th Century* (Capitol 1986)★★, *Born 2B Blue* (Capitol 1988)★★★, *Wide River* (1993)★★.

● COMPILATIONS: *Anthology* (Capitol 1972)★★★★, *Greatest Hits (1974-1978)* (Capitol 1978)★★★★, *A Decade Of American Music: Greatest Hits 1976-1986* (1987)★★★★, *The Best Of 1968-1973* (Capitol 1990)★★★★, *Box Set* (Capitol 1994)★★★★.

● VIDEOS: *Steve Miller Band Live* (Video Collection 1988).

MINDFUNK

This intense American thrash-funk quintet was formed in 1989 by vocalist Patrick R. Dubar and rhythm guitarist Jason Coppola. Adding John Monte (ex-Method Of Destruction; bass), Reed St. Mark (ex-Celtic Frost; drums) and Louis J. Svitek (ex-MOD; guitar), they signed to Epic Records and debuted with an aggressive and confident self-titled album the same year. Slayer, Red Hot Chili Peppers and Anthrax were obvious reference points, as were the hardcore origins of several of their membership. However, they were dropped by Epic shortly afterwards (a fact bitterly recalled in their second album's title), and Jason Everman (ex-Nirvana; Soundgarden) and Shawn Johnson joined in place of Coppola and St. Mark, respectively.

● ALBUMS: *Mindfunk* (Epic 1991)★★★, *Dropped* (Megaforce 1993)★★★.

MINDSTORM

Mindstorm is the rock vision of vocalist Travis Mitchell. The group is in essence the Canadian equivalent of Kingdom Come or Katmandu. Employing Al Rodgers (guitar), Bruce Moffet (drums), Russ Boswell (bass) and Gary Moffet (keyboards), the songs are immaculately constructed and delivered with aplomb. However, their credibility and creativity is compromised through the overwhelming sense of *déja vu* their recordings invoke. With aching riffs and thunderous drumming, Mindstorm careers along a well-worn rock 'n' roll path, with only the occasional musical detour. These include Eastern influences, simple acoustic bridges and brooding power ballads.

● ALBUMS: *Mindstorm* (Provogue 1987)★★, *Back To Reality* (Provogue 1991)★★.

MINISTRY

'The difference between Ministry and other bands is that we sold out before we even started.' Alain Jourgensen (b. Havana, Cuba) began producing music under the Ministry name in the early 80s in Chicago, but was unhappy with the Euro-pop direction in which his record company pushed him for *With Sympathy*, later describing it as 'that first abortion of an album'. Ministry took on a more acceptable shape for Jourgensen after *'Twitch'*, with the addition to Jourgensen's guitar, vocals and keyboards of Paul Barker (b. Palo Alto, California, USA) on bass and keyboards, and drummer Bill Rieflin. The band evolved their own brand of guitar-based industrial metal, considering *The Land Of Rape And Honey* to be their true debut, and employed a variety of guest musicians for both live and studio work, with regular contributions from ex-Rigor Mortis guitarist Mike Scaccia and ex-Finitribe vocalist Chris Connelly. Despite Jourgensen's dislike of touring, Ministry developed a stunning live show, with a backdrop of disturbing visual images to accompany the intense musical barrage, and the sinister figure of Jourgensen taking centrestage behind a bone-encrusted microphone stand. *In Case You Didn't Feel Like Showing Up (Live)* displayed the metamorphosis of the songs as the band extended themselves in concert. At this stage, Jourgensen and Barker were working on numerous other studio projects in a variety of styles, including Lard with Jello Biafra, but Ministry remained one of two main acts. The other, the outrageous Revolting Cocks, served as a more blatantly humorous outlet for the pair's creative talents, in contrast to the dark anger and socio-political themes of Ministry. As alternative culture became more acceptable to the mainstream, Ministry achieved major success with *Psalm 69* (subtitled *The Way To Succeed And The Way To Suck Eggs*), helped by the popularity on MTV of 'Jesus Built My Hotrod', featuring a guest vocal and lyric from Butthole Surfers' frontman

Gibby Haynes. The band were a huge draw on the 1992 Lollapalooza tour, playing second on the bill, and their debut European tour later that year was also a resounding success. In 1994 Rieflin was replaced by former Didjits drummer Rey Washam. Jourgensen was arrested on a drugs charge in August 1995. *Filth Pig* contained, in true Ministry fashion, a distorted and raucous version of Bob Dylan's beautiful love song, 'Lay Lady Lay'.

● ALBUMS: *With Sympathy* aka *Work For Love* (Arista 1983)★★, *'Twitch'* (Sire 1986)★★★, *The Land Of Rape And Honey* (Sire 1988)★★★, *The Mind Is A Terrible Thing To Taste* (Sire 1989)★★★, *In Case You Didn't Feel Like Showing Up (Live)* mini-album (Sire 1990)★★★, *Psalm 69* (Sire/Warners 1992)★★★, *Filth Pig* (Warners 1996)★★★.

Solo: Paul Barker as Lead Into Gold *Age Of Reason* (Wax Trax! 1992)★★.

● COMPILATIONS: *Twelve Inch Singles 1981-1984* (Wax Trax! 1984)★★★.

MINUTEMEN

Formed in 1980 in San Pedro, California, USA, and originally known as the Reactionaries, this influential hardcore trio initially comprised David Boon (guitar, vocals), Mike Watt (bass) and Frank Tonche (drums), but the latter was replaced by George Hurley prior to recording. Although the trio donated tracks to several independent compilations, notably for the pivotal Radio Tokyo Tapes and the Posh Boy and New Alliance labels, their association with SST Records resulted in some of the genre's most impressive recordings. The unfettered rage of their early work was less apparent on *Buzz Or Howl Under The Influence Of Heat* and *Project: Mersh EP* ('mersh' is San Pedro slang for 'commercial'), but *Double Nickels On The Dime* and *3-Way Tie (For Last)* showed an undeterred passion and commitment. The Minutemen came to a premature end in 1986 following the death of David Boon. Watt and Hurley decided to drop the group's name, and in its place formed Firehose with guitarist Ed Crawford.

● ALBUMS: *The Punch Line* (SST 1981)★★, *What Makes A Man Start Fires?* (SST 1983)★★, *Buzz Or Howl Under The Influence Of Heat* (SST 1983)★★★, *Double Nickels On The Dime* (SST 1984)★★★, *The Politics Of Time* (New Alliance 1984)★★★, *... Just A Minute Men* (Virgin Vinyl 1985)★★★, *Project: Mersh EP* (SST 1985)★★★, *3-Way Tie (For Last)* (SST 1985)★★★, *Ballot Result* (SST 1987)★★★.

● COMPILATIONS: *My First Bells 1980-1983* cassette (SST 1985)★★★, *Post-Mersh, Vol. 1* (SST 1987)★★, *Post-Mersh, Vol. 2* (SST 1987)★★★, *Post-Mersh, Vol. 3* (SST 1989)★★★.

MISERY LOVES CO.

Originally formed as a duo in January 1993, Swedish group Misery Loves Co. immediately attracted positive press coverage for their blend of intelligent 90s metal and strong songwriting. *Kerrang!* magazine led the chorus of approval, nominating them as 'the hottest new metal combo since the arrival of Machine Head'. Comprising Örjan Örnkloo (programming, guitar) and Patrik Wirén (vocals, guitar), the latter was formerly a member of thrash band Midas Touch (who recorded one album for Noise Records), while his partner played in the female dance band the Bikinis as well as collaborating with Graham Lewis of Wire. Electing to work together as a duo, they signed a Swedish contract with the MNW Zone label (also home to Clawfinger). They made their debut appearance on a compilation album, *Extreme Close Up*, before the release of a three-track EP, *Private Hell*, in January 1994. Their debut album was licensed to Earache Records in the UK, while live appearances saw the duo augmented by the addition of Jim Edwards (guitar), Marre (bass) and Boss (drums). By the time the group entered the studio for sessions for a second album they had become permanent members of the band. In the interim they released the *Happy* EP, which showed them cross-fertilizing standard industrial metal with techno and dance elements, including a CD-ROM track, claimed to be the first issued by a metal band.

● ALBUMS: *Misery Love Co.* (MNW Zone 1994/Earache 1995)★★★, *Not Like Them* (Earache 1997)★★★.

MISFITS

Like the Thirteenth Floor Elevators in the 60s and the New York Dolls in the early 70s, this US punk band was swiftly surrounded in a cloak of mythology and cult appeal. Long after their demise (they played their last live gig in 1983), their obscure US-only records were fetching large sums of money in collecting circles, among those fascinated by the band's spine-chilling mix of horror-movie imagery and hardcore. The Misfits were formed in New Jersey, New York, in 1977 by Gerry Only (bass) and Glenn Danzig (b. 23 June 1959, Lodi, New Jersey, USA; vocals) and, like many aspiring new wave acts, played in venues such as CBGB's, adding guitarist Bobby Steele and drummer Joey Image. Later that year, 'Cough Cool' became their first single on their own Plan 9 label. A four-track EP, *Bullet* (in a sleeve showing John F. Kennedy's assassination), was recorded before their debut album, and was followed by 'Horror Business'. A third single, 'Night Of The Living Dead', surfaced in 1979, the reference to the classic George A. Romero film revealing the Misfits' continued fascination with blood-and-guts horror. Then came an EP, *Three Hits From Hell*, recorded in 1980, but not issued until the following April, and a seasonal October single, 'Halloween'. Having lost Steele to the Undead, replaced by Jerry's brother Doyle, Googy (aka Eerie Von) stepped in on drums during a European tour with the Damned as Image's narcotic problems worsened. The Misfits rounded off 1981 by recording the seven-track mini-album *Evilive*, originally sold through the band's Fiend fan club, which also secured a German 12-inch release. The band's only original UK release was a 12-inch EP, *Beware*. Other Misfits releases included several patchy albums that failed to capture their live impact: 1982's *Walk Among Us*, *Earth A.D.* (aka *Wolfblood*) and the posthumous brace, *Legacy Of Brutality* and *Misfits*. Danzig issued his first solo single in 1981, 'Who Killed Marilyn?', later forming Samhain with Misfits drummer Eerie Von. He was subsequently venerated in heavy metal magazines in the late 80s as his eponymous Danzig vehicle gained ground. The other Misfits mainstays, brothers Jerry and Doyle, formed the hapless Kryst The Conqueror, who released one five-song EP with the help of Skid Row guitarist David Sabo. An ambitious 4-CD set was issued in 1996 in the shape of a coffin, and the following year the band re-formed, minus Danzig, releasing an album for Geffen Records.

● ALBUMS: *Beware* EP (Cherry Red 1979)★★★, *Walk Among Us* (Ruby 1982)★★★, *Evilive* EP (Plan 9 1982)★★★, *Earth A.D./Wolfsblood* (Plan 9 1983)★★★, *American Psycho* (Geffen 1997)★★★.

● COMPILATIONS: *Legacy Of Brutality* (Plan 9 1985)★★★, *The Misfits* (Plan 9 1986)★★★★, *Evilive* expanded version of 1981 mini-album (Plan 9 1987)★★★, *The Misfits* 4-CD box set (Caroline 1996)★★★★, *Static Age* (Caroline 1997).

MISSION

This UK rock band evolved from the Sisters Of Mercy, when Wayne Hussey (b. 26 May 1959, Bristol, England; ex-Walkie Talkies; Dead Or Alive) and Craig Adams split from Andrew Eldritch. They quickly recruited drummer Mick Brown (ex-Red Lorry, Yellow Lorry) and guitarist Simon Hinkler (ex-Artery). The original choice of title was the Sisterhood, which led to an undignified series of exchanges in the press between the band and Eldritch. In order to negate their use of the name, Eldritch put out a single under the name Sisterhood on his own Merciful Release label. Thus, the name the Mission was selected instead. After two successful independent singles on the Chapter 22 label, they signed to Mercury Records in the autumn of 1986. Their major label debut, 'Stay With Me', entered the UK singles charts while the band worked on their debut album. *God's Own Medicine* was the outcome, revealing a tendency towards straightforward rock, and attracting criticism for its bombast. A heavy touring schedule ensued, with the band's offstage antics attracting at least as much attention as their performances. A particularly indulgent tour of America saw Adams shipped home suffering from exhaustion. His temporary replacement on bass was Pete Turner. After headlining the Reading Festival, they began work on a new album under the auspices of Led Zeppelin bass player John Paul Jones as producer. *Children* was even more successful than its predecessor, reaching number 2 in the UK album charts, despite the customary critical disdain. 1990 brought 'Butterfly On A Wheel' as a single, providing further ammunition for accusations that the band were simply dredging up rock history. In February, the long-delayed third album, *Carved In Sand*, was released, revealing a more sophisticated approach to songwriting. During the world tour to promote the album, both Hinkler and Hussey became ill because of the excessive regime. Hinkler departed suddenly when they reached Toronto, leaving Dave Wolfenden to provide guitar for the rest of the tour. On their return, Paul Etchells took over the position on a more permanent basis. Hussey had meanwhile joined with the Wonder Stuff in proposing a fund-raising concert in London under the banner The Day Of Conscience, but the event self-destructed with a barrage of allegations about commercial intrusion. In a similar vein over the Christmas period, members of the band joined with Slade's Noddy Holder and Jim Lea to re-record 'Merry Xmas Everybody' for charity. However, 1992 brought numerous further personnel difficulties. Craig Adams returned to Brighton, while Hussey brought in Andy Hobson (bass), Rik Carter (keyboards) and Mark Gemini Thwaite (guitar). A reflective Hussey, promoting the *Sum And Substance* compilation, conceded: 'We had an overblown sense of melodrama. It was great - pompous songs, big grand statements. We've

never attempted to do anything that's innovative'.
● ALBUMS: *God's Own Medicine* (Mercury 1986)★★, *Children* (Mercury 1988)★★★, *Carved In Sand* (Mercury 1990)★★★, *Masque* (Mercury 1992)★★, *Neverland* (Neverland 1995)★★.
● COMPILATIONS: *The First Chapter* (Mercury 1987)★★, *Grains Of Sand* (Mercury 1990)★★, *Sum And Substance* (Vertigo 1994)★★★, *Salad Daze* (Nighttracks 1994)★★, *Blue* (Equator 1996)★★.
● VIDEOS: *From Dusk To Dawn* (PolyGram Music Video 1988), *South America* (Mish Productions 1989), *Crusade* (Channel 5 1991), *Waves Upon The Sand* (Channel 5 1991), *Sum And Substance* (1994).
● FURTHER READING: *The Mission - Names Are Tombstones Baby*, Martin Roach with Neil Perry.

MISUNDERSTOOD

One of psychedelia's finest groups, the Misunderstood originated in Riverside, California, USA, and evolved from a local surfing group, the Blue Notes. Their first line-up - Greg Treadway (guitar), George Phelps (guitar) and Rick Moe (drums) - was augmented by Rick Brown (vocals) and Steve Whiting (bass), before adopting their new name in 1965. Phelps was then replaced by Glenn Ross 'Fernando' Campbell, who played steel guitar. The quintet completed a single, 'You Don't Have To Go'/'Who's Been Talking?', before leaving for the UK on the suggestion of disc jockey John (Peel) Ravenscroft, then working in San Bernadino. Treadway was subsequently drafted, and his place was taken by Tony Hill (b. South Shields, Co. Durham, England). The group completed six masters during their London sojourn. 'I Can Take You To The Sun', a hypnotic, atmospheric and ambitious performance, was their only contemporary release, although the rousing 'Children Of The Sun' was issued after their break-up, in 1968. Campbell later re-established the name with several British musicians. Their two blues-cum-progressive singles shared little with the early, trail-blazing unit, and the latter-day version then evolved into Juicy Lucy.
● COMPILATIONS: *Before The Dream Faded* (1982)★★, *Golden Glass* (1984)★★.

MITCHELL, KIM

Having dissolved Max Webster in 1982, Mitchell was inspired to pursue a solo career. After signing with Anthem Records he released a mini-album that followed closely in the Max Webster tradition. He then took a break from music until he signed with Bronze Records. His next release was the excellent and slightly offbeat *Akimbo Alogo*, which also included the single 'Go For Soda'. At times reminiscent of the excesses of Frank Soda And The Imps and Neil Merryweather (*c*.1974), Mitchell's approach was, at times, misunderstood by the press, but there was no mistaking his obvious talent as a guitarist. He finally achieved critical acclaim with *Rockland*.
● ALBUMS: *Kim Mitchell* mini-album (Anthem 1982)★★★, *Akimbo Alogo* (Bronze 1985)★★★★, *Shakin' Like A Human Being* (Anthem 1987)★★★, *Rockland* (Atlantic 1989)★★★★.

MOBY GRAPE

The legend that continues to grow around this late 60s San Francisco group is mainly based on their magnificent debut album, which fans vainly willed them to repeat. This iconoclastic band was formed in September 1966, with the seminal line-up of Alexander Skip Spence (b. 18 April 1946, Windsor, Ontario, Canada; guitar, vocals), Jerry Miller (b. 10 July 1943, Tacoma, Washington, USA; guitar, vocals), Bob Mosley (b. 4 December 1942, Paradise Valley, California, USA; bass, vocals), Don Stevenson (b. 15 October 1942, Seattle, Washington, USA; drums) and Peter Lewis (b. 15 July 1945, Los Angeles, California, USA; guitar, vocals). With record companies queueing up to sign them, they decided to go with CBS Records and became marketing guinea pigs for an unprecedented campaign, whereupon 10 tracks (five singles plus b-sides) were released simultaneously. Not even the Beatles could have lived up to that kind of launch. Only one of the records dented the US chart: 'Omaha' reached a dismal number 88. Had the singles been released in normal sequence, they might all have been hits, as the quality of each song was outstanding. The band fell into immediate disarray, unable to cope with the pressure and hype. The resulting debut, *Moby Grape*, contained all these 10 tracks plus an additional three, and it deservedly reached the US Top 30 album charts. It is now recognized as a classic. The short, brilliantly structured, guitar-based rock songs with fine harmonies still sound fresh in the 90s. Their follow-up was a similar success (yet a lesser work), and made the US Top 20 album chart. As with their debut, CBS continued with their ruthless marketing campaign, determined to see a return on their investment, as the band had originally held out for a considerable advance. *Wow* sported a beautiful surrealistic painting/collage by Bob Cato, depicting a huge bunch of grapes mixed with an eighteenth-century beach scene, and came with a free album, *Grape Jam*. Additionally, one of the tracks was recorded at 78 rpm, forcing the listener to get up and change the speed only to hear a spoof item played by Lou Waxman And His Orchestra. Amidst this spurious package were some of their finest songs, including Spence's 'Motorcycle Irene', Miller's 'Miller's Blues', Mosley's 'Murder In My Heart For The Judge' and arguably their best track, 'Can't Be So Bad'. Penned by Miller and featuring his stinging guitar solo, this furiously paced heavy rock item is suddenly slowed down and sweetened by an outstanding five-part Mamas And The Papas-style harmony. The song failed to chart anywhere. Spence had departed with drug and mental problems by the release of *Moby Grape '69*, although his ethereal composition 'Seeing' is one of the highlights of this apologetic and occasionally brilliant album (the hype of the past is disclaimed by the 'sincere' sleeve notes). Other notable tracks included Lewis's hymn-like 'I Am Not Willing' and the straightforward rocker 'Truck Driving Man'. A disastrous European tour was arranged, during which the band was constantly overshadowed by the support act Group Therapy. Mosley left on their return to the USA, and allegedly joined the marines, leaving the rest to fulfil their contract by making a fourth album. He also made a solo album. Spence, who today lives in a men's hostel as a ward of the county, released the extraordinary *Oar*. This album has become a cult classic since its release in 1968, and is both painfully dark ('Diana') yet hopelessly light ('Lawrence Of Euphoria'). It does at least reflect Spence's condition as a paranoid schizophrenic. The poor-selling and lacklustre *Truly Fine Citizen* was badly received; the critics had already given up on them. The band then disintegrated, unable to use the name which was and still is owned by their manager, Matthew Katz. The remaining members have appeared as Maby Grope, Mosley Grape, Grape Escape, Fine Wine, the Melvills, the Grape, the Hermans and the Legendary Grape. During one of their many attempts at re-formation, Mosley and Miller actually released a record as Fine Wine. The original five reunited for one more undistinguished album in 1971, *20 Granite Creek*. Out of the mire, only Mosley's 'Gypsy Wedding' showed some promise. Skip Spence delivered the quirky 'Chinese Song', played on a koto, and the silk-voiced Lewis produced 'Horse Out In The Rain' with its unusual timing and extraordinary booming bass. A live album in 1978 delighted fans, and rumours abounded about various re-formation plans. Some of the band still play together in small clubs and bars, but the magical reunion of the five (just like the five Byrds) can never be. Spence, sadly, is in no fit state and, unbelievably, it was alleged that Mosley was also diagnosed as a schizophrenic and was living rough on the streets of San Diego. The myth surrounding the band continues to grow as more (outrageous) stories come to light. The debut album is one of the true rock/pop classics of the past 30 years (along with Love's *Forever Changes*), and their influence is immense. The 'grape sound' has shown up in many groups over the past 20 years including the Doobie Brothers, R.E.M., the Smithereens, Teenage Fanclub and Weezer, and Robert Plant is a long-term fan. They were, more than any other band from the Bay Area in 1967/8, the true embodiment of the music (but not the culture). Their appearance at Wetlands, New York, on 6 August 1997 was a delightful surprise. Mosley, Miller and Lewis performed as Moby Grape with ex-Big Brother And The Holding Company Sam Andrew replacing Spence and Randy Guzman replacing Stevenson.

● ALBUMS: *Moby Grape* (Columbia 1967)★★★★★, *Wow* (Columbia 1967)★★★, *Grape Jam* (Columbia 1967)★★, *Moby Grape '69* (Columbia 1969)★★★★, *Truly Fine Citizen* (Columbia 1969)★★★, *20 Granite Creek* (Reprise 1971)★★★, *Live Grape* (Escape 1978)★★★, *Moby Grape* (San Francisco Sound 1983)★★.
Solo: Bob Mosley *Bob Mosley* (Warner 1972)★★. Peter Lewis *Peter Lewis* (Taxim 1996)★★★.
● COMPILATIONS: *Great Grape* (Columbia 1973)★★★, *Vintage Grape* 2-CD box set with unreleased material and alternate takes (Columbia/Legacy 1993)★★★★★.

MOIST

Vancouver, Canada-based band, featuring David Usher (vocals) and Mark Makowy (guitar), who met at a party hosted by mutual friend and keyboard player Kevin Young. Makowy brought in bass player Jeff Pearce, and eventually drummer Paul Wilcox completed the line-up. Following a demo cassette in early 1993, the band went on to release a debut album on their own label in February of the following year. Picked up by EMI Music Canada just one month later, the record went platinum in their own country, mainly bolstered by a ferocious appetite for live appearances. Their most important early exposure in Europe came when they were invited to perform at the annual *Smash Hits* Poll Winners' Party as a token rock presence.
● ALBUMS: *Silver* (EMI 1994)★★★.

Molly Hatchet

This Lynyrd Skynyrd-style, blues-rock boogie outfit emerged from the US Deep South. The name derived from a tale of a woman in 17th-century Salem who beheaded her lovers with an axe after sleeping with them. The initial line-up comprised guitarists Dave Hlubek, Steve Holland and Duane Roland, plus bassist Bonner Thomas, vocalist Danny Joe Brown and drummer Bruce Crump. Their debut album, produced by Tom Werman (of Cheap Trick and Ted Nugent fame), was an instant success, with its three-pronged guitar onslaught and gut-wrenching vocals. Brown was replaced by Jimmy Farrar in 1980, before the recording of *Beatin' The Odds.* Farrar's vocals were less distinctive than Brown's, and an element of their identity was lost during the time that Farrar fronted the band. Nevertheless, commercial success ensued, with both *Beatin' The Odds* and *Take No Prisoners* peaking on the *Billboard* album chart at numbers 25 and 36, respectively. In 1982 Danny Joe Brown rejoined the band, while Thomas was replaced by Riff West on bass. *No Guts ... No Glory* emerged and marked a return to their roots: explosive guitar duels, heart-stopping vocals and steadfast rock 'n' roll. Surprisingly, the album flopped and Hlubek insisted on a radical change in direction. Steve Holden quit and keyboardist John Galvin was recruited for the recording of *The Deed Is Done.* This was a lightweight pop-rock album, largely devoid of the band's former trademarks. Following its release, the band retired temporarily to lick their wounds and reassess their future. In 1985 *Double Trouble Live* was unveiled, with a return to former styles. It included versions of their best-known songs, plus a Skynyrd tribute in the form of 'Freebird'. Founder-member Dave Hlubek departed, to be replaced by Bobby Ingram in 1989. They signed a new contract with Capitol Records and released *Lightning Strikes Twice.* This leaned away from their southern roots towards highly polished AOR. It featured cover versions of Paul Stanley's 'Hide Your Heart' and Miller/Burnette's 'There Goes The Neighbourhood', but was poorly received by fans and critics alike. Brown, meanwhile, continued to be plagued by illness as the result of diabetes.

● ALBUMS: *Molly Hatchet* (Epic 1978)★★★, *Flirtin' With Disaster* (Epic 1979)★★★, *Beatin' The Odds* (Epic 1980)★★, *Take No Prisoners* (Epic 1981)★★, *No Guts ... No Glory* (Epic 1983)★★★, *The Deed Is Done* (Epic 1984)★★, *Double Trouble Live* (Epic 1985)★★, *Lightning Strikes Twice* (Capitol 1989)★★, *Devil's Canyon* (SPV 1996)★★, *Silent Reign Of Heroes* (Koch 1998)★★.

● COMPILATIONS: *Greatest Hits* (Epic 1990)★★★.

Money, Eddie

Legend has it that Brooklyn native Eddie Mahoney was a New York police officer when first discovered by promoter Bill Graham (he was, in fact, a NYPD typist). Nevertheless, under Graham's managerial wing, Mahoney became Eddie Money and produced two hit singles in 'Baby Hold On' and 'Two Tickets To Paradise' from his self-titled debut, to begin a career that has seen him maintain arena-headlining status in America with a series of consistently fine R&B-flavoured AOR records. *Life For The Taking* produced two more hits, 'Rock And Roll The Place' and 'Maybe I'm A Fool', as Money built a strong live reputation that freed him from the constraining need for radio or MTV airplay to sell albums or concert tickets, although the hits continued to come. *Where's The Party?* saw a slight dip in form, but Money stormed back with perhaps his best 80s album, *Can't Hold Back*, producing three huge hits in the title track, 'I Wanna Go Back' and 'Take Me Home Tonight', where his warm, soulful vocals were augmented by Ronnie Spector's production. 1991's *Right Here* saw Money move away from the keyboard-dominated sound of preceding albums towards the rootsier feel of his early work, producing another hit in a cover version of Romeo's Daughter's 'Heaven In The Backseat'. While European success continues to elude him, Money's future in his homeland seems secure.

● ALBUMS: *Eddie Money* (Columbia 1977)★★, *Life For The Taking* (Columbia 1978)★★, *Playing For Keeps* (Columbia 1980)★★, *No Control* (Columbia 1982)★★, *Where's The Party?* (Columbia 1984)★★, *Can't Hold Back* (Columbia 1986)★★★, *Nothing To Lose* (Columbia 1988)★★, *Right Here* (Columbia 1991)★★.

● COMPILATIONS: *Greatest Hits: The Sound Of Money* (Columbia 1989)★★★.

● FILMS: *Americation* (1979).

Monroe, Michael

When Hanoi Rocks folded following the death of drummer Razzle in 1984, Monroe took several years' break before deciding to start again with a solo career. In 1988, *Nights Are So Long* emerged on the independent Yahoo label, featuring a mixture of originals and cover versions of songs by the Heavy Metal Kids, Johnny Thunders, MC5 and the Flamin' Groovies. This low-key comeback was a soul-cleansing process for Monroe, before he signed to Mercury Records, and threw himself back into the spotlight with all guns blazing. Recruiting Phil Grande (guitar), Tommy Price (drums), Kenny Aaronson (bass) and Ed Roynesdal (keyboards), he recorded *Not Fakin' It*, a streetwise selection of sleazy rock 'n' roll numbers, delivered in Monroe's inimitable, alley cat style. The album was well received and the tour to support it was a further triumph, proving easily the most successful of the Hanoi Rock spin-off projects.

● ALBUMS: *Nights Are So Long* (Yahoo 1988)★★★, *Not Fakin' It* (PolyGram 1989)★★★.

MONSTER MAGNET

This space-rock revivalist band was formed in New Jersey in 1989 by vocalist/guitarist David Wyndorf, with guitarist John McBain, bassist Joe Calendra and drummer Jon Kleinman. After a promising debut and the rather self-indulgent *Tab*, Monster Magnet suddenly found broad press and public support with *Spine Of God*, despite the back cover disclaimer that 'It's a satanic drug thing . . . you wouldn't understand'. The sound and songs drew on Wyndorf's obsession with late 60s psychedelia, music and culture, producing a hypnotic set that blended *Space Ritual*-era Hawkwind style with an MC5/Black Sabbath guitar barrage and a liberal sprinkling of drug references, all played with a 90s venom. The band were quick to capitalize, touring almost non-stop around Europe and the USA, and, following a US tour with Soundgarden, they lost McBain but gained a contract with A&M Records. The resultant *Superjudge*, with new guitarist Ed Mundell, was, if anything, more intense, and saw Monster Magnet pay tribute to Hawkwind with an affectionate blast through 'Brainstorm'. Their live shows remained an experience in themselves, with lighting engineer Tim Cronin's astral projection backdrop proving to be an essential component as the band whipped up a frenzy on stage, touring Europe with Paw and the USA with Raging Slab in 1994. *Dopes To Infinity* and *Powertrip* took space rock to perfection and established them as arguably the leaders of the genre.

● ALBUMS: *Monster Magnet* (Primo Scree 1991)★★★, *Tab* (Primo Scree 1991)★★★, *Spine Of God* (Primo Scree 1991)★★★, *Superjudge* (A&M 1993), *Dopes To Infinity* (A&M 1995)★★★, *Powertrip* (A&M 1998)★★★★.

MONTROSE

After working with Van Morrison, Boz Scaggs and Edgar Winter, guitarist Ronnie Montrose (b. Colorado, USA) formed Montrose in San Francisco in the autumn of 1973. Comprising vocalist Sammy Hagar (b. 13 October 1947, Monterey, California, USA), bassist Bill Church and drummer Denny Carmassi, they signed to Warner Brothers Records in 1973 and released their self-titled debut the following year. Produced by Ted Templeman, *Montrose* was an album that set new standards in heavy metal; the combination of Hagar's raucous vocals with the guitarist's abrasive guitar sound became a blueprint against which new bands judged themselves for many years to come. Including the classic recordings 'Bad Motor Scooter', 'Space Station No. 5' and 'Rock The Nation', the album still ranks as one of the cornerstones of the hard rock genre. Alan Fitzgerald replaced Bill Church on bass before the recording of the follow-up, *Paper Money*. Hagar was fired shortly after the tour to support the album was completed. Bob James and Jim Alcivar were drafted in on vocals and keyboards, but they never recaptured the magic of the debut release. Hagar and Ronnie Montrose, the principal protagonists, went on to solo careers, the latter joined by several ex-members of Montrose in Gamma. Carmassi, in addition, re-emerged in the 90s as drummer for the much hyped Coverdale Page project.

● ALBUMS: *Montrose* (Warners 1974)★★★★, *Paper Money* (Warners 1974)★★, *Warner Bros. Presents Montrose!* (Warners 1975)★★, *Jump On It* (Warners 1976)★★.

MONTROSE, RONNIE

After rock guitarist Ronnie Montrose (b. Colorado, USA) dissolved his own band, Montrose, in 1976, he decided to pursue a solo career. Switching styles from hard rock to jazz rock, he released *Open Fire*, an instrumental album that was unpopular with fans and critics alike. Disillusioned, he formed Gamma, who recorded three albums between 1979 and 1982. When Gamma ground to a halt in 1983, Montrose recorded *Territory*, another low-key solo set. In 1987 he teamed up with vocalist Johnny Edwards (later Foreigner) and drummer James Kottak (later of Kingdom Come), both ex-Buster Brown, and ex-Gamma bassist Glen Letsch. *Mean* was the result, an uncompromising hard rock record that had the guts and musical firepower of Montrose's debut, released 13 years previously. This line-up was short-lived, with Johnny Bee Bedanjek replacing Edwards and the addition of synthesizer player Pat Feehan, before *The Speed Of Sound* was recorded. Adopting a more sophisticated, melody-conscious approach, it lost much of the ground that had been recaptured by the previous album. Montrose decided to go solo again, producing *The Diva Station* in 1990. This was a semi-instrumental affair and incorporated rock, metal, jazz and soul influences, including an astonishing version of the old Walker Brothers hit, 'Stay With Me Baby'. Ronnie Montrose remains an extremely gifted guitarist, but as yet he has found it difficult to channel his energies in a direction that also brings commercial rewards. This situation has seen him devoting more time to production work.

● ALBUMS: *Open Fire* (Warners 1978)★★, *Territory* (Passport 1986)★★, *Mean* (Enigma 1987)★★★★, *The Speed Of Sound* (Enigma 1988)★★★, *The Diva Station* (Roadrunner 1990)★★★.

MOORE, GARY

b. 4 April 1952, Belfast, Northern Ireland. This talented, blues-influenced singer and guitarist formed his first major band, Skid Row, when he was 16 years old - initially with Phil Lynott, who left after a few months to form Thin Lizzy. Skid Row continued as a three-piece, with Brendan Shiels (bass) and Noel Bridgeman (drums). They relocated from Belfast to London in 1970 and signed a contract with CBS Records. After just two albums they disbanded, leaving Moore to form the Gary Moore Band. Their debut, *Grinding Stone*, appeared in 1973, but progress was halted the following year while Moore assisted Thin Lizzy after guitarist Eric Bell had left the band. This liaison lasted just four months before Moore was replaced by Scott Gorham and Brian Robertson. Moore subsequently moved into session work before joining Colosseum II in 1976. He made three albums with them, and also rejoined Thin Lizzy for a 10-week American tour in 1977 after guitarist Brian Robertson suffered a severed artery in his hand. Moore finally became a full-time member of Thin Lizzy, but he subsequently left midway through a US tour and formed a new band called G-Force, though this outfit soon foundered. Moore then resumed his solo career, recording a series of commercially ignored albums until he achieved hit singles in 1985 with 'Empty Rooms' and another collaboration with Phil Lynott, 'Out In The Fields'. His 1989 album *After The War* revealed a strong Celtic influence, and also featured guest artists such as Ozzy Osbourne and Andrew Eldritch (Sisters Of Mercy). However, his breakthrough to mainstream commercial acceptance came in 1990 with the superb, confident guitarwork and vocals of *Still Got The Blues*. Mixing blues standards and originals, Moore was acclaimed as one of the UK's foremost artists, a stature that the release of *After Hours* - featuring cameo appearances from B.B. King and Albert Collins - only confirmed. In 1994 with Jack Bruce and Ginger Baker as BBM, he released an accomplished and satisfying album, but personality conflicts meant that the collaboration was short-lived. In 1995 he released the excellent *Blues For Greeny*, an album of songs written by Peter Green and played on Green's Gibson Les Paul guitar, which had been a gift from Green to Moore many years earlier. *Dark Days In Paradise* had little blues on offer; instead, Moore attempted rock, AOR and pop. Just as his followers were becoming used to his recent style, he switched, and the album's tepid success no doubt reflected their rejection of his new approach.

● ALBUMS: as Gary Moore Band *Grinding Stone* (Columbia 1973)★★, *Back On The Streets* (MCA 1979)★★★★, *Corridors Of Power* (Virgin 1982)★★★, *Rockin' Every Night - Live In Japan* (Virgin 1983)★★★, *Live* (Jet 1984)★★★, *Run For Cover* (Ten 1985)★★★, *Wild Frontier* (Ten Ten 1988)★★★, *After The War* (Virgin 1989)★★★, *Still Got The Blues* (Virgin 1990)★★★★, *After Hours* (Virgin 1992)★★★, *Blues Alive* (Virgin 1993)★★★★, *Blues For Greeny* (Virgin 1995)★★★★, *Dark Days In Paradise* (Virgin 1997)★★.

● COMPILATIONS: *Anthology* (Raw Power 1986)★★★, *The Collection* double album (Castle 1990)★★★, *CD Box Set* (Virgin 1991)★★★, *Ballads + Blues 1982 - 1994* (Virgin 1994)★★★★.

● VIDEOS: *Emerald Aisles* (Virgin Vision 1986), *Video Singles: Gary Moore* (Virgin Vision 1988), *Gary Moore: Live In Sweden* (Virgin Vision 1988), *Evening Of The Blues* (Virgin Vision 1991), *Live Blues* (1993), *Ballads And Blues 1982-1994* (1995), *Blues For Greeny Live* (Warner Music Vision 1996).

MOORE, VINNIE

b. 1965, USA. This jazz-trained virtuoso guitarist was playing the guitar competently by the age of 12. Picked up by talent scout Mike Varney, he was introduced to the techno-thrash band Vicious Rumours, with whom he recorded *Soldiers Of The Night* in 1985. He left the band as soon as the album was released to concentrate on a solo career. *Mind's Eye* emerged in 1986, a self-written guitar instrumental collection. This combined a fusion of classical jazz, blues and hard rock that was heavily melodic and technically brilliant, earning comparisons to Joe Satriani's finest work. Two subsequent albums followed a similar pattern but were mellower still, after which he was employed by Alice Cooper as lead guitarist on his Hey Stoopid tour.

● ALBUMS: *Mind's Eye* (Shrapnel 1986)★★★★, *Time Odyssey* (Squawk 1988)★★★, *Meltdown* (Squawk 1991)★★★.

Morbid Angel

Formed in Florida, USA, in 1984, the band's original line-up consisted of Stering Von Scarborough (bass, vocals), Trey Azagthoth (guitar), Richard Brunelle (guitar) and Pete Sandoval (drums). They quickly gained a following on the underground death metal scene on account of their extreme, ultra-fast musical approach. The band recorded the self-financed *Abominations Of Desolation* in 1986. However, unhappy with the recordings, they decided not to release them, as had originally been intended, on their own Gorque Records label. They then underwent a personnel change, replacing the departed Scarborough with David Vincent (ex-Terrorizer), who gave the band much more of an identity with his strong, charismatic presence (he had previously produced *Abominations Of Desolation*). Morbid Angel continued to gain momentum and eventually attracted the attention of Earache Records, resulting in the band's official debut, *Altars Of Madness*, released in 1989, to great acclaim among death metal fans. By the release of *Blessed Are The Sick*, they had toured Europe extensively, establishing a strong following in the process. The album, like its forerunner, produced by Tom Morris, was once again a marked improvement on previous efforts, and strengthened their position within a growing fanbase. Owing to widespread bootlegging and the band's burgeoning popularity, Earache Records released the original recordings of *Abominations Of Desolation* in 1991. For 1993's *Covenant*, released through Giant/Warner in the USA, Flemming Rassmussen (Metallica, etc.) was drafted in to produce, and their rising profile was cemented by a US tour supporting Black Sabbath and Motörhead. 1994 saw the replacement of Richard Brunelle by Eric Rutan (ex-Ripping Corpse). His arrival seemed to revitalize Morbid Angel and 1995's *Domination* was a much more varied selection. While still undoubtedly death metal, songs such as 'Dawn Of The Agony' and 'Dreaming' touched on both classical and industrial traditions to expand the band's sound. Vincent left in June 1996 to pursue a solo career, in addition to working with Genitorturers.

● ALBUMS: *Altars Of Madness* (Earache 1989)★★★★, *Blessed Are The Sick* (Earache 1991)★★★, *Abominations Of Desolation* (Earache 1991)★★★, *Covenant* (Earache 1993)★★★, *Domination* (Earache 1995)★★★, *Entangled In Chaos* (Earache 1996)★★★★, *Formulas Fatal To The Flesh* (Earache 1998)★★★.

Mordred

Formed in San Francisco, USA, in 1985, Mordred were one of the first of a new breed of thrash metal bands that incorporated elements of funk into their high-speed onslaught. Comprising Scott Holderby (vocals), Danny White (guitar), James Sanguinetti (guitar), Art Liboon (bass) and Gannon Hall (drums), they signed to Noise Records and released *Fool's Game* in 1989. On their next album they recruited Aaron (Pause) Vaughn, a scratch disc jockey, to give their sound a new dimension. This approach was thought to offer enormous crossover potential, combining elements of Faith No More, Megadeth and Parliament, but so far the band have failed to gain a footing outside of a cult following.

● ALBUMS: *Fool's Game* (Noise 1989)★★★, *In This Life* (Noise 1991)★★, *Vision* (Noise 1992)★★★.

More

This New Wave Of British Heavy Metal band was led by guitarist Kenny Cox with Paul Mario Day (vocals), Laurie Mansworth (guitar), Brian Day (bass) and Frank Darch (drums). Wild live shows that ended with most of the audience on stage, coupled with a promising session for BBC Radio 1's *Friday Rock Show*, led to a contract with Atlantic Records as major N.W.O.B.H.M. acts such as Saxon and Iron Maiden began to make a serious impact. *Warhead* was a solid debut, but failed to match the live shows, and sales were poor despite a series of UK support performances that generally upstaged headliners Krokus, followed by an appearance in the opening slot of the 1981 Donington Festival. This lack of immediate success, plus record company problems, led to internal fighting, and by the release of *Blood And Thunder*, Cox had assembled an entirely new line-up of Nick Stratton (vocals), Andy John Burton (drums) and Barry Nicholls (bass). The album adhered faithfully to the riff-heavy style of *Warhead*, but without a UK release from a disinterested label, the band quickly faded.

● ALBUMS: *Warhead* (Atlantic 1980)★★★, *Blood And Thunder* (Atlantic 1982)★★★.

Morse, Steve, Band

Instrumental rock guitarist Steve Morse (b. Ohio, USA) took his primary influence, like so many others, from the Beatles. Expanding his listening to include prevalent rock bands such as the Yardbirds, Jimi Hendrix and Led Zeppelin, as well as a nascent interest in country music, Morse moved with his family to Georgia at the age of 13. There he was captivated by a live concert by classical guitarist Juan Mercadal, and he persuaded the artist to give him lessons. He went on to study with Mercadal at the University of Miami, while also assembling his first band, Dixie Dregs (aka the Dregs). Inspired by a campus performance from John McLaughlin's original Mahavishnu Quartet, he dedicated himself to exploring the conventions and frontiers of instrumental rock music. The Dregs, essentially a vehicle for these experiments, went on to record eight albums of bright, impressive fusion. Morse qualified as a pilot during this time, and flying remains his greatest passion outside of music. He also began his solo career after briefly joining Kansas for two albums. The Steve Morse Band's debut, *The Introduction*, continued to mine a particularly adept blend of instrumental rock fusion, with a guest role for guitarist Albert Lee. There was more of a vocal presence for *Stand Up*, which featured an appearance from another renowned guitarist, Eric Johnson. By the advent of *Southern Steel*, the Steve Morse Band was a core team of Morse, Berklee graduate Dave LaRue (bass) and Van Romaine (drums, ex-Blood, Sweat And Tears; Kansas; and Naughty By Nature). The acclaim surrounding Morse has rarely died down throughout his career - *Guitar Player* magazine made him ineligible for their Best Overall Guitarist poll after he won it five times in succession. He has also collaborated with artists including Eddie Van Halen, Steve Howe and Lynyrd Skynyrd, and accepted an invitation to join Deep Purple for a spell during the mid-90s. The Steve Morse Band's sixth album, *Structural Damage*, revealed an undiminished talent, and included the Celtic-influenced 'Sacred Ground' and the cinematic 'Dreamland'.

● ALBUMS: *The Introduction* (Elektra 1984)★★★, *Stand Up* (Elektra 1985)★★★, *High Tension Wires* (MCA 1989)★★★, *Southern Steel* (MCA 1991)★★★★, *Coast To Coast* (MCA 1993)★★★, *Structural Damage* (High Street 1995)★★★★.

● VIDEOS: *Highlights* (Warner Music 1995).

MORTA SKULD

Milwaukee-based four-piece Morta Skuld specialize in a provocative cocktail of death metal and noise, brewed by Dave Gregor (vocals, guitar), Jason Hellman (bass), Jason O'Connell (guitar) and Kent Truckebrod (drums). Their debut for Deaf Records was somewhat lacklustre, and several personnel difficulties erupted following its release, resulting in the band splitting in two. However, by the advent of a second long-playing set, the group had moved up a gear both in tempo and cohesion. The improvement was partially justified by the fact that, although their debut was released early in 1993, it had actually been written and recorded over a year earlier. The newer material, akin to a skinnier Obituary sound, brought good reviews in the metal press.

● ALBUMS: *Dying Remains* (Deaf 1993)★★, *As Humanity Fades* (Deaf 1994)★★★.

MOTHER LOVE BONE

This short-lived, Seattle-based quintet comprised Andrew Wood (vocals), Greg Gilmore (drums), Bruce Fairweather (guitar), Stone Gossard (guitar, ex-Green River) and Jeff Ament (bass, ex-Green River). Drawing influences from the Stooges, MC5 and the Velvet Underground, they specialized in heavy-duty garage rock laced with drug-fuelled psychotic overtones. Signing to Polydor Records, they debuted with *Apple* in 1990 to widespread critical acclaim. Their promising career was curtailed abruptly by the untimely death of vocalist Andrew Wood in March, shortly after the album was released. Gossard and Ament went on to enjoy further success with Temple Of The Dog and, to a much greater extent, Pearl Jam.

● ALBUMS: *Apple* (Polydor 1990)★★★★.

● COMPILATIONS: *Stardog Champion* (Polydor 1992)★★★.

MOTHER'S FINEST

Despite the 90s fixation with funk rock, Mother's Finest have long been considered the greatest in this musical field. Led by vocalist Baby Jean (b. Joyce Kennedy) and originating from Atlanta, Georgia, USA, the band boasts the talents of Moses Mo (b. Gary Moore; guitar), Glen Murdock (guitar, vocals), Mike (keyboards), Wizzard (b. Jerry Seay; bass) and B.B. Queen (b. B.B. Borden; drums). Formed in 1972, their music was basically funk with a metal edge, and Kennedy's vocals ranged from the sensual to all-out attack. The band never found great success in their homeland and only gained a cult following in Europe, although they were popular in Holland. In 1983, following the release of *Iron Age*, probably their hardest and most enduring record, the band disintegrated. Kennedy subsequently released two soul albums for A&M Records. Wizzard later linked up with

Rick Medlocke's Blackfoot. The original line-up re-formed in 1989 but the accompanying album failed to capture the fire and soul of earlier releases. Undaunted, they soldiered on and released a live recording, *Subluxation*, to critical acclaim. In its wake, and with a line-up boasting just three original members: Baby Jean, Murdock and Wizzard, they provided the agenda-setting *Black Radio Won't Play This Record*.

● ALBUMS: *Mother's Finest* (RCA 1972)★★★★, *Mother's Finest* (Epic 1976)★★★, *Another Mother Further* (Epic 1977)★★, *Mother Factor* (Epic 1978)★★★, *Live Mutha* (Epic 1979)★★, *Iron Age* (Epic 1982)★★★, *One Mother To Another* (Epic 1983)★★★, *Looks Could Kill* (Capitol 1989)★★, *Subluxation* (Capitol 1990)★★★★, *Black Radio Won't Play This Record* (Scotti Bros 1992)★★★.

MÖTLEY CRÜE

This heavy rock band was formed in 1980 by Nikki Sixx (b. Frank Faranno, 11 December 1958, California, USA; bass) and consisted of former members of several other Los Angeles-based groups. Tommy Lee (b. 3 October 1962, Athens, Greece; drums) was recruited from Suite 19; Vince Neil (b. Vince Neil Wharton, 8 February 1961, Hollywood, California, USA; vocals) from Rocky Candy; while Sixx himself had recently left London. Mick Mars (b. Bob Deal, 3 April 1956, USA; guitar) was added to the line-up after Sixx and Lee answered an advertisement announcing 'Loud, rude, aggressive guitarist available'. Their first single, 'Stick To Your Guns'/'Toast Of The Town', was issued in 1981 on their own Leathür label, followed by their self-produced debut, *Too Fast For Love*. The band signed to Elektra Records in 1982, and the album was remixed and reissued that August. The following year they recorded a new set, *Shout At The Devil*, with producer Tom Werman. He stayed at the helm for the two albums that broke them to a much wider audience in the USA, *Theatre Of Pain* (which sold more than two million copies) and *Girls, Girls, Girls*, which achieved the highest entry for a heavy metal album on *Billboard*'s album chart since *The Song Remains The Same* by Led Zeppelin in 1976. These albums refined the raw sound of earlier releases, without hiding the influence that Kiss and Aerosmith have exerted on their work. This change in style, which saw Mötley Crüe experimenting with organs, pianos and harmonicas in addition to their traditional instruments, has been described as a move from 'club-level metal glam' to 'stadium-size rock 'n' roll'. The band have not been without their setbacks: in 1984, Vince Neil was involved in a major car crash in which Hanoi Rocks drummer Razzle was killed. The subsequent *Theatre Of Pain* was dedicated to his memory, and this grim incident helped to inform the mood of the recording. Three years later, Nikki Sixx came close to death after a heroin overdose following touring with Guns N'Roses. Feuds with that same band, particularly between Neil and Axl Rose, later provided the group with many of their column inches in an increasingly disinterested press. The band survived to appear at the Moscow Peace Festival in 1989 before more than 200,000 people, and then in 1991 to issue *Dr. Feelgood*, which gave them their first US number 1 chart placing. Vince Neil was unexpectedly ejected from the band's line-up in 1992, establishing the Vince Neil Band shortly thereafter. His replacement for 1994's self-titled album was John Corabi (ex-Scream), although the band's problems continued with a record label/management split and a disastrous North American tour. Neil was working with the band again in autumn 1996. Lee became the focus of much press attention as a result of his explosive marriage to actress Pamela Anderson. Corabi was sacked in 1996 and the following year instigated litigation against the band members for damages arising from non-payment of monies owed to him. This action was taken as *Generation Swine* was released.

● ALBUMS: *Too Fast For Love* (Leathur 1981)★★, *Shout At The Devil* (Elektra 1983)★★, *Theatre Of Pain* (Elektra 1985)★★, *Girls, Girls, Girls* (Elektra 1987)★★★, *Dr. Feelgood* (Elektra 1989)★★★, *Mötley Crüe* (Elektra 1994)★★★, *Generation Swine* (Elektra 1997)★★★.

● COMPILATIONS: *Raw Tracks* (Elektra 1988)★★★, *Decade Of Decadence* (Elektra 1991)★★★★.

● VIDEOS: *Uncensored* (1987), *Dr. Feelgood, The Videos* (1989), *Decade Of Decadence* (1991).

● FURTHER READING: *Lüde, Crüde And Rüde*, Sylvie Simmons and Malcolm Dome.

MOTÖRHEAD

In 1975 Lemmy (b. Ian Kilmister, 24 December 1945, Stoke-on-Trent, Staffordshire, England; vocals, bass) was sacked from Hawkwind after being detained for five days at Canadian customs on possession charges. The last song he wrote for them was entitled 'Motörhead', and, after ditching an earlier suggestion, Bastard, this became the name of the band he formed with Larry Wallis of the Pink Fairies on guitar and Lucas Fox on drums.

Together they made their debut supporting Greenslade at the Roundhouse, London, in July. Fox then left to join Warsaw Pakt, and was replaced by 'Philthy' Phil Taylor (b. 21 September 1954, Chesterfield, England; drums), a casual friend of Lemmy's with no previous professional musical experience. Motörhead was a four-piece band for less than a month, with Taylor's friend 'Fast' Eddie Clarke (b. 5 October 1950, Isleworth, Middlesex, England) of Continuous Performance as second guitarist, until Wallis returned to the Pink Fairies. The Lemmy/Taylor/Clarke combination lasted six years until 1982, in which time they became the most famous trio in hard rock. With a following made up initially of Hell's Angels (Lemmy had formerly lived with their president, Tramp, for whom he wrote the biker epic 'Iron Horse'), the band made their official debut with the eponymous 'Motörhead'/'City Kids'. A similarly titled debut album charted, before the group moved over to Bronze Records. *Overkill* and *Bomber* firmly established the group's *modus operandi*, a fearsome barrage of instruments topped off by Lemmy's hoarse invocations. They toured the world regularly and enjoyed hits with 'Ace Of Spades' (one of the definitive heavy metal performances, it graced a 1980 album of the same name that saw the band at the peak of their popularity) and the number 5 single 'Please Don't Touch' (as Headgirl). Their reputation as the best live band of their generation was further enhanced by the release of *No Sleep 'Til Hammersmith*, which entered the UK charts at number 1.

In May 1982 Clarke left, citing musical differences, and was replaced by Brian Robertson (b. 12 September 1956, Glasgow, Scotland), who had previously played with Thin Lizzy and Wild Horses. This combination released *Another Perfect Day*, but this proved to be easily the least popular of all Motörhead line-ups. Robertson was replaced in November 1983 by Wurzel (b. Michael Burston, 23 October 1949, Cheltenham, England; guitar) - so-called on account of his scarecrow-like hair - and Philip Campbell (b. 7 May 1961, Pontypridd, Wales; guitar, ex-Persian Risk), thereby swelling the Motörhead ranks to four. Two months later and, after a final appearance on television's *The Young Ones*, Taylor left to join Robertson in Operator, and was replaced by ex-Saxon drummer Pete Gill. Gill remained with the band until 1987 and played on several fine albums including their GWR debut *Orgasmatron*, the title track of which saw Lemmy's lyric-writing surpass itself. By 1987 Phil Taylor had rejoined Motörhead, and the line-up remained unchanged for five years, during which time Lemmy made his acting debut in the *Comic Strip* film *Eat The Rich*, followed by other celluloid appearances including the role of a taxi driver in *Hardware*. In 1991 the group signed to Epic Records, releasing the acclaimed *1916*. The following year's *March Or Die* featured the American Mikkey Dee (ex-King Diamond) on drums and guest appearances by Ozzy Osbourne and Slash (Guns N'Roses). The title track revealed a highly sensitive side to Lemmy's lyrical and vocal scope in the way it dealt with the horrors of war. The idiosyncratic Lemmy singing style, usually half-growl, half-shout, and with his neck craned up at 45 degrees to the microphone, remained in place. On a more traditional footing they performed the theme song to the horror film *Hellraiser 3*, and convinced the film's creator, Clive Barker, to record his first promotional video with the band. Lemmy also hammed his way through insurance adverts, taking great delight in his press image of the unreconstructed rocker. Wurzel left the band and formed Wvkeaf in 1996. Now recording as a trio, the band released their nineteenth album (*Snake Bite Love*) in 1998.

● ALBUMS: *Motörhead* (Chiswick 1977)★★★, *Overkill* (Bronze 1979)★★★, *Bomber* (Bronze 1979)★★★, *On Parole* (United Artists 1979)★★★, *Ace Of Spades* (Bronze 1980)★★★★, *No Sleep 'Til Hammersmith* (Bronze 1981)★★★★, *Iron Fist* (Bronze 1982)★★★, *What's Words Worth?* 1978 recording (Big Beat 1983)★★★, *Another Perfect Day* (Bronze 1983)★★, *Orgasmatron* (GWR 1986)★★★★, *Rock'N'Roll* (GWR 1987)★★★, *Eat The Rich* film soundtrack (GWR 1987)★★★, *No Sleep At All* (GWR 1988)★★★, *Blitzkreig On Birmingham Live '77* (Receiver 1989)★★, *The Birthday Party* (GWR 1990)★★, *1916* (Epic 1991)★★★, *March Or Die* (Epic 1992)★★★, *Bastards* (ZYX 1993)★★★, *I* (SPV 1996)★★, *Overnight Sensation* (SPV 1996)★★★, *Snake Bite Love* (SPV 1998)★★★, *Live On The King Biscuit Flower Hour* recorded 1983 (King Biscuit 1998)★★.

● COMPILATIONS: *No Remorse* (Bronze 1984)★★★★, *Anthology* (Raw Power 1986)★★, *Born To Lose* (Castle 1986)★★, *Dirty Love* (Receiver 1990)★★, *Welcome To The Bear Trap* (Castle 1990)★★, *Best Of Motörhead* (Action Replay 1990)★★, *Lock Up Your Daughters* (Receiver 1990)★★, *From The Vaults* (Knight 1990)★★, *Meltdown* 3-CD box set (Castle 1991)★★★, *All The Aces* (Castle 1993)★★, *The Best Of Motörhead* (Castle 1993)★★★, *Protect The*

Innocent 4-CD box set (Essential 1997)★★★.
● VIDEOS: *Live In Toronto* (Avatar 1984), *Deaf Not Blind* (Virgin Vision 1984), *The Birthday Party* (Virgin Vision 1986), *The Best Of Motorhead* (Castle Music Pictures 1991), *Everything Louder Than Everything Else* (Sony Music Video 1991).
● FURTHER READING: *Motörhead: Born To Lose, Live To Win*, Alan Burridge. *Motörhead*, Giovanni Dadomo.

MOTT

This short-lived group was founded in 1975. Morgan Fisher (keyboards), Overend Watts (b. Peter Watts, 13 May 1947, Birmingham, England; bass, vocals) and Dale Griffin (b. 24 October 1948, Ross-on-Wye, England; drums), each formerly of Mott The Hoople, decided to drop the earlier suffix upon adding Nigel Benjamin (vocals) and Ray Major (guitar) to the line-up. Their albums proved sadly disappointing, provoking unfavourable comparisons with their previous, highly successful incarnation. The departure of Benjamin precipitated yet another change and, having invited ex-Medicine Head singer John Fiddler to join, the unit changed its name to British Lions.
● ALBUMS: *Drive On* (Columbia 1975)★★★, *Shouting And Pointing* (Columbia 1976)★★★.

MOTT THE HOOPLE

Having played in a number of different rock groups in Hereford, England, during the late 60s, the founding members of this ensemble comprised: Overend Watts (b. Peter Watts, 13 May 1947, Birmingham, England; vocals, bass), Mick Ralphs (b. 31 March 1944, Hereford, Herefordshire, England; vocals, guitar), Verden Allen (b. 26 May 1944, Hereford, England; organ) and Dale Griffin (b. 24 October 1948, Ross-on-Wye, England; vocals, drums). After dispensing with their lead singer Stan Tippens, they were on the point of dissolving when Ralphs sent a demo tape to Island Records producer Guy Stevens. He responded enthusiastically, and after placing an advertisement in *Melody Maker*, they auditioned a promising singer named Ian Hunter (b. 3 June 1946, Shrewsbury, Shropshire, England; vocals, keyboards, guitar). In June 1969 Stevens christened the group Mott The Hoople, after the novel by Willard Manus. Their self-titled debut album revealed a very strong Bob Dylan influence, most notably in Hunter's nasal vocal inflexions and visual image. With his corkscrew hair and permanent shades Hunter bore a strong resemblance to vintage 1966 Dylan and retained that style for his entire career. Their first album, with its M.C. Escher cover illustration, included pleasing interpretations of the Kinks' 'You Really Got Me' and Sonny Bono's 'Laugh At Me', and convinced many that Mott would become a major band. Their next three albums trod water, however, and it was only their popularity and power as a live act that kept them together. Despite teaming up with backing vocalist Steve Marriott on the George 'Shadow' Morton-produced 'Midnight Lady', a breakthrough hit remained elusive. On 26 March 1972, following the departure of Allen, they quit in disillusionment. Fairy godfather David Bowie convinced them to carry on, offered his assistance as producer, placed them under the wing of his manager, Tony De Fries, and even presented them with a stylish UK hit, 'All The Young Dudes'. The catchy 'Honaloochie Boogie' maintained the momentum but there was one minor setback when Ralphs quit to form Bad Company. With new members Morgan Fisher and Ariel Bender (b. Luther Grosvenor, 23 December 1949, Evesham, Worcestershire, England) the group enjoyed a run of further UK hits including 'All The Way From Memphis' and 'Roll Away The Stone'. During their final phase, Bowie's sideman Mick Ronson (b. 26 May 1945, Hull, Yorkshire, England, d. 30 April 1993) joined the group in place of Grosvenor (who had departed to join Widowmaker). Preparations for a European tour in late 1974 were disrupted when Hunter was hospitalized suffering from physical exhaustion, culminating in the cancellation of the entire tour. When rumours circulated that Hunter had signed a deal instigating a solo career, with Ronson working alongside him, the upheaval led to an irrevocable rift within the group, resulting in the stormy demise of Mott The Hoople. With the official departure of Hunter and Ronson, the remaining members carried on, working simply as Mott.
● ALBUMS: *Mott The Hoople* (Island 1969)★★★, *Mad Shadows* (Island 1970)★★★, *Wild Life* (Island 1971)★★, *Brain Capers* (Island 1971)★★★, *All The Young Dudes* (Columbia 1972)★★★, *Mott* (Columbia 1973)★★★★, *The Hoople* (Columbia 1974)★★★★, *Live* (Columbia 1974)★★★, *Original Mixed Up Kids: The BBC Recordings* (Windsong 1996)★★★.
● COMPILATIONS: *Rock And Roll Queen* (Island 1972)★★, *Greatest Hits* (Columbia 1975)★★★★, *Shades Of Ian Hunter - The Ballad Of Ian Hunter And Mott The Hoople* (Columbia 1979)★★★★, *Two Miles From Heaven* (Island 1981)★★★, *All The Way From Memphis* (Hallmark 1981)★★★, *Greatest Hits* (Columbia 1981)★★★★, *Backsliding*

Fearlessly (Rhino 1994)★★★, *All The Young Dudes: The Anthology* 3-CD box set (Sony 1998)★★★★.
● FURTHER READING: *The Diary Of A Rock 'N' Roll Star*, Ian Hunter.

Mould, Bob

b. 16 October 1960, Malone, New York, USA. The former guitarist, vocalist and co-composer in Hüsker Dü, Mould surprised many of that leading hardcore act's aficionados with his reflective solo debut, *Workbook*. Only one track, 'Whichever Way The Wind Blows', offered the maelstrom of guitars customary in his former group's work and instead the set was marked by a predominantly acoustic atmosphere. Cellist Jane Scarpantoni contributed to its air of melancholy, while two members of Pere Ubu, Tony Maimone (bass) and Anton Fier (drums; also Golden Palominos), added sympathetic support, helping to emphasize the gift for melody always apparent in Mould's work. Maimone and Fier also provided notable support on *Black Sheets Of Rain*, which marked a return to the uncompromising power of the guitarist's erstwhile unit. The set included the harrowing 'Hanging Tree' and apocalyptical 'Sacrifice Sacrifice/Let There Be Peace', but contrasted such doom-laden material with a brace of sprightly pop songs in 'It's Too Late' and 'Hear Me Calling', both of which echoed R.E.M. Mould also formed his own record company, SOL (Singles Only Label), which has issued material by, among others, William Burroughs. The artist abandoned his solo career in 1993, reverting to the melodic hardcore trio format with Sugar. By 1995, following the apparent demise of the band, he returned once again to his solo career. *Bob Mould* was an excellent album, although the ever perverse singer refused to undertake any promotional duties. Not surprisingly, it sounded like a cross between Hüsker Dü and Sugar, with sparkling tracks such as 'I Hate Alternative Rock' and the Tom Petty-esque 'Fort Knox, King Solomon'. Equally energetic was *The Last Dog And Pony Show*, with Mould still finding those memorable chord changes that lift the heart.
● ALBUMS: *Workbook* (Virgin 1989)★★★, *Black Sheets Of Rain* (Virgin 1990)★★★, *Bob Mould* (Creation/Rykodisk 1996)★★★★, *The Last Dog And Pony Show* (Creation 1998)★★★★.
● COMPILATIONS: *Poison Years* (Virgin 1994)★★★★.

Mountain

Mountain were one of the first generation heavy metal bands, formed by ex-Vagrants guitarist Leslie West (b. Leslie Weinstein, 22 October 1945, Queens, New York, USA) and bassist Felix Pappalardi (b. 1939, Bronx, New York, USA, d. 17 April 1983) in New York in 1968. Augmented by drummer N.D. Smart and Steve Knight on keyboards, they played the Woodstock Festival in 1970, releasing *Mountain Climbing!* shortly afterwards (with Corky Laing replacing Smart). Featuring dense guitar lines from West and the delicate melodies of Pappalardi, they quickly established their own sound, although Cream influences were detectable in places. The album was an unqualified success, peaking at number 17 in the *Billboard* album chart in November 1970. Their next two albums built on this foundation, as the band refined their style into an amalgam of heavy riffs, blues-based rock and extended guitar and keyboard solos. *Nantucket Sleighride* (the title track of which was later used as the theme tune to the UK television programme *World In Action*) and *Flowers Of Evil* made the *Billboard* charts at numbers 16 and 35, respectively. A live album followed, which included interminably long solos and was poorly received. The group temporarily disbanded to pursue separate projects. Pappalardi returned to producing, while West and Laing teamed up with Cream's Jack Bruce to record as West, Bruce And Laing. In 1974, Mountain rose again with Alan Schwartzberg and Bob Mann replacing Laing and Knight to record *Twin Peaks*, live in Japan. This line-up was short-lived as Laing rejoined for the recording of the disappointing studio album, *Avalanche*. The band collapsed once more and West concentrated on his solo career again. Pappalardi was shot and killed by his wife in 1983. Two years later, West and Laing resurrected the band with Mark Clarke (former Rainbow and Uriah Heep bassist) and released *Go For Your Life*. They toured with Deep Purple throughout Europe in 1985, but split again soon afterwards.
● ALBUMS: *Mountain Climbing!* (Windfall 1970)★★★, *Nantucket Sleighride* (Windfall 1971)★★★, *Flowers Of Evil* (Windfall 1971)★★★★, *Mountain Live (The Road Goes Ever On)* (Windfall 1972)★★, *Twin Peaks* (Columbia 1974)★★, *Avalanche* (Columbia 1974)★★, *Go For Your Life* (Scotti Brothers 1985)★★, *On Top* (Columbia 1992)★★, *Man's World* (Viceroy 1996)★★★.
● COMPILATIONS: *The Best Of Mountain* (Columbia 1973)★★★, *Over The Top* (Columbia/Legacy 1995)★★, *Super Hits* (Sony 1998)★★★.

MOURNEBLADE

London band whose main claim to fame was that one member was a British skateboarding champion. Formed in late 1984, the group comprised Derek Jasnock (keyboards), Richard Jones (guitar), Dunken Mullet (vocals), Jeff Ward (drums) and Clive Baxter (bass). They blended the heavier qualities of Hawkwind with the bass-driven power of Motörhead. In keeping with that tradition they took their name from a novel by Michael Moorcock, and signed to the Hawkwind-allied Flicknife Records. It was their tenuous links with the latter band that first brought them attention, and their debut album contained six excellent songs, though it failed to impress the Hawkwind fraternity or rock fans in general. They vanished from the music scene for a couple of years before regrouping in 1988, gaining a session on BBC radio's, then influential, *Friday Rock Show* in July of the following year. This saw them unveil a new sound, which had already been sketched more fully in January, when their second album had arrived. This contained further Hawkwind-inspired tracks, including 'Hall Of The Mountain King', but also grim tales such as 'Lolita' and 'Blonde Beautiful And Dead'. A few gigs and poor record sales later, they returned to obscurity.

● ALBUMS: *Times Running Out* (Flicknife 1985)★★★, *Live Fast, Die Young* (Plastic Head 1989)★★★.

MOVING TARGETS

This hardcore punk band, led by Kenny Chambers (vocals, lead guitar), formed in 1981 in Ipswich, Massachusetts, USA, a quaint fishing town just north of Boston. In keeping with their regional origins, Moving Targets would display a definite Mission Of Burma influence as their career progressed. They made their debut by recording three tracks for the Boston regional compilation *Bands That Could Be God*, alongside the likes of Salem 66 and Deep Wound (whose J. Mascis would later spearhead Dinosaur Jr). However, it was quite some time before anyone paid attention to their numerous demos and invited them into a 'proper' studio. In 1986 Lou Giordana (who had originally produced the compilation tracks) helped the band record 15 songs which finally persuaded Taang! Records to offer them a contract. *Burning In Water, Drowning In Flames* emerged in October 1986. A strong debut, the band's progress was nevertheless impeded when Chambers became involved in a variety of sidelines. These included Dred Foole And The Din (two albums), the Groinoids and Bullet Lavolta, with whom he toured. Moving Targets eventually re-formed with Pat Leonard (guitar) and Chuck Freeman (bass). During disagreements over the second album's direction, the group's original bass player returned. Chambers then recorded a solo album. A new line-up of Moving Targets, featuring two ex-members of Jones Very, Jeff Goddard (bass) and Jamie Van Bramer (drums), as well as guitarist Ben Segal, recorded *Fall*. Goddard had also appeared on Chambers' solo work.

● ALBUMS: *Burning In Water, Drowning In Flames* (Taang! 1986)★★★★, *Brave Noise* (Taang! 1989)★★★, *Fall* (Taang! 1991)★★★.

MR. BIG

Mr. Big (not to be confused with the 70s group of the same name) are a supergroup project, featuring bassist Billy Sheehan (ex-David Lee Roth), guitarist Paul Gilbert (ex-Racer X), drummer Pat Torpey (ex-Chris Impelliteri and Robert Plant) and vocalist Eric Martin (ex-Eric Martin Band). Signing to Atlantic Records, their self-titled debut was a high-energy blast of sophisticated hard rock. *Lean Into It*, released two years later, marked a considerable progression; the band had evolved their own style and sounded more comfortable together. Drawing on influences from a wider musical spectrum, the album was well received by the critics and charted on both sides of the Atlantic. The exposition of AOR that has graced the charts remains, however, in sharp contrast to their reputation for strong live performances. After his departure in 1997, Gilbert went solo and released *King Of Clubs* in 1998.

● ALBUMS: *Mr. Big* (Atlantic 1989)★★★, *Lean Into It* (Atlantic 1991)★★★★, *Live* (Atlantic 1992)★★, *Bump Ahead* (Atlantic 1993)★★★, *Hey Man* (Atlantic 1996)★★★.

● COMPILATIONS: *Big, Bigger, Biggest* (Atlantic 1997)★★★.

MR. BUNGLE

Originating in Eureka, California, USA, in the mid-80s, this bizarre punk-metal-jazz-*avant garde* amalgam was Mike Patton's first band prior to joining Faith No More, and the success of *The Real Thing* helped Patton to secure a record contract for his previous project. Patton and colleagues Trey Spruance (guitar), Trevor Dunn (bass) and Danny Heifetz (drums) adopted an oddly costumed image to match their eclectic musical style, with Patton and Spruance adopting the respective pseudonyms

Vlad Dracula and Scummy, enlisting jazz-noise experimentalist John Zorn to produce *Mr Bungle*. The album received surprisingly positive reviews considering its extreme, genre-hopping, improvisational format and strange lyrical themes, although Zorn's sympathetic production helped to focus the eccentricity. *Mr Bungle* sold respectably on the strength of Patton's name, but his Faith No More commitments kept live shows to a minimum. Spruance subsequently replaced Jim Martin in Faith No More for the recording of *King For A Day ... Fool For A Lifetime*, although he departed shortly afterwards.

● ALBUMS: *Mr Bungle* (Warners 1991)★★★★, *Disco Volante* (London 1995)★★★.

MSG

After stints with UFO and the Scorpions, guitarist Michael Schenker (b. 10 January 1955, Savstedt, Germany) decided to step out into the spotlight on his own in 1980. Enlisting the services of Gary Barden (vocals), Simon Phillips (drums), Mo Foster (bass) and Don Airey (keyboards), the Michael Schenker Group (later shortened to MSG) was born. Their approach, characterized by Schenker's screaming guitarwork, had much in common with both his previous bands. Schenker, now in complete control, hired and fired musicians at will, so the line-up of MSG has rarely been stable. Only Barden remained to record their second album; Cozy Powell (drums), Chris Glen (bassist, ex-Sensational Alex Harvey Band) and Paul Raymond (keyboards, ex-UFO) were the replacements. They enjoyed great success in the Far East, where they recorded a double live set at the Budokan Hall, Tokyo. This album went some way towards establishing the band in Europe. Graham Bonnet replaced Barden on *Assault Attack* and ex-Rory Gallagher drummer Ted McKenna was also recruited. Bonnet insisted on making a significant contribution to the compositions and his influence can clearly be heard on the album, which is far more blues-orientated than previous releases. Schenker fired Bonnet shortly after the album's launch and welcomed back former vocalist Gary Barden. The next two album releases were rigidly formularized. Old ideas were simply rehashed as the band remained stuck in a creative rut. Even the contribution of Derek St. Holmes (ex-Ted Nugent vocalist) could not elevate the very ordinary material. Barden left to form Statetrooper and MSG disintegrated. Schenker moved back to Germany and teamed up with singer Robin McAuley (ex-Grand Prix) to form the McAuley Schenker Group, still retaining the acronym MSG. They completed the new-look band, with Steve Mann, Rocky Newton and Bobo Schopf on keyboards, bass and drums, respectively. They also concentrated on a more melodic direction, as McAuley's prolific writing skills were, for once, accepted by Schenker. With the release of *Perfect Timing* and *Save Yourself*, they began to re-establish a solid fan base once more, though 1992's confusingly titled *MSG* was universally despised.

● ALBUMS: *The Michael Schenker Group* (Chrysalis 1980)★★★★, *MSG* (Chrysalis 1981)★★★★, *One Night At Budokan* (Chrysalis 1982)★★, *Assault Attack* (Chrysalis 1982)★★★, *Built To Destroy* (Chrysalis 1983)★★★, *Rock Will Never Die* (Chrysalis 1984)★★, *Perfect Timing* (EMI 1987)★★★, *Save Yourself* (Capitol 1989)★★★, *MSG* (EMI 1992)★★.

Mucky Pup

The rock group Mucky Pup was formed in New York, USA, in 1985, by John Milnes (drums), Dan Nastasi (guitar), Chris Milnes (brother of John; vocals) and Scott LePage (bass). Following the release of their debut album, 1988's *Can't Take A Joke*, LePage was replaced by David Neabore, who subsequently left to form the much-praised Dog Eat Dog with Dan Nastasi. However, as Chris Milnes revealed: 'The idea behind Mucky Pup has always been that I am the head of the band and the director, but every record and tour is with different people. It's fun always playing with different line-ups; kind of like a kaleidoscope, which is always the same, but by shaking it you end up with entirely new images.' Since the late 80s Mucky Pup have toured widely alongside bands including the Offspring, Primus, Live, Bad Religion and the Red Hot Chili Peppers, releasing a number of albums which have generally been overlooked by critics. Promotion for their debut album included a European tour of six countries, and they have returned to Europe on an almost six-monthly basis ever since. After the release of their second album, *A Boy In A Man's World*, Neabore's replacement on bass was Belgian native Mark D. Baker. A quick follow-up, *Now*, was issued in 1990. Two years were spent on the completion of the smoother-sounding *Act Of Faith*. Dan Nastasi contributed guitar to some of the album, but after his defection to Dog Eat Dog he was replaced by 'Junior'. This arrangement proved unsatisfactory, and for 1993's *Lemonade* John Milnes switched to guitar, his position as drummer taken by Kevin Powers. He returned to the drums for 1996's *Five Guys In A*

Really Hot Garage, by which time the line-up featured 'The Hinge' on guitar and Billy Joe Mama on bass. Recorded at Showplace Studios in New York, this offered a further glimpse of Mucky Pup's episodic but intriguing development.

● ALBUMS: *Can't Take A Joke* (SPV 1988)★★★, *A Boy In A Man's World* (SPV 1989)★★★, *Now* (SPV 1990)★★, *Act Of Faith* (SPV 1992)★★★, *Lemonade* (SPV 1993)★★★, *Alive & Well* (SPV 1994)★★, *Five Guys In A Really Hot Garage* (SPV 1996)★★★.

MUDHONEY

Mudhoney, forged from a host of hobbyist bands, can lay claim to the accolade 'godfathers of grunge' more legitimately than most - whether or not they desire that title. The band comprises brothers Mark Arm (b. 21 February 1962, California, USA; vocals) and Steve Turner (b. 28 March 1965, Houston, USA; guitar), plus Matt Lukin (b. 16 August 1964, Aberdeen, Washington, USA; bass) and Dan Peters (b. 18 August 1967, Seattle, Washington, USA; drums). Arm and Turner were both ex-Green River, the band that also gave birth to Pearl Jam, and the less serious Thrown Ups. Lukin was ex-Melvins, and Peters ex-Bundles Of Hiss. Mudhoney were the band that first took the sound of Sub Pop Records to wider shores. In August 1988 they released the fabulous 'Touch Me I'm Sick' single, one of the defining moments in the evolution of 'grunge', followed shortly by their debut mini-album. Contrary to popular belief, Turner chose the name *Superfuzz Bigmuff* after his favourite effects pedals rather than any sexual connotation. Early support included the admiration of Sonic Youth who covered their first a-side, while Mudhoney thrashed through Sonic Youth staple 'Halloween' on the flip-side of a split single. The first album was greeted as a comparative disappointment by many, though there were obvious stand-out tracks ('When Tomorrow Hits'). The EP *Boiled Beef And Rotting Teeth* contained a cover version of the Dicks' 'Hate The Police', demonstrating a good grasp of their 'hardcore' heritage. They had previously demonstrated an ability to choose a sprightly cover tune when Spacemen 3's 'Revolution' had appeared on the b-side to 'This Gift'. The band also hold the likes of Celibate Rifles and Billy Childish in high esteem. Members of the former have helped in production of the band, while on trips to England they have invited the latter to join as support. It was their patronage that led to Childish's Thee Headcoats releasing material through Sub Pop. Meanwhile, Mudhoney's shows were becoming less eye-catching, and progressively close to eye-gouging. Early gigs in London saw Arm invite every single member of the audience onto the stage, with the resultant near-destruction of several venues. *Every Good Boy Deserves Fudge* was a departure, with Hammond organ intruding into the band's accomplished rock formula. It demonstrated their increasing awareness of the possibilities of their own songwriting. Far from being wooden-headed noise dolts, the band members all have middle-class backgrounds, and while Arm is an English graduate, Turner has qualifications in anthropology. After much speculation, Mudhoney became the final big players in the Sub Pop empire to go major when they moved to Warner Brothers Records, though many argue that none of their efforts thus far have managed to reproduce the glory of 'Touch Me I'm Sick' or other highlights of their independent days. *My Brother The Cow*, however, revealed a band nearly back at its best. Released after extensive worldwide touring with Pearl Jam, highlights included 'Into Your Schtick', which reflected on the passing of one-time friend Kurt Cobain. Jack Endino's production, meanwhile, added lustre and managed effectively to capture the band's always compelling live sound. Mark Arm also plays with the trashy Australian garage rock band Bloodloss, who released their major label debut, *Live My Way*, in 1995.

● ALBUMS: *Superfuzz Bigmuff* mini-album (Sub Pop 1988)★★★, *Mudhoney* (Sub Pop 1989)★★, *Every Good Boy Deserves Fudge* (Sub Pop 1991)★★★, *Piece Of Cake* (Warners 1992)★★★, *Five Dollar Bob's Mock Cooter Stew* mini-album (Warners 1993)★★, *My Brother The Cow* (Warners 1995)★★★, *Tomorrow Hit Today* (Reprise 1998)★★★.

● COMPILATIONS: *Superfuzz Bigmuff Plus Early Singles* (Sub Pop 1991)★★★.

● VIDEOS: *Absolutely Live* (Pinnacle 1991), *No 1 Video In America This Week* (Warner Music Video 1995).

MURDER INC.

This *avant garde*/industrial metal band was formed in London during 1992 by ex-Killing Joke members and ex-Revolting Cocks vocalist Chris Connelly. Utilizing two drummers in Martin Atkins and Paul Ferguson, their style was inevitably dominated by a strong rhythmic element. Geordie Walker (guitar), Paul Raven (bass) and John Bechdel (guitar, keyboards) completed the line-up. Contracted to Music For Nations Records, the band debuted with a self-titled album in June 1992. This built on the brutal rhythms of Killing Joke's material, but, as with the other spin-off projects, it failed to inspire similar devotion to that enjoyed by the parent group.

● ALBUMS: *Murder Inc.* (Music For Nations 1992)★★★.

MURPHY'S LAW

Formed in 1985, New York, USA hardcore punk band Murphy's Law have endured a number of line-up shuffles over the ensuing decade. Jimmy 'G' Drescher has remained vocalist and leader in all subsequent incarnations, though he has dropped his original sobriquet of Jimmy Gestapo. Other members on the group's 1986 debut, *Murphy's Law*, were Pete Hines (drums), Pete Martinez (bass) and Alex Morris (guitar). However, by the advent of their fourth album in 1996, *Dedication*, Drescher had been joined by Todd Youth (guitar), Dean Rispler (bass) and Eric Arce (drums). Part of this change was forced - the group having lost bassist Chuck Valle in a fatal stabbing incident in 1994. The group's debut album included a cover version of Iggy Pop's 'I've Got A Right', which provided ample evidence of their influences. Subsequent efforts emphasized a predilection for what the group called 'party lyrics', in preference to the more dour and earnest hardcore groups. However, with *Dedication*, Valle's death proved to be a significant impact on Drescher's songwriting, resulting in songs such as 'Dysfunctional Family', 'Don't Bother Me' and 'Bitter'.

● ALBUMS: *Murphy's Law* (Rock Hotel 1986)★★★, *Back With A Bong!* (Rock Hotel 1989)★★, *Best Of Times* (Relativity 1991)★★★, *Dedication* (Profile 1995)★★★, *Dedicated* (Another Planet 1996)★★★.

MY DYING BRIDE

From Bradford, Yorkshire, England, My Dying Bride proffer an intriguing blend of full-blooded doom metal, with more poise than most and a rare experimental streak. Vocalist Aaron's lyrics also depart somewhat from the herd - although he often concerns himself with biblical and religious matters, his stance is neither that of Christian or Satanist: 'The Bible is a fantastic story...There's no heaven or hell as far as I'm concerned, it's just a nice story and I like to write about it because it affects so many people's lives.' After formation in 1990 they secured a contract with French label Listenable, through whom they provided their first official release, the 'God Is Alone' single. This was enough to interest UK label Peaceville, who released their debut EP, *Symphonaire Infernus Et Spera Empyrium*.

Their 1992 album, *As The Flower Withers*, followed shortly afterwards, featuring artwork by popular cult artist Dave McKean. My Dying Bride were already making a name for themselves as innovators in the doom genre, with a sound that combined the morbid grind of death metal with orchestral flourishes and haunting refrains. The resultant effect was one of grandiose tragedy. After recording another EP, *The Thrash Of Naked Limbs*, they took on their session violinist and pianist, Martin Powell, as a full member of the band, confirming their dedication to a path that combined classical and contemporary influences. A second album, *Let Loose The Swans*, saw Aaron singing, rather than growling in the traditional death metal style, and is their most distinctive and accomplished work to date. The vitality and colour of the band was enshrined in their 1994 release, the *I Am The Bloody Earth* EP, with the a-side featuring guest vocals from Ghost (of G.G.F.H.), while the b-side, 'Transcending (Into The Exquisite)', featured a challenging remix from local dance gurus Drug Free America. November 1994 saw the release of a box set containing their previous EPs, which sold out almost immediately, reflecting My Dying Bride's growing popularity. *The Angel And The Dark River* offered only six songs spanning 52 minutes, but it sacrificed immediacy for a deep-rooted evocation of sadness and loss. It revealed a band unafraid of exploring the boundaries of doom metal, although not all reviews were favourable. *Alternative Press* said that the band 'exaggerate their Jesus-in-spandex theatrics to laughable extremes'.

● ALBUMS: *As The Flower Withers* (Peaceville 1992)★★★, *Let Loose The Swans* (Peaceville 1993)★★★, *The Angel And The Dark River* (Peaceville 1995)★★, *Trinity* (Fierce/Futurist 1995)★★★, *Like Gods Of The Sun* (Music For Nations 1996)★★.

MYLES, ALANNAH

Toronto-based vocalist Myles spent much of her early career unsuccessfully shopping for a recording contract in her native Canada, but when she and writing partner Christopher Ward changed tack, targeting an American deal with a David Tyson-produced demo and a video for 'Just One Kiss', they met with almost instant success. Tyson produced *Alannah Myles*, an excellent commercial hard-rock debut on which the vocalist turned her deep, soulful voice to a variety of material, from gentle acoustic guitar-based ballads to raunchy rock 'n' roll. After the years of struggle, the debut ironically took off rapidly in Canada, with 'Love Is' helping Myles to achieve major status in just three months, but the slow, steamy raunch of 'Black Velvet' brought much wider success. She suddenly found herself topping the US singles chart and hitting the Top 3 in the UK as 'Black Velvet' became a worldwide hit. *Alannah Myles* subsequently became the most successful debut in Canadian music history, selling more than five million copies globally. Myles subsequently proved that she was no mere studio songbird, taking her band out on the road. Her most recent albums, *Alannah* and *Arrival*, failed to find favour beyond her cult following.

● ALBUMS: *Alannah Myles* (Atlantic 1989)★★★★, *Rockinghorse* (Atlantic 1992)★★★, *Alannah* (Atlantic 1995)★★, *Arrival* (El Dorado 1997)★★★.

MYTHRA

Judas Priest-influenced band from the north-east of England who came together in 1979 at the height of the New Wave Of British Heavy Metal and released one of the most outstanding records of the era. Yet the band - Vince High (vocals), Mick Rundel (guitar), Barry Hopper (drums), Maurice Bates (rhythm guitar) and Pete Melsom (bass) - never achieved the greatness a band that sells 15,000 singles in 20 days deserves. The EP, *Death And Destiny*, first released on Guardian Records, was quickly reissued on Street Beat Records to coincide with their appearance at the Bingley Hall festival with Motörhead. It, too, sold well and their battle cry of 'Death And Destiny' was sung by a thousand voices at the aforementioned gig. However, by 1981 their name was absent from the live listings, leaving the EP to command a high collectors' value and cult reputation. Metallica fans should track it down to see how much *Kill 'Em All* owes to this band.

N.W.O.B.H.M.

(see New Wave Of British Heavy Metal)

NAILBOMB

A side-project for Sepultura vocalist/guitarist Max Cavalera (b. Belo Horizonte, 4 August 1969) and Fudge Tunnel singer/guitarist Alex Newport, both residents of Phoenix, Arizona. Nailbomb arrived with the public thus: 'It was right after the last show on the Ministry tour. It was in San Diego and we were having a party. Me and Alex were talking 'cause the tour was over, the rest of the guys in Sepultura were going to Brazil, and I wasn't going because it was close to the time my son (Zyon) would be born. But I didn't want to stay and just do nothing in Phoenix...So I told Alex, "why don't we get together and do some songs, just for the hell of it". We didn't even think of recording anything'. Originally titled Hate Project, then Sickman, they eventually settled on Nailbomb because both partners wanted something 'real shocking'. A tape of the duo's demos reached Monte Conner at Roadrunner. He secured a larger budget, and the result was *Point Blank*, which improved on the quality of the original demos but maintained the punk sound (a cross between Big Black and Discharge) that they had developed together. Contributions came from Sepultura's lead guitarist Andreas Kisser and drummer Igor Cavalera, together with an appearance by Fear Factory's Dino Cazares on '24 Hour Bullshit'. A second album was essentially a live recording, although Cavalera's vocals begin to grate painfully by the end of the set.

● ALBUMS: *Point Blank* (Roadrunner 1994)★★★, *Proud To Commit Commercial Suicide* (Roadrunner 1995)★★.

NAKED RAYGUN

Formerly Negro Commander, a band whose life span extended to a single show, Chicago, Illinois, USA's Naked Raygun were their city's premier hardcore band of the early 80s. Despite appearances to the contrary, their name was chosen prior to the election of US President Ronald Reagan.

Dropping bass player Marco Pezzati for Camilo Gonzalez of the Wayouts at the same time as they lost their original name, the rest of the band comprised Jeff Pezzati (vocals) and Santiago Durango (guitar). No drummer featured in the original line-up until Jim Colao was recruited. Santiago then moved on to Big Black and Arsenal, and was replaced by John Haggerty who had already played saxophone at early shows. Their recording career had begun with the documentary 1981 Chicago live compilation, *Busted At Oz*, released on Autumn Records (it also featured the Effigies and Strike Under, from whom later members would come). New drummer Eric Spicer (ex-DVA) was drafted in 1983 as the group began to take shape. 'The old line-up didn't have a common, long-term goal. We just had practices, we just played some songs we had in our heads . . . We never talked about records, we played any show in Chicago we could get . . .' They played their first New York date at Gildersleeves later that year. It had taken the band three years to complete their first tour, after which they announced two further tours in 1984. Their first record release had been 1983's cacophonous *Basement Screams* EP on Ruthless Records (run by Big Black and the Effigies, and entirely different to the label of the same name operated by rapper Eazy E). However, their debut album was a vastly superior artefact in showcasing their talents, with individual songs of great quality including 'Surf Combat' and 'Gear', while 'Metastasis' benefited from Pezatti's trademark malevolent vocal inflections. The jazzy intonations of 'Libido', meanwhile, served as an early indication of a willingness to change their mode of address. In 1986 Pierre Kezdy deputized for Camillo on bass, and their *All Rise* album of that year proved to be their finest moment. The group moved from Homestead Records to set up their own Sandpunder label, before another shift to Caroline Records. Their admiration for the work of the Buzzcocks was compounded when they were joined onstage by a drunken Steve Diggle on their 1989 UK tour to promote *Understand?*. After an emotional final gig at Chicago's Maxwell's venue Haggerty left (to join Pegboy) to be replaced by Bill Stephens (ex-Product 19). However, his contribution to 1990's *Raygun ... Naked Raygun* failed to fill the gap adequately, and Naked Raygun subsequently ground to a halt.

● ALBUMS: *Throb Throb* (Homestead 1985)★★★, *All Rise* (Homestead 1986)★★★★, *Jettison* (Caroline 1988)★★★, *Understand?* (Caroline 1989)★★★, *Raygun ... Naked Raygun* (Caroline 1990)★★.

Naked Truth

This Atlanta, Georgia-based quartet originated in the local hardcore scene in 1988, although the individual band members arrived from far afield: vocalist Doug Watts came from Detroit, bassist Jeff from Harlem, New York, and drummer Bernard Dawson from Los Angeles, while Jimmie Westley was the only Georgia native, from Savannah. Life was initially tough for a black metal band in Georgia, but the dreadlocked group attracted the interest of former Clash manager Bernie Rhodes, and he helped the band sign to Sony and relocate to London. *Green With Rage* introduced Naked Truth's raw, aggressive sound, which was given an individual slant by jazz and funk influences, but the homesick Jeff departed, and was replaced by London-born Kwame Boaten for the *Read Between The Lines* EP. The band were fortunate to secure a UK tour with Little Angels after a Motörhead support slot was lost owing to a tour cancellation, and despite the obviously different styles, Naked Truth were well received. The band built up a varied following, boosted by a series of London residencies, before *Fight* appeared. The album demonstrated the band's ability to mix styles as diverse as jazz and death metal seamlessly and convincingly, while Watts supplied varied vocals, from rap to all-out hardcore rage, and intelligent lyrics. The band were impressive when they supported Living Colour around the UK, but they decided on a name change to Watts before releasing their second full album.

● ALBUMS: *Green With Rage* mini-album (Sony 1991)★★★, *Fight* (Sony 1993)★★★.

Napalm Death

This quintet from Birmingham, England, was formed in 1981. Dispensing with their original style by the mid-80s, they then absorbed punk and thrash metal influences to create the new subgenre of grindcore, arguably the most extreme of all musical forms. Side one of their debut album featured Justin Broadrick (guitar), Mick Harris (drums) and Nick Bullen (bass, vocals), but by side two this had switched to Bill Steer (guitar), Jim Whitely (bass) and Lee Dorrian (vocals), later replaced by Barney Greenway, with Harris the only survivor from that first inception (though that, too, had been subject to numerous changes). Broadrick went on to join Head Of David and Godflesh. *Scum* largely comprised sub-two-minute blasts of metallic white noise, overridden by Dorrian's unintelligible vocal tirade. The lyrics dealt with social and political injustices, but actually sounded like somebody coughing up blood. Their main advocate was Radio 1 disc jockey John Peel, who had first picked up on *Scum*, playing the 0.75 second-long track 'You Suffer' three times before inviting them to record a session for the programme in September 1987. This came to be acknowledged as one of the 'Classic Sessions' in Ken Garner's 1993 book on the subject, and introduced new bass player Shane Embury (also Unseen Terror, who split after one album in 1988). Elsewhere, Napalm Death were the subject of derision and total miscomprehension. They were, however, the true pioneers of the 'blast-snare' technique - whereby the tempo of a given beat is sustained at the maximum physical human tolerance level. They went on to attract a small but loyal cult following on the underground heavy metal scene. *From Enslavement To Obliteration*, consisting of no less than 54 tracks on the CD, was a state-of-the-art-less offering that easily bypassed previous extremes in music. However, following a Japanese tour in 1989 both Dorrian and Steer elected to leave the band, the former putting together Cathedral, the latter Carcass. Despite the gravity of the split, replacements were found in vocalist Mark 'Barny' Greenway (ex-Benediction) and US guitarist Jesse Pintado (ex-Terrorizer). To maintain their profile the band embarked on the European *Grindcrusher* tour (in their wake, grindcore had developed considerably and found mass acceptance among the rank and file of the metal world) with Bolt Thrower, Carcass and Morbid Angel, before playing their first US dates in New York. A second guitarist, Mitch Harris (ex-Righteous Pigs), was added in time for *Harmony Corruption*, which, along with the 12-inch 'Suffer The Children', saw Napalm Death retreat to a more pure death metal sound. During worldwide touring in 1992, sole surviving original member Mick Harris became disillusioned with the band and vacated the drum-stool for Danny Herrara, a friend of Pintado's from Los Angeles. A fourth album, *Utopia Banished*, celebrated the band's remarkable survival instincts, while the heady touring schedule continued unabated. By 1993 the band had played in Russia, Israel, Canada and South Africa in addition to the more familiar European and US treks. A cover version of the Dead Kennedys' 'Nazi Punks Fuck Off', issued as a single, reinstated their political motives. As *Fear, Emptiness, Despair* confirmed, however, they remain the antithesis of style, melody and taste - the punk concept taken to its ultimate extreme, and a great band for all the difficulty of listening to them. Greenway was sacked in October 1996 and replaced a few months later by Phil Vane, but both *Diatribes* and *Inside The Torn Apart* represented business as usual. Drummer Mick Harris has recorded two albums with Eraldo Bernocchi, 1997's *Overload Lady* and the following year's *Total Station*.

● ALBUMS: *Scum* (Earache 1987)★★, *From Enslavement To Obliteration* (Earache 1988)★★★, *The Peel Sessions* (Strange Fruit 1989)★★★, *Harmony Corruption* (Earache 1990)★, *Live Corruption* (Earache 1990)★, *Utopia Banished* (Earache 1992)★★, *Fear, Emptiness, Despair* (Earache 1994)★★, *Greed Killing* mini-album (Earache 1995)★★, *Diatribes* (Earache 1996)★★, *Inside The Torn Apart* (Earache 1997)★★, *Breed To Breathe* mini-album (Earache 1997)★★, *Bootlegged In Japan* (Earache 1998)★★.

● COMPILATIONS: *Death By Manipulation* (Earache 1992)★★.

● VIDEOS: *Live Corruption* (Fotodisk 1990).

NASTY IDOLS

This Swedish glam-metal quintet was formed in 1988 by vocalist Andy Pierce and guitarist Jonnie Wee, with Dick Qwarfort (bass), George Swanson (drums) and Roger White (keyboards) completing the line-up. They pursued a commercial hard rock direction in the style of Bon Jovi and Whitesnake, debuting with *Gigolos On Parole* to widespread indifference. Wee was soon replaced by Peter Espinoza on guitar, and his arrival marked a move towards a more glam-metal image, with Mötley Crüe and Hanoi Rocks influences taking over. *Cruel Intention* was the result, released in 1991. A marked improvement, it nevertheless failed to emulate this new set of influences in terms of commercial reward.

● ALBUMS: *Gigolos On Parole* (Black Mark 1989)★★, *Cruel Intention* (Black Mark 1991)★★★★.

NASTY SAVAGE

This heavy metal/thrash quintet was formed in Brandigan, Florida, USA, in 1983 by vocalist and professional wrestler Nasty Ronnie and guitarist Ben Meyer. Assisted by David Austin (guitar), Fred Dregischan (bass) and Curtis Beeson (drums), they made their debut via demo tracks that subsequently appeared on the *Metal Massacre IV* and *Iron Tyrants* compilations in 1984. This led to a contract with Metal Blade Records, producing four albums over the ensuing five years. From an initial hard rock base of Iron Maiden and Judas Priest styles, they gradually incorporated thrash elements into their music, drawing inspiration and ideas from Metallica, Anthrax and Slayer. They employed four bass players in as many years, with guitarist Richard Bateman assuming bass duties in 1988. Rob Proctor replaced Beeson on drums the following year. When they eventually sundered at the close of the decade, they were chiefly lamented for their spectacular live show, which featured their wild vocalist smashing television sets on stage and performing crude gymnastics.

● ALBUMS: *Nasty Savage* (Metal Blade 1985)★★★, *Indulgence* (Metal Blade 1987)★★★★, *Abstract Reality* (Metal Blade 1988)★★★, *Penetration Point* (Metal Blade 1989)★★.

NAZARETH

Formed in 1968 in Dunfermline, Fife, Scotland, Nazareth evolved out of local attractions the Shadettes. Dan McCafferty (vocals), Manny Charlton (guitar), Pete Agnew (bass) and Darrell Sweet (drums) took their new name from the opening line in 'The Weight', a contemporary hit for the Band. After completing a gruelling Scottish tour, Nazareth opted to move to London. *Nazareth* and *Exercises* showed undoubted promise, while a third set, *Razamanaz*, spawned two UK Top 10 singles in 'Broken Down Angel' and 'Bad Bad Boy' (both 1973). New producer Roger Glover helped to focus the quartet's brand of melodic hard rock, and such skills were equally prevalent on *Loud 'N' Proud*. An unlikely rendition of Joni Mitchell's 'This Flight Tonight' gave the group another major chart entry, while the Charlton-produced *Hair Of The Dog* confirmed Nazareth as an international attraction. Another cover version, this time of Tomorrow's 'My White Bicycle', was a Top 20 entry and although *Rampant* did not yield a single, the custom-recorded 'Love Hurts', originally a hit for the Everly Brothers, proved highly successful in the USA and Canada. Nazareth's popularity remained undiminished throughout the 70s but, having tired of a four-piece line-up, they added guitarist Zal Cleminson, formerly of the Sensational Alex Harvey Band, for *No Mean City*. Still desirous for change, the group invited Jeff 'Skunk' Baxter, late of Steely Dan and the Doobie Brothers, to produce *Malice In Wonderland*. While stylistically different from previous albums, the result was artistically satisfying. Contrasting ambitions then led to Cleminson's amicable departure, but the line-up was subsequently augmented by former Spirit keyboard player John Locke. Baxter also produced the experimental *The Fool Circle*, while the group's desire to capture their in-concert fire resulted in *'Snaz*. Glasgow guitarist Billy Rankin had now joined the group, but dissatisfaction with touring led to Locke's departure following *2XS*. Rankin then switched to keyboards, but although Nazareth continued to enjoy popularity in the USA and Europe, their stature in the UK was receding. Bereft of a major recording contract, Nazareth suspended their career during the late 80s, leaving McCafferty free to pursue solo ambitions (he had already released a solo album in 1975). *No Jive* was an impressive comeback album in 1992, but Nazareth unfortunately failed to capitalize on its success.

● ALBUMS: *Nazareth* (Mooncrest 1971)★★★, *Exercises* (Mooncrest 1972)★★★, *Razamanaz* (Mooncrest 1973)★★★★, *Loud 'N' Proud* (Mooncrest 1974)★★★, *Rampant* (Mooncrest 1974)★★★, *Hair Of The Dog* (Mooncrest 1975)★★★★, *Close Enough For Rock 'N' Roll* (Mountain 1976)★★★, *Play 'N' The Game* (Mountain 1976)★★, *Expect No Mercy* (Mountain 1977)★★, *No Mean City* (Mountain 1978)★★, *Malice In Wonderland* (Mountain 1980)★★, *The Fool Circle* (NEMS 1981)★★, *'Snaz* (NEMS 1981)★★, *2XS* (NEMS 1982)★★, *Sound Elixir* (Vertigo 1983)★★, *The Catch* (Vertigo 1984)★★, *Cinema* (Vertigo 1986)★★, *Snakes & Ladders* (Vertigo 1990)★★, *No Jive* (Mainstream 1992)★★, *Nazareth At The Beeb* (Reef 1998)★★★.
Solo: Dan McCafferty *Dan McCafferty* (1975)★★.

● COMPILATIONS: *Greatest Hits* (Mountain 1975)★★★, *20 Greatest Hits: Nazareth* (Sahara 1985)★★★, *Anthology: Nazareth* (Raw Power 1988)★★★.

● VIDEOS: *Razamanaz* (Hendring 1990).

NECROS

With a fluid line-up headed by Barry Henssler (vocals), with, at various times, Todd Swalla (drums), Andy (guitar), Brian Pollack (guitar), and at least four different bass players, this early 80s hardcore act from Maumee, Ohio, USA, released a number of records that continue to sell for high sums among modern collectors (they should not be confused with the Washington, DC band of the same name and musical genre). They are also one of the few Midwest outfits of their type who did not split up within a few years of their formation, essentially due to the strong friendships that existed within the band. Henssler, a minor legend in the alternative rock community, who once partied with Pink Floyd when they played the university at which his father was a professor, was always the band's focus. Much emphasis was placed on education in the Henssler family, and he continued to attend college throughout the band's career. Corey Rusk, one of their bass players from a slightly earlier period, later moved to Chicago, Illinois, and took over the running of the prestigious Touch And Go Records label. The humour of the Necros was always central to their appeal in a music scene noted for its puritanical world view; the b-side of 'Conquest For Death' featured a song about the rights of the disabled ('Take Em Up'), but actually turned out to be a swipe at the privileges awarded disabled drivers. Musically, they mixed thrash with unusual chord sequences, later moving over to a more straightforward hard rock sound. The further they progressed in their career, the more quickly they closed the dividing line between punk and metal, though the crisper production on *Tangled Up* made it the most accessible Necros record to date. Happily, before such compromise eclipsed their own style, Henssler left the band to form Big Chief.

● ALBUMS: *Conquest For Death* (Touch & Go 1983)★★★, *Tangled Up* (Restless 1987)★★★, *Live Or Else* (Medusa 1989)★★.

NEFILIM

The Nefilim's 1996 album, *Zoon*, announced the rebirth of former Fields Of The Nephilim singer Carl McCoy. By the advent of that group's final album, 1990's *Elizium*, McCoy was on the verge of despair, finding the old material he was playing 'tedious'. The critical revulsion McCoy has faced during his career, plus the various machinations concerning the end of his commercially successful former band (who renamed themselves Rubicon), doubtless informed some of the vitriol on *Zoon*. However, McCoy also took the opportunity to push his occultist and pagan influences to the fore (previous Fields Of The Nephilim material had thinly veiled references to literary works by H.P. Lovecraft as well as less clearly defined Sumerian mythologies). The product of four years' writing and experimentation, the album featured a variety of guest musicians and producers, none of whom were prominent mainstream names, as McCoy sought to establish the Nefilim as his own project. The album took its title from the Greek word for 'beast' or 'animal', but failed to find an audience outside of the pagan rock fraternity and die-hard Nephilim fans.

● ALBUMS: *Zoon* (Beggars Banquet 1996)★★.

NEIL, VINCE, BAND

Following his surprise sacking from Mötley Crüe, frontman Vince Neil (b. Vincent Neil Wharton, 8 February 1961, Hollywood, California, USA) wasted no time in establishing a solo career, contributing 'You're Invited But Your Friend Can't Come' (co-written with Damn Yankees duo Jack Blades and Tommy Shaw) to the *Encino Man* (*California Man* outside the USA) soundtrack. After this, he assembled a band with ex-Billy Idol guitarist Steve Stevens, ex-Fiona guitarist Dave Marshall, ex-Enuff Z'Nuff drummer Vikki Foxx, and bassist Robbie Crane, who had switched from rhythm guitar after original bassist Phil Soussan's departure. The Ron Nevison-produced *X-Posed* brought Neil a good deal of respect, demonstrating his songwriting ability on good-time arena metal that followed the direction in which he felt Mötley Crüe should have moved. The Vince Neil Band secured a high-profile opening slot with Van Halen, but throat problems for Neil held up subsequent live work, and Stevens departed, with Brent Woods replacing him. Rumours abounded of a Mötley Crüe reunion while Neil and his band worked towards a second album, but the acrimony surrounding the split made this unlikely. This was confirmed by the arrival of a second Vince Neil album, *Carved In Stone*, in July 1995. As well as introducing new guitarist Woods, it was produced by the Dust Brothers, the American production team more usually identified with the world of hip-hop.

● ALBUMS: *X-Posed* (Warners 1993)★★★, *Carved In Stone* (Warners 1995)★★★.

NELSON

The twin sons of early rock 'n' roll star Rick Nelson and wife Kris, Matthew and Gunnar Nelson were born on 20 September 1967, Los Angeles, California, USA. Musically inclined as children, the boys learned to play bass and drums as well as singing. Their father booked studio time for them on their 12th birthday, and they recorded a self-penned song with vocal backing by the Pointer Sisters. By the early 80s the twins had joined a heavy metal band called Strange Agents, which later changed its name to the Nelsons. In 1990, now simply called Nelson, the twins, both sporting waist-length blond hair (which saw them nicknamed the 'Timotei Twins'), signed with David Geffen's new DGC record label and recorded a self-titled pop-rock album. The first single release, '(Can't Live Without Your) Love And Affection', reached number 1 in the US charts, while the album made the US Top 20. Afterwards, however, press reaction remained hostile towards any return.

● ALBUMS: *Nelson* (DGC 1990)★★★, *Because They Can* (Geffen 1995)★★.

Neon Cross

This Californian 'white metal' quartet was formed in 1984 by David Raymond Reeves (lead vocals) and Don Webster (guitar). Enlisting the services of Ed Ott (bass) and Michael Betts (drums), it took another four years before the band made their debut with a track on 1988's *California Metal* compilation. A contract with Regency Records ensued and their self-titled debut album emerged as a competent amalgam of Stryper, Barren Cross and Bloodgood. It was, however, discredited somewhat by Reeves' limited vocal ability.

● ALBUMS: *Neon Cross* (Regency 1988)★★.

Neon Rose

This progressive rock group was formed in Sweden in 1973 by vocalist Roger Holegard and guitarist Gunnar Hallin. Augmented by Piero Mengarelli (guitar), Beno Mengarelli (bass, vocals) and Thomas Wilkund (drums), they signed to Vertigo the following year. Inspired by Iron Butterfly, Emerson, Lake And Palmer and Deep Purple, Neon Rose were an experimental quintet that indulged in long, esoteric and frequently blues-based workouts. They debuted with *A Dream Of Glory And Pride* in 1974, which showcased the band's instrumental capabilities, but also highlighted their vocal shortcomings. Two further albums were released, but the quality of material declined significantly. They disappeared from the scene in 1976.

● ALBUMS: *A Dream Of Glory And Pride* (Vertigo 1974)★★★, *Neon Rose Two* (Vertigo 1974)★★, *Reload* (Vertigo 1975)★★.

Neurosis

A multi-dimensional aural protest group from Oakland, California, USA, attached to the Alternative Tentacles Records label, Neurosis comprise Steve Von Till (vocals, guitar), Dave Edwardson (guitar, vocals), Jason Roeder (drums), Scott Terry (guitar, vocals) and Simon (keyboards). They began their career as a trio in 1986, before evolving musically and also expanding their personnel. They are highly regarded for their use of video, film and artwork in a live setting, with their performances invoking several mediums to articulate their deeply held suspicions about a modern consumerist society: 'It takes art and images to describe our concept. The words are just one part, it takes pictures and moving pictures and sound to create the whole, basically.' They made their debut in 1992 with *Souls At Zero*, a typically stark, uncomfortable recording that eschewed melody in favour of musical belligerence. Appropriately, it featured a still from the film *The Wicker Man* on its cover. As *Lime Lizard* journalist Nick Terry remarked, 'Nature imagery abounds in both lyrics and music, evoking a pagan fascination with fire, cold, earth, poison, blood and the natural cycle of decay.' Subsequent releases have maintained the band's restless fascination with social ills and sonic experimentalism, though on occasion their radicalism could alienate listeners - the grinding pace of *Enemy Of The Sun* failing to match the impact of their debut. 1995's *Pain Of Mind* marked a significant return to form, with the emphasis placed once more on spiritual and pagan themes, a fascination that continued with *Through Silver In Blood*. Rather than protest at what the band has long judged to be an impending apocalypse, this album struck a detectable note of resignation. The group also formed its own art collective at this time, the Tribes Of Neurot, who among their other activities have released albums of ambient experiments conducted in studio down-time.

● ALBUMS: *Souls At Zero* (Alternative Tentacles 1992)★★★★, *Enemy Of The Sun* (Alternative Tentacles 1994)★★, *Pain Of Mind* (Alternative Tentacles 1995)★★★★, *Through Silver In Blood* (ICR 1996)★★★.

New Bomb Turks

A loud but melodious US alternative rock band, New Bomb Turks' manifesto was to rid their genre of its more dour concerns, re-establishing the sheer adrenaline rush and hedonism of the music. They met while studying at Ohio State University, where each of them - Eric Davidson (vocals), Jim Weber (guitar), Matt Reber (bass) and Bill Brandt (drums) - read English. They first worked together as disc jockeys on campus radio station WSOR, gradually pulling together as a band and making their debut through a series of limited-issue 7-inch singles. It was with their debut album, however, that their arrival was recognized, with *Maximum Rock 'n' Roll* magazine calling it the 'album of the year, maybe of the last five years'. In its wake, New Bomb Turks sagged under the expectations of such hysterical praise, taking their time before preparing a follow-up set, then blasting through the recording sessions to produce *Information Highway Revisited* in just sixty hours. It was a recording that retained their spontaneity and established them as qualitative peers of Green Day and the Offspring, even if its sales profile was dwarfed by the success of those bands. *Pissing Out The Poison* reminded fans of their early days, being a double album comprising singles for labels including Sympathy For The Record Industry, eMpTy, Get Hip, Demo Derby, Bag Of Hammers and Damaged Goods, plus cover versions of material by the New York Dolls and Hawkwind. Subsequent albums, *Scared Straight* and *At Rope's End*, revealed the band to be back to their devastatingly noisy best.

● ALBUMS: *!!Destroy-Oh-Boy!!* (Crypt 1992)★★★, *Information Highway Revisited* (Crypt 1994)★★★, *Scared Straight* (Epitaph 1996)★★★★, *At Rope's End* (Epitaph 1998)★★★.

● COMPILATIONS: *Pissing Out The Poison* (Crypt 1995)★★★.

New England (UK)

This British hard rock quartet was formed in Deptford, London, in 1990 by original Atom Seed member Chris Huxter (bass). Enlisting the services of Paul McKenna (lead vocals), Dave Cook and Ian Winters (drums), they secured a contract with the independent Street Link label. *You Can't Keep Living This Way* emerged in 1991 and confused the critics; the music was awkward to tie down and not easily pigeonholed, fusing influences as diverse as Led Zeppelin, Faith No More, the Doors and Van Halen, with the attitude of punk not lagging far behind. However, this was not enough to gain them a place in metal's first division, and they collapsed soon afterwards.

● ALBUMS: *You Can't Keep Living This Way* (Street Link 1991)★★★.

New England (USA)

This American quartet comprised John Fannon (guitar, vocals), Jimmy Waldo (keyboards), Gary Shea (bass) and Hirsh Gardener (drums). Taken under the wing of Kiss's manager, Bill Aucoin, they purveyed sophisticated, melodic rock in a vein similar to Styx and Journey. In 1979 they were given the chance to impress on a major stage, landing the support slot on the American leg of the Kiss tour. Although competent, their music lacked individuality and the band themselves had a nondescript image. After a third album, produced by Todd Rundgren, the band disintegrated in 1981, with Waldo and Shea eventually going on to join Alcatrazz.

● ALBUMS: *New England* (Infinity 1979)★★★, *Explorer Suite* (Elektra 1980)★★, *Walking Wild* (Elektra 1981)★★.

New Frontier

This melodic US pop-rock group was formed in 1988 by ex-Billy Satellite vocalist Monty Byron and ex-Gamma bassist Glen Letsch. Adding David Neuhauser (keyboards) and Marc Nelson (drums), they successfully negotiated a contract with the newly formed Mika label. Their debut album was produced by Ritchie Zito (of Heart and Cheap Trick fame) and featured a collection of high-tech AOR numbers that were targeted at the *Billboard* charts. Failing to generate media interest, the band disintegrated shortly after the album's release. Letsch went on to play with Robin Trower.

● ALBUMS: *New Frontier* (Mika 1988)★★★.

New Idol Son

Formed in the artistic hothouse of the Bay Area of San Francisco during 1991, New Idol Son immediately saw the press compare them to a '90s rebirth of MC5 meets Black Sabbath'. Vocalist/guitarist Matt Hizendragzer first met drummer Brent Hagin at a Mookie Blaylock (who later transmuted into Pearl Jam) show. Eventually, Rich Carr (bass) and Mike Davis (guitar) were recruited via adverts in BAM magazine, with the band titled Difference Engine. Playing shows along the west coast as support to Downset, Fear Factory and others, they built a strong reputation among local press outlets until Pavement Music moved in for their signatures in 1994. However, at this point it was discovered that another band already held the rights to the name Difference Engine, and New Idol Son was born when Hizendragzer saw the legend on the back of a book in a second-hand store. Their debut album, *Reach*, offered crafted musical composition with emotive lyrics, sometimes imbued with quasi-religious overtones.

● ALBUMS: *Reach* (Bulletproof 1994)★★★.

New Wave Of British Heavy Metal

The names speak for themselves - Iron Maiden, Def Leppard, Saxon, Samson, Venom, Diamond Head, Girlschool and Praying Mantis. These represented only a handful of the bands who found success during the period 1979 to 1981. The phrase was first coined by Geoff Barton at *Sounds*, but much credit is also owing to DJ Neal Kay, whose help in giving bands such as Iron Maiden and Praying Mantis (as well as many others) their first break was crucial. EMI Records were quick off the mark and with Kay's help, they produced the compilation album *Metal For Muthas*, which put many bands on the road to fame, and others, including Toad The Wet Sprocket, on the road to obscurity. Well over 200 bands emerged during this period and many released records on their own labels - even more never made it past the rehearsal stage, while others remained strictly 'bedroom' bands. This enthusiasm also helped to revitalize older bands and some, including Gillan and Motörhead, became spearheads for the movement. However, by 1981 the corporate machine began to eat up the talent and American influences crept in, destroying the movement's identity. If, as has often been stated, the movement started with Iron Maiden's *Soundhouse Tapes* EP in 1979, then it would be equally true to suggest that the final nail in its coffin came in September 1981, when Paul Di'Anno left that band. Just like punk in 1977, the ideas and attitude fell victim to clean living and commerciality.

● COMPILATIONS: *Metal For Muthas Volume 1* (EMI 1980)★★★, *Metal For Muthas Volume 2 Cut Loud* (EMI 1980)★★, *Brute Force* (MCA 1980)★★, *New Electric Warriors* (Logo 1980)★★★, *The NWOBHM '79 Revisisted* (Vertigo 1990)★★.

NEW WORLD

US heavy metal band New World were formed in February 1992 by guitarist Mike Polak, who completed the line-up with the addition of seasoned musicians Martin Koprax (vocals), Bernd Fuxa (bass) and Thomas Fend (drums). Polak had been featured on Mike Varney's 'Guitar On The Edge' series and taught at the American Institute Of Music, Europe's biggest rock school, from where Fend was also drawn. An eight-track demo, *The World We Created*, sold out quickly on the underground rock network, and as a consequence, New World landed a contract with Rock The Nation Records. Their influences, ranging from jazz and classical to more conventional rock sources, saw comparisons to Dream Theater when their debut album was released in 1994.

● ALBUMS: *Changing Times* (RTN 1994)★★★★.

NEW YORK DOLLS

One of the most influential rock bands of the last 20 years, the New York Dolls predated the punk and sleaze metal movements that followed and offered a crash course in rebellion with style. Formed in 1972, the line-up stabilized with David Johansen (b. 9 January 1950, Staten Island, New York, USA; vocals), Johnny Thunders (b. John Anthony Genzale Jnr., 15 July 1952, New York City, New York, USA, d. 23 April 1991, New Orleans, Louisiana, USA; guitar), Arthur Harold Kane (bass), Sylvain Sylvain (guitar, piano) and Jerry Nolan (d. 14 January 1992; drums), the last two having replaced Rick Rivets and Billy Murcia (d. 6 November 1972). The band revelled in an outrageous glam-rock image: lipstick, high heels and tacky leather outfits providing their visual currency. Underneath they were a first-rate rock 'n' roll band, dragged up on the music of the Stooges, Rolling Stones and MC5. Their self-titled debut, released in 1973, was a major landmark in rock history, oozing attitude, vitality and controversy from every note. It met with widespread critical acclaim, but this never transferred to commercial success. The follow-up, *Too Much Too Soon*, was an appropriate title - and indicated that alcohol and drugs were beginning to take their toll. The album remains a charismatic collection of punk/glam-rock anthems, typically delivered with 'wasted' cool. Given a unanimous thumbs-down from the music press, the band began to implode shortly afterwards. Johansen embarked on a solo career and Thunders and Dolan formed the Heartbreakers. The Dolls continued for a short time before eventually grinding to a halt in 1975, despite the auspices of new manager Malcolm McLaren. The link to the Sex Pistols and the UK punk movement is stronger than that fact alone, with the Dolls remaining a constant reference point for teen rebels the world over. Sadly for the band, their rewards were fleeting. Jerry Nolan died as a result of a stroke while undergoing treatment for pneumonia and meningitis. Thunders had departed from an overdose, in mysterious circumstances, less than a year earlier. *Red Patent Leather* is a poor-quality and posthumously released live recording from May 1975 - *Rock 'N' Roll* offers a much more representative collection.

● ALBUMS: *New York Dolls* (Mercury 1973)★★★★, *Too Much Too Soon* (Mercury 1974)★★★, *Red Patent Leather* (New Rose 1984)★★.

● COMPILATIONS: *Lipstick Killers* (ROIR 1981)★★★, *Best Of The New York Dolls* (Mercury 1985)★★★, *Night Of The Living Dolls* (Mercury 1986)★★★, *Rock 'N' Roll* (Mercury 1994)★★★★.

● FURTHER READING: *New York Dolls*, Steven Morrissey.

NEXT STEP UP

Formed in 1991 in Baltimore, Maryland, USA, by Mike Ayres (guitar) and Aaron Martinek (bass, ex-Corrupted), Next Step Up experimented with numerous musicians before eventually settling on a line-up of Damon Stowell (drums, ex-Premonition), J.R. Glass (vocals) and Jon Sampson (bass). Sampson joined after Martinek had vacated his position immediately following sessions for their *Fall From Grace* album. Their gruff, intense combination of doom metal and hardcore had previously been documented on several compilations, an EP, *Intent To Kill*, and their debut album, *Heavy*. However, neither this nor the subsequent *Fall From Grace* offered anything of significant musical vitality, despite the production assistance of Drew Mazurek (Corrosion Of Conformity).

● ALBUMS: *Heavy* (Shadow 1993)★★, *Fall From Grace* (Gain Ground 1995)★★.

NIAGARA

This melodic rock group was formed in Madrid, Spain, during 1987 by Angel Arias (bass) and V. M. Arias (guitar). The line-up was completed with the addition of Tony Cuevas (lead vocals), Joey Martos (drums) and Ricky Castaneda (keyboards). Using English lyrics and concentrating on a style that embodied elements of Europe and Whitesnake, they built up a sizeable following on the European heavy rock scene. Produced by Baron Rojo guitarist Carlos de Castro, *Now Or Never* was an impressive debut that featured abrasive guitarwork, coupled with razor-sharp arrangements.

● ALBUMS: *Now Or Never* (Avispa 1988)★★★★.

NICE

Originally the back-up band to soul singer P.P. Arnold, the Nice became one of the true originators of what has variously been described as pomp-rock, art-rock and classical-rock. The band comprised Keith Emerson (b. 1 November 1944, Todmorden, Yorkshire, England; keyboards), Brian 'Blinky' Davison (b. 25 May 1942, Leicester, England; drums), Lee Jackson (b. 8 January 1943, Newcastle-Upon-Tyne, England; bass, vocals) and David O'List (b. 13 December 1948, Chiswick, London, England; guitar). After leaving Arnold in October 1967 the Nice quickly built a reputation as one of the most visually exciting bands. Emerson's stage act involved, in true circus style, throwing knives into his Hammond Organ, which would emit outrageous sounds, much to the delight of the audience. Their debut, *The Thoughts Of Emerlist Davjack*, while competent, came nowhere near reproducing their exciting live sound. By the time of the release of its follow-up, *Ars Longa Vita Brevis*, O'List had departed, being unable to compete with Emerson's showmanship and subsequently joined Roxy Music. The album contained their notorious single, 'America', from *West Side Story*. During one performance at London's Royal Albert Hall, they burnt the American flag on stage and were severely lambasted, not only by the Albert Hall authorities, but also by the song's composer, Leonard Bernstein. The band continued their remaining life as a trio, producing their most satisfying and successful work. Both *Nice* and *Five Bridges Suite* narrowly missed the top of the UK charts, although they were unable to break through in the USA. The former contained an excellent reading of Tim Hardin's 'Hang On To A Dream', with exquisite piano from Emerson. The latter was a bold semi-orchestral suite about working-class life in Newcastle-upon-Tyne. One of their other showpieces was an elongated version of Bob Dylan's 'She Belongs To Me'. *Five Bridges* also contained versions of 'Intermezzo From The Karelia Suite' by Sibelius and Tchaikovsky's 'Pathetique'. Their brave attempt at fusing classical music and rock together with the Sinfonia of London was admirable, and much of what Emerson later achieved with the huge success of Emerson, Lake And Palmer should be credited to the brief but valuable career of the Nice. With Emerson's departure, Jackson floundered with Jackson Heights, while Davison was unsuccessful with his own band, Every Which Way. Jackson and Davison teamed up again in 1974 to form the ill-fated Refugee.

● ALBUMS: *The Thoughts Of Emerlist Davjack* (Immediate 1967)★★★, *Ars Longa Vita Brevis* (Immediate 1968)★★★, *The Nice* (Immediate 1969)★★★★, *Five Bridges* (Charisma 1970)★★★★, *Elegy* (Charisma 1971)★★.

● COMPILATIONS: *Autumn 76 - Spring 68* (1972)★★★, *20th Anniversary Release* (1987)★★★, *The Best Of The Nice* (Essential 1998)★★★★.

NIGHT RANGER

This talented and sophisticated American pomp-rock group released a string of first-class albums between 1982 and 1988. Featuring Jack Blades (vocals, bass), Brad Gillis (guitar, ex-Ozzy Osbourne), Alan Fitzgerald (keyboards, ex-Montrose), Kelly Keagy (drums) and Jeff Watson (guitar), they gigged in and around their hometown of San Francisco as an extension of Gillis's club band, Ranger. They soon attracted the attention of promoter Bill Graham, who secured them support slots to Santana, Judas Priest and the Doobie Brothers. They also signed with Neil Bogart's short-lived Boardwalk label, though this decision had a major impact on their later career when Boardwalk was swallowed up by MCA, who had little sympathy for the band's rock roots. However, Night Ranger's first four albums made the *Billboard* Top 40 charts, with *Seven Wishes* reaching the Top 10 in June 1985. They also enjoyed two Top 10 single hits in the USA with 'Sister Christian' and 'Sentimental Street', peaking at numbers 5 and 8, respectively. *Man In Motion* saw the departure of Fitzgerald as the band adopted a rockier direction. Produced by Keith Olsen, the album was their first commercial failure. The band split shortly afterwards, with *Live In Japan*, featuring one of their 1988 concerts, emerging two years later. Jack Blades joined Damn Yankees with Ted Nugent, Tommy Shaw and Michael Cartellone. The name was resurrected in 1992 by Gillis and drummer/vocalist Kelly Keagy with new members, much to the disgust of Blades and Watson. It seemed unlikely that the new formation would add much to the existing Nightranger legacy of solid US AOR.

● ALBUMS: *Dawn Patrol* (Boardwalk 1982)★★★★, *Midnight Madness* (MCA 1983)★★★★, *Seven Wishes* (MCA 1985)★★★★, *Big Life* (MCA 1987)★★★, *Man In Motion* (MCA 1988)★★★, *Live In Japan* (MCA 1990)★★.

● COMPILATIONS: *Greatest Hits* (MCA 1989)★★★.

NIGHTWING

After the demise of UK band Strife in 1978, bassist/vocalist Gordon Rowley formed Nightwing, with Alec Johnson (guitar), Eric Percival (guitar), Kenny Newton (keyboards) and Steve Bartley (drums). They debuted in 1980 with *Something In The Air*, a grandiose AOR album in the style of Styx, Kansas or Journey. Percival quit shortly after its release, and the band continued as a four-piece to record *Black Summer*. This moved towards a more metallic style, in keeping with the New Wave Of British Heavy Metal. The band expanded once more to a five-piece with vocalist Max Bacon for the rawer *Stand Up And Be Counted*. Bacon's stay was short-lived as he moved on to Bronz, with Johnson also departing soon afterwards. Dave Evans and Glynn Porrino were swiftly recruited to fill in on vocals and guitar, but their compositional abilities failed to match those of Johnson. Consequently, *My Kingdom Come* represented the nadir of the band's creative capabilities. Nightwing finally resigned hope after the disappointing *Night Of Mystery, Alive!, Alive!*

● ALBUMS: *Something In The Air* (Ovation 1980)★★★, *Black Summer* (Gull 1982)★★★★, *Stand Up And Be Counted* (Gull 1983)★★★, *My Kingdom Come* (Gull 1984)★★, *Night Of Mystery, Alive!, Alive!* (Gull 1985)★★, *Natural Survivors* 80s recordings (Neat 1996)★★★.

NINE INCH NAILS

Trent Reznor (b. 17 May 1965, Mercer, Pennsylvania, USA), the multi-instrumentalist, vocalist, and creative force behind Nine Inch Nails, trained as a classical pianist during his small-town Pennsylvania childhood, but his discovery of rock and early industrial groups, despite his dislike of the 'industrial' tag, changed his musical direction completely. Following a period working in a Cleveland recording studio and playing in local bands, Reznor began recording as Nine Inch Nails in 1988. The dark, atmospheric *Pretty Hate Machine*, written, played and co-produced by Reznor, was largely synthesizer-based, but the material was transformed onstage by a ferocious wall of guitars, and show-stealing Lollapalooza performances in 1991. Coupled with a major US hit with 'Head Like A Hole', it brought platinum status. Inspired by the live band, Reznor added an abrasive guitar barrage to the Nine Inch Nails sound for *Broken* (a subsequent remix set was titled *Fixed*), which hit the US Top 10, winning a Grammy for 'Wish'. 'Happiness In Slavery', however, courted controversy with an almost universally banned video, where performance artist Bob Flanagan gave himself up to be torn apart as slave to a machine, acting out the theme of control common to Reznor's lyrics. Reznor also filmed an unreleased full-length *Broken* video, which he said 'makes "Happiness In Slavery" look like a Disney movie'. By this time, Reznor had relocated to Los Angeles, building a studio in a rented house at 10050 Cielo Drive, which he later discovered was the scene of the Tate murders by the Manson family (much to his disgust, due to eternal interview questions thereafter about the contribution of the house's atmosphere to *The Downward Spiral*). Occupying the middle ground between the styles of previous releases, *The Downward Spiral*'s multi-layered blend of synthesizer textures and guitar fury provides a fascinating soundscape for Reznor's exploration of human degradation through sex, drugs, violence, depression and suicide, closing with personal emotional pain on 'Hurt': 'I hurt myself today, To see if I still feel, I focus on the pain, The only thing that's real'. *The Downward Spiral* made its US debut at number 2, and a return to live work with Robin Finck (guitar), Danny

Lohneer (bass, guitar), James Woolley (keyboards) and Reznor's long-time friend and drummer Chris Vrenna drew floods of praise, with Nine Inch Nails being one of the most talked-about acts at the Woodstock anniversary show. The first non-Nine Inch Nails releases on Reznor's Nothing label appeared in 1994 (beginning with Marilyn Manson), and the band also found time to construct an acclaimed soundtrack for Oliver Stone's film *Natural Born Killers*. In the following year Reznor announced plans to record an album with circus 'freak show' specialist Jim Rose, stating with typical bombast: 'the record will confront just about every issue that upsets people. It will be non-PC in every way imaginable'. In 1996/7 Reznor worked with film director David Lynch on the music score for *Lost Highway*.

● ALBUMS: *Pretty Hate Machine* (TVT 1989)★★★, *Broken* mini-album (Nothing 1992)★★, *Fixed* mini-album (Nothing 1992)★★, *The Downward Spiral* (Nothing 1994)★★★★, *Further Down The Spiral* remix mini-album (Island 1995)★★★.

● FURTHER READING: *Nine Inch Nails*, Martin Huxley.

1994

This US melodic-rock quartet was formed in 1977 by ex-L.A. Jets duo Karen Lawrence (vocals) and John Desautels (drums). With the addition of Steve Schiff (guitar) and Bill Rhodes (bass), they signed to A&M Records and released a self-titled debut the following year. This was characterized by Lawrence's powerful vocals and a style that incorporated elements of Heart, Aerosmith and Foreigner. Guitarist Steve Schiff was replaced by Rick Armand on *Please Stand By*, which lacked the rough edges of their debut, and saw them move towards mainstream AOR. Success eluded the band and Lawrence left in 1980. After a decade of less than successful projects, which have included collaborations with Cheap Trick, Jeff Beck and Rod Stewart, it was rumoured that Lawrence might reform 1994. However, the only firm evidence of any such move was the guest appearance of Steve Schiff on her 1986 solo album.

● ALBUMS: *1994* (A&M 1978)★★★, *Please Stand By* (A&M 1979)★★.

Solo: Karen Lawrence *Rip & Tear* (FM Revolver 1986)★★.

Nirvana

Formed in Aberdeen, Washington, USA, in 1988, the Nirvana that the MTV generation came to love comprised Kurt Cobain (b. Kurt Donald Cobain, 20 February 1967, Hoquiam, Seattle, USA, d. 5 April 1994, Seattle, Washington, USA; guitar, vocals), Krist Novoselic (b. 16 May 1965, Croatia, Yugoslavia; bass) and Dave Grohl (b. 14 January 1969, Warren, Ohio, USA; drums). Grohl was 'something like our sixth drummer', explained Cobain, and had been recruited from east coast band Dave Brammage, having previously played with Scream, who recorded for Minor Threat's influential Dischord Records label. Their original drummer was Chad Channing; at one point Dinosaur Jr's J. Mascis had been touted as a permanent fixture, along with Dan Peters from Mudhoney. Having been signed by the Seattle-based Sub Pop Records, the trio completed their debut single, 'Love Buzz'/'Big Cheese', the former a song written and first recorded by 60s Dutch group Shocking Blue. Second guitarist Jason Everman was then added prior to *Bleach*, which cost a meagre $600 to record. Though he was pictured on the cover, he played no part in the actual recording (going on to join Mindfunk, via Soundgarden and Skunk). The set confirmed Nirvana's ability to match heavy riffs with melody and it quickly attracted a cult following. However, Channing left the group following a European tour, and as a likely replacement proved hard to find, Dan Peters from labelmates Mudhoney stepped in on a temporary basis. He was featured on the single 'Sliver', Nirvana's sole 1990 release. New drummer David Grohl reaffirmed a sense of stability. The revamped trio secured a prestigious contract with Geffen Records, whose faith was rewarded with *Nevermind*, which broke the band worldwide. This was a startling collection of songs that transcended structural boundaries, notably the distinctive slow verse/fast chorus format, and almost single-handedly brought the 'grunge' subculture overground. It topped the US charts early in 1992, eclipsing much-vaunted competition from Michael Jackson and Dire Straits and topped many Album Of The Year polls. The opening track, 'Smells Like Teen Spirit', reached the UK Top 10, further confirmation that Nirvana now combined critical and popular acclaim.

In early 1992 the romance of Cobain and Courtney Love of Hole was sealed when the couple married (Love giving birth to a daughter, Frances Bean). It was already obvious, however, that Cobain was struggling with his new role as 'spokesman for a generation'. The first big story to break concerned an article in *Vanity Fayre* that alleged Love had taken heroin while pregnant; this saw the state intercede on the child's behalf by not allowing the

Cobains alone with the child during its first month. Press interviews ruminated on the difficulties experienced in recording a follow-up album, and also revealed Cobain's use of a variety of drugs in order to stem the pain arising from a stomach complaint. The recording of *In Utero*, produced by Big Black/Rapeman alumnus Steve Albini, was not without difficulties. Rumours circulated concerning confrontations with both Albini and record company Geffen over the 'low-fi' production. When the record was finally released, the effect was not as immediate as *Nevermind*, although Cobain's songwriting remained inspired on 'Penny Royal Tea', 'All Apologies' and the evocative 'Rape Me'. His descent into self-destruction accelerated in 1994, however, as he went into a coma during dates in Italy (it was later confirmed that this had all the markings of a failed suicide attempt), before returning to Seattle to shoot himself on 5 April 1994. The man who had long protested that Nirvana were 'merely' a punk band had finally been destroyed by the success that overtook him and them. The wake conducted in the press was matched by public demonstrations of affection and loss, which included suspected copycat suicides. The release of *MTV Unplugged In New York* offered some small comfort for Cobain's fans, with the singer's understated, aching delivery on a variety of cover versions and Nirvana standards enduring as one of the most emotive sights and sounds of the 90s. Grohl formed the excellent Foo Fighters, alongside ex-Germs guitarist Pat Smear (who had added second guitar to previous touring engagements and the band's *MTV Unplugged* appearance), following press rumours that Grohl would be working with Pearl Jam (much to Courtney Love's chagrin) or Tom Petty. Novoselic formed Sweet 75 early in 1997.

● ALBUMS: *Bleach* (Sub Pop 1989)★★★★, *Nevermind* (Geffen 1991)★★★★★, *In Utero* (Geffen 1993)★★★★, *MTV Unplugged In New York* (Geffen 1994)★★★★.

● COMPILATIONS: *Incesticide* (Geffen 1992)★★★, *Singles* (Geffen 1995)★★★★, *From The Muddy Banks Of The Wishkah* (Geffen 1996)★★★★.

● VIDEOS: *Live! Tonight! Sold Out!!* (Geffen 1994), *Teen Spirit: The Tribute To Kurt Cobain* (Labyrinth 1996).

● FURTHER READING: *Route 666: On The Road To Nirvana*, Gina Arnold. *Nirvana And The Sound Of Seattle*, Brad Morrell. *Come As You Are*, Michael Azerrad. *Nirvana: An Illustrated Biography*, Suzi Black. *Nirvana: Tribute*, Suzi Black. *Never Fade Away*, Dave Thompson. *Kurt Cobain*, Christopher Sandford. *Nirvana: Nevermind*, Susan Wilson.

● FILMS: *Kurt And Courtney* (1998).

Nitzinger, John

b. Texas, USA. This energetic and highly talented guitarist/vocalist specializes in blues-based hard rock and boogie, and has worked with Bloodrock, Alice Cooper and Carl Palmer's P.M., supplying ferocious Ted Nugent-inspired guitar chords to each. Members of Bloodrock, for whom he also wrote songs, returned the favour by appearing on his solo material. His three albums on his own account are highly varied and explore a wider range of styles than might initially be imagined. Psychedelia, jazz, rock, blues and metal nuances have been integrated within his own extrovert approach, though since the mid-70s his recording career has taken a back seat to session work.

● ALBUMS: *Nitzinger* (Capitol 1971)★★★, *One Foot In History* (Capitol 1972)★★★, *Live Better...Electrically* (20th Century 1976)★★.

No Exqze

This melodic rock quartet from Holland was formed by ex-Vandenberg bassist Dick Kemper in 1987. Recruiting Geert Scheigrond (guitar), Leen Barbier (vocals) and Nico Groen (drums), they signed to Phonogram Records and debuted with *Too Hard Too Handle* in 1988. No Exqze allowed Kemper to indulge his writing talents, which had previously been suppressed in Vandenberg - not without good reason, it might be argued. Produced by Tony Platt, the album was dominated by Barbier's soulful vocals, which added depth and character to Kemper's rather average AOR-style compositions.

● ALBUMS: *Too Hard Too Handle* (Phonogram 1988)★★★.

No FX

No FX were formed in Los Angeles, California, USA, in 1983. Immediately, it was obvious that they were one of the few bands on the hardcore scene to embrace humorous lyrical fare to genuinely amusing effect. The band, whose present line-up features 'Fat' Mike (vocals, bass), Eric Melvin (guitar, vocals), El Hefe (guitar, trumpet) and Erik Sandon (drums), set their agenda with their debut EP for Mystic Records, *The PMRC Can Suck On This*. Afterwards, they addressed accusations about being on this most unfashionable of labels (which was completely injudicious in releasing material by any hardcore band that came its way) with the *So What If We're On Mystic* EP. It was via a contract with Epitaph Records and the *Ribbed* album that No FX became a productive unit in terms of worldwide sales. *Ribbed* featured a blemishless collection of genuinely funny songs, notably the male-hygiene-bonding epic, 'Shower Day'. The full musicianship and clean production only helped to illuminate their witty, everyday intrigues, with lyrics written by 'Fat' Mike, a graduate of San Francisco University. With the breakthrough of groups such as Offspring and Rancid, No FX, significantly older than either, became a mainstream group by the mid-90s, though in truth they had not altered musical direction since their inception. Instead, each album offered increasingly savage witticisms and a disciplined but flexible musical attack, able to vary pace from anything between outright thrash and ska.

● ALBUMS: *Liberal Animation* (Epitaph 1988)★★, *S+M Airlines* (Epitaph 1990)★★, *Ribbed* (Epitaph 1991)★★★, *White Trash, Two Heebs And A Bean* (Epitaph 1992)★★★, *Punk In Drublic* (Epitaph 1994)★★, *We Heard They Suck Live* (Epitaph 1995)★★, *Heavy Petting Zoo* (Epitaph 1996)★★, *So Long And Thanks For All The Shoes* (Epitaph 1997)★★.

No Sweat

This Dublin-based, six-piece melodic rock group comprised Paul Quinn (lead vocals), Dave Gooding (guitar), Jim Phillips (guitar), P.J. Smith (keyboards), Jon Angel (bass) and Ray Fearn (drums). Together they impressed Def Leppard vocalist Joe Elliot, who took over production on their debut album and helped them to secure a contract with London Records. The record company's public relations team subsequently launched an impressive and expensive campaign on their behalf. They supported Thunder on their 'Backstreet Symphony' tour in 1990 and were generally well received by the press. Paul Quinn's voice oozed emotion, but their material failed to stamp its own identity. Accusations of hype followed, and the band quietly dissolved a year later. Gooding later joined the mid-90s hard rock group b.l.o.w.

● ALBUMS: *No Sweat* (London 1990)★★.

Nocturnus

This innovative American death metal band was formed by drummer and vocalist Mike Browning following his departure from an early incarnation of Morbid Angel. *The Key* showed an original approach, mixing the frenzied yet intricate riffing of guitarists Sean McNenney and Mike Davis with the atmospheric keyboard washes of Louis Panzer. Critical acclaim abounded, but the sound proved rather too radical for much of the death crowd, and Nocturnus struggled to rise above cult status. *Thresholds* was recorded with new vocalist Dan Izzo, taking the pressure off Browning, with permanent bassist Emo Mowery being recruited after the sessions to replace touring bassist Jim O'Sullivan (Chris Anderson played on the album). However, with no upturn in the band's fortunes they parted company with Earache, re-emerging in 1994 with an EP for new label Moribund.

● ALBUMS: *The Key* (Earache 1990)★★★, *Thresholds* (Earache 1992)★★★.

Nokemono

This Japanese hard rock quintet was formed in 1978. Inspired by fellow countrymen Bow Wow, Yukihiro 'Ace' Nakaya (vocals) and Shigeo 'Rolla' Nakano (guitar) decided to put together a band along similar lines. Recruiting Bunzo 'Bunchan' Satoh (guitar), Masaaki 'Cherry' Chikura (bass) and Tadashi 'Popeye' Hirota (drums), they were picked up by the local SMS label. The resultant *From The Black World* combined Van Halen, Deep Purple and UFO influences. It was an impressive debut, somewhat marred by an inferior production. However, the band remained virtually unknown outside their own country and the album was their solitary contribution to Japanese metal.

● ALBUMS: *From The Black World* (SMS 1979)★★★.

NoMeansNo

An 'artcore' trio from Victoria, British Columbia, Canada, NoMeansNo have done much to expand the boundaries of the 'hardcore' genre, fusing funk and fuzz pop with a continually questioning lyrical stance. The first established line-up featured Andrew Kerr (guitar) and the brothers Rob Wright (bass) and John Wright (drums). Kerr joined shortly after their 1984 debut, *Mama*. Taking their name from the phrase commonly used in connection with the rights of rape victims, their lyrics explore the middle ground between the individual and society, often in tones of self-disgust: 'nobody knows you and nobody wants to' (from 'Body Bag'). Though some of their early efforts lose impact through their disjointed nature, by *Small Parts Isolated And Destroyed* the band had refined the approach into a more structured whole - despite the music veering from thrash jazz to *avant garde* experimentalism. *0+2=1* crystallized their determinedly resistant approach. Their rejection of the media, particularly their refusal to have press photos taken, has thus far limited their accessibility, though their extensive cult popularity in Europe provides adequate compensation. Following a collaboration with Alternative Tentacles Records head Jello Biafra (*The Sky Is Falling And I Want My Mommy*), in late 1991 Andy Kerr, a veteran of the band for eight years, departed to form Hissanol (with NoMeansNo producer Scott Henderson). Many of the songs for *Why Do They Call Me Mr. Happy?* were written by Rob for his solo act, Mr Happy, a pseudonym that saw him toy with authoritarian images such as policeman, cleric and Mafia leader. Some of the songs, notably 'The River', were remorselessly bleak. The Wright brothers also recorded 1992's quasi-comic *Gross Misconduct* as the Hanson Brothers. *The Worldhood Of The World (As Such)* was their first album to be recorded as a quartet, with guitar, keyboards and an additional drummer (whom they refused to credit, even on the liner notes, as had been the case with the guitarist they added before *Sex Mad*, who was replaced on this album by someone known only as Tommy). Despite such disorientating tactics and a consistent refusal to engage with the media, it was another superb instalment of fluent guitar rock and incisive, sarcastic lyrics.

● ALBUMS: *Mama* (Wrong 1984)★★★, *Sex Mad* (Psyche Industry/Alternative Tentacles 1986)★★★, *The Day Everything Became Nothing* mini-album (Alternative Tentacles 1988)★★★, *Small Parts Isolated And Destroyed* (Alternative Tentacles 1988)★★★, *Wrong* (Alternative Tentacles 1989)★★★, *Live + Cuddly* (Alternative Tentacles 1991)★★★, with Jello Biafra *The Sky Is Falling And I Want My Mommy* (Alternative Tentacles 1991)★★★, *0+2=1* (Alternative Tentacles 1991)★★★, *Why Do They Call Me Mr. Happy?* (Alternative Tentacles 1993)★★★, *The Worldhood Of The World (As Such)* (Alternative Tentacles 1995)★★★.

● COMPILATIONS: *The Day Everything Became Isolated And Destroyed* (Alternative Tentacles 1988)★★★.

NORUM, JOHN

Norum was formerly guitarist for the Swedish band Europe but left just as the band were on the verge of worldwide recognition with 'The Final Countdown'. After completing the recording of the *Countdown* album, he decided to break ranks, unhappy with the pop-metal direction that vocalist Joey Tempest was intent on pursuing. Turning to a solo career, he enlisted the help of Marcel Jacob (bass, ex-Yngwie Malmsteen), Peter Hermansson (drums, ex-220 Volts) and Goran Edman (vocals, ex-Madison) to record *Total Control* in 1987. Musically, this followed a similar path to that of his former employers, but featured more prominent rock guitarwork and less polished vocals. Following the release of a live album and a collaboration with Don Dokken, he moved to Los Angeles to work on sessions with Glenn Hughes (ex-Trapeze, Deep Purple), which resulted in *Face The Truth*.

● ALBUMS: *Total Control* (Columbia 1987)★★★, *Live In Stockholm* (Columbia 1988)★★, *Face The Truth* (Epic 1992)★★★.

NORUM, TONE

Tone is the younger sister of former Europe guitarist John Norum. She debuted in 1986 with *One Of A Kind*, an album written, arranged and played on by Joey Tempest (also of Europe) and her brother. The musical direction was very close to that of her sibling's concern: melodic pop-metal, with the occasional power ballad. *This Time* followed a similar pattern, but used session musicians and the Billy Steinberg/Tom Kelly writing team who had previously penned hits for Madonna and Whitney Houston. The result was a highly polished melodic rock album. *Red* saw Tone move away from AOR towards folk rock.

● ALBUMS: *One Of A Kind* (Epic 1986)★★★, *This Time* (Epic 1988)★★, *Red* (Epic 1989)★★★.

NOTORIOUS

This ill-fated pop-rock act seemed set to revive the careers of ex-Diamond Head singer Sean Harris and guitarist Robin George, but was aborted before it had a chance to get off the ground. With an expensively recorded debut for the relaunched Bronze label, with George contributing all instrumentation, the future seemed bright, but the duo were reluctant to recruit a touring band when pressed by the record company, as they viewed Notorious as a 'studio project'. The disagreement resulted in *Notorious* being deleted after only three weeks on release. The album itself was an underrated effort, with Robert Plant's solo work an obvious influence, and produced an excellent single in 'The Swalk'. Denied any real chance of success, the duo parted company, with Harris returning to a revived Diamond Head.

● ALBUMS: *Notorious* (Bronze 1990)★★.

NOTWIST

A German hardcore punk band comprising Martin Messerschmidt (drums), Markus Acher (vocals, guitar), Martin Grteschmann and Michael Acher (bass), Notwist first came to prominence when, in 1989, they submitted a demo recording of their song, 'I Don't Want To Sell Myself', to a Bavarian radio contest. Following the breakthrough of compatriots Blumfeld, by the mid-90s Notwist had secured a domestic following sufficient to provoke overseas interest. *12*, their fourth album, was the first to be released in the USA by the Zero Hour label. An unconventional take on punk electronica, with discordant twists akin to early Sonic Youth and Wire, the record also featured other unusual elements including bluegrass guitar (on 'The Incredible Change Of Our Alien'). Such eclecticism and adventurism reflects the brothers' varied musical interests - they additionally play in the spin-off groups Potawatome and Village Of Sangoona and write soundtrack music for friends' films.

● ALBUMS: *12* (Zero Hour 1997)★★★.

Nova, Aldo

b. Aldo Caparucio. Nova is a virtuoso guitarist of Italian descent. He arrived on the rock scene in 1982 with a self-titled debut of melodic AOR/pomp-rock that incorporated elements of Boston and Styx, with production offered by Blue Öyster Cult's Sandy Pearlman. Momentum was lost, however, with *Subject*, a disjointed and ultimately disappointing concept album. *Twitch* made amends somewhat, with a return to smooth, sophisticated and melody-conscious symphonic rock. Disillusioned by the lack of media response and complex legal wrangles and contractual commitments, he left the music business in 1985. After a six-year break, he was persuaded to return to the studio by his good friend Jon Bon Jovi (having guested on the latter's *Blaze Of Glory* solo project). Together they wrote the material for *Blood On The Bricks*, a stunning collection of hard rock songs, saturated with infectious hooks and inspired guitar breaks. The album was well received in the music press and drew comparisons with Bryan Adams, Europe and, unsurprisingly, Bon Jovi.

● ALBUMS: *Aldo Nova* (Portrait 1982)★★★★, *Subject: Aldo Nova* (Portrait 1983)★★★, *Twitch* (Portrait 1985)★★★, *Blood On The Bricks* (Polygram 1991)★★★★.

Nowherefast

This Californian melodic rock quartet was formed in 1981 by Steve Bock (vocals, bass) and Jeff Naideau (guitar, keyboards). Enlisting the services of Bob Frederickson (guitar) and Jimmy Hansen (drums), they soon secured a contract with the WEA/Scotti Brothers label. Incorporating elements of blues and funk into Kansas and Journey-like AOR, they delivered a self-titled debut in 1982. The album was unsuccessful and the band's name unfortunately provided a fair description of the impact they had made.

● ALBUMS: *Nowherefast* (Scotti Bros 1982)★★.

Nuclear Assault

Formed in New York, USA, in 1985, this extreme and influential group consisted of John Conelly (guitar, vocals), Anthony Bramante (guitar), Dan Lilker (bass) and Glenn Evans (drums). Lilker formed Nuclear Assault while still a member of Anthrax, making them one of the earliest thrash metal outfits. The sound of Nuclear Assault proved much more aggressive, however, merging the styles of hardcore and thrash with socially aware lyrics. Becoming popular through constant touring and a refusal to compromise in their recorded work, their audience grew steadily throughout the 80s. Lilker, however, left the band in 1993 to concentrate on a new project, Brutal Truth. Bramante was expelled around the same time, with the pair being replaced by Scott Metaxas and Dave DiPietro, respectively, both formerly of Prophet. The transitional *Something Wicked* failed to provide any conclusive proof of artistic rejuvenation.

● ALBUMS: *Game Over* (Music For Nations 1986)★★★, *The Plague* (Music For Nations 1987)★★★, *Survive* (Music For Nations 1988)★★★, *Handle With Care* (Music For Nations 1989)★★★, *Out Of Order* (Music For Nations 1991)★★, *Live At Hammersmith* (Music For Nations 1993)★★, *Something Wicked* (Music For Nations 1993)★★.

● COMPILATIONS: *Assault & Battery* (Receiver 1997)★★★.

● VIDEOS: *Radiation Sickness* (1988), *Handle With Care* (Strand 1996).

Nuclear Valdez

This unconventional AOR act was based in Miami, Florida, but drew from the members' ethnic origins for both musical and lyrical inspiration. Vocalist/guitarist Froilan Sosa's family originated in the Dominican Republic, while Jorge Barcala (lead guitar), Juan Diaz (bass) and Robert Slade LeMont (drums) are all of Cuban descent. The band incorporated the Latin influences in their backgrounds to give an unusual and unique flavour to their sound. Lyrically, the band were not content with the AOR conventions of love and heartache, but explored themes closer to their collective heart, such as the Castro regime and the homesickness of Cuban exiles, while their choice of band name, with its clever ecological overtones, served to confirm their more cerebral approach. *I Am I* established their characteristic rhythmic sound with classy guitarwork from Barcala and passionate, smoky vocals from Sosa, and also produced a US hit in 'Summer'. *Dream Another Dream* confirmed their abilities with further strong material; nevertheless, Nuclear Valdez remain a cult act.

● ALBUMS: *I Am I* (Epic 1990)★★★★, *Dream Another Dream* (Epic 1992)★★★.

NUDESWIRL

This band from New Jersey, New York, USA, was formed by guitarist/vocalist Shane M. Greene and guitarist Diz Cortright with drummer Woody Newland and bassist Christopher Worgo, specializing in an indie guitar-driven, heavy-rock style that prompted comparisons with acts as diverse as Soundgarden, Nirvana, the Pixies and Trouble. This was rather different to Greene and Cortright's occasional They Might Be Giants tribute band, known as They Might Be Vaginas, which played locally with Greene on vocals and accordion and Cortright on bass. Nudeswirl signed to Megaforce on the strength of chaotic live shows around the underground club circuit. *Nudeswirl* was a varied debut, with the band driving their weighty sound in a multitude of directions, with their use of Gretsch guitars lending the delivery a warm, earthy feel. However, the nuances of the album were somewhat lost in the live arena as the band toured Europe with Mindfunk and the USA with Flotsam And Jetsam, in addition to their own dates, producing some visually lifeless performances. The band's future seemed in doubt following the departure of Greene in mid-1994.

● ALBUMS: *Nudeswirl* (Megaforce 1993)★★★.

NUGENT, TED

b. 13 December 1949, Detroit, Michigan, USA. Inspired by 50s rock 'n' roll, Nugent taught himself the rudiments of guitar playing at the age of eight. As a teenager he played in the Royal Highboys and Lourds, but this formative period ended in 1964 upon his family's move to Chicago. Here, Nugent assembled the Amboy Dukes, which evolved from garage band status into a popular hard-rock attraction. He led the group throughout its various permutations, assuming increasing control as original members dropped out of the line-up. In 1974 a revitalized unit - dubbed Ted Nugent And The Amboy Dukes - completed the first of two albums for Frank Zappa's DiscReet label, but in 1976 the guitarist embarked on a fully fledged solo career. Derek St. Holmes (guitar), Rob Grange (bass) and Cliff Davies (drums) joined him for *Ted Nugent* and *Free For All*, both of which maintained the high-energy rock of previous incarnations. However, it was as a live attraction that Nugent made his mark - he often claimed to have played more gigs per annum than any other artist or group. Ear-piercing guitarwork and vocals - 'If it's too loud you're too old' ran one tour motto - were accompanied by a cultivated 'wild man' image, where the artist appeared in loin-cloth and headband, brandishing the bow and arrow with which he claimed to hunt for food. Trapeze stunts, genuine guitar wizardry and a scarcely self-deprecating image ('If there had been blind people at the show they would have walked away seeing') all added to the formidable Nugent persona. The aggression of a Nugent concert was captured on the platinum-selling *Double Live Gonzo*, which featured many of his best-loved stage numbers, including 'Cat Scratch Fever', 'Motor City Madness' and the enduring 'Baby Please Don't Go'. Charlie Huhn (guitar) and John Sauter (bass) replaced St. Holmes and Grange for *Weekend Warriors*, and the same line-up remained intact for *State Of Shock* and *Scream Dream*. In 1981 Nugent undertook a worldwide tour fronting a new backing group, previously known as the D.C. Hawks, comprising Mike Gardner (bass), Mark Gerhardt (drums) and three guitarists - Kurt, Rick and Verne Wagoner. The following year Nugent left Epic for Atlantic Records, and in the process established a new unit that included erstwhile sidemen Derek St. Holmes (vocals) and Carmine Appice (drums, ex-Vanilla Fudge). Despite such changes, Nugent was either unwilling, or unable, to alter the formula that had served him so well in the 70s. Successive solo releases offered little innovation and the artist drew greater publicity for appearances on talk shows and celebrity events. In 1989 Nugent teamed up with Tommy Shaw (vocals, guitar, ex-Styx), Jack Blades (bass, ex-Night Ranger) and Michael Cartellone (drums) to form the successful 'supergroup', Damn Yankees. After the Damn Yankees were put on hold in 1994, Nugent resumed his solo career for his first studio album in seven years. Reunited with Derek St. Holmes, *Spirit Of The Wild* also saw Nugent return to his usual lyrical posturing, including the pro-firearms 'I Shoot Back' and 'Kiss My Ass', a hate list featuring Courtney Love (of Hole) and the cartoon characters *Beavis And Butthead* among its targets.

● ALBUMS: *Ted Nugent* (Epic 1975)★★★, *Free For All* (Epic 1976)★★★, *Cat Scratch Fever* (Epic 1977)★★★★, *Double Live Gonzo* (Epic 1978)★★★, *Weekend Warriors* (Epic 1978)★★★, *State Of Shock* (Epic 1979)★★★, *Scream Dream* (Epic 1980)★★★, *Intensities In Ten Cities* (Epic 1981)★★★, *Nugent* (Atlantic 1982)★★, *Penetrator* (Atlantic 1984)★★, *Little Miss Dangerous* (Atlantic 1986)★★, *If You Can't Lick 'Em ... Lick 'Em* (Atlantic 1988)★★, *Spirit Of The Wild* (Atlantic 1995)★★.
● COMPILATIONS: *Great Gonzos: The Best Of Ted Nugent* (Epic 1981)★★★★, *Anthology: Ted Nugent* (Raw Power 1986)★★★.
● VIDEOS: *Whiplash Bash* (Hendring 1990).
● FURTHER READING: *The Legendary Ted Nugent*, Robert Holland.

NUTZ

This UK hard rock quintet was formed in 1973 by Dave Lloyd (vocals) and Mick Devonport (guitar). With the addition of Keith Mulholland (bass), Kenny Newton (keyboards) and John Mylett (drums), they gained a reputation as the ubiquitous support act. Playing competent, blues-based rock and boogie, their exuberant and high-energy live shows always overshadowed the drab and lifeless studio recordings. Their sexist album covers were typical of the genre, though less likely was Lloyd's contribution of a vocal to a *Crunchie* chocolate bar advertisement. Newton left to join Nightwing in 1978 while the band changed their name to Rage in a deliberate attempt to jump on the New Wave Of British Heavy Metal bandwagon.
● ALBUMS: *Nutz* (A&M 1974)★★★, *Nutz Two* (A&M 1975)★★, *Hard Nutz* (A&M 1976)★★★, *Live Cutz* (A&M 1977)★.

NYMPHS

This band originated in the Los Angeles club scene around volatile vocalist Inger Lorre (b. Laurie Wenning), a former model from New Jersey, with a line-up that eventually stabilized with drummer Alex Kirst, guitarists jet freedom (who prefers to have his initials expressed in lower case) and Sam Merrick, and bassist Cliff D. The Nymphs signed to Geffen in 1989, bolstered by a wave of hype that suggested that the band were a female-fronted Guns N'Roses (in truth their sound owed more to Lou Reed, the Stooges and Patti Smith). A period of limbo ensued as the band fought to record a debut on their own terms. Tales of drug abuse, rehabilitation and mental hospitals escalated as the tension of being contractually prohibited from playing live took its toll. These problems were exacerbated when producer Bill Price was commandeered by Guns N'Roses to mix their *Use Your Illusion* albums. Lorre expressed the feelings of the Nymphs by crushing five poppies (to represent the band members) and urinating on them, all on top of the desk of her label's A&R chief. *Nymphs* eventually emerged in February 1992 to a fanfare of critical praise; it was a darkly enthralling set that mixed punk and grunge with Lorre's lyrical images of death, drugs and sex (often drawn from personal experience). Subsequent live shows were of variable quality, with internal tensions abounding due to Lorre's eccentric behaviour, and following *A Practical Guide To Astral Projection*, it was no surprise when the Nymphs disintegrated spectacularly on stage in Miami in September of that same year. Lorre has reportedly since focused her attention on writing children's stories.
● ALBUMS: *Nymphs* (Geffen 1992)★★★, *A Practical Guide To Astral Projection* mini-album (Geffen 1992)★★★.

OBITUARY

This intense and disturbing death metal group originates from Brandon, Florida, USA, where they formed in 1985. After recording a single and contributing two tracks to *Metal Massacre* compilations as Xecutioner, they changed their name to Obituary. This was initiated by the appearance of another, inferior act, who also travelled under the Xecutioner banner. Signed to Roadrunner Records, the band comprised John Tardy (vocals), Allen West (guitar), Trevor Peres (guitar), David Tucker (bass) and Donald Tardy (drums). *Slowly We Rot*, unveiled in 1989, was characterized by their vocalist's gurgling, sewer-like vocals, primarily employed as a musical instrument rather than a means of imparting lyrics, over a maelstrom of crashing power-chords and demonic drumming.

Indeed, the indecipherable nature of John Tardy's outbursts helped to insure them against some of the hysterical criticisms levelled at other death metal pioneers. *Cause Of Death* saw the band refine their unique style, with ex-Death guitarist James Murphy and bassist Frank Watkins in place of West and Tucker, respectively. Obituary, however, continued to specialize in a hideous and brutal musical carnage, taking the death metal concept to its ultimate conclusion. West returned for *World Demise*, again recorded with long-time producer Scott Burns. This album revealed a more considered approach, with the occasional audible lyric from Tardy (a press statement from Peres noted, 'We're serious people, and we wanna be taken seriously'). Allen West also has his own side-project, Six Feet Under, a collaboration with Cannibal Corpse's Chris Barnes. A three-year gap elapsed before *Back From The Dead*, during which time the band had changed their style to hardcore/punk.

● ALBUMS: *Slowly We Rot* (Roadracer 1989)★★★, *Cause Of Death* (Roadracer 1990)★★★, *The End Complete* (Roadracer 1992)★★★, *World Demise* (Roadrunner 1994)★★★, *Back From The Dead* (Roadrunner 1997)★★★, *Dead (Live)* (Roadrunner 1998)★★★★.

OBSESSED

Spawned by the Washington, DC underground of the early 80s, the Obsessed were ranked alongside Minor Threat and Bad Brains in the vicinity, yet never made the immediate transition to nationwide renown that those two outfits achieved. Though more obviously metal-inclined than either, notwithstanding odes to mysticism and Black Sabbath riffs, the Obsessed - Scott 'Wino' Weinrich (vocals, guitar), Mark Laue (bass) and Ed Gulli (drums) - proved influential to two rival camps of supporters, who could be delineated by the length of their hair. They made their debut with a three-track EP (*Sodden Jackyl*) for their own Invictus label, but otherwise relied on live shows and the circulation of demo tapes to establish their reputation. After several years of attrition, Weinrich hooked up with Saint Vitus, replacing vocalist Scott Reagers (on the latter's request), and moving to Los Angeles. The group went on to cut several albums of ultra-heavy hardcore between 1986 and 1991. Towards the end of this stint, Saint Vitus's German label, Hellbound, approached Weinrich about the now-legendary Obsessed demos, and an eponymous album was released in 1990 (also referred to as *The Purple Album*). A fine collection that overcame the obvious budget limitations, it immediately drew the kind of attention that the band lacked during its infancy, but put into question Weinrich's tenure with Saint Vitus. Forced to make a choice by guitarist Dave Chandler, he elected to re-form the Obsessed with Scott Reeder (bass) and Greg Rogers (drums, ex-Poison 13). The raging *Lunar Womb* revealed a rejuvenated and ferocious band back at the peak of its powers. However, problems with Hellbound delayed progress, until Columbia Records stepped in to offer the Obsessed a recording contract, while Reeder (going on to join Kyuss) was replaced by part-time B.A.L.L./Scream member, Guy Pinhas. Despite signing with a major, however, the Obsessed, and Weinrich in particular, maintained an enviable status amongst their peers, the more high-profile of their supporters including L7's Jennifer Finch, Corrosion Of Conformity's Pepper Keenan, Fugazi's Ian MacKaye, Pantera's Phil Anselmo and Henry Rollins.

● ALBUMS: *The Obsessed* (Hellbound 1990)★★★★, *Lunar Womb* (Hellbound 1991)★★★, *The Church Within* (Columbia 1993)★★★.

OBSESSION

This Connecticut, USA-based outfit was formed in 1983 by vocalist Mike Vescara and guitarist Bruce Vitale. Adding Art Maco (guitar), Matt Karugas (bass) and Jay Mezias (drums), they made their debut with a track on the *Metal Massacre* compilation album in 1983. Combining Judas Priest, Venom and Anvil influences, they subsequently recorded the *Marshall Law* mini-album, a high-speed, dual guitar onslaught, accentuated by Vescara's piercing howl. A contract with Enigma ensued and the two albums that resulted showed the band diversifying into more melodic territory. In mid-1988 Maco and Mezias quit, but the band finally folded when Vescara accepted the position of frontman with Japanese rockers Loudness.

● ALBUMS: *Marshall Law* mini-album (Metal Blade 1984)★★★★, *Scarred For Life* (Enigma 1986)★★★, *Methods Of Madness* (Enigma 1987)★★.

OBUS

This Spanish melodic metal band was formed in 1980 by vocalist Fortu, guitarist Francisco Laguna, Fernando Sanches (drums) and Juan Luis Serrano. Though restricting their potential audience by singing in their native tongue, this undoubtedly helped the authenticity of their sound, which was otherwise unoriginal. Signing to the local Chapa Discos label, they recorded three amateurish albums that lacked fresh ideas, before dissolving in the mid-80s.

● ALBUMS: *Preparato* (Chapa Discos 1981)★★, *Podoroso Como El Trueno* (Chapa Discos 1982)★★, *El Que Mas* (Mausoleum 1984)★★.

Of Perception

Between 1979 and 1984, Deviant (b. Stuart Powell, Enfield, England; vocals, guitar, keyboards) and Jellyfish (b. Kevin Nicholson, Tottenham, London, England; bass, vocals, keyboards), were the mainstay of the New Wave Of British Heavy Metal band Tooth. After playing in various other groups, the two reunited in 1989 for a jam session with various friends and session men. Within a year they had assembled a stable line-up with ex-Swamp Angels guitarist Dave Williams and former lighting engineer Pete Smith. After a few gigs and two demos they found ex-Neil Christian bassist Arthur Anderson to record/produce and mix an entire album in 24 hours. The resulting *So Join Mr Dreams* offered a marriage of Doors, Motörhead and Hawkwind influences. It found little favour in the UK but an audience emerged in Europe. Dejected after a tour of Holland fell through at the last moment in 1992, they entered the studio to record a new album with producer Brian Martin. The resultant *Lords So Strange R* was a much more ambitious project, featuring the debut of female backing vocalist Jazz J. Soon afterwards they broke up, which turned out to be a blessing in disguise. Absent from the music scene, they attracted a cult following in Spain and Germany, as well as in 'underground' magazines around the world. The group re-formed late in 1994 minus Jazz J and Smith, and after initial studio work, were joined by session drummer 'Chops'.

● ALBUMS: *So Join Mr Dreams* (Hawke Park 1991)★★★, *Lords So Strange R* (Hawke Park 1992)★★★.

● VIDEOS: *Of Perception* (1991).

Offspring

Although they only found commercial fortune in the mid-90s, the Offspring had been a staple of the southern Californian punk community since 1984. Singer/guitarist Bryan 'Dexter' Holland (b. 29 December 1965) and bass player Greg Kriesel (b. 20 January 1965, Glendale, California, USA) announced their intention to form a band at a party where they heard TSOL's *Change Today* for the first time. Kriesel then joined Manic Subsidal, with former Clowns Of Death guitarist Holland, plus Doug Thompson (vocals) and Jim Benton (drums). When Thompson was forced out, Holland took over vocals, while Benton was replaced by Clowns Of Death drummer James Lilja. A third Clowns Of Death member, guitarist Kevin 'Noodles' Wasserman (b. 4 February 1963, Los Angeles, California, USA), joined later. Manic Subsidal was rechristened the Offspring in 1985. Shows supporting the likes of Econo Christ and Isocraces followed, at an average of one performance every two months. Their debut single, 'I'll Be Waiting', was released on their own Black Records. However, by 1987 Lilja was losing interest in the band, and was replaced for a Las Vegas show by Ron Welty (b. 1 February 1971, Long Beach, California, USA; ex-FQX - Fuck Quality X-Rays). He joined them permanently in July 1987, ironically during an Offspring show supported by FQX, whom he had now abandoned. A demo was recorded in 1988 and touted around punk labels, but Offspring were initially forced to gain recognition by advertising in the classifieds of underground magazines *Flipside* and *Maximum Rock 'n' Roll*. These songs were lifted and placed on compilation cassettes and albums, spreading the group's name in the process. By March 1989 they were ready to record their debut studio album, recruiting Dead Kennedys, TSOL and Iggy Pop veteran Thom Wilson. Via a contract with Nemesis Records the world was at last able to hear the Offspring's unique cross-matching of hardcore with Middle Eastern guitar from chief songwriter Holland. A six-week national tour followed, though Noodles was stabbed during their Hollywood anti-nuclear benefit. The *Baghdad EP* bore witness to the group's progression, with a less self-consciously punk musical dialogue, and the notable absence of some of the cluttered tempo changes of their debut. It was their last record for Nemesis, however, and by 1992 they were in Brett Gurewitz's West Beach Studio working on a new project for Epitaph Records (Gurewitz had initially rejected the band, as had practically every other underground label in the USA, only to change his mind on hearing a new demo tape). *Ignition*'s more relaxed pace, dropped in favour of bigger, memorable choruses, opened up Holland's lyrics to closer scrutiny. There was evident craftsmanship in songs such as 'Take It Like A Man' and 'No Hero', which concerned suicide. This reflected the sophistication of the music, with Holland's Arabic guitar breaks contrasting with Noodles' forceful blues licks. Its release coincided with individual academic success, with Kriesel finishing his finance degree, Welty his electronics degree and

Holland taking his masters (he went on to complete his doctorate in molecular biology). In June they toured Europe for the first time with labelmates No FX, preceding a two-week domestic stint with the Lunachicks on which Noodles was temporarily replaced by his friend, Rob Barton, who also helped out on the following tour with Pennywise. The group's third album, *Smash*, was completed in February 1994 with Thom Wilson again producing. Ever more adventurous, this time Offspring combined punk with ska and hard rock, with a cover version of the Didjits' 'Killboy Powerhead' as a concession to their roots. 'What Happened To You' eloquently addressed the subject of hard drugs (to which so many of their So-Cal hardcore compatriots had fallen victim), while 'Something To Believe In' and 'Self-Esteem' were more detached and introspective than before. By the end of 1994 the album had achieved platinum status as the result of extensive touring with labelmates Rancid and Dutch hardcore band Guttermouth, and the crossover success of MTV favourite 'Come Out And Play (Keep 'Em Separated)'. By 1995 *Smash* was accredited with quadruple platinum sales, and their recording of the Damned's 'Smash It Up', for the soundtrack of *Batman Forever*, was another major success. Much of 1995 was spent in dispute with their record company, with the group eventually signing with Columbia Records in 1996. *Ixnay On The Hombre* was well received in February 1997, but failed to establish Offspring as a commercial force.

● ALBUMS: *Offspring* (Nemesis 1989)★★, *Ignition* (Epitaph 1992)★★★, *Smash* (Epitaph 1994)★★★, *Ixnay On The Hombre* (Columbia 1997)★★★.

OMEN

This Los Angeles, USA-based, melodic power-metal outfit formed in 1984. Comprising J.D. Kimball (vocals), Kenny Powell (guitar, ex-Sacred Blade), Jody Henry (bass) and Steve Wittig (drums), they debuted with a track on the *Metal Massacre V* compilation. This led to a contract with Metal Blade and the release of *Battle Cry* the same year. This was a competent, if uninspired, collection of Iron Maiden-style rockers, which lacked distinction owing to Kimball's weak vocals. Three more albums followed a similar pattern, with 1987's mini-opus *Nightmares* being the most interesting (it featured a strong cover version of AC/DC's 'Whole Lotta Rosie'). Coburn Pharr replaced Kimball in 1988 and helped the band to produce *Escape From Nowhere*, their finest recorded work. Adding Rush-styled dynamics to their basic metal framework, it was characterized by Pharr's powerful and high-pitched vocals. Surprisingly, it failed to sell and Pharr left to join Annihilator in 1990. Kenny Powell emerged in the 90s with a new band, Step Child.

● ALBUMS: *Battle Cry* (Roadrunner 1984)★★, *Warning Of Danger* (Roadrunner 1985)★★★, *The Curse* (Roadrunner 1986)★★★, *Nightmares* (Roadrunner 1987)★★★★, *Escape From Nowhere* (Roadrunner 1988)★★★.

ONE HIT WONDER

From Long Beach, Orange County, California, and led by singer and principal songwriter Dan Root, One Hit Wonder additionally comprise Randy Bradbury (bass), Trey Pangborn (guitar) and Chris Webb (drums). Their self-titled debut EP in 1995, produced by alternative rock team the Robb brothers (Lemonheads, Buffalo Tom), consolidated the impression created by an initial batch of underground 7-inch singles for Lethal Records. The material on offer ('Break Your Heart', 'After Her Disasters') provided down-at-heel takes on life, backed by focused metal riffing with power-pop flourishes.

● ALBUMS: *Outfall* (Nitro 1997)★★★.

ONE MORE TIME

Comprising Peter Grönwall (the son of Abba's Benny Andersson), Nanne Nordqvist and Maria Radsten, the visual appearance of Sweden's One More Time evoked nothing so much as a reduced Heart when they made their debut in 1992. They enjoyed immediate success not only domestically but throughout Europe when 'Highland', a single taken from their debut album of the same title, announced their bombastic style. It brought them a clutch of international awards, included a Group Of The Year accolade in Belgium. Grönwall, an experienced symphonic instrument musician, remains the creative power behind One More Time, although the combined harmonies of the group's two female members are what gave *Highland* its immediacy.

● ALBUMS: *Highland* (CNR 1992)★★★.

ONLY CHILD

This US heavy rock group was formed by the multi-talented songwriter, vocalist and guitarist Paul Sabu in 1988. Featuring Tommy Rude (keyboards), Murril Maglio (bass) and Charles Esposito (drums), their self-titled debut consisted of melodic rock that partially justified the critical acclaim it received. The praise heaped upon the album by the UK's *Kerrang!* magazine, in particular, was rather premature, as the overtly commercial riffs and obvious hooks soon wore thin. This was borne out by the shortfall in anticipated sales. Esposito was replaced by Tommy Amato in 1989 and they were signed by Geffen Records to start work on new material, but thus far Only Child have remained quiet.

● ALBUMS: *Only Child* (Rampage 1988)★★.

ONSLAUGHT

This UK thrash quintet, originally conceived as a punk/metal hybrid, was formed in Bristol in 1983 by guitarist Nige Rockett and drummer Steve Grice. With the addition of vocalist Paul Mahoney and bassist Jason Stallord, they recorded *Power From Hell* on the independent Cor label in 1985. This opened the doors to a contract with Under One Flag, the thrash subsidiary of Music For Nations. *The Force* saw the band expand to a quintet, with the arrival of new vocalist Sy Keeler; Mahoney was relegated to bass and Stallord switched to rhythm guitar. The album was heavily reliant on the styles of Slayer, Metallica and Anthrax, with little original input. Mahoney was replaced by James Hinder on bass shortly after the album was released. Moving to London Records, *In Search Of Sanity* was their make-or-break album. Before it was completed, Steve Grimmett (ex-Grim Reaper) and Rob Trottman replaced Keeler and Stallord, respectively. After a series of delays, the album finally surfaced in early 1989. Producer Stephan Galfas had watered down their aggressive sound in an attempt to court commercial success. Even the cover version of AC/DC's 'Let There Be Rock' proved less strong than expected, and the material generally lacked distinction. They had moved away from hard-line thrash towards mainstream metal with negative results. The album was slated by the metal media and Grimmett quit in 1990. A replacement was found in the form of Tony O'Hara, but the band were dropped by their label soon after. Disillusioned, the members went their separate ways in 1991, with Grimmett forming Lionsheart.

● ALBUMS: *Power From Hell* (Music For Nations 1985)★★★, *The Force* (Music For Nations 1986)★★★, *In Search Of Sanity* (London 1989)★★.

ORAL

A rather sad four-piece all-female UK band comprising 'glamour' models and Stripagram girls, the line-up of Oral (a suitably childish reference point) consisted of Bev (vocals), Monica (guitar), Dee (drums) and Candy (bass). Candy had quit by the time their only album was released and as they played no gigs, it is questionable whether any of them could play at all. Evidently the whole thing was designed to further their day jobs, and they gained a little publicity thanks to song titles such as 'I Need Discipline' and 'Gas Masks Vicars And Priests'. Their debut album was entitled *Sex*, written so that anyone glancing at the sleeve would read simply 'Oral Sex'. Even the group's version of the Sex Pistols' 'Black Leather' was ill-advised.

● ALBUMS: *Sex* (Conquest 1987)★.

ORANGE

This Yugoslavian hard rock quintet was formed in 1981 by Zlato Magdalenic (vocals), Mijo Popovic (guitar), Tomaz Zontar (keyboards), Marko Herak (bass) and Franc Teropic (drums). Together they secured a contract with the local RTB label. Musically, they incorporated elements of AC/DC, Deep Purple and Accept, but added little creative input of their own. The band were known as Pomeranca in Yugoslavia and attracted a small but loyal cult following after the release of their debut album in 1982. This featured native lyrics and consequently excluded a large section of their potential audience. *Madbringer* saw the band using English lyrics for the first time, but their crude enunciation failed to enhance their appeal.

● ALBUMS: *Peklenska Pomaranca* (RTB 982)★★★, *Madbringer* (RTB 1983)★★.

ORGANIZATION

Formed from the remnants of Death Angel, the US band Organization comprise Rob Cavestany (vocals, guitar), Andy Galeon (drums, vocals), Dennis Pepa (bass) and Gus Pepa (guitar). The former band, while on tour supporting *Act III*, suffered a bus crash that seriously injured drummer and youngest member Galeon. When singer Mark Osegueda decided he was unable to wait for him to make a full recovery, Cavestany took over as singer and frontman and the Organization was born. Marking their arrival with an appearance at the Dynamo Festival in Europe in 1992, the members had learned enough about the music industry to act in a more independent fashion, setting up their own Unsafe Unsane Recordings for the release of *Free Burning* (licensed to Bulletproof/Music For Nations in the UK). However, reactions to the set were lukewarm after the positive press generated by their stage shows. Critical apathy also afflicted its 1995 follow-up, *Savor The Flavor*.

● ALBUMS: *Free Burning* (Unsafe Unsane

Recordings 1993)★★, *Savor The Flavor* (Unsafe Unsane Recordings 1995)★★★.

Orphan

This Canadian melodic heavy rock quartet was formed in 1982 by ex-Pimps duo Chris Burke Gaffney (vocals, bass) and Brent Diamond (keyboards). Enlisting the services of guitarist Steve McGovern and drummer Ron Boivenue, they negotiated a contract with the Portrait label the following year. Drawing inspiration from commercial rockers such as Bryan Adams and Queen, they debuted with *Lonely At Night*, a sophisticated collection of accessible AOR anthems. *Salute* saw Boivenue succeeded by Terry Norman Taylor and the guest appearance of guitarist Aldo Nova, but the songs lacked the impact of those on their debut release and the band's progress dissipated.

● ALBUMS: *Lonely At Night* (Portrait 1983)★★★★, *Salute* (Portrait 1985)★★★.

Osbourne, Ozzy

b. John Osbourne, 3 December 1948, Aston, Birmingham, England. In 1979 this highly individual and by now infamous vocalist and songwriter left Black Sabbath, a band whose image and original musical direction he had helped to shape. His own band was set up with Lee Kerslake, formerly of Uriah Heep, on drums, Rainbow's Bob Daisley (bass) and Randy Rhoads (b. Randall William Rhoads, 6 December 1956, Santa Monica, California, USA, d. 19 March 1982), fresh from Quiet Riot, on guitar. Rhoads' innovative playing ability was much in evidence on the debut, *Blizzard Of Oz*. By the time of a second album, Daisley and Kerslake had left to be replaced by Pat Travers drummer Tommy Aldridge and Rudy Sarzo (bass). Throughout his post-Black Sabbath career, Osbourne has courted publicity, most famously in 1982 when he had to undergo treatment for rabies following an onstage incident when he bit off the head of a bat. In the same year his immensely talented young guitarist, Rhoads, was killed in an air crash. In came Brad Gillis but, so close was Rhoads' personal as well as musical relationship to Osbourne, many feared he would never be adequately replaced. *Talk Of The Devil* was released later in 1982, a live album that included Sabbath material. Following a tour that saw Sarzo and Gillis walk out, Osbourne was forced to rethink the line-up of his band in 1983 as Daisley rejoined, along with guitarist Jake E. Lee. Aldridge left following the release of *Bark At The Moon*, and was replaced by renowned virtuoso drummer Carmine Appice (b. 15 December 1946, Staten Island, New York, USA). This combination was to be short-lived, however, Randy Castillo replacing Appice, and Phil Soussan taking on the bass guitar. Daisley appeared on *No Rest For The Wicked*, although Sabbath bassist Geezer Butler played on the subsequent live dates. The late 80s were a trying time for Osbourne. He went on trial in America for allegedly using his lyrics to incite youngsters to commit suicide; he was eventually cleared of these charges. His wife, Sharon (daughter of Don Arden), also became his manager, and helped Osbourne to overcome the alcoholism that was the subject of much of his work. His lyrics, however, continued to deal with the grimmest of subjects, including the agony of insanity, and 1986's *The Ultimate Sin* was concerned almost exclusively with the issue of nuclear destruction. In later years Osbourne has kept to more contemporary issues, rejecting to a certain extent the satanic, werewolf image he constructed around himself during the early 80s. In March 1989 he enjoyed a US Top 10 hit with a duet with Lita Ford, 'Close My Eyes Forever'. He embarked on a farewell tour in 1992, but broke four bones in his foot which inhibited his performances greatly. He also donated $20,000 to the Daughters Of The Republic Of Texas appeal to help restore the Alamo, and performed his first concert in the city of San Antonio since being banned for urinating on a wall of the monument in 1982. Predictably, neither retirement nor atonement sat too comfortably with the man, and by late 1994 he was announcing the imminent release of a new solo album, recorded in conjunction with Steve Vai. He also teamed up with Therapy? to sing lead vocals on the track 'Iron Man' for the Black Sabbath tribute album, *Black Nativity*. Far less likely was his pairing with Miss Piggy of *The Muppet Show* on 'Born To Be Wild', for a bizarre Muppets compilation album. He also confesssed that his original partner on his 1992 Don Was-produced duet with actress Kim Basinger, 'Shake Your Head', was Madonna, although he had not actually recognized her. Other strange couplings included one with the Scottish comedian Billy Connolly and the popular UK boxer Frank Bruno on the 'Urpney Song', written by Mike Batt for the cartoon series *Dreamstone*. *Ozzmosis* (1995) was arguably his best album to date, and was a major success. The line-up on the album was Geezer Butler (bass), Rick Wakeman (keyboards), Zakk Wylde, who co-wrote six tracks (guitar), and Deen Castronovo (drums). Osbourne is one hard-rocker who has tried every excess known and has survived. Amazingly, his work continues to sound inspired and exciting.

● ALBUMS: *Blizzard Of Oz* (Jet 1980)★★★, *Diary Of A Madman* (Jet 1981)★★★, *Talk Of The Devil* (Jet 1982)★★, *Bark At The Moon* (Jet 1983)★★, *The Ultimate Sin* (Epic 1986)★★, *Tribute* (Epic 1987)★★★, *No Rest For The Wicked* (Epic 1988)★★, *Just Say Ozzy* (Epic 1990)★★, *No More Tears* (Epic 1991)★★★, *Live & Loud* (Epic 1993)★★, *Ozzmosis* (Epic 1995)★★★★.

● COMPILATIONS: *Ten Commandments* (Priority 1990)★★, *The Ozz Man Cometh* (Epic 1997)★★★★.

● VIDEOS: *The Ultimate Ozzy* (Virgin Vision 1987), *Wicked Videos* (CIC Videos 1988), *Bark At The Moon* (Hendring Music Video 1990), *Don't Blame Me* (Sony Music Video 1992), *Live & Loud* (1993), *Ozzy Osbourne: The Man Cometh* (SMV 1997).

● FURTHER READING: *Ozzy Osbourne*, Garry Johnson. *Diary Of A Madman: The Uncensored Memoirs Of Rock's Greatest Rogue*, Mick Wall.

Ostrogoth

This Belgian hard rock outfit was formed in Gent, Belgium, during 1983, by guitarist Rudy Vercruysse and drummer Mario Pauwels. After a series of false starts, the line-up stabilized with the addition of Marc Debrauwer (vocals), Marnix Vandekauter (bass) and Hans Vandekerckhove (guitar). They debuted with a mini-album, *Full Moon's Eyes*, a competent if predictable rehash of Iron Maiden and Judas Priest riffs. This line-up recorded two further collections in the same vein, but received little recognition outside their native Belgium. The band splintered in 1985, with only Vercruysse and Pauwels remaining. They rebuilt Ostrogoth with Peter de Wint (vocals), Juno Martins (guitar), Sylvain Cherotti (bass) and Kris Taerwe (keyboards). In 1987 they produced *Feelings Of Fury*, which added a melodic slant to their previous enterprises. The group subsequently disbanded with Pauwels moving on to Shellshock and Hermetic Brotherhood.

● ALBUMS: *Full Moon's Eyes* mini-album (Mausoleum 1983)★★★, *Ecstasy And Danger* (Mausoleum 1983)★★, *Too Hot* (Mausoleum 1985)★★★, *Feelings Of Fury* (Ultraprime 1987)★★★.

Our Lady Peace

Comprising Raine Maida (vocals), Mike Turner (guitar), Chris Eacrett (bass) and Jeremy Taggart (drums), Our Lady Peace were formed in Toronto, Canada, in 1994. The unusual, eclectic nature of the band's music is as much a result of their varied experiences as their musical influences. Maida (b. *c.*1972, Canada) is a former criminology student at the University of Toronto, while Turner (b. *c.*1965, Canada), an English graduate, grew up in England during the punk explosion. Eacrett (b. *c.*1971, Canada) was studying marketing when he made initial contact with Maida and Turner. After meeting local producer Arnold Lanni they set about recording their first demos, which immediately attracted the attention of Sony Music Canada. The group's debut album, *Naveed*, took its title from 'the ancient Middle Eastern name for bearer of good news'. As Maida elaborated: 'We took the concept of Naveed and placed it into the dark optimism of our music. Naveed is a constant quest to obtain knowledge, possessed with the desire to grow mentally and spiritually.' The songwriting, which was undertaken before their stage debut, evolved out of a communal musical approach, with Maida supplying lyrics. *Clumsy* was a strong follow-up, showcasing a more mature songwriting approach.

● ALBUMS: *Naveed* (Sony Canada/Epic 1995)★★★, *Clumsy* (Columbia 1997)★★★.

Outside Edge

Formerly known as Blackfoot Sue and Liner, this UK band switched to the name Outside Edge in 1984 to pursue an AOR direction. Comprising Tom Farmer (vocals, bass), Eddie Galga (guitar), Pete Giles (keyboards) and Dave Farmer (drums), they signed to Warner Brothers Records and released a self-titled debut in 1985. This was Americanized melodic rock, but featured rough and ragged vocals from Farmer, in contrast to the musical stylization. *Running Hot* followed in 1986 and was produced by Terry Manning (of ZZ Top fame), but Outside Edge were still unable to break through on a commercial level. The Farmer brothers left in 1989 and the remaining duo recruited new members to become Little Wing.

● ALBUMS: *Outside Edge* (Warners 1985)★★★, *Running Hot* (10 1986)★★.

Overdose

First sighted contributing a track to the *Metal Massacre 9* compilation, Brazilian thrash band Overdose actually started their career alongside the better-known Sepultura, each band supplying one side to the *Brutal Devastation/Seculo XX* album in 1985. Afterwards, the fortunes of the two bands diverged, and it looked as though Overdose would become a mere footnote in the Sepultura story

(Overdose vocalist B.Z., a graphic artist, also designed their logo). Claudio David (guitar), Sergio Cichovicz (guitar), Eddie Weber (bass), Andre Marcio (drums) and B.Z. kicked their heels while contractual problems were sorted out. They sustained themselves with a rigorous South American touring schedule that helped to define their bombastic and potent sound. They also recorded profusely. *Progress Of Decadence* (1994) was their sixth album, but was the first to be released in Europe, the group having previously sustained themselves with a staunch following in their native territory.

● ALBUMS: *Progress Of Decadence* (Under One Flag 1994)★★★, *Scars* (Fierce 1996)★★★.

Overflash

Announcing his musical style as 'Cyberdeath', Overflash is the creation of Swedish-born 'musical deviant' Devo. Employing high-tech midi-computer technology in addition to his own screaming vocals, Overflash's musical output encompasses everything from baroque to techno and death metal. Calling on guitars, percussion instruments, strings, vocoder voice treatments and a wide variety of samples, his debut album was released on MNW Records in 1994 - though Overflash had originally been founded in 1986. Despite its eclecticism, *Threshold To Reality* was criticized for the artist's over-employment of pulp cyberpunk imagery that lacked lyrical dexterity.

● ALBUMS: *Threshold To Reality* (MNW 1994)★★.

Overkill

This thrash metal quartet was formed in New York, USA, in 1984 by vocalist Bobby 'Blitz' Ellsworth, guitarist Bobby Gustafson, bassist D.D. Vernie and drummer Sid Falck. Together they self-financed the recording of a mini-album. Desperately short of cash and exposure, they sold the rights to the small Azra label and made a net loss. They were soon picked up by Megaforce, however, and released their full debut album in 1985. *Feel The Fire* was a brutal speed-metal riff assault, but lacked the variation in light and shade to compete with groups such as Metallica and Anthrax. Three more albums followed a similar pattern, with *Under The Influence* raising their profile and generating comparisons to Testament. Following *The Years Of Decay*, Gustafson quit and was replaced by Rob Cannavino and Merritt Gant (ex-Faith Or Fear). Expanded to a quintet, the band recorded *Horrorscope*, their best work to date. Varying their approach, they only switched to hyperspeed at crucial moments, in order to maximize the impact. The album also featured an amazing version of Edgar Winter's 'Frankenstein'. Their reputation has continued to grow, following successful support slots on Helloween and Slayer tours, and another excellent album in *I Hear Black*. *W.F.O.* was packed with strong songs such as 'Where It Hurts' and 'New High In Lows', but was released only in mainland Europe. In 1995, shortly after releasing a 10th anniversary live triple album, guitarists Cannavino and Gant both left the band. Gustafson later appeared as a member of Grip Inc, Cycle Sluts From Hell and Skrew.

● ALBUMS: *Overkill* mini-album (Azra 1984)★★★, *Feel The Fire* (Megaforce 1985)★★, *Taking Over* (Megaforce 1987)★★, *Under The Influence* (Megaforce 1988)★★★, *The Years Of Decay* (Megaforce 1989)★★★, *Horrorscope* (Megaforce 1991)★★★★, *I Hear Black* (Atlantic 1993)★★★, *W.F.O.* (Atlantic 1994)★★★, *10 Years Of Wrecking Your Neck - Live* (Edel 1995)★★, *Fuck You And Then Some* (Megaforce 1995)★★★, *The Killing Kind* (CMC 1996)★★★, *From The Underground And Below* (CMC 1997)★★.

● COMPILATIONS: *Greatest Hits Live* (CMC 1995)★★★.

Oz

This Finnish heavy metal outfit was formed by The Oz (vocals) and Eero Hamalainen (guitar) in 1977. Complemented by Kari Elo (bass) and Tauno Vajavaara (drums), they adopted an approach that fused elements of Black Sabbath and Motörhead into a violent power-chord frenzy. It took five years before the band made their debut with *The Oz*, a heavy rock album that suffered from a low-budget production and weak vocals. Elo and Hamalainen were fired shortly after the album's release, with bassist Jay C. Blade and guitarists Speedy Foxx and Spooky Wolff recruited as replacements. The band relocated to Sweden and produced *Fire In The Brain*, a collection of tough and uncompromising power-metal songs not dissimilar to the work of Judas Priest. It served to bring them to the attention of RCA Records who offered them a European contract. The two albums that followed, however, were disappointing. Oz moved away from their metallic roots and experimented with a greater use of melody, and this approach did not suit. It came as no surprise when they lost their contract. Disillusioned, the band split up in 1987 before reforming two years later (with no original members). Comprising Ape De Martini (vocals), Mark Ruffneck (drums), T.B. Muen (bass), Michael Loreda (guitar) and Mike Paul (guitar), they entered the studio to start work on new material in vain pursuit of former glories.

● ALBUMS: *The Oz* (Kraf 1982)★★, *Fire In The Brain* (Wave 1983)★★★, *III Warning* (RCA 1984)★★★, *Decibel Storm* (RCA 1986)★★★.

Ozz

This American hard rock project was founded by vocalist Alexis T. Angel and guitarist Gregg Parker. Using session musicians to complete the band, they debuted with *Prisoners* in 1980. Produced by Andy Johns, Parker's guitarwork proved exemplary and provided the perfect foil for Angel's vocal acrobatics (comparisons to prime Led Zeppelin were frequently mooted). Parker then relocated to London in 1982 to form the short-lived Ninja, but interest in his former project remained strong enough to prompt the release of *Exploited*, a compilation of live material and studio out-takes.

● ALBUMS: *Prisoners* (Epic 1980)★★★, *Exploited* (Streamline 1983)★★.

P

P

This US celebrity rock band was formed by actor Johnny Depp and Gibby Haines of the Butthole Surfers in 1995. Depp, a film superstar of the 90s through films such as *Edward Scissorhands* and *Benny And Joon*, had previously played on Shane MacGowan And The Popes' debut album and had associated with several rock stars. He had actually harboured dreams of his own band ever since running away from home in Florida as a teenager, moving to Los Angeles in the hope of finding a deal for his then band. His ambitions were realized when Depp met Haines through a mutual friend, Sal Jenco, at the Viper Room club (owned by Depp). Jenco became the band's drummer, with Depp on vocals and bass, Haines on lead vocals and Bill Carter on guitar and bass. Their debut album was produced by Andrew Weiss (ex-Henry Rollins Band, currently of Ween) at Oceanway Studios in Los Angeles. The first single was 'Michael Stipe', a tribute to the R.E.M. leader, featuring the lyrics, 'I finally got to meet Michael Stipe/He touched my arm'. Also included was a cover version of Abba's 'Dancing Queen', on which Depp played sitar. After recording, however, Haines returned to work with the Butthole Surfers, leaving P's long-term future in doubt.

● ALBUMS: *P* (Capitol 1995)★★★.

Page, Jimmy

b. James Patrick Page, 9 January 1944, Heston, Middlesex, England. One of rock's most gifted and distinctive guitarists, Page began his professional career during the pre-beat era of the early 60s. He was a member of several groups, including Neil Christian's Crusaders and Carter Lewis And The Southerners, the latter of which was led by the popular songwriting team Carter And Lewis. Page played rousing solos on several releases by Carter/Lewis protégés, notably the McKinleys' 'Sweet And Tender Romance', and the guitarist quickly became a respected session musician. He appeared on releases by Lulu, Them, Tom Jones and Dave Berry, as well as scores of less renowned acts, but his best-known work was undertaken for producer Shel Talmy. Page appeared on sessions for the Kinks and the Who, joining an élite band of young studio musicians who included Nicky Hopkins, John Paul Jones and Bobby Graham. The guitarist completed a solo single, 'She Just Satisfies', in 1965, and although it suggested a frustration with his journeyman role, he later took up an A&R position with Immediate Records, where he produced singles for Nico and John Mayall. Having refused initial entreaties, Page finally agreed to join the Yardbirds in 1966 and he remained with this groundbreaking attraction until its demise two years later. The guitarist then formed Led Zeppelin, with whom he forged his reputation. His propulsive riffs established the framework for a myriad of tracks - 'Whole Lotta Love', 'Rock 'N' Roll', 'Black Dog', 'When The Levee Breaks' and 'Achilles Last Stand' - now established as rock classics, while his solos have set benchmarks for a new generation of guitarists. His acoustic technique, featured on 'Black Mountain Side' and 'Tangerine', is also notable, while his work with Roy Harper, in particular on *Stormcock* (1971), was also among the finest of his career. Page's recordings since Led Zeppelin's dissolution have largely been ill-focused. He contributed the soundtrack to Michael Winner's film *Death Wish II*, while the Firm, a collaboration with Paul Rodgers, formerly of Free and Bad Company, was equally disappointing. However, a 1988 release, *Outrider*, did much to re-establish his reputation, with contributions from Robert Plant, Chris Farlowe and Jason Bonham, the son of Zeppelin's late drummer, John. The guitarist then put considerable effort into remastering that group's revered back-catalogue. *Coverdale/Page* was a successful but fleeting partnership with the former Whitesnake singer in 1993, but it was his reunion with Robert Plant for the *Unledded* project, and an album of new material in 1998, that really captured the public's imagination. Page also achieved an unlikely UK hit single in August 1998, collaborating with Puff Daddy on 'Come With Me', from the *Godzilla* soundtrack.

● ALBUMS: *Death Wish II* film soundtrack (Swan Song 1982)★★, with Roy Harper *Whatever Happened To Jugula* (Beggars Banquet 1985)★★★, *Outrider* (Geffen 1988)★★, with David Coverdale *Coverdale/Page* (EMI 1993)★★★, with Robert Plant *Unledded/No Quarter* (Fontana 1994)★★★★, with Plant *Walking Into Clarksdale* (Atlantic 1998)★★★★.

● COMPILATIONS: *Jam Session* (Charly 1982)★★, *No Introduction Necessary* (Thunderbolt 1984)★★, *Smoke And Fire* (Thunderbolt 1985)★★.

● FURTHER READING: *Mangled Mind Archive: Jimmy Page*, Adrian T'Vell.

PAIN TEENS

The Pain Teens were an extraordinary US rock group, who were formed in the late 80s and comprised Scott Ayers (guitar, samples, drums), Bliss Blood (vocals, percussion), Kirk Carr (bass) and Frank Garymartin (drums). After two obscure albums for Anonmie Records at the turn of the decade the group moved to Trance Syndicate, the left-field label set up by King Coffey of the Butthole Surfers. The marriage was an obvious one, with the Pain Teens able to conduct their experimental approach to music without the hindrance of commercial expectation. Happily, this did not necessitate an unpleasant listening experience, though certainly the subject matter chosen by Pain Teens could be described as difficult. Samples drawn from television shows, especially the psychobabble of confessional talk shows, littered their albums of this period, the best of which was *Destroy Me, Lover*. A confrontational, multi-dimensional record, it was released in a classic 'pulp fiction' cover, the image of which (man assailing woman) took on a ghastly double meaning when Blood's vocals began to address the disturbing subject matter of 'Lisa Knew'. This exorcism of child abuse was accompanied by a complementary track, 'Body Memory', which explored the mind of an incest survivor. Some light relief was on offer with their string arrangement of Leonard Cohen's 'Story Of Isaac', but the title of the sweet pop track 'RU 486', was actually the serial number of an abortion pill. Not a band to spare anyone the truth of just how brutal life can be, the Pain Teens disbanded following the release of 1995's *Beast Of Dreams*.

● ALBUMS: *Pain Teens* (Anomie 1988)★★★, *Case Histories* (Anomie 1989)★★★, *Born In Blood* (Trance Syndicate 1990)★★★ *Stimulation Festival* (Trance Syndicate 1992)★★★, *Destroy Me, Lover* (Trance Syndicate 1993)★★★★, *Beast Of Dreams* (Trance Syndicate 1995)★★★.

PALAIS SCHAUMBURG

News of German band Palais Schaumburg gradually filtered through in 1981 via two singles on the Zick Zack label, 'Rote Lichter' and 'Telefon'. Frontman and bassist Holger Hiller (ex-Geister-Fahrer and Traneninvasion) was joined by drummer Ralf (ex-Abwarts, later replaced by Mufti), Thomas Fehlman (synthesizer) and Timo (bass/trumpet, ex-Immermanner), to create a dense, synthesized and at times experimental formula. A deal with the Kamera label in 1982 produced a one-off single, 'Wir Bauen Eine Neue Stadt', before Palais Schaumburg signed with Mercury Records. An album, *Lupa*, emerged later that year, but the band could only muster two further offerings. After 'Hockey' in 1983 and 'Beat Of Two' in the following year, Hiller left to pursue a solo career.

● ALBUMS: *Lupa* (1982)★★.

PALLAS

This UK progressive rock outfit was formed in Aberdeen, Scotland, in 1975, by Euan Lowson (vocals), Niall Mathewson (guitar), Ronnie Brown (keyboards), Graeme Murray (bass) and Derek Forman (drums). They toured the British club circuit for many years, receiving constant rejections from A&R departments. Undeterred, they decided to self-finance the recording of a demo album. This materialized in 1983 as *Arrive Alive*, a high-quality collection of melodic songs. The set's modest success led to a contract with EMI, the services of Yes producer Eddie Offord, and a large budget to record

The Sentinel in Atlanta, Georgia, USA. This was an ambitious and intricate concept album that betrayed the group's Marillion and Yes influences. Lowson left at this juncture, to be replaced by Alan Reed. *The Wedge* followed and represented the pinnacle of the group's creativity. However, its commercial failure led to EMI severing its links with the band. Despite this, Pallas remained together, but finally split when unable to find a new label sympathetic to their cause.

● ALBUMS: *Arrive Alive* (Kigg Cool 1983)★★★, *The Sentinel* (Harvest 1984)★★★★, *The Wedge* (EMI 1986)★★★.

PANDEMONIUM

This Alaskan heavy metal band was formed by the Resch brothers - Chris (vocals), Eric (bass) and David (guitar) - in 1981. They relocated to Los Angeles, California, and teamed up with Chris Latham (guitar) and Dave Graybill (drums) the following year. Making their debut on the first *Metal Massacre* compilation with 'Fighting Backwards', it opened the door to a full contract with Metal Blade Records. Three albums followed over the next five years, with each successive release becoming less formularized (despite displaying the continually strong influence of Van Halen), but to little commercial advantage.

● ALBUMS: *Heavy Metal Soldiers* (Metal Blade 1984)★★★, *Hole In The Sky* (Metal Blade 1985)★★, *The Kill* (Metal Blade 1988)★★.

PANDORA'S BOX

This one-off project was put together by US producer Jim Steinman to record his rock opera, *Original Sin*. The band featured Roy Bittan (piano), Jeff Bova (synthesizers), Jim Bralower (drums), Eddie Martinez (guitar) and Steve Buslowe (bass). Utilizing a series of guest vocalists, who included Elaine Caswell, Ellen Foley, Gina Taylor, Deliria Wild, Holly Sherwood and Laura Theodore, *Original Sin* was a grandiose concept album themed on sex. Featuring classical interludes, spoken introductions, atmospheric ballads and breathtaking rock 'n' roll, it was almost too ambitious. Despite state-of-the-art production (courtesy of Steinman), it never received the sort of recognition afforded his Meat Loaf projects.

● ALBUMS: *Original Sin* (Virgin 1989)★★★.

PANTERA

This Texan heavy metal quartet was formed in 1981. They initially comprised Terry Glaze (guitar, vocals), Darrell Abbott (guitar), Vince Abbott (drums) and Rex Rocker (bass). Drawing musical inspiration from Kiss, Aerosmith and Deep Purple, they debuted with *Metal Magic* in 1983. This well-received set led to prestigious support slots to Dokken, Stryper and Quiet Riot. *Projects In The Jungle* indicated that the band were evolving quickly and starting to build a sound of their own. The Kiss nuances had disappeared and the band sounded, at times, similar to early Def Leppard, with anthemic cuts such as 'Heavy Metal Rules' and 'Out For Blood' leading the charge. The membership altered their names at this juncture, with Glaze becoming Terence Lee, Darrell Abbott switching to Diamond Darrell and brother Vince emerging as Vinnie Paul. *Power Metal* was the first album on which Phil Anselmo took over lead vocals, but it lacked the depth and polish of previous efforts, and had yet to make the full conversion to heavy thrash that later became the band's trademark. Diamond Darrell turned down the offer to join Megadeth at this point, in order to concentrate on new Pantera material. The decision proved crucial, as a return to form was made with 1990's *Cowboys From Hell*. This was an inspired collection of infectious hard rock, played with unabashed fervour, with Anselmo growing as a creative and visual force. *Vulgar Display Of Power*, meanwhile, belied half of its title by invoking a sense of genuine songwriting prowess to augment the bone-crushing arrangements. Establishing a fierce reputation, it surprised few of the group's supporters when *Far Beyond Driven* entered both the UK and US album charts at number 1. Rock music had found powerful new ambassadors in the brutally honest and savagely executed thrash metal of Pantera. The key word here is 'loud', as *Official Live: 101 Proof* demonstrates without a doubt.

● ALBUMS: *Metal Magic* (Metal Magic 1983)★★★, *Projects In The Jungle* (Metal Magic 1984)★★★, *I Am The Night* (Metal Magic 1985)★★★, *Power Metal* (Metal Magic 1988)★★, *Cowboys From Hell* (Atco 1990)★★★★, *Vulgar Display Of Power* (Atco 1992)★★★★, *Far Beyond Driven* (East West 1994)★★★★, *Driven Downunder Tour '94 Souvenir Collection* (East West 1995)★★, *The Great Southern Trendkill* (East West 1996)★★★, *Official Live: 101 Proof* (East West 1997)★★.

● VIDEOS: *Vulgar Video* (Warner Vision 1994), *Watch It Go* (Warner Vision 1998).

PARADISE LOST

This Halifax, Yorkshire, England-based death metal quintet was formed in 1988, deriving their name from John Milton's epic poem. The band consisted of Nick Holmes (b. 7 January 1970, Halifax, Yorkshire, England), Gregor Mackintosh (b. 20 June 1970, Halifax, Yorkshire, England; guitar), Aaron Aedy (b. 19 December 1969, Bridlington, Yorkshire, England; guitar), Stephen Edmondson (b. 30 December 1969, Bridlington, Yorkshire, England; bass) and Matthew Archer (b. 14 July 1970, Leicester, Yorkshire, England; drums), and they were signed to the independent Peaceville label on the strength of two impressive demos. They debuted in 1990 with *Lost Paradise*, which was heavily influenced by Napalm Death, Obituary and Death. It featured indecipherable grunting from Holmes, over a barrage of metallic white noise. *Gothic* saw a major innovation in the 'grind-core' genre, with female vocals, keyboards and guitar lines that, for once, were not lost in the mix. Importantly, the tempo had also eased: 'We started to play more slowly because all the others were playing as fast as possible.' Many, notably Asphyx and Autopsy, followed suit. With indications in the early 90s of the metal subgenres becoming accepted within the mainstream, it came as no surprise when Paradise Lost found a wider audience with *Shades Of God*, their first effort for Music For Nations. Recorded with producer Simon Efemey (Diamond Head, Wonder Stuff), and with artwork from cult cartoonist Dave McKean, this release was heralded in the press as a 'coming of age'. Sell-out shows in Europe followed, before the group returned to Longhome studios in the UK, with Efemey once again in attendance. The *As I Die* EP gained a strong foothold on MTV, and gained approval from peers including Metallica, before *Icon* was released in September 1993. If previous offerings had seen the band's fanbase expand, *Icon* brought about an explosion of interest, and acclaim usually reserved for the US gods of death metal. Reactions to the band's live shows in the USA with Sepultura were equally strong. However, before sessions for a fifth album could begin, Archer amicably departed, to be replaced by Lee Morris, who joined for 1995's excellent *Draconian Times*, by which time Paradise Lost's popularity was such that several promotional concerts had to be performed under the alias the Painless. They subsequently signed to EMI Records.

● ALBUMS: *Lost Paradise* (Peaceville 1990)★★★, *Gothic* (Peaceville 1991)★★★, *Shades Of God* (Music For Nations 1992)★★★, *Icon* (Music For Nations 1993)★★★★, *Draconian Times* (Music For Nations 1995)★★★★, *One Second* (Music For Nations 1997)★★.

● COMPILATIONS: *The Singles Collection* 5-CD box set (Music For Nations 1997)★★★★, *Reflection* (Music For Nations 1998)★★★.

● VIDEOS: *Live Death* (1990), *Harmony Breaks* (1994).

PARADOX

This German thrash-metal outfit was formed in 1986 by ex-Warhead duo Charly Steinhauer (vocals, guitar) and Axel Blaha (drums). After a series of false starts and a track included on the *Teutonic Invasion Part 1* compilation, the line-up stabilized with the addition of Markus Spyth (guitar) and Roland Stahl (bass). Signing to UK label Roadrunner, they delivered *Product Of Imagination* in 1987, a collection of formulaic speed-metal material. *Heresy* saw a major personnel reshuffle and a marked improvement in their conversion of Metallica and Anthrax riffing. Stahl and Spyth had been replaced by Dieter Roth (guitar), Manfred Springer (guitar) and Armin Donderer (bass), with the expanded line-up allowing a greater degree of flexibility live and adding more depth to their studio sound.

● ALBUMS: *Product Of Imagination* (Roadrunner 1987)★★, *Heresy* (Roadrunner 1989)★★★★.

PARIAH (UK)

Formerly known as Satan, this Newcastle-upon-Tyne, England group became Pariah in 1988, feeling that their original name may have led to misconceptions concerning their style. They were never a true black-metal outfit, as their original moniker suggested, but were instead part of the New Wave Of British Heavy Metal scene. Pariah comprised Michael Jackson (vocals), Steve Ramsey (guitar), Russ Tippins (guitar), Graeme English (bass) and Sean Taylor (drums). Their first album was *The Kindred* in 1988, an album of hard, fast metal, characterized by the dual guitar onslaught of Ramsey and Tippins. Following *Blaze Of Obscurity*, Jackson quit and was replaced by Mark Allen, but there was no further significant progress in their career. Along with Demon, Pariah passed into history as one of the most talented metal acts of their generation to be lost to obscurity, save for mentions in reference books.

● ALBUMS: *The Kindred* (Steamhammer 1988)★★★, *Blaze Of Obscurity* (Steamhammer 1989)★★★.

PARIAH (USA)

This Florida, USA-based speed-metal quartet was formed in 1987 by the Egger brothers, with the full line-up comprising Garth Egger (vocals), Shaun

Egger (guitar), Chris Egger (drums) and Wayne Derrick (guitar). Unable to secure a record contract in the USA, they were finally signed to the Dutch Moshroom label in 1988, for whom they debuted with *Take A Walk*, a mixture of styles that alternated between derivative Anthrax/Metallica thrash and the characterless pop-metal of Europe and Bon Jovi.

● ALBUMS: *Take A Walk* (Moshroom 1988)★★.

PARIS, JEFF

This American vocalist/guitarist started his career in the jazz-rock group Pieces. He subsequently played with a number of similar bands on a short-term basis, and built up a reputation as a fine backing vocalist and talented songwriter. He worked with Cinderella, Y&T, Vixen and Lita Ford in this capacity and was offered a solo recording contract by Polygram in 1986. He debuted with *Race To Paradise* the same year, a highly polished and melodic collection of AOR anthems, similar in style to Michael Bolton and Eric Martin. *Wired Up* saw Paris toughen up his approach. The album was typical North American rock and drew comparisons with Bruce Springsteen and Bryan Adams. However, both sets failed commercially and Polygram terminated his contract in 1988.

● ALBUMS: *Race To Paradise* (Polygram 1986)★★★★, *Wired Up* (Polygram 1987)★★★.

PARR, JOHN

b. 18 November 1954. This vocalist, guitarist, composer and producer specializes in highly melodic AOR. Though British, his success had been drawn largely from the USA, where his recordings for Atlantic Records have been compared to Rick Springfield and Eddie Money. Parr composed the themes for the movies *American Anthem* and *St. Elmo's Fire*, the second of which made the UK Top 10 singles chart in 1985. The follow-up, 'Naughty Naughty', achieved a paltry number 58. He also duetted with Meat Loaf on 'Rock 'N' Roll Mercenaries', but this failed to embellish either artist's profile, stopping just short of the Top 30. Two solo albums, his self-titled debut in 1985 and *Running The Endless Mile* in 1986, both fared poorly with the critics. His finest moment remains the energetic 'St. Elmo's Fire (Man In Motion)'.

● ALBUMS: *John Parr* (Atlantic 1985)★★, *Running The Endless Mile* (Atlantic 1987)★.

PARTNERS IN CRIME

This short-lived UK 'supergroup' was put together by ex-Status Quo drummer John Coghlan. Enlisting the services of Noel McCalla (vocals, ex-Moon), Mark de Vanchque (keyboards, ex-Wildfire), Ray Major (guitar, ex-Mott) and Mac Mcaffrey (bass), they specialized in Americanized melodic rock. Debuting with *Organised Crime* in 1985, it was obvious that this set of seasoned musicians gelled together well. Produced by John Eden (Status Quo) and James Guthrie (Pink Floyd, Queensrÿche) it was a strong album in many respects, yet failed to stand out from the numerous other acts offering similar material. The band sundered soon after the album was released.

● ALBUMS: *Organised Crime* (Epic 1985)★★.

PATTO

Patto was formed in 1969 when four members of Timebox - Michael Patrick 'Patto' McGrath (b. 22 September 1942, Glasgow, Scotland, d. 4 March 1979; vocals), Peter 'Ollie' Halsall (b. 14 March 1949, Southport, Merseyside, England, d. 29 May 1992; guitar, vibes), Clive Griffiths (bass) and John Halsey (drums) - abandoned commercial constraints and embarked on a more progressive direction. Their debut, *Patto*, featured several of the group's most lasting performances. Although producer Muff Winwood opted for a rather rudimentary sound, the set contained a series of impressive songs, featuring complex signatures, excellent vocals and Halsall's superb guitar work. Sometimes frenzied, at other times restrained, his contributions enhanced an already outstanding collection. A second release, *Hold Your Fire*, exaggerated their jazz-rock persuasions, but retained the urgency and fire of their debut. Judicious overdubs ensured a fuller sound, yet Patto's interplay and empathy remained intact. Faced by commercial indifference, the group embarked on a third collection vowing to capture the irreverent side of their music. *Roll 'Em, Smoke 'Em, Put Another Line Out* was only partially successful, with 'Singing The Blues On Reds' and the compulsive 'Loud Green Song' being the stand-out tracks. The project fared no better than its predecessors and Patto broke up in 1973 when their label rejected a completed fourth album, *Monkey's Bum*. Mike Patto joined Spooky Tooth, appearing on their final album, *The Mirror*, in 1974. Halsall resurfaced in Tempest before forging a partnership with Kevin Ayers. He was reunited with Patto in 1975 as a member of Boxer, and subsequently worked alongside John Halsey in the Beatles spoof, the Rutles. The latter joined Patto in the ad hoc 'supergroup' Hinkley's Heroes, but the vocalist's career was cut short in March 1979 when he succumbed to throat cancer.

Halsall remained an in-demand session guitarist until his death in 1992. Griffiths was permanently hospitalized following a road accident. Three years later the group's original producer, Muff Winwood, compiled a remastered, double CD anthology of their best work.

● ALBUMS: *Patto* (Vertigo 1970)★★★, *Hold Your Fire* (Vertigo 1971)★★★, *Roll 'Em, Smoke 'Em, Put Another Line Out* (Vertigo 1972)★★★.

● COMPILATIONS: *A Sense Of The Absurd* 2-CD set of first two albums (Mercury 1995)★★★.

PAW

This Lawrence, Kansas, USA quartet formed in 1990 with brothers Grant (guitar) and Peter Fitch (drums) and bassist Charles Bryan, recruiting vocalist Mark Hennessy (b. Mark Thomas Joseph Brendan Hennessy, 6 May 1969, Kansas, USA) from local art-noise band King Rat, which Hennessy described as a period when 'I thought I was Nick Cave'. Paw were the leading local band, and picked up support gigs with Nirvana and the Fluid before recording their first seven-song demo at Butch Vig's Smart Studios in Wisconsin, which led to an enormous major label bidding war, won by A&M Records. *Newsweek* described Paw as 'the next Nirvana', but Hüsker Dü, Dinosaur Jr and the Replacements were probably better reference points for *Dragline*'s marriage of melody and raw guitar power, with a distinctive small-town story-telling aspect to the songs. 'Sleeping Bag' was perhaps the most poignant, telling the childhood story of a car crash that hospitalized the seriously injured Peter Fitch; when older brother Grant feared the worst, he slept in Peter's sleeping bag, 'as corny as it sounds, just to be a little closer to him'. *Dragline* deservedly received universal acclaim, and the band toured exhaustively, earning an excellent live reputation, touring Europe with Therapy? and Hammerbox, the UK with Tool, and both the UK and USA with Monster Magnet, as singles 'Sleeping Bag' and 'Couldn't Know' brought them a wider audience. The band returned to the studio in late 1994, but without Bryan, who had tired of the endless touring. The results were displayed on *Death To Traitors*, an assured album with some outstanding vocals from Hennessy.

● ALBUMS: *Dragline* (A&M 1993)★★★★, *Death To Traitors* (A&M 1995)★★★.

PEACE, LOVE AND PITBULLS

Comprising Joakim Thaström (music, lyrics, vocals), Niklas 'Hell' Hellberg (programming), Peter Puders (guitar) and Rikard Sporrong (guitar), the imaginatively named Swedish group Peace, Love And Pitbulls operate in musical territory somewhere between heavy metal and hardcore techno - Nine Inch Nails are an obvious influence. They formed around the central figure of Thaström. Previously a member of Ebba Grön - widely celebrated as Sweden's closest approximation of the Sex Pistols - in the 80s he concentrated on a solo career with mixed results. A two-year period of recuperation in Amsterdam preceded his return to Sweden to form Peace, Love And Pitbulls in 1992. The results were accurately portrayed to the press as 'a kind of vitriol reality'. Notably, the group's debut album was the first time Thaström had written lyrics in English. 'I needed to change languages because I wanted to be able to shout "Yeh, Baby!" in a song without sounding ridiculous', he told the press. Songs such as 'Do The Monkey', 'Hitch-Hike To Mars' and 'Reverberation Nation' confirmed that he lost none of his powers of outrage in translation.

● ALBUMS: *Peace, Love And Pitbulls* (MNW 1993)★★★.

PEARL JAM

This revisionist (or, depending on your viewpoint, visionary) rock quintet was formed in Seattle, USA, in the early 90s, by Jeff Ament (b. 10 March 1963, Big Sandy, Montana, USA; bass) and Stone Gossard (b. 20 July 1966, Seattle, Washington, USA; rhythm guitar). Gossard had played with Steve Turner in the Ducky Boys, the latter going on to perform with Ament in Green River. Gossard became a member when Mark Arm (like Turner, later to join Mudhoney) switched from guitar to vocals. Gossard and Ament, however, elected to continue working together when Green River washed up, and moved on to Mother Love Bone, fronted by local 'celebrity' Andrew Wood. However, that ill-fated group collapsed when, four weeks after the release of their debut album, *Apple*, Wood was found dead from a heroin overdose. Both Gossard and Ament subsequently participated in Seattle's tribute to Wood, Temple Of The Dog, alongside Chris Cornell of Soundgarden, who instigated the project, Soundgarden drummer Matt Cameron, plus Gossard's schoolfriend Mike McCready (b. 5 April 1965, Seattle, Washington, USA; guitar) and ex-Bad Radio vocalist Eddie Vedder (b. 23 December 1966, Evanson, Illinois, USA). He had been passed a tape of demos recorded by Ament, Gossard and McCready by Red Hot Chili Peppers drummer Jack Irons. Both Vedder and McCready eventually hooked up permanently with Ament and Gossard to become Pearl Jam, with the addition of drummer Dave Krusen (having originally dabbled with the name Mookie Blaylock). The band signed to Epic Records in 1991, debuting the following year with the powerful, yet melodic, *Ten*. A bold diarama, it saw the band successfully incorporate elements of their native traditions (Soundgarden, Mother Love Bone, Nirvana) with older influences such as the Doors, Velvet Underground, the Stooges and the MC5. The self-produced recording (together with Rick Parashar) showed great maturity for a debut, particularly in the full-blooded songwriting, never better demonstrated than on hit single 'Alive'. Dynamic live performances and a subtle commercial edge to their material catapulted them from obscurity to virtual superstars overnight, as the Seattle scene debate raged and Kurt Cobain accused them of 'jumping the alternative bandwagon'. In the USA *Ten* was still in the Top 20 a year and a half after its release, having sold over 10 million copies by the end of 1996 in that country alone. The touring commitments that followed, however, brought Vedder to the verge of nervous collapse. He struggled back to health in time for the Lollapalooza II tour, an appearance on *MTV Unplugged*, and Pearl Jam's cameo as Matt Dillon's 'band', Citizen Dick, in the Cameron Crowe film *Singles*. Vedder also fronted a reunited Doors on their induction into the Rock And Roll Hall Of Fame in Los Angeles at the Century Plaza hotel, performing versions of 'Roadhouse Blues', 'Break On Through' and 'Light My Fire'. The eagerly awaited 'difficult' follow-up was announced in October 1993, close on the heels of Nirvana's latest offering. While reviews were mixed, the advance orders placed the album on top of charts on both sides of the Atlantic. *Vitalogy* seemed overtly concerned with re-establishing the group's grass-roots credibility, a strong clue to which arrived in the fact that the album was available for a week on vinyl before a CD or cassette release (a theme revisited on 'Spin The Black Circle'). There were also numerous references, some oblique, others more immediate, to the death of Nirvana's Kurt Cobain. Ironically, 1994 also saw drummer Dave Abbruzzese dispensed with, amid unfounded rumours that former Nirvana drummer Dave Grohl would be invited into the ranks. This turmoil did not affect the quality of *No Code*, featuring more melody with grunge guitar replaced by steely acoustics. Jack Irons became the drummer, although he left the band temporarily in 1998.

● ALBUMS: *Ten* (Epic 1991)★★★★, *Vs.* (Epic 1993)★★★★, *Vitalogy* (Epic 1994)★★★, *No Code* (Epic 1996)★★★★, *Yield* (Epic 1998)★★★★.

● VIDEOS: *Single Video Theory* (Sony 1998).

● FURTHER READING: *Pearl Jam: The Illustrated Biography*, Brad Morrell. *Pearl Jam Live!*, Joey Lorenzo (compiler). *The Illustrated Story*, Allan Jones. *Pearl Jam & Eddie Vedder: None Too Fragile*, Martin Clarke. *Five Against One: The Pearl Jam Story*, Kim Neely.

PELL, AXEL RUDI

This German heavy metal guitar virtuoso left Steeler in 1988 to concentrate on a solo career. Influenced by Ritchie Blackmore, Yngwie Malmsteen and Tony Macalpine, he played explosive guitar pyrotechnics within a traditional metal framework. *Wild Obsession* featured Charlie Huhn (vocals), Bonfire member Jorg Deisinger (bass) and Jorg Michael (drums, ex-Rage). It was well received by the music press, but this did not translate into sales, partly owing to Pell's reluctance to take the band on tour. *Nasty Reputation* represented a major leap forward in songwriting. The heart of the music was still in the early 70s, but the guitar-work and the sheer energy of the delivery were quite remarkable. Bob Rock, now on vocals, gave the music great authority, with the expanded quintet also including Volker Krawczak (bass) and Kai Raglewski (keyboards). 1995's live album, *Made In Germany*, featured another new vocalist, with Jeff Scott Soto recruited from Yngwie Malmsteen's Rising Force.

● ALBUMS: *Wild Obsession* (Steamhammer 1989)★★★, *Nasty Reputation* (Steamhammer 1991)★★★★, *The Ballads* (Steamhammer 1993)★★★, *Made In Germany* (SPV 1995)★★.

PENTAGRAM

Among the best of the bands continuing the seminal heavy metal tradition of early Black Sabbath, the core of Pentagram was formed by Bobby Liebling (vocals) and Joe Hasselvander (drums) in the USA in 1978. Like Sabbath, their roots were in the lively white blues bands of the early 70s, which they translated into ominous, crunching riffs and dark, devilish lyrics. However, unlike Black Sabbath, who treated the infernal with ambivalence, Pentagram have always seemed much more comfortable with their Satanic themes. Their first album, *Pentagram*, was released in 1985, but by this time, Hasselvander had left, dismayed at the lack of label support, and joined Raven. Hasselvander (replaced by Stuart Rose), however, had already laid down most of the tracks for their next album, *Day of Reckoning*. Strong local and cult support was not enough to sustain Pentagram's increasingly unfashionable approach and they split in 1990. Nevertheless, this same cult appeal saw the rights for their first two albums (with their debut retitled as *Relentless*) bought by UK label Peaceville and re-released in 1993. Inspired by this renewed interest, Liebling re-formed the band with the classic line-up of Hasselvander (drums), Martin Swaney (bass) and Victor Griffin (guitar, keyboards), and released the new album *Be Forewarned.* While it is difficult to call Pentagram original, their sinisterly infectious riffs and fidelity to metal's darker roots certainly justify the band's enduring appeal.

● ALBUMS: *Pentagram* (1985)★★★, *Day Of Reckoning* (Peaceville 1987)★★★★, *Be Forewarned* (Peaceville 1994)★★★.

PERRY, JOE, PROJECT

b. Anthony Joseph Perry, 10 September 1950, Boston, Massachusetts, USA. Having severed an apprenticeship in the aspiring Jam Band, guitarist Perry then became a founder-member of Aerosmith. This durable hard rock act became one of the USA's leading attractions during the 70s, principally through the artist's exciting, riffing style and vocalist Steve Tyler's charismatic performances. Tension between the group's leading figures led to the former's departure in 1979. He subsequently formed the Joe Perry Project with Ralph Mormon (vocals), David Hull (bass) and Ronnie Stewart (drums), but neither *Let The Music Do The Talking* nor *I've Got The Rocks 'N' Rolls Again*, which featured new singer Charlie Farren, captured the fire of the guitarist's previous group. Perry then established a new line-up around Mach Bell (vocals), Danny Hargrove (bass) and Joe Pet (drums) for *Once A Rocker, Always A Rocker*, but once again the combination failed to generate commercial approbation. Former Aerosmith colleague Brad Whitford (guitar) was then added to the group, but it was disbanded in 1984 when a full-scale reunion of Aerosmith was undertaken. The ensuing *Done With Mirrors* featured the title song of the Project's debut album, but Aerosmith's successful rebirth brought Perry's external aspirations to a premature close.

● ALBUMS: *Let The Music Do The Talking* (Columbia 1980)★★★, *I've Got The Rocks 'N' Rolls Again* (Columbia 1981)★★★, *Once A Rocker, Always A Rocker* (MCA 1984)★★.

PERRY, STEVE

Following the success of *Escape* and *Frontiers*, the members of US band Journey took an extended break in order to pursue solo projects. Vocalist Steve Perry (b. 22 January 1953, Hanford, California, USA) assembled a team of respected session players to produce *Street Talk*, which displayed soul and R&B influences in both Perry's vocals and songwriting, and proved a superb showcase for his talents. *Street Talk* proved to be the most successful of the Journey solo efforts, producing an enormous US hit in 'Oh Sherrie', an emotive tribute to Perry's girlfriend, and its influence on the style of *Raised On Radio*, Journey's final album, was obvious. However, amid rumours of up to three follow-up records being scrapped, it was not until 1994 that *For The Love Of Strange Medicine* saw the resumption of Perry's career, with a more straightforward AOR style than on the previous album. Any doubts over the viability of the project after such a protracted absence were dispelled when the album made its US chart debut at number 15, and produced a US Top 10 hit with 'You Better Wait'.

● ALBUMS: *Street Talk* (Columbia 1984)★★★★, *For The Love Of Strange Medicine* (Columbia 1994)★★★.

PERSIAN RISK

The line-up of this heavy metal outfit, based in the north of England, was in a constant state of flux during their formative period in the early 80s. At one time Phil Campbell and Jon Deverill, later of Motörhead and the Tygers Of Pan Tang, respectively, were involved. The band debuted with a track on the *Heavy Metal Heroes Vol. 2* compilation, and later recorded a single for Neat Records. It took a further three years to record an album because of the regular line-up shuffles. *Rise Up* was made with the team now comprising Carl Sentance (vocals), Phil Vokins (guitar), Graham Bath (guitar), Nick Hughes (bass) and Steve Hopgood (ex-Chinatown; drums). Formularized and rather outdated, the songs were rooted in the early phase of the New Wave Of British Heavy Metal, which, unlike Persian Risk, had matured and progressed considerably since its inception. The album was unsuccessful and the band disintegrated when Bath and Hopgood left to join Paul Di'Anno's Battlezone.

● ALBUMS: *Rise Up* (Razor 1986)★★★.

PESTILENCE

This German speed/thrash metal quartet was formed by guitarists Randy Meinhard and Patrick Mameli in 1986. Enlisting the services of Marco Foddis (drums) and Martin van Drunen (vocals, bass), they debuted with a track on the *Teutonic*

Invasion II compilation (1987) on the Rock Hard label. A contract with Roadrunner ensued and they recorded *Mallevs Maleficarum*, a high-speed metallic blur reminiscent of Slayer and Testament. Meinhard quit soon after the album was released to form Sacrosanct. Ex-Theriac guitarist Patrick Uterwijk stepped in as replacement and the band entered the studio to record *Consuming Impulse*. This marked a distinct technical and musical improvement over their enthusiastic, but slightly amateurish, debut. Produced by Harris Johns, the album took off in the USA and Pestilence toured extensively with Death and Autopsy during 1990. However, van Drunen left shortly afterwards to front his own band, Asphyx (subsequently forming Submission and acting as guest vocalist on the second Comecon album), with Mameli taking over as vocalist. Pestilence finally split in 1994, with Mameli becoming increasingly hostile to the death metal fraternity that had devoured the band's work.

● ALBUMS: *Mallevs Maleficarum* (Roadrunner 1988)★★, *Consuming Impulse* (Roadrunner 1989)★★★, *Testimony To The Ancients* (Roadrunner 1991)★★, *Spheres* (Roadrunner 1993)★★★.

PET LAMB

Formed in Dublin in 1991, the four members of Pet Lamb are Dylan Phillips (guitar, vocals), Brian Mooney (guitar, vocals), Kevin Talbot (bass) and James Lillis (drums). Influenced by the hardcore assault of the Butthole Surfers and Jesus Lizard, with the songwriting shared between Phillips and Mooney, they admitted to their central inspiration being 'a mixture of lust, beer, frustration and boredom'. The group were first adopted by small independent imprint Blunt, a liaison that produced two EPs, and brought about support slots to the musically sympathetic Therapy?, NoMeansNo, Babes In Toyland and others. After a session for the John Peel programme, Roadrunner snapped up the band, packing them off to Dublin's Sonic Studios to record their debut for the label, 'Black Mask' - 'a kind of teenage sex and death fantasy, featuring Satan'. In its wake came a debut album, *Sweaty Handshake*, propelled by songs such as the defiant 'Insult To Injury' and self-loathing 'Fun With Maggots'.

● ALBUMS: *Sweaty Handshake* (Roadrunner 1995)★★★.

PETERIK, JIM

This US keyboardist/composer started his career as a session musician. His first taste of success came with 'Ides Of March' at the end of the 60s. It was 1977, however, before he finally recorded a solo album; *Don't Fight The Feeling* was a mature, melodic rock album that drew comparisons with Bob Seger, Bruce Springsteen and Michael Bolton. However, it made little headway and Peterik returned to session work, guesting on Sammy Hagar and .38 Special albums. In 1978 he formed Survivor with guitarist Frankie Sullivan and went on to multi-platinum success.

● ALBUMS: *Don't Fight The Feeling* (Scotti Bros. 1977)★★★.

PETRA

One of the first US Christian hard rock bands, Petra are an excellent musical unit who have never been swayed by passing trends and have adhered resolutely to their own ideals and beliefs. The group was formed in 1972 by vocalist Greg Volz and guitarist Bob Hartman, recruiting Mark Kelly (bass), John Slick (keyboards) and Louie Weaver (drums) to their cause. Petra specialized in a varied musical approach that incorporated elements of the Eagles, Joe Walsh, Kansas and Deep Purple. They have released well over a dozen high-quality albums to date, with their popularity having gradually waned from its peak in 1984. At this time, they appeared in the US Top 12 best-attended bands list in *Performance* magazine, while *Not Of This World* sold in excess of a quarter of a million units. John Schlitt (ex-Head East) replaced Volz after 1986's *Back To The Street* and the band adopted a heavier direction thereafter. John Lawry and Ronnie Cates replaced Slick and Kelly on keyboards and bass, respectively, in 1988. David Lichens (guitar) and Jim Cooper (keyboards) have also joined and departed. In 1996 the new line-up consisted of Pete Orta (lead guitar), Kevin Brandow (keyboards) and Lonnie Chapin (bass), together with long-standing members Weaver and Schlitt. Hartman is still part of the organization although he no longer tours, instead he prefers to take a role as writer and producer.

● ALBUMS: *Petra* (Myrrh 1974)★★, *Come And Join Us* (Myrrh 1977)★★, *Washes Whiter Than* (Star Song 1979)★★, *Never Say Die* (Star Song 1981)★★★, *More Power To Ya* (Star Song 1982)★★★, *Not Of This World* (Kingsway 1983)★★★, *Beat The System* (Kingsway 1985)★★★, *Captured In Time And Place* (Star Song

1986)★★★, *Back To The Street* (Star Song 1986)★★★, *This Means War* (Star Song 1987)★★★, *On Fire* (Star Song 1988)★★★, *Petra Means Rock* (Star Song 1989)★★★, *Petra Praise - The Rock Cries Out* (Dayspring 1989), *Beyond Belief* (Star Song 1990)★★★, *Petra Praise 22: We Need Jesus* (Word 1997)★★★.
● VIDEOS: *Captured In Time And Space* (1989).

PEZ BAND

This melodic US pop-rock outfit was formed in 1976 by vocalist Mimi Betinis and guitarist Tommy Gawenda. Enlisting the services of Mike Gorman (bass) and Mick Rain (drums), they made their debut with a self-titled album on the Passport label. The accent on the commercial dynamic was overt, with thin melodies and lightweight guitarwork. The album flopped and the band changed direction to hard-driving, blues-based rock. *Laughing In The Dark* was a remarkable improvement and featured highly engaging lead guitar, reminiscent of Gary Moore and Pat Travers. This, too, failed to find favour (perhaps because the band were already labelled as an unsuccessful pop act). Disillusioned by the lack of media response, they bowed out with a live mini-album, *30 Seconds Over Schaumberg*. The group re-formed temporarily in 1981, releasing *Cover To Cover*, but then disbanded for a final time.
● ALBUMS: *Pezband* (Passport 1977)★★, *Laughing In The Dark* (Passport 1978)★★★★, *30 Seconds Over Schaumberg* (Passport 1978)★★★, *Cover To Cover* (Passport 1981)★★★.

PHANTOM BLUE

This guitar-orientated melodic rock outfit were from Los Angeles, California, USA. The all-female line-up, comprising vocalist Gigi Hangach (vocals), guitarists Nicole Couch (guitar), Michelle Meldrum (guitar), Kim Nielsen (bass) and Linda McDonald (drums), was impressive on a technical, visual and musical level. Under the guiding hand of Shrapnel Records' guitar supremo, Mike Varney, the girls were introduced to Steve Fontano and Marty Friedman (later of Megadeth), who became responsible for producing and arranging their debut album. Comprising nine originals, *Phantom Blue* was a credible and rewarding bout of mature, individual rock that, with a sheen of production gloss to temper the screaming guitars, impressed widely. A second, long-delayed album, *Built To Perform*, saw Friedman guest once more, and included a cover version of Thin Lizzy's 'Bad Reputation', but much of the momentum had been lost. In 1994 Rana Ross replaced Nielsen on bass as the band attempted to regain lost ground.
● ALBUMS: *Phantom Blue* (Roadrunner 1989)★★★, *Built To Perform* (Roadrunner 1993)★★.

PHENOMENA

This ambitious video and musical project was co-ordinated by Tom Galley (brother of former Whitesnake guitarist Mel Galley) - the albums are concept affairs, centred on the theme of supernatural phenomena. However, utilizing an impressive list of guest musicians has not always guaranteed a good result, and Phenomena went some way towards proving this truism. With Neil Murray (bass), Cozy Powell (drums), Mel Galley (guitar) and Glenn Hughes (vocals) among the initial line-up, great things were evidently expected for *Phenomena*. However, the songs were often overtly complex and lacked a central melody line. *Dream Runner*, released two years later, suffered from similar problems, but the music was less of a disappointment. It featured an impeccable array of guests once more, with Ray Gillen, Max Bacon, Scott Gorham, Kyoji Yamamoto and John Wetton contributing in one form or another. The album received good reviews in the music media, but sold poorly. As a result, plans to make the Phenomena projects into films were aborted.
● ALBUMS: *Phenomena* (Bronze 1985)★★, *Phenomena II - Dream Runner* (Arista 1987)★★.

PHOENIX

This UK group rose from the ashes of Argent in 1975. A trio, the band comprised John Verity (vocals, guitar), Robert Henrit (drums) and Jim Rodford (keyboards, bass). They continued in much the same vein as before - hard rock infused with melody and a keen sense of dynamics - and debuted with a self-titled album in 1976, before landing the support slot to Ted Nugent's UK tour. The band proved an excellent live proposition, but this was never translated into album sales, and they split after just 12 months together. In 1979 Verity and Henrit re-formed Phoenix with Russ Ballard (keyboards, vocals), Bruce Turgon (bass), Ray Minnhinnett (guitar) and Michael Des Barres (vocals). This short-lived collaboration produced *In Full View*, a nondescript melodic rock album that sold poorly. The band disintegrated shortly afterwards, with Verity and Henrit joining Charlie and then later forming Verity, under the vocalist's own surname.
● ALBUMS: *Phoenix* (CBS 1976)★★★, *In Full View* (Charisma 1980)★★.

PICTURE

This Dutch heavy metal quartet was formed in 1979 by Ronald van Prooyen (lead vocals) and Jan Bechtum (guitar). With the addition of bassist Rinus Vreugdenhil and drummer Laurens 'Bakkie' Bakker, they modelled themselves on British bands, most noticeably Uriah Heep, Deep Purple and Motörhead. They went through numerous line-up changes during their seven-year, seven-album career, but produced consistently high-quality material throughout. Vocalists included Pete Lovell, Shmoulik Avigal and Bert Heerink (ex-Vandenberg), while Chris van Jaarsueld, Henry van Manen and Rob van Enhuizen were responsible for six-string duties at one time or another. The band folded in 1987, but played a one-off reunion concert the following year.

● ALBUMS: *Picture* (Backdoor 1980)★★★, *Heavy Metal Ears* (Backdoor 1981)★★★, *Diamond Dreamer* (Backdoor 1982)★★★★, *Eternal Dark* (Backdoor 1984)★★★, *Traitor* (Backdoor 1985)★★★, *Every Story Needs Another Picture* (Backdoor 1986)★★★, *Marathon* (Touchdown 1987)★★★.

PIGEONHED

Pigeonhed managed to develop a new, industrial spin on the grunge sound at a time when most observers were beginning to dismiss it. Both the full-time band members have an impressive pedigree in the Seattle-inspired scene, Shawn Smith (vocals) being an ongoing member of Brad (with Pearl Jam's Stone Gossard) and Satchel, and Steve Fisk (samples) having worked with Nirvana, Soundgarden and Screaming Trees. It is the sonic possibilities of Fisk's tape manipulation that allow the band to stand out from their more puritanically guitar-orientated colleagues, deploying influences as diverse as techno, gospel and p-funk among the usual noisy dynamics. Pigeonhed's second album amounted to a gathering of the post-Cobain clans, including contributions from Matt Chamberlain (Pearl Jam), Kim Thayil (Soundgarden) and Jerry Cantrell (Alice In Chains).

● ALBUMS: *Pigeonhed* (Sub Pop 1993)★★★, *The Full Sentence* (Sub Pop 1997)★★★.

PINK FAIRIES

The name 'Pink Fairies' was initially applied to a fluid group of musicians later known as Shagrat. The original Tolkien-inspired appellation was resurrected in 1970 when one of their number, Twink (b. John Alder, 1944, Colchester, Essex, England), erstwhile drummer in Tomorrow and the Pretty Things, joined former Deviants Paul Rudolph (b. USA; guitar, vocals), Duncan Sanderson (bass, vocals) and Russell Hunter (drums). The Fairies' debut album, *Never Neverland*, was a curious amalgam of primeval rabble-rousing ('Say You Love Me') and English psychedelia ('Heavenly Man'). It also featured 'Do It' and 'Uncle Harry's Last Freak Out', two songs that became fixtures of the group's live set as they became stalwarts of the free festival and biker circuits. Twink left the band in 1971 and the remaining trio completed the disappointing *What A Bunch Of Sweeties* with the help of Trevor Burton from the Move. Rudolph, later to join Hawkwind, was briefly replaced by Mick Wayne before Larry Wallis joined for *Kings Of Oblivion*, the group's most exciting and unified release. The trio split up in 1974, but the following year joined Rudolph and Twink for a one-off appearance at London's Chalk Farm Roundhouse. A farewell tour, with Sanderson, Wallis and Hunter, extended into 1977, by which time Martin Stone (ex-Chilli Willi And The Red Hot Peppers) had been added to the line-up. The Pink Fairies were then officially dissolved, but the original line-up, without Rudolph, but including Wallis, were reunited in 1987 for *Kill 'Em 'N' Eat 'Em* before going their separate ways again.

● ALBUMS: *Never Neverland* (Polydor 1971)★★★, *What A Bunch Of Sweeties* (Polydor 1972)★★, *Kings Of Oblivion* (Polydor 1973)★★★, *Live At The Roundhouse* (Big Beat 1982)★★, *Previously Unreleased* (Big Beat 1984)★★, *Kill 'Em 'N' Eat 'Em* (Demon 1987)★★.

● COMPILATIONS: *Flashback* (Polydor 1975)★★★, *Pink Fairies* (Polydor 1990)★★★, *Mandies & Mescaline Round At Uncle Harry's* (New Millennium 1998)★★★.

PITCH SHIFTER

Nottingham, England-based quartet comprising Jonathan Clayden (vocals), Jonathan Carter (guitar, programming), D (drums) and Mark Clayden (bass). In early 1991 they signed to Peaceville Records and launched their career with the release of *Industrial*. Among those impressed with the group's visceral guitar assault (at that time also featuring second guitarist Stuart Toolin, and no drummer) was disc jockey John Peel, who invited them to perform three tracks on his show in May 1991. Moving over to Earache Records, they recorded their debut for the label in January of the following year, with the *Submit* mini-album. For its full-length follow-up the group increased the ratio of technology, though its application remained studiously intense. The lyrics built on the themes of oppression and social injustice, while the use of samplers and sequencers offered an extra aural dimension. Touring with Treponem Pal, Consolidated, Neurosis and Biohazard ensued - and this musical melting pot produced the germ of an idea within the band. The resultant *The Remix Wars* saw the band revisiting their back catalogue, allowing access also to other sympathetic hands, including Therapy?, Biohazard and rappers Gunshot.

● ALBUMS: *Industrial* (Peaceville 1991)★★★★, *Submit* mini-album (Earache 1992)★★★, *Desensitized* (Earache 1993)★★★, *The Remix Wars* (Earache 1994)★★★★, *Infotainment* (Earache 1996)★★★, *www.pitchshifter.com* (Geffen 1998)★★★.

● VIDEOS: *Deconstruction* (1992).

PIXIES

This US group was formed in Boston, Massachusetts, by room-mates Charles Michael Kittridge Thompson IV aka Black Francis (b. Charles Francis Kitteridge III, 1965, Long Beach, California, USA; vocals, guitar) and Joey Santiago (guitar). A newspaper advertisement, requiring applicants for a 'Hüsker Dü/Peter, Paul And Mary band', solicited bassist Kim Deal (b. 10 June 1961, Dayton, Ohio, USA) who in turn introduced drummer David Lovering. Originally known as Pixies In Panoply, the quartet secured a recording contract on the UK independent label 4AD Records on the strength of a series of superior demo tapes. Their debut release, *Come On Pilgrim*, introduced the band's abrasive, powerful sound and Francis's oblique lyrics. *Surfer Rosa*, produced by Big Black's Steve Albini, exaggerated the savage fury of its predecessor and the set was acclaimed Album Of The Year in much of the UK rock press. The superlative *Doolittle* emphasized the quartet's grasp of melody, yet retained their drive, and this thrilling collection scaled the national Top 10, aided and abetted by the band's most enduring single, 'Monkey Gone To Heaven'. The Pixies were now a highly popular attraction and their exciting live performances enhanced a growing reputation, establishing clear stage favourites in 'Debaser', 'Cactus', 'Wave Of Mutilation' and 'Bone Machine'. 1990's *Bossanova* showed an undiminished fire with a blend of pure pop with 'Allison' and sheer ferocity in 'Rock Music'. The band found themselves the darlings of the rock press and were once again widely regarded for recording one of the top albums of the year. Kim Deal, meanwhile, attracted glowing reviews for her offshoot project, the Breeders. *Trompe Le Monde* was, if anything, an even harsher collection than those that had preceded it, prompting some critics to describe it as the 'Pixies' heavy metal album'. Following the rechristened Frank Black's departure for a solo career in early 1993 the band effectively folded, but the group's reputation continues to outshine any of the membership's concurrent or subsequent projects. Released in 1997, the excellent CD compilation *Death To The Pixies* confirmed the band's lasting influence.

● ALBUMS: *Come On Pilgrim* (4AD 1987)★★★, *Surfer Rosa* (4AD 1988)★★★★, *Doolittle* (4AD 1989)★★★★, *Bossanova* (4AD 1990)★★★, *Trompe Le Monde* (4AD 1991)★★★.

● COMPILATIONS: *Death To The Pixies 1987-1991* (4AD 1997)★★★★, *At The BBC* (4AD 1998)★★★.

PLANT, ROBERT

b. 20 August 1948, West Bromwich, West Midlands, England. Plant's early career was spent in several Midlands-based R&B bands, including the New Memphis Bluesbreakers and Crawling King Snakes, the latter of which featured drummer and future colleague John Bonham. In 1965 Plant joined Lee John Crutchley, Geoff Thompson and Roger Beamer in Listen, a Motown-influenced act, later signed to CBS Records. A cover version of 'You Better Run', originally recorded by the (Young) Rascals made little headway, and Plant was then groomed for a solo career with two 1967 singles, 'Laughing, Crying, Laughing' and 'Long Time Coming'. Having returned to Birmingham, the singer formed Band Of Joy in which his growing interest in US 'west coast' music flourished. This promising group broke up in 1968 and following a brief association with blues veteran Alexis Korner, Plant then joined another local act, Hobstweedle. It was during this tenure that guitarist Jimmy Page invited the singer to join Led Zeppelin. Plant's reputation as a dynamic vocalist and frontman was forged as a member of this highly influential unit, but he began plans for a renewed solo career following the death of John Bonham in 1980. *Pictures At Eleven* unveiled a new partnership with Robbie Blunt (guitar), Paul Martinez (bass) and Jezz Woodruffe (keyboards) and while invoking the singer's past, also showed him open to new musical directions. *The Principle Of Moments* contained the restrained UK/US Top 20 hit, 'Big Log' (1983), and inspired an ambitious world tour. Plant then acknowledged vintage R&B in the

Honeydrippers, an *ad hoc* group that featured Page, Jeff Beck and Nile Rodgers, whose mini-album spawned a US Top 3 hit in 'Sea Of Love'. Having expressed a desire to record less conventional music, Plant fashioned *Shaken 'N' Stirred*, which divided critics who either praised its ambition or declared it too obtuse. The singer then disbanded his group, but resumed recording in 1987 on becoming acquainted with a younger pool of musicians, including Phil Johnstone, Dave Barrett, Chris Blackwell and Phil Scragg. *Now And Zen* was hailed as a dramatic return to form and a regenerated Plant felt confident enough to include Zeppelin material in live shows. Indeed, one of the album's stand-out tracks, 'Tall Cool One', featured a cameo from Jimmy Page and incorporated samples of 'Black Dog', 'Whole Lotta Love' and 'The Ocean', drawn from their former group's extensive catalogue. The singer's artistic rejuvenation continued on *Manic Nirvana* and the excellent *Fate Of Nations*, before again joining up with Jimmy Page for the *Unledded/Walking Into Clarksdale* projects, satisfying those who would never have the vocalist forget his past.

● ALBUMS: *Pictures At Eleven* (Swan Song 1982)★★★, *The Principle Of Moments* (Swan Song 1983)★★, *Skaken 'N' Stirred* (Esparanza 1985)★★, *Now And Zen* (Esparanza 1989)★★★, *Manic Nirvana* (Atlantic 1990)★★★, *Fate Of Nations* (Fontana 1993)★★★, with Jimmy Page *Unledded/No Quarter* (Fontana 1994)★★★★, with Page *Walking Into Clarksdale* (Atlantic 1998)★★★★.

● VIDEOS: *Knebworth 90* (1990), *Mumbo Jumbo* (1991).

● FURTHER READING: *Robert Plant*, Michael Gross. *Led Zeppelin's Robert Plant Through The Mirror*, Mike Randolph.

PLEASURE BOMBS

Comprising Mark Lewis (guitar), Janet Daily (vocals), Bobby Nei (bass), Joey Crifo (drums) and David Matos (guitar), US heavy metal band Pleasure Bombs made their debut for Atco Records in 1991 with *Days Of Heaven*. The stand-out track on this collection of medium-paced, melodic hard rock was 'Summer's Over', the video for which achieved airplay on the UK's *Raw Power* television show. Despite good reviews, the group were compromised by a lack of media exposure, and this above-average record was never followed up.

● ALBUMS: *Days Of Heaven* (Atco 1991)★★★.

PLEASURE ELITE

Pleasure Elite were formed in winter 1990 in Seattle, USA, around pseudonymous musicians V. Blast (vocals), Lord Hoop De' Luv (guitar, vocals, sequencer), the Deacon (keyboards), Razor Monkey (drums) and Father Shark (guitar). Boasting a frenetic live show that won them early supports with KMFDM, Rage Against The Machine, Jesus Jones and Alien Sex Fiend, the band's lyrical concerns included media manipulation, lust and corruption. They made their debut with *Bad Juju* in May 1994, an album that delighted in crossing sundry musical frontiers including industrial metal and more traditional rock structures. With production by Pearl Jam associate Don Gilmore, the collection was promoted with the release of a strong attendant single, 'Media Feed'.

● ALBUMS: *Bad Juju* (Music For Nations 1994)★★★.

POINT BLANK

Essentially from the same mould as Texan blues boogie supremos ZZ Top, Point Blank's first two releases were produced by Bill Ham, who had also masterminded the latter band's rise to fame. Point Blank's line-up has been somewhat fluid, but in the main it featured John O'Daniel (vocals), Rusty Burns (guitar), Kim Davis (guitar), Bill Randolph (bass), Mike Hamilton (keyboards) and Buzzy Gren (drums). Their third venture into the recording studio resulted in *Airplay*, which saw a slightly less intensive boogie stance, but this was rectified on *The Hard Way*, a part-live release that saw the band in blistering form. Bobby Keith replaced John O'Daniel in 1981 and their last two albums reflected a more radio-friendly approach to their sound, but without commercial success.

● ALBUMS: *Point Blank* (Arista 1976)★★★, *Second Season* (Arista 1977)★★★, *Airplay* (MCA 1979)★★, *The Hard Way* (MCA 1980)★★★★, *American Excess* (MCA 1981)★★★, *On A Roll* (MCA 1982)★★★.

POISON

This heavy metal band was formed in Pennsylvania, USA, in the spring of 1983 by Bret Michaels (b. Bret Sychalk, 15 March 1962, Harrisburg, Pennsylvania, USA; vocals) and Rikki Rockett (b. Richard Ream, 8 August 1959, Pennsylvania, USA; drums). They were soon joined by Bobby Dall (b. Kuy Kendall, 2 November 1958, Miami, Florida, USA; bass) and Matt Smith (guitar). Legendarily, Slash from Guns N'Roses also auditioned at one point. The quartet played local clubs as Paris, before moving to Los Angeles and changing their name. It was at this point that Smith left the band and was replaced by C.C. Deville (b. 14 May 1963, Brooklyn, New York, USA; guitar). They were signed by Enigma Records in 1985 and released their first album in 1986, which went double platinum in America and produced three hits. *Open Up And Say...Ahh!* gave them their first US number 1, 'Every Rose Has Its Thorn'. Four other singles were also released, including a cover version of 'Your Mama Don't Dance' which was a major US hit for Loggins And Messina in 1972. Poison were originally considered a 'glam band' because of the make-up they wore, but by the release of *Flesh And Blood*, in 1990, this image had been toned down dramatically. That year they also played their first UK shows, and fans declared their love of songs such as 'Unskinny Bop' and 'Talk Dirty To Me' when the band made their official UK debut in front of 72,500 people at the Donington Monsters of Rock Festival on 18 August 1990. The following year saw Deville replaced on guitar by the much-travelled Richie Kotzen. *Native Tongue* added brass with the Tower Of Power Horns and established the band alongside Bon Jovi as purveyors of image-conscious, hard melodic rock. As well as many supporters, this inevitably also saw them pilloried by more purist elements in heavy metal fandom. In 1994 Michaels' face appeared on the news-stands once more when he dated *Baywatch* star Pamela Anderson, before being unceremoniously 'dumped'. Blues Saraceno replaced Smith in 1995. In 1996 Michaels began an acting career, taking a major role in *A Letter From Death Row*.

● ALBUMS: *Look What The Cat Dragged In* (Enigma 1986)★★★, *Open Up And Say ... Ahh!* (Capitol 1988)★★★★, *Flesh And Blood* (Capitol 1990)★★★★, *Native Tongue* (Capitol 1993)★★★.

● COMPILATIONS: *Greatest Hits* (Capitol 1997)★★★.

● VIDEOS: *A Sight For Sore Ears* (1990), *Flesh, Blood And Videotape* (1991), *7 Days Live* (1994).

POISON IDEA

These hardcore heavyweights' broad appearance (nearly all the band members could be generously described as obese) gave little credence to the harsh, speedy rock path they pursued. Formed in Portland, Oregon, USA, in late 1980, their first incarnation featured Jerry A. (vocals), Pig Champion (guitar), Chris Tense (bass) and Dean Johnson (drums). They debuted with the unwieldy EP *Pick Your King*, which contained no less than 13 tracks, packaged in a sleeve featuring Elvis Presley on one side and Jesus Christ on the other. By the time of *Kings Of Punk* they were slightly more tuneful, but no less belligerent. However, Johnson and Tense were both fired and replaced by Steve 'Thee Slayer Hippy' Hanford (drums) and Tim Paul (ex-Final Warning, now Gruntruck; bass). The sound was also filled out with additional guitarist Vegetable (ex-Mayhem). However, Tim Paul only lasted one abortive gig (just one song, in fact) before being replaced by the returning Tense. His tenure, though slightly longer, lasted only until the release of *War All The Time*, after which Mondo (also ex-Mayhem) joined. The line-up wars continued after 'Getting The Fear' was released, with Vegetable sacked on New Year's Eve, replaced by Kid Cocksman (ex-Gargoyle; guitar), and Mondo quit after the appropriately titled 'Discontent'. Myrtle Tickner (ex-Oily Bloodmen) then became the band's fourth bass player. Aldine Striknine (guitar, ex-Maimed For Life) stepped in for the next casualty, Cocksman (apparently sacked for being too thin), to record *Feel The Darkness*, after which Mondo returned once more, this time on second guitar. Despite the line-up confusions and obvious gimmickry, they produced a body of work of some substance, characterized by a lyrical preference for matters alcoholic and sexual, with some of the world's great song titles ('Record Collectors Are Pretentious Assholes', etc.). Live, they were both enormously impressive and impressively enormous. After *We Must Burn* Poison Idea disbanded, with Tense and Johnson going on to form Apartment 3G. In 1996 the band re-formed with Jerry A and Champion recruiting Johnson (drums) and Tense (bass), and releasing *Pig's Last Stand*.

● ALBUMS: *Kings Of Punk* (Pusmort 1986)★★★, *War All The Time* (Alchemy 1987)★★★, *Record Collectors Are Pretentious Assholes* (Bitzcore 1989)★★★, *Poison Idea* (In Your Face 1989)★★★, *Feel The Darkness* (Vinyl Solution 1990)★★★, *Pajama Party* (Vinyl Solution 1992)★★★, *Blank, Blackout, Vacant* (Vinyl Solution 1992)★★★, *We Must Burn* (Vinyl Solution 1993)★★★, *Pig's Last Stand* (Sub Pop 1996)★★★.

PORNO FOR PYROS

This theatrical rock act was formed by Jane's Addiction frontman Perry Farrell (b. 29 March 1959, Queens, New York, USA) in 1992, following the demise of his previous act. Enlisting former bandmate Stephen Perkins (b. 13 September 1967, Los Angeles, California, USA; drums), Martyn Le

Noble (b. 14 April 1969, Vlaardingen, Netherlands; bass) and Peter DiStefano (b. 10 July 1965, Los Angeles, California, USA; guitar), Farrell began developing his new band's direction during their low-key live debut on the Lollapalooza II second stage. With Farrell's creative input and Perkins' rhythmic talents, similarities between Porno For Pyros and Jane's Addiction's recorded output were inevitable, but the subtle shift in musical direction became more obvious in the live setting. Porno For Pyros' shows were closer in character to a carnival, with Farrell as ringmaster, than a traditional rock show, with the band augmented not only by Matt Hyde's keyboards but also by a cast of dancers and performance artists, from the ballerina pirouetting to 'Orgasm', to the sharp contrast of the fire-breathing stripper who appeared during 'Porno For Pyros'. The band subsequently headlined at the 1993 UK Reading Festival in spectacular fashion, and appeared at the Woodstock Anniversary show in 1994. Farrell had become a real star and great media fodder by the time their breakthrough album, *Good God's Urge*, was issued. DiStefano was diagnosed as having cancer in October 1996, and the band cancelled all work while he underwent chemotherapy. In 1997 Farrell announced the resurrection of Jane's Addiction for live dates, and not long afterwards it was reported that Porno For Pyros had disbanded.

● ALBUMS: *Porno For Pyros* (Warners 1993)★★★, *Good God's Urge* (Warners 1996)★★★.

● FURTHER READING: *Perry Farrell: Saga Of A Hypster*, Dave Thompson.

POSSESSED

Formed in San Francisco, California, USA, in 1983, this heavy metal band consisted of Jeff Beccarra (bass, vocals), Mike Tarrao (guitar), Larry Lalonde (guitar) and Mike Sus (drums). Through early demos and their inclusion on the *Metal Massacre VI* compilation album, released on Metal Blade Records in 1984, the band attracted the attention of Combat Records, who promptly signed them. This resulted in their debut, *Seven Churches*, released in 1985. Growling vocals and ultra-fast Slayer-influenced riffs were the order of the day and the band quickly made their mark on the death metal underground. The next album, produced by ex-Rods drummer Carl Canedy, was *Beyond The Gates*, released in 1986. The band toured throughout Europe building a strong following, and on their return to America they recorded and released a mini-album entitled *The Eyes Of Terror*. Produced by guitar maestro Joe Satriani, the album was, as expected, heavily guitar-orientated, but owing to internal wrangles, the band folded soon after its release.

● ALBUMS: *Seven Churches* (Roadrunner 1985)★★★★, *Beyond The Gates* (Under One Flag 1986)★★★★, *The Eyes Of Terror* mini-album (Under One Flag 1987)★★★.

POWELL, COZY

b. Colin Powell, 29 December 1947, England, d. 5 April 1998. Powell was a virtuoso drummer who played with the likes of Jeff Beck, Rainbow and Emerson, Lake And Powell. His musical career began in 1965 when he was a member of the Sorcerers, before working with Casey Jones And The Engineers for a couple of months, then returning to his first band, who changed their name first to Youngblood, and then to Ace Kefford Stand. Powell then moved on to Big Bertha. In 1971 Jeff Beck founded a new group consisting of Robert Tench (vocals), Max Middleton (keyboards), Clive Chaman (bass), and Powell. The Jeff Beck group was among the premier exponents of R&B jazz-rock, and Powell appears on two of the band's albums. It was after his work with Bedlam, the band he formed in 1972 with Frank Aiello (vocals), Dennis Ball (bass) and Dave Ball (guitar), that Powell came to the attention of producer Micky Most, resulting in lucrative session work for Most's RAK label. This gave Powell the opportunity to release hit singles such as 'Dance With The Devil' and 'The Man In Black'. This latter single was recorded while Powell was in Cozy Powell's Hammer, a group with Bedlam's Aiello as vocalist, along with newcomers Don Airey (keyboards), Clive Chaman (bass) and Bernie Marsden (guitar). This project came to an end in April 1975 when Powell decided to take a break and spend three months motor racing. Strange Brew was formed in July 1975, with Powell on drums, but this project lasted for little more than a month. He then joined Ritchie Blackmore's Rainbow, with whom he played until 1980, his farewell concert with them being at the first Donington Rock festival. In 1981 Powell appeared on the Michael Schenker Group's *MSG*, and in the mid-80s replaced Carl Palmer to become the third member of Emerson, Lake And Powell. He also released three solo sets in the early 80s, working with Gary Moore among other renowned musicians. The album he recorded with Emerson, Lake And Powell enjoyed little chart success and his tenure with the group was short, as was now becoming customary for the artist (he also played for two years in Whitesnake). In 1990

Powell appeared on and produced Black Sabbath's *Headless Cross*, and worked with Brian May. In the mid-90s he formed the Splinter Group with Nigel Watson and the legendary Peter Green, touring and releasing an album. Powell was about to record a solo album when he was killed in a car crash near Bristol in April 1998.

POWER

US quartet from New Jersey, New York, USA, built on the skills of Alan Tecchio (ex-Hades, Watchtower; vocals), Daniel Dalley (guitar), Mike Watt (drums) and Bill Krohn (bass). Watt had previously attended Boston's Berklee College Of Music, while acclaimed guitarist Dalley had released a solo instrumental album in 1989, as well as being a regular interviewee in musicians' magazines. However, frontman Tecchio was the best-known member, and was concurrently a member of Non-Fiction. Power signed to European label Rock The Nation Records for the release of *Justice Of Fire* in 1994, which typically addressed its thematic constructs against a background of riffing and power surges.

● ALBUMS: *Justice Of Fire* (RTN 1994)★★★.

PRAYING MANTIS

Formed in London, England, in 1977, Praying Mantis were at the forefront of the New Wave Of British Heavy Metal. The original line-up consisted of Tino 'Troy' Neophytou (guitar, vocals), Robert Angelo (guitar), Tino's brother Chris 'Troy' Neophytou (bass, vocals) and Mick Ransome (drums). Through early demo recordings the band attracted the attention of heavy-metal club DJ Neal Kay, who helped them to release an independent three-track EP, *The Soundhouse Tapes Vol. 2*, a title also used by Iron Maiden for their first release. The band's career can be closely linked with Iron Maiden during those early years as, in addition to both bands appearing on the *Metal For Muthas* compilation released by EMI Records in 1980, they also toured England together. Signing to Arista Records and replacing Robert Angelo (who joined Weapon in July 1981) and Mick Ransome with guitarist/vocalist Steve Carroll and ex-Ten Years After drummer Dave Potts, the band's debut, *Time Tells No Lies*, was released in 1981. It was not well received, owing to the lacklustre production and basic melodic rock sound. The band decided a line-up change was needed, replacing the departed Steve Carroll with ex-Grand Prix vocalist Bernie Shaw, and they also recruited keyboard player Jon Bavin. This line-up went on to record 'Turn The Tables' for a compilation album released on the Yet Records label in the mid-80s. Through a lack of media interest the band metamorphosed into Stratus, who specialized in standard melodic rock and also featured ex-Iron Maiden drummer Clive Burr. To celebrate the 10th anniversary of the N.W.O.B.H.M. the band re-formed early in 1990 to tour Japan as part of the British All Stars. This new line-up consisted of founder-members Tino and Chris Troy, ex-Iron Maiden vocalist Paul Di'Anno, ex-Iron Maiden guitarist Dennis Stratton and ex-Weapon drummer Bruce Bisland.

● ALBUMS: *Time Tells No Lies* (Arista 1981)★★, *Predator In Disguise* (1993)★★.

PRECIOUS METAL

This US glam-metal rock group was formed in Los Angeles, California, in the mid-80s. They came to the public's attention via their 1985 debut, *Right Here, Right Now*, which was produced by AOR producer and guitar-hero Paul Sabu. An all-female outfit, they featured Leslie Wasser (vocals), Janet Robin (guitar), Mara Fox (guitar), Alex Rylance (bass) and Carol Control (drums). Unfairly categorized alongside 70s female group the Runaways, Precious Metal set about forging an original style. They were hampered in this by the inability of the hard rock press to engage critically with female bands above and beyond obvious comparisons and cosmetic factors. Their second and third album releases demonstrated that, at the very least, there was more potential at work than they were being given credit for.

● ALBUMS: *Right Here, Right Now* (Polygram 1985)★★★, *That Kind Of Girl* (Chameleon 1988)★★★, *Precious Metal* (Chameleon 1990)★★★.

PRETTY MAIDS

This Danish heavy metal quintet was formed in 1981 by vocalist Ronnie Atkins and guitarist Ken Hammer. Taking their musical brief from British acts Deep Purple, Judas Priest and UFO, their style was such that enthusiasm often outweighed originality. The band has undergone numerous line-up changes, with the current outfit comprising Atkins and Hammer along with Ricky Marx (guitar), Allan Delong (bass) and Phil Moorhead (drums). Although competent musicians, at times their delivery, image, and song titles provoked Spinal Tap comparisons in the press. *Future World* from 1987 was the band's strongest release to date. The more recent Roger Glover-produced *Jump The Gun* failed to offer anything new, aside from affording the band the opportunity of working with one of their heroes.

● ALBUMS: *Pretty Maids* (Bullet 1983)★★★, *Red, Hot And Heavy* (CBS 1984)★★★, *Future World* (CBS 1987)★★★★, *Jump The Gun* (CBS 1990)★★.

PRIMUS

The vast majority of reviewers can generally agree on one word to describe Primus - weird. Formed in San Francisco in 1984 by former Blind Illusion bassist Les Claypool, seven drummers passed through before Tim 'Herb' Alexander settled in, with Claypool's Blind Illusion colleague, ex-Possessed man Larry Lalonde, replacing original guitarist Todd Huth shortly before the band recorded their debut. Musically, the band are highly talented and original, mixing funk, punk, thrash, metal and rock in their own intense manner, once described by Claypool as 'psychedelic polka'. Claypool and Alexander produce quirky, sometimes hypnotic rhythms, accentuating each other's playing, while former Joe Satriani pupil Lalonde creates and colours within the framework, although his playing owes more to Frank Zappa than to that of his old teacher. Claypool's vocals lean towards cartoonish narrative, with lyrics of a suitably abstract and humorous nature, drawing from both life and his film and literary influences. A common theme to all their albums is marine life, reflecting the band's passion for sea-fishing (they have played with fish-shaped covers on their vocal microphones). Their debut, *Suck On This*, was a self-financed live set successfully released on their own Prawn Song label, and much of the material was to feature on *Fizzle Fry*, an independent studio release that won a Bay Area Music Award and, helped by touring with Faith No More, Jane's Addiction, 24-7 Spyz and Living Colour, a major recording contract. *Sailing The Seas Of Cheese* further raised their profile, with their reworking of 'Tommy The Cat' from the debut (with a Tom Waits guest vocal) featuring in hit movie *Bill And Ted's Bogus Journey*. A lengthy world tour in support of Rush was then followed by stadium dates with U2. Any doubts as to the band being a sufficient draw for the closing (effectively headlining) slot on the 1993 Lollapalooza tour were dispelled when *Pork Soda* debuted in the US charts at number 7, producing a hit in 'My Name Is Mud'. Claypool would also hook up with Huth and former Primus drummer Jay Lane to form side-project Sausage, recording *Riddles Are Abound Tonight* for Interscope in 1994. *Tales From The Punch Bowl* was a major hit in the USA during 1995. Alexander was replaced by ex-Godflesh Brian Mantia in August 1996. In 1997 Primus provided the theme music to US animation series *South Park*.

● ALBUMS: *Suck On This* (Prawn Song 1990)★★, *Frizzle Fry* (Caroline 1990)★★★, *Sailing The Seas Of Cheese* (Interscope 1991)★★★, *Pork Soda* (Interscope 1993)★★★, *Tales From The Punch Bowl* (Interscope 1995)★★★★, *The Brown Album* (Interscope 1997)★★★, *Rhinoplasty* (Interscope 1998)★★★.

PRINCESS PANG

This New York-based rock quintet was formed in 1986 around the nucleus of Jeni Foster (vocals), Ronnie Roze (bass) and Brian Keats (drums). The line-up was finally completed a year later by the addition of guitarists Jay Lewis and Andy Tyernon. Signing to Metal Blade Records, they were introduced to Ron St. Germain (of Bad Brains fame) who eventually handled the production of their debut. Released in 1989, it was a gutsy hard rock album, full of tales of New York's low-life. Foster, with her aggressive delivery, drew comparisons to Guns N' Roses' Axl Rose, though the band failed to capitalize on the attentive press they initially received.

● ALBUMS: *Princess Pang* (Roadrunner 1989)★★★.

PRISM

This Canadian rock group has always proved difficult to categorize in terms of musical style, and major commercial success has proven similarly elusive. Their most stable line-up comprised Ron Tabak (vocals - replaced by Henry Small in 1981), Lindsay Mitchell (guitar), Al Harlow (bass) and Rocket Norton (drums). Their first two releases on the Ariola label were lightweight pop rock work-outs with layered keyboards fills, while *Armageddon* saw the band, now signed to the Capitol label, move towards a heavier, grandiose style. with several lengthy compositions. Their next two recordings saw further line-up changes and resulted in a more typical American rock sound, ideal for radio consumption. In the process they found considerable success as a live act on the US circuit. However, just as long-term rewards seemed within reach, Ron Tabak was killed in a car crash during 1984. Prism died with him.

● ALBUMS: *Prism* (Ariola 1977)★★★, *See Forever Eyes* (Ariola 1978)★★, *Armageddon* (Ariola 1979)★★★, *Young And Restless* (Capitol 1980)★★★, *Small Change* (Capitol 1981)★★, *Beat Street* (Capitol 1983)★★★.

● COMPILATIONS: *The Best Of Prism* (Phonogram 1988)★★★.

PRO-PAIN

This New York hardcore outfit was assembled by the former Crumbsuckers rhythm section of Gary Meskill (bass, vocals) and Dan Richardson (drums) after the demise of their old band. Tom Klimchuck provided the guitars on *Foul Taste Of Freedom*, a full-blooded and aggressive hardcore blast given a brutally heavy sound by producer Alex Perialas, and matched by typically challenging lyrics, an approach that drew Pantera and Biohazard comparisons. It also impressed Roadrunner Records sufficiently to gain the band a contract. However, Klimchuck departed shortly after the release to be replaced by Nick St Dennis, with a second guitarist in Mike Hollman (ex-Possessed) added later. He was in turn replaced by Rob Moschetti. Pro-Pain ran into problems over the original cover for *The Truth Hurts*, which depicted a stitched-up female torso after an autopsy, while the inner artwork featured a series of disturbing police photographs of street crime victims from the early 90s. Despite the fact that the cover was from an art exhibit in a prominent Indiana gallery and that the police photos were public domain, the cover was obscured by a large sticker in the USA, while it was replaced entirely in the UK, with the original available by mail order. The music, meanwhile, had acquired a new groove from the band's touring experience, while Meskil's lyrics remained true to his roots, with the social decay in his Long Island home a favourite subject.

● ALBUMS: *Foul Taste Of Freedom* (Energy 1992)★★★, *The Truth Hurts* (Roadrunner 1994)★★★, *Contents Under Pressure* (Edel 1996)★★, *Pro-Pain* (High Gain/Active 1997)★★★.

● COMPILATIONS: *The Best Of Pro-Pain* (High Again 1998)★★★.

PRONG

This US thrash-hardcore rock trio was formed in the mid-80s. Hailing from New York's lower east side, the band comprised Tommy Victor (vocals, guitar), Mike Kirkland (vocals, bass) and Ted Parsons (drums), and caused an immediate stir with their first release on the independent Spigot label. Emotionally angry, lyrically brutal, Prong partnered a relentless assault with some fierce guitar-riffing. Their second album for Epic Records, *Prove You Wrong*, in 1991, was their most significant work to date. By the advent of *Cleansed* the group had expanded to a four-piece. First they had added ex-Flotsam & Jetson bass player Tony Gregory, before recruiting Killing Joke musician Paul Raven, who had previously worked with the band on their *Whose Fist Is It Anyway* remix EP. John Bechdel of Murder Inc. additionally expanded the band's sound with his programming and sampling skills. A injury to Raven in 1996 prevented him from working and his replacement was Vince Dennis, loaned from World In Pain. Victor joined the 1996 line-up of Danzig.

● ALBUMS: *Primitive Origins* (Mr Bear 1987)★★, *Force Fed* (Spigot 1988)★★★, *Beg To Differ* (Epic 1990)★★★, *The Peel Sessions* mini-album (Strange Fruit 1990)★★★, *Prove You Wrong* (Epic 1991)★★★, *Cleansed* (Epic 1994)★★★, *Rude Awakening* (Epic 1996)★★★.

PULKAS

Led by intimidating vocalist Luke Lloyd, this purposefully extreme, hard-rocking four-piece was formed in the mid-90s when they met on a London Underground train. Guitarist Martin Bourne, bassist Jules McBride and drummer Rob Lewis, together with Lloyd, accepted a contract with Earache Records, despite other offers. The quarter joined the label's 1998 *NextGen* package tour before entering the studio with Colin Richardson, previously producer with Machine Head and Fear Factory. The result was *Greed*, which earned them a series of comparisons with Korn and Tool that the band resented. The cover of *Greed*, meanwhile, earned the band a certain notoriety, featuring as it did a picture of a sperm fertilizing an egg.

● ALBUMS: *Greed* (Earache 1998)★★★.

PUNGENT STENCH

A Viennese death metal band, Pungent Stench began as a musical project in February 1988. In this form they released a split album with the Disharmonic Orchestra and an EP entitled *Extreme Deformity* in 1989. Their increasing popularity among fans of extreme, grotesque music soon convinced them to become a permanent unit, comprising Alex Wank (drums), Jacek Perkowski (bass) and boisterous frontman Martin Schirenc (vocals, guitar). After an undistinguished first album they released *Been Caught Buttering*, a strong development in Pungent Stench's distinctive style. The death metal genre has always been fixated with blood and guts, but Pungent Stench took things further with a level of sickness that showed a certain morbid panache. They also have a rampant sense of humour that runs throughout their gross lyrics and nauseating artwork, while touring commitments with Type O Negative, Brutal Truth and Soldom helped to spread their warped messages around the world. Later releases, such as the 1993 EP *Dirty Rhymes and Psychotronic Beats*, highlighted the funk or even dance-related elements in their death metal cocktail. *Club MONDO BIZARRE For Members Only* revealed an increasing tendency towards material concerning sexual deviance (fitting, perhaps, for a band hailing from the same city as Freud).

● ALBUMS: *For God Your Soul ... For Me Your Flesh* (Nuclear Blast 1990)★★★★, remixed and re-released in 1993, *Been Caught Buttering* (Nuclear Blast 1991)★★★, *Club MONDO BIZARRE For Members Only* (Nuclear Blast 1994)★★★.

● COMPILATIONS: *Collection* (Nuclear Blast 1996)★★★.

● VIDEOS: *La Muerte* (1993).

PURE MANIA

While Stiff Little Fingers remain the best-known punk band to name themselves after a Vibrators song, Pure Mania took their name from the title of the Vibrators' debut album. Formed in Sweden in 1984, the group comprises Hans Spennare (guitar, vocals), Engan (vocals, bass), Benke (guitar, vocals) and Stahl (drums). After taking a few years to perfect their potent blend of new-wave power rock, the group began to record prolifically by the end of the decade. Although the essence of the group's sound, drenched in power chords and attitude, has remained ostensibly the same, the sequence of their albums reveals the growing influence of more experimental groups such as the Cult and Nomads. As one critic stated of their successful 1993 release, *Alibaba Baby*, 'If Vikings had the chance to plug their axes into a bank of Marshall amps, then maybe this is the sort of sound they'd have made.'

● ALBUMS: *6-Stringed Gun* (Rainbow 1988)★★, *Dirty Love* (Rainbow 1988)★★, *Back To The Junkyard* (Rainbow 1989)★★★, *Gasoline Queen* (Rainbow 1991)★★★, *Alibaba Baby* (Rainbow 1993)★★★.

PUSSYCAT

Although Pussycat were a soft rock band from Limburg in Holland, three of their members, Theo Wetzels, Theo Coumans and John Theunissen, were previously in hard rockers Scum. They joined with husband and wife Lou and Tony Wille plus Tony's two sisters Marianne Hewson and Betty Dragstra. Lou Wille was previously in Ricky Rendell And His Centurions, and later Sweet Reaction alongside Tony. Sweet Reaction signed to EMI (Holland) and producer Edy Hilberts changed their name to Pussycat. They recorded 'Mississippi', which became a surprise UK number 1 on Sonet Records. The follow-up, 'Smile', was a minor hit, after which the band failed to chart.

● ALBUMS: *First Of All* (1976)★★.

PYLE, ARTIMUS, BAND

Having replaced original drummer Boby Byrns in Lynyrd Skynyrd in 1975, Pyle spent two years touring and recording with that band before the fateful air crash in October 1977 which killed Steve Gaines and Ronnie Van Zant. He then formed the Artimus Pyle Band in the late 70s with a line-up consisting of Darryll Otis Smith (vocals), John Boerstler (guitar), Steve Brewington (bass) and Steve Lockhart (guitar, keyboards). The group continued in the Skynyrd tradition, playing a mixture of souped-up rock 'n' roll and heavy rock with a pronounced southern flavour. However, in the process he knocked several of the rough edges off his former group's sound. Despite the presence of numerous colleagues and co-writers, their self-titled debut and the follow-up collection (as APB, with Lockhart replaced by Russ Milner and new vocalist Karen Blackmon) failed to inspire sales beyond a loyal clique of diehard Skynyrd fans. *Night Caller* in particular was an obvious attempt to penetrate AOR radio without the songwriting substance necessary to do so. Lacking any real hope of a commercial breakthrough, it was no surprise that APB released no further albums.

● ALBUMS: *Artimus Pyle Band* (MCA 1982)★★★, as APB *Nightcaller* (MCA 1983)★★.

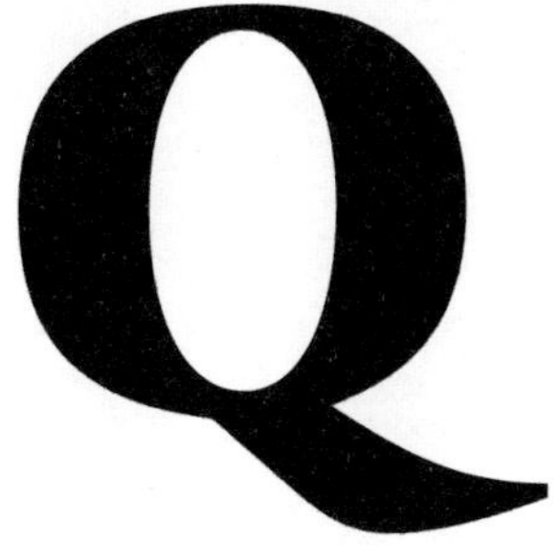

Q5

This US group was formed in Seattle, Washington, in 1983 by the innovative guitarist Floyd Rose. He is otherwise best known for being the inventor of the locking tremelo system, the now indispensable device that ensures the guitar stays in tune even after the heaviest of tremelo use. Joining Floyd Rose in Q5 were Jonathan K (vocals), Rick Pierce (guitar), Evan Sheeley (bass, keyboards) and Gary Thompson (drums), all previously with TKO. Signing to the small independent label Albatross Records, the band released their debut, *Steel The Light*, in 1984. It was later released in Europe on the Roadrunner Records label in 1985. The album was typically Americanized melodic hard rock and, in a glut of similar releases, passed largely unnoticed. Floyd Rose built his own recording studio at his home which the band then used for the recording of a second album. With virtually unlimited studio time available, *When The Mirror Cracks* was released on the Music For Nations label in 1986. Full of strong, melodic compositions, it did, however, tend to sound slightly over-produced. The band fell apart in 1987, and Floyd Rose will be remembered more for his contribution to guitar technology than his recordings with Q5.

● ALBUMS: *Steel The Light* (Albatross 1984)★★, *When The Mirror Cracks* (Music For Nations 1986)★★★.

QUARTZ

Quartz were formed in Birmingham, England, in 1974 by ex-Idle Race guitarist Mike Hopkins and local singer Mike Taylor, initially taking the name Bandylegs. Two years later they joined forces with Geoff Nichols (guitar, keyboards), Dek Arnold (bass, vocals) and Mal Cope (drums) to become Quartz. It was their friendship with Black Sabbath's Tony Iommi that helped to secure them a contract with Jet Records, and Iommi agreed to produce their first album as well as taking them on Sabbath's 1977 tour. *Quartz* should have been a stepping stone to stardom but the group were deluged with press accusations of plagiarism of their sponsors. By 1978 they had been dropped by Jet, and found themselves moving from label to label in search of commercial success. Indie imprint Reddingtons Rare Records offered a new bolthole in 1980 as Quartz had a crack at the singles market with their version of Mountain's classic, 'Nantucket Sleighride', which was used as the theme to UK television's *World In Action* current affairs programme. The band soldiered on, releasing a 12-inch red vinyl single, 'Satan's Serenade', also on Reddingtons, and had a track featured on EMI Records' *Mutha's Pride EP* showcase after becoming caught up in the New Wave Of British Heavy Metal. Jet reissued their debut album in a large brown paper bag with a competition that allowed the winning entrant to fill said receptacle at a famous record shop. This promotion was backed up with a mini-tour followed by support slots to Gillan on their UK tour. MCA Records finally picked up their contract and released *Stand Up And Fight*, which contained one of their best-loved numbers in 'Stoking Up The Fires Of Hell'. Nichols began to moonlight by playing keyboards for Black Sabbath and later joined them on a full-time basis when Quartz ground to a halt in 1984.

● ALBUMS: *Quartz* (Jet 1977)★★★, *Live Songs* (Logo 1980)★★, *Stand Up And Fight* (MCA 1980)★★★, *Against All Odds* (Heavy Metal 1983)★★★.

QUEEN

Arguably Britain's most consistently successful group of the past two decades, Queen began life as a glam rock unit in 1972. Astronomy student Brian May (b. 19 July 1947, Twickenham, Middlesex, England; guitar) and Roger Taylor (b. Roger Meddows-Taylor, 26 July 1949, Kings Lynn, Norfolk, England; drums) had been playing in Johnny Quale And The Reactions, Beat Unlimited and a college group called Smile with bassist Tim Staffell. When the latter left to join Humpty Bong (featuring former Bee Gees drummer Colin Petersen), May and Taylor elected to form a new band with vocalist Freddie Mercury (b. Frederick Bulsara, 5 September 1946, Zanzibar, Africa, d. 24 November 1991, London, England). Early in 1971 bassist John Deacon (b. 19 August 1951, Leicester, Leicestershire, England) completed the line-up. Queen were signed to EMI Records late in 1972 and launched the following spring with a gig at London's Marquee club. Soon after the failed single, 'Keep Yourself Alive', they issued a self-titled album, which was an interesting fusion of 70s glam and late 60s heavy rock (it had been preceded by a Mercury 'solo' single, a cover of the Beach Boys' 'I Can Hear Music', credited to Larry Lurex). Queen toured extensively and recorded a second album, which fulfilled their early promise by reaching the UK Top 5. Soon afterwards, 'Seven Seas Of Rhye' gave them their first hit single (UK number 10), while *Sheer Heart Attack* consolidated their commercial standing by reaching number 2 in the UK album charts. 'Killer Queen' from the album was also the band's first US hit, reaching number 12 in May 1975. The pomp and circumstance of Queen's recordings and live act were embodied in the outrageously camp theatrics of the satin-clad Mercury, who was swiftly emerging as one of rock's most notable showmen during the mid-70s. 1975 was to prove a watershed in the group's career. After touring the Far East, they entered the studio with their producer Roy Thomas Baker and completed the epic 'Bohemian Rhapsody', in which Mercury succeeded in transforming a seven-minute single into a mini-opera. The track was both startling and unique in pop and dominated the Christmas charts in the UK, remaining at number 1 for an astonishing nine weeks. The power of the single was reinforced by an elaborate video production, highly innovative for its period and later much copied by other acts. An attendant album, *A Night At The Opera*, was one of the most expensive and expansive albums of its period and lodged at number 1 in the UK, as well as hitting the US Top 5. Queen were now aspiring to the superstar bracket. Their career thereafter was a carefully marketed succession of hit singles, annual albums and extravagantly produced stage shows. *A Day At The Races* continued the bombast, while the catchy 'Somebody To Love' and anthemic 'We Are The Champions' both reached number 2 in the UK. Although Queen seemed in danger of being stereotyped as over-produced glam rock refugees, they successfully brought eclecticism to their singles output with the 50s rock 'n' roll panache of 'Crazy Little Thing Called Love' and the disco-influenced 'Another One Bites The Dust' (both US number 1s). Despite this stylistic diversity, each Queen single seemed destined to become an anthem, as evidenced by the continued use of much of their output on US sporting occasions. Meanwhile, *The Game* gave Queen their first US number 1 album in July 1980. The group's soundtrack for the movie *Flash Gordon* was another success, but was cited by many critics as typical of their pretentious approach. By the close of 1981, Queen were back at number 1 in the UK for the first time since 'Bohemian Rhapsody' with 'Under Pressure' (a collaboration with David Bowie). After a flurry of solo ventures, the group returned in fine form in 1984 with the satirical 'Radio Gaga' (UK number 2), followed by the histrionic 'I Want To Break Free' (and accompanying cross-dressing video). A performance at 1985's Live Aid displayed the group at their most professional and many acclaimed them the stars of the day, though there were others who accused them of hypocrisy for breaking the boycott of apartheid-locked South Africa. Coincidentally, their next single was 'One Vision', an idealistic song in keeping with the spirit of Live Aid. Queen's recorded output lessened during the late 80s as they concentrated on extracurricular ventures. The space between releases did not affect the group's popularity, however, as was proven in 1991 when 'Innuendo' gave them their third UK number 1, and the album of the same name also topped the UK charts. By this time they had become an institution. Via faultless musicianship, held together by May's guitar virtuosity and the spectacular Mercury, Queen were one of the great theatrical rock acts. The career of the group effectively ended with the death of lead singer Freddie Mercury on 24 November 1991. 'Bohemian Rhapsody' was immediately reissued to raise money for AIDS research projects, and soared to the top of the British charts. The song also climbed to US number 2 in March 1992 after featuring in the movie *Wayne's World* (it had originally reached number 9 in January 1976). A memorial concert for Mercury took place at London's Wembley Stadium on May 20 1992, featuring an array of stars including Liza Minnelli, Elton John, Guns N'Roses, George Michael, David Bowie and Annie Lennox (Eurythmics). Of the remaining members Brian May's solo career enjoyed the highest profile, while Roger Taylor worked with the Cross. Queen never announced an official breakup, so it was with nervous anticipation that a new Queen album was welcomed in 1995. The Mercury vocals were recorded during his last year while at home in Switzerland, and the rest of the band then worked on the remaining songs. While Mercury must be applauded for the way he carried his illness with great dignity, it is fair to say that May, Taylor and Deacon performed wonders in crafting an album from slightly inferior material. It will never be known whether all the tracks on *Made In Heaven* would have found their way onto an album had Mercury been with us today.

● ALBUMS: *Queen* (EMI 1973)★★★, *Queen II* (EMI 1974)★★★★, *Sheer Heart Attack* (EMI

1974)★★★★, *A Night At The Opera* (EMI 1975)★★★★, *A Day At The Races* (EMI 1976)★★★, *News Of The World* (EMI 1977)★★, *Jazz* (EMI 1978)★★, *Live Killers* (EMI 1979)★★, *The Game* (EMI 1980)★★★, *Flash Gordon* film soundtrack (EMI 1980)★★, *Hot Space* (EMI 1982)★, *The Works* (EMI 1984)★★★, *A Kind Of Magic* (EMI 1986)★★★★, *Live Magic* (EMI 1986)★★, *The Miracle* (EMI 1989)★★, *Queen At The Beeb* (Band Of Joy 1989)★, *Innuendo* (EMI 1991)★★★, *Live At Wembley '86* (EMI 1992)★★, *Made In Heaven* (EMI 1995)★★★.

● COMPILATIONS: *Greatest Hits* (EMI 1981)★★★★★, *The Complete Works* 14-LP box set (EMI 1985)★★★, *Greatest Hits II* (EMI 1991)★★★, *Queen Rocks* (EMI 1997)★★★.

● VIDEOS: *Queen's Greatest Flix* (PMI 1984), *We Will Rock You* (Peppermint Music Video 1984), *The Works Video EP* (PMI 1984), *Live In Rio* (PMI 1985), *Live In Budapest* (PMI 1987), *The Magic Years Volume One: Foundations* (PMI 1987), *The Magic Years Volume Two: Live Killers In The Making* (PMI 1987), *The Magic Years Volume Three: Crowning Glory* (PMI 1987), *Rare Live: A Concert Through Time And Space* (PMI 1989), *The Miracle EP* (PMI 1989), *Queen At Wembley* (PMI 1990), *Greatest Flix II* (PMI 1991), *Box Of Flix* (PMI 1991), *Champions Of The World* (PMI 1995), *Rock You* (Music Club 1995), *Made In Heaven: The Films* (Wienerworld 1996).

● FURTHER READING: *Queen*, Larry Pryce. *The Queen Story*, George Tremlett. *Queen: The First Ten Years*, Mike West. *Queen's Greatest Pix*, Jacques Lowe. *Queen: An Illustrated Biography*, Judith Davis. *Queen: A Visual Documentary*, Ken Dean. *Freddie Mercury: This Is The Real Life*, David Evans and David Minns. *Queen: As It Began*, Jacky Gun and Jim Jenkins. *Queen Unseen*, Michael Putland. *Queen And I, The Brian May Story*, Laura Jackson. *Queen: A Concert Documentary*, Greg Brooks. *Queen: The Early Years*, Mark Hodkinson. *The Complete Guide To The Music Of ...*, Peter Hogan. *Mercury - The King Of Queen*, Laura Jackson. *Queen Live*, Greg Brooks. *Freddie Mercury - More Of The Real Life*, David Evans and David Minns. *Queen Live: A Concert Documentary*, Greg Brooks.

QUEENSRŸCHE

Queensrÿche were formed in Seattle, USA, by Geoff Tate (vocals), Chris DeGarmo (guitar), Michael Wilton (guitar), Eddie Jackson (bass), and Scott Rockenfield (drums), from the ashes of club circuit band the Mob and, in Tate's case, the Myth. Immediately, Tate offered them a distinctive vocal edge, having studied opera - he had turned to hard rock because of the lyrical freedom it offered. A four-track demo tape recorded in the basement of Rockenfield's parents' house in June 1982 led to record store owners Kim and Diana Harris offering to manage the band. The tape itself took on a life of its own, circulating throughout the north-west of America, and in May 1983 the band launched their own 206 Records label to house the songs on a self-titled 12-inch EP (lead track, 'Queen Of The Reich', had long since given them their name). The EP caused quite a stir in rock circles and led to EMI Records offering them a seven-album contract. The record was quickly re-released and grazed the UK Top 75, although the band's sound was still embryonic and closer to Britain's New Wave Of British Heavy Metal than the progressive rock flavour that would become their hallmark. Their first full album for EMI, *The Warning*, was comparatively disappointing, failing to live up to the promise shown on the EP, particularly in the poor mix, which was the subject of some concern for both the record company and band. Only 'Road To Madness' and 'Take Hold Of The Flame', two perennial live favourites, met expectations. *Rage For Order* followed in 1986 and saw the band creating a more distinctive style, making full use of modern technology, yet somehow the production (this time from Neil Kernon) seemed to have over-compensated. Although a dramatic improvement, and the first genuine showcase for Tate's incredible vocal range and the twin guitar sound of DeGarmo and Wilton, the songs emerged as clinical and neutered. 1988 saw the Peter Collins-produced *Operation: Mindcrime*, a George Orwell-inspired concept album that was greeted with enthusiastic critical acclaim on its release. With some of the grandiose futurism of earlier releases dispelled, and additional orchestration from Michael Kamen, worldwide sales of over one million confirmed this as the album to lift the band into rock's first division. In the wake of its forerunner, there was something positively minimal about *Empire*, which boasted a stripped-down but still dreamlike rock aesthetic best sampled on the single 'Silent Lucidity', a Top 10 US hit in November 1991, which was also nominated for a Grammy. The album itself earned a Top 10 placing in America. Only single releases broke a four-year recording gap between *Empire* and 1994's *Promised Land*, the most notable of which was 1993's 'Real World', included on the soundtrack to the Arnold Schwarzenegger flop *Last Action Hero*. Although a more personal and reflective set, *Promised Land* continued the band's tradition of dramatic song structures, this time without Kamen's arranging skills. Well over a decade into a career that at first seemed of limited appeal, Queensrÿche's popularity continued to grow. However, they stumbled with 1997's *Hear In The New Frontier*, which experimented with a less grandiose style that confused both critics and record buyers.

● ALBUMS: *The Warning* (EMI 1984)★★, *Rage For Order* (EMI 1986)★★, *Operation: Mindcrime* (EMI 1988)★★★, *Empire* (EMI 1990)★★★, *Promised Land* (EMI 1994)★★★, *Hear In The New Frontier* (EMI 1997)★★★.

● COMPILATIONS: *Queensrÿche* includes *Queensrÿche* and *Prophecy* EPs (EMI 1988)★★★.

● VIDEOS: *Live In Tokyo* (PMI 1985), *Video Mindcrime* (PMI 1989), *Operation Livecrime* (PMI 1991/93), *Building Empires* (PMI 1993).

QUICKSAND

Comprising Walter Schreifels (vocals, guitar, ex-Youth Of Today; Gorilla Biscuits), Tom Capone (guitar), Sergio Vega (bass) and Alan Cage (drums), hardcore quartet Quicksand were formed in New York City, New York, in the early 90s. They instantly recalled the established traditions of CBGB's hardcore with a disciplined musical engine, adding a strong pop sensibility with compulsive hooks. They made their debut in 1993 with *Slip*, an insistent collection of passionate songs with staccato rhythms that recalled Fugazi. It was rigorously road-tested during 250 live shows. By 1994 Quicksand were playing major venues across the USA alongside Offspring, who invited them back the following year for their European tour. This coincided with the release of *Manic Compression*, another bracing collection of cerebral punk songs. Railing against apathy and injustice without ever descending to rhetoric, Quicksand's arrival was the next step forward for hardcore, their departure was less spectacular. Tom Capone joined Pete Mengede in his new band Handsome and Alan Cage joined Seaweed. Schreifels took on some projects as a record producer and in 1996 formed a new band, World's Fastest Car. In May 1997 there were rumours of a Quicksand re-formation, which were confirmed in 1998.

● ALBUMS: *Slip* (Island 1993)★★★, *Manic Compression* (Island 1995)★★★.

QUICKSILVER MESSENGER SERVICE

Of all the bands that came out of the San Francisco area during the late 60s Quicksilver typified most the style, attitude and sound of that era. The original band in 1964 comprised: Dino Valenti (b. 7 October 1943, Danbury, Connecticut, USA, d. 16 November 1994, Santa Rosa, California, USA; vocals), John Cipollina (b. 24 August 1943, Berkeley, California, USA, d. 29 May 1989; guitar), David Freiberg (b. 24 August 1938, Boston, Massachusetts, USA; bass, vocals), Jim Murray (vocals, harmonica), Casey Sonoban (drums) and, very briefly, Alexander 'Skip' Spence (b. 18 April 1946, Windsor, Ontario, Canada; guitar, vocals), before being whisked off to join the Jefferson Airplane as drummer. Another problem that later proved to be significant in Quicksilver's development was the almost immediate arrest and imprisonment of Valenti for a drugs offence. He did not rejoin the band until late 1969. In 1965 the line-up was strengthened by the arrival of Gary Duncan (b. Gary Grubb, 4 September 1946, San Diego, California, USA; guitar) and, replacing Sonoban, Greg Elmore (b. 4 September 1946, San Diego, California, USA). Murray departed soon after their well-received appearance at the Monterey Pop Festival in 1967. The quartet of Cipollina, Duncan, Elmore and Freiberg recorded the first two albums; both are important in the development of San Francisco rock music, as the twin lead guitars of Cipollina and Duncan made them almost unique. The second collection, *Happy Trails*, is now regarded as a classic. George Hunter and his Globe Propaganda company were responsible for some of the finest album covers of the 60s and *Happy Trails* is probably their greatest work. The live music within showed a spontaneity that the band were never able to recapture on subsequent recordings. The side-long suite of Bo Diddley's 'Who Do You Love' has some incredible dynamics and extraordinary interplay between the twin guitarists. Duncan departed soon afterwards and was replaced by UK session pianist and ex-Steve Miller Band member, Nicky Hopkins (b. 24 February 1944, London, England, d. 6 September 1994, California, USA). His contributions breathed some life into the disappointing *Shady Grove*, notably with the frantic 'Edward, The Mad Shirt Grinder'. *Just For Love* showed a further decline, with Valenti, now back with the band, becoming overpowering and self-indulgent. 'Fresh Air' gave them a Top 50 US hit in 1970.

Cipollina departed, as did Freiberg following his arrest in 1971 for drug possession (he found a lucrative career later with Jefferson Starship). Various incarnations have appeared over the years with little or no success. As recently as 1987, Gary Duncan recorded an album carrying the

Quicksilver name, but by then old fans were more content to purchase copies of the first two albums on compact disc.

● ALBUMS: *Quicksilver Messenger Service* (Capitol 1968)★★★, *Happy Trails* (Capitol 1969)★★★★★, *Shady Grove* (Capitol 1969)★★, *Just For Love* (Capitol 1970)★★, *What About Me* (Capitol 1971)★★, *Quicksilver* (Capitol 1971)★★, *Comin' Thru* (Capitol 1972)★★, *Solid Silver* (Capitol 1975)★★, *Maiden Of The Cancer Moon* recorded 1968 (Psycho 1983)★★, *Peace By Piece* (Capitol 1987)★★.

● COMPILATIONS: *Anthology* (Capitol 1973)★★★, *The Best Of Quicksilver Messenger Service* (Capitol 1990)★★★, *Sons Of Mercury (1968-1975)* (Rhino 1991)★★★★, *The Best Of Quicksilver Messenger Service* (CEMA 1992)★★★.

QUIET RIOT

Heavy metal band Quiet Riot had their 'five minutes' of fame in 1983 with a remake of a Slade song, 'Cum On Feel The Noize', and a US number 1 album, *Metal Health* - the first metal album to reach that position in the US charts. However, they were unable to maintain that momentum with subsequent releases. The band formed in 1975 with lanky vocalist Kevin DuBrow (b. 1955), Randy Rhoads (b. Randall William Rhoads, 6 December 1956, Santa Monica, California, USA, d. 19 March 1982; guitar), Drew Forsyth (drums) and Kelly Garni (bass), taking their name from a suggestion made by Status Quo's Rick Parfitt. They recorded two albums with that line-up, released only in Japan, that are now collector's items. Rudy Sarzo then replaced Garni. Rhoads left in 1979 to join Ozzy Osbourne and was later tragically killed in a plane crash in March 1982. At that point the band briefly split up, with some members joining the vocalist in a band called DuBrow, Sarzo also working with Osbourne. Quiet Riot regrouped around DuBrow, Sarzo, guitarist Carlos Cavazo and drummer Frankie Banali and signed to the Pasha label for their breakthrough album and single in 1983, their musical and visual style fashioned after the harder-rocking glam acts of the 70s. Friction within the group followed their quick success and resultant publicity affected sales of the 1984 follow-up, *Condition Critical*, which reached number 15 in the US charts but was considered disappointing. Sarzo was replaced by Chuck Wright in 1985. Quiet Riot recorded another album in 1986, which reached number 31 but showed a marked decline in the group's creativity. DuBrow and Wright were subsequently ejected from the band and a self-titled 1988 album, with new vocalist Paul Shortino (ex-Rough Cutt) and Sean McNabb on bass, barely scraped the charts. The group then disbanded, Banali later working with W.A.S.P. DuBrow put together a new version of the group in the 90s, releasing two lacklustre albums.

● ALBUMS: *Quiet Riot* (Columbia Japan 1977)★★, *Quiet Riot II* (Columbia Japan 1978)★★, *Metal Health* (Pasha 1983)★★★, *Condition Critical* (Pasha 1984)★★, *QRIII* (Pasha 1986)★, *Quiet Riot* (Pasha 1988)★, *Terrified* (Moonstone 1993)★★, *Down To The Bone* (Kamikaze 1995)★★.

● COMPILATIONS: *Wild Young And Crazee* (Raw Power 1987)★★★, *The Randy Rhoads Years* (Rhino 1993)★★★, *The Best Of Quiet Riot* (Sony 1996)★★★.

QUIREBOYS

After violent incidents at early live shows, this UK band altered their name from Queerboys to Quireboys, to avoid further trouble. Comprising Spike Gray (vocals), Nigel Mogg (bass; brother of Phil Mogg of UFO), Chris Johnstone (keyboards), Guy Bailey (guitar), Ginger (b. 12 December 1964, South Shields, Tyne & Wear, England; guitar) and Coze (drums), they were all originally drinking buddies in London pubs. Drawing musical inspiration from the Faces, Rolling Stones and Mott The Hoople, they specialized in bar-room boogie, beer-soaked blues and infectious raunch 'n' roll. Spike's rough-as-a-gravel-path vocal style, closely resembling Rod Stewart's, added fuel to accusations of the band being little more than Faces copyists. After releasing two independent singles they signed to EMI Records and immediately underwent a line-up reshuffle. Coze and Ginger (who went on to form the Wildhearts) were removed and replaced by Ian Wallace and Guy Griffin, respectively. They recorded *A Bit Of What You Fancy* in Los Angeles, under the production eye of Jim Cregan (former Rod Stewart guitarist). It was an immediate success, entering the UK album charts at number 2 in February 1990. 'Hey You', lifted as a single, also met with similar success, peaking at number 14 in January 1990. An eight-track live album followed, which duplicated most of the numbers from their first album, as a stop-gap measure to bridge the long period between successive studio releases. However, when *Bitter Sweet & Twisted* failed to ignite, Spike left to form his own band, God's Hotel, denying rumours that he had been invited to replace Axl Rose in Guns N'Roses (after having contributed to Slash's solo album). The Quireboys had come to a natural conclusion, or, as Spike prefers to put it, 'we were past our sell-by-date'. Bassist Nigel Mogg put together his own project, the Nancy Boys, in New York.

● ALBUMS: *A Bit Of What You Fancy* (Parlophone 1989)★★★, *Live Around The World* (Parlophone 1990)★★★, *Bitter Sweet & Twisted* (Parlophone 1992)★★.

● COMPILATIONS: *From Tooting To Barking* (Castle 1994)★★★.

● VIDEOS: *A Bit Of What You Fancy* (PMI/EMI 1990).

RABIN, TREVOR

b. 1955, South Africa. Trevor Rabin learned classical piano and guitar from an early age, forming his first band, Rabbit, when he was aged only 14. Rabbit were a short-lived teenybop sensation in South Africa during the early 70s, releasing two albums that attained gold status. Moving to England in 1977, he signed to Chrysalis Records and polished up some demos he had previously recorded in South Africa for release as his first solo album. This featured a mixture of styles, and included jazz, rock, blues and AOR numbers. Future releases pursued a more mainstream melodic rock approach, with *Wolf*, released in 1981, being his *tour de force*. He also ventured into production with Wild Horses and Manfred Mann. He accepted the invitation to join Yes in 1983, and it was not until there was a major conflict in this camp that he managed to find enough time to record another solo effort. *Can't Look Away*, surfacing in 1989, had more in common with Yes than with his previous solo work. In 1990 he contributed to Seal's big-selling debut album. A number of his musical soundbites have been used by Apple the computer company.

● ALBUMS: *Trevor Rabin* (Chrysalis 1978)★★★, *Face To Face* (Chrysalis 1979)★★, *Wolf* (Chrysalis 1981)★★, *Can't Look Away* (Elektra 1989)★★★.

RACER X

This Los Angeles, California, USA band earned a reputation for guitar-orientated melodic rock, delivered with precision despite the blurring speed. Featuring Jeff Martin (vocals, ex-Surgical Steel), Paul Gilbert (guitar), John Alderete (bass) and Harry Gschoesser (drums, ex-Nobros) they released *Street Lethal*, a high-tech fusion of relentless guitarwork and some memorable songs. Scott Travis (ex-Hawk) took over the drumstool and Bruce Bouillet was added as a second guitarist in 1986. By the time *Second Heat* was issued the following year the band had matured considerably, with the music more accomplished on several levels, most notably in arrangement and production. Paul Gilbert left in 1988 to join Mr. Big, and was replaced by Chris Arvan. Jeff Martin broke ranks shortly afterwards and Scott Travis understandably accepted the offer to join his heroes, Judas Priest. The band ground to a halt in 1990.

● ALBUMS: *Street Lethal* (Roadrunner 1986)★★★, *Second Heat* (Roadrunner 1987)★★★★, *Extreme Volume...Live* (Roadrunner 1988)★★, *Live...Extreme Vol. 2* (Roadrunner 1992)★★.

RAGE (GERMANY)

Formerly known as Avenger, this German power trio changed their name to Rage in 1985, to avoid confusion with the British Avenger (and thereby get confused with the British band Rage). A series of line-up changes ensued before the combination of vocalist Peavey Wagner, guitarist Manni Schmidt and drummer Chris Efthimiadis gelled. Their first two albums were rather one-dimensional, being competent, but uninspiring, techno-thrash affairs. With the recording of *Perfect Man*, they experimented more with song structures and had improved considerably as musicians. Future releases combined the technical prowess and subtle melodies of Rush with the unbridled aggression of Megadeth. Their reputation in Germany has grown rapidly, but they have yet to make any significant impression outside their homeland.

● ALBUMS: *Reign Of Fear* (Noise 1986)★★★, *Execution Guaranteed* (Noise 1987)★★, *Perfect Man* (Noise 1988)★★★★, *Secrets In A Weird World* (Noise 1989)★★★, *Reflections Of A Shadow* (Noise 1990)★★★, *Beyond The Wall* (Noise 1992)★★★, *Saviour* (Noise 1993)★★★, *XIII* (Gun 1998)★★.

Rage (UK)

A UK quartet of Dave Lloyd (vocals), Mick Devonport (guitar), Keith Mulholland (bass) and John Mylett (drums), Rage were formed in the early 80s from the remnants of Nutz, ostensibly in an attempt to capitalize on the emergent New Wave Of British Heavy Metal scene. Like Nutz before them, they managed to attract controversy for their sexist artwork, particularly their 1982 debut for Carrere Records, *Nice 'N' Dirty*. However, neither this nor the follow-up collection, *Run For The Night*, convinced any of their doubters in the metal press, and they broke up shortly thereafter.

● ALBUMS: *Nice 'N' Dirty* (Carrere 1982)★★★, *Run For The Night* (Carrere 1982)★★.

Rage Against The Machine

The name says everything about Rage Against The Machine. The aggressive musical blend of metal guitar and hip-hop rhythms is an appropriate background to the rap-styled delivery of angry, confrontational, political lyrics, addressing the band's concerns over inner city deprivation, racism, censorship, propaganda, the plight of Native Americans and many other issues as the group strive to offer more than mere entertainment. Formed in Los Angeles in 1991 by former Lock Up guitarist Tom Morello and ex-Inside Out vocalist Zack de la Rocha, with bassist Timmy C and drummer Brad Wilk, Rage Against The Machine signed a major record contract with, importantly, creative control on the strength of a demo tape and some impressive early live shows. Further live work with Pearl Jam, Body Count, Tool and Suicidal Tendencies ensued, with the band encountering trouble with the French government during the Suicidal tour over T-shirts that showed a genuine CIA instructional cartoon on how to make a Molotov cocktail, taken from documents made for the Nicaraguan Contra rebels. The T-shirts were confiscated and destroyed by French Customs. The band subsequently released a self-titled debut, with a stunning cover photograph of a Buddhist monk burning himself to death in protest at the Vietnam War, and rose rapidly to fame, Henry Rollins describing them as 'the most happening band in the US'. The album was a hit on both sides of the Atlantic, and Rage Against The Machine enjoyed single success with 'Killing In The Name', although de la Rocha was distinctly unhappy with a radio edit that removed all expletives and 'completely shut down the whole purpose of that song'. A sell-out UK tour in 1993 was followed by further powerful performances on the Lollapalooza festival tour in the USA. *Evil Empire* became a much more successful album, reaching number 1 in the USA. Tracks such as the highly political 'Vietnow' and 'Down Rodeo' showed the band at their angriest and most potent. Beyond the swearing are some of the most honest and powerful lyrical statements of the 90s.

● ALBUMS: *Rage Against The Machine* (Epic 1992)★★★, *Evil Empire* (Epic 1996)★★★★.

● VIDEOS: *Home Movie* (Sony Music Video 1997).

Raging Slab

Greg Strzempka (vocals, guitar) and Elyse Steinman (bottleneck guitar) formed Raging Slab in 1983, recruiting lead guitarist Mark Middleton and bassist Alec Morton while going through numerous drummers, including ex-Whiplash/Slayer percussionist T.J. Scaglione and future Warrior Soul frontman Kory Clarke. The three-guitar frontline gave a definite Southern rock flavour to the Slab's basic rock 'n' roll, but gigging around the New York hardcore scene of the 80s also added a hard, contemporary edge. The band made their debut with *Assmaster*, which was elaborately packaged with a comic drawn by friends at *Marvel Comics*, and was followed by *True Death* as the band supported themselves with constant touring before a major contract emerged. *Raging Slab*, with latest drummer Bob Pantella, was excellent, with 'Geronimo', a sensitive lament to the fall of the Native American nation, as its centrepiece. However, despite support tours with everyone from Mötley Crüe to the Butthole Surfers, it sold poorly. The band at last found a spiritual home and more creative freedom at Def American, and moved to a Pennsylvania farm where they built their own studio to record the acclaimed *Dynamite Monster Boogie Concert*. This was Raging Slab's most consistent work as they freely extended their talents in new directions, and finally felt at home with their 14th drummer, Paul Sheenan. The live shows were as hot as ever as the Slab toured America with Monster Magnet and undertook their first European tour. New drummer Scott Nesmith joined in time to play on *Sing Monkey Sing*.

● ALBUMS: *Assmaster* (Buy Our Records 1987)★★★, *True Death* mini-album (Buy Our Records 1988)★★★, *Raging Slab* (RCA 1989)★★★, *Dynamite Monster Boogie Concert* (Def American 1993)★★★★, *Sing Monkey Sing* (American 1996)★★.

RAINBOW

In May 1975 guitarist Ritchie Blackmore (b. 14 April 1945, Weston-Super-Mare, England; guitar) left Deep Purple, forming Rainbow the following year. His earlier involvement with American band Elf led to his recruitment of the latter's Ronnie James Dio (b. Ronald Padavona, 10 July 1940, New Hampshire, USA; vocals), Mickey Lee Soule, (keyboards), Craig Gruber on bass and Gary Driscoll as drummer. Their debut, *Ritchie Blackmore's Rainbow*, was released in 1975, and was undeservedly seen by some as a poor imitation of Deep Purple. The constant turnover of personnel was representative of Blackmore's quest for the ultimate line-up and sound. Dissatisfaction with the debut album led to new personnel being assembled. Soule left, while Jimmy Bain took over from Gruber and Cozy Powell (b. Colin Powell, 29 December 1947, England, d. 5 April 1998) replaced Driscoll. With Tony Carey (b. 16 October 1953, USA, on keyboards, *Rainbow Rising* was released, an album far more confident than its predecessor. Shortly after this, Bain and Carey left, being replaced by Bob Daisley (ex-Widowmaker) and David Stone, respectively. It was when Rainbow moved to America that difficulties between Dio and Blackmore came to a head, resulting in Dio's departure from the band in 1978. His replacement was Graham Bonnet, whose only album with Rainbow, *Down To Earth*, saw the return as bassist of Roger Glover, the man Blackmore had forced out of Deep Purple in 1973. The album was a marked departure from the Dio days, and while it is often considered one of the weaker Rainbow collections, it did provide an enduring single, 'Since You've Been Gone', written and originally recorded by Russ Ballard. Bonnet and Powell soon became victims of another reorganization of Rainbow's line-up. Drummer Bobby Rondinelli and particularly new vocalist Joe Lynn Turner brought an American feel to the band, a commercial sound introduced on *Difficult To Cure*, the album that produced their biggest hit in 'I Surrender'. Thereafter the group went into decline as their increasingly middle-of-the-road albums were ignored by fans (former Brand X drummer Chuck Burgi replaced Rondinelli for 1983's *Bent Out Of Shape*). In 1984 the Rainbow project was ended following the highly popular Deep Purple reunion. The group played its last gig on 14 March 1984 in Japan, accompanied by a symphony orchestra as Blackmore, with a typical absence of modesty, adapted Beethoven's 'Ninth Symphony'. A compilation, *Finyl Vinyl*, appeared in 1986, and (necessarily) featured several different incarnations of Rainbow as well as unreleased recordings. Since then the name has been resurrected in a number of line-ups. A new studio recording was issued in 1995. The present vocalist is Dougie White.

● ALBUMS: *Ritchie Blackmore's Rainbow* (Oyster 1975)★★★, *Rainbow Rising* (Polydor 1976)★★★★, *On Stage* (Polydor 1977)★★, *Long Live Rock And Roll* (Polydor 1978)★★★, *Down To Earth* (Polydor 1979)★★★, *Difficult To Cure* (Polydor 1981)★★, *Straight Between The Eyes* (Polydor 1982)★★, *Bent Out Of Shape* (Polydor 1983)★★, *Stranger In Us All* (RCA 1995)★★.

● COMPILATIONS: *Best Of* (Polydor 1983)★★★, *Finyl Vinyl* (Polydor 1986)★★, *Live In Germany* (Connoisseur 1990)★★.

● VIDEOS: *The Final Cut* (Polygram Music Video 1986), *Live Between The Eyes* (Channel 5 1988).

● FURTHER READING: *Rainbow*, Peter Makowski.

RAM JAM

Formed in the mid-70s, Ram Jam was an east coast US group best known for its one Top 20 single, 'Black Betty', in 1977. That song was the focus of a boycott by several groups who considered it offensive to black women, even though it had originally been written by Huddie 'Lead Belly' Ledbetter, the legendary black folk and blues singer. The group consisted of guitarist Bill Bartlett (b. 1949), bassist Howie Blauvelt (formerly a member of Billy Joel's early group the Hassles), singer Myke Scavone and drummer Pete Charles. Bartlett had earlier been lead guitarist with the Lemon Pipers. After leaving that group, Bartlett retired from music for some time, before recording a demo of the Lead Belly song. Released on Epic Records, it reached number 18, but the group never had another hit. In the UK they succeeded twice, first in 1977 (number 7), and then in 1990 a remix version made number 13, making them a quite extraordinary one-hit-wonder.

● ALBUMS: *Ram Jam* (Epic 1977)★★, *Portrait Of An Artist As A Young Ram* (Epic 1978)★.

RAMMSTEIN

Formed in Berlin, Germany, this confrontational alternative rock band first came to international prominence when film and television director David Lynch (*Twin Peaks*) declared his admiration and commissioned them to work with him. By this time, Rammstein's explosive, unhinged live shows had already made them famous throughout mainland Europe. The group comprises Till Lindemann (vocals), Richard Kruspe (guitar), Paul Landers (guitar), Christoph Schneider (drums), Oliver Riedel (bass) and Flake Lorenz (keyboards). Their pyrotechnics earned them comparisons to America's Kiss, but the group's frenzied industrial metal sound and dubious lyrics were less obviously commercial. Those lyrics, touching on subjects including child molestation and natural and man-made catastrophes, at first saw them attract a right-wing audience - although the group strenuously deny that this was their intention. Rammstein, named after the 1988 air show disaster that killed 80, made their debut in October 1995 with *Herzeleid*, produced in Sweden by Jacob Hellner (previously a veteran of work with Clawfinger) on a modest budget. Nevertheless, the record sold in excess of half a million copies in Germany alone, and established the group as a potent commercial force. By the time *Sehnsucht* followed in 1997, the group had extended its popularity via a clutch of headlining appearances at European festivals. Following Lynch's inclusion of two Rammstein songs on the soundtrack to his 1996 film *Lost Highway*, US gore-metal fans were also won over. Although they sing in German, all the group's lyrics are translated in accompanying CD liner notes, adding to their growing international appeal.

● ALBUMS: *Herzeleid* (Motor Music 1995)★★★, *Sehnsucht* (Motor Music 1997)★★★★.

RANCID

Guitarist Lars Frederiksen, drummer Brett Reed, bass player Matt Freeman and singer/guitarist Tim 'Lint' Armstrong provide street-level punk with their ideas informed and inspired by a youth of blue-collar poverty in Albany, California, USA. Armstrong and Freeman (often under the alias Matt McCall) had formed their first band, Operation Ivy, in 1987 with Dave Mello (drums) and Jesse Michaels (vocals). When that band split up in 1989, Freeman, Armstrong and Reed (ex-Smog) became Rancid. They made their debut in 1992 with a five-track 7-inch single, 'I'm Not The Only One'. After flirting with the idea of using Green Day's Billy Joe Armstrong as a second guitarist, Rancid were contacted by Brett Gurevitz's Epitaph Records, with a view to recording their debut album. During these sessions Reed met ex-Slip and UK Subs guitarist Fredericksen, and invited him to join the group. He did so, and Rancid's self-titled debut was released in April 1993, featuring more variety and composure than their debut single. In September they began their first national tour, followed by an extended European trek in November. Fredericksen made his debut at the beginning of the following year on the 'Radio Radio Radio' single, co-written with Green Day's Armstrong and released on Fat Wreck Chords, the label run by Fat Mike of No FX. February saw sessions begin on their next album, *Let's Go*. Comprising 23 songs, including the single 'Salvation', it saw the band, and Armstrong in particular, compared favourably with the early Clash sound, albeit taken at a more frenetic pace. The album quickly achieved gold then platinum status, alerting the major labels to Rancid's presence. An offer was made by Madonna's Maverick Records, allegedly accompanied by a nude picture of the singer, but was declined. More tempting was a one and a half million dollar advance contract from Epic Records (the Clash's US label) but this too was turned down in favour of staying 'with friends' at Epitaph. Rancid were now a very bankable attraction for a group whose visual image had never strayed from bondage trousers and mohawks. They returned to the studio after touring in March 1995, with ... *And Out Come The Wolves* the result. Returning to punk ska reminiscent of Operation Ivy at their peak and the Clash by their third album, as ever, the lyrics were written from earthy personal experience. Once again, it was a major seller. The ska theme continued with a collaboration with Mighty Mighty Bosstones vocalist Dicky Barrett for a track on 1998's *Life Won't Wait*.

● ALBUMS: *Rancid* (Epitaph 1993)★★★, *Let's Go* (Epitaph 1994)★★★, ... *And Out Come The Wolves* (Epitaph 1995)★★★, *Life Won't Wait* (Epitaph 1998)★★★.

RATCAT

Emerging in 1986 from Australia's thrash metal scene and based in Sydney, Ratcat relocated to the UK to promote their Ramones-tinged pop rock. The trio comprises Simon Day (vocals, guitar), Amr Zaid (bass and occasional vocals) and Andrew Polin (drums). If UK audiences were surprised to see them occupy support slots for INXS, it was less of a shock in their homeland, where they regularly top the charts and appear on the covers of teenage magazines. Despite the obvious commercial validity of the band, their music remains rooted in pure garage group aesthetics: 'We've always said that, at heart, we're basically scuzz rats. We're at our best when we're at our scuzziest'.

● ALBUMS: *Tingles* (1991)★★★, *Blind Love* (1991)★★.

RATT

This heavy metal group formed in Los Angeles, California, USA, and featured Stephen Pearcy (vocals), Robbin Crosby (guitar), Warren DeMartini (guitar), Juan Croucier (bass) and Bobby 'The Blotz' Blotzer (drums). They evolved out of 70s band Mickey Ratt, transmuting into their present form in 1983, with a hint of pop about their brand of metal similar to Cheap Trick or Aerosmith. They released a self-titled mini-album in 1983 on a local label, and struck up a close friendship with members of Mötley Crüe, which no doubt helped them to sign to Atlantic Records the following year. They made their breakthrough with their first full album, *Out Of The Cellar*, which stayed in the *Billboard* Top 20 for six months. They toured with Ozzy Osbourne before joining a Billy Squier jaunt where they were apparently 'thrown off' because they were more popular than the headline act. Their subsequent output has followed a familiar heavy metal route, but they have the ability to sell out concert halls and produce recordings that regularly received gold discs. *Decimater* featured several songs co-written with Desmond Child and proved their most adventurous recording to date, though Crosby would depart after *Rat 'n' Roll*. In 1993 Pearcy unveiled his new outfit, Arcade, and in 1996 he formed Vertex. However, the band were reunited to record the poorly received *Collage*.

● ALBUMS: *Ratt* (Time Coast 1983)★★, *Out Of The Cellar* (Atlantic 1984)★★, *Invasion Of Your Privacy* (Atlantic 1985)★★, *Dancing Undercover* (Atlantic 1986)★★, *Reach For The Sky* (Atlantic 1988)★★★, *Decimater* (Atlantic 1990)★★★, *Rat 'n' Roll* (East West 1991)★★★, *Collage* (DeRock 1997)★★.

● VIDEOS: *The Video* (1986).

RATTLESNAKE KISS

Birmingham, UK-based heavy metal quintet, formed in 1990 by vocalist Sean Love and guitarists Ralph Cardall and Bill Carroll. Influenced by American bands such as Queensrÿche, Van Halen and Rush, their speciality was in sophisticated and technically accomplished hard rock. The songs, which came over more powerfully in a live setting than in the studio, combined power with musical precision. Picked up by the Sovereign label they released a self-titled debut album in early 1992, though this did not fully reflect the band's musical prowess or energy as a result of thin production.

● ALBUMS: *Rattlesnake Kiss* (Sovereign 1992)★★★.

RAVEN

Formed in Newcastle in 1980, Raven were one of the first bands to be associated with the New Wave Of British Heavy Metal movement. The group comprised the Gallagher brothers, John (vocals, bass) and Mark (guitar), plus drummer Rob 'Wacko' Hunter. Unleashing a wall of noise punctuated by searing guitarwork and shattering vocals, they signed to local independent label, Neat Records. Their reputation grew with the release of a single, 'Don't Need Your Money', and the ensuing live shows that promoted it. John Gallagher's trademark high-pitched vocals and the group's then-innovative speed metal were heard to best effect on four albums for Neat Records, including the excellent *Live At The Inferno*. They then relocated to America and secured a contract with Atlantic Records. Adopting a more melodic approach, *Stay Hard* emerged in 1985 and sold well, but only in their adopted territory - the home-grown fanbase was left somewhat aghast. Since then the band has reverted to its former blitzkrieg style, releasing a string of competent, but rather dated and pedestrian albums. Drummer Rob Hunter moved into production work in 1988, to be replaced by Joe Hasselvander. Despite receiving plaudits from more commercially successful bands, *Glow* confirmed that their influence now lay firmly in the past.

● ALBUMS: *Rock Until You Drop* (Neat 1981)★★★, *Wiped Out* (Neat 1982)★★, *All For One* (Neat 1983)★★★, *Live At The Inferno* (Neat 1984)★★★★, *Stay Hard* (Atlantic 1985)★★★, *The Pack Is Back* (Atlantic 1986)★★, *Life's A Bitch* (Atlantic 1987)★★, *Nothing Exceeds Like Excess* (Under One Flag 1989)★★, *Glow* (SPV 1995)★★, *Everything Louder* (SPV 1997)★★.

● COMPILATIONS: *The Devil's Carrion* (Castle 1985)★★★★.

RE-ANIMATOR

Formed in Hull, England, in 1987, Re-Animator consisted of Kevin Ingleson (guitar, vocals), Mike Abel (guitar), John Wilson (bass) and Mark Mitchell (drums). Strongly influenced by the legacy of the New Wave Of British Heavy Metal, and armed with the new thrash metal musical attitude this had helped to inspire, the band signed to the Music For Nations subsidiary label, Under One Flag. Their debut, *Deny Reality*, was a harsh barrage of guitars that stood them in good stead for their full album debut, *Condemned To Eternity*. This offered no great departure in musical style but was still regarded as a solid statement. The release of *Laughing* in 1991 saw a major change in direction for the band. Gone were the guitar set-pieces as the band incorporated funk elements. Added to other stylistic experiments it resulted in an album that was neither one thing nor the other. However, the new approach gelled better on *That Was Then, This Is Now*.

● ALBUMS: *Deny Reality* mini-album (Under One Flag 1989)★★★, *Condemned To Eternity* (Under One Flag 1990)★★★, *Laughing* (Under One Flag 1991)★★★, *That Was Then, This Is Now* (Under One Flag 1993)★★★★.

Realm

This Milwaukee, USA-based hi-tech thrash metal quintet was formed by guitarists Takis Kinis and Paul Laganowski in 1985. By a process of trial and error they finally completed the line-up with Mark Antoni (vocals), Steve Post (bass) and Mike Olson (drums). Following a string of successful club shows they landed support slots to Wendy 'O' Williams and Megadeth tours in 1986. Signing to Roadracer Records, they released *Endless War* in 1988. This was a complex fusion of hard rock, thrash and jazz influences and included a remarkable cover version of the Beatles' 'Eleanor Rigby'. Their second album saw them becoming arguably too complex with a multitude of unnecessary time-changes, rendering much of the material incoherent and unmelodic.

● ALBUMS: *Endless War* (Roadracer 1988)★★★, *Suiciety* (Roadracer 1990)★★.

Reckless

This Canadian pop-metal act was formed by guitarist Steve Madden with Jan Melanson (vocals), Gene Stout (bass) and Gil Roberts (drums), originally under the name Harlow. *Reckless* emerged to a generally positive reception, with commercial guitar-led metal in a Van Halen vein given individual identity by Melanson's quirky vocal delivery. Coupled with the frontwoman's striking blond looks, this seemed to give Reckless a chance to stand out from the crowd. However, the album bombed, and the band broke up. Madden tried again with a new line-up featuring Doug Adams (vocals), Todd Pilon (bass) and Steve Wayne Lederman (drums), but while *Heart Of Steel* was another good effort based around Madden's stylish guitarwork, it lacked the distinctive qualities of its predecessor, and the band faded.

● ALBUMS: *Reckless* (EMI 1981)★★★★, *Heart Of Steel* (Heavy Metal America 1984)★★★.

Red Dogs

This blues-based UK rock 'n' roll quintet was formed in 1989 by Mickey 'The Vicar' Ripley (vocals) and Chris John (guitar). Enlisting the services of Mick Young (bass), Paul Guerin (guitar) and Stow (drums), the band signed to Episode Records the following year. They debuted with *Wrong Side Of Town*, a six-track offering that took the Rolling Stones as its primary influence. The Red Dogs raised their profile by supporting Cheap And Nasty and UFO on their 1991 UK tours. Taking their infectious brand of bar-room boogie to a larger stage initially proved successful, though afterwards they failed to heighten their profile significantly. Ripley departed and formed Josh in 1996.

● ALBUMS: *Wrong Side Of Town* mini-album (Episode 1989)★★★.

Red Fun

A band from Stockholm, Sweden, formed in 1992, Red Fun consist of four veterans of that country's metal/hard rock scene. Thomas Persson (vocals), whose mane of red hair gives the band their name, was formerly a member of Alien. Tobbe Moen (bass) is an experienced session player, while Freddy von Gerber (drums) had appeared in a number of groups including Intermezzo, Bam Bam Boys, Rat Bat Blue and Easy Action. Kee Marcello (guitar) was also a member of the last-named band, as well as, more famously, Europe. Red Fun recorded a debut album in 1992 as well as a promotional single, 'My Baby's Coming Back'. Their press statements of the time boasted that they would put 'some of the hedonism back' into hard rock, following its domination by grunge. Support slots to Guns N'Roses and Neil Young in the summer of 1993 ensured that Red Fun were set firm to appeal to traditionalists.

● ALBUMS: *Red Fun* (Cheiron/Music For Nations 1993)★★★.

Red Hot Chili Peppers

These engaging Hollywood ruffians mixed funk, punk and grunge in the mid-80s and encouraged a legion of other bands to regurgitate the formula. Led by 'Antwan The Swan' (b. Anthony Kiedis, 1 November 1962, Grand Rapids, Michigan, USA; vocals), the band's original line-up also featured 'Flea' (b. Michael Balzary, 16 October 1962, Melbourne, Australia; bass), Hillel Slovak (b. 31 March 1962, Israel, d. 25 June 1988; guitar) and Jack Irons (b. California, USA; drums). They began life as garage band Anthem before Balzary departed for seminal 80s punks Fear. When Irons and Slovak moved on to join the less notable What Is This?, the nails appeared to be firmly in place on the Anthem coffin. However, under their new name, the Red Hot Chili Peppers acquired a speculative recording contract with EMI Records America. Unfortunately, as Irons and Slovak were under contract with their new band, their debut album had to be recorded with Jack Sherman on guitar and Cliff Martinez (ex-Captain Beefheart; Weirdos) on drums. Production was handled, somewhat surprisingly, by the Gang Of Four's Andy Gill. The band set about building their considerable reputation as a live outfit, much of which was fuelled by their penchant for appearing semi-naked or worse. Slovak returned to guitar for the second album, this time produced by George Clinton. Also featured was a horn section comprising Maceo Parker and Fred Wesley, veterans of James Brown, among others. Martinez returned shortly afterwards to reinstate the original Anthem line-up, and their third album saw a shift back to rock from the soul infatuation of its predecessors. In 1988 they released the *Abbey Road EP*, featuring a pastiche of the famous Beatles album pose on the cover (the band were totally naked save for socks covering their genitalia). However, the mood was darkened when Slovak took an accidental heroin overdose and died in June. Deeply upset, Irons left, while the band recruited John Frusciante (guitar) and Chad Smith (b. 25 October 1962, St. Paul, Minnesota, USA; drums). After the release of *Mother's Milk*, the single 'Knock Me Down' was released as a tribute to Slovak. Of their most commercially successful excursion, 1991's *BloodSugarSexMagik*, they accurately diagnosed their motivation, and much of their attraction: 'Just recognizing that I was a freak, but knowing that was a cool place to be.' Producer Rick Rubin, usually associated with the harder end of the metal and rap spectrum (Slayer, Danzig), nevertheless brought out the Peppers' first ballads. Such sensitivity has done little to deter the vanguard of critics who have long since raged at what they saw as the band's innate sexism. Frusciante was replaced in June 1992 by Arik Marshall, who in turn was sacked one year later.

In 1994 new guitarist Dave Navarro (b. 7 June 1967, Santa Monica, California, USA; ex-Jane's Addiction) joined in time to participate in recording the excellent *One Hot Minute*, released in 1995. *BloodSugarSexMagik* had sold four million units in the USA by 1996. Navarro left the band in 1998 and was replaced by ex-member John Frusciante.

● ALBUMS: *Red Hot Chili Peppers* (EMI America 1984)★★★★, *Freaky Styley* (EMI America 1985)★★★, *Uplift Mofo Party Plan* (EMI Manhattan 1987)★★★, *Mother's Milk* (EMI America 1989)★★★, *BloodSugarSexMagik* (Warners 1991)★★★★, *One Hot Minute* (Warners 1995)★★★.

● COMPILATIONS: *What Hits!?* (EMI 1992)★★★, *Plasma Shaft* (Warners 1994)★★★, *Out In L.A.* (EMI 1994)★, *Greatest Hits* (CEMA/EMI 1995)★★★, *Essential Red Hot Chili Peppers: Under The Covers* (EMI 1998)★★.

● VIDEOS: *Funky Monks* (Warner Music Vision 1992).

● FURTHER READING: *True Men Don't Kill Coyotes*, Dave Thompson. *Sugar And Spice*, Chris Watts. *The Complete Story*, Spike Harvey.

Redd Kross

This Los Angeles, California, USA band was formed in 1979. Redd Kross melded elements of 70s glam-rock, 60s psychedelia and 80s heavy metal to become a popular 'alternative' act in the 80s. Originally called the Tourists, the band changed its name to Red Cross (they were later forced to change the spelling after the International Red Cross organization threatened to sue). At the beginning, the band consisted of 15-year-old Jeff McDonald as singer, his 11-year-old brother Steve on bass, Greg Hetson on guitar and Ron Reyes on drums. After gaining local recognition opening for such hardcore outfits as Black Flag, Red Cross made its first recordings in 1980 for a compilation album on the punk label Posh Boy Records. Shortly afterwards Hetson left to form the Circle Jerks and Reyes joined Black Flag. The band signed with manager John Silva, who went on to manage Nirvana and Sonic Youth following introductions by members of Redd Kross. Other musicians came and went throughout the band's history, the McDonald brothers being the only mainstay. The group's popularity grew steadily, particularly among those who listened to college radio stations, and by the end of the 80s they had recorded three albums in addition to the debut. Some featured cover versions of songs by such influences as the Rolling Stones and Kiss, while elsewhere the group's originals crossed 70s punk with the bubblegum hits of the 60s. The group resurfaced in the autumn of 1990 with *Third Eye*, their first album for a major label, Atlantic Records. However, it was 1993's *Phaseshifter* that brought about their commercial breakthrough, with the band continuing to record catchy post-punk homages to 70s kitsch, a ploy that was still proving popular by the time of 1997's exuberant *Showtime*.

● ALBUMS: *Born Innocent* (Smoke 7 1982)★★, *Teen Babes From Monsanto* (Gasatanka 1984)★★★, *Neurotica* (Big Time 1987)★★★, *Third Eye* (Atlantic 1990)★★, *Phaseshifter* (This Way Up/Mercury 1993)★★★, *Showtime* (This Way Up 1997)★★★, *Show World* (This Way Up 1997)★★★★.

REED, DAN, NETWORK

Along with Living Colour, this band led the way in the late 80s growth of funk-rock. Formed in Oregon, USA, the Network featured Dan Reed (vocals), Melvin Brannon II (b. 6 July 1962; bass), Brion James (lead guitar), Daniel Pred (drums), and Blake Sakamoto (keyboards). Signed to Mercury Records, they released their first, self-titled album in 1988, which contrasted the commercial rock of artists such as Bon Jovi with the funk rhythms of Prince. The album was enthusiastically received by those craving rock music with a difference, as tracks such as 'Get To You' and 'Ritual' soon became dancefloor hits at rock club bastions. That debut was followed by *Slam*, produced by Nile Rodgers of Chic fame, who gave the album a slightly harder edge while retaining the funk element of its predecessor. A single, 'Rainbow Child', provided the band with its first minor UK hit single, briefly entering the Top 40 in 1989. Prestigious support slots were gained in 1990 in Europe with Bon Jovi and the Rolling Stones, which helped to raise their profile and bring their music to much larger audiences. In 1991 *The Heat* was released, which saw them reunited with Bruce Fairbairn, producer of their first album. This included a highly original version of Pink Floyd's 'Money' as well as the singles 'Mix It Up' and 'Baby Now I', neither of which made an impression in the charts. In 1993 rumours of disquiet in the ranks emerged, exacerbated by Reed's decision to tour Sweden with a Swedish pick-up band under the slightly altered title Dan Reed And The Network. Afterwards Reed travelled to India to spend time with the exiled Tibetan spiritual leader, the Dalai Lama. This life-changing experience resulted in him retreating to his acting and theatre career when he returned to Portland. At this time it was stated by his representatives that it was unlikely that he would ever play music professionally again. Despite critical acclaim, support slots on major tours and a fair degree of radio exposure, the Dan Reed Network failed to achieve their big commercial break, while watching contemporaries such as Living Colour and Faith No More achieve platinum status.

● ALBUMS: *Dan Reed Network* (Mercury 1988)★★★★, *Slam* (Mercury 1989)★★★, *The Heat* (Mercury 1991)★★, *Live At Last* (Videomedia 1998)★★.

● COMPILATIONS: *Mixing It Up - The Best Of* (Mercury 1993)★★★.

REEF

Reef, originally titled Naked, were formed in England while students on a music course at West London Institute, though each member originated from Bath, Somerset. The line-up comprised Kenwyn House (b. 1 August 1970, Tiverton, Devon, England; guitar), Gary Stringer (b. 18 June 1973, Litchfield, Staffordshire, England; vocals), Dominic Greensmith (b. 2 June 1970, Denby, Derbyshire, England; drums) and Jack Bessant (b. 19 March 1971, Wells, Somerset, England; bass). They rose to fame via an advert for the Sony Mini-Disc portable stereo system. This depicted them as a heavy metal band touting for a contract, presenting their self-titled song, 'Naked', to an unimpressed A&R man, who throws the offending demo out of the window only for it to be retrieved and played by a passing skateboarder. It falsely gave the impression of them being a US band (the video was filmed in New York). Unsurprisingly signed to Sony Records, their first release was 'Good Feeling' in late 1994. The group were keen not to be seen as a one-song group and to this end initially declined to offer 'Naked' as a single release, often refusing to play it live. Their debut album was well received and hugely successful, although comparisons to Pearl Jam were widespread. *Glow* was the record that put them in the spotlight as a potentially major act, helped by the chart success of the anthemic single 'Place Your Hands'.

● ALBUMS: *Replenish* (Sony 1995)★★★, *Glow* (Additive 1996)★★★★.

REID, VERNON

Formerly the lead singer and guitarist with Living Colour, Reid (b. 22 August 1958, London, England) founded a new solo venture, titled Masque, in 1996. His debut solo album, *Mistaken Identity*, featured the full Masque band plus collaborators such as James Carter (saxophone), John Popper (of Blues Traveler), DJ Spooky and rapper Chubb Rock. Co-producers included Prince Paul and jazz legend Teo Macero. This represented his artistic rebirth after 10 years on the road with Living Colour, who disbanded in 1995. As Reid told *Rolling Stone*, 'Doing this album represents freedom for me. But freedom, as we know, is a responsibility. And part of what that responsibility calls me to do is not edit out what I'm feeling and thinking - and not to let anxiety and worry and market concerns infect the process.' Among the best tracks on view were 'Lightnin'', a tribute to Lightnin' Hopkins, and the dancehall reggae of 'Fresh Water Coconut'.

● ALBUMS: *Mistaken Identity* (Epic 1996)★★★.

REIGN

Reign are a thrash/doom metal band from South Shields in the north-east of England, influenced by bands including Paradise Lost and Carcass. Comprising John Cook (vocals, bass), Mark Robinson (rhythm and acoustic guitar), Ronnie McLean (drums) and Mick Storrie (rhythm and lead guitar), they initially rose to prominence via a final appearance in BBC Radio 1's *Rock War* competition, where they were unarguably the most extreme group on offer. Signing to European record label Mausoleum Records, the obvious next step was the recording of a debut album. *Embrace* combined brutal riffs with selective displays of melody. Positively reviewed in most of the genre magazines, Reign set about UK touring to promote the album during the spring of 1995.

● ALBUMS: *Embrace* (Mausoleum 1995)★★★, *Exit Clause* (Mausoleum 1996)★★.

REO SPEEDWAGON

Formed in Champaign, Illinois, USA, in 1970 when pianist Neal Doughty (b. 29 July 1946, Evanston, Illinois, USA) and drummer Alan Gratzer (b. 9 November 1948, Syracuse, New York, USA) were joined by guitarist and songwriter Gary Richrath (b. 10 October 1949, Peoria, Illinois, USA). Although still in its embryonic stage, the group already had its unusual name, which was derived from an early American fire-engine, designed by one Ransom E. Olds. Barry Luttnell (vocals) and Greg Philbin (bass) completed the line-up featured on *REO Speedwagon*, but the former was quickly replaced by Kevin Cronin (b. 6 October 1951, Evanston, Illinois, USA). The quintet then began the perilous climb from local to national prominence, but despite their growing popularity, particularly in America's Midwest, the band was initially unable to complete a consistent album. Although *REO Two* and *Ridin' The Storm Out* eventually achieved gold status, disputes regarding direction culminated in the departure of their second vocalist. Michael Murphy took his place in 1974, but when ensuing albums failed to generate new interest, Cronin rejoined his former colleagues. Bassist Bruce Hall (b. 3 May 1953, Champaign, Illinois, USA) was also brought into a line-up acutely aware that previous releases had failed to reflect their in-concert prowess. The live summary, *You Get What You Play For*, overcame this problem to become the group's first platinum disc, a distinction shared by its successor, *You Can Tune A Piano, But You Can't Tuna Fish*. However, sales for *Nine Lives* proved disappointing, inspiring the misjudged view that the band had peaked. Such impressions were banished in 1980 with the release of *Hi Infidelity*, a crafted, self-confident collection that topped the US album charts and spawned a series of highly successful singles. An emotive ballad, 'Keep On Lovin' You', reached number 1 in the USA and number 7 in the UK, while its follow-up, 'Take It On The Run', also hit the US Top 5. However, a lengthy tour in support of the album proved creatively draining and *Good Trouble* is generally accepted as one of REO's least worthy efforts. The quintet withdrew from the stadium circuit and, having rented a Los Angeles warehouse, enjoyed six months of informal rehearsals during which time they regained a creative empathy. *Wheels Are Turning* recaptured the zest apparent on *Hi Infidelity* and engendered a second US number 1 in 'Can't Fight This Feeling'. *Life As We Know It* and its successor, *The Earth, A Small Man, His Dog And A Chicken*, emphasized the group's now accustomed professionalism, by which time the line-up featured Cronin, Doughty, Hall, Dave Amato (b. 3 March 1953; lead guitar, ex-Ted Nugent), Bryan Hitt (b. 5 January 1954; drums, ex-Wang Chung) and Jesse Harms (b. 6 July 1952; keyboards). Too often dubbed 'faceless', or bracketed with other in-concert 70s favourites Styx and Kansas, REO Speedwagon have proved the importance of a massive, secure, grass-roots following.

● ALBUMS: *REO Speedwagon* (Epic 1971)★★★, *REO Two* (Epic 1972)★★★, *Ridin' The Storm Out* (Epic 1974)★★★, *Lost In A Dream* (Epic 1974)★★, *This Time We Mean It* (Epic 1975)★★, *REO* (Epic 1976)★★, *REO Speedwagon Live/You Get What You Play For* (Epic 1977)★★, *You Can Tune A Piano But You Can't Tuna Fish* (Epic 1978)★★, *Nine Lives* (Epic 1979)★★, *Hi Infidelity* (Epic 1980)★★, *Good Trouble* (Epic 1982)★★, *Wheels Are Turning* (Epic 1984)★★, *Life As We Know It* (Epic 1987)★★, *The Earth, A Small Man, His Dog And A Chicken* (Epic 1990)★★, *Building The Bridge* (Essential 1996)★★.

● COMPILATIONS: *A Decade Of Rock 'N' Roll 1970-*

1980 (Epic 1980)★★★, *Best Foot Forward* (Epic 1985)★★, *The Hits* (Epic 1988)★★★, *A Second Decade Of Rock 'N' Roll 1981-1991* (Epic 1991)★★.
● VIDEOS: *Wheels Are Turnin'* (Virgin Vision 1987), *REO Speedwagon* (Fox Video 1988).

Revolting Cocks

The history of the US rock group Revolting Cocks goes back to the mid-80s when Al Jourgensen (also Ministry) met Belgians Richard 23 and Luc Van Acker in a Chicago pool hall. Their first single was 'No Devotion', which made the PMRC's 'Naughty 9' list on account of its blasphemy. The British Home Secretary Douglas Hurd later tried to prevent them entering the country by refusing them work permits. The lyrical scope of the group's debut offered no respite. Subject matter included rioting soccer fans, sitcom junkies and industrial accidents. Joined in 1987 by multi-instrumentalist William Rieflin, the next single, 'You Often Forget', featured both 'malignant' and 'benign' versions in tribute to the media fascination of the time with Betty Ford's breasts. Richard 23 then departed for Front 242, and was replaced by Chris Connelly of Finitribe. Paul Barker of Ministry also played on and co-produced the half-live *You Goddamned Son Of A Bitch*, recorded at a Chicago show in September 1987. *Beers, Steers + Queers* was the group's second studio album, its title track a witty cod-machismo collision of cowboy kitsch and dialogue taken from the homosexual scenes in the film *Deliverance*. A cover version of Olivia Newton John's '(Let's Get) Physical' also featured - basically a loop of someone screaming the title. Afterwards the band left Wax Trax! Records (as had Ministry, from whom RevCo took Barker, Mike Scaccia and Louie Svitek - other part-time members have included Raven of Killing Joke and Nine Inch Nails' Trent Reznor). *Linger Ficken' Good* included a further bizarre cover version, this time Rod Stewart's 'Do You Think I'm Sexy'. Afterwards RevCo took a break from inflaming moral umbrage while Jourgensen concentrated on Ministry activities, leading him finally to concede in 1995 that 'we ran out of beer at the party'.
● ALBUMS: *Big Sexy Land* (Wax Trax! 1986)★★★, *You Goddamned Son Of A Bitch* (Wax Trax! 1988)★★★, *Beers, Steers + Queers* (Wax Trax! 1990)★★★, *Linger Ficken' Good ... And Other Barnyard Oddities* (Sire/Reprise 1993)★★★.

Rhinoceros

A rock band that promised more than it was able to deliver, Rhinoceros was an Elektra Records signing of the late 60s. The group looked a formidable line-up on paper with Michael Fonfara (ex-Electric Flag; keyboards), Billy Mundi (ex-Mothers Of Invention; drums), Doug Hastings (ex-Buffalo Springfield; guitar), Danny Weis (ex-Iron Butterfly; guitar) and John Finlay (vocals). The spectacular fold-out cover artwork on their debut by G. Sazaferin showed a brightly colourful, beaded Rhinoceros. Unfortunately the music was disappointing; only the Buddy Miles-influenced 'You're My Girl (I Don't Want To Discuss It)' and their 'greatest hit', the instrumental 'Apricot Brandy', stood out. The BBC adopted the latter as a Radio 1 theme. Two more albums followed, but by now the ponderous Rhinoceros had turned into a dodo.
● ALBUMS: *Rhinoceros* (Elektra 1968)★★★, *Satin Chickens* (Elektra 1969)★★, *Better Times Are Coming* (Elektra 1970)★.

Rhoads, Randy

Possibly one of the best hard rock guitarists to come out of America during the past two decades, Randy Rhoads (b. Randall William Rhoads, 6 December 1956, Santa Monica, California, USA, d. 19 March 1982) might, had his life not been so tragically curtailed in a freak aeroplane accident, have been talked about in the same breath as Eddie Van Halen and Jimmy Page. Certainly, there are many sterile technicians in the metal world whose celebrated virtuosity offers no match to Rhoads' flair. At an early age Rhoads began to study the guitar and in 1972 formed his first band, Quiet Riot, who, by 1975, with vocalist Kevin DuBrow and drummer Drew Forsyth, began to earn a good live reputation. By 1978 (when they were joined by bassist Rudy Sarzo), this had earned them a recording contract with Columbia Records, who pushed them (successfully) into the Japanese market. In October 1979 Sarzo joined American legends Angel and Rhoads became a guitar tutor. With Ozzy Osbourne finally free of Black Sabbath he began to put together a new band called Blizzard Of Ozz, having recruited a bassist and drummer. Osbourne then held auditions for a guitarist in Los Angeles. At the end of a day spent listening to rehashed Sabbath riffs he fell asleep. Later that evening he awoke to hear a gripping and original style. Half-conscious, he turned to his manager/wife Sharon and asked who the girl with the guitar was. From out of his mass of long blonde hair Rhoads appeared to take the post. It is with Osbourne that Rhoads is best remembered for his stunning live performances and excellence in the studio. The first Ozzy album contained his powerful signature on tracks such as

'Crazy Train' and 'Suicide Solution', as well as the more sensitive 'Dee', a track written by Rhoads for his mother. The title track of the second album, *Diary Of A Madman*, contains a superb mixture of acoustic and electric guitar, while 'You Can't Kill Rock And Roll' moved one reviewer to comment that 'Randy is at his most eloquent, spacey and rich'. Not satisfied with being merely a rock guitarist, Rhoads also concentrated on his masters degree in classical guitar, eventually hoping to meld the two styles to create new wonders. However, it was not to be. Whilst *en route* to Florida for further live shows, the tour bus made an unscheduled stop where the driver's friend had a small aeroplane. After taking up a couple of band members for a joy-ride, Rhoads and a make-up girl were persuaded to enlist. The pilot, high on cocaine, seemingly aimed the aircraft at the empty tour bus and all passengers were killed. Osbourne and his wife have never fully recovered from the tragedy. In 1987 Ozzy and Rhoads' mother put together a tribute album containing live recordings and a studio out-take of 'Dee'.

● ALBUMS: with Quiet Riot *Quiet Riot* (Columbia 1978)★★★, *Quiet Riot 2* (Columbia 1979)★★★; with Ozzy Osbourne *Blizzard Of Ozz* (Jet 1980)★★★, *Diary Of A Madman* (Jet 1981)★★; *Randy Rhoads Tribute Album* (Epic 1987)★★.

RIFF RAFF

Featuring Doug Lubahn (vocals, bass), Ned Lubahn (guitar, keyboards), Werner Fritzching (guitar) and Mark Kaufman (drums), this group from New York, USA, released just one album of above-average melodic heavy rock. *Vinyl Futures* represents a mixture of styles, the closest approximation of which might be early Rush crossed with Foreigner. They are not to be confused with the Finnish band of the same title. Lubahn would go on to work with Billy Squier when Riff Raff bit the dust.

● ALBUMS: *Vinyl Futures* (Atco 1981)★★★.

RIGGS

This Californian quartet was founded by vocalist/guitarist Jerry Riggs in 1981. With Jeremy Graf (guitar), David Riderick (bass) and Stephen Roy Carlisle (drums) completing the line-up, they specialized in hard-edged, metallic pop, with considerable crossover potential. Riggs on vocals was particularly distinctive, sounding not dissimilar to Bryan Adams. Their debut and only release remains an undiscovered gem of infectious and classy AOR. They were unfortunate in that they lacked a strong visual image and, without a strong promotional push, the project was doomed. Disillusioned, they disbanded, with Jerry Riggs later going on to play with Pat Travers.

● ALBUMS: *Riggs* (Full Moon 1982)★★★.

RIOT

Riot's career has forever been dogged by record company problems and a general lack of interest from press quarters - a surprising epitaph for a New York band who formed in 1976 and were the subject of a petition to get one of their albums released in Europe. Signed in 1977 to Ariola, the band comprised L.A. Kouvaris (guitar), Mark Reale (guitar), Peter Bitelli (drums), Jimmy Iommi (bass) and vocalist Speranza. Constant touring brought them little success and by 1979 Kouvaris was replaced by Rick Ventura. Capitol Records signed them and released *Narita* - still hailed as a hard rock classic, it brought them widespread attention in the UK, which led to an appearance at the Donington Festival in 1980. The following year they returned to the studio and recorded *Fire Down Under*. Capitol refused to release it and fans in the UK started the aforementioned petition to force their hand. Capitol stuck fast and dropped them, but Elektra were quick to recognize their potential. The album was eventually released to critical acclaim. However, Iommi and Bitelli quit, to be replaced by Kip Leming and Sandy Slavin, while former Rachel vocalist Rhett Forrester replaced Speranza. The next album, *Restless Breed*, was a mixed affair, but contained an excellent version of Eric Burdon's 'When I Was Young'. After a badly produced live album they were dropped by Elektra. They released one final album to a total absence of industry or fan interest in 1984. A brief but unsuccessful re-formation with most of the original line-up ensued in 1986, before Reale emerged with an all-new band, featuring Tony Moore (vocals), Don Van Stavern (bass) and Bobby Jarzombek (drums) and made an acclaimed comeback with *Thundersteel*, although *Privilege Of Power* and *Nightbreaker*, with new vocalist Michael Dimeo and guitarist Mike Flyntz, saw the band's sound fail to progress with the times. Forrester had a short-lived solo career before he too disappeared from view. It later emerged that he was murdered during an attempted robbery in January 1994.

● ALBUMS: *Rock City* (Ariola 1977)★★★, *Narita* (Capitol 1979)★★★, *Fire Down Under* (Elektra 1981)★★★★, *Restless Breed* (Elektra 1982)★★★, *Riot Live* (Elektra 1982)★★, *Born In America* (Grand Slam 1984)★★, *Thundersteel* (Columbia1988)★★★★, *Privilege Of Power*

(Columbia 1989)★★★, *Riot Live* 1980 recording (Columbia 1989)★★, *Nightbreaker* (Rising Sun 1994)★★★.

ROADHOUSE

This melodic UK hard rock quintet was assembled in 1991 around former Def Leppard guitarist Pete Willis. Utilizing the talents of Wayne Grant (bass), Richard Day (guitar), Paul Jackson (vocals) and Trevor Brewis (drums), the band were signed by Phonogram largely on the strength of the guitarist's connections. Their self-titled debut album was a major disappointment, however, featuring an average collection of commercial AOR-styled songs. The band lacked identity and have so far been unable to inject drive or spontaneity into their up-tempo numbers, while the ballads lacked sincerity, emotion or class.

● ALBUMS: *Roadhouse* (Phonogram 1991)★★.

ROBERTS, KANE

Kane Roberts first came to prominence as macho lead guitarist in Alice Cooper's band, during his mid-80s comeback, when he was lured from Lone Justice to add musical and visual muscle to Cooper's theatrical live shows. With the help of Cooper's management he secured a solo contract with MCA Records in 1987. His debut release, however, was somewhat at odds with his tough-guy image, featuring a collection of AOR and ballads. He quit Cooper's band the following year to concentrate on his solo career. Playing down the muscleman image, he teamed up with Desmond Child to write material for *Saints And Sinners*. This was a highly polished melodic rock album in a Bon Jovi-meets-Kiss vein, with John McCurry (guitar), Steven Steele (bass), Myron Grombacher (drums) and Chuck Kentis (keyboards) being recruited as permanent band members.

● ALBUMS: *Kane Roberts* (MCA 1987)★★★, *Saints And Sinners* (Geffen 1991)★★★.

ROCK CITY ANGELS

This blues-based hard rock quintet from the USA were formed by vocalist Bobby Durango and bassist Andy Panik in 1982. After a series of false-starts under the names the Abusers and the Delta Rebels, they settled on the title Rock City Angels, adding guitarists Doug Banx and Mike Barnes and drummer Jackie D. Jukes to complete the line-up. *Young Man's Blues* was an impressive debut. Utilizing full digital technology, it was a double album that featured a superb amalgam of earthy rockers and honest blues numbers. Durango's vocals have a southern twang to them, while the songs themselves combined elements of Lynyrd Skynyrd, Little Feat and the Georgia Satellites. Despite this the album failed commercially and, disillusioned, the band broke up in 1989. Durango immediately started a new band under his own name.

● ALBUMS: *Young Man's Blues* (Geffen 1988)★★★★.

ROCK GODDESS

Formed by sisters Jody and Julie Turner at the tender age of 13 and nine, respectively, even in such infancy Jody proved a good guitarist and Julie showed considerable promise as a drummer. Their father ran a music shop in Wandsworth, London, which had a rehearsal room next to it. The sisters, along with schoolfriend and budding bassist Tracey Lamb, soon started to put a set together. By 1981 they had recorded their first demo tape and began to play clubs in London, earning a reputation as schoolgirl rockers who could hold their own against more established outfits. They soon attracted the attention of Karine, singer with indie band Androids Of Mu, who invited them to contribute one track, 'Make My Night', which she produced, to the all-female compilation album, *Making Waves*. They then set out on tour with Androids Of Mu and the Gymslips, with their father now managing them. Through his efforts they acquired a contract with A&M Records, and spent most of 1982 writing songs and playing live. The following year they released their debut album, and a single entitled 'My Angel'. With Girlschool running out of steam they picked up much of their following and boosted their line-up with Kate Burbela on second guitar. Their follow-up album the same year was a better received product, yet Lamb decided to leave and was replaced by Dee O'Malley, who departed herself in 1986 to start a family. The final album was a good effort but interest in the band had long gone and Jody left to pursue a solo career. In 1988 Lamb joined Girlschool.

● ALBUMS: *Rock Goddess* (A&M 1983)★★★, *Hell Hath No Fury* (A&M 1983)★★★, *Young And Free* (Just In 1987)★★.

ROCKHEAD

Rockhead were put together by producer Bob Rock (b. Robert Jens Rock, 19 April 1954, Winnipeg, Canada), famed for his work with Bon Jovi, Aerosmith, Mötley Crüe and Metallica, with Steve Jack (vocals), Jamey Kosh (bass) and Chris Taylor (drums). Rockhead (the producer/guitarist's nickname) had little difficulty in finding a recording contract, with Richie Sambora and the Cult's Billy Duffy guesting on their debut, and landed a prestigious European tour support slot with Bon Jovi. All this made the band an easy target for sniping critics, but although *Rockhead* was hardly innovative, it was a solid and, naturally, superbly produced collection of stadium hard rock that translated well to the stage. The band proved to be a capable live act too, providing Bob Rock with a pleasant diversion from studio work.

● ALBUMS: *Rockhead* (EMI 1993)★★.

Rods

This New York power-trio exploded onto the heavy metal scene in 1980. Formed by ex-Elf guitarist David Feinstein, the line-up was completed by drummer Carl Canedy and bassist Stephen Farmer. Although heavily influenced by Kiss, Ted Nugent and Deep Purple, they transformed these influences into a unique sound that was at once aggressive, powerful and uncompromising. *Rock Hard*, released on the independent Primal label, was a terse and anthemic debut, which eventually led to the inking of a contract with Arista. Gary Bordonaro replaced Farmer before their first major label release (a remixed version of *Rock Hard*, with three additional tracks). *Wild Dogs* was a disappointing follow-up and sold poorly, which ensured the band would be dropped by their label. Consigned once more to the independent sector, *In The Raw* was a poorly produced collection of demos, while the live album suffered from muddy sound and uninspired performances. By this stage the band had largely alienated their original fanbase. *Let Them Eat Metal*, although a marked improvement, still failed to sell and they branched into more melodic rock, recruiting Andy McDonald (guitar), Rick Caudle (vocals), and Emma Zale (keyboards). In 1987 the band returned to a three-piece format again, with Craig Gruber (ex-Elf) replacing Bordonaro, before ex-Picture vocalist Shmoulic Avigal was added to record *Heavier Than Thou*. The third successive release to fail to make any impact, this increased existing internal pressures and the band imploded shortly thereafter.

● ALBUMS: *Rock Hard* (Primal 1980)★★★, *The Rods* (Arista 1981)★★★, *Wild Dogs* (Arista 1982)★★, *In The Raw* (Shrapnel 1983)★, *Live* (Music For Nations 1983)★★★, *Let Them Eat Metal* (Music For Nations 1984)★★★, *Heavier Than Thou* (Zebra 1987)★★★.

Rogue Male

Formed in London, England, in 1984, the band's original line-up consisted of Jim Lyttle (vocals, guitar), John Fraser Binnie (guitar; ex-Dirty Tricks), Kevin Collier (bass; ex-Le Griffe) and Steve Kingsley (drums). Signing to the Music For Nations label, their debut, *First Visit*, was full of fast, punk-influenced metal. With live gigs revealing Jim Lyttle to be a charismatic leader, they embarked on an ill-fated American tour. Blaming their US label Elektra Records for a lack of promotion, the band returned to England to begin work on a second album. At this point Steve Kingsley left to be replaced by session drummer Charlie Morgan, who played on the album recordings, but was replaced soon afterwards by Danny Fury. *Animal Man* was released in 1986 but the band dissolved soon after its release in the face of public indifference.

● ALBUMS: *First Visit* (Music For Nations 1985)★★★★, *Animal Man* (Music For Nations 1986)★★.

Rollins, Henry

b. Henry Garfield, 13 February 1961, Washington, DC, USA. Vocalist Rollins quickly returned to action following the break-up of Black Flag, releasing *Hot Animal Machine*, followed by the *Drive By Shooting* EP (under the pseudonym Henrietta Collins And The Wife Beating, Child Haters). The Rollins Band was eventually formed in 1987 with Chris Haskett (guitar), Andrew Weiss (bass) and Sim Cain (drums). The group developed their own brand of hard rock with blues and jazz influences, over several studio and live albums, building a considerable following with their heavy touring schedule. Rollins' lyrics deal with social and political themes, often unashamedly exorcizing personal demons from a troubled childhood. The sight of the heavily muscled and tattooed frontman on stage, dripping sweat and roaring out his rage, is one of the most astonishing, memorable sights in hard rock music, topping off an enthralling live act. Their commercial rise began with the opening slot on the first Lollapalooza tour, exposing the band to huge audiences for the first time. *The End Of Silence* was a deserved success, and contained some of Rollins' most strikingly introspective lyrics. 'Just Like You' narrated his difficulty in dealing with his similarities to an abusive father: 'You should see the pain I go through, When I see myself I see you'. Rollins' spoken word and publishing activities (his regime is one that allows for little more than a few hours' sleep each night) also drew major media interest. An accomplished and experienced spoken word performer with several albums to his credit, Rollins' often hilarious style is in direct contrast to his musical persona, and he has drawn comparisons to Lenny Bruce and Dennis Leary (although, in contrast, he implores his audience not to destroy themselves with poisons like alcohol and tobacco). Despite the humour there is a serious edge to his words, best animated in the harrowing story of the murder of his best friend, Joe Cole, within feet of him. Rollins' workaholic frame also levers his own publishing company, 2.13.61 (after his birthdate), which has grown from small beginnings in 1984 to publish a wide range of authors, including Rollins' own prolific output. He also has a music publishing enterprise Human Pittbull and co-owns a record label with Rick Rubin dedicated to classic punk reissues - Rollins himself having graduated from the infamous late 70s Washington DC 'straight edge' scene and bands such as SOA. He has additionally broken into film acting, appearing in *The Chase* and *Johnny Mnemonic*. Back with the Rollins Band, *Weight*, produced by long-time sound man Theo Van Rock, saw the first personnel change since the band's inception with Melvin Gibbs replacing Weiss, and adding a funkier spine to the band's still intense core. *Come In And Burn*, released in 1997, was adjudged to be a largely uninspiring collection. Rollins released a further spoken word recording, *Think Tank*, in 1998 and was also pursuing new acting opportunities, including an appearance in David Lynch's *Lost Highway*.

● ALBUMS: *Hot Animal Machine* (Texas Hotel 1986)★★, spoken word *Big Ugly Mouth* (Texas Hotel 1987)★★★, spoken word *Sweat Box* (Texas Hotel 1989)★★, spoken word *The Boxed Life* (Imago 1993)★★★, as the Rollins Band *Live* (Eksakt 1987)★★★, *Life Time* (Texas Hotel 1988)★★★, *Do It* (Texas Hotel 1988), *Hard Volume* (Texas Hotel 1989)★★★, *Turned On* (Quarterstick 1990)★★★, *The End Of Silence* (Imago 1992)★★★★, *Weight* (Imago 1994)★★★, *Get In The Van* (Imago 1994)★★★, *Everything* (Thirsty Ear 1996)★★, *Come In And Burn* (Dreamworks 1997)★★, spoken word *Think Tank* (1998)★★★.

● FURTHER READING: all titles by Henry Rollins *High Adventures In The Great Outdoors* aka *Bodybag. Pissing In The Gene Pool. Art To Choke Hearts. Bang!. One From None. See A Grown Man Cry. Black Coffee Blues. Now Watch Him Die. Get In The Van: On The Road With Black Flag. Do I Come Here Often (Black Coffee Blues Part Two). Turned On: A Biography Of Henry Rollins*, James Parker.

Romeo's Daughter

This UK AOR band were fronted by female vocalist Leigh Matty, expertly backed by songwriter and guitarist Craig Joiner, Tony Mitman on keyboards, Ed Poole on bass and drummer Andy Wells. The band came together under the direction of producer Robert 'Mutt' Lange in what seemed to be an attempt to recreate a similar project from the late 70s with his wife's band, Night. Lange, along with John Parr and Joiner, worked hard on the songs and production and, armed with a contract with Jive Records, issued the single 'Heaven In The Back Seat', a minor hit that brought together elements of both Heart and Belinda Carlisle while retaining an 'English' sound. 1989's self-titled album sold well and the band proved a popular live attraction, receiving much attention from Radio 1's *Rock Show* who broadcast live concerts and an exclusive session. 'Heaven In The Back Seat', meanwhile, also turned up on the soundtrack to *Nightmare On Elm Street 5: The Dream Child*. The band went to ground but resurfaced in 1993 with another single, 'Attracted To The Animal', followed by a major tour and an album on Music For Nations. By this time they had lost much of their earlier impact and by 1994 had left both management and label in search of new ideas, and were contemplating a change of name.

● ALBUMS: *Romeo's Daughter* (Jive 1989)★★★, *Delectable* (Music For Nations 1993)★★.

Rose Tattoo

This legendary Australian band was formed by former Buster Brown members Angry Anderson (b. Gary Anderson, Australia; vocals) and Mick 'Geordie' Leech (bass) with Peter Wells (slide guitar, vocals), Michael Cocks (lead guitar) and Dallas 'Digger' Royall (drums) in Sydney in 1977. They released their classic self-titled debut (known as *Rock 'N' Roll Outlaws* outside Australia) the following year. *Rose Tattoo* was an aggressive blues-rock masterpiece packed with excellent songs, and the band's electric live performances and tough tattooed image drew support from punks and rockers alike. Their European debut in 1981, supporting Rainbow, and an appearance at the Reading Festival caused quite a stir, but a poor sound on *Assault & Battery* rather dulled their impact. This was despite the quality of the material, with Anderson characteristically offering political comment and true story narrative against a straightforward boogie background. *Scarred For Life*, with Robin Riley replacing Cocks, had a stronger production and yet more high-quality songs, but the band fell apart on their first US tour with Aerosmith and Pat Travers over numerous personal problems. Anderson and Leech assembled a new line-up with Greg Jordan (slide guitar), Robert Bowron (drums) and John Meyer (guitar) for *Southern Stars*, but the band later split. *Beats From A Single Drum* was released for contractual reasons under the name Rose Tattoo, but was in fact Anderson's solo debut as he expanded his horizons into film and television. However, the legend remained strong, and Rose Tattoo were persuaded to re-form the original line-up (sadly without Royall, who had died in 1990) for an Australian support slot with Guns N'Roses (who had covered the group's 'Nice Boys' on their debut EP) in 1993, plus a small tour of their own, culminating in a biker festival headline slot. Despite an average age of around 45, Rose Tattoo proved that the old fire still burned brightly with dazzling performances.

● ALBUMS: *Rose Tattoo* (Albert 1978)★★★, *Assault & Battery* (Albert 1981)★★★★, *Scarred For Life* (Albert 1982)★★★, *Southern Stars* (Albert 1984)★★★, *Beats From A Single Drum* (Mushroom 1987)★★★.

● COMPILATIONS: *Nice Boys Don't Play Rock 'N' Roll* (Albert 1992)★★★★.

Rossington Collins

This US rock band was formed in 1979 by the four surviving members of the 1977 Lynyrd Skynyrd plane crash; Gary Rossington (guitars), Allen Collins (guitars), Billy Powell (keyboards) and Leon Wilkerson (bass), who joined with Dale Krantz (vocals), Barry Harwood (guitars) and Derek Hess (drums). They continued in the best traditions of Skynyrd, though the female lead vocals gave them a different sound. They broke up in 1983 after just two albums. Powell later joined the Christian rock band Vision, while Collins was paralyzed from the waist down in a car accident in the mid-80s, and died of pneumonia on 23 January 1990. Krantz married Rossington and both they and Powell took their places in the Lynyrd Skynyrd reunion tour of 1987.

● ALBUMS: *Anytime, Anyplace, Anywhere* (MCA 1980)★★★, *This Is The Way* (MCA 1982)★★.

Roth, David Lee

b. 10 October 1955, Bloomington, Indiana, USA. Roth, the former lead vocalist with Van Halen, first expressed his desire to go solo during a period of band inactivity during 1985. He subsequently recorded a mini-album, *Crazy From The Heat*, featuring a varied selection of material that was a departure from the techno-metal approach of Van Halen. The album was favourably reviewed and after much speculation, he finally broke ranks in the autumn of 1985. Roth soon found himself in the US Top 3 with an unlikely version of the Beach Boys' 'California Girls' (complete with a suitably tacky video) and an even stranger cover version of 'I Ain't Got Nobody'. This bizarre change must have baffled and bemused his fans, but he soon assembled an impressive array of musicians, notably guitar virtuoso Steve Vai (ex-Frank Zappa; Alcatrazz), bassist Billy Sheehan (ex-Talas) and drummer Greg Bissonette to record *Eat 'Em And Smile*. This featured an amazing selection of blistering rockers and offbeat, big production numbers. It proved that Roth was still a great showman; the album was technically superb and infused with an irreverent sense of 'Yankee' humour. *Skyscraper*, released two years later, built on this foundation, but focused more on an elaborately produced hard rock direction. Billy Sheehan departed shortly after its release to be replaced by Matt Bissonette. Brett Tuggle on keyboards was also recruited to expand the line-up to a five piece and add an extra dimension to their sound. Steve Vai left in 1989 to pursue a solo career, but was only temporarily missed as Jason Becker stepped in, a new six-string whizz kid of the Yngwie Malmsteen school of guitar improvisation. *A Little Ain't Enough* emerged in 1991 and, although technically faultless, it tended to duplicate ideas from his previous two albums. *Your Filthy Little Mouth* saw him relocate to New York. This time, amid the histrionics about girls and cars, were odes to the Los Angeles riots, and the unutterably horrible pseudo-reggae of 'No Big 'Ting'. In 1996 following Sammy Hagar's departure (sacking) from Van Halen, Lee Roth was falsely rumoured to be rejoining the band he had left 10 years earlier.

● ALBUMS: *Crazy From The Heat* (Warners 1985)★★★, *Eat 'Em And Smile* (Warners 1986)★★, *Skyscraper* (Warners 1988)★★, *A Little Ain't Enough* (Warners 1991)★★, *Your Filthy Little Mouth* (Warners 1994)★★.

● COMPILATIONS: *The Best* (Rhino 1997).

● VIDEOS: *David Lee Roth* (1987).

● FURTHER READING: *Crazy From The Heat*, David Lee Roth.

Rough Cutt

A typical mid-80s Los Angeles, California, USA rock band, Rough Cutt followed in the footsteps of Ratt and Quiet Riot but lacked originality. Led by vocalist Paul Shortino, they were proficient enough to gain support slots on American tours with Accept and Krokus, but generated little interest in the UK. Warner Brothers took a chance on them in 1985 and released the first of two average albums. In 1986 they were dropped by the company and Shortino left to join Quiet Riot, leaving the rest of the band - Amir Derakh (guitar), David Alford (drums), Matt Thor (bass) - to form Jailhouse.

● ALBUMS: *Rough Cutt* (Warners 1985)★★, *Wants You* (Warners 1986)★★.

Rough Diamond

This highly touted UK supergroup was formed to considerable fanfare in 1976. Dave Clempson (ex-Bakerloo; Colosseum; Humble Pie; guitar), Damon Butcher (keyboards; ex-Steve Marriot's All Stars), Willie Bath (bass) and Geoff Britton (ex-Wings; drums) joined former Uriah Heep singer David Byron, but their launch was undermined by a court case brought by another group claiming the same name. The delay undermined the quintet's confidence and the ensuing album proved disappointing. Its appearance during the punk explosion exacerbated problems and although the band looked to the USA for solace, friction between Byron and his colleagues proved insurmountable. The singer embarked on a solo career in October 1977 while the remaining members added Garry Bell and adopted a new name, Champion, releasing an album on Epic Records in 1978.

● ALBUMS: *Rough Diamond* (Island 1977)★★★.

Rough House

Originally named Ruff Haus, this hard rock band based in Dusseldorf, Germany, comprised Uwe Stedtler (vocals), Rolf Himmelman (guitar), Jens Schwarz (bass) and Gunter Zimmerman (drums). Formed in October 1978, they borrowed liberally from British and American traditions, though initially they confined their lyrics to German. Of the two albums they released, *Blitzkrieg* is widely considered the most proficient, including as it does their debut single, 'Putsch'. After the group's demise in 1982 the members returned to day jobs, Zimmerman continuing to work as a producer.

● ALBUMS: *Blitzkrieg* (Stanz 1979)★★★★, *Krankenhaus* (Stanz 1980)★★★.

Rough Silk

Comprising Jan Barnett (vocals, guitar), Herbert Harman (drums), Ferdy Doernberg (piano, keyboards), Hilmer Staacke (guitar) and Ralf Schwertner (bass), Hannover, Germany-based rock band Rough Silk represent part of the new wave of European rock music. With an easily detectable bent towards American AOR stylings, in the vein of bands such as Rainbow, Bon Jovi and REO Speedwagon, Rough Silk have struggled to throw off accusations of imitation. However, they are nevertheless competent at their craft, as has been proved by two albums for the Mausoleum label recorded at Dieter Dierks' German studio. The second of these was the better, with songs such as 'Toxical Roses' and 'One More For The Ride' demonstrating the group's ability to tackle contrasting material without losing momentum.

● ALBUMS: *Rough Silk* (Mausoleum 1993)★★★, *Walls Of Never* (Mausoleum 1995)★★★.

Rox

Hailing from Manchester, England, Rox were a glam rock band heavily influenced by Kiss and Angel, who sprang to life in 1981 (as Venom) with Mark Anthony (vocals), Red Hot Red (b. Ian Burke; guitar), Paul Diamond (b. Paul Hopwood; guitar), Gary Maunsell (bass) and Tony Fitzgerald (drums). They soon built up a loyal following and received a great deal of attention from *Sounds*. A year later Fitzgerald left and was replaced by Bernie Emerald (b. Bernard Nuttall). With the departure of Anthony they recruited their roadie, Kevin Read, who took on the name of 'Kick Ass' Kevin Kozak. After reported threats from Newcastle's black metal merchants of the same name they decided to change theirs to Rox. Maunsell was then replaced by Billy Beaman before they set out on tour. After the release of the EP *Hot Love In The City*, in August 1992 they signed to Music For Nations. The group released a 12-inch EP, *Krazy Kutz*, a year later, before a higher profile tour and album, *Violent Breed*. Soonwards after Kozak was replaced by Anthony again, this time using the name Mark Savage. Despite the fact that there were no new records to promote they managed to hitch a ride on the Quiet Riot tour of the UK in 1984. The following year Diamond quit and the band split up (Diamond later turned up in a new group, Torino).

● ALBUMS: *Violent Breed* (Music For Nations 1983)★★★.

Royal Court Of China

This Nashville, Tennessee quartet were formed in 1984 by Joe Blanton (vocals, rhythm guitar), Chris Mekow (drums), Robert Logue (bass) and Oscar Rice (guitar), taking their name from a reference to the highest form of Chinese opium, which had originally been the name chosen by Jimmy Page and Paul Rodgers for the group that became the

Firm. Impressive local gigging and the self-financed *Off The Beat 'n' Path* EP led to a contract with A&M, but with Logue and Rice's penchant for a folkier sound, the album tended more towards R.E.M. in style than the hard rock direction that the other two preferred, and following a tour with REO Speedwagon, the band split. Blanton and Mekow retained both name and contract, and recruited bassist Drew Cornutt and guitarist Josh Weinberg, although the latter was replaced by Jeff Mays when he failed to live up to expectations in the studio. *Geared And Primed*, produced by Vic Maile, was an impressively diverse album, following a harder direction while retaining the more rootsy guitar elements of their previous release, particularly on the lighter material. However, the album lacked the depth of quality material to make it a success, and the band faded from sight.

● ALBUMS: *The Royal Court Of China* (A&M 1987)★★★, *Geared And Primed* (A&M 1989)★★★.

RPLA

RPLA sprang to fame when they starred on an unlikely front cover of the UK heavy metal *Kerrang!* magazine, who marketed them as a 'Pretty Boy' band similar to Poison and Mötley Crüe. Not long after this appearance they emerged with a different image and admitted that they were a 'gay' rock band. While this should have made no difference at all it knocked the macho metal press off its stride and suddenly the rave write-ups and gig reviews disappeared, with the band suffering as a result. They became the subject of a news item on UK television about sexism/homophobia in rock and *Kerrang!* were singled out. Within a few weeks a small piece on them became conspicuous by its appearance in said magazine. Whatever their press relationship was, the band did themselves no favours because the music content was never strong enough to overcome even the mildest prejudice.

● ALBUMS: *Metal Queen Hijack* (EMI 1992)★★.

Rub Ultra

Dub metal crossover artists formed in London in August 1993, comprising Will (vocals), Steve (guitar), Charlie (bass), Sarah (vocals, percussion; sister of Will) and Pete (drums). Together they released two EPs in 1994, *Combatstrengthsoap* and *Cosmyk Fynger Tactik*, the latter's cover featuring a holiday snap of a camel's posterior. Following support slots with Headswim, S*M*A*S*H* and Therapy? (whose Michael McKeegan was prepared to roadie for the band) rumours began to circulate that their debut album for Virgin indie subsidiary Hut would have none other than John Leckie as producer.

● ALBUMS: *Liquid Boots And Boiled Sweets* (Hi Rise 1995)★★★.

Runaways

Formed in 1975, the Runaways were initially the product of producer/svengali Kim Fowley and teenage lyricist Kari Krome. Together they assembled an adolescent female group following several auditions in the Los Angeles area. The original line-up consisted of Joan Jett (b. Joan Larkin, 22 September 1960, Philadelphia, Pennsylvania, USA; guitar, vocals), Micki Steele (bass - later of the Bangles) and Sandy West (drums), but was quickly bolstered by the addition of Lita Ford (b. 23 September 1959, London, England; guitar, vocals) and Cherie Currie (vocals). The departure of Steele prompted several replacements, the last of which was Jackie Fox (b. Jacqueline Fuchs) who had failed her first audition. Although originally viewed as a vehicle for compositions by Fowley and associate Mars Bonfire (b. Dennis Edmonton), material by Jett and Krome helped to assert the quintet's independence. *The Runaways* showed a group indebted to the 'glam-rock' of the Sweet and punchy pop of Suzi Quatro, and included the salutary 'Cherry Bomb'. *Queens Of Noise* repeated the pattern, but the strain of touring - the quintet were highly popular in Japan - took its toll on Jackie Fox, who left the line-up and abandoned music altogether, becoming an attorney practising in intellectual property law. Personality clashes resulted in the departure of Cherie Currie, whose solo career stalled following the failure of her debut, *Beauty's Only Skin Deep*. Guitarist/vocalist Vicki Blue and bassist Laurie McAllister completed a revitalized Runaways, but the latter was quickly dropped. Subsequent releases lacked the appeal of the group's early work which, although tarred by novelty and sexual implication, nonetheless showed a sense of purpose. The Runaways split in 1980 but both Jett and Ford later enjoyed solo careers, the former engendering considerable commercial success during the 80s. In 1985 the mischievous Fowley resurrected the old group's name with all-new personnel. This opportunistic concoction split up on completing *Young And Fast*. In 1994 there were reports that Fowley was being sued by Jett, Ford, Currie and West over unpaid royalties. Fox was not involved in the action, presumably because she is now herself a practising lawyer.

● ALBUMS: *The Runaways* (Mercury 1976)★★★,

Queens Of Noise (Mercury 1977)★★, *Live In Japan* (Mercury 1977)★★, *Waitin' For The Night* (Mercury 1977)★★, *And Now ... The Runaways* (Phonogram 1979)★★, *Young And Fast* (Allegiance 1987)★.

● COMPILATIONS: *Rock Heavies* (Mercury 1979)★★★, *Flamin' Schoolgirls* (Phonogram 1982)★★, *The Best Of The Runaways* (Mercury 1982)★★, *I Love Playing With Fire* (Laker 1982)★★.

RUNNING WILD

This quartet from Hamburg, Germany, were strongly influenced by the New Wave Of British Heavy Metal Movement of the early 80s. Formed in 1983 by guitarist/vocalist Rockin' Rolf, a plethora of personnel changes occurred before Majik Moti (guitar), Jens Becker (bass) and Iain Finlay (drums) were recruited and a degree of stability was achieved. They initially pushed a black-metal image, but made little impact with their rigidly formularized, one-paced rantings. They changed course musically with their third album and tried to emulate the style of Iron Maiden, and also adopted a rather unfortunate swashbuckling pirate's image. However, Rolf's weak vocals and the repetitiveness of their material always hindered their chances of promotion to rock's upper echelons. 1998's *The Rivalry* saw a change in look - from pirate costumes to Napoleonic uniforms.

● ALBUMS: *Gates Of Purgatory* (Noise 1984)★★★, *Branded And Exiled* (Noise 1985)★★★, *Under Jolly Roger* (Noise 1987)★★★, *Ready For Boarding* (Noise 1988)★★★, *Port Royal* (Noise 1988)★★, *Death Or Glory* (Noise 1990)★★, *Blazin' Stone* (Noise 1991)★★★, *The Rivalry* (G.U.N. 1998)★★★.

● COMPILATIONS: *The First Years Of Piracy* (Noise 1992)★★★.

● VIDEOS: *Death Or Glory* (1992).

RUSH

This Canadian heavy rock band comprised Geddy Lee (b. Gary Lee Weinrib, 29 July 1953, Willowdale, Toronto, Canada; keyboards, bass, vocals), Alex Lifeson (b. Alex Zivojinovich, 27 August 1953, British Columbia, Canada; guitar) and John Rutsey (drums). From 1969-72 they performed in Toronto playing a brand of Cream-inspired material, honing their act on the local club and bar circuit. In 1973 they recorded a version of Buddy Holly's 'Not Fade Away' as their debut release, backing it with 'You Can't Fight It', for their own label, Moon Records. Despite failing to grab the attention as planned, the group pressed ahead with the recording of a debut album, which was remixed by Terry 'Broon' Brown. Brown would continue to work with the band until 1984's *Grace Under Pressure*. With no bite from the majors, once again this arrived via Moon, with distribution by London Records. However, at least the quality of the group's live appointments improved, picking up support slots with the New York Dolls in Canada and finally crossing the US border to play gigs with ZZ Top. Eventually Cliff Burnstein of Mercury Records (who would later also sign Def Leppard) heard the band, and his label would reissue the group's debut. At this point Neil Peart (b. 12 September 1952, Hamilton, Ontario, Canada; drums, ex-Hush), who was to be the main songwriter of the band, replaced Rutsey, and Rush undertook their first full tour of the USA. Rush's music was typified by Lee's oddly high-pitched voice, a tremendously powerful guitar sound, especially in the early years, and a recurrent interest in science fiction and fantasy from the pen of Neil Peart. Later he would also conceptualize the work of authors such as John Barth, Gabriel Garcia Marquez and John Dos Passos. This approach reached its zenith in the group's 1976 concept album, *2112*, based on the work of novelist/philosopher Ayn Rand, which had as its central theme the concept of individual freedom and will. Including a 20-minute title track that lasted all of side one, it was a set that crystallized the spirit of Rush for both their fans and detractors. However, the band's most popular offering, *A Farewell To Kings*, followed by *Hemispheres* in 1978, saw Peart finally dispense with his 'epic' songwriting style. By 1979 Rush were immensely successful worldwide, and the Canadian Government awarded them the title of official Ambassadors of Music. As the 80s progressed Rush streamlined their image to become sophisticated, clean-cut, cerebral music-makers. Some early fans denigrated their determination to progress musically with each new album, though in truth the band had thoroughly exhausted its earlier style. They enjoyed a surprise hit single in 1980 when 'Spirit Of Radio' broke them out of their loyal cult following, and live shows now saw Lifeson and Lee adding keyboards for a fuller sound. Lee's vocals had also dropped somewhat from their earlier near-falsetto. The best recorded example of the band from this period is the succinct *Moving Pictures* from 1981, a groundbreaking fusion of technological rock and musical craft that never relies on the former at the expense of the latter. However, their career afterwards endured something of a creative wane, with the band at odds with various musical innovations. Despite this, live shows were still exciting events for the large pockets of fans the band retained all over the world, and in the powerful *Hold Your Fire* in 1987 they proved they were still able to scale former heights. In 1994 the band agreed to a break for the first time in their career, during which Lifeson worked on his Victor side project. They returned in 1996 with *Test For Echo*. Often criticized for lyrical pretension and musical grandstanding - unkind critics have suggested that Rush is exactly what you get if you let your drummer write your songs for you - they nevertheless remain Canada's leading rock attraction.

● ALBUMS: *Rush* (Moon 1974)★★, *Fly By Night* (Moon 1975)★★, *Caress Of Steel* (Mercury 1975)★★, *2112* (Mercury 1976)★★, *All The World's A Stage* (Mercury 1976)★★, *A Farewell To Kings* (Mercury 1977)★★, *Hemispheres* (Mercury 1978)★★, *Permanent Waves* (Mercury 1980)★★★, *Moving Pictures* (Mercury 1981)★★★, *Exit: Stage Left* (Mercury 1981)★★★, *Signals* (Mercury 1982)★★★, *Grace Under Pressure* (Mercury 1984)★★, *Power Windows* (Mercury 1985)★★, *Hold Your Fire* (Mercury 1987)★★, *A Show Of Hands* (Mercury 1989)★★, *Presto* (Atlantic 1989)★★, *Roll The Bones* (Atlantic 1991)★★, *Counterparts* (Mercury 1993)★★, *Test For Echo* (Atlantic 1996)★★.

● COMPILATIONS: *Archives* 3-CD set (Mercury 1978)★★★, *Rush Through Time* (Mercury 1980)★★, *Chronicles* (Mercury 1990)★★★.

● VIDEOS: *Grace Under Pressure* (1986), *Exit Stage Left* (1988), *Thru' The Camera's Eye* (1989), *A Show Of Hands* (1989), *Chronicles* (1991).

● FURTHER READING: *Rush*, Brian Harrigan. *Rush Visions: The Official Biography*, Bill Banasiewicz.

S.A.D.O.

This German group achieved a degree of notoriety during the mid-80s with their Tubes-like stage show that incorporated a selection of scantily clad females in sado-masochistic uniform. Vocalist Andre Cook has been the only permanent member since the band's inception in 1983, losing original collaborators Matti Kaebs (drums), Wolfgang Eicholz (guitar), Matthias Moser (guitar) and Stepan Neumann (bass) - all of whom left to form V2 after the release of the inappropriately titled *Circle Of Friends*. Cook attempted to jump the thrash-metal bandwagon with *Dirty Fantasy*, attracting minimal attention, then adopted a more melodic AOR approach for *Sensitive*. Their final line-up included Cook, a returning Moser (guitar), Duncan O'Neill (bass) and Danny (drums), but all to little avail as the group disbanded shortly after the album's release.

● ALBUMS: *Shout* (Noise 1984)★★★, *Circle Of Friends* (Noise 1987)★★, *Dirty Fantasy* (Noise 1988)★★★, *Another Kind Of...* mini-album (Noise 1989)★★★, *Sensitive* (Noise 1990)★★.

SABBAT

Formed in England in 1986, this group comprised Martin Walkyier (vocals), Andy Sneap (guitar), Frazer Craske (bass) and Simon Negus (drums). It was a demo tape, *Fragments Of A Faith Forgotten*, that first brought Sabbat to the attention of the press and public in 1986. Part of a new wave of thrash metal bands, Sabbat stood out for their skilful live displays and musical flair, and earned a two-page spread in *Kerrang!* magazine before releasing any vinyl. Lyrically they were preoccupied with pagan arts, witchcraft and the dark ages, elements of which were incorporated into a bizarre and theatrical stageshow. Their brand of thrash, meanwhile, was complex but forceful, and they quickly became a cult attraction on the metal circuit. *History Of A Time To Come* emerged soon afterwards and was well received, reflecting the promise of earlier recordings. Its successor, *Dreamweaver*, was based on Brian Bates' novel *The Way Of Wyrd*, and demonstrated considerable musical development. After this Walkyier and Craske left, to replaced by Ritchie Desmond (vocals), Wayne Banks (bass) and extra guitarist Neil Watson. This line-up recorded the less taxing and ultimately inconsequential *Mourning Has Broken*. It was immediately followed by the break-up of Sabbat. Martin Walkyier has since formed Skyclad, while Sneap launched Godsend in 1996.

● ALBUMS: *History Of A Time To Come* (Noise 1988)★★★, *Dreamweaver (Reflections Of Our Yesterdays)* (Noise 1989)★★★★, *Mourning Has Broken* (Noise 1991)★★.

SABU

The son of actor Selar Sabu, vocalist and guitarist Paul Sabu (b. Burbank, California, USA) has carved out a successful career as a songwriter, producer/engineer and guitarist for a variety of major acts. He has also contributed to numerous film soundtracks, but his solo projects have been dogged by bad luck. The Sabu band, featuring bassist Rick Bozzo and drummer Dan Holmes, found some success with their soulful hard rock debut, but the album made no impression in America because Sabu also released a disco album at the same time on the Ocean label. Sabu turned to studio work, putting his band on ice until Motown subsidiary Morocco offered him a contract. As Kidd Glove, the band adopted a harder style, showcasing Sabu's vocals (reminiscent of a smokier Sammy Hagar) and guitarwork. However, the album did not take off, and when Morocco folded the band followed. Sabu was joined by Bozzo, Dan Ellis (keyboards) and Charles Esposito (drums) for the critically acclaimed *Heartbreak*, which did well until the label went into liquidation, and Sabu supported himself with an Arista songwriting contract while he put together his next project, Only Child. Sabu finally released a new solo album after a decade's wait in 1995, collaborating with ex-Baton Rouge guitarist Lance Boulen among others. The record was credited to Paul Sabu, and reawakened interest in an artist considered by many to be a unique guitar talent.

● ALBUMS: *Sabu* mini-album (MCA 1980)★★, *Heartbreak* (Heavy Metal America 1985)★★★, *Paul Sabu* (Now And Then 1995)★★★. Kidd Glove: *Kidd Glove* (Morocco 1984)★★, *Between The Light* (USG 1998)★★.

SACRED REICH

This Phoenix, Arizona, USA thrash band formed in 1985, with Jason Rainey (rhythm guitar) joined by Phil Rind (bass, vocals) and Greg Hall (drums), with Wiley Arnett replacing original lead guitarist Jeff Martinek in 1987. The band stayed together despite Flotsam And Jetsam wooing Arnett and Rind (who was also offered the Dark Angel vocal slot) and Slayer offering Greg Hall Dave Lombardo's then vacant drumstool, appearing on *Metal Massacre 8* before making a fine debut with *Ignorance*. This displayed considerable maturity and musicianship with hardcore political lyrics to match the ironic band name. Rind continued to work on political themes on *Surf Nicaragua*, while the band toured heavily, and the *Live At The Dynamo* EP followed an acclaimed 1989 performance at the Dutch festival. *The American Way* reaped the benefits of Sacred Reich's experience, with Hall's performance particularly outstanding, while Rind's lyrics ranged across ecology (on the brilliant 'Crimes Against Humanity', the original album title), intolerance, apartheid and the ills of US society ('Lady Liberty rots away, No truth, no justice, The American way'). The band also preached musical tolerance with '31 Flavors', the funk-rock album-closer. Hall, however, found the constant touring hard, and was later replaced by Dave McClain, who made his recording debut on *Independent*, ironically the band's first major label outing, which saw them stretch their musical abilities beyond straight thrash boundaries. *Independent* became US metal radio's choice as the best album of 1993. McClain was tempted away to join Machine Head in 1996.

● ALBUMS: *Ignorance* (Metal Blade/Enigma 1987)★★★★, *Surf Nicaragua* mini-album (Metal Blade/Enigma 1988)★★★, *The American Way* (Metal Blade/Enigma 1990)★★★, *Independent* (Hollywood 1993)★★★★, *Heal* (Metal Blade 1996)★★★, *Still Ignorant* (Metal Blade 1997)★★★.

SADNESS

Swiss extreme metal band Sadness take their primary influence from domestic forebears such as Celtic Frost and Coroner, but their sound also encompasses elements of baroque and classical composition in a manner close to that of the UK's My Dying Bride. Similarly they also draw on classical literature for much of their lyrical inspiration. A quintet led by guitarist Chiva, their 1994 debut album, *Oedipus*, concentrated on the darker elements of Greek Mythology, while the follow-up collection was a concept album geared towards specific parts of *Dante's Inferno* (notably *The Divine Comedy*). It was produced by Voco Fauz-Pas (a collaborator with the Young Gods, Treponem Pal and others) and Celtic Frost member Martin Eric Ain.

There was also a shift in language from the first album from German to a mixture of French, Spanish, German and English, with guest vocals from Christina Christine.

● ALBUMS: *Oedipus* (1994)★★★, *Danteferno* (1996)★★★.

SAGA

Drawing on a variety of influences from Rush to Emerson, Lake And Palmer, multi-talented musician Mike Sadler and drummer Steve Negus put together their first line-up in Toronto, Canada, in 1977, with the guitar/keyboard-playing brothers Jim and Ian Crichton. A self-financed album was then released on their own label. In 1980 they signed to Polydor Records and, with additional musicians, produced *Images At Twilight*, which continued the science fiction themes of their debut. A 12-inch EP was released in the UK to promote the album and, receiving a good deal of positive reaction, they set out on tour, supported for many shows by Magnum. Later that year they added another keyboard player, Jim Gilmore, and began work on the next album. Released in 1981, this elevated them into the major concert circuit where they proved a big attraction in America. Their record company lost interest, but Epic came to the rescue until a more lasting contract was set up with Portrait Records. However, the band lost direction and the founder-members became disillusioned and soon left to pursue a new venture. The rest of the group attempted to recapture former glories, and returned to the sci-fi concept for their 1989 album.

● ALBUMS: *Saga* (Maze 1978)★★, *Images At Twilight* (Polydor 1980)★★★, *Silent Knight* (Polydor 1980)★★★, *Worlds Apart* (Polydor 1981)★★, *In Transit* (Polydor 1982)★★, *Head Or Tails* (Epic 1983)★★, *Behaviour* (Portrait 1984)★★, *Wildest Dreams* (Atlantic 1987)★★, *The Beginners Guide To Throwing Shapes* (Bonaire 1989)★★, *Security Of Illusion* (1992)★★, *Steel Umbrellas* (1995)★★, *Generation 13* (Bonaire 1995)★★.

SALAS, STEVIE, COLORCODE

Guitarist/vocalist Stevie Salas was working in a Los Angeles recording studio when George Clinton turned him into a hot property by asking him to play on his 1986 album, *R&B Skeletons In The Closet*. Salas subsequently found himself in demand for his guitar and production skills, working with acts such as Was (Not Was), Andy Taylor, the Tubes and Eddie Money, and contributing to the *Bill And Ted's Excellent Adventure* soundtrack. A lucrative and enjoyable stint in Rod Stewart's touring band ensued before Salas was able to concentrate on his own project with bassist C.J. deVillar and drummer Winston A. Watson. *Stevie Salas Colorcode* was a sparkling debut, fusing raw hard rock and funk into excellent songs, from the anthemic 'Stand Up' to 'Indian Chief', a sensitive tribute to Salas's father. With airplay success for opening single 'The Harder They Come', the band were hotly tipped by the rock press. Live shows with Joe Satriani in the USA and 24-7 Spyz in the UK further enhanced Colorcode's reputation, but the momentum was lost, along with their recording contract, during the sale of Island Records to Polygram, when the majority of Island's hard rock acts were dropped. However, the band retained a Japanese deal, and released two further albums: *Stuff*, a collection of demo and live tracks with a superb acoustic reworking of 'Blind' from the debut, and the *Bootleg Like A Mug!!* live set, which displayed a distinct Hendrix influence with cover versions of 'Little Wing' and 'Hey Joe'. Salas went on to work with old friend Bootsy Collins and ex-Band Of Gypsys drummer Buddy Miles, releasing *Hardware* in 1992 under the Third Eye name (conversely packaged in the UK as *Third Eye Open* on Rykodisc by Hardware), before reuniting with the Colorcode band and a host of guest stars to record *Stevie Salas Presents The Electric Pow Wow*, a mixture of original material and largely obscure covers. The adaptable guitarist also played as part of Terence Trent D'Arby's live band. Salas then put Colorcode on ice for a time to work more closely with Sass Jordan on her *Rats* album, the pair having aleady collaborated on *Racine* and Salas's *Electric Pow Wow* set. Another Colorcode album, *Back From The Living Dead*, then emerged with the original line-up augmented by bassist T.M. Stevens, Pride And Glory/ex-Sass Jordan drummer Brian Tichy, and 24-7 Spyz bassist Rick Skatore, and the material and performances matched the quality of the debut.

● ALBUMS: *Stevie Salas Colorcode* (Island 1990)★★★, *Stuff* (Polystar 1991)★★★, *Bootleg Like A Mug!!* (Polystar 1992)★★★, *Stevie Salas Presents The Electric Pow Wow* (Polystar 1993)★★★, *Back From The Living Dead* (Polystar 1994)★★★, *Viva La Noise* (USG/East West 1998)★★★.

SALEM, KEVIN

Prominent New York-based rock singer-songwriter Kevin Salem (guitar, vocals) made best use of his dramatic surname by recruiting Dave Dunton (keyboards), Keith Levreault (drums; ex-Blood

Oranges, Roscoe's Gang), Todd Novak (guitar, vocals; ex-Dragsters) and Scott Yoder (bass; ex-Blue Chieftains) to provide a 'going concern' rock group. Salem himself hailed from Johnstown, Pennsylvania, before moving to Boston where he joined Dumptruck for their acclaimed 1987 album, *For The Country*. He would stay with that band until the early 90s, when frustrations and legal complications saw him depart. Relocating to New York, Salem performed with his own *ad hoc* band, also working as a sideman for Freedy Johnston and Yo La Tengo. His session contributions included tracks on Johnston's *Can You Fly*, the Pooh Sticks' *Million Seller* and Chris Harford's *Be Headed*. As well as recording with Miracle Legion, Salem also took the production mantle for Madder Rose's debut album. His first album under his own name was actually completed in 1992, after he had recorded 11 songs in a variety of New York studios, sneaking in after-hours to lay down the tracks when cash-flow problems arose. The resulting *Keep Your Crosses Fingered* was postponed, however. Instead, Salem concentrated on putting together the current line-up of his band, who recorded *Soma City* in five days at Hoboken's Water Music studios. It was helped in no small part by the production tutelage of Niko Bolas (best known for his work with Neil Young) who fitted in Salem for free between commissions from Billy Joel and Rod Stewart. It included one song, 'Forever Gone', that was co-written with Nirvana/Urge Overkill producer Butch Vig. *Glimmer* was further proof of his talent as Salem shapes up to sound like the US version of Ian McNabb.

● ALBUMS: *Soma City* (Roadrunner 1994)★★★, *Glimmer* (Roadrunner)★★★.

SALTY DOG

This Los Angeles-based band were put together in late 1986 by bassist Mike Hannon (b. Columbus, Ohio, USA) and drummer Khurt Maier (b. Sacramento, California, USA), enlisting Youngstown, Ohio-born vocalist Jimmi Bleacher and replacing their original guitarist (Scott Lane) with Canadian Pete Reveen in early 1987. The band developed a blues-based style that drew immediate Led Zeppelin comparisons, but owed more to a mixture of influences from old bluesmen such as Memphis Slim, 'Sonny Boy' Williamson and Willie Dixon to the more contemporary sounds of Black Flag and Motörhead. *Every Dog Has Its Day*, recorded in Rockfield Studios in Wales with producer Peter Collins, demonstrated that the Zeppelin references were most apt, owing to the sheer variety of styles within Salty Dog's bluesy framework, from the straightforward opener 'Come Along', through the smouldering 'Slow Daze', to the tongue-in-cheek acoustic blues of 'Just Like A Woman'. The album received a flurry of good reviews, but Salty Dog were unable to capitalize, as Bleacher departed shortly after its release. The band struggled to find a replacement, locating Dallas native Darrel Beach (ex-DT Roxx) in late 1991, but the loss of momentum proved crucial and Salty Dog faded.

● ALBUMS: *Every Dog Has Its Day* (Geffen 1990)★★★.

SAMHAIN

Samhain were Glenn Danzig's second major project and formed a bridge between the macabre exuberance of US punk legends the Misfits and the seductively menacing rock of his current band, Danzig. Samhain consisted of Danzig (b. 23 June 1959, Lodi, New Jersey, USA; vocals), ex-Misfits drummer Eerie Von (b. 25 August 1964, Lodi, New Jersey, USA; now bass), Steve Zing (drums), and Peter 'Damien' Marshall (guitars), with Lyle Preslar (ex-Minor Threat) and London May (drums) also recording under the banner. In Samhain Danzig stripped away a lot of the kitsch that had characterized the Misfits, and replaced it with a starker, less comic-book approach. Sinister and predatory, Samhain's music was an exercise in lean, evocative rhythm and bleak mood. As with the Misfits, the production was very uneven, and the sound often seemed too thin to sustain the bite the material demanded. Nevertheless, at their best, most notably on their strongest album, *November Coming Fire*, Samhain could be hauntingly hungry and morbidly resonant. Their last recording, *Final Descent*, features a remastered version of the *Unholy Passion* material compiled with another session from 1987 with future Danzig band guitarist John Christ.

● ALBUMS: *Initium* (Plan 9 1984)★★, *Unholy Passion* mini-album (Plan 9 1985)★★★, *November Coming Fire* (Plan 9 1986)★★★★.

● COMPILATIONS: *Final Descent* (Plan 9 1990)★★★.

SAMSON

This UK heavy metal group was formed in 1978 by guitarist Paul Samson, and has since been dogged by line-up changes, management disputes and record company problems. These have occurred at critical points in the band's career, just as major success seemed imminent. The first incarnation of the band comprised Paul Samson (guitar), Chris Aylmer (bass), Bruce Bruce (vocals) and Clive Burr (drums), the latter soon moving on to Iron Maiden and being replaced by the masked Thunderstick. Samson specialized in high-energy, blues-based rock and were among the leading lights of the New Wave Of British Heavy Metal movement, with each of their first four albums becoming minor classics of the genre. In 1981 Bruce Bruce and Thunderstick departed; the former assumed his real name, Bruce Dickinson, and joined Iron Maiden as lead vocalist. Thunderstick formed a new group under his own name. Nicky Moore (ex-Tiger) and Mel Gaynor (ex-Light Of The World) stepped in on vocals and drums, respectively, but Gaynor soon moved on to Simple Minds, with Pete Jupp filling in as replacement (who would in turn later join FM). *Before The Storm* and *Don't Get Mad, Get Even* are Samson's most accomplished works, with Moore's gritty and impassioned vocals giving the band a sound that was both earthy and honest. Chris Aylmer left in 1984 and was replaced by ex-Diamond Head bassist Merv Goldsworthy, before the recording of an excellent live album, *Thank You And Goodnight*. The band split soon afterwards, with *Head Tactics* being a posthumous release comprising remixes of tracks from *Head On* and *Shock Tactics*. Nicky Moore went on to form Mammoth, while Paul Samson released a solo effort, *Joint Forces*, in 1986. The band re-formed in 1988 and released *Refugee* two years later, a classy, if slightly dated, collection of bluesy, hard rock numbers.

● ALBUMS: *Survivors* (Lazer 1979)★★, *Head On* (Gem 1980)★★★, *Shock Tactics* (RCA 1981)★★★, *Before The Storm* (Polydor 1982)★★★★, *Don't Get Mad, Get Even* (Polydor 1984)★★★★, *Thank You And Goodnight* (Metal Masters 1984)★★★★, *Refugee* (Communique 1990)★★★, *Live At Reading* (Raw Fruit 1991)★★★, *Joint Forces* (1993)★★★.

● COMPILATIONS: *Head Tactics* (Capitol 1986)★★★, *Pillars Of Rock* (Connoisseur 1990)★★★, *Burning Emotion* (Magnum 1995)★★★.

● VIDEOS: *Biceps Of Steel* (1985).

SANCTUARY

Formed in Seattle, Washington, USA, in 1985, Sanctuary consisted of Warrel Dane (vocals), Lenny Rutledge (guitar, vocals), Sean Blosl (guitar, vocals), Jim Sheppard (bass) and Dave Budbill (drums, vocals). Through two early demo tracks included on a low-budget compilation, *Northwest Metal Fest*, the band attracted the attention of Megadeth guitarist Dave Mustaine, who offered to oversee their next recordings. With this recommendation behind them the band signed to CBS/Epic Records and Mustaine was duly enlisted as producer. *Refuge Denied* introduced Sanctuary's somewhat basic thrash sound, one of great intensity but with little direction or scope. After touring with Megadeth the band released *Into The Mirror Black*, but broke up shortly afterwards.

● ALBUMS: *Refuge Denied* (CBS 1987)★★, *Into The Mirror Black* (CBS 1990)★★★.

SANTERS

Canadian heavy metal trio with a strong blues influence, formed in 1980 by guitarist and vocalist Rick Santers and his brother Mark on drums, together with their friend, Rick Lazaroff, on bass. Aside from playing numerous concerts and recording their debut album in 1981, Rick Santers was in demand as a session player and, in particular, helped fellow Canadian Lee Aaron with her demos and first album. In 1982 Santers the band picked up a European licensing deal with Heavy Metal Records who released *Racing Time* in December. This featured some fine guitarwork, especially on the tracks 'Mistreatin' Heart' and 'Hard Time Loving You'. Their last album was released two years later, before Rick decided to return to session work.

● ALBUMS: *Shot Down In Flames* (Ready 1981)★★★, *Racing Time* (Ready/Heavy Metal 1982)★★★, *Guitar Alley* (Ready/Heavy Metal 1984)★★.

SARACEN

A quintet of Steven Bettney (vocals), Robert Bendelow (guitar), Richard Lowe (keyboards), Barry Yates (bass) and John Thorne (drums), Saracen originally broke through as part of the N.W.O.B.H.M. in the early 80s. Their debut album, *Heroes, Saints And Fools*, included set crowd-pleasers such as 'No More Lonely Nights' and attracted encouraging reviews. However, by the advent of their much-delayed second album, Saracen had changed styles to become a more pomp rock-orientated entity. As a result of inter-band turmoil over the new direction, only Bettney and Lowe remained from the group's original incarnation.

● ALBUMS: *Heroes, Saints And Fools* (Nucleus 1981)★★★, *Change Of Heart* (Neat 1984)★★.

SARAYA

Formed in 1987 by vocalist Sandi Saraya and keyboard player Gregg Munier, this US rock band originally travelled under the title Alsace Lorraine. With the addition of Tony Rey (guitar), Gary Taylor (bass) and Chuck Bonfarte (drums), they changed their name to Saraya. Fusing influences such as Heart, the Pretenders and Pat Benatar, they recorded a self-titled debut for Polygram; a melodic and highly polished collection of AOR numbers characterized by Sandi's hammy but infectious vocal style. Following internal disputes Rey and Taylor quit in 1990 and were replaced by Tony Bruno and Barry Dunaway, respectively. 1991's *When The Blackbird Sings* again failed to find success.

● ALBUMS: *Saraya* (Polygram 1989)★★★, *When The Blackbird Sings* (Polydor 1991)★★.

SARKOMA

Alternative metal band from the US Midwest staffed by 'a brotherhood of musicians' who include Brian Carter (vocals), Tony Chrisman (bass), Mike Hilleburg (guitar), Aaron Ingram (drums) and Stuart Johnson (guitar). Sarkoma made their debut in 1992 with the *Completely Different* EP, before regional and national touring. Lyrical content derived from the personal and imagined experiences of Johnson, including one song, 'Blue Horizon', written from a female perspective. Other issues explored on the group's debut album, *Integrity*, included evolution ('Universal Footsteps') and celebrity ('Mortamer'). With strong all-round songwriting it may not prove too long before the band are forced to become better acquainted with the latter sentiment.

● ALBUMS: *Integrity* (Bulletproof 1994)★★.

SATAN

Formed from the ashes of the band Blitzkrieg in Newcastle-upon-Tyne, England, in 1981, the original line-up of Satan comprised Trevor Robinson (vocals), Russ Tippins (guitar), Steve Ramsey (guitar), Graeme English (bass) and Andy Reed (drums). In 1981 the band recorded two tracks for a compilation, *Roxcalibur*, and a self-financed single entitled 'Kiss Of Death'. Soon after its release vocalist Robinson left the band to be replaced by Ian Swift who himself was soon supplanted by Brian Ross. Through numerous demos and a name built for themselves via the underground tape-trading scene, they attracted the attention of Noise Records. Their debut album, *Court In The Act*, followed in 1984. Typified by speed-metal riffs and strong lead guitarwork, this was again well received. However, the name of the band did not work to their advantage, and was atypical of their lyrical dimension. Not only did they alter the name to Blind Fury but once again changed vocalists, replacing the departed Ross with Lou Taylor. This line-up recorded one album using the Blind Fury appellation, *Out Of Reach*, in 1985. The band changed vocalists yet again, replacing Taylor with Michael Jackson and reverted to the name Satan shortly thereafter. A new demo attracted the interest of the German-based Steamhammer Records and *Into The Future* was released in 1986. The album's poor production was parried by the power and quality of the material. *Suspended Sentence* followed in 1987. However, once again the name was causing problems and record company and managerial pressure now saw it changed to Pariah. After two further albums, *The Kindred* and *Blaze Of Obscurity*, the band in all its myriad guises folded in 1990.

● ALBUMS: *Court In The Act* (Neat 1984)★★★, *Into The Future* (Steamhammer 1986)★★, *Suspended Sentence* (Steamhammer 1987)★★★.

SATRIANI, JOE

Joe Satriani grew up in Long Island, New York, USA, and is a skilled guitarist responsible for teaching the instrument to, among others, Kirk Hammett of Metallica, and Steve Vai. After travelling abroad extensively in his youth he returned to the USA to form the Squares. This project folded in 1984 through an abject lack of commercial recognition, giving Satriani the opportunity to concentrate on his experimental guitar playing. The outcome of this was the release of an EP, *Joe Satriani*. Following a spell with the Greg Kihn band, appearing on *Love And Rock 'N' Roll*, Satriani released *Not Of This Earth*, an album that was less polished than its successor, *Surfing With The Alien*. Despite offering no vocal accompaniment, this set was a major seller and brought mainstream respect to an artist often felt to be too clinical or technical for such reward.

In 1988 he was joined more permanently by Stu Hamm (bass) and Jonathan Mover (drums), also working for a spell on Mick Jagger's late 80s tour. Never afraid to push his considerable musical skills to the limit, Satriani has played the banjo and harmonica on his albums, as well as successfully attempting vocals on *Flying In A Blue Dream*. In 1993 he released *Time Machine*, a double CD that contained a mixture of new and previously unreleased tracks dating back to 1984, and also live material from his 1993 Extremist world tour. The guitarist then replaced Ritchie Blackmore in Deep Purple in 1994, while maintaining his own solo recording career with two further albums.

● ALBUMS: *Not Of This Earth* (Relativity 1986)★★★, *Surfing With The Alien* (Relativity 1987)★★★★, *Dreaming 11* (Relativity 1988)★★★, *Flying In A Blue Dream* (Relativity 1990)★★★, *Time Machine* (1993)★★★, *Joe Satriani* (Epic 1995)★★★, with Eric Johnson and Steve Vai *G3 In Concert* (Epic 1997)★★★★, *Crystal Planet* (Epic 1998)★★★.

SATYRICON

One of the leaders of the Norwegian black metal scene, Satyricon are as comically attired and deathly serious about their intent as peers such as Burzum and Mayhem. Led by the brooding blonde figure of vocalist and songwriter Satyr himself, with the aid of the similarly pseudonymous Kveldulv and Frost, Satyricon made their debut in 1994 with *Dark Medieval Times* for their own Moonfog Records label. This established the group's lyrical concerns - a patently nationalistic pride in Norse and Viking heritage as well as the atavistic belief that society is sliding towards Armageddon. This was also evident in their preceding demos (the second of which, 1994's *The Forest Is My Throne*, was later released as a split-CD with Enslaved). On their satanic/paganist position, Satyr proved himself both forthright and resigned: 'It would not be realistic to get rid of Christianity, I won't live that long anyway. At least I've contributed to the War.' The group's most high-profile release, 1996's *Nemesis Divina*, was promoted with a substantial European tour alongside Dissection and Gorgoroth.

● ALBUMS: *Dark Medieval Times* (Moonfog 1994)★★★, with Enslaved *The Forest Is My Throne* (Moonfog 1994)★★★, *Shadow Throne* (Moonfog 1995)★★, *Nemesis Divina* (Moonfog 1996)★★★.

SAVAGE

Formed in Mansfield, England, in 1978, Savage's line-up consisted of Chris Bradley (bass, vocals), Andy Dawson (guitar), Wayne Redshaw (guitar) and Mark Brown (drums). Their debut album, *Loose 'N' Lethal*, won critical acclaim for its ultra-heavy riffs and was firmly rooted in the New Wave Of British Heavy Metal. The band then toured Europe where they quickly gained popularity, especially in Holland. Similar success in their homeland was not as forthcoming. In 1984 the band signed a new recording agreement with Zebra Records who released an EP, *We Got The Edge*. This revealed an amended approach with a more mellow, cultured sound. Restraint was also in evidence on 1985's *Hyperactive*. After this, Savage seemed to lose both momentum and direction and they disbanded in 1986.

● ALBUMS: *Loose 'N' Lethal* (Ebony 1983)★★★★, *Hyperactive* (Zebra 1985)★★★, *Babylon* (Neat 1997)★★.

SAVAGE GRACE

No relation to the early 70s group who recorded for Reprise Records, this US power-metal quartet, originally titled Maquis De Sade, were formed in Los Angeles, California, in 1981. Since then they have enjoyed a chequered career hindered by unstable line-ups, the first of which featured Mike Smith (vocals), Chris Logue (guitar, vocals), Brian East (bass) and Dan Finch (drums). They were signed on the strength of a track included on the *Metal Massacre* series of compilations and a self-financed EP, *The Dominatress*, which the band had released in 1983. *Master Of Disguise*, their full debut from 1985, preceded their first line-up changes; ex-Agent Steel guitarist Mark Marshall was added, while Mike Smith's departure left Chris Logue to handle the lead vocals. Drummer Dan Finch also quit to be replaced by Mark Markum. This incarnation of the band managed to stay together long enough to record 1986's *After The Fall From Grace*. Savage Grace then toured Europe with Heir Apparent and swapped bassist Brian East for that band's Derek Peace before beginning work on recordings for a projected third album. However, the continual line-up shuffles had taken their toll and Peace rejoined Heir Apparent as Savage Grace disappeared late in 1988.

● ALBUMS: *Master Of Disguise* (Metal Blade 1985)★★★, *After The Fall From Grace* (Black Dragon 1986)★★★.

SAVATAGE

Previously known as Metropolis and Avatar, Savatage, a melodic, heavy rock quintet, were formed in Florida, USA, in 1983 by the Oliva brothers. The full band line-up comprised Jon Oliva (vocals, keyboards), Criss Oliva (guitar), Steve 'Doc' Wacholz (drums) and Keith Collins (bass), the latter eventually replaced by Johnny Lee Middleton. Their initial approach was strongly influenced by Judas Priest and Iron Maiden, a style demonstrated by their *City Beneath The Surface EP* from their year of formation. Savatage's first three albums also clearly reflect their influences, with a high-energy fusion of power-riffs and high-pitched vocals. *Fight For The Rock* marked a detour towards more melodic AOR, which was poorly received by their fans, before returning to their roots for the next album. Chris Caffery was added as a second guitarist in 1989, before the recording of *Gutter Ballet*. This, and *Streets*, represented the band's finest work to this point. Both were elaborate rock operas, featuring a mixture of dynamic hard rock and atmospheric ballads. Utilizing an orchestra and state-of-the-art production techniques, they also found themselves with a minor hit single on their hands in the shape of 'Jesus Saves'. Jon Oliva was then relegated to nominal backing vocals behind new frontman Zachary Stevens - having elected instead to concentrate on penning rock operas full-time and working as part of Doctor Butcher. Stevens was ex-White Witch, and joined in time for 1993's *Edge Of Thorns*. That year also brought tragedy when founding member and guitarist Criss Oliva was killed in October in a car crash near his home in Clearwater, Florida. For *Handful Of Rain* the group recruited ex-Testament guitarist Alex Skolnick, whose former band had toured with Savatage in support of Dio in 1989. The set included one notable tribute to the late guitarist, 'Alone I Breathed'.

● ALBUMS: *Sirens* (Music For Nations 1985)★★★, *The Dungeons Are Calling* mini-album (Music For Nations 1985)★★★, *Power Of The Night* (Atlantic 1985)★★, *Fight For The Rock* (Atlantic 1986)★★★, *Hall Of The Mountain King* (Atlantic 1987)★★★, *Gutter Ballet* (Atlantic 1990)★★★, *Streets* (Atlantic 1991)★★★★, *Edge Of Thorns* (Bullet Proof 1993)★★★, *Handful Of Rain* (Bullet Proof 1994)★★, *Dead Winter Dead* (Edel/Concrete 1995)★★★, *Live Devastation* (Metal Blade 1995)★★, *Ghost In The Ruins* (SPV 1996)★★★, *The Wake Of Magellan* (Edel/Concrete 1997)★★★, *Japan Live '94* (SPV 1998)★★★.

● COMPILATIONS: *From The Gutter To The Stage* (Edel 1997)★★★.

SAXON

Formed in the north of England in the late 70s, Saxon were originally known as Son Of A Bitch and spent their early days paying dues in clubs and small venues up and down the UK, with Peter 'Biff' Byford (vocals), Graham Oliver (guitar), Paul Quinn (guitar), Steve Dawson (bass) and Pete Gill (drums) building a strong live reputation. After the name switch they signed a contract with French label Carrere, better known for its disco productions than its work with heavy metal bands. During the late 70s many young metal bands were emerging in a UK scene that became known as the New Wave Of British Heavy Metal. These bands challenged the supremacy of the old guard of heavy metal bands, and Saxon were at the head of this movement along with Iron Maiden and Diamond Head. The first album was a solid, if basic, heavy rock outing, but the release of *Wheels Of Steel* turned the tide. Saxon's popularity soared, earning themselves two UK Top 20 hits with 'Wheels Of Steel' and '747 (Strangers In The Night)'. They capitalized on this success with the release in the same year of *Strong Arm Of The Law*, another very heavy, surprisingly articulate, metal album. A further Top 20 hit arrived with 'And The Bands Played On', drawn from the following year's *Demin And Leather*, which also produced 'Never Surrender'. They toured the USA to great acclaim and appeared at the Castle Donington 'Monsters Of Rock' Festival. By the time of 1982's *The Eagle Has Landed*, which gave Saxon their most successful album, reaching the UK Top 5, the group were at their peak. That same year, Pete Gill was replaced by drummer Nigel Glockler, who had previously worked with Toyah (Gill joined Motörhead in 1984). At this point Saxon counted among their rivals only the immensely popular Iron Maiden. The release of *Power And The Glory* enforced their credentials as a major rock band. The follow-up, *Innocence Is No Excuse*, was a more polished and radio-friendly production but it stalled just inside the Top 40. It heralded an uncertain time for the band and a resulting slide in their popularity. The departure of Steve Dawson contributed to their malaise. *Rock The Nations* was as punishing as old, but the chance to recapture former glories had now expired. In 1990 Saxon returned to the public eye with a UK tour that featured a set-list built on their popular older material. *Solid Ball Of Rock* was their most accomplished album for some time, but in early 1995 Oliver, Dawson and Gill played live together while contesting the rights to the name Saxon with Byford. The issue was soon resolved, however, and Byford was back in place for *Dogs Of War*, with Oliver having taken his leave. A workmanlike record harking back to the band's mid-80s propensity for epic choruses, it was neither awful nor progressive. Oliver, Dawson and Gill subsequently formed Son Of A Bitch.

● ALBUMS: *Saxon* (Saxon Carrere 1979)★★★, *Wheels Of Steel* (Saxon Carrere 1980)★★★, *Strong Arm Of The Law* (Carrere 1980)★★★, *Denim And Leather* (Carrere 1981)★★★, *The Eagle Has Landed* (Carrere 1982)★★★, *Power And The Glory* (Carrere 1983)★★★, *Crusader* (Carrere 1984)★★★, *Innocence Is No Excuse* (Parlophone 1985)★★, *Rock The Nations* (EMI 1986)★★,

Destiny (EMI 1988)★★★, *Rock 'N' Roll Gypsies* (Roadrunner 1990)★★, *Solid Ball Of Rock* (Virgin 1991)★★★, *Dogs Of War* (HTD/Virgin 1995)★★.
● COMPILATIONS: *Anthology* (Raw Power 1988)★★★, *Back On The Streets* (Connoisseur 1990)★★★, *Greatest Hits Live* (Essential 1990)★★, *Best Of* (EMI 1991)★★★★.
● VIDEOS: *Live Innocence* (1986), *Power & The Glory - Video Anthology* (1989), *Saxon Live* (1989), *Greatest Hits Live* (1990).

SCANNER

This German rock quintet rose from the ashes of Lion's Breed in 1987. Comprising Tom S. Sopha (guitar), Michael Knoblich (vocals), Wolfgang Kolorz (drums), Axel A.J. Julius (guitar) and Martin Bork (bass), their brand of metal-thrash identified them with fellow countrymen Helloween. Signing to Noise Records in 1988, Scanner released *Hypertrace*, a science-fiction concept album. The storyline revolved around extraterrestrial robots preventing war between the superpowers and, although far from original, it found an appreciative and appreciable audience. Knoblich quit the group in 1989 and was replaced by ex-Angel Dust vocalist S.L. Coe. They recorded *Terminal Earth*, another concept album, centred this time on the aforementioned robots' concern for planet Earth, and the damage that the human race has inflicted upon it. Not suprisingly, it bore a strong musical resemblance to its predecessor.
● ALBUMS: *Hypertrace* (Noise 1988)★★★, *Terminal Earth* (Noise 1990)★★, *Mental Reservation* (Massacre 1995)★★.

SCAT OPERA

Formed in the UK during the late 80s by Ernie Brennan (vocals), Steve Yates (guitar), John O'Reilly (bass) and Mark Diment (drums), Scat Opera recorded several well-received demos before picking up prestigious support slots with Faith No More in the autumn of 1989. Though comparisons to that band followed, in truth Scat Opera played at greater velocity and with more precise musical definition. The pieces, however, were not entirely in place until they signed a contract with Music For Nations in the spring of 1990. They made their debut a year later with *About Time*, recorded at Slaughterhouse Studios and produced by Colin Richardson. A UK tour as support to Gaye Bykers On Acid ensued, before returning to the studio (this time Windings Studio in Wales) with Richardson for a second set, *Four Gone Confusion*, to be released in October 1992. Again the music incorporated elements drawn from funk (particularly apparent in bass player O'Reilly's slapping technique), jazz and metal.
● ALBUMS: *About Time* (Music For Nations 1991)★★★, *Four Gone Confusion* (Music For Nations 1992)★★★.

SCATTERBRAIN

A New York, USA band who have experienced at first hand the swings and roundabouts of the modern music industry, Scatterbrain drew original members Tommy Christ (vocals) and Paul Nieder (guitar) from hardcore outfit Ludichrist. This group, who released two albums for Relativity, *Immaculate Deception* in 1987 and *Powertrip* in 1989, were never accepted by the hardcore community, whose low tolerance threshold for humour militated against Ludichrist's flippancy. Scatterbrain was consequently invoked as the duo's new home, featuring additional members Guy Brogna (bass) and Mike Boyko (drums). However, early songs such as 'Goodbye Freedom, Hello Mom' indicated that their sense of fun had not deserted them in the transition. Their debut, *Here Comes Trouble*, boasted two minor hits, 'Down With The Ship' and 'Don't Call Me Dude', both of which also had memorable videos. Touring the USA and Europe, Scatterbrain discovered a rich vein of support for their efforts in Australia, where 'Don't Call Me Dude' went Top 10. *Scamboogery* followed in 1991, though this was their last tenure with their label. For *Mundus Intellectualis* the group moved over to Music For Nations subsidiary Bulletproof Records, with opening track 'Write That Hit' addressing the group's problems with industry executives (some of the lyrics, including 'How about hip hop?', were legendarily taken from real suggestions made to them by their former record company).
● ALBUMS: *Here Comes Trouble* (In-Effect 1990)★★★, *Scamboogery* (In-Effect 1991)★★★, *Mundus Intellectualis* (Bulletproof 1994)★★.

SCHENKER, MICHAEL

b. 10 January 1955, Savstedt, Germany. Schenker began his musical career in 1971 at the age of 16, when, along with brother Rudolf, he formed the Scorpions. After contributing impressive guitarwork on the band's *Lonesome Crow* debut, he was offered the chance to replace Bernie Marsden in UFO. Schenker joined the group in June 1973 and their resultant musical direction swung to hard rock. *Phenomenon*, released in 1974, featured the metal classics 'Doctor, Doctor' and 'Rock Bottom', with Schenker's performance on his Gibson 'Flying V' hammering home the band's new identity. A series of strong albums followed before Schenker eventually quit in 1978 after the recording of *Obsession*. The split had been predicted for some time following personal conflicts between Schenker and vocalist Phil Mogg. The guitarist moved back to Germany and temporarily rejoined the Scorpions, contributing to *Lovedrive*, released in 1979. Soon afterwards he formed his own band, the Michael Schenker Group, which was later abbreviated to MSG. MSG's personnel has remained in a constant state of flux, with Schenker hiring and firing musicians seemingly at will. In 1991 Schenker also took time out between MSG albums to contribute to the Contraband project, a one-off collaboration between members of Shark Island, Vixen, Ratt and L.A. Guns.

● ALBUMS: as MSG *The Michael Schenker Group* (Chrysalis 1980)★★, *MSG* (Chrysalis 1981)★★, *One Night At Budokan* (Chrysalis 1982)★★, *Assault Attack* (Chrysalis 1982)★★, *Built To Destroy* (Chrysalis 1983)★★, *Rock Will Never Die* (Chrysalis 1984)★★, *Perfect Timing* (EMI 1987)★★, *Save Yourself* (Capitol 1989)★★, *MSG* (EMI 1992)★★, *BBC Radio One Live In Concert* 1982 recording (Windsong 1993)★★.

Schon And Hammer

This was a short-lived partnership between Journey's Neal Schon (b. 27 February 1954, San Mateo, California, USA; guitar, vocals) and Jan Hammer (b. 17 April 1948, Prague, Czechoslovakia; keyboards, drums). The fusion of styles between Schon's AOR and Hammer's jazz-rock produced *Untold Passion*, a record that largely consisted of virtuoso performances from both musicians duelling against each other. The innovative British electric jazz bassist Colin Hodgkinson, previously with Back Door, accompanied the duo in the studio on the first album and Schon's vocal contributions proved to be particularly satisfying. By the time of the second release many of Schon's comrades from Journey had been enlisted, resulting in a lighter collection of songs and a departure from Schon And Hammer's *raison d'être*. The partnership was soon dissolved, with Schon returning full-time to Journey and Hammer moving to television work, enjoying particular success with the *Miami Vice* series.

● ALBUMS: *Untold Passion* (CBS 1981)★★★, *Here To Stay* (CBS 1982).

School Of Violence

This New York hardcore quartet was formed in 1985 by Stegmon Von Heintz (guitar), Karl Agell (vocals), Rick Stone (bass) and M.S. Evans (drums). Their recorded debut came on a compilation album, *The People Are Hungry*. This led to a contract with Metal Blade Records and the release of *We The People* in 1988. Assimilating influences drawn from punk and thrash bands such as Bad Brains, Anthrax and D.O.A., it featured vitriolic lyrics addressing social and political injustices. The production was very ragged, however, and the messages were swamped beneath the drum and bass-laden tumult.

● ALBUMS: *We The People* (Metal Blade 1988)★★.

Schubert

Formed in Austria in 1987, soft rock band Schubert quickly rose to become their country's dominant musical force in that genre. Comprising ex-No Bros members Klaus Schubert (guitars) and Nikki P. Opperer (keyboards), plus ex-UB vocalist Lem Enzinger, their Bon Jovi-styled big ballads and up-tempo rockers were effectively realized on half a dozen domestic albums that assailed the Austrian charts. They made their pan-European debut in 1995 with *Toilet Songs*, so called to reflect their disillusionment at the world in general. The opening song, 'Reflections Of The Past', was the surprise in an otherwise seamless parade of AOR songs, with a distinctive industrial metal feel, but elsewhere it was business as usual. With Opperer's Hammond organ leading from the front, many critics detected an open debt to the Uriah Heep model of the mid-70s.

● ALBUMS: *Toilet Songs* (Mausoleum 1995)★★★.

Scorn

A synthesis of new technology and the traditional grindcore logarithms of pounding bottom end drums and bass, Scorn are a UK duo of ex-Napalm Death personnel Mick Harris (drums; also a member of Painkiller) and Nick Bullen (bass, vocals) - initially helped out by a further former member of that band, Justin Broadrick (guitar). A debut album and attendant single, *Vae Solis* and 'Lick Forever Dog', were produced by John Wakelin at Rhythm Studios in Birmingham. Setting out on the road with Cancer and Pitch Shifter to promote this primeval slab of white noise, the group were joined by Candiru guitarist Pat McCahan, who replaced Broadrick (now fully occupied with Godflesh). A five-track, 40-minute 12-

inch single emerged in October 1992, 'Deliverance', followed by the *White Irises Blind* EP. *Colossus* was the group's second full-length affair and once more saw them working with Wakelin. If anything, *Evanescence* surpassed previous exercises in extremity, with a bass sound so deep that the term dub was widely invoked. This sonic marginalism led them into contact with musicians outside of their own tribe, and 1995 saw the release of a remix album, with contributors including Coil, Scanner, Meat Beat Manifesto and Bill Laswell among others.

● ALBUMS: *Vae Solis* (Earache 1992)★★★, *Colossus* (Earache 1993)★★★, *Evanescence* (Earache 1994)★★★★, *Ellipsis* (Scorn 1995)★★★, *Logghi Barogghi* (Earache 1996)★★, *Zander* (KK 1997)★★★.

SCORPIONS

This German hard rock group was formed by guitarists Rudolf and Michael Schenker (b. 10 January 1955, Savstedt, Germany) in 1971. With Klaus Meine (b. 25 May 1948; vocals), Lothar Heinberg (bass) and Wolfgang Dziony (drums), they exploded onto the international heavy rock scene with *Lonesome Crow* in 1972. This tough and exciting record was characterized by Schenker's distinctive, fiery guitarwork on his Gibson 'Flying V' and Klaus Meine's dramatic vocals. Soon after the album was released, Heinberg, Dziony and Schenker left, the latter joining UFO. Francis Buchholz and Jurgen Rosenthal stepped in on bass and drums, respectively, for the recording of *Fly To The Rainbow*. Ulrich Roth was recruited as Schenker's replacement in 1974 and Rudy Lenners took over the drumstool from Rosenthal the following year. The following releases, *Trance* and *Virgin Killer*, epitomized the Scorpions' new-found confidence and unique style - a fusion of intimidating power-riffs, wailing guitar solos and melodic vocal lines. Produced by Dieter Dierks, the improvements musically were now matched technically. Their reputation began to grow throughout Europe and the Far East, backed up by exhaustive touring. *Taken By Force* saw Herman Rarebell replace Lenners, with the band branching out into anthemic power-ballads, bolstered by emotive production, for the first time. Although commercially successful, Roth was not happy with this move, and he quit to form Electric Sun following a major tour to support the album. *Tokyo Tapes* was recorded on this tour and marked the end of the first phase of the band's career. This was a live set featuring renditions of their strongest numbers. Mathias Jabs (ex-Fargo) was recruited as Roth's replacement, but had to step down temporarily in favour of Michael Schenker, who had just left UFO under acrimonious circumstances. Schenker contributed guitar on three tracks of *Lovedrive* and toured with them afterwards. He was replaced by Jabs permanently after collapsing on stage during their European tour in 1979. The band had now achieved a stable line-up, and shared the mutual goal of breaking through in the USA. Relentless touring schedules ensued and their albums leaned more and more towards sophisticated, hard-edged melodic rock. *Blackout* made the US *Billboard* Top 10, as did the following *Love At First Sting* which featured 'Still Loving You', an enduring hard rock ballad. *World Wide Live* was released in 1985, another double live set, but this time only featuring material from the second phase of the band's career. It captured the band at their melodic best, peaking at number 14 in a four-month stay on the US chart. The band took a well-earned break before releasing *Savage Amusement* in 1988, their first studio album for almost four years. This marked a slight change in emphasis again, adopting a more restrained approach. Nevertheless, it proved a huge success, reaching number 5 in the USA and number 1 throughout Europe. The band switched to Phonogram Records in 1989 and ended their 20-year association with producer Dieter Dierks. *Crazy World* followed and became their most successful album to date. The politically poignant 'Wind Of Change', lifted as a single, became their first million-seller as it reached the number 1 position in country after country around the world. Produced by Keith Olsen, *Crazy World* transformed the band's sound, ensuring enormous crossover potential without radically compromising their identity or alienating their original fanbase. Buchholz was sacked in 1992, at which time investigators began to look into the band's accounts for alleged tax evasion. His replacement was classically trained musician Ralph Heickermann, who had previously provided computer programming for Kingdom Come, as well as varied soundtrack work. Heickermann made his debut on a perfunctory 1995 live album, their third such venture. Allied to a lack of new material, *Live Bites* only served to heighten suspicions about the long-term viability and vitality of the band.

● ALBUMS: *Action/Lonesome Crow* (Brain 1972)★★★, *Fly To The Rainbow* (RCA 1974)★★★, *In Trance* (RCA 1975)★★★★, *Virgin Killers* (RCA 1976)★★, *Taken By Force* (RCA 1978)★★, *Tokyo*

Tapes (RCA 1978)★★, *Lovedrive* (EMI 1979)★★, *Animal Magnetism* (EMI 1980)★★, *Blackout* (EMI 1982)★★★, *Love At First Sting* (EMI 1984)★★★★, *World Wide Live* (EMI 1985)★★★, *Savage Amusement* (EMI 1988)★★★, *Crazy World* (Vertigo 1990)★★★, *Face The Heat* (Vertigo 1993)★★, *Live Bites* (Mercury 1995)★★, *Pure Instincts* (East West 1996)★★.
Solo: Herman Rarebell *Nip In The Bud* (Harvest 1981)★★.
● COMPILATIONS: *The Best Of The Scorpions* (RCA 1979)★★★, *The Best Of The Scorpions, Volume 2* (RCA 1984)★★, *Gold Ballads* (Harvest 1987)★★, *CD Box Set* (EMI 1991)★★, *Deadly Sting* (EMI 1995)★★.
● VIDEOS: *First Sting* (PMI 1985), *World Wide Live* (1985), *Crazy World Tour* (1991).

Scrap Iron Scientists

This all-black rock band, consisting of Richard Martin (vocals), Steve Wellington (guitar), Steve Liburd (bass) and Johann James (drums), was formed in London, England, in 1994, and rose to prominence in 1995 as support act on Body Count's UK tour. Their uncompromising rock sound was reminiscent of both Anthrax and Red Hot Chili Peppers. They performed at an anti-racist carnival on Plumstead Common, London, near the headquarters of the extreme right-wing British National Party. Further supports with Crown Of Thorns and Skunk Anansie followed, before they embarked on their first recording sessions.

Scream

Not to be confused with the Washington, DC punk band of the same name, this group took shape from the ashes of LA favourites Racer X when in-demand Philadelphian vocalist/guitarist John Corabi joined Bruce Bouillet (lead guitar) and John Alderete (bass) in that band's final line-up. With the departure of Scott Travis to Judas Priest, the drumstool was filled by Walt Woodward III (ex-Americade and Shark Island), and the band became the Scream. In contrast to the complex guitar-orientated metal of the old act, the Scream played in a variety of styles, from the gentle ballad, 'Father, Mother, Son' and the witty acoustic blues of 'Never Loved Her Anyway' to the electric hard rock of 'Outlaw' and the atmospheric 'Man In The Moon'. They even tackled funk-rock with 'Tell Me Why', revealing influences as diverse as the Rolling Stones, Van Halen, Led Zeppelin, Humble Pie and Aerosmith. However, the resultant debut, *Let It Scream*, was a highly cohesive work with a powerful Eddie Kramer production and a charismatic performance from Corabi. The album and subsequent live work were well received, and with priority backing from Hollywood Records, the Scream seemed set for stardom, until Corabi was tempted away to replace Vince Neil in Mötley Crüe. A lengthy search for a new singer ensued, with Billy Scott eventually being recruited, but the band subsequently changed their name to Stash, with a new direction reportedly in the vein of Sly And The Family Stone.
● ALBUMS: *Let It Scream* (Hollywood 1991)★★★.

Screaming Jets

Australian rock band the Screaming Jets originally comprised Dave Gleeson (vocals), Grant Walmsley (guitar), Paul Woseen (bass), Brad Heaney (drums) and Richard Lara (guitar). Their caustic, brutal rock and extravagant stage show brought early attention, which increased with the release of their debut album, *All For One*. After supporting Thunder on UK dates through 1992 a second collection followed, the similarly bombastic *Tear Of Thought*. Support spots with the Quireboys and their own headlining club dates ensued. Their popularity in Europe was climaxed by an appearance at the Rock Am Ring Festival in Germany in front of 50,000 rock fans. They returned home to Australia but in early 1994 lost the services of both Heaney and Lara, replaced by Craig Rosevear and Jimi Hocking, respectively. They continued to play around 300 shows a year on their domestic circuit, and enjoyed a surprise national chart success with a rare ballad, 'Helping Hand', in 1994. As a consequence both the group's first two albums were eventually certified platinum in Australia. They embarked on sessions for a third album in 1995, accompanied by producer Robbie Adams, whose track record included engineering two U2 studio albums.
● ALBUMS: *All For One* (RooArt 1990)★★★, *Tear Of Thought* (RooArt 1993)★★★, *Screaming Jets* (RooArt 1995)★★.

Screaming Trees

Hard-drinking rock band from the rural community of Ellensburg, near Seattle, USA. The Screaming Trees blend 60s music (the Beach Boys being an obvious reference point) with psychotic, pure punk rage. Not to be confused with the Sheffield, England synthesizer group of the same name who were also operational in the mid-80s, brothers Gary Lee Conner (b. 22 August 1962, Fort Irwin, California, USA; guitar) and Van Conner (b.

17 March 1967, Apple Valley, California, USA; bass) are among the largest men in rock, rivalled in their girth only by fellow Seattle heavyweights Poison Idea. The rest of the line-up comprises Mark Lanegan (vocals) and Barrett Martin (b. 14 April 1967, Olympia, Washington, USA; drums - replacing original incumbent Mark Pickerell in 1991). *Even If And Especially When*, the best of three strong albums for SST Records, included notable compositions such as the live favourite 'Transfiguration', which typified the group's blend of punk aggression and 60s mysticism. Major label debut *Uncle Anaesthesia* brought production from Terry Date and Soundgarden's Chris Cornell. By the time Screaming Trees moved to Epic Records they had embraced what one Melody Maker journalist called 'unashamed 70s Yankee rock', straddled by bursts of punk spite. Lanegan had by now released a solo, largely acoustic album, *The Winding Sheet*, for Sub Pop Records in 1990. This affecting, intensely personal collection included a cover version of Lead Belly's 'Where Did You Sleep Last Night', which Kurt Cobain would later employ as the trump card in Nirvana's *MTV Unplugged* session. Other extra-curricular activities included Gary Lee Conner's Purple Outside project, and his brother Van fronted Solomon Grundy (one album each in 1990). After four years they returned with *Dust*, comparatively mellow and highly commercial. The mellowness was induced by Lanegan's friendship with the late Kurt Cobain. This sadness is reflected in the lethargic 'Look At You', although the album's mantric 'All I Know' and 'Make My Mind' dispel any accusation of wallowing in self-pity.

● ALBUMS: *Clairvoyance* (Velvetone 1986)★★, *Even If And Especially When* (SST 1987)★★★, *Invisible Lantern* (SST 1988)★★★, *Buzz Factory* (SST 1989)★★, *Uncle Anaesthesia* (Epic 1991)★★★, *Sweet Oblivion* (Epic 1992)★★★, *Change Has Come* mini-album (Epic 1993)★★★, *Dust* (Epic 1996)★★★★.

Solo: Solomon Grundy *Solomon Grundy* (New Alliance 1990)★★★. Mark Lanegan *The Winding Sheet* (Sub Pop 1990)★★★, *Scraps At Midnight* (Sub Pop 1998)★★★★.

● COMPILATIONS: *Anthology: SST Years 1985-1989* (SST 1995)★★★.

SEA HAGS

Purveyors of all things degenerate and of definite 'wrong side of the tracks' orientation, Sea Hags were formed in San Francisco, California, in 1985. With a line-up comprising ex-rock photographer Ron Yocom (guitar, vocals), Frankie Wilsey (guitar), Chris Schlosshardt (bass) and Adam Maples (drums), their own manager would famously describe their trajectory thus: 'there's only so far you can get with three junkies and one alcoholic'. Their first and only album was recorded for Chrysalis by Guns N' Roses producer Mike Clink (after the Cult's Ian Astbury had expressed an interest). This collection, which aped the group's obvious inspiration, Aerosmith, riff for riff, caught the attention of the press, a situation exacerbated by the media-friendly antics of the subjects. However, the sadly predictable death of Chris Schlosshardt from a suspected drug overdose killed the band's momentum. Maples was briefly rumoured to be replacement for Steven Adler in Guns N'Roses, while Wilsey joined Arcade.

● ALBUMS: *Sea Hags* (Chrysalis 1989)★★★.

SEBADOH

Based in Boston, Massachusetts, USA, Sebadoh are led by Lou Barlow (b. *c*.1966; vocals, guitar). Before his well-publicized partnership with J. Mascis in Dinosaur Jr, Barlow had also played guitar to Mascis's drums in primal Boston hardcore group Deep Wound. However, as Dinosaur Jr worked their way out of the alternative/college rock circuit and into the mainstream, friendships within the band began to fray. The break came in 1989 when Barlow mistakenly let his bass feed back after missing his cue. Mascis's response was to walk over and hit Barlow over the head with his guitar, thereby irrevocably damaging their relationship. Afterwards Barlow was fired, and admitted to being 'just kind of lost, for a whole year'. When he eventually regrouped he began to record four-track demos with drumming friend Eric Gaffney. Sebadoh's early recordings led to them being heralded as kings of the US 'lo-fi' scene, which also encompassed Pavement and Guided By Voices. These cassette releases, untutored but full of the pop hooks with which Barlow would become identified, were dwarfed by the impact of 1991's *Sebadoh III*, at which time the duo was expanded with the addition of bass player/vocalist Jason Loewenstein. Seen by many as the ultimate 90s college rock album, *Sebadoh III* was composed of irony-laden indie folk rock with continually surprising pop twists. It remains the group's most enduring achievement. The UK-issued *Rockin The Forest* included the group's tongue-in-cheek 'Gimme Indie Rock' single and saw the band adopt a comparatively professional rock/pop sound. *Sebadoh Vs Helmet* included two Nick Drake cover versions as well as a revisited version of 'Brand New Love', originally issued on *Freed Weed* and recently released as a cover version by Superchunk. The group then joined Sub Pop Records for the deftly titled *Smash Your Head On The Punk Rock*, which was issued in the wake of Nirvana's global breakthrough. The group's prolific output of albums continued, forcing critics to reassess perceived notions of Barlow as a minor figure in Dinosaur Jr's success, and as a genuine talent in his own right. With Sebadoh now a group proper, Barlow still found time to write solo material which was credited to Sentridoh, and collaborate with John Davis as the Folk Implosion. In 1994 Eric Gaffney left the band, to be replaced by Bob Fay, although Gaffney had 'sort of' quit and been replaced at least three times previously. *Bakesale* was the band's first album to benefit from production at the celebrated Fort Apache Studios in Cambridge, Massachusetts. The greater depth of sound allowed the listener better access to the Sebadoh ethos, with Barlow's voice having developed a real empathetic edge on songs such as 'Careful' and Dreams'. As Barlow maintained: 'What's really important are the words. We play guitars so you can actually hear the texture of the music. As a songwriter, if you have anything to give at all, it's what your words are.' In 1996 Barlow made a surprise entry into the US Top 40 with a song written with his Folk Implosion partner John Davis. 'Natural One' was issued as a single after being featured on the soundtrack to the controversial film *Kids*. *Harmacy* seemed like an unintentional bid for pop stardom and was peppered with catchy riffs.

● ALBUMS: *Freed Man* (Homestead 1989)★★★, *Weed Forestin* (Homestead 1990)★★★, *Sebadoh III* (Homestead 1991)★★★, *Rockin The Forest* (20/20 1992)★★, *Sebadoh Vs Helmet* (20/20 1992)★★★, *Smash Your Head On The Punk Rock* (Sub Pop 1992)★★★, *Bubble And Scrape* (Sup Pop 1993)★★★, *4-Songs* (Domino 1994)★★, *Bakesale* (Sub Pop/Domino 1994)★★★★, ... *In Tokyo* (Bolide 1995)★★, *Harmacy* (Sub Pop 1996)★★★★.

● COMPILATIONS: *Freed Weed* (Homestead 1990)★★★.

2ND HEAT

Assembled in Bremerhaven, Germany, by Kai Braue (guitar), Marcel Robbers (vocals), Mathias Gonik (bass) and Frank Hoogestraat (guitar), 2nd Heat were formed in 1992 and soon earned their spurs on bills with Phantom Blue, Tigertailz, Lee Aaron and Saga. Soon afterwards, the group, who specialize in guitar-intensive traditional metal, raised their profile by recording a self-financed cassette, which went on to sell over 800 copies. This came to the attention of Rock The Nation Records, who signed the band and re-released the tape with the addition of a bonus track, 'Cyan Eyes', to generally strong reviews.

● ALBUMS: *Shreddervision* (RTN 1994)★★★★.

SEDUCER

This hard rock group was formed in Amsterdam, Netherlands, in 1980 by vocalists/guitarists Frans Phillipus and Jerry Lopies. After a series of false starts, the line-up stabilized with the recruitment of bassist Eppie Munting and drummer Rene van Leersum. Specializing in blues-based hard rock and boogie, the band contributed their first tracks to a compilation, *Holland Heavy Metal Vol. 1*, in 1982. A deal with the independent Universe label followed and a self-titled debut appeared in 1983. This was poorly received, and a line-up reshuffle ensued, with Van Leersum and Lopies departing in favour of ex-Hammerhead guitarist Erik Karreman, drummer Jan Koster and vocalist Thijs Hamelaers. They contributed two further numbers to the *Dutch Steel* compilation in 1984, but the group disbanded shortly afterwards as Koster and Karreman formed Highway Chile, while Hamelaers went on to Germane and later the Sleez Beez.

● ALBUMS: *Seducer* (Universe 1983)★★★, *Sin Speaks* (Waggletone 1997)★★.

SEGER, BOB

b. 6 May 1945, Detroit, Michigan, USA. Seger began his long career in the early 60s as a member of the Decibels. He subsequently joined Doug Brown and the Omens as organist, but was installed as their vocalist and songwriter when such talents surfaced. The group made its recording debut as the Beach Bums, with 'The Ballad Of The Yellow Beret', but this pastiche of the contemporaneous Barry Sadler hit, 'The Ballad Of The Green Beret', was withdrawn in the face of a threatened lawsuit. The act then became known as Bob Seger and the Last Heard and as such completed several powerful singles, notably 'East Side Story' (1966) and 'Heavy Music' (1967). Seger was signed by Capitol Records in 1968 and the singer's new group, the Bob Seger System, enjoyed a US Top 20 hit that year with 'Ramblin' Gamblin' Man'. Numerous excellent hard-rock releases followed, including the impressive *Mongrel* album, but the artist was unable to repeat his early success and disbanded the group in 1971. Having spent a period studying for a college degree, Seger returned to music with his own label, Palladium, and three unspectacular albums ensued. He garnered considerable acclaim for his 1974 single, 'Get Out Of Denver', which has since become a much-covered classic. However, Seger only achieved deserved commercial success upon returning to Capitol when *Beautiful Loser* reached the lower reaches of the US album charts (number 131). Now fronting the Silver Bullet Band - Drew Abbott (guitar), Robyn Robbins (keyboards), Alto Reed (saxophone), Chris Campbell (bass) and Charlie Allen Martin (drums) - Seger reinforced his in-concert popularity with the exciting *Live Bullet*, which was in turn followed by *Night Moves*, his first platinum disc. The title track reached the US Top 5 in 1977, a feat 'Still The Same' repeated the following year. The latter hit was culled from the triple-platinum album, *Stranger In Town*, which also included 'Hollywood Nights', 'Old Time Rock 'N' Roll' and 'We've Got Tonight'. By couching simple sentiments in traditional, R&B-based rock, the set confirmed Seger's ability to articulate the aspirations of blue-collar America, a feature enhanced by his punishing tour schedule. *Against The Wind* also topped the US album charts, while another live set, *Nine Tonight*, allowed the artist time to recharge creative energies.

He recruited Jimmy Iovine for *The Distance* which stalled at number 5. Among his later hit singles were the Rodney Crowell song 'Shame On The Moon' (1983), 'Old Time Rock 'n' Roll' (from the film *Risky Business*), 'Understanding' (from the film *Teachers*) and the number 1 hit 'Shakedown', taken from the soundtrack of *Beverly Hills Cop II*. Seger released his first studio album for five years in 1991. Co-produced by Don Was, it was a Top 10 hit in the USA, clearly showing his massive following had remained in place. A highly successful greatest hits collection issued in 1994 (with copious sleeve notes from Seger) also demonstrated just what a huge following he still has. *It's A Mystery* came after a long gap, presumably buoyed by recent success. It ploughed typical Seger territory with regular riff rockers such as 'Lock And Load' alongside acoustic forays such as 'By The River'. The most interesting track on the album was the title track, a great mantric rocker sounding less like Seger and more like Hüsker Dü. He followed the success of the album with a box-office record-breaking tour of America in 1996. Ticketmaster claimed that the concert in his home-town sold 100,000 tickets in 57 minutes.

● ALBUMS: *Ramblin' Gamblin' Man* (Capitol 1969)★★★, *Noah* (Capitol 1969)★★★, *Mongrel* (Capitol 1970)★★★, *Brand New Morning* (Capitol 1971)★★★, *Back In '72* (Palladium 1973)★★★, *Smokin' O.P.'s* (Palladium 1973)★★★, *Seven* (Palladium 1974)★★★, *Beautiful Loser* (Capitol 1975)★★★, *Live Bullet* (Capitol 1976)★★★★, *Night Moves* (Capitol 1976)★★★★, *Stranger In Town* (Capitol 1978)★★★★, *Against The Wind* (Capitol 1980)★★★, *Nine Tonight* (Capitol 1981)★★★, *The Distance* (Capitol 1982)★★★, *Like A Rock* (Capitol 1986)★★★, *The Fire Inside* (Capitol 1991)★★★, *It's A Mystery* (Capitol 1995)★★★.

● COMPILATIONS: *Bob Seger And The Silver Bullet Band Greatest Hits* (Capitol 1994)★★★★.

● FILMS: *American Pop* (1981).

SEND NO FLOWERS

The story of Bristol, England-based Send No Flowers is a prime example of the ruthlessness of the music industry. With the original name of Agent Orange, Steve Rendell (guitar), Dominic Gearon (bass), Matt Bradbury (vocals), Scott Leach (guitar) and Tom Broman (drums) formed the band in 1994 with a desire to introduce some originality to their local music scene. They moved collectively into a Bristol farmhouse in order to forge a coherent rock identity. Over several months the band worked on new material that owed a great deal to Seattle grunge bands such as Alice In Chains and Pearl Jam. The resulting demo achieved the desired results - they piqued the interest of the rock press and one of their tapes attracted a rave review from rock paper *Kerrang!* They built a steady following through touring, finally signing to EastWest Records, and work began on the sessions that formed their debut, *Juice*. While the grunge references were unmistakable, the band had managed to take the Seattle sound and create something of their own design. The songwriting was accomplished, with the crowning glory coming in the form of the self-indulgent 'Fireman', an eight-minute orgy of intense melody, stirring strings and sublime choruses. Having presented the British rock scene with one of the outstanding releases of the year, the band's fortunes took a downward turn. The album failed to sell, and they were unceremoniously dropped by their label and subsequently broke up – and no one sent flowers. Various members resurfaced as Shineola but the resurrection was very short-lived.

● ALBUMS: *Juice* (EastWest 1996)★★★.

SENSER

This multi-ethnic, seven-piece south London band was conceived in 1987. Their *métier* is the synthesis of numerous styles of music into a format that at once stimulates both the feet and grey matter. Fronted by Heitham Al-Sayed (raps, vocals, percussion), Senser proved the only band of their generation to see features in magazines dedicated to heavy metal, hip-hop and indie music - and few were in any way grudging. The other members of the band were Nick Michaelson (guitar), Andy 'Awe' (a DJ who once held the national high score on the Asteroids video game), Haggis (engineer), James Barrett (bass), John Morgan (drums) and Kersten Haigh (vocals, flute). This line-up was cemented in 1992, as they began the first of two tours supporting Ozric Tentacles, plus low-key squat and benefit gigs. The first seeds of the band were sown when Michaelson and Barrett met at a guitarist competition at the Forum, in London. Ex-schoolfriend Haigh fronted the band from 1988 onwards, before the Senser name had been invoked, bringing vocals inspired from her journeys in India. Wimbledon resident Al-Sayed joined in 1991 as a drummer, but soon progressed to rapping duties as the band attempted to tackle their own version of Public Enemy's 'She Watch Channel Zero'. Their 1993 singles, 'Eject' and 'The Key', brought rave reviews across dance and indie periodicals, with their ferocious musical clatter evading categorization. 'Switch', entering the UK Top 40, in turn announced a Top 5 debut album, *Stacked Up*, and a widely applauded appearance on the 1994 Glastonbury Festival stage. Al-Sayed, meanwhile, was particularly vocal in espousing the cause of the travelling community, under threat in 1994 from a new Criminal Justice bill. Although his throat problems prevented the band from building on their impact for much of 1994, *Stacked Up* went on to achieve over 80,000 sales. Al-Sayed, Morgan and Haggis all left the band early in 1996 to form Lodestar. Now fronted by just Haigh, the band returned in 1998 with the long overdue follow-up, *Asylum*.

● ALBUMS: *Stacked Up* (Ultimate 1994)★★★, *Asylum* (Ultimate 1998)★★★★.

● VIDEOS: *States Of Mind* (1995).

SENTINEL BEAST

This thrash metal group was formed in Sacramento, California, USA, in 1984 by bassist Mike Spencer, vocalist Debbie Gunn and drummer Scott Awes. Adding guitarists Barry Fischel and Mark Koyasako, they debuted with their theme tune, 'Sentinel Beast', on the *Metal Massacre VII* compilation in 1986. This opened the door to a full contract with Metal Blade Records and the emergence of *Depths Of Death* the same year. This was standard Anthrax-style heavy metal, poorly produced and notable only for the high-speed cover of Iron Maiden's 'Phantom Of The Opera'. The album was a commercial flop and founder-member Spencer left to join Flotsam And Jetsum soon after its release. The band subsequently disintegrated, with Debbie Gunn reappearing later in Znowhite and Ice Age.

● ALBUMS: *Depths Of Death* (Metal Blade 1986)★★★.

SEPULTURA

Formed in Belo Horizonte, Brazil, in 1984 by brothers Igor (b. 24 September 1970, Brazil; drums) and Max Cavalera (b. Belo Horizonte, 4 August 1969, Brazil; vocals, guitar), with Paulo Jnr. (b. 30 April 1969, Brazil; bass) and guitarist Jairo T, who was replaced in April 1987 by Andreas Kisser (b. 24 August 1968) of fellow Brazilian metal act Pestilence. Sepultura is the Portuguese word for grave, and this is a strong clue as to the nature of a music that deals with themes of death and destruction, originally influenced by bands such as Slayer and Venom. In 1985 Sepultura recorded an album with Brazilian band Overdose (whom Sepultura had supported on their very first gig), but this debut, *Bestial Devastation*, was of poor quality and had limited circulation. Their first solo effort, *Morbid Visions*, was released in 1986, followed a year later by *Schizophrenia*. The music on both was typified by speed, aggression and anger, much of which stemmed from the band's preoccupations with the poor social conditions in their native land. It was Monte Conner of American record label Roadrunner who brought the band to international notice in 1989 when they released *Beneath The Remains*, which had been recorded in Rio with Scott Burns as producer. In 1990 Sepultura played at the Dynamo Festival in Holland where they met Gloria Bujnowski, manager of Sacred Reich; their relationship with her led to the re-release of *Schizophrenia*. Despite European and American success, Sepultura have not deserted Brazil, and they played at the Rock in Rio festival in 1990. *Arise*, released in 1991, proved the best-selling album in the history of the Roadrunner label. The sessions for *Chaos A.D.* saw the group strip down their music in a more minimalist approach, which mirrored the punk ethos, especially evident on a cover version of New Model Army's 'The Hunt' (they had previously cut the Dead Kennedys' 'Drug Me' for an Alternative Tentacles compilation). In 1994 Cavalera branched out to release the *Point Blank* CD, working alongside Fudgetunnel's Alex Newport under the name Nailbomb. *Roots* was seen as their peak and an album that allowed them to create rather than imitate. Brazilian themes were explored, notably with the pulsating 'Ratamahatta' and the tribal 'Itsari'. Having hit a peak in 1996 it came as a shock when Cavalera left to form Soulfly, who released their self-titled debut in 1998. His replacement in Sepultura was American Derrick Green, who featured prominently on 1998's *Against*.

● ALBUMS: *Bestial Devastation* with Overdose (Cogumelo 1985)★★★, *Morbid Visions* (Cogumelo 1986)★★★, *Schizophrenia* (Cogumelo 1987)★★★, *Beneath The Remains* (Roadracer 1989)★★★, *Arise* (Roadracer 1991)★★★, *Chaos A.D.* (Roadrunner 1993)★★★. Max Cavalera in Nailbomb *Point Blank* (Roadrunner 1994)★★★, *Roots* (Roadrunner 1996)★★★★, *Against* (Roadrunner 1998)★★★.

● COMPILATIONS: *Blood-Rooted* (Roadrunner 1997)★★★.

● VIDEOS: *Third World Chaos* (Roadrunner 1995), *We Are What We Are* (Roadrunner 1997).

SERGEANT

This predominantly Swiss, six-piece group was formed from the ashes of the Steve Whitney Band. Comprising Pete Prescott (vocals), Rob Seales (guitar), Chrigi Wiedemeier (guitar), Urs Amacher (keyboards), Rolf Schlup (bass) and Gary Steimer (drums), they specialized in Americanized hard rock with melodic undercurrents. Signing to Mausoleum Records, they debuted in 1985 with *Sergeant*, a workmanlike rock record that paid respect to Van Halen, Kiss and Foreigner. *Streetwise*, released the following year, was a major disappointment, as it merely regurgitated and reprocessed the riffs of their debut. Disillusioned by the media and public response, the band went their separate ways shortly after the album was released. In 1988 Seales and Amacher re-formed the band with new members Romy Caviezel (vocals), Harry Borner (bass) and Urs Rothenbuhler (drums).

● ALBUMS: *Sergeant* (Mausoleum 1985)★★★, *Streetwise* (Mausoleum 1986)★★.

SEVENDUST

Formed in Atlanta, Georgia, USA, in 1994, extreme metal band Sevendust comprises vocalist Lajo, drummer Morgan Rose, bass player Vince Hornsby and guitarists Clint Lowery (brother of Corey Lowery of Stuck Mojo) and John Connolly. All were previously members of sundry local rock outfits, with Lajo recruited from a local bar blues/funk rock group. Said Rose: 'I knew from the moment I saw him that if we could put his voice on top of our music it would be a beautiful combination.' The quintet first became Rumblefish then Sevendust, recruiting former Twisted Sister member Jay Jay French as manager and signing to TVT Records (formerly home to Nine Inch Nails). A self-titled debut album followed. Buoyed by strong radio play and an intensive touring schedule throughout America, it hit the number 1 spot in the US metal charts and stayed there for 12 weeks. A small tour of England, sponsored by *Kerrang!* magazine, ensued.

● ALBUMS: *Sevendust* (TVT 1998)★★★.

SEVEN MARY THREE

US alternative rock band Seven Mary Three made their breakthrough when a copy of their debut CD, *Churn*, was passed to a disc jockey at WJRR, a commercial radio station broadcasting from Orlando, Florida. As a result of their championing of the track 'Cumbersome', Seven Mary Three were head-hunted and signed by Mammoth Records. Comprising Jason Ross (vocals, guitar), Casey Daniel (bass), both natives of Orlando, and Jason Pollock (guitar) and Giti Khalsa (drums), the group formed in 1992 when Ross and Pollock were attending the College Of William And Mary. After recruiting Daniel and Khalsa, Seven Mary Three embarked on a rigorous touring schedule, increasing their popularity in the Virginia and Florida regions. With a growing live reputation, the band elected to base their activities permanently in Florida. Their debut CD was independently produced after the group members pooled resources and borrowed money from friends. After Mammoth had offered the group a contract they entered Morrisound Studios in Tampa to re-record their debut as *American Standard*, an album that drew strong reviews throughout the American alternative rock press.

● ALBUMS: *Churn* (Independent 1995)★★★, *American Standard* (Mammoth 1996)★★★, *Rockcrown* (EastWest 1997)★★★.

707

US melodic pomp-rock group formed in 1979 by Kevin Russell (guitar, vocals), Jim McClarty (drums) and Phil Bryant (bass, vocals). However, the band's line-up was in a constant state of flux. Tod Howarth (keyboards, guitar, vocals), Felix Robinson (bass, ex-Angel) and Kevin Chalfant made important contributions during the group's lifetime. 707 debuted with a radio-friendly self-titled album, characterized by strong musicianship and instantly contagious hooklines and choruses. Their next two albums adopted a more metallic approach, with *The Second Album* deservedly reaching the lower reaches of the US *Billboard* chart. *Mega Force*, produced by Keith Olsen, also provided the theme tune for the film of the same name. Unfortunately, the creative ideas had started to run dry by this stage, while the songs duplicated earlier ideas and were generally less immediate. Internal disputes became more and more common, and the band finally fell apart in 1983. Howarth went on to play with Frehley's Comet, while Chalfant backed Kim Carnes and Night Ranger before co-founding The Storm in 1991.

● ALBUMS: *707* (Casablanca 1980)★★★, *The Second Album* (Casablanca 1981)★★★★, *Mega Force* (Broadwalk 1982)★★.

7 Year Bitch

US alternative rock band 7 Year Bitch formed in 1991 in Seattle, Washington, USA, and originally comprised Selene Vigil (guitar), Elizabeth Davis (bass), Valerie Agnew (drums) and Stefanie Sargent (guitar). Their rise to prominence was rapid; their debut single, 'Lorna', sold out of its initial pressing of 1,000 copies and captured ecstatic reviews in magazines from Seattle's *Hype* to the UK's *Melody Maker*. Shows in the north-west of America led to a Pearl Jam member asking them to take their place opening for the Red Hot Chili Peppers in February 1992. Confirmation of their ability arrived with an impressive appearance at that year's New Music Seminar. However, a month before the scheduled release of their debut album, guitarist Sargent died. The release was held in abeyance while the group considered whether or not to continue. They eventually decided to do so, releasing a limited edition 10-inch picture disc before *Sick 'Em* followed in October 1992. Comprising all their compositions to date (which included a variety of compilation appearances), it was dedicated to the memory of Sargent. A replacement guitarist, Roisin Dunne, brought the band back to full strength in November. 1993 and 1994 were spent touring widely, alongside such acts as L7, Cypress Hill and Rage Against The Machine, before a second album arrived in May 1995. *¡Viva Zapata!* again won favourable reviews from diverse sources (including the hard rock press), and preceded a move to a major label, Atlantic Records. Dunne left the band in July 1996 and was replaced by ex-Mudwimmin guitarist Lisa Faye.

●ALBUMS: *Sick 'Em* (C/Z 1992)★★★, *¡Viva Zapata!* (C/Z 1994)★★★, *Gato Negro* (Atlantic 1996)★★★.

Sex, Love And Money

Formed in Greenville, North Carolina, USA, by Chuck Manning (vocals, guitar), John Bateman (guitar), Jim Bury (bass) and Jon Chambliss (drums), this metal outfit took its name from a local expression: 'It's a term that people call other people around here - SLAM babies - their primary concerns are Sex, Love and Money. To us it's a deeper, darker, and more realistic view of what we think everybody's invisible engine is'. Bateman graduated from Greenville's highly regarded Art School, after spending much of his life in Columbia, South America. This bred an early interest in both metal and flamenco. He hooked up with the remaining members who were participating in a Ramones-influenced punk band in April 1991. Songwriting within the band is arranged on a democratic principle with each member writing their own parts in isolation, Manning adding the lyrics. This creative process first saw fruition in January 1995 with the release of a self-titled debut album for Music For Nations subsidiary Bulletproof Records.

● ALBUMS: *Sex, Love And Money* (Bulletproof 1995)★★★.

Shadow King

In 1990, vocalist Lou Gramm eventually departed hugely successful AOR group Foreigner, after pursuing an equally successful solo career with two late 80s albums for Atlantic Records. In 1991 his desire to be part of a band once more led to the formation of Shadow King. Named after one of the band's songs, and based on the description of a huge, decadent and apocalyptic city, the band is completed by Vivian Campbell (b. 25 August 1962, Belfast, Northern Ireland, guitar; ex-Dio and Whitesnake), Bruce Turgon (bass; ex-Black Sheep and Warrior) and Kevin Valentine (drums). They debuted with a self-titled album for Atlantic in 1991. This was a strong collection of hi-tech, hard-edged AOR characterized by Gramm's soulful vocals. Campbell's guitar work was economical and restrained, marking a distinct change from his previous flamboyant output. Superbly produced by

Keith Olsen, it was one of the year's most accomplished and mature rock releases. Afterwards Campbell moved on to join Def Leppard.
● ALBUMS: *Shadow King* (Atlantic 1991)★★★.

SHAH

Formed in Moscow, Russia, in 1985, Shah comprise Antonio Garcia (vocals, guitar), Anatoly Krupnov (bass) and Andrei Sazanov (drums). The group were pioneers of thrash metal in the USSR and attracted the attention of Velerie Gaina, guitarist with fellow Soviet band, Kruiz. Gaina helped Shah record their first demo, which he then took to the West and German independent label Atom H Records. Suitably impressed, the label signed the band, resulting in a debut collection, *Beware*, which betrayed the obvious influence of Anthrax. Bearing in mind the cultural and political hurdles the band had to overcome, it was a considerable achievement. In 1990 Shah played at the Public Against Violence Festival in Ostava, Czechoslovakia, along with German melodic rockers Bonfire and UK thrash metal band Talion, and were a huge success. They continue to perform regularly and extensively in their own country.
● ALBUMS: *Beware* (Atom H 1989)★★★.

SHAKIN' STREET

This rock 'n' roll quintet was influenced by the Stooges, Rolling Stones and Blue Öyster Cult, and took their name from a song by the MC5. Formed in Paris in 1975 by Fabienne Shine (b. Tunisia; vocals) and her songwriting partner, Eric Lewy (guitar, vocals), the group was completed by Mike Winter (bass), Armik Tigrane (guitar) and Jean Lou Kalinowski (drums). Signing to CBS Records, they debuted with the average *Vampire Rock*, a selection of predominantly up-tempo rockers, notable only for Shine's unusual vocals. Ross 'The Boss' Funicello (ex-Dictators) replaced Tigrane for the second album. This was a vast improvement, with a denser sound and more abrasive guitarwork brought through in the final mix. Ross The Boss subsequently left to form Manowar with Joey De Maio in 1981, but Shakin' Street carried on for a short time with ex-Thrasher guitarist Duck McDonald, before finally disbanding. Their second album proved an undiscovered classic of the metal genre and is much sought after by collectors.
● ALBUMS: *Vampire Rock* (Columbia 1978)★★★, *Shakin' Street* (Columbia 1980)★★★★, *Skin 'Em* (Virgin 1981)★★.

SHANGHAI

Formerly known as Spider, they changed their name to Shanghai in 1981 to avoid confusion with the other groups using the same name at the time. Signing to Chrysalis Records, the band comprised Amanda Blue (vocals), Keith Lentin (guitar), Beau Hill (keyboards, ex-Airborne), Jimmy Lowell (bass) and Anton Fig (drums). They debuted with a self-titled album in 1982, a keyboard dominated, melodic pop-rock opus that received favourable reviews at the time of release. The band soon splintered with Hill moving into the production side, Anton Fig worked with Glen Burtnick and Amanda Blue started a solo career under the guidance of Gene Simmons. Given time to develop, Shanghai could have been a major force on the American AOR scene.
● ALBUMS: *Shanghai* (Chrysalis 1982)★★★.

SHARK ISLAND

This five-piece, melodic hard rock group was formed in 1986 from the ashes of Los Angeles glam rockers the Sharks. Comprising Richard Black (vocals), Spencer Sercombe (guitar), Tom Rucci (bass), Michael Guy (guitar) and Walt Woodward (drums; ex-Americade), they recorded an album of demos in 1987 which saw A&M Records step in with a development deal. As a result of this, two of the band's songs were aired on the soundtrack to *Bill And Ted's Excellent Adventure*. Losing second guitarist Guy and replacing their rhythm section with Chris Heilman (ex-Bernie Tormé; bass) and Gregg Ellis (drums), they then moved over to Epic Records for a second album and first release proper in 1988. This showed the band to have matured considerably, with the material displaying new-found confidence in better production surroundings. Black had developed into an accomplished vocalist and songwriter, with a style that married the best elements of Jon Bon Jovi and David Coverdale (Whitesnake). It is an oft-repeated rumour that Axl Rose of Guns N'Roses leaned heavily on his style in developing his own delivery. Black was also involved in the Contraband project of 1991, which featured Michael Schenker and members of L.A. Guns, Ratt and Vixen. This one-off collaboration recorded an album of cover versions, including Shark Island's 'Bad For Each Other'. Sercombe would also work on various MSG dates.
● ALBUMS: *S'Cool Bus* (Shark 1987)★★★, *Law Of The Order* (Epic 1989)★★.

SHARMAN, DAVE

b. *c.*1970, England. Dave Sharman first rose to prominence in 1989 when he featured on a session for BBC Radio 1 DJ Tommy Vance's *Friday Rock Show*. Comprising four instrumental selections, this proved such a success that producer Tony Wilson was allegedly alerting labels during recording. His debut album, titled after its year of release, saw rave reviews from both the metal and musician fraternities, with US magazine *Guitar For The Practising Musician* declaring Sharman 'Guitar God In Waiting'. Later, he was invited on the 'Night Of The Guitars' tour, where he shared a stage with Rick Derringer, Ronnie Montrose and others. A second album, *Exit Within*, was conceived when the guitarist met ex-Whitesnake bass player Neil Murray at an Ian Gillan audition, the duo linking with German vocalist Thomas Brache. The resultant 'Trucker' and 'Frantic' tracks were utilized by Radio 1's *Rock Show* and used as theme music. A more solid band aggregation was sought for *Here 'N' Now*, with Sharman joined by Steve Wood (drums), Tom Jeffreys (bass) and a retained Brache on vocals. Titling the new band Graphic, they debuted with a set that comprised seven band compositions and three instrumentals.

● ALBUMS: *1990* (1990)★★★, *Exit Within* (1992)★★★. With Graphic: *Here 'N' Now* (Bleeding Hearts 1995)★★★.

SHARP NINE

Formed in Sweden in 1993, Sharp Nine consist of Jesper Starander (vocals), brother Joacim Starander (guitar), Andreas Jonasson (guitar), Dan Hansson (bass) and Frederick Lindehall (drums). After first honing their live set on popular hard rock covers they set about writing their own material, with all the members contributing to the songwriting process. After a heavy performance schedule in and around Stockholm, the group began work at Radiostudio 12 on their debut album. Produced by the band with Tommy Korge, the finished result owed much to the Seattle grunge boom, though there were also trace elements of industrial music and more conventional rock pop.

● ALBUMS: *Untimed* (Mausoleum 1995)★★.

SHAW, TOMMY

After Styx broke up in 1983 former vocalist Tommy Shaw embarked on a solo career. Signing to A&M Records, he released *Girls With Guns* the following year. This proved a big disappointment to Styx fans, who had high hopes for Shaw, and were not impressed with the strictly average melodic pop-rock on offer. The pomp and ceremony of old appeared to have vanished overnight. *What If* followed the same pattern and was another commercial disappointment. Moving to Atlantic Records, Shaw teamed up with ex-Charlie vocalist/guitarist Terry Thomas. This produced *Ambition* and marked a return to form, both in the standard of songwriting and the singer's delivery. Rather than build on this and develop a successful solo career, he declared his intention to become part of a band set-up once more. Teaming up with guitarist Ted Nugent, bassist Jack Blades (ex-Night Ranger) and drummer Michael Cartellone, he went on to multi-platinum success as part of Damn Yankees.

● ALBUMS: *Girls With Guns* (A&M 1984)★★, *What If* (A&M 1985)★★, *Ambition* (A&M 1987)★★★.

SHELLAC

Rock *enfant terrible* Steve Albini (ex-Big Black/Rapeman) formed this trio on an informal basis in 1993. Buoyed by the attention garnered in the wake of his producing *In Utero* for Nirvana, Albini (velocity), Bob Weston (mass) and Todd Trainer (time) issued 'The Rude Gesture A Pictorial History', the first of two limited-issue singles to appear on the trio's own label. It offered all the trademarks of Albini's previous groups - awkward time changes, thundering bass lines, screaming guitar and frantic vocals. Weston was ex-Volcano Suns, while Trainer had worked with Rifle Sport and Breaking Circus. 'Uranus' followed in similar, exciting fashion. A third single, 'The Admiral', came in a sleeve still showing Albini's caustic remarks referring to how it should be designed. A different version of the a-side appeared on *Shellac At Action Park*, which developed Albini's distinctive style without subverting its power. His work remained as challenging as ever on the follow-up, *Terraform*, which was recorded in 1996 but not released until two years later.

● ALBUMS: *Shellac At Action Park* (Touch And Go 1994)★★★, *Terraform* (Touch And Go 1998)★★★.

SHERRIFF

This Canadian melodic rock quintet was formed in 1981 by Arnold Lanni (vocals, keyboards) and bassist Wolf Hassel (bass). With the addition of Freddy Curci (vocals), Steve De Marchi (guitar) and Rob Elliot (drums), they signed to Capitol Records and released a self-titled debut the following year. Their approach was characterized by grandiose, sweeping melodies that drew inspiration from Kansas, Foreigner and Styx, but with a smattering of their own ideas to authenticate the songs. The album failed to attract the media's attention and the band members parted company. Lanni and Hassel later formed Frozen Ghost, while Curci and De Marchi teamed up in Alias. In 1988, quite unexpectedly, 'When I'm With You' from the debut Sherriff album became a number 1 US hit 5 years after it first charted (at number 61). The album was re-released and also did well; resulting in pressure to re-form Sherriff. Lanni and Hassel declined as they retained the rights to the name and wanted to continue with Frozen Ghost.

● ALBUMS: *Sherriff* (Capitol 1982)★★★.

SHIHAD

These inventive rockers from Wellington, New Zealand, originally formed in 1988. Established by founding members Jon Toogood (b. 9 August 1971; vocals/guitar), Phil Knight (b. 14 December 1972; bass) and Tom Larkin (b. 18 September 1971; drums), the Shihad line-up has featured so many bass players that they have prompted comparisons with Spinal Tap. The band's early days concentrated on honing their live sound and establishing an identity, and it was not until 1993 that they recorded their first album. Adding a distinctly industrial flavour to their hard-edged and largely tuneless fare, their debut, *Churn*, was produced by Killing Joke frontman Jaz Coleman. With such a heavy reputation, the band managed to secure a variety of support slots with the likes of Pantera and Misery Loves Co. *Killjoy* was essentially more of the same but attracted a great deal of critical acclaim in New Zealand, giving them four major awards at the 1995 Clear Music and Entertainment Awards, including top album and a shared award for top group. With their self-titled third album they took on yet another new bass player in Karl Kippenberger (b. 26 August 1973) and underwent a major stylistic change. Stripping away the industrial bluster, they opted for a leaner, more melodic pop-edged approach, utilizing the talents of top mixer Adam Casper, best known for his work with Soundgarden and R.E.M. The diversity of new material made the album far more accessible than previous outings and boasted mellow moments in 'Missionary', alongside heavy pop-punk tunes such as 'Outta Phase' and 'La La Land'. The only acknowledgement of their heavier past was on 'Yr Head Is A Rock', which nevertheless was permeated by melody. A series of high-profile support slots – including a stint with Silverchair – ensured that the newly streamlined Shihad received maximum exposure after the overhaul.

● ALBUMS: *Churn* (Noise 1993)★★★, *Killjoy* (Noise 1995)★★★★, *Shihad* (Noise 1996)★★★.

SHIRE

This American hard rock quartet was formed in 1983 by David Anthony (vocals), Alan St. Lesa (guitar), Mick Adrian (bass) and Steve Ordyke (drums). They secured a record contract with Enigma the following year. Influenced by Dokken, Kiss and Van Halen, their debut was a somewhat formularized collection of mid-paced rockers that ultimately lacked distinction. Produced by Don Dokken and Michael Wagner, the album was eagerly anticipated, but proved a major disappointment when it arrived. Little more was heard of Shire in its wake.

● ALBUMS: *Shire* (Enigma 1984)★★★.

SHIVA

This UK rock trio, which combined both progressive rock and metal traditions, was formed in 1981 by multi-instrumentalist John Hall (vocals, guitar, keyboards). Adding Andy Skuse (bass, keyboards) and Chris Logan (drums) they signed to Heavy Metal Records in 1982. Together they debuted with *Fire Dance*, a complex and inventive album that brought to mind memories of Rush, Deep Purple and Uriah Heep to its generally sympathetic reviewers. Instrumentally, the album was faultless, but the vocals were less impressive. Phil Williams replaced Logan in 1984, but this new line-up failed to record.

● ALBUMS: *Fire Dance* (Heavy Metal 1982)★★★.

SHOK PARIS

Hailing from Ohio State, USA, Shok Paris were formed in 1982 by the three-man nucleus of drummer Bill Sabo and guitarists Eric Manderwald and Ken Erb. With vocalist Vic Hix and bassist Kel Bershire completing the line-up, they debuted with 'Go Down Fighting' on the *Cleveland Metal* compilation. This opened the door to a deal with Auburn Records and they recorded *Go For The Throat* in less than two days. Musically, with their high-energy, aggressive songs they were very much in the Riot, Kiss and Accept mould. Jan Roll took over on drums on *Steel And Starlight*, but this proved to be simply a repeat performance, played under different titles with less conviction than the debut.

● ALBUMS: *Go For The Throat* (Auburn 1984)★★★, *Steel And Starlight* (Auburn 1987)★★.

Shortino, Paul

Former Quiet Riot vocalist Shortino found musical ambition early in life, coming from a talented family and taking vocal lessons before his teens. Later came a series of bands on Hollywood's Sunset Strip playing club gigs. It was on this scene that he first encountered Wendy and Ronnie Dio (of Dio), through whose auspices Shortino was engaged as vocalist for Rough Cutt. After that band sundered he joined Quiet Riot in 1989, but not before he had written songs for the television series *Fame*, and played the part of Duke Fame in *Spinal Tap*. The 90s saw him elect to pursue a solo career, joining with guitarist Jeff Northrup. The first results of this collaboration arrived with the release of the agenda-setting *Back On Track* in March 1994.

● ALBUMS: *Back On Track* (Bulletproof 1994)★★★.

Shotgun Messiah

This Swedish act began life as Kingpin, with Harry K. Cody (guitar), Tim Skold (bass) and Stixx Galore (drums) joined by ex-Easy Action vocalist Zinny J. San, releasing *Welcome To Bop City* in 1988. A subsequent relocation to Los Angeles, USA, saw a name change for both band and (remixed) album. *Shotgun Messiah* was set apart from other glam albums by the quality of musicianship, Cody evoking Steve Vai and Joe Satriani with his fluid soloing. San departed after touring was complete, with Skold taking the vocalist slot while Bobby Lycon joined as bassist for *Second Coming*, which offered promising songwriting progression and gruff, powerful vocals from Skold. However, the band failed to expand beyond their cult status despite enthusiastic press support, and both Lycon and Stixx left after *I Want More*, an EP of covers (Ramones, New York Dolls, Iggy Pop) and acoustic reworkings of older material. Cody and Skold (now bassist/vocalist) took the bold step of industrializing Shotgun Messiah, using drum machines, synthesizers and samples on *Violent New Breed*, and creating a new sound by blending commercial songwriting with abrasive delivery for an excellent album, although the transformation was viewed with cynicism in some quarters. However, this effort still could not enhance Shotgun Messiah's fortunes, and Cody and Skold called it a day soon afterwards.

● ALBUMS: *Shotgun Messiah* (Relativity 1989)★★★, *Second Coming* (Relativity 1991)★★★, *I Want More* mini-album (Relativity 1992)★★, *Violent New Breed* (Relativity 1993)★★★★.

Shy

This quintet was founded in Birmingham, England, and specialized in Americanized, melodic heavy rock. Formed in 1982, they released their debut album the following year on the independent Ebony label. The songs were excellent, characterized by the silver-throated purr of Tony Mills, but the album was let down by a slight production. New bassist Roy Stephen Davis joined in 1984, and along with vocalist Mills, guitarist Steve Harris, drummer Alan Kelly and keyboard player Pat McKenna, they secured a new contract with RCA Records. Two quality albums of sophisticated pomp-metal followed, with 1987's *Excess All Areas* being the band's finest work. This included a melodramatic version of Cliff Richard's 'Devil Woman' given a true heavy metal revision. They gained the support slot on Meat Loaf's 1987 UK tour, but the album still failed to sell in large quantities. RCA dropped the band, but they were rescued by MCA Records, which allocated a large budget to record *Misspent Youth*, with Roy Thomas Baker as producer. This album was a major disappointment as the band's naturally aggressive approach had been tempered. The songs were geared for Stateside FM-radio consumption and the group's identity was suffocated in the clinically sterile production. In 1993 new vocalist, Los Angeles-based, Birmingham-born John 'Wardi' Ward, replaced Tony Mills, who had departed in 1990. The new line-up played at the White Knights Festival in Russia in 1992, and signed to Parachute Records. They launched their comeback in 1994 with a cover version of the Rolling Stones' 'It's Only Rock 'n' Roll'.

● ALBUMS: *Once Bitten, Twice...* (Ebony 1983)★★★, *Brave The Storm* (RCA 1985)★★★, *Excess All Areas* (RCA 1987)★★★★, *Misspent Youth* (MCA 1989)★★, *Welcome To The Madhouse* (1994)★★.

Sick Of It All

Sick Of It All are long-standing members of the infamous hardcore community bred in New York City, New York, USA, in the late 80s. Even in a genre noted for its uncompromising aggression, they earned both rave notices and suspicion for what many perceived as the sheer hatefulness of their songwriting. Despite the criticism, they continue to stand by the ethos of their theme song, 'We Stand Alone'. They were also committed to the popular US abstention movement dubbed 'straight edge' (no drugs, cigarettes or alcohol). The band was formed by brothers Lou (vocals) and Pete Koller (guitar), who rearranged the original rhythm section after their 1989 debut album, bringing in Arman Majidi (drums) and Craig Setari (bass). This featured a spoken-word introduction by rapper KRS-1 and punishing, primal punk rock music. The aforementioned *We Stand Alone* mini-album featured one side of studio recordings and one live, including a cover version of Minor Threat's 'Betray' (interesting not least because Minor Threat had popularized the straight edge phenomenon). In 1994 the band were snapped up by a major label, Atlantic Records. A single lifted from their debut for the label included another tell-tale choice of cover version, Sham 69's 'Borstal Breakout'. In 1995 they contributed a track, 'Just A Patsy', to an album pieced together by Corrosion Of Conformity's Reed Mullin dedicated to ending the imprisonment of native American Leonard Peltier. They were also the victims of a concerted attack by baseball bat-wielding thugs while on tour in Manchester, England, allegedly orchestrated by bootleg T-shirt vendors.

● ALBUMS: *Blood, Sweat, And No Tears LP* (In-Effect 1989)★★★, *We Stand Alone* mini-album (In-Effect 1991)★★, *Just Look Around* (In-Effect 1992)★★★, *Scratch The Surface* (East West 1994)★★★, *Built To Last* (East West 1997)★★★.

SIEGES EVEN

This German 'techno-thrash' quartet was put together by vocalist Franz Herde and guitarist Markus Steffen in 1986. After recording three demos they were picked up by the Steamhammer label in 1988. They debuted with *Life Cycle*, a complex and inventive speed-metal fusion of jazz, rock and classical styles. The material was characterized by a multitude of quick-fire time changes, which ultimately fragmented the songs and made them difficult to distinguish from one another. The album was generally well received, but made little impact outside Germany.

● ALBUMS: *Life Cycle* (Steamhammer 1988)★★★.

SILENT RAGE

This Californian hard rock quartet was formed in 1986 by Mark Hawkins (vocals, guitar, synthesizer), Timmy James Reilly (vocals, guitar), E.L. Curcio (bass) and Jerry Grant (drums). They debuted with 'Make it Or Break It' on the *Pure Metal* compilation. This led to producer/guitarist Paul Sabu taking an interest in the band. He produced *Shattered Hearts* and co-wrote three numbers on the album. This collection followed a direction similar to Y&T, Kiss and Van Halen but featured extensive use of keyboards, which added a strong melodic undercurrent to the songs. Moving to Kiss bassist Gene Simmons' self-titled label, a subsidiary of RCA Records, *Don't Touch Me There* materialized in 1990. This built on the strong foundations of their debut and was well produced, but blatantly geared for Stateside FM radio playlists.

● ALBUMS: *Shattered Hearts* (Chameleon 1987)★★★, *Don't Touch Me There* (Simmons/RCA 1990)★★★.

SILVER MOUNTAIN

This melodic heavy metal group was formed in Malmo, Sweden, in 1978, taking their name from a song on Rainbow's debut album, 'Man On The Silver Mountain'. Not surprisingly, the band's sound proved to be an amalgam of Deep Purple, Rainbow and Judas Priest influences. Silver Mountain have been through an endless series of line-up changes, with the only constant being founder-member Jonas Hansson (guitar, vocals). It took almost five years before the band secured a contract, with Roadrunner Records. They went on to release four competent, if slightly dated, metal albums, and built up strong followings in Scandinavia, Greece and Japan. The most recent line-up comprised Johan Dahlstrom (vocals), Jonas Hansson (guitar, vocals), Erik Bjorn Nielsen (keyboards), Per Stadin (bass) and Kjell Gustavson (drums).

● ALBUMS: *Shakin' Brains* (Roadrunner 1983)★★★, *Universe* (Roadrunner 1985)★★★, *Live In Japan '85* (SMS 1986)★★, *Roses And Champagne* (Hex 1988)★★★.

SILVERCHAIR

When Australian rock trio Silverchair arrived on European shores in 1995, their press coverage concentrated firmly on the fact that each member was just 15 years old. However, Chris Joannou (b. 1979; bass), Daniel Johns (b. 1979; vocals/guitar) and Ben Gillies (b. 1979; drums) seemed quite capable of producing a noise in the best adult traditions of their primary influences, Pearl Jam and Nirvana. They actually formed three years previously in 1992 as Innocent Criminals, sharpening their skills in Joannou's parents' garage in Newcastle. Covers of material by Led Zeppelin, Kiss and Deep Purple soon evolved into a set of original songs. A few hesitant concerts later they entered and won a national Talent Quest contest, which allowed them to record a more polished demo and a promotional video. The single they chose to record, 'Tomorrow', was released by Sony Records and quickly became a national number 1. When Hole and Ministry toured Australasia, Silverchair were booked as support, further bolstering their reputation. Johns' lyrics were a naive trawl through social dilemmas informed by their author's viewing of documentaries on the SBS channel. Despite this, *frogstomp* quickly achieved double platinum status in Australia, and even hardened critics found it difficult to completely ignore the group's enthusiasm. In the USA where the album sold over 2 million, the band were often thought to be another band from Seattle. Their Cobain-inflenced lyrics of negativity and death were cited during a 1996 murder trial as two teenagers were accused of a family murder. Tracks from *frogstomp* were quoted during the trial.

● ALBUMS: *frogstomp* (Murmur/Epic 1995)★★★, *Freak Show* (Epic 1997)★★★★.

Silverhead

The first real band to be fronted by actor/singer Michael Des Barres, Silverhead formed in 1971 with Steve Forest (guitar), Rod Davies (guitar), Nigel Harrison (bass) and Pete Thompson (drums). They were signed to Deep Purple's record label in 1982 by Tony Edwards and their debut album soon followed. Although quite mild on record, their stage presence and raucous glam rock style won them a lewd reputation. This did little to help and Forest quit. Adopting a heavier approach they enlisted Robbie Blunt as Forest's replacement and recorded an album, *16 & Savaged*, and toured, mainly in America. By 1974 they had found an audience in Japan and in New York where glam had its home with the New York Dolls. It was during this time that Des Barres met up with 'super groupie' Pamela Miller, and not long afterwards, the band split. While Des Barres married Miller, Harrison joined Ray Manzarek from the Doors for his solo outings before they both formed Nite City (Harrison later found fame with Blondie), Blunt joined the re-formed Chicken Shack but would later be remembered for playing guitar on Robert Plant's hit single, 'Big Log'. Des Barres went on to Detective and a solo career. A little insight into Silverhead *circa* 1974 can be discovered in Pamela Des Barres' book, *I'm With The Band*.

● ALBUMS: *Silverhead* (Purple 1972)★★★, *16 & Savaged* (Purple 1973)★★★.

Simmons, Gene

One of the most charismatic characters in the world of heavy rock, Simmons (b. Chaim Witz, 25 August 1949, Haifa, Israel) is bass player with Kiss. Indeed, he was a founder-member of the band in 1971 along with Paul Stanley. Simmons' first involvement with the music industry was in producing radio jingles, but it was not long before Kiss became a worldwide phenomenon. Simmons, along with his bandmates, donned complete make-up (in his case a blood-dripping, fire-eating demon) and it was not until 1983 when Kiss unmasked that the 'real' Gene Simmons was revealed. Simmons has recorded some 20 albums with Kiss and has penned a great deal of the material either solely or in partnership with Paul Stanley. In 1978, while still in full demonic make-up, he released a credible solo album, as did all his then bandmates. A star-studded number of guest stars featured, including Bob Seger, Cher, Donna Summer, Helen Reddy and Cheap Trick guitarist Rick Nielsen, and it reached number 22 on the US chart. A single was released at the same time, 'Radioactive', which was marketed in red vinyl together with a free Gene Simmons Kiss mask. It reached number 41 in the UK charts. During the 80s Simmons expanded his talents into production, films and set up his own record label, Simmons Records. In 1989 he took rock vocalist King Diamond to court for using facial make-up similar to that he had worn in Kiss. Simmons won the case. The 90s sees Kiss still recording under the guidance of Simmons and Stanley while the former's other music business activities continue.

● ALBUMS: *Gene Simmons* (Casablanca 1978)★★★.

Simple Aggression

Formed on 1 October 1989 in the hills of Independence, Kentucky, USA, Simple Aggression subsequently relocated to Cincinnati to establish their reputation. Comprising Doug Carter (vocals), James Carr (guitar), Darrin McKinney (guitar), Dave Swart (bass) and Kenny Soward (drums), the group took a name that prophesied a high-velocity metal attack. However, the quintet were more than a simple 'thrash' band, preferring instead to work a steady groove at the core of their sound (the influence of the Red Hot Chili Peppers was certainly at work). A latent commercial instinct was also unveiled on their long-playing debut by the inclusion of a strong ballad, 'Of Winter'.

● ALBUMS: *Formulations In Black* (Bulletproof 1994)★★★.

SINNER

This German hard rock/thrash metal group was formed by Matthias Lasch in 1980. Lasch later became known as Mat Sinner, adding guitarists Wolfgang Werner and Calo Rapallo, drummer Edgar Patrik (later of Bonfire) and keyboardist Franky Mittelbach to complete the band's initial line-up. Influenced by Accept, Judas Priest, Iron Maiden and later Metallica, they released six workmanlike, but ultimately uninspiring, albums between 1982 and 1987. The personnel was in a constant state of flux, with Sinner the only constant. Their early career was dominated by New Wave Of British Heavy Metal-style material, reminiscent of Angelwitch and Tygers Of Pan Tang, then they moved towards a thrashier direction as Slayer and Anthrax arrived on the scene. The band have never made any impression outside Germany and after *Dangerous Charm* in 1987 they were dropped by their record company.

● ALBUMS: *Wild 'n' Evil* (SL 1982)★★★, *Fast Decision* (Noise 1983)★★★, *Danger Zone* (Noise 1984)★★, *Touch Of Sin* (Noise 1985)★★★, *Comin' Out Fighting* (Noise 1986)★★★, *Dangerous Charm* (Noise 1987)★★, *Bottom Line* (No Bull/Kock International 1995)★★★.

SIX FEET UNDER

This Swedish power-metal quintet modelled themselves on Deep Purple, Rainbow and Whitesnake. The band were formed in 1982 by vocalist Bjorn Lodin and guitarist Thomas Larsson. Recruiting Peter Ostling (keyboards), Kent Jansson (bass) and Claus Annersjo (drums), they signed to the Europa Film label the following year. This contract resulted in two albums which featured few original ideas. Larsson's guitar style was based almost exclusively on Ritchie Blackmore's, which imbued the songs with too strong a sense of *déjà vu*. Marcus Kallstrum took over on drums on *Eruption*, which sold fewer copies than their debut. Disillusioned, the band members went their separate ways in 1985. Their name, however, was revived in 1995 by a completely different group, formed by Cannibal Corpse vocalist Chris Barnes and Obituary guitarist Allen West.

● ALBUMS: *Six Feet Under* (Europa Film 1983)★★★, *Eruption* (Europa Film 1984)★★.

SIXTY SIX

Comprising Gabby Ramirez (ex-Willees; bass), Bill Longhorse (ex-Rumble; vocals, guitar), Nate Fowler (guitar, backing vocals) and Toby H. Sheets (drums), hard rock band Sixty Six formed in Dallas, Texas, USA, in 1994. With all the members veterans of a variety of Dallas groups, Sixty Six's professionalism was highlighted by the booking of major US tours within months of their formation. The group's debut album, released on the independent Steve Records label, featured 14 selections of their early songwriting, described in the press as 'Texas rock'. Several tracks also drew heavily on the local blues tradition, with Ramirez admitting the inspiration behind 'Burnin' Hell' was John Lee Hooker.

● ALBUMS: *Sixty Six* (Steve 1995)★★.

SKAGARACK

This Danish melodic hard rock quintet was formed in 1985 by vocalist Torben Schmidt and guitarist Jan Petersen. With the addition of Tommy Rasmussen (keyboards), Morten Munch (bass) and Alvin Otto (drums), they incorporated elements of Whitesnake, Night Ranger and Boston into their music. From AOR beginnings, they have gradually evolved into a heavier and more powerful group than their self-titled debut might have suggested. Schmidt's vocals are reminiscent of David Coverdale's: melodic, powerful and emotive, and Skagarak remain a fine band whose obvious potential has yet to cross the Scandinavian frontier.

● ALBUMS: *Skagarack* (Polydor 1986)★★★, *Hungry For A Game* (Polydor 1988)★★, *A Slice Of Heaven* (Medley 1990)★★★.

SKID ROW (EIRE)

This blues-based rock band was put together by Gary Moore (b. 4 April 1952, Belfast, Northern Ireland) in Dublin, Eire, in 1968, when the guitarist was only 16 years old. Recruiting Phil Lynott (vocals, bass), Eric Bell (guitar) and Brian Downey (drums) the initial line-up only survived 12 months. Lynott, Bell and Downey left to form Thin Lizzy, with Brendan Shiels (bass, vocals) and Noel Bridgeman (drums) joining Moore as replacements in a new power-trio. The group completed two singles, 'New Places, Old Faces' and 'Saturday Morning Man' - only released in Ireland - before securing a UK contract via CBS Records. Skid Row was a popular live attraction and tours of the USA and Europe, supporting Canned Heat and Savoy Brown, augured well for the future. Their albums were also well received, but Moore's growing reputation as an inventive and versatile guitarist outstripped the group's musical confines. He left in 1971 to work with the folk-rock band Dr. Strangely Strange and later on to the Gary Moore Band. Although Paul Chapman proved an able replacement, Skid Row's momentum faltered and the trio was disbanded the following year. Sheils has, on occasion, revived the name for various endeavours, while Chapman later found fame with UFO.

● ALBUMS: *Skid Row* (Columbia 1970)★★★, *34 Hours* (Columbia 1971)★★★, *Alive And Kicking* (Columbia 1978)★★.

● COMPILATIONS: *Skid Row* (Columbia 1987)★★★.

SKID ROW (USA)

Skid Row were formed in New Jersey, USA, in 1986 by Dave 'The Snake' Sabo (b. 16 September 1964; guitar) and Rachel Bolan (b. 9 February 1964; bass). Sebastian 'Bach' Bierk (b. 3 April 1968, Freeport, Bahamas; vocals, ex-Madam X), Scott Hill (b. 31 May 1964; guitar) and Rob Affuso (b. I March 1963; drums) completed the line-up. Influenced by Kiss, Sex Pistols, Ratt and Mötley Crüe, the band's rise to fame was remarkably rapid. The break came when they were picked up by Bon Jovi's management (Sabo was an old friend of Jon Bon Jovi) and offered the support slot on their US stadium tour of 1989. Bach's wild and provocative stage antics established the band's live reputation. Signed to Atlantic Records, they released their self-titled debut album to widespread critical acclaim the same year. It peaked at number 6 on the *Billboard* album chart and spawned two US Top 10 singles with '18 And Life' and 'I Remember You'. *Slave To The Grind* surpassed all expectations, debuting at number 1 in the US charts. Their commercial approach had been transformed into an abrasive and uncompromising barrage of metallic rock 'n' roll, delivered with punk-like arrogance. Afterwards, however, progress was halted by squabbling that broke the group following 1994's desultory *Subhuman Race*.

● ALBUMS: *Skid Row* (Atlantic 1989)★★, *Slave To The Grind* (Atlantic 1991)★★★, *B-Side Ourselves* mini-album (Atlantic 1992)★★, *Subhuman Race* (Atlantic 1994)★★.

● COMPILATIONS: *40 Seasons: The Best Of Skid Row* (Atlantic 1998)★★★.

● VIDEOS: *Oh Say Can You Scream?* (1991), *No Frills Video* (1993), *Roadkill* (1993).

SKIN

The collapse of Jagged Edge led Myke Gray (b. 12 May 1968, Fulham, London, England) to form Taste with Jagged Edge bassist Andy Robbins, ex-Kooga vocalist and guitarist Neville MacDonald (b. Ynysybwl, Pontypridd, Wales) and drummer Dickie Fliszar, previously with Bruce Dickinson's live band, in 1991. Rory Gallagher's previous use of the Taste name soon led to a name-change to Skin. The band were content to ignore grunge trends and instead developed a more traditional melodic hard rock style, at times reminiscent of mid-80s Whitesnake, but with a fresh, contemporary edge both musically and lyrically. Near-constant touring, including support stints with Thunder and Little Angels, helped the band develop a strong UK fanbase, and Skin built on this, with the *Skin Up* EP and 'House Of Love' both doing well before 'Money' pushed them into the UK Top 20. Their self-titled debut album displayed the band's songwriting and musicianship to the full, with strong, bluesy vocals from MacDonald, and it deservedly hit the UK Top 10. The band successfully transferred their electric live show to the second stage at Donington in 1994, and enjoyed another Top 20 single with 'Tower Of Strength', confirming their status as one of Britain's most popular rising rock bands. In 1995 they released a strictly limited edition (50 copies) album of classic rock 'n' roll cover versions, available solely to readers of British metal magazine *Kerrang!* Recorded live at the Borderline, London, in October 1994, the material included classics from Led Zeppelin, Van Halen, Montrose, Golden Earring, Beatles, Deep Purple, the Who and EMF. The long-standing live favourite, 'Take Me Down To The River', was also released in more conventional form.

● ALBUMS: *Skin* (Parlophone 1994)★★★, *Lucky* (1996), *Experience Electric* (Reef 1997)★★★★.

SKINNY PUPPY

Industrial band Skinny Puppy, from Vancouver, Canada, are widely regarded as a forceful influence on the development of the genre in the late 80s, counting Nine Inch Nails' Trent Reznor among their loudest advocates. The principals behind the band are cEVIN Key (as this multi-instrumentalist prefers to call himself) and Nivek Ogre (b. Kevin Ogilvie), the group's singer and lyricist, who is not related to their producer, Dave Ogilvie (later a full-time member of the band). They met in 1983, and quickly discovered a mutual taste in esoteric film music. Their first release was a cassette, *Back And Forth*, before the *Remission EP*, released on the Canadian label Nettwerk Records in 1984. This introduced their dark electronics, textured by synthesizers, samples and tape loops. It was followed by *Bites*, again reminiscent of Throbbing Gristle and Cabaret Voltaire's early experimentation and aural shock tactics. A more homespun component was the strong dance rhythms and sequences, which, while stopping some way short of convention, helped make these recordings more accessible. It featured Wilhelm Schroeder as collaborator, with one track, 'Assimilate', produced by Severed Heads' Tom Ellard. *Mind: The Perpetual Intercourse* continued previous threads but with superior production. It also introduced Dwayne Goettel (b. 1965, d. 23 August 1995) on keyboards and electronics, Schroeder's replacement, and formerly of another industrial unit named Psyche. His contribution to *Cleanse Fold And Manipulate* helped improve the group's aesthetic, though the appeal of the results was largely limited to an underground fanbase. The follow-up chose a slightly altered lyrical tack, with Ogre expanding on his environmental concerns ('Human Disease (S.K.U.M.M.)') and issue songs ('VX Gas Attack'). The anti-vivisection theme was also relocated to the stage, where Ogre would dramatize the roles of test animal, lab technician and consumer. Al Jourgensen of Ministry joined for the sessions that produced *Rabies*, adding metallic guitar runs to help bring Skinny Puppy to the attention of other musical sub-genres. *Too Dark Park* refined previous lyrical concerns, to produce a set of bunker-mentality belligerence and stark minimalism. *Last Rights* was to have featured spoken extracts from the 60s LSD-celebrity Timothy Leary, but although he gave permission his management blocked their use at the last moment. Its substitution with 40 seconds of silence caused a major fault on several thousand copies. Members of Skinny Puppy have also been involved in a number of side projects. Key worked with former pen pal Edward Ka-Spel of the Legendary Pink Dots as the more pop-orientated Teargarden. Various members of Skinny Puppy, including long-standing collaborator Alan Nelson, also played with Hilt, whose debut album was released in 1989. In 1990 a compilation of 12-inch versions was released, including Adrian Sherwood's remix of 'Addiction'. Goettel died from a heroin overdose in 1995. The band had recently completed an album for Rick Rubin's American Records, with the provisional title of *The Process*. Goettel had also formed a spin-off project, Download (also the title of a song from *Last Rights*), whose EP was released, posthumously, on the German label Off Beat Records in October 1995. In interviews to promote the new album at the beginning of 1996, the remaining members of the group announced their decision not to continue with the band. Download were formed by some ex-members in 1996.

● ALBUMS: *Back And Forth* cassette only (1983)★★★, *Bites* (Nettwerk 1985)★★★, *Mind: The Perpetual Intercourse* (Nettwerk/Capitol 1987)★★★, *Cleanse Fold And Manipulate* (Nettwerk/Capitol 1987)★★★, *VIVsectVI* (Nettwerk/Capitol 1988)★★★, *Rabies* (Nettwerk/Capitol 1989)★★★, *Too Dark Park* (Nettwerk/Capitol 1990)★★★, *Ain't It Dead Yet* live album (Nettwerk/Capitol 1991)★★★, *Last Rights* (Nettwerk/Capitol 1992)★★★, *The Process* (Subconscious/American 1995)★★★. Solo: with Teargarden *Tired Eyes Slowly Burning* (Nettwerk 1987)★★★, *The Last Man To Fly* (Nettwerk 1992)★★★, *Shelia Liked The Rodeo* (Nettwerk 1993)★★★. With Hilt *Call The Ambulance Before I Hurt Myself* (Nettwerk 1989)★★★, *Journey To The Centre Of The Bowl* (Nettwerk 1991)★★★. With Doubting Thomas *The Infidel* (Wax Trax! 1991)★★.

● COMPILATIONS: *Bites And Remission* (Nettwerk 1987)★★★, *Twelve Inch Anthology* (Nettwerk 1990)★★★, *Back And Forth Series Two* (Nettwerk 1993)★★, *Brap* (Off Beat 1996)★★★. With Teargarden *Bouquet Of Black Orchids* (Play It Again Sam 1994)★★★.

● VIDEOS: *Ain't It Dead Yet?* (1992).

SKREW

Austin, Texas, USA industrial metal group Skrew's unsettling take on atavism is concocted by Adam Grossman (vocals, guitar), Bobby Gustafon (guitar, ex-Overkill), Brandon Workman (bass), Mark Dufour (drums), Jim Vollentine (keyboards) and Doug Shappuis (guitar). The band's origins can be traced back to 1991 when they originally emerged as a duo, before expanding the group after the first album for live commitments. Singer, guitarist and lyricist Grossman remained the core of both incarnations. Tours with Corrosion Of Conformity and Prong in Europe followed, before a domestic tour prefaced studio work on a second album as a full sextet. *Dusted* thus incorporated a three-guitar base, with outstanding tracks including the sharpened hardcore of 'Jesus Skrew Superstar'. The equally disturbing 'Godsdog' took a more experimental avenue. The group's ability to cross stylistic borders at will was confirmed on 1996's *Shadow Of Doubt*, described in the sleeve notes as an analogy for 'the bleak inner recesses of our corrupt souls.' Alongside more conventional industrial metal tracks, it included 'Sam I Am' and 'Black Eye', two powerful songs geared more towards dance rhythms.

● ALBUMS: *Burning In Water, Drowning In Flame* (Devotion 1992)★★★, *Dusted* (Devotion

1994)★★★★, *Shadow Of Doubt* (Metal Blade 1996)★★★, *Angel Seed XXIII* (Metal Blade 1997)★★★.

SKULL

This US hard rock quartet was put together by ex-Meat Loaf guitarist Bob Kulick in 1991. Recruiting vocalist Dennis St. James, bassist Kjell Benner and drummer Bobby Rock, they adopted an approach that bridged the musical styles of Kiss and Styx. Signing to the independent Music For Nations label, they released *No Bones About It* to a mixed reception. The songs were strong and adequately performed, but were ultimately too derivative in their musical approach.

● ALBUMS: *No Bones About It* (Music For Nations 1991)★★.

SKUNK ANANSIE

This London, England-based quartet, formed in 1994, are led by the stunning black lesbian singer Deborah 'Skin' (b. Brixton, London, England). After attending a furniture design course at Teesside Polytechnic in Middlesborough, she returned to the capital and started meeting musicians on the local circuit. Her original band was shelved for being too 'rockist', but she retained the services of bass player Cass and began rehearsing with Skunk Anansie (who also include Ace, guitar, and Mark Richardson, drums) in January 1994. After signing to One Little Indian Records their debut single followed, 'Little Baby Swastikkka', available only through mail order from BBC Radio 1's *Evening Session* programme. The controversial 'Selling Jesus' was then followed by 'I Can Dream', which skirted the fringe of the UK Top 40, while the group toured with Therapy? and Senser and as part of the *New Musical Express*'s Bratbus coalition. They also appeared on the first edition of Channel 4's *The White Room* television programme. After collaborating with labelmate Björk on her 'Army Of Me' single, Skunk Anansie began work on the band's debut album with Andy Wallace. This contained the predicted brew of agit prop and funk metal, while Skin's lyrics remained forceful, but over the course of a full album, it was clear that there was a lack of development in style and in terms of the issue-led subject matter. This lack of progression was carried over to *Paranoid And Sunburnt*, which took a good idea and sound just 40 minutes too far. *Stoosh* was a harder-edged collection, characterized by metal-edged guitar and Skin spitting out her lyrics. Controversial lyrics can sometimes sound deliberately contrived, but on this collection, Skin sounds as though she means it. Her anger on the excellent opening track, 'Yes It's Fucking Political', is almost tangible.

● ALBUMS: *Skunk Anansie* (One Little Indian 1995)★★★, *Paranoid And Sunburnt* (One Little Indian 1995)★★★, *Stoosh* (One Little Indian 1996)★★★★.

● FURTHER READING: *Skunk Anansie: Skin I'm In*, Steve Malins.

SKYCLAD

This innovative UK thrash-folk-rock crossover group was put together in 1991 by former Sabbat vocalist Martin Walkyier. Enlisting the services of Steve Ramsey (guitar), Graeme English (bass) and Keith Baxter (drums), they were signed by European label Noise. The debut, *Wayward Sons Of Mother Earth*, combined pagan lyrics, crashing power-chords and electric violin (courtesy of Fritha Jenkins) to startling effect. Press descriptions included citing them as the 'heavy metal equivalent of Fairport Convention', but they certainly offered a welcome alternative to run-of-the-mill trad-rock. Both Baxter and recently recruited guitarist Dave Pugh were ejected from the band in 1995, to be replaced by two former members of Inner Sanctum - Dave Ray (guitar) and Jed Hawkins (drums). Pugh went on to form his own project, Load Stone. Skyclad's contract with Noise Records came to an end with *The Silent Whales Of Lunar Sea*, released a few months previously.

● ALBUMS: *The Wayward Sons Of Mother Earth* (Noise 1991)★★★, *A Burnt Offering For The Bone Idol* (Noise 1992)★★★, *Jonah's Ark* (Noise 1993)★★, *The Silent Whales Of Lunar Sea* (Noise 1995)★★★, *Irrational Anthems* (Massacre 1996)★★★, *Oui Avant-Garde A Chance* (Massacre 1996)★★, *The Answer Machine?* (Massacre 1997)★★★.

SLADE

Originally recording as the 'N Betweens, this UK quartet comprised Noddy Holder (b. Neville Holder, 15 June 1950, Walsall, West Midlands, England; vocals, guitar), Dave Hill (b. 4 April 1952, Fleet Castle, Devon, England; guitar), Jimmy Lea (b. 14 June 1952, Wolverhampton, West Midlands, England; bass) and Don Powell (b. 10 September 1950, Bilston, West Midlands, England; drums). During the spring of 1966 they performed regularly in the Midlands, playing an unusual mixture of soul standards, juxtaposed with a sprinkling of hard rock items. A chance meeting with producer Kim Fowley led to a one-off single, 'You Better

Run', released in August 1966. Two further years of obscurity followed until their agent secured them an audition with Fontana Records' A&R head Jack Baverstock. He insisted that they change their name to Ambrose Slade and it was under that moniker that they recorded *Beginnings*. Chaff on the winds of opportunity, they next fell into the hands of former Animals bassist-turned-manager, Chas Chandler. He abbreviated their name to Slade and oversaw their new incarnation as a skinhead group for the stomping 'Wild Winds Are Blowing'. Their image as 'bovver boys', complete with cropped hair and Dr Marten boots, provoked some scathing press from a media sensitive to youth culture violence. Slade persevered with their skinhead phase until 1970 when it was clear that their notoriety was passé. While growing their hair and cultivating a more colourful image, they retained their aggressive musicianship and screaming vocals for the bluesy 'Get Down Get With It', which reached number 20 in the UK. Under Chandler's guidance, Holder and Lea began composing their own material, relying on distinctive riffs, a boot-stomping beat and sloganeering lyrics, usually topped off by a deliberately misspelt title. 'Coz I Luv You' took them to number 1 in the UK in late 1971, precipitating an incredible run of chart success that was to continue uninterrupted for the next three years. After the average 'Look Wot You Dun' (which still hit number 4), they served up a veritable beer barrel of frothy chart-toppers including 'Take Me Bak 'Ome', 'Mama Weer Al Crazee Now', 'Cum On Feel The Noize' and 'Skweeze Me Pleeze Me'. Their finest moment was 1977's 'Merry Xmas Everybody', one of the great festive rock songs. Unpretentious and proudly working-class, the group appealed to teenage audiences who cheered their larynx-wrenching singles and gloried in their garish yet peculiarly masculine forays into glam rock. Holder, clearly no sex symbol, offered a solid, cheery image, with Dickensian side whiskers and a hat covered in mirrors, while Hill took tasteless dressing to marvellous new extremes. Largely dependent upon a young, fickle audience, and seemingly incapable of spreading their parochial charm to the USA, Slade's supremacy was to prove ephemeral.

They participated in a movie, *Slade In Flame*, which was surprisingly impressive, and undertook extensive tours, yet by the mid-70s they were yesterday's teen heroes. The ensuing punk explosion made them virtually redundant and prompted in 1977 the appropriately titled *Whatever Happened To Slade*. Undeterred they carried on just as they had done in the late 60s, awaiting a new break. An appearance at the 1980 Reading Festival brought them credibility anew. This performance was captured on the *Slade Alive At Reading '80* EP which pushed the group into the UK singles chart for the first time in three years. The festive 'Merry Xmas Everybody' was re-recorded and charted that same year (the first in a run of seven consecutive years, subsequently in its original form). Slade returned to the Top 10 in January 1981 with 'We'll Bring The House Down' and they have continued to gig extensively, being rewarded in 1983 with the number 2 hit, 'My Oh My', followed the next year by 'Run Run Away', a UK number 7 and their first US Top 20 hit, and the anthemic 'All Join Hands' (number 15).

Slade were one of the few groups to have survived the heady days of glitter and glam with their reputation intact and were regarded with endearing affection by a wide spectrum of age groups. However, it appears that their creative peak is way behind them, as highlighted by the derivative Slade II (minus Holder and Lea). Holder, meanwhile, has become a popular all-round television personality and hosts a regular 70s rock programme on radio. The compilation *Feel The Noize - The Very Best Of* in 1996 received outstanding reviews in the UK, heralding a mini-glam rock revival.

● ALBUMS: as Ambrose Slade *Ambrose Slade - Beginnings* (Fontana 1969)★★, *Play It Loud* (Polydor 1970)★★, *Slade Alive* (Polydor 1972)★★★, *Slayed* (Polydor 1972)★★★, *Old, New, Borrowed And Blue* (Polydor 1974)★★★, *Stomp Your Hands, Clap Your Feet* (Warners 1974)★★★, *Slade In Flame* (Polydor 1974)★★★, *Nobody's Fools* (Polydor 1976)★★★, *Whatever Happened To Slade?* (Barn 1977)★★★, *Slade Alive Vol. 2* (Barn 1978)★★, *Return To Base* (Barn 1979)★★, *We'll Bring The House Down* (Cheapskate 1981)★★, *Till Deaf Us Do Part* (RCA 1981)★★, *Slade On Stage* (RCA 1982)★★★, *Slade Alive* (Polydor 1983)★★, *The Amazing Kamikaze Syndrome* (RCA 1983)★★, *On Stage* (RCA 1984)★★, *Rogues Gallery* (RCA 1985)★★, *Crackers - The Slade Christmas Party Album* (Telstar 1985)★★, *You Boyz Make Big Noize* (RCA 1987)★★, as Slade II *Keep On Rockin'* (Total 1996)★★.

● COMPILATIONS: *Sladest* (Polydor 1973)★★, *Slade Smashes* (Barn 1980)★★★, *Story Of* (Polydor 1981)★★★, *Slade's Greats* (Polydor 1984)★★★, *Keep Your Hands Off My Power Supply* (Columbia 1984)★★★, *Wall Of Hits* (Polydor 1991)★★★, *Slade Collection 81-87* (RCA 1991)★★, *Feel The Noize - The Very Best Of* (Polydor 1996)★★★★.

● VIDEOS: *Slade In Flame* (Hendring 1990), *Wall Of Hits* (Polygram 1991).
● FURTHER READING: *The Slade Story*, George Tremlett. *Slade In Flame*, John Pidgeon. *Slade: Feel The Noize*, Chris Charlesworth.
● FILMS: *Slade In Flame* (1974)

SLASH'S SNAKEPIT

Guns N'Roses guitarist Slash (b. Saul Hudson, 23 July 1965, Stoke-on-Trent, Staffordshire, England) was not the first of the band's numerous personnel to pursue a solo career, but his results have arguably been the finest. His Snakepit band of rock veterans include one-time Guns N'Roses member Gilby Clarke (guitar), Brian Tischy (drums; ex-Pride And Glory), Eric Dover (vocals; ex-Jellyfish) and James Lomenzo (bass; ex-Pride And Glory). The idea first came to Slash when Guns N'Roses had just completed their monumental two-and-a-half-year tour to support *Use Your Illusion*. Having built his own home studio, he invited various parties around to jam, and when he and Axl Rose began to air their differences in public the rehearsal studio became something of an escape. Slash, Clarke and Guns N'Roses drummer Matt Sorum began to write material, while other visitors included Mike Inez from Alice In Chains. At this point Dover, out of work due to Jellyfish's demise, joined the party. Together with Slash he wrote 12 new songs in as many days. When Rose heard of the project he suggested that the songs be donated to the next Guns N'Roses album, but Slash refused, pointing out that he had already turned them down when they were presented to him in demo form. With this level of rancour, Sorum chose not to pursue the Snakepit project any further, leaving Slash to recruit the Pride And Glory rhythm section (ironic, given that their former guitarist, Zakk Wylde, was then inducted, briefly, into Guns N'Roses). After many delays Slash's Snakepit's debut album was finally released in April 1995 to strong reviews, Slash evidently revelling in the creative freedom it afforded him. It was followed by arena tours alongside Bon Jovi as well as a return to smaller, club-sized venues.
● ALBUMS: *It's Five O'Clock Somewhere* (Geffen 1995)★★★.

SLAUGHTER

When Vinnie Vincent's Invasion disintegrated in 1988, vocalist Mark Slaughter and bassist Dana Strum decided to start a new group under the name Slaughter. Recruiting guitarist Tim Kelly and drummer Blas Elias, they soon secured a contract with Chrysalis Records and recorded *Stick It To Ya*. With an approach that fused elements of Kiss, Mötley Crüe and Bon Jovi, their style was ultimately derivative, yet distinctive owing to the stratospheric-like vocals of Mark Slaughter. Three-minute blasts of memorable metallic pop, complete with rousing anthemic choruses was the usual recipe. Following support slots to Kiss on their American tour, the album took off and peaked at number 18 during its six-month residency on the *Billboard* album chart. A live mini-album followed, which featured live versions of songs from their debut release.
● ALBUMS: *Stick It To Ya* (Chrysalis 1990)★★★, *Stick It To Ya Live* (Chrysalis 1990)★★, *The Wild Life* (Chrysalis 1992)★★★.
● VIDEOS: *From The Beginning* (1991).

SLAVE RAIDER

Formed in America in 1987 around the antics of vocalist Chainsaw Caine and his cohorts Nicci Wikkid (guitar), Letitia Rae (bass), Lance Sabin (guitar) and a drummer who called himself The Rock. At best they could be described as a poor man's Twisted Sister but lacked the talent to move off the bottom rung. Having recorded their debut album, to be used as a demo, Jive Records picked them up and Caine set his sights on taking the UK by storm. This included live performances where he would 'chainsaw' in half a large cardboard cut-out of Rick Astley. As a stage *coup de grace* it was neither particularly funny nor particularly original. Jive, however, pushed them hard with promotional videos and press coverage, but to little avail. They then put them in a London recording studio with Chris Tsangarides, but even the legendary producer could do little to help them and soon after the release of their second album, Jive dropped them and they broke up.
● ALBUMS: *Take The World By Storm* (Jive 1988)★★★, *What Do You Know About Rock 'N' Roll* (Jive 1989)★★.

SLAYER

This intense death/thrash metal quartet was formed in Huntington Beach, Los Angeles, USA, during 1982. Comprising Tom Araya (bass, vocals), Kerry King (guitar), Jeff Hanneman (guitar) and Dave Lombardo (drums), they made their debut in 1983, with a track on the compilation *Metal Massacre III*. This led to Metal Blade signing the band and releasing their first two albums. *Show No Mercy* and *Hell Awaits* were undiluted blasts of pure white metallic noise. The band played at breakneck speed with amazing technical precision, but the intricacies of detail were lost in a muddy production. Araya's lyrics dealt with death, carnage, Satanism and torture, but were reduced to an indecipherable guttural howl. Rick Rubin, producer and owner of the Def Jam label teamed up with the band in 1986 for the recording of *Reign In Blood*. Featuring 10 tracks in just 28 minutes, it took the concept of thrash to its ultimate conclusion. The song 'Angel Of Death' became notorious for its references to Joseph Mengele, the Nazi doctor who committed atrocities against humanity (ironic, given that Araya has non-Aryan origins). They themselves admitted to a right-wing stance on matters of society and justice, despite being the subject of virulent attacks from that quarter over the years. *Hell Awaits* saw Rubin achieve a breakthrough in production with a clear and inherently powerful sound, and opened up the band to a wider audience. *South Of Heaven* represented Slayer applying the brakes and introducing brain-numbing bass riffs similar to Black Sabbath, but was delivered with the same manic aggression as before. The guitars of Hanneman and King screamed violently and Araya's vocals were comprehensible for the first time. *Seasons In The Abyss* pushed the band to the forefront of the thrash metal genre, alongside Metallica. A state-of-the-art album in every respect, although deliberately commercial, it is the band's most profound and convincing statement. A double live album followed, recorded in London, Lakeland and San Bernadino between October 1990 and August 1991. It captured the band at their brutal and uncompromising best and featured definitive versions of many of their most infamous numbers. However, it saw the permanent departure of Lombardo after many hints of a separation, with ex-Forbidden drummer Paul Bostaph stepping in. Lombardo went on to form Grip Inc., working with Death leader Chuck Shuldiner. 1994 saw the group work alongside Ice-T on a cover of the Exploited's 'Disorder' for the *Judgement Night* soundtrack, before the unveiling of their sixth studio album, *Divine Intervention*. Two years later, *Undisputed Attitude* demonstrated the band's punk influence and featured a particularly inspired version of the Stooges' 'I Wanna Be Your Dog'.

● ALBUMS: *Show No Mercy* (Metal Blade 1984)★★, *Hell Awaits* (Metal Blade 1985)★★, *Reign In Blood* (Def Jam 1986)★★★, *Live Undead* (Enigma 1987)★★, *South Of Heaven* (Def American 1988)★★★, *Seasons In The Abyss* (Def American 1990)★★★, *Decade Of Aggression-Live* (Def American 1991)★★★, *Divine Intervention* (American 1994)★★★, *Undisputed Attitude* (American 1996)★★★, *Diabolus In Musica* (Columbia 1998)★★★★.

● VIDEOS: *Live Intrusion* (American Visuals 1995).

SLEDGEHAMMER

Formed in Slough, Middlesex, England, by former schoolteacher Mike Cooke (guitar, vocals) in 1978, with Terry Pearce (bass) and Ken Revell (drums), the trio's first live appearance came as support to Motörhead. In 1979 they recorded the single 'Sledgehammer', which proved to be their only hit and was reissued at least three times on different labels. To promote the single they toured with April Wine and Budgie and played the Reading Festival. They re-recorded the track for the *Metal For Muthas* compilation album and then spent much of the year on the road with Def Leppard and various New Wave Of British Heavy Metal packages. Their debut album, released in 1984, had been recorded during 1981 with help from John McCoy (Gillan). This failed to sell, as did the single, 'In The Queue'. Again, both suffered from comparisons to 'Sledgehammer', with the band unable to shake off the 'one hit wonder' syndrome. They soon faded away from the landscape, though they turned to more serious matters a couple of years later with 'Porno Peat' (an anti-pornography single) and concentrated on raising both money and awareness for women's rape centres and child abuse groups.

● ALBUMS: *Blood On Their Hands* (Illuminated 1984)★★.

SLEEP

This San Jose, California doom metal trio draw from 60s and 70s influences, including Black Sabbath, Jimi Hendrix and Pink Floyd, to produce their own retro-styled brand of 'stoner' metal, a term derived from the band's smoking habits, even using suitably ancient amplifiers for an authentic early Sabbath sound. Al Cisneros (bass, vocals), Mat Pike (guitar) and Chris Hakius (drums) made their recorded debut with a cover of 'Snowblind' on the *Masters Of Misery* Sabbath tribute. After this they produced an awesomely heavy debut in *Sleep's Holy Mountain*, built on intense, weighty riffs and slow, lengthy song structures similar to early Sabbath, although, like contemporaries such as Monster Magnet and Cathedral, the delivery had a distinctly modern edge. Sleep's live performances continued the tradition of fearsomely heavy guitars as they toured the UK and Europe with Cathedral, Cannibal Corpse and Fear Factory, and played US dates with Nik Turner's Hawkwind Experience. A second album, *Dope Smoker*, was released in 1995, and, remarkably, is comprised of a single 37 minute-long track.

● ALBUMS: *Sleep's Holy Mountain* (Earache 1993)★★★, *Dope Smoker* (Earache 1995)★★★, *Jerusalem* (Dopesmoker 1998)★★★★.

SLICK, EARL, BAND

b. USA. A virtuoso hard rock guitarist of some standing, Earl Slick formed his own band in the mid-70s. Previous aggregations had not recorded, though Slick had already toured and recorded with artists of the stature of David Bowie. With Jimmie Mack (vocals), Gene Leppik (bass) and Bryan Madey (drums), the Earl Slick Band made its debut for Capitol Records in 1976 with a self-titled album of songs written by Slick and Mack. Immediately, the creative tension between the two parties was evident - Slick showcasing his guitar skills wherever possible, while Mack seemed to be more interested in integrated songwriting. This led to an inconsistent, although at times excellent recording. The schism had not been fully resolved by the advent of *Razor Sharp*, where Slick's guitar playing continued to dominate. After its release Slick returned to session work, notably with John Waite.

● ALBUMS: *Slick Band* (Capitol 1976)★★★, *Razor Sharp* (Capitol 1977)★★★.

SLOAN

This Canadian grunge band originated at the Nova Scotia College Of Art in Halifax, where drummer Andrew Scott and bassist Chris Murphy linked with Northern Ireland-born guitarist Patrick Pentland and guitarist/vocalist Jay Ferguson. Sloan developed their own sound from a mixture of hardcore and grunge influences, producing a guitar-fuelled battery of short, sharp songs, releasing the *Peppermint* EP, recorded at a friend's house in Halifax, through their own Murderecords label. A lively performance at Canada's East Coast Music Conference brought the band to the attention of Geffen Records, who liked the EP and promptly signed Sloan. *Smeared* impressed reviewers and public alike, with the pop songwriting and vocal melodies counterpointed by Pentland's raw, aggressive guitarwork. In spite of a low-key promotional approach, the record performed well as North American college radio picked up on 'Underwhelmed'. The band then broke up for a while and were dropped by their record company; the members subsequently reunited in 1996 and issued *One Chord To Another* locally on their own Murderecords label. It was later released on EMI throughout the rest of the world.

● ALBUMS: *Smeared* (Geffen 1992)★★★, *Twice Removed* (Geffen 1994)★★★, *One Chord To Another* (Murderecords 1996)★★★.

SMASHING PUMPKINS

Once widely viewed as poor relations to Nirvana's major label alternative rock, Chicago, USA's Smashing Pumpkins, led by vocalist/guitarist Billy Corgan (b. 17 March 1967, Chicago, Illinois, USA) have persevered to gradually increasing commercial acceptance and press veneration. Corgan's inspirations, the Beatles, Led Zeppelin, Doors and Black Sabbath, as well as a professional jazz musician father, add up to a powerful musical cocktail over which his lyrics, which frequently cross the threshold of normality and even sanity, float unsettlingly. The rest of the band comprised D'Arcy Wretzky (b. 1 May 1968, South Haven, Michigan, USA; bass), James Iha (b. 6 March 1968, Elk Grove, Illinois, USA; guitar) and Jimmy Chamberlain (b. 10 June 1964, Joliet, Illinois, USA; drums). Smashing Pumpkins made their official debut with a drum machine at the Avalon club in Chicago. Chamberlain was then drafted in from a ten-piece showband (JP And The Cats) to fill the percussion vacancy (Corgan had previously played in another local band, the Marked). The group made its debut in early 1990 with the release of 'I Am The One' on local label Limited Potential Records. Previously they had included two tracks on a Chicago compilation, *Light Into Dark*. This brought the band to the attention of influential Seattle label Sub Pop, with whom they released 'Tristessa'/'La Dolly Vita' in September 1990, before moving to Caroline Records. *Gish*, produced by Butch Vig, announced the group to both indie and metal audiences, and went to number 1 on the influential Rockpool College Radio Chart. Ironically, given the Nirvana comparisons, this came before Vig had produced *Nevermind*. However, it was *Siamese Dream* that launched the band to centrestage with its twisted metaphors and skewed rhythms. A Top 10 success in the US *Billboard* charts, it saw them joined by mellotron, cello and violin accompaniment to give the sound extra depth. However, these remained secondary to the pop hooks and rock atmospherics that have defined the band's sound. *Mellon Collie And The Infinite Sadness* was a bold project (the double CD contained 28 songs), yet the band managed to pull it off. With swirling strings, angst-ridden vocals and some beautifully spiteful guitar the album was a major achievement artistically and commercially. Their touring keyboard player, ex-Dickies Jonathan Melvoin (b. 6 December 196, Los Angeles, California, USA, d. 12 July 1996) died of a heroin overdose in July 1996. At the same time the band sacked their drummer Chamberlain after his continuing drug abuse. His replacement was Matt Walker, formerly with industrial band Filter, but he departed in late 1997 to form his own band. During frenetic preparations for the new Smashing Pumpkins album, Iha found time to release a surprisingly mellow solo set.

● ALBUMS: *Gish* (Caroline 1991)★★★, *Siamese Dream* (Virgin 1993)★★★★, *Mellon Collie And The Infinite Sadness* (Virgin 1995)★★★★, *Zero* (Hut 1996)★★, *Adore* (Hut 1998)★★★★.
Solo: James Iha *Let It Come Down* (Hut 1998)★★★.

● COMPILATIONS: *Pisces Iscariot* (Virgin 1994)★★, *The Aeroplane Flies High* 5 CD-box set (Virgin 1996)★★★.

● VIDEOS: *Vieuphoria* (Virgin Music Video 1994).

● FURTHER READING: *Smashing Pumpkins*, Nick Wise.

Snakepit Rebels

Comprising Ubbe Rydeslätt (vocals), Anton Solli (guitar), Kricke Zetterqvist (guitar), Lasse Lekberg (bass) and Mats Rydeslätt (drums), Swedish heavy metal act the Snakepit Rebels formed in 1987. From their visual appearance to their music the group owe a debt to Guns N'Roses, most readily detectable in Ubbe Rydeslätt's tortured vocals (his 'day job' is that of owner of a tattoo parlour). The group's musical power base is Solli, who before the formation of the Snakepit Rebels had worked widely in Europe as a session guitarist. The group's self-titled 1990 debut album was given a full European as well as a Japanese release, where the group have consistently proved highly popular. The follow-up, 1993's *Dustsucker*, was recorded at the legendary Abbey Road studios in England and included a dubious cover version of David Bowie's 'Life On Mars'.

● ALBUMS: *Snakepit Rebels* (Four Leaf Clover 1990)★★★, *Dustsucker* (Four Leaf Clover 1993)★★★.

SNFU

From Edmonton, Alberta, Canada, SNFU are a hardcore punk band who took obvious influence from both the Subhumans and D.O.A. Their line-ups have always centred around Mr Chi Pig (vocals) and Brent (guitar), with the rhythm section changing with almost every successive album. One of their early drummers, Jon Card, would later join D.O.A.. SNFU have persevered over the years with a formula encompassing largely headlong adrenaline rushes. The most significant interlude was *If You Swear You'll Catch No Fish*, slick titles such as 'Better Homes And Gardens' indicating a growing maturity in the way they conveyed their lyrical gaze. Previously, overtly obvious joke anthems such as 'Cannibal Cafe' had been their let-down. By the next album, they were speeding along at a furious rate once more, though some of the early angst had disappeared: 'It's hard to be angry when you live in an environment like this; the physical aspect of Edmonton is so comfortable'. They had definitely not grown in self-importance, however: 'We're still the same awful band we were in '81'. Still active, SNFU encapsulate the best traditions of Canadian hardcore; energy, verve and humour. They moved over to Epitaph in 1995 for another splintering punk rock album.

● ALBUMS: *And No One Else Wanted To Play* (BYO 1984)★★, *If You Swear You'll Catch No Fish* (BYO 1986)★★★, *Better Than A Stick In The Eye* (BYO 1988)★★, *Last Of The Big Time Suspenders* (Skullduggery 1992)★★, *The Ones Most Likely To Succeed* (Epitaph 1995)★★, *Fyulaba* (Epitaph 1996)★★.

Sniper

This Japanese heavy metal group was formed in 1981 by guitarist Mansanori Kusakabe. Enlisting the services of Shigehisa Kitao (vocals), Romy Murase (bass) and Shunji Itoh (drums), their brand of heavy metal drew strongly on the styles of UFO and Deep Purple. Debuting with the single 'Fire' in 1983, they contributed 'Crazy Drug' to the *Heavy Metal Forces* compilation album the following year. Their first album was recorded live at the Electric Ladyland Club in Nagoya in 1984 and featured new recruit Ravhun Othani (ex-Frank Marino Band) as a second guitarist. The album was a limited edition of 1,000, which sold out, only to be re-pressed twice, with similar success. The band disintegrated shortly after its release, but was resurrected in 1985 by Kusakabe. The new line-up included Noburu Kaneko (vocals), Takeshi Kato (keyboards), Tsukasa Shinohara (bass) and Toshiyuki Miyata (drums). They produced *Quick And Dead*, but it made little impact outside Japan. A proposed tour of Holland to support it was cancelled and the band have been inactive since.

● ALBUMS: *Open The Attack* (Electric Ladyland 1984)★★, *Quick And Dead* (Megaton 1985)★★.

Snowblind

This UK melodic hard rock quintet was formed in 1982 by guitarist Andy Simmons. With Tony Mason (vocals), Ross Bingham (guitar, keyboards), Geoff Gilesoie (bass) and Kevin Baker (drums) completing the line-up, they were one of the few non-speed metal/thrash bands signed to the Belgian Mausoleum label. Using Magnum, Rush and Grand Prix as their musical blueprint, they debuted with a self-titled album in 1985. This comprised grandiose epics, punctuated by explosive guitar runs in places. The only drawback was Mason's vocals, which lacked the necessary warmth and range to give the songs real distinction. The album fared badly and little has been heard from them since.

● ALBUMS: *Snowblind* (Mausoleum 1985)★★.

Social Distortion

Formed in Fullerton, Orange County, California, USA, in the summer of 1978, Social Distortion initially featured Mike Ness (guitar), Casey Royer (drums), and the Agnew brothers, Rikk (vocals, guitar) and Frank (bass). That line-up only lasted until the following year, at which point the Agnews and Royer departed for fellow Fullerton band the Adolescents. Dennis Danell then joined on bass, and Ness took over vocals (following experiments with a singer titled Dee Dee), and 'Carrott' replaced Royer. However, this remains a simplification of the band's early line-up shuffles, with other members including Tim Mag (later DI) and Danny Furious (ex-Avengers). After impressing Robbie Fields of Posh Boy Records at a party in Fullerton in 1981, the band booked studio time through him to record their 'Mainliner' 7-inch. This was a one-off affair, however, and afterwards the group moved on to their own 13th Floor Records label, also picking up a new and more permanent drummer and backing vocalist, Derek O'Brien (also DI). By this time Danell had switched to rhythm guitar, with Brent Liles becoming the new bass player (making the band a quartet once more). This line-up would last until 1984, spanning the recording of *Mommy's Little Monster*. A superb punk rock debut, this collection revealed more cohesion and tradition than the band's immediate peers, with a sound tracing its heritage back to the Rolling Stones as much as the Sex Pistols. It seemed that Social Distortion had all the ingredients to popularize hardcore ('Another State Of Mind' was achieving plays on MTV long before punk bands were fashionable in that medium), but their breakthrough was delayed by Ness's increasing use of hard drugs. The band practically disintegrated as a result. O'Brien joined DI permanently, while Liles fled for Agent Orange in 1985. Their replacements were John Maurer (bass) and Chris Reece (drums, ex-Lewd). After attending detoxification clinics, Ness finally made a comeback with 1988's *Prison Bound*. A mature, less strident effort, it saw the band flirt with country on tracks such as 'Like An Outlaw', returning to a revved-up Rolling Stones blueprint for a cover version of 'Backstreet Girl' as well as sharp original songs. It also signalled a move towards conventional blues rock that would come to fruition with successive albums for Epic and Sony Records. The best of these was 1992's *Between Heaven And Hell*, by which time the multi-tattooed Ness had moved into prime rockabilly mode, with lyrical inspiration taken from his battles with drink and drugs. Songs such as 'Born To Lose' undercut their potential for cliché with the kind of hard-hitting authenticity that had always surrounded the band. *White Light, White Heat, White Trash* featured a blistering version of the Rolling Stones' 'Under My Thumb' in addition to the (almost) radio-friendly single 'I Was Wrong'. Ex-Danzig drummer Chuck Biscuits joined the band in July 1996.

● ALBUMS: *Mommy's Little Monster* (13th Floor 1983)★★★, *Prison Bound* (Restless 1988)★★★, *Social Distortion* (Epic 1990)★★★, *Between Heaven And Hell* (Sony 1992)★★★, *White Light, White Heat, White Trash* (Epic 1996)★★★★, *Live At The Roxy* (Time Bomb 1998)★★.

Soda, Frank

This eccentric Canadian vocalist/guitarist is widely known for his warped sense of humour. He appeared on stage attired in strange outfits and the climax of the show usually involved making a television set explode on his head. Backed by the Imps, a two-piece rhythm section comprising Charles Towers (bass) and John Lechausser (drums), he recorded two hard rock albums characterized by frenzied, Frank Zappa-like guitar and Soda's shallow vocals. *Saturday Night Getaway* used session musicians instead of the Imps and featured four cuts from *In The Tube*, with the remaining new songs sounding second-rate in comparison. He built up a small but loyal cult following in Canada, but failed to make an impression elsewhere. He did, however, help singer Lee Aaron launch her career in 1982.

● ALBUMS: *In The Tube* (Quality 1979)★★★, *Frank Soda And The Imps* (Quality 1980)★★★,

Saturday Night Getaway (Quality 1981)★★★, *Adventures Of Sodaman* (Visual 1983)★★.

SODOM

This black metal/thrash trio was formed in 1983 by Angel Ripper (bass, vocals), Aggressor (vocals, guitar) and Witchhunter (drums). They drew inspiration from bands such as Motörhead, Anvil and Venom, making their debut with an agenda-setting EP, *Sign Of Evil*. By the time *Obsessed By Cruelty* emerged in 1986, Aggressor had quit to be replaced firstly by the similarly pseudonymous Grave Violator, then Destructor and finally Blackfire. *Persecution Mania* followed in 1987 and marked a vast improvement over their debut, though lyrics had not moved on from obsessions with war, bloodlust and the black arts. Produced by Harris Johns, it had a crisp and powerful sound and was to become their best-selling release. They toured Europe in 1988 with Whiplash and recorded *Mortal Way Of Life*, the first ever double live thrash album. *Agent Orange* followed in 1989 and they were supported by Sepultura on a European tour to help promote it. Michael Hoffman was recruited as the new guitarist when Blackfire left for Kreator in 1990.

● ALBUMS: *Obsessed By Cruelty* (Steamhammer 1986)★★, *Persecution Mania* (Steamhammer 1987)★★★, *Mortal Way Of Life* (Steamhammer 1988)★★★, *Agent Orange* (Steamhammer 1989)★★★, *Ausgebombt* (Steamhammer 1990)★★, *Better Off Dead* (Steamhammer 1991)★★★, *Tapping The Vein* (Steamhammer 1993)★★.

● COMPILATIONS: *Ten Black Years* (Steamhammer 1997)★★★.

SOJOURN

This US melodic rock quintet was formed in 1983 by Kevin Bullock (vocals, guitar, keyboards) and Doug Robinson (guitar, vocals). Enlisting the services of Kevin Stoker (keyboards), Doug Pectol (bass) and Dane Spencer (drums), they secured a contract with the Mad Cat label in 1985. They debuted with *Lookin' For More*, a melodic rock album with rough edges. It incorporated abrasive guitarwork within a pomp-rock framework, and drew comparisons with Triumph, Journey and UFO. *Different Points Of View* consolidated their style, but nothing was heard from them afterwards.

● ALBUMS: *Lookin' For More* (Mad Cat 1985)★★★, *Different Points Of View* (Mad Cat 1988)★★★.

SOLITUDE

Solitude were formed by Mike Hostler (drums) and Dan Martinez (guitar) in Delaware, USA, in 1985. With the addition of Keith Saulsbury (vocals, guitar) and Rodney Cope (bass) they released their first demo, *Focus Of Terror*, in 1987, their second, *Sickness*, following a year later. Increasingly strong reviews were maintained by their third and final demo, *Fall Of Creation*. Red Light then stepped in and signed the band in 1993 (Music For Nations offering a UK contract). *From This Life*, their debut album, saw them combine diverse influences, taking Black Sabbath, Slayer and Pantera as a traditional metal foundation, but also adding elements of blues and progressive rock. Lyrically, targets included the death of communism ('After The Red'), betrayal ('In This Life') and growing old ('The Empty'), all dealt with in bold, primary colours and language. Touring with Death Angel, Sacred Reich, Forbidden and Celtic Frost has not helped them to escape the death metal category, which somewhat inadequately describes their sound.

● ALBUMS: *From This Life* (Red Light 1994)★★★.

SOLITUDE AETURNUS

Formed in 1988 by Texan guitarist John Perez, Solitude Aeturnus set out to revive the 'heavy groove orientated' style of Black Sabbath. The results were slow, epic, guitar-based heavy metal with a definite ethereal edge. Solitude Aeturnus secured a contract in 1991 and released *Into The Depths Of Sorrow*. This established them as part of the doom metal movement, which was a more atmospheric, grinding counterpart to the frantic aggression of death metal. While many of the bands in the doom genre were interested in creating sweeping vistas of tragic horror, Solitude Aeturnus have a more grandiose, dreamlike quality. Much of this is due to the semi-operatic vocals of Robert Lowe which contrast effectively with the maudlin power of the lumbering guitar riffs of John Perez and Edgar Rivera (the rhythm section comprises Lyle on bass and Wolf on drums). Unfortunately, while they are good at what they do, Solitude Aeturnus have a tendency to be somewhat one-dimensional. Their third album, *Through The Darkest Hour*, followed a label change and saw the band's material develop a little more punch.

● ALBUMS: *Into The Depths Of Sorrow* (Roadracer 1991)★★★, *Beyond The Crimson Horizon* (Roadracer 1992)★★★, *Through The Darkest Hour*

(Bullet Proof 1994)★★★★, *Adagio* (Massacre 1998)★★★★.

SONIC YOUTH

A product of New York's experimental 'No-Wave' scene, Sonic Youth first recorded under the auspices of *avant garde* guitarist Glenn Branca. Thurston Moore (b. 25 July 1958, Coral Gables, Florida, USA; guitar), Lee Ranaldo (b. 3 February 1956, Glen Cove, New York, USA; guitar) and Kim Gordon (b. 28 April 1953, Rochester, New York, USA; bass) performed together on Branca's *Symphony No. 3*, while the group debuted in its own right on his Neutral label. *Sonic Youth* was recorded live at New York's Radio City Music Hall in December 1981 and featured original drummer Richard Edson. Three further collections, *Confusion Is Sex*, *Sonic Death* and a mini-album, *Kill Yr Idols*, completed the quartet's formative period, which was marked by their pulsating blend of discordant guitars, impassioned vocals and ferocious, compulsive drum patterns, courtesy of newcomer Jim Sclavunos, or his replacement, Bob Bert. *Bad Moon Rising* was the first Sonic Youth album to secure a widespread release in both the USA and Britain. This acclaimed set included the compulsive 'I'm Insane' and the eerie 'Death Valley '69', a collaboration with Lydia Lunch, which invoked the horror of the infamous Charles Manson murders. Bob Bert was then replaced by Steve Shelley (b. 23 June 1962, Midland, Michigan, USA), who has remained with the line-up ever since. In 1986 the group unleashed *Evol*, which refined their ability to mix melody with menace, particularly on the outstanding 'Shadow Of A Doubt'. The album also introduced the Youth's tongue-in-cheek fascination with Madonna. 'Expressway To Yr Skull' was given two alternative titles, 'Madonna, Sean And Me' and 'The Cruxifiction Of Sean Penn'. Later in the year the band were joined by Mike Watt from fIREHOSE in Ciccone Youth, which resulted in a mutated version of 'Into The Groove(y)' and 1989's *Ciccone Youth*, which combined dance tracks with experimental sounds redolent of German groups Faust and Neu. Sonic Youth's career continued with the highly impressive *Sister*, followed in 1988 by *Daydream Nation*, a double set that allowed the group to expand themes when required. Once again the result was momentous. The instrumentation was powerful, recalling the intensity of the Velvet Underground or Can, while the songs themselves were highly memorable. In 1990 Sonic Youth left the independent circuit by signing with the Geffen Records stable, going on to establish a reputation as godfathers to the alternative US rock scene with powerful albums such as *Goo* and *Dirty*. Thurston Moore was instrumental in the signing of Nirvana to Geffen Records, while Kim Gordon was similarly pivotal in the formation of Hole. Steve Shelley would also work closely with Geffen on a number of acts. Successive stints on Lollapalooza tours helped to make Sonic Youth the nation's best-known underground band, while the group's members continued to collaborate on music and soundtrack projects to a degree that ensured the continuation of an already vast discography. Moore also runs his own underground record label, Ecstatic Peace! The *Syr* mini-albums and 1998's full-length *A Thousand Leaves* documented the band's restless experimentalism.

● ALBUMS: *Confusion Is Sex* (Neutral 1983)★★★, *Kill Yr Idols* mini-album (Zensor 1983)★★, *Sonic Death: Sonic Youth Live* cassette only (Ecstatic Peace! 1984)★★, *Bad Moon Rising* (Homestead 1985)★★★, *EVOL* (SST 1986)★★★★, *Sister* (SST 1987)★★★★, *Daydream Nation* (Blast First 1988)★★★★, *Goo* (Geffen 1990)★★★, *Dirty* (Geffen 1992)★★★★, *Experimental Jet Set, Trash And No Star* (Geffen 1994)★★★, *Washing Machine* (Geffen 1995)★★★, *Made In USA* film soundtrack 1986 recording (Rhino/Warners 1995)★★, *Syr 1* mini-album (Syr 1997)★★★, *Syr 2* mini-album (Syr 1997)★★★, with Jim O'Rourke *Syr 3* mini-album (Syr 1997)★★★, *A Thousand Leaves* (Geffen 1998)★★★★.

Solo: Lee Ranaldo *From Here To Infinity* (SST 1987)★★. Thurston Moore *Psychic Hearts* (Geffen 1995)★★★.

● COMPILATIONS: *Screaming Fields Of Sonic Love* (Blast First 1995)★★★.

● VIDEOS: *Goo* (DGC 1991).

● FURTHER READING: *Confusion Is Next: The Sonic Youth Story*, Alec Foege.

SORTILEGE

This French heavy metal band was formerly known as Blood Wave. Sortilege were formed in 1981 by vocalist Christian Augustin and guitarist Stephanne L'Anguille Dumont. Adding Didier Dem (guitar), Daniel Lapp (bass) and Bob Snake (drums) they secured a contract with the Dutch Rave On label in 1983. They specialized in a persistent metallic boogie. *Metamorphose* was also released as *Metamorphosis*, complete with English lyrics, but it still failed to make any impact outside France. *Hero Tears* saw the band running short of ideas. They broke up shortly after its release.

● ALBUMS: *Sortilege* (Rave On 1983)★★★,

Metamorphose (Steamhammer 1984)★★★, *Hero Tears* (Steamhammer 1985)★★.

Soul Asylum

Originally a Minneapolis, Minnesota, USA garage hardcore band, Soul Asylum spent their early years under the yoke of comparisons with the more fêted Replacements and Hüsker Dü. Indeed, Bob Mould has been known fondly to describe Soul Asylum as 'our little brothers', and was on hand as producer for their first two long-playing sets. Their roots in hardcore are betrayed by their original choice of name, Loud Fast Rules. Their first formation in 1981 centred around the abiding creative nucleus of Dave Pirner (b. 16 April 1964, Green Bay, Wisconsin, USA; vocals, guitar) and Dan Murphy (b. 12 July 1962, Duluth, Minnesota, USA; guitar), alongside Karl Mueller (b. 27 July 1963, Minneapolis, USA; bass) and Pat Morley (drums). Together they specialized in sharp lyrical observations and poppy punk. Morley left in December 1984 to be replaced, eventually, by Grant Young (b. 5 January 1964, Iowa City, Iowa, USA), who arrived in time for *Made To Be Broken*. As their music progressed it became easier to trace back their heritage to the 60s rather than 70s. *Hang Time*, their third album proper, was their first for a major. It saw them move into the hands of a new production team (Ed Stasium and Lenny Kaye), with a very apparent display of studio polish. The mini-album that was meant to have preceded it (but ultimately did not), *Clam Dip And Other Delights*, included their dismantling of a Foreigner song, 'Jukebox Hero', and a riotous reading of Janis Joplin's 'Move Over'. When playing live they have been known to inflict their renditions of Barry Manilow's 'Mandy' and Glen Campbell's 'Rhinestone Cowboy' on an audience. Though *The Horse They Rode In On* was another splendid album, the idea of Soul Asylum breaking into the big league was becoming a progressively fantastic one (indeed, band members had to pursue alternative employment in 1990, during which time Pirner suffered a nervous breakdown). However, largely thanks to the MTV rotation of 'Somebody To Shove', the situation was about to change. In its aftermath they gained a prestigious slot on the *David Letterman Show* before support billing to Bob Dylan and Guns N'Roses, plus a joint headlining package with Screaming Trees and the Spin Doctors on the three-month Alternative Nation Tour. Soon they were appearing in front of a worldwide audience of 400 million at the 1993 MTV Awards ceremony, where they were joined by R.E.M.'s Peter Buck and Victoria Williams for a jam of their follow-up hit, 'Runaway Train'. With Pirner dating film starlet Winona Ryder, the profile of a band who seemed destined for critical reverence and public indifference could not have been more unexpectedly high, and *Grave Dancers Union* was a major success. However, in 1995 the band announced that their next studio sessions would avoid the overt commercial textures of their previous album, although subsequent reviews of *Let Your Dim Light Shine* were mixed. They also recruited their fourth drummer, Stirling Campbell, to replace Grant Young; however, Campbell left the band in 1997. Pirner and Murphy's side project is Golden Smog, together with the Jayhawks' Gary Louris (guitar) and Marc Perlman (bass). They reconvened Soul Asylum for 1998's *Candy From A Stranger*, their most relaxed and intimate recording to date.

● ALBUMS: *Say What You Will* (Twin Tone 1984)★★★, *Made To Be Broken* (Twin Tone 1986)★★★, *While You Were Out* (Twin Tone 1986)★★★, *Hang Time* (Twin Tone/A&M 1988)★★★, *Clam Dip And Other Delights* mini-album (What Goes On 1989)★★★, *Soul Asylum And The Horse They Rode In On* (Twin Tone/A&M 1990)★★★★, *Grave Dancers Union* (A&M 1993)★★★, *Let Your Dim Light Shine* (A&M 1995)★★★, *Candy From A Stranger* (Columbia 1998)★★★.

● COMPILATIONS: *Time's Incinerator* cassette only (Twin Tone 1984)★★★, *Say What You Will Clarence, Karl Sold The Truck* (Twin Tone 1989)★★★.

Soul Coughing

Formed in New York City, New York, USA, Soul Coughing comprise M. Doughty (guitar, vocals, lyrics), composer Mark de Gli Antoni (keyboards, samples), Sebastian Steinberg (double bass, ex-Marc Ribot) and Yuval Gabay (b. Israel; drums). Their origins can be traced back to 1993 when Doughty was working on the door at the New York *avant garde* jazz club the Knitting Factory. There he gradually recruited the group's members from the club's clientele, and together they set out on a path of 'shared musical adventure'. Their debut album, *Ruby Vroom*, received universal critical acclaim, and preceded their first major touring commitments. It is in the live arena that they are best observed - in performance they regularly adopt and adapt the jazz predilection for extended improvisation. As Doughty told the press, 'This band lives to play live. We lose our minds sitting at home.' *Irresistible Bliss* was another successful marriage of hip-hop beats, mechanical noise and expansive musicianship, with each of the 12 songs thematically linked to day-to-day life in New York. As Doughty insisted, the contents were 'mostly paranoid love songs about hoping desperately someone will call you, while at the same time being incredibly afraid of the sound of the ringing phone.' Produced by Tony Bennett associate David Kahne and Steve Fisk, it was recorded in the same sessions that saw the band complete compositions for the *Blue In The Face* and *X-Files* film soundtracks.

● ALBUMS: *Ruby Vroom* (Slash/London 1994)★★★★, *Irresistible Bliss* (Slash/London 1996)★★★.

SOULFLY

Formed by singer Max Cavalera (b. Belo Horizonte, 4 August 1969, Brazil), previously vocalist with Sepultura prior to their acrimonious separation, Soulfly additionally comprises Jackson Bandeira (aka Lucio, guitar), Roy Mayorga (drums) and Marcello D Rapp (bass). The group was formed in Los Angeles, California, USA, in 1997. Bandeira was previously a member of Brazilian group Chico Science (with whom Cavalera once shared a stage). Mayorga had been in bands including Agnostic Front, Shelter and Nausea. Marcello, meanwhile, was formerly part of Sepultura's road crew, and had his own band, Mist, who recorded three albums between 1987 and 1992. Soulfly's debut single, 'Bleed', released in 1998, dealt with the death of Cavalera's stepson Dana Wells in a gang-related car crash. The rest of the self-titled album that accompanied its release also touched on the illness of Cavalera's two children (the band is managed by his wife Gloria Cavalera) and his conversion to Christianity. Produced by Ross Robinson, *Soulfly* featured a number of high-profile guest appearances - Chino Moreno of the Deftones ('First Commandment'), Christian Wolbers of Fear Factory ('Bumba' and 'No'), Fred Durst of Limp Bizkit (who co-wrote 'Bleed') and Benji from Dub War ('Prejudice' and 'Quicombo').

● ALBUMS: *Soulfly* (Roadrunner 1998)★★★★.

SOUND BARRIER

Formerly known as Colour, Sound Barrier were a black heavy metal band from the USA formed in 1980 by Spacey T. (guitar), Bernie K (vocals), Stanley E. (bass) and Dave Brown (drums), who signed to MCA Records in 1982. They debuted with *Total Control*; a highly complex fusion of metal, soul, funk and blues influences that defied simple pigeonholing. Despite or because of this, it sold poorly and they were subsequently dropped by their label. They bounced back with a mini-album on the independent Pitbull label, which consolidated the style laid down on their debut release. This led to a contract with Metal Blade, but *Speed Of Light* adopted a simpler mainstream approach that proved unsuccessful in widening their appeal. Emil Lech had taken over on bass by this stage, but the band splintered shortly after the album's release. Bernie K. went on to Masi, Spacey T. and Stanley E. joined Liberty, while Emil Lech teamed up with Joshua.

● ALBUMS: *Total Control* (MCA 1983)★★★, *Born To Rock* (Pit Bull 1984)★★★, *Speed Of Light* (Metal Blade 1986)★★.

SOUNDGARDEN

This Seattle-based US quartet fused influences as diverse as Led Zeppelin, the Stooges, Velvet Underground and, most particularly, early UK and US punk bands into a dirty, sweaty, sexually explicit and decidedly fresh take on rock 'n' roll. The group, Chris Cornell (b. 20 July 1964, Seattle, Washington, USA; vocals, guitar), Kim Thayil (b. 4 September 1960, Seattle, Washington, USA; guitar), Hiro Yamamoto (b. 20 September 1968, Okinawa, Japan; bass) and Matt Cameron (b. 28 November 1962, San Diego, USA; drums), proffer a sound characterized by heavy-duty, bass-laden metallic riffs, which swings between dark melancholia and *avant garde* minimalism. Cornell's ranting vocal style and articulate lyrics complete the effect. The group's first recording, the *Screaming Life* EP, was the second release on the hugely influential Sub Pop label, and marked out their territory. Indeed, Thayil had brought together the label's owners Bruce Pavitt and Jonathan Poneman in the first place. After signing to SST Records and releasing *Ultramega OK*, they attracted the attention of A&M Records and eventually released *Louder Than Love*, one of the most underrated and offbeat rock albums of 1989. This also meant that they were the first of the Sub Pop generation to sign to a major. After its release Cameron and Cornell also participated in the two million-selling Temple Of The Dog album, which co-featured Pearl Jam members Eddie Vedder, Stone Gossard and Jeff Ament laying tribute at the door of deceased Mother Love Bone singer Andrew Wood. However, following the recording sessions for *Louder Than Love*, Yamamoto was replaced by Jason Everman (ex-Nirvana), though he played on only one track, a cover version of the Beatles' 'Come Together', before departing for Mindfunk via Skunk. His eventual replacement was band friend Ben 'Hunter' Shepherd. *Badmotorfinger* built on the group's succesful formula but added insistent riffs, the grinding but melodious guitar sound that would come to define 'grunge', and their own perspectives on politics, religion and society. Among its many absorbing moments was the MTV-friendly single 'Jesus Christ Pose'. Landing the support slot on Guns N'Roses' US *Illusions* tour deservedly opened up Soundgarden to a much wider audience. *Superunknown* capitalized on this, and debuted at number 1 on the *Billboard* chart on 19 March 1994. Produced by Michael Beinhorn (Soul Asylum, Red Hot Chili Peppers, etc.) and the band themselves, it was a magnum opus, clocking in at more than 70 minutes and featuring 15 songs. Eventually selling over three million copies, it was promoted by an Australasian tour in January 1994, headlining the 'Big Day Out' festival package above the Ramones, Smashing Pumpkins and Teenage Fanclub, before moving on to Japan. *Down On The Upside* was another fine album, recorded during Cornell's allegedly serious drug problems; the record belies the band's internal strife with intense but highly melodic heavy rock. With continuing unrest in the camp, the band decided to fold in April 1997.

● ALBUMS: *Ultramega O.K.* (SST 1989)★★★, *Louder Than Love* (A&M 1990)★★★, *Screaming Life/FOPP* (Sub Pop 1990)★★, *Badmotorfinger* (A&M 1991)★★★★, *Superunknown* (A&M 1994)★★★★, *Down On The Upside* (A&M 1996)★★★.

● COMPILATIONS: *A-sides* (A&M 1997)★★★★.

● VIDEOS: *Motorvision* (1993).

● FURTHER READING: *Soundgarden: New Metal Crown*, Chris Nickson.

Spanos, Danny

This American vocalist/composer performed and recorded under his own name, always preferring the services of hired hands to a conventional band set-up. He recorded three albums during the early 80s, using a variety of session musicians, including Earl Slick, Rick Derringer, Carmine Appice, Dana Strum and Frankie Banali. His style fell somewhere between Jimmy Barnes and Bryan Adams - easily accessible hard rock with gritty vocals and infectious hooklines. Ultimately, the songs lacked real character and he failed to break into the big time.

● ALBUMS: *Danny Spanos* (Windsong 1980)★★★, *Passion In The Dark* (Epic 1983)★★, *Looks Like Trouble* (Epic 1984)★★.

Spartan Warrior

This UK heavy metal group was formed in 1983 by Dave Wilkinson (vocals) Neil Wilkinson (guitar), Paul Swaddle (guitar), Tom Spencer (bass) and Gordon Webster (drums), making their debut with two cuts on the *Guardian* compilation in 1984. This opened the door to a contract with Roadrunner Records, which resulted in two nondescript, poorly produced metal albums. These incorporated elements of Rush, Deep Purple and Led Zeppelin, but few original ideas of their own. Failing to make any impact, the band returned to their day jobs in 1986.

● ALBUMS: *Spartan Warrior* (Roadrunner 1984)★★★, *Steel 'N' Chains* (Roadrunner 1985)★★.

Speedway Boulevard

This short-lived US group featured a *pot-pourri* of musical styles. Formed in 1979, the band comprised Ray Herring (vocals, piano), Gregg Hoffman (guitar, vocals), Jordan Rudes (keyboards), Dennis Feldman (bass, vocals) and Glenn Dove (drums). They debuted on Epic Records with a self-titled album that defied simple categorization. It featured a solid foundation of heavy-duty symphonic rock, modified by blues, funk, soul and Caribbean influences. In places, it courted comparisons with Led Zeppelin's more experimental phases. Sadly, the band broke up before their true potential could be realized. Feldman went on to play with Balance and later Michael Bolton. Rudes guested on Vinnie Moore's *Time Odyssey*.

● ALBUMS: *Speedway Boulevard* (Epic 1980)★★★.

Spellbound

This Swedish metal quintet was assembled in 1984 by Hans Froberg (vocals), J.J.Marsh (guitar), Al Strandberg (guitar, keyboards), Thompson (bass) and Ola Strandberg (drums), making their debut with a track on Sonet's *Swedish Metal* compilation. This led to a full contract, with the band delivering *Breaking The Spell* in 1984. Their style, based on an amalgam of Van Halen, Led Zeppelin and Europe, was given some distinction by Froberg's powerful vocals. *Rockin' Reckless* followed, a carbon copy of their debut, and suggested that the band were running out of ideas after just one album. Their association with Sonet ended in 1987, and nothing has been heard from them since.

● ALBUMS: *Breaking The Spell* (Sonet 1984)★★★, *Rockin' Reckless* (Sonet 1986)★★.

SPIDER (UK)

This British boogie group was formed on Merseyside in 1976 by the Burrows brothers. The band comprised bassist/vocalist Brian Burrows, drummer Rob E. Burrows and guitarists Sniffa and Col Harkness. After incessant gigging around the north-west, they relocated to London and were eventually signed by RCA Records in 1983. They debuted with *Rock 'N' Roll Gypsies*, a fuel-injected collection of boogie-based rockers, identical in almost every respect to the style of Status Quo. From then on, they were regarded as a poor-man's Quo. The album sold miserably and RCA dropped them. Picked up by A&M Records, they released *Rough Justice*, a semi-concept affair concerning a courtroom trial. Spider were the defendants, being accused of playing heavy metal rock 'n' roll. Another flop, it left the band without a label once more. Undaunted they plodded on, with Stu Harwood replacing Sniffa on guitar in 1986. Moving to the Mausoleum label, they produced *Raise The Banner* the same year. Musically they had not progressed, and the market for low-tech, three-chord boogie proved an ever contracting one. Outdated, and out of luck, they broke up shortly after the album was released. Brian Burrows is now a cartoonist and record sleeve designer.

● ALBUMS: *Rock 'N' Roll Gypsies* (RCA 1983)★★★, *Rough Justice* (A&M 1984)★★★, *Raise The Banner* (Mausoleum 1986)★★.

SPIDER (USA)

Prior to the formation of Spider in New York during 1978, Amanda Blue (vocals), Keith Lentin (guitar) and Anton Fig (drums) had worked together six years earlier in the South African-based Hammak. Adding keyboardist Holly Knight and ex-Riff Raff bassist Jimmy Lowell, they soon signed with the Dreamland label. This was made possible by Ace Frehley's (Kiss guitarist) recommendation, following Fig's appearance on the guitarist's solo album. Specializing in commercial American rock, with pop-rock overtones, they released two classy albums and achieved minor US single successes with 'New Romance' and 'Better Be Good To Me'. They changed name to Shanghai in 1982 to avoid confusion with the British group of the same name.

● ALBUMS: *Spider* (Dreamland 1980)★★★, *Between The Lines* (Dreamland 1981)★★★.

SPINAL TAP

The concept for Spinal Tap - a satire of a fading British heavy metal band - was first aired in a late 70s television sketch. Christopher Guest, formerly of parody troupe *National Lampoon*, played the part of lead guitarist Nigel Tufnell, while Harry Shearer (bassist Derek Smalls) and actor Michael McKean (vocalist David St. Hubbins) had performed with the Credibility Gap. Their initial sketch also featured Loudon Wainwright III and drummer Russ Kunkel, but these true-life musicians dropped out of the project on its transformation to full-length film. *This Is Spinal Tap*, released in 1984, was not a cinematic success, but it has since become highly popular through the medium of video. Its portrayal of a doomed US tour is ruthless, exposing incompetence, megalomania and sheer madness, but in a manner combining humour with affection. However, rather than incurring the wrath of the rock fraternity, the film has been lauded by musicians, many of whom, unfathomably, claim inspiration for individual scenes. Contemporary UK comedy team the Comic Strip used elements of Spinal Tap's theme in their second film, *More Bad News*. Spinal Tap reunited as a 'real' group and undertook an extensive tour in 1992 to promote *Break Like The Wind*, which featured guest appearances by Jeff Beck, Nicky Hopkins and Slash (Guns N'Roses). At this stage it seems that Spinal Tap's jokes at metal's expense are too deeply rooted in truth ever to wear thin.

● ALBUMS: *This Is Spinal Tap* (Polydor 1984)★★★, *Break Like The Wind* (MCA 1992)★★★.

● VIDEOS: *This Is Spinal Tap* (1989).

● FURTHER READING: *Inside Spinal Tap*, Peter Occhiogrosso.

● FILMS: *This Is Spinal Tap* (1984).

SPLIT BEAVER

This heavy metal quartet was formed in Wolverhampton, England, during 1982 by Darrel Whitehouse (vocals), Mike Hoppet (guitar), Alan Rees (bass) and Mick Dunn (drums). They signed to the local Heavy Metal Records label the same year. The band specialized in plodding and clichéd British rock, influenced by Deep Purple and Thin Lizzy but with neither the wit nor technique. They debuted with *When Hell Won't Have You*, a pedestrian and disappointing collection of up-tempo rockers, after which they split up. It seems Hades was not the only place unwilling to entertain Split Beaver.

● ALBUMS: *When Hell Won't Have You* (Heavy Metal 1982)★★.

SPOOKY TOOTH

Formed in 1967 as a blues group, they quickly moved into progressive rock during the heady days of the late 60s. Formerly named Art, they released a ponderous version of Buffalo Springfield's 'For What It's Worth' as 'What's That Sound'. The original band comprised Gary Wright (b. 26 April 1945, Englewood, New Jersey, USA; keyboards, vocals), Mike Kellie (b. 24 March 1947, Birmingham, England; drums), Luther Grosvenor (b. 23 December 1949, Evesham, Worcestershire, England; guitar), Mike Harrison (b. 3 September 1945, Carlisle, Cumberland, England; vocals) and Greg Ridley (b. 23 October 1947, Cumberland, England; bass). Their hard work on the English club scene won through, although their only commercial success was in the USA. They combined hard-edged imaginative versions of non-originals with their own considerable writing abilities. *Its All About* was a fine debut; although not a strong seller it contained their reading of 'Tobacco Road', always a club favourite, and their debut single, 'Sunshine Help Me', which sounded uncannily similar to early Traffic. It was *Spooky Two*, however, that put them on the map; eight powerful songs with a considerable degree of melody, this album remains as one of the era's finest heavy rock albums. Their self-indulgent excursion with Pierre Henry on *Ceremony* was a change of direction that found few takers, save for the superb cover painting by British artist John Holmes. *The Last Puff* saw a number of personnel changes: Ridley had departed for Humble Pie, Gary Wright left to form Wonderwheel and Grosvenor later emerged as 'Ariel Bender' in Stealers Wheel and Mott The Hoople. Three members of the Grease Band joined; Henry McCullough (b. 1943, England), Chris Stainton and Alan Spenner. The album contained a number of non-originals, notably David Ackles' 'Down River' and a superb version of Elton John's 'Son Of Your Father'. The band broke up shortly after its release, although various members, including Foreigner's Mick Jones, Bryson Graham (drums), Mike Patto and Ian Herbert (bass) eventually regrouped for three further albums which, while competent, showed no progression and were all written to a now dated formula. Judas Priest recorded 'Better By You, Better Than Me', which resulted in a court case following the deaths of two fans. The band were accused of inciting violence, causing the two fans to shoot themselves.

● ALBUMS: *It's All About* (Island 1968)★★★, *Spooky Two* (Island 1969)★★★★, *Ceremony* (Island 1970)★★, *The Last Puff* (Island 1970)★★★★, *You Broke My Heart So I Busted Your Jaw* (Island 1973)★★, *Witness* (Island 1973)★★, *The Mirror* (Good Ear/Island 1974)★★.

● COMPILATIONS: *That Was Only Yesterday* (1976)★★★, *The Best Of Spooky Tooth* (Island 1976)★★★★.

SPREAD EAGLE

This New York metal band came together when vocalist Ray West joined Paul DiBartolo (guitar), Rob DeLuca (bass) and Tommi Gallo (drums), who had previously been together in a Boston band. The band were signed at a very early stage, and were forced to complete their songwriting in the studio while recording their debut. *Spread Eagle* comprised wonderfully raucous and raw metal built on vicious chainsaw guitar, although some typically sex-orientated lyrics provoked criticism, despite their tongue-in-cheek nature. The band tended to be slow starters live, taking time to build up a real head of steam, but otherwise their raw power and aggression transferred well to the stage. *Open To The Public* was more refined, as the band had matured and were able to spend more time on songwriting and recording, although much of the drumming was provided by session players as Gallo flitted in and out of the band. However, Spread Eagle have yet to improve upon their minor league status.

● ALBUMS: *Spread Eagle* (MCA 1990)★★★★, *Open To The Public* (MCA 1993)★★★.

SPY

This six-piece symphonic US rock group was formed in 1979 by David Nelson (guitar), John Vislocky (vocals), Danny Seidenberg (violin), Michael Visceglia (bass), Dave Le Bolt (keyboards) and Rob Goldman (drums). Spy were a highly versatile and talented band in the Boston, Styx and Kansas vein. Their self-titled debut, released in 1980, was an undiscovered classic of the pomp-rock genre. Saturated with keyboards, stunning vocal harmonies and fluid guitarwork, it is still difficult to explain why the album sold so poorly. They had more songs in preparation, but CBS dropped them before they could be completed. Spy disintegrated as most of the band members returned to session work.

● ALBUMS: *Spy* (Kirshner 1980)★★★★.

SPYS

This US pomp-rock quintet was formed in 1981 by ex-Foreigner duo Al Greenwood (b. New York, USA;

keyboards) and Edward Gagliardi (b. 13 February 1952, New York, USA; bass). Enlisting the services of John Blanco (vocals), John Digaudio (guitar) and Billy Milne (drums), they signed to EMI Records the following year. They debuted with a self-titled album, produced by Neil Kernon (of Dokken and Michael Bolton fame). This featured some upfront, punchy guitarwork amid the sophisticated, keyboard-dominated arrangements. On *Behind Enemy Lines*, they became a little self-indulgent, utilizing a Russian male voice choir on several tracks. The album flopped and with growing legal and contractual problems, Spys disintegrated in 1983. Greenwood went on to work with Joe Lynn Turner and later N.Y.C.

● ALBUMS: *The Spys* (EMI America 1982)★★★, *Behind Enemy Lines* (EMI America 1983)★★.

SQUADRON

This American glam-rock quartet was formed in 1981 by Kevin (guitar, vocals) and Shawn Duggan (guitar, vocals). With the addition of bassist Bob Catalano and drummer John Blovin, they drew inspiration from the New York Dolls, Marc Bolan and Mötley Crüe. Dressed in red plastic clothes, with their hair sprayed grey, the visuals were always more interesting than the music. They released one album but disbanded soon after its release.

● ALBUMS: *First Mission* (1982)★★.

SQUIER, BILLY

Having gained valuable experience as guitarist in the power-pop group Sidewinders, Billy Squier (b. Boston, USA), who had also appeared in the less celebrated Magic Terry and the Universe, formed his own band under the name of Piper and recorded two albums for A&M during the late 70s. He dissolved Piper in 1979 and signed a solo contract with Capitol Records. *Tale Of The Tape* was released the following year and helped to establish Squier's reputation as a sophisticated and talented songwriter and guitarist. Drawing inspiration from Led Zeppelin, Queen, Fleetwood Mac and Genesis amongst others, he has continued to release quality albums of hard rock/pop crossover material. In the UK Squier has largely been ignored, even though he toured with Whitesnake in 1981 and played the Reading Festival. The story in the USA is entirely different. There he has enjoyed major successes with *Don't Say No* and *Emotions In Motion*, both of which made number 5 in the *Billboard* album chart. The former also produced hit singles in 'The Stroke' and 'My Kinda Lover'. By the time he released his eighth studio album, *Tell The Truth*, in 1993, Squier could reflect on worldwide sales of over 11 million records.

● ALBUMS: *Tale Of The Tape* (Capitol 1980)★★★, *Don't Say No* (Capitol 1981)★★★, *Emotions In Motion* (Capitol 1982)★★★, *Signs Of Life* (Capitol 1984)★★★, *Enough Is Enough* (Capitol 1986)★★★, *Hear And Now* (Capitol 1989)★★, *Creatures Of Habit* (Capitol 1991)★★, *Tell The Truth* (Capitol 1993)★★★.

● COMPILATIONS: *Reach For The Sky* (Polygram Chronicles 1996)★★★.

● VIDEOS: *Live In The Dark* (1986).

SQUIRREL BAIT

From Louisville, Kentucky, USA, Squirrel Bait were a highly amusing and captivating second-generation hardcore band of the mid-80s. Comprising Peter Searcy (vocals), Ben Daughtry (drums; replacing Britt Walford), David Grubbs (guitar), Brian McMahan (guitar) and Clark Johnson (bass), their two albums for Homestead Records are pithy blasts of youthful aggression and humour. Inspired by Hüsker Dü and the Replacements, *Skag Heaven* in particular sounded as fresh as anything of its genre and period. It promised a great future that never materialized. College careers beckoned and Squirrel Bait disbanded, though several members duly formed or joined other groups. Daughtry enjoyed the highest profile by teaming up with Evan Dando in the Lemonheads, and is currently a percussionist for the cabaret band Love Jones. Grubbs made three solo albums for Homestead as Bastro, also working with Bitch Magnet before joining the re-formed Red Crayola. McMahan formed Slint and then the Palace Brothers. Searcy at first joined a Violent Femmes cover band before establishing the Big Wheel on a more permanent footing.

● ALBUMS: *Squirrel Bait* (Homestead 1985)★★★, *Skag Heaven* (Homestead 1987)★★★.

ST. PARADISE

This short-lived US hard rock group was formed in 1978 by ex-Ted Nugent band duo Derek St. Holmes (vocals, guitar) and Rob Grange (bass, vocals). Recruiting ex-Montrose drummer Denny Carmassi, the line-up looked very promising. Signed by Warner Brothers, they released a self-titled debut in 1979. Comprising of power-metal, the album lacked both drive and individuality and compared unfavourably with everything with which the band's members had previously been associated. Following a European tour supporting

Van Halen, which failed to win new fans for St. Paradise, the band disintegrated. Carmassi joined Gamma and St. Holmes worked with Aerosmith's Brad Whitford for a short time, before rejoining Nugent once more.

● ALBUMS: *St. Paradise* (Warners 1979)★★★.

STABBING WESTWARD

Comprising Christopher Hall (vocals, guitar), Walter Flakus (keyboards, programming, guitar), Jim Sellers (bass) and Andy Kubiszewski (drums, guitar, programming), Stabbing Westward made their debut for Columbia Records in 1994 with the searing intensity of *Ungod*. A collision of technology with ferocious metal riffs, it was promoted by a year of touring with acts as disparate as Prong, Alice Donut, Killing Joke and Depeche Mode. The tour climaxed with a main-stage appearance at the UK's Reading Festival. Despite their seemingly meteoric arrival on the scene, however, Stabbing Westward had nearly a decade of musical history behind them. They were formed in 1986 by Hall and Flakus in the small town of Macomb, Illinois, USA, after they had spent time 'floating in and out of other people's bands'. The duo moved to Chicago in 1986 and added a guitarist. They were temporarily joined by Nine Inch Nails' drummer Chris Vrenna, who had previously worked with Hall as part of the Die Warzau touring ensemble. Replaced by David Suycott on drums, Stabbing Westward expanded to a five-piece band with the addition of guitarist Stuart Zechman and bass player Sellers. Despite their increasing technical and musical proficiency, they found it difficult to secure a major recording contract until, in the early 90s, Columbia was impressed by the depth of their sound. The label flew the group to London, England, to record their debut album with producer John Fryer (Nine Inch Nails, Love And Rockets, Cocteau Twins). *Ungod* was widely acclaimed by reviewers in the metal and alternative press, but before a follow-up collection could be recorded, the line-up shuffled once more, with Nine Inch Nails, The The and Crowded House collaborator Kubiszewski replacing Suycott. *Wither Blister Burn & Peel* was a particularly rewarding album, with songs such as 'Crushing Me' and 'What Do I Have To Do?' impressing with their inward-focused lyrics and intense musicianship. Lead singer Hall described *Darkest Days* as an album 'more like a ride through the life of a depressed person'.

● ALBUMS: *Ungod* (Columbia 1994)★★★★, *Wither Blister Burn & Peel* (Columbia 1996)★★★, *Darkest Days* (Columbia 1998)★★★.

STAGE DOLLS

This melodic power-trio emerged from Trondheim, Norway. Formed in 1983, the original line-up comprised Torstein Flakne (vocals, guitar, ex-Kids), Terje Storli (bass) and Erlend Antonson (drums, ex-Subway Sect), the latter eventually replaced by Steinar Krokstad. Their three albums combine high-tech production with superbly crafted AOR, the songs heavily infused with melody and a keen sense of dynamics. 'Love Cries', lifted as a single from their self-titled 1988 album, became a minor US hit in 1989. On the strength of this, they secured the support slots on the Blue Murder and Warrant USA tours the same year, but failed to build on the initial momentum.

● ALBUMS: *Soldier's Gun* (PolyGram 1985)★★★, *Commandoes* (PolyGram 1986)★★★★, *Stage Dolls* (Polydor 1988)★★★.

STAMPEDE

This melodic UK hard rock band was formed in 1981 by ex-Wild Horses trio Reuben Archer (vocals), Laurence Archer (guitar) and Frank Noon (drums). Recruiting bassist Colin Bond, they signed to Polydor Records the following year. Noon left for Tormé and was replaced by Eddie Parsons before they debuted with *The Official Bootleg*, recorded live at the Reading Festival. Their music at this point incorporated elements of Deep Purple and UFO, particularly the guitar style of Laurence Archer which appeared to be a composite of the techniques of Michael Schenker and Ritchie Blackmore. *Hurricane Town* followed, but was a disappointment. It featured disposable, mid-paced rockers reminiscent of Thin Lizzy. Unable to attract media attention, Stampede split up in 1983. Laurence Archer joined Grand Slam and later recorded a solo album, *L.A.*

● ALBUMS: *The Official Bootleg* (Polydor 1982)★★, *Hurricane Town* (Polydor 1983)★★★.

STANFORD PRISON EXPERIMENT

Formed in Los Angeles, California, USA, in the early 90s, Stanford Prison Experiment comprise Mike Starkey (guitar, vocals), Mario Jiminez (vocals), Mark Fraser (bass) and Davey Latter (drums). Matching the energy of punk with rock riffs and construction, the band's quick rise followed the release of a strong debut album. Its follow-up, *The Gato Hunch*, produced by Ted Nicely (Girls Against Boys, Fugazi), followed six weeks of touring alongside close friends Quicksand, with whom they also released a joint single in 1995.

They moved to Island Records in 1997 and released their debut for the label in 1998.

● ALBUMS: *Stanford Prison Experiment* (World Domination 1993)★★★, *The Gato Hunch* (World Domination 1995)★★★, *Wrecreation* (Island 1998)★★★.

STARCASTLE

This AOR rock group was formed in Illinois, USA, in 1972 by Stephen Hagler (guitar, vocals), Herb Schildt (keyboards) and Gary Strater (bass). The six-piece line-up was completed by ex-REO Speedwagon vocalist Terry Luttrell, guitarist Matt Stuart and drummer Steve Tassoer. After being championed by the local WGPU Radio Station in Champaign, Illinois, they were signed by Epic Records in 1974. Their music, which incorporated elements of Yes, Emerson, Lake And Palmer and Rush, was characterized by multi-vocal harmonies and complex, but carefully executed time-changes. They released four albums before splitting up, but never achieved the recognition their talents deserved.

● ALBUMS: *Starcastle* (Epic 1975)★★★, *Fountains Of Light* (Epic 1977)★★★, *Citadel* (Epic 1978)★★, *Reel To Reel* (Epic 1979)★★.

STARCHILD

This Canadian hard rock quartet was formed in 1977 by Richard Whittie (vocals), Robert Sprenger (guitar), Neil Light (bass) and Gregg Hinz (drums). Influenced by Triumph, Rush and Styx, their sole album was characterized by Sprenger's inventive guitarwork and Whittie's distinctive vocals. Hinz quit to join Helix shortly after the album's release, with ex-Lone Star drummer Dixie Lee stepping in as replacement. The band split up before any further recordings were made.

● ALBUMS: *Children Of The Stars* (Axe 1978)★★★.

STARFIGHTERS

This UK hard rock/boogie quintet was formed in 1980 by ex-Suburban Studs vocalist Steve Burton and guitarist Stevie Young (cousin of AC/DC's Angus Young). With Pat Hambly (guitar), Doug Dennis (bass) and Steve Bailey (drums, ex-Holly And The Italians) completing the line-up, they were picked up by Jive Records in 1981, after having toured with AC/DC. Produced by Tony Platt, their debut album was characterized by raunchy rock 'n' roll, with abrasive, up-front guitarwork from Young. However, at best they were a poor man's AC/DC, specializing in second-hand riffs, hackneyed vocals and a predictable backbeat. On *In Flight Movie*, they tried desperately to move away from this approach, concentrating instead on more traditional blues-based hard rock. Unfortunately this new style had even less to commend it, and they broke up soon after the record's release.

● ALBUMS: *Starfighters* (Jive 1981)★★★, *In Flight Movie* (Jive 1983)★★.

STARSHIP

(see Jefferson Starship; Jefferson Airplane; Hot Tuna)

STARR, JACK

After quitting the heavy metal band Virgin Steele in 1984, guitarist Jack Starr teamed up with ex-Riot vocalist Rhett Forrester and former Rods rhythm section Gary Bordonaro and Carl Canedy. They delivered *Out Of The Darkness* in 1984, a subtle combination of aggression, melody and dynamics. Starr dissolved the band soon after the album came out, preferring instead to use a new set of backing musicians on each subsequent release. Over the next four albums he moved away from his metallic roots, towards more commercial, arena-style rock typified by Bon Jovi and Dokken. Starr is one of the more original new-style, techno-wizard guitarists, but has yet to receive the recognition his talents undoubtedly deserve. He has recently opted to record under the band name of Burning Starr.

● ALBUMS: *Out Of The Darkness* (Music For Nations 1984)★★★★, *Rock The American Way* (Passport 1985)★★★, *No Turning Back* (US Metal 1986)★★★, *Blaze Of Glory* (US Metal 1987)★★★, *Burning Starr* (US Metal 1989)★★★.

START

This Icelandic pop-rock group was formed in 1980 by vocalist Petur Kristjansson and guitarist Kristjan Edelstein. Enlisting the services of Eirikur Haukson (guitar, vocals), Nikulas Robertson (keyboards), Jon Olafsson (bass, vocals) and David Karlsson (drums), they signed to the Steinar label the following year. They debuted with *En Hun Snyst Nu Samt*; a predictable collection of soft-rock anthems with Icelandic vocals. They disappeared into oblivion, after representing Iceland in the Eurovision Song Contest.

● ALBUMS: *En Hun Snyst Nu Samt* (Steinar 1981)★★★.

STARZ

New York band formed in 1975 by guitarist Brendan Harkin, drummer Joey X Dube and bassist Peter Sweval. Whilst looking for musicians to complete their line-up they worked as session men and also recorded a soundtrack to the porn film *Divine Obsession*. The following year they recruited guitarist Richie Ranno and vocalist Michael Lee Smith and signed to Capitol Records, who released the hit single, 'She's Just A Fallen Angel', and the album *Starz*. Two more albums followed in 1977 before Harkin and Sweval left to be replaced by Bobby Messano and Orville Davies, respectively. This line-up recorded the monumental *Colisseum Rock* set which took them to a worldwide audience. What followed was two years of touring but no new recordings. After a farewell tour they split in 1980. Ranno and Dube formed a new band with bassist Oeter Scance. A year later Ranno and Scance reunited with Smith and together with ex-Prism drummer Doug Madick, formed Hellcats. This band continued in the Starz vein of anthemic rock with melody. Indeed, they even included much Starz material in their live set, their success leading to a series of Starz live albums and compilations being released. Messano had spent his time working with various bands associated with Atlantic Records including Fiona, and in 1989 formed his own band.

● ALBUMS: *Starz* (Capitol 1976)★★★, *Violation* (Capitol 1977)★★★, *Attention Shoppers* (Capitol 1977)★★, *Colisseum Rock* (Capitol 1978)★★★★.

● COMPILATIONS: *Live In America* (Violation 1983)★★★, *Live In Canada* (Heavy Metal 1985)★★★, *Piss Party* (Heavy Metal 1985)★★★, *Brightest Starz* (Heavy Metal 1985)★★★, *Starz To Colisseum Rock* (Heavy Metal 1985)★★★, *Do It With The Lights On* (Performance 1987)★★, *Live In Action* (Roadrunner 1989)★★★. As the Hellcats: *Hellcats* (King Klassic 1982)★★★, *Hellcats Kids* (King Klassic 1987)★★. Bobby Messano: *Messano* (Strategic 1989)★★.

STATETROOPER

After leaving UK band MSG vocalist Gary Barden formed Statetrooper in 1986 with Martin Bushell (guitar), Jeff Summers (guitar, ex-Weapon), Steve Glover (keyboards), Jeff Brown (bass, ex-Wildfire) and Bruce Bisland (drums, ex-Wildfire; Weapon). They debuted the following year with a self-titled album of melodic AOR, which featured extensive keyboards with a production from Phil Chilton. It courted comparisons with Foreigner, Styx and Thin Lizzy, but lacked consistency in terms of songwriting. The album sold poorly and following a short period with Brian Robertson (ex-Motörhead and Thin Lizzy) on guitar, the band broke up.

● ALBUMS: *Statetrooper* (FM Revolver 1987)★★★.

STATUS QUO

The origins of this durable and now-legendary attraction lie in the Spectres, a London-based beat group. Founder-members Mike (later Francis) Rossi (b. 29 May 1949, Peckham, London, England; guitar, vocals) and Alan Lancaster (b. 7 February 1949, Peckham, London, England; bass) led the act from its inception in 1962 until 1967, by which time Roy Lynes (organ) and John Coughlan (b. 19 September 1946, Dulwich, London, England; drums) completed its line-up. The Spectres' three singles encompassed several styles of music, ranging from pop to brash R&B, but the quartet took a new name, Traffic Jam, when such releases proved commercially unsuccessful. A similar failure beset 'Almost But Not Quite There', but the group was nonetheless buoyed by the arrival of Rick Parfitt aka Rick Harrison (b. 12 October 1948, Woking, Surrey, England; guitar, vocals), lately of cabaret attraction the Highlights. The revamped unit assumed their 'Status Quo' appellation in August 1967 and initially sought work backing various solo artists, including Madeline Bell and Tommy Quickly. Such employment came to an abrupt end the following year when the quintet's debut single, 'Pictures Of Matchstick Men', soared to number 7 in the UK. One of the era's most distinctive performances, the song's ringing, phased guitar pattern and *de rigeur* phasing courted pop and psychedelic affectations. A follow-up release, 'Black Veils Of Melancholy', exaggerated latter trappings at the expense of melody, but the group enjoyed another UK Top 10 hit with the jaunty 'Ice In The Sun', co-written by former 50s singer Marty Wilde. Subsequent recordings in a similar vein struggled to match such success, and despite reaching number 12 with 'Down The Dustpipe', Status Quo were increasingly viewed as a *passé* novelty. However, the song itself, which featured a simple riff and wailing harmonica, indicated the musical direction unveiled more fully on *Ma Kelly's Greasy Spoon*. The album included Quo's version of Steamhammer's 'Junior's Wailing', which had inspired this conversion to a simpler, 'boogie' style. Gone too were the satin shirts, frock coats and kipper ties, replaced by long hair, denim jeans and plimsolls. The departure of Lynes *en route* to Scotland - 'He just got off the train and that was the last we ever saw of him' (Rossi) - brought the unit's guitar work to the fore, although indifference from their record company blighted progress. Assiduous live appearances built up a grass-roots following and impressive slots at the Reading and Great Western Festivals (both 1972) signalled a commercial turning point. Now signed to the renowned Vertigo label, Status Quo scored a UK Top 10 hit in January 1973 with 'Paper Plane' but more importantly, reached number 5 in the album charts with *Piledriver*. A subsequent release, *Hello*, entered at number 1, confirming the group's emergence as a major attraction. Since that point their style has basically remained unchanged, fusing simple, 12-bar riffs to catchy melodies, while an unpretentious 'lads' image has proved equally enduring. Each of their 70s albums reached the Top 5, while a consistent presence in the singles chart included such notable entries as 'Caroline' (1973), 'Down Down' (a chart-topper in 1974), 'Whatever You Want' (1979), 'What You're Proposing' (1980) and 'Lies'/'Don't Drive My Car' (1980). An uncharacteristic ballad, 'Living On An Island' (1979), showed a softer perspective while Quo also proved adept at adapting outside material, as evinced by their version of John Fogerty's 'Rockin' All Over The World' (1977). That song was later re-recorded as 'Running All Over The World' to promote the charitable *Race Against Time* in 1988. The quartet undertook a lengthy break during 1980, but answered rumours of a permanent split with *Just Supposin'*. However, a dissatisfied Coughlan left the group in 1981 in order to form his own act, Diesel. Pete Kircher (ex-Original Mirrors) took his place, but Quo was then undermined by the growing estrangement between Lancaster and Rossi and Parfitt. The bassist moved to Australia in 1983 - a cardboard cut-out substituted on several television appearances - but he remained a member for the next two years. Lancaster's final appearance with the group was at Live Aid, following which he unsuccessfully took out a High Court injunction to prevent the group performing without him. Rossi and Parfitt secured the rights to the name 'Status Quo' and re-formed the act around John Edwards (bass), Jeff Rich (drums) and keyboard player Andy Bown. The last-named musician, formerly of the Herd and Judas Jump, had begun his association with the group in 1973, but only now became an official member. Despite such traumas Quo continued to enjoy commercial approbation with Top 10 entries 'Dear John' (1982), 'Marguerita Time' (1983), 'In The Army Now' (1986) and 'Burning Bridges (On And Off And On Again)' (1988), while *1+9+8+2* was their fourth chart-topping album. Status Quo celebrated its silver anniversary in October 1991 by entering *The Guinness Book Of Records* having completed four charity concerts in four UK cities in the space of 12 hours. This ambitious undertaking, the subject of a television documentary, was succeeded by a national tour which confirmed the group's continued mass-market popularity. They achieved another number 1 single in 1994 with 'Come On You Reds', a musically dubious project recorded with football club Manchester United.

The much-loved Status Quo have carved a large niche in music history by producing uncomplicated, unpretentious and infectious rock music. An ill-chosen version of 'Fun Fun Fun' in 1996 had the Beach Boys relegated to harmony backing vocals and did little for either Quo's or the Beach Boys' reputation. At the same time the group attempted to sue BBC Radio 1 for not playlisting the single or their latest album (*Don't Stop*). Francis Rossi released a solo single, 'Give Myself To Love', in July 1996, followed by an album, *King Of The Doghouse*. As expected, they lost the case against Radio 1. That incident aside, their track-record is incredible: worldwide sales of over 100 million, and even with the dubious 'Fun Fun Fun', they have racked up 50 UK hit singles (more than any other band).

● ALBUMS: *Picturesque Matchstickable Messages* (Pye 1968)★★★, *Spare Parts* (Pye 1969)★★, *Ma Kelly's Greasy Spoon* (Pye 1970)★★★★, *Dog Of Two Head* (Pye 1971)★★★, *Piledriver* (Vertigo 1972)★★★★, *Hello* (Vertigo 1973)★★★, *Quo* (Vertigo 1974)★★★, *On The Level* (Vertigo 1975)★★★, *Blue For You* (Vertigo 1976)★★, *Status Quo Live!* (Vertigo 1977)★★, *Rockin' All Over The World* (Vertigo 1977)★★★, *If You Can't Stand The Heat* (Vertigo 1978)★★★, *Whatever You Want* (Vertigo 1979)★★★, *Just Supposin'* (Vertigo 1980)★★★, *Never Too Late* (Vertigo 1982)★★, *1+9+8+2* (Vertigo 1982)★★, *Back To Back* (Vertigo 1983)★★, *In The Army Now* (Vertigo 1986)★★★, *Ain't Complaining* (Vertigo 1988)★★★, *Perfect Remedy* (Vertigo 1989)★★, *Rock 'Til You Drop* (Vertigo 1991)★★, *Live Alive Quo* (Vertigo 1992)★★, *Thirsty Work* (Polydor 1994)★★, *Don't Stop* (PolyGram 1996)★★.

● COMPILATIONS: *Status Quo-tations* (Marble Arch 1969)★★★, *The Best Of Status Quo* (Pye 1973)★★★, *The Golden Hour Of Status Quo* (Golden Hour 1973)★★★, *Down The Dustpipe* (Golden Hour 1975)★★★, *The Rest Of Status Quo* (Pye 1976)★★, *The Status Quo File* (Pye

1977)★★★, *The Status Quo Collection* (Pickwick 1978)★★★, *Twelve Gold Bars* (Vertigo 1980)★★★, *Spotlight On Status Quo Volume 1* (PRT 1980)★★★, *Fresh Quota* (PRT 1981)★★★, *100 Minutes Of Status Quo* (PRT 1982)★★★, *Spotlight On Status Quo Volume 2* (PRT 1982)★★★, *From The Makers Of...*(Phonogram 1983)★★★, *Works* (PRT 1983)★★★, *To Be Or Not To Be* (Contour 1983)★★★, *Twelve Gold Bars Volumes 1 & 2* (Vertigo 1984)★★★, *Na Na Na* (Flashback 1985)★★★, *Collection: Status Quo* (Castle 1985)★★★, *Quotations, Volume 1* (PRT 1987)★★★, *Quotations, Volume 2* (PRT 1987)★★★, *From The Beginning* (PRT 1988)★★★, *C.90 Collector* (Legacy 1989)★★★, *B-Sides And Rarities* (Castle 1990)★★★, *The Early Works 1968 - '73* CD box set (Essential 1990)★★★, *The Other Side Of ...* (Connoisseur 1995)★★★, *Whatever You Want - The Best Of Status Quo* (Vertigo 1997)★★★★, *The Singles Collection 1966-73* (Castle 1998)★★★★.

● VIDEOS: *Live At The NEC* (PolyGram Music Video 1984), *Best Of Status Quo, Preserved* (Channel 5 1986), *End Of The Road 1984* (Channel 5 1986), *Rocking All Over The Years* (Channel 5 1987), *The Anniversary Waltz* (Castle 1991), *Rock Til You Drop* (PolyGram Music Video 1991), *Don't Stop* (PolyGram Music Video 1996).

● FURTHER READING: *Status Quo: The Authorized Biography*, John Shearlaw. *Status Quo*, Tom Hibbert. *Status Quo: Rockin' All Over The World*, Neil Jeffries. *25th Anniversary Edition*, John Shearlaw. *Just For The Record: The Autobiography Of Status Quo*, Francis Rossi and Rick Parfitt.

STEEL FOREST

This Dutch quintet was formed in Amsterdam during 1981 by Sunny Hays (vocals), Fred Heikens (guitar), Appie van Vliet (keyboards), Ron Heikens (bass) and Joop Oliver (drums). They negotiated a deal with the Dureco label the following year. They made their debut with *First Confession*, a clichéd and formularized Euro-rock opus, which failed to find an audience. Hays was replaced by Thijs Hamelaers (later of Sleez Beez) and William Lawson (ex-Angus) took over the drumstool after the album was released, but this line-up disintegrated before entering the studio.

● ALBUMS: *First Confession* (Dureco 1982)★★.

STEEL POLE BATHTUB

Formed in Bozeman, Montana, USA, in 1988, Steel Pole Bathtub soon relocated to San Francisco in order to pursue their highly personal take on hardcore music. Employing samples and unusual chord progressions and rhythms in order to twist their dense, atmospheric rock music into new shapes, the group released its debut album, *Lurch*, in 1990. Herein the group members - Dale Flattum (bass, vocals), Mike Morasky (guitar, vocals) and Darren Mor-X (drums) - first established their penchant for left-field rock dynamics and lyrics dealing with obsession, confusion and mental instability. Long before the advent of the Seattle grunge bands, there was also an obvious debt to Black Sabbath as well as punk forebears such as Flipper. Subsequent albums refined their style while their sonic experimentalism brought frequent comparisons to the Butthole Surfers. In addition to appearing on a number of underground compilation albums, they have also collaborated with Jello Biafra (ex-Dead Kennedys). In the 90s they were among a batch of alternative rock groups to secure a recording contract with a major label, in this case Slash/London Records.

● ALBUMS: *Lurch* (1990)★★★, *The Miracle Of Sound In Motion* (1993)★★★, *Some Cocktail Suggestions* (Slash/London 1994)★★, *Live* (Slash/London 1994)★★★, *Scars From Falling Down* (Slash/London 1996)★★★.

STEELE, CHRISSY

This Canadian 'heavy metal goddess' linked up with former Headpins guitarist and songwriter Brian MacLeod to concoct *Magnet To Steele* in 1991. The album was recorded on Macleod's yacht whilst cruising around British Columbia. Steele has a powerful and characteristic style, but the derivative and commercial structure to the material did her no favours. The bravado and sexual imagery of the press releases appeared more interesting than the actual music.

● ALBUMS: *Magnet To Steele* (Chrysalis 1991)★★.

STEELER (GERMANY)

This German heavy metal quintet, formerly known as Sinner, emerged as Steeler in 1981. The band were formed in Bochum, Westphalia, by Peter Burtz (vocals) and virtuoso guitarist Axel Rudi Pell. With the addition of Volher Krawczak (bass), Bertram Frewer (backing vocals) and Volker Jakel (drums), they signed to the independent Earthshaker label in 1984. They debuted the same year with a self-titled album of up-tempo hard-rockers that recalled the Scorpions. However, the strong material was discredited somewhat by the budget production. After *Rulin' The Earth*, the band moved to Steamhammer Records and replaced Krawczak with new bass player Herve Rossi. *Strike*

Back saw the band move towards an Americanized arena-rock approach, typical of Ratt, Dokken and Kiss. After *Undercover Animal* a series of line-up changes ensued, with Pell leaving to build a solo career. In consequence, the future of the band was sealed, and no further releases accrued.

● ALBUMS: *Steeler* (Earthshaker 1984)★★★, *Rulin' The Earth* (Earthshaker1985)★★★, *Strike Back* (Steamhammer 1986)★★, *Undercover Animal* (Steamhammer 1988)★★.

STEELER (USA)

This US hard rock quartet was formed in Nashville, Tennessee, in 1982 by vocalist Ron Keel. Recruiting Rik Fox (bass) and Mark Edwards (drums), the line-up was completed when Shrapnel label boss Mike Varney introduced Swedish guitarist Yngwie Malmsteen to the band. They relocated to Los Angeles and gigged incessantly on the bar and club circuit. Varney offered them a contract and they delivered a self-titled debut the following year. It was pure Americana bar-rock - chest-beating anthems, punctuated by shrill guitarwork. Malmsteen quit just as the album was released, joining Alcatrazz and later forming his own outfit, Rising Force. Keel formed a new outfit under his own name, while Fox formed Sin.

● ALBUMS: *Steeler* (Shrapnel 1983)★★★.

STEEPLECHASE

This nondescript melodic US rock quartet was formed in 1980 by Joe Lamente (vocals), Tony Sumo (guitar), Bob Held (bass) and Vinny Conigliaro (drums). They were signed to the local BCR label the following year. Drawing inspiration from the Midwest rock scene, their music incorporated elements of Petra, Starz and Spy. Their debut and sole album failed to take off and the band disintegrated soon after its release. Lamente joined Shelter and later recorded the solo set, *Secrets That You Keep*, in 1986.

● ALBUMS: *Steeplechase* (BCR 1981)★★.

STEINMAN, JIM

American songwriter, producer and musician Steinman first came to the public's attention in 1975 as musical arranger for the comedy company *National Lampoon*. He was also a playwright and it was at an audition that he first met Dallas singer/actor Meat Loaf. Together they conceived one of the biggest rock albums of all time, *Bat Out Of Hell*. Steinman's unique Wagnerian production technique was later to grace songs from countless other artists, from Bonnie Tyler ('Total Eclipse Of The Heart') to Barry Manilow. With Meat Loaf unable to record a follow-up, Steinman grew impatient and decided to record the album himself. Released in 1981, *Bad For Good* lacked the vocal impact of Meat Loaf and was not a bestseller - it was, however, still a superb album, featuring Todd Rundgren as guitarist and co-producer. Many of the songs would later appear on the *Bat Out Of Hell II* album which heralded a reunion with Meat Loaf, having parted company after the latter's *Deadringer* set, also from 1981. Perhaps the most stunning track from *Bad For Good* was a spoken-word piece titled 'Love And Death And An American Guitar', where Steinman proclaims in a style reminiscent of Jim Morrison's 'Horse Latitudes', that 'I once killed a Fender guitar'. He was also the mastermind behind the 1990 project *Original Sin*, a concept piece based on sexuality - at times almost operatic in construction, it was not taken seriously and so he returned to production work where he remains most in demand. Steinman produced Bonnie Tyler's *Free Spirit* in 1996, the same year that he negotiated a long-term publishing contract with PolyGram. One of the first fruits was the rock opera *Dance Of The Vampires*. That year he also worked with Andrew Lloyd Webber on a musical based upon the 60s movie *Whistle Down The Wind*, which was eventually staged in London's West End in summer 1998.

● ALBUMS: *Bad For Good* (Epic 1981)★★★, *Original Sin* (Virgin 1990)★★.

STEPPENWOLF

Although based in southern California, Steppenwolf evolved out of a Toronto act, the Sparrow(s). John Kay (b. Joachim F. Krauledat, 12 April 1944, Tilsit, Germany; vocals), Michael Monarch (b. 5 July 1950, Los Angeles, California, USA; lead guitar), Goldy McJohn (b. 2 May 1945; keyboards), Rushton Moreve (bass) and Jerry Edmonton (b. 24 October 1946, Canada; drums) assumed their new name in 1967, inspired by the novel by cult author Herman Hesse. John Morgan replaced Moreve prior to recording. The group's exemplary debut album included 'Born To Be Wild' which reached number 2 in the US charts. This rebellious anthem was written by Dennis Edmonton (Mars Bonfire), guitarist in Sparrow and brother of drummer Jerry. It was featured in the famous opening sequence of the film *Easy Rider*, and has since acquired classic status. Steppenwolf actively cultivated a menacing, hard rock image, and successive collections mixed this heavy style with blues. 'Magic Carpet Ride' and 'Rock Me' were also US Top 10 singles yet the group deflected the criticism attracted by such temporal success by addressing contemporary issues such as politics, drugs and racial prejudice. Newcomers Larry Byrom (guitar) and Nick St. Nicholas (b. 28 September 1943, Hamburg, Germany; bass), former members of Time, were featured on *Monster*, Steppenwolf's most cohesive set. A concept album based on Kay's jaundiced view of contemporary (1970) America, it was a benchmark in the fortunes of the group. Continued personnel changes undermined their stability, and later versions of the band seemed content to further a spurious biker image, rather than enlarge on earlier achievements. Kay dissolved the band in 1972, but his solo career proved inconclusive and within two years he was leading a reconstituted Steppenwolf. The singer has left and re-formed his creation several times over the ensuing years, but has been unable to repeat former glories.

● ALBUMS: *Steppenwolf* (Dunhill 1968)★★★, *The Second* (Dunhill 1968)★★★, *Steppenwolf At Your Birthday Party* (Dunhill 1969)★★★, *Early Steppenwolf* (Dunhill 1969)★★, *Monster* (Dunhill 1969)★★★★, *Steppenwolf 'Live'* (Dunhill 1970)★★, *Steppenwolf 7* (Dunhill 1970)★★, *For Ladies Only* (Dunhill 1971)★★★, *Slow Flux* (Mums 1974)★★, *Hour Of The Wolf* (Epic 1975)★★, *Skullduggery* (Epic 1976)★★, *Live In London* (Attic 1982)★★, *Wolf Tracks* (Attic 1982)★★, *Rock & Roll Rebels* (Qwil 1987)★★, *Rise And Shine* (IRS 1990)★★.

● COMPILATIONS: *Steppenwolf Gold* (Dunhill 1971)★★★★, *Rest In Peace* (Dunhill 1972)★★★, *16 Greatest Hits* (Dunhill 1973)★★★★, *Masters Of Rock* (Dunhill 1975)★★★★, *Golden Greats* (MCA 1985)★★★★.

STERLING COOKE FORCE

This Jimi Hendrix-inspired US group was put together by guitarist/vocalist Sterling Cooke in 1983. Recruiting Gino Cannon (vocals), Harry Shuman (bass) and Albie Coccia (drums), they recorded two unspectacular albums during the mid-80s. *Force This* saw Cooke rescind the vocals to Cannon and the music adopted a more melodic and restrained style. Second-hand riffs, bridges and solos were the order of the day, which left the band with a serious identity crisis. After losing their recording contract they were consigned to the status of minor club circuit band from then on.

● ALBUMS: *Full Force* (Ebony 1984)★★★, *Force This* (Ebony 1986)★★.

STEVENS', STEVE, ATOMIC PLAYBOYS

Steve Stevens first attracted attention as lead guitarist in Billy Idol's band, where his flash and fiery style brought Idol's hard rock to life. Stevens also accompanied Michael Jackson on 'Dirty Diana' and has worked with Ric Ocasek of the Cars, Steve Lukather of Toto and the Thompson Twins. He broke ranks from Idol's band in 1988 to form Steve Steven's Atomic Playboys with vocalist Perry McCarty, drummer Thommy Price and keyboard player Phil Ashley. Released in 1989, their self-titled debut was a major disappointment. With the exception of the title-cut, the songs were derivative and overtly commercial. Following an unsuccessful US club tour in 1990, the band split up.

● ALBUMS: *Steve Steven's Atomic Playboys* (Warners 1989)★★★.

STILLBORN

Pretenders to the title of 'Sweden's heaviest band', Stillborn formed in 1988 and comprise Henke (vocals), Kim (guitar), Henning (guitar), Sam (bass) and Peter (drums). The description of their sound was given to them by Sweden's biggest-selling newspaper after their Scandinavian tour of 1992 as a reference to their powerful live authority and doom-obsessed lyrics. The group was originally started as a quartet in 1988, and *Necrospirituals* quickly established their abrasive, threatening sound. Expanded to a five-piece unit by 1990, that year's *Permanent Solution* was a more polished but still powerful effort. A great deal of press and broadcast attention followed, which was enough to persuade Roadrunner Records to license the record throughout Europe. *State Of Disconnection* was just as brutal as previous albums but saw the group penetrate the international market for the first time, with excellent reviews appearing in US metal magazines as well as their European equivalents.

● ALBUMS: *Necrospirituals* (Radium 1989)★★★★, *Permanent Solution* (Radium/Roadrunner 1990)★★★, *State Of Disconnection* (Radium/Roadrunner 1992)★★★.

STILTSKIN

Authors of the most distinctive riff of 1994, few knew who Stiltskin were at the time, yet millions recognized the instrumental section of 'Inside' that accompanied a lavish Levi's television advertisement. Picked up by the jeans manufacturer when it was overheard playing at the group's publishers, 'Inside' shot to number 1 in the UK charts when finally released as a single in the summer of 1994. The band had actually formed in 1989 when Peter Lawlor (guitar) and James Finnigan (bass) met for the first time in London. Finnigan had previously spent two years working alongside the Kane brothers in Hue And Cry, before electing to pursue a rockier direction. His new partner, meanwhile, had just returned from New York, dismayed with the dominance of dance and rap music. The duo began working on songs together in Lawlor's demo studio, recruiting an old friend of Finnigan's, Ross McFarlane, as drummer. However, unable to find a suitable singer or arouse record company interest, McFarlane relocated to Glasgow to drum with several bands, including Slide and Fireball. There were few further developments until the summer of 1993, when Lawlor and Finnigan were driving along the M8 between Edinburgh and Glasgow and passed a figure 'frantically retrieving objects which resembled guitars from a van engulfed in flames on the motorway's hard shoulder'. That distressed figure was Ray Wilson, who accepted an offer of a lift from the pair in order to make the gig he was playing that night. When he walked offstage, Lawlor and Finnigan offered him the job as Stiltskin vocalist. The new formation persuaded McFarlane to return to the fold, shortly after which they were approached to use 'Inside'. Their management team set up White Water records to house their releases, with a second single, 'Footsteps', also charting, before a debut album appeared in late 1994. Forever overshadowed by their albatross, 'Inside', Stiltskin joined a long list of one-hit wonders. Wilson went on to become lead singer with Genesis following Phil Collins' departure.

● ALBUMS: *The Mind's Eye* (White Water 1994)★★★.

STINGRAY

This South African melodic heavy rock group was formed in 1978 by Dennis East (vocals), Mike Pilot (guitar), Danny Anthill (keyboards), Allan Goldswain (keyboards), Eddie Boyle (bass) and Shaun Wright (drums). Together they based their style firmly on American rock giants such as Styx, Boston, Kansas and Journey. They released two technically excellent albums, characterized by the heavy use of keyboards and multi-part vocal harmonies, but failing to attract attention outside their native South Africa, the band broke up in 1981.

● ALBUMS: *Stingray* (Carrere 1979)★★★, *Operation Stingray* (Nitty Gritty 1980)★★★.

STONE FURY

Moving from Hamburg, Germany, to Los Angeles, USA, in 1983, vocalist Lenny Wolf teamed up with Bruce Gowdy (guitar) to form Stone Fury. Adding Rick Wilson (bass) and Jody Cortez (drums), they signed to MCA Records and debuted the following year with *Burns Like A Star*. The album offered traditional blues-based hard rock, similar in construction to Led Zeppelin. Wolf's vocals were modelled very closely on Robert Plant's, both in pitch and phrasing, which provoked accusations of imitation. *Let Them Talk* was more restrained and employed a greater use of melody and atmospherics. Unable to make a breakthrough in the USA, Wolf went back to Germany and later formed Kingdom Come on his return to the USA in 1987. Gowdy, in the meantime, formed World Trade.

● ALBUMS: *Burns Like A Star* (MCA 1984)★★★★, *Let Them Talk* (MCA 1986)★★★.

STONE TEMPLE PILOTS

The Stone Temple Pilots are the result of a chance meeting between vocalist Weiland (b. Scott Weiland, 27 October 1967, Santa Cruz, California, USA) and bassist Robert DeLeo (b. 2 February 1966, New Jersey, USA) at one of Black Flag's final shows in Los Angeles. After discovering that they both went out with the same girl, a songwriting partnership led to the formation of a full band, originally known as Mighty Joe Young, and later renamed Stone Temple Pilots, with drummer Eric Kretz (b. 7 June 1966, Santa Cruz, California, USA) and DeLeo's guitarist brother Dean (b. 23 August 1961, New Jersey, USA) joining the duo. Moving away from the Guns N'Roses-crazed Los Angeles scene of the time to San Diego, the band were able to play club shows and develop hard rock material given an alternative edge by their varied influences. Although the sound of the band brought many others to mind, from Led Zeppelin to Seattle bands such as Pearl Jam and Alice In Chains, and Weiland's deep voice bore a passing resemblance to that of Eddie Vedder, it was very much Stone Temple Pilots' own sound, and there was no denying the quality of *Core*. The dense wall of muscular guitar over a tight, precise rhythm section provided a powerful setting for Weiland's emotive vocals and challenging lyrics. 'Sex Type Thing', perhaps the band's best-known song, deals with sexual harassment from the viewpoint of a particularly brutish male, and the singer was initially concerned that the message would be misinterpreted. His fears proved unfounded and, helped by heavy touring, *Core* would reach the US Top 20 by the summer of 1993, eventually selling over four million copies in the USA. The follow-up, *Purple*, debuted at number 1 in the US album charts, staying there for three weeks. This time the band purposely avoided any material that could be construed as derivative of Pearl Jam, having tired of the unfair criticism. Their second effort proved to be an atmospheric and rewarding experience, as STP produced a quasi-psychedelic sound that confirmed their own identity and considerable talents. In May 1995, Weiland was arrested in Pasadena, California, and was charged with possession of heroin and cocaine, a misdemeanour that carried with it a possible four-year jail sentence. In early 1996 their best album to date was released amid rumours of serious drug abuse during the recording sessions. *Tiny Music . . . Songs from The Vatican Gift Shop* was indeed a powerful record, but its success was tainted by Weiland being ordered by the courts to be confined to a drug rehabilitation centre. To have this happen at such a crucial time in the band's career (when the new album was still in the US Top 20) was a severe blow and raised serious questions about the group's future. However, by the end of 1996, Weiland had been cleared of the drugs charges and the band were back on the road. In 1998 Weiland released his solo debut and announced the band would record another album. Shortly afterwards, however, he was arrested in New York and charged with heroin possession.

● ALBUMS: *Core* (Atlantic 1992)★★★, *Purple* (Atlantic 1994)★★★, *Tiny Music . . . Songs From The Vatican Gift Shop* (Atlantic 1996)★★★.
Solo: Scott Weiland *12 Bar Blues* (East West 1998)★★★.

● FURTHER READING: *Stone Temple Pilots*, Mike Wall and Malcolm Dome.

STOOGES

Purveyors, with the MC5, of classic, high-energy American rock, the Stooges' influence on successive generations is considerable. They were led by the enigmatic James Jewel Osterberg (aka Iggy Stooge and Iggy Pop, b. 21 April 1947, Ann Arbor, Michigan, USA) who assumed his unusual sobriquet in deference to the Iguanas, a high-school band in which he drummed. Iggy formed the Psychedelic Stooges with guitarist Ron Asheton. Scott Asheton (drums) and Dave Alexander (bass) completed the line-up, which quickly became a fixture of Detroit's thriving underground circuit. By September 1967, the group had dropped its adjectival prefix and had achieved a notoriety through the onstage behaviour of its uninhibited frontman. The Stooges' first album was produced by John Cale although the group's initial choice was veteran soul svengali Jerry Ragovoy. This exciting debut matched its malevolent, garage-band sneer with the air of nihilism prevalent in the immediate post-summer of love era. Iggy's exaggerated, Mick Jagger-influenced swagger swept over the group's three-chord maelstrom to create an enthralling and compulsive sound. The band were augmented by saxophonist Steven Mackay for *Funhouse*. This exceptional release documented a contemporary live set, opening with the forthright 'Down On The Street' and closing with the anarchic, almost free-form 'LA Blues'. This uncompromising collection proved uncommercial and the Stooges were then dropped by their record label. A second guitarist, Bill Cheatham joined in August 1970, while over the next few months two bassists, Zeke Zettner and Jimmy Recca, passed through the ranks as replacements for Dave Alexander. Cheatham was then ousted in favour of James Williamson, who made a significant contribution to the ensuing Stooges period. Long-time Iggy fan David Bowie brought the group to the Mainman management stable and the singer was also responsible for mixing *Raw Power*. Although it lacked the purpose of its predecessors, the set became the Stooges' most successful release and contained two of their best-known performances, 'Gimme Danger' and 'Search And Destroy'. However, the quartet - Iggy, Williamson and the Asheton brothers - were dropped from Mainman for alleged drug dependence. In 1973, Scott Thurston (keyboards) was added to the line-up, but their impetus was waning. The Stooges made their final live appearance on 9 February 1974 at Detroit's Michigan Palace. This tawdry performance ended with a battle between the group and a local biker gang, the results of which were captured on *Metallic KO*. Within days a drained Iggy Pop announced the formal end of the Stooges. *Rubber Legs* and *Open Up And Bleed* are both collections of rough mixes and live recordings, for collectors and serious fans only.

● ALBUMS: *The Stooges* (Elektra 1969)★★★★, *Funhouse* (Elektra 1970)★★★★, as Iggy And The Stooges *Raw Power* (Columbia 1973)★★★★, *Metallic KO* (Skydog 1976)★★, *Rubber Legs* rare recordings from 1973/4 (Fan Club 1988)★★, *Open Up And Bleed* (Bomp 1996)★★.

● COMPILATIONS: as Iggy Pop And James Williamson *Kill City* (Bomp 1977)★★, *No Fun* (Elektra 1980)★★, as Iggy And The Stooges *I'm*

Sick Of You (Line 1981)★★, *I Gotta Right* (Invasion 1983)★★.

Storm

This Los Angeles-based quartet, formed in 1978 by Jeanette Chase (vocals), Lear Stevens (guitar), Ronni Hansen (bass) and David Devon (drums), played hi-tech hard-rock, characterized by Lear's Brian May-like guitar sound and the powerful vocals of Chase. They incorporated elements of Queen, Van Halen and Styx within complex, and at times classically styled, arrangements. Their second album moved more towards AOR, with the inclusion of more lightweight material and even folk influences. *Eye Of The Storm* was AOR for the 90s, immaculate yet familiar riffs and gorgeous structures that are ultimately bland but impossible to fault.

● ALBUMS: *Storm* (MCA 1979)★★★, *Storm* (Capitol 1983)★★★, *Eye Of The Storm* (Music For Nations 1996)★★★★.

Stormbringer

This Swiss quintet was formed in 1984 by Dave Barreto (vocals), Angi Schilero (guitar), Fabian Emmenger (keyboards), Urs Hufschmid (bass) and Laurie Chiundinelli (drums). Taking their name from Deep Purple's 1974 album, they specialized in melodic power-metal, evidently based on the works of the latter group. However, it proved to be a rather nondescript tribute, and attracted few supporters. Disillusioned by the lack of media and public response, they split up soon after the album was released. Schilero went on to play with China for a short time, before starting his own band.

● ALBUMS: *Stormbringer* (Musk 1985)★★★.

Stormtroopers Of Death

More commonly known as S.O.D., this band initially came into existence as a one-off side project for Anthrax musicians Scott Ian (guitar) and Charlie Benante (drums). Taking time out during the recording of Anthrax's *Spreading The Disease* in 1985, they asked Nuclear Assault bassist Dan Lilker (originally a member of Anthrax) and roadie Billy Milano (vocals, ex-Psychos) to join them, to make use of three days' free studio time. The result was *Speak English Or Die*, a manic fusion of thrash and hardcore styles, that had both humour and considerable crossover appeal. Milano went on to form Method Of Destruction, using exactly the same musical blueprint (indeed, some of Scott Ian's S.O.D. lyrics would be re-used in this project). A posthumous release, *Live From Budokan*, emerged in 1992, while sporadic reunions have also occurred over recent years.

● ALBUMS: *Speak English Or Die* (Megaforce 1985)★★★★, *Live From Budokan* (Megaforce 1992)★★.

Stormwitch

This German heavy metal quintet, who employed a strong satanic/gothic horror image, were formed by guitarist Lee Tarot (b. Harold Spengler) in 1981, together with Andy Aldrian (vocals), Steve Merchant (guitar), Ronny Pearson (bass) and Pete Lancer (drums). These were all fellow Germans, who nevertheless altered their names in order to sound American. Their first three albums offered undistinguished Euro-metal, reminiscent of Running Wild, and made little impact outside Germany. A lack of success saw them change direction on 1987's *The Beauty And The Beast*, adopting a more straightforward hard rock approach - all to little avail, however, with the band disintegrating shortly afterwards.

● ALBUMS: *Walpurgis Night* (Powerstation 1984)★★★, *Tales Of Terror* (Powerstation 1985)★★, *Stronger Than Heaven* (Powerstation 1986)★★★, *The Beauty And The Beast* (Gama 1987)★★★.

Stradlin, Izzy, And The Ju Ju Hounds

Tired of the pressures of working with one of the world's high-profile acts, Stradlin left Guns N'Roses in the autumn of 1991 to work on a solo project. With himself on guitar and lead vocals, and the former Burning Tree rhythm section of Mark Dutton and Doni Grey, Stradlin added a Ju Ju Hounds line-up of former Georgia Satellites guitarist Rick Richards, ex-Broken Homes bassist Jimmy Ashhurst, and drummer Charlie Quintana, for the band's 1992 recording debut. Axl Rose's description of the band as 'Izzy's Keith Richards thing' was apt, as the influence of the Rolling Stones guitarist on Stradlin's songwriting and vocal style was obvious, even incorporating their shared taste for reggae with a furious cover version of Toots And the Maytals' 'Pressure Drop'. However, far from being a mere homage, the album was excellent, and generally well received. Subsequent live shows were electric affairs, with Stradlin appearing more relaxed, and Richards, in particular, contributing some stunning slide/lead guitar work, and vocals. Somewhat surprisingly, Stradlin made a brief return to the Guns N'Roses camp for some open-air European shows in the summer of

1993, ironically standing in for his replacement, Gilby Clarke, after the latter broke his wrist.

● ALBUMS: *Izzy Stradlin And The Ju Ju Hounds* (Geffen 1992)★★★, *117 Degrees* (Geffen 1998)★★★.

STRANGER

This melodic pop-rock quartet was formed in Florida, USA, during 1981 by Greg Billings (vocals), Ronnie Garvin (guitar), Tom Cardenas (bass) and John Price (drums). With the line-up stabilized, they signed to CBS Records the following year. Produced by Tom Werman (of Ted Nugent and Mötley Crüe fame), their debut album was a highly impressive collection of anthemic rockers, punctuated by some fiery guitarwork from Garvin. Despite its seemingly obvious commercial potential the album failed to make an impact, and little was heard of the band until a second album, a full nine years later.

● ALBUMS: *Stranger* (Epic 1982)★★★★, *No Rules* (Thunderbay 1991)★★.

STRANGEWAYS

This Scottish quartet was put together in 1985 by brothers Ian (guitar) and David Stewart (bass). With Jim Drummond (drums) and Tony Liddell (vocals), they debuted with a self-titled album in 1985. This offered a blend of Americanized, melodic AOR comparable with the work of Boston, Journey or Kansas. Produced by Kevin Elson (of Journey fame), it surpassed many expectations, but was ignored by the British public. Terry Brock (from Atlanta, USA) replaced Liddell on *Native Sons*, which saw the band consolidate their style and progress significantly as songwriters. It remains one of the sadly neglected albums of the pomp-rock/AOR genre. *Walk In The Fire* was not as immediate, with Brock's vocals sounding hoarse and less sophisticated. He left to audition for Deep Purple in 1989, but was unsuccessful. Strangeways have been inactive since.

● ALBUMS: *Strangeways* (Bonaire 1986)★★★, *Native Sons* (RCA 1987)★★★★, *Walk In The Fire* (RCA 1989)★★.

STRAPPING YOUNG LAD

Rock singer/guitarist Devin Townsend chose Strapping Young Lad as his pseudonym for his solo career in the mid-90s. Previously he had worked with both Steve Vai and the Wildhearts, before both ventures ground to a halt. Possibly alienated by his experiences with volatile musicians, Townsend took matters into his own hands on *Heavy As A Heavy Thing* - including playing nearly all the instruments, and writing and producing the collection himself. This was a wide-ranging, esoteric collection, straddling industrial noise and semi-operatic, pomp rock at its extremes. Also included in this strangely affecting set was a cover version of Judas Priest's 'Exciter'. He set out on tour to promote the album with a backing band that included guitarists Mike Sudar and Jed Sinion, bass player Ashley Scribner and drummer Adrian White (who had contributed a few percussion pieces to the album). Townsend also found time to collaborate with Black Sabbath bass player Geezer Butler, and played on Front Line Assembly's 1995 album.

● ALBUMS: *Heavy As A Heavy Thing* (Century Media 1995)★★★★, *City* (Century Media 1997)★★★, *No Sleep 'Till Bedtime* (Century Media 1998)★★★.

STRAPPS

This UK hard rock quartet was formed in 1975 by Ross Stagg (vocals, guitar), Noel Scott (keyboards), Joe Read (bass) and Mick Underwood (drums), and were picked up by EMI Records the following year. Drawing their inspiration from Deep Purple, Thin Lizzy and Uriah Heep, they released four albums over a five-year period. These met with very limited success, except in Japan, where they maintained a cult following. Strapps never graduated from support act status in Europe, which was a fair summation of their true potential. The band disintegrated in 1979, when Underwood joined Gillan.

● ALBUMS: *Strapps* (EMI 1976)★★★, *Secret Damage* (EMI 1977)★★★, *Sharp Conversation* (EMI 1978)★★, *Ball Of Fire* (EMI 1979)★★.

STRATUS

When former Iron Maiden drummer Clive Burr joined Praying Mantis in 1985 the new band became known as Stratus - the remaining personnel comprising Bernie Shaw (vocals), Tino Troy (guitar), Alan Nelson (keyboards), and Chris Troy (bass). Moving away from the formularized New Wave Of British Heavy Metal approach, Stratus employed the extensive use of keyboards and multi-part vocal harmonies. They debuted with *Throwing Shapes*, a lacklustre pomp-rock album lacking both in energy and quality songs. The album fared badly and the band split up soon after it was released. Bernie Shaw went on to join Uriah Heep.

● ALBUMS: *Throwing Shapes* (Steeltrax 1985)★★.

STRAY DOG
This blues-based US heavy metal group started life as a power-trio in 1973. Formed by Snuffy Walden (vocals, guitar), Alan Roberts (bass, vocals) and Leslie Sampson (b. 1950; drums), their style incorporated elements of Jimi Hendrix and Led Zeppelin. Timmy Dulaine (guitar, vocals) and Luis Cabaza (keyboards) were added in 1974, with rather negative results. The aggression and power of the three-piece had been dissipated by needlessly intricate arrangements. *While You're Down There* was another disappointment and following management and contractual problems, the band went their separate ways in 1975. Walden later reappeared as theme composer to popular US television soap opera *30 Something*.
● ALBUMS: *Stray Dog* (Manticore 1973)★★★, *While You're Down There* (Manticore 1974)★★.

STREETS
This melodic US heavy rock quartet was formed in 1982 by ex-Kansas vocalist Steve Walsh and Mike Slamer (guitar; ex-City Boy). Drafting in Billy Greer (bass) and Tim Gehrt (drums), they adopted a much more straightforward AOR approach than their former employers, concentrating on infectious hooklines and memorable choruses, rather than intricate keyboard fills and complex arrangements. Their self-titled debut was received very favourably by the music media, but failed to win over a large audience, partly due to poor promotion. *Crimes In Mind* saw the band maturing as songwriters, but Atlantic Records were guilty of indifference once more, and the album failed to take off. Disillusioned, Streets broke up in 1986, with Walsh and Greer joining the revamped Kansas.
● ALBUMS: *Streets* (Atlantic 1983)★★★, *Crimes In Mind* (Atlantic 1985)★★★.

STRESSBALL
New Orleans sludge metal specialists, formed in 1989, whose name is derived from drummer and part-time chef Joe Fazzio's own 'stressball' - 'it takes batteries and it's supposed to be like a paperweight or something, and when you get pissed off, you throw it at the wall and it sounds like glass breaking'. The rest of the group comprises Lennon Laviolette (guitar), Steven Gaille (vocals) and Eddy Dupuy (bass). Fazzio is also a good friend of Pantera's Phil Anselmo, and the two play together in the side-band Both Legs Broken (along with Kirk Windstein from Crowbar and Mark Schultz from Eyehategod). Stressball was inaugurated while Fazzio and friends practised at a 100-year-old warehouse in the centre of New Orleans, from where bands such as Graveyard Rodeo (who practically invented the slow, torturous sound associated with the scene), Eyehategod and stablemates Crowbar also emerged. Fazzio himself had previously played in a band called Crawlspace with Michael Williams from Eyehategod, with whom they have toured widely.
● ALBUMS: *Stressball* (Pavement 1993)★★★.

STRIFE
Blues-based British hard rock trio who formed in 1972. The band - John Reid (vocals, guitar), Gordon Rowley (bass, vocals) and David Williams (drums, vocals) - gigged incessantly and earned a reputation as a perennial support act, but lacked the individuality to reach headline status. Strife built up a small but loyal cult following during the mid-70s, with their honest, no-frills, good-time rock 'n' roll. They released two average rock albums, with *Back To Thunder* featuring Don Airey on keyboards and Paul Ellison in place of Williams on drums. After one last stab at success with the EP *School*, the band gave up in 1979. Rowley went on to form Nightwing.
● ALBUMS: *Rush* (Chrysalis 1975)★★★, *Back To Thunder* (Gull 1978)★★.

STRIKER
This versatile hard rock quartet was formed in 1977 by the multi-talented Rick Randle (vocals, keyboards, guitar). Enlisting the services of Scott Roseburg (vocals, bass, guitar), Rick Ramirez (guitar) and Rick Taylor (drums, vocals), Striker signed with Arista Records the following year. Their music incorporated rock, funk, boogie, blues and soul influences, and although this eclecticism avoided press pigeon-holing, it also limited their potential audience. Their album featured impressive guitar and vocal harmonies, but lacked identity because of the varied styles employed. Failing to win an appreciative audience, Randle dissolved the band in 1979. Rick Ramirez went on to join Bruzer.
● ALBUMS: *Striker* (Arista 1978)★★★.

STRYPER
Christian heavy metal quartet from Los Angeles, California, formed by the Sweet brothers in 1981. Originally known as Roxx Regime, this group featured Michael Sweet (vocals), Robert Sweet (drums), Timothy Gaines (bass) and Oz Fox

(guitar), playing standard, Americanized hard rock. Devising a carefully constructed image and marketing strategy, they subsequently changed their name to Stryper and dressed in matching yellow and black outfits. They were now a band with a mission - to spread the word of God through rock music, and become the total antithesis of the satanic metal movement. Signing to Enigma Records, they attracted widespread media attention, which generally focused on the 'novelty' factor of their spiritual inclinations. A debut mini-album, *Yellow And Black Attack*, featured standard hard rock, with simple lyrics and high-pitched harmonies, while live shows climaxed with the band throwing bibles into the audience. By their third album they had built up a loyal army of fans and the excellently produced melodic rock contained within widened their appeal. *To Hell With The Devil* peaked at number 32 on its three-month stay on the *Billboard* album charts. *In God We Trust* saw the band mellow, with more emphasis on pop-rock singalong numbers and the resultant exclusion of driving rock. The album was a commercial disappointment, failing to build on the success of the previous release. It did reach number 32, but only stayed on the *Billboard* chart for five weeks. The band took time off for a radical rethink, before entering the studio again. Oz Fox ventured into production during this time and oversaw the recording of the debut album by fellow Christian-rockers Guardian. *Against The Law* emerged in 1990, marking a return to a more aggressive style. The yellow and black stage costumes had been jettisoned and the lyrics were considerably less twee. However, by this time, most of their original fans had moved on and the album sold poorly. When Michael Sweet quit in 1992 it seemed only divine intervention could rescue Stryper.

● ALBUMS: *The Yellow And Black Attack* (Enigma 1984)★★★, *Soldiers Under Command* (Enigma 1985)★★★, *To Hell With The Devil* (Enigma 1986)★★★★, *In God We Trust* (Enigma 1988)★★★, *Against The Law* (Enigma 1990)★★★.

● VIDEOS: *Live In Japan* (1988).

STUPIDS

Formed in Ipswich, Suffolk, England, the Stupids merged the post-punk sound of the early to mid-80s UK scene with a hardcore adrenaline rush imported from America. The group were active from 1985 to 1989, though by the latter stages of their career they had relocated to London. Membership was fluid and typically hidden by pseudonyms, but the main contributors were Tommy Stupid (vocals, guitar, drums), Pauly Pizza (bass), Marty Tuff (guitar) and Ed Wenn (bass). The early stage of their career was documented by two albums and a 7-inch EP for Children Of The Revolution Records, by which time their sub-two-minute thrashes and spontaneous humour were familiar to many through the BBC disc jockey John Peel. He aired every track on their first two albums, recording three sessions for the programme over the years. He also wrote extensively about the Stupids' idiosyncratic appeal in his *Observer* newspaper column. Greater distribution via Vinyl Solution Records allowed their releases to find international approval, including a split 10-inch EP with Australian band the Hard-Ons. They also appeared on the covers of both the *New Musical Express* and *Sounds*, as the most visible and vital band in a new hardcore scene developing principally in the east of England. Later high-profile guitar groups such as the Senseless Things and Ned's Atomic Dustbin grew up seeing the Stupids. Although they eventually collapsed in 1989, by the time they did so they had produced a significant volume of work, much of it hilarious, toured both the USA and Australia, broken the lower reaches of the national charts and all without ever having the backing of a major record company.

● ALBUMS: *Peruvian Vacation* (Children Of The Revolution 1986)★★★, *Retard Picnic* (Children Of The Revolution 1986)★★★, *Van Stupid* (Vinyl Solution 1987)★★★, *Jesus Meets The Stupids* (Vinyl Solution 1987)★★★.

STYX

This Chicago-based quintet are widely believed to be responsible for the development of the term pomp-rock (pompous, overblown arrangements, with perfect-pitch harmonies and a very full production). Styx evolved from the bands Tradewinds and T.W.4, but renamed themselves after the fabled river from Greek mythology, when they signed to Wooden Nickel, a subsidiary of RCA Records, in 1972. The line-up comprised Dennis De Young (vocals, keyboards), James Young (guitar, vocals), Chuck Panozzo (bass), John Panozzo (b. 20 September 1947, USA, d. 16 July 1996, Chicago, Illinois, USA; drums) and John Curulewski (guitar). Combining symphonic and progressive influences they released a series of varied and highly melodic albums during the early 70s. Success was slow to catch up with them; *Styx II*, originally released in 1973, spawned the Top Ten *Billboard* hit 'Lady' in 1975. The album then made similar progress, eventually peaking at number 20.

After signing to A&M Records in 1975, John Curulewski departed with the release of *Equinox*, to be replaced by Tommy Shaw. This was a real turning point in the band's career as Shaw took over lead vocals and contributed significantly on the writing side. From here on Styx albums had an added degree of accessibility and moved towards a more commercial approach. *The Grand Illusion*, released in 1977, was Shaw's first major success, peaking at number 6 during its nine-month stay on the *Billboard* album chart. It also featured the number 8-peaking single, 'Sail Away'. *Pieces Of Eight* and *Cornerstone* consolidated their success, with the latter containing 'Babe', the band's first number 1 single in the USA. *Paradise Theater* was Styx's *tour de force*, a complex, laser-etched concept album, complete with elaborate and expensive packaging. It generated two further US Top 10 hits in 'The Best Of Times' and 'Too Much Time On My Hands'. The album became their most successful ever, and also stayed at number 1 for three weeks on the album chart. *Kilroy Was Here* followed, yet another concept album, which brought them close to repetition. A watered-down pop-rock album with a big-budget production, its success came on the back of their previous album rather than on its own merits. *Caught In The Act* was an uninspired live offering. They disbanded shortly after its release. Styx re-formed in 1990 with the original line-up, except for pop-rock funkster Glenn Burtnick, who replaced Tommy Shaw (who had joined Damn Yankees). *Edge Of The Century* indicated that the band still had something to offer, with a diverse and classy selection of contemporary AOR. As one of the tracks on the album stated, the group were self-evidently 'Not Dead Yet'.

● ALBUMS: *Styx* (Wooden Nickel 1972)★★, *Styx II* (Wooden Nickel 1973)★★★, *The Serpent Is Rising* (Wooden Nickel 1973)★★★, *Man Of Miracles* (Wooden Nickel 1974)★★★, *Equinox* (A&M 1975)★★★, *Crystal Ball* (A&M 1976)★★★, *The Grand Illusion* (A&M 1977)★★★, *Pieces Of Eight* (A&M 1978)★★★, *Cornerstone* (A&M 1979)★★★, *Paradise Theater* (A&M 1980)★★★★, *Kilroy Was Here* (A&M 1983)★★★, *Caught In The Act/Live* (A&M 1984)★★, *Edge Of The Century* (A&M 1990)★★★, *Return To Paradise* (CMC International 1997).

● COMPILATIONS: *The Best Of Styx* (A&M 1979)★★★, *Classics Volume 15* (A&M 1987)★★★.

● VIDEOS: *Caught In The Act* (1984), *Return To Paradise* (BMG 1997).

SUBHUMANS

Influential Vancouver hardcore band who did much of the groundwork for later Canadian left-field outfits. However, the Subhumans are possibly more famous for their contribution to and inclusion in 'ecological terrorism' activities. Charges included bombing a plant that made guidance systems for nuclear missiles, dynamiting a hydro-power station and fire-bombing pornography shops. Gerry 'Useless' Hannah (bass) was the band member implicated and tried, along with four others, and received a 10-year custodial sentence. The Subhumans had already marked out their ability to challenge the conventions of the punk movement with *Incorrect Thoughts*' 'Slave To My Dick', an indictment of male stupidity that went against the grain of the macho ethos of 'hardcore' music. The rest of the original band featured Brian 'Wimpy Boy' Goble (vocals, ex-Skulls), Mike Graham (guitar) and Greg 'Dimwit' James (drums). James was replaced by Jim Iwagama on drums when he joined Pointed Sticks, until he returned when that band split. Gerry Useless would quit the band after his sentence as he became more interested in environmental issues (he wanted to become a forest warden). Iwagama also chose this moment to depart, for reasons of pure lethargy. The returning James was joined by a new bass player, Ron, again from Vancouver. Goble and James would go on to pursue a lengthy career in D.O.A.. James is the elder brother of original D.O.A. drummer Chuck Biscuits (later Circle Jerks, Black Flag, Danzig, etc.). Historically, the 'guerrilla' activities overshadowed the career of one of the few hardcore bands capable of writing bracing, fully realized songs with a rare lyrical poignancy.

● ALBUMS: *Incorrect Thoughts* (Friends 1980)★★★, *No Wishes, No Prayers* (SST 1983)★★★.

SUGAR

In the aftermath of Nirvana's commercial breakthrough unhinging a flood of loud, powerful and uncompromising USA-based music, Bob Mould (b. 16 October 1960, Malone, New York, USA; guitar, vocals) found himself subject to the somewhat unflattering representation 'Godfather of Grunge'. The ex-Hüsker Dü songwriter earned this accolade on the back of his former group's considerable influence, but with Sugar he seemed set to continue to justify the critical plaudits that have followed his every move. Joined by David Barbe (b. 30 September 1963, Atlanta, USA; bass, vocals, ex-

Mercyland) and Malcolm Travis (b. 15 February 1953, Niskayuna, New York, USA; drums, ex-Zulus), he found another powerful triumvirate to augment his own muse. Barbe proved particularly complementary - a talented songwriter in his own right, his presence as a forthright and intelligent counterpoint mirrored the contribution Grant Hart made to Hüsker Dü. Sugar's breakthrough, most visibly in the UK, came with the arrival of *Copper Blue* in 1992. Populated by energetic, evocative, and determinedly melodic pop noise, the album found critics grasping for superlatives. The Hüsker Dü comparisons were inevitable, but Mould was now viewed as an all-conquering prodigal son. Singles such as 'Changes' tied the band's musical muscle to a straightforward commercial skeleton, and daytime radio play became an unlikely but welcome recipient of Sugar's crossover appeal. The legendarily contrary Mould responded a few months later with *Beaster*; in which the melodies and hooks, though still present, were buried under layers of harsh feedback and noise. Ultimately as rewarding as previous work, its appearance nevertheless reminded long-term Mould watchers of his brilliant but pedantic nature. *F.U.E.L.* offered a hybrid of the approaches on the two previous albums, and again saw Mould venerated in the press, if not with the same fawning abandon that *Copper Blue* had produced. Afterwards, however, Mould ruminated widely about his doubts over the long-term future of Sugar, suggesting inner-band tensions between the trio. Mould confirmed this in spring 1996, stating that 'it wasn't fun anymore'. Travis joined Customized and Barbe was standing in with Buzzhungry. Mould wasted no time in recording and issuing another excellent solo album in April 1996.

● ALBUMS: *Copper Blue* (Creation 1992)★★★★, *Beaster* mini-album (Creation 1993)★★★★, *F.U.E.L. (File Under Easy Listening)* (Creation 1994)★★.

● COMPILATIONS: *Besides* (Rykodisk 1995)★★.

SUGAR RAY

One of an increasing number of US bands in the 90s to combine hip-hop beats with heavy metal riffs following Rage Against The Machine's breakthrough, Sugar Ray comprise Mark McGrath (vocals), Rodney Sheppard (b. *c.*1966; guitar), Murphy Karges (b. *c.*1966; bass), Stan Frazier (b. *c.*1968; drums) and DJ Homicide (b. Craig Bullock, *c.*1971; turntables). Their lyrical concerns can be gauged by the fact that their debut album's title was based on an advertisement in a pornographic magazine. Or, as McGrath put it: 'We're meat-eating, beer-drinking pigs from America.' Heavily promoted by their record company on both sides of the ocean, their songs were undoubtedly punchy and charismatic in a grubby, Beastie Boys-styled fashion, but beyond its effortless vulgarity there was little musical innovation to distinguish it from their peers.

● ALBUMS: *Lemonade And Brownies* (Atlantic 1995)★★, *Floored* (Atlantic 1997)★★★.

SUGARCREEK

This top-class pomp-rock group emerged from North Carolina, USA. The band were formed in 1981 by vocalist Tim Clark and guitarist Jerry West. Recruiting Rick Lee (keyboards), Robbie Hegler (bass) and Lynn Samples (drums), they drew inspiration from the popular AOR rock artists of the day (Journey, Styx and Kansas). They made a significant breakthrough with *Fortune*, a highly melodic album swathed in keyboards and silky-smooth vocal harmonies. Michael Hough was added as a second guitarist for *Rock The Night Away*, which marked a more commercial slant to the band's songwriting. He quit shortly after the album was released and the band subsequently shortened their name to Creek in 1986.

● ALBUMS: *Live At The Roxy* (Beaver 1981)★★★, *Fortune* (Beaver 1982)★★★★, *Rock The Night Away* (Ripete 1984)★★★, *Sugarcreek* (Music For Nations 1985)★★★.

SUICIDAL TENDENCIES

Vocalist Mike Muir formed Suicidal Tendencies in the early 80s in the Venice Beach area of Los Angeles, California, USA, enlisting Grant Estes (guitar), Louiche Mayorga (bass) and Amery Smith (drums). Despite an inauspicious start, being voted 'worst band and biggest assholes' in *Flipside* magazine's 1982 polls, the band produced a hardcore classic in *Suicidal Tendencies*, and although they initially fell between hardcore punk and thrash stools, MTV's support of 'Institutionalized' helped the group take off. *Join The Army* was recorded with respected guitarist Rocky George and drummer R.J. Herrera replacing Estes and Smith, and the skateboarding anthem, 'Possessed To Skate', kept the group in the ascendancy. *How Will I Laugh Tomorrow...When I Can't Even Smile Today?* marked the debut of Mike Clark (rhythm guitar) as the group's sound exploded, extending from a balladic title track to the furious 'Trip At The Brain'. This progression continued on *Controlled By Hatred/Feel Like Shit...Deja Vu*, but as the band's stature increased, so did their problems. Their name and image were easy targets for both the PMRC and the California police, with the former blaming teenage suicides on a band who were unable to play near their home-town due to performance permit refusals from the police, who feared Suicidal Tendencies were an LA gang. Naturally, the outspoken Muir fought vehemently against these bizarre accusations and treatment. Talented bassist Robert Trujillo, with whom Muir formed Infectious Grooves in tandem with Suicidal, made his debut on the excellent *Lights...Cameras...Revolution*, which produced hits in the defiant 'You Can't Bring Me Down' and 'Send Me Your Money', a vitriolic attack on television evangelist preachers. The band also re-recorded their debut during these sessions for release as *Still Cyco After All These Years*. The Peter Collins-produced *The Art Of Rebellion*, with new drummer Josh Freece, was a more ambitious, diverse work, and rather more lightweight than previous albums. Any fears that the band was mellowing were dispelled by furious live shows. *Suicidal For Life*, with Jimmy DeGrasso (ex-White Lion/Y&T) replacing Freece, emphasized the point as the band returned in fast-paced and profanity-peppered style, while continuing to extend individual talents to the full. Shortly after its release, in 1995 news filtered through that the band were no more. However, in 1997, Muir returned with new material and a revamped line-up, featuring Mike Clark and Dean Pleasants (guitars), Josh Paul (bass) and Brooks Wackerman (drums).

● ALBUMS: *Suicidal Tendencies* (Frontier 1983)★★★, *Join The Army* (Caroline/Virgin 1987)★★★, *How Will I Laugh Tomorrow...When I Can't Even Smile Today* (Epic 1988)★★★, *Controlled By Hatred/Feel Like Shit...Deja Vu* (Epic 1989)★★, *Lights...Camera...Revolution* (Epic 1990)★★★, *The Art Of Rebellion* (Epic 1992)★★★, *Still Cyco After All These Years* (Epic 1993)★★★, *Suicidal For Life* (Epic 1994)★★★.

● COMPILATIONS: *FNG* (Virgin 1992)★★★, *Prime Cuts* features two new tracks (Epic 1997).

SUN CITY GIRLS

Formed in the early 80s in Phoenix, Arizona, USA, this wildly eclectic and disorientating trio evolved from a local band named Paris 1984 (who also featured Maureen Tucker of the Velvet Underground). Sun City Girls was officially formed in 1982 by brothers Alan and Rick Bishop and percussionist Charles Gocher. Their name derived from a projected retirement community close to Phoenix. In common with other counter-culture theorists such as Negativland and Consolidated, the trio have embarked on a career clouded by misinformation and media pranks. Their first performance came as support to hardcore band Black Flag before a bemused punk rock crowd - it would not be the last audience they would confound. In addition to the albums listed, the group have issued over a hundred 7-inch singles and over 20 cassettes for their own Cloaven tape label. Their productions have incorporated, at various times, acid rock, experimental jazz, sound collage, chants, surf, folk and world music. Stage performances feature mock Kabuki theatre, extended comic sketches (such as their 1994 San Francisco show where they appeared as tramps singing around a campfire) and deranged rants at their audiences. Their subjects have included Nancy Reagan, Napoleon, space travel and dinosaurs. In the early 90s the group relocated to Seattle, founding their own record label, Abduction Recordings. They also immersed themselves in soundtrack work, though the films concerned are so obscure even members of the group's inner circle claim not to have seen them. With a catalogue of nearly a thousand songs, only two Sun City Girls CDs are currently available, a testament to the group's missionary devotion to vinyl and their utter lack of concern at fiscal probity.

● ALBUMS: *Sun City Girls* (Placebo 1984)★★★, *Grotto Of Miracles* (Placebo 1986)★★★, *Midnight Cowboys From Ipanema* (Amarillo 1986)★★★, *Horse Cock Phepner* (Placebo 1987)★★★, *Torch Of The Mystics* (Tupelo 1990)★★★, *Dawn Of The Devi* (Majora 1991)★★★, *Live From Planet Boomerang* (Majora 1992)★★, *Bright Surroundings Dark Beginnings* (Majora 1993)★★★, *C.O.N. Artists* (Poon Village 1993)★★★, *Valentines From Matahari* (Majora 1993)★★★, *Kaliflower* (Abduction 1993)★★★, *Juggernaut* film soundtrack (Abduction 1993)★★, *Piasa ... Devourer Of Men* film soundtrack (Abduction 1994)★★.

SUNNY DAY REAL ESTATE

Formed in Seattle during 1992, this rock quartet was yet another excellent hopeful from this fertile area of the West Coast. The band comprised Dan Hoerner (b. 13 May 1969, Seattle, Washington, USA; guitar, vocals), Jeremy Enigk (b. 16 July 1974, Seattle, Washington, USA; guitar, vocals), Nate Mendel (b. 2 December 1968, Seattle, Washington, USA; bass) and William Goldsmith (b. 4 July 1972, Seattle, Washington, USA; drums). They financed a debut single, 'Song Number 8/Song Number 9', on their own One Day I Stopped Breathing label and eventually signed with Sub Pop Records in 1994. Their debut, *Diary*, was locally acclaimed but shortly after its release Mendel and Goldsmith defected to form the Foo Fighters and the band effectively collapsed. In October 1995 a self-titled belated second album was released with a minimalist cover design that seemed to deliberately discourage any sales. The ghastly plain pink cover had the band's name printed in minuscule type. Inside, apart from the track listing, was a small picture of a fly. The music, however, was quite excellent, blending Seattle grunge with melodic pop.

● ALBUMS: *Diary* (Sub Pop 1994)★★★, *Sunny Day Real Estate* (Sub Pop 1995)★★★.

SURFACE

This Birmingham, England-based hard rock group was formed in 1986 by Gez Finnegan (vocals), Mark Davies (guitar), Loz Rabone (guitar), Dean Field (keyboards), Ian Hawkins (bass) and Jamie Hawkins (drums). They styled themselves on the successful US AOR formula of groups such as Journey, and signed to the independent Killerwatt label, where they debuted with *Race The Night*, which was recorded live. The album failed and the band returned to their former part-time status.

● ALBUMS: *Race The Night* (Killerwatt 1986)★★.

SURGIN

This US melodic hard rock group was founded in 1984 by former Rest members Tommy Swift (drums) and Jack Ponti (guitar, vocals). Enlisting the services of Russel Arcara (vocals), John Capra (keyboards), Gay Shapiro (keyboards) and Michael King (bass, vocals), they debuted in 1985 with *When Midnight Comes*. This featured the Bon Jovi track, 'Shot Through The Heart', which was written by Ponti and Jon Bon Jovi, while they were both part of Rest. Elsewhere the album was comprised of infectious hard rock anthems, underscored by strong melody lines, and was critically acclaimed at the time of release. In spite of tours supporting Aerosmith and Ratt, Surgin failed to achieve commercial success. As Ponti concentrated on session work and composing for other artists, Surgin became redundant.

● ALBUMS: *When Midnight Comes* (Music For Nations 1985)★★★.

SURRENDER

This Canadian hard rock quintet was formed in 1978 by Alfie Zappacosta (vocals, guitar), Steve Jenson (guitar), Peter Curry (keyboards), Geoff Waddington (bass) and Paul Delaney (drums). Incorporating elements of Rush, Triumph and Yes in their music over the course of two excellent albums characterized by extended guitar-keyboard interplay, they nevertheless failed to find an appreciative audience. Curry and Waddington quit in 1983 and the remaining trio continued as Zappacosta.

● ALBUMS: *Surrender* (Capitol 1979)★★★★, *No Surrender* (Capitol 1982)★★★★. As Zappacosta: *Zappacosta* (Capitol 1984)★★, *A To Z* (Capitol 1987)★★.

SURVIVOR

This sophisticated melodic US rock group was put together by guitarists Jim Peterik (formerly of Ides Of March) and Frankie Sullivan in 1978. Recruiting vocalist Dave Bickler, they recorded their self-titled debut as a three-piece. This featured a *pot-pourri* of ideas that had no definite direction or style. They expanded the band to a quintet in 1981, with the addition of Marc Doubray (drums) and Stephen Ellis (bass). From this point on, the band were comparable in approach to the AOR rock styles of Styx, Foreigner and Journey, but never achieved the same degree of recognition or success. Their first short-lived flirtation with glory came with the song 'Eye Of The Tiger', used as the theme to the *Rocky III* film. The single, with its heavy drumbeat and rousing chorus, became a worldwide number 1 hit, and is still a staple of FM radio and various advertising campaigns. Unfortunately, the rest of the songs on the album of the same name were patchy in comparison. Nevertheless, the work succeeded on the strength of the title cut, peaking at numbers 2 and 12 on the US and UK album charts, respectively. *Caught In The Game*, released the following year, was a more satisfying album. It adopted a heavier approach and featured a more up-front guitar sound from Sullivan, but did not find favour with the record-buying public. Bickler was fired at this stage and replaced by ex-Cobra vocalist Jimi Jamison, whose vocals added an extra, almost soulful dimension to the band. The resulting *Vital Signs* gave the band their second breakthrough. It enjoyed a six-month residency on the *Billboard* album chart, reaching number 16 as its highest position, and also spawned two Top 10 hits with 'High On You' and 'The Search Is Over'. They recorded 'Burning Heart' (essentially a re-tread of 'Eye Of The Tiger') as the theme song to *Rocky IV* in 1986 and achieved another international hit, reaching number 5 on the UK singles chart. Surprisingly, the song was not included on *When Seconds Count*, which pursued a heavier direction once more. The band had contracted to a three-piece nucleus of Jamison, Sullivan and Peterik at this juncture and had used session musicians to finish the album. *Too Hot To Sleep* was probably the most consistent and strongest album of the band's career, featuring a collection of commercially minded, hard rock anthems. The album made little commercial impact and the group finally disbanded in 1989.

● ALBUMS: *Survivor* (Scotti Bros 1979)★★, *Premonition* (Scotti Bros 1981)★★, *Eye Of The Tiger* (Scotti Bros 1982)★★, *Caught In The Game* (Scotti Bros 1983)★★, *Vital Signs* (Scotti Bros 1984)★★★, *When Seconds Count* (Scotti Bros 1986)★★, *Too Hot To Sleep* (Scotti Bros 1988)★★★.
● COMPILATIONS: *Best Of* (Scotti Bros 1989)★★★.

SVEN GALI

This Toronto, Canada-based group was formed in 1988 by guitarists Dee Cernile and Frank Cernile, vocalist Dave Wanless (b. London, England), and bassist Shawn Maher after the members had accumulated professional experience as backing musicians for a number of Canadian acts, but had tired of their anonymous status. Enlisting New York session drummer Gregg Gerson, the band spent their formative years on the domestic club circuit, honing an accessible, yet raw, metal sound that would serve them well. Their self-titled debut and ensuing live shows, including a UK tour with Wolfsbane, drew comparisons to Skid Row (USA) in style, delivery and stage performance. *Sven Gali* went on to sell over 100,000 copies in Canada alone. The group's second album featured new drummer Mike Ferguson and production from Kelly Gray, whose previous successes included Candlebox's debut. It also included guest appearances from Chris Thorn (Blind Melon), and Kevin Martin and Scott Mercado of Candlebox. It was a marked departure from the debut, which was unsurprising given the material for that album had originaly been written as far back as 1990. However, for a band once captioned as 'surmounting the difficulties facing traditional metal in post-grunge times', it was strange to hear songs so redolent of Soundgarden and Alice In Chains. Drummer Mike Ferguson joined in 1995. Their second album recorded in Seattle featured guest appearances from members of Blind Melon, Candlebox and Sweaty Nipples.

● ALBUMS: *Sven Gali* (Ariola/BMG 1993)★★★★, *Inwire* (RCA 1995)★★★.

SWANS

Like many early 80s American bands determined to stretch the boundaries of musical cacophony, the Swans were drawn to the thriving New York underground that has also produced Jim Thirlwell (Foetus), Lydia Lunch and Sonic Youth. Although the band have endured numerous line-up changes, the Swans always centred on singer Michael Gira and, later, Jarboe. After a raucous debut EP in 1982, *Speak*, the band released the influential *Filth* on the German Zensor label, which attracted a strong European audience. In 1984 came *Cop* on their own Kelvin 422 label, their first record to appear in the UK. Although *Cop* was awash with harsh guitars and awkward, dirge-like sounds, it was more readily accessible than *Filth*. So too, despite the title, was the subsequent EP, *Raping A Slave*, in March 1985. 'Time Is Money (Bastard)' began 1986 with a typically uncompromising title, preceding *Greed* in February. Themes of depravity, sex, death and the more sinister aspects of human nature prevailed, further explored on *Holy Money* and 'A Screw' later that year. In 1987 the band moved to Product Inc. for a double album, *Children Of The God*, although another less official effort, *Public Castration Is A Good Idea*, also surfaced that year. Most of 1987 was taken up with Jarboe's new project, Skin (who released three albums), although there was a limited German-only Swans release, *Real Love*. Another double album, 1988's *Feel Good Now*, emerged on the Rough Trade Records-distributed Love label. Meanwhile, a sinister cover version of Joy Division's 'Love Will Tear Us Apart' climbed the indie charts in June, resulting in a contract with MCA Records. 'Saved', the Swans' first single for the major label in April 1989, revealed a definite shift towards mainstream rock, further evident on *The Burning World*: The sombre approach was still there, but the ingredients were more aurally palatable. The band also seemed to have worked out of their collective system their monstrous live assaults on audiences, which were generally too painful and horrifically loud to be anything other than an exercise in art-house shock tactic indulgence. 'Can't Find My Way Home' was far more melodic than earlier singles and it seemed that Swans were on the brink of crossing over to a much wider audience. However, for the next two years they concentrated on reissues of early material on Gira's own Young God label. In May 1991 the band issued *White Light From The Mouth Of Infinity*, which was both commercial and innovative, illustrating the way in which Gira and companions could always command the attention of those willing to experiment a little in their listening tastes. In 1995 Gira released his first book, *The Consumer And Other Stories*, through Henry Rollins' 21/3/61 publishing house, in tandem with the Swans' latest recording venture, a relatively restrained and accessible collection dubbed *The Great Annihilator*. It was accompanied by Gira's debut solo album, *Drainland*. Following a tour in support of 1996's *Soundtracks For The Blind*, however, the Swans announced their demise.

● ALBUMS: *Filth* (Zensor/Neutral 1983)★★★, *Cop* (K.422 1984)★★, *Greed* (PVC 1986)★★★, *Holy Money* (PVC 1986)★★★, *Children Of The God* (Product Inc/Caroline 1987)★★★★, *Feel Good Now* (Love 1988)★★★, *The Burning World* (Uni-MCA 1989)★★★, *White Light From The Mouth Of Infinity* (Young God 1991)★★★, *The Great Annihilator* (Young God 1995)★★★, *Die Tur Ist Zu* (Rough Trade 1996)★★★, *Soundtracks For The Blind* (Young God 1996)★★★.
Solo: Michael Gira *Drainland* (Young God 1995)★★★, *Swans Are Dead* (Release 1998)★★.

● FURTHER READING: *The Consumer And Other Stories*, Michael Gira.

SWEATY NIPPLES

Unattractively titled heavy metal band, whose name legendarily arrived from the following scenario: 'The temperature was 198 degrees in a bakery. Olga, a 240lb dominating boss, had just finished chastising Davey, Brian and Dave for makig bread loaves in a phallic form when her shirt sleeve got caught in a mixer'. This hapless misogynistic tale continues until it results in Dave (rechristened Davey Nipples; bass) burrowing his head into the lady's mammaries to disengage her from the machine. An inauspicious start for the band, which also featured the aforementioned Brian Lehfeldt (vocals, percussion) and Dave Merrick (vocals, samples), as well as Ryan Moore (guitar). The group have built a healthy following in their native north-west America on the back of compulsive live performances not seen in that region since the heyday of Poison Idea. In the process they have picked up awards at the 1991 Portland Music Association ceremony (best alternative/metal act) and the 1992 PMA equivalent for best live show. With this behind them they joined the North West leg of the 1992 Lollapalooza tour, sharing a stage with Faith No More, Bad Brains and others. Their debut album was recorded for Nastymix (predominantly a rap outlet) with Rick Parashar (Alice In Chains, Pearl Jam) and Kelly Gray (Candlebox) at the controls. Scheduled for release in October 1991, Nastymix subsequently entered receivership and the resulting mire of lawyers and officialdom placed Sweaty Nipples in stasis. They persevered by playing live and adding two new members, Scott Heard (vocals, guitar) and Hans Wagner (drums), eventually gaining a new deal with Megaforce (Music For Nations in the UK). After an eponymous single, the group made their long-playing debut with *Bug Harvest*. This, despite the group's grisly moniker, weighed in with a highly effective, and somewhat fearsome three guitar/two drummers attack.

● ALBUMS: *Bug Harvest* (Megaforce 1994)★★★.

SWEET SAVAGE

This melodic hard rock quartet was formed in Belfast, Northern Ireland, in 1979 by guitarists Vivian Campbell and Trevor Fleming. Recruiting bassist David Haller and drummer David Bates, they achieved their first break by landing the support slots on 1981 tours by Motörhead and Wishbone Ash. Debuting the same year with 'Take No Prisoners'/'Killing Time', the future looked very bright for the band. A UK tour supporting Thin Lizzy was followed by an impressive session on UK DJ Tommy Vance's *Friday Rock Show* ('Eye of The Storm' appeared on the compilation, *Friday Rock Show II*). Two further singles, 'Straight Through The Heart' (1981) and 'The Raid' (1981), were released, before Campbell accepted the offer to join Ronnie James Dio. Four rewritten Sweet Savage tracks appeared on Dio's *Holy Diver*. The band continued with Ian Wilson as Campbell's replacement. However, he proved an inadequate substitute and the band folded in 1984, after the re-release of 'Straight Through The Heart'.

● ALBUMS: *Rune* (Neat Metal 1998)★★★.

SWEET SISTER

Spanish heavy metal band formed in 1990 with a line-up of Tete (vocals, guitar), Pedro (guitar, keyboards), Toni (bass) and Jordi (drums). They recorded their first demo in 1992. Two others followed before they entered the studio in 1994 to record 22 tracks, of which 12 were selected for their debut album with Music For Nations subsidiary Under One Flag. Reflecting varied musical tastes running from the Cure to Guns N'Roses via U2, the album attracted a degree of press support but sales were limited outside of their homeland.

● ALBUMS: *Flora And Fauna* (Under One Flag 1994)★★★.

SWORD

This Canadian heavy metal quartet was formed in Montreal in 1981 by vocalist Rick Hughes and drummer Dan Hughes. Augmented by Mike Plant (guitar) and Mike Larock (bass), it took the band five years to secure a recording contract. Finally signing to Aquarius Records in 1986, in the same year they released *Metalized*, which paid respect to both the early 80s British scene and older groups such as Black Sabbath and Rainbow. Sword then secured support slots on the Alice Cooper and Metallica tours of 1987, regaling audiences with a primal example of early power metal. *Sweet Dreams*, released in 1988, consolidated this approach: monstrously aching riffs and gut-wrenching guitar breaks, encased within dynamic and melodic arrangements. Sword were an excellent unit, but through a lack of image and record company backing, their commercial prospects were ultimately compromised, and they broke up in 1991.

● ALBUMS: *Metalized* (Aquarius 1986)★★★, *Sweet Dreams* (Aquarius 1988)★★.

SYE

This Canadian hard rock group was formed in 1981 by Phillipino-born vocalist/guitarist Bernie Carlos. Based in Toronto, Carlos joined forces with bassist and fellow countryman Phillipino Gunner San Augustin. The duo joined the Metal Blade label and debuted with *Turn On The Night* in 1985. Session musician Ray Cincinnato played drums on the album, but Steve Ferguson was recruited as a permanent addition after the work was released. Sye's music featured some impressive guitar parts, but was ultimately hampered by the weak and indistinct vocals. It would be four years before a follow-up appeared, by which time their name had largely been forgotten.

● ALBUMS: *Turn On The Fire* (Metal Blade 1985)★★★, *Winds Of Change* (Loudspell 1989)★.

SYMPOSIUM

London-based Symposium were at the forefront of the wave of adolescent power-pop bands signed up on the back of Ash's success. Formed at school in Kensington, West London, the band comprise ex-choirboys Wojtek Godzizsz (bass), Ross Cummins (vocals), Joe Birch (drums), Will McGonacle (guitar) and Hagop Tehaparian (guitar). Originally known as the Jump Puppets, they built up an exciting live reputation on the strength of a few gigs, selling out the 100 Club in July 1996 barely a month after they had finished their education. Support slots for Ash and Bis followed, along with several bans on account of their fans' tendency to vandalize venues.

After signing to Ash's label, Infectious, they released their debut single, 'Farewell To Twilight', followed by the euphoric 'Drink The Sunshine'. Despite suffering the setback of having Andrew Lloyd-Webber declare them his favourite pop group, the band continued to be championed by the music press, and played on the *New Musical Express*'s Brats tour in January 1997. Following their third top 40 single, 'The Answer To Why I Hate You', Cummins managed to break his leg during an overly energetic performance. The release of their debut mini-album in November 1997 ensured more glowing press coverage. With production by Clive Langer and Alan Winstanley (Madness, Morrissey, Elvis Costello), the eight-song set captured the raw vigour and youthful enthusiasm of their live shows in all its noisy, tuneful glory. Their debut full-length album was more refined, indicating that the band were beginning to mature musically.

● ALBUMS: *One Day At A Time* mini-album (Infectious 1997)★★★, *On The Outside* (Infectious 1998)★★★.

T

T-Ride

This innovative trio originated in Santa Clara, California, where childhood friends Eric Valentine (drums) and Dan Arlie (bass, vocals) linked up with guitarist Jeff Tyson to produce an effective blend of musical influences and styles. Signed to Hollywood Records, the band rejected the label's offers of major production names such as Eddie Kramer in favour of their drummer, who had already amassed considerable production experience with a variety of acts, in addition to producing the excellent demo that clinched their contract. Valentine duly made a sterling job of *T-Ride*. The band were compared most obviously to Queen and Van Halen owing to the sheer variety of the material, high-quality musicianship and songwriting, and stunning vocal harmonies, but the delivery also had sufficient humour and individuality to give the band their own identity. The debut attracted a succession of positive reviews, moving Joe Satriani to describe the band as the future of metal, and T-Ride were equal to the task of transferring their songs to the live arena. However, the album simply disappeared, and the band have been quiet since.

● ALBUMS: *T-Ride* (Hollywood 1992)★★★.

T.A.S.S.

German heavy metal trio who combine the industrial approach of Front 242 with more conventional metal riffing for a result not unlike that produced in recent years by Machine Head. Formed in Berlin by ex-Voodoo Club members 'The Voodoo' and 'Dr. Rabe', they expanded to a trio in the summer of 1992 with the addition of American singer and lyricist Collier. Their combination of monolithic guitars, pounding dance rhythms and intelligent sampling recalled Nine Inch Nails at their most pummelling.

● ALBUMS: *Maniafesto* (Gun 1994)★★★, *Suck* (Gun 1996)★★★★.

Tad

The monolithic noise engine that is Tad was formed in Seattle, USA, in 1988, by Tad Doyle (b. Idaho; vocals, guitar) and Kurt Danielson (bass), who had previously been working together with the delightfully titled Bundles Of Piss. Fellow miscreants Gary Thorstensen (guitar) and Josh Sinder (drums) joined later. With the rise of the American north-west and the Sub Pop label in particular, Tad became pre-eminent among that label's bands - though in truth there was always a strong metallic undercurrent that set them aside from the traditional hardcore-rooted sound of grunge. Lyrically too, as *God's Ball* all too clearly demonstrates, they were closer in style to Black Sabbath than Black Flag (song titles included 'Nipple Belt' and 'Satan's Chainsaw'). Whatever, the career of Tad has always proved entertaining. Sharing a touring van with Nirvana in 1989 on their first European jaunt they were ideally placed to see the destruction of the Berlin wall, though on a later European excursion they were offered the perfect contrast when the Belfast hotel in which they were staying was bombed by the IRA (the explosive device malfunctioned). *Salt Lick* saw production from Steve Albini (Big Black, Rapeman, Shellac) and, understandably, was even noisier as a result. *8-Way Santa* earned much of its notoriety from a sleeve that featured a man fondling a woman's breast - an endearing picture found in a garage-sale photo album. However, this prompted a legal suit in 1991 by the woman concerned (and her second husband) that forced its removal. That was hardly the end of the group's travails, however. On their US tour with Primus in the summer of the same year they narrowly missed being struck by lightning. The following year in Canada, further calamity was averted when a mountain boulder descended and crashed through their van, just behind the driver's seat. Moving to Music For Nations for 1993's *Inhaler*, bad-tempered songs such as 'Grease Box' and 'Lycanthrope' suggested little compromise in attitude. Tad Doyle, meanwhile, enjoyed minor celebrity status with a small part in Cameron Crowe's *Singles* film, before his band made their debut for a major label with 1995's *Infrared Riding Hood*.

● ALBUMS: *God's Balls* (Sub Pop 1989)★★★, *Salt Lick* (Sub Pop 1990)★★★, *8-Way Santa* (Sub Pop 1991)★★★, *Inhaler* (Music For Nations 1993)★★★, *Live Alien Broadcast* (Music For Nations 1994)★★, *Infrared Riding Hood* (East West 1995)★★★.

TAFFOLA, JOEY

b. *c*.1965, USA. Beginning his career on the guitar at the age of 14, Joey Taffola served his apprenticeship with the unremarkable speed-metal outfit Jag Panzer. In 1987 he left the band and returned to California to take instruction from guitar guru Tony Macalpine. Moving to the Guitar Institute Of Technology, Taffola studied jazz, rock and classical styles alongside Paul Gilbert (later of Racer X). After recording a series of demos, Shrapnel boss Mike Varney signed Taffola to produce a guitar instrumental album. With the help of former Jag Panzer drummer Reynold Carlson and ex-Rising Force bassist Wally Voss, *Out Of The Sun* appeared in 1987. Although the album featured guest appearances by Paul Gilbert (guitar) and Tony Macalpine (keyboards), it lacked both direction and individuality. Taffola's style proved a characterless hybrid of Yngwie Malmsteen's, Macalpine's and Vinnie Moore's styles. After an aborted band project featuring ex-Rising Force vocalist Mark Boals, Taffola started work on his second album, *Infa Red*.

● ALBUMS: *Out Of The Sun* (Roadrunner 1987)★★, *Infa Red* (Roadrunner 1991)★★★.

TALAS

This US hard rock outfit was masterminded by bass virtuoso Billy Sheehan. Enlisting the services of former Chain Reaction vocalist Phil Naro, guitarist Mitch Perry and drummer Mark Miller, they specialized in melodic, guitar-orientated rock with a strong commercial edge. After the release of a self-financed debut album in 1980 the band began to build up a small, but loyal fanbase. This attracted the attention of Food For Thought Records. Enjoying a larger budget, Talas delivered *Sink Your Teeth Into That* in 1982. This was a showcase for Sheehan's amazing bass work and featured 'Shyboy', which he later re-recorded with David Lee Roth. At this point the band were put on hold, as Sheehan helped out UFO on their European tour. After a fruitless association with Steve Stevens, Sheehan put Talas back on the road and recorded *Live Speed On Ice* in 1983. The album did not sell and the band became redundant as Sheehan then left to join Roth's band and later formed Mr. Big.

● ALBUMS: *Talas* (Relativity 1980)★★★, *Sink Your Teeth Into That* (Food For Thought 1982)★★★★, *Live Speed On Ice* (Important 1983)★★.

● COMPILATIONS: *The Talas Years* (Combat 1990)★★★.

TALION

This UK speed-metal quartet, formerly known as Trojan, formed in 1988, the line-up comprising Graeme Wyatt (vocals), Pete Wadeson (guitar), Phil Gavin (bass) and Johnny Lee Jackson (drums). Influenced by Metallica, Megadeth and Judas Priest, their niche was uninspired and at times amateurish speed metal. Signed to the independent Major Records, they debuted with *Killing The World* in 1989. This was a fairly lacklustre recording that ensured that the band did not progress beyond pub-rock status.

● ALBUMS: *Killing The World* (Major 1989)★★.

TALISMAN

This Swedish melodic heavy metal band was founded in 1989 by ex-Rising Force bassist Marcel Jacob. Recruiting vocalist Jeff Scott Soto and guitarist Christopher Stahl, they joined Airplay Records and made their debut the following year with a self-titled album, incorporating elements of Europe, Yngwie Malmsteen and TNT. High-pitched vocal harmonies and bursts of fiery guitar were the band's trademarks, but they failed to make an impression outside Sweden.

● ALBUMS: *Talisman* (Airplay 1990)★★★, *Life* (Now & Then 1995)★★★.

TALL STORIES

This cult AOR band was formed in New York, USA, in 1988 by vocalist/guitarist Steve Augeri. The Tall Stories line-up settled with the addition of lead guitarist Jack Morer and the experienced rhythm section of Tom DeFaria (drums) and Kevin Totoian (bass). The latter had replaced Anthony Esposito (bass), who would join Lynch Mob, while numerous early drummers included the Damn Yankees' Michael Cartellone. The band's abilities developed as they played the clubs around the tri-state area of New York, New Jersey and Connecticut, and they were signed by Epic Records. The Frank Fillipetti-produced *Tall Stories* was universally hailed as an AOR classic, with an artful guitar-based delivery reminiscent of Tyketto. Augeri's vocals evoked Journey's Steve Perry and Strangeways' Terry Brock in addition to Tyketto's Danny Vaughn. However, like many good 90s AOR albums, *Tall Stories* remains an undiscovered gem, and the band have been quiet since. Augeri departed to join Tyketto in 1995.

● ALBUMS: *Tall Stories* (Epic 1991)★★★★.

TANGIER

This US hard rock outfit have adopted a different style on each of their albums to date. Formed in 1984 by vocalist Bill Matson and guitarist/songwriter Doug Gordon, they initially played blues-based hard rock, which paid respect to Free, Molly Hatchet and Bad Company. With Rocco Mazella (guitar), Mike Kost (bass) and Mark Hopkins (drums) completing the line-up, they toured frequently but failed to make a breakthrough. Five years after formation, Matson and Gordon returned with Gari Saint (guitar), Garry Nutt (bass) and Bobby Bender (drums) to record *Four Winds*. The first act to be signed to Atco, the band offered a sophisticated sound that leaned towards mainstream AOR with blues undercurrents. Matson and Saint quit in 1990, with Mike Le Compte taking over vocal duties and the band contracting to a four-piece in the process. *Stranded* emerged the following year and saw the band diversifying their approach and toughening their act. The hybrid was a little awkward at times, but more often achieved the desired end result of producing radio-friendly material with memorable choruses.

● ALBUMS: *Four Winds* (Atco 1989)★★★, *Stranded* (Atco 1991)★★★.

TANK

This UK band, led by Algy Ward (bass, vocals, ex-Damned) with brothers Peter (guitar) and Mark Brabbs (drums), were dogged throughout their career by a reputation as Motörhead copyists stemming from their *Filth Hounds Of Hades* debut. The band's early power trio stance obviously owed much to Motörhead, although their songwriting style and sense of humour set them apart, and they were given a very hot reception by the notoriously intolerant Motörhead crowd on the *Iron Fist* tour. *Power Of The Hunter* showed distinct progression and included a fun cover version of the Osmonds' 'Crazy Horses', but the collapse of Kamaflage Records shortly after the release was a setback. Undaunted, Tank emerged as a quartet with ex-White Spirit guitarist Mick Tucker on *This Means War*, an impressive concept album but this too was unsuccessful, and the Brabbs brothers departed. Tank recorded two further albums, adding Cliff Evans (guitar) and drummers Graeme Crallan (on *Honour And Blood*) and Gary Taylor (on *Tank*) without any upturn in their fortunes. Tucker departed prior to the release of the latter, and the band split in 1989 after an ill-fated US club tour.

● ALBUMS: *Filth Hounds Of Hades* (Kamaflage 1982)★★★, *Power Of The Hunter* (Kamaflage 1982)★★★★, *This Means War* (Music For Nations 1983)★★★★, *Honour And Blood* (Music For Nations 1985)★★, *Tank* (GWR 1988)★★.

TANKARD

Formed in 1982, German thrash metal band Tankard are determined to live up to their country's reputation as a nation of beer drinkers. Heavy drinking while on tour, relaxing, or in the studio is hardly uncommon in the rock world, but Tankard's interest in alcohol borders on the obsessive. Always light-hearted and loud, typical song titles include 'The Morning After' and 'Beermuda', which are delivered in a drunken assault of punk-influenced thrash guitars. While they are something of an institution on the European mainland, this has never translated into acceptance in the UK or US markets. *Tankwart* is an oddity, released only in their domestic market, consisting of covers of traditional German drinking songs. The previous year's *Two Faced* had seen the band take a more conventional approach to their craft with the intention of producing 'serious' music. It was not a happy compromise.

● ALBUMS: *Zombie Attack* (Noise 1985)★★★, *Chemical Invasion* (Noise 1987)★★★, *The Morning After* (Noise 1988)★★★, *Hair Of The Dog* (Noise 1990)★★, *The Meaning Of Life* (Noise 1990)★★★, *Fat, Ugly, Live* (Noise 1991)★★, *Stone Cold Sober* (Noise 1992)★★★, *Alien* (Noise 1993)★★★, *Two Faced* (Noise 1993)★★, *Tankwart* (Noise 1994)★, *Disco Destroyer* (Century Media 1998)★★★.

TASTE

A popular blues-rock attraction, Taste was formed in Cork, Eire in 1966 when Eric Kittringham (bass) and Norman Damery (drums) joined Rory Gallagher (b. 2 March 1949, Ballyshannon, Co. Donegal, Eire, d. 15 June 1995), erstwhile guitarist with the Impact Showband. The new group became a leading attraction in Ireland and in Germany, but in 1968 Gallagher replaced the original rhythm section with Charlie McCracken (bass) and John Wilson (ex-Them) on drums. The new line-up then became a part of London's burgeoning blues and progressive circuit. Their debut, *Taste*, was one of the era's most popular releases, and featured several in-concert favourites, including 'Same Old Story' and 'Sugar Mama'. *On The Boards* was another commercial success, and the group seemed poised to inherit the power-trio mantle vacated by Cream. However, the unit broke up in October 1970 following a rancorous split between

Gallagher and his colleagues. The guitarist then began a fruitful solo career until his untimely death in 1995.

● ALBUMS: *Taste* (Polydor 1969)★★★, *On The Boards* (Polydor 1970)★★★★, *Live Taste* (Polydor 1971)★★, *Live At The Isle Of Wight* (Polydor 1972)★★.

● COMPILATIONS: *The Greatest Rock Sensation* (Polydor 1985)★★★.

TATTOO RODEO

Previously known as White Sister, an ultra-sophisticated funk-tinged hard-rock outfit, the band switched name and changed image somewhat during 1991, in order to secure a major recording contract. With acoustic and blues influences replacing the soul/funk elements, the band aimed at the same market as Tesla, Bon Jovi and Def Leppard. Comprising Dennis Churchill-Dries (vocals, bass), Rick Chadock (guitar), Michael Lord (keyboards) and Rich Wright (drums), the band specialize in highly infectious and melodic song structures, characterized by an impassioned vocal delivery. Picked up by Atlantic, they debuted with *Rode Hard, Put Away Wet* and received a positive, if slightly guarded, media response. This comprised 13 blues-based rock anthems that had both guts and style. Their image was rather understated and as a result, they failed to attract the degree of attention that their talents deserved.

● ALBUMS: *Rode Hard, Put Away Wet* (1991)★★★, *Skin* (Mausoleum 1995)★★★.

TATTOOED LOVE BOYS

This UK rock quartet was formed in 1987 by vocalist Gary Mielle and drummer Mick Ransome (ex-Praying Mantis). With Chris 'CJ' Jagdhar (guitar) and Darayus Z. Kaye (bass) completing the line-up, they drew inspiration from the New York Dolls, Ramones and Hanoi Rocks. *Bleeding Hearts And Needle Marks* in 1988 proved they could write instant, if ultimately disposable, sleazy rock anthems that possessed a degree of naïve charm. The album sold poorly and the band disintegrated in 1989. Jagdhar went on to join the Wildhearts. They were resurrected in 1991 with the nucleus of Ransome and Mielle plus new recruits Dean Marshall (bass), Nick Singleton (guitar) and Chris Danby (rhythm guitar). *No Time For Nursery Rhymes*'s attempt at a more sophisticated approach did not work. The result was an amateurish affair that hinted at plagiarism of Guns N'Roses. Ransome resurfaced in 1995 in a new band called the Gang Show, which also featured former members of Dogs D'Amour and Motörhead.

● ALBUMS: *Bleeding Hearts And Needle Marks* (Razor 1988)★★★, *No Time For Nursery Rhymes* (Music For Nations 1990)★★.

TEA PARTY

Formed in Canada in 1990, the Tea Party comprise Jeff Martin (guitars, vocals), Stuart Chatwood (bass, backing vocals) and Jeff Burrows (drums, percussion). The group's climactic, highly atmospheric debut album of 1993, *Splendor Solis*, produced immediate comparisons with both the Doors and Led Zeppelin. Well-crafted musical compositions complemented Martin's singing style, which was based on his early appreciation of blues artists such as B.B. King and Howlin' Wolf. His detached, broody lyrics also added to the record's sense of doomed adventure. It later achieved platinum status in Canada. The follow-up collection, *The Edge Of Twilight*, used over 31 instruments in the studio, notably eastern-flavoured strings and percussion. As *Melody Maker* commented, it was a 'ravaged, bluesy, shamanic holler that bleeds decadence and sex'. The introduction of world music into their otherwise hard rock songs seemed to invite further Led Zeppelin comparisons. Full of sophisticated musicianship and technical ability, *The Edge Of Twilight* was an interesting contrast to rock's mid-90s flirtation with punk minimalism.

● ALBUMS: *Splendor Solis* (Chrysalis 1993)★★★, *The Edge Of Twilight* (Chrysalis 1995)★★★, *Transmission* (Atlantic 1997)★★.

TEDDYBEARS STHLM

While Sweden has long been renowned for its output of metal and hard rock bands, Teddybears STHLM can claim to be the country's first genuine hardcore punk act to have made an international impression. Based in Stockholm, the group was founded in 1991 by Pat Scab (vocals), Jocko Apa (bass), Glenn (drums) and Klas Åhlund (guitar). Their debut single, 'Women In Pain', was released in that year, and helped to establish a strong underground following for the group's abrasive punk songs. Support slots to bands such as Rage Against The Machine and Faith No More furthered their reputation, though their appearance at the Hultsfred Rock Festival prompted one noted rock critic to describe them as the worst band he had ever seen. Offered a recording contract by a multinational record label days after the festival, Teddybears STHLM typically turned it down in favour of staying with the Swedish independent MNW Records. Their 1993 debut album, *You Are*

Teddybears, condensed 17 songs into 37 minutes. It also proved that the group could extend their music beyond a basic hardcore framework, with flourishes of psychedelia and jazz (taking its cue from the Minutemen's 80s work). Scab is also an accomplished painter, with his work having been exhibited in a number of Stockholm art galleries. Drummer Glenn is also a proficient cartoonist, with a long track-record of published work behind him.

● ALBUMS: *You Are Teddybears* (MNW 1993)★★★.

TEMPEST, JOEY

b. 19 August 1963, Stockholm, Sweden. The former lead vocalist of the heavy rock group Europe, his distinctive voice being internationally known from the success of 'The Final Countdown' in 1986. His self-titled debut was issued in 1995 and contained a selection of good-quality songs, most of which contained at least one melodic hook. Well-produced, well sung, well played - but it all added up to little. Tempest had taken a more mainstream pop direction that some of his followers found too retro. Tracks such as 'We Come Alive' and 'Pleasure And Pain' were instantly appealing, but had little aftertaste.

● ALBUMS: *A Place To Call Home* (Polygram 1995)★★★.

TEN YEARS AFTER

Formed in Nottingham, England, as the Jaybirds in 1965, they abandoned their pedestrian title for a name that slotted in with the booming underground progressive music scene. The quartet of Alvin Lee (b. 19 December 1944, Nottingham, England; guitar, vocals), Chick Churchill (b. 2 January 1949, Mold, Flint/Clywd, Wales; keyboards), Ric Lee (b. 20 October 1945, Cannock, Staffordshire, England; drums) and Leo Lyons (b. 30 November 1943, Bedford, England; bass) played a mixture of rock 'n' roll and blues that distinguished them from the mainstream blues of Fleetwood Mac, Chicken Shack and Savoy Brown. Their debut album was largely ignored and it took months of gruelling club work to establish their claim. The superb live *Undead*, recorded at Klooks Kleek club, spread the word that Lee was not only an outstanding guitarist, but he was the fastest by a mile. Unfortunately for the other three members, Lee overshadowed them to the extent that they became merely backing musicians in what was described as the Alvin Lee show. The band began a series of US tours that gave them the record of more US tours than any other UK band. Lee's furious performance of 'Goin' Home' at the Woodstock Festival was one of the highlights, although that song became a millstone for them. Over the next two years they delivered four solid albums, which all charted in the UK and the USA. *Ssssh*, with its Graham Nash cover photography, was the strongest. 'Stoned Woman' epitomized their sound and style, although it was 'Love Like A Man' from *Cricklewood Green* that gave them their only UK hit (number 10, June 1970). *A Space In Time* saw them briefly relinquish guitar-based pieces in favour of electronics. By the time of *Rock 'N' Roll Music To The World* the band were jaded and they rested from touring to work on solo projects. This resulted in Lee's *On The Road To Freedom* with gospel singer Mylon LeFevre and a dull album from Chick Churchill, *You And Me*. When they reconvened, their spark and will had all but gone and remaining albums were poor. After months of rumour, Lee admitted that the band had broken up. In 1978 Lee formed the trio Ten Years Later, with little reaction, and in 1989 the original band reformed and released *About Time*, but only their most loyal fans were interested. The band was still active in the early 90s.

● ALBUMS: *Ten Years After* (Deram 1967)★★★, *Undead* (Deram 1968)★★★★, *Stonedhenge* (Deram 1969)★★★, *Ssssh* (Deram 1969)★★★★, *Cricklewood Green* (Deram 1970)★★★★, *Watt* (Deram 1970)★★★, *A Space In Time* (Chrysalis 1971)★★★, *Rock 'N' Roll Music To The World* (Chrysalis 1972)★★, *Recorded Live* (Chrysalis 1973)★★, *Positive Vibrations* (Chrysalis 1974)★★, *About Time* (Chrysalis 1989)★★.

● COMPILATIONS: *Alvin Lee & Company* (Deram 1972)★★★, *Goin' Home! - Their Greatest Hits* (Deram 1975)★★★, *Original Recordings Volume 1* (1987)★★★, *The Essential* (Chrysalis 1992)★★★★, *Solid Rock* (Chrysalis 1997)★★★.

TERRAPLANE

Terraplane evolved in the early 80s in south London as Nuthin' Fancy, the post-school band of Danny Bowes (vocals) and Luke Morley (guitar). By 1983 they had evolved into Terraplane with the addition of Nick Linden (bass) and Gary James (drums). The band soon became fixtures on the London circuit, playing at the Reading Festival before releasing an independent single, 'I Survive'. Suitably impressed, Epic Records signed Terraplane, but the young band perhaps took too much notice of advice about image and style from their label and management, who chose to emphasize a poppier direction, away from the band's melodic hard rock roots. When the debut finally emerged, the humorous original title of *Talking To God* (later *You*) *On The Great White Telephone* had been replaced by the bland *Black & White*. While the quality of Morley's songwriting was obvious, the production resulted in a slick pop sound in contrast to the band's rockier live appraoch, given a heavier edge with the addition of rhythm guitarist Rudi Riviere (ex-Sapphire). *Black & White* was only a moderate success but failed to break the lucrative pop market, and *Moving Target*, recorded without the departed Riviere (to America and session work), was rather directionless, with the band folding a year later. Morley, Bowes and James regrouped with much greater success in Thunder, perhaps demonstrating what might have been for Terraplane had the band been left to develop in their own right.

● ALBUMS: *Black & White* (Epic 1986)★★, *Moving Target* (Epic 1987)★★.

TERRORIZER

This American quartet were more of a project than a real band, featuring the Morbid Angel rhythm section of Pete Sandoval (drums) and David Vincent (bass, vocals), in collaboration with the Californian-based duo of Oscar Garcia (vocals) and Jesse Pintado (guitar). Terrorizer broke up when Morbid Angel's emergence from the underground death metal scene meant that Sandoval and Vincent no longer had time to spare. *World Downfall*, however, was a definitive grindcore album, given a fierce sound by producer Vincent and engineer Scott Burns. Sandoval and Vincent produced their customary tight performance to ensure effective delivery of often highly paced material, while Pintado showed the ability and aggression that was to lead to his subsequent recruitment to the Napalm Death ranks - which just left Garcia to growl and spit outrage through largely politicized, hardcore-influenced lyrics. A second album remains unreleased.

● ALBUMS: *World Downfall* (Earache 1989)★★★.

TERRORVISION

This quartet from Bradford, England formed in 1986 as Spoilt Bratz, and quickly fused rock, funk and thrash influences into an infectiously upbeat pop-metal style. Singer Tony Wright (b. 6 May 1968, Yorkshire, England), guitarist Mark Yates (b. 4 April 1968, Bradford, Yorkshire, England), Leigh Marklew (b. 10 August 1968, England; bass), and Shutty (b. 20 March 1967, England; drums) were signed by EMI Records on the strength of their 'Pump Action Sunshine' demo, and negotiated the formation of their own label name, Total Vegas. Two remixed demo tracks, 'Urban Space Crime' and 'Jason', appeared on the *Thrive* EP as Terrorvision followed a hectic touring schedule prior to the release of *Formaldehyde*. The debut produced minor hits in 'American TV' and 'New Policy One', and was backed by UK and European tours with the Ramones and Motörhead, respectively, while Def Leppard frontman Joe Elliott was sufficiently impressed to invite Terrorvision to open Leppard's 1993 show at Sheffield's Don Valley Stadium. 1994 proved to be quite a year for Terrorvision, beginning with their UK Top 30 breakthrough with 'My House'. *How To Make Friends And Influence People* emerged to rave reviews and entered the UK Top 20, bringing the band their first silver disc, and produced four more Top 30 singles in 'Oblivion', 'Middleman', 'Pretend Best Friend' and 'Alice, What's The Matter?'. They also played both the Reading and Donington Festivals, in addition to two sold-out UK tours and a series of European dates, before moving on to work on a new album in 1995. Major critical acclaim and healthy sales accompanied their most commercial and assured work to date with *Regular Urban Survivors*. Exactly 10 years after they were formed as the Spoilt Bratz, Terrorvision finally made the big screen.

● ALBUMS: *Formaldehyde* (Total Vegas 1992)★★★, *How To Make Friends And Influence People* (Total Vegas 1994)★★★★, *Regular Urban Survivors* (Total Vegas 1996)★★★★, *Shaving Peaches* (Total Vegas 1998)★★★★.

● VIDEOS: *Fired Up And Lairy* (PMI 1995).

TESLA

Originally known as City Kid, Tesla are a five-piece, blues-based, hard rock quintet from Sacramento, California, USA. Named after the scientist Nikola Tesla, the current line-up came together in 1985. The band comprises Jeff Keith (vocals), Tommy Skeoch (guitar, vocals), Frank Hannon (guitar, keyboards, vocals), Brian Wheat (bass, vocals) and Troy Lucketta (drums, ex-Eric Martin Band; Breathless). They signed to Geffen Records in 1986 and recorded *Mechanical Resonance*, a universally acclaimed debut that ranks alongside that of Montrose's first album in terms of setting new standards. The title was taken from one of Tesla's theories and combined raunchy metallic rock with blues and rock 'n' roll influences. Jeff Keith's impassioned vocals gave the material an added dimension, as the songs alternated between passionate, gut-wrenching ballads and crazy, fuel-injected rockers. The album eventually took off in the USA, reaching number 32 on the *Billboard* chart. *The Great Radio Controversy* saw the band rapidly maturing, with a highly polished, but no-less energetic collection of songs that were saturated with infectious riffs and subtle hooklines. The ballad, 'Love Song', became a Top 10 hit, while the album climbed to number 18 on the US charts. Tesla's third collection created something of a precedent, a live album that was totally acoustic and included a number of inspired cover versions. It highlighted the band's humour, technical excellence and ability to entertain. *Psychotic Supper* showed they could easily switch back to power-mode, with a near 70-minute onslaught of high-energy hard rock numbers. Tesla defy convention and have no gimmicks, nor do they conform to any particular image, choosing instead to tour relentlessly (for over a year to support *Psychotic Supper*, playing over 138 shows in the process). *Bust A Nut*, meanwhile, included a cover version of Joe South's 'Games People Play', and offered a further blast of superbly declaimed traditional, neo-purist, heavy metal.

● ALBUMS: *Mechanical Resonance* (Geffen 1986)★★★, *The Great Radio Controversy* (Geffen 1989)★★★, *Five Man Acoustical Jam* (Geffen 1990)★★★, *Psychotic Supper* (Geffen 1991)★★★★, *Bust A Nut* (Geffen 1994)★★★.

● COMPILATIONS: *Time's Makin' Changes: The Best Of Tesla* (Geffen 1995)★★★.

● VIDEOS: *Time's Making Changes - The Videos And More* (1995).

TESTAMENT

This US thrash act was one of the first to emerge from San Francisco's Bay Area in Metallica's wake in the 80s. Originally formed as Legacy in 1983, becoming Testament two years later, the line-up included vocalist Steve Souza alongside Alex Skolnick (lead guitar, replacing original guitarist Derek Ramirez), Eric Peterson (rhythm guitar), Greg Christian (bass), and Louie Clemente (drums). However, Souza soon departed for Exodus and was replaced by giant frontman Chuck Billy. *The Legacy* was a ferocious introduction, quickly establishing Testament at the forefront of the burgeoning thrash scene. Following a live mini-album recorded at Holland's Dynamo Festival, *The New Order* consolidated their popularity with improved songwriting, producing the classic 'Disciples Of The Watch'. Skolnick, however, was losing interest in pure thrash, extending his undoubted talents by moonlighting in Stuart Hamm's touring band at one point, and his influence brought a more considered melodic power metal approach to *Practice What You Preach*, which worked superbly. However, *Souls Of Black* was rushed to coincide with the European Clash Of The Titans tour with Slayer, Megadeth and Suicidal Tendencies, and was consequently disappointing. After *The Ritual*, Skolnick joined Savatage and Clemente also departed. *Return To Apocalyptic City* introduced Glen Alvelais (guitar, ex-Forbidden) and John Tempesta (b. 1964, New York, USA; drums, ex-Exodus), but Alvelais' tenure was short-lived, with journeyman guitarist James Murphy (ex-Death, Obituary, Disincarnate, Cancer) stepping in for *Low*, which saw a return to their previous thrashing style. Tempesta subsequently joined White Zombie, and was replaced by John Dette (ex-Evil Dead). 1994's *Low* was the group's last record with Atlantic Records. A live album was released in 1995 on Eric Peterson's own Burnt Offering Records. Issued to raise funds to finance a new studio collection, it was followed by the band's appearance in the film *Strange Days* in which they performed a new song, 'New Eyes Of Old'. Dette left in 1996 to join Slayer and the band's future looked bleak.

● ALBUMS: *The Legacy* (Megaforce 1987)★★★★, *Live At Eindhoven* mini-album (Megaforce 1987)★★★, *The New Order* (Megaforce 1988)★★★★, *Practice What You Preach* (Megaforce 1989)★★★★, *Souls Of Black* (Megaforce 1990)★★, *The Ritual* (Atlantic 1992)★★★, *Return To Apocalyptic City* mini-album (Atlantic 1993)★★★, *Low* (East West 1994)★★★, *Live At The Fillmore* (Burnt Offerings 1995)★★, *Demonic* (Music For Nations 1997)★★★.

● COMPILATIONS: *Signs Of Chaos: The Best Of Testament* (Mayhem 1998)★★.

THE AGE OF ELECTRIC

This Canadian four-piece rock band was driven to early commercial and critical recognition on the strength of approving comments from producer Bob Rock, of Bon Jovi and Metallica fame. They formed in Maple Leaf, Regina, Canada, in 1989, around two sets of brothers; Todd Kearns (guitar, vocals), John Kearns (bass), Ryan Dahle (guitar) and Kurt Dahle (drums). They soon moved to the more receptive rock circuit in Vancouver, and released two independent CDs. The first was 1991's *The Latest Plague* album, followed by 1994's *Ugly* EP. Both were housed on their own God's Teeth Ethel label. *Ugly*, which had been written nearly three years previously but was delayed by the lack of interest from record companies, entered the Canadian Top 10 after Rock stepped in to produce and finance. 'The fact that it did so well was vindication for us that maybe we were doing the right thing after all', said Todd Kearns, which was the same conclusion reached by Mercury Records. They signed The Age Of Electric in 1995, but not before the group's second collection had already appeared on Cargo Records. A fine collection of power pop and astute, idiosyncratic lyrics, this mature collection confirmed the wisdom of Rock's original judgement and promised a high commercial profile for their major label debut, which they had already begun to write.

● ALBUMS: *The Latest Plague* (God's Teeth Ethel 1991)★★★, *The Age Of Electric* (God's Teeth Ethel/Cargo 1995)★★★.

THERAPY?

Northern Irish hard rock/indie metal trio comprising Andy Cairns (guitar, vocals), Michael McKeegan (b. Belfast; bass) and Fyfe Ewing (drums). Cairns and Ewing first met by chance at a charity concert in the late 80s. At that time both were playing in covers bands, but decided to begin writing together. McKeegan was drafted in for live support (having originally lent his bass to the duo's bedroom sessions) and the enduring Therapy? line-up was in place. They played their first gig supporting Decadence Within at Connor Art College in the summer of 1989, by which time they had already composed some 30 songs. After two demos failed to ignite attention from suitable labels, the band released their debut single, 'Meat Abstract'/'Punishment Kiss', on their own Multifuckingnational imprint. Following approving plays from John Peel the group found their way on to Wiiija Records, via the intervention of Silverfish's Leslie Rankine. Their debut single was then added to new material for a mini-album, *Baby Teeth*. This was followed in short order by a second abbreviated set, *Pleasure Death*. Both these collections went to number 1 in the UK indie charts, but the band remained hamstrung by lack of finance from their record company. Therapy? signed to A&M Records in 1992, and collected a much bigger budget for a new album, *Nurse*, and touring. However, at best the press were neutral about the record, which featured more complex arrangements and themes than the punk-descended speed burn-outs of earlier releases. The band's career was revitalized in March 1993 when 'Screamager' made the UK Top 10. Almost a year later *Troublegum* was unveiled, which returned to more familiar Therapy? elements - buzzsaw guitar, harsh but persistent melodies and musical adrenalin - aided by a cleaner, leaner production than had previously been the case. Nominated for the Mercury Music Prize - alongside the Prodigy, easily the most extreme record to be offered as a candidate - it enshrined Therapy?'s progress as the most commercially successful British band working in their territory. In 1995, *Infernal Love* offered a significant departure. Alongside the trademark grinding hardcore sound came ballads, string quartets and upbeat lyrics, indicating a band able to shed their old skins musically and lyrically, where it might have been easier to retread former glories. Ewing left the band in January 1996 and was eventually replaced by ex-My Little Funhouse Graham Hopkins (b. 1976). The band was further augmented by cellist Martin McCarrick. After a protracted absence they released *Semi-Detached*, an excellent return to their roots.

● ALBUMS: *Baby Teeth* mini-album (Wiiija 1991)★★, *Pleasure Death* mini-album (Wiiija 1992)★★★, *Nurse* (A&M 1992)★★★, *Troublegum* (A&M 1994)★★★★, *Infernal Love* (A&M 1995)★★, *Semi-Detached* (A&M 1998)★★★.

THIN LIZZY

Formed in Dublin, Eire, in 1969, this fondly remembered hard-rocking group comprised Phil Lynott (b. 20 August 1951, Dublin, Eire, d. 4 January 1986; vocals, bass), Eric Bell (b. 3 September 1947, Belfast, Northern Ireland; guitar) and Brian Downey (b. 27 January 1951, Dublin, Eire; drums). After signing to Decca Records, they issued two albums, neither of which charted. A change of fortune occurred after they recorded a novelty rock version of the traditional 'Whiskey In The Jar'. The single reached the UK Top 10 and popularized the group's blend of Irish folk and strident guitarwork. The group then underwent a series of line-up changes during early 1974. Bell was temporarily replaced by Gary Moore (b. 4 April 1952, Belfast, Northern Ireland), after which two more short term guitarists were recruited, Andy Gee and John Cann. The arrival of guitarists Brian Robertson (b. 12 September 1956, Glasgow, Scotland) and Scott Gorham (b. 17 March 1951, Santa Monica, California, USA) stabilized the group as they entered their most productive phase. A series of UK concerts throughout 1975 saw the group make considerable headway. 1976 was the breakthrough year with the acclaimed *Jailbreak* hitting the charts. The driving macho celebration of

'The Boys Are Back In Town' reached the UK Top 10 and US Top 20 and was voted single of the year by the influential *New Musical Express*. In early 1977 Robertson was forced to leave the group due to a hand injury following a fight and was replaced by the returning Moore. Another UK Top 20 hit followed with the scathing 'Don't Believe A Word', drawn from *Johnny The Fox*. Moore then returned to Colosseum and the recovered Robertson took his place. Both 'Dancin' In The Moonlight' and *Bad Reputation* were UK Top 10 hits and were soon followed by the excellent double album, *Live And Dangerous*. The torturous line-up changes continued apace. Robertson left in August 1978 and joined Wild Horses. Moore returned and helped record *Black Rose*, but within a year was replaced by Midge Ure (formerly of Slik and the Rich Kids).1979 saw the group scaling new commercial heights with such Top 20 singles as 'Waiting For An Alibi' and 'Do Anything You Want To', plus the best-selling *Black Rose*. By late 1979, the peripatetic Ure had moved on to Ultravox and was replaced by Snowy White. In early 1980, Lynott married Caroline Crowther, daughter of the television personality Leslie Crowther. After recording some solo work, Lynott reunited with Thin Lizzy for *Chinatown*, which included the controversial Top 10 single, 'Killer On The Loose'. The heavily promoted *Adventures Of Thin Lizzy* maintained their standing, before White bowed out on *Renegade*. He was replaced by John Sykes, formerly of the Tygers Of Pan Tang. One more album, *Thunder And Lightning*, followed before Lynott split up the group in the summer of 1984. A posthumous live album, *Life-Live*, was issued at the end of that year. Its title took on an ironically macabre significance two years later when Lynott died of heart failure and pneumonia after a drugs overdose. Four months later, in May 1986, Thin Lizzy re-formed for the Self Aid concert organized in Eire by Bob Geldof, who replaced Lynott on vocals for the day. The 90s found Brian Robertson touring with tribute band, Ain't Lizzy, while the original group's name remained on the lips of many young groups as a primary influence.

● ALBUMS: *Thin Lizzy* (Decca 1971)★★, *Shades Of A Blue Orphanage* (Decca 1972)★★, *Vagabonds Of The Western World* (Decca 1973)★★★, *Night Life* (Vertigo 1974)★★★, *Fighting* (Vertigo 1975)★★★, *Jailbreak* (Vertigo 1976)★★★★, *Johnny The Fox* (Vertigo 1976)★★★, *Bad Reputation* (Vertigo 1977)★★★, *Live And Dangerous* (Vertigo 1978)★★★★, *Black Rose* (Vertigo 1979)★★★, *Renegade* (Vertigo 1981)★★, *Thunder And Lightning* (Vertigo 1983)★★, *Life-Live* double album (Vertigo 1983)★★, *BBC Radio 1 Live In Concert* 1983 recording (Windsong 1992)★★★.

● COMPILATIONS: *Remembering - Part One* (Decca 1976)★★, *The Continuing Saga Of The Ageing Orphans* (Decca 1979)★★, *Rockers* (Decca 1981)★★, *Adventures Of Thin Lizzy* (Vertigo 1981)★★★, *Lizzy Killers* (Vertigo 1983)★★★, *The Collection* double album (Castle 1985)★★★, *The Best Of Phil Lynott And Thin Lizzy* (Telstar 1987)★★★, *Dedication - The Best Of Thin Lizzy* (Vertigo 1991)★★★★, *The Peel Sessions* (Strange Fruit 1994)★★, *Wild One - The Very Best Of ...* (Mercury 1995)★★★★.

● VIDEOS: *Live And Dangerous* (VCL 1986), *Dedication* (PMV 1991), *The Boys Are Back In Town* (Eagle Rock Entertainment 1998).

● FURTHER READING: *Songs For While I'm Away*, Philip Lynott. *Thin Lizzy*, Larry Pryce. *Philip*, Philip Lynott. *Thin Lizzy: The Approved Biography*, Chris Salewicz. *My Boy: The Philip Lynott Story*, Philomena Lynott with Jackie Hayden. *The Ballad Of The Thin Man*, Stuart Bailie.

THIRD EYE BLIND

Formed in the Bay area of San Francisco, California, USA, contemporary rock band Third Eye Blind are led by singer-songwriter Stephan Jenkins (b. USA). Said to be influenced equally by the Geto Boys and Joy Division, they began to attract a following through a series of high-profile performances, including a support slot to Oasis in San Francisco, before they were signed. They also took over the headliners' billing when Tim Booth of James was forced to cancel a series of concerts because of illness. Their first single, 'Semi-Charmed Life', duly became a number 1 hit on *Billboard*'s Modern Rock chart. It was a typical effort, in that, beneath the slick-surface pop sound, the lyrics portrayed 'a storm brewing'. Their self-titled debut album, produced by Jenkins and Eric Valentine, reached the *Billboard* Top 100 following its release in April 1997.

● ALBUMS: *Third Eye Blind* (Elektra 1997)★★★★.

38 SPECIAL

38 Special were formed in 1977 by guitarist and vocalist Donnie Van Zant (brother to Johnny of the Van Zant Band and Lynyrd Skynyrd's Ronnie), with Jeff Carlisi (guitar), Don Barnes (guitar), Larry Junstrom (bass) and drummers Steve Brookins and Jack Grodin. In keeping with fraternal tradition the band proffered Southern boogie/rock, though their

sound later slipped into AOR. Signed to A&M Records they had little impact outside of the southern states, but in 1979 scored a minor hit with 'Rocking Into The Night', which was followed by an album and major tour. With fame eluding them (despite further single success in 1980 with 'Hang On Loosely'), they dropped out of the scene in 1984, but made a comeback in 1986 and recorded the film theme to *Revenge Of The Nerds 2*. Barnes left soon afterwards, as did Brookins, both in attempts to launch their own bands. Danny Chauncey joined on guitar while Brookins was replaced by keyboard player Max Carol. 1988's *Rock N Roll Strategy* earned strong reviews, but after release the group lost their contract with A&M. *Bone Against Steel*, meanwhile, saw them return to a southern boogie framework without the AOR trappings and won many new supporters.

● ALBUMS: *38 Special* (A&M 1977), *Special Delivery* (A&M 1978), *Rockin' Into The Night* (A&M 1979), *Wild-Eyed Southern Boys* (A&M 1980), *Special Forces* (A&M 1982), *Tour De Force* (A&M 1983), *Strength In Numbers* (A&M 1987), *Rock N Roll Strategy* (A&M 1988), *Bone Against Steel* (Charisma 1991).

THOR

b. Jon-Mikl Thor. This body builder turned singer who took his name from a Marvel comic character, was a former Mr. Teenage USA, Mr. Canada and Mr. North America. His band consisted of vocalist Pantera (b. Rusty Hamilton, a former model), Steve Price (guitar), Keith Zazzi (bass) and Mike Favata (drums). Their debut release, *Keep The Dogs Away*, appeared on the Three Hats Record label in 1978. This album was an uneventful affair of basic hard rock/heavy metal which, even at the time of its release, sounded dated. Thor then took a long break until returning with the release of a mini-album, *Unchained*, in 1984. Then came Thor's most successful album, *Only The Strong*, released on Roadrunner in 1985. Much attention was paid to Thor's live party-piece - where, by blowing into it, he expanded and burst a rubber hot-water bottle (often with the claim 'let's see Michael Jackson do this'). Other 'theatricals' included staged clashes between Norse gods, with Thor resplendent in spiked body armour, wielding a mighty (plastic) sword or bearded axe - all conducted without the tiniest trace of irony, and an almost camp machismo from the group's frontman. 1985 proved an eventful year for Thor as not only did he have two singles, 'Let The Blood Run Red' and 'Thunder On The Tundra' (both from *Only The Strong*), released, but also a live album, *Live In Detroit*. That year also saw him enter the film world, appearing in and writing the soundtrack for *Recruits*. Part of the soundtrack formed the basis for Thor's next release, *Recruits: Wild In The Streets*. That marked the end of Thor's musical aspirations as he once again turned his attention to the movie business by appearing in *Zombie Nightmare* alongside original *Batman* star Adam West.

● ALBUMS: *Keep The Dogs Away* (Three Hats 1978)★★, *Unchained* mini-album (Ultra Noise 1984)★★★, *Only The Strong* (Roadrunner 1985)★★★, *Live In Detroit* (Raw Power 1985)★★, *Recruits: Wild In The Streets* (Roadrunner 1986)★★★.

● VIDEOS: *Live In London* (1985).

THOUGHT INDUSTRY

From Michigan, USA, Thought Industry comprise Brent Oberlin (vocals, bass), Dustin Donaldson (drums), Paul Enzio (guitar) and Chris Lee (guitar). Though often wrongly classified within the 'industrial' metal fraternity (the result not just of their name but also tours with Godflesh and Skinny Puppy), Thought Industry's sound is too relentlessly individual for either that or another pigeonhole, metal: 'To me most 'metal' bands rehash cliched musical/lyrical ideas and are very conservative in their output and viewpoints. We use the power of metal or punk without its parody or redundancy'. Any satisfactory description of the band's music would be hard pressed to deny the strong metallic undercurrent, however, which their dual guitar approach epitomizes. Critical guesses over *Songs For Insects* spanned the Jesus Lizard, Voivod and Primus, with lyrics that dealt with hallucinogenic drugs, violence and social alienation. For the lugubriously titled follow-up, subjects would be dealt with inside a more personal framework, but the musical onslaught continued unabated.

● ALBUMS: *Songs For Insects* (Music For Nations 1993)★★★, *Mods Carve The Pig: Assassins, Toads And God's Flesh* (Music For Nations 1994)★★★, *Black Umbrella* (Metal Blade 1997)★★★, *Recruited To Do Good Deeds For The Devil* (Metal Blade 1998)★★.

THRASHER

In June and July 1984 the US heavy metal label Combat funded a super session and enlisted Carl Canedy (drums) to write and produce an album's worth of material. Canedy formed a writing partnership with guitarist Andy MacDonald and they put the 'Thrasher' band together at the Music America Studios in New York. An impressive line-up was amassed: Kenny Aaronson (bass; Derringer, HSAS), Dickie Peterson (vocals; Blue Cheer), Billy Sheehan (bass; Talas), Mars Cowling (Pat Travers Band; bass), Maryann Scandiffio (Black Lace; vocals), Dan Spitz (guitar; Anthrax), Jack Starr (guitar; Virgin Stee), Rhett Forrester (vocals; Riot), Kim Simmonds (guitar; Savoy Brown), Gary Bordonaro (bass; Rods) and additional vocalists James Rivera, Leslie Dunn and Jackie Kenyon.

● ALBUMS: *Thrasher* (Music For Nations 1985)★★★.

3 Colours Red

Formed in London, England, in 1994, uninhibited hard rock band 3 Colours Red earned immediate comparisons to the Wildhearts, whom they duly supported through 1995. Comprising Pete Vuckovic (b. 16 February 1971, Tiveton, Devon, England; vocals, bass), Chris McCormack (b. 21 June 1973, South Shields, Tyne & Wear, England; guitar, and brother of Danny McCormack of the Wildhearts), Ben Harding (b. 31 January 1965, Stoke-On-Trent, England; guitar) and Keith Baxter (b. 19 February 1971, Morecombe, Lancashire, England; drums), their early stage show combined the earnest ferocity of the best garage rock with memorable pop hooklines. Despite this, the group were not quite as fresh to the rock scene as many had assumed - Vuckovic was formerly a member of the groundbreaking Diamond Head in their later period. Backed by a major management company, the group found themselves a further notable support slot in 1996 as 'first on the bill' to the Sex Pistols at the latter's re-formation concert at Finsbury Park, London. Doubtless this came as a result of McCormack and Baxter's work on Glen Matlock's 1996 solo album, *Who's He Think He Is When He's At Home?* At the same time their debut single, 'This Is My Hollywood', was released on *New Musical Express* journalist Simon Price's Fierce Panda label. Creation Records signed the band in late 1996 and Alan McGee was suitably modest when he claimed '3 Colours Red are the second best band in Britain' (after Oasis). The debut album, *Pure*, attempted to consolidate on the modest success of their chart singles.

● ALBUMS: *Pure* (Creation 1997)★★★.

311

Formed at high school in Omaha, Nebraska in 1990, hip-hop/rock crossover group 311 then relocated to Los Angeles, California, USA. There Nick Hexum (vocals, guitar), Timothy J. Mahoney (guitar), P-Nut (bass), SA Martinez (vocals, turntables) and Chad Sexton (drums) set about establishing their reputation. With the Red Hot Chili Peppers and Rage Against The Machine having popularized a cross-genre rock hybrid, 311 seemed to be a ripe commercial prospect. Unfortunately, neither of their initial album releases provided them with any commercial reward. Instead they concentrated on live work, playing with groups as diverse as Kiss and Cypress Hill. Their fortunes were transformed when 'Down' was released as a single in 1995 and was given rotation play on MTV. The single was housed on the group's self-titled third album, which as a consequence sold over a million copies.

● ALBUMS: *Music* (Capricorn/Mercury 1993), *Grassroots* (Capricorn/Mercury 1994), *311* (Capricorn/Mercury 1995), *Transistor* (Capricorn 1997).

Throbs

This short-lived band took shape in mid-1988 when Canadian vocalist Ronnie Sweetheart moved to New York to link up with Danny Nordahl (bass), Ronnie Magri (drums) and Swedish guitarist Roger Ericson. The Throbs were signed by Geffen Records after only their third live show in New York, and experimented with adding a second guitarist to the line-up, including one show with future Wildhearts mainman Ginger shortly after his departure from the Quireboys, before recording their debut as a quartet. The production team of one-time Alice Cooper collaborators Bob Ezrin and Dick Wagner was highly suited to the project, as the band clearly drew influences from the sleazier US rock of the early 70s along with later contemporaries such as Hanoi Rocks, although they lacked Cooper's sly lyrical wit. However, despite some enthusiastic reviews for the record, the ensuing live shows, which included a UK tour with Mr. Big, were poor, with the Throbs' performances failing to live up to their image. The band continued to work on the road for a while after losing their recording deal, but eventually disintegrated, with Ericson and Nordahl going on to form the Vibes.

● ALBUMS: *The Language Of Thieves And Vagabonds* (Geffen 1991)★★★.

Thunder

This UK hard rock quintet was heavily influenced by Bad Company and the Rolling Stones. Thunder evolved from the ashes of Terraplane, with the surviving nucleus of Danny Bowes (vocals), Luke Morley (guitar) and Gary James (drums) recruiting Mark Luckhurst (bass) and Ben Matthews (guitar) to complete the line-up. Moving away from the melodic power-pop of their former incarnation, they teamed up with producer Andy Taylor (ex-Duran Duran) to record *Backstreet Symphony*, a stunning album of bluesy rockers and atmospheric ballads, which received widespread critical acclaim. Their style is characterized by a dual guitar attack of alternating riffs and lead breaks, with Bowes' gritty and emotional vocals adding charisma and distinction. Live, the icing on the cake is drummer Gary James' erratic behaviour, which has included appearing in a tutu or offering impromptu Frank Sinatra impersonations. They landed the opening slot at Donington in 1990 and were the surprise success of the day. In 1991 they concentrated on the American market, touring extensively in an attempt to make the all-important breakthrough. However, though another strong collection, *Laughing On Judgement Day* was not the album to do it. 1993 saw Luckhurst (who would go on to join the David Coverdale/Jimmy Page touring band) depart in acrimony to be replaced by Mikael Hoglund (ex-Great King Rat). The title of their excellent third album, *Behind Closed Doors*, proved appropriate as the group had spent over 12 months recording the set in the USA with the aid of Aerosmith/AC/DC producer Mike Fraser. Thunder have retained the spirit of great hard rock bands of the 60s and 70s (Free, Bad Company) without sounding remotely dated. They are arguably the present leaders of the pack.

● ALBUMS: *Back Street Symphony* (EMI 1990)★★, *Laughing On Judgement Day* (EMI 1992)★★★, *Behind Closed Doors* (EMI 1995)★★★★, *Live Circuit* (EMI 1995)★★, *The Thrill Of It All* (B. Lucky Music 1996)★★★★, *Thunder Live In England* (Eagle 1998)★★★.

● COMPILATIONS: *Their Finest Hour (And A Bit): The Best Of Thunder* (EMI 1995)★★★.

● VIDEOS: *Back Street Symphony: The Videos* (PMI 1990), *Live* (Eagle Rock Entertainment 1998).

THUNDERHEAD

After an unsuccessful audition with Victory, American vocalist Ted Bullet met ex-Viva guitarist Henrik Wolter and ex-Talon bassist Ole Hempleman in a Hanover bar, and with the addition of drummer Alex Scotti to complete this German-based band, recorded a demo that quickly prompted a contract with Intercord. *Behind The Eight Ball* was recorded when the band had hardly played a live date, but was a reasonable debut in a basic metal style similar to the Almighty's early work, and sold well on the German market as the group played with Victory and Uriah Heep in the USA and in the UK and Europe with Motörhead. *Busted At The Border* and *Crime Pays* followed in the traditional metal footsteps of the debut, although Thunderhead became a more cohesive band as a result of their live work, with more power metal overtones to their heavily guitar-based sound. They maintained their level of success in Germany, undoubtedly helped by their frontman's English vocals and outrageous onstage demeanour, but they remained a minor act in global terms.

● ALBUMS: *Behind The Eight Ball* (Intercord 1989)★★★, *Busted At The Border* (Intercord 1990)★★★, *Crime Pays* (Intercord 1991)★★★.

THUNDERS, JOHNNY

b. John Anthony Genzale Jnr., 15 July 1952, New York City, New York, USA, d. 23 April 1991, New Orleans, Louisiana, USA. Johnny Thunders first gained recognition as a member of the New York Dolls, an aggregation that built a reputation for its hard R&B-influenced rock sound and glam/punk appearance in the early 70s. First calling himself Johnny Volume, the guitarist joined the high school band Johnny And The Jaywalkers, then a local band called Actress, which included in their line-up two other future Dolls members, Arthur Kane and Billy Murcia. Actress evolved into the New York Dolls in late 1971. Genzale, now renamed Johnny Thunders, recorded two albums for Mercury Records with the Dolls. After leaving the band in 1975 along with drummer Jerry Nolan, the pair formed a new band alongside ex-Television guitarist Richard Hell called the Heartbreakers. This line-up was completed with the addition of guitarist Walter Lure. Hell left the group soon afterwards to form the Voidoids, with Billy Wrath replacing him. Thunders and the Heartbreakers recorded prolifically for US and UK labels such as Track and Jungle Records. The group achieved greater popularity in the UK, where they were accepted as peers by early punk-rock bands that had idolized the Dolls. Thunders earned a reputation for his shambling stage performances owing to an excess of drugs and alcohol, and he often made unscheduled guest appearances with other artists. His first solo collection, *So Alone*, found him supported by many UK musicians, including Phil Lynott, Peter Perrett (Only Ones), Steve Jones and Paul Cook (Sex Pistols), Steve Marriott (Humble

Pie/Small Faces) and Paul Gray (Eddie And The Hot Rods/Damned). Thunders later gigged with fellow junkie Sid Vicious, in the Living Dead. The Heartbreakers broke up and re-formed numerous times, recording their last album together in 1984. Thunders then produced an album of 50s and 60s R&B/pop cover versions with singer Patti Palladin and an album with ex-MC5 guitarist Wayne Kramer. The latter featured a group called Gang War formed by Thunders and Kramer in the late 80s and early 90s. Despite the promise of all this activity, Thunders was found dead in a hotel room in New Orleans, Louisiana in mysterious circumstances in 1991. He was 38. Despite Thunders' notorious drug dependency, the autopsy failed to reveal the cause of death although later reports cited a heroin overdose.

● ALBUMS: *So Alone* (Real 1978)★★★★, *In Cold Blood* (New Rose 1983)★★★, *Too Much Junkie Business* cassette only (ROIR 1983)★★★, *Hurt Me* (New Rose 1984)★★★, *Que Sera Sera* (Jungle 1985)★★★, *Stations Of The Cross* cassette only (ROIR 1987)★★, with Patti Palladin *Copy Cats* (Restless 1988)★★★, *Gang War Featuring Johnny Thunders And Wayne Kramer* (Zodiac 1990)★, *Bootlegging The Bootleggers* (Jungle 1990)★★, *Live At Max's Kansas City '79* (ROIR 1996)★★★, *Have Faith* (Mutiny 1996)★★.

● COMPILATIONS: *Hurt Me* (Dojo 1995)★★★, *The Studio Bootlegs* (Dojo 1996)★★.

● FURTHER READING: *Johnny Thunders: In Cold Blood*, Nina Antonia.

THUNDERSTICK

Barry Graham, aka Thunderstick, began drumming for Iron Maiden in 1977; a year later he joined Samson where he spent the next three years as the New Wave Of British Heavy Metal's most controversial figure - the man in the rapist's mask. The image was indeed offensive and did little to elevate either his or Samson's career, but he was still a powerful drummer in the Keith Moon mould. Aside from appearing on Samson's three albums, *Survivors*, *Head On* and *Shock Tactics*, he also appeared on the Gillan set, *For Gillan Fans Only*. After Samson he teamed up with Gillan guitarist Bernie Torme in the Electric Gypsies, where he remained until forming Thunderstick the band in 1982. Adopting a more theatrical mask and outfit, he put together this Screaming Lord Sutch/Alice Cooper-styled outfit with Neil Hay (bass), Ben K. Reeve (guitar), Colin Heart (guitar) and Vinnie Monroe (vocals). In November 1983 they released a 12-inch EP entitled *Feel Like Rock 'N' Roll*, with a line-up featuring American singer Jodee Valentine and guitarists Wango Wiggins and Cris Martin replacing Heart, Monroe and Hay (the latter joining Julia Fordham's backing band), while Reeve switched to bass. Most press interest seemed to revolve around Valentine who played the 'pin up' role. The music was consequently largely forgotten and when their album came out in 1984, there was more concern about the pending marriage between Valentine and Graham. The band hacked away for another two years before splitting up (which was also what happened to the newlyweds). Graham later rejoined Paul Samson on two more projects but today he is more involved with music management.

● ALBUMS: *Beauty & The Beasts* (Thunderbolt 1984)★★★.

TIGERTAILZ

Tigertailz are a UK band renowned for their outrageous glam-rock looks as much as their music, which is also strongly influenced by 70s glam-rockers such as T. Rex and the Sweet. Formed in South Wales during 1984, they built up a loyal and vociferous following throughout the UK with a line-up featuring Stevie James (aka Steevi Jaimz; vocals), Jay Pepper (guitar), Pepsi Tate (bass) and Ace Fincham (b. USA; drums). The last-named pair had both worked in N.W.O.B.H.M. act Treason, and also Crash KO. Their first release, *Young And Crazy*, met with little critical acclaim, although their eternally loyal fans lapped it up. Stevie James departed soon afterwards in somewhat acrimonious circumstances, and went on to form St Jaimz. His replacement was Kim Hooker (ex-Rankelson) who provided vocals on the much stronger *Bezerk*. This release showcased Tigertailz as an equal to American acts such as Mötley Crüe in terms of penning instantly memorable, glam-rock anthems. Continuing to develop a loyal following, particularly in Japan, the writing was nonetheless on the wall when Finchum departed in 1992. The remaining trio (Tate, Pepper and Hooker) re-emerged a year later with a new band, Wazbones.

● ALBUMS: *Young And Crazy* (Music For Nations 1987)★★★★, *Bezerk* (Music For Nations 1990)★★★.

TOO MUCH JOY

From Westchester County in New York, USA, an affluent neighbourhood devoid of the ghetto culture celebrated in much rap parlance, Too Much Joy still managed to attract controversy in 1990. By performing cover versions of 2 Live Crew songs at a concert in Miami, Florida, they became the subjects of an obscenity case (later dismissed by jury). In the process they became rap's least likely victims of censorship. Their debut album, 1988's uninspiring *Son Of Sam I Am*, included a version of LL Cool J's 'That's A Lie'. However, by the advent of *Cereal Killers* they had performed what some critics termed 'a Beastie Boys in reverse' - moving from their hardcore hip hop roots into the hardcore punk of early Hüsker Dü.

● ALBUMS: *Son Of Sam I Am* (Alias 1988)★★★, *Cereal Killers* (Alias 1991)★★★.

TOOL

One of the leading new heavy metal acts of the 90s, Tool were formed in Los Angeles, USA, in 1990 by guitarist Adam Jones, vocalist Maynard James Keenan, bassist Paul D'Amour and drummer Danny Carey. All four band members are Lachrymologists, and the influence of this very personal and cathartic religion is evident in both the pained intensity of their music and lyrics based on personal experience and feelings. The mini-album, *Opiate*, was a powerful introduction to Tool's densely rhythmic style, with 'Hush' helping establish a buzz for the band; the accompanying video graphically displayed the song's anti-censorship slant of 'I can't say what I want to/Even if I'm not serious' as the band appeared naked with their mouths taped shut. European dates with friends Rage Against The Machine and a US tour with the Rollins Band helped to sharpen Tool's live performances. Their increased confidence was evident on *Undertow*, which featured a guest vocal from Henry Rollins on 'Bottom'. While the band retained their angry intensity and penchant for difficult lyrical subjects, their songwriting became more adventurous, culminating in the experimental ambient closer, 'Disgustipated' - lyrically, however, the track displayed a sense of humour that belied Tool's miserable image by protesting about a carrot's right to life, satirizing the politically correct movement. *Undertow* reached platinum status as the band toured extensively, including a stint on the 1993 Lollapalooza tour. *Aenima* was their most assured and most successful album, narrowly missing the top of the *Billboard* album chart in November 1996.

● ALBUMS: *Opiate* (Zoo 1992)★★, *Undertow* (Zoo 1993)★★★, *Aenima* (RCA 1996)★★★★.

TORMÉ, BERNIE

Irish guitarist who formed punk band Urge in 1976, came to London a year later to join Scrapyard and subsequently put together the Bernie Tormé band. In 1978 he appeared on the NEMS punk compilation, *Live At The Vortex*, which helped to raise his profile, and later he earned himself a solo contract with Jet Records. After three solo singles and numerous live appearances it was announced that he was to join the Ian Gillan Band where he remained until 1981, playing on three albums - *Mr Universe* (Acrobat 1979), *Glory Road* (Virgin 1980) and *Future Shock* (Virgin 1981). After Gillan he formed the Electric Gypsies with drummer Frank Noon (Def Leppard/Next Band) and Everton Williams on bass (formerly of punk group Bethnal). After one single, 'Shoorah Shoorah', Noon left and was briefly replaced by Thunderstick (Samson and his own, eponymous band). In March 1982 he flew to America to join Ozzy Osbourne's band as a replacement for the recently deceased Randy Rhoads. Two months later he returned to the UK and re-formed the Bernie Tormé band with Ron Rebel (Iron Maiden/McCoy) on drums, and bassist James C. Bond (Stampede). This line-up lasted until 1984 when he formed 'Tormé' with ex-Girl vocalist Phil Lewis. After a number of records the band split having gained little ground, and both Tormé and Lewis relocated to America. Lewis collaborated with members of W.A.S.P. and Guns N'Roses in L.A. Guns while Tormé joined ex-Twisted Sister vocalist Dee Snider in Desperados, where he remained for a year, eventually quitting due to the band's inactivity. Since then he has worked on various projects, though none have proved fruitful.

● ALBUMS: *Turn Out The Lights* (Kamaflage 1982)★★★, *Electric Gypsies* (Zebra 1983)★★★, *Live* (Zebra 1984)★★, *Back To Babylon* (Zebra 1985)★★★, *Die Pretty Die Young* (Heavy Metal 1987)★★★, *Official Bootleg* (Onsala International 1987)★★, *Are We There Yet* (Heavy Metal 1991)★★★.

TORONTO

By 1979 guitarist Brian Allen and drummer Jim Fox had broken away from the Canadian band Rose, with whom they had been since 1976, together with American bassist Nick Costello from Centaurus. This formed the nucleus of a band whose locality also lent them their name. The line-up was soon completed with Scott Kreyer (keyboards), Sheron Alton (guitar) and vocalist Holly Woods. Although they produced solid AOR material they never made it outside of their home country, despite both A&M Records and MCA Records releasing their albums in Europe. Costello and Fox had left by 1983 and the band were now more often billed as Holly Woods & Toronto. A final album was very much in the Lee Aaron vein and saw a marked improvement, but with falling sales, even at home, they folded.

● ALBUMS: *Lookin' For Trouble* (Solid Gold 1980)★★★, *Head On* (Solid Gold 1981)★★★, *Get It On Credit* (Solid Gold 1982)★★, *Girls Night Out* (Solid Gold 1983)★★, *Assault And Flattery* (Solid Gold 1984)★★★.

TOUCH

This cult AOR/pomp rock act evolved from American Tears, a band who released three albums in the USA in the mid-70s, when bassist/vocalist Doug Howard joined Craig Brooks (vocals, guitar), Glenn Kithcart (drums) and songwriter Mark Mangold (keyboards, vocals). Their self-titled debut has long been regarded as a neglected classic of the genre, featuring a strong collection of songs and a sound dominated by superb vocal harmonies and Mangold's impressive keyboard work. The band opened the bill for the inaugural Donington Festival in 1980, and passed into Donington folklore when Howard accidentally swallowed a bee while having a drink at the end of the set. Their best-known track, 'Don't You Know What Love Is', appeared on the compilation of live recordings from that day, *Monsters Of Rock*, but despite all the good press, the debut failed to sell significantly. A follow-up effort was recorded, with Todd Rundgren at the production helm, but the band split before it could be released, disenchanted with their record company and management. Two tracks from these sessions were included on a 1990 reissue of *Touch*. Mangold became a session musician, working with Brooks on Michael Bolton's early solo albums, before forming Drive, She Said with Al Fritsch.

● ALBUMS: *Touch* (Ariola 1980)★★★.

TRANCE SYNDICATE RECORDS

Trance Syndicate was formed in Austin, Texas, USA, in 1990, by King Coffey, drummer with the Butthole Surfers. It has quickly grown from humble origins to become one of the most cultish logos on the US underground. The label's sound reflects both the Buttholes' fondness for drugs-inspired mind adventures, lyrical oddness and sonic confrontation, as well as recalling an earlier generation of Texas groups, such as the Thirteenth Floor Elevators, whose Roky Erickson signed to the label in the mid-90s. Trance Syndicate has continued to operate on a contract-free basis, with financial and manufacturing support from Chicago's Touch & Go Records. Some of the best releases on the label have been from established stars the Pain Teens (Houston), My Dad Is Dead (Cleveland), Bedhead (Dallas), Sixteen Deluxe (Austin) and Starfish (Austin).

● ALBUMS: various *Cinco Anos!* (Trance Syndicate 1995)★★.

TRAPEZE

Formed in Wolverhampton, England in 1968, Trapeze were one of several local acts signed to the Moody Blues' label, Threshold Records. John Jones (vocals), Mel Galley (guitar, vocals), Terry Rowley (guitar), Glen Hughes (b. 21 August 1952, Cannock, Staffordshire, England; bass) and Dave Holland (bass) recorded a self-titled debut album, before Jones and Rowley were dropped from the line-up. Trapeze completed the Neil Slaven-produced *Medusa* and *You Are The Music* as a trio before Hughes replaced Roger Glover in Deep Purple in June 1973. However, the three musicians were latterly reunited, although the bassist dropped out in the midst of an ill-fated tour of the USA and embarked on a solo career. Galley and Holland then recruited Rob Kendrick (guitar) and Pete Wright (bass), issuing two albums for Warner Brothers Records before Pete Galby replaced Kendrick for a final Trapeze release entitled *Hold On/Running*.

● ALBUMS: *Trapeze* (Threshold 1970)★★★, *Medusa* (Threshold 1970)★★★, *You Are The Music...We're Just The Band* (Threshold 1972)★★, *Hot Wire* (Threshold 1974)★★★, *Trapeze* (Threshold 1975)★★, *Hold On/Running* (Threshold 1978)★★★, *Live In Texas* (Aura 1981)★★.

● COMPILATIONS: *Final Swing* (Threshold 1974)★★★, *Live In Texas: Dead Armadillos* (See For Miles 1997)★★★★.

TRAVERS, PAT, BAND

Canadian guitarist Pat Travers began his career playing in his brother's band. Having moved to London, he set up a group of his own consisting of Peter 'Mars' Cowling (bass) and drummer Roy Dyke (of Ashton, Gardner And Dyke). In 1976 they played at the Reading Rock Festival, and this led to greater recognition of their debut, *Pat Travers*. In 1977 Nicko McBrain, who subsequently joined Iron Maiden, replaced Roy Dyke. Travers himself turned his talents to songwriting, his music taking a more experimental turn, and being aided by other artists, including Scott Gorham. During their 1977 tour, Clive Edwards replaced McBrain, and

Michael Dycke added another guitar. Guitarist Pat Thrall, who had been a member of Automatic Man, and Tommy Aldridge (drums), formerly of Black Oak Arkansas, were recruited to work on *Heat In The Street*, an extremely powerful album. Their relationship with the band was short-lived, however. After the tour to support *Crash And Burn*, Thrall and Aldridge departed in order to work with Ozzy Osbourne. Subsequent recordings featured Sandy Gennaro (drums) and Michael Shrieve (ex-Santana), and were notable for their solid, blues-like sound. In 1984 the line-up of Pat Marchino (drums), Barry Dunaway (bass), Jerry Riggs (guitar) and Travers released *Hot Shot*, an album that was not a commercial success. There was then a lengthy break in Travers' recording career until 1990 when he released *School Of Hard Knocks*. The following year Travers was working again with Thrall, Aldridge and Cowling, touring Japan along with Jerry Riggs and Scott Zymowski, and planning a reunion album. After this came a series of blues-orientated albums, including the well-received *Blues Tracks* and *Blues Magnet*.

● ALBUMS: *Pat Travers* (Polydor 1976)★★★, *Makin' Magic* (Polydor 1977)★★★, *Putting It Straight* (Polydor 1977)★★★, *Heat In The Street* (Polydor 1978)★★★, *Go For What You Know* (Polydor 1979)★★★, *Crash And Burn* (Polydor 1980)★★★, *Radio Active* (Polydor 1981)★★★, *Black Pearl* (Polydor 1982)★★★, *Hot Shot* (Polydor 1984)★★★, *School Of Hard Knocks* (Razor 1990)★★★, *Boom Boom* (Essential 1991)★★★, *Just A Touch* (1993)★★★, *Blues Tracks* (1993)★★★, *Blues Magnet* (Provogue 1994)★★★, *Halfway To Somewhere* (Provogue 1995)★★★, *Lookin' Up* (Provogue 1996)★★★.

● COMPILATIONS: *Anthology Volume 1* (Polydor 1990)★★★★, *Anthology Volume 2* (Polydor 1990)★★★★.

● VIDEOS: *Boom Boom* (1991).

TRESPASS

Formed in Suffolk, England during 1976 by the Sutcliffe brothers, Mark (guitar) and Paul (drums). It was during 1979 that, along with Steve Mills (vocals), Cris Linscott (bass) and Dave Crawte (rhythm guitar), they released 'One Of These Days', on their own Trial label. The single remains one of the undiscovered classics of the era and the band should have made a more lasting impression with their blend of traditional hard rock and 'new' heavy metal. A second single, 'Jealousy', passed by without comment, but live they were getting noticed. In 1981 Linscott left to be replaced by Robert Irving and Mark took over vocal duties from Mills. Later a new vocalist, Robert Ekland, joined, and they then recorded an album and the *Bright Lights* EP. Receiving a degree of critical acclaim the major labels remained blind to their talents and the band faded away. In 1988 Crawte, now playing bass, and the brothers formed Blue Bludd, with Phil Kane (vocals) and Robert Ariss (keyboards). They adopted an American sound, drawing comparisons to White Lion and Ratt, and signed with Music For Nations for two albums, *The Big Noise* and *Universal Language*.

● ALBUMS: *Trespass* (Trial 1981)★★★.

TRIBE AFTER TRIBE

This 'African acid rock' trio developed from vocalist/guitarist Robbi Robb's Asylum Kids, who were major pop stars in their native South Africa. However, a lyrical move towards anti-apartheid politics meant trouble for the band - bassist Robby Whitelaw's left cheek and jaw were left permanently paralyzed after a vigilante beating - and Robb and Whitelaw were forced to flee the country with the help of Amnesty International, relocating to Los Angeles in 1987. Recruiting drummer PK, Tribe After Tribe created an innovative and atmospheric sound, mixing rock with traditional African styles and Robb's emotive political lyricism. An uncompromising outfit, they had difficulty in finding a sympathetic ear at a record company until Megaforce signed them in 1990, when the band were on the verge of releasing their debut independently. In the event further studio time with producer Bob Johnston enhanced the basic tracks. *Tribe After Tribe* was a haunting debut, attracting many admirers, including Pearl Jam's Eddie Vedder, who invited Tribe After Tribe to support on their 1992 US tour. *Love Under Will*, with new drummer Chris Frazier (ex-Steve Vai), continued the development of the band's uniquely spiritual style as they persisted in ignoring the marketing men. They also extended their political stance by campaigning in support of the Rock The Vote movement in their adopted country, their own background adding weight to the argument.

● ALBUMS: *Tribe After Tribe* (Megaforce 1991)★★★★, *Love Under Will* (Megaforce 1993)★★★, *Pearls Before Swine* (Music For Nations 1997)★★★.

TRIUMPH

This Canadian power-trio formed in Toronto during 1975. The band share many similarities to Rush aside from geographical location, as they are all highly accomplished musicians who have experimented with many facets of high-tech melodic rock. Comprising Rik Emmett (guitar, vocals), Gil Moore (drums) and Mike Levine (bass, keyboards), they nevertheless follow a rockier road than their fellow countrymen. Interest built slowly, but the band finally made a breakthrough with *Progressions Of Power*, their fourth album, released in 1980. *Allied Forces* and *Never Surrender* saw the pinnacle of their success, with both albums attaining gold status in the USA. Their music is characterized by Emmett's high-pitched vocals and intricate guitarwork, supplemented by keyboard fills and a thunderous rhythm section. *Thunder Seven*, a CD-only release, was a disjointed collection, while the live album that followed suffered from a wooden sound and flat production. In live settings the band frequently used Rick Santers as an extra guitarist to overcome the limitations of a three-man line-up. Again like Rush, their concerts were renowned for their sophisticated special effects rather than the actual music, and featured every conceivable pyrotechnic device available, plus the ultimate in computerized, laser-lighting rigs. *The Sport Of Kings* saw the band move in a blatantly commercial direction, but *Surveillance* marked a return to their roots: an aggressive and well-produced hard rock album. Emmett left the band in 1988 and was replaced by guitarist Phil Xenides. The vocals were taken over by Moore, but much of the group's character left with Emmett.

● ALBUMS: *Triumph* (Attic 1976)★★, *Rock 'N' Roll Machine* (RCA 1977)★★, *Just A Game* (RCA 1979)★★, *Progressions Of Power* (RCA 1980)★★★, *Allied Forces* (RCA 1981)★★★, *Never Surrender* (RCA 1982)★★★, *Thunder Seven* (RCA 1984)★★, *Stages* (MCA 1985)★★, *The Sport Of Kings* (MCA 1985)★★, *Surveillance* (MCA 1987)★★★, *Edge Of Excess* (1993)★★.

● COMPILATIONS: *Classics* (RCA 1989)★★★.

● VIDEOS: *Night Of Triumph Live* (1988), *Triumph At The US Festival* (1988).

TROJAN

Formed in Wigan, England, in 1982, Trojan's original line-up consisted of Dave Kenyon (vocals), Pate Wadeson (guitar), Andy J. Halliwell (guitar), Brian Bentham (bass) and Mick Taylor (drums). The band first became noticed on the heavy metal underground scene with a hastily recorded five-track cassette. This credible offering was a blend of high-speed thrash metal with a punk attitude. The band contributed a track to a budget compilation, *Metal Maniaxe*, released on Ebony Records in 1982. However, owing to a relative lack of record company promotion, coupled with a yearning by various members of the band to pursue other musical directions, they dissolved. Determined to carry on, Wadeson underwent lengthy auditions to re-form the band. By 1984 a new line-up was confirmed, featuring Graeme Wyatt (vocals), Eddie Martin (bass) and Sam Hall (drums). *Chasing The Storm* was released on Roadrunner Records in 1985 and was well received, with its sound firmly rooted in the N.W.O.B.H.M. The group toured extensively at home and abroad, culminating in an appearance at the Whiplash Festival in Belgium in 1986. Through managerial and personal problems the band split up for a final time in 1988, at which time Wadeson and Wyatt went on to form the melodic thrash band Talion.

● ALBUMS: *Chasing The Storm* (Roadrunner 1985)★★★.

TROUBLE

This influential quintet was formed in Chicago, USA, in 1979, when vocalist Eric Wagner and guitarists Bruce Franklin and Rick Wartell were joined by Sean McAllister (bass) and Jeff Olson (drums). Trouble's early material drew strong Black Sabbath comparisons with a doom-laden, riff-heavy approach, and *Trouble* (later renamed *Psalm 9* to prevent confusion with their fourth album) was a stunning debut. *The Skull* added a darker air to their epic style. However, McAllister was fired and Olson left to become a minister, while Ron Holzner (bass) and Dennis Lesh (drums) came in for *Run To The Light*, where the shorter, punchier material was let down by weak production. Lesh was subsequently replaced by ex-Zoetrope drummer Barry Stern. A deserved major contract with Def American followed, and Trouble duly reached new creative heights, incorporating Beatles and Pink Floyd influences for a broader, more psychedelic yet still heavy sound on *Trouble*. The superb *Manic Frustration* continued the progression as Trouble's most mature and accessible work to date, but despite colossal critical praise, the band remained a cult phenomenon. Parting company with their label, Trouble returned to their underground roots, touring heavily and selling self-financed recordings on the road before signing to Bulletproof/Music For Nations in late 1994. *Plastic Green Head* was a typically strong and diverse selection, elegantly traversing everything from doom rock to hard pop and psychedelia. The band broke up in August 1996.

● ALBUMS: *Trouble/Psalm 9* (Metal Blade

1984)★★★★, *The Skull* (Metal Blade 1985)★★★, *Run To The Light* (Metal Blade/Enigma 1987)★★★, *Trouble* (Def American 1990)★★★, *Manic Frustration* (Def American 1992)★★★★, *Plastic Green Head* (Bulletproof/Music For Nations 1995)★★★.

Trout, Walter, Band

b. 6 March 1951, Atlantic City, New Jersey, USA. This highly talented and experienced blues guitarist finally formed and recorded with his own band in 1989 after a lengthy spell with John Mayall and Canned Heat. With a line-up of Jim Trapp (bass), Leroy Larson (drums) and Dan Abrams (keyboards), he debuted with *Life In The Jungle* in 1990. This showcased Trout's remarkable feel and dexterity and courted Jimi Hendrix, Robin Trower and Gary Moore comparisons. Klas Anderhill took over on drums for *Prisoner Of A Dream*, on which the band moved into a more commercial mainstream rock direction. Much of the soulful passion was replaced for a heavier approach more akin to bands such as Europe, Whitesnake and Bon Jovi. Trout moved away from his blues roots with *Transition*, although his remarkable ability as a guitarist shone through an album of patchy songs. Following a live album Trout moved to Silvertone Records, presumably in the hope of expanding his market to a wider audience. *Tellin' Stories* was an exciting set of crisply recorded rock/blues yet surprisingly it was not the anticipated commercial success. A year later he was back with Provogue, having now replaced Larson and Abrams with Bernard Pershey and Martin Gerschwitz, respectively. *Breaking The Rules* was a quieter and more introspective album, with Trout's contentment with life seemingly apparent from the lyrics. *Positively Beale Street* mixed together all of Trout's previous styles and on this collection his guitar playing was exemplary. The slow, gospel-influenced ballad 'Let Me Be The One', written by Dave Williams and Mick Parker, was the album's highlight.

● ALBUMS: *Life In The Jungle* (Provogue 1990)★★★★, *Prisoner Of A Dream* (Provogue 1991)★★★, *Transition* (Provogue 1992)★★, *Live, No More Fish Jokes* (Provogue 1992)★★, *Tellin' Stories* (Silvertone 1994)★★★, *Breaking The Rules* (Provogue 1995)★★★, *Positively Beale Street* (Provogue 1997)★★★.

Trower, Robin

b. 9 March 1947, London, England. Guitarist Trower spent his early career in the Paramounts, a popular Southend, Essex-based R&B/beat group who completed five singles between 1963 and 1965. Having briefly worked with a trio dubbed the Jam, he joined several colleagues from his earlier act in Procol Harum. Trower remained in this much-praised unit until 1971, when his desire to pursue a tougher musical style proved incompatible with their well-established grandiose inflections. He initially formed the short-lived Jude with Frankie Miller (vocals), Jim Dewar (bass, vocals) and Clive Bunker (drums, ex-Jethro Tull), but having retained Dewar (formerly with Lulu and Stone The Crows), founded the Robin Trower Band with drummer Reg Isidore. *Twice Removed From Yesterday* and *Bridge Of Sighs* explored a melodic, guitar-based path, redolent of the late-period Jimi Hendrix, whom Robin was often criticized for merely aping. His lyrical technique, offset by Dewar's gritty delivery, nonetheless proved highly popular and the trio achieved considerable success in the USA. Although ex-Sly And The Family Stone drummer Bill Lordan replaced Isidore in 1974, *For Earth Below* and *Long Misty Days* maintained the same musical balance. However, Trower's desire for a purer version of R&B resulted in his inviting black producer Don Davis to collaborate on *In City Dreams* and *Caravan To Midnight*. The new style alienated the guitarist's rock audience, while the rock-based *Victims Of The Fury* was bedevilled by weaker material.

In 1981 he and Lordan formed BLT with bassist Jack Bruce, but within two years Trower had reconvened the Robin Trower Band with Dewar, David Bronze (bass), Alan Clarke and Bobby Clouter (both drums). *Back It Up* failed to repeat former glories and the artist was then dropped by long-time label, Chrysalis Records. The well-received *Passion*, released independently, engendered a new contract with Atlantic Records, for whom a new line-up of Trower, Bronze, Davey Pattison (vocals) and Pete Thompson (drums) completed *Take What You Need*. Trower is also heavily involved in record production.

● ALBUMS: *Twice Removed From Yesterday* (Chrysalis 1973)★★★, *Bridge Of Sighs* (Chrysalis 1974)★★★★, *For Earth Below* (Chrysalis 1975)★★★, *Robin Trower Live* (Chrysalis 1976)★★★★, *Long Misty Days* (Chrysalis 1976)★★★, *In City Dreams* (Chrysalis 1977)★★, *Caravan To Midnight* (Chrysalis 1978)★★, *Victims Of The Fury* (Chrysalis 1980)★★, *Back It Up* (Chrysalis 1983)★★★, *Beyond The Mist* (Music For Nations 1985)★★★, *Passion* (Gryp 1987)★★★, *Take What You Need* (Atlantic 1988)★★★, *In The*

Line Of Fire (Atlantic 1990)★★, *Someday Blues* (Demon 1997)★★★.
● COMPILATIONS: *Portfolio* (Chrysalis 1987)★★★.

TRULY

Formed in the mid-90s in Seattle, Washington, USA, Truly struggled initially to separate themselves from two assumptions - first, that they were a 'supergroup', and second, that they had anything to do with the grunge movement. The group features former Soundgarden bass player Hiro Yamamoto, Screaming Trees drummer Mark Pickerel and former Storybook Krooks vocalist/guitarist Robert Roth. Yamamoto was the founding force behind the group - though after his experiences with Soundgarden he was disenchanted enough with the music industry to have taken a sabbatical working in a bicycle store. Roth's songs offered a similar level of alienation - informed both by his recent split with his girlfriend of nine years and the Storybook Krooks' brief flirtation with the music industry. The group's sound then evolved into something stylistically different to anything in which the participants had previously been involved. Instead of the familiar stop-start song construction patented by the Seattle grunge bands, Truly chose to write longer, more experimental pieces, redolent of an energized version of the progressive rock bands. They made their debut with *Fast Stories ... From Kid Coma* in 1995, a hard-hitting, insistent record that occasionally overreached in its attempts to distance itself from its contemporaries. Its UK release was delayed until 1996, though the band did play their first shows in the UK in December 1995.
● ALBUMS: *Fast Stories ... From Kid Coma* (Parlophone 1995)★★★.

TRUST

This French metal band was formed in the late 70s by vocalist Bernard Bonvoisin and guitarist Norbert 'Nono' Krief, with drummer Jean-Emile 'Jeannot' Hanela and bassist Raymond Manna. The band were musically influenced by AC/DC, but their lyrics reflected the anti-establishment punk ethos. *Trust* was an enormous domestic success, and the outstanding 'L'Elite' stimulated international interest. Yves 'Vivi' Brusco replaced Manna and guitarist Mohammed 'Moho' Chemlekh was added shortly after the recording of *Repression*, a superb effort that caused controversy in France due to the sympathetic treatment of infamous French criminal Jaques Mesrine in 'Instinct De Mort' and 'Le Mitard', the latter using Mesrine's lyrics. An English language version, with lyrics translated by Sham 69's Jimmy Pursey, attracted a good reaction from outside France, although Bonvoisin sounded slightly uncomfortable and much of the lyrical edge was lost. Trust were a popular support to Iron Maiden on their *Killers* UK tour, subsequently appearing at the 1981 Reading Festival. *Marche Ou Creve* saw Nicko McBrain take over on drums, and was another solid release, featuring a tribute to late AC/DC vocalist Bon Scott in 'Ton Dernier Acte'. However, the band lost some credibility when 'Misere', which attacked the Thatcher government, was omitted from the English language version (retitled *Savage*). A drummer 'swap' with Iron Maiden saw Clive Burr replace McBrain for 1983's *Trust*, before Farid replaced him. Inner tensions broke Trust apart after the disappointing *Rock 'N' Roll*, with Bonvoisin recording two solo albums while Krief worked with Johnny Hallyday. Renewed interest following Anthrax's cover versions of 'Antisocial' and 'Sects' stimulated a re-formation, with Brusco on rhythm guitar and new bassist Frederick, a union that produced a live album.
● ALBUMS: *Trust* (Columbia 1979)★★★★, *Repression/Repression Version Anglaise* (Columbia 1980)★★★, *Marche Ou Creve* (Epic 1981)★★★, *Trust* (Epic 1983)★★★, *Man's Trap* (Epic 1984)★★★, *Rock 'N' Roll* (Epic 1984)★★, *Live - Paris By Night* (Celluloid 1989)★★.
● COMPILATIONS: *Best Of* (Premier 1988)★★★.

TUFF

This US rock quartet was formed in 1990 by Stevie Rachelle (vocals), Jorge Desaint (guitar), Todd Chase (bass) and drummer Michael Lean. They signed to Atlantic Records and debuted with *What Comes Around, Goes Around* in 1991. The influences here were evidently Poison, Warrant and Bon Jovi, yet they displayed just enough energy to maintain a level of credibility. However, reviews were not kind and afterwards the group remained quiet.
● ALBUMS: *What Comes Around, Goes Around* (Atlantic 1991)★★★.

TUNGSTEN

Duo formed in Chalmette, Louisiana, USA, a small town on the edge of New Orleans, in the early 90s. Al Hodge (guitar, bass, vocals) and Mark Talamo (drums, electronics) became friends in high school a decade previously, sharing interests in both traditional heavy metal and technology. However, unlike many of the groups caught in its nets by the diversity of the 90s, Tungsten were not afraid of the term metal: 'There are so many bands out there that are almost embarrassed to say that. I'd rather be called a metal band than be a 60s hippie-wanna-be band that hails from the trend land of Seattle'. Lyrically their debut articulated Hodge's frustrations with failed relationships and a sense of betrayal, particularly virulent on tracks such as 'Born XY' or 'Just Fades Away'. It was recorded at Talamo's own 16-track digital studio, where he has also engineered albums for Crowbar and Down.

● ALBUMS: *183.85* (Music For Nations 1994)★★★.

TURA SATANA

(see Manhole)

TURNER, JOE LYNN

American vocalist who first came to prominence in 1977 with the band Fandango, who played typical AOR music. The band also featured a guitarist called Rick Blakemore which, with hindsight, may have been a good omen. Turner's radio-friendly vocals graced all four of their albums between 1977 and 1980. In 1981 he was invited by guitarist Ritchie Blackmore to replace Graham Bonnet in Rainbow. Blackmore was looking to change the sound of the band and aim it squarely at the American market. Turner's vocals were perfect for this and helped to secure the band further airplay with singles 'I Surrender' and 'Street Of Dreams', but Rainbow remained more popular in the UK and the rest of Europe. Consequently, after three excellent albums - *Difficult To Cure* (1981), *Straight Between The Eyes* (1982) and *Bent Out Of Shape* (1983) - Blackmore finished the band and re-formed Deep Purple. Turner then obtained a contract with Elektra Records and released one underrated album in 1985. Through lack of publicity the album flopped and Turner took a rest until he teamed up with Swedish guitar hero Yngwie Malmsteen and Rising Force. In 1988 a single, 'Heaven Tonight', became a hit and Turner looked like he was back on track, but a degree of criticism about his live performance from some quarters damaged sales of *Odyssey*. The band set out on a world tour and played to packed halls in Russia where they recorded and filmed concerts in Leningrad released in 1989 as *Trial By Fire*. Turner was replaced later in 1989 and returned to writing new material and guesting with various other artists. A year later Ritchie Blackmore contacted him again and suggested that he replace Ian Gillan in the re-formed Deep Purple. Turner accepted and appeared on 1990's *Slaves And Masters* and toured with them. Things quietened down with the band and by 1993 he had been replaced by Gillan again. His second solo album (on the Music For Nations label) was an excellent effort.

● ALBUMS: *Rescue You* (Elektra 1985)★★★, *Nothing's Changed* (Music For Nations 1995)★★★★.

21 GUNS

This melodic hard rock quartet was assembled in 1991 by ex-Thin Lizzy guitarist Scott Gorham (b. 17 March 1951, Santa Monica, California, USA). Recruiting fellow Americans Leif Johansen (bass), Michael Sturgis (drums) and Tommy La Verdi (vocals) to complete the line-up, they were soon offered a contract by RCA Records. They debuted in the summer of 1992 with *Salute*, a highly polished album that met with positive reviews in the press. Influences such as Foreigner, White Lion and Journey were prevalent throughout the album, though Gorham's distinctive style held in check any accusations of plagiarism.

● ALBUMS: *Salute* (RCA 1992)★★★.

24-7 SPYZ

This multifaceted South Bronx, New York hardcore quartet formed in 1986, initially playing a mixture of ska, punk and funk. They gradually began to incorporate hardcore aggression in the manner of Fishbone and Bad Brains, progressing, like the former in particular, towards an eclectic but accessible sound. Comprising founder Jimi Hazel (guitar), Peter Fluid (vocals), Rick Skatore (bass) and Anthony Johnson (drums), the band made its debut with *Harder Than You*, mixing rap and reggae into their funk and thrash melting pot, with stunning performances from the Jimi Hendrix-worshipping Hazel and the energetic Fluid. *Gumbo Millenium* continued in similar genre-blending fashion as the band began to attract press attention for their wild live act, but musical differences saw both Fluid and Johnson depart when touring ended. Jeff Broadnax (vocals) and Joel Maitoza (drums) made their debut on *This Is ... 24-7 Spyz*, with the band unexpectedly maintaining a continuity of style, both live and in the studio, despite the drastic line-up changes. *Strength In Numbers* featured 24-7 Spyz's most consistent material, but, like Fishbone, the band's diversity seemed to hold them back, and commercial success remained a distant prospect. A reunion of the original line-up was mooted in mid-1994, but only Fluid returned for the ensuing*Temporarily Disconnected*.

● ALBUMS: *Harder Than You* (In-Effect

1989)★★★★, *Gumbo Millenium* (In-Effect 1990)★★★, *This Is ... 24-7 Spyz* mini-album (East West 1991)★★★★, *Strength In Numbers* (East West 1992)★★★, *Temporarily Disconnected* (Enemy 1995)★★★, *Heavy Metal Soul By The Pound* (What Are Records? 1996)★★★.

TWISTED SISTER

Formed in 1976, this New York quintet's original purpose was to provide the antidote to the disco music that was saturating the airwaves during the mid-70s. Featuring Dee Snider (vocals), Eddie Ojeda (guitar), Mark 'The Animal' Mendoza (bass, ex-Dictators), Jay Jay French (guitar) and Tony Petri (drums) they had a bizarre image that borrowed ideas from Kiss, Alice Cooper and the New York Dolls. Musically they combined sexually provocative lyrics and dumb choruses with heavy-duty, metallic rock 'n' roll. A.J. Pero (ex-Cities) took over on drums before the recording of their debut, *Under The Blade*. This was picked up from the independent Secret label by Atlantic Records, following a successful UK appearance at the Reading Festival and a controversial performance on *The Tube* television show in 1982. The band never lived up to their initial promise, with successive albums simply regurgitating earlier ideas. Their greatest success was *Stay Hungry*, which cracked the Top 20 album charts on both sides of the Atlantic. It also included the hit single, 'I Am, I'm Me', which peaked at number 18 in the UK. Their audience had become bored with them by the time *Come Out And Play* was released and the tour to support it was also a flop. Pero quit and returned to his former outfit, Cities; Joey 'Seven' Franco (ex-Good Rats) was drafted in as replacement. Snider steered the band in a more melodic direction on *Love Is For Suckers*. The album was still-born; Atlantic terminated their contract, and the band imploded in 1987. Snider went on to form Desperado, with ex-Gillan guitarist Bernie Tormé (subsequently evolving, more permanently, into Widowmaker). Looking back on his days dressing up with his old band, Snider would conclude: 'All that flash and shit wears thin. There's gotta be something beyond it. And there wasn't with Twisted Sister'.

● ALBUMS: *Under The Blade* (Secret 1982)★★, *You Can't Stop Rock 'N' Roll* (Atlantic 1983)★★, *Stay Hungry* (Atlantic 1984)★★★, *Come Out And Play* (Atlantic 1985)★★, *Love Is For Suckers* (Atlantic 1987)★★, *Live* (Music For Nations 1994)★★.

2 TRIBES

This funk metal crossover aggregation was formed in London during 1990, the multiracial line-up giving them their name. The band, who, predictably, were often described as the UK's answer to Living Colour, comprised Ashton Liburd (vocals), Paul Gold (bass), Rod Quinn (b. Dublin, Eire; drums) and John McLoughlin (guitar). The group's efforts were spearheaded by a single, 'The Music Biz', which featured that same legend scrawled across a pig on its cover picture. Their uncompromising live sets, meanwhile, included a cover version of Public Enemy's '911 Is A Joke', the American rap stars' vicious attack on emergency response times in black communities, prompted by the death of a relative after having waited three hours for an ambulance. Signed to Chrysalis subsidiary Compulsion, they made their long-playing debut in early 1992, with a self-titled album that met with a degree of enthusiasm from the rock press. Especially notable was the agenda-setting 'File Under Rock (Bite The Hand That Bleeds Us)' single, which bemoaned the fact that their records were always categorized under the 'black' sections in stores, despite 2 Tribes being an authentic rock act - it included the line: 'This ain't Soul II Soul, It's rock 'n' roll'. However, despite earning a Single Of The Week plaudit in the UK weekly *New Musical Express*, it was not enough to avert their descent into obscurity, with the band splitting soon after its release.

● ALBUMS: *2 Tribes* (Compulsion 1992)★★.

TYGERS OF PAN TANG

This hard rock band was formed in Whitley Bay, Newcastle-upon-Tyne, England, in 1978, as part of the New Wave Of British Heavy Metal. The four-piece line-up comprised Jess Cox (vocals), Rob Weir (guitar), Rocky (bass) and Brian Dick (drums). Their debut EP was the first rock release on Newcastle's Neat label, and it quickly topped all the metal charts. On the back of their first flush of success they moved to MCA Records. However, after one album Cox departed to be replaced by Jon Deverill (from Cardiff, Wales; vocals) and John Sykes (guitar). Sykes later left (to join Thin Lizzy and then Whitesnake) and was replaced by former Penetration guitarist Fred Purser. *The Cage* broke the band in the USA, before two years of disputes with MCA held up their career, and only compilation albums were released during this period. Guitarist Steve Lamb joined in 1985, and a year later former vocalist Cox formed Tyger Tyger in order to try to recapture past glories.

● ALBUMS: *Wild Cat* (MCA 1980)★★★, *Spellbound* (MCA 1981)★★, *Crazy Nights* (MCA 1981)★★, *The Cage* (MCA 1982)★★, *The Wreck-Age* (Music For Nations 1985)★★, *First Kill* (Neat 1986)★, *Burning In The Shade* (Zebra 1987)★. Solo: Jess Cox *Third Step* (Neat 1983)★.

● COMPILATIONS: *The Best Of The Tygers Of Pan Tang* (MCA 1983)★★.

TYKETTO

Following the demise of Waysted in 1987, American vocalist Danny Vaughn set about forming his own band, with drummer Michael Clayton, bassist Jimi Kennedy and guitarist Brooke St. James, with Vaughn's former Waysted colleague Jimmy Dilella (guitar, keyboards) also briefly involved. Taking the name Tyketto from some 'tagging' on a graffiti-covered Brooklyn wall, the band were signed by Geffen Records in 1989. The Richie Zito-produced *Don't Come Easy* was a classic slice of melodic hard rock, with Vaughn's immaculate vocals enhancing an already strong collection of songs, which were given a rootsy flavour by the mix of acoustic and electric guitars. Conditions were difficult for the band in their recession-hit homeland, but they proved themselves on a UK tour with White Lion, and seemed to be destined for stardom. However, the album title proved somewhat prophetic. Kennedy departed, with James Lomenzo (ex-White Lion) filling in before a permanent replacement was found in Jaimie Scott. *Strength In Numbers* was recorded in 1992, but the release was delayed by over a year when Geffen surprisingly dropped Tyketto, despite the fact that the label had already sent out advance tapes and prepared two possible sleeves. Retaining only a Japanese deal, the band signed to Music For Nations in Europe in December 1993, and the album was finally released, albeit to a cooler reaction than that afforded the debut. However, excellent live performances dispelled any doubts, and with American label interest, the future again seemed bright for this genuinely talented band. Further drama came with the departure of Vaughn although he was replaced by Steve Augeri from Tall Stories, who debuted on *Shine*.

● ALBUMS: *Don't Come Easy* (Geffen 1991)★★★, *Strength In Numbers* (Music For Nations 1994)★★★, *Shine* (Music For Nations 1995)★★, *Take Out And Served Up Live* (Music For Nations 1996)★★.

TYPE O NEGATIVE

From the carcass of controversial nihilist New York act Carnivore, vocalist and bass guitarist Peter Steele formed Type O Negative in 1988. Fusing elements of heavy metal, gothic rock, industrial music and psychedelia, Type O Negative are a four-piece that explore the darker edges of the human soul with caustic irony. Their second release, The *Origin Of The Feces*, was a typical act of media terrorism. Mixed by the band to sound like a live recording from hell, it features chants of 'You Suck' and slow-handclapping from the audience, while Steele cynically drawls to the band 'Let's get this over with'. The sleeve featured a close up of a sphincter, while the band photos inside each have a 'turd' lovingly laid upon them. Despite such truculence, success beckoned as Type O Negative secured tours with influential bands such as Nine Inch Nails, Jackyl, Danzig and Mötley Crüe. *Bloody Kisses* proved a surprise success, with its effective blend of musical velvet and razor blades, leading to the re-release of *Origin Of The Feces* (in less offensive packaging). The current line-up consists of Peter Steele (vocals, bass), Josh Silver (keyboards), Kenny Hickey (guitar) and Johnny Kelly (drums). Steele hit the headlines in 1995 when he posed naked in *Playgirl* magazine.

● ALBUMS: *Slow, Deep, Hard* (Roadrunner 1991)★★★, *Origin Of The Feces* (Roadrunner 1992)★★, *Bloody Kisses* (Roadrunner 1993)★★★★, *October Rust* (Roadrunner 1996)★★★.

● VIDEOS: *After Dark* (Roadrunner Video 1998).

UFO

This well-regarded UK rock band formed in 1969 when Andy Parker (drums) joined Phil Mogg (b. 1951, London, England; vocals), Pete Way (bass) and Mick Bolton (guitar) in Hocus Pocus. With a name change to UFO and a musical style that fused progressive space-rock and good-time boogie, they released three albums that were successful only in Germany and Japan. In 1974 Bolton quit, to be replaced by Larry Wallis (ex-Pink Fairies), followed by Bernie Marsden (later of Whitesnake) and finally Michael Schenker (b. 10 January 1955, Savstedt, Germany). Securing a contract with Chrysalis Records they recorded *Phenomenon*, a powerful hard rock album that featured the classics 'Rock Bottom' and 'Doctor, Doctor'. Schenker's presence helped to forge their new sound, as he strangled the hard-edged metallic riffs out of his Flying V. A series of strong albums followed, and the band expanded to a five-piece in 1976, with the addition of a keyboardist, initially Danny Peyronel (ex-Heavy Metal Kids) and later Paul Raymond (formerly of Savoy Brown). *Lights Out* and *Strangers In The Night* consolidated the band's success, the latter a superb double live album recorded on their sell-out US tour of 1977. After long-running internal disagreements, Schenker quit in 1978 to rejoin the Scorpions and later form MSG. Paul Chapman (ex-Lone Star) was offered the guitarist's vacancy, having played with the band for short periods on two previous occasions. From this point on, they never recaptured the level of success and recognition they had attained with Schenker. A string of uninspiring albums followed, which lacked both aggression and the departed guitarist's riffs. Paul Raymond joined MSG in 1980, with Neil Carter (ex-Wild Horses) taking his place. Pete Way left after the release of *Mechanix*, eventually forming Waysted and ex-Eddie And The Hot Rods/Damned bassist Paul Gray took over his position. *Making Contact* represented the nadir of the band's creativity, being dated and devoid of the old energy. A farewell UK tour was undertaken in 1983, but it was a sad end for what was originally a fine band. Two years later Mogg resurrected the name with Raymond and Gray, plus ex-Magnum drummer Jim Simpson and the Japanese guitarist Atomic Tommy M. They recorded *Misdemeanor*, which unsuccessfully rekindled the old flame, with forceful guitars and hard and insistent melodies. Success eluded them and they disbanded again. In 1991, UFO were reborn once more. This time the line-up featured the nucleus of Mogg and Way, plus guitarist Laurence Archer (ex-Grand Slam) and drummer Clive Edwards (ex-Wild Horses). *High Stakes And Desperate Men* attempted to recapture the halcyon days of 1974-78, with limited success, but talk in 1993 of a full-scale reunion, including Schenker, was what really fuelled fan interest. In 1995 the speculation was finally ended when the band's 'classic line-up' (Mogg, Schenker, Way, Raymond and Parker) re-formed to record *Walk On Water*, initially released in Japan only.

● ALBUMS: *UFO 1* (Beacon 1971)★★, *UFO 2 - Flying* (Beacon 1971)★★, *UFO Lands In Tokyo - Live* (1972)★★★, *Phenomenon* (Chrysalis 1974)★★★, *Force It* (Chrysalis 1975)★★★, *No Heavy Pettin'* (Chrysalis 1976)★★★★, *Lights Out* (Chrysalis 1977)★★★★, *Obsession* (Chrysalis 1978)★★, *Strangers In The Night* (Chrysalis 1979)★★★, *No Place To Run* (Chrysalis 1980)★★, *The Wild, The Willing And The Innocent* (Chrysalis 1981)★★, *Mechanix* (Chrysalis 1982)★★, *Making Contact* (Chrysalis 1983)★★, *Misdemeanor* (Chrysalis 1985)★★★, *Ain't Misbehavin'* (FM Revolver 1988)★★★, *High Stakes And Desperate Men* (Essential 1992)★★★, *BBC Live In Concert* (Windsong 1992)★★★, *Lights Out In Tokyo: Live* (Castle 1993)★★★, *Walk On Water* (Zero 1995)★★★, *Parker's Birthday* (Griffin 1996)★★, *On With The Action* 1976 recording (Zoom 1998)★★.

● COMPILATIONS: *Headstone - The Best Of UFO* (Chrysalis 1983)★★★, *The Collection* (Castle 1985)★★★, *The Best Of The Rest* (Chrysalis 1987)★★★, *The Essential UFO* (Chrysalis 1992)★★★★, *The Decca Years* (Decca 1993)★★, *Doctor, Doctor* (Spectrum/Polydor 1995)★★★, *X-Factor: Out There & Back* (Snapper 1998)★★★.

● VIDEOS: *Misdemeanor Live* (Hendring Music Video/Castle Communications 1985).

Ugly Kid Joe

Formed in Isla Vista, California, USA, in 1989 by Whitfield Crane (vocals), Klaus Eichstadt (guitar) and drummer Mark Davis, adding second guitarist Roger Lahr, and bringing in bassist Cordell Crockett (whose father owns *Guitar Player* magazine) in early 1991, the band flirted with several names before settling on Ugly Kid Joe, coined for a support slot in order to satirize headliners Pretty Boy Floyd. The band made their debut with a mini-album, *As Ugly As They Wanna Be*, which was an almost instant success, selling over two million copies in the USA on the back of the poppy hit 'Everything About You', a humorous number featured in the enormously popular *Wayne's World* film. The song rather belied the true musical nature of the band, in reality much heavier with funk influences, drawing comparisons with both Mötley Crüe and Faith No More from reviewers. Dave Fortman (ex-Sugartooth) replaced Lahr on guitar for *America's Least Wanted*, which produced further hits in the shape of 'Neighbor' and 'Cats In The Cradle'. Given a powerful sound by Mark Dodson, the album established the band's credibility without sacrificing their sense of humour, and live shows, including a support slot on Ozzy Osbourne's farewell US tour, further helped the band to shake off their novelty tag. Sessions for a second album proper began in 1994 at a rented house in Santa Ynez, California, with drummer Shannon Larkin (ex-Wrathchild America; Souls At Zero) replacing Davis. The release of the band's second album, *Menace To Sobriety*, was preceded by a series of AIDS benefits on a tour of US ski resorts, and another offbeat single, 'Milkman's Son'. However, there was also a concerted effort by their management and label to market the band as serious rock artists - including an 'approved photographs only' contract not seen since Guns N'Roses were at the height of their collective paranoia. The band returned to independent status when they released 1996's *Motel California* on their own Evilution label.

● ALBUMS: *As Ugly As They Wanna Be* mini-album (Stardog 1992)★★, *America's Least Wanted* (Stardog 1992)★★★, *Menace To Sobriety* (Mercury 1995)★★★, *Motel California* (Evilution 1996)★★.

ULTRAVIOLENCE

UK extreme rock band featuring Johnny Violent, who introduced himself via the scorching 'Shout' single, which sold out within one week and drew the attention of UK radio presenter John Peel. A session on his radio programme resulted in 1992, which drew further journalistic gasps as the band traversed the sonic boundaries between industrial metal and techno. In its wake Ultraviolence signed with EMI subsidiary Food Records, but few concessions to the mainstream were advanced on the subsequent *Vengeance* EP. This low-fi but high bpm encounter brought the marriage with Food to an abrupt end, with Violent sustaining himself via live outings with Eskimos And Egypt, Hyperhead and others. Ultraviolence then found a more natural home at Earache Records, debuting with 'I Destructor' and 'Johnny Is A Bastard' (as Johnny Violent). Ever more musically outlandish, the resultant album, *Life Of Destructor*, was a bruising affair, but one with some method in its mayhem. In the light of its favourable response Violent was invited to remix for diverse names including Terrorvision, G.R.O.W.T.H. and Laibach. They then guested with the Orb at a New York show - an appearance guaranteed to startle the assembled onlookers out of their ambient daydreams. A collaboration with television host 'Krusher' and Wurzel of Motörhead in 1995 was followed by *Shocker*, a Johnny Violent release. The Ultraviolent moniker returned for 1998's *Killing God*.

● ALBUMS: *Life Of Destructor* (Earache 1993)★★★★, *Psycho Drama* (Earache 1995)★★★, *Killing God* (Earache 1998)★★★.

UNCLE SAM

Formed in 1987, Uncle Sam were the brainchild of guitarist Larry Millar. With the recruitment of fellow New Yorkers David Gentner (vocals), Bill Purol (bass) and Jeff Mann (drums), they signed with the independent Razor Records. Influenced by both the punk and thrash movements, their songs were short, frantic and sometimes devoid of melody. Gentner's vocals were monotonous, while the back beat lacked depth and colour. At best they came across as an updated but pale version of the Stooges or MC5, and there were few mourners when the band collapsed in the 90s.

● ALBUMS: *Heaven Or Hollywood* (Razor 1988)★★, *Letters From London* (Razor 1990)★★.

UNDERSTAND

Formed in Southend, Essex, England, in 1992, alternative rock band Understand grew from the ashes of local group Stand Off (other members of that band, Hallam Foster and Tony Maddocks, went on to work with Above All). Comprising Dom Anderson (vocals), John Hannon (guitar), Rob Coleman (guitar), Stuart Quinnell (bass) and Andy Shepherd (drums), they continued Stand Off's 'straight edge' creed of abstinence from drink and drugs, with their musical influences clearly American. Fugazi, the leaders of the 'emo-core' (emotional hardcore) and straight edge scenes, are their obvious chief influence. Their debut self-titled EP was recorded with noted hardcore producer Don Fury in his studio in 1994, but failed to garner sympathetic press coverage - though earlier reviews of their demos and live shows had been much more positive. Their debut album for East West Records, *Burning Bushes And Burning Bridges*, proved much more popular. Produced by Chris Sheldon, best known for his work on Therapy?'s *Troublegum*, this was a more disciplined, powerful showcase for their work. The songs that attracted most attention were 'Southend', a tribute to the group's seaside home-town, and 'The Rudeness We Encounter', a plea for the return of a very old-fashioned English concept - politeness.

● ALBUMS: *Burning Bushes And Burning Bridges* (East West 1996)★★★★.

UNSANE

A trio of Chris Spencer (vocals, guitar), Charlie Ondras (drums) and Peter Shore (bass, vocals), founded at college in 1988 in New York City, New York, USA, Unsane are one of America's most brutal bands. After playing 'the usual East Coast firetraps' they signed to Minneapolis independent label Treehouse Records who released their debut single, 'This Town', in 1989. The cover art featured San Francisco's Zodiac serial killer, establishing a pattern of controversial packaging that has continued since. A debut album was recorded with Wharton Tieres for Circuit Records but was never released. Instead the group released singles for Glitterhouse, PCP and Sub Pop Records, before a self-titled album for Matador Records in 1991. In 1992 the group's hectic touring schedule was interrupted by the death of drummer Ondras from a drug overdose. His replacement, Vinnie Signorelli (formerly of the Swans and Foetus), joined at the end of 1992. As well as two compilations (a singles package and a document of the group's three sessions for disc jockey John Peel), the group embarked on sessions for 1994's *Total Destruction*. Co-produced by Martin Bisi (who had formerly worked with Sonic Youth, Swans and Cop Shoot Cop), their major label debut for Atlantic Records, *Total Destruction*, refused to compromise the group's sound for a mainstream audience, staying true instead to Unsane's primary strengths - volume and aggression.

Tours with Biohazard and 7 Year Bitch followed through 1994 and 1995, leading to the release of *Scattered, Smothered And Covered*, which featured a police photograph from Mexico of a mother who 'had a terminal disease and was bludgeoned to death by her daughter'. On 'Alleged' it also included one of the few instances of harmonica playing (from Chris Spencer) in modern hardcore music.

● ALBUMS: *Unsane* (Matador 1991)★★, *Total Destruction* (Matador/Atlantic 1994)★★★★, *Scattered, Smothered And Covered* (Amphetamine Reptile 1995)★★★, *Occupational Hazard* (Lockjaw 1998)★★★.

● COMPILATIONS: *Singles 1989-92* (Matador 1992)★★★★, *The Peel Sessions* (Matador 1994)★★★★.

UPPER CRUST

Who exactly was behind the recording of the Upper Crust's *Let Them Eat Rock* debut remains something of a mystery - the participants disguising themselves behind the sobriquets Lord Bendover (guitar, vocals), Lord Rockingham (guitar, vocals), The Duc d'Istortion (lead guitar), The Marquis De Roque (bass) and Jackie Kickassis (drums). The record doubtless involved some of the premier alternative rock stars from Boston, Massachusetts, USA, while at least producers (Paul) Kolderie And (Sean) Slade were owning up to their real names. *Let Them Eat Rock* proved to be that rare artefact - a winning, high-comedy concept album. Taking riotous punk rock guitars as their starting point the group chose to invert class hatred in a series of barbed lyrics describing their targets as 'peasants'. They themselves appeared on the cover resplendent in restoration wigs and powdered make-up. A succession of songs followed abusing starving people for not having a job, discussing the merits of manservants and the problems of choosing the correct garment in the morning. The hilarious 'Friend Of A Friend Of The Working Class' was the stand-out track, rivalling the Monochrome Set's 'The Ruling Class' as the definitive parody of the aristocracy.

● ALBUMS: *Let Them Eat Rock* (Upstart 1996)★★★.

URBAN DANCE SQUAD

A group who deliberately blur the boundaries between rock, rap and dance music, Amsterdam, Netherlands' Urban Dance Squad originally comprised Rude Boy (b. Patrick Remington; rapper, singer) plus the pseudonymous Magic Stick (drums), DJ DNA (programming), Silly Sil (bass) and Tres Manos (b. Rene van Barneveld; guitar). Their 1989 debut album for Arista Records, *Mental Floss For The Globe*, included the hit single 'Deeper Shade Of Soul', which peaked at number 21 in the US charts, and was a Top 40 entry in several other countries. Their debut album, with its combination of riveting guitar lines, samples and rapping, was an obvious precursor to 90s crossover acts such as

Rage Against The Machine. Their impact on the charts looked to be a fleeting one, however, until they re-emerged in 1994 with an accomplished collection for the Virgin Records-backed Hut imprint. For this the group eschewed the sample-heavy style of old, having slimmed down to a quartet with the departure of DNA. By the advent of 1996's *Planet Ultra*, the group had moved towards writing in a more traditional vein, with Rude Boy preferring to sing rather than rap. Many of the contents were written during jams while the group toured the USA to promote *Persona Non Grata*. The keyboards on *Planet Ultra* were provided by Belgium's Wizards Of Ooze, and production by Phil Nicolo of the Butcher Brothers.

● ALBUMS: *Mental Floss For The Globe* (Arista 1989)★★★★, *Life 'N Perspectives Of A Genuine Crossover* (Arista 1991)★★★, *Persona Non Grata* (Hut 1994)★★★, *Planet Ultra* (Virgin 1996)★★★.

URGE OVERKILL

Formed in 1986 in Chicago, Illinois, USA, Urge Overkill are led by National 'Nash' Kato (b. 31 December 1965, Grand Forks, North Dakota, USA; vocals) and his co-vocalist and drumming partner Blackie 'Black Caesar' Onassis (b. Johnny Rowan, 27 August 1967, Chicago, Illinois, USA). The line-up is completed by bass player Eddie 'King' Roeser (b. 17 June 1969, Litchfield, Minnesota, USA). They took their name from an old Funkadelic song, and combined the upfront rock riffs of AC/DC with the pop of the Raspberries and Cheap Trick. After releasing a lacklustre debut 12-inch, the *Strange, I...* EP, Urge Overkill went on to record four albums for seminal Chicago punk label Touch & Go Records, and supported Nirvana. With producers that included Steve Albini and Butch Vig, no one could contest their punk rock credentials. However, such product placement proved misleading They covered Neil Diamond's 'Girl, You'll Be A Woman Soon', stating that he was more important to their development than any late 70s band. As they revealed, 'We come from the fine tradition of James Brown and the soul bands, for whom looking good was paramount.' As if to confirm their lack of sympathy for the growing punk movement Urge Overkill took delight in wearing outlandish ethnic clothes, touring Chicago in an open-top car, with chilled champagne nestling in the boot. They also flew in the face of grunge fashion by filming videos about picnics, yachting and their second most-favoured form of transport - the horse-drawn carriage. Such behaviour won them few friends within the tightly knit Chicago scene, the most public demonstration of their rejection coming from Albini (he cited them as 'freakish attention-starved megalomaniacs'). *The Supersonic Storybook* saw the band trade in overblown images of Americana, resenting the new austerity that had swept the nation and deprived its teenagers of opportunities for excess - in particular, the band's favoured drug, the hallucinogenic artane. *Stull* was inspired by a visit to the ghost town of the same name, situated exactly at the mid-point of the USA, 40 miles away from Kansas. *Saturation*, their debut record for major label Geffen Records, was produced by hip-hop duo the Butcher Brothers, once again revealing a much more gaudy, vaudeville and escapist outlook than other Chicago bands. *Exit The Dragon* was an equally impressive follow-up. Their version of 'Girl, You'll Be A Woman Soon' became a chart hit in 1994 as a result of its use on the soundtrack to Quentin Tarantino's *Pulp Fiction*.

● ALBUMS: *Jesus Urge Superstar* (Touch & Go 1989)★★, *Americruiser* (Touch & Go 1990)★★, *The Supersonic Storybook* (Touch & Go 1991)★★★, *Stull* mini-album (Touch & Go 1992)★★, *Saturation* (Geffen 1993)★★★★, *Exit The Dragon* (Geffen 1995)★★★★.

URIAH HEEP

The critics have scoffed and generally poured derision on Uriah Heep over the years, but the band have sold millions of records and have had five US Top 40 albums. A technically brilliant heavy rock band, they deserve most credit for continuing despite almost 30 personnel changes and two deaths along the way. David Byron (b. 29 January 1947, Epping, Essex, England, d. 28 February 1985; vocals) formed the group with Mick Box (b. 8 June 1947, Walthamstow, London, England; lead guitar, vocals). The pair had teamed up in the Stalkers during the mid-60s, and after the group split they assembled another called Spice. This then evolved into Uriah Heep when the duo were joined by Ken Hensley (b. 24 August 1945, London, England; guitar, keyboards, vocals) and Paul Newton (b. 1946, Andover, England; bass). Hensley, a talented musician, had previously played guitar with Kit And The Saracens and the soul group Jimmy Brown Sound. Before Uriah Heep were bonded under the experienced management of Gerry Bron, Hensley had played alongside Mick Taylor (later to become a member of the Rolling Stones) in the Gods. He had also played on an album by Toe Fat which included Cliff Bennett. The rota of drummers started with former Spice man Alex

Napier, followed by Nigel Olsson (later with Elton John). Finding a permanent drummer was to remain one of the band's problems throughout their early years. Their debut, *Very 'eavy, Very 'umble*, in 1970, was a simplistic, bass-driven passage from electric folk to a direct, harder sound. They auditioned numerous drummers before offering the job to Keith Baker (ex-Bakerloo), who recorded *Salisbury* before deciding that the tour schedule was too rigorous for his liking. *Salisbury* was a drastic development from the debut, with many lengthy, meandering solos and a 16-minute title track embellished by a 26-piece orchestra. The group were near the forefront of a richly embossed, fastidious style of music later to become dubbed 'progressive rock'. During 1971 the line-up was altered again when Lee Kerslake, another former member of the Gods and Toe Fat, replaced Ian Clarke. An ex-member of the Downbeats and Colosseum, Mark Clarke, superseded Paul Newton on bass guitar but lasted just three months before Gary Thain (b. 15 May 1948, Wellington, New Zealand, d. 19 March 1976; ex-Keef Hartley Band) took over. Gerry Bron had formed Bronze Records by 1971 and *Look At Yourself* became the group's first entry in the UK charts when it reached number 39 in November. The stability of the new line-up enabled the band to enter their most successful period during the early 70s when the fantastical, eccentric nature of their lyrics was supported by a grandiose musical approach. The quintet recorded five albums, beginning with *Demons And Wizards*, their first to enter the US charts. The musical and lyrical themes continued on *The Magician's Birthday*, the double set *Uriah Heep Live*, *Sweet Freedom*, *Wonderworld* (their last Top 40 entry in the US chart) and *Return To Fantasy* as the band revealed a rare thirst for tough recording and performance schedules. Gary Thain was asked to leave in February 1975 after becoming too unreliable. He died of a drug overdose the following year. John Wetton, formerly of King Crimson, Family and Roxy Music was expected to provide the impetus needed when he took over the bass guitar in March 1975. However, many observers considered that he had taken a retrogressive step in joining a group that was quickly becoming an anachronism. The union, celebrated on *Return To Fantasy*, failed on a creative level although it marked their first and last appearance in the UK Top 10. Wetton left after just over a year to back Bryan Ferry. Early in 1976, Uriah Heep were set to fold when internal arguments broke out and they found the previously winning formula had become archaic and undeniably staid. In Ken Hensley's own words, they were 'a bunch of machines plummeting to a death'. There had been an earlier, brooding row when Thain suffered a near-fatal electric shock in Dallas and said he had not been shown enough regard for his injuries. Hensley walked out during a tour of the USA in the summer of 1976 and in a subsequent power-struggle, Byron was forced to leave. Byron soon afterwards joined Rough Diamond and after their brief lifespan released a series of solo albums before his death in 1985. Hensley had already embarked upon a short, parallel solo career, releasing two albums in 1973 and 1975. John Lawton, previously the singer with Lucifer's Friend, debuted on *Firefly*. The new bassist was David Bowie's former backing musician, Trevor Bolder. The singer's position underwent further changes during the late 70s and early 80s as the group found themselves playing to a cult following that was ever decreasing. Ex-Lone Star singer John Sloman performed on *Conquest*, after which Hensley left the group, leaving original member Mick Box to pick up the pieces. A brief hiatus resulted and a new Uriah Heep that included Box, Kerslake, John Sinclair (keyboards), Bob Daisley (bass, ex-Widowmaker) and Peter Galby (vocals, ex-Trapeze) was formed. Daisley would later quit in 1983 and be replaced by the returning Bolder. Bronze Records collapsed in 1984 and the band signed with Portrait Records in the USA. Their earlier extensive touring allowed them to continue appearing at reasonably sized venues, especially across the USA, and in 1987 they had the distinction of becoming the first western heavy metal group to perform in Moscow. Inevitably, there were more personnel changes with the new additions of Bernie Shaw (vocals) and Phil Lanzon (keyboards), both formerly of Grand Prix. Despite seeming out of time with all other developments in hard rock, 1995's *Sea Of Light* offered another evocative slice of the band's trademark melodic rock, maintaining their high standards in fashioning superior AOR. Their European tour of the same year saw them reunite with former vocalist John Lawton as a temporary measure, with Bernie Shaw suffering from a throat problem. *Sonic Origami* contained some of the band's best work since the classic Byron days.

● ALBUMS: *Very 'eavy, Very 'umble* (UK) *Uriah Heep* (USA) (Vertigo 1970)★★, *Salisbury* (Vertigo 1971)★★, *Look At Yourself* (Bronze 1971)★★★, *Demons And Wizards* (Bronze 1972)★★★, *The Magician's Birthday* (Bronze 1972)★★, *Uriah Heep*

Live (Bronze 1973)★★, *Sweet Freedom* (Bronze 1973)★★★, *Wonderworld* (Bronze 1974)★★★, *Return To Fantasy* (Bronze 1975)★★★, *High And Mighty* (Bronze 1976)★★★, *Firefly* (Bronze 1977)★★★, *Innocent Victim* (Bronze 1977)★★, *Fallen Angel* (Bronze 1978)★★, *Conquest* (Bronze 1980)★★, *Abnominog* (Bronze 1982)★★, *Head First* (Bronze 1983)★★, *Equator* (Bronze 1985)★★, *Live In Europe 1979* (Castle 1987)★★, *Live In Moscow (Cam B Mockbe)* (Legacy 1988)★★, *Live At Shepperton '74* (Castle 1988)★★, *Raging Silence* (Legacy 1989)★★, *Different World* (Legacy 1991)★★, *Sea Of Light* (HTD 1995)★★★, *Spellbinder* (1996)★★, *King Biscuit Flower Hour Presents In Concert* recorded 1974 (King Biscuit 1997)★★, *Sonic Origami* (Eagle 1998)★★★.

● COMPILATIONS: *The Best Of Uriah Heep* (Bronze 1975)★★★★, *Anthology* (Raw Power 1986)★★★, *The Collection* (Castle 1989)★★★, *Still 'Eavy, Still Proud: Two Decades Of Uriah Heep* (Legacy 1990)★★, *Rarities From The Bronze Age* (Sequel 1992)★★★, *The Lansdowne Tapes* (Red Steel 1993)★★, *Free Me* (Spectrum/PolyGram 1995)★★, *Lady In Black* (Spectrum/PolyGram 1995)★★, *A Time Of Revelation: 25 Years On* 4-CD box set (Essential 1996)★★★★, *Classic Heap: An Anthology* (PolyGram 1998)★★★.

● VIDEOS: *Easy Livin'* (Virgin Vision 1988), *Raging Through The Silence - Live At The Astoria* (Virgin Vision 1988), *Live Legends* (Castle Music Pictures 1990), *Gypsy* (Hendring Video/Castle Communictaions 1990).

VAI, STEVE

b. 6 June 1960, Long Island, New York, USA. Vai began his musical career at the age of 13, forming his first rock band, Rayge, while still at school. At this time he was tutored by Joe Satriani, who was to have a profound effect on his style for years to come. He studied jazz and classical music at the Berklee College Of Music in Boston, Massachusetts, before relocating to Los Angeles, California, in 1979. He was recruited by Frank Zappa as the lead guitarist in his backing band, while he was still only 18 years old. By 1984 he had built his own recording studio and had begun experimenting with the fusion of jazz, rock and classical music. These pieces were eventually released as *Flex-able*, and were heavily influenced by Zappa's offbeat and unpredictable style. In 1985 Vai replaced Yngwie Malmsteen in Alcatrazz, then moved on to even greater success with Dave Lee Roth and later Whitesnake. *Passion And Warfare*, released in 1990, was the album that brought Vai international recognition as a solo performer. It welded together jazz, rock, funk, classical and metal nuances within a melodic instrumental framework. It climbed to number 18 on the *Billboard* album chart, earning a gold disc in the process. *Alien Love Secrets* further highlighted his extraordinary style with guitars sounding like horses on 'Bad Horsie' and a Venusian vocal on 'Kill The Guy With The Ball' created by utilizing massive EQ, his left foot and a digital whammy bar. Vai takes the instrument into new realms but still makes it sound like a guitar, most of the time. *Fire Garden* was half-instrumental/half-vocal, and contained a bizarre mix of stunning guitar pyrotechnics, together with one of his most evocative compositions, 'Hand On Heart'.

● ALBUMS: *Flex-able* (Akashic/Relativity 1984)★★, *Flex-able Leftovers* (Relativity 1984)★★, *Passion And Warfare* (Relativity 1990)★★★; as Vai *Sex & Religion* (Relativity 1993)★★★, *Alien Love Secrets* (Relativity 1995)★★★, *Fire Garden* (Epic 1996)★★★, with Joe Satriani and Eric Johnson *G3 In Concert* (Epic 1997)★★★★.

VAIN

This band was formed in San Francisco, USA, in 1985 by songwriter Davy Vain, with James Scott (lead guitar), Danny West (rhythm guitar), Ashley Mitchell (bass), and Tom Rickard (drums). Early shows with Poison and Guns N'Roses, before either was a major act, and a series of impressive demos aroused considerable interest before a contract with Island Records was signed. *No Respect* was crammed with atmospheric driving metal with its own particular ambience owing to the live-in-the-studio recording technique. While the lyrics were largely sexually orientated, Davy Vain eschewed the usual glam perspective by drawing inspiration from his own relationships. *No Respect* and attendant single, 'Beat The Bullet', did well, particularly in the UK, where Vain toured triumphantly with Skid Row. Davy Vain had by this time also been employed in the unlikely capacity of producer to San Francisco neighbours Death Angel on their *Frolic In The Park* album in 1988. However, the band ran into problems when *All Those Strangers* was rejected after a management/ownership change at Island, and Vain were dropped. Davy Vain, Scott and Mitchell worked briefly with ex-Guns N'Roses drummer Steven Adler (b. 22 January 1965, Cleveland, Ohio, USA) in Road Crew, which fell apart during Adler's divorce and litigation with his old band, before re-forming Vain with West and ex-Kill City Dragons drummer Danny Fury, making an impressive return with *Move On It*. The original band's unreleased second album, its title now changed to *Fade*, was released in Japan in 1995, and internationally two years later.

● ALBUMS: *No Respect* (Island 1989)★★★, *Move On It* (Heavy Metal 1993)★★★★, *Fade* (Revolver 1997)★★★.

VAN HALEN

The origins of this, one of America's most successful heavy metal bands, date back to Pasadena, California, in 1973. Edward (Eddie) Van Halen (b. 26 January 1957, Nijmegen, Netherlands; guitar, keyboards), Alex Van Halen (b. 8 May 1955, Nijmegen, Netherlands; drums) and Michael Anthony (b. 20 June 1955, Chicago, Illinois, USA; bass) who were members of the Broken Combs, persuaded vocalist David Lee Roth (b. 10 October 1955, Bloomington, Indiana, USA) to leave the Real Ball Jets and become a member. After he consented they changed their name to Mammoth. Specializing in a mixture of 60s and 70s covers plus hard rock originals, they toured the bar and club circuit of Los Angeles virtually non-stop during the mid-70s. Their first break came when Gene Simmons (bassist of Kiss) saw one of their club gigs. He was amazed by the energy they generated and the flamboyance of their lead singer. Simmons produced a Mammoth demo, but surprisingly it was refused by many major labels in the USA. It was then discovered that the name Mammoth was already registered, so they would have to find an alternative. After considering Rat Salade, they opted for Roth's suggestion of simply Van Halen. On the strength of Simmons' recommendation, producer Ted Templeman checked out the band, was duly impressed and convinced Warner Brothers Records to sign them. With Templeman at the production desk, Van Halen entered the studio and recorded their self-titled debut in 1978. The album was released to widespread critical acclaim and compared with Montrose's debut in 1974. It featured a unique fusion of energy, sophistication and virtuosity through Eddie Van Halen's extraordinary guitar lines and Roth's self-assured vocal style. Within 12 months it had sold two million units, peaking at number 19 in the *Billboard* chart; over the years this album has continued to sell and by 1996 it had been certified in the USA alone at 9 million sales. Eddie Van Halen was named as Best New Guitarist Of The Year in 1978, by *Guitar Player* magazine. The follow-up, simply titled *Van Halen II*, kept to the same formula and was equally successful. Roth's stage antics became even more sensational - he was the supreme showman, combining theatrical stunts with a stunning voice to entertaining effect. *Women And Children First* saw the band start to explore more musical avenues and experiment with the use of synthesizers. This came to full fruition on *Fair Warning*, which was a marked departure from earlier releases. *Diver Down* was the band's weakest album, with the cover versions of 60s standards being the strongest tracks. Nevertheless, the band could do no wrong in the eyes of their fans and the album, as had all their previous releases, went platinum. Eddie Van Halen was also a guest on Michael Jackson's 'Beat It', a US number 1 in February 1983. With *1984*, released on New Year's Day of that year, the band returned to form. Nine original tracks reaffirmed their position as the leading exponents of heavy-duty melodic metal infused with a pop sensibility. Spearheaded by 'Jump', a *Billboard* number 1 and UK number 7, the album lodged at number 2 in the US chart for a full five weeks during its one-year residency. This was easily his most high-profile solo outing, though his other select engagements outside Van Halen have included work with Private Life and former Toto member Steve Lukather. Roth upset the applecart by quitting in 1985 to concentrate on his solo career, and ex-Montrose vocalist Sammy Hagar (b. 13 October 1947, Monterey, California, USA) eventually filled the vacancy. Retaining the Van Halen name, against record company pressure to change it, the new line-up released *5150* in June 1986. The album name was derived from the police code for the criminally insane, as well as the name of Eddie Van Halen's recording studio. The lead-off single, 'Why Can't This Be Love', reached number 3 in the *Billboard* chart and number 8 in the UK, while the album became their first US number 1 and their biggest seller to date. *OU812* was a disappointment in creative terms. The songs were formularized and lacked real direction, but the album became the band's second consecutive number 1 in less than two years. *For Unlawful Carnal Knowledge*, written as the acronym *F.U.C.K.*, stirred up some controversy at the time of release. However, the music on the album transcended the juvenile humour of the title, being an immaculate collection of gritty and uncompromising rockers. The band had defined their identity anew and rode into the 90s on a new creative wave - needless to say, platinum status was attained yet again. A live album prefigured the release of the next studio set, *Balance*, with Van Halen's popularity seemingly impervious to the ravages of time or fashion. It is unusual for a greatest hits compilation to debut at number 1 but the band achieved this on the *Billboard* chart in 1996 with *Best Of Volume 1*. Hagar departed in 1996 after rumours persisted that he was at loggerheads with the other members. Fans immediately rejoiced when it was announced that the replacement would be David Lee Roth, although not on a full-time basis. A few months later, Roth issued a statement effectively ruling out any further involvement. The vacancy went to Gary Cherone (b. 26 July 1961, Malden, Massachusetts, USA) soon after Extreme announced their formal disbanding in October 1996. The first album to feature Cherone, *Van Halen III*, was universally slated.

● ALBUMS: *Van Halen* (Warners 1978)★★★★, *Van Halen II* (Warners 1979)★★★★, *Women And Children First* (Warners 1980)★★★, *Fair Warning* (Warners 1981)★★★, *Diver Down* (Warners 1982)★★★, *1984 (MCMLXXXIV)* (Warners 1984)★★★★, *5150* (Warners 1986)★★★★, *OU812* (Warners 1988)★★★★, *For Unlawful Carnal Knowledge* (Warners 1991)★★★, *Live: Right Here Right Now* (Warners 1993)★★★, *Balance* (Warners 1995)★★★, *Van Halen III* (Warners 1998)★★.

● COMPILATIONS: *Best Of Volume 1* (Warners 1996)★★★★.

● VIDEOS: *Live Without A Net* (WEA 1987), *Live: Right Here Right Now* (1993), *Video Hits Volume 1* (Warner Music Video 1996).

● FURTHER READING: *Van Halen*, Michelle Craven. *Excess All Areas*, Malcolm Dome.

VAN HALEN, EDDIE

b. 26 January 1957, Nijmegen, Netherlands. Van Halen is highly regarded as one of rock music's more distinctive guitarists. The group Van Halen's debut album was considered by many to be one of the greatest heavy rock albums ever released. A short guitar-only track, 'Eruption', epitomized Eddie Van Halen's guitar pyrotechnics. Together with fellow Van Halen bandmate, extrovert showman David Lee Roth, their stage show was an incredible spectacle. Eddie Van Halen not only proved to be a superb musician but he always exuded an air of total enjoyment. He has recorded numerous albums with Van Halen the band, and although they have not all been as fiery and dynamic as the first release, they all display his versatile guitar style. Matters have not, however, always gone according to plan and in 1984 he fell out with colleague Roth over musical direction, resulting in Roth departing the ranks and Sammy Hagar joining. This marked a new era for the band who continue to enjoy considerable success. To date, Eddie Van Halen has not recorded a solo album, although he has guested on several including those by Private Life (whom he has also produced) and Steve Lukather (ex-Toto). Perhaps his most famous guest contribution to date is his guitar solo on Michael Jackson's 1983 number 1 single 'Beat It', taken from the phenomenally successful *Thriller*.

VANDENBERG

This Dutch hard rock act was a vehicle for the talents of Adrian Vandenberg (b. 31 January 1954, Holland), formed by the experienced guitarist after the collapse of his previous band, Teaser, and an unsuccessful spell rehearsing with Thin Lizzy. The group, which was completed by Bert Heerink (vocals), Dick Kemper (bass; ex-Turbo) and Jos Zoomer (drums), quickly signed to Atlantic Records on the strength of an impressive demo, enabling Vandenberg to give up the session work and super-realist art that had financially supported him. The self-produced *Vandenberg* had a heavy sound reminiscent of the Scorpions and Judas Priest, and contained sparkling performances from Vandenberg and Zoomer. The former's songwriting and guitar-playing, compared at the time to Michael Schenker, interested David Coverdale, who twice asked the guitarist to join Whitesnake. However, with the album and 'Burning Heart' single enjoying considerable success in the USA, Vandenberg declined. *Heading For A Storm* benefited from the band's wider experience, with Heerink particularly improved, but failed to maintain the previous momentum of US success, despite a tour supporting Kiss. *Alibi*, however, saw the band regain much of the lost ground with a better production and more fiery fretwork from Vandenberg, but the departure of Heerink the following year for Picture unfortunately signalled a downward slide for the band, which dissolved in 1987 when Vandenberg finally accepted a further offer from the persistent Coverdale.

● ALBUMS: *Vandenberg* (Atco 1982)★★★, *Heading For A Storm* (Atco 1984)★★★, *Alibi* (Atco 1985)★★★.

● COMPILATIONS: *The Best Of Vandenberg* (Atlantic 1990)★★★.

VANILLA FUDGE

This US rock group was formed in December 1966 and comprised Mark Stein (b. 11 March 1947, New Jersey, USA; organ), Vince Martell (b. 11 November 1945, Bronx, New York, USA; guitar), Tim Bogert (b. 27 August 1944, Richfield, New Jersey, USA; bass) and Joey Brennan (drums). All were previously members of the Pigeons, a New York-based group modelled on the (Young) Rascals. Brennan was latterly replaced by Carmine Appice (b. 15 December 1946, Staten Island, New York, USA), and having established a style in which contemporary songs were imaginatively rearranged, the unit was introduced to producer Shadow Morton, who had a reputation for melodramatic pop with the Shangri-Las. Dubbed Vanilla Fudge by their record label, the quartet scored an immediate success with an atmospheric revival of the Supremes' hit, 'You Keep Me Hanging On'. The slowed tempo, studious playing and mock-gospel harmonies set a precedent for the group's debut album, which featured similarly operatic versions of the Impressions' 'People Get Ready', Sonny And Cher's 'Bang Bang' and the Beatles' 'Eleanor Rigby' and 'Ticket To Ride'. The audacity of this first selection was impossible to repeat. A flawed concept album, *The Beat Goes On*, proved overambitious, while further selections showed a group unable to create original material of the calibre of the first album. Subsequent records relied on simpler, hard-edged rock. When Vanilla Fudge split in 1970, the bassist and drummer remained together in Cactus before abandoning their creation in favour of Beck, Bogert And Appice. Stein worked with Tommy Bolin and Alice Cooper before forging a new career composing advertising jingles, while Martell later appeared in the Good Rats, a popular Long Island bar-band. The group briefly re-formed in 1983, releasing *Mystery* which failed to make any impact.

● ALBUMS: *Vanilla Fudge* (Atco 1967)★★★, *The Beat Goes On* (Atco 1968)★★, *Renaissance* (Atco 1968)★★, *Near The Beginning* (Atco 1969)★★, *Rock And Roll* (Atco 1970)★★, *Mystery* (Atco 1984)★★.

● COMPILATIONS: *The Best Of The Vanilla Fudge* (Atco 1982)★★, *Psychedelic Sundae - The Best Of* (Rhino 1993)★★★.

VARDIS

Taking their central influence from mid-70s Status Quo and adding heavier guitar, *Fireball XL5* fan Steve Zodiac formed Quo Vardis in his home-town of Wakefield, England, in 1978, with bassist Alan Selway and drummer Gary Pearson. Zodiac, usually barefoot and bare-chested, with long blonde hair, guitar and screaming vocals, cut the perfect heavy metal stereotype. In 1979, dropping Quo from their name, the group released the *100 M.P.H. EP*, and then set out on tour. By 1980 they had built a major live reputation, yet their second single, 'If I Were King', lacked that live aggression. Logo Records remained impressed and signed them up. Realizing that performance was their strongest medium, their debut album arose from a live taping. In 1981 they gigged with Hawkwind and released their own version of 'Silver Machine', and an album, *Worlds Insane*, which may be the only heavy metal album ever to feature bagpipes (played by Judd Lander, on a track entitled 'Police Patrol'). This gained them much publicity (appearing naked with bagpipes for photos, etc.), while a further tenuous Status Quo link was achieved by having Andy Bown play keyboards on the album. From this point on they remained firm live favourites but falling record sales saw them dropped by Logo. In 1983 Selway quit and Terry Horbury (ex-Dirty Tricks) replaced him and played on their final album. Like most of the New Wave Of British Heavy Metal bands, they eventually faded away rather than burning out.

● ALBUMS: *Worlds Insane* (Logo 1981)★★★★,

Quo Vardis (Logo 1982)★★, *The Lion's Share* (Razor 1983)★★, *Vigilante* (Raw Power 1986)★★.
● COMPILATIONS: *The Best Of Vardis* (British Steel 1997)★★★.

VENOM

This influential English black metal band, who were a major influence on thrash pioneers Metallica, Slayer and Possessed, as well as the satanic fraternity, were formed in Newcastle Upon Tyne by Cronos (b. Conrad Lant; bass, vocals), Mantas (b. Geoff Dunn; guitar) and Abaddon (b. Tony Bray; drums). Their debut was 1981's legendary *Welcome To Hell*, a raw collection of brutal songs filled with dark, satanic imagery. *Black Metal* was much better in terms of playing and production, and remains Venom's best album, containing the atmospheric 'Buried Alive' amid the more customary speed bursts. *At War With Satan*, a semi-concept album, and numerous singles followed - BBC Radio 1 DJ Tommy Vance paid £100 to charity when Mike Read played 'Warhead' on his breakfast show for a bet - and Venom played numerous major shows worldwide (club dates were precluded by the nature of Venom's pyrotechnics, which tended to cause structural damage in enclosed spaces), proudly refusing to be anything but headliners. However, the poor *Possessed* and a spate of unofficial live and compilation releases hurt the band, and Mantas left as the *Eine Kleine Nachtmusik* live set emerged. Mike Hickey and Jimmy C. were recruited for live commitments, and this line-up produced the commendable power metal of *Calm Before The Storm* before Cronos left, taking both guitarists for his Cronos band. Mantas, however, rejoined Abaddon, bringing rhythm guitarist Al Barnes, and the new Venom was completed by ex-Atomkraft bassist/vocalist Tony 'The Demolition Man' Dolan. *Prime Evil* harked back to the early Venom approach, albeit with rather more professionalism, and contained a good cover of Black Sabbath's 'Megalomania'. Barnes left after 1991's *Temples Of Ice*, and the remaining trio temporarily recruited guitarist Steve White and keyboard player VXS. Subsequent releases failed to emulate the standards of the earlier albums, but Cronos returned to the band in 1996, replacing Dolan. 1997's *Cast In Stone* featured new and re-recorded material, and was followed by a world tour. Venom, already the subject of a tribute album, remain among the most important of all heavy metal acts, having originated a style that became a template for much of the music's modern practitioners.
● ALBUMS: *Welcome To Hell* (Neat 1981)★★★, *Black Metal* (Neat 1982)★★★★, *At War With Satan* (Neat 1984)★★, *Possessed* (Neat 1985)★★, *Eine Kleine Nachtmusik* (Neat 1985)★★, *Calm Before The Storm* (FilmTrax 1987)★★★, *Prime Evil* (Under One Flag 1989)★★★, *Tear Your Soul Apart* (Under One Flag 1990)★★, *Temples Of Ice* (Under One Flag 1991)★★, *The Waste Lands* (Under One Flag 1992)★★, *Cast In Stone* (SPV 1997)★★★.
● COMPILATIONS: *The Singles '80 - '86* (Raw Power 1986)★★★, *New, Live And Rare* (Caroline 1998)★★.

VICIOUS RUMORS

This San Francisco power metal band formed in 1979, making their debut on *US Metal III* after linking with guitar guru Mike Varney. However, by the release of *Soldiers Of The Night*, only one of the original line-up, guitarist Geoff Thorpe, remained, alongside bassist Dave Starr, drummer Larry Howe, and vocalist Gary St Pierre. Unable to find a suitable guitar partner, Thorpe drafted in Vinnie Moore, and his blistering guitar solo contributions brought the band considerable attention, although he never became a permanent member, with Terry Montana joining for live work. However, *Digital Dictator* saw the line-up stabilize with the addition of guitarist Mark McGee and vocalist Carl Albert (b. 13 May 1962, d. 22 April 1995) in place of Montana and St Pierre, respectively, and the new guitar partnership gelled superbly to produce a more song-based record. The band duly signed a major contract with Atlantic Records, producing two albums of high-quality power metal in *Vicious Rumors* and *Welcome To The Ball*, built on excellent musicianship and Thorpe-McGee guitar interplay, which the band reproduced easily on stage. However, the material lacked the commercial edge to cross over into the mainstream and the band were dropped, although they maintained their popularity in Japan, and returned to independent territory for the Queensrÿche-influenced *Word Of Mouth*. However, in 1995 lead singer Carl Albert died from injuries sustained in a car crash after returning from rehearsal sessions.
● ALBUMS: *Soldiers Of The Night* (Roadrunner 1986)★★★, *Digital Dictator* (Roadrunner 1988)★★, *Vicious Rumors* (Atlantic 1990)★★★, *Welcome To The Ball* (Atlantic 1991)★★★, *Word Of Mouth* (SPV 1994)★★★, *Cyberchrist* (Massacre 1998)★★.

VICTOR

Taken from W.H. Auden's poem of the same name, Victor is the enigmatic title given to Rush guitarist Alex Lifeson's first solo project. In 1994, for the first time in their career, the trio agreed to take a break from their established work regime and Lifeson took the opportunity to put together his first solo album. Recorded over 10 months at his home studio, just north of Toronto, the result was a very dark, diverse and aggressive album. Much of the recording was completed by himself, with an impressive list of guest musicians including guitarist Bill Bell, bassist Pete Cardinali, drummer Blake Manning and Primus bassist Les Claypool. Most of the vocals were handled by Lifeson, with contributions from Edwin of I Mother Earth and acclaimed Canadian vocalist/songwriter Dalbello. By Lifeson's own admission, the lyrical fare is based on relationships and love, subjects already covered a million times over, but the altogether heavier and fiercer intent and execution made Victor sound harder than the smooth art-rock so many fans associated with modern Rush. If anything, the prominence of some of the guitar work recalled Rush's rockier period of the 70s and early 80s; the inclusion of Dalbello's powerful vocals, sounding spookily like Rush bassist/vocalist Geddy Lee, on 'Start Today' completed the illusion. As a diversion from the usual output from Rush, Victor provided a fascinating glimpse into their guitarist's inventive solo abilities.

● ALBUMS: *Victor* (Atlantic 1996)★★★.

VIKSTRÖM, TOMAS

b. Sweden. Vikström's father, Sven-Erik Vikström, is a widely reputed Swedish opera singer. Thomas too has followed that path, but he has also recorded to greater success as a rock singer. His popular music career began with the Swedish rock group Talk Of The Town, who enjoyed a degree of domestic success with their song 'Free Like An Eagle'. After that group collapsed he returned to the theatre and took starring roles in two rock operas - *Barefoot Life* and *The Adventures Of Hoffman*. The latter was a major production in Stockholm that ran for several months and earned him tumultuous acclaim. However, the lure of rock 'n' roll once again tempted him away and he took over as vocalist for one of Sweden's longest-running (and most extreme) rock bands - Candlemass. With Vikström at the helm Candlemass won the prestigious Zeppelin Prize, awarded by a special jury of musicians and journalists. In 1993 he opted for a solo career, releasing *If I Could Fly* for Virgin Records. Guests included many celebrated names drawn from the Swedish rock firmament, and the album was successful throughout Europe. Noticeably more commercial than his work with Candlemass, it earned comparisons with mainstream rock artists including Jackson Browne and Bryan Adams.

● ALBUMS: *If I Could Fly* (Virgin 1993)★★★.

VINCENT, VINNIE

b. Vincent Cusano. Vincent began his musical career as guitar/vocalist in the melodic rock band Treasure in 1977. In 1982 he accepted the offer to join Kiss and contributed to *Creatures Of The Night* and *Lick It Up*, the latter featuring the band without make-up on the cover for the first time. After two years with Kiss, Vincent left to form the autonomous Vinnie Vincent Invasion. Recruiting Robert Fleischmann (ex-Journey; vocals), Dana Strum (ex-Ozzy Osbourne group; bass) and Bobby Rock (drums), they secured a contract with Chrysalis Records in 1985. Their self-titled debut album, released the following year, was a critical success. Fleischman was replaced by Mark Slaughter immediately after the album was released, and the cohesion of the band was lost. *All Systems Go* followed a similar pattern to its predecessor, but was not widely purchased by metal fans. Frustrated by the lack of success, Slaughter and Strum left to form Slaughter. Vincent was dropped by Chrysalis, but in 1990 he teamed up with Fleischmann again to work on a solo project.

● ALBUMS: *Vinnie Vincent Invasion* (Chrysalis 1986)★★★, *All Systems Go* (Chrysalis 1988)★★★.

VIOLENCE

This Bay Area thrash band (also known as Vio-Lence because of their logo) formed as Death Penalty in San Francisco in 1985, with a line-up of guitarists Phil Demmel and Troy Fua, Eddie Billy (bass), Perry Strickland (drums) and vocalist Jerry Burr, who was replaced in 1986 by Sean Killian; Robb Flynn (b. 19 July 1968, Oakland, California, USA) and Deen Dell had replaced Fua and Billy, respectively, before Violence signed a one-album deal with Mechanic. *Eternal Nightmare* was typically riff-heavy Bay Area thrash, with excellent Demmel-Flynn guitar interplay, but Killian's vocals were an acquired taste, and aggressive marketing, which included pre-release demo giveaways and the infamous 'vomit' bag for the 'Eternal Nightmare' single (the 'vomit' was in fact a mixture of vegetable soup and vinegar), produced only moderate sales. *Oppressing The Masses* was an impressive effort, but was delayed as Atlantic Records were unwilling to distribute the album due to Killian's lyrics for 'Torture Tactics', inspired by a horrifying documentary on the use of torture as a political weapon by oppressive regimes around the world; the offending track was removed and later released on an independent EP. Violence struggled to broaden their appeal, and after the tired-sounding *Nothing To Gain*, the band faded, only for Flynn to emerge to almost instantaneous success with Machine Head.

● ALBUMS: *Eternal Nightmare* (Mechanic 1988)★★★, *Oppressing The Masses* (Megaforce 1990)★★★, *Nothing To Gain* (Bleeding Hearts 1993)★★.

VIRGIN STEELE

Comprising David DeFeis (vocals, keyboards), Jack Starr (guitar), Joe O'Reilly (bass) and Joey Ayvazian (drums), US rock band Virgin Steele were always likely to appeal to heavy metal purists. Like Manowar, they eschewed any considerations of subtlety in favour of excess - be it in musicianship or stage appearance. The group made its debut for Music For Nations in 1983, the first record to be released on that increasingly dominant independent, with a self-titled collection that established their *modus operandi*. It also brought them considerable acclaim in the heavy metal press. Over subsequent albums, however, Virgin Steele became subject to internal rifts, with Starr opting for a solo career in 1984. None of their subsequent releases managed to recreate the spirit of their first three records and by the early 90s they had broken up.

● ALBUMS: *Virgin Steele* (Music For Nations 1983)★★★★, *Guardians Of The Flame* (Music For Nations 1983)★★, *A Cry In The Night* (Music For Nations 1984)★★★, *Noble Savage* (Cobra 1986)★★, *Age Of Consent* (SPV 1989)★★.

VIXEN

Not to be confused with the Yorkshire, England-based Vixen, this glossy, female US rock quartet was put together in 1986 by former Madam X drummer Roxy Petrucci. The line-up initially featured Steve Vai's wife Pia Koko on bass, but she was succeeded by Share Pederson before the band signed to EMI Records. With Janet Gardner handling vocals and Jan Kuehnemund on guitar, the band had a wealth of musical ability and a strong visual image. Their debut album included material by outside writers, most notably Richard Marx and Jeff Paris. *Rev It Up* was largely self-penned and launched the band in the USA. Marketed as the female equivalent of Bon Jovi, they specialized in four-minute pop/rock anthems and the occasional obligatory power-ballad, with memorable choruses including 'Cryin'' and 'How Much Love', plus the Marx-composed epic 'Edge Of A Broken Heart'. Petrucci would later work with Lorraine Lewis (ex-Femme Fatale) in a new all-female outfit. Petrucci and Gardner reunited in 1998 to release *Tangerine*, on which they were backed by Maxine Petrucci and Gina Stile (ex-Poison Dollys).

● ALBUMS: *Vixen* (EMI 1988)★★★, *Rev It Up* (EMI 1990)★★★, *Tangerine* (Eagle 1998)★★★.

VOIVOD

Formed in Canada in the early 80s, Voivod consisted of Denis Belanger (vocals), Denis D'Amour (guitar), Jean-Yves Theriault (bass) and Michel Langevin (drums). The release of their first album made them one of the first thrash metal bands to make a name for themselves worldwide. The sound of this debut was highly unconventional, with an almost *avant garde* feel at times. A second album continued in this tradition with noisy, neo-industrial elements, and helped them become popular in metal underground circles. Progression was evident on *Killing Technology* which showcased improved musicianship and lyrics. However, on *Dimension Hatross* they left behind much of their thrash roots, and there was now much more to their sound than that basic attack. This trend continued on *Nothingface*, which contained little that could be labelled thrash metal, and *Angel Rat*, which also saw the departure of Jean-Yves Theriault. Influences such as progressive rock were increasingly taking hold of song construction and twisting the band's narratives into new and occasionally brilliant shapes. The strength of their ideas and the depth of their musical skills and interpretation has helped them to grow steadily and transcend thrash roots while still retaining a strong fanbase right across the metal spectrum. *Negatron* marked the recording debut of new bass player/vocalist Eric Forrest. Jim Thirwell (Foetus) guested on one track, 'DNA', while 1997's *Phobos* featured a track, 'M-Body', co-written with Jason Newsted of Metallica.

● ALBUMS: *War And Pain* (Metal Blade 1984)★★★★, *RRROOOAAARRR* (Noise International/Combat 1986)★★★, *Killing Technology* (Noise International/Combat 1987)★★★★, *Dimension Hatross* (Noise International 1988)★★★, *Nothingface* (Mechanic/MCA 1989)★★★, *Angel Rat* (Mechanic 1991)★★★, *The Outer Limits* (Mechanic/MCA 1993)★★★, *Negatron* (Mausoleum 1995)★★★, *Phobos* (Hypnotic 1997)★★★.

● COMPILATIONS: *The Best Of Voivod* (Futurist/Mechanic 1992)★★★.

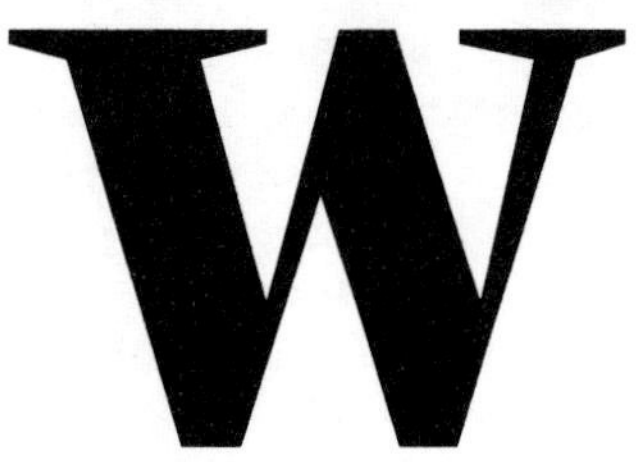

W.A.S.P.

This theatrical shock-rock troupe was formed in the early 80s in Los Angeles, USA; their name was apparently an acronym of We Are Sexual Perverts. Outrageous live performances included throwing raw meat into the audience and the whipping of a naked woman tied to a 'torture rack' as a backdrop to a primitive metal attack. The band, led by bassist/vocalist Blackie Lawless (b. 4 September 1956) with guitarists Chris Holmes (b. 23 June 1961) and Randy Piper and drummer Tony Richards, were snapped up by Capitol Records, who then refused to release their debut single, the infamous 'Animal (Fuck Like A Beast)', on legal advice. It was subsequently licensed to independent labels. *W.A.S.P.* was an adequate basic metal debut, although it lacked 'Animal', while *The Last Command*, with new drummer Steve Riley (ex-B'zz), consolidated W.A.S.P.'s status with a more refined approach, producing the excellent 'Wild Child' and 'Blind In Texas'. W.A.S.P. became a major US concert draw, albeit with a stageshow much toned down from the early days. *Inside The Electric Circus* in 1986 continued in this vein, and saw the debut of bassist Johnny Rod (ex-King Kobra), with Lawless replacing Piper on rhythm guitar, while live shows saw Lawless's trademark buzzsaw-bladed codpiece replaced by a remarkable flame-throwing version. *Live ... In The Raw* was a decent live set, but once again lacked 'Animal', which remained the centrepiece of W.A.S.P.'s repertoire. That song, and the band's outrageous approach, made them a constant target for the PMRC, whom Lawless successfully sued for unauthorized use of copyrighted material. As Lawless became a tireless free speech campaigner, he moved the band towards a serious stance on *The Headless Children*, with Quiet Riot drummer Frankie Banali replacing the L.A. Guns-bound Riley. The socio-political and anti-drug commentary was backed by vivid imagery in the live setting, but Holmes departed after the tour, the split catalyzed by his drunken appearance in the film *The Decline And Fall Of Western Civilisation Part II: The Metal Years*. Lawless used session musicians to record *The Crimson Idol*, a Who-influenced concept effort, and toured with Rod, Doug Blair (guitar) and Stet Howland (drums), but went solo after compiling the *First Blood ... Last Cuts* retrospective. *Still Not Black Enough* promised to be their most commercial record and was preceded by two tracks issued together, 'Black Forever' and 'Goodbye America'. Their flagging career was further marred by the release of the listless *W.A.S.P.* in 1995, which featured Bob Kulick, who appeared on *The Crimson Idol*, on guitar. Following 1997's equally forgettable *Kill, F**k, Die* the concert set *Double Live Assassins* served as a timely reminder that the group were still a potent live act.

● ALBUMS: *W.A.S.P.* (Capitol 1984)★★, *The Last Command* (Capitol 1985)★★★, *Inside The Electric Circus* (Capitol 1986)★★★, *Live ... In The Raw* (Capitol 1987)★★, *The Headless Children* (Capitol 1989)★★, *The Crimson Idol* (Parlophone 1992)★★★, *Still Not Black Enough* (Raw Power 1995)★★★, *W.A.S.P.* (Castle 1995)★★, *Kill, F**k, Die* (Raw Power 1997)★★, *Double Live Assassins* (Snapper 1998)★★★.

● COMPILATIONS: *First Blood ... Last Cuts* (Capitol 1993)★★★.

● VIDEOS: *Live At The Lyceum* (PMI 1985), *W.A.S.P.: Videos In The Raw* (PMI 1988).

Waite, John

b. 4 July 1955, Lancaster, Lancashire, England. Waite is a singer, bassist and occasional harmonica player who has found greater fame and fortune in the USA than in his native land. A former art student, he began playing in bands in the late 60s and in 1976 formed the Babys with Mike Corby, Tony Brock and Walter Stocker. The Babys split in 1981 after five albums and Waite embarked on a solo career. His debut single, 'Change', was not a chart hit and he had to wait until 'Missing You' was released from his second album for a breakthrough. In the UK the record made a respectable number 9 but in the USA it went to the top. Waite formed the No Brakes band, joined by former David Bowie guitarist Earl Slick, to promote the new album, but did not scale the same heights again. Instead he formed the ill-fated Bad English in 1989, before resuming his solo career in the mid-90s. In 1995 he had his first hit for several years with the power ballad 'How Did I Get By Without You'. The album *Temple Bar* was more in the folk-rock line and included covers of songs by Hank Williams and Bill Withers.

● ALBUMS: *Ignition* (Chrysalis 1982)★★, *No Brakes* (EMI America 1984)★★, *Mask Of Smiles*

(Capitol 1985)★★, *Rovers Return* (EMI America 1987)★★, *Temple Bar* (Imago 1995)★★.
● COMPILATIONS: *The Essential* (EMI America 1992)★★★.

WALSH, JOE

b. 20 November 1947, New Jersey, USA. Guitar hero Walsh started his long and varied career in 1965 with the G-Clefs. Following a spell with local band the Measles, he found major success when he joined the James Gang in 1969. Walsh's growling, early heavy metal guitar technique was not unlike that of Jeff Beck's, and the Walsh sound had much to do with the achievements of the James Gang. He left in 1972 and formed Barnstorm with Joe Vitale (drums) and Kenny Passarelli (bass). The self-titled album promised much and made a respectable showing in the US charts. Despite the follow-up being credited to Joe Walsh, *The Smoker You Drink The Player You Get* was still Barnstorm, although the band broke up that same year. *Smoker* became his first gold album and featured some of his classic songs such as 'Meadows' and 'Rocky Mountain Way'. On the latter he featured the voice bag, from which his distorted voice emitted after being sung into a plastic tube. Walsh, along with Peter Frampton and Jeff Beck popularized this effect in the early 70s.

In 1974 he produced Dan Fogelberg's classic album *Souvenirs* and guested on albums by Stephen Stills, the Eagles and B.B. King. *So What* in 1975 was another gold album and featured the Walsh classic, 'Turn To Stone'. During the summer he performed at London's Wembley Stadium with the Beach Boys, Elton John and the Eagles. Five months later Walsh joined the Eagles when he replaced Bernie Leaden and became full-time joint lead guitarist with Glen Frey. His distinctive tone contributed greatly to their milestone *Hotel California*; his solo on the title track is one of the highlights. Additionally he retained his autonomy by continuing his highly successful career and released further solo albums including the excellent *But Seriously Folks ...* which featured the humorous autobiographical 'Life's Been Good'. The song dealt with his fortune and fame in a light-hearted manner, although there was a degree of smugness attached, for example: 'I have a mansion, forget the price, ain't never been there, they tell me its nice'. Such was Walsh's confidence that at one point he announced he would stand for President at the next election. He was wise to have maintained his solo career, as the Eagles only made one further album. Walsh shrewdly kept his best work for his own albums. In 1980 Walsh contributed to the best-selling soundtrack *Urban Cowboy* and was rewarded with a US Top 20 hit 'All Night Long'. Both *There Goes The Neighborhood* and *You Bought It - You Name It* maintained his profile and although his 1987 album, *Got Any Gum?* was uninspiring, his career continues to prosper as a solo and session player. In 1992 he was playing with Ringo Starr on the latter's comeback tour. By 1995 a rakish and fit-looking Walsh was once again playing in front of vast audiences as a member of the reunited Eagles.
● ALBUMS: *Barnstorm* (ABC 1972)★★★, *The Smoker You Drink, The Player You Get* (ABC 1973)★★★★, *So What?* (ABC 1975)★★★★, *You Can't Argue With A Sick Mind* (ABC 1976)★★, *But Seriously Folks ...* (Asylum 1978)★★★, *There Goes The Neighborhood* (Asylum 1981)★★, *You Bought It - You Name It* (Warners 1983)★★, *The Confessor* (Warners 1985)★★, *Got Any Gum?* (Warners 1987)★★, *Ordinary Average Guy* (Epic 1991)★★, *Robocop - The Series Soundtrack* (Essential 1995)★★.
● COMPILATIONS: *The Best Of Joe Walsh* (ABC 1978)★★★, *All The Best* (Pickwick 1994)★★, *Look What I Did! - The Joe Walsh Anthology* 2-CD (MCA 1995)★★★.

WARFARE

Taking their cue from Venom and Motörhead, this three-piece band was formed in Newcastle in 1984 by former Angelic Upstarts drummer Paul Evo, who also took on vocal duties, guitarist Gunner and bassist Falken. With Algy Ward (Saints; Damned; Tank) at the production helm they recorded an album for Neat Records and put together an excellent set of punk/metal standards. They also recorded one track with their friends, Venom, entitled 'Rose Petals Fall From Her Face', one of the world's most obnoxious songs (the album that housed it ran under the banner *Pure Filth*). Their next recording was a 12-inch single, a wickedly satirical version of Frankie Goes To Hollywood's 'Two Tribes', which brought them to public attention and even secured national airplay. In 1985 they set off on a tour of Europe and enhanced their anarchic image with wild live performances. The only new recording came as another 12-inch single, the *Total Death EP*, which contained interesting numbers such as 'Rape', Destroy' and 'Metal Anarchy'. The latter gave them a title for their second album, produced by Lemmy, which also featured a guest appearance from fellow Motörhead man Wurzel on guitar. They continued in the same vein for 1987's *Mayhem Fuckin'*

Mayhem, but soon after release Falken left to be replaced by Zlaughter. The following year's *Conflict Of Hatred* had some surprise guests, with Mart Craggs (Lindisfarne) on saxophone and Irene Hume (Prelude) joining the more predictable supporting cast, which included an appearance from Mantas (Venom). They resurfaced in 1990, announcing their intention to record a tribute album to Hammer Horror Films' 49th birthday celebration. An ambitious and ultimately unsuccessful project, this featured many samples of classic Hammer films. After one big promotional concert they were faced with a barrage of press criticisms and announced that they would no longer perform live, stating as an epitaph: 'If our fans want to see us they will have to buy a video'. Since then they have remained largely inactive.

● ALBUMS: *Pure Filth* (Neat 1984)★★, *Metal Anarchy* (Neat 1986)★★★, *Mayhem Fuckin' Mayhem* (Neat 1987)★★★, *Conflict Of Hatred* (Neat 1988)★★, *Hammer Horror* (Hammer Film Music/FM Revolver 1990)★★★.

● VIDEOS: *A Concept Of Hatred* (Jettisoundz 1988).

WARHORSE

Warhorse was formed in 1970 by bassist/vocalist Nick Simper, formerly of Johnny Kidd And The Pirates. Between 1967 and 1969 Simper had been a member of Deep Purple and the influence of this group can be heard clearly on *Warhorse*. Ashley Holt (vocals), Ged Peck (guitar), Frank Wilson (piano; ex-Velvett Fogg) and Mac Poole (drums) completed a line-up which enjoyed a European hit single with 'St. Louis'. This spirited version of the Easybeats' number typified the group's early style. Peter Parker replaced Peck for *Red Sea*. He introduced a new dimension to the Warhorse sound which became more guitar-orientated. However, despite considerable success on the Continent, Warhorse split up in 1974. Simper subsequently formed Nick Simper's Fandango, Holt later worked with Rick Wakeman and in 1980 Gale formed Dirty Looks.

● ALBUMS: *Warhorse* (Vertigo 1970)★★★, *Red Card* (Vertigo 1972)★★★.

● COMPILATIONS: *The Warhorse Story Volume 1* (RPM 1997)★★★, *The Warhorse Story Volume 2* (RPM 1997)★★.

WARLOCK

After two years of constant gigging, the German band Warlock - Doro (b. Dorothee Pesch, 3 June 1964, Dusseldorf, Germany; vocals), Peter Szigeti (guitar), Rudy Graf (guitar), Frank Rittel (bass) and Michael Eurich (drums) - finally released an album. Signed to the independent Mausoleum label, they issued *Burning The Witches*, which boasted a sound typical of German bands such as the Scorpions and Accept, but with the vocals of Doro sounding strangely like Ronnie James Dio. The album, and the presence of their striking blonde-haired vocalist brought them to notice in the rest of the world and they were signed by Vertigo Records, who released *Hellbound* a year later. By 1986 the emphasis on the band was focused mainly on Pesch. Graf left to be replaced by Niko Arvantis and the next single, 'You Hurt My Soul', was withdrawn (the tracks turned up later on a 12-inch EP). *True As Steel* suffered from over-production and Americanization. Pesch then relocated the band to New York where they dissolved. A new line-up, with Eurich the only surviving member, added Tommy Bolan (guitar), Tommy Henriksen (bass) and, eventually, a re-hired Arvantis. The resulting album, *Triumph And Agony*, was definitely the latter, and again the band split. *Force Majeure*, credited to Doro And Warlock, was essentially a solo effort. Bobby Rondinelli, formerly of Rainbow, played drums on that set. A year later Warlock were confined to history as Pesch fully adopted the American sound and pushed herself forward as a new Lee Aaron or Lita Ford.

● ALBUMS: *Burning The Witches* (Mausoleum 1984)★★★, *Hellbound* (Vertigo 1985)★★★★, *True As Steel* (Vertigo 1986)★★, *Triumph And Agony* (Vertigo 1987)★★★.

● VIDEOS: *Metal Racer* (Hendring Video/Castle Communications 1990).

WARRANT

A product of the late 80s Los Angeles club scene, Warrant comprised John 'Jani' Lane (b. 1 February 1964, Akron, Ohio, USA; vocals), guitarists Erik Turner (b. 31 March 1964, Omaha, Nebraska, USA) and Joey Allen (b. 23 June 1964, Fort Wayne, Indiana, USA), Jerry Dixon (b. 15 September 1967, Pasadena, California, USA; bass) and Steven Sweet (b. 29 October 1965, Wadsworth, Ohio, USA; drums). A clever self-promotion campaign and sterling live work turned the band into LA's hottest unsigned outfit, and Columbia Records were quick to step in. *Dirty Rotten Filthy Stinking Rich* was a solid debut, and 'Down Boys', coupled with exhaustive touring made it a hit (US number 27 in April 1989). However, sales went through the roof as MTV favourite 'Heaven' rose to number 2 in the US charts three months later. This success, along with that of another ballad, 'Sometimes She Cries', and the band's looks, led to image problems, with Warrant unjustly viewed as a manufactured act in some quarters of the press. The tongue-in-cheek pop metal title track of *Cherry Pie*, written by Lane in 45 minutes to round off the album, was another enormous US hit (number 10 in September 1990), but did little to redress the band's credibility problems, although further hits 'I Saw Red' (which also reached number 10) and 'Uncle Tom's Cabin' undoubtedly helped. The band's UK debut supporting David Lee Roth had little chance to impress the British press, as the dates had to be abandoned when Lane fell and cracked a rib on the first night. *Dog Eat Dog* was a credible attempt at a heavier approach, but during the grunge era it sold dramatically less than either of its multi-million-selling predecessors. Lane went solo, with Columbia reducing both parties to demo deals, and although he later rejoined, Allen and Sweet departed, the latter leaving the music business altogether. Former Kingdom Come duo Rick Steier and James Kottak, who had worked on Lane's solo project, replaced them. *Ultraphobic* earned them strong reviews at a time when the band's career was seemingly on the wane.

● ALBUMS: *Dirty Rotten Filthy Stinking Rich* (Columbia 1989)★★★, *Cherry Pie* (Columbia 1990)★★, *Dog Eat Dog* (Columbia 1992)★★★, *Ultraphobic* (CMC International/Music For Nations 1995)★★★, *Belly To Belly* (CMC International 1996)★★, *Warrant Live 1986-1997* recorded 1997 (CMC International)★★★.

● COMPILATIONS: *The Best Of Warrant* (Sony Legacy 1996)★★★.

WARRIOR

Formed in 1982, Los Angeles, California, USA band Warrior occupied a space somewhere between the barbarian machismo of Manowar and the grandiose pomp rock of Queen. The line-up originally comprised Perry McCarty (vocals), Tommy Asakawa (guitar), Joe Floyd (guitar), Rick Bennett (bass, keyboards) and Liam Jason (drums). The band spent time playing the local clubs and refining their style before recording a three-track demo that led to sold-out local shows and record deals with MCA Records in the USA and 10 Records in Europe. They subsequently endured considerable technical problems during the recording of *Fighting For The Earth* and lost both Bennett and Jason following the sessions, with Bruce Turgon (bass, ex-Black Sheep) and Jimmy Volpe (drums) replacing them. It was a reasonable debut, built on a dense, rhythmic guitar barrage and thunderous drums overlaid by McCarty's near-operatic vocals. Lyrics included some entertaining if daft sub-Nietzschean fantasy scenarios. Similarities to Judas Priest were obvious, although Warrior tended to avoid dual lead guitar work, and the band's stage image, although leather-clad, was in a futuristic armour style befitting their name. However, a bemused public showed little interest and the rock press, convinced they were being sold an industry-hyped act, treated them with disdain. In 1986 the band split leaving the members to join other acts (McCarty joined Steve Steven's Atomic Playboys, while Turgon found himself a job with Shadow King).

● ALBUMS: *Fighting For The Earth* (MCA 1985)★★★.

WARRIOR SOUL

This psychotic art-rock quartet from New York is the brainchild of poetry-reading, one-time video DJ and L7 (the Detroit, rather than the all-female Los Angeles, version) drummer Kory Clarke. With the help of Pete McClanahan (bass), John Ricco (guitar) and Paul Ferguson (drums), *Last Decade, Dead Century* was released in 1990, with Clarke leading from the front with vocals and lyrics that took few prisoners: 'At that time everybody was hooked on Hollywood and the whole vibe of 80s Republican morality. But all that lame ass shit had no content'. Influences as diverse as the Doors, Metallica, the Stooges and Joy Division were combined to produce a dark, intense, angst-ridden debut album. Lyrically it criticized the establishment's inability to solve contemporary social problems, with references to political and police corruption, the homeless and narcotics. Mark Evans took over as drummer on *Drugs, God And The New Republic*, which built on previous themes, but increased the musical intensity of their delivery, honed on US supports to Queensrÿche, whose philosophical, if not musical, angle they echoed. Alex Arundel then replaced Ricco on guitar. The message for *Salutations From The Ghetto Nation* was succinct if not polite. These works received considerable critical acclaim, but it would be *Chill Pill* and *Space Age Playboys* that converted this into album sales. If anything, *Chill Pill* was more resentful and hate-filled than previous offerings, but by *Space Age Playboys* the band looked to have exhausted this avenue. What listeners received instead was an 'up' record, which maintained Clarke's political allegiances, but allied them to a collage of images and events that eschewed the earlier didacticism. Arundel and McClanahan left in 1995 leaving doubts about the band's future.

● ALBUMS: *Last Decade, Dead Century* (Geffen 1990)★★★, *Drugs, God And The New Republic* (Geffen 1991)★★★, *Salutations From The Ghetto Nation* (Geffen 1992)★★★, *Chill Pill* (Geffen 1993)★★★, *Space Age Playboys* (Music For Nations 1994)★★, *F**ker* (Music For Nations 1996)★★.

WATCHTOWER

This experimental four-piece Texan outfit married the power of Metallica with the intricate and sophisticated arrangements of Rush, via the musicianship of Alan Tecchio (vocals), Ron Jarzombek (guitars), Doug Keyser (bass) and Rick Colaluca (drums). Watchtower's playing was of a high order and their songs contained multiple time-changes, including Jarzombek's exemplary performances on lead, acoustic and even reverse-taping guitar. The group's brand of electro-charged techno-thrash did not earn them the widespread attention that seemed their due.

● ALBUMS: *Watchtower* (Noise 1988)★★★, *Control And Resistance* (Noise 1989)★★★.

WATT, MIKE

Watt's bass contributions to hardcore experimentalists Minutemen and Firehose have passed into US indie rock legend, but it was not until 1995 that he recorded as a solo artist. As soon as he did, the array of alternative rock stars willing to help out was proof of his and his bands' influence. Participants included Eddie Vedder (Pearl Jam), Evan Dando (Lemonheads), Chris and Curt Kirkwood (Meat Puppets), Thurston Moore and Lee Ranaldo (Sonic Youth), Dave Grohl and Krist Novoselic (Nirvana), Gary Lee Connor and Mark Lanegan (Screaming Trees), Pat Smear (Germs), Flea (Red Hot Chili Peppers), Henry Rollins, Dave Pirner (Soul Asylum), Zander Schloss (Circle Jerks/Weirdos), Epic Soundtracks (Swell Maps), Paul Roessler (Twisted Roots/DC3), Joe Baiza (Saccharine Trust), Adam Horovitz and Mike D. (Beastie Boys), Frank Black and J. Mascis (Dinosaur Jr). One track, 'Intense Song For Madonna To Sing', which failed to secure that particular star's input, was an obscure reference to an ancient Minutemen song, 'Political Song For Michael Jackson To Sing'. Although by its very nature a mixed bag, which occasionally lapsed into an unfocused celebrity jam session, the album did have several strong moments, notably Vedder's vocals on 'Against The 70s' and the electric jazz flourish of 'Sidemouse Advice'.

● ALBUMS: *Ball-Hog Or Tugboat* (Columbia 1995)★★★★, *The Engine Room* (Columbia 1997)★★★.

WAYSTED

Waysted were formed in 1982 by ex-UFO bassist Pete Way after he failed to get Fastway off the ground with 'Fast' Eddie Clarke. He subsequently set about putting this band together in America, where he was helping out Ozzy Osbourne, and soon found Ronnie Kayfield (ex-Heartbreakers), who was teaching guitar at the time. Returning to the UK, he further enlisted Frank Noon (Def Leppard/Next Band) on drums, UFO guitarist/keyboard player Paul Raymond and vocalist Ian 'Fin' Muir (ex-Flying Squad). Chrysalis Records (home to UFO) showed interest and signed them to a one-album contract. The resulting *Vices* featured several excellent compositions including 'Toy With The Passion', 'Love Loaded' and a cover of Jefferson Airplane's 'Somebody To Love'. However, the line-up instabilities that plagued the band began when Raymond was fired on the eve of a UK tour supporting Dio. Guitarist Barry Benedetta (himself about to audition for UFO) was added before a famously riotous US tour with Osbourne and Mötley Crüe, but he, old friend Kayfield and Noon were all sacked afterwards as Waysted and Chrysalis parted company. Ex-Jess Cox guitarist Neil Shepherd barely lasted beyond the recording of *Waysted*, which featured ex-UFO drummer Andy Parker, before he was in turn replaced by another UFO refugee, Paul Chapman, as Waysted toured the UK with Iron Maiden. The album was produced by ex-Ten Years After member Leo Lyons and also featured contributions from former Angelic Upstarts drummer Decca Wade. *The Good, The Bad, The Waysted* proved to be the band's best album as Way and Chapman blended perfectly to provide a weightier blues-rock sound that suited Fin's smoky vocals, but line-up changes continued with the addition of ex-Fastway drummer Jerry Shirley and temporary keyboard/guitar player Jimmy DiLella, formerly with Chapman's D.O.A. band. Any hopes of stability vanished when Fin was replaced by ex-D.O.A. vocalist Danny Vaughn and Johnny DiTeodora joined on drums, but the band gained a new contract with Parlophone Records for *Save Your Prayers*, which saw Waysted move towards classic UFO in style, with Vaughn's vocals smoothing out the rough edges of his predecessor. The revitalized Waysted embarked on a UK and European tour supporting Status Quo and US tour with Iron Maiden, but Chapman subsequently departed and was replaced by 17-year-old

American Erik Gamans, who displayed a startling talent on his debut live shows. However, Vaughn quit, forming Tyketto, and the clearly declining band returned to the UK, recording demos with Martin Chaisson (b. Martin Smith) with guest vocals from the Quireboys' Spike Gray, before recruiting ex-Tygers Of Pan Tang vocalist Jon Deverill, but the band finally split in late 1987. Way rejoined Phil Mogg in a revamped UFO, DiTeodora joined Britny Fox, and Gamans reappeared in Cold Sweat.

● ALBUMS: *Vices* (Chrysalis 1983)★★★, *Waysted* mini-album (Music For Nations 1984)★★★, *The Good, The Bad And The Waysted* (Music For Nations 1985)★★★★, *Save Your Prayers* (Parlophone 1986)★★★.

● COMPILATIONS: *Completely Waysted* (Raw Power 1985)★★★.

WEAPON

This sadly neglected metal act was formed in March 1980 by guitarist Jeff Summers (ex-Snatch) and vocalist Danny Hynes, along with Bruce Bisland on drums (ex-Lip Service) and bassist Barry 'Baz' Downes (ex-Inner City Unit; Snatch). After only a handful of gigs they were spotted by 'Fast' Eddie Clarke from Motörhead, who offered them the support slot on their Ace Up Your Sleeve tour. Weapon accepted and rushed into the studio to record two tracks, 'It's A Mad Mad World' and 'Set The Stage Alight', to be released as a single through Virgin Records. After the tour they recorded enough demos for an album but found no record company interest. Live, however, they excelled, with strong material such as 'Take It Away' and 'Remote Control'. In 1981 Bisland left and was replaced by Jon Phillips who had been playing with Megaton, and the line-up was also boosted by ex-Iron Maiden/Praying Mantis guitarist Robert Angelo. After a series of rehearsals at a studio in Lotts Road they set out on tour but became dogged by problems - these came to a head at the Granary in Bristol where the audience could see the group in its death throes as the set progressed. Summers joined Bisland with ex-More members in Wildfire, Angelo returned to the club circuit with High Roller and later Nitro Blues, while Hynes surfaced in 1986 with ex-Sweet members in Paddy Goes To Hollyhead. In 1986 Summers and Bisland joined Statetrooper before later going to Japan as part of the British All Stars/Praying Mantis supergroup.

WEST, LESLIE

b. Leslie Weinstein, 22 October 1945, Queens, New York, USA. West, who from an early age suffered from a glandular disorder that affected his weight, began his rock 'n' roll career as a member of the Vagrants, a mid-60s hard rock grouping who released several singles to little commercial recognition. In 1969 he formed Mountain with bass player Felix Pappalardi. Together they would go on to create some of the most timeless power blues compositions of the period, notably 'Mississippi Queen', drawn from their first album, *Mountain Climbing*. Their third gig was in front of nearly half a million people at Woodstock, and they went on to release three more albums (two of which went gold). After Pappalardi's defection in 1971, West put together a three-piece with Jack Bruce and Mountain's Corky Laing on drums, recording as West, Bruce And Laing. Mountain were re-formed for two further albums following Bruce's departure, but West took the hint and turned solo (having released his first such set in 1969, produced by Pappalardi, which served as a catalyst to the formation of Mountain). Forming the Leslie West Band, he released *The Great Fatsby* and *The Leslie West Band*, the latter pairing him with Mick Jones of Foreigner. West then retired from music to sort out various substance addictions, before reforming Mountain in 1985 with Laing and bassist Mark Clarke. The group split up shortly after touring throughout Europe, and West returned to his solo career. *Theme For An Imaginary Western* reunited him with Bruce, while *Alligator* saw him working with bassist Stanley Clarke and vocalist Johnette Napolitano of Concrete Blonde. He also appeared on two IRS compilations of guitar virtuosos, *Guitar Speak* and *Night Of The Guitars* (also a tour). He went on to work as musical director with DJ Howard Stern, and through him was introduced to comedian Sam Kinison (leading to West arranging the latter's version of 'Wild Thing'). After appearing on four cuts on Billy Joel's *River Of Dreams*, West also made his screen debut in *The Money Pit*, as the lead singer of a cross-dressing rock band, Lana And The Cheap Girls. However, he returned to the studio and the rock scene with his first album in over four years, *Dodgin' The Dirt*. With the backing of journeymen Steve Hunter (guitar, ex-Lou Reed; Peter Gabriel), Kevin Neal (drums, ex-Pat Travers) and Randy Coven (bass), it proved an honest attempt to re-establish himself within what he considered to be his natural market. West then joined Noel Redding in a reformed Mountain, recording two tracks for 1995's *Over The Top* compilation.

● ALBUMS: *Leslie West: Mountain* (Windfall 1969)★★★, *The Great Fatsby* (RCA 1975)★★★, *The Leslie West Band* (RCA 1976)★★, *Theme For An Imaginary Western* (Passport 1988)★★★, *Alligator* (IRS 1989)★★, *Lesley West Live!* (Shrapnel 1993)★★, *Dodgin' The Dirt* (Shrapnel/Blues Bureau 1993)★★.

● COMPILATIONS: *Blood Of The Sun: 1969-1975* (Raven 1996)★★★.

West, Bruce And Laing

This US trio was formed in 1972 by Leslie West (b. Leslie Weinstein, 22 October 1945, Queens, New York, USA; guitar, vocals) and Corky Laing (drums) following the demise of Mountain, a heavy rock group renowned, as critics wrote, for sounding 'more like Cream than Cream'. There was thus a sense of inevitability when the latter group's bassist, Jack Bruce (b. John Symon Asher, 14 May 1943, Glasgow, Lanarkshire, Scotland), joined the duo for this short-lived venture. West, Bruce And Laing completed two disappointing studio albums, neither of which matched the fire and purpose of the musicians' previous conglomerations, despite aping their constituent parts. A disillusioned Bruce abandoned the project in the summer of 1973, although a posthumous live set was issued the following year. West and Laing remained together in Leslie West's Wild West Show, before West reformed Mountain in 1974. Bruce, meanwhile, resumed his maverick career.

● ALBUMS: *Why Doncha* (Columbia 1972)★★, *Whatever Turns You On* (RSO 1973)★★, *Live 'N' Kickin'* (RSO 1974)★★★.

Whale

The outlandish rock band Whale, from Stockholm, Sweden, are led by vocalist Cia Berg, famed for delivering songs such as 'Young, Dumb 'n' Full Of Cum' without a trace of self-consciousness. She formed the band in the early 90s in collusion with guitarist, semi-professional comedian and one-time fiancé Henrik Schyffert. They first met when Schyffert, a veteran of several punk bands such as Ubangi, was producing a Swedish pop show, *Topp E Pop*. He invited Berg to become the show's host. Also part of the new team was hip-hop producer and bass player Gordon Cyrus, who originally provided the show with its background music. Their initial intention, in addition to writing radio jingles together, was to release just one single as Whale. However, when MTV began to play the resultant artefact, the typically salacious 'Hobo Humpin' Slobo Babe' (concerning a rich girl who 'gets off' on sleeping with tramps), their career change was made permanent. The following singles, 'Pay For Me' and 'I'll Do Ya', were also heavily endorsed by MTV. Live, the combination of conventional heavy metal (they cite old-school rockers Saxon and Judas Priest as a major influence) was skewered on Cyrus's hip-hop beats and funk grooves, providing a platform for Berg's animated, sexually themed vocals. *We Care*, which included a guest appearance from Tricky on two tracks, provided a more restrained, yet still vibrant version of that sound. It was recorded in a small studio in the Spanish countryside owned by manager Cameron McVey, who lives there with his wife Neneh Cherry. In 1998, augmented by three new members, the band released the vibrant *All Disco Dance Must End In Broken Bones*.

● ALBUMS: *We Care* (Hut 1995)★★★, *All Disco Dance Must End In Broken Bones* (Hut 1998)★★★.

White Lion

This US group was formed in Brooklyn, New York, during 1983, by Mike Tramp (lead vocals, ex-Mabel) and Vito Bratta (guitar, ex-Dreamer). After a series of false starts, they signed to Elektra Records with Felix Robinson (bass, ex-Angel) and Dave Capozzi (drums) completing the line-up. However, the label were unhappy with the recording of *Fight To Survive* and after refusing to release the album, terminated their contract. RCA Records picked up the release option and the album finally surfaced in Japan in 1984. By this stage, James Lomenzo and Gregg D'Angelo had taken over bass and drums, respectively, on a permanent basis. The album did in fact meet with favourable reviews, some critics comparing Mike Tramp to David Lee Roth and Vito Bratta to Eddie Van Halen, others likening the songs to those of Europe, Dokken or Journey. Signing to Atlantic Records, they released *Pride*, which developed their own identity, in particular Mike Tramp's characteristically watery falsetto style. The album catapulted them from obscurity to stardom, climbing to number 11 during its year-long stay on the *Billboard* album chart. It also spawned two US Top 10 hits with 'Wait' (number 8, February 1988) and 'When The Children Cry' (number 3, November 1988). *Big Game* was a disappointing follow-up. Nevertheless, it still made the US charts, peaking at number 19. *Mane Attraction*, released in 1991, saw the band recapture lost ground over the course of a strong melodic rock collection.

Lomenzo and D'Angelo quit owing to 'musical differences' shortly after the album's release and were replaced by Tommy 'T-Bone' Caradonna (bass, ex-Alice Cooper) and Jimmy DeGrasso (drums, ex-Y&T). The group eventually broke-up, with Tramp going on to form Freak Of Nature.

● ALBUMS: *Fight To Survive* (Grand Slam 1984)★★, *Pride* (Atlantic 1987)★★★, *Big Game* (Atlantic 1989)★★, *Mane Attraction* (Atlantic 1991)★★.

● COMPILATIONS: *The Best Of* (Atlantic 1992)★★★.

WHITE SPIRIT

Formed in Hartlepool, England, in 1975 by guitarist Janick Gers (b. Hartlepool, Lancashire, England) and drummer Graeme Crallan, they put together various line-ups before settling in 1979 with Phil Brady (bass), Malcolm Pearson (keyboards) and Bruce Ruff (vocals). In 1980 they signed to Neat Records, who subsequently released a debut single, 'Backs To The Grind'. This was followed by tours with Iron Maiden and Budgie. MCA Records were quick to sign them for a second single, 'High Upon High'. A tour with Gillan was planned and Gillan's bassist, John McCoy, produced their album, timed to come out at the same time as the tour. *White Spirit* would, unsurprisingly, offer strong echoes of past bands such as Deep Purple. From this point on the group failed to capitalize on their initial success and by 1982 Gers had been invited to replace Bernie Tormé in Gillan. This effectively killed off the band and Ruff also quit. One final attempt to crack the big time offered itself in 1983 with Brian Howe on vocals and Mick Tucker on guitar. This line-up failed to generate any interest and White Spirit joined the large graveyard of New Wave Of British Heavy Metal bands. Howe went on to join Bad Company, Tucker joined Tank and Gers later joined Iron Maiden.

● ALBUMS: *White Spirit* (MCA 1980)★★★.

WHITE ZOMBIE

This theatrical metal band was formed in 1985 in the Lower East Side of New York City, New York, USA, and were named after a horror film. Led by Rob 'Zombie' Straker (b. 1966) and female bassist Sean Yseult (b. 1966), with drummer Ivan DePlume and guitarist Tom Guay, White Zombie released two albums of noisy metal on their own label while they played chaotic shows around local clubs to increasing acclaim from the underground press. John Ricci replaced Guay on guitar for *Make Them Die Slowly*, and the band's more focused approach helped rid them of the art-noise label that had been placed upon their earlier albums. However, Bill Laswell's production still failed to capture the band's raw onstage power. Musical differences meant that Ricci was replaced by Jay Yuenger (b. 1967, Chicago, Illinois, USA), who made his debut on the *God Of Thunder EP*, a cover of the Kiss classic (rumoured legal action from Gene Simmons over the use of his copyrighted make-up image on the sleeve never materialized). The Andy Wallace production on their major label debut, *La Sexorcisto: Devil Music Vol. 1*, finally did White Zombie justice, with Rob Zombie sounding positively demonic as he roared his bizarre stream-of-consciousness lyrics against a monstrous instrumental barrage punctuated by sampled B-movie dialogue. This also proved to be their breakthrough album as White Zombie toured the USA ceaselessly, extending their tours continually as MTV played 'Thunder Kiss 65' and 'Black Sunshine' regularly, with further support coming from cartoon critics *Beavis And Butthead*. As *La Sexorcisto* took off, Philo replaced DePlume, only to be sacked as the touring finally ended, reinstated, and then replaced by ex-Exodus/Testament drummer John Tempesta (b. 1964, New York, USA) as White Zombie returned to the studio. The long-delayed *Astro Creep 2000* was greeted with enthusiasm in the American rock community, selling over a million copies in a few weeks. The single, 'More Human Than Human', also became a major hit, with plays on mainstream radio stations that had previously shunned the band. They continued to tour widely, now with a Rob Zombie-designed stage set designed as a replica of a junkyard. Yuenger also involved himself in two notable collaborative projects. The first, with bandmate Yseult, was work with Dave Navarro (Red Hot Chili Peppers), Keith Morris (Circle Jerks) and Greg Rogers (ex-Obsessed), masquerading as Zombie All Stars for a Germs tribute album. He also formed a punk-inspired side group, Bull Taco, with Morris, Navarro, Chad Smith (Red Hot Chili Peppers) and Zander Schloss (Circle Jerks). *Supersexy Swingin' Sounds* in 1996 was very well received, although as a marketing tool the 60s easy listening hammock style cover was a total contradiction to the music within. Rob Zombie released his solo debut in 1998, retaining Tempesta on drums.

● ALBUMS: mini-album *Psycho-Head Blowout* (Silent Explosion 1987)★★, *Soul Crusher* (Silent Explosion 1988)★★★, *Make Them Die Slowly* (Caroline 1989)★★★, *La Sexorcisto: Devil Music*

Vol. 1 (Geffen 1992)★★★★, *Astro Creep 2000: Songs Of Love, Destruction And Other Synthetic Delusions Of The Electric Head* (Geffen 1995)★★★★, *Supersexy Swingin' Sounds* (Geffen 1996)★★★.
Solo: Rob Zombie *Hellbilly Deluxe* (Geffen 1998)★★★.

WHITESNAKE

This UK-based heavy rock band was led throughout its career by David Coverdale (b. 22 September 1951, Saltburn-By-The Sea, Cleveland, England). The lead vocalist with Deep Purple since 1973, Coverdale left the group in 1976 and recorded two solo albums, *Whitesnake* and *Northwinds*. Shortly afterwards, he formed a touring band from musicians who had played on those records. Entitled David Coverdale's Whitesnake, the group included Mick Moody (b. August 30, 1950; guitar, ex-Juicy Lucy), Bernie Marsden (guitar, ex-Babe Ruth), Brian Johnston (keyboards), Neil Murray (bass) and David Dowell (drums). Pete Solley replaced Johnston shortly before the band recorded their debut EP, *Snake Bite*, which reached UK number 61 in June 1978. For much of the late 70s the group toured in the UK, Europe and Japan (the first US tour was in 1980). During this period there were several personnel changes, with ex-Deep Purple members Jon Lord (b. 9 June 1941, Leicester, England) and Ian Paice (b. 29 June 1948, Nottingham, Nottinghamshire, England) joining on keyboards and drums. Whitesnake's first British hit was 'Fool For Your Loving' (number 13 in May 1980), composed by Coverdale, Marsden and Moody, and the double album, *Live ... In The Heart Of The City* (named after the Bobby Bland song 'Ain't No Love In The Heart Of The City' featured on stage by Coverdale) reached number 5 the same year. *Come An' Get It* climbed to number 2 in the UK album charts in April 1981, with 'Don't Break My Heart Again' reaching number 17 the same month. At this point, the illness of Coverdale's daughter and tension among the members caused a hiatus in the group's career. When Whitesnake reformed in 1982 only Lord and Moody remained from the earlier line-up. The new members were Mel Galley (b. 8 March 1948; guitar), ex-Back Door and Alexis Korner bassist Colin Hodgkinson (b. 14 October 1945, Peterborough, England) and Cozy Powell (b. Colin Powell, 29 December 1947, England, d. 5 April 1998; drums). However, this configuration lasted only briefly and by 1984 the long-serving Moody and Lord had left, the latter to join a regenerated Deep Purple. While Coverdale remained the focus of Whitesnake, there were numerous personnel changes in the following years, including the return of Murray. These had little effect on the band's growing reputation as one of the leading exponents of heavy rock, with unambiguously sexist record sleeves marking out their lyrical and aesthetic territory. Frequent tours finally brought a million-selling album in the USA with 1987's *Whitesnake* and Coverdale's bluesy ballad style brought transatlantic Top 10 hits with a re-mixed 'Here I Go Again' (US number 1, UK number 9) and 'Is This Love' (US number 2, UK number 9). They were co-written with ex-Thin Lizzy guitarist John Sykes, a member of Whitesnake from 1983-86. His replacement, Dutch-born Adrian Vandenberg (b. 31 January 1954, Holland), was co-writer with Coverdale on the band's 1989 album, co-produced by Keith Olsen and Mike Clink. Ex-Dio guitarist Vivian Campbell was also a member of the band in the late 80s. Despite headlining the Donington Festival in August 1990, Coverdale put the group on ice at the end of the year. He later joined forces with Jimmy Page for the release of *Coverdale/Page* in early 1993, but when Whitesnake's contract with Geffen Records in the USA expired in 1994, it was not renewed. Coverdale returned with a new album in 1997 with Vandenberg, Guy 'Starka' Pratt (bass), Brett Tuggle (keyboards) and Denny Carmassi (drums). *Restless Heart* was a mellow (by Whitesnake standards) recording that emphasized just what a terrific voice and range Coverdale has.

● ALBUMS: *Trouble* (United Artists 1978)★★★, *Love Hunter* (United Artists 1979)★★★, *Live At Hammersmith* Japanese release (United Artists 1980)★★, *Ready An' Willing* (United Artists 1980)★★★, *Live ... In The Heart Of The City* (United Artists 1980)★★★, *Come An' Get It* (Liberty 1981)★★★, *Saints & Sinners* (Liberty 1982)★★, *Slide It In* (Liberty 1984)★★★, *Whitesnake* (Liberty 1987)★★★★, *Slip Of The Tongue* (EMI 1989)★★★, *Restless Heart* (EMI 1997)★★★.
● COMPILATIONS: *Best Of* (EMI 1988)★★★★, *Greatest Hits* (MCA 1994)★★★★.
● VIDEOS: *Fourplay* (PMI/EMI 1984), *Whitesnake Live* (PMI/EMI 1984), *Trilogy* (PMI/EMI 1988).
● FURTHER READING: *Illustrated Biography*, Simon Robinson. *Whitesnake*, Tom Hibbert.

WHITNEY, STEVE, BAND

This Euro-rock group was formed in 1975 by Chrigi Wiedemeier (guitar), Rolf Schlup (bass), Mick Hudson (vocals), Andy Lindsay (guitar) and Pete

Leeman (drums) - with absolutely no sign of a Steve Whitney. They debuted in 1980 with *Hot Line*, an overtly commercial melodic rock album that lacked conviction. Gary Steimer and Rob Seales replaced Leeman and Lindsay, respectively, on *Night Fighting*, which marked a change in direction. This saw them drop the poppy harmonies and switch to blues-based hard rock in the classic AC/DC mould. Mick Hudson then quit and the remaining four members continued as Sergeant.

● ALBUMS: *Hot Line* (EMC 1980)★★★, *Night Fighting* (EMC 1982)★★★.

WICKED MARAYA

Formed in New York, USA, in the early 90s, Wicked Maraya comprises Lou Falco (vocals), Michael Iadevaio (guitar), Dan Malsch (guitar), John Iadevaio (bass) and Mike Nach (drums). With a sound located somewhere between the pomp rock of Queensrÿche, Fates Warning and Savatage, the group's debut album was an impressive example of modern progressive metal. With intelligent, supple songwriting, and a fine production gloss courtesy of Jim Morris (a veteran of work with Savatage and Crimson Glory), *Cycles* boded well for their long-term career. To promote it the group set about a European tour with Metal Church.

● ALBUMS: *Cycles* (Mausoleum 1995)★★★.

WIDOWMAKER (UK)

A minor 'supergroup' formed in 1975 by Steve Ellis (vocals, ex-Love Affair), Luther Grosvenor aka Ariel Bender (b. 23 December 1949, Evesham, Worcestershire, England; guitar, ex-Spooky Tooth; Mott The Hoople), Bob Daisley (bass, ex-Chicken Shack; Broken Glass), Paul Nichols (drums, ex-Skip Bifferty; Lindisfarne) and Huw Lloyd Langton (guitar, ex-Hawkwind; Leo Sayer). They soon signed to Jet Records, and set up a tour in America. Also popular in the UK, although records failed to chart, they appeared on *The Old Grey Whistle Test*, soon after which Ellis left to be replaced by John Butler, who was at that time fronting his own band. Together they recorded their second and slightly heavier album, *Too Late To Cry*, released in April 1977. It suffered from the media preoccupation with punk, and in July they split up. Daisley went on to work with Ozzy Osbourne, Rainbow and Uriah Heep, while Langton rejoined Hawkwind in November 1979, where he stayed until 1989 when he went solo.

● ALBUMS: *Widowmaker* (Jet 1976)★★, *Too Late To Cry* (Jet 1977)★★.

WIDOWMAKER (USA)

Entirely separate from the UK band of similar name, this Widowmaker were formed in 1991 by former Twisted Sister clothes horse/vocalist Dee Snider. Between 1983 and 1987, Twisted Sister sold over 8 million albums, and Snider became one of metal's most distinctive and easily recognizable figureheads. Widowmaker sought to blend 90s innovations with 'classic' 80s rock style, Snider bringing along Joe Franco (drums, ex-Good Rats; Leslie West; Doro; Vinnie Moore), Al Pitrelli (guitar, ex-Danger, Danger; Alice Cooper; Great White; Asia) and Marc Russell (b. London, England; bass, ex-Beki Bondage). Their debut album was released on an independent label before the band signed to CMC International (Music For Nations in the UK). A second set, *Stand By For Pain*, caught the 90s bug for writing about serial killers ('Killing Time'), with other stand-out tracks such as 'Protect And Serve' lambasting corruption in the legal system. Though Snider had hardly been away since the death of Twisted Sister, devising and presenting MTV's *Heavy Metal Mania* (now *Headbanger's Ball*) and hosting *Metal Nation* on radio station WRCN, his former fans were glad to have him back - fronting a thoroughly rock 'n' roll rock 'n' roll band.

● ALBUMS: *Blood And Bullets* (Music For Nations 1991)★★★, *Stand By For Pain* (CMC International 1995)★★★.

WILD HORSES

This melodic hard rock quartet was formed in 1978 by bassist Jimmy Bain (ex-Rainbow) and guitarist Brian Robertson (b. 12 September 1956, Glasgow, Scotland; ex-Thin Lizzy). Deriving their name from a song on the Rolling Stones' *Sticky Fingers*, they enlisted the services of drummer Clive Edwards (ex-Pat Travers) and second guitarist/keyboard player Neil Carter. The line-up never lived up to expectations; Bain's weak vocals did not give the band enough identity, while the material was too derivative of Thin Lizzy and UFO. Live, the band were a different proposition and exuded a raw energy and aggression not evident in their studio work. John Lockton and Dixie Lee (ex-Lone Star) replaced Carter and Edwards for *Stand Your Ground*, which followed a much more blues-orientated direction. The band finally fell apart in 1981 with Bain going on to work with Ronnie James Dio (in Dio), and Robertson joining Motörhead after a period of session work.

● ALBUMS: *Wild Horses* (EMI 1980)★★★, *Stand Your Ground* (EMI 1981)★★★.

WILD TURKEY

Bass-player Glenn Cornick (b. 24 April 1947, Barrow-in-Furness, Cumbria, England), then known as Glenn Barnard, began his musical career as a member of the mid-60s group, Joey And The Jailbreakers. He also worked with a number of similarly underachieving outfits, such as the Vikings, Formula One, the Hobos and the Executives. Eventually he graduated into Blackpool's John Evan's Smash, soon to become known as Jethro Tull. Famous as much for his psychedelic costumes as his musicianship, Cornick spent three successful years with the group until quitting in 1970. Cornick recruited Jon Blackmore (guitar), Graham Williams (lead guitar), John 'Pugwash' Weathers (b. 2 February 1947, Carmarthen, Glamorganshire, Wales; drums, later Gentle Giant) and Gary Pickford Hopkins (guitar, vocals, ex-Eyes Of Blue/Big Sleep) to become Glenn Cornick's Wild Turkey. However, within months of the group's first rehearsals, Williams and Weathers had both defected to Graham Bond's group. Their replacements were Man's original drummer, Jeff Jones, and lead guitarist Alan 'Tweke' Lewis. The group had also shortened its name simply to Wild Turkey by the time its debut, *Battle Hymn*, was released for Chrysalis Records in 1972. Reviews were good and the band seemed to be in the ascendancy as they played regularly to audiences of up to 20,000 as support to Black Sabbath. Soon after a successful support to Jethro Tull in America, Jon Blackmore deserted the group for a writing career with the *New Musical Express*, and Cornick recruited former roadie Steve Gurl (keyboards) and Mick Dyche (drums). The group's only single, 'Good Old Days', preceded the release of *Turkey* in 1973. However, it failed to match the impact of the group's debut and the group imploded. Lewis joined Man, and was temporarily replaced by future Whitesnake guitarist Bernie Marsden. Jones was replaced on drums by Kevin Currie, but no third album was forthcoming. Until, that is, in 1996, when a phone call from Barry Riddington of HTD Records encouraged Cornick to reassemble Wild Turkey, with Pickford Hopkins and Lewis also taking part in the reunion.

● ALBUMS: *Battle Hymn* (Chrysalis 1972)★★★, *Turkey* (Chrysalis 1973)★★, *The Stealer Of Years* (HTD 1996)★★★.

WILDHEARTS

Following his sacking from the Quireboys and a brief tenure with the Throbs, UK guitarist/songwriter Ginger (b. 12 December 1964, South Shields, Tyne & Wear, England) set about forming the Wildhearts around the nucleus of himself plus ex-Tattooed Love Boys guitarist Chris 'CJ' Jagdhar, with the duo taking on vocal duties after the departure of ex-Torbruk frontman Snake. The line-up stabilized with the recruitment of former Dogs D'Amour drummer Bam Bam and bassist Danny McCormack (ex-Energetic Krusher), and the quartet signed to East West Records in late 1989. Contractual difficulties meant that the Wildhearts' debut EP, *Mondo Akimbo A-Go-Go*, was delayed until early 1992, but the poor production could not obscure the quality of the songs or the band's original style, mixing pop melodies with aggressive, heavy riffing. A Terry Date-remixed version was released as a double-pack with the *Don't Be Happy ... Just Worry EP* (later reissued as a single album). This had much greater impact, and the band's following increased as they undertook a succession of support tours. Bam rejoined his old group during this period, with his predecessor Andrew 'Stidi' Stidolph filling the gap. *Earth Vs The Wildhearts* was recorded in a mere seven days, but turned out to be one of the best British rock albums for years, mixing metal, punk and pop into an adrenalized collection of songs, with their commercial appeal tempered only by the liberal use of expletives in the song titles. Stidolph was ousted shortly afterwards in favour of ex-Radio Moscow drummer Ritch Battersby, and following an acclaimed tour with the Almighty, the band broke into the UK Top 40 in February 1994 with 'Caffeine Bomb'. Subsequent headline dates saw the sound augmented by the keyboards of ex-Grip frontman Willie Dowling, while the summer of 1994 saw guitarist Jagdhar ousted. He would later re-emerge with a new band, Honeycrack, which also featured Dowling. Later that year an exclusive 40-minute mini-album, available only through the Wildhearts' fan club, was released (still featuring CJ on guitar). *Fishing For Luckies* revealed new dimensions to the Wildhearts, stretching even to Pogues influences on 'Geordie In Wonderland', and the commercially available single, 'If Life Is Like A Love Bank I Want An Overdraft', brought a UK number 31 hit in January 1995, but the band delayed their second album proper until their line-up was restored to a quartet. Auditions for a replacement were held in November, after using Steve Vai guitarist Devin Townsend as a stand-in. Despite the unsettling lack of a second guitarist, *P.H.U.Q.* was widely applauded as the band's strongest collection to date, with Ginger maturing as a lyricist and the group producing a much more accessible sound. Jagdhar was eventually replaced by Jeff Streatfield. They countered accusations of pandering to a new audience with typically uncomplicated statements to the media such as: 'There's nothing wrong with playing a short snappy song that's got a chorus you can sing along to. What's accessible mean?'. This was justified by 'I Wanna Go Where The People Go' reaching UK number 16 in May 1995. Media speculation that Senseless Things guitarist Mark Keds would be recruited permanently was confirmed in 1995, but when he joined his former band for dates in Japan and failed to return in time for the Wildhearts' appearance at the Phoenix Festival, the venture soured into acrimony on both sides. By July they were still auditioning for a new singer and guitarist, despite the release of 'Just In Lust' (UK number 28), with Keds making his sole Wildhearts appearance on the b-side. Confusion was rife during the autumn of 1995: had the band broken up or not? They attempted to qualify the rumour by saying that they would break up if they failed to secure a new recording contract. They were in dispute with East West over the re-release of an expanded *Fishing For Luckies*, and when the record company released *Fishing For More Luckies* the band made a great deal of noise in opposing it and urged fans not to buy it. Ironically, it was an excellent album and one that fans were keen to own. The following year the restless band achieved their highest charting single, when 'Sick Of Drugs' (on Round Records) reached number 14 in April. The band signed a new contract with Mushroom Records in April 1997, releasing the lacklustre *Endless, Nameless* later that year amid more rumours of a split. The departed bassist Danny McCormack formed the Yo-Yo's in 1998.

● ALBUMS: *Earth Versus The Wildhearts* (East West 1993)★★★, *Don't Be Happy...Just Worry* (East West 1994)★★★, *Fishing For Luckies* mini-album (Fan Club 1994)★★★★, *P.H.U.Q.* (East West 1995)★★★★, *Fishing For More Luckies* (East West 1995)★★★★, *Fishing For Luckies* (Round Records 1996)★★★★, *Endless, Nameless* (Mushroom 1997)★★★, *Anarchic Airwaves - The Wildhearts At The BBC* (Kuro Neko 1998)★★★.

● COMPILATIONS : *The Best Of The Wildhearts* (East West 1996)★★★.

WILDSIDE

This Los Angeles-based glam rock quintet was formed in 1991 by vocalist Drew Hannah and guitarist Brent Wood, with Benny Rhynestone (guitar), Marc Simon (bass) and Jimmy D. (drums) completing the line-up. Contracted to Capitol Records, *Under The Influence* emerged in July 1992 to a lukewarm reception. Although professionally competent and technically without fault, the material proved to be both derivative and uninspired.

● ALBUMS: *Under The Influence* (Capitol 1992)★★, *Wildside* (Tony Nicole Tony 1995)★★.

WILLARD

Named after a character from James Herbert's book, *The Rats*, Willard were formed in Seattle, USA, in 1991, by Johnny Clint (vocals), Mark Spiders (guitar), Steve Wied (drums), Otis P. Otis (guitar) and Darren Peters (bass). They were picked up by Roadracer Records the same year. Subtitled *The Sound Of Fuck!*, their debut album, *Steel Mill*, released in July 1992, was a powerful and uncompromising debut, with influnces ranging from traditional metal sources such as Black Sabbath to the more hardcore-derived output of Nirvana and Henry Rollins.

● ALBUMS: *Steel Mill* (Roadracer 1992)★★★.

WINGER

This melodic US hard rock act was formed by experienced session musicians Kip Winger (bass, vocals) and Paul Taylor (keyboards, guitar) following their work together on Alice Cooper's *Constrictor* tour. Enlisting lead guitarist Reb Beach and drummer Rod Morgenstein (ex-Dixie Dregs), the quartet chose the name Sahara, but were forced to change to Winger at the last moment - the original name still appeared on a corner of the debut sleeve. *Winger* proved to be an immediate success, producing US Top 30 singles in 'Seventeen' (number 26, February 1989) and 'Headed For A Heartbreak' (number 19, June 1989), while the vocalist's rugged good looks turned him into a major sex symbol. This rather worked against the band in press terms, and Winger were never really taken seriously by the UK rock press in particular, despite abilities which kept them in demand for musician-type magazines and a genuinely impressive debut. *In The Heart Of The Young* consolidated Winger's US success, producing another enormous hit in 'Miles Away' (number 12, October 1990), and the band were well received on their debut European shows, but the heavy touring schedule proved too much for Taylor, who subsequently departed, later working with Steve Perry. The band adopted a heavier approach on the commendable *Pull* to compensate for the lack of keyboards, recruiting a second touring guitarist in John Roth, but were unable to swim against the grunge tide to emulate their earlier successes. After a lengthy US club tour, the band was put on ice while Winger pursued a solo career.

● ALBUMS: *Winger* (Atlantic 1988)★★★, *In The Heart Of The Young* (Atlantic 1990)★★★★, *Pull* (Atlantic 1993)★★★.
Solo: Kim Winger *Made By Hand* (Domo 1998)★★★.

WITCHFINDER GENERAL

This Midlands-based New Wave Of British Heavy Metal group are rather better remembered for two controversial album covers than for any of their actual music. Formed in 1979 by vocalist Zeeb and guitarist Phil Cope, with a name taken from a classic horror film, the initial line-up settled with a rhythm section of Toss McCready (bass) and Steve Kinsell (drums). Their debut single, 'Burning A Sinner' (also jokingly known as 'Burning A Singer'), revealed a primitive, Black Sabbath-influenced doom metal style, and was quickly followed by the *Soviet Invasion EP*, and a track on the *Heavy Metal Heroes* compilation. Saxon producer Peter Hinton was drafted in for *Death Penalty*, recorded in three days with a session drummer - this position remained unstable - and bassist Rod Hawkes replaced the departed Kinsell and McCready. The album showed promise, although it suffered from the rushed recording process. Most attention centred on its sleeve, which featured a mock-sacrifice scene photographed in a graveyard, with a well-known topless model and friend of the band, Joanne Latham, appearing semi-nude. The subsequent publicity reached the UK tabloids, and the band attempted to repeat the formula with *Friends Of Hell*, with the sleeve featuring several semi-naked models daubed with theatrical blood in a similar sacrifice scene, this time photographed in front of a church. This cynical effort succeeded only in losing what little support the band had garnered, and they quickly faded.

● ALBUMS: *Death Penalty* (Heavy Metal 1982)★★★, *Friends Of Hell* (Heavy Metal 1983)★★.

WITCHFYNDE

This early UK satanist heavy metal band were formed in the late 70s, and came to prominence with the 'Give 'Em Hell' single, followed by an album of the same name. The quartet of Montalo (guitar), Steve Bridges (vocals), Andro Coulton (bass) and Gra Scoresby (drums) produced a fast and furious brand of Judas Priest and Black Sabbath-influenced metal, mixing heavy riffs with occult lyrics and imagery. *Stagefright*, a live set, followed, but the band were dissatisfied with the level of their record company's support, and took a lengthy break before finding a new label. Witchfynde resurfaced with new members Luther Beltz (vocals) and Pete Surgey (bass) on *Cloak & Dagger*. Although the album was recorded quickly with a low budget, the material again showed genuine quality, and produced the popular 'I'd Rather Go Wild'. However, the long spell of inactivity meant that the band had fallen far behind such early contemporaries as Iron Maiden and Def Leppard, and they were unable to sustain this success without major label backing. A final double set, *Lords Of Sin*, coupled with a live mini-album, *Anthems*, was released before the band disappeared.

● ALBUMS: *Give 'Em Hell* (Rondelet 1980)★★★, *Stagefright* (Rondelet 1981)★★, *Cloak & Dagger* (Expulsion 1983)★★★, *Lords Of Sin/Anthems* (Mausoleum 1985)★★★.

WOLFSBANE

This UK quartet from Tamworth, Staffordshire, UK, employed a strong biker image to augment their incendiary heavy metal anthems. Featuring Blaze Bayley (b. 1963, Birmingham, West Midlands, England; vocals), Jason Edwards (guitar), Steve 'Danger' Ellet (drums) and Jeff Hately (bass), they incorporated elements of Van Halen, Iron Maiden and Zodiac Mindwarp into their own high-energy and, at times, chaotic style. Picked up by Rick Rubin's Def American label, they released *Live Fast, Die Fast* as an opening philosophical statement. The album failed to match the manic intensity of their live shows and was let down by weak production. Their next two releases saw some development on the songwriting front, with the addition of sci-fi and b-movie imagery, to supplement the well-worn themes of sex, booze and rock 'n' roll. After three albums their style remained loud, aggressive and, to a degree, derivative. In 1993, they separated both from P Grant Management and Def American, and by the following year Bayley quit to replace Bruce Dickinson in Iron Maiden. The remaining members soon abandoned their former name to become Stretch, signing with Cottage Industry Records in the summer of 1995.

● ALBUMS: *Live Fast, Die Fast* (Def American 1989)★★, *All Hell's Breaking Loose Down At Little Kathy Wilson's Place* (Def American 1990)★★★, *Down Fall The Good Guys* (Def American

1991)★★★, *Massive Noise Injection* (Bronze 1993)★★★.

WORLD WAR III

This short-lived American quartet came together when vocalist Mandy Lion and guitarist Tracy G were joined by the former Dio rhythm section of Jimmy Bain (bass) and Vinnie Appice (drums). Their sole, self-titled album displayed an impressive traditional metal style, with Tracy's G's superb guitar work complemented by a thunderous backing from the Bain/Appice team, although Lion's gruff vocals and a lyrical preoccupation with his own sexual exploits and fantasies tended to detract a little from the overall effect. The album met with limited success, and the band dissolved, with Appice returning briefly to Black Sabbath with Ronnie James Dio before being reunited with Tracy G in a revamped Dio band. Lion later turned up in Jake E Lee's post-Badlands group, Wicked Alliance.

● ALBUMS: *World War III* (Hollywood 1991)★★.

WRATHCHILD

Formed in 1980 in Evesham, Worcestershire, England, as a Black Sabbath-influenced band, it was another two years before Wrathchild emerged at the forefront of the new glam rock scene. Original members Rocky Shads (vocals) and Marc Angel (bass) were joined by ex-Medusa personnel Lance Rocket (guitar) and Eddie Starr (drums). They subsequently released an EP on Bullet Records and toured heavily to promote it. By 1983 they had developed a melodramatic live show and perfected their Kiss/Angel influences, while retaining an 'English' quality. A year later their hard work paid off with a deal with Heavy Metal Records, but a bad choice of producer (Robin George) led to a slick but flat sound that was not at all representative. Soon afterwards they entered into a long-running legal battle with the company, which almost killed off the group. During this time indie label Dojo released a compilation of early material that was far superior to the official album - it also contained the definitive version of live favourite and title track, 'Trash Queens'. In 1988 they made their comeback with the aptly titled *The Bizz Suxx*. 'Nukklear Rokket' was also released and was followed with a tour that lacked the early aggression and visual drama. The follow-up album in 1989 fared badly against the more established glam rock bands such as Mötley Crüe, and the group once again entered a legal battle, this time to stop an American thrash metal band using their moniker. They won, and their namesakes appended America to their tag. However, they disappeared from view shortly thereafter.

● ALBUMS: *Stakk Attakk* (Heavy Metal 1984)★★, *Trash Queens* (Dojo 1985)★★★, *The Bizz Suxx* (FM Revolver 1988)★★★, *Delirium* (FM Revolver 1989)★★.

● VIDEOS: *War Machine* (Hendring Video/Castle Communications 1988).

WRATHCHILD AMERICA

This US heavy metal quartet from Baltimore, USA seemed set for great things with the release of *Climbing The Walls*, which displayed quality Metallica-influenced thrash infused with melody, although the production did not quite convey the band's live guitar firepower. However, the good press accrued by Brad Divens (bass, lead vocals), Jay Abbene (guitar), Terry Carter (guitar, vocals) and Shannon Larkin (drums, vocals) went to waste as they became bogged down in litigation over the use of the Wrathchild name with the UK glam outfit of the same title. When the debut finally emerged, with America tagged onto the band's name, the pre-release publicity was long forgotten. *3D* proved the band's abilities again with a punchier sound, but stood little chance in a dwindling thrash market. The band lost their recording contract, and subsequently changed their name to Souls At Zero, pursuing a darker direction, although they later lost Larkin to Ugly Kid Joe.

● ALBUMS: *Climbing The Walls* (Atlantic 1989)★★★★, *3D* (Atlantic 1991)★★★, as Souls At Zero *A Taste For The Perverse* (Concrete 1995)★★★.

XENTRIX

Originally known as Sweet Vengeance, this UK rock band was formed in Preston, Lancashire, in 1986, and originally featured Chris Astley (vocals, guitar), Kristian Havard (guitar), Paul Mackenzie (bass) and Dennis Gasser (drums). The group had done little until signing to Roadrunner Records on the strength of their *Hunger For* demo tape in 1988 (they had already recorded one track, 'Blackmail', for inclusion on the Ebony Records compilation album, *Full Force*, under the Sweet Vengeance moniker). It was their debut album, *Shattered Existence*, that brought them to the wider public's attention. Combining Metallica-style power riffs with Bay Area thrash pretensions, the band became popular on the UK club circuit and recorded a cover version of the Ray Parker Jnr. track 'Ghostbusters', a stage favourite, for their first single release. They had problems with the track, however, as they had used the *Ghostbusters* film logo for the cover without Columbia Pictures' permission. The resulting press did the band no harm and the single was released with a new cover in 1990. *For Whose Advantage* was musically similar to previous releases, but it still did much to enhance their profile. With *Dilute To Taste* and *Kin* the band took a more traditional power metal approach that augured well. A full three-year gap preceded the release of *Scourge* in 1996, by which time vocalist/guitarist Astley had been replaced by Simon Gordon (vocals) and Andy Rudd (guitar).

● ALBUMS: *Shattered Existence* (Roadrunner 1989)★★★, *For Whose Advantage* (Roadrunner 1990)★★★, *Dilute To Taste* (Roadrunner 1991)★★★, *Kin* (Roadrunner 1992)★★★, *Scourge* (Heavy Metal 1996)★★.

XYZ

This French-American Los Angeles-based hard rock act, led by vocalist Terry Ilous with Marc Richard Diglio (guitar), Patt Fontaine (bass) and Paul Monroe (drums), played initially in a blues-based style, but their sound was moulded in the studio by producer Don Dokken into an almost exact replica of Dokken, with Ilous in particular sounding like the producer himself. *XYZ* was not without merit, containing some high-quality songs with fiery axework from Diglio, although this inevitably led to George Lynch comparisons. However, the debut was reasonably successful as the band toured the USA with Enuff Z'Nuff and Alice Cooper, and Capitol Records signed XYZ for *Hungry*. With George Tutko's production the band established a more characteristic sound with a much heavier approach, also reflecting their bluesier influences with a cover of Free's 'Fire And Water', but the album was a commercial failure, and the band eventually broke up.

● ALBUMS: *XYZ* (Enigma 1989)★★, *Hungry* (Capitol 1991)★★★.

Y&T

This San Francisco-based band formed in the mid-70s as Yesterday And Today, but David Meniketti (vocals, lead guitar), Joey Alves (rhythm guitar), Phil Kennemore (bass vocals) and Leonard Haze (drums) failed to make any real impact until they released *Earthshaker* as Y&T. *Earthshaker* was a classic hard rock record built on a blistering guitar barrage, Haze's thunderous rhythms and a superb collection of songs, catapulting the band into the public eye, but it also proved to be something of an albatross around the collective Y&T neck. *Black Tiger* was excellent, but subsequent records failed to maintain the standards set on *Earthshaker*. The *Open Fire* live set stopped the rot, and *Down For The Count* signalled a return to form, albeit in a more commercial direction. 'Summertime Girls' was picked up by US radio, but a disenchanted Y&T split with both their record label and drummer, feeling that Haze's image left a lot to be desired. Jimmy DeGrasso made his drumming debut on *Contagious* and Stef Burns replaced Alves for *Ten*, which were both credible hard rock albums, but the band's fortunes were waning and Y&T split in late 1990, with Burns moving on to Alice Cooper's band, DeGrasso joining White Lion and then Suicidal Tendencies, and Meniketti working with Peter Frampton. A brief Y&T reunion came to nothing.

● ALBUMS: As Yesterday And Today: *Yesterday And Today* (London 1976)★★, *Struck Down* (London 1978)★★. As Y&T: *Earthshaker* (A&M 1982)★★★★, *Black Tiger* (A&M 1983)★★★, *Mean Streak* (A&M 1983)★★, *In Rock We Trust* (A&M 1984)★★, *Open Fire* (A&M 1985)★★★, *Down For The Count* (A&M 1985)★★★, *Contagious* (Geffen 1987)★★★, *Ten* (Geffen 1990)★★★, *Yesterday And Today Live* (Metal Blade 1991)★★.

● COMPILATIONS: *The Best Of Y&T (1981-1985)* (A&M 1990)★★★, *Anthology* (Castle 1992)★★★.

Young Gods

This heavily experimental trio originated from Geneva, Switzerland, and specialized in hard electronic rock and rhythm. The main artistic engine was Franz Treichler (vocals), alongside original collaborators Cesare Pizzi (samples) and Frank Bagnoud (drums). Although singing mainly in French, they found an audience throughout Europe via the premier outlet for 'difficult' music, Play It Again Sam Records. Notable among their releases were 'L'Armourir', a version of Gary Glitter's 'Hello Hello I'm Back Again', and *The Young Gods Play Kurt Weill*, which stemmed from a commission to provide a tribute performance of the composer's works. They had already been awarded a French Government Arts grant to tour the USA in 1987, where they maintain cult popularity. *T.V. Sky* was sung entirely in English, but *Only Heaven*'s ambient direction was a disappointing sidetrack. In the 90s Treichler worked with drummer Üse Hiestand and sampler/mixer Alain Monod, alongside his longstanding producer and co-songwriter Roli Mosimann.

● ALBUMS: *The Young Gods* (Product Inc./Play It Again Sam 1987)★★★, *L'Eau Rouge* (Play It Again Sam 1989)★★★, *The Young Gods Play Kurt Weill* (Play It Again Sam 1991)★★★, *T.V. Sky* (Play It Again Sam 1992)★★★, *Live Sky Tour* (Play It Again Sam 1993)★★★, *Only Heaven* (Play It Again Sam 1995)★★, *Heaven Deconstruction* (Paradigm 1997)★★.

Youth Brigade

Formed in Los Angeles, California, USA, in the late 70s from the ashes of the Extremes, Youth Brigade initially comprised Shawn Stern (guitar, vocals), Adam Stern (bass, vocals), Mark Stern (drums, ex-No Crisis; Sado Nation) and Greg Louis Gutierrez (guitar). One of Los Angeles' finest hardcore bands of the period, they also formed the BYO label as a direct response to the Ellis Lodge riot of 1979 when bands including the Go-Go's played at a gig that was violently curtailed by riot police. BYO was housed at Skinhead Manor, an eight-bedroomed mansion in the heart of Hollywood, rented by an assortment of mavericks intent on creating an alternative media base (including fanzines, pirate radio, live shows, etc.). It was named in honour of the visiting Sham 69. Youth Brigade had started out as part of the Skinhead Manor collective, originally as a six-piece group with two singers. They soon crystallized into a line-up made up solely of the Stern brothers. Another band of the same name was born in Washington, DC, at the same time (playing the same type of aggressive punk music), but this group faded from view before too much confusion arose. Often compared to the Ruts because of their integration of reggae with punk pop, Youth Brigade's debut album was easily one of the most accessible of the 'So-Cal Hardcore' scene. *Sound And Fury I* demonstrated the group's potential with a wide variety of music employed even at this early stage in their career. 'Men In Blue', for example, included a rap, and the group also tackled the doo-wop classic 'Duke Of Earl'. They embarked on a major tour playing at over 100 venues in 1983 and 1984, covering much of the USA, Europe and Canada, but always using non-mainstream outlets to book the shows. In 1986 they shortened their title to Brigade to accommodate 'a further progression in style'. The new line-up featured bass player Bob Gnarly, formerly of Plain Wrap (Gutierrez had long since joined Salvation Army and then the Three O'Clock). Their first album as the Brigade, *The Dividing Line*, featured a cameo appearance from Jane Wiedlin on 'The Hardest Part'. Stern's lyrics were evolving and taking in matters spiritual and emotional as well as social, but Brigade never took themselves too seriously, raps and break-dancing continuing to be a feature of their live shows. However, their previous audience remained unimpressed by what they saw as Brigade's conversion to conventional hard rock. The group disbanded, with Stern subsequently forming That's It with Tony Withers (ex-Stupids).

● ALBUMS: as Youth Brigade *Sound And Fury*; as the Brigade *The Dividing Line*.

Z

Zappa, Dweezil

b. 5 September 1969, USA. Dweezil is the son of the legendary Frank Zappa. However, it was not his father that prompted Dweezil to form a band, but Eddie Van Halen. Unfortunately, this obsession led to an almost direct copy of his hero's style, right down to wielding identical guitars and dressing the same. However, Dweezil still built up a small cult following with early releases, breaking into the mainstream via the album and video, *My Guitar Wants To Kill Your Mama*, one of his father's old tunes given the Van Halen treatment. The video achieved mass viewing figures on MTV and music programmes all over the world. The album was completed with Bobby Blotzer (drums; Ratt), Steve Smith (drums; Journey), and Fiona (vocals). For *Shampoo Horn* the videos took on a much more surreal nature. Dweezil's brother Ahmet helped out on vocals, but that Van Halen ghost still lurked.

● ALBUMS: *Havin' A Bad Day* (Rykodisc 1987)★★★, *My Guitar Wants To Kill Your Mama* (Chrysalis 1988)★★★, *Confessions* (Chrysalis 1991)★★, *Shampoo Horn* (Chrysalis 1993)★★★.

● VIDEOS: *My Guitar Wants To Kill Your Mama* (1988).

Zed Yago

Founded in Germany by blues singer Jutta Weinholt (ex-Breslau) in 1985, Zed Yago were a traditional rock concern very much in keeping with the sound pioneered by fellow nationals, Warlock. Jutta's vocal style owed much to Doro from Warlock, but also saluted American singer Ronnie James Dio. Her band comprised Jimmy and Gunnar on guitar, Tach on bass and a larger-than-life bald powerhouse of a drummer known as Bubi. They first attracted mainstream attention in May 1989 with the release of 'Black Bone Song'. This was followed by their second album and a tour - one concert of which was broadcast live on BBC Radio 1. They vanished in 1990 having failed to make any lasting impact.

● ALBUMS: *From Over Yonder* (SPV 1988)★★★, *Pilgrimage* (BMG 1989)★★.

Znowhite

Standard American power metal team, with the notable exception that it boasted multiracial membership, who came together in late 1983 in Chicago, Illinois, with brothers Ian and Sparks Tafoya on guitar and drums and vocalist Nicole Lee. They spent much of the following year gigging in the Bay Area of San Francisco with Metallica, and supported Raven on their US tour. Their first album was released thanks to the help of influential friends Johnny Z and Doc McGhee, whose better-known credits include Anthrax and Mötley Crüe. A second collection again followed the power metal mantra, but in 1988 they adopted a higher profile when they signed to Roadrunner Records and played gigs outside of the San Francisco scene. Musically they became much heavier and eagerly joined the thrash metal bandwagon - though with results that hardly compared to those of their new peer group. Following disappointing sales, the group sundered just after the close of the decade, with members drifting off into a new conglomeration, Cyclone Temple.

● ALBUMS: *All Hail To Thee* (Enigma 1984)★★, *Kick 'Em While They're Down* (Enigma 1985)★★★, *Act Of God* (Roadrunner 1988)★★★.

Zodiac Mindwarp And The Love Reaction

Formed in 1985, Zodiac Mindwarp And The Love Reaction projected an image encompassing everything from sex maniacs and party animals to leather-clad bikers. Put together by Zodiac (b. Mark Manning), a former graphic designer, their image and attitude was always more interesting than their music. With twin guitarists Cobalt Stargazer and Flash Bastard, plus Trash D. Garbage and Slam Thunderhide on bass and drums, respectively, they were the ultimate science-fiction garage band, influenced by Alice Cooper, Motörhead and the Stooges. After releasing the mini-album *High Priest Of Love*, on the independent Food label, they were signed by Mercury Records, who funded the recording of *Tattooed Beat Messiah*. Although rigidly formularized, it spawned the hits 'Prime Mover' and 'Back Seat Education', which were accompanied by expensive and controversial videos. The creative juices soon ran dry, however. Zodiac's backing band disintegrated and Mercury dropped him from its roster in 1989.

In 1991 he re-formed the band with Stargazer, Thunderhide and new bassist Suzy X, releasing the single 'Elvis Died For You'. Despite signing to

European label Musidisc, little further progress was made. Manning later lived up to his reputation by collaborating with the KLF's Bill Drummond in 1994 on the semi-pornographic work, *A Bible Of Dreams*.

● ALBUMS: *High Priest Of Love* (Food 1986)★★★, *Tattooed Beat Messiah* (Mercury 1988)★★★, *Hoodlum Thunder* (Musidisc 1992)★★, *The Friday Rock Show Sessions At Reading '87* (Windsong 1993)★★.

● VIDEOS: *Sleazegrinder* (Channel 5 Video 1989).

● FURTHER READING: *A Bible Of Dreams*, W. Drummond and M. Manning.

ZZ Top

Formed in Houston, Texas, USA, in 1970, ZZ Top evolved out of the city's psychedelic scene and consist of Billy Gibbons (b. 16 December 1949, Houston, Texas, USA; 6-string guitar, vocals, ex-Moving Sidewalks), Dusty Hill (b. Joe Hill, 19 May 1949, Dallas, Texas, USA; bass, vocals) and Frank Beard (b. 11 June 1949, Houston, Texas, USA; drums), the last two both ex-American Blues. ZZ Top's original line-up - Gibbons, Lanier Greig (bass) and Dan Mitchell (drums) - was also the final version of the Moving Sidewalks. This initial trio completed ZZ Top's debut single, 'Salt Lick', before Greig was fired. He was replaced by Bill Ethridge. Mitchell was then replaced by Frank Beard while Dusty Hill subsequently joined in place of Ethridge. Initially ZZ Top joined a growing swell of southern boogie bands and started a constant round of touring, building up a strong following. Their debut album, while betraying a healthy interest in blues, was firmly within this genre, but *Rio Grande Mud* indicated a greater flexibility. It included the rousing 'Francine' which, although indebted to the Rolling Stones, gave the trio their first hit and introduced them to a much wider audience. Their third album, *Tres Hombres*, was a powerful, exciting set that drew from delta music and high energy rock. It featured the band's first national hit with 'La Grange' and was their first platinum album. The group's natural ease was highly affecting and Gibbons' startling guitarwork was rarely bettered during these times. In 1974, the band's first annual 'Texas-Size Rompin' Stompin' Barndance And Bar-B-Q' was held at the Memorial Stadium at the University Of Texas. 85,000 people attended: the crowds were so large that the University declined to hold any rock concerts, and it was another 20 years before they resumed. However, successive album releases failed to attain the same high standard and ZZ Top took an extended vacation following their expansive 1976/7 tour. After non-stop touring for a number of years the band needed a rest. Other reasons, however, were not solely artistic, as the group now wished to secure a more beneficial recording contract.

They resumed their career in 1979 with the superb *Deguello*, by which time both Gibbons and Hill had grown lengthy beards (without each other knowing!). Revitalized by their break, the trio offered a series of pulsating original songs on *Deguello* as well as inspired recreations of Sam And Dave's 'I Thank You' and Elmore James' 'Dust My Broom'. The transitional *El Loco* followed in 1981 and although it lacked the punch of its predecessor, preferring the surreal to the celebratory, the set introduced the growing love of technology that marked the group's subsequent releases. *Eliminator* deservedly became ZZ Top's best-selling album (10 million copies in the USA by 1996). Fuelled by a series of memorable, tongue-in-cheek videos, it provided several international hit singles, including the million-selling 'Gimme All Your Lovin'. 'Sharp Dressed Man' and 'Legs' were also gloriously simple yet enormously infectious songs. The group skilfully wedded computer-age technology to their barrelhouse R&B to create a truly memorable set that established them as one of the world's leading live attractions. The follow-up, *Afterburner*, was another strong album, although it could not match the sales of the former. It did feature some excellent individual moments in 'Sleeping Bag' and 'Rough Boy', and the cleverly titled 'Velcro Fly'. ZZ Top undertook another lengthy break before returning with the impressive *Recycler*. Other notable appearances in 1990 included a cameo, playing themselves, in *Back To The Future 3*.

In 1991 a greatest hits compilation was issued and a new recording contract was signed the following year, with BMG Records. *Antenna* was the first album with the new company. Over the years one of their greatest strengths has been their consistently high-standard live presentation and performance on numerous record-breaking (financially) tours in the USA. One of rock's maverick attractions, Gibbons, Hill and Beard have retained their eccentric, colourful image, dark glasses and stetson hats, complete with an almost casual musical dexterity that has won over hardened cynics and carping critics. In addition to having produced a fine (but sparse) canon of work they will also stay in the record books as having the longest beards in musical history (although one member, the inappropriately named Frank Beard, is clean-shaven). Whether it was by design or chance, they are doomed to end every music encyclopedia.

● ALBUMS: *ZZ Top's First Album* (London 1971)★★, *Rio Grande Mud* (London 1972)★★★, *Tres Hombres* (London 1973)★★★★, *Fandango!* (London 1975)★★, *Tejas* (London 1976)★★, *Deguello* (Warners 1979)★★★★, *El Loco* (Warners 1981)★★★, *Eliminator* (Warners 1983)★★★★, *Afterburner* (Warners 1985)★★★★, *Recycler* (Warners 1990)★★★★, *Antenna* (RCA 1994)★★★, *Rhythmeen* (RCA 1996)★★★★.

● COMPILATIONS: *The Best Of ZZ Top* (London 1977)★★★, *Greatest Hits* (Warners 1991)★★★★, *One Foot In The Blues* (Warners 1994)★★★.

● VIDEOS: *Greatest Hits Video Collection* (Warner Music Video 1992).

● FURTHER READING: *Elimination: The ZZ Top Story*, Dave Thomas.

INDEX

C

D

E

H

I

L

N

O

P

Q

R

S

T

U

V

W

X

Y

Z